The World Today Series®

Stryker-Post Publications
Harpers Ferry, WV
USA

Latin America

by Robert T. Buckman

2005

39th EDITION

Next Publication Date, August 2006

Robert T. Buckman . . .

A journalism professor at the University of Louisiana at Lafayette, he graduated from Texas Christian University where he earned his bachelor's and master's degrees in journalism and political science. He holds a doctorate in journalism from the University of Texas. His writings on Latin America have been widely published in books, newspapers, magazines, and scholarly journals. He has lived and worked in Chile, where he served a Fulbright Fellowship in 1991, Panama, and Paraguay. A former lieutenant colonel in the U.S. Army Reserve, he was reserve military attaché to Colombia until his retirement in 1998.

Adapted, rewritten and revised annually
from a book entitled *Latin America 1967*,
published in 1967 and succeeding years by

Stryker-Post Publications
P.O. Drawer 1200
Harpers Ferry, WV 25425
Telephones: 1–800–995–1400 (U.S.A. and Canada)
  Other: 1–304–535–2593
  Fax: 1–304–535–6513
  www.strykerpost.com
VISA–MASTERCARD–AMERICAN EXPRESS

The World Today Series has thousands of subscribers across the U.S. and Canada. A sample list of users who annually rely on this most up-to-date material includes:

Public library systems
Universities and colleges
High schools
Federal and state agencies
All branches of the armed forces & war colleges
National Geographic Society
National Democratic Institute
Agricultural Education Foundation
Exxon Corporation
Chevron Corporation
CNN

International Standard Book Number: 1–887985–66–2

International Standard Serial Number: 0092–4148

Library of Congress Catalog Number 73–647061

Cover design by Lisa Filar

Cartographer: William L. Nelson

Typography by Barton Matheson Willse & Worthington
Baltimore, MD 21244

Printed in the United States of America by
United Book Press, Inc.
Baltimore, MD 21207

Photographs used to illustrate *The World Today Series* come from many sources, a great number from friends who travel worldwide. If you have taken any which you believe would enhance the visual impact and attractiveness of our books, do let us hear from you.

ACKNOWLEDGMENTS

Un montón de gracias to various people who helped ensure the quality of this volume: Michael Nix, who volunteered to offer his time to pore over the book to look for typos, awkward syntax and inaccuracies; Mario Antonio Sandoval of Guatemala and Orlando López of Paraguay, who always review those countries' chapters to offer suggestions or corrections; Davie Sessoms of the U.S. Army Special Warfare Center at Fort Bragg, who always keeps me updated on new titles for the bibliography; and Sherre Amire, who shows extraordinary patience and offers encouragement every spring during the intense revision process.

This just in . . .

Even an annually revised reference book has a deadline sometime. After this book was set in type, but before final proofing was completed, several breaking events occurred that supersede some of the information contained in various chapters of this year's book.

In the U.S.-Latin American Relations and Brazil chapters, for example, we report on Brazil's quest, along with Germany, India and Japan, for permanent seats on the U.N. Security Council, which they want expanded from 15 to 25 seats. At present, there are five permanent members: the United States, Britain, France, Russia and China. The 10 non-permanent members have rotating two-year terms; Latin America has two non-permanent seats. Permanent members of the council have veto power.

On July 17, foreign ministers of the four aspirant countries met at the United Nations with representatives from Nigeria, South Africa, Libya and Egypt, representing the African Union, which has 53 members, whose votes will be crucial to obtaining the changes. However, the African countries want the Security Council expanded to 26 members with two permanent seats for Africa. The two sides could not reach an agreement, but were planning to meet again in late July. For the change to be effected, it will require a two-thirds majority in the General Assembly, or 128 of the 191 members. Mexico, Argentina and Colombia oppose a permanent seat for Brazil. Obviously, Pakistan opposes a permanent seat for India and will probably be backed by Muslim countries, so the chances for passage were still cloudy when this book finally went to press.

The postal-congressional bribery scandal investigation in Brazil was continuing to unfold, and claimed another high-ranking casualty, although not for corruption. Mauro Marcelo de Lima e Silva, head of the Brazilian Intelligence Agency, submitted his resignation after he made an injudicious remark in which he called the congressional investigators "circus beasts performing in a ring." Opinion polls suggested that the developing scandal has not affected the popularity of President da Silva—yet.

On the subject of polls, Socialist Michelle Bachilet appears within striking distance of winning a first-round victory in Chile's presidential election in December. Bachilet is the candidate of the *Concertación*, the center-left coalition that has won every presidential election since Chile's return to democracy in 1989. The conservative opposition, once thought to have an excellent shot at winning the presidency for the first time, is now fragmented by the rival candidacies of Joaquín Lavín of the ultra-rightist Independent Democratic Union *(UDI)*, who narrowly lost the 2000 runoff, and Sebastián Piñera of the center-right National Renewal *(RN)*. A survey published on July 14 by the respected polling firm Center for Public Studies *(CEP)* gave Bachilet 47%, to 21% for Lavín and 14% for Piñera. The margin of error was 2.7 percentage points.

The day before that poll was released, the Chilean Congress approved a historic constitutional amendment that shortens the presidential term from six to four years and at last eliminates the 10 non-elected senators, a fixture of the 1980 constitution imposed during the Pinochet dictatorship. The change leaves the Senate with 38 members, all elected.

In Colombia, the Constitutional Court is now expected to rule by mid-November 2005 on the constitutionality of Congress' approval of a law that would allow President Alvaro Uribe to run for a second consecutive term. A Gallup Poll released on July 16 continues to show Uribe virtually unbeatable, with an approval rating of 69%. Former President César Gaviría of the Liberal Party, a potential candidate, was far behind with an approval rating of 35%. Gaviría is a harsh critic of Uribe, and has called him "messianic."

In strife-torn Haiti, the so-called Council of Sages, the influential but unelected body that chose the interim president, recommended on July 16 that the *Lavalas* Party of exiled President Jean-Bertrand Aristide be barred from the upcoming elections in October and November on the grounds that it promotes violence (which it does). However, the Provisional Electoral Council responded that all parties would be entitled to field candidates.

Also in Haiti, there was another shocking reminder of the country's lawless, violent climate. Jacques Roche, culture editor of the daily newspaper *Le Matin* and host of a television talk show, was abducted by unknown kidnappers on July 10. His bullet-riddled body, which bore signs of torture, was found four days later. His kidnappers had demanded $250,000 ransom. They later reduced it to $10,000, which Roche's fans raised and paid, but he was slain anyway. It is unclear whether the murder was a common kidnapping, which is commonplace in Haiti, or was politically motivated. The interim culture minister blamed Roche's death on Aristide supporters.

In Mexico, the Institutional Revolutionary Party *(PRI)* scored two important gubernatorial victories on July 3. It retained the governorship of the state of Mexico, the country's most populous, and reclaimed the state of Nayarit, which it had lost to an opposition coalition in 1999. In Mexico state, the *PRI*'s Enrique Peña Nieto received a winning plurality 47.6% of the vote against a divided opposition. In Nayarit, the *PRI*'s Ney González won with a plurality of 46%; Miguel Angel Navarro of the Party of the Democratic Revolution *(PRD)* received 42.7%.

As expected, *PRI* party president Roberto Madrazo, former governor of Tabasco and leader of the party's so-called "dinosaur" faction, formally announced his presidential candidacy on June 26. The *PRI* decided at a party convention on July 12 to allow all Mexican voters, regardless of party affiliation, to participate in the *PRI*'s presidential primary, which was expected to be held before the end of the year.

In another major change in Mexican politics, the Congress on June 28 approved a long-sought law that will allow Mexican citizens living abroad to vote. There are an estimated 12 million Mexicans who live outside Mexico, 98% of them in the United States. It was unclear, however, how many of them will be able to obtain the necessary voting credentials from the Federal Electoral Institute in time for the *PRI* primary or the July 2, 2006 presidential election.

There was also a potentially major development in the on-going and bloody drug war in Mexico. A man believed to be Vicente Carillo Fuentes, former head of the notorious Juárez Cartel, was arrested in a shopping mall in Mexico City on July 4 under an assumed name and in disguise. Carillo Fuentes' family insisted it was not he; federal authorities said they were virtually sure it is. It still had not been confirmed at press time.

CONTENTS

Stone piece, Tiahuanaco culture, Bolivia

The UN has received into its ranks many small countries, such as those of the Caribbean region. The purpose of this series is to reflect *modern world dynamics*. Thus, we mention only briefly the beautiful nations of the Lesser Antilles and concentrate our attention on the growth of the larger, developing countries.

São Paulo, Brazil, in 1930 . . .

. . . and today

Latin America Today

Latin America, always a land of color and conflict, is undergoing the most dramatic changes of its post–colonial history. These changes—political, economic, technological and cultural—are accelerating as the 21st century begins. It is an understatement to say that Latin America at the dawn of the 21st century bears little resemblance to the Latin America of 1900. Despite some notable exceptions, Latin America gave rise to a stereotype that persists to this day of tropical republics mired in squalor, ruled by self-serving autocrats and lagging decades if not centuries behind the economically advanced societies of Europe and North America.

Such a view ignores the fact that Argentina at the turn of the 20th century was an industrialized and agriculturally rich society boasting a higher standard of living than that of France. Sadly, however, as is true of many stereotypes, there was enough element of truth throughout the rest of the region to reinforce the perception of dictators, destitution and depression. Since World War II, this picture has been slowly, painfully, and sometimes violently evolving into a collection of societies entering the modern world. Some have evolved more than others, but the trend is inexorable. This evolution involves four discrete elements: a democratic revolution; economic diversification and expansion; technological acceleration; and cultural growth and projection.

Democratic Revolution

The sudden collapse of communism and the emergence of democracy in Eastern Europe at the beginning of the 1990s was one of the watershed events of world history. Less dramatic but no less historic was the slow, inexorable shift of Latin America away from its past of *caudillo* strongmen, military juntas and revolving-door regimes and toward constitutionally elected civilian governments. As recently as 1977, only three of the 20 true "Latin" American republics had genuinely democratic systems with free elections involving two or more political parties and peaceful transfers of power from one to another: Colombia, Costa Rica and Venezuela.

Two other nations had what could be charitably described as imperfect civilian democracies. Mexico had enjoyed civilian rule since the promulgation of its 1917 constitution and peacefully transferred power from one president to another like clockwork every six years, with re-election strictly forbidden. But until 2000, all those presidents were of one party, the *Partido Revolucionario Institucional (PRI)*, which held government at all levels in a vise–grip and was not above rigging elections to quash the aspirations of upstart opposition parties. In the Dominican Republic, the late President Joaquín Balaguer was elected in 1966, 1970 and 1974 and attempted to hang onto power indefinitely through extra-constitutional means.

Fourteen other republics were governed by military juntas; even the once–envied democracies of Chile and Uruguay had opted for order over chaos in 1973. Finally, Cuba was—and still is—distinguished by the peculiar totalitarian experiment of Fidel Castro, a model that was viewed then as a beacon by guerrilla movements and left–wing political parties throughout the region.

Democracy in Latin America, it seemed, was a concept that was unfeasible at best and unwanted at worst. But in 1978, the tide slowly began to turn, until by the late 1980s it had become a tidal wave in favor of duly elected civilian government. In the Dominican elections that year, Balaguer ordered troops to halt the vote–counting when it became apparent the opposition was winning. Under pressure from the administration of U.S. President Jimmy Carter, Balaguer was forced to honor the opposition victory and grudgingly yielded power. After two intervening presidents, Balaguer returned in 1986 for three more terms, retiring as a blind, feeble old man in 1996 and turning over power to a freely elected president of the opposition.

This transition to democracy in all but one of the Latin American Republics is described in detail in the sections on each nation, together with an indication of things to come.

Lest this picture of emerging democracy be misconstrued as overly rosy, it must be noted that two or more consecutive elections, no matter how honest in the eyes of international observers, do not in and of themselves guarantee that the mortar of democratic institutions will set properly. It often takes generations before adherence to liberal principles becomes woven into a nation's social fabric. True democracy flowers best in a climate characterized by such principles as co-equal executive, legislative and judicial branches; tolerance of opposition viewpoints, whether expressed on the floor of a congress, in free and independent mass media or in the streets; unquestioned civilian control over the military; workable constitutions that endure

1

Latin America Today

A beautiful example of Peruvian designed fabric

more than a decade or two; eschewal of the temptation to resort to political violence; and public confidence in the integrity of governmental institutions and leaders. Most Latin American countries are still lacking in this regard.

In fairness, however, Latin America should be cut some slack. There is not yet a Utopian society anywhere on Earth. Even in the United States, which has long held a paternal attitude toward its wayward Latin American neighbors, political assassinations and attempted assassinations have occurred with alarming frequency, and local pockets of political corruption, complete with vote fraud, influence peddling and kickbacks, are legendary.

But the United States, Canada and the English-speaking states of the Caribbean enjoyed an advantage over their Latin American neighbors in having had a colonial master that had experienced its Glorious Revolution in 1688. The Enlightenment came late, if at all, to Spain, Portugal and France. The abuses of George III that Jefferson enumerated in the Declaration of Independence seem little more than nitpicks in contrast to the absolute power wielded by divine right by the monarchs of the other colonial powers. When Great Britain granted independence to its colonies, whether voluntarily or involuntarily, it left in place viable political institutions rooted in parliamentary democracy and common law upon which they could build. Washington and Jefferson learned much in the House of Burgesses of colonial Virginia. Spain, Portugal and France, by contrast, bequeathed a legacy of power concentrated in the hands of one man. To put it another way, no Spanish king ever signed a Magna Carta.

Thus, although the newly independent Latin America emulated the U.S. Constitution with its three branches of government and checks and balances, in practice the executive enjoyed disproportionate power. Latin America became the living embodiment of the adage that absolute power corrupts absolutely, and such traditions are not easily discarded. In just the past few years, despite the aforementioned advances in Latin American democracy, we have witnessed attempts by several elected presidents to play fast and loose with constitutional rights in the name of expediency. We also have seen the murders of prominent political reformers in Colombia, Mexico and elsewhere.

Another troubling factor is the willingness of democratically elected presidents to employ legal and extralegal measures once employed by their dictatorial predecessors to curtail press freedom, especially critical editorials and investigative reporting. In Peru, for example, Alberto Fujimori flouted the constitution in using a bureaucratic technicality to revoke the Peruvian citizenship of an Israeli-born television station owner in 1997 after the station became too aggressive in reporting abuses of human rights by the government. Also in 1997, Panamanian President Ernesto Pérez Balladares, using the labor law as a pretext, attempted to expel a Peruvian citizen who was associate editor of the country's principal daily, which had been ferocious in reporting on the Pérez government's shortcomings. The president backed down only in the face of intense international pressure from press and human rights groups, pressure to which Fujimori proved immune.

Colombian President Ernesto Samper's congressional allies enacted a broadcast law that required all independently produced news programs on the government– owned network to apply for new licenses at the end of 1997, a move aimed at *QAP*, a nettlesome "60 Minutes"–like news show. Presidents Alvaro Arzú and Alfonso Portillo of Guatemala and Rafael Caldera of Venezuela were openly hostile to the media, and all three applied pressure on businessmen to pull ad-vertising from media that failed to support their governments, pressure that included threats of tax audits. Caldera unsuccessfully attempted at the Ibero-American summit in Venezuela in November 1997 to impose a region–wide regulation that would guarantee "truthful reporting" and impose sanctions on media that violated these government-set standards of "truth." His successor, Hugo Chávez, succeeded in having just such a "truth" guarantee inserted into the new Venezuelan constitution approved by voters in December 1999—with the government, of course, to define "truth."

Under the Spanish legal system, the principle of *desacato* is often used as a cudgel against journalists by thin-skinned public officials offended by critical reporting or editorials—truth is not a defense. In Chile, a Supreme Court justice used a section of an archaic national security law in 1999 to order the arrest of the author of an unflattering book on the country's court system. The publisher and editor were jailed, all copies of the book were confiscated from bookstores and warehouses, and the author fled to the United States. She could not return until 2001, after Congress finally repealed that section.

The following year, the editor of a crusading weekly newspaper in Venezuela was forced into exile in Costa Rica after a powerful friend of President Chávez sued him for defamation for accusing him of influence peddling; the judge in the case refused to allow the editor's lawyer to present evidence showing that his accusations were true. In 2004, Chávez implemented a restrictive new broadcast law that basically cows independent radio and television stations into practicing self-censorship.

In Portuguese-speaking Brazil, President Luiz Inácio da Silva ordered the visa of the *New York Times* bureau chief in Rio

Veracruz, Mexico: The largest of the colossal heads found from the Olmec civilization

de Janeiro revoked in May 2004 after he wrote an article quoting sources as saying the president has a drinking problem. There was a domestic and international outcry, the Supreme Court blocked the revocation to determine its constitutionality, and da Silva backed down and rescinded the revocation.

Another tactic for dealing with aggressive journalists remains widespread in Latin America: murder. According to the Inter American Press Association (IAPA), 287 journalists were martyred in the performance of their duties in the Americas from October 1988 to April 2005, including 118 in Colombia, 48 in Mexico, 27 in Brazil, 18 in Guatemala, 18 in Peru, and 14 in El Salvador. Fifteen journalists were murdered just between April 2004 and April 2005. Many of the murders can be linked to drug traffickers or guerrillas, but a suspicious number—almost all of them unsolved and unpunished—were of journalists who were investigating official corruption or who had written critical editorials or interpretative articles. Independent journalism in Latin America remains a high-risk occupation, and until it can be practiced without fear, true democracy cannot take root.

The Declaration of Chapultepec, promoted by the IAPA and signed in Mexico City in 1994 by representatives of 22 nations of the hemisphere, acknowledges the importance of freedom of the press and freedom of expression for democratic societies and denounces acts of violence against journalists. Yet, the other 13 countries of the hemisphere have not signed, and abuses continue to occur even in the signatory countries. The plight of the media is serious enough that it appeared on the agenda of the second Summit of the Americas in Santiago, Chile, in April 1998. The 34 hemispheric leaders (Castro was not invited) agreed to establish an office within the Inter-American Commission for Human Rights to investigate attacks against journalists.

There have been encouraging signs during the past few years that executive branches, and the once-omnipotent military establishments, no longer wield unchecked power. Two presidents, Brazil's Fernando Collor and Venezuela's Carlos Andres Pérez, were impeached and removed from office by their congresses for political corruption. In Paraguay, President Raúl Cubas was impeached by the Chamber of Deputies for abuse of power in 1999 and resigned and went into exile in the face of certain conviction and removal by the Senate.

The leaders of the former Argentine junta were prosecuted for human rights abuses committed during the "dirty war" of 1976–83. Jorge Serrano's attempt to stage a Fujimori–style self–coup in Guatemala in 1993 failed because the army remained loyal to the constitution, and he fled into exile. A coup attempt by a Paraguayan army general, Lino Oviedo, also fizzled out for lack of support in 1996. During the constitutional crisis over the 1998 removal, justifiable or not, of Ecuador's President Abdalá Bucaram, the military remained in its barracks and allowed the civilians to effect a reasonably smooth transition.

Not all signs have been encouraging, however. There were the 1991 military coup that toppled the elected government of Jean-Bertrand Aristide in Haiti; the temporary suspension of constitutional guarantees in 1992 by Peru's Fujimori for reasons of expediency, and his shamelessly rigged "reelection" in 2000; the probably unconstitutional removal by Congress of Ecuador's Bucaram in 1998 on the ostensibly justifiable (but unproven) charge of "mental incompetence;" the unquestionably unconstitutional barracks revolt in Ecuador that overthrew President Jamil Mahuad in January 2000 for the unjustifiable reason that his public popularity was too low; the dissolution of Parliament by Haitian President René Préval in 1999; and the rigged election in Haiti in December 2000 that brought Aristide back to power.

Another disturbing antidemocratic trend has been the use of mob violence to force the resignations of democratically elected presidents who have subsequently become unpopular. In just the past five years, there were the violent street protests in Argentina that led to the resignation of the elected president, Fernando de la Rua, in December 2001 and his eventual replacement with the man who lost the election, Eduardo Duhalde; the almost successful military coup in Venezuela in April 2002 that had President Chávez under house arrest for 24 hours; the violent demonstrations in Bolivia that forced President Gonzalo Sánchez de Lozada from office in October 2003, just 14 months into his five- year term, and forced his successor, Carlos Mesa, to step down in June 2005 after 19 months; and the street protests that forced Congress to remove President Lucio Gutiérrez in April 2005 after 27 months in office.

Two other presidents forced from office by public protests evoke less sympathy: Fujimori of Peru in November 2000 and Aristide in Haiti in February 2004. Both had been re-elected fraudulently.

A possible indicator of growing self-confidence in the viability of these new democratic institutions is a willingness to permit reelection of popular, successful presidents. In a region with its tradition of Stroessners and Balaguers, who remained in control through orchestrated elections, virtually all of these new democracies, and some of the old ones, incorporated a prohibition against reelection, or at least immediate reelection, into their constitutions. Since then, however, the congresses of Peru, Argentina, Brazil and Venezuela amended their constitutions to permit the reelections of Presidents Fujimori, Menem, Cardozo and Chávez. Yet, in Panama, when President Pérez Balladares called a referendum in 1998 to seek approval for a second term, a resounding 64% of the voters rejected the idea. The Dominican Republic, which had banned immediate re-election in 1994 after Balaguer's last term, reinstituted it in 2002 at the urging of President Hipólito Mejía, but he was so unpopular he was defeated for re-election anyway. In 2004, the far more popular Colombian President Alvaro Uribe was calling for a constitutional amendment that would permit him to seek a second term, and in mid-2005 it appeared the measure would be approved.

A bus crosses a shallow river in Colombia

Latin America Today

On the down side, it appears some of the old dangers may be resurfacing. After Peru and Argentina opened the door to reelection, Fujimori and Menem began making plans for Rooseveltian third terms. When Peru's electoral court rejected that idea as unconstitutional, Fujimori made an end-run around the judiciary, maintaining that his first election in 1990 was under the pre-1993 constitution and thus did not count. Opinion polls showed overwhelming sentiment against a third term, but when Fujimori's opposition in Congress attempted to call for a referendum to decide the issue as was done in Panama, Fujimori's allies squelched the initiative. Fujimori was "reelected" in May 2000 in an election that was so blatantly fraudulent that the opposition chose to boycott it and international observers withdrew rather than participate in a flawed vote count. Fujimori was inaugurated for his third term in July 2000, but public indignation and mounting evidence of scandal forced him to resign in November, paving the way for a new presidential vote in April and June 2001, which international observers pronounced fair.

In Argentina, Menem declared in February 1998 that he would not seek a third term, then coyly hinted that he would accept a draft, then aggressively began pushing for a constitutional amendment. It was a moot issue, however, because not only did Menem's Justicialist Party lose its majority in Congress in 1997, but polls were showing that Menem had become so unpopular that he would be badly beaten even if he could run. At the end of 1998, Menem pragmatically disavowed another

run in 1999, but bombastically began vowing a comeback in 2003. He tried, but received only 24% of the vote and dropped out. He lived in self-imposed exile in Chile with his young, former beauty queen wife, fighting extradition to face corruption charges. He returned to Argentina in December 2004 when a judge lifted the arrest warrant against him, and at 77 was vowing to retake the presidency from President Néstor Kirchner, a fellow Peronist, in the 2007 election.

Another curious trend is the public's fascination in several countries with former military strongmen or charismatic military figures who have entered the political arena. In Bolivia in 1997, former strongman Hugo Banzer was elected to the presidency by the Congress after he won a plurality of the popular vote. He resigned after four years because of cancer, but he respected democratic institutions while in power.

In Guatemala, opinion polls once showed that the most popular political figure in the country was former military dictator Efraín Ríos Montt, a pariah in human rights circles for his alleged massacre of thousands of Indian peasants during his 1982-83 regime. He was barred by the constitution from serving again as head of state, but he successfully appealed that restriction and ran for president in 2003. When push came to shove, however, the Guatemalan people decided they weren't all that nostalgic for his jack-booted rule after all, and he ran a poor third.

A similar situation occurred in Paraguay. Former General Lino Oviedo, who had attempted a coup in 1996 and who

was convicted and placed under house arrest, won the Colorado Party nomination for president over the opposition of incumbent civilian President Juan Carlos Wasmosy—himself of the Colorado Party. Polls indicated that Oviedo, who could not even leave his quarters to campaign, would win the May 1998 election handsdown, causing Wasmosy to threaten to postpone the vote. The Supreme Court intervened and declared Oviedo's candidacy illegal, whereupon his running mate, Raúl Cubas, was elected president. Cubas then ordered the release of Oviedo, widely seen as the power behind the throne, a move that sparked a governmental crisis. The public's fascination with Oviedo, however, dimmed after the assassination in March 1999 of Vice President Luis María Argaña, Oviedo's leading opponent within the Colorado Party. The day after President Cubas' subsequent resignation, Oviedo fled to Argentina, then to Brazil, where he was arrested in June 2000. The Supreme Court ordered his release in 2001, and he vowed to return to Paraguay and run for the presidency. Faced with imminent arrest, however, he remained in Brazil and again ran a surrogate candidate in 2003. This time, however, his stand-in received only 13.5% of the vote, finishing fourth.

The most dramatic case of a would-be *caudillo* continues to unfold in Venezuela. Former Lieutenant Colonel Hugo Chávez, who spent two years in prison for leading a failed attempt to overthrow President Carlos Andres Pérez in 1992, capitalized on public disgust with the corruption of the two traditional parties to run for president as an independent populist. In December 1998, after the two desperate parties agreed on a unity candidate, Chávez won a landslide victory. Upon assuming office in February 1999, he expressed his contempt for the legislative and judicial branches, then called for an election for a constituent assembly to rewrite the 1962 constitution. His adherents won 90% of the seats in that assembly, which then forged a new organic law that would allow Chávez to serve for two consecutive six-year terms, besides granting him broad new powers. Voters overwhelmingly approved the new constitution in December 1999, whereupon Chávez called for a new presidential election for May 2000, postponed at the last minute until July. Chávez won with 59% of the vote, an even greater landslide than in December 1998. An open admirer of Cuba's Fidel Castro, Chávez has openly expressed contempt for freedom of the press and the voices of dissent. He has voiced the familiar siren song of *caudillos* past who assume dictatorial powers: It is the only way to solve the country's problems. Mounting opposition to Chávez's

The Tikal Altar Stone, Guatemala

4

View of Montevideo, Uruguay

heavy-handed methods erupted into violence in April 2002, which led to an abortive military coup. Within 48 hours, however, additional violence by pro-Chávez mobs effected his return to power. Ironically, Chávez, like Argentina's Juan Perón, is an elected autocrat, a political oxymoron if there ever was one. Chávez, increasingly unpopular, became the target of a recall campaign. In June 2004, his opponents succeeded in collecting more than the 2.4 million signatures needed for the recall election, which was was held in August 2004, but Chávez emerged stronger than ever when 59% of the voters chose not to remove him.

A Chávez-like phenomenon then occurred in troubled Ecuador, where Lucio Gutiérrez, a flamboyant colonel who spent six months in jail for his role in overthrowing Mahuad in 2000, was decisively elected president in November 2002 on a platform to clean up corruption and effect social justice. But then Gutiérrez fell from public favor when he himself came under suspicion for corruption. In the face of mounting street protests demanding Gutiérrez's resignation, Congress removed him from office in April 2005 and sent him into exile in Brazil, the third Ecuadorian president to be removed either by Congress or the military within eight years.

There is nothing new about people in struggling societies turning to a strong-willed, charismatic leader who promises to bring order out of chaos, in Latin America or elsewhere. It evokes memories of the infamous explanation by an Italian woman for why Mussolini remained popular for so long: "Because he made the trains run on time." The fact that a former military leader is elected president in a free, honest popular vote does not in and of itself represent a threat to democracy; Brazil's Getulio Vargas and Chile's Carlos Ibáñez both were returned to power in free elections. Indeed, it is the very manifestation of the people's will. It can be argued that the United States has elevated a number of military heroes to the presidency—most recently in 1952 and 1956—without under-

mining its democracy. But the United States and Latin America have vastly different traditions where military presidents are concerned, and the question that remains unanswered at this juncture is whether military men who win power through the ballot box are committed democrats or Trojan horses who will disregard the democratic process if it becomes inconvenient to them.

But even when civilians are elected, Latin Americans have shown themselves incredibly impatient with new presidents who do not prove themselves to be Supermen who can solve all their countries' problems quickly. Public protests forced Presidents Mahuad and Gutiérrez of Ecuador, de la Rua of Argentina and Sánchez de Lozada of Bolivia to depart partway through their terms, bringing all three countries perilously close to mob rule. Opposition to Venezuela's Chávez led to violent street demonstrations, a coup and counter-coup, a general strike and a bitter recall election, all of which have polarized the country and left it on the brink of civil warfare.

Alejandro Toledo of Peru, now four years into his five-year term, is a pariah with an approval rating in the single digits. If he is forced from office like the others, will his successor be any more acceptable to the pot-bangers in the streets? In Bolivia, President Carlos Mesa, who as vice president succeeded Sánchez de Lozada, was far more popular than his predecessor, but left-wing Indian parties sponsored protests that drove him, too, to resign in June 2005.

An ambitious periodic 17-nation survey begun in 1996 by the Chilean polling firm Latinobarómetro for the British newsmagazine *The Economist* on Latin Americans' attitudes toward their young democracies gives cause for both cheer and alarm. Respondents were asked whether they agree with the statements, "Democracy is preferable to any other kind of government," and "In certain circumstances, an authoritarian government can be preferable to a democratic one." The Dominican republic became the 18th nation in the survey in 2004. There was less cause for cheer in the 2004 survey than in the 2003 survey. In nine of the 18 countries, 50% or more of respondents agreed that democracy is the best form of government; in 2003, it was 11 countries. Not surprisingly, the highest support was 78% in traditionally democratic and stable Uruguay, while the lowest was 35% in Guatemala, which has had a succession of disappointing elected presidents. By contrast, however, in only four countries did more than 20 percent agree that authoritarian government is sometimes preferable to democracy; the highest percentage was 39% in Paraguay, compared with 7% in Costa Rica and Uruguay.

The bad news was that support for democracy was down since 1996 in 13 of the countries. Nicaragua and Paraguay showed the most precipitous drop, 20 percentage points each. Surprisingly, Venezuela, which has experienced some of the hemisphere's most turbulent politics since 1996, was one of the three countries that showed an increase, from 62% to 74%. Chile rose from 54% to 57%, while desperately poor Honduras rose from 42% to 46%. Mexico remained unchanged at 53%. Between 2003 and 2004, support for democracy increased in six countries, declined in seven and remained unchanged in four. The year before, however, support for democracy had decreased in 11 countries.

In only five countries, however, has tolerance of authoritarianism as a substitute for democracy increased since 1996—Argentina, Bolivia, Ecuador, Paraguay and Peru. It remained unchanged—at 7%—in stable, prosperous Costa Rica. In Paraguay, acceptance of authoritarianism rose by 13 percentage points, tying with those who preferred democracy to any other form of government, at 39% each.

Overall, when the Latin America of 2005 is compared with the Latin America of 1977, there can be no disputing the advances that have been made toward de-

PER CAPITA INCOME		
Bahamas	$17,000	(2002)
Barbados	$12,000	(2002)
Trinidad-Tobago	$6,490	(2002)
Chile	$6,000	(2004)
Mexico	$5,945	(2003)
Venezuela	$4,400	(2004)
Panama	$4,320	(2004)
Costa Rica	$4,193	(2003)
Argentina	$3,486	(2003)
Grenada	$3,391	(2004)
Uruguay	$3,300	(2003)
Belize	$3,237	(2002)
Brazil	$2,840	(2003)
Cuba	$2,800*	(2003)
Jamaica	$2,771	(2001)
Peru	$2,305	(2004)
El Salvador	$2,258	(2003)
Ecuador	$2,118	(2003)
Guatemala	$2,068	(2002)
Dominican Rep.	$1,896	(2003)
Colombia	$1,844	(2003)
Suriname	$1,671	(2001)
Paraguay	$1,019	(2003)
Honduras	$920	(2002)
Bolivia	$914	(2004)
Guyana	$760	(1999)
Haiti	$425	(2002)
Nicaragua	$370	(2002)

*Purchasing parity

SOURCE: U.S. Department of State

Latin America Today

mocracy, so in fairness, the Latin American glass should be viewed as four-fifths full rather than one-fifth empty. The long-range prospects for democracy ultimately will depend on economic stability and development—and the patience of the Latin Americans themselves.

Economic Diversification and the Trend Toward Free Trade

For more than a hundred years, most of the post-colonial Latin American countries languished in the economic doldrums while North America experienced robust economic growth and prosperity. Only Argentina experienced growth similar to that of the United States and Canada. Several factors condemned Latin America to the poverty from which it is only now beginning to emerge.

To begin with, just as Spain, Portugal and France had failed to bequeath a democratic tradition to their former colonies, neither did they leave behind sound economic infrastructures. Sadly, these colonial powers were more concerned with exploitation than with development. Spain in particular was obsessed with how much precious metal could be extracted from the ground, not with agriculture or with building roads, schools or financial institutions. Granted, the Jamestown colonists had come in search of gold, but when it became apparent that there was no gold in Virginia, the English recognized that the fecund soil offered other opportunities. The demand created for tobacco and later cotton generated the

Panamanian equestrian Fernando Senderos

wealth that gold did not. Subsequent English immigrants to the New World, whether to escape prison or religious persecution, came prepared to exploit the wealth of the soil or to engage in mercantilism. This fostered an independent, entrepreneurial spirit that was carried over into the post–independence period.

In addition, the Industrial Revolution was exported successfully from Britain to America. Industry, agriculture and the advent of public education led in the 19th century to the rise of a literate middle class of independent farmers and merchants with political rights sandwiched between those who amassed great wealth and those left behind in destitution. The unique concept of homesteading, providing free title to land in return for working it, further broadened the base of the independent-minded middle class in the English colonies. The opportunities it offered for self-advancement also sparked a wave of immigration that brought with it new zeal and new ideas.

There was no corresponding industrialization, democratization or mass education in Spain or Portugal or in most of their erstwhile colonies in the 19th century. The result was a dual class structure in which a tiny, educated, wealthy elite, a disproportionate number of them Caucasian, held absolute economic and political power over a mass of desperately poor, illiterate Indian and *mestizo* peons. This structure was enforced in some countries for decades by a lone dictator, such as Paraguay's Rodrigo Gaspar de Francia or Mexico's Porfirio Díaz. Thus, social inequality enforced at bayonet point and usually condoned by the Catholic Church, became the second major obstacle to Latin American development. Industrial growth requires a literate workforce.

The third major obstacle was monocultural dependency, the reliance of a country's economy on a single resource for export. This handicap persisted throughout the late 19th century and in some cases well into the 20th century. Thus, Brazil and Colombia depended on coffee, Bolivia on tin, Chile on copper, Peru on guano fertilizer, Cuba and the Dominican Republic on sugar, Venezuela on petroleum and Ecuador and the Central American republics on bananas. The derogatory term "banana republic" is another unfortunate Latin American stereotype, but again it had some basis in fact. The products upon which these countries depended for foreign exchange were at the mercy of the world market. To use an old analogy, when the world tin market sneezed, Bolivia caught pneumonia.

Compounding this situation was a fourth obstacle, undercapitalization that could only be overcome by surrendering

control of the nation's one valuable resource to those who *did* have capital: foreign investors. Consequently, foreign-owned companies, mostly British and U.S., came to dominate these underdeveloped economies, exercising considerable political influence over their host governments. Probably the most egregious example was that of the United Fruit Company of the United States, which treated the Central American countries as private fiefs.

These deplorable conditions persisted decade after decade, as those with the power and money were able to maintain the status quo through force if necessary. Those lacking power could only submit. In those countries where democracy did manage to gain a temporary foothold in the late 19th and early 20th centuries—Argentina, Brazil, Chile and Uruguay—it is not surprising that socialist, communist and anarchist movements won adherents, much as they did in the United States during the same era. If misery existed under a capitalist system, the logic went, capitalism must be the enemy. Foreign capitalists were especially popular whipping boys. Expropriation of foreign holdings came into vogue, beginning with Mexico's nationalization of the oil industry in 1938. Guerrilla movements also targeted foreign companies.

Latin American intellectuals, from the 1960s until the early '90s, almost universally followed like sheep a school of thinking known as "dependency theory," which held that Latin America was economically and culturally "dependent" upon the developed countries, especially the United States. Occasionally even reform-minded military officers would seize power with a promise to redress social wrongs, such as the military government in Peru from 1968–80 that sought to impose a socialist system based on the Yugoslav model. Marxism came to power by force of arms in Cuba in 1959 and in Nicaragua in 1979 and through the ballot box in Chile in 1970. Fidel Castro was an enticing role model. Even conservative military regimes created state-owned corporations to run utilities, airlines, railroads, ports, mines and oil refineries. The realization that a cumbersome bureaucracy was a woefully inefficient way to provide reliable telephone or electrical service came slowly.

Other economic experiments were aimed at what were seen as sinister outside forces: high protective tariffs and regional trade blocs. Alas, these also proved a disappointment. Tariffs designed to protect fledgling local industries often created bloated monopolies that produced substandard and overpriced products. Trade blocs such as the Central American Common Market and the Andean Pact proved ineffectual because the member countries were not producing products for export that the other members wanted to import.

The right-wing Pinochet government in Chile proved to be the regional maverick when it withdrew from the Andean Pact and scuttled its protective tariffs to create a free-market economy based on the theories of Nobel Prize-winning U.S. economist Milton Friedman. Many of Pinochet's economic brain trust studied under Friedman at the University of Chicago, earning them the sobriquet, "Chicago Boys." The initial result was a disastrous recession as local businesses proved unable to compete with better and cheaper foreign imports. But gradually the economy equalized, showing real growth with single-digit inflation, something unattainable under the Marxist government of Salvador Allende. Pinochet also broke Chile's dependency on copper exports, promoting the export of fresh fruits. Chile's free-market strategy proved so successful that Pinochet's civilian successors have left it in place and it has been emulated by its neighbors.

Not long after the creation of Chile's free-market model, the Soviet Bloc collapsed, taking down with it the discredited notion of a state-run economy. Like a chain of dominos, Latin American countries began privatizing decades-old, state-owned corporations: Argentina, Brazil, Mexico, Peru and others. New policies, some of them draconian, also permitted Argentina, Brazil, Mexico and Peru to tame the hyperinflation that had become a seemingly permanent fixture throughout the 1970s and '80s. Two presidents who were the very embodiments of Latin America's conversion from public sector to private sector dominance were Brazil's Fernando Henrique Cardoso (1995–2003), an erstwhile Marxist economist and leading dependency theorist, and Argentina's Carlos Saúl Menem (1989–99), a Peronist who steered the country on a course 180 degrees from that set by his patron saint, Juan Perón.

By the mid-1990s, Latin America was in the midst of an economic boom that had U.S. and European economists predicting that the region could repeat the success story of the robust export-oriented economies of Asia. This expectation was heightened by the catastrophic collapse of the Asian stock markets in late 1997. Mexico was welcomed into the North American Free Trade Agreement (NAFTA) in 1993, while Argentina, Brazil, Paraguay and Uruguay formed *Mercosur,* a trade bloc that showed moderate signs of success. The bloc almost collapsed in the wake of the economic crises in Argentina and Brazil, but now is showing signs of revitalization. So is the Andean Pact, composed of Bolivia, Colombia, Ecuador, Peru

and Venezuela. In mid-2004, the two blocs were on the verge of creating a South American free-trade area.

No longer seen as bogeymen, foreign investors were not only welcome but openly courted, and the political stability spreading through the region makes it an attractive target for investment. In addition, tourism continues to expand, providing jobs and a pollution-free source of foreign exchange.

Following up on the concept of NAFTA and *Mercosur,* U.S. President Bill Clinton invited the Western Hemisphere's heads of state, minus Cuba's Fidel Castro, to Miami in 1993 for the first Summit of the Americas. There, the idea of establishing a hemisphere-wide Free Trade Area of the Americas (FTAA), with membership limited to democratic countries, was first advanced. In 1997, Clinton suffered a setback when an odd coalition of Republicans and pro-labor Democrats blocked the president's request for so-called "fast-track" authority to negotiate trade pacts.

Nonetheless, at the second Summit of the Americas in Santiago, Chile, in 1998, the 34 heads of state (once again, Castro was not invited), approved blueprints to establish the FTAA by 2005. Also recognizing that true economic development is dependent upon an educated workforce, the summit's communiqué called for the expenditure of $6.1 billion over three years to improve education. It also set a goal that 100% of the hemisphere's children would have access to elementary education and 75% would have access to secondary education by 2010.

The third Summit of the Americas was held in Quebec City, Canada, in April 2001, and once again the FTAA was the top agenda item. The 34 heads of state from democracies in the hemisphere again attended. The new U.S. president, George W. Bush, appeared to be an even more enthusiastic advocate of the FTAA than had Clinton, and Congress grudgingly granted him fast-track authority. The heads of state set a target date of January 1, 2005, for establishment of what would become the world's largest free-trade bloc, encompassing 800 million people and accounting for an estimated $15 trillion in trade. The concept was not without its naysayers, however. In the streets of Quebec, protesters representing labor unions, environmental groups and various anti-capitalist organizations engaged in violent clashes with police in an attempt to break up the summit. Inside the summit, Venezuelan President Hugo Chávez charged that the lofty goals of the Miami and Santiago summits of reducing poverty had not been met, while Brazilian President Cardoso complained about U.S. anti-dumping laws.

A harbinger of possible doom for the FTAA came at a meeting of the World Trade Organization in Cancun, Mexico, in September 2003, which collapsed largely because of the opposition of Latin American members. Two months later, a ministerial summit in Miami hammered out a compromise agreement for a "two-tiered" FTAA that would have a basic accord but with the flexibility for signatories to make separate agreements with one another.

The next Summit of the Americas took place in Monterrey, Mexico, in January 2004, but it focused primarily on such issues as democracy and corruption. The major change from the previous summit was that Chávez was joined by two powerful new anti-FTAA allies, Luiz Inácio "Lula" da Silva of Brazil and Néstor Kirchner of Argentina. Besides the anti-dumping issue, these three leaders also demanded a reduction in U.S. agricultural subsidies so their imports can compete. The United States, meanwhile, has been pressing for greater protection for intellectual property. The January 1, 2005 target date was not made official, not in Monter-

CORRUPTION PERCEPTION INDEX		
Country	World rank (1–145)	Score (0–10)
Finland	1	9.7
Canada	12	8.5
United States	17	7.5
Chile	20	7.4
Barbados	21	7.3
Uruguay	28	6.2
Costa Rica	41	4.9
Suriname	49	4.3
El Salvador	51	4.2
Trinidad -Tobago	51	4.2
Brazil	59	3.9
Belize	60	3.8
Colombia	60	3.8
Cuba	62	3.7
Panama	62	3.7
Mexico	64	3.6
Peru	67	3.5
Jamaica	74	3.3
Dominican Rep.	87	2.9
Nicaragua	97	2.7
Argentina	108	2.5
Ecuador	112	2.4
Honduras	114	2.3
Venezuela	114	2.3
Bolivia	122	2.2
Guatemala	122	2.2
Paraguay	140	1.9
Haiti	145	1.5
Bangladesh	145	1.5
Guyana:	Not rated	

Source: Transparency International

Latin America Today

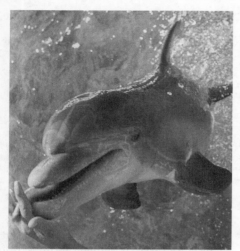

A trainer with a playful porpoise in Nassau, Bahamas . . .

rey nor in a subsequent ministerial summit in Puebla, Mexico, in April. Meanwhile, *Mercosur* embarked on concluding free-trade pacts with the Andean Pact, Mexico, and the European Union, though the talks with the EU broke down. The target date for the FTAA quietly passed, and the idea appears moribund.

By the late 1990s, Latin America was experiencing regional economic growth that averaged a healthy 3% per year. In September 1998, however, uncertainty over the Russian ruble caused a chain-reaction market panic that hit the United States, the major Asian stock markets, and then Brazil, Argentina and Mexico. The crisis worsened in January 1999 when the bottom dropped out of the Brazilian stock market; its government allowed its currency, the *real*, to float, and it lost 46% of its value. The panic spread to neighboring stock markets, and for a time it appeared a massive regional recession was likely. The market crisis coincided with a dramatic drop in the world market price of petroleum, which affected the economies of Venezuela, Ecuador and Mexico. The situation eventually stabilized.

As with the trend toward democracy, however, the dramatic improvement in the Latin American economy has had its negative aspects, as well as nagging, unremedied problems: the continued gap between the very wealthy and the very poor; endemic corruption; environmental pollution; overpopulation; and an underground economy based on the illegal traffic of drugs.

According to a report released in September 1996 by the U.N. Economic Commission for Latin America and the Caribbean, one third of Latin Americans lived in poverty and 18 percent of them lived in *dire* poverty, earning less than $1 a day. Even in comparatively affluent countries such as Uruguay, the wealthiest 10 percent of the population had access to 15 times the resources of the poorest 10 percent; in Honduras and Peru, the figure was 80 times.

In these emerging democracies, however, these destitute masses do have access now to something else—the ballot box. Latin America may be seeing a rebirth of the now-discredited movements of the left, with their siren song of help for the underprivileged. The election of Chávez in Venezuela in 1998 was followed by the elections of such populists as da Silva in Brazil and Lucio Gutiérrez in Ecuador in 2002, of Kirchner in Argentina in 2003 and of Tabaré Vásquez in Uruguay in 2004.

Such newly industrialized countries as Mexico, Argentina, Brazil and Chile are learning quickly what it took the United States and other developed economies more than a century to discover: that industrialization carries an expensive environmental price tag. The air pollution in Mexico City, Santiago and São Paulo is notorious, as well as a serious health hazard. Rivers and coastlines have become dumping grounds for the toxic waste byproducts of heavy industry. Brazil, meanwhile, only began to take action in 1998 to slow the destruction of its rain forests in the name of agriculture, an environmental rape that had raised international concerns for its exacerbation of global warming. Yet, in most of these still-underprivileged countries, this is a price they have been willing to pay in order to provide jobs for growing urban populations. But unless some solutions are found soon, those who are "lucky" enough to find work in the major cities may find that they have condemned themselves and their children to early graves.

Unchecked population growth has been problematical in countries ranging from industrial giants such as Mexico and Brazil to desperately poor agrarian Haiti. Too often social scientists in developed countries, many of whom apparently never visit Latin America, are too quick to single out the Roman Catholic Church's ban on contraception as the primary culprit. Although this is a factor, one would find that the urban middle classes in Latin America are just as willing to practice birth control in defiance of the pope as Roman Catholics in North America or Europe. Most of the population growth occurs in the lower economic strata, but not because they are more devout Catholics.

There are long-standing cultural factors at play as well. The *macho* ethic holds that the number of children a man sires is an outward manifestation of his virility, his very manhood. Moreover, as is the case in Africa and Asia, poor Latin Americans dependent upon agriculture for their existence see children as future fieldhands, someone to help them carry their burdens as they themselves age. Also, it is believed, a large brood is one way to guarantee security for one's old age. Such traditions cannot be overcome by government decree, but until some way is found to ensure that the number of new job-seekers does not exceed supply, Latin America's newly affluent cities will continue to be ringed by slums populated by those with high expectations, waiting their turn for a better life that may never come.

The drug trade has created in some areas the illusion of prosperity. In reality, it has brought back the monocultural dependence of poor farmers on a single cash crop. In the cities, it has brought fabulous wealth to a tiny cadre of drug lords, wealth which has trickled down in droplets to the veritable army of lab processors, transporters, security personnel and others who have been enticed away from legitimate pursuits by the promise of quick, if venal, wealth.

It has been estimated that the Rodríguez Orijuela brothers, Gilberto and Miguel, the leaders of the Cali Cartel of Colombia who were extradited to the United States in 2004, are worth $250 billion. But the wealth drugs generate is illusionary—there is so much of it there is nothing left on which to spend it. Further, the real economies within which the drug trade operates cannot officially incorporate it. Governments cannot tax billions in revenue that is not legal and not claimed. Moreover, it proves a drain on the economy because governments must spend millions on enforcement that proves futile, while the very governmental institutions that seek vainly to bring this illicit industry to bay are themselves corrupted from the top down by the drug barons.

The futility is exacerbated by the rather naive counter-narcotics policies of the consuming countries of the north. For years the hope has been that somehow impoverished peasants can be made to see that they are endangering lives in Los Angeles or Chicago and that they can be persuaded to substitute cultivating coca with another cash crop—whose yield per hectare may be one tenth as much. Unless the insatiable demand for narcotics can be curbed in the consuming countries, there will be poor Latin Americans willing to run the risks to cultivate, process and transport drugs.

Technological Emergence

Yet another stereotype of Latin America, persistently reinforced by Hollywood, is of a backward region with muddy streets and antiquated technology. In the rural areas, that is still too often the case. But in the major cities, the economic boom has led inevitably to investment in modernizing the technological infrastructures. The impetus is the very essence of free-market capitalism: the necessity to compete. Visitors to even the poorer capital cities of most Latin American capitals will find computers literally everywhere, in hotels, banks, newspapers, universities and even small businesses. To ignore computerization is to fall behind the competition.

The communications revolution also has pervaded Latin America. For example, the tallest structure on the Santiago, Chile, skyline, just two blocks from the Moneda (presidential) Palace along Avenida Bernardo O'Higgins, is the Entel Tower, bristling with antennas and satellite dishes linking Santiago with the interior and with the rest of the world. Guests at even mid-priced hotels in a country like Guatemala may be surprised to find CNN and HBO on their television sets. Again, competition demands this.

As is the case in developed countries, the technological revolution has been an upward spiral, with innovation breeding innovation. Some of these countries, such as Brazil and Chile, now manufacture their own computer hardware and software. Free–trade agreements facilitate the transfer of technology across international boundaries.

If there is a negative picture at all in the technological emergence of Latin America, it is that there is still a long way to go. If public investment is made in upgrading public transportation, perhaps with modern subway systems such as Santiago's, it could help lessen the air pollution crises in the capital cities; as bad as Santiago's air quality is, it would be worse if the subway had not supplanted hundreds of buses belching oily exhaust from the combustion of cheap fuel. Despite advances in medical technology, more funds need to be invested in that sector to acquire state–of–the–art equipment. If the current economic expansion continues, it is inevitable that technological expansion will continue in its wake.

Cultural Growth and Projection

There is no more a "Latin American culture" than there is a homogenous U.S. or European culture. Which music, for example, is indicative of U.S. culture: jazz, blues, country-western, bluegrass, rock 'n' roll, rap, or grunge rock? The answer, of course, is all of the above. Is there a typically European art, literary style, music, architecture, fashion or cuisine? They vary, of course, from country to country. Latin American culture—or better described, cultures—also are regionalized.

The stereotype of the Latin American as a devout Catholic *mestizo* who speaks Spanish, wears white *campesino* cotton clothing, listens to mariachi music and eats spicy food is as far from reality as the Latin American stereotype of the "typical" gringo as a rich, Anglo-Saxon Protestant who wears Calvin Klein jeans, listens to rock and eats nothing but steak or hamburgers. (All right, maybe there's a kernel of truth to the rock and hamburger part.)

The North American view of Latin America understandably has been geographically influenced by neighboring Mexico. As Don Podesta of the *Washington Post* wrote a few years ago, Mexico is "a prism through which all Latin culture is viewed." But it is a woefully distorted view. In reality, the majority of the South American population are Portuguese-speaking Brazilians. Chile has a Lutheran minority of more than 10% stemming from German immigration in the 19th century, while nearly 40% of Guatemalans are converts to evangelical Protestantism. Mariachi music is no more, nor less, representative of Latin America than are Argentina's tango, Brazil's samba, the salsa of the Caribbean countries, the flute music of the Andean highlands, Chile's *huaso* music or the harp–based folk music of Paraguay. An Argentine accustomed to his bland meat–and–pasta diet would probably gag on chili-pepper-laced *ceviche*, a concoction of raw fish and lime juice peculiar to the Pacific coast countries.

Ethnically, the Hispanic colonies evolved far differently from their counterparts in North America, or for that matter, in Brazil. The English colonizers pushed the Indian tribes back beyond the ever-expanding frontier, or simply extermi-

nated them, while for manual labor in the fields they imported black slaves from West Africa. The Portuguese followed a roughly similar policy in Brazil. The Spanish, meanwhile, enslaved the Indian populations they found there, pressing them into service in the mines and on the *haciendas*. But while miscegenation was limited between the English on the one hand and the Indians and black slaves on the other, it was widespread in Brazil and the Spanish colonies, producing a mixed race of *mestizos* in the Hispanic realm, and of *mulattos* in Brazil.

This ethnic mosaic was not woven evenly, however, which resulted in the cultural discreteness of today. The Argentines, like their counterparts in the United States, followed a shameless policy of genocide against the indigenous inhabitants, with the result that its culture is preponderantly Caucasian-European. So is that of Costa Rica, but there the white settlers found the land largely uninhabited. In Guatemala, Peru and Bolivia, the undiluted Indian races are in the majority. Perhaps the most diversified cultural tapestry is that of Panama, where apart from whites, *mestizos* and Indians there are the descendants of black laborers brought from the Caribbean early in this century to construct the canal, and Orientals who came later.

Just as the Anglo-Saxon stereotype is fading in the United States, so is the Hispanic stereotype no longer *apropriado* in Latin America, and for the same reason: successive waves of massive immigration beginning in the late 19th century and continuing to the present. Roughly half of all Argentines, for example, are of Italian lineage, descendants of migrant farm-

. . . while silvered dolphins decorate the fountain in a flower–filled patio in mid–town Port–of–Spain, Trinidad

Latin America Today

workers who came to harvest grapes because of the reversed seasons and decided to stay. Germans, British and other Europeans also flocked to Argentina, Uruguay and Chile, as did European Jews seeking escape from persecution. Spanish Republicans seeking refuge after their defeat in the 1936–1939 civil war settled throughout the region.

Most Latin American countries also have unassimilated colonies of Arabs, Gypsies, blacks, and Orientals. To underscore just how much of a melting pot Latin America has become, we have only to consider the surnames of some of the recent elected presidents in more than one half of the former Spanish colonies: Sanguinetti in Uruguay (Italian); Fujimori in Peru (Japanese); Aylwin in Chile (Welsh); Frei in Chile (Swiss); Wasmosy in Paraguay (Hungarian); Menem in Argentina, Bucaram and Mahaud in Ecuador and Saca in El Salvador (Arab); Fox in Mexico (English), Kirchner in Argentina (German) and Berger in Guatemala (Belgian). By contrast, of its 42 presidents, the United States has had but six without Anglo-Saxon surnames: Van Buren and the two Roosevelts (Dutch), Kennedy and Reagan (Irish) and Eisenhower (German).

Language, religion and ethnicity may be the roots of a culture, but its flowers are thoughts, ideas and expressions. In this regard, Latin America represents a veritable cultural nursery, one that finally has begun achieving recognition from the rest of the world. To be sure, U.S. and European cultural influences are much in evidence, ranging from Coca-Cola, McDonald's and Calvin Klein to the *plan europeo* practiced by the hotels and the architecture that makes cities like Buenos Aires, Rio de Janeiro and Santiago appear like New World copies of Madrid, Milan or Lisbon. The dependency theorists who warned that Latin America was economically subjugated by the United States also wrung their hands over perceived U.S. cultural intrusion; for some reason, they never seemed threatened by European influences. However, despite Coca-Cola, McDonald's, Calvin Klein, Rambo, rock music and the ubiquitous "I Love Lucy" reruns, the *dependentistas* wasted a great deal of bile for nothing. The Latin American cultures not only were not supplanted, Latin American art, music, literature, cinema and television have grown into distinctive genres in their own right, and these cultural expressions have been projected to the developed world.

Five Latin Americans have received the Nobel Prize for Literature: Gabriela Mistral of Chile (1945), Miguel Angel Asturias of Guatemala (1967), Pablo Neruda of Chile (1971), Gabriel García Márquez of Colombia (1982), and Octavio Paz of Mexico (1990), all of whose works have been translated into several languages.

Because Latin American art, music, literature and cinema are so individualistic according to nation, they are described more fully under the "Culture" section of each nation contained in this book.

Latin American television development lagged well behind that of the United States and Europe, and because of its higher price tag it was usually the governments that led the way. This made television, like radio, an important political tool and a pawn in the quest for power. An exception was in Chile, where the first three stations were licensed to major universities. In recent years, state–owned television stations have yielded increasingly to privatization; in some countries, as in Britain, privately owned stations compete with the government station. In its early days, television programming in Latin America was crude, unreliable and heavily dependent on translated imported programs from the United States, which were cheaper than producing programs locally. This reality lent grist to the argument of the cultural dependency theorists.

That has changed dramatically since the 1970s, however, with Mexico, Brazil, Argentina, Venezuela, Colombia and Chile all producing that uniquely Latin American soap opera, the *telenovela*, both for domestic consumption and for export. Variety shows are reminiscent of those of the United States in the 1950s and 1960s. One that reaches a hemispheric audience is *Sábado Gigante*, transmitted every Saturday from Miami but emceed by a Chilean, Mario Krutzberger, better known by the stage name Don Francisco.

Latin America has embraced U.S.-style sitcoms and news magazine shows, and some U.S. imports are still in evidence, but the dependency theorists' fears that they would outpace demand for programs produced in the native language have not been realized.

Looking Forward . . .

In attempting to digest this description of the political, economic, technological and cultural realities of Latin America today, one must invariably return to the analogous glass that is half full rather than half empty. Much cheer can be taken from the advances that have been made, while the remaining shortcomings must be acknowledged and addressed.

Another indicator of hope is Latin America's seeming abandonment of its policy of paranoia vis-à-vis its neighbor to the north. Granted, the United States did much to warrant paranoia with its policy of gunboat diplomacy and CIA-sponsored intrigue. A sardonic joke underscored the Latin American view of the United States: Why are there never military coups in the United States? Because they don't have an American Embassy!

The most recent U.S. intervention in the region, in Haiti in 1994, however well intentioned it may have been, inevitably raised eyebrows anew in Latin American capitals. For that reason, virtually all Latin American governments opposed in principle the U.S. invasion of far-off Iraq in 2003. Still, the United States is not seen quite as the bogeyman it once was, and country after country has elected presidents who earned undergraduate or graduate degrees in the United States, something that is no longer a political stigma.

Meanwhile, the relationship of old that bordered on praetorianism has yielded to one of a more equitable partnership in terms of trade. The stubborn resistance of Venezuela, Brazil and Argentina to the FTAA underscores the region's growing independence.

Another encouraging sign of growing Latin American independence from the United States since the advent of democracy has been the trend toward regional cooperation and integration. In 1986, 19 democratic countries established the so-called Rio Group—17 of the Spanish-speaking republics (less Cuba), Brazil and Guyana. Unlike the Organization of American States (see U.S.-Latin American Relations), the United States is not a signatory. The Rio Group was created to promote democracy within the region, but its annual summits, the most recent of which took place in Rio de Janeiro in November 2004, have provided the heads of state

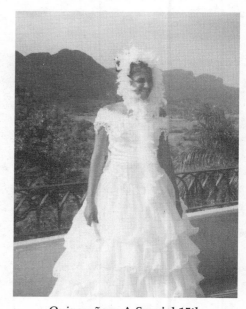

Quinceañera, **A Special 15th birthday celebration**

Photo by Gary Seldomridge

of these nations with an opportunity to discuss issues of mutual concern, including all those listed in the previous paragraph plus regional trade, drug trafficking, terrorism and political unrest. Education and the troubling situation in Haiti—which is not a member of the group—dominated the Rio summit in 2004. Guyana will host the next summit.

An even newer organization, the South American Community of Nations, was established in Cuzco, Peru, on December 8, 2004. The presidents of six countries and foreign ministers of six others signed the accord: the 10 Spanish- or Portuguese-speaking countries of South America, plus Guyana and Suriname. The group was the outgrowth of talks between South America's two free-trade blocs, *Mercosur* and the Andean Pact, to create a continent-wide free-trade zone, which has a combined gross domestic product of about $1 trillion. The summit did not set a timetable, however. The presidents of Brazil and Peru also announced their countries would collaborate to construct the first east-west highway across the continent from ocean to ocean, which they said would further integration even more. The new community is largely the brainchild of Brazilian President da Silva. Citing the European Union as a model, da Silva said he envisions, eventually, a unified continent with a central government, one foreign policy and a common currency.

Other issues must be addressed, however, if Latin America is to continue to develop democratically, socially and economically. Mob rule to force out duly elected presidents must be eschewed. Otherwise, political anarchy will lead to the type of instability that invites a return to authoritarianism. Press freedom must be respected as an independent check on would-be autocrats. Environmental pollution, that inevitable by-product of development, threatens the health of the next generation. Institutionalized corruption is still a political and economic leech on the lifeblood of almost all the countries of the region. Hygiene and health care still lag far behind those of the developed world. Most importantly, that next generation needs to be provided with better education. Latin America continues to trail the developed world and the emerging countries of Asia in educational quality. The next generation must be more than merely literate; it must join the computer age.

The hemisphere's greatest remaining blight, the anachronistic totalitarian system in Cuba, must inevitably acquiesce to the weight of history. A false hope was raised with Pope John Paul II's historic visit to Cuba in January 1998, an event that Castro marked by allowing a revival of religious expression and by releasing some of his political prisoners. Alas, since then, Castro has continued to imprison dissenters—78 alone in the crackdown of March and April 2003, bringing the total to more than 300—and to resist international calls for reform. In response to the "Varela Project," a petition signed by 11,000 courageous dissenters in 2002 that called for a referendum on free elections and freedom of expression, Castro responded with a "petition" of his own, signed by a suspicious 8.2 million people, for a constitutional amendment that would make his dogmatic Marxist system "untouchable." The National Assembly dutifully passed this constitutional amendment-to-outlaw-constitutional amendments, 557-0. Castro, who turned 79 in August 2005, thus threw down his gauntlet before the domestic and international chorus for reform, raising the specter of a violent struggle for power when he finally dies.

The overall trend in Latin America toward greater political freedom, economic affluence, technological expansion, cultural individuality and regional integration is evident. There have inevitably been setbacks. There will be more. But for the moment, Latin America appears to be investing in its future, and its stock is clearly on the rise.

Robert T. Buckman
Lafayette, Louisiana, June 2005

The home of Nobel Laureate Pablo Neruda (1904–73) at Isla Negra, Chile, is now a museum visted by tens of thousands of Chilean and foreign visitors a year. Neruda, whose poetry has been translated into several languages, was one of five Latin Americans to have won the Nobel Prize in Literature.

Photo by the author

The Early Americans

THE GEOGRAPHICAL FACTOR

The development of few civilizations have been so influenced by geographical factors as those in Latin America. Contrary to long held beliefs, the land of Central and South America is neither young nor generally fertile. Old and trampled by several civilizations, large territories had already been abandoned by the Indians, even before the arrival of the Spaniards. The Mayas probably exhausted their initial homeland, and the Incas called the vast desert regions between Peru and Chile "the land of hunger and death." Furthermore, the continent had few and scattered ports and is internally divided by rugged mountains, jungles, turbulent rivers and arid zones, which constitute formidable obstacles for communication or exploitation of natural resources.

Thus, since pre–Columbian times, human societies developed in sort of isolated clusters having little contact with other communities. The Spanish policy of building cities as centers of political power increased this basic pattern of concentration and regionalism. Consequently, once the unifying authority of the Spanish king collapsed, it was impossible to keep all those remote and distant cities under a common authority. Immediately, almost every important urban center felt capable of demanding and asserting its own independence.

Geography not only contributed to this fragmentation, but also greatly determined the acceleration of two negative social trends which continue to hinder Latin American progress: (1) the abnormal growth of cities, especially capitals, constantly attracting masses of impoverished peasants—Mexico City's population jumped from less than 5 million in 1963 to 13.1 million in 2000—and (2) the lack of balance in the national population distribution. In almost every Latin country, the population is concentrated in one–third to one–half of its national territory, leaving large zones almost totally uninhabited. Such conditions make the exploitation of the hinterland's resources a difficult and costly enterprise.

Indian Civilizations

When the Spaniards and other Europeans reached the New World, they found the native Americans in various stages of cultural development. Thinly scattered nomadic tribes of hunters and fishermen who also practiced simple farming populated much of the region. In contrast, three groups of natives—the Mayas, the Aztecs and the Incas—developed comparatively sophisticated and complex civilizations. They constructed large cities with imposing architectural styling, organized empires, acquired a knowledge of mathematics and astronomy and worked in precious stones and metals. The majority of these Indian civilizations had a sort of fatalistic concept of life and the universe; their worship halls and temples were full of terrifying gods who incessantly demanded sacrifices, usually human. Their societies were stratified by class division and were based more on communal interest and units than on individual achievements. Furthermore, vast distances and geographical obstacles hindered enlightening inter–cultural relations, while the absence of horses, cows or any pack animals limited their economic expansion or mass mobility. Perhaps because of such limitations, only one of these civilizations, the Mayas, developed some form of primitive writing, while none discovered the practical use of the wheel. In spite of intense research by scientists and archaeologists, we don't have yet a clear picture of the intricate aspects of the social systems and collective beliefs of pre–Columbian Indian society. Many questions remain to be answered.

The Mayas (Guatemala, Mexico, Belize, Honduras, El Salvador)

As the most advanced and sophisticated of the early American civilizations, Mayan culture flourished for more than 1,000 years, reaching the peak of its development in the 7th and 8th centuries A.D. Mayan life was sustained by a single basic crop: corn, which grew in such abundance that it allowed them time to engage in a multitude of activities other than raising food, thus raising their lifestyles above that of the other Indian societies which remained tied to the soil in order simply to exist. Apparently the Mayas lived mostly in independent city states, tied together by an extensive road system and a common culture. A warlike people, the Mayas placed most political power in the hands of an extended royal family and priests. Mayan religion was based on the worship of many gods, but the practice declined with the growing sophistication of the society. Initially, religious ceremonies called for frequent human sacrifices. Art and architecture were not greatly inferior to that of Europe at the time. As pioneers in the use of mathematics and astronomy, the Mayas refined an advanced calendar as early as the 4th century B.C. They also devised the mathematical concept of *zero* and developed a highly complex form of writing based on hieroglyphics (picture writing) which until today remains partially undeciphered.

Among the greatest achievements of the Mayas was art, including sculpture, pottery and textiles. Foremost was architec-

ture. Major reminders of the Mayan civilization survive today in the form of thousands of monumental temples, soaring pyramids and majestic palaces. Many of these impressive structures have been discovered only recently, enveloped in the lush, tropical jungles of Central America and southern Mexico. These vestiges of the past, however, have yet to reveal why the Mayas suddenly abandoned their great cities long before the arrival of the Spaniards. Was it due to massive crop failure? Was it pestilence? Military defeat? Rebellion by slaves? The answer to this question is slowly being revealed—it probably involved the split-up of a large empire because of rivalries, followed by succession of unnumbered small states each with its own fortification and the fascination of the people with constant warfare. The techniques of siege were probably perfected, and they killed each other off to an extent that those remaining simply disappeared into the thick foliage to live as primitives.

The Aztecs (Mexico)

When Hernán Cortés landed on the Mexican coast in 1519, the Aztec empire

Aztec goddess *Coatlicue*

was at the very height of its power and development. Assimilating the knowledge and achievements of previous civilizations such as the Olmecs and the Toltecs, the Aztecs developed into a harsh and efficient military society which allowed them to conquer all of central Mexico from the Atlantic to the Pacific. This brutal form of domination provoked constant rebellions among the tribes they subjugated, from whom they extracted slaves and human victims for sacrifice to their gods. In one especially dry season, Montezuma I, claiming that "the gods are thirsty," sacrificed 20,000 human beings on Aztec altars.

The Aztec social system rested on a rigid class structure with most manual work being performed by slaves captured during military campaigns. The economy was based on corn. Aztec architecture was impressive and their capital city of Tenochtitlán, now the site of Mexico City, was described by the conquering Spaniards as being equal to any in Europe. Although not as advanced as the Mayas had been in the use of science, mathematics or writing, the Aztecs did develop a more cohesive empire, even though it was based on force. The widespread resentment among enslaved neighboring groups was shrewdly exploited by Cortés to topple the Aztec empire.

Incas (Peru, Ecuador, Bolivia)

The empire carved out of the rugged Andes by the Incas reached its greatest level of development about a century before the arrival of the Spaniards. Through conquest of weaker Indian tribes in the region, the Incas expanded their realm from Peru through southern Colombia, Ecuador and Bolivia, and northern Chile—

Mayan ruins at Tikal, Guatemala

The Early Americans

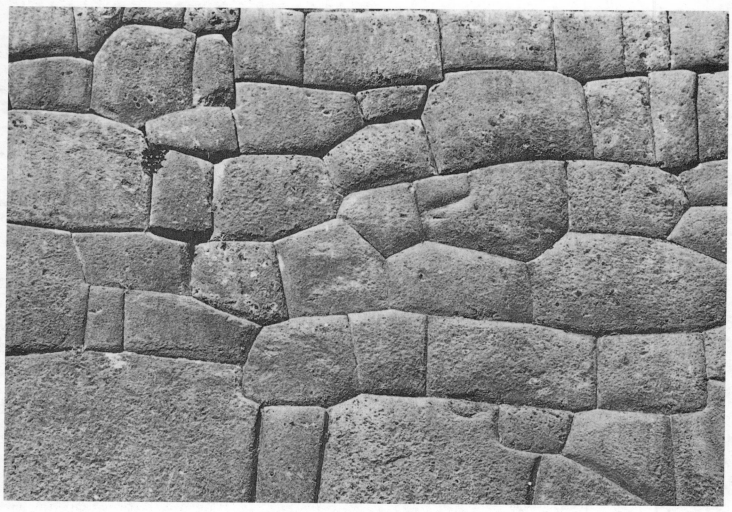

Detail of an Inca stone wall in Cuzco, Peru

a combined area of more than 350,000 square miles. Facilitated by an efficient administrative command, a courier communications network and an impressive road system rivaling that of the Roman Empire, the Incas were able to weave their vast domain into the most highly organized and efficient civilization of all the native Americans.

At the head of the entire system was the ruling god–emperor called Inca. Under him was a highly structured noble class and priests, followed by lower level officials. The rigid chain of command permeated every corner of the empire. The Incas integrated newly conquered tribes into the realm by imposing a single language, *Quechua,* religion and social structure. Except for the highly rigid caste system of the ruling elite, the Inca state came close to being a totalitarian socialist state. All property was owned by the state and all work was organized on a communal basis. Through a system called "mita" (which the Spaniards later immediately

adopted in the region) all members of the lower classes were obliged to work free for the empire for a period of four months every year. In return, the empire provided for the needs of its citizens. The result was a rather dull life for the masses—with little incentive, capability or effort to rebel.

The heart of the empire was the capital of Cuzco (literally "navel" in Quechua). A magnificent city by almost any standard, Cuzco glistened with enormous palaces and temples (many of which were lavishly decorated with gold) and other imposing dwellings which housed the elite. Even today, some of these structures are still in use, having withstood for centuries the abuses of man and the elements.

Although the Incas were less developed than the Mayas in the skills of writing, mathematics and astronomy, they surpassed the Mayas in architecture, water works, stonework and engineering. Indeed, some lengthy Inca suspension bridges were found when the Europeans reached the area and remained in use un-

til the middle of the 19th century. Inca systems of irrigation, pottery, textiles, medicines and even surgical techniques were remarkable. The Incas' greatest gift to the world, however, was the potato, which in time would save tens of thousands of Europeans from starvation. Despite its vast power, the Inca empire quickly fell to the *conquistadores.* The reasons for the sudden collapse of America's greatest Indian civilization were numerous: the Spaniards possessed superiority in firearms, employed advanced military tactics, exploited the advantage of horses and were relentlessly driven onward by the lure of gold. In contrast, the Inca empire was mortally weakened by a rigid social system in which the vital administrative structure was paralyzed once the top Inca was captured. In addition, a devastating war of succession between two royal Inca brothers had left the empire exhausted and divided. As a result, the Incas fell easy prey to a band of only 184 conquerors led by a cunning Francisco Pizarro.

The Early Americans

Major Native Cultures About 1500

Other Indian civilizations that reached a high level of development were the Chibchas of northern Colombia and the Pueblo Indians of New Mexico. Indeed, the 16th century Spanish conquerors of Latin America—in contrast to the 17th century English, French and Dutch settlers in North America—encountered civilized natives whose social level was not greatly inferior to their own.

The impact of the conquest destroyed the Indian civilizations and looted their priceless treasures. To this was added the seizure of their valuable lands, forced labor and the spread of diseases unknown to the Indians, which decimated their population. The Spanish intermarried with the women of the former Indian ruling classes and built their empire on the social and economic foundations of the vanquished civilizations. Unsuited to plantation labor, especially in the tropics, the Indians were replaced by slaves imported from Africa and indentured laborers from Asia.

One of the most impressive and lasting achievements of the Spaniards was the conversion of the Indians to Catholicism. Devoted missionaries, still imbued with the religious fervor of the "glorious crusade" which had expelled the Arabs from Spain, risked their lives to preach the new faith among the Indians, learned their languages and defended them from the greed of the *conquistadores* and even the Spanish crown. Thanks to their examples and sacrifices, Catholic religion, or at least some variation of Catholicism, penetrated deeply among the Indian masses, transforming the Church into a powerful and influential institution in Latin America from the colonial period; its influence is

waning as Indians migrate to the larger cities.

Scattered remnants of Indian civilization retreated from Spanish influence to the mountains of Guatemala, Ecuador, Peru and Bolivia, while the majority remained under Spanish rule. Until recent times, many of the Indians have succeeded in preserving their ancient communal life and customs. Today, the Quechua–speaking Indians still number some 6 million in Bolivia and 2 million in Ecuador. Although their living conditions have scarcely improved since Pizarro's time, Andean Indians have remained detached and suspicious of meager government efforts to incorporate these survivors of the Inca Empire into a modern social and economic structure.

Efforts to modernize traditional Indian lifestyles have also been painfully slow in Central America and Mexico. In Guatemala, the descendants of the Mayas have largely continued to cling to their traditional customs despite government programs to encourage change. Even in Mexico, the most *mestizo* country in Latin America, many of Aztec and Mayan ancestry, particularly in the southern area, still have only marginal contact with the

20th century—even though modernization of Indian lifestyles has been a nominal objective of the Mexican government.

The process of social change has accelerated since World War II with the aid of modern communications—particularly the transistor radio—which have helped to penetrate the isolation that has allowed outmoded social, economic and political conditions to persist in the remote hinterlands.

Recently some Latin American governments, particularly those of Mexico and Peru, have begun to show an increasing appreciation of the contributions and heritage of the early American civilizations. This growing interest has not been without cost. The rising appeal for Indian art has led to large–scale looting of ancient monuments and graves. In Central America and in the Andes, art thieves have stolen priceless stonework, jewelry and pottery—irreparably damaging some of it in the process—in an effort to satisfy the modern demand for genuine ancient art. In that sense, today's art thieves are continuing the same traditions of the *conquistadores* who plundered the early American Indian civilizations.

The ruins of Machu Picchu, the remote mountainous retreat of the Inca rulers, so well hidden that it was not until discovered in 1911.

15

Conquest, Colonization, and the Challenge of Independence

Cortés and the ambassadors of Moctezuma

Cortés began his conquest of Mexico in 1519; Pizarro invaded Peru in 1531 and Quesada and others began the conquest of Colombia in 1536. The Spaniards' superiority in weaponry and cavalry does not fully explain the victory of so few over so many. The decisive factor was the different character of the contending armies. Based on individual initiative, the Spanish regiments could face and fight formidable odds no matter what the losses. Based on strict authority and command, the Indian armies usually disintegrated when the general or high priest was captured or killed. In the battle of Otumba, Cortés had no gunpowder and only sixteen horsemen, while the Aztecs were 20,000 strong. When a desperate Spanish charge killed the Aztec commander, the Indian army remained paralyzed while Cortés and his small group marched toward the safety of Tlaxcala, the capital of a powerful Indian tribe which had become Cortés' ally.

The conquest and colonization of Brazil followed a different pattern. By the Treaty of Tordesillas of 1494, Spain and Portugal divided South America between them along the 45th Meridian—Spain to the west, Portugal to the east. As early as April 22, 1500, Admiral Pedro Alvares Cabral established Portugal's authority over the region, but as further explorations found no traces of gold and silver, and since Portugal was then fully engaged in its profitable Asian trade, Brazil received scant attention. For many years, colonists occupied only a narrow belt of coastal land. The *"bandeirantes,"* rough adventurers and *mestizos* organized in groups called "bandeiras," were the ones who in their search for Indians and wealth slowly opened the interior of Brazil, pushing the nomadic Indian tribes into further remote areas. Portugal's declining Asian trade ultimately stimulated emigration to Brazil. In 1549, after the appointment of the first royal governors, a better system of land distribution was established and the Jesuits opened their first schools.

The strategic position and potential of Brazil attracted foreign attacks. French and Dutch attempts to hold Brazilian territories failed, however, and by 1645 the expanding colony was under Portugal's firm control. Initially sugar production flourished in the north, but the discovery of gold in what is today the state of Minas Gerais made the south the economic and political center of the colony, a position consolidated by subsequent discoveries of diamonds and precious stones. At the beginning of the 19th century, Brazil was a growing but still basically rural colony, with a vast and untouched hinterland.

During the colonial period, Spain created a highly centralized government, with most power concentrated in the monarch, and an internal balance of power which functioned remarkably well for three centuries. The region was divided into four viceroyalties: New Spain (capital, Mexico City), New Granada (capital, Bogotá), Peru (capital, Lima), and Rio de la Plata (capital, Buenos Aires). Several captains–general ruled less important territories. All judicial matters were dealt with by the *audiencias,* and the designation of ecclesiastical posts remained in the king's hands. At the end of his term, every viceroy had to submit to a *juicio de residencia,* a sort of trial where everyone could accuse him of improprieties or abuses of power. Although initially some authority had been granted to city councils *(cabildos),* eventually their autonomy was greatly reduced by royal control. Conse-

Conquest, Colonization, and the Challenge of Independence

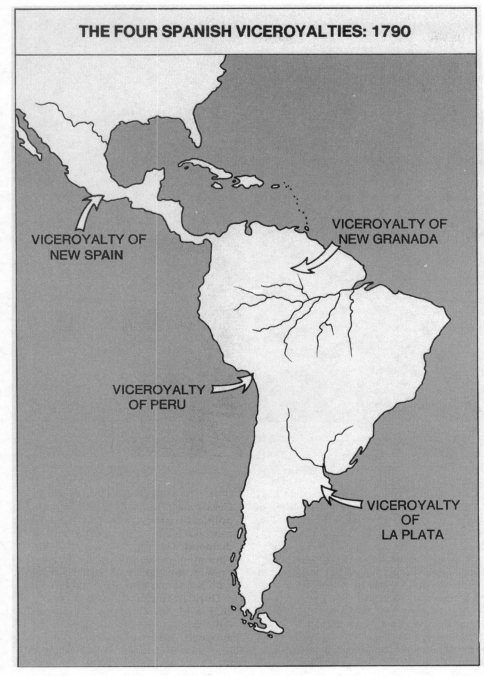

THE FOUR SPANISH VICEROYALTIES: 1790

VICEROYALTY OF
NEW SPAIN

VICEROYALTY OF
NEW GRANADA

VICEROYALTY
OF PERU

VICEROYALTY
OF
LA PLATA

oles to be treated as equals and to share political power intensified the friction between the two groups. Aware of Spain's and Portugal's decline as European powers, the creoles turned to France for cultural guidance.

Thus, the French Revolution had more impact in Latin America than did the American one. In Haiti, the division of the French white ruling elite brought about by France's political turmoil, sparked a rebellion of the black slaves under Toussaint L'Overture, which after a bloody and devastating war, ended with the liberation of the island. In the rest of Latin America, though, the creoles were far from being *Jacobins* (revolutionaries). A minority sympathized with the Declaration of Human Rights, but the majority was aware of the dangers which an open rebellion against Spain and Portugal could bring. Fearful of the surrounding masses of Indians and *mestizos*, most of the creoles wanted reforms, not revolution. Only the collapse of the Iberian monarchies could prompt them into action. In 1808 Napoleon gave them the opportunity. Invading the Iberian peninsula, he imprisoned the Spanish king and forced the Braganças, Portugal's royal family, to escape to Rio de Janeiro. Confronted with this political crisis, the creoles were forced to act.

Independence and Its Aftermath

While the Spanish people rebelled against Napoleonic armies, and the Brazilians proudly received their sovereigns, Hispanoamericans were left in a political vacuum. Their initial reaction was to swear fidelity to Ferdinand, the captured Spanish king. Soon, however, *they* realized their power. Deprived of legitimacy and without hope of receiving reinforcements from

quently, the colonies gained little experience in self–government or administration of public affairs.

The Church was in charge of education, but private religious orders, especially the Jesuits, made determined efforts to modernize learning. Nevertheless, a humanistic, non–scientific type of education became traditional in Ibero–America. Under the patronage of the Church and the Crown, architecture and schools of painting flourished, and the Baroque style, perfectly suited to dazzle the masses, became dominant in all artistic expression. By the middle of the 18th century, while Brazil,

whose development was much slower, had only scattered rural towns, Hispanic America displayed important cities like Mexico and Lima, impressive cathedrals, a few universities and even famous writers like Sor Juana Inés de la Cruz and Carlos de Siguenza y Gongora.

At the beginning of the 18th century, the ruling elite became increasingly divided between the *criollos*, or creoles (those born in America) and the *peninsulares* (mainly functionaries recently arrived from Spain or Portugal). The creoles generally controlled the land, the *peninsulares* wielded political power. The aspiration of the cre-

Cathedral of Cuzco, built about 1535

Conquest, Colonization, and the Challenge of Independence

General José de San Martín proclaims Peru's independence, July 1821

Spain, colonial authorities were practically paralyzed. By 1810 the creoles had moved from tentative autonomy to open independence. Significantly, Mexico and Peru, the two viceroyalties where Indian population was in greater proportion, remained under Spanish control. Immediately, regionalism and individualism began to fragment colonial unity. In the principal cities of the continent, hastily formed governments adopted republican constitutions and strove to extend their shaky authority over the surrounding territories.

In 1814, Napoleon's defeat brought absolutist Ferdinand back to the Spanish throne. The prestige of the restored king, and some military reinforcements, gave the colonial authorities the upper hand. By 1816, with the exception of Buenos Aires, including the Viceroyalty of Rio de la Plata, Spanish rule had been reestablished over most of the empire. Absolutism, however, could no longer appeal to the creoles. Furthermore, Spain's political troubles had not ended: in 1820 a poorly equipped army destined to fight in America rebelled against the king, occupied Madrid and imposed a liberal constitution. In the meantime, inspired by the leadership of Simón Bolívar and José de San Martín, the creoles renewed the war. After organizing an army in Argentina,

San Martín crossed the Andes and defeated the Spaniards in Chile. Bolívar obtained similar victories in Venezuela and Colombia. After invading Peru and meeting Bolívar, San Martín abandoned the struggle and retired to France, the first in a long list of disillusioned liberators. Bolívar marched into Peru and on December 9, 1824, his best commander, Antonio José de Sucre, defeated the last royalist army in the battle of Ayacucho.

Two years before that decisive battle, with less violence, Mexico and Brazil achieved independence. In Mexico, the successive rebellions of two priests, Father Miguel Hidalgo and Father José María Morelos, backed mostly by Indians and *mestizos*, had been defeated by an alliance of conservative creoles and Spanish forces. In 1820 the proclamation of a liberal constitution in Spain induced those conservative allies to seek independence. Their instrument was a creole army officer, Agustín de Iturbide, whose mission was to defeat the remnant republican guerrillas and to proclaim a conservative empire. Instead, Iturbide gained popularity by appealing to *all* factions, entered Mexico City in triumph and was proclaimed Emperor Agustín I. In Brazil, Portugal's liberal revolution produced similar consequences. The new government in Lisbon recalled

the king, and tried to reduce Brazil back to a colonial status. Before departing Brazil, the king designated his son Pedro as regent and gave him sound advice: if the Brazilians want independence, don't *oppose* them, *lead* them. Shortly after his father's departure Pedro received a peremptory summons from the Lisbon parliament. Encouraged and supported by the Brazilians, he refused to go. When Portugal sent him a rash ultimatum, Pedro answered by proclaiming the independence of Brazil. On December 1, 1822, he was crowned emperor of Brazil. By 1825, Portugal had lost its American colony and only Cuba and Puerto Rico remained under Spanish rule.

The Challenge of Independence

The first 50 years of independence were marked by political turmoil, regional confrontations and economic decline. The only exceptions to this were Chile, where a small territory and a rather homogenous population allowed the creole elite to develop a strong and stable government, and Brazil, where the monarchy provided a moderate unifying force. In the rest of Latin America, the lack of concensus on who should rule, massive ignorance, racial differences and a tradition of

18

ACTA DE INDEPENDENCIA
DEL
IMPERIO MEXICANO,
PRONUNCIADA POR SU JUNTA SOBERANA,
CONGREGADA EN LA CAPITAL DE EL, EN 28 DE SETIEMBRE DE 1821.

La Nacion Mexicana, que por trescientos años, ni ha tenido voluntad propia, ni libre el uso de la voz, sale hoy de la opresion en que ha vivido.

Los heróicos esfuerzos de sus hijos han sido coronados, y está consumada la empresa, eternamente memorable, que un génio, superior a toda admiracion y elogio, amor y gloria de su patria, principió en Iguala, prosiguió y llevó al cabo, arrollando obstáculos casi insuperables.

Restituida, pues, esta parte del Septentrion al ejercicio de cuantos derechos le concedió el Autor de la naturaleza, y reconocen por inenagenables y sagrados las naciones cultas de la tierra, en libertad de constituirse del modo que mas convenga á su felicidad, y con representantes que puedan manifestar su voluntad y sus designios, comienza á hacer uso de tan preciosos dones, y declara solemnemente, por medio de la Junta Suprema del imperio, que es Nacion soberana é independiente de la antigua España, con quien, en lo sucesivo no mantendrá otra union que la de una amistad estrecha, en los términos que prescribieren los tratados: que entablará relaciones amistosas con las demas potencias, ejecutando, respecto de ellas, cuantos actos pueden y están en posesion de ejecutar las otras naciones soberanas: que va a constituirse con arreglo a las bases que en el plan de Iguala y tratado de Córdoba estableció sabiamente el primer gefe del ejército imperial de las tres garantías; y en fin, que sostendrá a todo trance, y con el sacrificio de los haberes y vidas de sus individuos, si fuere necesario, esta solemne declaracion, hecha en la capital del imperio a veintiocho de setiembre del año de mil ochocientos veintiuno, primero de la independencia mexicana.

Mexico's Declaration of Independence with Iturbide's signature, top left–hand corner

Conquest, Colonization, and the Challenge of Independence

authoritarianism, opened the doors for *caudillos*, strong leaders who temporarily commanded the loyalty of armed groups and imposed their authority over congresses and constitutions. There were *caudillos* of all sorts: enigmatic men like Gaspar Rodríguez de Francia, who closed Paraguay to foreign influences; barbarians like Bolivian Mariano Melgarejo, who "executed" his uniform for hurting his neck; ultra Catholics like Ecuadorian García Moreno and liberals like Venezuelan Gusmán Blanco. But almost all of them, even Argentine Juan Manuel de Rosas, represented more a consequence than a cause. They filled a political vacuum and, to a certain extent, contributed to uniting the nations they ruled.

Around 1870, Latin America entered a period of political stability and economic progress. In Argentina, Buenos Aires' liberal oligarchy finally imposed its authority over the provinces. Brazil became a republic in 1889 and even Mexico, a land plagued by internal dissension and foreign military interventions, attained political stability under the firm control of dictator Porfirio Díaz. Almost simultaneously, expanding European markets, especially England's, which had become the dominant economic power in Latin America, increased the demands for Latin American products, ushering in a period of growth and economic dependence.

During this period, waves of European immigrants poured into Argentina, Brazil, Chile and, in lesser numbers, into other Latin American nations. Political parties appeared, government control over the remote territories expanded thanks to better communication and the creation of professional armies, and large towns like Buenos Aires, Rio de Janeiro and Mexico became burgeoning cities.

In 1898, the United States intervened in the Cuban war of independence, defeated Spain and occupied Cuba and Puerto Rico. Cuba became "independent" in 1902, while the following year, Panama severed itself from Colombia (an event orchestrated by the United States) and signed a treaty with Washington authorizing the construction of a canal in an "American" territorial zone that was to extend from the Atlantic to the Pacific, physically dividing Panama. In spite of those ominous notes, which sent a wave of anti-imperialism throughout Latin America, at the beginning of the 20th century a mood of optimism reigned in the hemisphere.

Many of the old problems, though, remained unsolved. Unequal distribution of wealth, economic dependence, landless peasants, regional concentration of power, all hampered genuine development. Very soon, hemispheric and international events demonstrated the fragility of Latin American political stability. In 1910, the Mexican Revolution began; four years later, World War I exposed the vulnerability of the hemispheric economies; after the Russian Revolution of 1917, Communist parties appeared in almost every Latin American country. Another economic crisis shook the continent in 1919; thus, the 1920s were years of political turmoil crowned by the devastating economic crisis of the worldwide depression of 1929–1939.

Few Latin American governments survived the impact of the Great Depression. Only World War II and the emergence of

U.S. troops camp in front of the Presidential Palace in Havana, 1898

Conquest, Colonization, and the Challenge of Independence

View of the Zocalo, Mexico City's main square

the United States as a global power temporarily revitalized the economy of the hemisphere. But the period after the war also brought the economic competition of new underdeveloped nations, the decline of Latin exports, and, finally, with Cuba's revolution, the entrance of Latin America into the ideological struggle between the U.S. and the Soviet Union.

In 1961, Castro's Cuba, the first socialist regime in the Western Hemisphere, launched a continental offensive under Marxist banners. The emergence of Castroite guerrillas in almost every corner of the continent disrupted the slow but steady progress toward democracy experienced in the 1950s, when military regimes were toppled in Argentina, Venezuela, Colombia, Brazil, Guatemala and Peru. Threatened by this new enemy, Latin American armies, occasionally backed or tacitly supported by equally alarmed civilians, responded with a series of military coups, which reduced the number of democratic governments

to only four. Simultaneously, Washington initiated an ambitious "Alliance for Progress" to lessen Latin American economic and social problems, and increased its military aid to the armies. By 1975, the guerrillas had been defeated, but dictatorial regimes dominated most of the continent. Under new authoritarian economic guidelines, there was some progress toward industrialization and agricultural development. In the 1970s Latin America spent more money on education (in relative terms of national budgets) than any other region in the world.

The stormy economic winds of the early 1980s brought a sudden halt to that effort. The oil crisis, accompanied by the subsequent economic recession in the United States and Western Europe, hit Latin America hard. With astronomical external public debts, plummeting prices for its products and sources for further loans drying up, Latin America plunged into its worst economic crisis of the last five de-

cades. While austerity measures triggered popular protests in several countries, the emergence of the Marxist-oriented *Sandinista* regime in Nicaragua brought forth an oblique U.S. intervention.

By the end of the 1980s, however, military regimes had yielded to elected civilian governments in Argentina, Bolivia, Brazil, Chile, Ecuador, El Salvador, Guatemala, Honduras, Paraguay, Peru and Uruguay, while Mexico initiated political reform that led to a pluralist party system in place of one-party dominance.

Latin America entered the 21st century in the midst of impressive economic expansion that was giving rise at long last to a middle class. But it also was experiencing political growing pains as the young democracies sought to cope with perennial woes such as widespread poverty, drug trafficking and institutionalized corruption. Developing strong, viable democratic institutions for the future remains the challenge for the present.

U.S.–Latin American Relations

The history of the relationship between the United States and Latin America can be divided into five relatively distinct periods: **1820–80**, the era of the Monroe Doctrine and U.S. paternalism; **1880–1934**, the era of open U.S. imperialism, intervention, and the policies of gunboat diplomacy and the "big stick;" **1934–45**, the "Good Neighbor Policy;" **1945–90**, the Cold War, the Alliance for Progress, the Cuban and Nicaraguan revolutions and U.S. support for anti–communist dictators; and **1990– present**, the post Cold War era, the emergence of democracy in Latin America and a growing U.S.–Latin American trade partnership.

Even a brief summary of U.S.–Latin American relations usually begins by mentioning how the example of American independence stirred rebellious ideas among the creole elites in colonial Latin America. Actually, geographical, cultural and political barriers greatly reduced the impact of American "revolutionary" wars in the southern hemisphere. Only the tiny minority of cultivated creoles had some notion of what had happened in North America. Beyond the general satisfaction of witnessing the defeat of England and a vague reverence toward the figures of George Washington and Thomas Jefferson, it is difficult to find concrete traces of North American influence among the Latin American elite of the 18th century.

For a long time, the United States, following President Washington's isolationist policy, remained indifferent to the affairs of the southern neighboring nations. While Latin America struggled and achieved independence, the United States concentrated on purchasing Florida from Spain in 1821 and avoided any act or declaration that could endanger those negotiations.

In 1823, President Monroe delivered his famous message to Congress, quickly raised to the rank of a "doctrine," warning European powers that any attempt to extend their system to any portion of this hemisphere would be considered as a threat to the United States. In spite of its significance, the Monroe Doctrine was a U.S. unilateral declaration which did not imply any concern or interest in Latin American problems. When three years later Simón Bolívar, dreaming of unifying the newly born Latin American states, convened the ill-fated first Pan-American Congress, the United States reacted with little enthusiasm. The United States did not invoke the Monroe Doctrine in 1833 when England occupied the Falkland Islands claimed by Argentina nor in 1838–40 when France took military actions against Mexico and Buenos Aires. In 1848, a victory in its war with Mexico allowed the United States to acquire vast territories from that country and extend its territory to the Pacific Ocean.

Historical circumstances prevented Latin America from expressing any strong criticism of the United States during Mexico's debacle. Fragmented into several fledgling states, facing almost continuous internal political turmoil and poorly informed of international events, Latin America was not ready for any continental or racial solidarity. Furthermore, during almost the entire 19th century the dominant power in Latin America was Great Britain, not the United States. By 1880 the situation had changed. Political stability and economic progress in Latin America coincided with the emergence of expansionist or imperialist trends in the United States.

In 1889 the United States showed its growing economic interest in the southern regions by holding in Washington the first Pan-American Conference and establishing the basis for an inter-American regional system under U.S. domination. Shortly after that conference, American expansionism transformed the image of the United States from a "model" to be copied by Latin America into an aggressive "Colossus of the North," bent on dominating the entire continent.

In 1898 the United States intervened in the Cuban rebellion against Spain, defeated Spain and occupied Puerto Rico and the Philippines. Cuba proclaimed its independence in 1902 only after accepting an amendment in its constitution (the Platt Amendment) that gave the United States the right to intervene on the island under certain conditions (determined by the United States). The acquisition of the Panama Canal and the Roosevelt Corol-

International Conference of American States, Washington, D.C., 1889

lary to the Monroe Doctrine, by which the United States acquired the right to decide when a "flagrant wrongdoing" had occurred in a Latin America state that merited "preventive intervention," defined a new imperialist U.S. policy.

Woodrow Wilson, a self-professed progressive on domestic policy, soon proved that he could be as jingoistic as Theodore Roosevelt in the name of imposing his vision of democratic morality on the nations to the south. After the odious Victoriano Huerta overthrew and murdered the democratic reformer Francisco Madero in Mexico just days before Wilson's inauguration in March 1913, Wilson soon signaled that it would be U.S. policy to promote democracy in Mexico and elsewhere. When U.S. intelligence determined that a shipment of German arms was bound for Veracruz, Wilson ordered U.S. Marines to seize the Mexican port in 1914 to prevent the guns from reaching Huerta, a move that backfired by causing Mexican public opinion to rally around the dictator. After Huerta was toppled in 1915, Wilson threw his support behind the new president, Venustiano Carranza, who was opposed by such rebel leaders as Emiliano Zapata in the south and Francisco "Pancho" Villa in the north. Wilson could do little in the south, but he allowed Carranza's troops to use U.S. railroads to outflank Villa. Enraged, Villa attacked the town of Columbus, New Mexico, in 1916, killing 19 Americans and prompting Wilson to dispatch Gen. John J. Pershing on a "punitive expedition" into Mexico to pursue Villa. Once again, the U.S. intervention had the effect only of galvanizing the various Mexican warring factions against the *gringo* invaders. The expedition was a total failure, and even long after the end of the Mexican Revolution, Mexico's distrust of its trigger-happy northern neighbor lingered.

Also during his first term, before he became more preoccupied with the threat from Germany that led to U.S. entry into World War I, Wilson sent the Marines at one time or another to occupy Nicaragua, Honduras, Costa Rica, the Dominican Republic and Haiti. The Marines remained in Nicaragua throughout much of the 1920s, battling a rebel leader who was to become a martyr and would lend his name to a Marxist movement 50 years later: Augusto César Sandino. The occupation of Haiti endured for 19 years, under five presidents of both parties, until 1934.

World War I diminished Great Britain's influence and facilitated U.S. economic expansion in the hemisphere. Between 1913 and 1920 U.S. commerce with Latin America increased by 400%. In 1929, U.S. investment in the region amounted to over $5 billion, exceeding Britain's by almost $1 billion. Latin American bitterness, how-

The President of Colombia addresses the OAS conference, Bogotá, March 1948.

ever, worried Washington. By 1928, the time of the sixth Conference of American States in Havana, Nicaraguan guerrilla leader Sandino, then fighting the Marines in his country, had become a Latin hero and the United States began to reconsider the wisdom of the "big stick" policy. The economic crash of 1929 increased interest in a policy change. In 1933, President Franklin Roosevelt proclaimed the Good Neighbor Policy.

From 1933 until 1945, U.S.–Latin relations experienced a considerable improvement. Economic recovery and better trade agreements, the rise of fascism, adoption by the Communist parties of a conciliatory tactic known as the "popular front" and the spirit of solidarity provoked by World War II contributed to raise the Good Neighbor Policy and Panamericanism to a real level of continental unity.

Roosevelt died in 1945, the war ended, and the United States once more relegated Latin America to a secondary position. From the end of World War II to the Cuban Revolution, U.S.-Latin American relations steadily declined. While Washington concentrated its attention on Europe and on meeting the Soviet global challenge, Latin America confronted old and pressing economic and social problems. Population growth, unstable economies, populist movements and military interventions agitated the continent. The United States seemed exclusively interested in creating a solid anti–communist bloc in the hemisphere.

In 1954, when the elected but "leftist" government of President Jacobo Arbenz in Guatemala posed a perceived threat to the unity of the bloc, the United States used the first conference of the new Organiza-

U.S.–Latin American Relations

tion of American States (OAS), created in Bogotá in 1948, to pressure Latin delegates into an anti–Guatemalan declaration. After a vague anti-communist declaration was issued, the American delegation paid little attention to the rest of the agenda. A few months later, Arbenz was toppled by a U.S.-backed invasion from Honduras.

Democratic leaders and parties in Latin America expressed their criticism of what they considered U.S. favoritism toward anti-communist dictators. This criticism found a favorable echo when a powerful upsurge of democratic movements seemed to be sweeping the continent. The *MNR (Movimiento Nacionalísta Revolucionario)* came to power in Bolivia in 1952; in 1955, Juan Perón fell in Argentina, and in the following years, Generals Odría, Rojas Pinilla and Pérez Jiménez were toppled in Peru, Colombia and Venezuela, respectively. "Democracy is on the march," proclaimed Costa Rican leader José Figueres in 1959. That year, General Fulgencio Batista was forced to abandon Cuba as Fidel Castro entered Havana in triumph, hailed as a democratic hero. Contrary to general expectations in and outside the island, the Cuban revolution moved radically to the left, creating an entirely new situation in Latin American history.

Immediately after seizing power, Castro demonstrated his decision to revolutionize the entire Latin continent by encouraging and aiding guerrilla groups in several countries. This policy, the rapid socialization of the revolutionary regime and increasing anti-American propaganda, strained relations with the United States. In the summer of 1960, President Eisen-

hower reduced the Cuban sugar quota allowed to enter the United States, the Soviet Union announced its intention to purchase the total amount of the reduction, and arms from the communist bloc began pouring into Cuba. In January 1961, after several conflicts and mutual recriminations, the United States, which was already preparing a military operation against Castro, broke diplomatic relations with Cuba.

John F. Kennedy was inaugurated just days later and inherited from Eisenhower a CIA plan for an invasion of Cuba by anti-Castro exiles. The force of 1,200 men had been training clandestinely in Guatemala, again governed by a president friendly to the United States. At the last minute, however, Kennedy withdrew crucial air support for the operation, fearing a Soviet response. The Bay of Pigs invasion ended in a disaster, raising Castro to the level of an international hero in the eyes of some, and damaging the United States' reputation as a military power.

Emboldened by this U.S. failure, the Soviets secretly began placing nuclear missiles in Cuba capable of striking deep inside the continental United States. A dangerous Soviet-American confrontation followed. In October 1962, the United States imposed a naval "quarantine" around Cuba to prevent the delivery of any more missiles, and demanded the removal of those already there. The world teetered closer to the brink of nuclear war than at any time during the Cold War. After a tense standoff, the Soviets pulled the missiles out of Cuba, but at the same time, obtained a guarantee from Washington that no further aggressive action would be

taken against Castro. The U.S. anti-communist bloc in the Western Hemisphere seemingly had been broken.

Protected by the U.S.-Soviet pact, Castro increased his guerrilla campaign in Latin America. The United States, which had managed to isolate Cuba diplomatically in 1961, answered with the Alliance for Progress, to promote economic progress in Latin America, and with renewed military aid to Latin American armies. The second aspect of the strategy proved more successful than the first. While few economic advantages were accomplished by the Alliance for Progress, Latin American armies defeated the guerrillas everywhere in the region. Unfortunately, victory was usually preceded or followed by military coups. By the end of the 1960s, only a few democracies had survived the military onslaught.

The guerrillas' defeat, and the continuous deterioration of Cuba's economy, saved and sustained by increasing Soviet aid, forced Castro to abandon his independent guerrilla path and accept Soviet control of Cuba. From 1973 to 1975, U.S.-Cuban relations seemed to be improving. Many Latin American nations reestablished relations with Cuba, while several influential voices in the United States asked for an end to the commercial embargo imposed on the island. In 1975, the conciliatory trend was halted when Castro sent troops to Angola to aid a faltering socialist regime, and publicly denounced American "colonialism" in Puerto Rico.

Castro was not the only crisis facing the United States in Latin America during the 1960s. In January 1964, less than two months after Lyndon Johnson succeeded the assassinated Kennedy, riots erupted in Panama when foolhardy American high school students in the U.S.-controlled Canal Zone tore down the Panamanian flag which, under a decree from President Eisenhower, flew beside the U.S. flag in the Zone. U.S. troops opened fire on the rioters as they spilled over into the Zone; a total of 22 Panamanians and six Americans were killed in the bloodshed. Panama still honors its slain citizens on every anniversary of the riots, and Fourth of July Avenue in Panama City was renamed "Avenue of the Martyrs."

The following year, the left-wing Juan Bosch came to power in the Dominican Republic, sparking civil unrest, and an alarmed Johnson feared that the country would become "another Cuba." He dispatched the 82nd Airborne Division to restore order, but not before there was considerable fighting and loss of life. When an adviser suggested that the OAS assume the peace-making role in the Dominican Republic, the earthy LBJ was reported to have commented, "Those people couldn't pour

U.S.–Latin American Relations

piss out of a boot if they had instructions written on the heel." True or not, it epitomized what Latin Americans regarded as U.S. arrogance and condescension.

The back-to-back incidents of U.S. military force in Panama and the Dominican Republic reinforced Latin America's distrust of its powerful neighbor, and greatly enhanced Castro's prestige among left-leaning, anti-U.S. movements in the region.

In 1967, Johnson enjoyed a modest triumph with a CIA operation to train a Bolivian ranger battalion that ultimately tracked down and killed the legendary revolutionary Ernesto "Che" Guevara.

Republican President Richard Nixon did little to dissipate Latin American distrust in 1970 when the CIA made a clumsy attempt to bribe Chilean congressmen into blocking the election of the Marxist Salvador Allende as president after he had received a narrow plurality, but not a majority, of the vote. As another example of both the prevailing Cold War mentality and traditional U.S. arrogance toward Latin America, National Security Adviser Henry Kissinger reportedly said, "I see no reason to allow a country to go communist because of the irresponsibility of its own people."

Allende was elected, and he promptly nationalized most U.S. businesses. Nixon responded with an economic embargo against Chile, which brought Allende sympathy even from non–Marxist Latin Americans. Like Castro, he was viewed as a heroic David standing up to the American Goliath. It wasn't revealed until 1975 that Nixon's CIA also waged a clandestine effort to destabilize the Allende government by instigating public protests and strikes by independent truck drivers. The CIA also was tangentially involved in the military coup that overthrew Allende in 1973. Allende died in the bloody coup, and although it was not clear whether it was by his own hand or at the hands of the military, another anti–U.S. martyr had been created.

That same year, the Uruguayan military overthrew that country's long-standing democracy, which had proven incapable of dealing with the *Tupamaros*, an urban revolutionary movement. U.S. complicity was also suspected in the Uruguayan coup. The military regime succeeded in crushing the *Tupamaros*—along with Uruguayan democracy in the process.

Democratic President Jimmy Carter reversed long–standing U.S. policy of sup-

porting military dictatorships in the name of anti-communism and embarked on a moralistic crusade reminiscent of Woodrow Wilson's. He appointed ambassadors who aggressively confronted the generals in Brazil, Chile, Argentina, Uruguay, El Salvador, Nicaragua and Paraguay for alleged human rights violations and curtailed or cut military aid to those countries. He also strained relations with Brazil just weeks into his presidency in 1977 by condemning its nuclear program, which provoked Brazil into canceling its mutual-defense treaty with the United States. At the same time, Carter sought to ameliorate long-standing distrust of the United States by signing the historic Panama Canal treaties—somewhat hypocritically—with a dictator, Omar Torrijos. The signing ceremony at OAS headquarters in Washington in 1977 was a major hemispheric event, with all the Latin American heads of state except Castro in attendance.

The *Sandinistas* toppled strongman Anastasio Somoza—a West Point graduate—in Nicaragua on Carter's watch in 1979, but they exhibited little gratitude to the United States for withdrawing its traditional support for Somoza. They vilified the United States, turned to Cuba and the

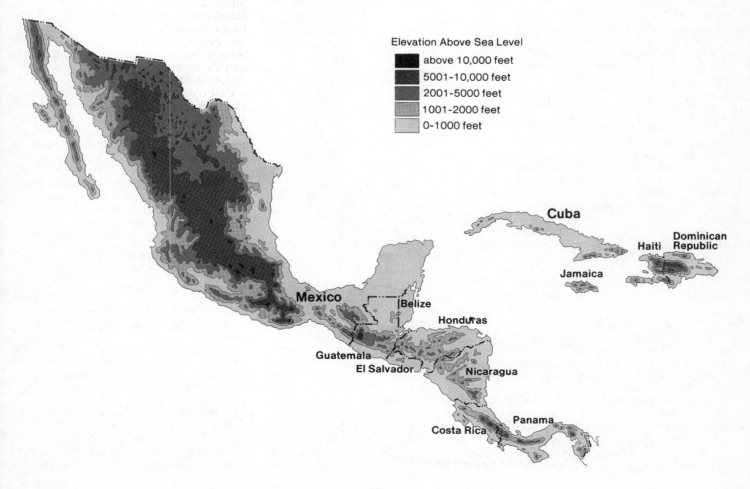

Elevation Above Sea Level

- above 10,000 feet
- 5001-10,000 feet
- 2001-5000 feet
- 1001-2000 feet
- 0-1000 feet

U.S.–Latin American Relations

Soviet Union for support and began establishing a Marxist state with little regard for the human rights that Carter seemed to cherish.

Carter faced another Latin American crisis in 1980 with the so-called Mariel boatlift, named for a small Cuban port. When Castro declared that anyone who wished to leave Cuba was free to do so, thousands of boats owned by Cuban-American expatriates in Florida sailed to Cuba in a Dunkirk-like evacuation and carried about 125,000 Cubans to the United States. Too late was it discovered that thousands of them were common criminals and lunatics Castro had removed from prisons and asylums and forced onto the boats. Carter's inept handling of the crisis was a major issue in the 1980 election.

In that election, Republican Ronald Reagan defeated Carter in a landslide and immediately ordered a 180-degree course change in Latin American policy. He reversed Carter's human-rights policy and began patching up relations with the military strongmen. He restored military aid and enlarged the training programs for Latin American officers and NCOs at the U.S. Army's School of the Americas (which Carter had relocated from Panama to Georgia) to combat Marxist insurgencies. Despite congressional objections, he lavished military aid on the military regime in El Salvador to combat that insurgency, and he fired the Carter-appointed ambassador there who had the audacity to criticize the regime after four American nuns were murdered by right-wing death squads.

In October 1983, Reagan ordered U.S. forces into the Caribbean island nation of Grenada after its Marxist president, Maurice Bishop, was overthrown and murdered by a cabal of pro-Cuban, Marxist-Leninist soldiers. The invasion, all too reminiscent of the era of gunboat diplomacy, was denounced throughout Latin America, even by the anti-communist strongmen Reagan had been courting. Moreover, Reagan provided military and financial aid to the Nicaraguan *Contras*, who were battling to topple the *Sandinistas* and whom Reagan praised as "the moral equivalent of our founding fathers." All this was part of Reagan's overall strategy of defeating the Soviet Union and winning the Cold War with a massive military buildup and confronting the Soviets vicariously with surrogate warriors on such far-flung battlefields as Afghanistan, Angola and Central America.

Reagan's support for the *Contras* almost proved the undoing of his presidency, however. When the Democratic-controlled Congress prohibited any further aid to the *Contras*, Reagan's minions made an end-run around Congress by secretly selling

Elevation Above Sea Level

- above 10,000 feet
- 5001–10,000 feet
- 2001–5000 feet
- 1001–2000 feet
- 0–1000 feet

arms to Iran, then at war with Iraq, and diverting the profits to the *Contras*. When the deal became public in late 1986, a major scandal erupted that lingered until Reagan left office in 1989. By then, however, Reagan's strategy of spending the Soviet Union into oblivion was well on its way to success.

With the collapse of the Soviet Union, Reagan's successor, Republican George Bush, had the opportunity to usher in a new era of mutual understanding and cooperation between the United States and Latin America without the old issue of communism vs. anticommunism hanging over both parties. During his first few months in office, he attended an anti-drug summit in Cartagena, Colombia, and promised closer ties with Latin America

in return for its cooperation on drug control. However, Bush's military intervention in Panama in December 1989, no matter how justifiable in light of strongman Manuel Noriega's provocations, was denounced throughout the hemisphere as just another example of the United States' application of naked power to enforce its will in Latin America.

Another obstacle in U.S.-Latin American relations left over from the Reagan era was effectively eliminated when the *Sandinistas* finally were removed from power—by free election—in 1990.

Toward the end of his single term in office, Bush negotiated the North American Free Trade Agreement (NAFTA) with Canada and Mexico, and he openly advocated a hemisphere-wide free trade zone.

U.S.–Latin American Relations

By the time Democrat Bill Clinton came to office in 1993, virtually all the dictatorships had been replaced by democratically elected civilian governments. He had to contend neither with gross abuses of human rights, as Carter had, nor with the problem of communist insurgencies, as Reagan had. In his first year in office, Clinton invited the heads of state of all the nations of the hemisphere except Cuba to a Summit of the Americas in Miami. There, he resurrected Bush's proposal for a Free Trade Area of the Americas (FTAA), open to any country with a democratic form of government. Toward that end, he made a state visit to Brazil, Uruguay, Argentina and Chile in 1997.

Meanwhile, however, Clinton found himself in the position of resorting to armed intervention just as his two Republican predecessors had. After the military strongmen who had overthrown the democratically elected Haitian President Jean-Bertrand Aristide refused to acquiesce to international pressure to restore Aristide, Clinton ordered in the 82nd Airborne Division in September 1994 to keep order and to effect the transition back to democracy. Although this invasion was a benevolent one and there was minimal loss of life, the televised images of American paratroopers landing in Haiti in full battle dress evoked the old specter of Theodore Roosevelt's "big stick." The Americans withdrew in 1995 and were replaced by United Nations peacekeepers.

Clinton was able to turn his attention again toward the upcoming second Summit of the Americas in Santiago, Chile, but in late 1997 the Congress blocked his request for "fast-track" authority to negotiate trade agreements on his own initiative. Nonetheless, when the 34 hemispheric leaders (once again, Castro had been excluded) met in Santiago from April 17–19, 1998, they issued a communiqué that called for establishment of the FTAA by 2005. Clinton praised Latin America's advances in democracy, but called for "a second generation of reforms" to consolidate the region's fragile democracies.

Although the Santiago summit was marked by unprecedented good will between the U.S. president and his Latin American counterparts, there were still some nagging complaints about U.S. hegemony. Among these were the continued U.S. embargo against Cuba, with which nearly all the Latin American countries now have diplomatic and trade relations, and the U.S. policy of "certifying" countries as cooperating allies in the war against drugs as a condition for financial aid, which the Latin Americans saw as demeaning. The drug issue as a whole continues to strain North-South relations today, with the United States pushing for

support at eradicating coca, marijuana and heroin poppy cultivation at their sources, while Latin America argues that there would be no market for illegal drugs if the United States would curb the demand for them at home. Both sides, of course, have a point.

Clinton's successor in January 2001, Republican George W. Bush, has shown a greater interest in, and sensitivity toward, Latin America than most of his predecessors, including his father. In fact, he declared he wants to see the 21st century "the century of the Americas." A former governor of Texas, he is fluent in Spanish and openly courted Hispanic votes in the 2000 presidential race. Indeed, the Cuban-American vote in Florida provided the narrow victory in that state that gave him an Electoral College victory over the Democratic candidate, Al Gore.

Accustomed to dealing with Mexican authorities as governor, Bush made a state visit to Mexico weeks after his inauguration to meet with the newly inaugurated President Vicente Fox; in the past, new U.S. presidents made their first trip abroad to Western Europe. Both conservatives, Bush and Fox got on well. Bush also hosted Chilean President Ricardo Lagos and Brazilian President Fernando Henrique Cardoso at the White House soon after the visit to Mexico.

In April 2001, Bush attended the third Summit of the Americas in Quebec, where he conversed in Spanish with his Latin American counterparts and voiced his strong commitment to the FTAA. The leaders agreed to a target date of January 1, 2005, and made adherence to representative democracy a condition for participation. The only major opposition came from Cardoso, who accused the United States of protectionism, and Venezuela's Hugo Chávez, who said the FTAA would do nothing to alleviate poverty.

Much of Bush's hope for expanded free trade in the hemisphere depended on Congress granting him what it had denied Clinton: fast-track trading authority, renamed trade promotion authority, or TPA. The Republican-controlled House of Representatives, which had denied that authority to Democrat Clinton, approved it for Republican Bush in late 2001—by one vote. The Senate, in which the Democrats had a one-seat majority, finally approved TPA in August 2002, 64-34. Armed with his new authority, Bush finally concluded a free-trade pact with Chile in June 2003, which was seen as a precursor to the FTAA. He also began pushing for a free trade agreement with Central America; in December 2004, El Salvador became the first country to sign on.

A few months after Quebec, U.S. Secretary of State Colin Powell flew to Lima,

Peru, to attend the periodic summit of OAS foreign ministers, ostensibly to emphasize again the Bush administration's commitment to regional integration and democracy.

The date: September 11, 2001. Within hours of his arrival, Powell made a hasty departure for Washington to deal with the crisis of the terrorist attacks on New York and Washington. Although his Latin American colleagues were sympathetic and understanding, there could have been no more symbolic reminder of where U.S. priorities lay in the world.

Perhaps mindful of the need to mend fences in the wake of the shift of global priorities after September 11, Bush made a whirlwind, four-day tour of Mexico, El Salvador and Peru in March 2002. In Mexico, he attended a U.N. summit on poverty in Monterrey, to assure Latin America and other developing regions that the United States was concerned with more than the war on terrorism. In El Salvador, he held a summit with several Central American presidents to assure them of his commitment to a U.S.-Central American free-trade pact. In Lima, Bush told his Andean counterparts that he was trying to get a recalcitrant Democratic-controlled Senate to reinstate preferential tariffs that had expired the month before, and he urged their continued cooperation on combating terrorism and drug trafficking. On all three stops, he reiterated his support for democracy.

Despite Bush's wooing of Latin America, however, more and more Latin American leaders have begun sharing Brazil's and Venezuela's skepticism toward the FTAA. In December 2001, Argentine President Fernando de la Rua, an advocate of the FTAA, was forced to resign because of an economic crisis and deadly riots. He was replaced by an interim president, Eduardo Duhalde, who was cool to the FTAA; his elected successor, Néstor Kirchner, is frigid toward it. Brazil's current president, Luiz Inácio da Silva, elected in 2002, is a longtime critic of the FTAA, more critical even than his predecessor, Cardoso. Da Silva and Kirchner have instead called for strengthening the *Mercosur* trade bloc (Argentina, Brazil, Uruguay and Paraguay) and for increased regional economic integration in preference to the FTAA, which they argue would be dominated by the United States. Even Mexico's Fox, despite his conservatism and warm relations with Bush, met with da Silva at the Rio Group summit in Peru in 2002 and came away committed to greater Mexican trade with *Mercosur*.

In July 2002, the 10 presidents from South America's two major trading blocs, *Mercosur* and the Andean Pact, (Bolivia, Colombia, Ecuador, Peru and Venezuela)

U.S.–Latin American Relations

met in Guayaquil, Ecuador; the president of Chile, an associate member of *Mercosur*, also attended. It was the second such summit between the two trade blocs; the first was held in September 2000. In the so-called "Guayaquil Consensus," the presidents agreed that strengthened trade between the two South American blocs must precede implementation of the FTAA, and there was more grumbling that the United States preaches free trade while practicing protectionism. In August 2003, Peru joined Bolivia and Chile as associate members of *Mercosur*. On December 8, 2004, 12 countries signed an accord in Cuzco, Peru, creating the South American Community of Nations.

No progress toward the FTAA was made at the Summit of the Americas in Monterrey, Mexico, in January 2004 (see Latin America and the World), where Bush raised a few eyebrows by suggesting raising the bar for participation in the FTAA by blackballing "corrupt" countries as well as undemocratic Cuba. A cynic might well ask which country would then qualify—including the United States, given the much-publicized corporate scandals of 2003. The January 1, 2005 deadline for establishing the FTAA came and went, and its prospects appear more remote than they did at the Quebec Summit of 2001.

Bush has continued the war on drugs, including the highly unpopular and offensive policy of "certifying" countries as allies. Despite Bush's declaration of "the century of the Americas," drug certification and four other things have strained U.S.-Latin American relations on his watch and called into question the depth of his administration's commitment to Latin America in general or to its democratization in particular.

The first was the abortive military coup in Venezuela in April 2002 that had President Hugo Chávez under house arrest for 48 hours. Chávez had long been a thorn in the side of the United States because of his close ties to Cuba, Iraq, Iran and Libya and for his opposition to the FTAA (see Venezuela). The statements emanating from the State Department within hours of the coup clearly conveyed the idea that the Bush administration regarded the overthrow of Chávez, who had twice been elected by overwhelming majorities, as the will of the Venezuelan people. The administration said, essentially, that Chávez had it coming. When Chávez was reinstalled two days later, President Bush's national security adviser, Condoleezza Rice, said in a televised interview that she hoped Chávez had learned something from his experience. The message regarding U.S. policy toward Latin America was unmistakable: We're all for democracy—

as long as you don't elect someone we don't like.

The second has been what is apparently the official policy of the Bush administration to have its ambassadors openly electioneer for presidential candidates it favors, a stunning breach of diplomatic protocol. The first such instance came in the Nicaraguan campaign in October 2001, when U.S. Ambassador Oliver Garza appeared at functions for the Liberal candidate, Enrique Bolaños, whose opponent was the former *Sandinista* president, Daniel Ortega. The ambassador even invited Bolaños to distribute U.S. food aid, and he actually warned Nicaraguan voters that U.S. aid could be jeopardized if Ortega won. Bolaños won the election. A few months later, U.S. Ambassador Manuel Rocha used the same tactics in Bolivia, where one of the candidates was Evo Morales, leader of the coca farmers, who had pledged to reverse the incumbent administration's coca-eradication policy. Like Garza, Rocha appeared at campaign rallies for the favored U.S. candidate, former President Gonzalo Sánchez de Lozada, and he publicly hinted that a Morales victory could jeopardize U.S. aid. This time, however, this clumsy policy almost backfired. Bolivians were justifiably furious over this interference in their internal political affairs. The result: Morales, whom polls had predicted would receive no more than 12% of the vote, was catapulted into second place, with about 21% (see Bolivia). Congress then had to choose between Morales and Sánchez, and the Bolivian press reported that Rocha was lobbying members of Congress to vote for Sánchez. Sánchez ultimately won, but Rocha's interference left a bitter taste in the mouths of a good many Bolivians.

The third was the U.S. intervention in Iraq in 2003, which for many Latin American countries was just too reminiscent of U.S. gunboat diplomacy. Even those countries morally opposed to Saddam Hussein's regime and generally friendly to the United States, such as Mexico and Chile, publicly criticized the war; Chile's opposition on the U.N. Security Council briefly delayed the U.S.-Chilean free-trade agreement. Four countries—the Dominican Republic, El Salvador, Honduras and Nicaragua—did send contingents of several hundred troops each to participate in the coalition in Iraq, assigned to various missions. All but El Salvador decided to pull their troops out, however, after Spain withdrew its troops from Iraq in the wake of the Madrid terrorist bombings in March 2004.

The fourth has been the practice—which in fairness did not originate with Bush—to send lower-echelon representatives to the inaugurations of democratically elected

presidents. When a dozen or more heads of state from Latin America, and sometimes elsewhere, attend an inauguration and the United States sends a cabinet secretary who happens to have a Hispanic surname—as it did in Argentina—or an unpopular trade representative—as it did in Brazil—the contrast does not go unnoticed and can only be seen as offensive. Fidel Castro, meanwhile, regularly attends inaugurations. An encouraging change was Powell's attendance at the inauguration of Panamanian President Martín Torrijos on September 1, 2004.

This souring of U.S.-Latin American relations was acutely evident in June 2003, when Powell once again attended the OAS foreign ministers' summit, in Santiago, Chile. He urged his 33 colleagues to denounce Cuba's crackdown on dissent in April (see Cuba) and to support the transition to a democratic Cuba. Powell's plea met an icy reception; only the Canadian foreign minister was supportive. Just a month earlier, the United States had failed to get the OAS to adopt a resolution condemning the crackdown, winning support from only 17 of the 34 member countries. Even countries opposed to Castro's dictatorship also oppose the U.S. trade embargo against Cuba. The rejection of the U.S. position against Cuba appeared to be a case of Latin American blood being thicker than Western Hemisphere water and general resentment against a paternalistic U.S. attitude.

Another indication of this is the fact that the Ibero-American summits (see Latin America and the World), which include Cuba but exclude the United States, have been far more critical of Cuba's human rights record than has the OAS. In other words, Latin America seems to be saying, we don't need you to tell us what to do.

Bush traveled to Santiago, Chile, in November 2004 for the annual summit of the 21-member Asia-Pacific Economic Cooperation (APEC) group, and he reportedly hoped to use the opportunity to mend fences with his Latin American counterparts at the meeting. Instead, he caused ill feelings when his Secret Service detail demanded that all guests at a planned state dinner pass through metal detectors, causing Chilean President Ricardo Lagos to downgrade the event to a working dinner of just the heads of state and their wives. Even then, Bush's Secret Service agents became involved in a shoving match with Chilean security guards who tried to prevent them from entering the dinner, causing Bush to personally intervene to escort the agents inside. The incident was shown on television in Latin America and around the world. Bush stopped in Cartagena, Colombia, en route home to confer with President Alvaro Uribe.

Bush's new secretary of state, Condoleezza Rice, made a visit to Chile, Brazil Colombia and El Salvador in April 2005 in yet another attempt to sooth ruffled feathers in the region, to discuss the war on terrorism and to reiterate U.S. support for democracy.

In September 2004, the pro-U.S. Miguel Angel Rodríguez, who served as president of Costa Rica from 1998–2002, was elected secretary-general of the OAS. Just two weeks later, however, Rodríguez resigned in the face of allegations that as president he took a $400,000 payoff from the government of Taiwan and a kickback of $510,000 from a French telecommunications firm. This reopened the jockeying for the leadership of the hemispheric body, which lasted six months. The United States let it be known its preferred candidate was Mexican Foreign Secretary José Luis Derbez—which may have doomed his candidacy. When the first vote on April 11, 2005, ended in a 17–17 tie between Derbez and Chilean Interior José Miguel Insulza., Derbez dropped out in the interest of unity. Rice declared she was pleased with the selection of Insulza, who has stressed his commitment to promoting democracy in the region.

The 2005 annual meeting of the OAS foreign ministers was held June 7-9 in Fort Lauderdale, Florida, the first time the meeting had been held on U.S. soil since 1971. Both Bush and Rice addressed the meeting, urging the OAS to grant the secretary-general greater power to deal with countries drifting back toward authoritarianism. Venezuela responded that the idea was obviously directed at it. Bush and Rice diplomatically resisted the temptation to say, "If the shoe fits." But most members agreed the language had Venezuela in mind, and in a major rebuff of the United States the final resolution on the issue, advanced by Brazil and Chile, was a watered-down version that stressed "the right of self-determination and the principle of non-intervention" over worries about would-be dictators.

In sum, the United States is still sending mixed signals to its Latin American neighbors—just as it has for 200 years—and Latin America is responding accordingly.

Latin America and the World

One of the most dramatic changes taking place in Latin America is its progressive integration into the rest of the world. Almost totally isolated during most of the 19th century and until World War II under the tutelage first of Britain and then of the United States, Latin America has since then experienced a progressive "opening to the world."

After 1960, Canada increased its economic and cultural ties with Latin countries, principally Brazil, Cuba and, with NAFTA in 1994, Mexico. The most important nations of Western Europe, especially Germany, Italy and Spain, reinforced their influence in the hemisphere through economic aid, cultural programs and support for political groups or parties attuned to their predominant ideologies.

During the Cold War, the Soviet Union eagerly sought to extend its influence, and enjoyed some degree of success. The Cuban socialist regime, which transformed the island into a formidable military base, opened the door for further Soviet influence in Latin America. The Peruvian military regime of 1968-80 enjoyed close ties with the Soviet Union, which re-equipped the Peruvian army with T-62 tanks and its air force with MiGs. The Nicaraguan army under the *Sandinistas* also became equipped with Soviet weapons, including tanks, helicopter gunships and other modern armaments. Every year, thousands of Latin American students received grants to study in Moscow, and Marxist publications multiplied on the continent. Latin America, a region once relegated by the Kremlin to a secondary position, became one of its top priorities (as foretold by Lenin before his death). But one factor was overlooked by most observers: the Soviet largess directed at Latin America was at the expense of the Soviet workers. With the fall of communism, Russia has maintained warm relations with Latin America, though trade has been negligible.

In recent decades, there has been increased Japanese interest in investment in Latin America. With its huge surplus from a favorable balance of foreign trade for years, the supply of money is ample. Needless to say, the Japanese insist on control and security of their investments and, above all, efficiency, productivity and competitiveness. Nothing could be healthier for Latin America; local entrepreneurs may decide to adopt Japanese styles of production, which would greatly assist in long–term solutions to chronic economic ills.

During much of the Cold War, Latin American countries other than Cuba joined the United States in recognizing the Nationalist Chinese government on Taiwan as the legitimate government of China. Mexico recognized the communist regime in Beijing in 1971, seven years before the United States did. One by one, most other Latin American countries also recognized Beijing. However, of the 23 nations that still maintain full diplomatic relations with Taiwan, 10 are developing nations of the Western Hemisphere that have benefited greatly from Taiwan's generosity with foreign aid: Belize, Costa Rica, the Dominican Republic, Guatemala, Haiti, Honduras, Nicaragua, Panama and Paraguay.

In the past few years, however, the economically resilient People's Republic of China has greatly expanded its political and economic influence among the other Latin American nations. Trade between China and Latin America increased roughly four-fold between 1997 and 2004. Chinese President Hu Jintao made an unprecedented state visit to Chile, Argentina and Brazil in November 2004, signing letters of intent to invest tens of billions of dollars in those countries' infrastructures and to greatly expand trade. China, meanwhile, has great demand for Chilean copper and South American agricultural products, especially Argentine soybeans. Venezuelan President Hugo Chávez visited Beijing in December 2004; China pledged to invest in Venezuela's oil industry and to double bilateral trade.

Latin America has two rotating seats on the 15-member U.N. Security Council, but in May 2005 Brazil joined with Germany, Japan and India in sponsoring a resolution to expand the council to 25 members and make those four countries permanent members along with the United States, Russia, Britain, France and China. Permanent members have veto power.

Latin America also has played a leading role in the so-called G-15, a group of developing countries, most of them rich in natural resources or with large industrial bases, that was organized in 1989 as a counterpart to the G-7 (now G-8) group of highly industrialized countries. Originally the bloc had 15 members, but has expanded to 19. Thirteen Latin American or Caribbean countries belong to the G-15: Argentina, Brazil, Chile, Colombia, Jamaica, Mexico, Peru and Venezuela. The other members are Algeria, Egypt, India, Indonesia, Iran, Kenya, Malaysia, Senegal, Sri Lanka and Zimbabwe. Venezuela hosted the 2002 G-15 summit.

Overlapping with the G-15 is the G-21, an organization of developing countries designed to present a unified stance in trade negotiations with the developed countries, particularly over the thorny issue of agricultural subsidies in the developed countries, which developing countries complain is hypocritical and makes their agricultural exports uncompetitive. The organization's 21 countries encompass half the globe's population and most of its farmers. Thirteen of those countries are Latin American: Argentina, Bolivia, Brazil, Chile, Colombia, Costa Rica, Cuba, Ecuador, Guatemala, Mexico, Paraguay, Peru and Venezuela. The others are China, Egypt, India, Indonesia, Nigeria, Pakistan, the Philippines, South Africa and Thailand. The G-21 countries were a major factor in the collapse of the World Trade Organization summit in Cancun, Mexico, in September 2003.

U.S.–Latin American Relations

At the G-8 summit in France in June 2002, the leaders of Latin America's two largest economies—Brazil's da Silva and Mexico's Fox—attended for the first time—but probably not for the last.

Mexico, Peru and Chile are among the 21 countries with robust economies around the Pacific Rim that comprise the so-called Asia-Pacific Economic Cooperation (APEC) group. Other members include the United States, Canada, Japan, China, South Korea, Thailand, Malaysia and Australia. Chile hosted the annual summit in November 2004, where the United States advanced the idea of a free-trade zone that would dwarf the European Union or the ill-fated FTAA. Such a bloc is far in the future, however.

Since 1991, the heads of government and key ministers of Spain, Portugal and the 19 Latin American countries they once colonized have met every November for the Ibero-American Summit. Unlike the OAS and the Summits of the Americas, the United States is not included but Cuba is. The agendas usually include such topics as trade and human rights. Although these summits have accomplished little of substance, such as persuading Cuba to clean up its human rights act, they have provided a forum for a healthful exchange of ideas of mutual importance to the Latin American leaders and their Iberian counterparts. They also have helped give Latin America a toehold in European trade, as Spain and Portugal are both members of the European Union. At the 2001 summit in Lima, Peru, the agenda was expanded to include the Argentine financial crisis, drug trafficking and terrorism, which was of importance to both Spain, with its Basque terrorist group *ETA*, and Colombia, plagued by both left-wing guerrillas and right-wing paramilitaries. The final resolution condemned the terrorist attacks on the United States as "barbarian acts" and a "threat to democracy." Cuba's Fidel Castro, usually the central attraction at these summits, did not attend because of Hurricane Michelle. He also failed to attend the 2002 summit in the Dominican Republic, where the heads of state again chided Cuba for its human rights record. The chaotic situation in Haiti, even though as a former French colony it is not included in the summits, dominated the 14th annual meeting in San Jose, Costa Rica, in 2004.

As an outgrowth of the Ibero-American summits, the first summit of leaders of the European Union, Latin America and the Caribbean was held in 1999. Spain hosted another two-day summit in Madrid in May 2002, which was attended by about 50 heads of government and their foreign and economy ministers. Trade and terrorism dominated the agenda. As one of the major accomplishments, the EU and Chile ended their "association" agreement, the first step to beginning a free-trade agreement that was signed in November 2002; Mexico already has such an agreement with the EU. In its final declaration, the EU pledged to initiate separate free-trade talks with the Andean, Caribbean and Central American trade blocs. *Mercosur* then entered into an "association" agreement with the EU like the one Chile had. The EU also acceded to a request from the Colombian president to add the Revolutionary Armed Forces of Colombia *(FARC)* to its list of terrorist organizations.

The third EU-Latin American-Caribbean summit, held in Guadalajara, Mexico, in May 2004, proved more political and more contentious. The major agreement between the two sides of the Atlantic was a resolution calling for a strengthening of the United Nations, which the delegates said should be the sole entity responsible for solving international conflicts. It was seen as an oblique criticism of U.S. intervention in Iraq. Less obliquely, the delegates condemned the abuse of Iraqi prisoners by U.S. forces. As often happens at these get-togethers, however, Cuba introduced a note of discord by complaining that the resolution condemning prisoner abuse wasn't harsh enough, by attacking the EU for allegedly blocking a resolution against the U.S. economic embargo and by being the only nation of the 58 represented to withhold its approval of the summit's final declaration. Back in Havana, the Cuban government issued a statement referring to the EU as "a flock of sheep" that follows the U.S. lead. EU President Romano Prodi chided Cuba for its confrontational attitude toward the EU. Also at the summit, representatives of the EU and *Mercosur* fine-tuned some of the points for a free-trade agreement, which would have represented $40 billion in trade. The fourth summit is to be held in Vienna in 2006.

The EU and *Mercosur* concluded a free-trade agreement in early 2004 that was expected to go into force by October 31, but it soon became unraveled as the two blocs quibbled over a wide array of issues. *Mercosur* wanted greater access to Europe for its agricultural products, while the EU wanted greater access for its industrial goods. The two sides pushed back the deal until an undisclosed date in 2005, but barring a breakthrough the deal appeared as dead as the FTAA.

Even as the EU door was closing, however, a new window of opportunity opened with the first South American-Arab Summit in Brasilia, Brazil, May 10–11, 2005. Heretofore, trade between Latin America and the Middle East has been meager, despite the blood ties that date back to the Moorish occupation of the Iberian Peninsula before 1492 and, more recently, to 19th and 20th century Arab emigration to Latin America (see Latin America Today). An estimated 17 million Latin Americans are of Arab descent, and they have achieved economic success and influence disproportionate to their numbers. The summit, organized and hosted by Brazilian President da Silva, brought together representatives of 12 South American and 22 Arab countries of the Middle East and North Africa. Many of those were heads of state, including new presidents Mahmoud Abbas of the Palestinian Authority and Jalal Talabani of Iraq (in reality a Kurd, not an Arab).

In economic terms, a tangible result of the summit was an agreement between the four-nation *Mercosur* and the six-nation Gulf Cooperation Council (Bahrain, Kuwait, Oman, Qatar, Saudi Arabia and the United Arab Emirates) to initiate negotiations for a free-trade agreement. Da Silva said Brazil alone expects to double its trade with Arab countries to $15 billion in three years. But in political terms, the summit may have had more far-reaching results as a forum for the disdain both regions harbor toward U.S. economic and military hegemony. Da Silva, in fact, rejected a U.S. request for observer status at the summit. The Declaration of Brasilia did denounce terrorism and expressed support for Iraq's battle against insurgents, but it also endorsed resistance to "foreign occupation," seen as a thinly veiled reference to the United States and Israel. The declaration called for a sovereign Palestinian state and called on Israel to withdraw to its pre-1967 borders and to dismantle its settlements in Palestinian territory, including East Jerusalem. The declaration embraced the concept of free trade, but said it should be geared toward the benefit of the world's poor and should not widen the gap between developed and developing nations.

The potential for trade agreements between Latin America on the one hand and the EU, the Middle East or China on the other is enormous. They also signal a lessening of Latin America's traditional dependence on the United States and its increasing involvement in world affairs.

The Republic of Argentina

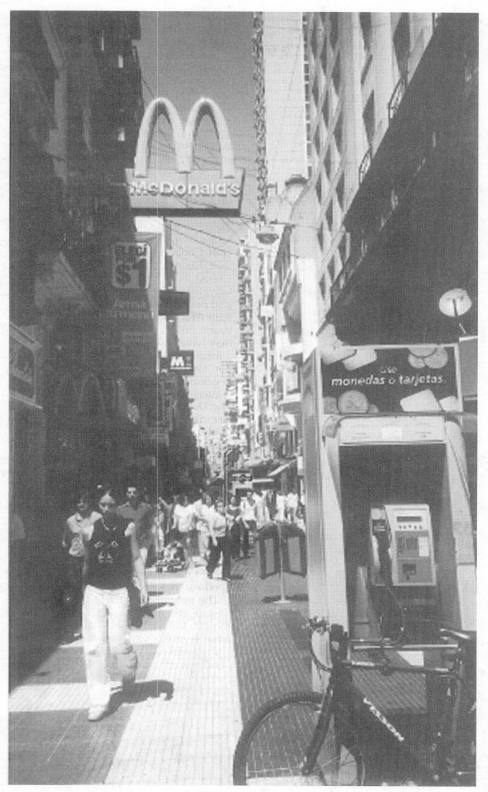

Downtown Buenos Aires

Capital City: Buenos Aires (Pop. 13 million, including suburbs)

Climate: The northern *Chaco* region is wet and hot; the central plains, or *Pampas*, are temperate with moderate rain-fall; southern Patagonia is arid, becoming wet and cold in the southernmost part

Neighboring Countries: Uruguay and Brazil (East); Paraguay and Bolivia (North); Chile (West)

Official Language: Spanish

Other Principal Tongues: English, German, Italian

Ethnic Background: European (predominantly Spanish and Italian) 98%; *Mestizo* (mixed Spanish and Indian ancestry) 2%

Principal Religion: Roman Catholicism

Chief Commercial Products: Meat, grain, oilseed, hides, wool

Currency: Peso (replacing the former *Austral*)

Gross Domestic Product: U.S. $127.6 billion in 2032, reflecting peso devaluation since 2001 ($3,486 per capita)

Former Colonial Status: Spanish Crown Colony (1580–1816)

Independence Date: July 9, 1816

Chief of State: Néstor Kirchner (b. February 25, 1950), president (since May 25, 2003)

National Flag: Sky blue, white and sky blue equal horizontal stripes with "the sun of May" centered in the white stripe.

Argentina varies widely in terrain and climate. Four main regions are generally recognized. The northern region (*Chaco*) is heavily forested, low, wet and hot; the central plains (*Pampas*) are flat, fertile and temperate, well watered along the coast and increasingly dry to the west; the southern region (*Patagonia*) is an arid, windswept plateau, cut through by grassy valleys; the fourth region (Andes) runs the length of the Argentine-Chilean frontier—the mountains are low and glaciated in the south, high and dry in the central part and gradually widen into the high plateau of Bolivia in the north.

Argentina's most important river is the Paraná, with tributaries that flow into the Río de la Plata estuary north of Buenos Aires. A 25-mile-long bridge connecting Argentina and Uruguay, reaching a height of 1,200 feet over the shipping lane, is now under construction. Three-quarters of Argentina's land is too dry for cultivation without irrigation. The capital city and adjoining *Pampas* have 98% of the population. Temperatures vary from the hot, humid *Chaco* to the cold and damp Patagonia in the south.

History: The Río de la Plata estuary was first visited in 1516 by Spanish explorers who were driven off by hostile Indians. Magellan visited the region in 1520 and

Area: 1,072,745 sq. mi. = 2,771,300 sq. km. Argentina claims 1,084,120 square miles, including the Falkland Islands, in dispute with Great Britain, and other territories claimed by Chile

Population: 37.9 million (2004 est.)

Argentina

Spain made unsuccessful efforts to establish colonies on the Paraná River in 1527 and 1536. The Spanish moved up river to the Paraná's junction with the Paraguay River, where they founded Asunción, the center of Spanish operations in southeastern South America for the succeeding 50 years. In 1573, an expedition from Asunción established a settlement in the vicinity of modern Buenos Aires and subsequently Spain transferred its base of colonial government from Asunción to the new town.

Argentina was settled by two main streams of colonists: one crossed the Andes from Peru and occupied the fertile oases along the areas on the eastern slopes of the Andes, founding Córdoba and Tucumán; the other arrived directly from Europe and settled in and around the port of Buenos Aires. Thus, from the start, two distinct groups of Argentine people developed. The people of the interior, a mixture of Spanish and Indian heritage, were dependent on the grazing of cattle on the plains of the central *Pampas* and upon small home manufactures. Far removed from any aid, these people developed a rude, self-sufficient civilization fiercely resistant to encroachment and disdainful of the ruling authority established in Buenos Aires by urban intellectuals.

The people of Buenos Aires, a mixture of Europeans (Spanish, French, English, Italian and German) who came to the port for trade, to defend the region or to govern it, had little interest in the Latin Americans and sought to re-create in Buenos Aires the standards of living of the European cities from which they originated. The nobility, which governed the defending military, and the clergy, retained special privileges; they could neither be tried in the local courts nor be held accountable to the people for their actions.

Under the Spanish colonial system, Latin America was held by a few people who administered their grants as feudal holdings. Far removed from the restraints of the Spanish court, the Argentine people

evolved into a somewhat wild and free civilization that allowed the development of community and regional pride. In 1806 and 1807, British expeditions attacked and temporarily occupied Buenos Aires; in both cases, almost without Spanish aid, the creoles rallied and defeated the British. The following year, Napoleon's invasion of Spain turned the British into allies, but the exhilaration of those victories did much to imbue self-confidence among the creoles.

On May 25, 1810, the *cabildo* of Buenos Aires declared it would govern the viceroyalty of La Plata in the name of the deposed King Fernando VII; rebel envoys and armies were sent to the provinces to forge national unity, but, as in the rest of Hispanic America, attempts to hold the former viceroyalty's territories under Buenos Aires' control were far from successful. A provincial assembly eventually declared independence on July 9, 1816. Paraguay proclaimed its own independence and Uruguay, under the guidance of its popular hero José Manuel Artígas, insisted on autonomy, ushering in a long period of Brazilian-Argentine conflict over the region, which culminated in a pre-

City Hall in Buenos Aires, 1846

urban leadership, the fertile *Pampas* lands were seized and distributed to large estate holders, a policy which continued for several years; the governments used the army "to open" the interior of Argentina, eliminating Indians and *gauchos* and gaining further territories. For a considerable period after independence, Argentina was simply a cattle-raising country, importing all manufactured goods and even food from Europe.

In the late 19th century, the demand for chilled beef led to changes in the meat industry, requiring better cattle and grains for both cattle-feeding and human consumption. Despite the changes in production, however, Argentine economic and political power remained in the hands of a small group of planters, cattle raisers and the merchants in the port city.

Contemptuous of the cattle-herding *gauchos*, the *porteños*, residents of the port, Buenos Aires, opened the doors of Argentina to European immigrants. From 1852 to 1895, hundreds of thousands of Italians, Spanish, Germans and British poured into the nation. In 1852, of a total population of 1,200,000, non-Argentines were less than 5%, but by 1895 of almost 4 million inhabitants, over 1 million were foreigners. By the beginning of the 20th century, the demands for political equality of this mass of immigrants transformed the political scene. The Radical Party had become the most popular among the immigrants and emerged into the first really populist party of Argentina. Organized by an enigmatic leader, Hipólito Irigoyen, the Radical Party has maintained its influence, in one form or another, up to the present day.

carious Uruguayan independence in the 1840s. Even in the interior of what is today Argentina, the provinces constantly rebelled against Buenos Aires. The first 50 years of Argentine history is the history of the struggle between Buenos Aires and the provinces, and of political turmoil in the capital, where different types of government were tried in a desperate search for stability.

Argentina's greatest hero, General José de San Martín, refused to be dragged into such internecine disputes and concentrated on organizing an army to invade and liberate Chile. Like Bolívar in the north, San Martín was convinced that independence could not be assured until no Spanish stronghold remained in South America. Subsequently he crossed the Andes with his army, battling the Spanish into submission in Chile. He then turned to Peru, fighting his way to the north of that country where he met the liberator of northern South America, Simón Bolívar. Disappointed by Bolívar's refusal to take command of the two armies, San Martín, feeling that his presence as a military man might adversely affect the Peruvian revolution, retired and left for France, where he remained for the rest of his life.

Argentina started its independent history with great territorial losses and a division between its social groups—those of the port and the interior, the metropolis and the countryside. The elimination of Spanish control created a series of conflicts among the regional contenders for power. There was immediate strife between the ranchers controlling large estates on the coast and the merchants in Buenos Aires, who insisted that all trade pass through

the port, with duties and taxes used for the capital city rather than for the country. The interior provinces in turn demanded a federal form of government, with autonomous sovereign states and a national capital outside Buenos Aires.

To foster economic development, the leaders of Buenos Aires wanted to promote agriculture and expand European immigration to farm the land as was being done in the United States. The coastal ranchers, knowing that small farms would destroy their great *estancias*, made common cause with the interior to overthrow the Buenos Aires leaders and installed their own leader in 1835, Juan Manuel de Rosas. In the name of federalism, he brutally imposed "national unity" and stubbornly opposed French and British intervention in Río de la Plata, preserving Argentina for future generations. Unfortunately, his enemies belonged to one of the most brilliant generations in Argentine history, one that produced quantities of great literature. These eminent writers included Domingo Faustino Sarmiento and Bartolomé Mitre, both destined to become presidents of the republic (see Culture). A combination of Brazilian forces and Argentine caudillos finally overthrew Rosas' government in 1852.

A constitution of 1853 provided for a federal system and moved the seat of government to Paraná, 150 miles north of Buenos Aires. The former capital seceded from the union, was defeated, renewed the war and was again defeated by national forces. In 1861 the provinces accepted Buenos Aires' supremacy and the first constitutional president, Bartolomé Mitre, assumed office. During the years of the non-

General José de San Martín

Argentina

General Bartolomé Mitre

Industrialization came late to Argentina and was largely due to British investment during the last half of the 19th century. Concentrated in Buenos Aires and in the hands of a few large investors, industry centered on the supply of local needs and the transportation and processing of Argentina's export commodities. Although industrialization changed the ratio of national earnings from agriculture and cattle raising to include industrial products, it provided little increase in total earnings.

The formation of labor unions, largely through the efforts of immigrants, posed the first threat to the historic domination of the country by landed interests and industrialists, both Argentine and foreign. The unions also included displaced agricultural laborers and were initially disorganized and effectively excluded from participation in political or economic power until the first decades of the 20th century. The ruling elite chose compromise: in 1912 electoral laws were democratically modified, providing for a secret ballot and minority party representation. The first elections held under this system in 1916 resulted in a Radical Party victory under Irigoyen and the defeat of the large land-owners' and industrialists' Conservative Party. The populist Radical Party ruled Argentina from 1916 to 1930. Its programs included expansion of the democratic system and social reforms to benefit workers, but these fell short of expectations. Political and social unrest soon appeared—in 1918 there was a rebellion of students at the University of Córdoba

and a year later widespread strikes provoked bloody confrontations with the police. Social unrest soon caused the downfall of the Radical Party. A restless army, weary of turmoil and fascinated by Italian dictator Benito Mussolini and his totalitarian efficiency, found its opportunity in 1930 when the international depression gripped the country. An elderly Irigoyen was deposed and the armed forces seized the government "to save the nation from chaos." The "saviors" remained in or behind power for more than *five decades* and remain a force to be reckoned with to this day. The Conservative Party was restored to power. For the next 13 years, a combination of landowners, bankers, merchants and generals controlled the government. But in 1943, a group of pseudo-fascist army officers, who feared the government's progressive inclinations toward the Allied powers, used "official corruption" as a pretext to seize power. Lacking a program, and with limited leadership abilities, the government failed to cope with internal problems and mismanaged foreign relations.

The Perón Eras

From the rubble of political confusion there emerged a new leader, Colonel Juan Domingo Perón, a classic charismatic *caudillo* who, wittingly or unwittingly, united forces which had resisted conservative efforts to reestablish political dominance. He brilliantly saw that no government could exist in Argentina without the support of the middle classes, which had grown substantially, and, more important, the lower laboring class.

Attaining the office of labor minister under the conservative military government, he devoted his efforts toward seizing control of the labor unions from the Radical and Conservative parties. Tremendous assistance came from popular radio announcer Maria Eva Duarte. The military-conservative element sensed too late that he had acquired an immense power base. When an attempt was made to remove Perón in 1945, masses rallied to his support and forced the government to desist. In the elections of 1946, Perón became president with a substantial majority of the vote.

Perón married the glamorous and even more charismatic radio announcer, who became popularly called "Evita," and they used their abilities well, gaining firm control of labor and creating a popular mass organization called the *Descamisados* ("shirtless ones") which some erroneously identified with the Fascist Italian regime. Despite the fact that Perón threatened conservative interests, he was able to gain and hold vital army support through pay

raises and military expenditures. He also received support of the clergy through advocacy of programs of religious education and by adopting a moderate position on church-state relations.

While Perón and Evita built their strength through propaganda and blatant patronage, certain of their accomplishments were significant. The working class was brought into the political arena and made aware of its massive power. Evita's charitable social works provided health and welfare benefits to the poor that could not be withdrawn (all, of course, widely publicized). The increased wages paid to labor and the practice of "featherbedding" in the government of Buenos Aires was deceiving, as rising prices canceled the increased earnings of the people. Mass housing, schools and hospitals and a flood of labor laws favorable to the workers dominated Perón's programs. Costly and often inefficient industries were created to provide jobs for the thousands streaming into the cities. Agriculture, the backbone of the economy, was taxed heavily to pay for disorderly industrialization. The natural result was a drop in farm output which in turn caused a drop in exports and foreign trade. The problem of importing more than is exported is one that persists in Argentina to this day.

Perón's handling of foreign relations was astute and restored Argentina's international prestige; however, his efforts to establish Argentine political leadership in Latin America were resented and resisted by most of the other nations of the continent. The death of Evita in 1952 from cancer marked the beginning of the decline of Perón's power. Within a short time the bankrupt state of the economy became apparent and thereafter the moral bankruptcy was difficult to hide. Resorting to repression to silence opposition to his regime, Perón alienated the Church and coerced opposition businessmen and landowners into burying their complaints against his rule. Popular unrest and increasing economic problems gave the armed forces, which had resisted Perón's attempts to control them, an opportunity to intervene. In September 1955, a military insurrection ended his rule.

The army seized the government and installed a provisional president. Honest, but timid, he was unable to cope with the overwhelming problems inherited from Perón. After serving for two months, he was replaced by another general who was able to restore civil order and hold elections in 1958.

Arturo Frondizi, elected in 1958, was capable, but also was a stern disciplinarian; he sought to repair the damage created by the Perón regime. He lasted until 1962 when he was overthrown and replaced by

President and Mrs Perón

the military. His replacement, Dr. Arturo Illia, lasted until mid-1966 when he was deposed by another military coup.

Lieutenant General Carlos Onganía was installed as the next president; known as "El Caño" (The Pipe), he was said to be straight on the outside but hollow within. His solution for Argentine problems was to ban political parties, dismiss the Congress and neutralize the courts. It was not long before he envisioned a regime modeled after that of Mussolini with himself (of course) as permanent head. By late 1969, however, his dream turned into a nightmare, replete with riots, strikes and general unrest.

Three years of near-anarchy and frequent changes in military government leadership ensued. The generals ordered elections which were set for March 1973 and most political parties were legalized, including Perón's *Justicialista* movement. Long-standing criminal charges against the former leader were dropped to permit his return from Spain where he had been in exile, maintaining control of his movement by balancing one rival faction against another and issuing vague political statements.

When the military refused to permit Perón to run for the presidency, he instructed his party to nominate Héctor J. Cámpora, a colorless party worker. Campaigning on the slogan "Cámpora to the presidency, Perón to power," the *Justicialistas* gained 49.5% of the vote, plus large majorities in congressional and provincial races.

Inaugurated in May 1973, Cámpora pledged to revitalize the economy, increase benefits for labor and seek closer ties with "neutralist" countries. However, Cámpora's efforts to cooperate with the restive leftists within the party quickly alienated its conservative members. Street fighting between rival factions became common; when one bloody shootout left 25 dead and hundreds wounded at an airport reception for Perón, Cámpora and his entire cabinet were forced to resign after only 49 days in power. The son-in-law of Perón's private secretary was named interim president and new elections were set for September. With anti-Perón military leaders having been forced into retirement, Perón was free to run for president.

Ironically, many of those who supported *El Líder* included such former enemies as the military, the large landowners and business leaders—all of whom welcomed his increased conservatism. Perón's main support, however, came from his traditional base of power: organized labor. As his running mate, Perón chose his wife, Isabel, a 42-year-old former cabaret dancer. Certain of victory, he ran a leisurely campaign based on vague promises of national unity. Election results gave him 61.9% of the vote, while the candidate of the opposition Radical Civic Union received 24.3%. A third center-right coalition candidate won less than 15%.

The problems facing Perón were immense. The economy was plagued with low growth and high inflation; leftist terrorism was rampant and his own political movement was badly divided. As President, Perón concocted an unrealistic mixture of a leftist foreign policy and a conservative domestic program. He sought closer economic and political ties with "Marxist" and "Third World" countries and even hoped to make an official visit to Moscow. Huge credits ($1.2 billion) were offered to Cuba; at the same time, greater restrictions were placed on foreign private investments in Argentina.

Perón's domestic policies, however, were staunchly conservative. He openly courted right-wing union and political leaders. At his direction, liberal government and school officials were dismissed and leftist publications closed. He publicly berated leftist *Peronista* youths as "mercenaries at the service of foreign forces." These conservative policies merely widened the rift within his political movement. Having played an important role in bringing Perón back to power through their struggles with the military government, the leftists now refused to be pushed out of the *Peronista* movement. Instead, left-wing guerrillas continued their attacks against conservative union leaders, right-wing government officials and foreign businessmen. Conservatives responded with counter-terror. The basic functions of the government ground to a halt as the rift between the right and the left, as well as between *Peronistas* and anti-*Peronistas*, polarized the nation.

Perón's hapless plight was perhaps best seen in his 1974 May Day speech: while he was calling for "peace and conciliation" among his followers, rival *Peronista* factions broke into bloody street fighting even before his speech was ended. The continued jockeying for position became even more intense as Perón's health began to fail; in hindsight, he was senile when he returned from Spanish exile. Each faction hoped to be able to seize control of the party should *El Líder* die in office.

By 1973, the aging Perón, almost 78, tired easily and had difficulty concentrating for more than brief periods. In November he suffered a mild heart attack from which he never recovered; death came from heart failure in July 1974.

With the passing of Juan Domingo Perón, most national leaders quickly pledged their *oral* support for constitutional government and the new president, María Estela Martínez de Perón, widely known simply as "Isabel" or "Isabelita." However, a crucial difference existed between the loyalty the people toward *El Presidente Perón* on the one hand and *La Presidente Perón* on the other. She lacked

Argentina

his personal magnetism and the immense power base formerly he had held, and she was totally unimaginative. Moreover, Argentines could not help but draw unfavorable references between her and the much more popular and charismatic Evita. Actually, Isabel's husband had selected her as his running mate only to allow him additional time to choose a more likely successor.

Occupying the highest office ever held by a woman in the Western Hemisphere, Isabel held conservative views that were bitterly opposed by leftists, while old-line *Peronistas* resented her because she was not Evita. More ominous, the old guard regarded her background as a nightclub dancer with a sixth-grade education as woefully inadequate—which it was. The upper classes dismissed her as a commoner, as they had Evita. Feeling herself thus isolated from traditional sources of power, Isabel began to rely heavily on the advice and counsel of José López Rega, minister of social welfare, a close confidant of the late president and somewhat mysterious practitioner of the occult. He, too, favored staunch conservative measures which, needless to say, were opposed by moderates and bitterly resisted by leftists.

Frail and reclusive, Isabel delegated broad power to López Rega and other key officials in the hope of pulling the nation

La Presidente **Isabela Perón**

out of an economic nosedive caused by (1) runaway inflation (2) growing shortages of industrial and consumer goods, (3) a thriving black market, (4) huge budget and foreign trade deficits, (5) declining domestic and foreign investments and (6) a disastrous drop in farm output. Part of the fiscal plight was caused when Isabel permitted large wage increases in violation of an earlier wage-price freeze. Although the move was popular with the large labor movement, it triggered widespread business losses which, in turn, led to a fresh round of price increases and a further escalation of inflation, which by 1975 was at an annual rate of 330%.

During the same period, the government policies of overtaxing farmers to subsidize the immense urban population had caused a major decline in farm exports which traditionally furnished the bulk of Argentina's foreign exchange earnings. As a result, the nation faced a trade deficit of $600 million in 1975. Worse, some $2 billion in foreign debts were due the same year; although foreign reserves stood at $1 billion when the *Peronistas* took office in 1973, they plummeted to an all-time low of only $2 million by early 1976. To finance the government, the money supply was expanded by 200%.

In spite of further attempts at austerity (which failed) the economic picture worsened until there was virtual paralysis. Political conditions also declined—violence became the worst in the nation's history. Assassinations by leftist and right-wing terrorists claimed 1,100 lives during 1975. One leftist group, the *Montanaros*, collected huge fees by kidnapping business leaders. A single kidnapping netted the guerrillas $60 million!

Although the *Peronistas* scored well (46.5%) in regional elections in the normally conservative province of Misiones, the victory did not hide the disintegration of the *Peronista* movement. During the 21 months she was in office, Isabel reorganized the cabinet 10 times. The conservative labor movement—long a pillar of support for Perón—continued to increase the distance between itself and Isabel. The loss of this vital support paved the way for the collapse of the Perón presidency. Increasingly erratic, *La Presidente* took a leave of absence from her job in the latter part of 1975. Compounding the economic and political malaise was a growing public resentment against increasing reports of widespread political corruption. Among those implicated was Isabel, who was accused of transferring half a million dollars from a public charity to her own bank account. A formal congressional probe of the incident was averted, however, only after the *Peronista*-controlled legislature voted along strict party lines to drop the inquiry.

Lt. Gen. Jorge Rafael Videla

Government corruption, rising terrorism, a reeling economy and disintegrating government control of national affairs prompted a long expected military coup on March 24, 1976—the sixth within the prior 21 years. Army Lieutenant General Jorge Rafael Videla, 50, was named president and head of the three-man *junta*.

The "Dirty War"

To combat Argentina's mounting problems, the generals vowed to fight for three key goals: an end to political terrorism, a drastic cut in the inflation rate and economic development.

To control inflation, wages were frozen, taxes increased and prices were allowed to rise to their natural levels. Also, the peso was devalued by 70%, government spending was reduced and farm prices raised to stimulate agricultural growth. These measures helped cut inflation from 35% *a month* to about 10% by early 1978. Political corruption was a special target, and the *junta* moved swiftly to prosecute those who profited illegally under the *Peronista* government; Isabel Perón was so charged and placed under house arrest.

Upon seizing power, the military rulers were able to boast of dramatic improvements in the national economy. Foreign reserves jumped from $20 million in 1976 to $10 *billion* by mid-1980. Farm output also grew, paced by a 52% rise in wheat production during the 1978–79 season over the previous harvest. Oil and natural gas exploration was increased as the government sought to attain self-sufficiency in energy by 1982.

Such rapid economic expansion carried a high price tag, as the liberalization of monetary policies helped to undermine confidence in the peso. The cost in human lives was even greater. Hoping to improve domestic stability—and thereby stimulate economic investments—the government unleashed a campaign of terror against the leftists. Between 1976 and 1981, some 6,000–15,000 persons simply disappeared after having been arrested by security forces. To protest these human rights abuses, the Carter administration suspended military aid to Argentina.

In doing this, the U.S. administration failed to realize that there are two sides to every conflict. The leftists didn't have the words "human rights" in their vocabulary. Summary executions of military personnel by leftists using clandestine, terrorist and guerrilla tactics were ordinary occurrences in Argentina at the time.

Retaliation by the military was equally grisly. It was revealed in 1995 that a naval school used as a prison was the point of departure for many imprisoned by the military. A prison guard wielding a hypodermic loaded with a hypnotic drug would inject a shackled prisoner. When he became unconscious, he was loaded aboard an airplane which flew over the Atlantic for an appropriate distance. The unconscious (but not dead) prisoner would be unceremoniously dumped overboard. Dissidents thus did indeed disappear, without a trace. The school also served as a torture center.

Economic Woes

The nation's impressive economic boom proved short-lived, and by mid-1981 the country was mired in a recession and disenchanted with military rule. To enhance its public image, the *junta* tried several moves. In July 1981, the government bowed to the demands of the *Peronistas* and freed Isabel; she promptly took up a luxurious and quiet exile in Spain.

ARGENTINAZO: ¡LAS MALVINAS RECUPERADAS!

ACCION CONJUNTA DE NUESTRAS FUERZAS ARMADAS; MARCHAN AVIONES Y BARCOS EN GRAN OPERATIVO; EL TIEMPO CONSPIRA

Buenos Aires' *Cronica* (April 2, 1982) hails Argentina's "recovery" of the Malvinas (Falkland Islands)

Still, the opposition to military rule persisted. In December 1981 the *junta* fired moderate President Roberto Viola, replacing him with hardline Army Commander Leopoldo F. Galtieri. In contrast to Viola, who attempted to deal with the banned political parties, the new president sought to reaffirm the military's control of the government and its commitment to free-market economic policies. Although Galtieri pledged to deal more firmly with the nation's economic problems, the recession intensified, driving the inflation rate to 130% and unemployment to 13–16%. Argentina was in its worst economic crisis of the century. By March 1982, labor unrest was spreading throughout the land and the outlawed political parties were agitating for a return to constitutional government.

The Falkland Islands War

At that point, Galtieri and some top military commanders made a momentous decision. Taking advantage of a dispute between Argentina and Britain over some rather worthless islands, the Falklands (*Malvinas* to the Argentines), the president ordered the armed forces to seize them in April 1982. So, after an absence of 149 years the Argentine flag once again flew

General Leopoldo F. Galtieri

Argentine troops man the Falkland beaches

Argentina

over this disputed territory. Overnight, Galtieri and his military conquerors were the heroes of Argentina. For the next 74 days, Argentina was at war.

The dispute over the Falkland Islands started in the 1500s. On the basis of initial occupation, the Argentine historical claim does seem to have somewhat greater validity.

Despite treaties, the British did establish colonies on the islands in the 1770s, but they were soon abandoned. The Spanish claims to the islands were transferred to Argentina when the nation achieved independence from Spain in 1816. Four years later, Argentina reaffirmed its sovereignty over the archipelago as parts of the islands were settled and land grants were awarded. Apparently the Argentines also used the territory as a penal colony.

At the urging of the U.S. consulate in Buenos Aires, the British forcibly occupied the islands in January 1833. At that time, all Argentine residents were deported. For the next 149 years, Argentines were prevented from living on the islands, and until 1999 Argentine citizens had to buy a round-trip ticket before they were even allowed to *visit* the islands. Since 1851 the islands have been largely controlled by the Falkland Islands Company, a London-"based firm that owns 40% of the main two islands.

Economically, the Falklands have little to offer except offshore oil deposits. Charles Darwin called them "the miserable islands" when he visited them in 1833. Most of the residents today are engaged in sheep ranching and associated production of wool.

The Argentine invasion of 1982 *did* violate two basic principles of international law: (1) use of force to settle international disputes and (2) the right of self-determination. As a result, the United Nations Security Council voted to demand that they withdraw. There is widespread sentiment in Latin America in favor of returning the islands to Argentina and the United Nations also voted overwhelmingly in the 1960s and 1970s to ask Great Britain to negotiate on the islands' "decolonization."

The British position in 1982 was for 25 more years of control over the islands. Argentina warned that it might seek "other means" to resolve the dispute. It was this frustration with diplomacy that set the stage for the invasion by Argentina. The conflict quickly escalated to include a British nuclear submarine. Ten weeks later, there had been 1,700 Argentine casualties, including 650 dead or missing. The beaten Argentines left enormous amounts of military equipment worth millions of dollars. There were 11,000 war prisoners held by the British. After a lengthy delay they were returned to remote ports in Argen-

tina where they were received amid great security (in part to prevent media coverage) and with little fanfare. The battle cost the British $2 billion—$1 million for each Falklander.

For Argentina, the war was a disaster. The army was humiliated, the military dictatorship was discredited and the economy was pushed toward bankruptcy. In Buenos Aires, angry crowds marched on the Plaza de Mayo demanding to nail "Galtieri to the wall!" The writing was already on the wall for the dictator. In order to prevent elimination of its power, the *junta* promptly fired the president. That was the easy part.

For the next week, the government remained virtually paralyzed while the three armed forces quarreled over a successor. Having just lost on the battlefield, the army—the largest of the three services—had no intention of going down in defeat on the home front as well. Unable to reach an agreement, it finally named one of its own to the presidency: retired Major General Reynaldo Benito Antonio Bignone, age 58. In dismay, the navy and air force said they would not actively participate in the new government.

The United States was put in an awkward position by the conflict. Its endorsement of a 1947 Inter-American Treaty of Mutual Defense (better known as the Rio Treaty) appeared questionable when it refused to side with Argentina. By supporting the British, the significance of the Monroe Doctrine came into question in the minds of many Latin Americans. When it cut off military aid to Argentina, its reliability as a supplier of weapons became questionable. Argentina's support of U.S. efforts against communists in Nicaragua and El Salvador was terminated.

Democracy

Demoralized by defeat and besieged by monumental social and economic problems, the Argentine military government had no other expedient but to allow the electoral process to run as fast and smooth as possible while attempting a rear guard action to protect the power of the armed forces from future judicial action. Encouraged by political freedom, human rights activists demanded more information about the *desaparecidos* (disappeared ones) during the "Dirty War" and stern punishment for those responsible for the crimes. The military *junta* answered with (1) a declaration that the *desaparecidos* should be considered dead and (2) in September 1983 with a law granting amnesty to military security personnel involved in the anti-terrorist campaign of 1976–1982. An outraged public opinion forced the presidential candidates to announce they

would repeal the law as soon as civilian authority was reestablished.

One military officer was sentenced to 10 years imprisonment for "illegal association." Many of those sentenced to prison were quietly released within a few months or years.

On October 30, 1983, general elections were held. The winner, Raúl Alfonsín of the Radical Civic Union (*UCR*), represented a more moderate tendency in the Argentine political spectrum. The *Peronistas*, poorly organized, were waiting for Isabel to return, but she preferred her more peaceful life in Spain.

The new democratic government, which ended an eight-year period of military rule, faced a multiplicity of urgent problems, but three appeared as the most pressing: control of the armed forces, labor demands and a depressed economy. The full extent of the military's crackdown became clear in late 1985 when nine military leaders, including Videla, Viola and Galtieri were placed on trial. Furious with an attempt by the military to whitewash the gruesome activities of elite military and paramilitary units, the civilian courts assumed jurisdiction. The trial furnished lively media material describing in detail methods of torture and execution. The defense presented by the generals was predictable: (1) they were fighting a war against a subversive enemy financed from abroad and (2) they did not know the extent of the excesses being perpetrated by those under their control. Further, in typical military fashion, lesser officers and personnel claimed they were simply following military orders.

General Videla and Admiral Emilio Massera (Navy member of the Videla *junta*) were sentenced to life for 62 murders; three others were given nominal sentences. Galtieri and two other principals were acquitted, but Galtieri was sentenced by a court martial to 12 years imprisonment for "negligence" in directing the armed forces during the Malvinas war. His son, killed in the conflict, was buried on one of the islands. Human rights activists numbering 3,000, led by the Mothers of the Plaza de Mayo, who sought information as to their absent loved ones, paraded to protest the leniency of the sentences. This illustrated a well-known fact about the military in Argentina—the country cannot exist without it and cannot stand living with it. Nevertheless, court action against thousands of former military and police strongmen was commenced in 1986, with orders that they be expedited. This, however, led to extreme unrest and in 1987 a serious threat of revolt by the military. To dispel this, President Alfonsín requested the legislature to grant amnesty to all military personnel below the rank of colonel—an action which the liberals (but not the *Peronistas*) denounced. The president was obviously under heavy pressure from the military when this move was made in May. The net result was that of 7,000 potential defendants who could have been tried for atrocities, perhaps 50 actually were charged; there were few convictions.

The year 1985 also marked action against former *Montanaro* leaders (*Peronista*) who had touched off the "Dirty War" of the 1970s. The defense to charges of murder and kidnapping was also predictable: the organization was only exercising political rights and responsibilities. Labor demands were temporarily appeased by some concessions and appeals to democratic patriotism. But it was on the international economic front where Argentina gained its most impressive, even if quite indecisive, battle. Under the burden of a public debt estimated at about $48 billion, Argentina threatened to ignore

Raúl Alfonsín

a March 31, 1984, deadline for paying $500 million in interest to creditors around the world. After several complicated maneuvers, the alarmed bankers agreed to new terms and better payment conditions. Argentina temporarily gained an essential respite and showed other debtor nations that they were not without bargaining power.

The program of austerity, which was necessary to support economic reorganization on even a modest level, sharply lowered living standards in Argentina. A basic problem involved investment funds. There was and is an annual trade surplus which was eaten up by the need to pay interest. It was necessary to borrow additional funds to pay that interest, pushing the external debt to $64 billion.

Although Alfonsín initially appeared to be an astute politician, his knowledge of economic policy was low and this showed quite visibly. Further, he had no competent advisers. The result was hyperinflation caused by spiraling wages and prices (as much as 400% per month!). A new currency, the *austral*, was introduced, but it was devalued so many times it became meaningless.

Alfonsín tried repeated wage-price freezes that didn't work. Strikes became commonplace. Although the country could have been self-sufficient in oil production, he demanded 50% of production from potential foreign producers as the price of exploration.

The *Peronista* movement splintered into two factions, but loosely reconsolidated in 1987 and in 1988 it nominated Carlos Saúl Menem, popular governor of the impoverished province of La Rioja in the northwest, for president. His running mate was Eduardo Duhalde, from Buenos Aires. Years later, they would become bitter rivals for control of the party.

Menem, who is of Syrian descent, proved to be a most colorful candidate, promising everything to everybody. One of his campaign posters showed him reclining on a couch in a bikini bathing suit. He was known for his love of movie starlets and fast cars. He trounced his opponent from Alfonsín's *UCR*, receiving 47.4% of the vote to 32.5%. Alfonsín had vowed to serve until the end of his term in November, but, beset with riots and a host of unsolvable problems, he stepped down in July; Menem was sworn in. He was faced with a debt of $69 billion.

The Menem Presidency

What those attending the inaugural heard was quite different from that which they heard before the election. "I do not bring easy or immediate promises . . . I can only offer my people work, sacrifice and hope," he said, sounding rather Churchillian. "We must tell the truth, once and for all: Argentina has broken down." He forthwith announced a number of controversial measures calculated to bring order to the country.

Prices went up, restaurants emptied and pasta became a disliked meat substitute. By the end of 1989 all military were pardoned, including Galtieri and later, Videla, infuriating many; 1 million signed a resolution of protest. Menem normalized relations with the British. His popularity plummeted sharply. He took an ominous step in March 1990, signing a decree authorizing the military to act in the event of "social upheaval." Further, it would command all state and local police in such an event. The economy continued

Carlos Saúl Menem

its downward spiral and the middle class became poor.

In an ingenious move, he announced the privatization of about 90 state monopolies. Part of the purchase price was the purchase of a portion of Argentina's external debt, worth about 30 cents to the dollar. The first to go was the antiquated telephone system, which fetched more than $1.8 billion in hard currency. In early 1992 he effectively tied the latest Argentine currency, again called the peso, to the U.S. dollar to encourage North American and European investment.

Under Menem's programs the economy turned sharply upward, at least on the surface. The improvement did not involve all sectors, however. In a hurry to placate union workers and the economic elite, the government tended in the 1990s to overlook the small business sector and the white-collar workers. Privatization took its toll among relatives and party favorites—as economists express it, "redundancies"—were sharply pared. In other words, unless a person actually did something productive, he or she was fired. In the past, this was unheard of; favoritism was not limited to the elite owner class; unions also benefited. The result was the same: low productivity.

Investors from abroad were unwilling to provide funds in such a setting, so Menem energetically set about changing age-old employment patterns. The result spoke for itself. Both the gross national product and the annual per capita income more than *doubled* after 1990. Inflation was in single digits.

At the same time, however, scandals and corruption involving Menem's in-

Argentina

Edición
Internacional
Vía Aérea

LA NACION

Una selección
de la semana

Año 120 - Nros. 42.255 al 42.261 - Ed. Int. Nº 1562 - Año 28   Buenos Aires, lunes 3 de julio de 1989   Bouchard 557, C. P. 1106, Tel. 313-1003, 1453 y 312-3021/9

Menem dispondría la libertad de militares

Lo reveló implícitamente, al sostener que no puede ver encerrados "ni a los pájaros"; viajará a los EE. UU., en septiembre, por el problema de la deuda externa

Por César Ivancovich

(Enviado especial de LA NACION)

Jueves 29

LA RIOJA.— El presidente electo, Carlos Menem, reiteró que hay que cerrar las heridas entre militares y civiles y reveló implícitamente que todos los hombres de armas condenados por la Justicia recuperarán su libertad, al utilizar la expresión: "Yo no puedo ver encerrados ni a los pájaros".

También anunció que viajará en septiembre próximo a los Estados Unidos, en un intento por revertir la "extrema dureza" advertida en los medios financieros internacionales respecto de la Argentina.

"No hay vuelta que darle, todo pasa por allí", comentó el todavía gobernador riojano al justificar la aceptación del convite formulado por el presidente norteamericano, George Bush.

Menem no sólo se refirió a las dificultades que enfrenta la economía en el plano externo –en su reciente viaje a Washington, el canciller-designado, Domingo Cavallo, se estrelló contra una dura muralla construida por los centros financieros–, sino también en el ámbito local.

–Admitió, por ejemplo, que esos 2500 millones de dólares que según versiones aportarían empresas locales para el arranque de su plan económico son, por ahora, algo así como un espejismo en el medio del desierto. Nadie sabe, empero, si al seguir avanzando la imagen corresponderá efectivamente a un oasis.

Por lo que dicen los allegados de

Lo que sí dijo ayer el presidente electo es que la dureza que implica va a ser mayor después de los cien días que al comienzo de su gestión. Cree que las medidas de shock por aplicarse de entrada serán efectivas para bajar la inflación, pero que las requeridas para mantenerla en ese nivel, después de los tres primeros meses, podrían llegar a ser mucho más duras.

Este enviado le preguntó si creía que los operadores retirarían su capital del circuito financiero para invertirlo en la producción. "Si. Los especuladores deberán replegarse, pues habrá créditos baratos para la producción. Las mesas de dinero tendrán que adaptarse o desaparecer", sentenció el futuro presidente.

Formalizaron sus renuncias Alfonsín y Víctor Martínez

Las presentaron en el Congreso; serán aceptadas el 8, antes de que jure Menem

Sábado 1

El presidente Raúl Alfonsín y el vicepresidente Víctor Martínez presentaron ayer al Parlamento sus renuncias, para que la Asamblea Legislativa del 8 del actual las acepte momentos antes de que preste juramento como nuevo mandatario el doctor Carlos Saúl Menem.

Se formalizaron así las dimisiones anunciadas por Alfonsín en su discurso del 12 de junio, cuando anticipó su decisión de resignar el cargo a partir de ayer.

El sobre lacrado con la renuncia del jefe del Estado llegó al Congreso en manos del secretario general de la Presidencia, Carlos Becerra, quien lo entregó a Víctor Martínez en su carácter de titular del Senado.

Al recibir la renuncia –en una breve ceremonia realizada en su despacho– Martínez sumó la suya, también en sobre cerrado. Ambos fueron entregados al secretario parlamentario de la Cámara alta, Antonio Macris, y sólo serán

a la formalidad o un mensaje extenso con consideraciones o pronunciamientos políticos.

"Misión histórica"

"Presentar la renuncia me apena un poco, pero nos complace saber que esto lo hacemos en beneficio del país", dijo Víctor Martínez a los periodistas tras el acto en su despacho.

Becerra, por su parte, declaró que se sentía "muy honrado por esta misión histórica que me encomendó el Presidente: este acto cierra el capítulo de la consolidación de la democracia".

Agregó que el radicalismo acompañará "con alta responsabilidad" la nueva etapa política que comienza el 8 del actual.

Alfonsín en el Congreso

Martínez confirmó, asimismo, que pasado mañana Alfonsín concurrirá al Congreso, a las 17, para saludar protocolarmente al nuevo titular provisional

La Nación headlines two watershed events on July 3, 1989: President–elect Menem's declaration that he would release jailed military officers as a gesture of reconciliation, and the resignations of President Alfonsín and Vice President Martínez, which allowed Menem to take office five months early.

---

laws (and therefore attributed to him) tarnished his image (although he never pretended to be an angel). When a dispute arose with his wife in 1990, he simply threw her out of the presidential palace. She provided exciting copy for the media, particularly the tabloids.

Desiring that the positive work he had started continue, Menem began in 1993 to devise a way to circumvent the constitutional limitation that forbade a president more than one consecutive term. His constitutional six-year term was to end in 1995. In order to have it changed, it was necessary to have the cooperation of the *UCR*. This was made possible in part by the election of former President Alfonsín as leader of the party in November 1993. A deal was made (the Olivos Pact) between Menem's *Justicialista* Party and the *UCR* for a constituent assembly, the prime purpose of which was to enable Menem to run for a second term. The two parties had a majority (211 of 305 seats) adequate to adopt a proposed constitutional amendment in August 1993 allowing the president to run for a second term in 1995. The bill also reduced the presidential term to four years, created the office of prime minister and gave the president the power to nominate Supreme Court justices, subject to a two-thirds vote in the Senate.

Having won the right to seek reelection, Menem was blessed with incredibly favorable political and economic timing. He

easily won his historic reelection bid in May 1995 with about 50 percent of the vote, thus avoiding a runoff. Vice President Duhalde left the ticket to win the governorship of Buenos Aires Province. No sooner did Menem win his reduced second term than the effects of the Mexican peso devaluation struck Argentina, plunging it into recession. Unemployment soared to 18%.

Menem kept his campaign promises to modernize the economy through privatization and other free-market reforms, and he accomplished the unthinkable by keeping inflation to single-digits. Still, the painful remedies cost Menem his popularity. In June 1996, the *Peronistas* were dealt a severe blow when Fernando de la Rua, the *UCR* candidate for mayor of Buenos Aires, won a decisive victory in that *Peronista* stronghold. In 1997, the Radicals entered into an opposition alliance with *Frepaso*, a *Peronist* splinter group, to contest the October congressional elections. The Alliance wisely chose not to attack Menem's successful free-market policies, because the economy was still growing at a robust 8%. Instead, the Alliance hit the president where he was most vulnerable: the rampant corruption within his administration, which had grown so bad that Economy Minister Domingo Cavallo, the architect of the new economic miracle, resigned in disgust in 1996. In the elections for 127 of the 257 seats in the lower house,

the *Peronistas* suffered another serious setback by losing their absolute majority, dropping from 131 seats to 119; their share of the popular vote plummeted from 43% in 1995 to 36%. The Alliance won 106 seats, while other parties held 32 seats and the balance of power.

There was a hostile relationship between Menem and the press. Unlike years past, the Argentine media now enjoy unprecedented freedom and they dutifully exposed scandal after scandal in the Menem government. In January 1997, José Luis Cabezas, an investigative photographer who was probing alleged police corruption, was found beaten, shot and burned to a cinder in his car. The crime shocked the nation and brought international pressure on Menem to bring the killers to justice. The scandal reached a head in May 1998 when the wife of one of two policemen arrested in connection with Cabezas' murder publicly revealed that they had been hired by Alfredo Yabrán, a powerful, influential and secretive tycoon who was rumored to have Mafia ties and who for good measure was a close friend of Menem's. Cabezas had surreptitiously taken the first published photographs of the reclusive Yabrán, who, like Menem, was of Arab descent. As police closed in on Yabrán's *estancia* to arrest him for Cabezas' murder, the tycoon apparently shot himself to death. There was no autopsy, and he wasn't even buried before

Argentina

rumors circulated that the Mafia had murdered him to silence him. Quipped the U.S. ambassador: "Yabrán committed suicide, but we don't know who did it yet."

Yabrán's mysterious death was not to be the last to rivet the attention of the press and public. In August 1998, former navy Captain Horacio Estrada, who had just been subpoenaed to testify in controversial and illegal arms sales to Ecuador and Croatia, was found dead in his apartment with a gunshot wound to his head. In October 1998, businessman Marcelo Cattaneo, who was expected to appear in court in connection with another high-profile scandal involving alleged bribes by Banco Nación and the U.S. computer firm IBM, was found hanged on a communications tower. Both deaths were ruled suicides, but the press raised allegations of organized crime connections. A defensive Menem responded, "We can't jump to conclusions."

Ghosts from the Past

The past came back to haunt Argentina in 1998, beginning with controversial statements by two former naval officers that scraped open the still-healing wounds of the Dirty War. One, Adolfo Scilingo, voluntarily traveled to Spain, where he was wanted for human rights violations against Spanish citizens in Argentina, and served three months in jail. Upon his release, he openly expressed remorse in a press interview that he had participated in the so-called "death flights," in which naked prisoners were thrown to their deaths into the ocean from aircraft. He called for war-crimes trials for his fellow officers.

The other officer, Alfredo Astiz, was arrogant and unrepentant. Astiz had been sentenced to life in prison by France in absentia in 1990, and was also wanted by Spain and Italy for Dirty War atrocities against nationals of those countries. He, too, admitted in a magazine interview that he had killed prisoners, but justified the killings as necessary. His remarks sparked a public outcry, and Menem ordered him jailed. He was soon released, still defiant, but Menem stripped him of his former rank. In 2001, Astiz was arrested at the request of Sweden, which wanted him extradited to stand trial for the death of a Swedish girl during the Dirty War.

The Astiz incident prompted *Frepaso* to introduce legislation repealing the amnesty granted to military officers after the return to civilian rule, but this caused a strain between the Alliance coalition partners because the amnesty had been adopted during the administration of the Radicals' Alfonsín. In the end, Congress passed a watered-down version. Almost

simultaneously, the public expressed outrage over Menem's plan to raze the Navy Mechanics School, the most notorious of the military's torture centers during the Dirty War, and replace it with a park containing a memorial to the victims. Most Argentines evidently preferred to convert the school into a museum, much like the museums dedicated to Holocaust victims. In March 1998, a judge issued an injunction against plans to demolish the building, not on sentimental grounds but on the pretext that destruction might destroy criminal evidence.

The past again came crashing down on the present on June 10, 1998, when former President Videla was arrested on charges he participated in selling the babies of "disappeared" dissidents to adoptive parents. Videla's 1990 pardon on war crimes charges did not cover these new allegations. The so-called "baby-stealing" probe widened after Videla's arrest. In November, former Admiral Emilio Massera, navy chief during the Dirty War, was arrested after DNA tests showed that two women adopted as babies were children of parents who had disappeared after being arrested; one of them was adopted and raised by an aide of Massera's. In January 1999, former President Reynaldo Bignone was arrested for possible involvement in the baby kidnapping scheme but was not charged with a specific crime. Since then, several more officers have been detained in the baby-stealing investigation. In November 1999, Spanish Judge Baltasar Garzón, the same judge who had requested the arrest of former Chilean strongman Augusto Pinochet by the British in 1998, charged 98 former Argentine officers with alleged human rights abuses.

In March 2001, three weeks before the 25th anniversary of the 1976 coup that presaged the "Dirty War," a federal judge ruled in a case brought against army officers in the disappearance of a young couple in 1978 that the amnesty laws absolving the military of wrongdoing in human rights cases are unconstitutional. Six months later, a judge ordered the arrest of 12 former military men and six civilians at the request of Judge Garzón. In July 2002, former President Galtieri and 41 others were detained in connection with the disappearance of 20 *Montanaro* suspects during his presidency.

These ghosts continue to haunt Argentina (see Recent Developments).

The Elections of 1999

Eduardo Duhalde, the Peronist governor of Buenos Aires Province, regarded himself as the logical heir apparent to Menem and began running for the party's presidential nomination. But Menem

shocked the country—and infuriated Duhalde—by coyly hinting in early 1998 that he would be amenable to a constitutional amendment permitting him to run for a third term. For most it seemed a moot point because the Peronists had lost their majority in the Chamber of Deputies, but Menem nonetheless began talking more and more like a man running for reelection. Yet, faced with increasing opposition within the party, a chorus of criticism from the press, the near-impossibility of pushing such an amendment through Congress and opinion polls showing him running in the single digits, Menem subsequently declared that he would not run. But in October 1998 he boasted to a French newspaper that he would return to power in the 2003 election. Meanwhile, he ramrodded through a vote in a party conference that would keep him as leader of the party until 2002, even if another Peronist were to be elected president of the republic. In February 1999, a court invalidated that vote.

By early 1999, Menem was hinting *again* that he would accept a "draft." Tension between Menem and Duhalde mounted, and Duhalde pulled off an astute political maneuver by scheduling a referendum in Buenos Aires Province for March 28, 1999, on whether or not the constitution should be amended to allow Menem to run again. It was a classic poker player's bluff; it could have backfired if the vote were yes, but Duhalde was confident the vote would go against Menem. Menem realized it, too, and folded. He definitively withdrew from the race, Duhalde canceled the referendum, and the party postponed the date of the party primary to select the presidential candidate from April 11 to July 4. Duhalde won easily and selected a former pop music star, Palito Ortega, as his running mate.

The Alliance, meanwhile, had a schism of its own between two sexagenarians, the *UCR*'s Fernando de la Rua, 61, mayor of the city of Buenos Aires, and *Frepaso*'s Senator Graciela Fernández Meijide, 68, mother of one of the "disappeareds" of the Dirty War. In the Alliance's primary election in November 1998, de la Rua handily defeated her 63% to 36%. About 2 million people voted. To keep the Alliance intact, de la Rua chose as his running mate a *Frepaso* strategist, Carlos Alvarez. As a consolation, Fernández Meijide became the Alliance's candidate to succeed Duhalde as governor of Buenos Aires Province. Her opponent was Menem's retiring vice president, Carlos Ruckauf.

The disgruntled Domingo Cavallo, Menem's erstwhile economic adviser, launched an independent candidacy for president.

The ensuing campaign was the most dramatic the country had seen since the

41

Argentina

. . . and the socially elite at the glittering Colón Theater in Buenos Aires

restoration of democracy 16 years earlier. The lead see-sawed back and forth between de la Rua and Duhalde in the polls. But 10 years of Peronist rule, coupled with nagging public concerns over official corruption and an alarming 14.5% unemployment rate, proved too much of an encumbrance for Duhalde. In the balloting on October 24, de la Rua scored a decisive first-round victory, receiving 48.5% of the vote to Duhalde's 38% and Cavallo's 10.2%. With characteristic bombast, Menem declared on election night, "I could have won easily," a claim that was highly debatable. Nonetheless, the president graciously telephoned de la Rua to congratulate him. The Alliance's victory carried over into the elections for the Chamber of Deputies. It increased its number of seats from 106 to 123, just six short of a majority, while the *Justicialistas* fell from 122 seats to 101, their worst showing since they won 97 seats in the 1985 off-year elections. The *Justicialistas* could console themselves with victories for a number of governorships, among them that of Buenos Aires; Ruckauf defeated Fernández Meijide 48.3% to 41.5%. Moreover, they still controlled the Senate,

which required de la Rua to govern by consensus.

In July 1999, Foreign Minister Guido di Tella and British Foreign Secretary Robin Cook signed a bilateral agreement that in effect ended the diplomatic hostilities over the Falkland Islands. Argentine nationals were once again permitted to visit the islands.

Even before he took office, de la Rua also found himself involved in foreign affairs. He and Menem both denounced Spanish Judge Garzón's charges against 98 former Argentine officers (see Ghosts from the Past as an infringement on Argentine sovereignty and refused to recognize them. (In August, Menem had also demonstrated his disagreement with Spain over the Pinochet arrest by joining Chile in boycotting the Ibero-American summit in Cuba.)

Faced with a strained relationship with an old European friend, de la Rua made an effort to further improve relations with a long-time European foe. While in Paris in November to represent the Alliance in the Socialist International convention, he held a 20-minute dialogue with British Prime Minister Tony Blair. The two men

reportedly discussed mostly economic and trade issues, but they agreed in principle to expand upon the bilateral agreement reached in July on the Falkland Islands. Prince Andrew, a Falklands War veteran, represented Britain at de la Rua's inauguration.

De la Rua's Aborted Presidency

De la Rua was sworn in on December 10, 1999. The new president soon demonstrated that his administration represented not merely a change in parties and personalities but in style as well. Breaking with Menem's image as a flamboyant spendthrift, de la Rua announced he would sell Tango 1, the ostentatious presidential jet, a Boeing 757 that cost Argentine taxpayers $66 million and a small fortune to fly and maintain as well. De la Rua took trips by commercial jet.

De la Rua advocated a stinging $2.5 billion tax increase to reduce the $7.1 billion budget deficit. The IMF expressed its approval over the tax hike by extending a $7.4 billion loan, but the tax increase was far less popular with the Argentine public. Nonetheless, polls taken two months into his term showed that while his government had only a 42% approval rating, the president's was 63%. That would soon change.

De la Rua then introduced a far more controversial labor reform bill that would allow more flexibility in labor contracts, a move seen as a gesture to wary foreign investors but also to satisfy IMF expectations. Among its provisions were a reduction in employer contributions to payroll deductions, an increase in the probation period for new employees from 30 to 90 days and decentralization of collective bargaining. It was essentially an Argentine analogy to the Taft-Hartley Act of 1947 in the United States, and it had a similar effect of waving a red flag at the still-powerful trade unions, which took to the streets to protest the new measure after it passed the Chamber of Deputies. In April 2000, union militants surrounded the Congress and clashed with police, who used truncheons and rubber bullets to disperse them. It was merely a taste of what was to come.

The Peronist majority in the Senate temporarily delayed discussion of the bill, but a week later the upper chamber passed, 57-4, a compromise version that precluded salaries from being reduced in collective bargaining. Organized labor found itself split over the modified plan, reportedly because de la Rua slyly promised entrenched labor bosses that he would not probe their operations if they would support the bill. The measure then returned to the lower house to resolve the dispari-

Fernando de la Rua

ties in the two versions, as unions called a one-day general strike on May 5. It disrupted traffic, but not the functioning of the country as organizers had hoped. The Chamber of Deputies passed the bill on May 11 by a vote of 121-84.

Just two days after the one-day strike, de la Rua and the Alliance received an important vote of confidence. The Alliance candidate to succeed de la Rua as mayor of Buenos Aires, Anibal Ibarra of the Radicals' left-of-center *Frepaso* coalition partner, defeated the still-disgruntled Domingo Cavallo, 49.4% to 33.1%. On election night, Cavallo lashed out at the victor, charged that the election was tainted by fraud and boasted that he would overtake Ibarra in the runoff. The following day, however, faced with the brutal reality of mathematics, a contrite Cavallo apologized for his intemperate remarks and withdrew from the race, handing the mayoralty to Ibarra.

Fissures soon appeared in the Radical-*Frepaso* Alliance after de la Rua announced $938 million in budget cuts and reductions of from 12% to 15% in the salaries of civil servants. This time, 14 *Frepaso* members of Congress revolted against the president, as did the *Frepaso*'s moral guardian, Graciela Fernández Mejía, the social development minister.

Another one-day work stoppage was called for June 9, which was much more widely observed than the stoppage of May 5 and represented the most serious expression of public disapproval yet of de la Rua's austerity measures, which the public nicknamed "*el Ajuste*," or, the Adjustment.

Left-wing members of the Alliance also were grumbling over what they regarded as undue influence on de la Rua by his close friend Fernando de Santibañes, a prominent and conservative banker whom de la Rua had named head of the National Intelligence Service (*SIDE*).

In mid-2000, the executive and legislative branches became embroiled in a scandal; accusations arose that the government had paid $10 million in bribes to 11 senators to secure passage of the labor reform bill. There was no substantive evidence, but the scandal droned on for months before finally dying out. Despite the lack of concrete evidence, a poll indicated that 70% of the corruption-jaded Argentine public believed the charges were true; chief among the critics was none other than the reform-minded Vice President Carlos Alvarez of *Frepaso*, who presided over the Senate.

De la Rua shuffled his cabinet in October. But when he retained Santibañes and promoted Labor Minister Alberto Flamarique to presidential chief of staff— both men had been implicated in the bribe scandal—Vice President Alvarez resigned in protest. Alvarez delivered a stinging denunciation of corruption in government, but insisted that he and his party would remain loyal to de la Rua. Flamarique also resigned, although Fernández Mejide remained as social development minister, preserving for a time the illusion that *Frepaso* was a partner in the government. Alvarez's resignation would confront Argentina with a constitutional crisis 14 months later. Meanwhile, the role of Economy Minister José Luis Machinea was strengthened to deal with the recession.

At year's end, de la Rua publicly admitted that the country's economic performance had been disappointing again in 2000, with GDP down by 5% and unemployment remaining stubbornly around 15%. About the only bright spot was a $40 billion economic rescue package approved by the IMF. Among the terms of the package: Argentina had to reduce its budget deficit from more than $9 billion to $6.5 billion by the end of 2001.

In March 2001, de la Rua appointed a new economy minister, a conservative technocrat, Ricardo López Murphy, trusted by investors but detested by the Peronists and *Frepaso*. He would last only two weeks. During his brief tenure, he provoked the last remaining *Frepaso* cabinet members, including Fernández Mejide, to resign by announcing $4.5 billion in budget cuts. A desperate de la Rua stunned the country—but delighted the international financial markets—by resurrecting the irrepressible Domingo Cavallo to replace López.

Over the next several months, Cavallo came up with a series of offbeat ideas designed to placate the IMF and, in theory, to jumpstart the flagging economy. One such proposal: Granting emergency powers for one year to the president—in reality, to Cavallo—to deal with the economic crisis by decree. Congress approved these "superpowers," and the IMF expressed its immediate approval.

In April, Cavallo came up with another offbeat idea: Instead of pegging the peso solely to the dollar, the inflation-busting technique he had fathered a decade earlier, he proposed pegging the peso to the average of the dollar and the euro, the European Union's new monetary unit. Although Cavallo argued that it would add stability to the peso, the *bolsa* and international markets reacted negatively, and the proposal caused consternation in Brazil, Argentina's leading trading partner. On April 22, a Sunday, Argentina suspended issuance of $700 million in treasury bills, and its international risk rating jumped more than 10% to 1,049—a rate worse than Russia's. Cavallo went before the television cameras to reassure investors that his recovery plan was "on track."

In a separate development, a federal prosecutor accused Menem of being the intellectual author of illegal arms sales in 1991 to Ecuador, then in a virtual state of war with Peru, and to Croatia, then under a United Nations arms embargo. Peronists rallied to the defense of their former chief, who denied the charges. Always flamboyant, the 70-year-old Menem splashed back into the international deadlines on May 26, 2001, by marrying Cecilia Bolocco, a 36-year-old former Miss Universe from Chile. He made headlines again on June 7 when he was placed under house arrest on the arms sale charges. He was formally indicted in July, but in November the Supreme Court threw out the charges.

In July, de la Rua announced his seventh painful austerity plan to cut the budget deficit and stave off defaulting on Argentina's foreign debt, which at that point was $128 billion. The plan included a 13% pay cut for civil servants, which sparked labor protests. Argentina's country risk indicator jumped to 1,616 points—worse than Ecuador's! However, the 13 Peronist governors rallied around the austerity plan and pledged to balance their provincial budgets as well, and Congress approved it in late July. The IMF responded with another $8 billion loan.

The austerity plan may have pleased the IMF, but it proved highly unpopular to the Argentines, especially the restriction on savings withdrawals. By October 2001, de la Rua's approval rating was 18% and Cavallo's was 16%. It was bad timing for the Alliance. In the October 14 elections for the entire Senate and half the Chamber of Deputies, the Peronists strengthened their majority in the upper

Argentina

chamber and increased from 102 to 116 in the lower chamber, replacing the Alliance as the largest bloc. The *UCR* dropped from 84 seats to 71, while *Frepaso* dropped from 23 to 17; Cavallo's party dropped from 12 to nine seats. In the popular vote, the Peronists received 40%, the Alliance only 23%. Duhalde remained politically viable by winning a Senate seat from Buenos Aires. But 30% of Argentines angrily cast blank ballots or nullified them by writing in names like Bart Simpson or Mickey Mouse. The public mood was dangerously ugly.

Less than a week after the election, de la Rua's political woes were compounded when the last *Frepaso* cabinet resigned after Cavallo cut his department's budget by 75%.

For the next two months, de la Rua and Cavallo desperately tried to deal with the deepening economic crisis and to avoid default on the national debt, which had increased to $132 billion; it would be the largest default in history, one that threatened to generate global shock waves. To do it, de la Rua had to appease the IMF by trying to balance the budget in the face of declining revenues while trying to sell the idea of greater belt-tightening to a Peronist-dominated Congress, powerful Peronist state governors, the trade unions and domestic and foreign investors. In November, he announced a "debt swap," that traded $95 billion worth of existing bonds that paid 11% for longer-term bonds that paid only 7%; for investors, it was a no-brainer. Then the Peronist governors dealt the president a setback by rejecting his proposed reduction in federal remittances to the state governments, something he needed to meet the terms for a $22 billion international rescue plan.

Descent into Chaos

By December 2001, fears of an imminent Argentine default and economic meltdown had Argentines in a near-panic. De la Rua infuriated his countrymen by reducing the monthly limit on savings withdrawals from $1,500 to $1,000. The IMF did not help matters on December 5 by freezing a scheduled $1.3 billion installment on its $22 billion line of credit because of displeasure with the government's lack of progress in meeting demands on deficit reduction and because it felt the peso had become unreasonably overvalued by the dollar peg.

Events then exploded in chain reaction. On December 11, the government pleaded for consensus with the Peronists to cut the budget from $49.6 billion to $42.5 billion—a whopping 14% decrease—to obtain the desperately needed help from the IMF. The budget deficit was $11 bil-

Rounding up sheep for market

lion, about double what de la Rua had assured the IMF it would be by year's end. The Peronists demanded de la Rua's resignation as their price for cooperation. On December 13, there was a massive general strike to protest the 18.3% unemployment rate. On December 14, the government announced it had allayed defaulting on the debt by making a loan payment of more than $700 million, but the good news was muted by the sudden resignation of the deputy finance minister, ostensibly for personal reasons but which embarrassed the president. The same day, a new poll showed that a majority of Argentines wanted Cavallo, whose appointment they had cheered nine months earlier, to resign. For the next six days, Argentina was a powder keg. On Wednesday, December 19, it exploded.

The spark was a demonstration by mostly middle-class Argentines, frustrated over the decline in their living standards and weary of their financial insecurity. The demonstrations began peacefully with the traditional banging on pots and pans, but soon there were violent clashes

with police. Full-scale rioting erupted in the capital and several cities in the interior. Rioters looted grocery stores. Five people were killed that first day, and de la Rua declared a 30-day state of siege—the first since the riots of 1989 that shortened the Alfonsín presidency. The riots continued on Thursday, December 20. Demonstrators tried to storm de la Rua's office. More people were killed, as de la Rua pleaded for calm. With the republic literally falling apart, the entire cabinet, including Cavallo, resigned in a vain attempt to quell the violence. The number of rioters in Buenos Aires alone was estimated at 20,000. Simultaneously, thousands of people rushed to banks to withdraw their monthly limit.

That evening, de la Rua himself resigned, two years and 10 days after he was inaugurated, and at sunset he was ignominiously whisked away from the Casa Rosada by helicopter, a scene eerily like that in 1976 when the military overthrew Isabel Perón. The mobs cheered the news, but it was a hollow celebration at best. By Thursday night, the death toll had climbed to 22, many of them looters shot not by police but by shopkeepers defending their property.

Despite de la Rua's resignation, the rioting continued, as a leaderless government desperately tried to cope with the violence as well as with a constitutional crisis. With the vacancy in the vice presidency caused by Alvarez's resignation 14 months earlier, de la Rua's constitutional successor was the Senate president, Ramón Puerta, a Peronist. But Puerta, feigning ill health, let it be known that he had no stomach for his constitutional mandate, which he said made him president for only 48 hours. It was hard to blame him, because that same day the Economy Ministry delivered still more bad news: GDP for the third quarter declined by 4.9% compared with the third quarter of 2000.

Thus, Argentina was quite literally on the brink of anarchy by Saturday, December 22, when Congress called new elections for March 3 and the Peronists tapped their governor of San Luis, Adolfo Rodríguez Sáa, as their choice for interim president until then. He was elected on a 169-138 vote in a joint session of Congress and sworn in on Sunday, December 23. Rodríguez Sáa lifted the state of siege, suspended payment on the foreign debt, and channeled the money instead into the creation of 1 million new jobs, the first 24,000 to be public service jobs.

It seemed that the country at least was no longer rudderless, as calm temporarily returned; the final death toll from the riots was 27, with hundreds more injured or arrested. Seven deaths alone had taken place in the Plaza de Mayo, in front of the Casa Rosada. Plans were announced to issue a new currency in January, the *argentino*, to circulate alongside the peso and the dollar. The idea was abandoned within a week because of speculation.

On Saturday, December 29, pot-beating protesters took to the streets again to protest Rodríguez Sáa's decision to continue the limit on savings withdrawals. Again, the protests turned violent, although not deadly. Protesters coined a popular new slogan that summed up the national mood: *Que se vayan todos!* (Throw all of them out!) They tried to storm their way into the Casa Rosada and the Congress, but were expelled by riot police.

If Rodríguez Sáa had thought he would have more success than de la Rua at achieving a consensus, he was soon disappointed. He desperately urged the Peronist leaders to offer solutions that might quell the popular uprising without worsening the economic crisis and to reach a consensus on how to select the Peronist candidate for the March 3 election. They could not—or would not.

On Sunday, December 30, after exactly one week in office, Rodríguez Sáa resigned in disgust, bitterly lashing out at the members of his own party for failing to support him on the tough decisions that had to be made. Mob rule, it seemed, was close to prevailing in Argentina.

With Puerta out of the running, the next hapless interim president was Eduardo Carmoña, speaker of the Chamber of Deputies, who like Puerta would keep the presidential chair warm for 48 hours until a joint session of Congress met on New Year's Day 2002 to select the nation's fifth president in 12 days. Meanwhile, on New Year's Eve, Congress canceled the March 3 election and decided to appoint an interim president. The initial plan was for the interim president to fill out de la Rua's term, which would have expired December 10, 2003.

Caretaker Government

The unfortunate "winner" of the January 1 balloting: The former vice president, Buenos Aires governor and newly elected senator from Buenos Aires, Eduardo Duhalde, 60, the Peronist presidential candidate who lost to de la Rua in 1999. The vote was 262–21, with 18 abstentions. Duhalde was sworn in on Wednesday, January 2, 2002. He told the Congress and the nation that he was scrapping the "exhausted model" of free markets and neoliberal economic policies that he blamed for the country's plight and that he would "recreate the conditions" to attract investors. "Argentina is bankrupt," he bluntly told his countrymen, "Argentina is destroyed. This model destroyed everything." He thus was calling for a return to the pre-Menem Peronist ideals of populism and protectionism. Duhalde urged Argentines "never to doubt even for a minute that Argentina has a future." He promised to guarantee deposits to prevent further panic—or violence. He also continued the moratorium on foreign debt payments. But he avoided mention of the two most sensitive topics—a possible peso devaluation and whether he would lift the detested restriction on bank withdrawals, which Argentines had nicknamed *"el corralito,"* or little corral.

Duhalde appointed a bipartisan cabinet but with the key posts going to Peronists. As economy minister, he named Jorge Remes Lenicov, an internationally respected economist who had served as economy minister of Buenos Aires province under Governor Duhalde. As foreign minister Duhalde appointed the current Buenos Aires governor—and another former vice president—Carlos Ruckauf.

Duhalde and Remes immediately submitted to Congress an emergency economic plan which, among other provisions, granted Duhalde and Remes *carte blanche*, authorized devaluation of the peso and froze job layoffs for six months. Meanwhile, on January 3, Argentina missed an interest payment on a $28 billion loan; the country was officially in default. The Chamber of Deputies quickly approved it on January 5, and the Senate followed the next day. That night, Remes announced that the decade-old peg of the peso to the dollar had ended. He devalued the peso 40%, but said it would be allowed to float freely to find its levels on international exchanges.

An angry IMF board of directors sent a letter criticizing Duhalde's economic plan as incoherent. Deputy Economy Minister Jorge Todesca angrily responded that the letter was "offensive to Argentina." The IMF was not alone in its criticism, however. In a speech to the OAS in Washington on January 17, President Bush warned that Argentina would face a "bleak and stagnant future" if it returned to the old Peronist protectionism and called on Duhalde to come up with a coherent, long-term recovery plan.

On February 2, the Supreme Court got into the act by declaring the restrictions on savings unconstitutional, presenting Duhalde with yet another complication. Remes responded with another bank holiday on February 5, as depositors began arming themselves with court orders directing the banks to give them their money. Remes also declared that the peso would be allowed to float freely and that bank withdrawals and government transactions would henceforth be in pesos. This announcement led to even more violent demonstrations on February 19. (A year later, the Supreme Court ruled the conversion of bank accounts from dollars to pesos was an unconstitutional infringement of private property rights.)

On February 27, Duhalde succeeded in persuading the powerful Peronist governors to agree to a revenue-sharing plan that the IMF had demanded. But the economic situation worsened. The unemployment rate increased to an alarming 23.8% in April 2002—about what it was in the United States during the depths of the Great Depression. The peso hit an all-time low of 4.00 to the dollar. The percentage of Argentines living below the $200-a-month poverty line mushroomed to 57%. Then, suddenly, another old enemy returned: Inflation. In April 2002 alone, prices rose 10%, and for the first seven months of 2002, inflation was 35%. The combination of double-digit unemployment and double-digit inflation defied the laws of economics and created a climate of desperation.

In April, Remes abruptly resigned after Congress rejected his proposed bank re-

Argentina

form plan, adding to the turmoil. Duhalde then appointed Roberto Lavagna, a trade expert and former ambassador to the European Union and the World Trade Organization, as economy minister—the country's sixth in 14 months.

In a separate, unrelated development, former Economy Minister Cavallo was arrested in connection with the alleged sale of illegal arms to Ecuador and Croatia that had implicated Menem. At the same time, an appeals court ordered the presiding judge in the case to reopen the investigation of Menem and several others.

The government tried to come up with a plan to allow depositors to withdraw savings without bankrupting the banking system. It devised a scheme requiring depositors to accept five- and 10-year bonds in exchange for some accounts. Needless to say, depositors reacted with fury.

In May, Duhalde received the best news he had had in his first four months: Horst Köhler, the managing director of the IMF, agreed to give Argentina another year to pay a $136 million loan that was due.

Protests continued throughout May and June 2002, while Duhalde tried to persuade the Congress and the 14 Peronist governors to enable him to take the same difficult austerity measures to guarantee additional IMF support that had brought down de la Rua; he reportedly threatened to resign at one point unless they cooperated. On June 26, one protest turned deadly when riot police opened fire, killing two demonstrators.

Meanwhile, negotiations with the IMF dragged on. In September, the IMF agreed to postpone a $2.8 billion loan payment, but the IMF rejected Argentina's request for an aid package unless several reforms were adopted. The talks broke down altogether in October, with the IMF choosing to delay further talks until the election of Duhalde's successor. In November, Argentina was to make a $805 million payment on a World Bank loan, but was able to make only a $79.2 million payment for interest. Finally, in January 2003, the IMF relented and agreed to a $6.8 billion loan to help Argentina avoid default on its foreign debt, then $141 billion, which would have had global financial repercussions that nobody wanted.

The Election of 2003

On July 2, 2002, a frustrated Duhalde advanced the presidential elections by six months, from September to March 2003. Congress already had enacted open party primaries in November to select the candidates. The new law would have allowed independents to participate in the primaries, but a federal judge nullified the law as unconstitutional. Duhalde resorted

Eduardo Duhalde

to an executive decree to set December 15 as the date for the party primaries, but a constitutional court ruled that maneuver unconstitutional as well, finding that the president could not require all the parties to hold their primaries on the same day.

The separate parties thus were left to their own nomination machineries, although the Justicialist Party was the only one with a chance of winning the next election, which had been rescheduled for April 27. For the first time, a runoff would be held on May 18 if no candidate received a majority. The new president would be inaugurated on May 25.

An intra-party turf battle quickly erupted again between the Menem and Duhalde factions over who the Peronist candidate would be. In October, much to the annoyance of the Menem faction, a meeting of 585 Peronist leaders acceded to Duhalde's request to delay the party primary until January 19, 2003. Menem grumbled—with an element of truth—that Duhalde was stalling until he could field a candidate strong enough to stop Menem.

In January 2003, in a power struggle reminiscent of the referendum controversy of 1999, Duhalde succeeded in getting party backing to scrap the Peronist primary altogether, obviously because he knew Menem might well win it. Instead, the presidential election became a free-for-all, with rival Peronists and independents winding up on the same ballot. Menem's faction, of course, bitterly opposed the elimination of a primary they thought they could win. Soon, the ballot began filling up. Rodríguez Sáa declared his candidacy, as did a dark horse, Néstor Kirchner, the populist Peronist governor of Santa Cruz Province in remote, sparsely populated Patagonia. As his running mate he chose Duhalde's tourism and sports minister, Daniel Scioli. Duhalde threw his support behind Kirchner, which infuri-

ated both Menem and Rodríguez Sáa. Kirchner scored points with the voters by promising to retain the popular Lavagna as economy minister. With three strong candidates, who were already slinging mud at each other, it seemed the Peronists were in the process of disemboweling themselves.

The opposition was fragmented, too, however. Former Economy Minister Ricardo López Murphy, a Radical who survived his association with de la Rua with his reputation intact, announced as an independent and became the preferred choice of the country's business sector. Another new face, Elisa Carrió, elected to Congress as a Radical, launched a new movement with an anti-corruption platform, not unlike *Frepaso*. The poor discredited *UCR*, meanwhile, offered up a political lightweight named Leopoldo Moreau as its sacrificial lamb.

The vote totals stunned everyone:

Menem	4,686,646	24.36%
Kirchner	4,232,052	22.0%
López Murphy	3,144,528	16.34%
Carrió	2,720,692	14.14%
Rodríguez Sáa	2,715,799	14.12%
Moreau	450,489	2.34%

Far from feeling elated over his first-place showing, the once-popular Menem was shocked that he had failed to poll even a fourth of the vote. He was shocked even more over the next two weeks when polls showed that Kirchner would humiliate him by more than 2-1 on May 18. Faced with his first-ever electoral defeat, what Menem did next was generated by pure ego: On May 14, he withdrew from the runoff and made Kirchner president by default. It was more than just an egotistical move designed to avoid electoral humiliation, however; it was pure Machiavellian politics, Menem-style. Kirchner, denied an electoral victory, would have to govern for four years—if he lasts—on a shaky second-place mandate from only 22% of the voters. Menem, meanwhile, would be reminding Argentines of that every step of the way.

Kirchner Shakes Up the System

Kirchner, 53, a lawyer, was sworn in on May 25, 2003. Shaky mandate or not, he soon began rattling the country's institutions and its foreign policy. At least 12 Latin American presidents attended the inauguration, including Cuba's Fidel Castro, Venezuela's Hugo Chávez and Brazil's new president, Luiz Inácio da Silva—all critics of the U.S.-supported Free Trade Area of the Americas. Kirchner repeated his opposition to the FTAA after he was

President Néstor Kirchner

sworn in, and the inauguration was viewed as something of a festival of the Latin American left. Neither Duhalde nor Kirchner, incidentally, had condemned Castro's crackdown on dissent the month before (see Cuba). Kirchner also let it be known he sided with da Silva in stressing regional Latin American integration, and touted a concept he called "national capitalism." The Bush administration did little to help matters, snubbing Kirchner, as it had da Silva four months earlier, by sending a third-string representative, this time the secretary of housing and urban development, Mel Martínez.

Just three days into his term, Kirchner forced 27 army generals and 13 navy admirals into retirement. The upper echelons of the armed forces reacted angrily, but meekly complied. What else could they do? They obtained little sympathy from the senior field-grade officers who stood in line for promotion to general and admiral as a result of the shakeup. Then Kirchner began cashiering top-ranking federal police officers as well.

The same month, Kirchner turned on the judicial branch, asking Congress to impeach "some" of the nine Supreme Court justices. In unusually blunt language in a nationally televised address, Kirchner accused the justices of corruption and cronyism and of holding the nation "hostage" through its decisions that hamstrung many of Duhalde's economic reform plans. The Argentine justice system is notoriously corrupt, and Duhalde had tried unsuccessfully to impeach the justices. Kirchner focused on justices appointed by, and still loyal to, Menem; he cited Supreme Court President Julio Nazareno by name. Nazareno resigned in

July. By July 2004, three more Menem appointees chose to resign in the face of likely impeachment.

Days later June 17, Kirchner shook up taxpayers by announcing a crackdown on tax evasion—a time-honored tradition in Argentina. Reliable estimates indicate that revenue could be increased by 50% if all the tax cheaters paid what they owe.

Kirchner simultaneously made a splash in international circles. In June 2003, U.S. Secretary of State Powell belatedly visited Argentina after the OAS foreign ministers' meeting in Santiago, Chile. Kirchner assured Powell he wanted amicable relations with the United States, but also insisted that Washington maintain a respectful distance. The next day, Kirchner flew to Brasilia, where he and da Silva repeated their call for greater Latin American integration. On June 16, Kirchner suddenly reiterated Argentina's claim of sovereignty over the Malvinas (Falkland Islands), and called on Britain to resume talks on the islands' future. Britain summarily rejected the suggestion.

Horst Köhler, managing director of the IMF, came to Buenos Aires for his first face-to-face talks with Kirchner and Lavagna June 23–24 on the conditions for restructuring Argentina's debt. Kirchner bluntly told Köhler that he would not agree to any further conditions that would cause his countrymen any more suffering, and Köhler just as bluntly told the president that the Argentines' suffering would end only when there is an economic climate that once again attracts foreign investors and encourages Argentines to bring their money back from the foreign accounts where they have been stashing it for safekeeping. In a news conference afterward, Köhler admitted, "Argentina needs to deepen and broaden its structural reforms, but this cannot be done in six months." Köhler also agreed that some of the reforms demanded by the IMF, such as raising fees for public services, could be delayed a little longer. In the end, the two sides agreed to start negotiations within a few weeks on a three-year plan to repay the $13.5 billion that would be coming due between September 2003 and September 2006. Köhler left saying he was "impressed" with Kirchner and promising that the IMF would continue working with Argentina.

It seemed Kirchner had succeeded in easing strained relations with the IMF. But on September 9, 2003, Argentina defaulted on a $3 billion payment to the IMF on its $90 billion debt, the largest single missed payment in IMF history. A day later, he negotiated a deal with the IMF that allowed Argentina to restructure payment of $21 billion of the debt over three years. On September 25, Kirchner was in New

York addressing the United Nations, where he laid part of the blame for the failure to repay the debt at the feet of the IMF itself and of developed nations that block the exports of developing nations.

Relations with the IMF had improved immeasurably by January 2004, when the IMF announced that it was satisfied with Argentine compliance with the September agreement. But in August 2004, Kirchner suddenly and inexplicably canceled the agreement with the IMF. For good measure, Kirchner defiantly informed the holders of the $102.6 billion in outstanding Argentine bonds that he would exchange them for new bonds worth only about 30–35% of the value of the originals and, in essence, told them to take it or leave it. Creditors screamed foul and demanded that Kirchner compromise on a less painful figure. He refused. Faced with recovering 30 cents on the dollar or nothing, more than 70% of the bondholders had decided to take it when the deadline for the so-called debt-swap deal expired on February 25, 2005. Officially, the world's largest debt default in modern history was over. One effect of the reneging on Argentina's debt obligations has been a huge budget surplus, which Kirchner has been investing in infrastructure and social programs, which in turn has solidified his popularity.

Recent Developments

Although his actions and his rhetoric have made Kirchner a pariah to the IMF board, he remains enormously popular—for the time being—with the Argentines. In addition, he is the first president since Menem who can boast of an improving economy (see Economy). His popularity proved decisive in the victory of several of his allies in provincial elections in September 2003, among them Buenos Aires Mayor Anibal Ibarra, an independent, and Buenos Aires provincial Governor Felipe Sola, a Peronist. In 2004, his approval rating dropped from a phenomenal 80% to 60%—still phenomenal by Argentine and Latin American standards.

Kirchner also has created institutional shock waves by accelerating the investigations into, and arrests for, human rights abuses committed during the "Dirty War" of 1976–83 (see Ghosts from the Past). At Kirchner's urging, both houses of Congress in August repealed two of Alfonsín's amnesty laws that had blocked further prosecutions of military officers.

In July 2003, a federal judge ordered the arrests of 45 former officers. Forty of them had been charged by Spanish Judge Baltasar Garzón and Spain sought their extradition to stand trial there, but Kirchner's government rejected the extradition re-

Argentina

quest in order to bring them to justice in Argentina. They were released pending trial, though one, former army General Luciano Benjamín Menéndez, was re-arrested in September. The notorious Alfredo Astiz, the former navy officer known as "the Blond Angel of Death," also was arrested in September. Astiz was under indictment in France for the alleged murder of two French nuns and France sought his extradition. But his indictment in Argentina on May 20, 2004, served notice that he would face an Argentine court.

In October, Kirchner recalled the Argentine attaché to Italy, Horacio Losito, in connection with the massacre of 22 dissidents in Chacó in 1976. Also in October, a retired brigadier general and two retired colonels were arrested as part of the investigation into torture centers operated in Buenos Aires during the Dirty War, including the notorious Navy Mechanics School. A provincial deputy in Tierra del Fuego was arrested in January 2004 on suspicion of having tortured prisoners at the mechanics school. In February 2004, Kirchner had the school turned into a human rights museum. Kirchner also ordered police files opened and an investigation into whether the army was continuing abuse of prisoners three years after the return to democracy.

Another of the most notorious human rights suspects, former navy Captain Adolfo Scilingo, who had voluntarily surrendered to Spanish authorities and had admitted participation in the "death flights," finally went on trial in Madrid in January 2005. Scilingo abruptly recanted his confession, but in April the court found him guilty of 30 counts of murder and of torture and illegal detentions. He was sentenced to 640 years.

By mid-year 2004, however, Argentines were far less worried about the crimes of the past than they were about the crimes of the present. A crime wave, much of the it attributed to increasingly organized gangs of unemployed or homeless people, had the capital in a grip of fear. Residents took to the streets again in mass demonstrations to demand that something be done. The law-and-order demonstrators have shown they are not much better than the criminals. In July 2004, hundreds of them stormed city hall in Buenos Aires and held it for several hours before police finally acted. Kirchner sacked the police chief for not acting more expeditiously. When the president's justice minister publicly criticized the chief's firing, the pugnacious president fired him as well.

Another potential crisis in the making is an acute energy shortage, blamed on frozen electricity rates that led to increased demand. The foreign-owned utility companies have complained that inflation has made the current rates unrealistic

Carlos Gardel

and prevents further investment, but Kirchner has steadfastly refused to raise the rates on residential customers. The water supply system also is affected, and the freeze has strained relations with France, because the French company Suez owns a 40% share of Aguas Argentinas. Unless solutions are forthcoming, Argentina may experience the kind of blackouts and energy rationing that Brazil experienced in 2001. Some local blackouts already have occurred.

Former President Menem, the perennial bad penny of Argentine politics, remains a force his detractors, including Kirchner, cannot ignore. On April 20, 2004, an Argentine judge issued an arrest warrant for Menem, who was living in Chile with his Chilean wife and their baby, for allegedly embezzling $60 million from two prison construction projects. Argentina formally requested his extradition. In May, a Chilean judge rejected the petition, ostensibly because the stated reason for the extradition, Menem's failure to appear in court, is not an extraditable offense. In December, two Argentine judges rescinded the arrest warrants, and the flamboyant Menem triumphantly and with great media fanfare returned to Argentina on December 22, vowing to run against and defeat his fellow Peronist Kirchner in 2007.

Culture: Unlike most of the South American colonies, Argentina did not develop a

mestizo race (European-Indian) because the indigenous inhabitants were driven ever westward beyond the expanding frontier or were exterminated outright. This military policy, which bordered on genocide, extended into the late 19th century. While the United States and neighboring Brazil imported African slaves, what was to become the laboring class in Argentina stemmed from a wave of European immigrants, chiefly from Spain and Italy, who were attracted during the 19th century by work on the cattle ranches and in the wheat fields, vineyards and emerging industries.

Consequently, Argentina's ethnic makeup today is almost wholly European, with Italian descendants accounting for nearly half the population. This also has given Argentine Spanish a distinctly Italian inflection, an unmistakable accent that is the butt of jokes in other Latin American countries. Lesser influxes of British and German settlers, many of them well-to-do investors, also have colored Argentina's social fabric, as have Jews, Arabs and Gypsies.

Which is not to say that Argentina lacks a rich cultural heritage of its own. As occurred in the United States, the romanticism associated with the conquest of the frontier and the development of vast stretches of rich farming and grazing lands of the *Pampas* gave rise to a uniquely Argentine folk hero: the *gaucho*, or cowboy. As with the North American cowboy, it is difficult to separate myth from reality, but unquestionably the raw-boned *gauchos* with their baggy cotton pants, sheepskin chaps and *bolas*, (the device used to ensnare the legs of running calves) greatly shaped Argentine culture and folklore. Their drum-based music, *malambo*, is as identifiable with Argentine culture as the tango.

One of the great works of the so-called golden age of Argentine literature of the late 19th and early 20th centuries was the epic poem *El gaucho Martín Fierro*, written by José Hernández in two installments in 1872 and 1879. Martín Fierro occupies much the same place in Argentine folklore as do Paul Bunyan or Pecos Bill in the United States. It is not uncommon to see truck stops in northern Argentina today named for this folk hero. The legacy of the *gauchos* also is exploited today for tourist purposes in such Buenos Aires steakhouses as *La Estancia*, where waiters dress in traditional *gaucho* garb and *malambo* groups provide live music.

The wealth of the *estancias*, or ranches, also shaped Argentines' meat-based diets. The most popular eating places in Argentina, except perhaps for the ubiquitous pasta bars, are *parrilladas*, which specialize in assorted meats grilled over wood embers; often an entire goat is staked out on a metal frame and roasted in front of a *fogón*, or bonfire. The most common social gathering is the *asado*, a barbecue on a massive scale in which sometimes dozens of guests consume a variety of meats and wash them down with copious amounts of domestic wine, which can be excellent.

The relative enlightenment that followed the Rosas dictatorship in the mid-19th century allowed a rich literary tradition to take root. Two of the greatest writers of this period also were leaders in the struggle for democracy. Bartolomé Mitre served as president of the republic during the pivotal period of 1862–68, and two years after leaving the presidency he founded the daily newspaper *La Nación,* still published by his descendants today and regarded as one of the world's great newspapers. Domingo Faustino Sarmiento was forced into exile during the Rosas era and nettled the dictatorship from neighboring Chile, where he edited *El Mercurio*, then based in Valparaiso. Sarmiento's writings proved inspirational not only for Argentines but for other Latin Americans saddled with dictatorship, and he is revered as one of the premier figures of Latin American letters. He succeeded Mitre in the presidency, serving from 1868–74. Another great newspaper of record, *La Prensa*, was established in 1869; it served as a conduit for the poems, stories and essays of the great writers of the golden age. Both it and *La Nación* also developed a reputation for resisting the will of dictators; *La Prensa*, published by several generations of the Gainza and Paz families, was closed by Perón from 1951–55.

This tradition continued into the 20th century, when *La Nación* made space available for the verse of a blind man acknowledged as Argentina's greatest poet: Jorge Luis Borges (1899–1986). His reputation was global, although the Nobel Prize eluded him all his life. Like many of Latin America's great writers, artists and musicians, he spent much of his career in Europe, in part because of Argentina's periodic reversions to dictatorship and the chilling effect that invariably had on the arts. He died in Switzerland in 1986.

Other notable 20th century Argentine writers include Julio Cortázar (1914–84), a novelist, playwright and poet, perhaps best remembered for the plays *Los reyes* (1949) and *Bestiario* (1951) and the novels *Los premios* (1960), *Rayuela* (1963), *62/Modelo para armar* (1968), and *Libro de Manuel* (1973); and Ernesto Sábato (b. 1911), a renowned essayist and author of three memorable novels: *El túnel* (1948), *Sobre héroes y tumbas* (1961), and *Abbadón el exterminador* (1974). Both Cortázar and Sábato achieved recognition throughout the Spanish speaking— and reading—world, and their works have been translated into numerous other languages. Manuel Puig (1932–90), wrote a tale of two political prisoners sharing a cell that was adapted to the stage and the screen: *El beso de la mujer araña* ("The Kiss of the Spider Woman.") Another Argentine writer, Adolfo Pérez Esquivel, received the Nobel Peace Prize in 1980 for his courageous opposition to military rule.

In music, Argentina has produced its share of classical composers, the most renowned being Alberto Ginastera (1916–83). Argentina also has partial claim to Carlos Kleiber (1930–2004), one of the world's most eminent 20th century composers. His father, Erich Kleiber, also a noted composer, emigrated from Austria to Argentina in 1935 to escape the Nazis. Carlos Kleiber divided his career between Argentina and Europe, where he died and is buried.

But when one thinks of Argentine music, one thinks of the tango. The dance and music that has become synonymous with Argentina emerged as an erotic art form in the sleazy nightclubs and brothels of La Boca, the port district of Buenos Aires. Its contagious rhythm and sexual innuendo won it ready acceptance in the *avantegarde* circles of Paris during the 1920s, and from the Left Bank its popularity spread throughout the bistros and cabarets of Europe and the Prohibition-era U.S. nightclubs and speakeasies. Ironically, the tango composer and singer who came to be most identified with the genre was an immigrant from France at age 3: Carlos Gardel (1890–1935). Killed in a plane crash in Colombia at age 45, Gardel even today is the center of an Elvis-like cult following in Argentina. Posters of the forever-young Gardel, his slick black hair parted in the middle, are a ubiquitous symbol of the nation's cultural identity.

Eventually, through the talents of the internationally renowned composer Astor Piazzolla (1921–92), the tango emerged into a classical form acceptable in polite society. One literally cannot escape the sounds of the tango in Argentine restaurants, so ingrained is it in the life of the nation. Two U.S.-made movies, "Scent of a Woman" and "Evita," have revived interest in the tango abroad. In fact, the tango performed in "Scent of a Woman" was *Por una cabeza*, written by Gardel and Alfredo Le Pera shortly before they perished together in Colombia.

Argentine cinema, established in the 1930s, enjoyed something of a boom during the first Perón era, but lapsed into mediocrity during subsequent military regimes, particularly that of 1976–83, when political repression and artistic censorship forced many leading actors and directors into exile. Since 1983 it has enjoyed a renaissance and has won some international accolades. The film *La historia oficial,* ("The Official Story") an account of a middle-aged housewife who comes to realize that her adopted daughter was taken from two slain dissidents during the "Dirty War," won the Golden Palm at the Cannes Film Festival.

Radio in Argentina enjoyed a golden age in the 1920s and '30s, just as it had in the United States, the exception being that tango enjoyed equal billing with that of the Big Band sounds. Soap operas were popular, and provided the boost to stardom of an ambitious young actress named Eva Duarte—later Eva Perón. Television began as a state venture and wallowed in mediocrity for decades for much the same reason as did the cinema: the flight of talent from the censorship of military regimes. The result was a dependence on dubbed imported programs, mostly from the United States. Today's less-encumbered Argentine television has seen a boom in locally produced programs, many of them the ever-popular telenovelas, which often are exported.

Economy: Argentina is well-endowed with some of the richest farmland in the world and as a result, the economy has traditionally been based on agriculture, primarily cattle, wheat and wine. A favorable balance of trade led to industrialization as well, and at the turn of the 20th century, Argentina was one of the four wealthiest nations in the world.

Argentina

After World War II, the economy was plagued by the fiscal policies of the first Perón administration. When he took office in 1946, reserves stood at a respectable $1.5 billion. By 1955 that surplus had vanished and the nation was deeply in the red. Every government since then has added to the debt. Agriculture was penalized in order to promote industrialization. Food prices were held artificially low and taxes were placed on farm exports in order to finance the construction of factories. The government role in the economy also expanded. The state controlled more than half of all heavy industry—most of which has been inefficient, overstaffed and unprofitable. Because of a lack of capital investment in newer techniques, it became the equivalent of the "rust belt" industry of the northeast United States, which has been undergoing replacement by facilities erected in the southern United States because of onerous taxes, wages and workers' benefits in the North.

Argentina has for the last 50+ years enjoyed the most evenly distributed and largest per capita income in Latin America. Much of this wealth, however, was eroded by runaway inflation, particularly during the 1980s. Perón taught the nation to live beyond its means, printing more and more pesos, establishing a precedent which was repeated over and over.

Once the *Peronistas* returned to power in 1973 the economy was harassed by widespread strikes, a shortage of consumer goods and high job absenteeism. Even more damaging was the disastrous drop in farm exports, which usually had counted for 70% of the nation's foreign earnings. Although poor weather was a contributing factor, most farm problems stemmed from government policies which maintained low food prices for the people of Buenos Aires and the cities, where 80% of the nation lives. Beef exports dropped to their lowest level of the century when the European Common Market reduced imports of Argentine meat. At the same time, beef consumption rose because of lowered prices. By 1975 Argentines consumed 220 pounds of beef per person annually, twice the U.S. figure.

The major customer for Argentine wheat was the former Soviet Union, but this has been questionable since it dissolved. Agreements provided that Argentina had to import substantial amounts of Soviet goods, most of which were of poor quality. The successors of the Soviet Union have no hard currency reserves and are now haunted by galloping inflation. Having no money to pay for Argentine grain, the Russians are getting it from the United States, using credits (loans) that have been generously granted to further U.S. interest in keeping the state afloat in Moscow.

Industrial output fell in Argentina, partially due to a shortage of parts, frequent strikes and low capital reinvestment. The nation's once-mighty auto industry also broke down, with eight foreign-owned assembly plants losing $160 million on their Argentine operations in 1975. During that period, the growth in the nation's gross national product dropped to zero. It went as low as –9% in the late 1980s.

Controlling of the country from 1976–83, the military rulers sought to return Argentina to a free-market system—a dramatic about face from the state planning which had dominated the economy since Perón first took office. The impact of the changes was limited—partly because 60% of the economy was under government control or ownership.

The worst depression, coupled with hyper-inflation, corruption, overspending, a bulging bureaucracy in Buenos Aires and the provinces, and the excessive demands of labor unions, all took the starch out of the economy during the presidency of Raúl Alfonsín, of the Radical Civil Union (1983–89). One observer noted, "In the U.S. and Europe, things are either automatic or predictable. Here, nothing is automatic or predictable." Riots forced Alfonsín to relinquish power to his successor several months early.

Under Peronist President Carlos Menem (1989–99), things at last began changing (although a bitter pill for many). In 1992, he announced he was pegging the peso to the U.S. dollar, one-to-one. The effect was almost immediate. Inflation dropped from 40% per month to less than 10% per year, which enabled Argentina at last to engage in intelligent financial planning. It also attracted foreign investment in substantial quantities that was vitally necessary for continued growth. Menem also abandoned protectionism and embraced free-market economics, which for a Peronist was heretical. But there was no questioning its success.

Capital which used to migrate abroad began staying within Argentina, and funds began returning there from overseas. The return on investment was attractive in the 1990s, and Argentina imposed fewer and fewer restrictions on withdrawal of profits by investors, in stark contrast to much of the rest of Latin America.

The devaluation of the Mexican peso in 1994 presented a major threat to Argentine economic stability since it, just as Mexico, had been presumed to be a place for safe investment. Menem responded energetically to preserve Argentina's reputation, and did so successfully. He almost immediately instituted an austerity program to reduce imports and wages, two unpopular moves which had to be made just before the May 1995 elections. The program

enabled Argentina's banking system to defend its currency.

By early 1998, Argentina was experiencing a negative aspect of globalizing its economy. It had successfully overcome the effects of the 1994–95 Mexican peso crisis, only to begin feeling the effects of the crisis in the Asian markets. Growth was still in the neighborhood of 8%, and though unemployment was down it was still an uncomfortable 13%. Inflation for 1998 was a mere 1%. Overall, these were the best economic times Argentina had seen in decades. But it was not to last.

Foreseeing a coming slump, the IMF approved a three-year, $2.8 billion loan for Argentina in February 1998. Nonetheless, the country slid into recession. Meanwhile, in a surprise move apparently aimed at shoring up his traditional support among the once-powerful labor unions, Menem swung the pendulum back from his policy of appeasing the needs of big business by proposing new labor regulations that essentially left in place the *Peronistas'* liberal severance benefits. It also nullified a 1995 law that allowed companies greater leeway in hiring part-time workers without paying payroll taxes.

Responding to renewed fears of inflation, the head of the central bank announced in January 1999 that he favored a monetary treaty with the United States that would actually make the dollar the official currency of Argentina, as it is in Panama, within three years. Former President Alfonsín scoffed at the suggestion, saying it would make Argentina an economic vassal of the United States, like Puerto Rico.

Year-end figures for 1999 graphically demonstrated the severity of the recession incoming Radical President Fernando de la Rua had inherited from Menem. Real GDP declined by 3.5%, and unemployment was 14.5%. About the only good news was that once-feared inflation *declined* by 2%. De la Rua's painful austerity measures and the labor reform bill were needed to obtain funds from the IMF, but experts warned that it could be some time before the benefits were felt. Those experts proved correct. De la Rua made an ill-advised prediction in mid-2000 that Argentina would end the year with positive growth of 3.5% to 4%, a prediction that returned to haunt him and cost him even more of his credibility and popularity Argentina's economy *shrank* another 0.5% in 2000; the only cheer came from the fact that it was a fraction of the decrease of 1999. Unemployment was still a troubling 14.7%, and it has grown steadily worse since then.

Under de la Rua, there was no further talk of embracing the dollar as Ecuador

50

did in early 2000. Instead, de la Rua publicly called for *Mercosur* to emulate the European Union by adopting a common currency for the trade bloc. He predicted monetary union could be in place within three years, but financial experts said it could take 10. De la Rua also was an advocate of the Free Trade Area of the Americas (FTAA).

In late 2001, the recession deepened as unemployment grew to 18.3% and de la Rua sought desperately to meet the deficit-reduction goals he had set to ensure continued IMF support so Argentina could avoid default on its $132 billion foreign debt. When he imposed strict limits of $1,000 a month on savings withdrawals, angry Argentines took to the streets. The demonstrations erupted in violence that left 27 people dead and forced de la Rua to resign. After three interim presidents proved unwilling or incapable of dealing with the crisis, Congress elected a Peronist, Eduardo Duhalde, on January 2, 2002 as interim president until the next elections (see History).

Within days, the new president pushed an emergency economic reform package through Congress, after which he revoked Menem's 10-year-old dollar-parity plan. In March, the free-floating peso hit an all-time low of 4.00 to the dollar.

The economic crisis had plunged more and more Argentines into poverty. In March 2000, a study by the Social Development Ministry had reported that 37% of Argentines lived below the poverty line of $200 a month. By 2002, that figure was a staggering 57%, and in mid-2003 it had increased to 58.5%; 28% were classified as living in extreme poverty, double the percentage from before the meltdown. Bartering has become commonplace in the cash-strapped economy, as has eking a living by scavenging from garbage dumps.

GDP growth for 2001 was down 1%, but the political and economic turmoil caused GDP growth in 2002 to drop by a near-cataclysmic 13.6% before it finally bottomed out. Other signs of hope: unemployment abated to 18%, still high, and the peso rebounded to about 2.8 to the dollar.

The newly elected president, Néstor Kirchner, who took office on May 25, 2003, still had an economic nightmare to deal with. He rejected Menem's free-market approach and returned to the populism of Juan Perón. He also joined forces with Brazil's new center-left president, Luiz Inácio da Silva, in calling for a revival of the *Mercosur* trade bloc

Kirchner's hard-ball tactics in negotiating with the IMF bore fruit with an agreement reached in early 2004 (see History), but Kirchner canceled the agreement the following August. In a bold maneuver, he bluntly made a take-it-or-leave it offer

to creditors to exchange $102.6 billion in Argentine bonds for new ones worth only about 35% of the original indebtedness, and he gave them a deadline of February 25, 2005, to decide. Unhappy creditors had little choice but to accept and take the loss; those who did accounted for 76% of the debt.

Without a doubt, the diversion of resources from debt servicing has led to a dramatic resurgence in the economy. After a 10.9% decrease in GDP in 2002, Argentina showed growth in 2003 for the first time in five years, a robust 8.7%, and for 2004 it was up another 8.8%. Of course, this just recovers the ground lost during the crisis of 2000-02. The poverty rate dropped from 58% in 2002 to 44% in 2004. Unemployment, however, was still about 16% for both 2003 and 2004, a dramatic improvement from 2002, but gangs of unemployed people were regularly disrupting traffic in Buenos Aires with roadblocks. Inflation also threatened to become a problem again. In the first quarter of 2005, consumer prices rose 4%, and the projection for the year was 17%, the highest since 1992 if the 2002 peso devaluation is discounted.

The Future: In the space of 17 months, Argentina went from an inept elected president ejected from office by mob rule, to a series of ephemeral presidents with no stomach for the job, to an unelected caretaker, to an unpredictable populist "elected" by only 22% of the voters.

Néstor Kirchner, armed with that flimsy mandate handed to him by default when

Carlos Menem chose ego over electoral defeat and Machiavellian intrigue over the good of the nation, has been forced to govern a nation that is still beset with a crushing debt and high unemployment. Yet, his no-nonsense approach toward Menem, the IMF, the United States, the Supreme Court, the military and the police have been impressive, if brash at times. He can boast of something that no president since Menem in the early 1990s could: an improving economy and a high popularity rating, about 60% at the end of 2004.

His take-it-or-leave-it debt swap deal was, on the surface, a master stroke. He forced holders of more than $100 billion worth of Argentine bonds to accept new bonds worth only 30% of the originals. Grumbling, most did. What remains to be seen, however, is how Argentina, now a black sheep in international financial circles, will obtain more capital when it needs it—which it inevitably will. Another question is whether other debt-strapped nations may decide to employ the same tactic. If so, it will be a matter of time before the international financial system collapses from the losses.

Meanwhile, Kirchner's arch-nemesis, former President Menem, has returned from self-imposed exile in Chile now that he is not threatened with jail. He has vowed to run for his old job in 2007, when he would be 79, and boot out Kirchner, his fellow Peronist. Judging from recent polls, it would be a quixotic quest, as Kirchner is far more popular than Menem is.

The combative president is also involved in a turf battle with another former Peronist president, his old mentor Eduardo Duhalde. The two men are involved in a power struggle for the selection of congressional candidates in Buenos Aires, which is regarded as Duhalde's turf. There is speculation that Kirchner's wife, in Hillary Clinton style, may challenge Duhalde's own candidate for a Senate seat from Buenos Aires in the October 2005 elections. Those elections will provide a proving ground for the strength of the three Peronists and for what is left of the opposition.

If past experience proves a guide, Kirchner's greatest adversary may turn out to be neither the IMF nor Menem, nor Duhalde, nor even himself, but the Argentine people he leads. Despite Kirchner's current popularity, Argentines are not known for their patience with their elected leaders. They are like a spoiled, irresponsible adolescent from an affluent, privileged family, and it is time for them to grow up, to accept their responsibilities, and to work to realize their potential, which is considerable. If they ever can, Argentina once again could enter a Golden Age.

Belize

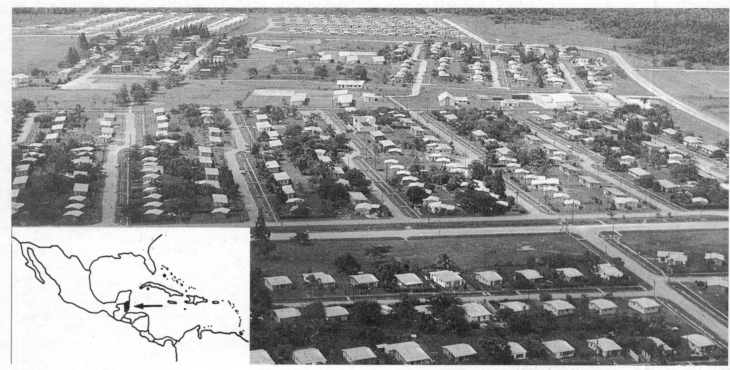

Aerial view of Belmopan

(pronounced Beh–lees)

Area: 8,866 sq. mi., somewhat larger than Massachusetts.

Population: 266,440 (estimated in 2003).

Capital City: Belmopan (Pop. 4,000, estimated).

Climate: Hot and humid.

Neighboring Countries: Mexico (North); Guatemala (West); Honduras lies 50 miles to the southeast across the Gulf of Honduras.

Official Language: English.

Other Principal Tongues: Spanish and some Indian dialects.

Ethnic Background: African (65%); Mestizo, Creole and those of Mayan ancestry, European.

Principal Religions: Roman Catholicism, Anglican Protestant Christianity.

Chief Commercial Products: Sugar, citrus fruit, lobster, shrimp, forest products.

Currency: Belize Dollar.

Gross Domestic Product: U.S. $1.28 billion in 2003 ($4,804 per capita).

Former Colonial Status: British Colony (1862–1981).

National Day: September 21 (Independence Day).

Chief of State: Queen Elizabeth II of Great Britain, represented by Colville Young, Governor General.

Head of Government: Said Musa, Prime Minister (since August 1998).

National Flag: A white circle on a blue field, with red horizontal bars at top and bottom. The circle shows two workers and symbols of agriculture, industry and maritime activity.

Wedged between Mexico's Yucatán Peninsula to the north and Guatemala to the west and south, and calmed by placid waters of the Caribbean Sea on its eastern coastline, Belize is a warm to hot and humid country about 174 miles long and 69 miles wide at its widest point. Flat and swampy on the coast, but mercifully relieved by pleasant sea breezes, the beaches are unspoiled and beautiful. The terrain slowly rises toward the interior to about 3,000 feet above sea level into pine forests and pasturelands. At lower altitudes, tropical growth predominates.

Some 15 miles offshore there is the longest barrier reef in the Western Hemisphere, stretching 190 miles, offering a spectacular variety of tropical fish and coral formations, a delight for the experienced snorkel diver. The land is thinly inhabited; the largest town is Belize City with a population of about 50,000—which, however, has an international airport.

History: Originally settled about 1638 by bands of British woodcutters illegally harvesting the timber in Spanish domains, Belize settlers managed their own affairs and

government, although the Spanish tried many times to eject them. In 1786 Britain finally appointed a superintendent for the territory; in 1840 it was termed a colony, called British Honduras, although it was not officially a colony until 1862 when it was made subordinate to Jamaica. In 1884 it was made a separate crown colony.

Colonial status continued until 1964 when the colony was granted full internal self-government. In June 1973, its name was changed to Belize. Following an outbreak of rioting, the colony was given its independence in September 1981.

Guatemala long had claimed Belize as an integral part of its territory. It loudly protested the granting of independence and refused to recognize it. Britain maintained a force of some 1,800 troops to maintain Belize's security. Guatemalan President Vinicio Cerezo generally conceded that Belize's independence was negotiable, provided Guatemala obtained access to the Atlantic via one or more of its ports. The dispute was settled in late 1992 when such rights were granted, and Guatemala formally recognized Belize.

Government consists of a 29-member House of Representatives and an eight-member appointed Senate. The People's United Party (PUP) of George Price held power from independence until 1984, when it was defeated by the United Democratic Party (UDP) led by Manuel Esquivel, running on a free-trade platform. But in late 1989, the Price and the PUP returned to power by a narrow margin of 15 to 14, later increased to 16-13 when a UDP member deserted his party.

Price made many friends during almost three decades of public service—particularly popular was his "clinic day" on Wednesdays, whereby any Belizean could drop in his office in Belize City and tell him of his concerns. His successors have continued this popular tradition.

In early 1993 Britain announced that it would withdraw its force from Belize within 15 months, which created quite a stir. Price, hoping to gain from the recent years of prosperity, mandated elections to be held in June 1993, 15 months before they were due.

But security was the main issue. Guatemala had repudiated the treaty recognizing Belize. The UDP seized the issue, typified by a song: "We don't want no Guatemala!" It won narrowly, 16 to 13 seats, and Esquivel again became prime minister.

The new UDP government charged that Price's party attempted to bribe two members to cross over party lines to aid in a takeover. Governor-General Minita Gordon was accused of being involved, and of interfering in the government and was asked to leave. The treaty with Guatemala was repudiated by Belize. British troops departed on January 1, 1994, and security became the responsibility of the Belize Defense Force. There is at present a British team designated a "jungle training" unit.

The UDP government, alleging mismanagement by the PUP, began raising taxes early in its five-year mandate. Most controversial was a 15% value-added tax; the government also raised utility rates. These unpopular measures returned to haunt Esquivel, and in the general election of August 28, 1998, the pendulum swung sharply back to the PUP, which had chosen Said Musa, a former attorney general under Price, as its standard bearer. Musa is on Palestinian descent.

In the campaign, Musa denounced Esquivel's "killa taxes," which he said were frightening away foreign investors. He pledged to cut utility rates and to create 15,000 new jobs. The appeal paid off; the PUP won in a landslide, taking 23 of the 29 seats in the lower house. The PUP carried some districts by 3–1. This time, Esquivel would not be around as leader of the opposition; he was defeated in his own district by the mayor of Belize City, José Coye. He was replaced by Dean Barrow, who is of African descent.

The PUP became the first party since independence to win two consecutive mandates, albeit with a slightly reduced majority, winning 21 of the 29 seats in the general elections on March 5, 2003. Since then, Musa's popularity has waned because of alleged corruption in the government. The most serious surfaced in August 2004 when it was disclosed that $3 million had been taken from the country's social security fund to cover the debts of a company owned by the finance minister. Seven cabinet ministers resigned, demanding that Musa fire the finance minister, which he did. Musa then assumed the finance portfolio himself.

Then, in January 2005, Musa did the same thing he had denounced Esquivel for doing in 1998—proposed a dramatic tax increase, as well as a cut in services. He said the measures were necessary to service the country's staggering debt, one of the highest in the world as a percent-

A sleepy weekday in Belize City   *Photo by Karen Bubenheim*

Belize

age of GDP (see Economy). Under Musa alone, the debt has risen from 41% of GDP to 93%. Demonstrations outside the House of Representatives during the tax debate turned violent, a rarity in Belize.

The violence became worse in April and May because Musa announced plans to sell the government's shares in the telephone company, BTL, to U.S. interests. Saboteurs, apparently union workers, cut down telephone poles and severed power lines, disrupting the country's power and communications grids. Looting broke out in Belize City that left one man dead, 27 people injured and 100 arrested. Teachers and civil servants staged strikes. Three UDP leaders were arrested in confrontations with police. The UDP demanded that Musa resign, but he has steadfastly refused.

Culture: Belizeans normally are friendly and warm-hearted people, about 65% of whom are of African origin, about 25% of Mayan and *mestizo* background. Most of the remainder is primarily of European extraction; a colony of German-speaking Mennonites produces almost all the country's dairy products. There also are colonies of Taiwanese, Sri Lankans and Arabs in this harmonious ethnic gumbo; Prime Minister Said Musa is of Palestinian descent.

Belmopan, the capital city, was built in 1971 in the center of the country about 50 miles west of Belize City, which is the largest urban area with a population of about 50,000. For the tourist, the city is not safe for a lone pedestrian, especially after dark. This also is true of those traveling alone to remote tourist facilities. Armed robbery and muggings are growing in number in spite of efforts by the government to control crime.

U.S. baseball is immensely popular; both men and women spend hours watching games and the cancellation of the 1994 World Series caused great disappointment. Excellent fishing, sailing, scuba diving and other sports abound. A Teacher's College provides a two-year intramural program followed by a year of supervised internship in the classroom.

There are roughly 700 Mayan ruins about 1,000 years old, which can be seen on guided tours, and unusual wildlife is prolific. The result has been that Belize has become a popular destination for adventuresome tourists.

Economy: Until recent times, forestry was the most important activity in Belize, but as the timber supply grew sparse, sugar cane growing took on more importance and now is the leading industry. Although the country has a great deal of land which is well suited for agriculture, only a small portion is farmed, and it is necessary for Belize to import millions of dollars in foodstuffs. Belize's major trading partners are the United States and the United Kingdom—about two thirds of its exports and imports are with these nations. It is a member of the Caribbean Community (CARICOM).

The lush lower altitudes of Belize, with their tropical climate, are favorable locations for two crops: marijuana and oranges for juice. The first presented a problem both to Belize and the United States in the 1980s. Production rose quickly to more than 1,000 tons annually and Belize became the second-largest supplier to U.S. dealers. After 1984 this was curtailed and virtually eliminated by a spraying program, but not before a high government official was arrested and indicted in Miami (1985) on charges of conspiring to export 30,000 tons annually to the United States. Production is now closely monitored and is less than 100 tons per year.

Cocaine proved to be a far more serious problem. As alternative routes of transportation from Colombia to the United States were restricted, Belize took up the slack. Small airplanes would land on rural roads for refueling. In order to stop this, the government erected poles on the sides of the roads to break the wings of the craft. Local people bent the poles to eliminate their effectiveness.

The Coca-Cola Company was lured to Belize by its potential for citrus crops, primarily oranges, for production of concentrated juice. A relatively enormous tract was purchased for about $172 an acre, but local opposition, coupled with that of Florida citrus growers, made the project impossible. Most of the land was donated to conservationists after opposition groups proclaimed that Coca-Cola sought to destroy 700,000 acres of virgin rain forest to plant orange trees.

Belize is relatively more prosperous than its Spanish-speaking neighbors, with an estimated per capita GDP of about $4,804 in 2003. Real GDP in 2003 was estimated at $1.28 billion. Real economic growth has averaged 4–5%, thanks largely to tourism. But a succession of governments has sought to boost the economy with drunken-sailor spending and heavy borrowing. The public debt now stands at about $1 billion, or about 93% of GDP, the 10th highest in the world. Standard & Poor's downgraded Belize's bonds and called the country's financial situation "dire."

The Future: It is tempting to draw an analogy between Belize and the American frontier of the 19th century. Belize harks back to an earlier, less hurried time, a place where "civilization" has not yet taken over with fast-food chains and computers. Tourists and immigrants have flocked here to take advantage of the legendary scuba diving in the longest coral reef in the Western Hemisphere, to enjoy the unspoiled beaches, to soak up the culture of the Mayan ruins, to experience the unique ecological wonders. But the real allure is that Belize is an anachronism, a laid-back, English-speaking enclave in the tropics just two hours by air from Houston, a place that has eschewed the frenetic pace of the 21st century, where visitors can "get away from it all" for a few days and settlers can find a new life in an unspoiled, underpopulated paradise.

But there is trouble in paradise Corruption, drug trafficking, a crushing public debt and, more recently, political upheaval threaten Belize's greatest asset: its peacefulness. Greater transparency would go a long way toward establishing confidence in governmental institutions, but political cronyism is entrenched in both parties. Ironically, Belize is hampered by the very thing that has made it so appealing: resistance to change.

Prime Minister Said Musa

The Republic of Bolivia

Nestled in the rugged mountains is a shimmering Andean lake

Area: 424,052 sq. mi.

Population: 9.2 million in 2005 (projected)

Capital Cities: La Paz (Pop. 1.25 million, estimated) and Sucre (110,000, estimated)

Climate: The eastern lowlands are hot all year round; they are wet from November through March, dry from May through September. The highland climate varies greatly with the altitude. The high plateau, or *altiplano*, is dry and cold all year round.

Neighboring Countries: Brazil (North and East); Paraguay (Southeast); Argentina (South); Chile (Southwest); Peru (Northwest).

Official Language: Spanish

Other Principal Tongues: Quechua, Aymara and Guaraní

Ethnic Background: Indian (70%); *mestizo* (mixed European and Indian (25%); European (5%)

Principal Religion: Roman Catholic Christianity

Chief Commercial Products: Tin, lead, zinc, silver, tungsten, gold, natural gas, agricultural products. Coca production, used to make cocaine, is a major source of income.

Currency: Bolivian Peso (subject to erratic valuation)

Gross Domestic Product: U.S. $8.1 billion in 2003 ($914 per capita)

Former Colonial Status: Spanish colony known as Upper Peru (1538–1825)

Independence Date: August 6, 1825

Chief of State: Eduardo Rodríguez Veltzé (b. March 2, 1956), interim president (since June 9, 2005).

National Flag: Equal red, yellow and green horizontal stripes.

Bolivia, the fifth-largest nation in South America, is landlocked. Stretching 1,000 miles from north to south and 800 miles east to west, it is divided into two highly contrasting regions—the *altiplano* (a high mountain plateau) and the eastern lowlands. The Andean mountain range reaches its greatest width—some 400 miles—in Bolivia. The *Western Cordillera*, which separates Bolivia from Chile and Peru, contains

Bolivia

snowy peaks of 19,000 to 21,240 feet, with numerous rough volcanoes along the crest. The narrow passes to the Pacific coast exceed 13,000 feet in altitude. The *altiplano*, lying to the east of the *Western Cordillera*, is an arid, windswept, treeless plateau some 85 miles wide and 520 miles in length and much of it is above 13,000 feet.

Split into basins by spurs from the *Western Cordillera*, the southern portion is parched desert, uninhabited except for mining camps; the northern portion, containing chilly Lake Titicaca (3,400 square miles at 12,500 feet), has many small settlements along the river flowing into the lake, and around the shore there is a large and prosperous Indian farming population. The eastern *cordillera*, separating the *altiplano* from the lowlands, reaches 20,000 feet in the north, but is much lower in the south.

The mountains drop sharply to the northeast and the hot, humid Amazon basin. Further to the south they form a stepped descent to a region called the *Puno* and then into the *Chaco* plains of Paraguay and Argentina. The valleys that cut into the eastern slopes of the mountains are fertile, semi–tropical and densely inhabited. These valleys, called *yungas*, produce a wide variety of cereals and fruits, but the task of transporting them to the cities of the *altiplano* is formidable. The lowland tropical plains of the northeast, once heavily populated, are now largely abandoned because of their inaccessibility.

History: The Aymara Indians living in the Lake Titicaca region had a relatively high level of development between 600 and 900 A.D. This civilization disappeared from some undetermined disaster and the Quechua–speaking Inca invaders found the surviving Aymaras living among monuments and ruins which they could not explain. Bolivia was still in Inca hands when the Spaniards arrived from Peru in 1538.

The Spanish development of Bolivia began with the discovery of a silver mountain at Potosí in 1545, followed by additional discoveries at Oruro. The capital, Sucre, was founded in 1539. La Paz (the actual capital), founded in 1548, was an important terminal for treasure convoys preparing for the difficult passage to Peru. The Inca social and economic organizations were abandoned in a mad effort to extract and process the metallic wealth of the mountains—tin, silver, lead and zinc. Jesuit missionaries penetrated into the

tropical lowlands, gathering the Indians into prosperous farming communities which endured into the 18th century. However, they aroused little interest on the part of the Spanish authorities and had even less influence on the social and political development of the country. The Spaniards intermarried with the Indians and a large group of multi–ancestry *mestizos* was the result, which would affect the course of Bolivian history.

Revolutionary movements against Spanish rule began early in Bolivia—revolts by *mestizos* broke out in La Paz in 1661 and at Cochabamba in 1730. Indian revolts occurred in Sucre, Cochabamba, Oruro and La Paz from 1776 to 1780. The University of San Francisco Xavier in Sucre issued a call in 1809 for the liberation of all colonies from Spain. Although several attempts were made to free Bolivia in the years following, they were unsuccessful until 1825, when Simón Bolívar sent General Antonio José de Sucre to free Upper Peru. Independence was declared on August 6 of that year.

No other South American nation faced greater initial handicaps than Bolivia. There were few competent patriotic leaders among the landed aristocracy and there was no middle class. The apathetic Indians

Exacting Inca stonework

and the *mestizos* were simply pawns in a game they did not under-stand. The military, which had been trained in the campaigns of San Martín and Bolívar, seized power. The history of independent Bolivia's first fifty years is a dismal recitation of misrule and violence as jealous rivals struggled for power. Following its defeat in The War of the Pacific (1879–1883), Bolivia lost its Pacific provinces to Chile and became a landlocked nation.

During the 1880s and 1890s several able men occupied the presidency. Silver mining was revived, a few schools were opened and political parties were developed. Traditional Liberal and Conservative titles were adopted, but their memberships represented little more than opposing factions of the nation's ruling elite. One of the principal Liberal demands was for the transfer of the capital from Sucre to La Paz. After seizing the presidency by revolt, a Liberal regime made La Paz the seat of government.

Under Liberal leadership, Bolivia achieved a degree of stability in the first two decades of the 20th century. Economic reforms were undertaken, disputes with Chile and Brazil were resolved—with losses of territory but with receipt of indemnities—mining was expanded and the building of roads and railroads was pushed. The motive behind this limited "modernization" was the increasing world demand for tin, a mineral that quickly became Bolivia's basic export, transforming the small group who controlled its extraction—the "tin barons"—into powerful international millionaires. In the 1920s a party carrying the label Republican came to power. Foreign capital was sought for mining and petroleum interests, attracting U.S. investors.

By the 1930s, United States interests controlled most of Bolivia's mineral concessions. While some of the investment capital went into roads, railroads and agriculture, much of it was wasted in irresponsible spending. When the world depression of the 1930s hit Bolivia, its economy collapsed, the treasury defaulted on its bonds and the Republican president was ousted.

In 1931 elections, Daniel Salamanca, a competent businessman, became president amid hopes that he could bring order out of chaos. This optimistic mood was shattered the following year with the outbreak of war with Paraguay. Blame for this senseless conflict lies with the miscalculation of the leadership of both countries. Humiliated by a long series of military disasters, both nations overestimated their own capabilities and underestimated those of the other. Though ostensibly more powerful than Paraguay, Bolivia, in a monumental display of military incompetence, suffered a crushing defeat in which 52,000 of its soldiers were killed. Fought to exhaustion on both sides, the war ended with Paraguay in possession of the disputed *Chaco* region in 1935. Soldiers returning home, angered by their shabby treatment during the war, joined with university students and labor agitators in demanding reforms.

In 1936, a group of socially conscious military officers led by Colonel David Toro overthrew the civilian government and proclaimed Bolivia a "socialist republic." This short–lived government established the first labor ministry and expropriated the holdings of Standard Oil. After only a year and a half, Toro was overthrown by an even more radical officer, Colonel Germán Busch, a hero of the Chaco War. He implemented the first labor code, encouraged organization of the tin miners and imposed governmental control over the tin companies. Busch died suddenly in 1939, and it remains an enduring mystery whether he died by his own hand or those of conservative economic interests alarmed by the pace of his reforms. At any rate, his death temporarily brought social reform to an abrupt halt.

Conservative military elements took control of the ballot boxes in 1940 elections and installed their man as president. For the next three years, the country was ruled by these right–wing elements, but during this period there arose a number of civilian–based political parties and movements, ranging from Trotskyite on the left to the Bolivian Falange, modeled after the movement of Spain's Generalisimo Francisco Franco, on the right. The one that was to have the most profound impact on the country, however, one that endures to this day, was the Revolutionary Nationalist Movement, or *MNR*, led by Víctor Paz Estenssoro, who had been an economic adviser to Busch. When another group of military reformers overthrew the conservatives in 1943 and installed Major Gualberto Villarroel as president, they invited the *MNR* to participate in the new government. Although Villarroel was enlightened in his treatment of the Indian population and was sympathetic to the miners, he proved too conservative for ultra–leftwing elements that overthrew him and publicly hanged him in 1946.

The 1952 Revolution

The following six years were marked by exceptional political turbulence and instability, even for Bolivia. The end of this volatile period, in which Bolivia was ruled by a wearisome series of military *juntas*, was marked by the beginning of what scholars regard as one of Latin America's four genuine social revolutions, along with those of Mexico, Cuba and Nicaragua.

In 1952, the *MNR* led a revolt that left about 3,000 dead and led to the installation of Paz Estenssoro as president. His revolutionary government took three re-

A Bolivian miner gazes into the icicled entrance of a tin mine near La Paz

57

Bolivia

View of La Paz

markable steps: it temporarily abolished the army and replaced it with armed militias of Indians and tin miners; it extended universal suffrage to the illiterate masses, giving them genuine political power for the first time, and it implemented true land reform, breaking up huge estates and giving Indian peasants title to their own plots. The *MNR* also established itself within the unions and Indian communities, making it then, as now, the country's premier civilian political force.

The revolution was hampered by a lack of trained administrators, inadequate financial resources, opposition from both internal and external elements and, above all, by a steady decline in tin prices that put Bolivia in chronic economic crisis. Nonetheless, for its first 12 years the revolution gave power to the powerless and brought an end to revolving–door governments. When Paz Estenssoro's four–year term expired in 1956, he was succeeded by another *MNR* leader, Hernán Siles Suazo. Paz Estenssoro, however, returned to power in the 1960 election, but when he made overtures toward reelection in 1964, the newly organized revolutionary army proved as skillful at staging a *coup d'etat* as had its predecessors. The vice president and former air force commander, General René Barrientos, came to power in November 1964, and Paz Estenssoro was forced into exile. Despite the *MNR's* failure to retain power, its 12 years of revolution proved to be a *fait accompli* from which there was no turning back to the "old order."

The flamboyant and charismatic Barrientos proved a highly popular president, and he was given a resounding mandate

in a 1966 election. The following year, a U.S.-trained counterinsurgency battalion captured and executed the legendary Argentine-born revolutionary, Ernesto "Che" Guevara, who had attempted to launch a Cuban-style revolution among Bolivia's rural Indians. Barrientos was fond of making personal visits to the interior by helicopter, and on one such trip, in April 1969, he died when his helicopter crashed. He was succeeded by his vice president who was quickly overthrown by General Alfredo Ovando, a leftist and nationalist who expropriated the holdings of Gulf Oil Co. He was in turn overthrown by the even more left-wing General Juan José Torres in 1970. Torres replaced the Congress with a Soviet-style "People's Assembly" and forged a coalition of Marxist intellectuals and tin miners. However, he failed to win the support of the peasants, as Barrientos had, or most workers. Even worse, he alienated the U.S. Embassy.

Coup No. 187 (the best estimate) in 145 years of independence ensued in 1971, bringing to power a more conservative military strongman, Colonel Hugo Banzer Suárez. By 1975, Banzer had fended off 13 coup attempts, and by 1978, after seven years, he had held power continuously longer than any Bolivian president of the 20th century. The formula for his longevity was a three–point strategy: elimination of major political opposition, economic improvement and increased emphasis on foreign affairs to divert popular attention from unsolved domestic problems. Perhaps the best example of this last strategy was Bolivia's renewed demand for access to the sea through Chile.

In July 1978 Banzer called for an open presidential election in which he had intended to relinquish power to his hand–picked successor, Colonel Juan Pereda Asbún. But in the balloting, former President Siles Suazo won a plurality, while Pereda ran a poor third. Congress was to decide the outcome, but rather than risk the anti–military Siles Suazo coming to power, Banzer suddenly resigned as Pereda proclaimed himself president. Banzer's departure thus created a power vacuum that was to return Bolivia to political turmoil for two years.

The usurpation of power lasted only four months. General David Padilla, the latest reform–minded military officer, overthrew Pereda in November and pledged to pave the way for yet another free election in July 1979. In that contest, Siles Suazo again polled a plurality but not a majority, throwing the decision to the Congress. Under the watchful eye of the jittery military, Congress opted for a compromise choice for president: Walter Guevara Arce, a civilian leader of the 1952 revolution who later split from the *MNR* and therefore was acceptable to conservative military elements. This good–faith effort at restoring civilian rule also would last only until November 1979, when an overly ambitious colonel, Alberto Natusch Busch, led a successful coup.

His motive for seizing power apparently was for personal gain rather than any lofty reform goals; he immediately found himself faced with overwhelming domestic and international opposition to his naked power play. After only 19 days in power, he was forced to resign and he fled into exile, taking an undetermined amount of cash from the national treasury with him. Congress then chose Lidia Gueiler as Bolivia's first woman president. She had no sooner taken office, of course, before speculation began as to when she would be overthrown and by which officer. She called still another election in June 1980 to choose a president, and once again the victor was Siles Suazo. Coup No. 191 took place and General Luis García Meza seized control of the government.

Thus, in the 24 months between Banzer's resignation in July 1978 and García Meza's coup in July 1980, Bolivia had had a total of seven presidents.

García Meza's 13 months in power marked the harshest crackdown on personal freedom in Bolivia's modern history. Hundreds were arrested, some labor leaders were murdered and strict censorship was imposed on the press. The new military regime seemed determined to muzzle—and if possible to exterminate—the opposition in the labor movement. Reports held that 500 to 2,000 political prisoners were jailed. The Carter Admin-

Bolivia

General García Meza

istration suspended all aid to the country and Bolivia had to turn to neighboring military governments for assistance.

Seeking to consolidate his control over the government, García Meza jailed his opponents and allegedly bribed key members of the armed forces with payoff money from drug traffickers.

Such heavy–handed tactics combined with depressed economic conditions fomented widespread opposition to the military. In August 1981, reformist military officers forced García Meza to resign. The coup was rather gentlemanly by Bolivian standards; as a consolation prize, the discredited strongman was allowed to live in the Presidential Palace for a month following his ouster. An attempt to bring García Meza and his collaborators to trial before the Bolivian Supreme Court in 1986 had to be aborted within two days—two justices died, the prosecutor claimed five others were closely associated with the defendants and the defense attorney claimed that other justices were communists.

Named as the new head of the three–man military *junta* was General Celso Torrelio Villa. Political conditions remained unstable as the nation chafed under harsh military rule. In November, tin workers mounted widespread strikes to demand a return of their union and political rights which the *junta* suspended in 1980. Hoping to ease criticism of the regime, Torrelio promised to (1) reduce human rights violations, (2) slow the rampant flow of illegal cocaine out of the country and (3) to reduce the state's role in the economy while expanding the opportunities for private enterprise.

Although such policies pleased the United States, which resumed full diplomatic ties after a 16–month delay, the promises prompted skepticism at home. Efforts to impose austerity measures touched off widespread strikes in early 1982. When the peso was allowed to float, it promptly fell 76% to a new rate of 44 to the U.S. dollar. This was only a precursor of that which was to come.

Return to Democracy

To reduce growing criticism, the *junta* promised to lift its ban on political activity and to hold elections for a constituent assembly early in 1983, but as the national economic crisis worsened and popular agitation spread, the government was forced to lift the ban on the activities of political parties and labor unions. The president resigned in mid–1982 and the remainder of the junta decided to shorten the political process by recalling the democratically elected Congress of 1980, which confirmed the results of those elections which had been won by Hernán Siles Suazo; in late 1982 he and Jaime Paz Zamora, a Socialist, were officially proclaimed as president and vice president of Bolivia.

The situation inherited by the civilian government bordered on total chaos. The public debt amounted to about $3 billion, inflation was utterly out of control, unemployment was rampant and the corruptive influence of the drug traffic had reached alarming proportions. During the first months of 1983, the government made brave, but disorganized, attempts to impose a program of economic austerity and public honesty. Its partial success immediately provoked opposition and social unrest.

By the middle of 1984, battered by worker strikes and interminable rumors of impending military coups, the civilian government had managed to survive against formidable odds. Exemplifying the extent of the regime's troubles, in mid–1984 President Siles Suazo encouraged private sectors to invest in the country, rejected a demand for a 500% rise in worker' wages, proclaimed a new war against drug dealers, promised to reduce inflation to 45%, reaffirmed his confidence in the loyalty of the armed forces and appealed to international institutions to lend more money to Bolivia to save the nation from a "desperate economic situation."

The president was abducted one month later and held for some hours before being released in what appeared to be a clumsy attempt to stage a military coup.

Social unrest, several more labor strikes and inflation, which at the beginning of 1985 was running at an astronomical annual rate of 24,000%, led Siles Suazo to advance presidential elections to 1985. It appeared that General Hugo Banzer would win, and he actually received more votes than the runner–up in an election riddled with corruption, particularly in the La Paz area. Although former President Paz Estenssoro, age 77, received 26.4% of the vote, about 2% less than Banzer, he was elected president by the new Congress, in which Paz Estenssoro's party received more seats than that of Banzer.

Paz Estenssoro successfully undertook renegotiation of Bolivia's foreign debt when he took office in August 1985 (it had reached $4.9 billion); he reduced the value of the peso by 1 million to one. (It had been traded on the black market at 1.4 million per $1 U.S.) He promised decentralization of the economy, particularly the state mining and petroleum monopolies. As might have been expected, these moves and others increased food prices tenfold and provoked strikes and violence which led to the declaration of a state of siege. About 1,500 hunger–striking trade unionists were arrested and sent into internal exile. Surprisingly, Banzer and his supporters joined in the efforts of Paz Estenssoro for economic reform. As a result of dramatic change, the International Monetary Fund, the World Bank, the United States, Japan, China and European countries were willing to resume loans to Bolivia.

The years 1985–1988 were not kind to Bolivia. Part of this was because of internal human factors, but most were natural or external in nature. The bottom dropped out of world tin prices in 1985. The basic causes were a vast stock oversupply (one year) and, more ominously, increased substitution of aluminum. Further complicating Bolivia's problems was the discovery of Brazilian deposits which can be mined with much greater ease. Bolivia wound up in the position of marketing tin for less than one third the price of production. By 1989, a single province of western Brazil was producing more tin than all of Bolivia, using modern technology in contrast to Bolivia's antiquated methods.

The government had no choice but to close the most inefficient mines, causing unemployment to rise to 32%. Huge numbers of workers marched in opposition ("March for Life").

Heavy flood damage in early 1986 occurred because of heavy rains and rising waters of Lake Titicaca, leaving 150,000 Aymara Indians destitute.

Finally, the United States decided to tackle its growing cocaine problem by destroying (hopefully) the sources. Coca production, from which cocaine is derived, produces more revenue for Bolivia than any other source. At first, a mild approach was attempted: an offer of $350 for every hectare of coca leaf taken out of production was made. Since up to $10,000 per hectare can be made by cultivating the narcotic leaf, the plan was not only poorly received, it was actively resisted by farmers who threatened violence. Then, in "Operation Blast Furnace," the United States persuaded the Bolivian government to cooperate in destroying the facilities used to process the coca into cocaine with the assistance of American helicopters and armaments.

Bolivia

The operation was approved, but was carried out in an incredibly clumsy way. Clusters of U.S. helicopters and military appeared at major Bolivian airports and sat idle for four days while "planning" went on. Needless to say, no one was home when they ultimately reached their target. The result: crowds demonstrated in front of the U.S. Embassy shouting *"Viva coca!"*

U.S. efforts against coca from 1986 to 1997 were hampered for several reasons. First, there was a demand for cocaine. If Bolivian coca production went down, it rose in neighboring nations. Second, coca production was an informal government industry. It successfully functioned because of an elaborate, ever-changing system of bribery which had even invaded the Supreme Court. Third, paid informants were useless because drug figureheads had counter-informants up to the highest level of the military and police.

Coca production underwent two important changes. First, it was no longer a "cottage" industry—plantations were used for production, which hired help at low wages for the menial work (they would otherwise be unemployed). The growers could raise large crowds for anti-government demonstrations quite easily. Second, instead of producing coca "paste" using kerosene and shipping it to Colombian cartels, Bolivia had a tremendous number of "factories" producing the treasured final product—white powder. This latter transformation reflected a local desire for immense profits formerly reaped by Colombian cartels, not because those elusive organizations have been seriously damaged by U.S. efforts to control cocaine production.

May 1989 presidential elections produced two top candidates out of nine—Gonzalo Sánchez de Lozada, 58, candidate of the *MNR*, received 23% of the vote and Banzer received 22%. Jaime Paz Zamora, nephew of Paz Estenssoro, but a leftist, received 19.5%. Three months of meetings in smoke–filled rooms ensued. Finally, in August the doors opened and number three was declared the new president. How? Number two, Banzer, who while in power had jailed and exiled Paz Zamora in the 1970s, threw his support behind his former arch foe in exchange for 10 out of 17 cabinet posts and virtually assured his control of the government.

Paz Zamora pledged to continue the style of government of his uncle and did so. Unrest did not cease; his term was typified by a nationwide teacher's strike and a murky plot to assassinate him, the chief drug enforcement officer and the U.S. ambassador in late 1990. Drug raids with U.S. assistance were only moderately successful and highly resented by Bolivians.

The next elections were held in mid-1993. Cabinet ministers resigned from government to support Banzer. In spite of this, Sánchez de Lozada won a plurality of 36%; Banzer then threw his support to his rival, making a runoff election unnecessary. The Congress decreed Sánchez de Lozada president in August 1993.

Like many other Latin American presidents of the 1990s, Sánchez de Lozada undertook a pragmatic program of privatizing cumbersome state-owned enterprises, including the national airline, the oil company and the telecommunications infrastructure. He also sought to decentralize power, placing unprecedented control in the hands of the departments. He also began welcoming foreign investors to Bolivia with red-carpet incentives.

Faced with strikes and protests by the majority Indian community for this seeming betrayal of the 1952 revolution, Sánchez reached a new land-reform agreement with Indian leaders in October 1996, the most significant such law since the transcendental land-reform law of 1952. Unlike the earlier law, the new statute not only gave peasants title to their land but also permitted them to sell it. Previously, they could only bequeath it to their children, with the result that individual plots became too small to be economically viable.

Banzer Returns to Power

The reforms proved to be the leading issue of the June 1, 1997 presidential elections, which drew 10 candidates and were marked by the stunning political comeback of the former strongman Banzer, now 71. All the major candidates embraced Sánchez's reforms, but Banzer capitalized on the discontent among the poor by running on a foggy populist platform which included his promise to "humanize" the reforms, whatever that meant. Nevertheless, the ploy worked, and Banzer, now a zealous democrat who pledged to respect human rights, emerged as the front runner with 22% of the vote. The *MNR* candidate was second with 18% and former president Paz Zamora was third with 17%. There was a 70% turnout of 3.2 million voters.

Because no one received a majority, Congress again was required to select the president, but this time Banzer's Nationalist Democratic Alliance (*ADN*) forged an unusual alliance with populist and left-wing parties to assure him of victory. In the balloting on August 5, Banzer received the necessary majority of 79 of the 157 deputies after only two thirds of them had voted. The new vice president was Jorge Quiroga, 37, a previous finance minister under Paz Zamora, a former IBM executive and an engineering graduate of Texas A&M who was married to a Texan. They

Hugo Banzer Suárez

were sworn in the next day, Independence Day, for a term that had been constitutionally extended from four to five years.

Though not specified in his inaugural address, Banzer soon issued a controversial pledge to eradicate Bolivia's coca production before the end of his term in 2002. Though the news gladdened the Clinton administration, the Republican-controlled U.S. Congress nonetheless began making noises that it would increase drug–control aid to Colombia while reducing Bolivia's aid from $34 million to $12 million. This prompted a visit to Washington in March 1998 by English–speaking Vice President Quiroga. He met with Clinton's drug policy adviser Barry McCaffrey, who assured him the Clinton administration wanted to increase the aid to $45 million.

Back at home, the powerful Confederation of Bolivian Workers (*COB*) soon began engaging in the country's second most popular pastime after soccer: general strikes. The *COB* was demanding an increase in the monthly minimum wage from the admittedly paltry $45 to an unreasonable and inflationary $667. The government made an offer of $54, which the *COB* predictably rejected. It called three 48–hour general strikes between August 1997 and March 1998, which were observed mostly by teachers, cleaning workers and some miners. When the government still refused to budge, an open–ended strike began in early April. Coupled with this, coca–growing peasants in the Chapare region, furious over the government's decision to eliminate their livelihood, joined the strike by setting up roadblocks on the Santa Cruz–Cochabamba highway. Hundreds of troops and police were dispatched to disperse them, and violence erupted.

Meanwhile, the negotiations between the government and the *COB* broke down when the government refused to accept the participation of Evo Morales, the leader of the coca growers, who had been elected to Congress in 1997. Morales made the seemingly reasonable argument that the government should offer incentives for the peasants to switch to alternative crops, which, in fact, already has been done, and non–traditional crops in Chapare now outnumber coca acreage three-to–one. The government also has paid farmers up to $2,500 per hectare—almost all of it provided by the United States, of course—to uproot coca plants, but the incentive program was not to be extended beyond 1998. Cooperate now and get paid, or be an outlaw, was the strategy. Miffed, Morales accused Banzer of having had ties to drug traffickers, which the president vehemently denied. The strike turned violent, and before it died out, 18 people were killed. But in the test of wills between the strong–willed Banzer and the strong–willed Morales, the president prevailed. He reported to Congress that of the estimated 40,000 hectares of coca cultivation, 7,000 were eradicated in 1997 and 11,620 in 1998. Critics maintained that new cultivation reduced the net eradication in those years to 2,000 and 8,000, respectively. Moreover, Morales and younger, less moderate spokesmen for the growers complain that the ostensible markets for the alternative crops do not exist.

Banzer faced another challenge in late 1998 when former President Sánchez de Lozada called for an investigation into Banzer's role in the human rights abuses committed during his military regime, when an estimated 200 people were killed. The call no doubt was inspired by the arrest in London days earlier of former Chilean strongman Augusto Pinochet and by the ongoing investigation of Argentine military men for atrocities committed during the "Dirty War." Banzer justifiably accused the *MNR* of hypocrisy and called on the opposition party to examine its own complicity with military regimes. Bolivian public opinion seemed to concur with Banzer that this was little more than political sour grapes on Sánchez's part.

In September 1999, the government announced even more impressive figures in the coca-eradication program than it had the year before. According to the information minister, the army and police had removed 11,670 hectares from cultivation, slightly more than the entire number of hectares for 1998, and predicted that another 14,000 hectares would be removed by the end of the year, which would leave only 16,000 hectares under cultivation.

General strikes continued to plague the country. In September 1999, both La Paz and Sucre were shut down for a day by a peaceful strike protesting increases in bread, fuel and transportation prices. But in April 2000, a seemingly routine local protest in Cochabamba against an increase in water prices turned violent and presented Banzer with his gravest domestic crisis to date. Before the unrest subsided nine days later, the protests had spread to five of the nine departments, five people were killed and 40 injured, dozens were arrested, and the president issued a 90-day state of siege, the seventh since the restoration of democracy.

The unrest was sparked by a $70 million contract to a London-based engineering firm to build a tunnel that would bring water across the Andes to Cochabamba, which would have required an increase of from 20% to 80% in water rates. In February, the New Republican Force (NFR), one of the members of Banzer's congressional coalition, had opposed the price increases, prompting the president to expel the group from the coalition. Public discontent in Cochabamba over the price increase soon escalated into violence fueled by general frustration over the depressed economy in the wake of coca eradication. Clashes erupted between soldiers and protesters in several locations, none more violent than in the town of Achacachi on April 10, where two soldiers and three protesters were killed. One of the soldiers, a captain, was dragged by a mob from a hospital room and killed in the town square. The protesters also looted government offices.

The unrest quickly spread, as angry farmers erected roadblocks in five departments. In one town, even policemen, angered by their low pay, seized their station; in La Paz, other policemen fired on soldiers. After Banzer declared the state of siege, which suspended basic civil liberties, the *COB* sought to mount a nationwide general strike. However, Banzer's pragmatic decision to cancel the water project contract, coupled with negotiations between the government and the protesters mediated by the Catholic Church, largely defused the crisis, and by April 13 the protests had lost their steam.

New, more broadly based protests flared up again in September 2000, principally by coca farmers protesting Banzer's eradication programs, but they were joined by other peasant farmers, teachers and transport workers. Banzer's response to the protests, which consisted mainly of blockading main roads, was relatively measured, leaving "only" about 10 people dead. The protests forced him to cancel a state visit to Japan. By April 2001, it was street vendors in La Paz who began demonstrating to protest new regulations on them. Those protests, while noisy, were nonviolent.

Shortly before Christmas 2000, Banzer officially declared the successful culmination of the coca eradication program, claiming 40,000 hectares had been removed from cultivation. Under the government's program, only 12,000 hectares in Yungas are allowed to be cultivated for "traditional" purposes, a concession to the sentiments of local Indians. Still, the peasants complained that other crops, such as coffee, earn them only a fraction of what they made from coca.

A new variable was added into the Bolivian political equation in November 2000, when a new Indian-based political party, *Movimiento Indígeno Pachacuti* (the Aymara word for "revival"), was established on the site of the execution by the Spanish in 1783 of Tupac Katari, the leader of an Indian revolt. Its leader is Felipe Quispe, the head of a peasant labor confederation, who is also known by the sobriquet Mallku, which means condor.

Perhaps in response to this new movement, as well as to the frequent protests, Banzer pushed through Congress in February 2001 an ambitious, 50-point constitutional reform to broaden, in principle at least, Bolivian democracy. The reforms took aim at election fraud by removing local elections from the control of local kingpins, providing for referenda, and empowering the Supreme Court rather than Congress with the decision to revoke congressional immunity in corruption investigations. The opposition *MNR* grudgingly supported the plan, but accused Banzer of having political motives.

A political era came to an end in Bolivia on June 7, 2001, when four-time former president Paz Estenssoro, the intellectual author of the 1952 revolution, died at 93 on the 59th anniversary of the founding of the *MNR*. His funeral in Tarija attracted thousands of peasants, who mingled with the elite of various parties who came to pay tribute to the man and his legacy.

The incumbent president would soon follow him. On July 1, 2001, Banzer, a heavy smoker, was admitted to Walter Reed Hospital in Washington; six days later he was diagnosed with lung and liver cancer and his condition was reported as "grave." Banzer resigned effective August 6, Independence Day and the fourth anniversary of his inauguration, and Vice President Quiroga was sworn in the following day for the remaining year of his term. Banzer, 75, succumbed in Santa Cruz on May 5, 2002. Thousands filled the streets to pay homage to this dictator-turned-democrat as his funeral cortege passed.

A lame duck from the start, Quiroga, known to Bolivians by the nickname "Tuto," nonetheless seemed determined to make a mark during his brief occu-

Bolivia

Former President Jorge Quiroga

pancy of the presidential palace. He pledged to continue Banzer's coca eradication policy, and he pushed several reform measures through Congress, including a civil service, non-partisan electoral courts, expanded powers for the comptroller-general and financial accountability for public officials. In October 2001, a member of Congress was stripped of his legislative immunity from prosecution for allegedly mishandling $60 million in public funds. Armed with his new power, the comptroller-general began investigating other congressmen and other public officials without regard to party. One problem that still has gone unaddressed, however, is the rampant corruption in the national police.

In November, when Quiroga issued a decree that prohibited the drying, shipping or sale of coca leaves in open markets, something that heretofore had been legal, Morales denounced the decree as unconstitutional. When police attempted to close such a market near Cochabamba in January 2002, the protests flared into three days of violence that left seven people, including four of the policemen, dead. A congressional panel then sought to strip Morales of his seat for allegedly inciting the violence. That sparked still more violence, in which two more people died. In the end, Quiroga and Morales reached a compromise on the decree.

Quiroga boycotted a summit meeting on terrorism and drugs in Peru with the presidents of the United States, Peru, Ecuador and Colombia in March 2002 in a fit of pique over a U.S. State Department report that Bolivia had not been doing enough to crack down on coca cultivation

in Chapare Department. Quiroga fired back a letter that claimed that 8,000 hectares of coca had been taken out of cultivation in the seven months since he assumed office.

The Elections of 2002

The presidential race of 2002 was the usual free-for-all. Two former presidents, Gonzalo Sánchez de Lozada of the *MNR* and Jaime Paz Zamora of the Movement of the Revolutionary Left (*MIR*) entered the race. As Quiroga was barred from running, the *ADN* nominated Ronald Mac-Lean. Morales entered the race as the candidate of the Movement to Socialism (*MAS*), while Felipe Quispe, as expected, ran as the candidate of the Pachacuti Indigenous Movement (*MIP*). Rounding out the cluttered field of major contenders was the long-time mayor of Cochabamba and a former army captain, Manfred Villa Reyes, the standard-bearer of populist-oriented New Republican Force (*NFR*).

Early polls showed Sánchez and Paz the two frontrunners, but then Reyes surged ahead of Paz into a statistical tie with Sánchez, with Morales a distant fourth. Sánchez, 72, pledged to continue free-market reforms and to make Bolivia more attractive to investors, initiatives he had taken as president. Paz and Morales both denounced free-market capitalism. Paz said he would return some of the country's vast natural gas wealth to state control, while Morales, 42, who chewed coca leaves at his rallies as a political statement, vowed to discontinue the coca eradication program and bombastically declared he would expel the *"yanquis."* Reyes, 46, offered only vague generalities, other than to say he would double the size of the armed forces—although what or whom they would be fighting against was unclear.

Then, just five days before the June 30 election, U.S. Ambassador Manuel Rocha, in a stunning breach of diplomatic protocol, warned during a ceremony he attended with President Quiroga that voting for Morales could jeopardize continued U.S. aid. The reaction was immediate and ferocious, as Bolivians of all political stripes denounced this U.S. intrusion into domestic politics. (Many Bolivians already were sensitive to U.S. intrusion, as the first lady, Virginia Gillum de Quiroga, still held U.S. citizenship.) Rocha's importune remark was to boomerang in a way he neither wanted nor expected.

The vote tabulation was electoral drama at its highest, as the count proved agonizingly slow and tantalizingly close. Sánchez de Lozada, as expected, forged into an early lead that was slim but unchanging, with Reyes Villa close behind. But to everyone's surprise—and to the conster-

nation of the loose-mouthed Ambassador Rocha and the Bush administration—Morales surged into a convincing third place, several points ahead of Paz Zamora. For nine days, the country—and the Bush administration—held their breaths. After the votes trickled in from the remote altiplano—coca-growing country—Morales finished in second place just 721 votes ahead of Reyes! The effect was as stunning as that of ultra-rightist Jean-Marie LePen's unexpected placing in the French presidential runoff the month before.

A total of 2,993,708 Bolivians had voted, a respectable turnout of 72.04%. The complete official count gave Sánchez 624,126 votes, or 22.46%; Morales, 581,884 votes, or 20.94%; Reyes, 581,163, or 20.91%; Paz, 453,375, or 16.31%; Quispe, 169,737, or 6.09%; Johnny Fernández of the Civic Solidarity Union (*UCS*), 153,175, or 5.51%; MacLean of the *ADN* had a pitiful 94,333, or 3.4%. Sánchez and Morales each carried four of the nine departments; Paz carried one, Reyes Villa none.

Congress, as usual, then had to choose a president from between Sánchez and Morales, and frantic jockeying began. Reyes Villa's *NFR* decided to remain in the opposition in the new Congress. The *MNR* eventually negotiated a coalition with Paz's *MIR*, the *UCS* and the *ADN*, which constituted a slight congressional majority. The press reported again that Ambassador Rocha was thrusting himself into domestic politics by actively participating in an inter-party meeting and that he was applying "pressure" on behalf of Sánchez and against Morales.

For his part, once his second-place finish was established, Morales suddenly began sounding more conciliatory. Interviewed by the Spanish-language edition of CNN, he insisted that there was a difference between coca cultivation and narcotrafficking, which he said he has always opposed, but he blamed the problem on the demand for cocaine in the developed countries. He also pragmatically made conciliatory remarks about the World Bank and the IMF, as radicals who suddenly find themselves on the brink of power often do.

But by then the outcome was a foregone conclusion. On August 4, Congress elected Sánchez de Lozada, known to Bolivians as "Goni," over Morales, 84-43.

An Abortive Presidency

Sánchez's inauguration on August 6, 2002, was attended by Spain's Prince Felipe and seven Latin American presidents, including Venezuela's Hugo Chávez, but despite all the intense U.S. interest in the outcome of the election, it sent only President Bush's drug policy adviser, John Walters, as its highest representative, which offended many Bolivians. Carlos Mesa was sworn in as vice president. In his address, Sánchez made conciliatory overtures to the Indian-based movements that constituted much of the congressional opposition for the first time, promised to launch massive public works projects to create jobs and warned his countrymen that they must "choose between progress and collapse."

With his shaky 22% mandate, there was little Sánchez could accomplish, however, and even that meager base of support soon began to erode. Long-simmering tensions over the coca eradication program erupted into violence again on January 14, 2003, when troops sought to clear roadblocks that angry farmers had erected on the La Paz-Cochabamba highway. The farmers kept the highway closed for two weeks, and the resulting violence left 10 civilians and two soldiers dead before the government and the farmers agreed to negotiate. But the worst was yet to come.

On February 9, Sánchez announced plans for a new progressive income tax of up to 12.5% to augment the value-added tax, in order to meet IMF demands to reduce the budget deficit from 8.5% to 5.5%. The reaction was immediate, negative and violent. First, 7,000 La Paz police officers, who were already demanding a 40% salary increase, went on strike to protest the new tax. On February 12, they were joined by thousands of other protesters, who laid siege to the presidential palace. Protesters chanted, "Resign or die, those are your choices," apparently a parody of Sánchez's inaugural address. Sánchez called out the troops. Policemen and soldiers confronted each other. The army fired tear gas at the police; the police fired tear gas back; the army then opened fire. In the ensuing exchange of gunfire, 14 people were killed. Chaos erupted in the capital as the protesters rioted. Some mobs looted and burned department stores, others occupied or set fire to 12 government buildings, including the vice president's office. The fires raged out of control as firefighters joined the striking policemen. Other riots broke out in Cochabamba and other cities.

Sánchez himself escaped from the presidential palace in an ambulance. Shaken, he agreed to rescind the income tax. After two days of violence, the striking policemen agreed to return to work and order was restored. The final toll was 32 dead and at least 102 injured, the worst civil violence since the implementation of democracy in 1982. There was a peaceful mass protest on February 17 to demand Sánchez's resignation, and the president responded two days later by purging his cabinet of his most unpopular ministers

and reduced the number of ministries from 18 to 13 to reduce expenditures. The IMF subsequently moderated its budget deficit demand to 6.5%.

At mid-year 2003, Sánchez's approval rating was 19%, the lowest of any Latin American leader except Peruvian President Alejandro Toledo; it would plummet still lower. Bolivia remained a powder keg, which exploded again in September 2003.

**Former President
Gonzalo Sánchez de Lozada**

The spark was something that should have been heralded as a major boost to the economy: a $5 billion pipeline to Chile by which natural gas could be sold for export to the western United States. Nationalists, however, were furious that the pipeline would pass through the territory that Bolivia lost to Chile in the War of the Pacific of 1879–84, and Morales and other leftist peasant leaders objected to selling Bolivia's natural resources to the hated *yanquis*, who had virtually destroyed their livelihood from coca cultivation. They argued that it harked back to the time when Spaniards came into Bolivia to exploit silver, and when British and American companies came to mine tin, letting little of the wealth trickle down to the Indians who labored in the mines. (The pipeline would have been built, ironically, by a Spanish-British consortium.)

Clashes between peasants and security forces on September 20 and 21 left seven people dead, and angry peasants once again rushed to throw up roadblocks around La Paz. Sánchez offered to negotiate with the peasants, but Quispe rebuffed the offer. Teachers and street vendors in La Paz joined the protests on September 30, and the miners joined a day later. Their demand: Sánchez's resignation.

The crisis lumbered on for two more weeks, during which another 16 people were killed, five of them in the impoverished El Alto suburb of La Paz; El Alto was placed under martial law. On October 12, a desperate Sánchez agreed to cancel the pipeline project, which would have created hundreds of badly needed jobs and brought in $1.5 billion a year in even more desperately needed foreign exchange. The cancellation failed to placate the protesters, however, and on October 13 La Paz was paralyzed by a transportation strike. Fifteen people died in clashes in La Paz, El Alto and Santa Cruz that day, two of them soldiers. Morales added his voice to the chorus of those demanding that Sánchez resign, and in a stunning development, Vice President Mesa publicly withdrew his support for the president because of the use of deadly force against the protesters and urged him to change course. Sánchez's development minister resigned in protest.

The embattled president, whose approval rating had dropped to a pitiful 9%, addressed the nation, but in unconciliatory language he refused to resign and blamed the unrest on "foreign" elements, apparently a reference to Venezuela's Hugo Chávez and Libya's Muammar Qadhafi, with whom Morales has close ties. The speech seemed only to further inflame the situation.

On Tuesday, October 14, thousands of miners marched on La Paz to join protesters who had effectively laid siege to the capital with burning tires and rock barricades; the death toll mounted. Reyes Villa, who had become a key Sánchez ally, joined those calling for resignation. Morales called the president and his cabinet "butchers," and Quispe went into hiding, claiming his life was in danger.

On Friday, October 17, with his allies abandoning him, the death toll at 74 and the country on the brink of chaos, Sánchez grudgingly and bitterly submitted his resignation to Congress. He and his wife flew to Miami. The violent street protests were transformed immediately into mass celebrations.

Mesa Seeks Consensus

Hours later, Mesa, a 50-year-old historian and a respected newspaper, radio and television journalist, was duly sworn in as Bolivia's 82nd president, providing some constitutional trappings to the third overthrow by mob rule of an elected South American president in less than four years. Addressing Congress after the presidential sash was placed on his shoulders, Mesa pledged a "period of historic transition" and said he would appoint a nonpartisan cabinet. He sounded a populist

Bolivia

note, saying that Bolivia must "overcome discrimination and put an end to divisions between first- and second-class citizens." He advocated resolving the gas pipeline issue through a popular referendum; the gas-producing areas that stood to benefit from it were solidly in favor of its construction.

Morales, widely seen as the man who orchestrated Sánchez's downfall, suddenly became statesmanlike and pledged to give Mesa a grace period to try to restore order.

Mesa, who constitutionally was entitled to serve out the remainder of Sánchez's five-year term, at first said he would serve only as interim president until he called a new election. But by January 2004 he had changed his mind and decided to last out his term. Few seemed to object; by May, his approval ratings were above 70%, a dramatic contrast to the detested Sánchez. One ingredient for his early success apparently was his non-partisan and transpartisan approach to governing. He also pleased his countrymen when he took advantage of the Summit of the Americas in Monterrey, Mexico, in January 2004 to call upon his Chilean counterpart, Ricardo Lagos, to give Bolivia an outlet to the sea. An uncomfortable Lagos could reply only that the summit was not the appropriate place to discuss the issue.

Mesa was under pressure from Morales and other Indian leaders to call a constituent assembly to revise the country's constitution. Mesa agreed in principle, but suggested delaying it until after departmental and municipal elections in November. Always impatient for immediate results, some of the Indian groups declared an indefinite general strike in May 2004, but it was largely ineffectual. Also in late May, the government successfully reached an agreement with workers at the Caracoles tin mine, ending a two-week strike.

As Mesa dexterously was building a consensus government to defuse the violent protests, one problem he did not need or count on was a rebellious military. Throughout the crisis that brought down Sánchez, the armed forces remained dutifully loyal to the civilian president and did not intervene, as it had so often in the past. But on May 8, the Supreme Court overturned the acquittal by a military tribunal of four officers who were tried in connection with the death of a nurse killed during the violence of February 2003. The Supreme Court ruled that the officers must be tried in civilian courts, which provoked outrage in the armed forces. Commanders ordered their troops to remain in their barracks as a symbolic protest, a chilling reminder that Bolivia's democracy is still pubescent. Mesa

adroitly agreed to name a commission to seek a legal solution to the issue, and the armed forces pledged to adhere to the constitution.

Recent Developments

Mesa held the promised referendum on the gas pipeline on July 18, 2004. Voters approved all five issues on the ballot, one of them by 92%, handing the president a major vote of confidence. The referendum, a new experience for Bolivians, increased taxes at the wellhead for the foreign companies and trimmed some of their rights.

But that still did not defuse the gas issue. The left was still pushing for either re-nationalization of the oil and gas companies or at least greater state control. Meanwhile, the gas-producing provinces of Santa Cruz and Tarija had stood to benefit greatly from the pipeline deal. On November 11, there was a 24-hour general strike in the two departments to demand autonomy from La Paz so they could go through with the deal themselves.

Former President Carlos Mesa

On December 30, 2004, Mesa announced price increases of 23% for diesel fuel and 10% for gasoline. The reaction was immediate, especially in already restive Santa Cruz and in El Alto, the huge, impoverished suburb of La Paz that had been the center of the protests that had brought down Sánchez de Lozada. There was a peculiar, short-lived coalition between the indigenous groups and the local elite, mostly of European descent, in Santa Cruz, which demanded that Mesa rescind the price hikes. Mesa argued that subsidized Bolivian fuel was already priced half of what it was in neighboring countries. Up went the roadblocks again, causing widespread commercial disruption for more than two weeks. Mesa kept his promise not to resort to armed confrontation as had his predecessor. Instead, he agreed to cut six percentage points from the increases. To assure the pacification of El Alto, he also agreed to cancel the government's contract with a French-owned water company, which residents

complained was price gouging and failing to install new lines as promised. The reality was that when the government rejected the company's request for a rate hike, it was forced to raise the installation fee to $450, which few El Alto residents could afford. But Mesa turned water supply over to the government, which, coupled with the fuel price rollback, placated the El Alto protesters.

Not so the still angry residents of Santa Cruz. Although they could afford a price hike much more easily than the residents of El Alto, they demanded a complete rollback and renewed their demands for autonomy. Tens of thousands poured into the streets to shout anti-Mesa slogans, but there was no violence. An autonomy movement called for a town-hall meeting for January 28 to demand popular election of the local governor; at present, the president appoints departmental governors. Tarija Department, where 85% of the gas reserves are located, also backed the separatist movement. This, however, provoked a warning from the armed forces that they fully supported the constitutional president and would not sit idly by to watch the country break apart. Once again, the conciliatory Mesa acceded to the *cruzeños'* demand rather than risk bloodshed. He agreed to elections for all nine departmental governors in August 2005, and he said he would call another referendum, this one to decide the autonomy issue.

The next flash point was a controversial energy bill, stemming from the referendum the previous July. Morales and his congressional allies advocated raising the royalty on oil and gas extraction from 18% to 50%. Mesa responded with a compromise that would put a 32% maximum tax on top of the 18% royalty, making the tax proportionate to the size of the gas field and making the tax deductible from other corporate taxes. Morales and the various indigenous groups arrogantly rejected the compromise, erected roadblocks again and precipitated yet another crisis that came to a head on March 7, when Mesa announced he would resign unless the disruptive demonstrations ended. Morales' *MAS* refused the conditions, and Mesa submitted his resignation to Congress. If he was bluffing, it worked. Thousands of pro-Mesa demonstrators converged on the Congress, which unanimously rejected the resignation on March 8. Even Morales admitted he did not want Mesa to quit.

Mesa relented and agreed to continue serving, but on condition that the roadblocks be dismantled, that Congress pass his energy bill, and that it approve an early presidential election for August 28 to choose his successor, as well as elections for a new Congress. Mesa warned that Bolivia was headed toward "collective suicide," but again vowed he would not use violence to break up the protests. Another week went by. Congress passed a compromise energy bill that deleted many provisions that Mesa advocated, such as the tax deduction, and rejected his call for an early election, calling it unconstitutional. Meanwhile, the roadblocks continued. On March 15, for a second time, Mesa said he would have to resign. After a tense two days, however, an obviously exhausted Mesa went on national television to declare, "I will not run away from my responsibilities."

By the first week of May, both houses of Congress had passed the contentious energy bill. At first, Mesa indicated he would sign it as the price for domestic peace. But on May 11, he stunned the country by refusing to either sign or veto it. The indigenous movements reacted with the predictable protests, including a 125-mile march on the capital. On May 13,

a car bomb exploded outside the La Paz offices of Petrobras, the Brazilian firm which, together with Repsol of Spain and British Petroleum, exploits most of Bolivia's gas deposits. There were no casualties. Mesa had kept his promise not to use deadly force, but he threatened again to resign if the protests turned violent.

On May 17, the Senate president signed the bill into law, as provided for in the constitution. Morales continued to demand a 50% tax, and an "indefinite" strike began in El Alto on May 22 to demand outright nationalization and, most recently, dissolution of Congress. By May 24, tens of thousands of protesters had essentially laid siege to La Paz, blocking major highways from the city and besieging the plant that supplies gasoline to the city. Police began firing tear gas and rubber bullets, injuring six, but not live ammunition. Protesters began arming themselves with sticks of dynamite. Health and air-

port workers went on strike. Police sealed off Murillo Plaza, site of the presidential palace, while in a sudden change of tactics, Mesa now proclaimed that he would serve out the remainder of his term and not cave in to pressure. It was ominously reminiscent of October 2003.

As the protests continued, the inevitable rumors of a military coup began circulating, spurred by the irresponsible statements of two lieutenant colonels to local media that a civilian-military government should replace Mesa and implement the protesters' demands. The defense minister and the chief of the armed forces disavowed the statements, proclaimed their support for Mesa and said the two officers would be prosecuted. Morales further inflamed an already tense situation by threatening to occupy the oilfields.

Meanwhile, in Santa Cruz, the autonomy movement was revived when Congress failed to call for a referendum. Lead-

Bolivia

ers of the movement called a referendum for August 12.

With Congress deadlocked on resolving the crisis, Mesa signed a decree on June 2 that sets October 16 as the date for an election for members of a constituent assembly that would rewrite the constitution to give more power to the Indian communities, one of the militants' key demands. Mesa also set the same day for a referendum to resolve the issue of greater departmental autonomy. Changing his mind yet again, Mesa said he would resign if the crisis continued. Neither side was placated, however. The militants refused to call off their siege of La Paz, while Santa Cruz separatist leaders said they would go ahead with plans for their own referendum on August 12. Both U.N. Secretary-General Kofi Annan and Pope Benedict XVI urged Bolivians to resolve the crisis peacefully.

On Monday night, June 6, Mesa went on national television to announce his resignation for a second time. He suggested that neither of the presidents of the Senate or Chamber of Deputies, who were next in the line of succession, should accept the presidency, which would require a new election within 150 days. Only the electoral process, Mesa warned, could save the nation, which he said was "on the brink of civil war."

The Congress abandoned the besieged capital for an emergency session in the administrative capital of Sucre. Protests quickly erupted there as well. On June 9 Congress voted to accept Mesa's resignation. Even if Mesa had not suggested it, Morales said that his party would refuse to recognize either Senate President Hormondo Vaca Diez—who is from Santa Cruz—or Chamber President Mario Cossio. Consequently, both men refused to accept the presidency. Under the constitution, that left Supreme Court Chief Justice Eduardo Rodríguez Veltzé, next in line. Rodríguez was sworn in late that night as Bolivia's 83rd president—and the fourth in less than two years.

Rodríguez, 49, is a respected figure who has both a law degree and a master's degree in public administration. On his first day, he announced he would call early elections. Morales pledged his support to Rodríguez as interim president until the new elections, in which Morales was certain to run for president again. The next day, June 11, the protesters declared a "truce" and lifted the siege of La Paz, where life slowly returned to normal. Clearly, Morales is the new power in Bolivia. That same day, the so-called "Paris Club," composed of the eight largest creditor nations, announced it was canceling $40 billion in Bolivian debt.

At the end of June, the various factions in Congress appeared stalemated over new elections and constitutional reform, and the Indian groups were threatening to return to their barricades. On July 2, however, the factions compromised and set December 4, 2005, as the date for elections for president and the departmental governors, and July 2, 2006, as the date for elections for the constituent assembly. Vaca Diez heralded the agreement as "a new period of harmony," a statement which may prove premature. When this book went to press, it had not been decided whether the December 4 election would also include the Congress.

Culture: The Spanish conquerors and settlers of Bolivia built new cities and tended to concentrate there, leaving the interior to the indigenous Aymara Indians. Today, the majority of Bolivians still speak Aymara as their first language, learning Spanish as a necessity to conduct official business. A substantial minority of the population also speaks Quéchua, the ancient tongue of the Incas. The populations of the cities of La Paz and Potosí are about 70% indigenous Indian, 25% *mestizo* and only 5% European.

Bolivian culture, consequently, remains essentially Indian with only a thin veneer of European Christianity superimposed upon it. Bolivia has produced few cultural figures of international note, although the flute–based folk music of the *altiplano* has become internationally popular. It is not unusual to see *altiplano* flute bands in colorful Indian dress playing on street corners from New Orleans to New York to Paris to Venice. Bolivians insist that the Brazilians "stole" the music for the megahit dance *Lambada* from Bolivia.

Because of the abysmally low literacy rate, Bolivia never developed a strong literary tradition. There were two newspapers of note, however, both published in La Paz: *El Diario*, founded in 1904, and *Presencia*, established by the Catholic Church during the revolutionary year 1952. *Presencia* ceased publication in 2001. Other current dailies now include *Los Tiempos*, *El Deber*, *La Prensa* and *La Razón*.

Economy: Bolivia's economy has been based on the extraction of its mineral wealth for more than 400 years. The vast sums produced have been exported, with little or no benefit accruing to the Bolivian people. Mismanagement and the decline of world demands for its minerals have resulted in the *de facto* bankruptcy of the Bolivian government. While the 1952 revolution largely ended serfdom, a lack of technical and financial resources limits a more even distribution of wealth and income. The nation's major source of income, the tin mines, are largely a thing of the past and has been replaced at least in part by exports of petroleum and natural gas.

The other mainstay of the Bolivian economy is coca leaf. President Banzer's program to eradicate coca cultivation was largely successful, but it created social unrest among the impoverished peasants who depend on it for their livelihood. The government's proposal to replace coca with alternative crops has a hollow ring, as any crop suitable for the humid Bolivian plains, such as soybeans or peanuts, will bring only a fraction of the price of illegal coca. The United Nations reported that production of coca leaf increased 35% between 2003 and 2004.

Bolivia remains one of the hemisphere's poorest nations, and its agricultural- and

Interim President Eduardo Rodríquez

mineral-based economy has shown but modest growth in recent years. Growth fell from 4.2% in 1997 and 4.7% in 1998 to 2.0% in 1999, 2.5% in 2000 and 1.5% in 2001. It was back up to 3.5% in 2004. Even the reduced growth of 1999 could have been worse, considering its three much more prosperous neighbors—Brazil, Argentina and Chile—slid into severe recessions. GDP stood at $8.1 billion in 2004. Per capita income surpassed the $1,000 mark for the first time in 1999, but it dropped back to $953 in 2002 and to $914 in 2004.

President Sánchez de Lozada sought to boost the economy with the potentially lucrative sale of natural gas to the United States. Bolivia has estimated gas reserves of 53.4 trillion cubic feet, second only to Venezuela in South America. However, even this positive move encountered furious opposition from the left, both because of anti-Americanism and because the gas would be exported through the Chilean port of Arica, which offended the sensibilities of many Bolivians still rankled by the loss of the Pacific coast to Chile in 1884. Public protests against the planned construction of a $5 billion gas pipeline to a Chilean port led to Sánchez's resignation in October 2003 and to the resignation of his successor, Carlos Mesa, in June 2005 (see History).

The Future: Bolivia is perilously close to mob rule. Carlos Mesa was something of an anomaly in South America: a popular president who kept threatening to resign, instead of an unpopular one who refuses to. In the end, the same mobs who once cheered when they forced Gonzalo Sánchez de Lozada to resign and when Mesa replaced him, now have cheered Mesa's own resignation. What has this accomplished? Sánchez and his running mate, Mesa, were elected on a flimsy electoral mandate of only 22%. But the new president, former Chief Justice Eduardo Rodríguez, has no electoral mandate at all. Will the mobs allow him to govern even for the five months before new elections? And after the elections, then what? If Evo Morales does come to power, and Santa Cruz votes to go its own way, civil war is a frighteningly genuine possibility.

The oppressed Indian majority has legitimate grievances, and the Indians' demand for a share of power after four centuries is a just one. But the self-destructiveness of their hatred of the foreign gas companies and the Caucasian elite is irrational and is preventing what could lead to an economic boom, as neighboring Brazil and Argentina are energy hungry. Now that they have succeeded in forcing the resignation of a second constitutional president, can Bolivian democracy long endure? The alternatives are a return to the military dictatorships of the past—or anarchy. Do they really want to risk either?

Apparently, a lot of Bolivians do. According to the annual *Latinobarómetro* survey published by the British newsmagazine *The Economist,* the percentage of Bolivians who believe that democracy is preferable to any other form of government plummeted from 64% in 1996 to 50% in 2003 (when Sánchez fell) to just 45% in 2004. The 19-point drop in support for democracy over eight years was exceeded only by the 20-point drops in Paraguay and Nicaragua. The percentage of Bolivians who believe that authoritarian government is sometimes preferable to democracy under certain circumstances rose from 17% in 1996 to 22% in 2003; in 2004 it was still 19%, the fifth-highest percentage in Latin America.

When the constitutional convention Morales and others are demanding is eventually held, some other reforms are advisable. They should scrap the congressional election of presidents when no candidate receives a majority and adopt the *segunda vuelta,* or runoff, between the top two contenders that most Latin American countries have to ensure that their president has a mandate of an absolute majority. This would prevent any more shaky 22% mandates, as Sánchez had, and provide Bolivian presidents with unquestioned legitimacy. Another would be to adopt the model of Costa Rica and other Latin American countries and have more than one elected vice president. In the case of Bolivia, four or five might be a good idea, given recent experience. These changes may not in themselves guarantee the survival of Bolivia's fragile democracy, especially against rabble-rousers who skillfully exploit the long-festering resentments of the Indians, but they would be steps in the right direction.

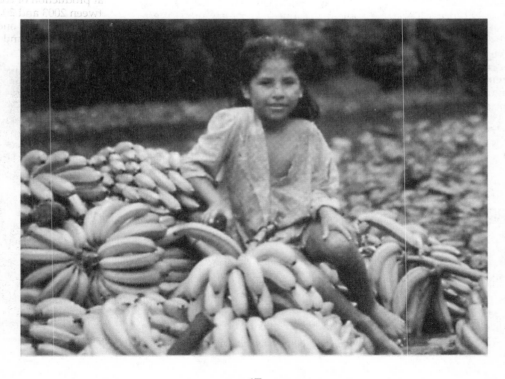

The Federative Republic of Brazil

Iguazu Falls (Brazil, Argentina, Paraguay)

Area: 3,286,500 square miles

Population: 177 million (2003 estimate).

Capital City: Brasilia (Pop. 2.3 million, estimated).

Climate: The northern lowlands are hot, with heavy rainfall; the central plateau and northeastern regions are subtropical and dry; the southern regions are temperate with moderate rainfall.

Neighboring Countries: French Guiana, Suriname, Guyana, Venezuela, Colombia (North); Peru, Bolivia (West); Paraguay, Argentina, Uruguay (Southwest).

Official Language: Portuguese.

Other Principal Tongues: English, French, German and other European languages.

Ethnic Background: Black African/Mulatto (48%), European White (48%); Other (3%); Native Indian (1%).

Principal Religion: Christianity (Roman Catholic 75%, Protestant Evangelical 20%).

Chief Commercial Products: Coffee, refined metal ores, chemicals, cacao, soybeans, sugar, cotton, wood, automobiles and parts, shoes.

Currency: Real (established July 1, 1994).

Gross Domestic Product: U.S. $508.6 billion in 2003 ($2,840 per capita).

Former Colonial Status: Colony of Portugal (1500–1815); Kingdom of the Portuguese Empire (1815–1822).

Independence Date: September 7, 1822.

Chief of State: Luiz Inácio "Lula" da Silva (b. October 27, 1945), president (since January 1, 2003).

National Flag: Green, with a yellow lozenge enclosing a blue sphere with 21 stars, five of which form the Southern Cross, and the motto *Ordem e Progresso* (Order and Progress).

Brazil occupies almost half of the South American continent and is almost as large as the continental United States. It stretches some 2,700 miles from the Guiana highlands in the North to the plains of Uruguay in the South and an equal distance from the "hump" on the Atlantic Coast to the jungles of Bolivia and Peru in the West. Almost half of this area is the hot, humid basin of the mighty Amazon River and its thousands of winding tributaries.

The northeast Bahia region, the interior of the "hump," is a semi-arid region; to the south and inland is a plateau drained to the northeast by the São Francisco River. This is a region of forests and plains which attracts migrants from other parts of Brazil and from abroad. The plains of the extreme south drain into the Paraná River valley. The southern states from Minas Gerais to Rio Grande do Sul comprise the effective Brazil, where approximately 90% of the population lives on less than 30% of the land. In an effort to draw settlers into other areas of the interior, the capital was moved in 1960 from pleasant and coastal Rio de Janeiro to inland and not so pleasant Brasilia. A modern city as planned, the capital is now surrounded by outlying shantytowns with almost one million people within 12 miles of the central area.

History: Pedro Alvares Cabral first raised the Portuguese flag in Brazil on April 22, 1500 after having been blown off course while enroute (he thought) from Portugal to India. The Portuguese government, preoccupied with its India trade, took little interest in the American claim until 1530 when it established a colony at Rio de Janeiro and in 1532 founded São Vincente. The land was quickly divided into vast estates with a frontage on the Atlantic Ocean and ran west to the line of demarcation between Spanish and Portuguese areas for discovery and colonization—approximately the 45th meridian west, set by the Treaty of Tordesillas in 1494. These estates, called *capitanias*, were granted as feudal holdings to the nobles who were to build towns and forts, explore, settle colonists and (most importantly) enrich the mother country. Thirteen of these estates were laid out, but the poor quality of the colonists sent out and the oppressive climate gave them a poor start.

In spite of this, several towns were founded—Olinda in 1535, Santo Amaro, Itamarca and Pernambuco in 1536, Bahia in 1549—and from these towns expeditions explored the interior.

From 1580 to 1640, Brazil was under Spanish control—Philip II of Spain had inherited the Portuguese throne. During this period, explorations were pushed beyond the demarcation line, but few towns were established in the dense interior. From 1630 to 1654, the Dutch briefly held the northeast coast from Pernambuco to Parnaiba. During most of its colonial period, Brazil was in reality a coastal colony with an immense, unexplored interior. That the colonies prospered and remained under Portuguese control was largely due to the politics of Europe and to the efforts of two capable leaders—General Tomé de Souza and General Mem de Sá—and to the efforts of a few Jesuit missionaries.

For almost one and a half centuries following Spanish rule, Brazil was neglected by the Portuguese government. It did, however, benefit from the liberal policies of the Marquis of Pombal, the Portuguese prime minister under Joseph I (1749–1777), who did much to improve the public services. In general, Brazil's communities were ruled by the municipal councils with little interference from the Portuguese monarchs. By the end of the colonial period, cities had developed power and prestige reminiscent of the feudal ones of Europe. The smaller municipalities were at the mercy of the militia commanders, and the great estates were under the absolute rule of their owners.

Probably the most cohesive force in the Brazilian colonies was the Catholic Church, and the most influential of the churchmen were the Jesuits. The Portuguese church had been influenced by modifying cultures at home, both Moslem and Oriental, and was subject to still more change in Brazil because of the primitive Indian and African Negro cultures. The Jesuits took as their first responsibility the protection of the Indians. Despite the opposition of the planters, who needed labor, the fathers gathered their charges into fortified villages, taught them useful arts and crafts, and improved methods of agriculture simultaneously with the fundamentals of Christianity.

The ouster of the Jesuits in 1759 was simply political reaction to the fact that they were so successful in their work of protecting the native Indians that they were bad for the colony's businessmen.

The settling of Brazil's interior was the work of a few pioneers, the celebrated *bandeirantes*, the boldest of whom were the missionaries and the slave raiders of São Paulo. The latter were foremost in establishing Portuguese rule in the interior; their raids forced the remaining Indians to withdraw deeper inland and served as a counter-force against Spanish penetrations. In their wake came planters and, later, gold prospectors. As African Negro slaves were introduced, the slave raiders turned to commerce and industry, making São Paulo the most prosperous of the Brazilian states. The colonial economy was based on sugar and forest products until the end of the 17th century, when the lure of gold depopulated the plantations as owners with their slaves migrated to Minas Gerais. Gold was also found in Mato Grosso and Goiás; about the same time it was learned that the bright stones found in Minas Gerais were diamonds. This wealth brought an influx of immigrants and pushed the frontier further inland. In 1763 the capital of Brazil was transferred from the north to Rio de Janeiro.

The cities furnished only the middlemen, the brokers and the hucksters in the

development of colonial Brazil. Its theoretically rigid class society was in fact for many decades a bizarre mixture of aristocracy, democracy and anarchy. At the top was the ruling class from Portugal; next came those of Portuguese origin born in Brazil—which included a majority of the estate owners; then followed in descending order mixed bloods, slaves and native Indians.

Actually, the system was elastic. The mulatto children born of the owner and his slaves might be reared equally with his legitimate children, and the Negro with the capacity to win wealth or influence took precedence with the elite. By the end of the colonial period, the whites had declined in number and influence, while those of mixed ancestry showed strength and a high degree of adaptation to the Brazilian environment. Brazil's society was tolerant, and the freedom from interference from Portugal allowed it to develop a one-class people—Brazilians.

Brazil's history as an independent state may be divided into two periods: Empire and Republic, and these in turn have their subdivisions. Certainly, loyalty to the crown kept the regional factions from creating small states, as happened in the Spanish states of Gran Colombia and Central America.

Brazil

Rio de Janeiro about 1825

Empire and Republic

In 1822, Pedro I, crown prince of Portugal and titular prince of Brazil, refused an order to return to Portugal and on September 7 declared Brazil independent. Surviving republican and separatist movements, he was able to create a constitutional monarchy. With his father's death in 1826, he inherited the throne of Portugal, which he renounced in favor of his five-year-old daughter to appease those Brazilians who feared a reunion with Portugal. However, through mismanagement and corruption, Pedro alienated the Brazilians, who in 1831 forced his abdication in favor of his five-year-old son, Pedro II. Fortunate in his tutors and regents, Pedro II proved to be a capable leader who retained the affection of the Brazilian people for a period of 49 years.

Although the abdication of Pedro I left Brazil on the verge of anarchy, the regents who governed during the minority of Pedro II were able to suppress rebellions. They made many liberal changes in the constitution, and Brazil avoided the series of tyrannical dictatorships experienced by many of the former Spanish colonies.

From his coronation in 1841 until 1850, Pedro II was occupied with establishing his authority to rule. The Brazil of this era consisted of population centers at Rio de Janeiro, Minas Gerais, São Paulo and Pernambuco. The population numbered some 7 million—between 1 and 2 million whites, 3 to 4 million Negro slaves, a million free Negroes and people of mixed blood and a half million Indians. The immense Amazon River basin was largely unexplored and while the cattle-raising south and the states of São Paulo and Minas Gerais were showing progress, the remainder of Brazil was still little more than a fringe of Atlantic coast settlements.

Although Pedro II's government was patterned after that of Great Britain, it lacked the popular base of the British government; the illiterate mass of Brazilians had no vote, and effective control fell to landowners, merchants and the learned men of the cities. Pedro's government was conducted by his ministers, while he exercised the role of arbitrator. The period of the 1840s was devoted to the suppression of separatist movements and consolidation of the nation; the 1850s and 1860s were spent in resolving Brazil's foreign disputes and in enlarging the national territory. The 1870s and 1880s were marked by much liberal legislation, the growth of republican ideas, the abolition of slavery and the end of the Empire.

From the 1850s to the 1870s, Brazil's economy expanded in a manner similar to that of the United States. Railroads, industry, agriculture and land speculation attracted large amounts of capital and a stream of immigrants who brought technical skills missing from Brazil's own population. By the mid 1870s, Brazil was earning a net profit of some $20 million from its foreign trade. During this period, Pedro II fostered education and Brazilian cultural expression developed. Through the 1860s his popularity and support were such that he could have governed under any title—king, emperor or president.

Liberal in his religious views, he respected freedom of worship; when in 1865 the pope published a ban against Free-masonry, Pedro refused to permit its adoption in Brazil. Despite his stand, the conflict between church and Masonry grew to the point that he personally became involved, losing support from the church and the clergy without satisfying the Masons. Following the Paraguayan War (1865–70) the Emperor became involved in a dispute between the army and the Liberal Party; while keeping the army under civilian control, he insisted upon supporting its legitimate needs for maintaining professional competence. These measures satisfied neither group and cost him the

Dom Pedro II, Emperor of Brazil

70

support of the elements whose interests he was defending.

The support of landowners was lost when slavery was abolished in 1871; the law also safeguarded the owners' economic interests and provided for the training of the emancipated slaves. Again, neither side was satisfied with Pedro's moderation and he was forced to abdicate in 1889 in the face of an impending military coup.

General Deodoro da Fonseca announced by decree the creation of the Federative Republic of Brazil, composed of 20 states. Pledged to recognize and respect the obligations created under the empire, the new government won popular acclaim. A constitution based on that of the United States was imposed on the country by decree in 1891. Although theoretically founded under democratic principles, the constitution gave less voice to the populace than it had under Pedro II. Fonseca later proved to be an inept leader and was replaced in 1893 by Marshal Floriano Peixoto, an even more capricious figure who provoked the navy into a rebellion which was followed by a short-lived civil war.

A reign of terror followed the rebellion—previously unknown in Brazil; in 1894 Peixoto peacefully turned the government over to a more moderate Civilain president, Prudente de Morais Barros, the first of three consecutive presidents from São Paulo.

The government was badly demoralized, and had an empty treasury, and people were widely split in a military-civilian standoff. Further complicating the scene were the conselheiros, a group of fanatics in the northeast who held out against the army until the last man was killed. The president was able to spend his last year in office in peace.

The years to 1910 saw the republic develop under a series of three capable presidents. Two decades of turmoil ensued, which tested the strength of the federal republic. Problems centered around political meddling by the military, anarchic regionalism and an ailing economy, all of which were complicated by World War I. The military-civilian division worsened and continued for some 20 years; in the states, state loyalty was greater than national loyalty and was compounded by various militia loyal to local political leaders.

The Vargas Era

Asian rubber production, the decline of coffee prices and the loss of foreign markets, rubbed salt in already sore wounds. Foreign debts and unwise fiscal policies in Brazil brought it to the verge of bankruptcy. The world-wide depression of the 1930s and political blunders of the government brought on military intervention

and the installation of Getulio Vargas, who ruled as dictator for 15 years. He combined a shrewd sense of politics with managerial ability and personal honesty. Sometimes compared with the Jesuits who defended the Indians against the landlords, Vargas posed as a defender of Brazil against the military and the powerful state governors, while trying to unify the laboring classes and grant the right to vote to the entire population.

Vargas rehabilitated the economy and forced state cooperation with the new national government. A new pseudo-fascist constitution in 1934 enfranchised women and provided social legislation to protect workers. Peace endured for a year, but was followed by communist and fascist attempts to seize power. Profiting from the scare, Vargas suspended the constitution, extended his term and ruled by decree. An amiable but forceful dictator, he

Getulio Vargas, 1934

selected capable men to administer government services and accomplished much to improve the living standards of the poor. His management of the national economy was sound and Brazil made notable progress in industrialization and in production. He also brought Brazil into the war on the side of the Allies and sent troops to fight in Italy. Despite the generally popular nature of his rule, by the end of World War II, opposition had developed to the point that Vargas could only retain his position by the use of force. On October 29, 1945, a committee of military officers persuaded Vargas to resign. Vargas already had ordered free elections for December, in which General Eurico Gaspar Dutra won the presidency by a decisive margin. Colorless and inept, he was unable to control the economy. Overspending and corruption and inflation spelled the end of his career.

In the elections of 1950, Vargas entered the competition as a candidate of the Labor Party and announced himself to be the champion of democratic government. The National Democratic Union was unable to stop his demagogic appeal. But his new term in office was not impressive; his appointees were largely incompetent and many were corrupt.

By 1954, general discontent was highly apparent; both the military and civilian elements were in a mood to unseat Vargas—events were triggered by an attack on the editor of a leading Rio newspaper. Faced with the evidence that his own bodyguard was implicated, and under military pressure for his resignation, Vargas instead committed suicide.

His successor proved to be no solution; by the time Juscelino Kubitschek finished his term, there was a flurry of strikes and refusals of the International Monetary Fund and Washington to advance further sums to an extravagant Brazil. Campaigning on a platform of austerity and competent government, Jãnio Quadros won the 1960 elections by the largest plurality of any president in Brazilian history. However, he was embarrassed by a last-minute round of wage increases granted by his predecessor and the election of a controversial leftist, João Goulart, as vice president. Quadros faced staggering problems, including large foreign debts, mounting inflation, widespread opposition to his plan for trade with the communist bloc and moderation toward Cuba. This led to feelings of frustration and his sudden resignation in August 1961.

Goulart was permitted to take office the following month only after agreeing to demands by conservative military officials to a drastic limitation of presidential powers. Brazil thus became a rudderless ship, headed by a president with no authority and a congress bitterly divided among 12 political parties. Faced with a stagnant economy, growing inflation which had reached an annual rate of 100% by 1964 and deepening social division, the president fought for and obtained greater power through a plebiscite in 1963. Relying increasingly on leftist support, he sought to divide the military and use mass demonstrations to intimidate his opposition.

Military–ARENA Rule, 1964–1985

Fearing the nation might be plunged into chaos, the armed forces ousted him on April 1, 1964, and replaced him with General Humberto Castelo Branco. This began a series of military governments that altered the political and economic face of Brazil.

Regarding themselves as authentic "revolutionaries," the military imposed a

Brazil

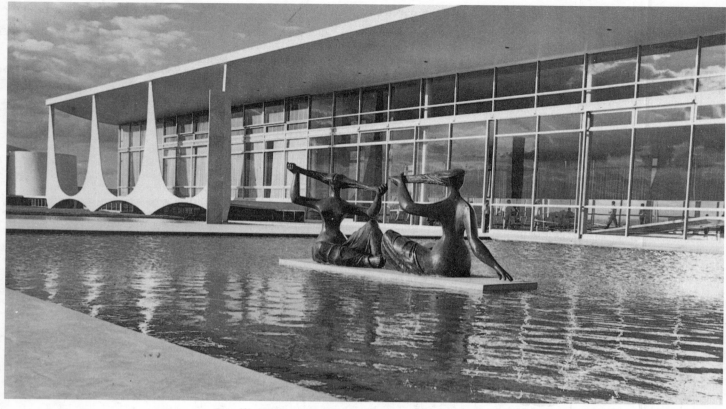

Brasilia's Alvorada Palace, the presidential residence

presidential government controlled by the high command of about 12 top officers better known as the *Estado Maior* or general staff. Their basic goal was not a social revolution, but an industrial revolution to enable Brazil to become a major world power. Relying heavily on technicians, the military government was relatively honest and nonpolitical. Indeed, the traditional politicians were suspect, "social" programs had low priority and human rights were respected only when they did not interfere with the "revolution."

The military quickly imposed austere economic measures to control inflation. In addition, all political parties were disbanded and replaced by two new ones: the Alliance for National Renovation (*ARENA*), and the Brazilian Democratic Movement (*MDB*).

In theory, *ARENA* was to be the dominant, government party, while the *MDB* was to furnish token opposition. In reality, both parties were powerless to challenge the military. After assuming dictatorial powers, ruling by decree, the military saw to it that *ARENA* won a large majority in carefully supervised 1966 elections. Following instructions, legislators then chose as the next president Marshal Arthur da Costa e Silva in 1967. In late 1968 he dissolved Congress, instituted press censorship and jailed prominent po-

litical opponents, including Kubitschek. In addition he suspended judicial "interference" with prosecution for "crimes against the state."

When Costa e Silva suffered a paralyzing stroke in mid-1969, General Emilio Garrastazu Médici was named president. Prosperity and repression were the two prominent traits of his regime, which believed that the first is possible only because of the latter. Under his tutelage, Brazil developed a prosperous economy, forcing even critics to admit that the "Brazilian miracle" economically compared with the post-war boom in Germany and Japan, albeit at tremendous loss of liberty.

The expanding economy helped finance ambitious government projects in education, health and public works. The mammoth Trans-Amazonian highway linked Brazil's Atlantic coast with the Peruvian border, hacked 3,250 miles through vast empty stretches of the national heartland. (A continuing battle with the encroaching jungle has been waged since that time.) The cost of economic boom was high; industrial growth was financed largely through exploitation of workers. During the first 10 years of military rule, the economy grew by 56% while real wages dropped by 55%. The result was a severe decrease in purchasing power for the lower classes. In the

same period, government expenditures for education were reduced by half and investments in health and social services also declined in real terms. While the upper 5% of the population saw its share of the national wealth jump by 9% to a total of 36%, the lower half's share dropped by 4% to a total of 14%. Although Brazilian business executives were among the world's best paid, the bottom 40% of the people were underfed. Government officials said this squeeze on the masses was necessary to raise exports. Foreign investments were attracted by the fixed low wage scale of less than 50 cents an hour.

The political situation was even more rigidly controlled—the 1967 constitution, imposed by the military, provided for a strong executive and a powerless congress. Through the Institutional Acts Nos. 5, 13 and 14, the regime systematically silenced its critics. Torture of political opponents was condemned by the Human Rights Commission of the Organization of American States. Despite ironclad censorship of the arts and media, some criticism of the regime was evident. Most outspoken was the Catholic Church. The regime in turn charged that church work with the poor was communist-oriented. Paramilitary government secret police frequently raided church offices, seizing property and harassing leaders. The regime conducted a major crackdown in 1973 on church activities that offended it.

Unknown to many Brazilians, presidential elections were held in early 1974. The official government candidate—selected by the military high command—was retired Army General Ernesto Geisel, a portly 68-year-old former head of the Brazilian oil monopoly, Petrobras. The only opposition candidate was denied meaningful access to the press and television during the campaign; he could not speak out against the regime, but he called the election a "farce." There was no direct vote for president in Brazil; the "electoral college" formalized the selection of the new president by a vote of 400 to 76.

Although he promised a degree of moderation, at the same time he cautioned that

social reform must wait until the nation's economic problems were solved. Nevertheless, press censorship was greatly reduced, although not eliminated, and police repression was also less evident. Efforts were made to improve strained relations with the Catholic Church and organized labor; small steps were taken to increase wages for the workers.

After allowing politicians a greater voice in national affairs, despite objections from hardliners within the ruling military councils, Geisel went ahead with plans to hold elections in late 1974. The results proved to be a disaster for the regime and its ARENA organization. The opposition MDB received twice the vote of the military-backed slate. As a result, the MDB picked up 16 of 22 Senate seats and a third

of the Chamber of Deputies. The military favored a return to the "good old days" while the civilian population appeared more restless after a decade of military rule. Geisel tried to walk a tightrope between the two sides—he decided not to overturn the election results, but at the same time he appeared to have placated the conservative military by permitting a rise in right-wing "vigilante" acts against suspected leftists and petty criminals. Reports of torture of political opponents continued to circulate; most of this activity was conducted by the government's Intelligence Operations Detachment (DOI). The president also appeared to have turned on his critics—in 1976 he revoked the political rights of three opposition legislators who charged that Brazil was be-

STATES AND TERRITORIES

Brazil

ing run by "an aristocracy wearing uniforms." The regime also brought charges against 21 critical journalists.

Economic decline had a dramatic impact on Brazil's foreign policy—in mid-1975 it became the first nation in Latin America (aside from Cuba) to recognize the Soviet- and Cuban-backed revolutionaries in the Angolan civil war.

This surprising move by the staunchly anti-communist regime was largely due to economics, as Brazil hoped to buy Angolan oil and wanted to include that country in an international coffee cartel to raise the price of that commodity. It also viewed this Portuguese-speaking African nation as a potential customer for Brazilian products.

Although Brazil always had maintained cordial relations with the United States, there was a strain in 1975—in addition to recognizing Angola, Brazil voted in the UN to equate Zionism with racism. (Brazil imports much of its oil from Arab states).

Further questions centered around development of atomic power based on West German technology. Although Brazil said it would not build the bomb, the United States and other countries feared Brazil's entry into the nuclear field would accelerate the race for nuclear weapons then shaping up in the "Third World." The final upsetting factor was Brazil's growing alignment with Third World economic aims. This centered on a belief that the price of raw materials from developing nations had not kept pace with the price of machines from industrialized states. Brazil's trade deficit with the United States steadily mounted to crisis proportions.

When the Carter administration reduced military aid until Brazil showed greater respect for human rights and called on Brazil to terminate its nuclear program, the response was cancellation of the entire 25-year-old military pact with the United States. Geisel faced serious conflict with the business community, which openly complained that it was being elbowed aside by huge, state-run industries and fast-growing multi-national corporations. Small farmers (as in the United States) were forced off their land by huge farm combines and other modern agricultural techniques. Political tensions mounted. After the Congress abruptly dismissed Geisel's proposal for judicial changes in 1977, the president dismissed the legislature for two weeks. By decree, he ordered changes that made Brazil a one-party state. Under the plan, the president, all state governors and a third of the Senate would be elected indirectly, and in a manner so as to force them to remain under permanent control of *ARENA* and the military. The measure further gave the president another year in office.

President Geisel chose his successor, announcing in early 1978 that General João Baptista de Oliveira Figueiredo, head of the national intelligence agency, would become the next chief executive. There followed an almost meaningless presidential campaign. Virtually unknown to the public at the time of his nomination, the new president sought to project the image of a Harry Truman style "man in the street"— a campaign model which sharply contrasted with Brazil's normally stern and colorless military leadership. The obedient electoral college, with the military

looking over its shoulder, officially named Figueiredo to a six-year term. In contrast, unusually free congressional elections were held throughout the nation in late 1978. To the chagrin of the military, the opposition *MDB* won a majority of the 45 million popular votes, largely because of big margins in urban areas. Nevertheless, since Brazilian law prohibited any opposition party from winning control of Congress, *ARENA* wound up with 231 of the 420 seats in the lower house and 42 of the 67 Senate seats. All 21 state governors and most city mayors were appointed directly by the military.

Installed in March 1979, the new president pledged to "open this country up to democracy"—a promise that dismayed some army officers who distrusted civilian government. This was not empty political talk. Under a new plan, free, direct elections were to be held for every office except the president. Brazil suddenly came alive with political activity. For the first time, government opponents were allowed access to the news media and the last political prisoner was released. At least six parties fielded candidates, compared to only one official and one opposition party permitted to exist under the old order. The plan put all Chamber of Deputies seats and one-third of the Senate seats up for grabs.

Maintaining the government-proclaimed policy of gradually returning the country to democratic rule, on November 15, 1982, peaceful elections were held for 479 seats in the Chamber of Deputies, one third of the seats in the Senate, the state governorships and assemblies, and the municipalities. Five parties participated—one pro-government, the Partido Democratico Social (*PDS*), and four opposition groups, the most important of which is the Partido Movimento Democratico Brasileiro (*PMDB*). The *PDS* gained an overall victory in the elections, retaining vital control of Congress, but the opposition, mainly the *PMDB* and the Partido Trabalhista Brasileiro (*PTB*)—Brazilian Labor Party—managed to win the state governorships of the three most important states: São Paulo, Rio de Janeiro and Minas Gerais.

However, expressed in intense (but sporadic) demonstrations of dissatisfaction and unrest in the principal cities, public attention was focused on the presidential elections. The majority of the opposition leaders expressed the will of the people shown in the rallies: direct presidential elections. The military-backed *PDS* convention in Brasilia nominated Paulo Salim Maluf, a wealthy businessman of Lebanese heritage. At the same time, a coalition of the *PMDB* and dissident *PDS* delegates calling itself the Democratic Alliance

Cattle–drawn cart

met and selected a widely known and revered public figure, Dr. Tancredo Neves. This elderly gentleman had the unique ability to attract the support of not only military elements, but communists and leftists. José Sarney, who had recently resigned as head of the *PDS*, was selected as vice presidential candidate of the alliance. The government opposed direct elections, arguing that they would break constitutional provisions. Instead, President Figueiredo proposed an amendment to the constitution which, while holding to indirect elections in 1985, would allow direct popular elections for the presidential period 1988–92. As the electoral college meeting drew close, political allegiances hardened. Charges (probably true) were made that Maluf had bribed and bought the nomination of the *PDS*. Popular support for Dr. Neves grew by leaps and bounds—the public sensed correctly that he was a person of great dedication and integrity. President Figueiredo, beset with illness and the military, correctly foreseeing a victory of Neves, made peace with him in an unwritten agreement. Sensing the tide running against him, Maluf attempted to make party allegiance binding on all delegates of the electoral college. The effort failed.

Return to Democracy

In early January 1985, indirect presidential elections were held, and an electoral college formed by 686 members representing most political parties elected Neves by a majority of 480 to 180 for Maluf; the majority included the dissatisfied members of the *PDS*.

Neves would have been sworn into office on March 15, officially ending a period of military rule of 21 years. Popular celebrations were cut short by the sudden illness of the president-elect, who was rushed to the hospital the day before his inauguration; after multiple operations he died on April 21, 1985, plunging the country into mourning.

Vice President Sarney, who had been acting president during Neves' illness, assumed the presidency and proclaimed that he would follow "the ideas and plans of Tancredo Neves." He inherited a coalition of Neves' center-left *PMDB* and a numerically smaller rightist Liberal Front Party (*PFL*) formed by a faction of the *PDS* of which party Sarney had been president before his resignation prior to the elections. Bickering between the two factions erupted almost immediately. Sarney initially ruled somewhat timidly and it appeared that he lacked the leadership necessary to move Brazil forward.

Labor unrest was rampant—a strike by a half million truckers, who in early 1986

Former President and Mrs. Figueiredo

blocked highways, threatened the food supply of the cities. This was topped by 1985 strikes by 2 million other workers, many under the leadership of a trade union firebrand destined to play a major role in Brazilian politics for the next two decades: Luiz Inándio da Silva, better known by his sobriquet "Lula."

Sarney did nothing to lessen governmental corruption which existed for a century and grew worse under the military. He spent the nation into virtual bankruptcy but did nothing for the immense number of poor.

Nature was not kind to Brazil in the last quarter-century. A killing frost in the 1970s destroyed millions of coffee trees; as soon as the industry had recovered, a murderous drought killed or stunted the plants, reducing production by 50%. Floods in the northeast and southeast in the 1980s followed by a five-year drought in the northeast left more than a million homeless. In late 1994, killing frosts again hit the coffee trees, resulting in a 100% rise in the price of Brazil's favored Arabica coffee. These natural disasters increased migration of unskilled, penniless people to the cities.

Economic Reforms and External Debt

Sarney's only attempt to rid the country of its economic unevenness and chronic programs was "The Cruzado Program." Prices were frozen, and wage increases of 20% in many sectors were decreed. Violators of the price freeze not only had to face the law, but vigilante committees. The cruzeiro was abolished and the cruzado took its place, worth

1,000 units of the former currency. A freeze on government hiring was commenced (in name only) at both the federal and state level. The staggering foreign debt (the largest in the world at $108 billion) was hesitantly rescheduled by the "Paris Club," a group of creditor nations representing commercial and national banks which had loaned money to Brazil. Sarney announced that Brazil would not "pay its foreign debt with recession, nor with unemployment, nor with hunger," but that is precisely what happened. The IMF, accustomed to inspections of and "recommendations" to debtor nations, was told it had to keep these activities at a minimum in Brazil.

A four-year moratorium was announced on income tax refunds. An ambitious land reform plan, however, had to be watered down to include only a distri-

Former President José Sarney

Brazil

Glamorous Rio de Janeiro from the ocean . . .

bution of government-owned acreage. Although the plan had originally included the purchase of sub-marginal producing land, the landowners hired gunmen in many areas to drive out the peasants who had resettled. "Liberation theology" priests and bishops of the Roman Catholic Church who supported the poor were infuriated and fomented unrest. Pope John Paul II had to remind the National Conference of Brazilian Bishops that the clergy had to stay out of politics, although he, too, supported land reform in Brazil.

High interest rates were established to discourage the flight of capital from Brazil. Taxes were raised on just about everything, including the purchase of U.S. dollars (25%). Additional taxes were imposed on the purchase of cars, and compulsory "loans" to the government were part of the purchase arrangement. Although there were loud murmurs of discontent from both the wealthy sector and from the labor movement, these sweeping reforms were generally greeted with initial acceptance by a country which had been sapped economically for too many years. But the maharajas—persons with low or non-existent work at government "jobs"—continued in a leech-like fashion to suck the economic blood out of the country.

The *PMDB* and *PFL* increased their majority in the Chamber of Deputies in late 1986 elections to a combined total of 374 out of 487 seats; the largest losses were incurred by the labor-supported *PTB*.

Due to inflation and currency instability, a vigorous black market in just about everything developed in which most consumer goods were bought and sold. Currency reform in 1988 was useless—it was followed by numerous devaluations. A price freeze was tried, and lifted after it failed. Brazil sank into actual bankruptcy; Sarney made it official in early 1987: Brazil would suspend payment of principal and interest on its foreign debt indefinitely.

Of course, all international credit instantly ended. The moratorium lasted a year and cost far more than had been gained. Further, the moratorium worsened economic chaos within Brazil to the extent that there was a genuine threat of resumed military control. Western banks responded by extending repayment of existing debt over 20 years and lowered interest rates.

Although heavily indebted, nevertheless Brazil became number 10 of the industrial nations of the world. It developed a lively business in aircraft and armaments worldwide, selling products of good quality and easily repairable. It surpassed Bolivia's tin production and experimented in enriched nuclear fuels, while avowing not to develop weapons. Nevertheless, it insisted on classifying itself as an underdeveloped nation of the "Third World." One observer likened it economically to a "hulking teenager." To this might be added "with a huge allowance, 24-hour use of the family car and little ambition."

Brazil's only hope was to get rid of at least half of the top-heavy government bureaucracy, at least half of the armed forces, punish government and union corruption with heavy penalties and make its currency non-exchangeable with any other currency except through a single, honestly managed central bank. Private banks should have been nationalized. Brazil should have gone even further: allow foreign enterprise to come into the country according to capitalist principles—i.e. the investor keeps the profits, not Brazil.

Fernando Collor de Mello

After five years of economic chaos under Sarney, capped by an inflation rate of 1,700% in 1989, it was inevitable that the 1989 elections would center around the economy. Although 30 candidates entered the fray, three emerged as the frontrunners. Because candidates of the left-wing *PTB* had been so successful in municipal elections during 1988, its leader, "Lula" da Silva, was initially the frontrunner. Leonel Brizola of the also leftist Democratic Worker's Party was second. Both were quickly outpaced by Fernando Collor de Mello, of the hastily organized, right-of-center National Reconstruction Party (*PRN*).

This wealthy, handsome, 6'1" governor of poverty-stricken Alagoas State on the central Atlantic Coast, trained as an economist, began his career as a reporter and went on to own a number of media organizations. He contrasted sharply with da Silva, a lathe operator with a fifth-grade education and a bad case of fractured grammar. While governor, Collor had undertaken an energetic program to fire almost half of the bureaucracy, particularly the maharajas, in order to bring solvency to the state. His action was reversed by the state Supreme Court. He quickly was able to gain the confidence of the owner of the largest private television network and the battle began. He made a bold promise: economic measures would ensure a 7% annual growth in the economy. If there was anything left over, it would be used to retire foreign debt.

The campaign was dirty and spirited. Personal attacks were the rule of the day.

When the dust settled, Collor had 28.5% of the vote and da Silva 16%. About 17% cast blank ballots (voting is compulsory over the age of 18 in Brazil). After an equally heated runoff, Collor won 43% to da Silva's 38%. He took office on March 15, 1990.

He inherited a Brazil in which sleaze had become so much a part of the very culture of the country. The work ethic of government employees (arrive late, if at all, take a long break for lunch and leave early, keeping any activity resembling work at a minimum) had been about as bad as can be imagined. Many jobs were "make work" situations distributed as patronage among relatives.

If the people thought Collor's campaign promises were stiff medicine, they gasped when decrees started to issue from the presidential palace. All banks were closed for three days and all savings accounts were limited to withdrawals of the equivalent of $1,200. Industries were allowed to

withdraw only enough to pay current salaries; this resulted in wholesale layoffs. Although this initially landed about $88 billion, it quickly dwindled to about $16 billion through corruption. The cruzeiro was reconstituted the national currency at a vastly increased value (they could not be printed in advance, lest the consequences of Collor's plans be revealed). Much of Brazil reverted to a barter economy because of currency shortages. But, oddly, 80% of the people stood solidly behind Collor although undergoing personal sacrifices.

The president had vowed to get rid of 360,000 unneeded government workers. He reached the figure of 260,000, but stumbled badly when the Supreme Court overturned him. Civil "servants" had tenure under the constitution and could not be fired. Collor oversaw the sale of 4,675 government limousines, formerly seen idling daily in the cafe district of Brasilia with waiting chauffeurs.

Things began to fall apart in 1992, however. As it later became apparent, Collor was caught up in a four-part storm which had no precedent and hopefully will have no repetition.

First, the unprecedented righteousness he displayed in his election campaign inflamed the passions of his supporters to a degree he never anticipated. Second, his loose-cannon younger brother decided to play to the tabloid media in a series of exposés starting in the spring of 1992 which were sensationalized and reprinted tirelessly by supposedly responsible media sources. They had no concern for truth or honest judgment, but only wished to sell as many newspapers as possible and command as wide an audience as they could on Brazil's TV networks.

Even more shabby, a series romanticizing anti-government teenage fighters replete with oriental karate skills appeared for late spring-early summer fare, inflaming Brazil's youth to an incredible degree. Third, Collor had virtually no support in either house of the legislature, and his cabinet turned out to have the loyalty of hyenas. Finally, he had used about $2.5 million in campaign contributions for personal purposes, including the luxurious remodeling of his mansion's back yard in Brasilia. The stage was set for the disgracing of a popular public figure (except in the eyes of political traditionalists).

The attacks by non-Collor-owned media were so vicious that Collor literally did not know what had hit him. The alleged offenses he was charged with were commonplace and overlooked in Brazil for more than a century. But incited particularly by a TV national network, popular demonstrations against Collor became commonplace.

. . . seen from Corcovado crowned by Christ the Redeemer, and then to . . .

Brazil

... the city's dark side where poverty and desperation live side by side in the favelas

Collor was removed by Congress in 1992, which some felt was like the pot convicting the kettle. He resigned rather than face a televised, months-long trial, but was convicted of "lack of decorum" (whatever that is). Criminal charges were dismissed by the Supreme Court because of "insufficient evidence," the legal language for a "fix." He benefited from the unwritten Brazilian law that no former political leader is convicted—of anything.

Itamar Franco

Collor's successor, Itamar Franco, was an unintelligent, colorless, temperamental hack who had bubbled to the top of the Brazilian political cauldron. His career was noted for utter silence on anything important and nit-picking on everything of little or no consequence. He showed poor judgment in personal matters while in office, permitting himself to be shown on TV holding hands with and kissing a young pornography actress during the 1994 Carnaval celebration.

During most of the 27 months of Franco's tenure, Brazil went from disorganized to chaotic. Inflation neared 40% per month, devaluing the currency to the point that it was virtually worthless. About half the people lived outside the wage economy. The authority of the state disappeared. Murder, which had been frequent, became ordinary. The killing of homeless "street children" in Rio and other large cities reached dreadful levels. They were almost all black and were kicked out of their homes as early as age 6 because there is not enough to feed them. Prostitution at age 8 is common. Shanty towns around the cities (favelas) were, and still are, controlled largely by drug gangs.

An effort was made in 1994 to assert control by sending the military with armored vehicles into areas close to Rio de Janeiro, which has the third largest slums in Latin America. This was done when it became apparent that innocent people were being frequently killed during police forays in pursuit of drug criminals. The operation lasted a day and a half and when it ended, drug gangs set off firecrackers to announce they were back in business.

The Congress wallowed eyeball deep in its own scandals; with Collor disposed of, the media turned on it, reporting generally at the level of U.S. tabloids. Indifferent to all criticism, it sat only on Wednesdays, if at all. The judiciary and police were openly corrupt.

After wearing out four finance ministers, Franco appointed Fernando Henrique Cardoso in 1994. It was an unlikely choice; Cardoso was a longtime Marxist economist and one of the loudest of the *dependentistas*, who viewed foreign investments as a threat to national identity. His book, *Dependency and Underdevelopment in Latin America*, was the Koran of dependency theorists. When it was published, Cardoso was exiled by the military government. Once in office as finance minister, however, and equipped with power rather than theories, Cardoso underwent a conversion as dramatic as that of St. Paul on the road to Damascus. He pragmatically replaced the inflation-riddled and devaluation-prone *cruzeiro* with a new currency, the *real*, which like Argentina's new currency was pegged to the U.S. dollar. Cardoso also began welcoming foreign investors and dismantling inefficient and costly state-owned utilities and other enterprises. Under Cardoso's guidance, inflation plummeted from 2,500% annually to double-digit levels. He became a national hero, an economic David who had slain the Goliath of hyperinflation. In October 1994, Cardoso was the presidential candidate of a coalition of his own Social Democratic Party and Franco's larger *PMDB*. He handily defeated da Silva, the perennial candidate of the left.

The Cardoso Era

Cardoso was inaugurated before an enthusiastic crowd in January 1995, and he forged a record as, arguably, the most able and effective democratic president of the 20th century. His economic measures stabilized the *real* and provided real GDP growth that was a steady 3–4% throughout his first term. He also fol-

Former President Itamar Franco

lowed through with his privatization program, as billions in foreign investment flowed into the country. At the end of 1997, unemployment was a mere 4.84%.

On the negative side, corruption remained ingrained, resisting attempts to combat it from the top. The problem was spotlighted further in late 1995 when Pelé, the former soccer star who had become a sports minister, declared that politicians were corrupt, that the Congress was full of thieves and that Brazil is a "decadent country."

An important political development in 1996 was the election of Celso Pitta as the first black mayor of São Paulo, although his administration, too, would be marred by corruption.

Riding a crest of popularity, Cardoso persuaded Congress in 1997 to amend the constitution to allow him to seek a second term, arguing that no president could successfully deal with the country's prodigious problems in one four-year term. His popularity was only marginally affected by the impact of the Asian market crisis that October that caused him to impose a tough, painful austerity plan to shore up the *real*. Even so, unemployment shot up sharply in January 1998.

Former President Franco sought the nomination of the *PMDB* for president in the October 4, 1998 elections. But in March, Franco's party opted to nominate Cardoso; Franco charged later that Cardoso had "bought" the nomination with promises of pork-barrel projects. That left da Silva, again, as his only major opponent.

Cardoso also came under fire in 1998 for alleged inaction in dealing with the fires in Roraima state (see Economy) and insensitivity to the victims of the El Niño-related drought in the northeast. The campaign between Cardoso and da Silva took a nasty

turn when da Silva accused Cardoso of offering to sell off the state-owned communications firm, Telebras, below market value: Cardoso responded by filing a defamation suit against his opponent.

Then, in early September, the world financial jitters, stemming from the previous year's Asian market crisis and uncertainty over the Russian ruble and debt payments, suddenly came crashing down on Brazil. Rumors spread that Brazil would devalue the *real*, which caused a market panic in São Paulo. On one day, the market dropped 13%, and the panic quickly spread to the markets in Argentina, Mexico, Venezuela and Colombia; shock waves also were felt in New York, Europe and Asia.

To defend the *real*, the government began selling off its reserves of dollars; in September alone, dollar reserves dropped by $30 billion. Interest rates were drastically raised, from 29.75% to 49.75%. On September 25, Cardoso boldly reacted to the crisis by pledging an austerity program to reduce the huge budget deficit, a move sure to reassure the IMF and nervous foreign investors, but highly risky for a politician just nine days away from an election.

Yet, on October 4, voters gave their president a resounding mandate to continue for another four years. Cardoso crushed da Silva 53% to 32%. He reiterated his determination to impose an austerity program, but put off the details until the crucial governor's races on October 25. The outcome of those races tempered Cardoso's elation over his presidential landslide. A friend and ally, Mario Covas, was reelected in

**Former President
Fernando Henrique Cardoso**

São Paulo, but two leftists were elected in Rio de Janeiro and Rio Grande do Sul. More ominous for Cardoso, former President Franco, Cardoso's erstwhile boss and now a bitter enemy, was elected governor of Minas Gerais.

Days later, Cardoso announced a $23.5 billion austerity plan of tax increases and spending cuts. On December 23, nine days before his inauguration, Cardoso announced his selection of a cabinet, which was little changed from the existing one except for the creation of a new development ministry.

The 1999 Economic Crisis

Cardoso was inaugurated for his second term on January 1, 1999; the same day, Franco was inaugurated as governor of Minas Gerais. Cardoso's austerity plan seemed to have quieted the fears of foreign investors and lending institutions. The slide of the *real* had stopped, and it was still pegged to the dollar; sanity had returned to the stock market, and inflation had remained under control.

Suddenly, the willful Franco, known to be consumed with jealousy against Cardoso because his former minion had received all the credit for rescuing Brazil from economic chaos, decided to toss a boulder into this tranquil pond and precipitated a financial crisis with global repercussions. On January 6, Franco announced a 90-day moratorium on the payment of his state's $13.5 billion debt, triggering another market panic that far surpassed the one in September. Wall Street responded negatively to the crisis, as did other markets around the world. International condemnation was heaped upon Franco, who actually seemed to relish the attention. It was to backfire on him, however; the World Bank froze $209 million in development loans for Minas Gerais.

This time, the central government could not keep propping up the *real* by selling dollars. On January 15, the government was forced to abandon the five-year-old *Real* Plan—which Franco and Cardoso had introduced together—and announced that the *real* would be allowed to float against foreign currencies. The reaction was immediate; at one point, the *real* plummeted 46% in value, before beginning a slow climb. The devaluation raised the specter of renewed inflation. On the other hand, it pleased manufacturers by making Brazilian exports more attractive.

The crisis continued for two months, as Brazil slid into a recession. By March, however, international fears that the Brazilian economy, burdened by the huge budget deficit, would collapse proved unfounded. Cardoso's painful austerity mea-

Brazil

sures dragged down his approval rating in the polls, especially as unemployment remained stubbornly high.

When Cardoso presented his budget in August 1999, he predicted that the economy would show a 1% decline for 1999 but would record a 4% growth rate in 2000, with 8.5 million new jobs. The old economic wizard proved close to the mark: the economy shrank by .4% in 1999, not as bad as he had predicted, and grew by 2.6% in 2000. In April 2000, Brazil paid off the last of the $41.5 billion of the international loan package the IMF and other institutions had advanced during the January 1999 market panic. Clearly, the economy was back on track.

There was a significant governmental restructuring in 1999 that had historic overtones. Cardoso created a new defense ministry, consolidating the three armed services and placing them under a civilian minister for the first time. The three chiefs of the uniformed services simultaneously were removed from the cabinet. Cardoso reportedly intended for the change to show how far the country had emerged from the 1964-85 dictatorship.

On April 22, 2000, Brazil observed the 500th anniversary of the landing of Portuguese sailor Pedro Alvares Cabral in Brazil in 1500. But what Cardoso had intended as a major celebration of Brazilian national identity and unity turned into an ugly spectacle when nearly 200 Indian tribes protested the event as an insult to their own cultural identity. They had a point; there were 6 million indigenous inhabitants when Cabral landed, but there were only 700,000 left. One of their banners asked a logical question: "Who says Brazil was discovered?" The Indians were soon joined by some African Brazilians, who said that to celebrate the Portuguese arrival was to celebrate the legacy of slavery. About 3,000 Indians descended on the town of Porto Seguro, near Cabral's landfall, to stage a "countercomemoration." Five thousand policemen were called out to discourage disruption of the planned celebration. Cardoso patiently acknowledged the Indians' right to protest, but warned against violence. Still, the police and the Indians inevitably clashed. The police used clubs and tear gas to break up the demonstration, and 140 Indians were arrested. Cardoso cut short his appearance in Porto Seguro, his carefully planned party in ruins.

On the heels of the protests against the 500th anniversary celebrations came an even more violent confrontation between authorities and landless peasants who squatted on unused lands and even forcibly occupied government buildings in Brasilia. About 30,000 peasants of the Landless Rural Workers Movement, or

Dancing in the streets . . . then after Carnaval

MST, took part in the protests, which left one peasant dead and 47 injured in clashes with security forces. Cardoso organized a special police force to deal with illegal squatters, but at the same time he acceded to some of their demands, agreeing to parcel out 5 million more acres in addition to the 40 million that already had been distributed during his administration. The landless issue remains volatile in Brazil.

Brazilian voters went to the polls on October 1 and 29, 2000, to elect mayors and councilmen in more than 5,500 municipalities, a closely watched quadrennial bellwether of the public mood midway between presidential elections. For the first time, reelection was permitted. If there was a clear victor, it was da Silva's Workers Party (*PT*), which increased its share of the popular vote from 10.6% in 1996 to 14.1% and the number of mayors from 112 to 174. In the 31 cities holding runoffs on October 29, the *PT* won 13 of the 16 that it contested. None created more excitement than the landslide victory in São Paulo of Marta Suplicy, 55, a former television sex psychologist in the 1980s who later served in Congress. She is popular with housewives because of her frank talk about sex and abortion and with homosexuals be-

cause of her advocacy of gay rights. She received nearly 59% of the vote against veteran former mayor and governor Paulo Maluf of the conservative Brazilian Progressive Party. She was aided greatly by the rampant corruption that had occurred during the administration of the incumbent, Celso Pitta, who was so tarnished that he chose not to stand for reelection. The *PT* also retained the mayoralty of Porto Alegre and won control of Goiania and Recife. In Rio de Janeiro, Cesar Maia of the Brazilian Labor Party scored an upset victory over incumbent Luis Paulo Conde of the conservative Liberal Front Party (*PFL*). Overall, however, the *PFL*, one of the four parties in Cardoso's governing coalition, strengthened its holdings of mayors from 962 to 1,027. Another coalition party, the *PMDB*, dropped from 1,323 to 1,253. Despite the impressive showing of the left-wing opposition, coalition parties still controlled most local governments.

For the remainder of Cardoso's term, his political troubles came not from the opposition but from scandals within his coalition that left stains on the coalition's reputation. The powerful and influential Senate president, Antonio Carlos Magalhães of the *PFL*, desperately sought to block the election of his arch-rival, Jader Barbalho of the *PMDB*, as his successor. Barbalho won, and apparently miffed that Cardoso had done nothing to block Barbalho's election, Magalhães publicly alleged high-level corruption in the executive branch. Cardoso sacked two *PFL* ministers for alleged disloyalty. This further infuriated Magalhães, who then accused Cardoso of harboring corrupt officials in the executive branch. The opposition *PT* called for a full congressional investigation.

Cardoso urged Congress against embroiling itself in an investigation that would delay his economic reform measures. Just as it seemed Cardoso would prevail, two separate scandals unfolded that ultimately would bring down both Magalhães and Barbalho. First, a news magazine reported leaked tapes that supported Magalhães' allegation that Barbalho had enriched himself with funds earmarked for *SUDAM*, an Amazon development agency, while he had served as governor of Para state. A newly appointed *SUDAM* director fueled the scandal with the revelation that $820 million was unaccounted for. Barbalho found himself testifying before the Senate ethics committee. Cardoso abolished the agency. In June 2001, new charges surfaced in the press that Barbalho was involved in the sale of $4 million in government notes in 1988 while he was agrarian reform minister. In September, he resigned as Senate president, and in October, he resigned from the body altogether. In February 2002, Barbalho was formally arrested and jailed, precipitating the breakup of the governing coalition.

Magalhães could not savor his triumph over his hated rival. In April 2001, a Senate report alleged that he and floor leader Jose Roberto Arruda had accessed a list showing how senators had voted on the expulsion of Senator Luiz Estevão in June 2000 for misconduct. Senate votes are secret, and rules violations are grounds for expulsion. Both Magalhães and Arruda vehemently denied the report, but irrefutable evidence surfaced against them. Arruda resigned as floor leader, and four days later made a tearful public confession that he had accessed the list. In May, both Magalhães and Arruda resigned their Senate seats.

In other matters, Congress approved a long-debated revision to the country's archaic 1916 civil code in August 2001. The revised code legitimizes the civil status of people born out of wedlock, lowers the age of majority for marrying or signing contracts from 21 to 18, and eliminates the preferential legal status of men over women. Previously, for example, a man could annul his marriage if he discovered his bride was not a virgin. Under the new code, neither spouse can go into debt without the consent of the other, and divorced fathers have equal custody rights with mothers. In May 2002, Cardoso endorsed a bill before Congress that would legalize homosexual unions, a move that probably was politically motivated to steal some thunder from da Silva's *PT*, which has long advocated gay rights.

Meanwhile, Brazil's alarming crime problem, and the methods being used to deal with it, remained in the international spotlight. Reports of extrajudicial executions of criminal suspects, especially youths in the country's squalid *favelas*, are commonplace. In 2001, the London-based human rights group Amnesty International issued a report alleging that torture was still a widespread practice by Brazilian security forces nearly two decades after the end of military rule. Yet, so desperate are Brazilians for a solution to a crime problem that has them living in abject fear for their persons and properties, that they tend to turn a blind eye to such abuses. They were reminded again of the evil nature of the problem in early June 2002 when Tim Lopes, an award-winning investigative reporter for the *Globo* network, was murdered while conducting an undercover investigation into sex abuse and drug use in a Rio de Janeiro *favela*. His burned and desecrated corpse was found in a cave. The killing outraged the country. Four people were arrested, including a drug lord.

The Elections of 2002

By the end of 2001, da Silva had declared his fourth candidacy for the presidency, and this time the polls consistently showed him in the lead with about a third of the votes against a field of lesser known candidates. Among those candidates were Health Minister José Serra, of the *PSDB* and Cardoso's acknowledged choice as his successor; Rio de Janeiro State Governor Anthony Garotinho of the Brazilian Socialist Party, a mellowed Marxist and a former agnostic who became an evangelical Presbyterian after surviving an automobile accident; former President Itamar Franco of the *PMDB*, then governor of Minas Gerais but still a pariah nationally; Ciro Gomes of the moderate-left Popular Socialist Party, a former governor of Ceará and a finance minister under Franco; and Maranhão State Governor Roseana Sarney, daughter of former President José Sarney of the *PFL*, then still part of the governing coalition.

At year's end, Sarney's candidacy was clearly on the ascendancy, and she edged into second place for the runoff spot; in January 2002 polls showed her with 25%, just two points behind da Silva. But then, as often happens in Brazilian politics, everything suddenly came unraveled.

Two weeks after Barbalho's arrest in February 2002, as part of the on-going investigation into the *SUDAM* scandal, police raided the office of a company owned by Sarney's husband, Jorge Murad, who also served as her state planning

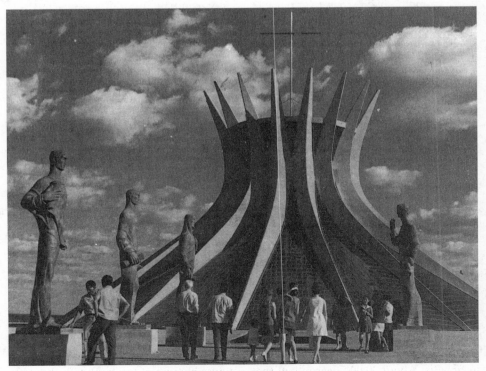

The Cathedral, Brasilia

Brazil

Fishing in the waters of the mighty Amazon River near Manaus

minister, and discovered 1.34 million *reais* ($570,000) in cash. Murad made several feeble and contradictory attempts to explain the source of the money, finally confessing that it was money he had raised illegally for his wife's presidential campaign; under the law, candidates cannot start raising money until the June before the election. Sarney's standing in the polls began dropping like mercury after a cold front, and in March she withdrew from the race. Bitterly, she accused Cardoso of staging the raid to damage her candidacy and to aid Serra's. Her brother, Jose Jr., resigned as Cardoso's environment minister, and two other *PFL* cabinet ministers also resigned in protest; the four-year-old coalition officially was no more. Cardoso denied complicity in the raid, noting that it had been carried out by state police, but there is no question that Serra was the chief beneficiary of Sarney's withdrawal.

Serra moved for a time into the undisputed second-place spot for the October 6 election, and he received a major boost in June when the *PMDB* endorsed him.

Meanwhile, the increasing possibility of a da Silva victory sent a chill through international financial markets, prompting the candidate and his party to engage in some frantic public relations maneuvering. The *PT* pointed to the sound fiscal records of the states and municipalities under its control, and da Silva pledged to continue Cardoso's rational policies and to continue servicing the $274 billion debt; he even began wearing suits and ties at his campaign appearances! Moreover, in a bold shift toward the political center, the *PT* entered

into an alliance with the center-right Liberal Party in June, and da Silva named Jose Alencar, a Liberal senator, as his running mate. It was a masterful, if unlikely, political stroke; the *PT* already has close ties with the progressive wing of the Catholic Church, while the Liberal Party draws support from the Universal Church of the Kingdom of God, a large evangelical congregation that controls a television network and claims an estimated 4 million followers. Nonetheless, two days later market jitters caused the *real* to drop to its second-worst showing ever of 2.84 against the dollar, leading da Silva to state that he would consider appointing people from outside the party as finance minister and central bank president.

The campaign then took more twists and turns than an amusement park ride. Until mid-July, it seemed inevitable that da Silva and Serra would square off in an October 27 runoff. But suddenly and inexplicably, Gomes surged past Serra, who slid just as dramatically. In August, after a televised debate among the top four candidates, in which the charismatic Gomes far outshone the lackluster Serra, Gomes soared to 32%, just two points behind da Silva, while Serra dropped to a pitiful 10%, Garotinho remained in fourth place.

Then, in early September, Gomes suddenly began to drop and Serra began rising dramatically, until the two were virtually tied in all major polls at about 17–20%. As the front-running da Silva wisely kept his mouth shut and remained above the fray, campaigning on a vague but safe platform of "peace and love," Serra and Gomes launched into mudslinging attacks against each other. The result: in the second half of September, da Silva rose to 42% for the first time, while Serra and Gomes both languished in the teens. Serra then began aiming his TV commercials at da Silva rather than at Gomes, accusing the *PT* of having advocated violent protests.

Da Silva, now sensing a chance to win the election without a runoff, largely ignored the attacks and decided to play the statesman. Seeking again to dispel his international image as a leftist bogeyman, he reiterated his promise that Brazil would service its foreign debt, but he said that Brazil must rely less on the IMF and more on its own potential. He scored points with the job-hungry electorate when he pointed out that *Petrobras* had contracted to have a huge oil platform built abroad, when the project could have employed 25,000 Brazilians. He vowed to cancel the contract if elected. In an interview with the leading newsmagazine, *Veja,* he insisted that he was sincere in his shift to the political center, and that the *PT* had "matured." Some pundits already had begun calling the new da Silva "Lula

Light." Despite the assurances, on September 22 the *real* fell to a record low of 3.57 to the dollar, while the stock exchange fell more than 3%. That same day, President Cardoso abandoned his neutrality and warned of dire economic consequences if da Silva or Gomes were elected.

Da Silva's bandwagon then began attracting latecomers. A faction of Cardoso's own *PMDB* in Rio de Janeiro State suddenly switched its support from Serra to da Silva, causing the president to predict—incorrectly—that da Silva would win a first-round victory. Da Silva received another unexpected boost when the Rev. Jesse Jackson came to Rio de Janeiro to urge Brazil's Protestants to vote for him, saying da Silva had been "touched by God." In his response, da Silva said that Jesus Christ was one of history's greatest revolutionaries. The sudden rush of supporters to what appeared to be the winning candidate even spawned a new verb: *Lular.*

On October 6, the polls were shown to be remarkably accurate, but there was no first-round knockout. A respectable 82.2% of the 115.1 million registered voters in the world's fourth-largest democracy turned out. The results:

Da Silva	39,443,876	46.44%
Serra	19,700,470	23.20%
Garotinho	15.175.776	17.87%
Gomes	10,167,650	11.97%

The three-week campaign for the runoff was largely anticlimactic, and Da Silva's bandwagon quickly took on the appearance of an M-1 tank. Gomes enthusiastically urged his backers to vote for da Silva and Garotinho quickly followed suit. The *PMDB* in Minas Gerais then transferred its support from Serra to da Silva. Not everyone was enthusiastic, however: The *real* fell to 4 to the dollar for the first time.

Serra bravely continued, insisting he would do the better job of rescuing the stagnant economy and predicting a return to hyperinflation if da Silva won. But polls showed his efforts were quixotic, giving da Silva a 2–1 lead. Even Cardoso began distancing himself from his own candidate. Da Silva, meanwhile, began sounding presidential, and he began attempting to lower the expectations of his supporters for dramatic changes. Their final televised debate was almost dull it was so gentlemanly.

The voters gave da Silva the expected present for his 57th birthday on October 27:

Da Silva	52,777,919	61.28%,
Serra	33,354,230	38.72%

Turnout was 79.5%. Serra graciously conceded defeat in a telephone call to his

President Luiz Inácio da Silva

rival, as congratulations poured in from Cardoso, George W. Bush and other world leaders. Millions of da Silva's supporters poured into the streets for a Carnaval-like celebration.

Brazil Under Lula

On January 1, 2003, the one-time shoeshine boy, metal lathe operator and trade union leader who never went beyond the fifth grade finally realized the goal that had eluded him in three previous elections as he was sworn in as president of Brazil. He was the first avowed leftist to serve as president since Goulart, who was overthrown by the military in 1964, and the first one elected directly. Brazilians, and the world, waited anxiously to see whether he would prove to be another statesman like South Africa's Nelson Mandela—or another loose cannon like Venezuela's Hugo Chávez.

His first day in office made some wonder if he were moving in the latter direction; he had breakfast with Chávez and dinner with Fidel Castro, both of whom he professes to admire. The United States did little to counterbalance the presence of Castro and Chávez, however. As the latest example of the Bush administration's unwise, and offensive, practice of sending third-string representatives to Latin American inaugurations, the U.S. representative was trade negotiator Robert Zoellick, even though about a dozen heads of state attended. That choice was especially nettlesome because Zoellick had offended Brazilian sensibilities the year before by remarking that if Brazil did not sign on to the FTAA it would be left trading only with Antarctica. Still, da Silva is not unmindful of the importance of har-

monious relations with the United States, and as president-elect he had met with President Bush in the White House in December for an amicable 45-minute dialogue that both men termed as fruitful.

In his first six months in office, da Silva performed a dexterous balancing act between the fire-breathing leftists in his own party on the one hand and the IMF, the Brazilian business community and the conservative opposition in Congress on the other. He had little choice but to try to govern by consensus; his *PT* has only 91 seats in the 513-member Chamber of Deputies, although that is the largest bloc in the lower house, and 14 in the 81-member Senate. The *PFL* has 84 in the lower house and 19 in the Senate, the *PMDB* has 74 and 19, respectively, and the *PSDB* has 71 and 11. In one of his first acts of statesmanship, da Silva struck an unlikely deal with former President Sarney of the *PSDB,* once the target of da Silva's strikes, by which Sarney became president of the Senate. Da Silva hammered together a loose coalition of nine of the 16 parties in the Congress, but the opposition still enjoyed a comfortable majority in both houses. The opposition, however, opted for cooperation to confrontation.

Early on, da Silva made some decisions calculated to mollify his core constituency on the left. He led his entire cabinet on a fact-finding visit to one of Rio's worst *favelas.* He delayed for one year a contract to purchase 12 new jet fighters for the air force. He hosted the assembly of the left-wing World Social Forum in Porto Alegre in January, bringing the 75,000 participants to their feet. He created a Council for Economic and Social Development, a town-hall-style body the *PT* has successfully employed at the local level to forge a consensus among government, business and labor leaders, which has given organized labor unprecedented access to high-level decision-making. And he made elimination of hunger his top priority through the establishment of *Fome Zero* (Zero Hunger), an ambitious nutrition program that incorporates governmental and non-governmental social organizations. He has carried his anti-hunger message to major international meetings, including the World Economic Forum, an organization of the world's richest countries, in Davos, Switzerland in January and the G-8 summit in France in June, 2003.

Although he toned down his rhetoric on the FTAA, which he once said would amount to U.S. "annexation" of Latin America, he continued to insist on greater "reciprocity" in U.S.-Latin American trade and indicated his intention to try to reinvigorate *Mercosur* as a regional alternative. On the same tour that took him to meet with Bush in Washington as president-elect,

he also visited Argentina, Chile and Mexico to promote his regional agenda. The new Argentine President, Néstor Kirchner, who is philosophically akin to da Silva, came to Brasilia in June to discuss *Mercosur's* future and wider regional integration.

At the same time, da Silva successfully downplayed his bogeyman image. In November, three weeks after his election, he had an upbeat meeting with IMF representatives regarding a $30 billion loan package, and the IMF people left pleased with what they heard. His key appointments were far from frightening: As chief of staff he appointed José Dirceu, the *PT* president who engineered the party's move to the center; as finance minister he appointed Antônio Palocci, a physician, who has pursued a Reaganesque fiscal policy that has exceeded IMF expectation on the budget surplus and stressed higher interest rates to ward off inflation; as foreign minister he named a career diplomat, Celso Amorim; and as head of the Central Bank he named Henrique Meirelles, former director of global banking for FleetBoston Financial Corporation. Even as he has promoted his anti-hunger campaign, da Silva has pragmatically undertaken critically needed reforms in taxation and the cumbersome public pension system, which caused grumbling on the left but which were straining public finances. In mid-June, he flew to Washington again to meet with Bush, and the two leaders got on so amicably that one would never had suspected their earlier ideological antipathy.

Despite the predicted complaints from both far right and far left, da Silva enjoyed a 75% approval rating after his first 100 days in office.

In the second half of 2003, da Silva pushed for two major reforms. One was a restructuring of the overly generous civil service pension system, which was $19 billion in debt and had become a luxury Brazilians couldn't afford to continue in its present form. The president skillfully forged a consensus with centrist parties to obtain the necessary three-fifth majority in both houses of Congress in August and December. The financial markets responded favorably, but fringe elements within da Silva's own party, and the civil service union that had long supported the *PT,* did not. In December, the *PT* expelled three deputies and one senator for their public opposition to pension reform, which did not say much for the party's commitment to freedom of expression.

The other major reform was an overhaul of the cumbersome and complex tax system that had confusing overlaps between the states and the federal government. The reform did not make much difference in revenue collections, but it greatly simplified the process.

Brazil

In January 2004, da Silva reshuffled his cabinet and brought the *PMDB* into the governing coalition. The civil servants were not the only traditional Lula allies who have been alienated by his pragmatic approach, which has differed little from Cardoso's. The Landless Movement *(MST)*, which helped elect da Silva by curtailing its activities during the campaign, charged in early 2004 that their onetime champion had reneged on his campaign promise to give titles to 60,000 families in his first year in office. Indeed, the government itself admitted it had given titles to only 36,000 families. Peasants invaded more than 200 parcels of land in 2003, and 63 of them were killed in the resulting clashes with the landowners' hired militias; it was the bloodiest year since 1990.

To defuse a possible resurgence of the *MST's* militant tactics, da Silva pledged to provide land to 115,000 families in 2004 and to 400,000 before the end of his term (Cardoso resettled 526,400 families in eight years). Instead, the promise merely emboldened the landless peasants, and squatters began invading parcels of unused land, mostly in the impoverished northeast, including da Silva's home state of Pernambuco. The government's own ministry in charge of the land program exacerbated the problem by giving priority to peasants in existing camps on unused land, which served as an incentive for more invasions.

By May 2005, only 117,500 families had received land, and 12,000 landless farmers staged a 125-mile, 17-day protest march from Goiania to Brasilia to demand the pace be accelerated. The march ended in violent clashes with police in Brasilia in

which 50 people on both sides were injured. The Pastoral Land Commission reported that the number of violent incidents stemming from land disputes was the highest in 20 years and had grown from 925 in 2002 to 1,690 in 2003 to 1,801 in 2004. The commission put the number of people killed in land disputes since democracy was restored in 1985 at 1,400. Meanwhile, the centrist parties in da Silva's governing coalition have applied pressure on da Silva to show more backbone against the *MST*. Clearly, the president is *entre a cruz e a espada*, as the Brazilians say.

It has not been da Silva's only dilemma. By early 2004, the *PT* found itself embroiled in two corruption scandals, something the self-righteous party once boasted it was above. One involved the *PT* mayor of a town in São Paulo state, who was murdered in January 2002. In December 2003, one of his friends was arrested for his murder. The ostensible motive was to stop the mayor from breaking up a lucrative kickback scheme involving government contracts; some of the money allegedly found its way into party coffers.

The other scandal had far greater impact. Da Silva's chief of staff, José Dirceu, had appointed the head of Rio de Janeiro's state lottery, Waldomiro Diniz, to be deputy secretary of parliamentary affairs. In February 2004, a video surfaced, reproduced in a magazine, showing Diniz apparently accepting campaign funds from a local numbers racketeer in exchange for political favors when he was head of the lottery. Diniz was fired, and Dirceu offered to resign, but da Silva rejected the offer. Da Silva responded to the scandal with a seemingly silly bill to outlaw bingo

parlors, a retaliation against gambling bosses seen as responsible for the scandal. The Senate rejected the bill, dealing da Silva his first major defeat.

In international affairs, da Silva has sought to give Brazil an ever-higher profile. He visited Washington again in August 2003 to meet with President Bush, and again the two men spoke glowingly of the warmth of their relationship. That is remarkable, given the on-going battle over U.S. tariffs, Brazil's leading role in the collapse of the World Trade Organization summit in Cancun, Mexico in September 2003, da Silva's close friendships with Cuba's Castro and Venezuela's Hugo Chávez, and da Silva's outspoken criticism of the U.S. invasion and occupation of Iraq.

In May 2004, da Silva made a six-day state visit to China, which is expected to become Brazil's second-largest trading partner after the United States. At the end of the visit, the two countries announced they would launch their third joint satellite and concluded a $5 billion deal for China to purchase Brazilian iron ore.

Brazil's own fledgling space program, meanwhile, has been plagued by technical failures and, in August 2003, a disaster. A 100-foot VLS-3 rocket exploded on the launch pad at the Alcantara Launch Center on the Atlantic Coast, three days before it was to have been launched. Twenty-one people were killed. Da Silva insisted the space program remains a priority.

Recent Developments

In May 2004, Brazil contributed a force of 1,200 troops to the U.N. peacekeeping mission in Haiti. It is the largest national contingent, and the peacekeeping mission is under Brazilian command.

Brazil's nuclear program sparked an international controversy beginning in April 2004 when *The Washington Post* reported that Brazil had denied U.N. inspectors access to a new uranium enrichment facility under construction at Resende. Brazil is the world's sixth-largest producer of uranium, but must send it abroad for enrichment. The new centrifuges will permit Brazil to enrich its own uranium for its Angra I and II nuclear power plants, which provide 4.3% of Brazil's electricity. There are plans to make a third plant operational by 2014.

Brazil denied the report and said it would allow inspectors access to part of the facility, but not to the centrifuges on the grounds that it would compromise industrial secrecy. The international media kept on the story. Anonymous diplomats told the Associated Press that Brazilian Science and Technology Minister Eduardo Campos announced at a closed-door con-

A rural church in Curitiba   World Bank Photo

ference of the International Atomic Energy Agency in Vienna in September 2004 that Brazil would abide by the Nuclear Non-proliferation Treaty, which it had finally signed in 1997, only if all atomic weapons everywhere were dismantled. Back in Brasilia, Campos said he had struck an accord with the IAEA whereby its inspectors would examine the pipes leading to the centrifuges, but would not make a visual inspection of the centrifuges. The IAEA inspection was required before enrichment could begin. The IAEA said its inspection was to ensure that no material has been removed illegally and to ensure that no weapons-grade fuel can be produced. Brazil insisted that it has no intention of producing weapons-grade fuel.

In October, the influential newspaper *O Estado de São Paulo* published a story quoting a former U.S. Defense Department source that the IAEA suspected Brazil had obtained a centrifuge on the black market from a notorious Pakistani scientist who has sold nuclear technology to rogue states like Iran, Libya and North Korea. Days later, U.S. Secretary of State Colin Powell visited Brasilia and expressed his confidence that Brazil does not intend to build nuclear weapons. It seemed the controversy would die down after the inspection was conducted on October 18. Within a week, the U.S. magazine *Science* reported that the enrichment facility would provide Brazil with enough weapons-grade fuel to produce six warheads per year and 63 per year by 2014. The head of Brazil's national atomic energy commission labeled the article "frivolous." An IAEA team visited the Resende plant again in November, after which the agency gave the green light for Brazil to begin enriching fuel. The plant was still in the testing stage at mid-year 2005.

Da Silva found himself at the center of another international incident in May 2004. *The New York Times'* bureau chief in Rio de Janeiro, Larry Rohter, wrote an article quoting da Silva's 1998 running mate, Leonel Brizola, and others as saying da Silva has a drinking problem that may affect his performance. Da Silva angrily denounced the article as "slander" and, in a fit of ill-advised pique, revoked Rohter's work visa for "offending the honor of the president." It would be the first time a foreign journalist had been expelled since the military regime was in power. The domestic and international reaction from human rights and journalism organizations was swift. Even some of da Silva's adversaries, including Cardoso, regarded the article as unfair, but they labeled da Silva's over-reaction as undemocratic. The Supreme Court intervened to block the revocation until it could determine its constitutionality. A day later, a chastened da Silva rescinded the revocation.

In August 2004, da Silva again raised doubts about his commitment to press freedom after magazines reported leaked documents suggesting that Henrique Meirelles, head of the central bank, had evaded taxes. Da Silva angrily introduced a bill to Congress to create a national press council that would require licenses to practice journalism, would impose a code of conduct and would have the power to discipline journalists who violate the code. The council also would prevent leaks and require reporters to show respect for people they write about and to do nothing "contrary to human values." In short, the council would prevent the press from reporting freely, as guaranteed in the constitution. The media organs lashed out at the idea as a throwback to the military regime, which had once jailed da Silva; one newspaper called da Silva's attempt to muzzle the press "Stalinist." But even José Genoino, president of da Silva's own *PT*, called the bill ill-advised and urged the president to rescind it. A month later, in the face of massive domestic and international condemnation, he did.

The closely watched quadrennial elections for the 5,562 municipalities were a muted victory for da Silva's *PT*. In the first round of voting on October 3, 2004, the *PT* more than doubled its number of mayoralties from 187 to 389, including six of the 26 state capitals. But it lost the biggest prize of all when São Paulo Mayor Marta Suplicy was trounced for reelection by former presidential candidate José Serra of the *PSDB*. Serra led her 43.5% to 35.8% on October 3, then finished her off with 55% in the October 31 runoff. (A São Paulo electoral court judge fined da Silva $18,000 for using his speech at the dedication of a public works project to endorse Suplicy.) The *PT* won 11 of the cities contested in the runoff, but it lost 12, including Belem, Curitiba and even the stronghold of Pôrto Alegre, which the *PT* had governed for 16 years.

Ghosts from the military dictatorship returned to haunt Brazil and presented da Silva with a minor crisis in October 2004, when newspapers published gruesome pictures purported to be the body of Vladimir Herzog, a Communist journalist slain by the military in a 1975 incident that garnered worldwide attention. Without consulting Defense Minister José Viegas, the army responded with an ambiguously worded statement that seemed to justify the repression that led to Herzog's death. Human rights groups, heretofore one of da Silva's core constituencies, reacted angrily.

Da Silva met with Viegas and the army commander to try to defuse the controversy. The army retracted its statement and da Silva's government maintained that the pictures were not of Herzog. Viegas resigned in protest on October 22, but it was not announced until November 4. Apparently seeking to maintain amicable relations with the armed forces, da Silva appointed Vice President Alencar as the new defense minister; he remained vice president. Alencar is himself a defense contractor, and his appointment raised questions about conflict of interest. To mollify the human rights groups, da Silva issued a decree in December to permit declassification of files from the dictatorship era, when about 400 dissidents were killed. Cardoso had ordered them classified forever.

But the human rights abuses of the past soon took a back seat to new ones in the long-simmering dispute between Brazilian farmers of the Amazon region and the indigenous tribes there. The government had acceded to many of the Indians' demands by guaranteeing them enclaves from which white settlers would be excluded. In November 2004, a band of about 40 farmers torched three Indian villages, one of them in a 6,370-square-mile enclave in the Sun Fox Mountains that was to be presented to five tribes totaling 15,000 people. The presentation was formally made in April 2005.

On February 12, 2005, Sister Dorothy Stang, a 73-year-old American nun who had championed the rights of Indians and landless peasants of Para state and had opposed ranching and illegal logging in the Amazon rain forest, was shot six times with a revolver following a dispute with a rancher. Her death generated international shock waves, and she became a martyr overnight. Da Silva threw the weight of his government into the investigation of the murder and dispatched 4,000 troops into the area to enforce order. Three men were initially arrested and charged with killing Stang. Also charged was the rancher who allegedly ordered the murder, who went into hiding, but surrendered six weeks later. A fourth alleged accomplice was arrested later. A Senate committee conducted hearings and concluded that there was a far wider conspiracy involved.

In March 2005, Amnesty International issued a scathing report accusing the government of not doing enough to protect Indian rights. In a remarkable ceremony at the presidential palace on April 19, Indian Day, the da Silva government officially apologized to the Indians for all past abuses and injustices. The Indians, apparently, were not impressed. On April 26, Indians in one new enclave took four federal policemen hostage, and in another they blocked highways, complaining that the enclaves were merely a government plan to deprive them of access to health care and economic opportunities.

Da Silva suffered a major political blow in December 2004 when two key parties withdrew from his coalition, including the

Brazil

Destruction of the Amazon: A global catastrophe

During the late 1990s, it seemed Brazil was finally willing to take action to deal with a problem that had brought it international condemnation for more than a decade: the destruction of the Amazon rain forest, which encompasses 1.6 million square miles and is believed to be home to 30% of the world's plant and animal species. But the wholesale destruction of this priceless resource is continuing at an alarming pace.

In their zeal to foster growth, a succession of Brazilian presidents, both military and civilian, gave agricultural development of the vast, virgin Amazon Basin a high priority. Developers were given *carte blanche* to use slash-and-burn methods to cut away trees to make room for cultivation, despite protests by national and international ecologists that the destruction of the rain forest could have a global impact. The clearing of vast areas of oxygen-producing trees, they argued, would further contribute to the world-wide buildup of greenhouse gases and contribute to global warming.

One Brazilian environmental activist, Chico Mendes, was murdered in 1988 for his high-profile efforts to save the forest, while president after president ignored the issue in the name of economic development.

In 1998, the Cardoso government released a report with the bittersweet finding that deforestation had reached its peak in 1995 of 11,621 square miles, double the 5,958 square miles cleared in 1994, and had begun tapering off. The rate in 1996 was down to 7,200 square miles, and 5,200 in 1997. Since 1978, the report said, 200,000 square miles, or one eighth of the forest, had been lost.

Days later, Congress approved legislation giving the federal environmental agency legal power to enforce environmental protection laws and providing criminal penalties for violators. Ironically, the law was no sooner on the books when a devastating fire in Roraima state, exacerbated by an El Niño-related drought, burned out of control for weeks, destroying the forest at a pace even more rapid than man's.

In 2001, it was estimated that another 6,095 square miles of rain forest had been lost through logging or fires. The Cardoso government banned ma-hogany logging altogether, and in 2002 it made operational a huge, $1.4 billion radar network, called the System for the Vigilance of the Amazon, or *SIVAM*, designed to maintain surveillance to thwart drug trafficking and illegal logging and mining.

It does not seem to have had the desired effect. A report released in 2003 by a group of environmental experts stated that deforestation accelerated by an alarming 40% in 2002, to 9,840 square miles, the worst year since 1995. The government's own official figures for 2002 were 8,983 square miles. The loss did slow dramatically in 2003, according to the government, to 2.1%, which still meant an overall increased loss of 9,496 square miles.

The government's figures for 2004 were even grimmer: 10,088 square miles, an accelerated increase of 6.2%, the second-worst loss on record. That means that an area the size of New Jersey has been lost each year for the past three years. The seven members of the Green Party in the lower house of Congress withdrew from the governing coalition in May 2005 to protest the government's failure to stop the destruction. The party complained that while the government has set aside preserves, it also has promoted dams, roads and farming.

According to the World Wildlife Fund, 17.3% of the Amazon rain forest has now been destroyed.

A report released by the International Center for Forestry Research in Indonesia in April 2004 blamed much of the increased deforestation on cattle ranching, while a report in December 2004 by the group Friends of the Earth cited construction of a highway through the Amazon, BR-163, which illegal loggers have been using to gain access. Still others blame soybean farming; Blairo Maggi, the governor of Mato Grosso state, where three fourths of the destruction has taken place, is the world's largest soybean producer.

The government acknowledged in a report in December 2004 that burning of the rain forest accounted for three fourths of Brazil's greenhouse gas emissions, while Brazil accounted for 3% of the world's greenhouse gases.

Environmentalists had another martyr in February 2005 when Dorothy Stang, an American nun who agitated against ranching and illegal logging in the rain forest, was murdered in a dispute with a rancher in Para state (see History). Largely in response to Stang's murder, the government of President Luiz Inácio da Silva mandated a reserve of 32,000 square miles of rain forest west of BR-163 in Para, Mato Grosso and Roraima states that would be off-limits to illegal loggers and ranchers; controlled logging would be strictly monitored. An estimated 350 logging companies now operate in the Amazon.

The international environmental organization Greenpeace hailed the move as historic, but also faulted da Silva's government for failing to do more to stop the destruction. The organization whimsically nominated da Silva, his chief of staff, his finance and agriculture ministers and the governors of Mato Grosso and Para for its first annual "Golden Chainsaw" award. The "winner," announced on June 20, 2005, was Governor Maggi.

But in a positive and dramatic development on June 2, federal investigators arrested 90 people, about half of them officials of the federal environmental protection ministry, *Ibama,* and the rest businessmen, in a crackdown on bribery by illegal logging companies. Environmental activists had alleged for years that environmental protection officials were corrupt. Among those arrested was the environmental secretary for Mato Grosso, but Governor Maggi himself was not implicated. The officials are accused of accepting bribes in return for documents certifying that trees had been cut legally. Much of the illegal logging had taken place on Indian enclaves and in national parks. The federal government halted the shipment of all wood from the Amazon for 30 days. It also announced all logging companies would be inspected for 60 days, while four logging companies in Mato Grosso were ordered to suspend operations. It is not difficult to understand why companies are willing to resort to bribery; the value of wood harvested illegally since the early 1990s is estimated at $370 million.

PMDB, the largest party in Congress. The other was the Popular Socialist Party (*PPS*). Many of the *PMDB* legislators, however, indicated they would continue to support the government as they saw fit. Da Silva was dealt a worse setback in February 2005 when his chosen candidate for speaker of the Chamber of Deputies was upset by Silverino Cavalcanti of the small Progressive Party. It was the first time the chamber had elected a speaker who was not the government's choice. In April, Cavalcanti placed himself squarely at odds with da Silva, saying the president had abused his authority by issuing temporary decrees and threatened not to place such decrees high on the chamber's agenda.

The seven Green Party members of the lower house withdrew from the governing coalition in May 2005 to protest the government's failure to slow down the destruction of the Amazon rain forest (see box).

Also in May, Brazil joined Germany, Japan and India in introducing a U.N. resolution that would expand the 15-member Security Council to 25 and make those four countries permanent members along with the United States, Russia, China, Britain and France. But Brazil's regional rivals, Argentina and Mexico, oppose a permanent seat for Brazil, as do Colombia and Costa Rica. Preliminary discussions on the expansion at the United Nations ended inconclusively, and Secretary-General Kofi Annan said the issue needed further study.

Da Silva could boast a robust 5.2% growth in GDP for 2004, a dramatic turnaround from the .2% loss in 2003, while inflation declined from 12.5% in 2003 to 7.6% in 2004, largely because of interest rate hikes. Although Da Silva's approval rating in the polls has taken a rollercoaster ride for his first two and a half years in office, overall he remains one of the few South American presidents whose popularity is consistently above 50%.

That may or may not change as a result of twin scandals that began unfolding as this book went to press. In May, the respected newsmagazine *Veja* accused a postal manager of accepting a bribe in exchange for a construction contract. It published images of him accepting the money. The magazine also accused Roberto Jefferson, leader of the *PT*, of involvement in the scheme.

Jefferson lashed back by publicly alleging that the *PT* had paid monthly "allowances" totaling $12,000 to certain unnamed lawmakers in return for their participation in the shaky coalition. Congress launched an investigation into what amounted to an admission of bribery. Pressed for details, Jefferson admitted that he didn't have proof and said da Silva himself was unaware of the payments, but that Dirceu was. Dirceu adamantly denied the charges, but he resigned on June 16 to return to his congressional seat. At Dirceu's first appearance there, the lower house erupted into a shouting match.

Da Silva went on the offensive, addressing the nation on television on June 23. In a comment reminiscent of Richard Nixon's "I am not a crook" speech, da Silva angrily insisted that his government "has not swept dirt under the rug," challenged his party's accusers to produce evidence and pledged to fight corruption. Both the vote-buying and postal scandals remained the subjects of congressional and media scrutiny in July.

Culture: Brazil is culturally unique among the Latin American republics, with its mix of Portuguese and African accents in religion, music, architecture and food. There was little interplay between the invading Portuguese colonizers and the indigenous Indians, and what scattered tribes remain are isolated and unassimilated in the vast interior Amazon rain forest. It was the influx of African slaves that shaped modern Brazil's ethnic and cultural composition.

It can be argued that Brazilian culture today is tripartite. In the far southern temperate zone, characterized by wheat farming, cattle ranching and coffee production, the population is predominantly Caucasian, a cross-current of European immigration. As in Argentina, the cattle culture produced a distinct sub-culture with a meat-based diet. The Brazilian equivalent of the Argentine *asado* is the *churrasco*, a variety of grilled meats and sausages. This region is the home of Brazil's national dish, *feijoada*, a culinary orgy traditionally served on Wednesdays and Saturdays and consisting of various smoked meats and sausages, black beans (*feijão*), rice, greens and orange slices.

In the northeast, on the "hump" of Brazil, the population is predominantly black and the culture has its roots in Africa, a mere 1,000 miles across the Atlantic. Despite the ostensible dominance of the Roman Catholic Church in Brazil, blacks still practice *macumba*, a voodoo-like tribal religion based on black magic. In this equatorial climate, there is little cattle ranching, and the diet is based more on seafood and the universal Brazilian staples, black beans and rice. The Bahian style of cooking is characterized by stewing fish, shellfish or chicken in dende oil, derived from a palm nut, and coconut milk. Perhaps the region's greatest contribution to Brazilian culture, however, is its music. Here is where the samba was born, and like Argentina's tango it began in the slums and won mainstream acceptance and an international following.

The third element of Brazilian culture is in the cosmopolitan and industrial urban centers, chiefly Rio de Janeiro and São Paulo, where the other two cultures converge. Here, Catholicism and *macumba* have intertwined to give the world one of its most distinctive cultural offerings: *Carnaval*, the Brazilian version of *Mardi Gras*, the great explosion of revelry and hedonism before the onset of the somber season of Lent.

Officially, Brazil is the largest Roman Catholic country in the world, and there was speculation that a Brazilian cardinal, Claudio Hummes, would be elected pope when Pope John Paul II died in April 2005. However, census figures show that the number of practicing Catholics has declined from 84 million in 1991 to 74 million in 2000, while the number of evangelical Protestants has soared from 9 million to 15 million in the same period. Recent polls indicate that 125 million Brazilians still consider themselves Catholic, even though they do not attend Mass, but an overwhelming majority of them disagree with the church on contraception and abortion.

One of Brazil's great social and cultural anomalies is that although racial tolerance has been practiced for generations and intermarriage between whites and blacks is relatively commonplace, the country's social elite and its political power structure remain virtually entirely Caucasian, while blacks still occupy a disproportionate share of the bottommost rung of Brazil's social and economic ladder. Mulattos are caught somewhere in between.

While the Portuguese influence is most keenly felt in Brazil's architecture and literature, the African contribution has been greatest to Brazilian folklore, art and music. Moreover, there was considerable French influence during the immediate post-independence period. During the reign of Emperor Dom Pedro I (1825–31), the French-founded Royal School of Science, Arts and Crafts was incorporated into the Academy of Fine Arts. French influence on Brazilian art was especially strong.

Nineteenth century Brazilian literature also was influenced by French naturalism. The two leading Brazilian representatives of this style were Aluísio de Azevedo, author of the novels *Ó mulato* and *O Cortico (The Slum)*; and the mulatto novelist, poet, playwright and story writer Joaquim Maria Machado de Assis. In the early 20th century were published two novels that remain classics of Brazilian—and Latin American—literature: *Os sertões*, by Eucliudes da Cunha, and *Canaã*, by Jose Pereira de Graça Aranha, for whom one of Brazil's modern literature prizes is named.

Arguably the country's most internationally renowned writer of the 20th century was Jorge Amado, (1912–2001), whose novels *Terra do sem fin, Dona Flor e seus dois maridos* and *Gabriela, cravo e canela*, have been translated and marketed worldwide. His death on August 6, 2001, four days before his 89th birthday, was a cause for national mourning, and his passing was noted around the world. Other noteworthy contemporary writers include the poet and essayist Carlos Drummond de Andrade and playwright Nelson Rodrigues.

In music, the samba and other styles of African origin bridge the gap between folk and popular. Brazilian classical composers whose works incorporated Brazilian folk styles included Claudio Santoro and the better-known, and internationally renowned, Heitor Villa-Lobos (1887–1959).

Brazil

Villa-Lobos is best remembered for his 14 *Chôros*, composed while working in *avant-garde* Paris from 1925–1930. *Chôros* were popular street serenades in Rio de Janeiro in the early 20th century, and they inspired Villa-Lobos' classical compositions much the way the tango inspired those of Astor Piazzolla in neighboring Argentina or jazz influenced those of George Gershwin in the United States.

Brazilian popular music, or *MPB* as it is called in the press, is a major domestic industry. Perhaps the best known abroad were Sergio Mendes, whose group Brasil 66 was especially popular in the United States in the 1960s during the *Bossa Nova* craze, and Antonio Carlos Jobim, (1927–1994) who wrote such internationally popular tunes as *Desafinado, Meditacão, Insensatez (End of a Love Affair), Garota de Ipanema (Girl from Ipanema)* and *The One-Note Samba.* Brazilian pop singers whose popularity spread throughout Latin America included Roberto Carlos and the late Elis Regina. Regina's daughter, Maria Rita, splashed onto the international scene in 2005 when she was named best new artist in the Latin Grammy Awards ceremony in Los Angeles.

Internationally known Brazilian artists included Waldemar Cordeiro, sculptor Mario Carvo Jr., and the naturalist painter Candido Portinari. In the field of architecture Brazil boasts the internationally famous Oscar Niemeyer, whose most enduring creation is Brazil's futuristic capital city, Brasilia, constructed in the 1950s during the presidency of Juscelino Kubitschek.

The Brazilian film industry, one of the region's oldest, received an impetus in the 1960s and 1970s through the creative genius of director Glauber Rocha and his *Cinema Novo* movement. Brazilian films, long exported to other Latin American countries and to Portugal, have won increasing critical acclaim elsewhere. Two outstanding examples are the comedy *Dona Flor e seus dois maridos*, adapted from the Jorge Amado novel, and *Pixote*, a dark film about the lives of Brazil's street children, which won actress Marilia Pera the New York Film Critics' Award for best actress in 1982.

After that, Brazilian cinematic creativity went into a slump that lasted nearly a decade. After the state-owned firm *Embrafilme* was abolished in 1990, ending government subsidies, only a handful of films was produced each year in the 1990s and only 1% of the films shown in Brazil were domestically produced, compared with 40% during the era of *Cinema Novo*. But in the late 1990s, a new law allowed film companies a tax write-off if they invested up to 3% in new films.

The incentive helped spark a revival. Thirty films were produced in 2000, and

Brazil has seen a new generation of directors achieve international acclaim. For example, *O Quatrilho*, a story about Italian immigrants to Brazil directed by Fabio Barreto, and *O Que E Isso Companheiro*, whose English title is *Four Days in September*, the true story of the kidnapping of a U.S. ambassador directed by Barreto's brother, Bruno, were nominated for Oscars in 1996 and 1998. In 1999, *Central do Brasil (Central Station)*, a story of an elderly woman who befriends an orphan boy directed by Walter Salles, was nominated for Best Foreign Film and its star, Fernanda Montenegro, was nominated for Best Actress. *Eu, Tu, Eles (Me, You, Them)*, a true story of polygamy in the Brazilian outback directed by Andrucha Waddington, received widespread acclaim at the 2001 Cannes Film Festival and won prizes at festivals in Cuba and the Czech Republic.

In 2002–03, another Brazilian film that won box office success at home and critical acclaim abroad was *Cidade de Deus (City of God)*, the name of an infamous Rio de Janeiro *favela*, or slum. Adapted from a novel by Paulo Lins and directed by Fernando Meirelles, the film examines the drug gang culture there. It received four Oscar nominations in the United States in 2004. The Brazilian Culture Ministry selected the film "Olga," by Jayme Monjardi, as Brazil's entry for best foreign film in the 2005 Oscars, but it was not nominated. It is the true story of Olga Benario, a German Jew who emigrated to Brazil, married a Communist activist and was deported back to Germany, where she died in a concentration camp in 1942

A different sort of phenomenon was the 2004 film "Mary, Mother of the Son of God," directed by the charismatic Catholic priest and pop music sensation Marcelo Rossi. It had the same sort of impact as Mel Gibson's "The Passion of the Christ" in the United States, and by March had been seen by 2.5 million Brazilians. Columbia, the distributor, planned to translate it into Spanish.

Brazilian radio and television developed along U.S. lines, though in its early days Brazilian television depended heavily on U.S. imports. That has changed, and Brazil now exports its translated *telenovelas* throughout Latin America. The mammoth *Globo* Network, with 75 million viewers, claims the largest audience of any network in the world.

Educational reform was late in coming to Brazil, and it lags behind some of its neighbors in literacy and newspaper readership per 1,000 people. For decades Brazil's most respected daily has been *O Estado de São Paulo*, owned by the Mesquita family, which resisted the press controls imposed by both Getulio Vargas and the military regimes of 1964–85. Rio's two elite

newspapers are *Jornal do Brasil*, founded in 1891, and the circulation leader, *O Globo*, which also owns the like-named television network. Numerous tabloid newspapers boast large circulations throughout the country. There are several high-quality magazines, including *Manchete, Veja* and *Isto É.*

Economy: Brazil currently boasts the world's ninth-largest economy. Occupying half the continent, Brazil has immense natural wealth, including a diverse agricultural sector in which tropical and subtropical products flourish. A significant cattle industry in the south provides meat for domestic consumption and leather for export. With the exception of petroleum, the country also has been blessed with mineral wealth, including gold, iron, manganese, chromium and tin. Brazil also is the world's third-leading producer of bauxite, the raw material from which aluminum is refined. Manufacturing began early in the 20th century, but domestic industry, protected from imports by high tariffs, failed to match that of neighboring Argentina. Like many Latin American countries, Brazil adopted a quasi-socialist mixed economic system characterized by public sector control of utilities and transportation. Brazil's economic growth has long been hamstrung by one of the world's highest birthrates, which largely accounts for the high percentage of people living below the poverty line.

The military governments that ruled the country from 1964–1985 reversed policy in the late 1960s by inviting foreign investors into Brazil, offering attractive tax incentives. The resulting capitalization led to a boom that international economists referred to as the "Brazilian economic miracle." Foreign automobile manufacturers put Brazil on wheels, and Volkswagen remains the country's largest manufacturer today. An aggressive effort was made to increase nontraditional exports, including automobiles, tractors, military vehicles, weapons, aircraft and shoes. In 1967 the government declared the port of Manaus near the mouth of the Amazon a free-trade zone, which still produces about $10 billion worth of goods, mostly consumer items for export.

The miracle abruptly halted in 1974–75 because of a dual blow. The first was OPEC's quadrupling of petroleum prices, which sparked a worldwide recession that was felt especially keenly in Brazil, which imported 90% of its oil. The second blow was a devastating frost in the south that virtually destroyed Brazil's coffee crop, still the leading export item. The military rulers sought a two-fold solution. Because coffee trees require seven years to produce marketable beans, farmers were encouraged to replant much of the destroyed coffee acreage with soybeans, an annual crop that provided immediate export earnings. The second was to begin manufacturing automobiles designed to burn pure alcohol, distilled from domestically grown sugar cane. Exploitation of newly discovered offshore oil deposits also helped ease Brazil's dependence on foreign oil, and with the drop in petroleum prices in the mid-1980s, alcohol became more expensive than gasoline.

As in neighboring Argentina, efforts by the military to deal with the recession sparked hyperinflation, which continued into the post-military period. Inflation peaked in 1994, when then-Finance Minister Cardoso implemented the *"Real Plan,"* named for the new currency unit. Inflation dropped to double-digit, then single-digit levels by 1997, when the Asian economic crisis forced President Cardoso to adopt a drastic austerity plan that included a 40% increase in interest rates and $18 billion worth of public savings, paid for through a combination of spending cuts and tax increases. Still, unemployment in January 1998 jumped to 7.25%, the highest in 13 years. In order to further shore up the real and prevent a flight of foreign capital, Cardoso urged congress to streamline the civil service and make social security cuts, which sparked violent protests in the capital.

Despite the economic advances of recent years, however, Brazil's economy remains perhaps the least equitable of any industrialized country. According to a U.S. State Department report issued in January 1998, the top 10% of Brazil's 163 million people account for 48% of the income, while the bottom 10% make only 1%. An estimated 17% of the work force earns less than the minimum wage of $105 a month. This situation is not likely to improve markedly until some effort is made to keep Brazil's burgeoning birthrate lower than the ability of the economy to absorb new workers, but producing babies is an inherent part of the male-oriented culture.

The Brazilian market collapse of September 1998 is reflected in the figures for real GDP growth: 2.8% in 1996, 3.2% in 1997, only .7% in 1998—and that was before the market meltdown of January 1999. Unemployment has risen steadily over the same period: 5.4% in 1996, 6.0% in 1997 and 8.0% at the end of 1998. The economic malaise has at least had one positive effect: inflation was only 2.0% in 1998, down from 4.3% in 1997 and 9.1% in 1996.

By mid-2000, there were clear signs that Brazil had weathered the crisis. It finished 1999 with a slight GDP growth of about 1%, which was far better than the predictions of deep recession. The growth rate for 2000 was an encouraging 4.5%, but in

2001 in dropped back to 3% and in 2002 it fell even further to 1.5%, barely enough to keep up with the growth in the workforce. The real appears to have stabilized, though it experienced dramatic fluctuations in the first half of 2001. Its fall against the dollar in March 2001—the lowest since the 1999 market crisis—nonetheless proved a boon for Brazilian exporters. As another positive indicator, the Central Bank announced in April 2000 that it was repaying $10.5 billion of the $41.5 billion emergency loan package the IMF had extended in 1999 to rescue the economy, bringing to $18.2 billion the amount that had been repaid.

Unemployment remained stubbornly high at 8% in 1999, 7.9% in 2000 and 8% in 2001 and 2002, although urban unemployment still was only half that of neighboring Argentina. Inflation, meanwhile, moderated from 5.9% in 2000 to 4% in 2001.

President Cardoso hosted the *Mercosur* summit in Rio de Janeiro in May 2000 and created a stir by suggesting the trade bloc could adopt a common currency, as the European Union had done, possibly within five years. But just two days later Cardoso's own finance minister threw cold water on the idea, saying it would take much longer.

Cardoso met with new U.S. President George W. Bush at the White House in late March 2001. Both men are enthusiastic free-trade advocates, and Bush proposed a U.S.-Brazilian free-trade pact, but a skeptical Cardoso questioned Bush's sincerity by pointing out protectionist U.S. anti-dumping measures aimed at Brazilian steel and produce. Cardoso repeated his criticism at the Summit of the Americas in Quebec in April. The steel dispute worsened in March 2002 when Bush, yielding to demands from domestic steelmakers, imposed a 30% tariff on most steel imports. In June, Brazil protested the U.S. tariff before the World Trade Organization.

Periodic drought in 2000 and 2001 led to an acute power shortage as the nation's hydroelectric dams became unable to meet national demand. The energy crisis, very similar to that then facing the state of California, led President Cardoso to impose power rationing that included mandatory blackouts of up to four hours per day beginning June 1, 2001. The goal was to cut electricity usage by 20% the first month. The rationing was lifted in September 2001, after rains began refilling the lakes, although some states were still plagued by power shortages. To cope with the crisis, the Cardoso government announced a short-term plan to build 55 new thermoelectric plants by 2003 to provide 21,000 megawatts and a long-term plan for eight new hydroelectric plants over seven years. The crisis was becoming a political issue as the 2002 presidential

election campaign got underway. The energy crunch probably was a factor that slowed economic growth in 2001.

Brazil's unusually high population growth of 1.3% annually, coupled with the economic slowdown of 1999–2001, has led to a dramatic drop in per capita GDP, from $3,600 in 2000 to $3,100 in 2001 to $2,820 in 2002.

By June 2002, polls showing the former socialist union leader Luiz Inácio da Silva, universally known by his nickname "Lula," with a strong lead for the October 6 presidential election led to concerns among international lenders and investors that as president da Silva could default on payments of Brazil's huge $274 billion debt. Despite assurances by the candidate that he had abandoned his erstwhile Marxist thinking (as had Cardoso before him), the jitters continued, affecting Brazil's bond rating. In response, the Cardoso government announced it would draw down $10 billion from an IMF loan to stabilize the markets and reassure foreign investors. On June 20, U.S. Treasury Secretary Paul O'Neill made an injudicious comment, saying Brazil's problems were more political than economic and questioning the wisdom of U.S. aid to stabilize the economy. The next day, the *real* dropped to 2.84 against the dollar, its second-worst showing on record; O'Neill hastily retracted his comment the following day and insisted he believed the Cardoso government was "implementing the right economic policies."

Despite worries about da Silva, the IMF took him at his word and approved a new $30 billion loan package shortly before the election. Da Silva won the election in a landslide and took office on January 1, 2003. He has carefully followed a pragmatic economic policy not unlike that of Cardoso's, which is ironic given that he twice ran against Cardoso and vilified his policies. As finance minister he named a physician, Antônio Palocci, who has not just met but exceeded IMF demands on a budget surplus, and as head of the Central Bank he appointed Henrique Meirelles, a former executive with FleetBoston Financial Corporation. In April 2003, the new U.S. treasury secretary, John Snow, visited Brasilia for harmonious talks with Palocci and Meirelles and came across as far less abrasive than had O'Neill. By mid-June 2003, the *real* had rebounded and stabilized at about 2.85 to the dollar.

Da Silva had little to boast about on the economy at the end of his first year, however. GDP, which had increased by 1.9% in 2002, declined by 0.2% in 2003, the economy's worst showing in a decade. Moreover, unemployment at year-end stood at 12.2%, while inflation was 9%. In April 2004, unemployment in São Paulo hit a record 20.6%. GDP growth for 2004

Brazil

had rebounded to an impressive 5.2%, which boosted da Silva's popularity. He also enjoyed a huge budget surplus, much of which was used in 2004 to create dead-end public service jobs. The government promised to invest more of the surplus in infrastructure in 2005.

Da Silva has placed greater emphasis on the *Mercosur* trade bloc and has been instrumental is trying to forge a merger of *Mercosur* with the Andean Pact and a free-trade agreement with the European Union. Negotiations for the latter collapsed in 2004.

The Future: "Lula" da Silva's stewardship of the world's fourth-largest democracy and the ninth-largest economy has been impressive. He has performed a delicate high-wire act, attempting to placate his natural constituency on the left with ambitious social programs while reassuring the right and center by keeping the shaky economy on at least an even keel by continuing Cardoso's pragmatic policies. In the process, he has made enemies on both sides—something that statesmen sometimes must do. But polls show that he still enjoys the approval of a clear majority of Brazilians, even while public confidence in his government lags far behind.

On the world stage, Lula seems to have become something of a grandstander, and he obviously relishes the spotlight. He has been the key force behind the new South American Community of Nations, and he envisions a European Union model for the continent, with one foreign policy, one currency—and Brazilian leadership (see Latin America Today). He has promoted his anti-hunger campaign at international forums, and he is lobbying for Brazil, China and India to turn the G-8 into the G-11. He has steadfastly defended Brazil's nuclear program in the face of justifiable international concerns.

So visible have Lula and Brazil become on the global stage that even Lula's friend and fellow populist, Argentine President Néstor Kirchner, publicly grumbled about it in an interview with a Buenos Aires daily. "If there is a job open at the World Trade Organization, Brazil wants it. If there is a space at the United Nations, Brazil wants it. If there is a job at the United Nations Food and Agriculture Organization, Brazil wants it. They even wanted to have a Brazilian pope," Kirchner said. The Brazilian media responded angrily to Kirchner's remarks.

At the South American-Arab summit meeting in May, the two friends appeared to have smoothed things over. But a week later, Brazil joined Germany, Japan and India in introducing a draft resolution at the United Nations for the four countries to be given permanent seats on an expanded 25-member Security Council. Lula made a state visit to Japan in May and discussed that goal in an address to the Japanese Diet. Clearly, Lula plans to ensure that Brazil has global visibility—and so will he.

As da Silva serves out the second half of his term, speculation has begun as to his possible challengers in 2006. A rematch with José Serra, the triumphant new *PSDB* mayor of São Paulo, is a distinct possibility. Two *PSDB* state governors, Geraldo Alckmin of São Paulo and Aécio Neves of Minas Gerais, have been widely mentioned. The conservative Liberal Front Party has already nominated the flamboyant three-term mayor of Rio de Janeiro, Cesar Maia, as its candidate. At mid-year 2005, polls suggest Lula is unbeatable, but Brazilian politics are notorious for their vicissitudes.

The da Silva presidency is historic in Latin America: an elected leftist who has not caused even a stir within the ranks of the armed forces. Of course, much has changed in Brazil since the military overthrew the last leftist president in 1964. But then, da Silva has changed, too, since he led strikes against the military government in the 1980s. By dragging the *PT* to the political center, he brought it out of the political wilderness to respectability and to victory, much as Tony Blair did with Britain's long-discredited Labour Party. If da Silva keeps on the cautious and balanced course he is on, he could very well succeed where Juan Perón, Fidel Castro, Salvador Allende and Hugo Chávez failed: by bringing about genuine social reform without causing economic disaster or political upheaval or both. If he can, he may be destined to hold a revered place in Brazilian and Latin American history, and other struggling Third World countries may seek to embrace the Lula Alternative.

Grinding corn to be used for Pamonha, a typical dish in Minas Gerais.   Clotilde Soares Guilbeau

The Republic of Chile

La Moneda (presidential palace) in Santiago

Area: 286,322 square miles.
Population: 15.1 million in 2003.
Capital City: Santiago (Pop. 5.1 million, estimated).
Climate: Northern coastal lowlands are very hot and dry; the central valley is warm and dry from October through April and mild and damp through September; the southern regions are wet and cold.
Neighboring Countries: Peru (Northwest); Bolivia (Northeast); Argentina (East);
Official Language: Spanish
Other Principal Tongues: German, Quechua and Araucanian.
Ethnic Background: The majority are mestizo (mixed European and Indian).
Principal Religion: Roman Catholic Christianity.
Chief Commercial Products: Copper, nitrates, iron, steel, foodstuffs, processed fish, agricultural products.
Currency: Peso.
Gross Domestic Product: U.S. $94.1 billion in 2004 ($6,0000 per capita).
Former Colonial Status: Spanish Crown Colony (1541–1818).
Independence Day: September 18, 1810.
Chief of State: Ricardo Lagos Escobar (born March 2, 1938), president (since March 11, 2000).

National Flag: White, blue and red, with a white star in the blue stripe.

Chile, which has a name derived from an old Indian word meaning "land's end," sixth in size among the South American countries, is a strip of land 2,600 miles long and averaging 110 miles wide, lying between the Andes and the Pacific Ocean. Nearly one-half of this territory is occupied by the Andes Mountains and a coastal range of peaks. Because of its north-south length, Chile has a wide range of soils and climates; the country's frontier with Peru runs from Arica on the Pacific coast east to the crest of the Andes. The frontier with Bolivia and Argentina follows the crest of the Andes—18,000 feet high in the north, rising to 23,000 feet in the center and dropping to 13,000 feet in the south. The coastal range runs from the north to deep south, dropping abruptly into the sea with few ports. The heartland of Chile is the central valley between the two ranges.

Chile is divided into five natural regions. The northern, extending 600 miles south from the Peruvian border to Copiapo, is one of the driest regions of the world. Here are found rich nitrate deposits and major copper mines for which Chile has been famous. From Copiapo 400 miles south to Illapel, there is a semi-arid

region; however, there is sufficient rainfall to permit the raising of crops in the valleys. Chile's iron ore is found in this region. From Illapel 500 miles south to Concepción is the fertile area of the lush, green central valley. With adequate rainfall in the winter (May to August) the valley is intensively cultivated. Here also are the three principal cities and the major portion of the population. From Concepción to Puerto Montt there is a forest region, with large, sparkling lakes and rivers where rainfall is oppressively heavy during the fall and winter. The fifth and last zone stretches south 1,000 miles from Puerto Montt. This is an almost uninhabited wild region of cold mountains, glaciers and small islands. Rainfall is torrential and the climate stormy, wet and chilling.

History: Prior to the arrival of the Spaniards, Chile was the home from time immemorial of the Araucanian Indians, a loosely grouped civilization of primitive people who were completely isolated from the rest of mankind.

In the early 15th century, the Incas pushed across the desert and conquered the northern half of the fertile valley where present-day Santiago is located; however, they were unable to penetrate south of the river Maule. The Spaniards later occupied the area held by the Indi-

Chile

ans and founded Santiago in 1541, but their efforts to extend their holdings further south were fiercely and successfully resisted by the Araucanians. About a century later, the Indians entered into a treaty with the Spanish to retain the land south of Concepción. Despite the treaty, war continued between the Araucanians and their would-be conquerors until late in the 19th century.

During the conquest, the land was divided into great estates among the army officers; soldiers and settlers married Araucanian women captives, producing a mestizo population with qualities of both conquerors and the conquered. The colonial period was one of savage warfare and internal dissension. Particularly sharp were clashes between landowners and the clergy over the practice of holding Indians in slavery. During the 17th century, slavery was replaced by a system of sharecropping which only recently has abated.

To the wars and dissensions which marked Chile's history must be added a long list of natural disasters. Earthquakes and tidal waves have repeatedly destroyed its cities. An additional difficulty was presented by the fact that from the end of the 16th century until independence in 1817, Chile's coasts were infested with British and French pirates.

For the entire Spanish period, Chile was part of the Viceroyalty of Peru, governed from Lima; trade with areas other than the colony was forbidden, which led to whole-sale smuggling. Reports of the early 18th century indicated some 40 French ships engaged in illegal trade with Chile. Not until 1778 was trade permitted between Chile and Spain. Neglected by both Spain and Lima, the landowning aristocracy felt little loyalty to their own over-

General Bernardo O'Higgins

lords and developed their estates as semi-independent fiefs.

Chile declared its independence from Spain on September 18, 1810, which was followed by seven years of bitter war between the Chileans and Spanish forces. Finally, victory was achieved in 1817 when

Punta Arenas, the only city on the Strait of Magellan

Courtesy: Mr. & Mrs. Schuyler Lowe

General José de San Martín led an army from Argentina across the Andes to help the Chileans. The Chilean revolutionary hero, General Bernardo O'Higgins, became the first president of the republic—under his leadership the first constitution was drafted. Almost revolutionary in its liberal democratic ideas, it served as a model for the famous constitution later adopted in 1833.

Opposition of the landowners to O'Higgins' efforts concerning the distribution of land to small farmers, the separation of church and state and the encouragement of free education, resulted in his ouster in 1823. For nearly 100 years, the country was ruled by a small oligarchy of landowners, or *latifundistas* who still own the major share of valuable land. Conservatives, advocating a strong central government, dominated the political scene until 1861. Their autocratic rule enlarged the economy and united the country; however, the repression of the Liberal Party laid the basis for years of bitter conflict.

Liberals came to power in 1861 and were successful in modifying some of the more restrictive measures of the conservative regime. However, they made little progress against the landowners or the church. Liberals ruled until 1891, during which time longstanding disputes with Peru and Bolivia led to the War of the Pacific (1879–1883). Although unprepared for war, Chile quickly defeated Bolivia, overran the disputed nitrate fields and occupied Lima from 1881 to 1884.

Dictating the victor's terms, Chile took possession of both Bolivian and Peruvian provinces and the ports Arica and Antofagasta. Liberal José Balmaceda, elected to the presidency in 1886, decided the time was ripe for major reforms to improve the lot of the poor and curb the power of the landlords and the church. By 1890, he had created a crisis in urging these programs and in 1891 the Congress voted to depose him and installed a naval officer to head a provisional government. With the support of the army, Balmaceda resisted the action; the result was a civil war resulting in the deaths of some 10,000, with widespread damage. Balmaceda was ultimately forced to seek asylum in the Argentine Embassy, where he committed suicide.

Balmaceda's death also marked the death of the Liberal era and ushered in the phenomenon of congressional rule that predominated over the executive—definitely an anomaly for Latin America. The conservative oligarchy wielded virtually unchecked control for the next three decades through a political machine known as *La Fronda*. This same period, however, witnessed a proliferation of political parties that supplanted the traditional Liberals and Conservatives: Radical, National,

Democratic, Socialist and Communist, among others. Moreover, there was an industrial revolution that led to greater agitation for reform by organized labor movements. World War I saw a boom in the demand for Chilean nitrates, although the wealth that flowed into the country, as usual, failed to trickle down to the lower economic strata. At the end of the war, the same social ferment that led to the Bolshevik Revolution in Russia erupted in Chile in the form of strikes. Revolution seemed imminent.

Alessandri and Ibáñez

In 1920, a so-called Liberal Alliance of Radicals, Democrats, some Liberals and other factions, coalesced behind the nomination of Arturo Alessandri Palma for president. Like Franklin D. Roosevelt and John F. Kennedy, Alessandri was a handsome, wealthy patrician with a charismatic personality who convinced the working classes that he had their interests at heart. His message paralleled that of President Hipólito Irigoyen in neighboring Argentina, whose social reforms had defused a revolution there and caught the fancy of Chileans. Alessandri advocated separation of church and state, women's suffrage and increased taxes on the wealthy, including an income tax, to fund social welfare programs. Alessandri's popular appeal was such that he eked out a narrow plurality despite the *latifundistas'* control of the rural vote. Faced with the prospect of a genuine revolution, such as the one that had just unfolded in Mexico, the oligarchy's representatives in Congress pragmatically realized that Alessandri represented the lesser of two evils and voted to ratify his victory.

It was a largely hollow victory, however, because although the Liberal Alliance controlled the Chamber of Deputies, the right still controlled the Senate and frustrated virtually all of Alessandri's reform measures save the income tax; it was a situation uncannily similar to the gridlock in Chile's Congress today. Congress' obstinance, however, was to prove its undoing, because one of the measures that was tied up was the army's appropriation, always a mistake in Latin America. In September 1924, a band of officers invaded Congress and not so subtly demanded that it approve Alessandri's reform package (as well as their back pay). The officers then demanded that the president sign the measures. He complied, but to protest this undemocratic intervention, he resigned and left for self-imposed exile, first to Argentina, then to his parents' native Italy.

A power vacuum resulted, into which stepped in January 1925 a young colonel who would have a direct or indirect influ-

ence on Chilean government for more than 30 years: Carlos Ibáñez del Campo. Ironically, it was this military man who would implement much of the remainder of the reforms Alessandri had called for in 1920, and he somehow did so without alarming the oligarchy. Moreover, he promulgated the 1925 constitution, largely inspired by Alessandri, that returned power to the executive and served as the cornerstone for a reborn but shaky democracy that would last until 1973. Hardly a democrat himself, however, Ibáñez ruled from behind the throne for two years until he was "elected" in a highly suspect election in 1927. Although he enjoyed widespread public approval for a time, not even this military strongman could control events in New York. With the Stock Market Crash of 1929, the world price of copper plummeted, dragging Chile into the Great Depression. Ibáñez was overthrown in 1931, and there was a bewildering succession of revolving-door governments, including a socialist one, for the next 15 months. During this period of chaos, Alessandri returned from Italy and his leadership-starved countrymen returned him to the presidency for a six-year term in October 1932.

The Alessandri of the 1930s, however, was a changed man from the fiery reformer of the 1920s. His exile in Benito Mussolini's Italy had taught him the value of order and stability. Nonetheless, women's suffrage became a reality in 1935. He skillfully placated the discrete elements of the power structure—the military, the church, the wealthy landowners and industrialists, the middle class—when necessary; he resorted to a heavy hand to keep the social ferment from exploding. He once dissolved Congress, and he threw strike leaders in jail, causing the Socialists and Communists to break away and form a European-style Popular Front then in vogue.

The Popular Front's presidential candidate in 1938, Pedro Aguirre Cerda, an intellectual, won by a narrow plurality. His government was responsible for the creation of Latin America's most comprehensive social welfare program, made possible largely by the jump in copper and nitrate prices caused by the outbreak of World War II, and it became something of a model for the left-wing reformers in Latin America and Europe. It also proved a training ground for a generation of left-wing politicians at home; Aguirre Cerda's minister of health, for example, was a young physician named Salvador Allende. The war also caused a breakup of the Popular Front because of the nonaggression pact between Hitler and Stalin.

President Aguirre died in 1941 and a Radical, Juan Antonio Ríos, defeated

Chile

Ibáñez, the candidate of the right, in the ensuing election. Ríos, who was considerably to the right of his predecessor, oversaw a booming wartime economy and, largely because of German influence, maintained a neutral course until just before the end of the war, when Chile declared war on the all-but-defeated Axis.

Ríos, too, died in office, and in the election to choose a successor in 1946 the vote was fragmented among several candidates. Congress then selected another Radical, Gabriel González Videla, who unwisely formed a coalition government that included Socialists and Communists. Not only did the United States exert pressure on González Videla because of the Communist influence, but the Communists began engaging in intrigues aimed at seizing absolute power. In 1948 González Videla purged the Communists not only from his cabinet but from Congress, including the world-renowned poet and future Nobel Laureate, Pablo Neruda.

Chile swung even farther to the right in the election of 1952 when Ibáñez, then 75, finally succeeded in finishing in first place in another fragmented election. Labeling himself above politics, this quasi-fascist managed to draw votes from poor laborers and farm workers. Congress, following its tradition to ratify the top vote-getter, returned him to power. Despite fears that he would seek to become another Juan Perón, whom he admired, Ibáñez presided over a largely do-nothing government for six years. When he failed to take strong action to deal with spiraling inflation, the populace became bitterly disillusioned with this once-dynamic leader.

In 1958, the Socialists and Communists, in their most determined effort, united behind the candidacy of Salvador Allende, a committed Marxist. The Liberals and Conservatives rallied behind a moderate, Jorge Alessandri, son of Arturo, while a new force, the Christian Democrats, nominated Eduardo Frei Montalva. Alessandri finished just 1% ahead of Allende, giving the establishment a scare. Alessandri proved quite conservative, and although he helped stabilize the economy, he failed to address the perennial social ills that were providing grist for the far left.

By 1964, it seemed the impatience of the lower classes for some remedies to their plight could well give Allende a plurality of the popular vote and, if Congress followed tradition, the presidency. Fearing that eventuality, the rightists gradually abandoned their own candidate and rallied behind the Christian Democrats' Frei, who represented a middle course of reform without revolution. Frei easily defeated Allende with 55% of the vote, the first time in decades that a candidate had

won with an absolute majority. Frei made good on many of his promises, initiating land reform and making the first steps toward nationalization of the foreign-owned copper mines. But he found himself in a damned-if-you-do-damned-if-you-don't dilemma. The right vilified him for going too far, the left for not going far enough.

Allende and Pinochet

In 1970, Allende was again a candidate, this time of a Socialist-Communist-Radical coalition called Popular Unity. But this time the right split with the Christian Democrats and nominated former President Alessandri, by then quite elderly, while the Christian Democrats nominated a left-of-center candidate, Rodomiro Tomic, who tried unsuccessfully to steal Allende's thunder. Polls showed the race a tossup between Allende and Alessandri, and the world watched with expectation to see if Allende would usher in the world's first democratically elected Marxist government. Ironically, only 29% of the electorate turned out for what would become the most fateful election in Chile's history. Allende won by an eyelash, 36.4% to Alessandri's 35.2%. Under the 1925 constitution, the choice fell again to Congress. Despite a

clumsy attempt by the CIA to bribe Christian Democratic congressmen to vote for Alessandri, Congress confirmed Allende, and Frei placed the presidential sash over the shoulders of his Marxist successor on November 3, 1970.

The victory of Popular Unity seemed to have caught even Allende and his dogmatic supporters by surprise. Despite their shaky mandate, they set off to turn Chile into a Marxist state, gradually alienating the centrist Christian Democrats who initially provided them with the congressional votes they needed to pass legislation. The government implemented a hastily devised economic program that nationalized the U.S.-owned copper mines and telephone system, which resulted in economic sanctions by the Nixon Administration. The Soviet Union and China, for a time, willingly came to Chile's economic rescue. In other action, the government increased wages and froze prices, which temporarily created the illusion of prosperity; Chileans went on a spending spree, and in 1971 municipal elections voters expressed their gratitude by giving Popular Unity 49% of the vote.

Old Marxists were suspicious in spite of the apparent economic success; some foresaw the disaster that lay ahead. The Soviet Union started to worry about being bur-

View of downtown Santiago

94

Chile

Salvador Allende

General Augusto Pinochet Ugarte

dened with the support of an expensive second Latin American nation. Fidel Castro warned Allende in 1973 during a state visit that Chile's economic plans were the opposite of Marxism, in which consumption is held to a minimum. Allende replied that he was working in a system where he had to win reelection until a "dictatorship of the proletariat" could be established, and rejected Castro's advice.

Although general disintegration of the economy was well underway by the time of 1973 congressional elections, thirst for continued consumerism resulted in an increased share of the vote for Allende's coalition to 44%. Voter enthusiasm could not save the economy, which was experiencing a "domino" style collapse in which one sector would bring down others. First to fall were the retail stores. With prices fixed and wages raised, stores could not afford to restock sold items; when everything on the shelves was gone, the stores closed, idling thousands.

The result in agriculture was the same. Instead of orderly land redistribution, Allende simply broke up plantations of wealthy persons regardless of productivity. Owners refused to plant crops which would be harvested by others. Political cronies were appointed to administer the nationalized farms; as production dropped by 20% it became necessary for Chile to increase food imports.

The government seized the copper mines owned by large U.S. companies to end what Allende termed foreign exploitation. Virtually no compensation was offered. Spurred on by widespread public support for his expropriation of the mines, Allende then ordered the nationalization of other key industries—including those owned by Chileans. Taking their cues from the government, workers (and outside agitators) began seizing farms and

factories throughout the country. To the great dismay of Allende's economic planners, workers did not hesitate to strike against newly expropriated state industries. These work stoppages—combined with inept management of nationalized firms, led to a catastrophic decline in economic output.

Allende isolated Chile in foreign affairs and trade. The availability of loans from non-communist nations and institutions predictably disappeared. The Soviets and Chinese heaped praise on Chile, but offered precious little monetary support. The United States even declined Chilean offers to buy food for cash.

The people found themselves wasting hour upon hour in lines to buy what few consumer goods were left. As the government continued to "finance" itself by printing more money, inflation ran absolutely wild. Food was scarce, spare parts for machinery were nonexistent; only the black market flourished. Strikes and street fights between rival political factions became common. Political bickering in the Congress froze all constructive activity.

As things crumbled, the opposition became more unified. The right-wing National Party and the fascist Fatherland and Freedom Party began to sabotage operations of the government. The culmination of resistance came when a two-month strike by the nation's truck owners opposing nationalization—a strike a U.S. congressional inquiry later determined to have been partly financed by the CIA—virtually cleared the roads at the same time protesting housewives were filling the streets. With civil war imminent, the military staged its long-expected coup on September 11, 1973. Quickly seizing control, they announced that Allende had allegedly killed himself with a machine gun given to him as a gift by Fidel Castro.

During his brief but stormy term as president, Allende left a lasting mark on the nation. He sought to increase the living standards of the poor, to distribute farms to those who worked the land and to provide a full spectrum of social and economic benefits. He might possibly have succeeded if a unified, workable plan had first been developed and if at the same time he had been given enough time and had control of his followers.

Although Allende was unable to control his supporters, civil liberties were largely respected. A small number of political opponents was sent into exile, but none was harmed. The vigorous opposition press (two-thirds of the total) remained free. Opposition parties thrived while critics of the government spoke out without fear of reprisal. Congress and the courts continued to function normally. Yet his administration was a disaster. When the Congress

and courts opposed his policies, Allende felt free to ignore them.

Allende never received a majority of votes in any election, thus he lacked the necessary public support for changes that were so radical. He came to power because of a divided opposition rather than because of his own popularity.

Once it decided to move against the Allende government, the *junta* left no holds barred. Leftists and suspected opponents of the *junta* were promptly exterminated or rounded up in huge detention centers. Catholic Church officials in Chile estimated that one out of every 100 Chileans was arrested at least once during the 16½ years the military held power. Many, according to the government, were "shot while trying to escape." Others simply disappeared while under detention. Other opponents of the regime were expelled from the country. By 1980, though, the government allowed many to return safely.

Even General Carlos Prats, Pinochet's predecessor as army commander and who had opposed the coup, went into self-imposed exile in Argentina. A year later, he and his wife were killed in a car bombing that two decades later was linked to Pinochet's infamous National Intelligence Directorate, or *DINA*. Another prominent exile, Orlando Letelier, who had served as Allende's defense and foreign ministers, was killed in an almost identical car bombing in Washington, D.C. in 1976. That assassination, also linked to *DINA*, strained relations with the United States. Four men, including one American, ultimately were convicted of Letelier's death.

A major victim of military repression was Chile's long-standing tradition as a pioneering Latin American democracy. Upon seizing power the *junta* immediately closed Congress and pointedly used its chambers to store records of political pris-

Chile

oners. The constitution was suspended and the courts neutralized. Freedom of the press disappeared and suspected books and publications were destroyed. Schools, factories and the nation itself, were placed under rigid control to discourage dissent and—most importantly—to "root out Marxism."

Political parties (except selected right-wing groups) were placed "in suspension." The large Christian Democratic Party newspaper was closed and its leader, former President Frei, was forced to muzzle his biting criticism. Not surprisingly, Marxists suffered most. Socialist and communist leaders were arrested, killed, exiled or forced into hiding.

The only group which continually dared to speak out against the generals was the Catholic clergy. The *junta* responded by banning some religious festivals and arresting priests and nuns suspected of leftist sympathies. At one point, the church's prisoner relief agency was ordered to discontinue its attempts to locate persons who disappeared following their arrest by security agents. The church disregarded the directive and reported 750 such disappearances in 1975.

When the Catholic Church published a book by former President Frei in 1976 calling for a return to democracy, the government quickly outlawed public discussion of it. In his sermons, Raúl Cardinal Silva Henríquez boldly criticized the regime's rigid austerity program, which he said was pushing the nation's impoverished masses to the edge of starvation.

A major goal of the military rulers had been to pull Chile out of an economic tailspin caused by the Allende administration. Skilled managers were sent to farms and factories while property seized by the previous government was returned. Taxes and interest rates were increased and the amount of currency in circulation was reduced by cuts in government spending of 15% to 20%. Strikes were strongly "discouraged," while the nation's high unemployment rate in the months following the coup forced wage levels downward.

To increase farm output and industrial production, prices of consumer goods—including food—were allowed to rise to their natural levels. Soaring food costs, however, threatened fully a third of the nation with hunger in the months following the coup. To prevent starvation, the government provided the most destitute with limited food handouts and low-paying public works jobs.

Although the *junta* consisted of four military men, real power was in the hands of General Augusto Pinochet Ugarte. Pinochet initially said that democracy could not be restored during his lifetime or the lifetime of his successor. Military

rule, he had insisted, could not be lifted until "the ills of democracy" had been erased. On freedom of expression, Pinochet was once quoted as saying, "We're not against ideas; we're just against people spreading them." In terms of human rights, the cure appeared to be worse than the disease. But economically, it was a tremendous success. Pinochet surrounded himself with a clique of civilian economic technocrats, many of whom had studied under free-market guru Milton Friedman at the University of Chicago, and who quickly won the monicker, "los Chicago Boys" (see Economy).

Chileans surged to the polls in January 1978 to give a simple "sí" or "no" vote in a plebiscite testing support for the military rulers. The *junta* received a lopsided 75% approval. Elated at the "solid support," President Pinochet declared that no further elections needed to be held for 10 years.

Even as Pinochet savored his electoral triumph, however, he was confronted with a serious threat from abroad. Neighboring Argentina suddenly revived an old territorial claim over three rocky, uninhabited islands at the mouth of the Beagle Channel in faraway Tierra del Fuego. At Argentina's suggestion, the two countries submitted their competing claims to the islands—Lennox, Picton and Nueva—to the British Crown for arbitration. The British ruled that Chile had legitimate sovereignty over all three islands, whereupon the Argentine military government of General Jorge Rafael Videla renounced the decision it itself had sought and threatened to seize the islands by force. By December 1978, both countries were on a war footing, and hostilities appeared imminent. Literally at the 11th hour, the two military strongmen, who after all were bound philosophically by their hatred of communism and democratic institutions, agreed to a second arbitration, this time by the Vatican. The Italian cardinal assigned to review the matter also concluded that Chile had the stronger claim. Despite occasional saber-rattling, Argentina eventually dropped the matter. But Pinochet had the last laugh. When Argentina foolishly invaded the Falkland Islands in 1982, precipitating war with Britain, Pinochet secretly allowed the Royal Navy to use Chilean territorial waters and islands, even as Chile was echoing the denunciation of other Latin American countries of the perceived British aggression against their sister republic.

Despite widespread national and international criticism of its harsh political and rigid economic policies, the *junta* could point to some dramatic successes: the inflation rate dropped from 600% per year in 1973 to just under 10% in 1981—one of

the lowest in Latin America. In addition, foreign investment rose rapidly.

Repression had also been reduced. The regime became increasingly tolerant of public criticism, and arrests of political opponents declined. At the same time, a limited number of Chileans sent into exile following the coup were allowed to return home.

Another "sí" or "no" plebiscite was put before the voters in September 1980. By a two-to-one margin, they approved President Pinochet's desire to remain in power for another eight years. Some observers charged that the balloting was rigged. His term was technically scheduled to end in 1990 after an election to choose his successor. But the strongman still enjoyed an added insurance policy: the *junta* had the power to reappoint him for *another* eight years—which in theory could stretch his term until 1997, the year that constitutional safeguards were slated to become effective. His intentions were made known in July 1986 when he scheduled another "yes" or "no" plebiscite to be held in October 1988. A yes vote would have returned him to power for another eight years.

Human rights violations by Chile's military rulers touched off widespread international protest and complicated relations with the United States. After Chilean secret police were linked with the 1976 as-

Entrance of La Moneda, the presidential palace

96

Chile

sassination of Allende supporter Orlando Letelier in Washington, the Carter administration cut off most military aid to the Pinochet regime in 1979. When a member of the military involved in the murder identified the masterminds of the plot in 1986 the subject came up again as demand for their extradition to the U.S. was made; it was ignored by Pinochet.

But the Reagan administration, favorably impressed with the *junta's* anticommunist leanings, sought to improve ties between the two countries. Thus, in 1981, some trade barriers were removed and the United States invited Chile to participate in joint naval exercises. The U.S. Senate voted in 1981 to resume military aid to Chile—on the condition that Santiago complies with "internationally recognized standards of human rights."

The economy, though, continued to deteriorate. Chile suffered the worst slump in all of Latin America in the recession of 1981–82, resulting in a reduction of about 13% in the gross domestic product and forcing the government to intervene in private enterprise to prevent an increasing number of bankruptcies. By May 1983, it was estimated that 21% of the urban force was unemployed. The following month a strike of truck drivers and copper miners—the first important labor challenge to the military government since 1973—appeared to be the beginning of a deep social crisis. The government's swift reaction, combining repression with conciliation, defused the danger.

When the *Alianza Democrática* (Democratic Alliance), a group of five opposition parties formed in 1983, tried in late 1984 to expand tenuous dialogue with the government and to pressure Pinochet for more political concessions, the government answered by declaring a stage of siege (the first in its 11 years in power), imposing a curfew and tightening its control over the media. By June 1985, however, it appeared as if the regime had softened its stand and was willing to listen to the group's more moderate members. Another attempt at reconciliation was attempted, this time spearheaded by "liberation theology" Catholic priests and bishops, a movement which ripened into the National Assembly of Civil Society, a gathering of professional associations, academics, students, teachers, bus drivers, shopkeepers and two large union groups.

In order to reinforce its demands for a return to democracy, the organization called for a general strike on July 2–3, 1986. Although the leader of the organization called the strike a "gigantic success," (which it was) it proved to be a mistake— the equivalent of tweaking the tiger's tail. The strike resulted in several deaths, many wounded and more than 1,000 arrests.

The regime's forces claimed to have discovered over 70 tons of munitions in 1986, allegedly from the Vietnam war period, including Soviet-bloc manufactured items and U.S. M-16 rifles. The caches of arms had been unloaded from Cuban trawlers for use by insurgents and guerrillas trained in insurrection in Cuba and Nicaragua, according to Chilean intelligence sources. For several months, conditions were unsettled, with leftist groups resorting to widespread terrorism and the military regime responding in kind. As one astute politician stated (rough translation): "it is open season on everyone." Right-wing terrorists felt quite justified in shooting and bombing leftist radicals and vice versa.

In September 1986, Pinochet narrowly escaped death in an ambush by left-wing terrorists on his motorcade that left five of his bodyguards dead. The radical Manuel Rodríguez Patriotic Front (*FPMR*) claimed credit for the deed; predictably, Pinochet responded with a new 90-day state of siege and announced he would "expel or lock up all those people talking about human rights and all those things."

In keeping with his intention to schedule a 1988 plebiscite to install himself in office for another eight years, in an effort to bolster sagging relations with the United States and to placate moderate politicians at home, Pinochet announced the legalization of political parties in March 1987 (except Marxists). But there was a catch: no party could be affiliated with one that had existed before. During a visit by Pope John

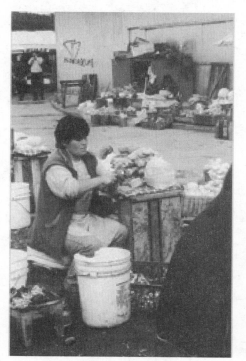

Fish market in Puerto Montt

Paul II in 1987, there was widespread violence, with clashes between dissidents and forces of the regime virtually every day.

Return to Democracy

As the time for the October 7, 1988 plebiscite drew near, Pinochet underwent a marked change. Instead of his former elitist, aloof style, he tried, with some success, to promote the image of a kindly old grandfather-figure. He counted on the division of the opposition (17 parties) and actually believed he would win. In August, after changes were made in the *junta*, it voted him in for another eight-year term as provided for in the questionable 1980 constitution. This met with widespread disfavor. The numerous political parties were highly united into The Command for No by a single ambition: to oust Pinochet.

The voting was relatively close because of a single reason: economic prosperity. By 1988 inflation had descended to 8% and Chile enjoyed a trade surplus of more than $1.5 billion. The outcome was 54% to 43% against Pinochet. The country held its breath, wondering what the elderly leader would do. Somewhat hesitantly, he announced that as provided for by law, elections would be held in December 1989.

Patricio Aylwin, a centrist Christian Democrat who had been a senator when the 1973 coup occurred, was the presidential candidate of a coalition of 17 center-left parties called the *Concertación*. The Communists were not part of the coalition but gave tacit support to Aylwin. In a three-way contest, Aylwin received 55% against Hernán Büchi, a former civilian finance minister during the military regime and Pinochet's hand-picked candidate, who received only 29%, and Francisco Javier Errázuriz, an enigmatic, Ross Perot-style tycoon who polled 15% as an independent. Election night saw an outpouring of jubilation as *Concertación* supporters filled the streets to celebrate the end of 17 years of authoritarian rule. On March 11, 1990, Pinochet placed the presidential sash on the shoulders of his civilian successor, marking a major milestone in the life of the country.

Not surprisingly, however, friction soon developed between the two over the issue of civilian control. Aylwin asked Pinochet to resign as army commander, but the general steadfastly refused, saying his presence provided stability for the transition to democracy. There was little Aylwin could do, as the 1980 constitution permitted Pinochet to remain in command until the end of 1997, and the *Concertación* lacked the votes in Congress to amend the constitution. In fact, the constitution also allowed Pinochet to name nine permanent "institutional" senators to the 47-member

97

Chile

upper house of Congress when he left office, which has given the conservative opposition a narrow majority and consequent veto power over legislation passed by the *Concertación*-controlled Chamber of Deputies. The opposition also enjoys a disproportionate number of elected seats in both houses because of the peculiar double-member districts, in which the top two vote-getters are both elected. It is classic gridlock. Among other things, the opposition-controlled Senate repeatedly blocked executive branch efforts to abolish the national holiday for September 11, the anniversary of the coup. The holiday was finally abolished in 1999.

Aylwin was heavily pressured to try all major military figures responsible for disappearances for so many years. A valid question was posed to him without being stated: if the military was to be tried, why also should not the left-wing, anti-military subversives also be tried? Lacking an answer, in the style of a skilled politician, he appointed a commission to investigate and study the matter.

The commission found that 3,197 people had been killed outright or disappeared at the hands of the military following the coup, but in the midst of prosperity, most Chileans seem to prefer to let the past rest in peace and not fan the flames of renewed conflict.

The Supreme Court, in an unusual and imaginative decision, heard a case involving the validity of the amnesty laws that protected the military against charges of alleged crimes. It was argued that because Chile was in fact at war, criminal charges could not be sustained. The court agreed about the state of war, but held that even so, the terms of the Geneva Convention forbidding the murder of prisoners was applicable.

The continuing dispute vividly illustrates an ongoing problem of today's world: how can law and justice during times of unlawfulness and injustice be applied retroactively? The question first arose at the Nuremburg trials following World War II. Pinochet summed up the dilemma very tersely, saying, "During wars, crimes are always committed."

Chile prospered under Aylwin, and for a time saw its economy expand at a rate approaching an average of 10% per year. It still had a thorny problem with the perpetually poor, but the government attempted to tackle that problem, too. Prosperity and growth were the products of free trade (few, if any tariffs) and foreign investment, the latter flowing in at a rate of more than U.S. $1 billion a year.

In December 1993, voters affirmed their satisfaction with the status quo by electing Eduardo Frei Ruiz-Tagle, son of the president who preceded Allende, to the

presidency by a resounding 59 percent of the vote against five opponents. Almost simultaneously, Congress extended the presidential term from four to six years, as it was before the military coup. Like Aylwin, Frei was a Christian Democrat who was the candidate of the *Concertación*. The two conservative opposition parties, National Renewal (*RN*) and the ultra-rightist Independent Democratic Union (*UDI*), bickered until just two months before the election before agreeing on a single candidate, Arturo Alessandri, grandson and namesake of the president of the 1920s and 1930s and nephew of the late President Jorge Alessandri, predecessor of Frei's father. Conservative unity came too late, however, as Alessandri polled only 29 percent, only slightly more than Pinochet's hand-picked candidate in 1989.

**Former President
Eduardo Frei Ruiz–Tagle**

One of the most historic aspects of this election, however, was that the once-mighty Communist Party received only about 3 percent. The *Concertación* retained its majority in the lower house, but the eight remaining "institutional senators" named by Pinochet (one had died) allowed the conservative opposition to keep control of the upper chamber and serve as a brake on the majority.

Frei, an engineer by training rather than a politician, had been elected to the Senate in 1989 and as president of the Christian Democratic Party two years later. Following the counsel of a group of influential advisers, Frei wisely kept the successful economic policies in effect, and Chile's economic growth continued to be the envy of Latin America. The combination of stable civilian government and free-market economics made Chile a favorite target of foreign investors, who have increasingly sought new opportuni-

ties in the region as they once did in the Pacific Rim countries of Asia. Frei also emerged as a leader of regional importance, hosting a Latin American summit in Santiago in 1996 and visiting with President Clinton at the White House in 1997 for trade talks. Clinton included Chile in his four-nation tour of South America in October 1997.

Like Aylwin before him, Frei experienced friction with Pinochet, who successfully resisted efforts to curtail the extraordinary authority granted to him in his personalized 1980 constitution. The general further annoyed the president, and generated great public controversy, by postponing his promised retirement from the announced date of January 26, 1998. Pinochet finally retired as army commander, at age 82, on March 10 in a fanfare-filled ceremony in which he tearfully bade farewell to the troops he had commanded for nearly 25 years and to the institution to which he had belonged for more than 60. He was succeeded by Major General Ricardo Izurieta, 53, a cavalry officer and former chairman of the National Defense Council.

But Pinochet's long-awaited retirement did not mean he was withdrawing from public life—or from the controversy that continues to follow him. The day after his retirement ceremony, and still adhering to a right given to him in the constitution as a former head of state, he put on a civilian business suit and assumed a lifetime seat in the Senate, joining the other non-elected "institutional senators" who give the conservative opposition a majority. Pinochet's transfer to the Senate angered left-wing lawmakers, and there were public demonstrations to protest such an antidemocratic measure. Efforts to block Pinochet by judicial means failed, as did an impeachment motion in the Chamber of Deputies, which was rejected in an unusual secret ballot 62–52. Once again the aging general demonstrated he was still a force to contend with, whether his detractors liked it or not.

Congressional elections in December 1997 failed to alter the balance of power, but voters sent some confusing signals. The lineup in the Chamber of Deputies remained 70–50 in favor of the *Concertación*, although its popular vote dropped to 50.5%. It also lost one Senate seat, giving it 20 of the elected seats to 18 for the conservatives. With the "institutional" senators, including Pinochet, the opposition held a commanding seven-seat majority. The Christian Democrats remained the largest party in Congress, but their popular vote fell from 27% to 23%. The Christian Democrats' main coalition partner, the center-left Party for Democracy (*PPD*), broke even. There were two major surprises: the ultra-rightwing *UDI* became the second ranking party in the Senate, moving ahead of its opposition partner, the *RN*. And on the left, the Communists showed their first modest gains since they abandoned their adherence to Marxism-Leninism. Perhaps most troubling for Chile's reborn democracy was that one sixth of eligible voters registered to vote and only 83% of registered voters turned out, even though voting is mandatory.

The Pinochet Case

Chilean government and society were suddenly thrust into turmoil in October 1998 when Pinochet flew to London for back surgery. On October 16, as he was recuperating in a clinic, the British government formally placed him under arrest, acting on an extradition request from Spain. A Spanish judge, Baltasar Garzón, acting largely on his own initiative, requested Pinochet's extradition to account for Spanish citizens tortured and killed during the military regime. But the warrant eventually was broadened to take advantage of the 1988 International Convention Against Torture, promulgated by the United Nations, by which a country can seek the arrest in a second country of someone accused of torture committed in a third country. Judges in Switzerland and France soon submitted similar extradition requests for Pinochet, while Chilean exiles-by-choice in France, Denmark, Italy and Belgium also filed petitions accusing Pinochet of human rights abuses.

The news of Pinochet's arrest made headlines around the world, particularly in Chile, where the news was greeted with glee by Pinochet's detractors and with outrage by his supporters. But the Spanish warrant and the British arrest also struck at the core of Chilean nationalism, and moderate Chileans, even some Pinochet-haters, denounced the action as a violation of Chilean sovereignty.

President Frei, despite his own personal animosity to the general, dutifully added his voice to those urging Pinochet's release on the grounds that as a member of the Chilean Senate he enjoyed diplomatic immunity from arrest. Rumors circulated that the military might take action if the government did not, a reminder of the Sword of Damocles that continues to hang above Chile's civilian rulers. In a case of delicious irony, Foreign Minister José Miguel Insulza, who himself had been arrested after the coup and spent years in exile, was dispatched to London to plead Pinochet's cause.

The Pinochet case then began a torturous (no pun intended) 16-month journey through the British court system. Pinochet, under house arrest in a rented mansion near London, won the first legal skirmish when the London High Court ruled that as head of state when the crimes were committed, Pinochet was immune to arrest in Britain, but declined to release him pending an appeal.

The case was heard before a panel of five Law Lords, jurists who are members of the House of Lords, Britain's court of last resort. While this hearing was underway, the Spanish cabinet called for Pinochet's extradition, prompting Frei to recall Chile's ambassador from Madrid for consultation. On November 25—Pinochet's 83rd birthday—the Law Lords voted 3–2 that Pinochet's arrest was legal. The decision then fell upon Home Secretary Jack Straw whether to grant Spain's extradition request.

Pinochet's lawyers then asked for a new hearing because one of the five Law Lords and his wife were active in the human rights group Amnesty International. The following day, the proud general was required to undergo the ignominy of appearing in court for a bail hearing. He huffily declared in Spanish that he did not recognize the jurisdiction of a non-Chilean court, and the judge remanded him on bail. The House of Lords agreed that Pinochet was entitled to a new hearing before a seven-judge panel.

On March 24, 1999, the Law Lords ruled 6–1 that Pinochet's arrest was legal and that the extradition request could proceed, but they agreed with Pinochet's lawyers that he could not be held accountable for any crime allegedly committed before September 29, 1988—the date that Britain incorporated the international torture convention into its criminal laws. This effectively dismissed 29 of the 32 charges in the Spanish warrant. The general remained under arrest on the other three counts. Judge Garzón began raising new allegations of cases committed after 1988.

In April 1999, Straw decided to proceed with the extradition request.

A hearing was held the following September. Pinochet's lawyers argued that Spain lacked jurisdiction to try the general for alleged crimes that occurred in Chile and also that he was too ill to stand trial. The magistrate rejected Pinochet's arguments and declared that he could be extradited. Once again, the decision fell upon Straw, who found himself in the unenviable position of choosing between releasing what the international community regarded as a war criminal or sending a feeble old man to Spain, where in all likelihood he would die in captivity.

Straw vacillated three months before ordering that Pinochet undergo a series of medical examinations to determine whether he were too ill to be extradited. The general, who turned 84 on November 25, 1999, underwent the exams in January 2000, and the Santiago daily *El Mercurio* carried a large front-page picture of Pinochet seated in the back seat of his limousine, obviously exhausted after the seven-hour ordeal. The picture did little to ameliorate Chilean public opinion toward the British or Spanish. On January 13, Straw decided that Pinochet was indeed too ill to be extradited, setting off a torrent of outrage by human rights groups.

A Chilean air force plane was dispatched to Britain, and on March 3, 2000, the once-proud Pinochet returned to his native soil—in a wheelchair.

His travails continued, however, and in May 2000 the Santiago Court of Appeals voted 13-9 to strip him of his legislative immunity as senator-for-life to allow him

Torres del Paine

Chile

BIENVENIDO
GENERAL PINOCHET
LIBERTADOR DE CHILE

GRACIAS POR DERROTAR AL
COMUNISMO Y EVITAR QUE NOS
CONVIRTIERAMOS EN UNA
SEGUNDA CUBA

Movimiento Vitalicio Augusto Pinochet.

BIENVENIDO HIJO
DE PUTA ASESINO!!
EL PUEBLO NO
OLVIDA TUS
CRÍMENES

The Chilean public's divided welcome to Pinochet as shown in leaflets showered on the crowds awaiting his arrival in Santiago . . . Courtesy of Zoubir Ouarti

to stand trial. Pinochet's lawyers immediately appealed to the Supreme Court, arguing once again that he was too frail and ill to stand trial. Moreover, the U.S. government announced in March it planned to investigate whether Pinochet were the intellectual author of the 1976 car bomb assassination of Orlando Letelier, a former Allende cabinet minister; Letelier's secretary, a U.S. national, also died in the blast.

That August, the Supreme Court voted 14-6 to uphold the lower court's decision to strip Pinochet of his legislative immunity. Judge Juan Guzmán, who had been appointed to handle the domestic complaints against Pinochet, found a loophole around the amnesty law that protected members of the military from being tried for atrocities committed following the coup. He decided to try him for the kidnappings, not murders, of 18 prisoners who disappeared and were never accounted for during the infamous "Caravan of Death," a helicopter-borne squad of soldiers that scoured the country after the coup and carried dissidents away to

their deaths. Kidnappings are not covered by the amnesty law.

Guzmán generated headlines around the world by announcing that Pinochet would stand trial and ordering him placed under house arrest. An appeals court quickly overturned his order, on the grounds that Guzmán never interrogated Pinochet before arresting him. Pinochet's lawyers, meanwhile, continued to argue that their client was too frail to stand trial, whereupon Guzmán ordered Pinochet to undergo more medical testing. At first, the proud Pinochet refused, but in January 2001, he yielded to his lawyers' advice and subjected himself to the exams. Later, Pinochet again ignored his lawyers and agreed to be interrogated in his seaside home by Guzmán. As a result, the judge declared Pinochet mentally competent to stand trial. Guzmán again issued an arrest warrant, which was served on Pinochet at his home. In July, an appeals court ruled that Pinochet was mentally incompetent to stand trial. But in August, the Supreme Court voted to overturn that decision.

For 11 more months the lawyers wrangled, until the Supreme Court ruled 4-1 in July 2002, that Pinochet was mentally incompetent to stand trial. Three days later, Pinochet resigned his lifetime Senate seat. His 29-year political career, and an era in Chilean history, were over.

But Pinochet's legal problems have persisted. Just a month after the Supreme Court declared him incompetent, Argentina requested his extradition in connection with the 1974 car bomb assassination there of the exiled General Carlos Prats and his wife. In October, the Supreme Court, citing its incompetence ruling, blocked the request.

Then, in November 2003, Pinochet granted an interview to a Spanish-language network in Miami, in which he laid the blame on the human rights abuses on his subordinates. In the interview, Pinochet came across as quite lucid. Suddenly, he was facing charges again, not only for the Prats assassination, but for nine kidnappings and one murder committed as part of the so-called "Operation Condor," a joint effort by South American military regimes of the 1970s to kill or imprison leftists.

In a 14–9 decision in May 2004 that stunned both sides, the Santiago Court of Appeals stripped Pinochet of his immunity, leaving him vulnerable not only to prosecution but to about 200 civil lawsuits. His lawyers appealed to the Supreme Court, which upheld the appeals court in a 9–8 ruling that August. His lawyers again appealed on the grounds that Pinochet was mentally incompetent to stand trial, and in September Pinochet was examined by three doctors: one appointed by Pinochet's lawyers, one by the families of victims, one by Judge Guzmán. In their report, released in October, the doctors appointed by the judge and the defense agreed Pinochet was incompetent, while the third said he was competent. In December, Judge Guzmán decided to go with the doctor who said he was competent and issued an indictment against Pinochet on December 13 in the Condor case. Five days later, Pinochet was hospitalized with a stroke. On January 4, 2005, a panel of the Supreme Court upheld the indictment, this time by a 3–2 vote.

Making this already complex series of legal twists and turns even more bewildering, the Santiago Court of Appeals voted on December 2 to strip Pinochet of immunity from prosecution in the Prats assassination, but on March 24 a different panel of Supreme Court justices overruled the appeals court in a 15–4 vote. After five years, the Chilean courts still cannot agree on what to do with Pinochet.

As if Pinochet didn't have enough worries from the human rights charges, in September 2004 he suddenly found himself facing international charges for money laundering (see Recent Developments).

Precio: $ 250
Regiones I-II: $ 330; XI y XII: $ 400

TIEMPO EN LA CAPITAL
Mín. 11 Máx. 29

UNIDAD DE FOMENTO
$ 15.087,36

la TERCERA

Lunes 17 de enero de 2000, Año 50, Número 18.112

Conéctese hoy a
www.tercera.cl
ELECCIONES: Descargue el resultado electoral ↳
ENCUESTA: ¿Volverá Pinochet esta semana? ↳
MOUSE: Guía de libros de computación ↳

Todo sobre la victoria de Lagos

PRESIDENTE2000

The front page of the Santiago daily *La Tercera* the morning after the January 16, 2000, presidential runoff shows the victorious Ricardo Lagos, right, with his defeated opponent, Joaquín Lavín, in a display of gracious goodwill.

The armed forces had been caught in a dilemma with their former commander's arrest. Although the military had protested vigorously, it seemed to realize that it is a new day in Chile, and that it would be bad public relations to undermine a duly elected government. Moreover, the military has felt compelled to own up to the whereabouts of the bodies of many of the "disappeared." Once a death is confirmed, it is covered by the amnesty law and can no longer be treated as a kidnapping. Alas, the military has acknowledged that many victims were dumped at sea.

101

Chile

President Ricardo Lagos
Photo by the author

The Lagos Presidency

As the Pinochet drama unfolded during 1999, Chileans prepared to elect their third president since the restoration of democracy. At first it seemed the *Concertación* might break apart if the Christian Democrats and the *PPD*, the *PDC*'s main coalition partner, could not agree on a candidate. In a coalition primary election, the *PPD*'s Ricardo Lagos, 61, a neo-socialist economist, defeated Andrés Zaldivar, a moderate Christian Democrat, with 70% of the vote. The *PDC* leadership rallied around Lagos, who had served as education minister under Aylwin and public works minister under Frei and who had spent most of the Pinochet regime in self-imposed exile on a faculty in North Carolina.

Meanwhile, the two right-wing opposition parties, *RN* and the *UDI*, also held a joint primary, and the overwhelming winner was the *UDI*'s Joaquín Lavín, 46, also an economist and a former mayor of the affluent Santiago suburb of Los Condes. During the Pinochet regime, Lavín had been one of the "Chicago Boys," the University of Chicago-educated economists who engineered Chile's free-market economic miracle. The Communist Party leader Gladys Marín mounted a separate candidacy, while three lesser candidates completed the field.

At mid-year, all the polls agreed that Lagos would win without a *segunda vuelta,* or runoff. But by late 1999, Chile found itself in its first recession in 15 years, Lagos' standing in the polls dropped. Moreover, like Aesop's tortoise, Lavín campaigned energetically and soon made inroads among conservative and moderate Christian Democrats who were leery of both Lagos' socialist past and his agnosticism. Lavín, by stark contrast, not only is a de-

vout Roman Catholic but is a member of the conservative Catholic organization Opus Dei. Lavín had another powerful asset: Lagos himself, who proved cold and stuffy as a candidate.

The results of the first round on December 12 were breathtakingly close: 3,359,679, or 47.96 percent, for Lagos, to 3,328,652, or 47.52 percent, for Lavín; the tortoise almost pulled it off. Marín received only 223,000 votes, or 3.2 percent, but those votes would prove crucial in the January 16, 2000 runoff.

This author spent two weeks in Chile observing the runoff campaign as a freelance journalist. By then, Lagos had heeded the advice of his advisers and was beginning to campaign in a more laid-back style, addressing crowds without a coat, although he couldn't quite bring himself to remove his tie. Both candidates tried to outdo each other with lavish, U.S.-style campaign promises that left analysts wondering how they expected to pay for them.

An amusing spectacle of the campaign was the devoutly Catholic Lavín and the agnostic Lagos pleading for votes from evangelicals, who now comprise 7 percent of the population.

Fortunately for Lagos, by election day the unemployment rate had ameliorated to 10.5%, hinting that a recovery was beginning. Still, the runoff was almost as dramatic as the first round had been: 3,677,968 or 51.31% for Lagos, to 3,490,561, or 48.69% for Lavín. The loser stunned the winner by coming personally to his hotel to congratulate him, then the two of them

went to the balcony together where, to the delight of the cheering Lagos supporters, Lavín magnanimously pledged his support to the president-elect. It was a refreshing conclusion to what had at times been a bruising battle. Lagos was inaugurated on March 11, 2000.

The first major litmus test of the Lagos government's popularity came in the municipal elections of October 29, 2000, for 341 local governments. The *Concertación* polled 52% of the popular vote nationwide, down from 56% in the 1996 municipal elections. Moreover, it lost about 40 cities and towns to the opposition. In the Santiago mayor's race, Lavín, who had narrowly lost the presidency just nine months earlier, handily defeated Marta Larraechea, wife of former President Frei, 62% to 28%. The *Concertación* also lost control of Concepción and Viña del Mar.

The next major showdown came in the congressional elections of December 16, 2001. The *Concertación* received 51.4% of the 1.7 million votes cast, compared with 44% for the conservative coalition *Alianza para Chile* and 2.6% for the Communists. But in the tabulation of seats, the *Concertación* lost ground. Even with former President Frei assuming a lifetime Senate seat, and the continued absence of Pinochet, the election resulted in a tie in the upper chamber. In the Chamber of Deputies, the *Concertación* dropped from 70 to 63 deputies. The Christian Democrats fell from 16 to 14 Senate seats and from 38 to 24 deputies. The major winners were Lagos' *PPD*, which increased its number of

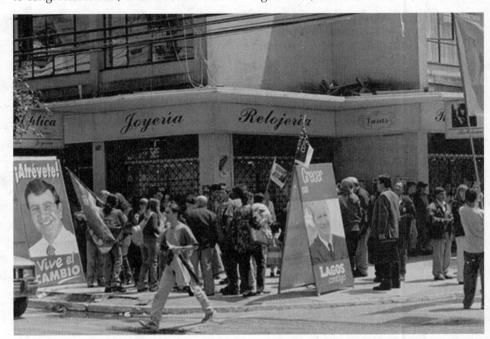

Supporters of rival presidential candidates Ricardo Lagos and Joaquín Lavín compete for space on the same street corner in downtown Puerto Montt in January 2000.
Photo by the author

senators from three to four and its number of deputies from 16 to 21; and the right-wing *UDI*, which increased its showing from 10 to 11 senators and from 24 to 35 deputies, eclipsing its coalition partner, the *RN*.

In late 2002 and early 2003, Chile was shaken by something far rarer than one of its frequent earthquakes: Corruption scandals, definitely an aberration in Chile, which unlike most other Latin American countries prides itself in the rectitude of its public institutions, both civilian and military. Indeed, Transparency International, an international corruption watchdog organization, rates Chile the 20th least corrupt country in the world.

First, in September, a newspaper exposé alleged that a cabal of officers from the Pinochet era was actively interfering in the investigation of human rights abuses. Revelations that a mid-ranking air force officer had in fact destroyed evidence of such abuses led to the resignation in October of General Patricio Ríos, commander of the air force. It was hailed as a major victory for civilian authority, which still lacked the constitutional power to fire officers.

Then, in November, a deputy transportation minister was charged with accepting a $21,000 bribe (in other countries, a $21,000 bribe would not even raise eyebrows) and four other officials were arrested. The Lagos government meekly acknowledged the apparent wrongdoing. The influence-peddling scandal exploded even louder in January 2003 when the Supreme Court stripped five *Concertación* members of the Chamber of Deputies of their legislative immunity amid allegations that they had been instrumental in channeling lucrative government contracts to companies in exchange for campaign contributions. Among those implicated was Juan Pablo Letelier, a Socialist deputy and son of Orlando Letelier, the exiled former cabinet minister assassinated by Pinochet's intelligence service in a car bombing in Washington in 1976. One other deputy was a Socialist, two were Christian Democrats and one was from Lagos' *PPD*.

In January 2003, Chile suddenly found itself in the world spotlight when it assumed one of the rotating seats on the 15-member U.N. Security Council just as debate began over the proposed U.S. resolution to authorize the use of force against Iraq. Chile steadfastly opposed the war resolution, straining relations with the United States, with which it had just concluded a long-sought free-trade agreement (see Economy).

Another indicator of how far Chile has come since the 1973 coup came in March 2003 with the election of Isabel Allende, daughter of the late Marxist president, as president of the Chamber of Deputies. She

is a distant cousin of her namesake, the famous novelist Isabel Allende (see Culture).

By late 2003, polls suggested that Lavín could well win the next presidential contest in 2005. But suddenly, it came the opposition's turn to confront a scandal. If corruption scandals are rare in Chile, lurid sex scandals are even rarer. In October, police arrested a wealthy, politically connected gymnasium owner, Claudio Spiniak, and charged him with operating a pedophile ring in which street children of both sexes were procured to provide pleasure for his friends at orgiastic parties.

At first, it seemed like just a sensational news story. But then Deputy Pía Guzmán of the *RN*, a children's rights advocate, declared at a news conference that three senators were among those who frequented Spiniak's parties, two from the *UDI* and one from the *Concertación*, although she declined to name them. Guzman's allegation caused a rift between the *RN*'s president, Sebastián Piñera, and Pablo Longueira, the *UDI* president. Longueira lashed out wildly at the media and against Guzmán, claiming the scandal was all a plot to undermine the *UDI*. The squabbling between Longueira and Piñera became so caustic that in December Lavín took the bold, and risky, step of announcing that he would pursue a presidential candidacy independent of the two parties.

Meanwhile, *"el Caso Spiniak"* became a veritable media circus, which this author witnessed first-hand during an eight-day visit to Chile in December. Political columnists and think-tank analysts began speculating on the damage the schism between the two conservative coalition partners may have on Lavín.

By early 2004, polls showed Lavín losing ground to two female cabinet ministers seen as potential *Concertación* candidates: Defense Minister Michelle Bachelet of the Socialist Party, and Foreign Minister Soledad Alvear, a Christian Democrat.

History was made in May 2004 when the Congress finally passed, and Lagos signed into law, a bill legalizing divorce in Chile, the last Latin American country to prohibit it.

Recent Developments

Still stunned by the Spiniak scandal, Chileans were shocked again in August 2004 when a U.S. Senate committee report alleged that the Washington-based Riggs Bank had allowed Pinochet and his wife to illegally stash $8 million in accounts there from 1994–2002. Although most Chileans had come to accept the reality that Pinochet was the intellectual author of the human rights abuses committed during his regime, it was widely believed, even by some of his opponents, that he was per-

sonally honest. The Chilean government quickly compared the amount of money Pinochet had stashed abroad and the amount he claimed for taxes; they didn't add up, and the government sued him for back taxes. In September, Pinochet's longtime nemesis, Spanish Judge Baltasar Garzón (see the Pinochet Case), charged the Pinochets and eight others with money laundering. The Chilean government, meanwhile, froze $5 million of Pinochet's assets. Pinochet, whose lawyers had been arguing that he was not mentally competent to stand trial, was lucid enough in February 2005 to offer to pay the government $5 million in back taxes in the hopes of having the freeze lifted. The government rejected the offer, an appeals court upheld the freeze, and the investigation is ongoing under Judge Sergio Muñoz, who also investigated the Spiniak scandal.

An institutional change of historic proportions occurred in October 2004 when the opposition-controlled Senate agreed to reform Pinochet's 1980 constitution to abolish the eight appointed senators, to repeal the provision giving former presidents Senate seats for life and to give the president the power enjoyed in other democracies to remove the heads of the armed forces. Still in place, however, is the double-member district system that guarantees the opposition virtual parity in both houses. The Chamber of Deputies, as expected, also approved the reforms, which should take effect in late 2005.

Virtually as historic was the remarkable statement issued in November by General Juan Emilio Cheyre, commander of the army, acknowledging for the first time the army's institutional responsibility for the "morally unacceptable actions of the past." Lagos praised the army's decision, and said it represented the army's "integration into today's democratic Chile." A presidential commission had interviewed 35,000 people and issued a definitive report in December 2004 in which the government admitted that torture was state policy during the military regime and that 28,000 people had been tortured. Chile, it seemed, was finally beginning to come to terms with its past and to heal old wounds.

Lagos hosted the annual summit of the Asia-Pacific Economic Cooperation (APEC) group in November 2004, and he called for a free-trade agreement by 2020 of the 21 signatories, which represent 60% of the world's economy. Lagos had an amicable meeting in La Moneda with President Bush during the summit, but the summit was marred later by a scuffle between Chilean security guards and Bush's Secret Service agents before a dinner for the heads of state and their wives. Bush personally intervened to escort his agents into the dinner in violation of Chilean security procedures.

Chile

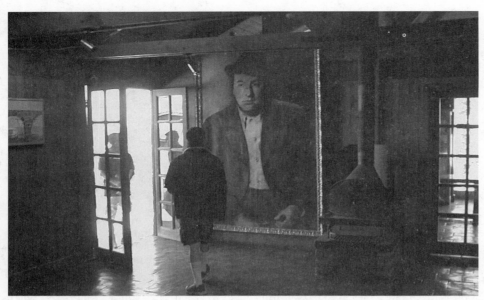

A visitor to the Pablo Neruda museum adjacent to his home in Isla Negra gazes at a larger-than-life portrait of the Nobel-laureate poet.
Photo by the author

The incident was broadcast on television, offending the sensibilities of Chileans.

Responding to opposition complaints that Foreign Minister Alvear and Defense Minister Bachelet were campaigning for president on company time, Lagos replaced both of them in September 2004. Polls have consistently shown Bachelet, a physician and a Socialist who was once jailed during the military regime, beating all possible opponents, including Lavín. Nonetheless, on October 31 the *Concertación* made its poorest showing to date in municipal elections. In the popular vote, it led the opposition coalition *Alianza* 45% to 39%, and it won 199 of the 345 municipal governments. Although the government claimed the elections were a triumph, it was the first time the *Concertación* had failed to poll a majority in municipal elections, and its six-point winning margin was half of what it was in 2000. Moreover, the *Alianza* retained the mayoralty of Santiago under the candidacy of Raúl Alcaíno, whom Lavín had hand-picked as his successor. Lavín decided not to run so he could focus on his presidential candidacy.

Two separate polls in April 2005 gave Bachelet 45% and 43%, Lavín 25% and 23%, and Alvear 14% and 11%. Suddenly, two major developments in May changed the electoral landscape—perhaps permanently. On May 14, the long-simmering opposition rivalry between the *UDI* and *RN* came to a head. Instead of endorsing Lavín's candidacy again as expected, *RN* abruptly voted to run its leader, Sebastián Piñera, as its candidate. On May 24, Alvear dropped out of the race, assuring that Bachelet would be the *Concertación* candi-date. The split in the opposition increases the likelihood that the election will be thrown into a runoff (see The Future).

Culture: One of Spain's least-developed colonies, since independence Chile has made cultural contributions far out of proportion to its size, particularly in literature. During the 19th century, Chile's intellectual climate produced not only outstanding writers but attracted others seeking greater freedom of expression. Two outstanding examples are Venezu-ela's Andrés Bello, whose statue stands in front of the University of Chile, which he founded, and Argentina's Domingo Faustino Sarmiento, who spent several years in exile as editor of *El Mercurio* during the dictatorship of Juan Manuel de Rosas in his native land. During this era Chile produced a number of its own realist prose writers, the best known of whom was probably the novelist Alberto Blest Gana, author of such enduring classics as *El niño que enloqueció de amor.* The late 19th century also produced a golden age in art, though it was heavily influenced by contemporary French impressionism.

In the 20th century, Chile enjoyed the distinction of being the only Latin American country to have produced two Nobel Prize-winning poets, Lucía Godoy Alcayaga (1886–1957) and Naftalí Reyes (1904–73). But the world does not remember them by the names with which they were born; it remembers them as Gabriela Mistral and Pablo Neruda. Both achieved international acclaim, and both represented Chile abroad for a time as diplomats. Mistral taught for several years in the United States. Their verse has been translated into several languages, and Neruda especially has become a global icon. The centennial of his birth on July 12, 2004, was marked by observances in Chile and throughout the Spanish-speaking world. His home overlooking the Pacific at Isla Negra is a popular pilgrimage destination for his admirers.

Chile's poetic tradition remains strong. Gonzalo Rojas, a contemporary of Neruda's, received Spain's prestigious Cer-

A wooden, totem-like sculpture titled *"Participación"* by Roberto Pohlhammer frames the Chilean Congress building in Valparaiso.
Photo by the author

104

vantes Prize in Literature in December 2003 at the age of 85. Another Chilean poet, Jorge Edwards, won the award several years earlier.

Two of Chile's best-known prose writers today are the novelist Isabel Allende, a distant cousin of the Marxist president, who now lives in California, and Ariel Dorfman. Two of Allende's novels, *La casa de los espiritus,* and *De amor y sombras,* were adapted for the English-language films *The House of the Spirits* and *Of Love and Shadows.* Dorfman's play, *La muerte y la doncella,* was adapted for the U.S. movie *Death and the Maiden.*

Probably the premier figure in music in the 20th century was the internationally renowned concert pianist Claudio Arrau (1903–91), who spent most of his career in Europe. In popular music, a folk singer who achieved cult-legend status much as Elvis Presley did in the United States was Violeta Parra (1917–67), like Arrau born in Chillán but who remained in Chile. Probably best remembered for the song, *Gracias a la vida,* Parra committed suicide over an unhappy love affair in 1967. Like Neruda, her likeness is still seen everywhere in Chile, and her voice or her songs remain popular throughout the Hispanic world.

Chile's folklore is grounded in the tradition of the *huaso,* a trans-Andean version of Argentina's gaucho. Its guitar-based music is similar to Mexican ranchero. Distinctly Chilean, however, is the national folk dance, the *cueca,* which traditionally is performed in conjunction with Chilean independence day on September 18 but is performed in touristy cafes year-round.

Chile's reputation as a haven for political and artistic expression disappeared during the 1973–90 military regime. Many of its own artistic, literary and musical figures were either killed or exiled. One of Chile's best-known popular singers, Victor Jara, was killed in the Santiago stadium after the 1973 coup. Film director Miguel Littín fled to Cuba. After 1990 many such artists returned, but a new generation emerged, less tied to the Marxist traditions of its predecessors. A promising young film director is Ricardo Larraín, whose 1991 movie, *La frontera,* won international acclaim.

Television came to Chile in 1960, but rather than the first stations being private or government-owned as in other Latin American countries, the first three stations were put on the air by the University of Chile, Catholic University of Santiago and Catholic University of Valparaíso; these universities still operate the stations today. The government launched *TV Nacional* in 1967. It wasn't until the early 1990s that the first two private franchises were awarded. Chilean television has become increasingly less dependent on for-eign programming and has produced a number of creditable programs of its own, some of which are exported to other Latin American countries.

Chile was the birthplace of the Latin American press. The region's first regularly published newspaper, *La Aurora de Chile,* appeared in 1810 and lasted nearly a decade. The press used to print it is on display in the National Library. Chile also is the home of the oldest continually published newspaper in Latin America, *El Mercurio,* which began as a weekly in Valparaiso in 1837, became a daily a few years later, and began publishing in Santiago in 1900. Today six dailies are published in the capital, and the provincial press also flourishes.

Economy: Few countries in the world have been whipsawed as violently from one political or economic extreme to another as has Chile. The country was long dependent on copper for foreign exchange, which as late as the 1970s still accounted for 60 percent of exports. As with Bolivia's dependence on tin, fluctuations in the world copper market often led to recessions in Chile. Moreover, the copper mines, as well as many of the country's utilities, were owned by foreign corporations, a fact that provided the Communist and Socialist parties with election-year ammunition. The elder Eduardo Frei tried to steer Chile on a middle course between Marxism and capitalism in the 1960s, an effort rewarded by President Lyndon Johnson, who lent Chile substantial foreign aid. Frei's halfway economic and social reforms proved of limited success, however, and in the end were criticized by the right as too radical and by the left as inadequate.

Gabriela Mistral

The result was the narrow minority victory of Salvador Allende's Popular Unity coalition in 1970, which jerked the country abruptly to the left. Allende quickly nationalized the copper mines and utilities, moves that were applauded even by Allende's conservative opponents at first because of nationalist pride. But signing a decree nationalizing an industry is one thing; running it efficiently and profitably proved to be quite another. The result was one of the many economic disasters of the Allende regime. Another was land reform, through the breaking up of the huge *latifundias* of wealthy and often absentee owners. On the surface, such reform seemed a long-overdue application of social justice. In reality, it destroyed agricultural operations that often were operating well, replacing them with small communal plots which were not commercially useful and run by peasants with little or no knowledge of efficient agricultural techniques. Marxist distribution policies also resulted in severe, Cuban-

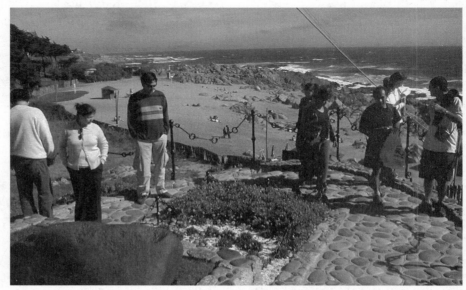

Visitors pay their respects at the graves of Pablo Neruda and his third wife, Matilde Urrutia, at his home overlooking the Pacific at Isla Negra. *Photo by the author*

Chile

style shortages, which eroded what little confidence the regime still enjoyed. To compound its woes, the regime was beset by hyperinflation of 1,000 percent annually. It was with the country on the verge of social and economic chaos that the military intervened on September 11, 1973.

The military government of General Pinochet moved quickly to restore order, and it reversed virtually every policy of the Marxist experiment. Land holdings were restored to their original owners, although a new homesteading law was implemented to provide land to small farmers who were able to demonstrate they planned to make it produce something beyond the basic needs of their families. For a time, nationalized industries were run by the state, but by the 1980s they were privatized.

The Pinochet government made it clear it intended a dramatic break with the past, that it would not merely restore the status quo ante Allende. With the government's encouragement, Chilean entrepreneurs began to exploit the wealth that had lured the first permanent Spanish settlers to the out-of-the-way colony: the extraordinarily rich, nitrate-laden soil. Because of the reversal of seasons in the Southern Hemisphere, Chile began exporting enormous quantities of produce to the United States, Europe and Japan during the Northern Hemisphere winter. By the time Pinochet relinquished power in 1990, agricultural exports exceeded those of copper, thus breaking the traditional dependence on that mineral. Yet, even copper began contributing to the Chilean economy as never before in the 1990s as exports from other copper-mining countries, such as Zaïre and Zambia, declined because of inefficiency and instability.

The most dramatic economic transition of the Pinochet regime, however, was the move to almost pure free-market economics. Pinochet surrounded himself with a "kitchen cabinet" of civilian economic technocrats, many of whom had been schooled under Milton Friedman at the University of Chicago. Thus, the press quickly dubbed this team of economists "los Chicago Boys." Chile withdrew from the Andean Pact in the late 1970s and slashed its high protective tariffs, which led to a flood of cheap imported goods. At the same time, government subsidies that had kept inefficient domestic industries afloat were eliminated, forcing them to sink or swim; more than a few sank. After a brief period of seeming prosperity, the new policies plunged Chile into a severe recession in 1981. Large and small industries, unable to compete with foreign imports, foundered. So did many banks. The economic crisis lasted more than three years before the new economic realities took hold.

New Chilean industries proved capable of holding their own in the international marketplace. One such example was Chile's new arms industries, born out of necessity from the cutoff of U.S. military aid because of Pinochet's human rights violations. Chilean wineries are another international marketing success story, and there even are beginning computer hardware and software industries.

By 1990, when Pinochet turned over power to Patricio Aylwin, Chile was in the midst of an economic boom. Ironically, while the new civilian government publicly reviled Pinochet for his human rights abuses, it grudgingly acknowledged the success of his free-market policies by retaining them. It was an especially bitter pill for the Socialists who were part of the governing coalition. The result, however, was an economy that for several years was the envy of Latin America—and the world. Real GDP growth between 1990 and 1997 has averaged a dazzling 8% annually, exceeding 12% in 1992 and 10% in 1995. Contributing to Chile's success, and to its attractiveness to foreign investors, are wage costs lower than Mexico's or South Asia's and an educated workforce; the literacy rate is 96%, compared with Brazil's 83%. In addition to robust growth, inflation was trimmed to 6% and unemployment to 4%. Chile also is widely admired for its private pension system, implemented during the Pinochet era and continued since, which has provided retirees far greater returns than the government's social security system. Even U.S. congressmen have been eyeing Chile's retirement system as a possible model.

Chile is an associate member of the four-nation *Mercosur* free-trade pact (Argentina, Brazil, Uruguay and Paraguay), but because its tariff policies differ so sharply from the other four, it has opted against full membership for the moment. Chile was expected to become the fourth member of NAFTA. President Eduardo Frei discussed the issue with President Clinton during a state visit to Washington in February 1997, but his pitch to the U.S. Congress was to a mostly empty chamber. The two presidents discussed the issue again during Clinton's visit to Santiago the following October. But in late 1997 the Republican-controlled U.S. Congress denied Clinton's request for "fast-track" trade authority, which effectively scuttled Chile's membership. Still, Chile already has free-trade agreements with the other two NAFTA members, Canada and Mexico, and the three countries have greatly expanded their trade.

A major success story in recent years has been wine, long recognized for its quality wine exports skyrocketed 5,000%, from $10.9 million in 1985 to $526 million

in 1999, accounting for 5.4% of total exports. The trend, though plateauing, continues upward, as large new tracts in the central region are planted with grapes.

In 1997, the economy became a victim of its own success. Frei was twice forced to raise interest rates to prevent the economy from overheating and to keep inflation under control. Two unforeseen external factors soon helped cool down the economy: a drop in the price of copper, which despite diversification still accounts for 42% of export earnings, from $1.19 to 75 cents a pound, and the October market panic in Asia, which buys about a third of Chile's exports.

The fallout of the Asian market crisis was still being felt in 1998. In September, Frei addressed the nation and announced that the 1999 budget would increase only 1.5% in real terms and called on the private sector to restrict pending. Frei predicted a 5% rise in GDP for 1998 and only 3.8% for 1999, but that was before the Brazilian market meltdowns of September 1998 and January 1999. Chile weathered that crisis better than Argentina, Venezuela or Mexico, but Frei's prediction for 1998 still fell short; the growth rate turned out to be only 3.3%, compared with the steamroller of 7.1% in 1997 and 7.2% in 1996. Worse still, the economy shrank 2.8% in the last quarter of 1998 and 2.3% in the first quarter of 1999 compared with the same quarters the previous years, meaning Chile officially was in recession for the first time in 15 years.

Year-end figures for 1999 hit just as Chileans were voting in the two rounds of the presidential election, and the recession almost proved the undoing of the ruling *Concertación*. Real GDP declined by 2.7% compared with 1998, when it had grown by 3.3%, while unemployment leaped from 6% to 11% and per capita income fell slightly from $5,100 to $5,000. Reflecting the recession, inflation was only 2.4%, compared with 4.7% the year before.

President Ricardo Lagos of the *Concertación* had reason to celebrate his first year in office: real GDP growth snapped back from the negative column to a healthy 4.3% for 2000, later revised to 5.4%; it was up 4.0% in 2001 but only 2.1% in 2002, reflecting the economic crisis in neighboring Argentina and the recession in the United States, the leading market for its exports.

Like Brazil's Fernando Henrique Cardoso, the one-time socialist Lagos underwent a dramatic conversion to free-market principles and has followed an economic course that has been so conservative that the opposition has had little to quibble with. He traveled to Quebec in April 2001 for the third Summit of the Americas and embraced the concept of a Free Trade Area of the Americas. While the U.S. Congress hesitated at approving a free-trade agreement with Chile, Lagos concluded a $9 billion free-trade accord with the 15-nation European Union in May 2002, which was signed the following November. Once President Bush received fast-track trade authority in 2002, the United States and Chile resumed free-trade talks that had begun 11 years earlier under Bush's father. After reaching some difficult compromises over environmental issues and capital investment outflows among others, the two sides finally reached an agreement in December 2002. The $6 billion trade agreement, seen as an important step toward a Free Trade Area of the Americas, was signed in Miami on June 6, 2003. In February 2003, Chile also concluded a $1.1 billion free-trade agreement with South Korea. In 2004 he was seeking to conclude similar deals with China, Singapore and New Zealand.

Growth for 2003 was 3.3%, and in 2004 it doubled to 6.1%, the best showing since 1997, largely because of a high international market price for copper. Inflation has declined steadily in recent years, from 4.5% in 2000 to 3.5% in 2001 to 2.8% in 2002. In 2003, it was only 1.1%, the lowest rate since 1935. Unemployment, however, has remained steady at 9% in 2004.

The Future: This author covered the 1989, 1993 and 1999–2000 presidential elections as a free-lance journalist and spent a semester in Chile as a Fulbright Scholar in 1991. In 1989, I had been struck by the lingering hatred between right and left, even by Chileans who had been born after the Allende period. The bitterness I heard in conversations with scores of Chileans from all classes and political persuasions reminded me of the century-long resentment of Southerners after the U.S. Civil War, which I experienced as a boy in Texas.

Now, at last, things seem to be changing. On my visit to Santiago in December 2003, I saw something that once would have been unthinkable: a statue of Salvador Allende in the *Plaza de la Constitución*, right across the street from the Moneda, where he died.

The army's dramatic confession of its sins during the dictatorship, and the government's come-clean report on torture, were transcendental. The money laundering charges against Pinochet have sullied what little remained of his reputation. If he makes it, he will turn 90 in November 2005. His passing, when it finally comes, should accelerate national reconciliation even more.

For the past several years, I have written in this section that even if Chileans move beyond the bitterness of the past, they must still purge the antidemocratic elements from Pinochet's 1980 constitution, such as the unelected "institutional senators" and the president's lack of authority to fire the heads of the armed forces. Now, those reforms are in the works, with the cooperation of the conservative opposition, which also is making concerted efforts to erase its past association with the military regime.

Chile elects its next president in December 2005. Polls show the favorite to be former Defense Minister Michelle Bachelet, 53, a doctor and a Socialist who was once tortured during the dictatorship. She did what was once unimaginable given her past—establish an excellent working relationship with the armed forces she led. Perhaps it was because she herself is the daughter of an air force general—even if he did oppose the 1973 coup and was arrested and tortured to death. Her standing in the polls in this conservative, *macho* society is even more remarkable because she is an atheist, the mother of three children by two different men and is separated from her husband.

The *Concertación's* primary is in July, but the withdrawal of former Foreign Minister Soledad Alvear, a Christian Democrat, in May clinched Bachelet's nomination. With the shifting winds of Chilean politics, Joaquín Lavín of the ultra-concervative Independent Democratic Union *(UDI)* was once favored to win the presidency on his second attempt, as happens frequently in Latin America. Then came the Spiniak scandal, from which the *Alianza* seems never to have recovered, and the dramatic and unexpected defection of the *UDI*'s coalition partner, National Renewal *(RN)*, which now is backing the candidacy of its keader, Sebastián Piñera. One player will not be on the field this go-around: Gladys Marín of the Communist Party. She died of cancer in March 2005.

The winds could shift again by December. Many of Alvear's fellow Christian Democrats will no doubt prefer the moderate Piñera, who unlike Lavín is not identified with the Pinochet dictatorship, to Bachelet, a Socialist, an atheist and a separated single mother. The real race will be between Lavín and Piñera to make it into the runoff with Bachelet. If Piñera does make it into the runoff by the grace of disaffected Christian Democrats, Lavín's disgruntled voters then will have to choose between backing a man they regard as a spoiler if not a traitor, or staying home; voting for Bachelet is not an option for them.

Of course, Bachelet could score a first-round victory over both of them. With a booming economy, (growth in 2004 was 6.1%), voters may decide not to rock the boat. No matter the outcome, the 2005 election will be a milestone: Chile's first woman president, or the *Concertación's* first presidential defeat.

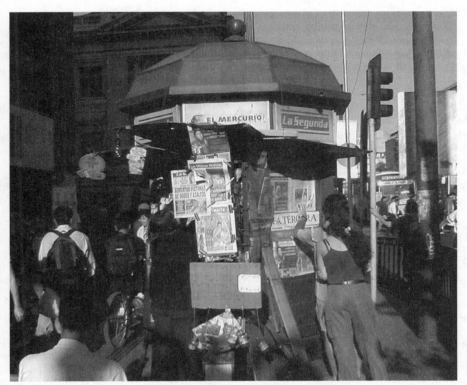

The ubiquitous news kiosks in Santiago and all Chilean cities and towns boast a wide variety of daily and weekly newspapers and magazines. *Photo by the author*

The Republic of Colombia

Area: 439,405 square miles.

Population: 45 million (2004 estimate).

Capital City: Bogotá (Pop. 7 million, estimated).

Climate: The lowlands are generally hot, with heavy rainfall except for the Guajira Peninsula, which is arid. Highland climate varies with altitude, becoming quite temperate and pleasant in the higher elevations.

Neighboring Countries: Venezuela (East and Northeast); Brazil (Southeast); Peru and Ecuador (South); Panama (Northwest).

Official Language: Spanish.

Other Principal Tongues: Isolated Indian dialects.

Ethnic Background: *Mestizo* (mixed European and Indian, 58%), European (20%) Mulatto (mixed Black and White, 14%), Negro (4%), Mixed Negro-Indian and Indian (4%).

Principal Religion: Roman Catholic Christianity.

Chief Commercial Products: Refined cocaine, a technically illegal export worth over $10 billion U.S., coffee, petroleum, cotton, tobacco, sugar, textiles, bananas, fresh-cut flowers.

Currency: Peso.

Gross Domestic Product: U.S. $83 billion in 2004 ($1,844 per capita). This does not include money from drug trafficking, which, if included, would increase this figure by an estimated 25%.

Former Colonial Status: Spanish Crown Colony (1525–1819)

Independence Date: July 20, 1810.

Chief of State: Alvaro Uribe Vélez, (b. July 4, 1952), president (since August 7, 2002).

National Flag: Yellow, blue and red horizontal stripes.

Colombia is the fourth largest state in South America and the only one with both Atlantic and Pacific coasts. The high Andes mountains divide the country into four ranges from the *Pasto Knot* just north of the border with Ecuador and occupy about two fifths of the land. To the east of the mountains are the great, seemingly endless plains (*llanos*) and the western tip of the Guiana Highland. The majority of Colombia's population is concentrated in the green valleys and mountain basins that lie between the ranges of the Andes.

Eleven of Colombia's 14 urban centers are in the mountain valleys; the remainder are on the Caribbean coast. The vast plains along the base of the eastern range contain cattle ranches, but the extensions of the plains into the jungle-filled Amazon Basin are almost unpopulated. The northern ends of the mountain valleys, which fan out to the Caribbean coast, are wet, hot and almost uninhabited.

Because travel between the populated areas is difficult, Colombia's people live in quite distinctive communities that vary from white, Indian and black populations to combinations of mixed ancestry. The rivers of Colombia have been its most important means of communication—the Magdalena is navigable for nearly 1,000 miles and still is the principal means of transporting cargo to and from the vicinity of Bogotá. The second great river is the Cauca, not important for transportation but for furnishing water for irrigation and power for industry in the Cauca Valley. In recent years a major construction program, similar to that of the Tennessee Valley project, has been undertaken to further develop the Cauca Valley's resources. As in all countries near the Equator, altitude is the principal factor, modifying an otherwise oppressive climate. Throughout the country rainfall is ample—there are no seasons applicable to the whole country. Summer is generally considered the dry season and the rainy season is winter; however, in some regions along the Pacific, rains, either violent thunderstorms or warm, steady showers, fall every day in the year. From sea level to

3,000 feet the climate is tropical; from 3,000 to 6,500 feet it is temperate; above 6,500 feet it is chilly. Crops are grown at elevations up to 10,000 feet, but above this level trees thin out and tall peaks are covered by snow year around.

History: The Spaniards first discovered the coast of Colombia about 1500, but the Indians proved so hostile that the explorers quickly withdrew. The first settlement was later established at Santa Marta in 1525, and Cartagena was subsequently founded in 1533. The interior was not penetrated until 1536 when Gonzalo Jiménez de Quesada explored the Magdalena River seeking its source. Climbing the eastern range, he found the Chibcha Indians in several of the mountain valleys, conquered them and founded Bogotá, the present capital. The Chibchas were sedentary, agricultural people who had developed a fairly high level of civilization.

More or less simultaneously, an expedition from Ecuador under Sebastián de Belalcazar discovered the Cauca Valley and founded Pasto, Popayán and Cali in 1536. Nicolaus de Federmann led an expedition toward the site of Bogotá from Venezuela.

Belalcazar reached Bogotá in 1538 and came into contact with Federmann in 1539. Similar to other conquests, the period of settlement was marked by conflict among the various groups of conquerors. Sugarcane, wheat, cattle, sheep and horses were introduced by the Spaniards and a royal government was established at Bogotá in 1550 for the administration of most of the land in modern Colombia.

Gold was discovered in Antioquía about 1550, rapidly reducing further interest in the agricultural regions around Bogotá and Cali. Almost simultaneously with the start of gold shipments to Spain, English and Dutch pirates started their attacks on Spanish shipping and the Caribbean ports. However, the interior of the country was at peace and, unmolested, gradually developed. Descendants of the conquerors amassed large estates, worked by Indian or black slaves and established a semi-feudal system of agriculture that still persists in the remote parts of Colombia.

During the colonial period, what is modern-day Colombia was part of the viceroyalty of New Granada. The movement for independence from Spain started in the 1790s following publication of the French Revolution's Declaration of the Rights of Man. This was not a popular movement, but rather one of young intellectuals from the aristocratic families of Bogotá. Revolts erupted in Venezuela in 1796 and 1806, followed by an abortive attempt to set up an independent government at Bogotá. However, the provinces were divided and the Spanish reestablished control. When news reached New Granada in 1810 that Spain's King Fernando VII had been deposed by Napoleon, the restive creoles revolted again. This time they seized Cartagena, then town after town in the Cauca and Magdalena valleys. On July 20, 1810, today observed as independence day, the *cabildo* in Bogotá arrested the viceroy and assumed control. Independence came after eight years of see-saw warfare in which Simón Bolívar and his generals, José Antonio Páez, Francisco de Paula Santander and Antonio José de Sucre victoriously marched and countermarched across Colombia, Venezuela and Ecuador. Following the defeat of the Spanish forces at the Battle of Boyacá, the Republic of Gran Colombia was proclaimed December 17, 1819, incorporating Venezuela, Colombia and Ecuador in a political union.

The allies in the war for independence divided over the form of government that should be established for the new state; Bolívar wanted a strong central government while Páez and Santander pressed for a federation of sovereign states. Later, this discord would be expressed by two political parties which developed and

Bolívar crossing the Andes

which still control the country today: the Conservatives, in favor of central government and close relations with the Catholic Church, opposed by the Liberals, favoring a federation of states and separation of church and state. The Republic of Gran Colombia lasted only 10 years. Venezuela separated from the union in 1829 and Ecuador declared its independence a year later; the remaining provinces took the name of New Granada. The name Colombia was restored in 1861 as the United States of Colombia and became the Republic of Colombia in 1886.

From its inception, the new republic was torn with dissent. Bolívar sought to create a "Great Colombia;" Santander believed there was little hope for uniting diverse people with few common interests into an effective union. Dissent grew during the period of the wars of liberation of Peru and Bolivia (1822–1824). In 1826, Bolívar assumed dictatorial power. By 1830, opposition to him led to revolt; the republic was broken up and the *el Libertador* died on his way into exile.

Santander became the actual founder of Colombia. Recalled from exile in 1832, he brought a degree of order from the chaos of war. Despite his own championing of democratic ideas, he imposed a strict discipline on the country, organized its finances and set up central government services with an iron hand. He and his successor pursued moderate policies concerning the church and the differences between the Conservatives and Liberals on the form of government. However, the radicals of both sides, as well as regional inter-

ests, sought their goals by force of arms; from 1839 to 1842 civil war was waged intermittently by constantly changing forces. By 1840 the gap between the Conservative and Liberal views had widened; the Liberals were characterized as blasphemous and disorderly while the Conservatives gained power as defenders of order, godliness and good government. The Conservatives (as usual during this period) represented an alliance of the landowners, the church and the army. From 1840 to 1880, the two parties alternated in power, each using its position to persecute the other and generally provoking recurrent strife bordering on civil war. In spite of this turmoil, by 1880 the economy had broadened, the population had doubled since independence, communication and trade were improved and Colombia had few international problems.

The election of Rafael Núñez in 1880 marked a major change in Colombia's history. A long-time Liberal, he united the moderates of his party with the more moderate Conservatives and formed the National Party. Surviving another Conservative-Liberal civil war in 1884–85, Núñez secured adoption of Colombia's 10th constitution and brought order to the country. The Liberal regime became progressively conservative and subsequently dictatorial—the privileges of the church were restored, peace was maintained and political dissent was suppressed. His death in 1899 left the government in the hands of conservatives without a leader capable of avoiding the consequences of 20 years of repression. Civil war raged for

Colombia

three years as Liberals sought to oust Conservatives. The so-called Thousand Day War left more than 100,000 dead, widespread destruction, a ruined economy and a demoralized people. These losses were soon followed by the revolt of the province of Panama in 1903 (arranged by the United States; see Panama).

The Colombians demanded a leader capable of reuniting the country and rebuilding the economy. A Conservative seemed to fit the bill; a proud and energetic man, Rafael Reyes assumed dictatorial powers. His five-year term was stormy—despite an empty treasury and a bitter people, he was able to reorganize the national finances, restore Colombia's credit, initiate the construction of roads and railroads and encourage the development of the coffee industry. Opposition forced his resignation in 1909.

Five Conservative presidents followed him (1909–1930). This era was marked by advances in political realism and cooperation. Elections became more honest, a semblance of a two-party government was developed and censorship of the press was reduced. During the same period, the economy improved, production rose, petroleum was discovered and business grew with the boom years of the 1920s. The ready money brought on an expansion of industry: railroads and power plants were built and coffee production expanded. The affluence also corrupted public officials and led to over expansion and inflation.

The break in world prices in 1929 associated with the rampant depression produced a financial disaster which discredited the Conservatives, and in 1930 a Liberal government came to power.

The peaceful transfer of power in 1930 was in marked contrast to the violence found in other parts of Latin America and to Colombia's past. So, too, the Liberals of 1930 were quite distinct from their predecessors. Most of the issues which had produced the civil wars of the previous century were dead or no longer important. The Liberal Party of 1930 was interested in economic and social reforms to protect the interests of labor and of the growing middle class.

The first of three elected Liberal presidents who would govern for the next 16 years, Enrique Olaya Herrera (1930–34), satisfied reform-minded Liberals while his moderation reassured Conservatives. The second, Alfonso López (1934–38), a wealthy publisher and intellectual, was far more outspoken and dynamic. To secure needed social reforms, he implemented radical changes in the constitution that frightened Conservatives. However, he tempered their fears with more moderate legislation. His successor, Eduardo Santos (1938–42), publisher of the influential Liberal daily *El Tiempo*, moved the country sharply back to the right, bringing denunciation from López and creating the first signs of the growing schism between the left and right wings of the party.

López returned to power in the 1942 election and brought the country into World War II on the side of the Allies, much to the displeasure of pro-Axis Conservatives and neutralists within his own party. Compounding López's problems, a corruption scandal erupted during his second administration that embroiled members of his own family. Increasingly, moderate Liberals joined with Conserva-

tives in Congress to block his proposals. There were numerous plots against him, and he faced discontent from underpaid government employees. Under mounting pressure, he resigned in 1945 and was replaced by an interim president until the 1946 election.

La Violencia

The Liberal split led to the election of a Conservative, Mariano Ospina Pérez, in 1946 with a plurality of 42% of the vote. A timid man in the wrong job at the wrong time, he was incapable of controlling either the growing militancy of the Liberal left or the fanaticism of the crypto-fascists in his own party. Bloodshed erupted between elements of these two political extremes, and there were revolts in several departments.

The murder in April 1948 of Jorge Eliécer Gaitán, a popular leader of the Liberal left, touched off a riot in the capital of such violence that the term *Bogotazo* was coined to describe a situation in which a whole people rioted. Some 2,000 deaths resulted as mobs roamed the streets, burning, looting and shooting. The conflict spread to the country as Liberals and Conservatives fought for control of villages and rural communities. The president declared martial law and gradually restored an appearance of order. It was in this atmosphere that the elections of 1950 were held. The Liberal Party, badly split, expected trouble at the polls and stayed away; the Conservatives elected their candidate, Laureano Gómez.

President Gómez was an admirer of Franco and Hitler, and installed an ultra-rightist regime. Ruling as a dictator, he used the army and police to hunt down and exterminate the Liberals. From his regime there developed an undeclared civil war that caused an estimated 200,000 deaths and a way of life known as *La Violencia* (The Violence). In 1953, he was ousted by a military coup, and General Gustavo Rojas Pinilla was installed as president. The change, accompanied by an amnesty, brought a lull in the fighting. However, his administration proved cruel and incompetent. The sole redeeming feature of his rule was that he did not discriminate between Liberals and Conservatives, forcing these enemies to arrange a truce in order to oust him in 1957.

Democracy Takes Root

There followed a Liberal-Conservative coalition that agreed to alternate Liberal and Conservative presidents for 16 years. A Liberal, Alberto Lleras Camargo, took office on August 7, 1958. Having to cope not only with the conflict between the par-

Coffee plantation

ties but with the equally bitter internal party strife, Lleras Camargo nonetheless succeeded in separating the political antagonists from rural bandits who were capitalizing on a continuing reign of terror. He pursued moderate policies in social and economic matters while attempting the political union of Colombia. His moderation restored a degree of stability to Colombia, but the political party in Congress and government imposed by the coalition soon showed its basic weakness. The government, lacking a majority, was unable to enact any of the needed reform measures; the people, unable to influence their destiny by political effort, lost interest in the democratic process.

His Conservative successor in 1962, Guillermo León Valencia, unable to obtain legislative cooperation for even the routine functions of government, was forced to rule by decree.

The Liberal regime that followed from 1966 to 1970 was forced to use the same system. Under President Carlos Lleras Restrepo, Colombia enjoyed a comfortable rate of economic growth and continued decline in traditional rural banditry and violence that had racked the nation for nearly three decades. The Liberal-Conservative truce, known as the National Unity Agreement, served to postpone renewed competition between the political factions. Misael Pastrana Borrero, a Conservative, was elected by a slim 1.5% majority over former dictator Rojas Pinilla in the 1970 elections. A politically unknown Conservative economist, Pastrana sought to diversify the nation's farm-based economy. Although exports soared and certain sectors of the economy improved, runaway inflation and increasing unemployment became major issues in the 1974 election campaign.

With the National Unity Agreement expiring at the presidential level in 1974, Colombians voted in the nation's first open election in more than 20 years. Alfonso López Michelsen, a Liberal, was elected with 52% of the vote. In second place was the Conservative candidate, while Rojas Pinilla's daughter ran a strong third as an independent. Although the Liberals also had won large majorities in both houses of Congress, the Constitution required that all appointive offices be divided equally between the Liberals and Conservatives until 1978; this requirement was extended informally through 1986.

To carry out his program, the president declared a "national economic emergency" just five weeks after taking office in mid-1974. Permitted under a 1968 law, the action allowed López to bypass the slow-moving Congress and institute by decree certain economic reforms. Highlights of the plan included raising the

daily wage by 40% to $1.50 a day, imposing a hefty tax increase on the wealthy and on luxury imports and instituting a special tax on idle farmland to encourage greater agricultural output. In addition, various steps were taken to cut the inflation rate from 30% in 1974 to an estimated 20% in 1976.

These bold economic measures met stiff opposition. Conservatives charged that the new business and personal taxes were causing a recession and discouraged new investments. On the other extreme, leftists demanded even more radical change, particularly in the rural sector. The top 4% of the population owned 68% of the farmland while the bottom 73% of the people held just 7%, consisting of small plots that provide a living only for a small family. Largely as a result of such a wide difference in living conditions, fully two thirds of the nation's youth suffered from malnutrition.

During his final year in office, President López Michelsen maintained a firm grip on the presidency—even though his administration was troubled by labor unrest, corruption charges, cabinet shuffles, guerrilla terrorism, high unemployment and inflation.

The Liberal Party candidate, Julio César Turbay Ayala, defeated his Conservative opponent in 1978 by a mere 140,000 votes. He immediately implemented his law-and-order promises by ordering an all-out military campaign against political violence, drug smuggling and general lawlessness.

Harsher tactics against guerrillas led to worldwide charges of violation of human rights. Yet the M-19 guerrilla front continued its sensational terrorism throughout 1980: seizure of 15 diplomats, murder of an American missionary and a 300-man attack on two provincial towns punctuated violence. In a murderous shoot-out with government troops in March 1981 in which much of the M-19 high command died, more than 400 people were killed.

Although the Liberal Party captured a majority of seats in the Congress and provincial assemblies in 1982, party dissent ultimately resulted in a Conservative victory in the 1982 presidential election. The new president, Belisario Betancur, quickly adopted an internal populist policy to help the lower classes, and a foreign policy more independent of the United States. The government was able to persuade some guerrillas to become part of the lawful political process.

Return to *La Violencia*

The next several administrations found themselves trying to deal with escalating violence from guerrillas, drug traffickers

and right-wing paramilitary elements that was to make Colombia one of the most dangerous countries on Earth. President Betancur ordered a crackdown on rampant drug trafficking in 1984. The powerful Colombian drug barons retaliated against the judiciary, contributing heavily to the various guerrilla movements active in the country. When the president in turn authorized the extradition of the drug lords to the United States for trial, the cocaine producers hired guerrillas to wipe out the judges involved in such proceedings.

During the 1980s, about 100 revolutionary groups and/or coalitions were active, all dedicated to terrorism. The terrorist threat was amply illustrated in 1985 when the M-19 stormed the Palace of Justice using mortar fire and grenades. Betancur ordered the army to storm the building, resulting in the deaths of 11 Supreme Court justices together with a large group working on extradition cases. After the event, one Colombian judge said, "You either have the choice of accepting a $500,000 bribe from these people or be killed." In all, 350 judges and prosecutors were killed during the 1980s. Frozen with fear, the Colombian Supreme Court ruled the extradition treaty unconstitutional.

The next president, Virgilio Barco, a Liberal (1986–90), also declared war on the drug barons. Fearful of being extradited, the drug cartels paralyzed efforts to control leftist guerrillas. They bribed or killed uncounted local police and eluded the national police and army. Crusading journalists also were assassinated. When a leading candidate for president was gunned down, Barco responded by reinstating the extradition laws. The terrified justice minister resigned, going into hiding in the United States with her son, fearful for their lives.

However, the lives of *Los Extraditables* also was hell on Earth. They knew that the army was always in pursuit of them and they stood little chance of escaping death on the spot if caught. Anyone who saw them was capable of informing the authorities (for a suitable price). There was no point in having hundreds of millions of dollars if one cannot have the pleasure of spending them. They increasingly became interested in a trial in Colombia and the possibility that bribes and favors would produce a lenient sentence in a country-club prison. In the interim, their drug business could be operated by their lieutenants.

Disillusioned by events in the former Soviet Union and Eastern Europe, M-19 guerrillas began laying down their arms in 1989. Presidential elections were held in May 1990, and the notoriously bloodthirsty Medellín Cartel of Pablo Escobar disposed of another candidate. Yet an-

Colombia

other candidate, Carlos Pizarro, a former guerrilla commander, was assassinated by right-wing elements. Although traditional spirited rallies in the principal cities and towns were the custom, this campaign was conducted on television—it was too dangerous to venture out. Running on a promise to continue the war on drug leaders, César Gaviria of the Liberal Party won with less than a majority.

The war on the cartels was costly—there were 40 or more murders a day in Colombia. The cost of having a policeman killed was $4,000 and a judge was $20,000—pocket change for the wealthy drug barons. All officials traveled in armored vehicles in motorcades. The drug cartels proclaimed a unilateral truce in mid-1990 and the level of violence abated sharply. Gaviria did not wait for a scheduled 1991 constitutional convention: he decreed that any drug baron who surrendered and confessed would (1) not be extradited to the United States and (2) would have his Colombian jail sentence cut in half. These promises would prove to be costly.

In early 1991 several of the drug kingpins (Escobar and the Ochoa brothers) surrendered. Escobar was allowed to build his own luxurious "jail" close to Medellín, his home town. It was virtually an open house. Rated as one of the wealthiest men in the world, he enjoyed the company of 11 of his associates, claiming that the walls of the "jail" were in

place to keep his enemies out. A deal obviously had been struck.

But even these pleasant conditions bored Escobar. He started running his cocaine business from the "jail," and used it as a site for the execution of real and imagined rivals. This was too much for the government and, exasperated, it sent a government force to seize the "jail" and its prime occupant. But Escobar was forewarned by one of his agents in the police and departed in July 1992 before the force arrived. He was "at large" but in misery until December 1993, pursued not only by federal forces, but by an impromptu group of former henchmen turned into reward-seekers (the United States and Colombia had posted $8.7 million for his capture). Loosely organized, they were known as *"Pepes"* (People Persecuted by Pablo Escobar). Weary, he offered to surrender in the spring of 1993, but the terms were impossible. He hid for several weeks in Medellín in late 1993, but was located by means of a traced telephone call. He and his bodyguard "offered resistance" and were shot dead on December 2 trying to elude pursuers on the rooftop of the building in which he had hidden. His funeral was sheer pandemonium as thousands sought to pay him tribute; he had "given generously" to many people and causes during his lifetime who wished to remember him. The fact is that he had a huge surplus of money that *had* to be given away.

The reward money was divided in unknown quantities between the police and survivors of Escobar's countless victims—he always had ample money for assassinations, crude torture and bombings. He was well-known for recruiting very young boys to carry out death sentences.

After 1990, Cali replaced Medellín as the center of the cocaine with its own cartel of drug overlords, chiefly the Rodríguez Orejuela brothers. It now controls 80% of the world's cocaine production and trade. Its leadership has changed several times in theory. When jailed, the drug kingpins operate from cells and their orders are carried out by an army of lieutenants, the membership of which is constantly changing. An elaborate system of distribution and money laundering is in place and functions smoothly. The profits are enormous, and now no longer being made by distribution using small aircraft. There are ample airports in Mexico where a 747 can land and quickly unload during the wee hours of the night on a remote pad. It leaves quickly, averting interception.

This is known to U.S. authorities, who are powerless to do anything to prevent such shipments. An elaborate and sophisticated radar system is now in operation showing such flights. Mexico is now the route of transport of an estimated 70% of the cocaine entering the United States.

A new prosecutor general was appointed, Gustavo de Greiff, under the constitution adopted in 1991, with wide pow-

A view of Medellín

ers and discretion calculated to deal with the drug kingpins. He initially appeared to be a source of hope that basic changes could be made to make the law effective in dealing with the Cali Cartel, but in 1994 this turned sour (or realistic, in the opinion of some). There had been close cooperation between the U.S. authorities and his office until it became obvious that either his office had been penetrated by drug cartel informants or he was becoming too accommodating with regard to drug trafficking. When the names of witnesses were disclosed to his office in early 1994 by the United States, their close relatives were murdered.

De Greiff was no stranger to controversy during his term. He angered both U.S. Attorney General Janet Reno and many Colombian officials by suggesting that the legalization of drugs be given serious consideration. He met with three kingpins of the Cali Cartel to discuss a plea bargain whereby none of them would receive more than five years in prison—and a country-club prison at that. U.S. and Colombian officials again were dismayed when the details of the meeting leaked out. De Greiff resigned when he reached the mandatory retirement age in August 1994 and the Supreme Court named as his replacement Alfonso Valdivieso. The new special prosecutor's tenure thus began at precisely the same time as a new president's, one who was shrouded with scandal even before taking office and who never shook it off.

The Samper Presidency

Ernesto Samper, the candidate of the Liberal Party in 1994, bragged in his presidential campaign that he bore 11 bullet wounds from an assassination attempt by drug traffickers. Indeed, he had survived an attempt on his life in 1989 by the Medellín Cartel. He emerged the frontrunner in the first round of voting in May 1994, and he was elected president in the June runoff by a razor-thin margin over his Conservative opponent, Andrés Pastrana. Between his election victory and his inauguration in August, however, a series of audio tapes of telephone conversations between Samper or members of his campaign staff and kingpins of the Cali Cartel were leaked to the press, which quickly dubbed them the "narcocassettes." Thus, Samper was sworn into office under a cloud. In his first year in office, his defense minister, who had been his campaign manager, was arrested and admitted that the Samper campaign had accepted about $6 million in assistance from the Cali Cartel. Samper became a pariah to the United States, and in March 1996 the Clinton Administration revoked Colombia's certification as an ally in the war against drugs.

Samper, just midway through his term, also was under pressure at home to resign because of the embarrassing revelations. When he refused, the lower house of Congress brought impeachment charges. But in June 1996, the House of Representatives voted decisively not to remove Samper from office; even the opposition Conservatives voted by a two-vote margin against impeachment. Why? Some observers contended that the House of Representatives was fearful of the political turmoil that would result from removing a president from office. Still others believed that the Congress wanted to send a signal to the United States not to interfere in Colombia's internal affairs.

Whatever the reason, the exoneration of Samper, despite convincing evidence against him, infuriated the United States. U.S. Ambassador Myles Frechette opened an almost daily war of words, not only against the president but the Colombian government as a whole. For example, within days of the congressional vote, he accused the Colombian intelligence agency of tapping his telephone, a charge the intelligence director hotly denied. The United States took an extraordinary step in July when it revoked Samper's visa to visit the United States, a stunning rebuke of a sitting chief of state. In September, Samper was again humiliated when a stash of heroin was discovered on the presidential aircraft just as it was about to take the president to New York to address the United Nations—on the war against drugs! Authorities impounded his plane, and he had to fly to New York on a commercial aircraft. (The following May, three Colombian Air Force soldiers were

charged with having smuggled the heroin onto the aircraft.) In 1997, the Clinton Administration again refused to certify Colombia as an ally in the drug war. Still, Samper hung tough, and vowed to serve until the end of his term in 1998.

Meanwhile, Valdivieso began to enjoy some success in his campaign against the Cali Cartel. In early 1996, the Rodríguez Orejuela brothers, Gilberto and Miguel, surrendered separately to authorities and were incarcerated in La Picota, a country-club prison, to await trial. A third Cali Cartel kingpin, José Santacruz Londoño, also surrendered but later opted to escape. He subsequently was gunned down, ostensibly by a rival drug gang. In January 1997, a judge sentenced Gilberto Rodríguez Orejuela to 10½ years in prison; Miguel subsequently was sentenced to terms of 9 and 22 years. Both the U.S. and Colombian governments expressed outrage over the lightness of the sentences for men who had smuggled hundreds of tons of cocaine into the United States and other countries. The sentences were another factor in the continued decertification of Colombia as an ally in the drug war. Another major kingpin, Helmer "Pacho" Herrera, was sentenced in March 1998 to six years and eight months in prison. Herrera was murdered in his jail cell in November 1998, apparently in a contract killing by a rival drug gang.

U.S.-Colombian relations began to improve dramatically in October 1997 with the resignation of Ambassador Frechette. He was replaced in March 1998 by Curtis Warren Kammen, a career diplomat seen as far less combative than Frechette. Foreign Minister María Emma Mejía labeled

Plaza de Bolívar, Bogotá

Colombia

the change "a breath of fresh air." A month after Frechette's departure, the Colombian Congress extended an overture of its own by acceding to a long-standing U.S. request to repeal the ban on extradition of Colombian nationals. It was only half a loaf for the United States, however, because the law was not made retroactive and thus exempted the Rodríguez Orejuela brothers. Nonetheless, the thaw in bilateral relations accelerated in December 1997 when the Clinton administration lifted its ban on military aid, suspended because of alleged human rights abuses by the army and the paramilitary groups it was accused of supporting. The United States attached some peculiar strings to the $37 million it promised, however; it could be used only for operations against guerrillas suspected of dealing with narcotics traffickers, and those operations were to be confined to a classified area in the south referred to as "the Box." But the most dramatic improvement in strained relations came in February 1998, when for the first time in three years the Clinton administration "certified" Colombia as an ally in the drug war. It was certified again in 1999, 2000 and 2001.

Guerrilla Warfare Stalemates

Coupled with the Colombian government's inability to come to grips with drug trafficking has been its stalemated war against the guerrilla groups, principally the Revolutionary Armed Forces of Colombia (*FARC*) and the National Liberation Army (*ELN*). Another once-nettlesome group, *M-19*, abandoned its armed struggle to participate in the electoral system, with minimal success. The *FARC* and *ELN* continue to hold sway over vast areas of the rugged interior of the country, but with a new twist. There is increasing evidence that in the wake of the collapse of the Soviet Union the two groups have become motivated less by ideology and more by greed, and that they have become mercenary forces in the hire of the drug traffickers. As one U.S. Embassy official put it, they have become common outlaws, much as Jesse James and other former Confederate guerrillas did after the U.S. Civil War.

The engagements have been bloody, grimly reminiscent of the guerrilla warfare in Vietnam, only more protracted. More than 35,000 people, military and civilian, have been killed since the insurgency erupted in the early 1960s. The rebels have disrupted the country's vital oil pipeline to the Caribbean coast regularly, they continue to assassinate local, state and national officials, and they frequently kidnap domestic and foreign businessmen for astronomical ransoms

that help them purchase sophisticated arms on the international black market. Unlike Vietnam, however, the rebels cannot rely on the support of a foreign power any longer and lack the military strength to take Bogotá by storm, although they operate freely in its environs. What is occurring at present, in short, is a classic military stalemate.

The Colombian army suffered a major humiliation in a *FARC* attack on its base at Las Delicias in Putumayo Province in August 1996, in which 26 soldiers were killed and another 70 taken prisoner. They were held for 10 months before Samper agreed, against the bitter opposition of the army, to the ignominious conditions to demilitarize a large area of Caquetá Department and to exchange the soldiers for *FARC* prisoners. The victory was a major boost for the *FARC*'s international prestige and credibility. Samper responded to the vocal criticism of his armed forces chief by sacking him in 1997.

More embarrassments were to come. In September 1997, the army launched a major offensive, called Destructor II, with 3,000 men in the south-central region. The

military expended 84,000 rounds of ammunition and more than 300 bombs, but it killed only nine Indian civilians and 40 cows, while taking one suspected guerrilla prisoner. Then, in early October, the armed forces commander himself narrowly escaped death when guerrillas ambushed his car. The army suffered another setback in December when the *FARC* killed nine soldiers and took 18 prisoners in an attack on a mountaintop communication outpost at Cerro de Patascoy in Nariño Department.

But the worst was yet in store for the beleaguered army. During the first week of March 1998, the *FARC* launched a Tet-like offensive designed to disrupt the congressional elections. The rebels inflicted the worst defeat to date on the army in the heaviest fighting in 30 years of warfare. The brunt of the fighting took place along the Caguan River in Caquetá, near the town of El Billar. According to both sides, the combat was at close quarters, sometimes hand-to-hand. At least 83 soldiers were killed and another 61 were captured. Compounding the army's humiliation, 43 of the prisoners were members of an elite

Bogotá, Colombia

114

Colombia

counterinsurgency unit. The army claimed it was attacked by 700 rebels and killed 40 of them; the *FARC* responded that it had committed only 300 men and had lost only six dead. The truth probably was somewhere in between.

The guerrillas and the armed forces are not the only key players in this protracted guerrilla war. Another is the various right-wing paramilitary groups that have committed numerous atrocities against civilians, mostly peasants, who are suspected of rebel sympathies. International human rights groups have alleged that these groups have the tacit support of the army, which the army continues to deny. In April 1997, Carlos Castaño, leader of the most notorious of these groups, brought 5,000 paramilitary fighters together under the umbrella of the so-called United Self-Defense Forces of Colombia (*AUC*). In 1997 and 1998, the *AUC* was responsible for several civilian massacres in different departments, many of which brought reprisals from the guerrillas. By 2003, the *AUC* was believed to have 10,000 fighters under arms.

Pastrana Seeks Peace

Colombian politics proved as volatile as ever as the country neared the two rounds of the 1998 presidential election on May 31 and June 21. In municipal elections on October 26, 1997, guerrillas murdered dozens of candidates and frightened hundreds of others into withdrawing. Tens of thousands of voters, intimidated by rebel threats of violence, stayed home.

In January 1998, the Liberals formally nominated President Samper's hand-picked candidate, former Interior Minister Horacio Serpa, for president. But Serpa's nomination threatened to split the party as anti-Samper reformers, led by Representative Ingrid Betancourt of the so-called Liberal Oxygen faction, denounced the nomination. The Conservatives, meanwhile, renominated Andrés Pastrana, who narrowly lost to Samper in 1994, while retired General Harold Bedoya, whom Samper had sacked the previous July, launched an independent candidacy, as did Noemí Sanín, who had served as a cabinet minister under both Betancur and Gaviria.

The congressional elections on March 8 should have been cause for jubilation for the Liberals, who won 53 of the 102 Senate seats to 27 for the Conservatives and about the same proportion of seats in the 161-member House of Representatives. Moreover, turnout was a higher-than-expected 44%, despite the backdrop of a guerrilla offensive and the usual voter apathy. But the party regulars were stunned when the maverick Betancourt won her Senate seat by the largest majority of any candidate.

Former President Andrés Pastrana

Polls leading up to the first round on May 31 all showed Pastrana with a strong lead. But on election day, which this author observed first-hand, Serpa defied all the predictions with a razor-thin first-place finish of 34.3% to Pastrana's 34.0%. Only 26,000 votes separated the two men. Sanín drew 26.6%, the largest vote for an independent candidate since Rojas Pinilla in 1970. The guerrillas behaved themselves this time, permitting a record turnout of 10.7 million voters.

In the June 21 runoff, the polls this time showed Serpa with a strong lead, and they might have been right but for two dramatic last-minute developments. Four days before the election, the media reported that a Pastrana representative had met with Manuel "Tirofijo" Marulanda of the *FARC*, who declared that Pastrana was the candidate with the greater chance of negotiating peace. This crippled Serpa, whose slogan was "The road to peace." In a record turnout of 12 million voters, 59% of those eligible, Pastrana won with 50.4% to Serpa's 46.5%, almost the identical margin by which Pastrana had lost to Samper four years before. The remaining 3.1% cast blank ballots in protest.

Pastrana, 44 when he took office on August 7, 1998, was the son of former President Misael Pastrana. He was schooled as a lawyer but eschewed that profession in favor of broadcast journalism, which he practiced until he was elected to the Bogotá city council in the 1980s. He was elected mayor in 1988 and a senator in 1991.

Shortly after his inauguration, Pastrana met again with Marulanda. Much to the army's displeasure, Pastrana agreed to the demand the *FARC* had made to Samper to demilitarize an area the size of Switzerland in Caquetá Department as a pre-condition

to peace talks. Pastrana fired the army commander because of his opposition. Pastrana rejected, however, a guerrilla proposal to exchange captured soldiers and policemen for 452 rebel prisoners.

Those who had hoped for a cessation of hostilities in anticipation of the peace talks were cruelly disillusioned on November 1, 1998, when the *FARC* launched its biggest push since the Caguan offensive in March, this time in coca-rich Vaupes Department in the southeast. An estimated 800 rebels overran the departmental capital, Mitu, near the Brazilian border, killing 60 policemen and 10 civilians; another 40 policemen were taken prisoner. This came even as the army was complying with the ordered demilitarization in Caquetá. The army suffered heavy casualties retaking the now-destroyed town. Despite the rebel offensive, the army meekly completed the demilitarization in Caquetá.

In a separate surprising development, the U.S. Congress in December tripled the amount of aid to the Colombian police for its drug-fighting efforts, from $88.6 million in 1998 to $289 million in 1999. In February, the Clinton administration, which had not requested the dramatic increase in counter-drug aid, recertified Colombia as an ally in the drug war.

The peace talks began on schedule on January 7, 1999, but days later the killed 130 alleged guerrilla sympathizers. Pastrana flew to Havana and on January 17 met with Fidel Castro and Venezuelan President-elect Hugo Chavez to solicit their intercession with the guerrillas. Nonetheless, the *FARC* broke off the talks three days later, demanding that Pastrana clamp down on the paramilitaries.

Perhaps as part of an effort to placate the *FARC* and jump-start the peace talks, Prosecutor General Alfonso Gómez announced on March 31 the arrest of an army lieutenant colonel in connection with the grisly July 1997 massacre by paramilitary forces of about 30 peasants in the town of Mapiripán, in Meta Department. He was the highest-ranking officer ever arrested for alleged paramilitary ties. Pastrana also cashiered two army brigadier generals whom the guerrillas and human rights groups had accused of paramilitary links. Another general was arrested in July 2001 and formally charged with organizing paramilitary forces in Antioquía Department.

Despite Pastrana's concessions, both the peace talks and the fighting dragged on simultaneously. In November 1999, government and *FARC* representatives met in Sweden, and Pastrana held out an olive branch by suggesting a cease-fire for the holiday season. Within days, the *FARC* responded with one of its largest offensives in months, launching coordinated attacks

Colombia

in six outlying departments that left 10 soldiers or policemen dead. Pastrana angrily denounced the attacks as "demented" and said they amounted to a betrayal. Despite the renewed fighting, government and *FARC* representatives met again at the Vatican in February 2000 with a representative of Pope John Paul II, with inconclusive results. By May, a frustrated, angry Pastrana was threatening to break off the talks. The *FARC*'s blasé response: If you want to.

Meanwhile, in April 2000, the *FARC* announced the creation of a new political group, the Bolivarian Movement for a New Colombia, which claimed to reach out to all disenchanted sectors of society. It was unclear whether the new group was designed as a political party to compete for power within the system, or whether it the *FARC* was attempting to establish a parallel national government within the large area it controlled. The *FARC* began passing "laws" and imposing taxes in the area it controlled.

The talks sputtered off and on for several more months, until in November 2000 the *FARC* suspended them indefinitely, ostensibly to protest the government's failure to curtail army involvement with the right-wing paramilitaries. Pastrana offered to extend the terms of the euphemistically named demilitarized zone—in reality a safe haven for the highly militarized guerrillas—if the *FARC* would return to the bargaining table. Pastrana met with Marulanda again in the jungle and agreed to an eight-month extension of the safe haven and a purging of the army's ranks of suspected collaborators with the *AUC*.

In February 2001, an army tribunal convicted a brigadier general of failing to stop the 1997 Mapiripán massacre. He was sentenced to only 40 months, but the conviction was nonetheless historic. Pastrana also pushed through a law mandating that armed forces personnel accused of human rights violations would henceforth be tried in civilian, not military, courts.

Yet, the killing continued. Although the armed forces scored a few impressive tactical victories, they also suffered some humiliating setbacks at the hands of the *FARC*. In October 2000, as the talks were still in progress, the *FARC* attacked a town, in Urubá Department with 800 guerrillas. Five of the much-touted Blackhawk helicopters brought elite troops to the rescue. One was shot down by ground fire, killing all 22 men on board; a second was grounded by mechanical failure; the other three reached their landing zone, but the 60 troops were annihilated after they landed. In March 2001, the *FARC* killed 17 marines in an attack on a vital telecommunications tower in the south. In

another incident, the *FARC* "executed" 13 policemen it had taken prisoner after capturing the town of Roncesvalles in July 2000. Apparently, the *FARC* was competing with the *AUC* to seize the moral low ground.

A prisoner exchange occurred on June 6, 2001, when the *FARC* released a badly wounded police colonel and three other officers. In exchange, the government released 73 ill prisoners. On June 28, the *FARC* released 242 more prisoners, leaving only an estimated 42 still in its hands. Some hailed the exchange as the most positive product of the two and a half years of "peace" talks, while some skeptics claimed that the *FARC* was only ridding itself of a logistical burden.

The public had good reason to be skeptical. A report released by the president's human rights office showed that in the first four months of 2001 the number of killings by non-governmental forces had actually *increased* by 75% over the previous year. Of those deaths, 529 were attributed to the *AUC*, 190 to the *FARC* and 50 to the *ELN*.

For its part, the *ELN* began reminding the government that it was still a force to be reckoned with. The *ELN* demanded that the government create a demilitarized zone for it in the north as it had for the *FARC* in the south, although it was more modest in its demand: "only" 2,300 square miles. Amazingly, despite the failure of the concessions to the *FARC* to bring peace, Pastrana announced in April that he was agreeing to demilitarize three municipalities in Bolívar and Antioquía departments, a total of about 1,800 square miles, as a precursor to peace talks with the *ELN*.

The government and *ELN* representatives met in Geneva in July 2000, but the talks were unproductive. Pastrana at first refused to yield to the demands for a safe haven, but after the *ELN* staged some spectacular kidnappings as a show of force, the jelly-spined Pastrana acquiesced in February 2001, agreeing to a reduced area of about 1,100 square miles, still larger than Rhode Island. Residents in the area, spurred in part by the *AUC*, protested their government's surrendering them and their lands to the *ELN*'s control in exchange for—nothing. The local army commander complained that he was on the verge of capturing the *ELN* headquarters in Bolívar when he was ordered to withdraw. The *AUC* launched an offensive in April against the *ELN*; seven guerrillas and four paramilitaries died. The *ELN* suspended the talks in April 19.

The other major player in the conflict, the *AUC*, was actually strengthened, in part perhaps because of the government's willingness to make concessions to the

guerrillas that many rank-and-file Colombians regarded as too much in exchange for too little. Its strength was estimated at 8,000 in 2001. It flouted the rules of warfare, preferring massacres of civilians to achieve its nebulous goals. One such atrocity was a raid on the town of Naya in Cauca state on April 14, 2001, in which 32 civilians were reported killed; the arms of a 17-year-old girl were severed with a chain saw. That same month, the U.S. government formally declared the *AUC* a terrorist organization, and in September it added it to the list of terror organizations to which Americans may be prosecuted for contributing money. Also in 2001, the Colombian army launched a crackdown against the paramilitaries called "Operation Dignity."

A milestone for the *AUC* came with Castaño's supposed resignation in August 2001, ostensibly because he could not control the more bloodthirsty elements. But in reality he merely yielded the *AUC*'s military command to Salvatore Mancuso, scion of an affluent Italian immigrant family, who is perceived as more of a hardliner than Castaño, even advocating attacks against army troops as well as against guerrillas. Days after Mancuso assumed command, the *AUC* massacred 11 people in Tolima Department. A month later, they massacred 24 more in Valle del Cauca Department, and 12 in Magdalena Department. In an interview with the Associated Press at a mountain hideout in February 2002, Mancuso boasted that the *AUC* numbered 14,000 effectives and promised even greater bloodshed.

The *FARC* found itself with a public relations problem in late September after it had kidnapped Consuelo Araujo, Pastrana's former culture minister, a prominent and highly popular patron of the arts, in a highway abduction. Her body was found a few days later, and the crime outraged the nation. Suddenly, the *FARC* announced on October 5 that it would desist from highway kidnappings and negotiate seriously for a cease-fire. Still grasping for his peace straw, and against the advice of his generals, Pastrana unwisely reciprocated the gesture just when the *FARC* was reeling, extending the safe haven for another three months, until January 2002.

The *ELN* declared a truce for Christmas and New Year's, which it kept. Not so the *FARC*, which launched attacks on several towns in Cauca at New Year's.

On January 10, 2002, Pastrana announced the *FARC* had broken off talks again and gave it 48 hours to abandon the demilitarized zone. He then dispatched troops into the area. The *FARC* responded with a 14-point negotiating plan, which Pastrana at first rejected, but then acqui-

Santuario (sanctuary) de las Lajas in Nariño State in southwestern Colombia, partially built into the rock of the mountain

Courtesy: Embassy of Colombia

Colombia

esced again. The *FARC* responded to the president's show of good faith by setting off bombs in a town 30 miles from Bogotá and by attacking a prison and freeing 39 rebels; four soldiers were killed in the attacks. Despite this perfidy, on January 20 caved in again and agreed to resume cease-fire negotiations, to be brokered by the United Nations, setting a deadline of April 7. The *FARC* responded by bringing urban terrorism to the capital. On January 25, it set off a car bomb in Bogotá that killed five people; on January 29, it dynamited 50 electrical towers and the dam that provides Bogotá with its water supply. The next day, thousands of residents of the capital poured into the streets for a mass demonstration against the *FARC*, banging on pots and pans, a traditional Latin American form of nonviolent protest.

Events then began to explode in a dramatic and violent chain reaction. On February 20, after the *FARC* hijacked a domestic airliner and forced it to land, kidnapping a prominent senator who was on board, Pastrana finally realized the futility of attempting to negotiate with people of bad faith and broke off the peace talks. He sent the army into the safe haven

and ordered the air force to bomb and strafe *FARC* base camps and landing strips in the zone; the military met surprisingly feeble resistance as the zone was "remilitarized." Apparently in retaliation and as a show of defiance, the *FARC* committed another outrage on February 24 by kidnapping independent presidential candidate Ingrid Betancourt. She remains a hostage. For the next two months, the *FARC* went on a rampage of assassinations, bombings and kidnappings. On April 14, it made an unsuccessful attempt to assassinate the front-running presidential candidate Alvaro Uribe, who was calling for a military victory over the *FARC* (see The Elections of 2002). On April 21 it kidnapped the governor of Antioquía. But the worst was yet to come.

In May 2002, about 1,000 *FARC* and 600 *AUC* fighters engaged in a bloody battle for the village of Bella Vista, in the district of Bojaya, in Chocó Department near the Panamanian border. More than 500 civilians were huddled in a church for safety during the battle when a *FARC* gas-cylinder mortar shell crashed through the roof and exploded, killing and dismembering 117 people, including 40 children and a

woman who was nine months pregnant. The *FARC* admitted it had fired the mortar round but claimed the church had been hit by accident. It cynically blamed the *AUC* for the appalling death toll, saying the civilians should not have been in the town—where they lived. It took the army eight days to reach the area. The Bella Vista atrocity shocked an already numbed Colombia, as well as the international community. The U.N. human rights representative to Colombia initially called it a "war crime."

Pastrana asked a U.N. human rights investigating team to visit the area, but he was not prepared for the scathing report it issued a few weeks later. It concluded the *FARC* was directly responsible for the deaths, but it blamed the *AUC* for putting the civilians in harm's way and it assailed the Pastrana government for ignoring warnings the United Nations had given it in April that a violent confrontation was imminent. It also castigated the army for its tardiness in reaching the town. The U.S. Congress, meanwhile, demanded to know why the army, which was the beneficiary of so much U.S. aid, had responded so slowly.

Once again, the *FARC* found itself with a public relations nightmare. In early June, the European Community finally acceded to a request from Pastrana to follow the U.S. lead in declaring the *FARC* a terrorist organization. Yet, the bloodletting continued

The guerrilla war began souring Colombia's relations with neighboring Venezuela. In February 2001, the government of President Hugo Chávez, long suspected of being sympathetic to the Colombian guerrillas anyway, admitted it had captured, then released, an *ELN* member suspected in a 1999 airplane hijacking. Pastrana and Chávez met at the remote Venezuelan mining town of Puerto Ordaz on March 24. By then Venezuela had rearrested the hijack suspect, and Pastrana was pressing for his extradition. The two presidents announced that Venezuela would serve as an active partner in the negotiations between the Colombian government and the guerrillas and that their two armed forces would exchange intelligence information. However, Colombian intelligence was aware that aircraft regularly flew between Venezuela's border region and the *FARC* safe haven.

A potentially important new variable was added to this already complex equation in February 2002 when the Bush administration asked Congress to approve additional military aid for Colombia. In a major policy shift, Secretary of State Colin Powell said the aid should be used against the guerrillas, not just against the drug traffickers. The U.S. government is especially concerned about security for the vital Caño

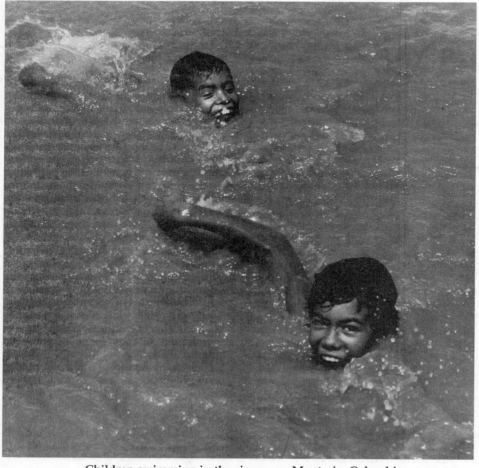

Children swimming in the river near Monteria, Colombia

Limón oil pipeline, which the *FARC* and the *ELN* have attacked nearly 1,000 times. Moreover, the United States sees the *FARC* as just another international terrorist organization to be included in its war on terrorism in the wake of the September 11, 2001 attacks. The *FARC's* alleged international links had been spotlighted the previous August when three suspected members of the Irish Republican Army were arrested in Colombia, accused of providing the *FARC* with terror training. In fact, the *FARC's* bombings in Bogotá in January had distinct IRA fingerprints.

"Plan Colombia"

As the peace talks and the fighting both droned on, Pastrana outlined a six-year, $7.5 billion plan to destroy the drug trade. Called *"Plan Colombia,"* it included expanded enforcement as well as incentives to farmers to plant alternative crops. The Clinton administration asked Congress in 2000 for $1.6 billion for aid to both the Colombian police and army for their counter-drug operations. Among the hardware included for *Plan Colombia* were 30 sophisticated Blackhawk helicopters. As usual, the administration insisted that the new aid money for the army would be used only against drug traffickers, not against the guerrillas, thus seeking to perpetuate the myth that the two were distinguishable and unrelated.

The House of Representatives approved the measure to which the Colombian aid was attached, but it hit a snag in the Senate. Pastrana personally flew to humbly plead for the aid money. Eventually, the Senate approved a drastically reduced $934 million aid package, which also replaced the 30 sophisticated Blackhawks with 60 aging Hueys. In the end, the two houses agreed on a $1.3 billion aid package, which Clinton quickly signed into law. Colombia thus became the third-largest recipient of U.S. military aid after Israel and Egypt. Days later, Clinton met with Pastrana in Cartagena.

U.S. Special Forces, or "Green Berets," trained a special counter-drug brigade of three battalions, totaling 3,000 men. The brigade received 16 Blackhawks and 25 SuperHueys. The *FARC* denounced *Plan Colombia*, using it as a convenient pretext for scuttling the peace talks, and in February 2002 it demanded that it be ended and foreign military advisers withdrawn. Clearly, they were feeling the pinch.

The new U.S. president, George W. Bush, upped the ante for *Plan Colombia*. In mid-2001, Congress approved an additional $676 million to battle the Colombian drug trade, a 50% increase. However, with all that money, some of it was bound to go bad. In May 2002, the U.S. Congress

partially suspended further aid for the drug war when Colombian media and the U.S. Embassy reported that $2 million had disappeared. The commander of the national police's anti-drug unit, General Gustavo Socha, fired six officers believed responsible. Days later, Socha was himself demoted and subsequently resigned, being replaced by General Jorge Linares.

A major event in the drug war occurred in September 2001 when Fabio Ochoa, an alleged kingpin of the old Medellín cartel, was extradited to the United States. It was a major departure for Colombia, which had not extradited such a notorious suspect in more than 10 years. Ochoa was convicted in Miami in May 2003.

There was some statistical evidence that *Plan Colombia* was showing signs of success. According to the U.N. Drug Control Program, the number of hectares under coca cultivation in Colombia declined by 11% from 2000 to 2001, to 145,000, and by another 30% in 2002. There were even greater inroads under the new government of President Alvaro Uribe, who took office in August 2002. The White House Office for National Drug Control Policy put the number of hectares at 114,000 in 2003, but it 2004 it had not changed.

The Elections of 2002

Meanwhile, the hapless president's Conservative Party proved a spectacular failure in the departmental and municipal elections in October 2000, a bellwether for the presidential contest on May 26, 2002. The Conservatives failed to win a single governorship, while the Liberals and independents each won 15. Independents also won the mayor's races in four of the five largest cities, including Bogotá. There, Antanas Mockus, a flamboyant and somewhat eccentric philosophy professor who served as mayor in 1995–97 and once mooned a heckler, won the post again. The campaigns were marked by the usual violence and intimidation; more than 20 candidates were killed either by left-wing guerrillas or right-wing paramilitaries, others were kidnapped and another 100 withdrew.

In the presidential race, the Liberals again nominated Horacio Serpa, who lost narrowly to Pastrana in 1998, hoping he would make the same sort of comeback Pastrana had after his 1994 defeat. The Conservatives nominated Juan Camilo Restrepo, who had been Pastrana's finance minister and ambassador to France. Once again, there were several independent candidates, seemingly assuring the race would be thrown into a runoff again: Noemí Sanín, who polled over a fourth of the vote as an independent in 1998; Senator Ingrid Betancourt, a prominent Liberal

renegade who had supported Pastrana in 1998; and Alvaro Uribe, a former Liberal governor of Antioquía, candidate of a movement called *Primero Colombia,* who pledged to get tough with the guerrillas. Rounding out the field was Luis Eduardo Garzón of the far-left Social and Political Front. It looked like Colombian politics as usual. But the 2002 election would not be usual.

Serpa, who had promised to continue peace talks with the guerrillas, led in early polls, but as the peace talks droned on and the *FARC* outrages continued, Uribe suddenly broke from the pack by promising to double the size of the military and seek an all-out victory over the guerrillas. His campaign slogan was *"mano firme, corazón grande"* (firm hand, big heart). After the peace talks collapsed on February 20 and Betancourt was kidnapped on February 24, he soared to 59% in the polls.

There was another bellwether of the public mood on March 10, when Colombians voted for a new Congress. The turnout was 44%, despite the usual rebel threats. The Liberals retained their majorities in both houses, but at least 27 new senators publicly declared their support for Uribe (the *AUC* claimed that 35% of the new Congress were its sympathizers, a claim that could neither be verified nor discounted). Voters clearly were in a get-tough mood.

On March 12, Restrepo, who had been receiving only 1–2% in the polls, dropped out. It left the Conservative Party without a presidential candidate for the first time since it was founded in 1849. He made no endorsement.

Uribe's tough anti-*FARC* rhetoric was not lost on the guerrillas. On April 13, they attempted to assassinate the candidate by setting off a remote-controlled

President Alvaro Uribe Vélez

Colombia

bomb under a bridge on a highway near Barranquilla as his motorcade passed. He escaped unhurt, but three bystanders were killed and 15 injured. Ignoring the danger, he stopped and offered comfort to the injured. For Uribe, the attack was *déjà vu;* in 1983, his father had been killed when he resisted a *FARC* kidnap attempt.

The assassination attempt backfired on the *FARC*; not only did their nemesis survive, but the attempt on his life boosted his standing in the polls. Desperately trying to regain his early momentum, Serpa alleged that Uribe was drawing support from the right-wing paramilitaries, a charge that Uribe denied. Even if it had been true, with the mood the Colombian voters were in, it probably would have helped him further.

The results on May 26 were a veritable landslide, not just a mandate in favor of the hawk, Uribe, over the dove, Serpa, but a repudiation of the guerrillas. A total of 11.2 million Colombians voted, a turnout of 46.3%. Uribe scored a decisive first-round victory with 5.7 million votes, or 52.9%; Serpa received 3.5 million, or 31.7%. Garzón was a distant third, followed closely by Sanín; Betancourt, still in *FARC* captivity, was a poor fifth.

A day after his election, the president-elect sounded far more conciliatory than the truculent candidate had been, saying he still favored a U.N.-brokered peace with the guerrillas. Uribe also said he was willing to engage in peace talks with the paramilitaries, something his predecessors had eschewed. He further promised to continue the war against drugs, to reduce corruption and increase efficiency in government, and somehow to increase social spending. A Harvard-educated lawyer, who turned 50 on July 4, 2002, Uribe had a positive record as an efficient governor of Antioquía. Three weeks after the election, the president-elect held talks in Washington with President Bush and other senior officials and in New York with U.N. Secretary-General Kofi Annan. Back home, he advocated a constitutional amendment to allow him to declare a state of emergency to deal with the guerrillas, a proposal that gave chills to human rights advocates.

Uribe Gets Tough

Uribe was inaugurated on August 7, 2002—indoors for security reasons. Pastrana, an Andean version of Neville Chamberlain, left office a pitiful failure, with an approval rating of 20%. The *FARC* launched a mortar attack near the National Palace in an attempt to disrupt the inauguration, killing 19 people and injuring 60.

The new president soon made it clear he would be as tough as Pastrana had been spineless. Within a week of his inauguration, Uribe declared a 90-day state of emergency to crack down on the guerrillas, the paramilitaries and the narco-traffickers, though human rights advocates feared an erosion of civil liberties. Indeed, roadblocks, ID checks and warrantless arrests became commonplace, and some parts of the country were placed under martial law. The state of emergency was extended in November for another 90 days, then for a final 90 days in February 2003.

Uribe proposed equipping 1 million citizens with two-way radios so they could report guerrilla activity; recruiting for volunteers was brisk. Uribe also introduced an emergency war tax to pay for his promised military buildup. Visiting his home department of Antioquía in late August, he gave the local military commanders a dressing down—reported on national television—for failing to take action against reported guerrilla activity in the area, in effect telling them to shape up and fight or resign. By early 2003, he had begun the training of young farmers to create a rural militia to number 12,000 by the end of the year.

The first major battles between the army and the *FARC* since Uribe's inauguration came in early September in Meta and Tolima departments. Both were decisive army victories that left 100 guerrillas dead in Meta and 22 in Tolima. Two weeks later, separate clashes near Bogotá and in Antioquía left another 21 guerrillas dead. Army casualties were reported light in all the encounters.

In September 2002, Uribe made a second visit to Washington to lobby for $450 million in military and counternarcotics aid, assuring liberal senators that he would respect human rights on his watch. He also visited again at the United Nations with Annan, who admonished him to clean up Colombia's human rights act. Soon thereafter, the U.S. State Department raised some eyebrows in human rights circles by certifying that Colombia passed muster under a U.S. law that denies aid to countries that violate human rights, and it released the first $41.6 million in aid. The United States already had announced in August it would step up its training of Colombian officers and NCOs and a new brigade for pipeline security.

Secretary of State Colin Powell visited Bogotá in December and sent mixed signals by praising Uribe's get-tough policy, while warning Colombia that the United States would not tolerate human rights abuses. In January 2003, in fact, the State Department banned aid to the 1st Air Combat Command for allegedly lying

about its role in an accidental bombing in 1998 that killed 17 civilians. Possibly to convince the United States and the world that Colombia was serious about human rights, a general was arrested in March 2003 for failing to prevent the 1997 Mapiripán massacre.

Uribe's policy was not to negotiate with the *FARC*, the *ELN* or the *AUC* as long as they were engaging in combat, but he held out the promise of renewed talks to any group that declared a unilateral cease-fire. In November, the policy began to bear fruit when the *AUC* declared a unilateral cease-fire beginning December 1.

The *AUC* leadership was beginning to feel the heat not only of the Colombian army and the *FARC*, but of the U.S. Justice Department. In September 2002, U.S. Attorney General John Ashcroft unsealed indictments against Castaño and Mancuso, alleging they were instrumental in the shipment of 17 tons of cocaine to the United States since 1997 and calling them a threat to U.S. national security. Castaño denied the charges and wrote U.S. Ambassador Anne Patterson that he was willing to surrender to U.S. authorities to establish his innocence; he did not, however.

Talks between the government and the *AUC* got underway, although at least 1,500 *AUC* renegade members refused to participate. Castaño warned them that they face "annihilation" if they did not. The talks broke down in June 2003, however, after the *AUC* accused the army of "massacring" 12 *AUC* members. The army said they were killed in an ambush.

The *AUC* suffered another blow in June 2003 when one of its most notorious commanders, Said Sepulveda, believed responsible for the deaths of 450 people, was captured by the army. In July, Mancuso announced that the *AUC* would lay down its arms because of the army's successes against the *FARC*, promising a complete demobilization by the end of 2005.

The *FARC* and *ELN* have remained in the field, although tenuous lines of communication to the government have been kept open through third parties—France for the *FARC*, Cuba for the *ELN*.

On February 7, 2003, the *FARC* demonstrated it was still in the urban terrorism business, setting off a powerful car bomb that gutted El Nogal, a 10-story social club in Bogotá frequented by the capital's elite. The death toll of 35 included six children; another 168 people were injured, many of them children, and certainly not all of them wealthy members of the club. It was the worst act of terrorism in Bogotá since the bloody days of Pablo Escobar a decade earlier, and it sparked national outrage against the guerrillas. Seven days later, rebels set off a bomb when police raided a house in Neiva in southern Colombia to investigate a plot to assassinate Uribe. Fifteen people, including eight policemen, were killed.

Another *FARC* atrocity, which turned into an international incident, came on February 15 when a small counterdrug aircraft carrying four American "contractors" for the U.S. Southern Command and one Colombian crashed behind *FARC* lines. The Colombian sergeant and one American were apparently executed by the rebels, who took the other three Americans prisoner. The Colombian government bristled, however, when the Bush administration sent a reported 150 troops to search for the three Americans, calling it an interference in Colombia's internal affairs. It was an incredible windfall for the *FARC*. The *FARC* announced it was holding the Americans as "prisoners of war" and said they would be released in exchange for dozens of rebel prisoners and they remain captives.

In an even bolder act, the *FARC* executed 10 hostages, including former Antioquía Governor Guillermo Gaviría, who had been kidnapped in 1997, when the army attempted a raid to rescue them in May 2003. The army and air force retaliated in June, bombarding *FARC* positions in Cauca and Meta and killing 67 rebels.

The government claimed a major political victory over the *FARC* in April when Rafael Rojas, commander of the *FARC*'s 46th Front, surrendered to the government and, in a nationally televised event with Uribe in Cartagena, urged his former comrades to do the same.

Meanwhile, the already tense relations with Venezuela over President Chávez's alleged support for the guerrillas were strained even further when Colombian peasants reported that Venezuelan air force jets and helicopters crossed the border on March 21, 2003, providing close air support for *FARC* rebels battling paramilitaries in North Santander Department. Uribe ordered an investigation, and confronted Venezuela with the evidence. Venezuelan Vice President José Vicente Rangel dismissed the reports as "an arsenal of lies." He countered that Venezuelan troops had been attacked by right-wing Colombian paramilitaries in the Venezuelan province of Zulia, and even accused the Uribe government of complicity with the *AUC*. That sparked an indignant rebuke from Bogotá. Uribe and Chávez met face-to-face in Puerto Ordaz, Venezuela, on April 23, but the meeting produced little of substance.

The war was not the only thing occupying Uribe's attention. A low-ranking judge suddenly created an international incident in November 2002 when he ordered the release of Gilberto and Miguel Rodríguez Orejuela, the imprisoned leaders of the Cali cocaine cartel, after they had served only about half their terms. Outraged, Uribe tried to block their release by appealing to another court. That judge ordered that Miguel, 59, be retained in prison (a separate judge tacked another four years to his term), but agreed that Gilberto, 63, should be released for "good behavior." This infuriated Uribe—and U.S. authorities who had long sought the notorious brothers' extradition—even further. They could do little but watch helplessly as the elder kingpin walked free. However, he was rearrested in March 2003 on an outstanding charge that he shipped 330 pounds of cocaine to the United States—in 1995. Both have since been extradited to the United States, Gilberto in December 2004 and Miguel in February 2005.

Colombia and the United States agreed in May 2003 to resume drug interdiction flights that the United States had suspended in 2001 when a Peruvian air force jet accidentally shot down a plane carrying missionaries. Uribe also had expanded the program of aerial spraying of coca fields with glyphosphate, which supposedly is environmentally benign. The number of hectares sprayed in 2002 was 121,000, compared with 94,000 in 2001, an increase of about 30%.

In a major development in the guerrilla war—and possibly a sign that Uribe's crackdown was having an effect—the *FARC* and the *ELN* announced in August 2003 that they were re-establishing an alliance that had dissolved nearly 20 years before and that they would engage in joint military actions against the Uribe government.

But since then, the momentum has clearly been on the side of the army, which continued to win victories in the field. In January 2004, the *FARC*'s Ricardo Palmera, alias Simón Trinidad, was arrested in Ecuador, the highest-ranking *FARC* leader to be captured to date. In addition, it appears that Manuel (Tirofijo) Marulanda may be dying of prostate cancer in Brazil, which could lead to a bitter internecine struggle to assume his mantle. Undaunted, the *FARC* marked its 40th anniversary in May 2004 with a bombastic pledge to fight on until victory. It had a hollow sound. At the same time, Uribe made a new peace overture to the *ELN*, probably hoping to drive a wedge between the two guerrilla movements.

Meanwhile, the security forces continued to inflict battlefield losses on the paramilitaries as well, even as negotiations continued. In November 2003, 800 *AUC* effectives laid down their arms in Medellín, and in May 2004, the *AUC* signed an agreement with the government's peace negotiator, Luis Carlos Restrepo, by which they would move into a 230-square-mile safe haven as a first step toward demobilization. The inducement was a generous amnesty offer and even cash rewards, which had human rights groups protesting that some of the *AUC* leaders should be tried for war crimes. The United States, meanwhile, wanted some of them extradited for drug trafficking. In April, Uribe compromised and agreed that *AUC* members could be tried for atrocities before a special war crimes tribunal and would face five to 10 years in prison. But he did not agree to extraditing them to the United States.

One *AUC* leader the United States wanted extradited was Castaño, but he mysteriously vanished in April 2004 and was believed killed by a rival faction that opposed demobilization. A similar fate befell former *AUC* leader Carlos Mauricio García, who had opposed the *AUC*'s involvement in drug trafficking. He was gunned down in a Bogotá neighborhood in May 2004. Not all paramilitaries, meanwhile, have been meekly demobilizing. Renegade paramilitaries massacred 11 peasants in Arauca Department in May 2004 for alleged collaboration with the guerrillas.

Defense Minister Jorge Alberto Uribe, no relation to the president, announced in January 2004 that 16,000 members of the *FARC*, *ELN* or *AUC* had been killed or captured or had surrendered during 2003. According to a Bogotá think-tank, the security forces fought more than 2,300 battles with the three outlaw armies in 2003, compared with 1,300 in 2002, and killed 2,930 of them while losing 523. Moreover, the murder rate in 2003, though still high by most international standards, was the lowest since 1986.

Uribe also could claim a major victory in the "third war," the war on drugs. In September 2003, the U.N. Office on Drugs and Crime stated in a report that in the first seven months of 2003, 81,500 acres of coca had been destroyed, mostly through the U.S. fumigation program, an increase of 32% from the acreage destroyed in 2002.

These successes have understandably bolstered Uribe's popularity; his approval rating rose from 75% in October 2003 to 80% in December, something most of his South American counterparts must envy.

Nonetheless, the Colombian electorate dealt Uribe unexpected dual setbacks on October 25 and 26, 2003. The first vote was a confusing referendum on a package of 15 Uribe-sponsored reforms. All obtained overwhelming majorities, but failed for the lack of a required 25% voter turnout. Among the proposals was one to reduce the size of Congress.

On October 26, opposition parties did better than expected in municipal elections. A major winner—and a probable

Colombia

presidential contender—was Lucho Guzmán of the moderate left movement Democratic Pole, who was elected mayor of Bogotá. The Senate dealt the politically wounded Uribe another blow on October 28 by rejecting a proposed constitutional amendment that would have allowed him to seek re-election.

Uribe also is less than popular with human rights advocates. A group of 80 human rights organizations issued a scathing report in September 2003 titled "The Authoritarian Curse," which accused Uribe of sanctioning human rights abuses and of undermining civil liberties. Uribe lashed back at his critics, accusing them of being sympathetic to "terrorists." He defended his approach to combating the guerrillas and narcos in a speech to the U.N. General Assembly.

But in March 2004, in its annual report, the Office of the U.N. High Commissioner for Human Rights called the human rights situation in Colombia "critical." However, the report also praised the government for restoring law and order in wide areas once held by the guerrillas, and it also assailed the guerrillas and the paramilitaries for their lack of humanitarian standards. In May 2004, Jan Egeland, the U.N. under-secretary for humanitarian affairs, delivered a much harsher assessment of the situation in Colombia, calling it a "humanitarian catastrophe." Egeland noted that the number of displaced persons had risen to 1 million, third highest in the world behind Congo and Sudan. Uribe also came under criticism from the European Union.

The United States, however, continued to voice support for Uribe. The Bush administration then asked Congress to increase aid to Colombia by nearly $700 million, and in March 2004 the Pentagon asked Congress to double the limit on military and civilian advisers to Colombia to 800 each.

Recent Developments

In mid-2004, another constitutional amendment was introduced to Congress to allow Uribe to stand for re-election in 2006. A poll indicated that 72% of Colombians favored it, and both major parties endorsed it. The amendment faced a total of eight votes in the Senate and Chamber of Representatives, and the tedious process was finally completed in November. The amendment then was submitted to the Constitutional Court, which still had not approved it when this book went to press in mid-2005. In May, Uribe announced he would establish a new party, which would also field candidates for Congress. The established parties reacted to the news predictably, and said it smacked of personalismo. A poll in March 2005 showed that 67% of voters wanted Uribe reelected, a phenomenal popularity for a South American president.

There was good reason for his popularity. Even though the latest annual report by the U.N. High Commissioner for Human Rights in April 2005 again termed the Colombian situation "critical," it noted that the murder rate had dropped from 65 per 1,000 people in 2003 to 44 in 2004 and the number of massacre victims had decreased from 1,400 to 259. The number of new displaced persons had been reduced by nearly two thirds, from 400,000 in 2003 to 160,000 in 2004. The report also said that although the rebels and the paramilitaries remain the main culprits for rights violations, there was an increase in incidents of abuse of authority, including warrantless searches and detentions, torture and extrajudicial executions. In March, the U.N. human rights office in Bogotá called for an investigation of local claims that the army had massacred eight civilians, including three children, and hacked them to pieces near Apartado, in the northwest. The Defense Ministry countered that there were no troops in that area at the time. Judging from Uribe's poll numbers, Colombians apparently feel occasional rights violations are worth the price to reduce the violence.

The armed forces still appear to be making gains in the wars against the guerrillas and the paramilitaries, although victory remains elusive. Indeed, James LeMoyne, the U.N. negotiator who had been trying since 2001 to negotiate an agreement between the government and the FARC, finally gave up in frustration in January 2005 and left the country.

The army launched "Plan Patriot" in late 2003, an offensive to go after the FARC and its cocaine operations in its former safe haven in Caquetá and Guaviare departments. A similar offensive, "Operation Emperor," was launched in Meta Department in February 2005. In one three-week period, the army claimed to have killed 70 rebels while losing five soldiers. The government claimed that guerrilla casualties were up 15% in one year and that the FARC had been reduced from 18,000 effectives to 12,000 through casualties, captures and desertions.

True or not, the FARC proved it could still strike back. In February 2005 it attacked a naval base in Nariño Department with home-made missiles, killing 14 marines, its most ambitious and deadly attack in a year. The same month, 19 army soldiers were killed in Antioquía. In April, it attacked an army convoy in the northeast, killing 17 soldiers.

Another 450 paramilitaries laid down their weapons and accepted amnesty in late 2004. This is causing friction with the United States, which wants some of the AUC leaders extradited to face drug trafficking charges. Human rights groups, meanwhile, want some of them to face charges for the massacres they perpetrated. A major FARC leader, Ricardo Palmera, was extradited to the United States in January 2005 to face drug charges.

There have been major developments in the ongoing drug war as well. The notorious leaders of the Cali Cartel, Gilberto Rodríguez Orejuela and his brother Miguel, were finally extradited to the United States, Gilberto in December 2004 and Miguel in February 2005. Simultaneously, a judge ordered the assets of the cartel seized. Also in December, police arrested Dagoberto Florez, one of the leaders of the Norte del Valle Cartel. He, too, is wanted by U.S. authorities, who had posted a $5 million reward. On May 12, 2005, Colombian authorities discovered a cache of 13.8 tons of cocaine worth $400 million in a wooden underground chamber near the Pacific coast, the largest seizure of cocaine ever on Colombian soil. Even more remarkably, it turned out that some of the cocaine belonged to the FARC and some to the AUC; the two battlefield rivals had actually contracted with the same trafficker! On the down side, the White House Office for National Drug Control Policy admitted that the number of hectares of coca eradicated in 2004, 114,000, was essentially unchanged from 2003, although it is still one third less than in 2001. Moreover, the street value of cocaine in the United States and Europe has actually decreased, suggesting that supply has not been affected, which in turn suggests that if the number of hectares in Colombia has not decreased, new fields are being planted in Colombia or in other Andean countries.

Relations between the governments of Uribe and Venezuelan President Chávez grew tense again in December 2004 after Colombia announced the capture of Rodrigo Granda, the FARC's foreign affairs representative. The announcement claimed that Granda had been arrested in Cucuta, a Colombian town near the Venezuelan border. Soon, however, Colombian and Venezuelan newspapers reported that Granda had, in fact, been abducted in Caracas by Colombian agents together with the aid of some Venezuelans. Chávez called for an investigation, and in January Uribe acknowledged that Granda had been captured in Caracas. An angry Chávez denounced the violation of Venezuelan sovereignty, canceled bilateral trade agreements, recalled his ambassador to Colombia and demanded that Uribe apologize, without offering an explanation of why or how Granda was in Venezuela in the first place and was given Venezuelan citizenship. Uribe did not apologize, and relations remain as sour as ever (see Venezuela).

Culture: The blend of the European and Indian races was more thorough in Colombia than in the nations of the southern areas of Latin America. Moreover, refugee blacks from the Caribbean settled along the northern coast and, as elsewhere, have made their contribution to Colombian music and art. However, the so-called Bolivarian countries of the northwestern tier of South America, those liberated by Simón Bolivar, have not been characterized by the comparative freedom of expression and political stability of the countries of the southern part of the continent.

Colombia's long history of dictatorship, political turmoil and domestic violence conspired to retard its cultural development until the latter half of the 20th century. The overthrow of the Rojas Pinilla dictatorship, and the truce reached between the warring Liberal and Conservative parties in 1958, marked a watershed in Colombian cultural expression. Bogotá's self-proclaimed title of "the Athens of South America" is a bit boastful, but there is no question that the country has made a regional impact.

This is especially true in the plastic arts, as a visit to the top floor of the *Museo Nacional* in Bogotá will attest. As in Chile, the influence of France on 19th century Colombian art is unmistakable, but in the late 20th century a number of talented Colombian painters and sculptors have won international reputations. Perhaps the three best known are Edgar Negret, the abstractionist Alejandro Obregón and Fernando Botero.

The premier figure of Colombian literature remains Gabriel García Márquez, who received the Nobel Prize in 1982. His landmark novel was *Cien años de soledad,* but later novels that have won international critical acclaim include *Crónica de una muerte anunciada* and *El Amor en los tiempos de cólera.* In 2002, he released the first of three installments of his memoirs, *Vivir para conratla (Live to Tell It).* García Márquez's leftist policies have brought him controversy. He is a close friend of Fidel Castro's and maintains a residence in Havana as well as in Paris. Despite his international prestige, he was denied a visa to visit the United States during the Reagan Administration.

A newer, if older, star among Colombian writers is Alvaro Mutis, a novelist and poet who has achieved acclaim in the Spanish-speaking world with the fictitious character, Maqroll el Gaviero; such novels as *La última escala del Tramp Steamer* and *Amirbar*; and the book of poetry, *La mansión de Araucaíma.* At the age of 79, he

received Spain's coveted Cervantes Prize in April 2002, becoming the first writer from any country to win all three of Spain's most prestigious literary awards.

Bogotá and the major provincial capitals of Medellín, Cartagena, Cali and Barranquilla have active theatrical and musical communities, though much is still borrowed from abroad. Colombian popular music has definite Caribbean influence.

Colombian cinema is still in the developmental stage, compared with the more established industries of Mexico, Brazil and Argentina, but a few feature-length films are produced each year. Colombian television has become largely self-sufficient in programming, and some of its *telenovelas* are exported.

In popular music, the beautiful young singer Shakira has won international renown in recent years, including in the United States. Colombia's leading recording artist, however, remains Diómedes Díaz, popularly known as "El Jefe," despite his conviction in 2002 of the wrongful death by cocaine overdose of his 22-year-old lover.

The Colombian press, like so much else in the country, has been shaped by the Liberal-Conservative rivalry and in recent years has been the target of drug-related violence. Involvement of newspaper owners in politics has been commonplace, most notably former Presidents Laureano Gómez, who established the Conservative mouthpiece *El Siglo,* and Eduardo Santos, whose family still publishes the prestigious pro-Liberal daily *El Tiempo.* Ironically, these two rival newspapers both were intimidated by the Rojas Pinilla dictatorship, forcing them to collaborate editorially against the dictator. The dean of the Colombian press and its circulation leader is another pro-Liberal paper, *El Espectador,* which has won international plaudits for its courageous editorial attacks against the drug cartels. Its editor, Guillermo Cano, was murdered by the Medellín Cartel in 1986, just one of scores of Colombian journalists who have given their lives in the line of duty. Several high-quality news magazines are published, the most widely read being *Cromos* and *Semana.*

Economy: The informal economy of Colombia is based on production and smuggled export of refined cocaine and far outweighs the formal economy based on agriculture. The coca leaves are not generally grown in Colombia, but come from Peru, Ecuador and Bolivia, where an acre can yield $10,000 a year. The final stage of processing takes place in Colombia, which traditionally has had but loose control over illicit activities. Small "factories" are easily moved, and with police

double-agents abounding, when there is a raid on a facility, no one is home.

Most of the population, however, was employed in agriculture, which is handicapped by inefficient techniques and misuse of resources—produce and labor. Rural violence is common and has stimulated migration to the cities since 1948 where many of the newcomers are unemployable because of lack of education and skills. Now, only 1.7% of the people work the land. An estimated 60% are engaged in the cocaine traffic in one capacity or another. The resources of Colombia are capable of supporting the growing population without the cocaine industry, but numerous problems, principally poor distribution of wealth, must be resolved before there can be major economic gains.

Government programs were undertaken to end the traditional dependence on coffee exports, and by 1973 other goods and products produced more foreign income than coffee. Manufactured goods are slowly gaining a larger share of total exports.

The López administration sought to revitalize the rural sector through agrarian reform and government investment. Tighter controls over foreign-owned firms and banks, together with new taxes on the wealthy increased government revenues 50%. High unemployment (17%) persists and a relatively high population growth rate of 2.3% annually also hampers progress.

Colombia has a thriving coal industry; it is not only self-sufficient in oil, but is a major exporter. Honda makes motorcycles here, with production exceeding 50,000 units per year.

One bright spot for the economy in 1996, albeit a temporary one, was a disastrous frost in Brazil that destroyed much of its coffee harvest. The result was skyrocketing coffee prices on the world market, much to the benefit of Colombia, whose coffee growers already had embarked on an aggressive marketing campaign with its "Juan Valdez" character in the industrialized countries.

The overall economic picture in Colombia has been bleak for several years. Chronic high unemployment, along with the endemic corruption within the Samper government, was one of the major issues in the 1998 presidential election that saw an end to 12 years of Liberal rule. The jobless rate that year was 16%, second only to Haiti among the 20 Latin republics, while inflation also was among the highest in the region at 18%. Real GDP for 1998 was $96.9 billion, up 3% since 1997. Growth in 1999 was 4.3%, which dropped to 2.8% in 2000 and bottomed out at 1.9% in 2002. Growth was 3.2% in 2003 and 4% in 2004.

Colombia

The dismal unemployment picture has steadily worsened: 18.1% in 1999, 19.7% in 2000 and 20.5% in 2001, the worst in Latin America. At the end of 2003, it was down to 14%. Inflation moderated slightly, from 9.2% in 1999 to 8% in 2001.

The combination of sluggish economic growth, population increase, joblessness and inflation have steadily dragged down Colombians' living standards. Per capita GDP declined from $2,440 in 1997 to $2,087 in 2001. In 2003, it plummeted to $1,844.

A major development has been a free-trade agreement Colombia signed with the *Mercosur* trade bloc in April 2004, which went into effect on July 1. It will gradually give Colombian exports duty-free entry to Brazil and Argentina over eight to 10 years, while tariffs will be eliminated on those countries' exports to Colombia over a period of 12 to 15 years. Meanwhile, Colombia and the United States began bilateral trade talks in May, which could make Colombia the second South American country after Chile to reach a free-trade agreement with the United States.

The Future: The contrast between the hapless, spineless Pastrana and the aggressive, no-nonsense Uribe has been dramatic. Uribe has both the *FARC* and the *ELN* on the defensive, inflicting heavy losses and forcing them into an alliance for the first time in two decades. The *AUC* is in the process of demobilizing. His approval rating remains about 70%, something phenomenal for a Latin American president after three years.

Uribe may also be responsible for reversing the slide of public confidence in Colombia's 47-year-old democracy, according to the two latest annual surveys by the Chilean firm *Latinobarómetro* published in the British newsmagazine, *The Economist.* In 2002, the year Uribe assumed office, the survey showed that only 39% of Colombians believed that democracy was preferable to any other form of government, compared with 60% in 1996. In the 2003 and 2004 surveys, that figure was back up to 46%. At the same time, 20% of Colombians in 1996 said in the survey that authoritarianism was sometimes preferable to democracy. In 2002, that was down to 11%, but in 2003 it had increased to 14%. It was back down to 12% in 2004.

The criticism Uribe has come under from the United Nations and domestic human rights groups for his "democratic security" program is akin to the debate in the United States over the Patriot Act, passed in the wake of the 9-11 terrorist attacks. It should be remembered that the U.S. Constitution permits the president to suspend the right of *habeas corpus* during times of invasion or rebellion, and Abraham Lincoln did just that during the Civil War. Yet, he is remembered as the Great Emancipator, not as a violator of human rights. Uribe is dealing with the guerrillas and the paramilitaries, who are the real threat to Colombia's democracy, in the only manner they understand, and he is showing signs of success.

However, the other side has a valid point, as do opponents of renewal of the Patriot Act. Once civil liberties have been chipped away in the name of security, no matter how justifiable the reason at the moment, can they ever be restored once the danger is past? In December 2003, Congress approved a law giving the military search, arrest, interrogation and judicial power for four years to combat "terrorism," which can be interpreted loosely. Much depends on the scruples of Uribe and his successors. Is he a Lincoln? Or, if he is allowed to serve a second term, could he become a Fujimori? Thus far there have been no serious infringements on freedom of the press or of expression, apart from Uribe's intolerant and injudicious likening of his human rights critics to terrorists. But the potential for abuse is there, if not by Uribe then by some future president who may not be as committed to civil liberties or tolerance of criticism.

Plan Colombia is beginning to show some signs of success after $3 billion in U.S. aid. Coca cultivation is down dramatically, forcing the kingpins to cultivate the leaf in other countries. At best, however, the war on drugs will remain on a treadmill. Why? As the Latin Americans have complained for years, U.S. and European demand for illegal drugs is insatiable, making the trafficking of them an endeavor too lucrative to abandon and so lucrative to make it worth the risks.

How can demand be reduced? One way could be through more effective public education in the consuming countries, something far more effective than Nancy Reagan's "Just say no" campaign. This author was the Army Reserve attaché to Colombia from 1994–1998, and I learned a great deal about cocaine production. The three principal ingredients needed to refine coca leaves into that coveted, exorbitant powder that addicts need so desperately are gasoline, powdered cement and hydrochloric acid. Public service messages that show in graphic detail the disgusting process of how cocaine is actually made ought to persuade any reasonable person never to try it—and maybe even to give it up.

Exiting Colombia on the Pan-American Highway into Ecuador, one encounters highland travelers.

Photo by Katie Thompson

The Republic of Costa Rica

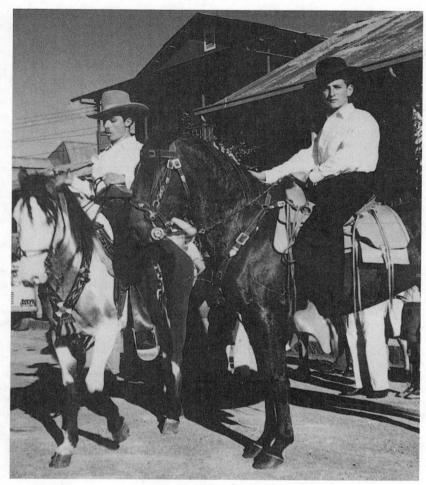

Costa Rican cowboys—campesinos

Area: 19,647 square miles.
Population: 3.96 million (2004 estimate).
Capital City: San José (Pop. 800,000, estimated).
Climate: The coastal lowlands are hot and tropical, with heavy rains from April to December. The valley of the central highlands is temperate, with moderate rains during the wet season.
Neighboring Countries: Nicaragua (North); Panama (Southeast).
Official Language: Spanish
Ethnic Background: Overwhelmingly Spanish European descent, blended with some Indian lineage. A few Indians with African heritage are found along the Atlantic coast; some pure-blood Indians live in the highlands.
Principal Religion: Roman Catholic Christianity.
Chief Commercial Products: Coffee, bananas, sugar and cacao.
Currency: Colon.
Gross Domestic Product: U.S. $16.7 billion in 2002 ($4,193 per capita).
Former Colonial Status: Spanish Crown Colony (1522–1821).
Independence Date: September 15, 1821.

Chief of State: Abel Pacheco de la Espriella (b. December 22, 1933), president (since May 8, 2002).
National Flag: Blue, white and red horizontal stripes.

Costa Rica, literally *Rich Coast*, is next to the smallest of the Central American republics. Lying between Nicaragua and Panama with coasts on both the Atlantic and Pacific oceans, the distance from ocean to ocean varies from 75 to 175 miles.

The country is divided into three distinct regions: the Atlantic coastal plains, the central highlands and the Pacific coast. The central highlands are part of a chain of scenic mountains rising in Nicaragua and running southeast through Costa Rica into Panama. They contain lofty peaks reaching 12,500 feet and several steep-sided inter-mountain valleys. The green central valley, some 40 miles wide and 50 miles long, lying between 3,000 and 6,000 feet above sea level, is the most densely populated part of Costa Rica.

The two principal cities, San José and Cartago, share the valley with four volcanoes, two of which are still violently ac-

tive. Mount Irazú, close to the capital, littered the city with ashes and cinders in 1962. Arenal erupted in 1998.

Costa Rica's coffee is grown on the slopes of the hills and volcanoes which rim the valley. The Atlantic coastal plains are moist and low, heavily forested and sparsely settled. Costa Rica's main port in the east is Puerto Limón, the only city of commercial importance in the area.

The Pacific lowlands, drier than the Atlantic plains, are quite narrow except for the Nicoya and Osa peninsulas. Thinly settled, the region produces bananas and fiber on large plantations. The port of Golfito on the Pacific coast handles most of the country's exports. Lying in the tropical rainbelt, Costa Rica has more than abundant rainfall, particularly in the rainy season from April to December of each year. Some parts of the oppressive Atlantic coast region have rain during 300 days of the year.

History: The Spaniards discovered the Nicoya Peninsula in 1522, settling in the Central Valley, where a few sedentary Indian farmers were found. They organized into a *hacienda* system of independent farm communities. The Spaniards intermarried with the Indians, who were assimilated into the Spanish culture. Cartago was founded in 1563, but no expansion of this settlement occurred for 145 years, during which time the Costa Ricans evolved as a community of small farmers. With the assimilated Indians and a few slaves, the Costa Rican worked his own land, developing a system of small, efficient and independent land-owners and a tradition of industry not usually found in Hispanic society. Settlers from Cartago founded Heredia in 1717 and San José in 1737; by 1750 the population had reached approximately 2,500, divided into some 400 family groups.

Independence from Spain was achieved on September 15, 1821 as a result of actions in Guatemala, Mexico and other colonies. Costa Rica fell victim to the civil wars which followed the separation of the Central American Republics from the short-lived Mexican Empire. However, remoteness from the scene of the bitter quarrels between conservatives and liberals in Guatemala and El Salvador minimized the effects of the civil war in Costa Rica. The most significant events of Costa Rica's history as an independent state have been its efforts to develop the economy to provide the revenues required to support the people.

The government encouraged the production of coffee in 1825, offering free land for development. From 1850, the coffee trade attracted new settlers and inspired the development of roads and the settlement of areas outside the central val-

Costa Rica

ley. The building of railroads between the 1870s and 1890s introduced banana growing to provide traffic for the new system. At the same time, West Indians were brought in to build the railroads, clear the forests and to work the Atlantic coast plantations.

Subsequently, irrigated banana plantations were developed on the Pacific coast, resulting in the building of ports at Golfito and Puntarenas. On the Nicoya Peninsula and in the northwest, cattle raising became and remains an important industry.

Politically, the Costa Rican experience was tranquil. The first experiments in government were hardly more than gentlemanly agreements among the principal families. The constitution of 1848 abolished the army and replaced it with a civil guard. Costa Rica has had only one major experience with dictatorial government. Tomás Guardia came to power in 1870 and ruled as an undisguised dictator until 1882. Exiling opposition leaders and spending money with a lavish hand, he broke up the traditional parties, installed his friends in office and undertook to modernize the rural agricultural state. During his term of office, roads, railroads, schools and public buildings were constructed; the production of sugar and coffee was increased and international trade was encouraged.

Costa Rican political freedom was recovered in elections of 1889 which were free and honest. Three subsequent attempts were made to seize the government: in 1917, which lasted two years, an unsuccessful attempt in 1932 and a communist—inspired effort in 1948 was ended by a brief civil war. José Figueres, a hero of the civil war, won election in 1953; a capable farmer and businessman, he did much to renew public works and increase government revenues. An outspoken critic of Caribbean dictatorships, he was denounced as a communist and an invasion force from Nicaragua moved to unseat him.

An appeal to the Organization of American States ended the conflict; Figueres disbanded the force he had raised for defense and pressed for both economic and social development. Subsequent presidents representing conservative and liberal parties have maintained the tradition of responsible, democratic government which was the ideal of Figueres. Like most countries dependent upon agricultural exports for its revenues, Costa Rica has had its economic problems, but also has shown a remarkable ability to handle them peacefully.

Between 1945 and 1974 the presidency alternated between conservatives and liberals while the single-chamber legislature was dominated by the liberal National Liberation Party (*PLN*). This pattern was reversed with the election of Daniel Oduber Quirós to succeed President Figueres.

With 42% of the vote, Oduber's victory was credited to the superior organization of the *PLN* and to the divided opposition of seven other candidates. The new president, a former head of the legislature, promised agrarian reform and constitutional changes to increase the power of the executive branch. However, in 1978, voters ousted the ruling *PLN*, electing Rodrigo Carazo of the Democratic Renovation Party. He won by 50% to 49% over the *PLN* candidate, former union organizer Luís Alberto Monge Alvarez.

The right-of-center president soon found his administration beset by scandals and fiscal problems. For years, Costa Ricans imported more than they exported and spent more than they earned. Somehow, it worked until 1980, when the nation's imported oil bills and international interest charges skyrocketed while earnings from exports nosedived.

Rather than impose needed austerity measures (the government subsidizes food, fuel and luxury imports), Carazo sought to stave off disaster by printing more paper money. International lenders responded by cutting off credit.

The crisis exacted another toll: Carazo became the most unpopular president in recent years. In 1982 presidential elections, voters rejected his Unity coalition in favor of Monge 56, who this time took 58% of the vote. During his years in office, his popularity remained high in spite of an unpleasant task: austerity measures to bolster a sagging economy.

By mid-1984, democratic Costa Rica appeared besieged by several problems. The armed conflicts in neighboring Nicaragua and El Salvador threatened to interfere with the national political process at a time when economic conditions in the nation reached a dangerously low level; the national public debt increased to $4.4 billion by 1986, placing the government on the brink of bankruptcy. Significantly, in mid-1984 the government asked the United States for $7.3 million in order to improve its military capability to resist increasing *Sandinista* pressure on its Nicaraguan border. By the middle of 1985, the first U.S. military advisers were already training the Costa Rican National Guard.

In 1986, voters elected Oscar Arias Sánchez of the *PLN* president by a majority of 52.3%. A highly educated and respected man, he performed admirably in the face of adversities which surrounded the country and which it had been experiencing from communist infiltration of the labor movement from within. His performance was mostly steady, but sometimes erratic. During a visit to Washington in mid-1987 he strongly urged President Reagan to discontinue aid to the *contras* of Nicaragua, stating that they were fomenting unrest in Central America. But a few days later, he declared that so long as the *Sandinista* re-

126

gime of Nicaragua existed, there would be a danger that communism would spread throughout Central America.

Arias was the architect in late 1987 of a peace plan for Central America, a scheme that was immediately embraced by liberals in the U.S. House of Representatives who had been trying to end aid to the anti-communist *contras*. He received the Nobel Peace Price for his efforts.

With the demise of the Soviet Union, the *Sandinistas* found the economic rug being abruptly yanked out from under their regime, and out of sheer desperation, accepted the Arias plan, which included democratization of that country.

Arias was not eligible under law for a second term, and was succeeded by 40-year-old Rafael Angelo Calderón, a lawyer from the Social Christian Unity Party (*PUSC*). He significantly cut the number of civil employees and undertook a number of measures to modernize the economy.

In the 1994 election, the *PLN* returned to power with the candidacy of José María Figueres, son of the former president. He narrowly defeated Miguel Angel Rodríguez of the *PUSC*, despite the cloud hanging over Figueres that he may have been involved in a murder when he was a teenager and charges, dismissed because of a statute of limitations, of corruption while he was a government minister. Figueres' campaign also was helped by a Washington-based political consulting firm, which ran U.S.-style television commercials that smeared Rodríguez as a shady businessman who once was forced to file for bankruptcy.

Although the Harvard-educated Figueres was elected on a promise to retain the Uruguayan-style social welfare system his father had engineered, once in office he did what so many other Latin American presidents have done in recent years. Confronted with economic reality, including a cumbersome public debt of $3.5 billion that represented 40% of GDP, he abandoned his party's idealistic social principles and sought pragmatic solutions to the country's economic woes. His greatest feat was in touting Costa Rica's low labor costs and highly literate work force to persuade transnational high-tech firms to locate assembly plants in Costa Rica. His major prize was Intel Corp., which agreed to build a $300 million assembly plant that has since exported $3 billion per year in Pentium processors. Among Figueres' other economic successes, he lowered the unemployment rate from 6.2% in 1996 to 5.4% in 1997, cut inflation to 11.2% in 1997, the lowest in four years, and oversaw a robust GDP growth rate of 4% in 1997. Yet, Figueres proved the most unpopular president since Carazo. Despite his economic successes, Costa Ricans still grumbled that

Oscar Arias Sánchez

their glass was half empty rather than half full. The Figueres administration was plagued by a number of low-level scandals, hardly more than peccadillos by Latin American standards but which undermined public confidence in his government. The public also was concerned over an alarming increase in common crime, including violent crime, once rare. Finally, Figueres was faulted for neglecting the nation's infrastructure, especially the sorry condition of streets and highways.

The time was ripe for the *PUSC*'s Rodríguez to make a Nixon-like comeback in the February 1, 1998 elections. The *PLN* candidate, former soccer star José Miguel Corrales, sought to distance himself from the unpopular Figueres by attempting to seize the moral high ground and purging the party of congressional and municipal candidates with allegedly questionable backgrounds. This move merely alienated Corrales from the rank and file of his own party. While Corrales made grand promises to pay housewives a minimum wage and to provide more free bonds for private home construction, Rodríguez's campaign strategy might well have been summed up, "It's the potholes, stupid." Indeed, at times he sounded more like a candidate for county commissioner than for president, promising to repave highways, to expand water purification systems, even to remove the hated turnstiles from the front of buses and to allow passengers to exit from the rear. The outcome was closer than the polls had predicted, with Rodríguez winning by a 46–43% margin over Corrales and 11 other candidates.

Rodríguez managed to do something unusual for a Latin American president: keep his promises. He expanded the San

José airport and embarked on an ambitious road-building program. He also was aggressive in luring more foreign investors, an initiative that appeared to pay off (see Economy). However, Rodríguez was met with vigorous street protests when he attempted to privatize state-owned companies as has been done in virtually every other Latin American country except Cuba and Uruguay. Rice farmers also protested his free-trade initiatives.

The 2002 election reflected Costa Ricans' growing disenchantment with what they regarded as a lack of choice between the two major parties. For the first time in Costa Rica's venerable 53-year-old democracy, a third-party candidate emerged who threatened the traditional parties' power monopoly. In 2001, Otton Solís, a 48-year-old economist and *PLN* dissident, formed the Citizen Action Party (*PAC*). The *PUSC* nominated a 68-year-old psychiatrist and congressional deputy, Abel Pacheco, while the *PLN* nominated Rolando Araya, 54, a chemical engineer. Both Pacheco and Araya had high name recognition from having been television commentators. Solís attacked what was widely perceived as the two main parties' corruption; Pacheco pledged to crack down on common crime, which has become a major problem and a threat to the all-important tourist industry; Araya placed his emphasis on improving education. Polls showed the three candidates at one point in a statistical three-way tie. In the balloting on February 3, 2002, however, the two major parties won the upper hand, but Solís prevented either of them from receiving the necessary 40% to avoid a second round. Pacheco finished first with 38.5%, Araya was second with 30.9% and Solís was a strong third with 26.3%. Besides throwing the election

President and Mrs. Abel Pacheco

Costa Rica

into a runoff for the first time, Solís' *PAC* also emerged as the kingmaker in the new Congress with 14 seats; the *PUSC* won 19 and the *PLN*, 17. Voter turnout was 69%, as anemic as it had been in 1998.

In Costa Rica's first-ever runoff, Araya attempted to win over Solís' voters by pledging a crackdown on official corruption, but he had little success because of the bitter attacks he had made on Solís in the first round to move up from third place in the polls. Araya also attempted unsuccessfully to portray Pacheco as a neoliberal; in truth, both candidates adhered to the popular sentiment against privatization of government-owned enterprises like telecommunications and insurance. In the April 7 runoff, Pacheco won with a resounding mandate of 58%. It was the first time the *PUSC* had won two successive elections. Pacheco was inaugurated on May 8, 2002

In January 2004, Costa Rica belatedly agreed to join El Salvador, Guatemala, Honduras and Nicaragua in creating a Central American Free Trade Agreement with the United States. Costa Rica initially had balked at opening up its state-owned insurance and telecommunications industries to competition with U.S. firms. Under a compromise reached with the United States, those two sectors would not become fully competitive until 2011.

Costa Ricans were stunned when a series of events began unfolding in August 2004 that implicated the current and three former presidents, from both major parties, in alleged financial improprieties.

In August, there were 13 days of street protests when it was reported that the lucrative contract for vehicle inspections was awarded to a Spanish firm in which a political adviser of President Pacheco had part ownership. But this relatively mild appearance of conflict of interest was nothing compared to the bombshells that exploded simultaneously in October.

First, on October 8, prosecutors announced that they were investigating two payments from the government of Taiwan totaling $400,000 in 2001 and 2002 to a company controlled by former President Rodríguez, who just two weeks earlier had been elected secretary-general of the Organization of American States. At the same time, the former head of the state-owned power and telephone company, *ICE*, testified that he had accepted a $2.4 million "prize," a euphemism for kickback, from the French firm Alcatel for a $149 million cell phone contract in 2001 and that he had passed $550,000 of it to then-President Rodríguez. Rodríguez resigned his OAS post and returned to Costa Rica to answer the charges. He was briefly handcuffed and jailed, then sentenced to house arrest, then jailed again pending trial.

On October 22, former President Calderón was also jailed, accused of taking $9 million in kickbacks from a $39 million loan from Finland for medical equipment to upgrade the state health care system. He allegedly brokered the deal in 2001, seven years after leaving office. Calderón and Rodríguez are both of the *PUSC*.

Next it was the turn of former President Figueres of the *PLN*, who had become head of the World Economic Forum, a Swiss-based think tank. He was accused in Costa Rica of failing to report as income about $1 million he received from Alcatel for supposed "consulting fees." Figueres admitted receiving the money, which violated the terms of his contract with the WEF. He resigned and returned to Costa Rica to face possibe tax evasion charges.

Almost simultaneously, Pacheco then stood accused of illegally accepting foreign campaign contributions for his 2002 presidential campaign. The investigation was briefly dropped because of a procedural error, then reopened in December. Moreover, nine officials resigned from Pacheco's government between August and October; the public works minister was caught running a loan shark operation.

In March 2005, judges agreed to release both Calderón and Rodríguez, who had complained of health problems, from jail and placed them under house arrest pending trial. Rodríguez had to post $430,000 in bond and Calderón, $500,000. All four investigations were ongoing when this book went to press.

At the height of the scandals, Oscar Arias, the only recent president *not* to be under investigation, announced in January 2005 that he would run for president again in 2006.

Pacheco, who had suffered a stroke two years before he was elected, was hospitalized briefly with chest pains in February 2005. He also suffers from diabetes and high blood pressure. Now 71, he insisted he is healthy enough to serve out the remainder of his term—unless he is impeached first.

Culture: Costa Ricans are predominantly Roman Catholic. Basically they are of European, primarily Spanish, ancestry; the country has the lowest percentage of Indians and *mestizos* of any Central American country. Early in the colonial era, the few Indians native to the area were assimilated into a uniform, friendly society of middle class merchants and small farmers. The pure Spanish descendants emerged as a small, rich elite controlling the wealth of Costa Rica.

Popular cultural expression is found in music and dance. The most characteristic art expression is the brilliantly decorated ox carts like those still found in rural

Spain and Portugal; they are accepted as a national symbol, although they have been replaced by trucks and tractors in the national economy. Through energetic promotion of education, Costa Rica has achieved the highest literacy rate in Central America—93%—greater than that of the United States. There is a vigorous free press. The country's newspaper of record is *La Nación*. Fifteen television stations provide a wide variety of entertainment.

This is one of the most pleasant of the Central American countries to visit. The train journey from San José to Limón is scenically spectacular. Of course, the usual precautions against thievery must be taken where there is great disparity in wealth, particularly in the bustling city of Limón.

Economy: Costa Rica's sources of external income are coffee and bananas. Industrial activity once was limited to processing agricultural products for market and the production of import substitutes for domestic consumption. In recent years, foreign firms have established assembly plants, such as Motorola and Intel.

Improved economic conditions have encouraged the upper class to retain more capital funds within Costa Rica, which before would have been invested abroad. There is no immediate threat to the economy, and there is also a growing sense within the elite that the wealth of the nation must be shared more widely.

Tourism is a rapidly growing industry, thanks to beautiful beaches on both coasts and a number of rain forest reserves. Costa Rica also has proven an ideal site for a relatively luxurious retirement at a modest cost for U.S. citizens. Stability and lower prices for everything but imported goods are attractive to persons with reasonable but not unlimited means and annual income. Costa Rica advertises itself in U.S. media as an excellent place for individual (not communal) retirement, attracting widespread interest. About 30,000 Americans already have settled here.

There was a major disappointment in 1998 when Motorola announced it would begin scaling back the output of its Costa Rican plant, but the impact was more than neutralized by the opening of Intel's Pentium processor plant. The plant's $2 billion in exports in 1999 gave Costa Rica a $93 million trade surplus, compared with a $702 million deficit in 1998, its first surplus in 13 years. It also generated a disproportionate growth in real GDP of 8.2%, the highest in Latin America, but experts warned that it would drop when the Intel plant was fully operational in 2000. It did; growth for 2000 was a meager 1.4%, only .7% in 2001, and 3.0% in 2002.

Costa Rica

These positive factors, plus political stability, an educated labor force and the Rodríguez administration's eight-year tax exemption for manufacturers of export products, have proven attractive to foreign investors. One target: the cumbersome government-owned electricity and telecommunications company, which Rodríguez attempted unsuccessfully to privatize. Costa Ricans have proven stubbornly reluctant to dismantle the quasi-socialist public sector, apparently out of fear of the unknown and despite the privatization trend that has swept Latin America. Even cellular telephone service and insurance are state-owned in Costa Rica. In the next few years, high-tech and ecotourism are expected to transform the Costa Rican economy, replacing the far more market-sensitive coffee and bananas as the mainstays of the economy.

In 2003, GDP growth was back up to 5.6%. Unemployment was only 6.7% in 2003, while inflation was a manageable 9.4%.

The Future: Although Costa Ricans had been grumbling for years about suspected corruption by their politicians, they were nonetheless boastful that their political system was still far more circumspect than those of most other Latin American countries. Indeed, Transparency International gave Costa Rica a score of 4.9 in its 2004 corruption perception index, ranking it 41st out of 144 countries; in Latin America, only Chile and Uruguay were regarded as less corrupt (see Latin America Today).

The jailing of former Presidents Calderón and Rodríguez in 2004, and the investigations against President Pacheco and former President Figueres, have shaken Costa Ricans' pride in their country's perceived rectitude. They are now like parents who thought their teenage daughter had done nothing worse than smoke cigarettes and drink beer, only to discover she had been smoking marijuana and charging the soccer team for sexual favors. Even before the scandals broke, the annual *Latinobarómetro* survey showed a 10-point drop from 2003 to 2004 in the percentage of Costa Ricans who believed democracy is preferable to any other form of government, from 77% to 67%; in 1996 it was 80%. Only Nicaragua showed a more precipitous one-year drop. The scandals have been, to use a cliché, a wake-up call, and voters are likely to engage in some political tough love in the February 2006 elections.

Former President Oscar Arias (1986–90), the respected Nobel Peace laureate and the only president in the past 16 years who is not accused of some shenanigans, has announced he plans to run again next year. His reputation may help him pull it off, but he has the handicap of being identified with the *PLN*, which like the *PUSC* has been sullied by the scandals. The greatest beneficiary of the scandals could well be Otton Solís of the Citizen Action Party, who ran a strong third in 2002 with an anti-corruption platform and can now campaign on the theme, *"Les dije!"* ("I told you so!). Voters will almost certainly be more receptive to his message this time around.

Typical Costa Rican ox cart

129

The Socialist Republic of Cuba

Señores Imperialists: We are not in the least afraid of you!

Photo by Sheila Curtin

Area: 44,217 square miles; with the Isle of Youth, 45,397 square miles.

Population: 11 million.

Capital City: Havana (Pop. 2.4 million, estimated).

Climate: Tropical with little daily or seasonal change. Cuba is buffeted by occasional tropical hurricanes from July to October.

Neighboring Countries: Cuba is an island, the largest and most westerly of the Greater Antilles islands, lying 90 miles south of Florida and separated from Hispaniola by 40 miles.

Official Language: Spanish.

Ethnic Background: Mulatto (mixed black and white), 51%; white, 37%; black, 11%; other, 1%.

Principal Religion: Roman Catholic.

Chief Commercial Products: Sugar, minerals and tobacco.

Currency: Peso.

Gross Domestic Product: U.S. $18.6 billion in 1999 ($1,531 per capita, 2001 est.). These figures are estimates derived from various factors and may be the result of government distortion or exaggeration. No reliable estimate is possible.

Former Colonial Status: Spanish Crown Colony (1492–1898).

Independence Date: May 20, 1902. (Spanish rule ended on December 10, 1898).

Chief of State: Fidel Castro Ruz (b. August 13, 1926), president (since January 1, 1959)

National Flag: Three blue and two white horizontal stripes; a white star in a red triangle at the staff.

Cuba, an island 745 miles long and not over 90 miles wide at any point, lies east and west across the Gulf of Mexico, 90 miles south of Key West, Florida. Cuba is gifted with moderate temperatures, adequate rainfall and excellent soils. While the general impression of Cuba is one of rolling hills, it is in fact quite mountainous in parts. To the west of Havana is the Sierra de los Organos, with elevations of up to 2,500 feet; toward the center of the island are the Trinidad Mountains rising to 3,700 feet; in the east the Sierra Maestra has peaks reaching 6,500 feet. About one sixth of the land is forested. The rough, stony headlands east of Guantanamo Bay are semi-arid and the source of copper, nickel, chrome and iron ores.

History: Cuba was discovered by Columbus in 1492 and conquered by the Spanish in 1511. Indians offered little resistance and, decimated by hard labor and epidemics, disappeared fairly rapidly. By the end of the 16th century only small, dwindling groups survived in the mountainous areas of the island.

The Spanish conquest of the continent relegated Cuba and the other islands in the Caribbean to a secondary position in the rapidly expanding empire. Lured by the news of gold and glory coming from Mexico and Peru, Spanish immigrants abandoned Cuba to join further exploration and conquests. Two factors, though, compelled Spain to pay special attention to Cuba: its strategic geographical location, dominating the entrance to the Gulf of Mexico, and the increasing attacks by pirates which forced Spain to concentrate its naval resources in "convoys," or fleets, for better protection of its rich cargoes. These fleets, one departing from Veracruz, Mexico, and the other from Cartagena, Colombia, joined in Havana and then, under the protection of the Spanish navy, sailed for Europe. Consequently the port of Havana had to be extremely well fortified, and the sporadic presence of these fleets allowed for a flourishing degree of commerce.

During the 18th century the development of the island gained some momentum. The decline of gold and silver production on the continent convinced many Spaniards that they should remain on the island. Garrisons were kept to protect several ports besides Havana; smuggling with other islands—principally Jamaica and Haiti, by then British and French possessions—increased trade. The rising demand for the island's first valuable export, tobacco, created favorable conditions for steady economic growth. The strategic importance of Cuba was highlighted in 1762 when Havana was attacked and captured by a large British expeditionary force. The British did not expand their occupation beyond the port, and they stayed less than two years. However, the attack jolted Spain. More fortifications were built along the shores of the island, more capable officials were sent to govern the colony and a program of road construction began into the interior of Cuba. Almost simultaneously, the island's sugar production began to demonstrate its rich potential.

The independence of the United States in 1783 opened a close and expanding market, and the collapse of Haiti's sugar production in 1799–1801 following its devastating war for independence gave Cuba a truly golden opportunity. In the first three decades of the 19th century the island changed rapidly from a slowly developing "factory" into the world's leading sugar producer.

The production of sugar, however, required a growing number of black slaves. Fearing a repetition of Haiti's experience, and enjoying unhindered prosperity—the Napoleonic wars and affairs in South America had kept Spain occupied in other areas—Cubans were not eager to risk all in an attempt to break with the mother country. After 1830, however, this situation began to change. Concentrating her attention on Cuba, Spain increased taxation, imposed arbitrary rules for its own benefit and completely alienated the creoles (native born Cubans of mixed ancestry), by denying them any voice in the government. Seeking annexation to the United States, a now powerful nation where slavery was accepted, many slave owners promoted armed expeditions from southern American ports, but the North's resistance to the incorporation of more slave territories into the Union, and the eventual defeat of the South in the American Civil War, put an end to those efforts. By 1865 the majority of the creoles still held hopes of obtaining reforms from Spain. Only a minority proclaimed the necessity of fighting for independence. An international economic crisis which hit the island in 1866 and Madrid's dismissal in 1867 of a Cuban delegation demanding reforms set the stage for the *independentistas*. In 1868, in the town of Yara, Carlos Manuel de Céspedes raised the banner of independence.

Using guerrilla tactics, and under the guidance of able military leaders, the Cubans fought valiantly against an increasing number of Spanish troops for 10 years. Their failure to invade the rich western provinces (the struggle was limited to the eastern regions), internal dissension, exhaustion of resources and renewed Spanish promises of reforms, brought peace in 1878. But in spite of the Cuban Autonomist Party's efforts, few reforms materialized. By 1890, Cuban discontent was growing and a new, exceptional leader had appeared: José Martí. Poet, essayist and patriot, Martí managed to unite almost all Cuban exiles, organized a conspiracy on the island and prepared to renew the struggle. He dreamed of a short, popular war which would avoid the destruction of wealth, the rise of military *caudillos* and U.S. intervention. In 1895 the war began and Martí was killed in one of its first skirmishes.

U.S. Domination

From 1895 until 1898 the Cubans fought Spain's military might. This time, able to carry the war throughout the entire island, the rebels burned and destroyed most of Cuba's wealth. Increasingly alarmed, and stimulated by imperialist groups and a "yellow" (sensationalist) press, the United States finally intervened in 1898 when the explosion of the battleship *Maine* in Havana harbor raised to a peak the clamor for war. The "splendid little war" against an exhausted Spain lasted a few months and ended with the military occupation of Cuba. After reorganizing a country ravaged by war and disease, the U.S. military forces abandoned the island in 1902. That year, the Cuban people proclaimed a constitution which (through the Platt Amendment by the U.S. Congress) gave the United States the right to intervene in case of crisis, and elected its first democratic president, Tomás Estrada Palma.

Estrada Palma's honest administration was marred by political turmoil when the president sought reelection in 1906—reluctantly, the United States was forced to again occupy the island for two years. After building a Cuban army and watching the election of Liberal José Miguel Gómez, the United States once more pulled out its

Cuba

President Batista deposits his ballot

military forces. The next 20 years witnessed rapid expansion of sugar production, increased American investment, persistent political corruption and economic instability of a one-product economy. Nevertheless, the republic progressed in many areas. Education improved, communication was expanded and a new nationalistic awareness matured. An economic crisis of 1919–21 resulted in a rising crescendo of popular demands for the abrogation of the Platt Amendment and strong protests against official corruption.

Liberal Gerardo Machado was elected president in 1925 and initiated a vast program of national regeneration and public construction. His popularity declined in 1928 when he imposed his candidacy for reelection on the Cuban people—it plunged after the economic collapse of 1929–30. Faced with widespread misery and violent opposition spearheaded by university students as well as a secret organization known as A.B.C., Machado responded with brutality. By 1933, in spite of increased terrorism on the part of the government, the struggle had reached a stalemate; the opposition had no realistic hopes of toppling Machado and the government was unable to eliminate its opponents. It was time for Washington again to intervene.

Constrained by his own "Good Neighbor Policy" which precluded the use of military force, the recently elected President Roosevelt sent his trusted aide Sumner Welles to seek a legal solution for Cuba; his mission was to prevent a revolution and avoid American military intervention. Posing as a mediator, Welles pressured Machado into making conces-

sions, encouraged the opposition and eroded the army's loyalty to the president. In 1933 a general strike decided the issue: Machado fled the island. Immediately Welles organized a provisional government with the cooperation of the A.B.C. and the majority of the opposition. But the revolutionary momentum disrupted his plan. There was a purely military insurrection of Army sergeants, headed by Fulgencio Batista, which was transformed by university students into a revolutionary movement that toppled the provisional government. For four turbulent months under a temporary president, the students and the sergeants (by then *colonels*) tried to enforce a radical and ambitious program of social reforms. Sternly opposed by Welles, the government collapsed in January 1934 when Batista shifted to the opposition. As soon as a moderate president was installed, Washington abrogated the Platt Amendment. For the following decade, *real power* centered around Batista.

Batista was not a bloody dictator or a counter-revolutionary. A man of humble origins, both shrewd and ambitious, he preferred bribery and corruption over brutality. Well aware of the importance of the nationalistic and social forces unleashed by the revolutionary episode of 1933, he tried to use them for his own benefit. Encouraging the emergence of political parties and the return to the island of political exiles, he quickly restored stability. Labor unions were legally protected, social legislation approved and a modest plan for national recovery announced. After Batista harshly repressed a general strike in 1935, the Cuban political atmosphere became calm. Supported by several

parties, including the Communist Party, Batista convened a Constitutional Assembly, and in 1940 one of the most advanced social constitutions in all of Latin America was issued. That same year Batista was elected president.

With the price of sugar climbing, Batista's term of office coincided with a return of economic prosperity. In 1944 Batista crowned his accomplishments by

The U.S. and Cuba
1902–1959

Despite the unevenness of U.S.–Cuban relations politically, the two nations developed close economic ties during the post–independence period through the 1959 Cuban Revolution. U.S. investment was encouraged and protected, and in fact became a mainstay of the Cuban economy. In spite of domestic Cuban upheavals, there was an unwritten understanding that neither U.S. investments nor Cuban tourist facilities calculated to attract Americans would be disturbed.

Some aspects of this relationship were resented by many Cubans, particularly the common U.S. notion that Cuba was a paradise for those seeking sexual adventures not explicitly described, but well–known. Many "French" postcards (pornography, judged by then–prevailing standards in the United States) had their origin in Cuba. Numerous films "for private exhibition" were produced and made in the island nation. Tourists relished in the decadence offered by the casinos and nightclubs, many controlled by organized crime figures, chief among them Meyer Lansky.

Havana and other coastal resorts and towns were favored ports of call for resort and cruise ships and there was regular steamship service catering to vacationers. A luxurious train regularly departed from New York—"The Havana Special"—which ran down the east coast through Miami and went on to Key West over a rail causeway. From there, the cars were loaded onto seagoing ferries which took them to their ultimate destination, loaded with fun–seeking vacationers. This ended in 1936 when a devastating hurricane wiped out the causeway.

As airline traffic came into its own after World War II, Havana was a favorite destination of tourists and vacationers. This pleasant state of affairs continued right up to 1960, with all political considerations being put aside.

allowing free elections. Ramón Grau San Martín, hero of 1933 and head of the *Autentico* Party, obtained the overwhelming majority of the votes. The *Autenticos* ruled from 1944 to 1948, with a positive record of benefits for the workers, respect for democratic values, a more equitable distribution of wealth, continuing economic recovery and rising living standards, but was tarnished by public corruption on an unprecedented scale. Grau was succeeded in 1948 by a fellow *Auténtico*, Carlos Prío Socarrás, who proved equally venal. Before the people could repudiate the *Auténticos* in 1952 elections, Batista disrupted the political process with a military coup.

Trying to keep up appearances, Batista promised elections in 1954. But the illegitimacy of the government prompted political parties and numerous sectors of the population to demand a return to "true democracy." Soon more radical opponents appeared. The students organized violent acts and on July 26, 1953—now a holiday in Cuba—a group of young men under the leadership of Fidel Castro made an unsuccessful attack on the military barracks at Santiago de Cuba. The sheer brutality of its repression mobilized popular support for the rebels. With Castro and his surviving group in prison, Batista renewed his effort to gain legitimacy.

Elections were held in 1954; Batista was elected to the presidency and he allowed *all* political prisoners to go free—including young Fidel Castro. But opposition to Batista increased. While a Student Revolutionary Federation resorted to terrorism to achieve Batista's overthrow, Castro, who had been in self-exile in Mexico, landed an expedition of 80 young men in Oriente Province in December 1956 and took immediate refuge in the Sierra Maestra mountains of eastern Cuba.

Weakened by adverse propaganda and its own corruption, with a demoralized army incapable of mounting any serious operation, the regime consistently lost ground. When in 1958 Washington showed its disapproval by proclaiming an arms embargo, Batista was doomed. On December 31 he fled the island (with millions of dollars stashed safely in Swiss banks), and Fidel Castro entered Havana in triumph on January 8, 1959.

The Cuban Revolution

For the vast majority of the Cuban people, Batista's downfall represented the end of an illegitimate and violent episode in their history and a quick return to the democratic process. Fidel Castro, and other leaders of the 26th of July Movement (named after the attack on the Moncada Army Barracks) had repeatedly promised the restoration of the 1940 con-

Ché Guevara, 1959

stitutional freedom of expression, elections within 18 months and an end of political corruption. Thus, the young leader, enhanced by his heroic image, received the almost unanimous applause of the Cuban people. Batista had fallen into such disrepute in the United States that Castro was considered to be a liberating hero of Cuba; there was widespread discussion and speculation about how firm and friendly ties with the new government on the island could be forged, together with enhanced U.S. investment. Castro, however, had other ideas.

The son of a wealthy Spanish landowner who studied for a time in a Jesuit seminary, Castro had very early shown inclinations toward violence and unlimited ambition: he wanted unrestricted, absolute power. Increasing his power with a series of laws which, at least temporarily, benefited the masses—agrarian reform, increased wages, a reduction of the cost of public services—he simultaneously used his popularity, or his charisma, as a weapon to crush his opponents. The Student Directory was reduced to a secondary role through a pointed television campaign; Dr. Manuel Urrutia, the same man he had appointed president six months before, was forced to resign under a barrage of insults in mid-1959. Soon a new slogan appeared: "Revolution first, elections later!" Special tribunals dealt harshly with *Batistianos* and later with anyone accused of counter-revolution; about 550 were executed by firing squads. In late 1959, one of the heroes of the revolution, Major Huber Matos, resigned to protest an increasing communist influence in the government. He was sentenced to 20 years in prison. By the end of that year, almost all of the media was under government control. Ominously, another slogan proclaimed that "to be anti-communist was to be counter-revolutionary." Quietly, Castro began building a formidable military apparatus, commanded by his brother,

Raúl. He also appointed his former revolutionary comrade, the Argentine dentist Ernesto "Che" Guevara, as minister of industry. Guevara embarked on a disastrous plan to communize Cuba's means of production. Tens of millions of dollars worth of U.S. land and business holdings were expropriated, further souring bilateral relations. In 1960, the United States retaliated with an economic embargo of the Castro regime, still in effect four decades later, and in January 1961 the outgoing Eisenhower administration severed diplomatic relations.

Meanwhile, there was widespread disillusionment in Cuba. Thousands left the island (with their descendants, the figure is now more than 2 million); others organized a resistance. Anti-communist guerrillas appeared in the central mountains and acts of sabotage became common.

Encouraged by this show of resistance, the U.S. CIA and Cuban exiles in Florida hatched up a scheme to have Cuban expatriates invade the island. The people, supposedly fed up with Castro, were anticipated to join the invaders in a groundswell movement that would envelop and suffocate the newborn regime. In April 1961, an expedition of about 1,200 Cuban exiles invaded at the *Bahia Cochinos* (Bay of Pigs) on the southern coast of Cuba. Although the size of the force, the anticipated response by Castro's forces and the terrain involved, all mandated the use of air support, no provision in the plans had been made for this. Further, no coordination had been undertaken with internal Cuban resistance forces, which had little,

Fidel pursuing his passion for baseball, 1960

Cuba

if any, organization. The invasion force was a sitting duck target for Castro's army. The whole plan was, in the words of Sir Winston Churchill, "a wretched half-measure." About 100 of the invaders were killed and the remainder captured.

Castro triumphantly announced that total victory had been won against "American imperialism," and he proceeded to wipe out all remaining internal resistance and to pose as a conquering hero. Defiantly, he proclaimed Cuba a socialist state. Emboldened by what appeared to be an indication of U.S. weakness, the Soviet Union, which until then had refrained from any military commitment, began sending vast amounts of military equipment to Cuba—including intermediate-range ballistic missiles with nuclear warheads.

In October 1962, President John F. Kennedy, still smarting from the Bay of Pigs fiasco, blockaded the island, placed U.S. military forces on alert and demanded withdrawal of the missiles. For 13 days, the world teetered on the brink of thermonuclear war. Soviet Premier Nikita Khrushchëv, furious, nevertheless complied with the U.S. demands, but only after obtaining a costly oral promise of vast significance from Kennedy: the U.S. would never invade Cuba. Kennedy thus verbally abrogated a cornerstone of U.S. Latin American policy—the long-standing Monroe Doctrine. Protected by that assurance, Castro embarked on a series of continental revolutionary adventures.

Castro's formula for revolutionary success was guerrilla warfare modeled on the Cuban experience. From 1962 to 1968, Havana became a center of support for leftist revolutionaries who spread their activities from Mexico to Argentina. Nevertheless, the formula failed. Opposed by communist parties which rejected *any* revolution they did not control as the "vanguard of the proletariat," and confronted by armies much better trained than Batista's, the guerrillas were defeated everywhere. In 1967, "Che" Guevara was killed in Bolivia, thus becoming an international Marxist icon. A dangerous deterioration of Cuba's economy forced Castro to fold the guerrilla banner and to accept the orthodox communist line demanded by the Soviet Union. Significantly, in 1968 Castro applauded the Soviet invasion of Czechoslovakia and publicly criticized China's Mao Tse-tung.

Communism in Cuba

Nothing resembling the structures of government envisioned in the tortured writings of Karl Marx came about in Cuba, nor did anything similar to the dual party-government structure of the Soviet Union emerge under Castro. Three stated goals of 20th century communism were achieved with remarkable success: the eradication of illiteracy, universal medical care and public housing. The centrally planned economy of the Soviet Union did not appear. Even though he had no skills in economics, Castro nevertheless waded in without hesitation, wrecking the economy with record speed.

Erratic planning, concentration of total power in Castro's hands and burgeoning bureaucracies, capped by the maintenance of a huge military force (once about 450,000) resulted in declining sugar productivity and failure to develop other resources for trade and income. The United States imposed an economic blockade in 1960, effectively isolating the island from the only significant source of foreign income and investment.

Increasing Soviet aid became vital for the survival of the revolution. When in 1968 Moscow was forced to apply a minimum of economic pressure to avoid pouring increasing amounts of economic aid into what seemed to be an endless chasm, Castro had to surrender more of what had become Cuba's limited independence. He made an urgent effort in 1970 to obtain desperately needed hard currency by mobilizing urban people, sending thousands of them into the fields to bring in the sugar cane, hoping for a 10-million-ton crop. The effort failed; the mobilization totally disrupted the economy for months. In the next year, Castro ostensibly began a process of "institutionalization" (creating organizations theoretically capable of

Cuban militia woman, 1960

sharing his power) while at the same time yielding increasing control over economic planning to Soviet advisers.

The Cuban debt to the Soviet Union, in spite of its annual purchases of the sugar crop at a level above the prevailing world price, increased at a rate of $2 billion annually, a figure which gradually rose to more than $5 billion. In an effort to repay the Soviets, Castro was receptive to a request for the use of his troops for international communist adventures. In 1975, 20,000 soldiers left for Angola to try to prop up its tottering communist regime; by 1989 this force had grown to almost 60,000. Having no stake in the outcome of Angola's ongoing struggle, Cubans turned out to be poor fighters, not caring to expose themselves to the cost of open warfare. They were overwhelmingly black; their return to Cuba, many infected with AIDS, and without a "victory," ended an unfortunate chapter in communist adventurism. Further Cuban involvement in Ethiopia, Yemen, Nicaragua, El Salvador and Guatemala also occurred during the 1970s and 1980s.

Both the United States and Cuba were humiliated in early 1980. Hundreds of Cubans stormed into the compound of the Peruvian Embassy in Havana, begging for political asylum. In a bold and unprecedented move, Castro suddenly announced that any Cuban who wished to leave the country was free to do so. The result was a frantic exodus, as thousands of small privately owned boats crossed the Florida Straits to the port of Mariel to pick up refugees in a Dunkirk-like evacuation. About 125,000 so-called *Marielitos* departed the island. Most were honorable and were assimilated into the Florida Cuban community as well as in other places. But a significant number were lunatics, and criminals, some forced onto the waiting boats at gunpoint, who wound up in already overcrowded U.S. federal prisons. Many others were homosexuals, considered undesirable in Cuba.

It had been a master stroke by Castro, a means of emptying his prisons and asylums as well as getting rid of potentially troublesome dissenters. But even he realized that he had overplayed his hand. After tedious indirect negotiations with the United States, Castro finally agreed to accept the undesirables back. Many of the prisoners rioted, however, preferring life as detainees in the United States to life in Cuba. The so-called "Mariel Boatlift" became a political issue in the 1980 U.S. presidential campaign, a foreign policy disaster of President Jimmy Carter that contributed to the victory of Ronald Reagan.

There followed eight years of increased bilateral hostility and U.S. military opposition to Cuban adventurism in Nicara-

"We are dignified and revolutionary Cubans." Propaganda in Viñales

Photo by Wayne Thompson

gua, El Salvador and Grenada, among other places. The U.S. invasion of Grenada in 1983 and the increasing presence of American advisers and troops in Central America made Castro more cautious. As a further demonstration of its submission to the Soviets, Cuba declined to attend the 1984 Summer Olympics in Los Angeles. Relations with the United States appeared to thaw briefly in 1984, but then resumed their frozen state when "Radio Martí" started broadcasting from Miami with U.S. government support. Cuba quickly jammed it.

Changes in the Cuban Politburo since 1966 have occurred twice, and although minorities were included, such as blacks, women and younger people, they were in fact meaningless. Castro's performances at party congresses in 1986 and 1991 were long, boring and virtually identical. First, he heaped praise on the achievements of Cuba under socialism. Then his mood turned to one of rage—he berated the assemblage, delivered a withering attack on the shortcomings of the Cuban people, made a devastating attack on capitalism and then vented his anger on the United States, the trade embargo in particular, Americans in general and then zeroed in on U.S. presidents from Kennedy to Clinton, with particular enmity expressed towards Nixon, Reagan and Bush (not in that particular order). All problems of Cuba were blamed on these sources, but never associated with poor Cuban leadership. Later added to his list of pariahs was the former Soviet Union and its ex-president, Mikhail Gorbachëv.

Cuba's foreign interests were identical to those of the Soviet Union when the latter existed. Now they are centered upon Cuban survival and include the cautious wooing of capitalist nations perceived not to be an imminent threat to Castro's continuation in power.

Its foreign ventures, financed by the Soviets, were costly. For reasons difficult to explain, Castro decreed that Cuban troops in Angola would not leave until *apartheid* was ended in South Africa and Namibia was independent. Cuban activities in Central America alienated most of Latin America, although a few nations with no communist threat preferred to play a "see no evil, hear no evil" attitude that was shortsighted. Both communism in general and Castro in particular have been stones around Cuba's neck for more than four decades.

A costly adventure in air piracy from the late 1960s through the 1970s gave Cuba (and its Soviet patron) an unnecessary and unprofitable black eye. It led to sharply increased security measures, with attendant inconveniences and delays at most U.S. airports, and left a sour taste in the perceptions of many potential friends that exists to this day and will continue into the foreseen future, even if things ultimately improve on the island.

In 1993, Caribbean tourist trade totaled more than $60 billion annually. Cuba's share: a paltry 2%. Even much smaller Jamaica earned twice as much from tourist visits as does Cuba. This limitation in tourist income was largely the product of the U.S. embargo, which prohibits Americans from spending dollars in Cuba except under very tight conditions. This effectively halted tourist trade, although there are loopholes available by traveling through the Dominican Republic, Mexico and Canada. But the bottom line is punitive: the United States will not guarantee the safety of its citizens who venture onto the island, although there is a United States interests section attached to the Swiss Embassy in Havana.

Fall of the Soviet Benefactor

The ascension to power of Mikhail Gorbachëv in the Soviet Union marked the beginning of the end for communist Cuba. Things began to deteriorate in 1986, as Soviet trade terms became tougher, and subsidies started to shrink. Soviet aid to Cuba had been as much as $6 billion a year. But in 1989, Gorbachëv visited the island. He had already concluded that overlaying the Castro regime with Soviet technicians and advisers simply had not been working and would not work in the future. More important, the Soviets were by that time having to borrow money from Western banks and import food from the United States. The Soviets sought additional sugar, which was by then rationed in Moscow. No increase could be delivered—crop production was down in Cuba because of corruption and inefficiency. The deterioration accelerated rapidly and by 1991–92 Cuba was in the grip of economic disaster.

Castro's response was to get rid of all elements of dissent, particularly Carlos Aldana, formerly No. 3 in the Cuban hierarchy, who represented a moderate trend corresponding to the Soviet Union's *glasnost* and *perestroika*.

Between 1989 and 1992, Cuba's annual purchasing power had descended from $8.1 billion a year to $2.2 billion. Sugar production descended to 7 million tons even with rationing and dispatching urban workers to harvest the cane by hand (there was no fuel). The 1992 harvest was 4.2 million tons and less was produced in 1993–94.

The administration of President George Bush decided to tighten the 1960 embargo in late 1992 with the Torricelli Law. No U.S. company, affiliate or subsidiary in this country or abroad, may trade with Cuba in any form. All U.S. ports are closed to any ship of any nation or registry that has, within the previous six months, called at a Cuban port. These tightened screws, together with the disappearance of $300 million a year in Soviet aid, has left the Cuban people in near destitution. The average Cuban is estimated to consume only 1,900 calories a day, compared with the 2,600 minimum recommended by the World Health Organization (the Castro regime claims the country's calorie consumption is 3,500, about that of the normal obese American). The result has been that increasing numbers of Cubans have attempted to flee the island in flimsy boats or inner-tube rafts. There may never be an accurate accounting of how many

Cuba

have drowned, died of dehydration or been eaten by sharks in a desperate attempt to escape their misery.

The 1990s brought some basic changes, brought on by the economic prostration of Cuba. Possession of the U.S. dollar was legalized in August 1993 and for 11 years was virtually the only hard currency on the island (see Economy). The peso officially traded at 1:1 with the dollar, but it took more than 100 pesos to buy a dollar on the open market. With the advent of the dollar came a system of black markets that still pervades everything. Few people bother with the lines and empty shelves of state stores, even though the black market means paying two to 10 times more for an article.

Persons in certain trades and professions were allowed to become "self-employed" in a variety of enterprises, but only if they first secured a government permit from an inefficient bureaucracy. Of course, a permit that is granted can be revoked. Small enterprises have bloomed, particularly in urban areas. A large number of "Mom and Pop" restaurants are known for delicious food in Havana, for fees payable in U.S. dollars. Bicycle repair, plumbing, and all similar services are by contract with one of the entrepreneurs. Physicians are not allowed the same freedom.

Several events occurred in 1994 that suggested, falsely, that basic change was on the horizon. Cuba decided to use the threat of a renewed flood of refugees to lessen or abate the U.S. embargo. Severe shortages of just about everything led to increased pressures to migrate to the United States. When these were resisted,

there was an anti-government riot in and near Havana. The Clinton administration, dealing with a flood of Haitian refugees, tried to discourage the Cubans, but refused to budge on removal of the tight embargo. A stop-gap "solution" of interning refugees in the territory of Guantanamo Bay was devised, but failed; conditions in the camps set up there were *worse* than in Cuba. The attempts to leave Cuba for Florida resulted in the loss of many lives. Castro threatened to unleash another wave of boat people in the summer of 1995; this was averted by a U.S. plan to gradually admit the Cubans remaining at Guantanamo.

Both Mexico and Canada, following the example set by the UN in 1993, urged that the U.S. embargo of Cuba be abandoned. It has been revealed that Cuba was sustained in large part during 1994 by funds arriving from Mexico (drug money, top level government personnel and banking investment) and from Spain (hotel construction). With the Salinas government of Mexico a thing of the past and the economic collapse of Mexico in late 1994, receipts dropped considerably.

On February 24, 1996, in an unexplainable and stupid act, Cuban air force jets shot down two unarmed small aircraft that were patrolling the waters off the coast of Cuba to protect the "boat people" from mishap. Three men, who were members of the Miami-based exile organization Brothers to the Rescue, were killed. There was an immediate outcry in the U.S. Congress; the result was the Helms-Burton Act, strengthening the already-existing embargo. Now, any foreign firm doing business with Cuba can be penalized in the United States. The avowed purpose is to stifle even minuscule investment and loans to Cuba.

In some respects, the Helms-Burton Act has backfired on the United States in that it appears to have done more to anger traditional U.S. allies, Canada in particular, than to genuinely punish Cuba economically.

Both Castro and his revolution marked a milestone in August 1996 when the dictator, his beard now fully gray, observed his 70th birthday. It was a reminder that both the revolution and its leader now are living on borrowed time. Almost as though to demonstrate that age has mellowed him, the once-flamboyant revolutionary made a number of state visits, including a tour of Europe and to the Latin American summit in Chile, dressed in stylish business suits rather than the fatigue uniform of old. While in Rome, the avowed athiest visited Pope John Paul II, and the two announced that the pontiff would visit Cuba for the first time in 1998.

A visit to Havana in 1996 by Democratic U.S. Representative Bill Richardson of New Mexico succeeded in winning release of a number of political prisoners. As a further sign of an easing of tensions, the White House approved a request by 10 U.S. news organizations to establish bureaus in Cuba, but in early 1997 Castro had approved only one: the Cable News Network, which he praised for its "objectivity."

No foreign media, however, were allowed to cover Castro's seven-hour speech on October 8, 1997, before the Fifth Communist Party Congress, the first in six years. In that speech, the aging dictator squelched any hopes that Cuba would deviate any further from its dogmatically Marxist course. He also placed the blame squarely on the United States for a series of terrorist bombings at Cuba's tourist-oriented hotels in September, accusing the Clinton administration of trying to undermine the Revolution by frightening away badly needed foreign tourists (see Economy). Castro tied the congress to a public relations stunt that brought Cuba renewed international attention: the weeklong ceremony to rebury the skeletal remains of Che Guevara that had been recovered from the Bolivian jungle after 30 years. On the eve of the congress, however, four dissidents, among them Vladimoro Roca, a former air force pilot and son of revolutionary hero Blas Roca, attempted to rain on Castro's parade by issuing a document titled "Homeland for Us All," which ridiculed the congress for focusing on the past glories of the revolution without offering solutions for the problems of the present. All four were arrested and subsequently sentenced to prison terms.

Varadero Beach—a protected area that the Cuban government would like all to believe is "typical."
Photo by Sheila Curtin

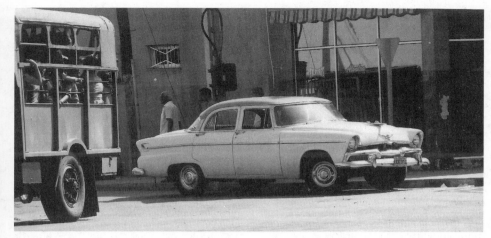

Transportation in Cuba: bus (left) or rare private automobile *Photo by Katherine Dickson*

The Papal Visit of 1998

Another public relations gimmick was even more stunning: Castro's invitation to Pope John Paul II to visit Cuba, which the Pope accepted. This was a major gamble for Castro, because he would not be able to censor this strong-willed pope the way he controls his own people's thinking. On the other hand, he apparently reasoned, the gesture might bring a relaxing of the U.S. trade embargo. Enigmatic as ever, Castro declared in November 1997 at the Ibero-American Summit in Venezuela that Cuba would never deviate from its revolutionary course, rejecting calls from Argentina's Carlos Menem and Nicaragua's Arnoldo Alemán for more respect for human rights. Yet, in December, as a gesture to the pope, Castro permitted the first Christmas holiday Cubans had had since 1969 (the declaration of atheism as official state doctrine had been rescinded in 1992). Even more unthinkable, he eased the restrictions on religious worship, and suddenly the Catholic churches were filled for Mass; other sects began receiving increased interest as well from a people starved for spirituality, including young people born after the Revolution.

Between Christmas and the Pope's arrival in January, however, Cuba suffered another public relations disaster with the defection of the talented pitcher Orlando "El Duque" Hernández, half-brother of the Florida Marlins' Livan Hernández, who had just been named the most valuable player of the 1997 World Series. Livan Hernández himself had defected in Mexico in 1995, and in 1996, his half-brother was banned from playing baseball when it was feared he, too, would leave to, quite literally, seek his fortune in the United States. "El Duque" and seven others left the island in a tiny boat and turned up a few days later in the Bahamas, where they sought political asylum. From there they went to Costa Rica, where the pitcher was eventually given a U.S. visa and was immediately recruited into the majors. It was yet another humiliation for the baseball-loving Castro. So was the much-publicized request of his 41-year-old daughter, Alina Fernández-Revuelta, for political asylum in Spain during the papal visit.

The pope's four-day visit to Cuba from January 21–25, 1998, was truly historic, with hundreds of thousands of Cubans attending open-air masses. Castro, true to his word, welcomed the pontiff at the airport and even attended a Mass; he also addressed John Paul as "holy father" and recalled that he had been schooled by Jesuits. Hundreds of Cuban exiles were granted special permission to enter the country for the event, many of whom were reunited with loved ones they had not seen for nearly 40 years. The pope's public declarations must have made Castro cringe at times. He denounced human rights violations and the denial of religious freedom, and called for the release of political prisoners. At the same time, he noted that the Vatican and the Cuban Revolution find common ground in their concern for the poor. More importantly for Fidel, he lamented the human suffering on the island and called for a lifting of the U.S. embargo. The pope privately presented Castro with the names of 270 jailed dissidents and requested their release (some human rights groups claim there are as many as 500 "prisoners of conscience"). In February, all were released but 70, who remained jailed for "security reasons." At the same time, the government reiterated that the laws against political dissent remain in effect, raising doubts as to whether there has been any meaningful move toward greater freedom of expression.

Nonetheless, Castro's gamble at least partly paid off. After the dissidents were freed, President Clinton announced a resumption of sales of medical goods and of airline service that had been severed after the 1996 downing of the two unarmed planes flown by Cuban exiles. He also renewed permission for dollars to be sent to Cuba. Since then, however, U.S.-Cuban relations resumed their usual roller coaster course, while continued repression on the island brought even more international condemnation.

Dissent and Baseball Diplomacy

The government implemented a new sedition law in 1998, aimed primarily at independent journalists and political dissidents. One of its first victims was journalist Mario Viera, who sent abroad a column, "Morals in Underwear," that lampooned the Cuban justice system and poked fun at Foreign Minister José Peraza Chapeau's participation in a meeting in Rome dealing with the establishment of an international criminal court. Viera was jailed for "defaming" Peraza Chapeau, and his trial in November 1998 drew about a dozen courageous protesters.

Still another independent journalist, Jesús Joel Díaz Hernández, was jailed in January 1999 and sentenced the following day to four years for "dangerous social behavior." The New York-based Committee to Protect Journalists named Castro as one of the world's 10 "enemies of the press." Unfortunately, a less scrupulous independent journalist gave the government the excuse it needed for a propaganda coun-

The bicycle is the only sure method of transportation in this gas–and–car starved nation. *Photo by Sheila Curtin*

Cuba

From a street scene in Old Town Havana, to . . .

terattack in 1998. An unnamed Cuban correspondent for the Madrid daily *ABC* dispatched an ostensible interview with Cuban Cardinal Jaime Ortega that turned out to be phony; the cardinal himself denied giving the interview. The official daily mouthpiece *Granma*—itself hardly a paragon of truth—denounced the "falsehoods" of the independent journalists and branded them as "mercenaries."

The so-called "Group of Four," meanwhile, was sentenced on March 25, 1999, to jail terms ranging from three and a half to five years for issuing the 1997 document criticizing the party congress. The sentences sparked protests on the island and brought denunciations from human rights groups abroad. National Assembly President Ricardo Alarcón defended the harsh sentences, calling the dissidents "subversives" and saying that the sentences were "not that severe."

Cuban dissidents continued their courageous activities, which are reminiscent of the non-violent movements of Gandhi and Martin Luther King Jr. In September 1999, they opened a "school" for teaching the tactics of civil disobedience. Later that month, two opposition movements, the Socialist Democratic Current and Democratic Solidarity, boldly delivered to the Council of State a document that detailed plans for a peaceful transition to a democratic Cuba. In November, Dr. Oscar Elías Biscet, a well-known physician and dissi-

dent, was arrested and subsequently sentenced to three years in prison for "public disorder and instigating crime." His offense: He hung three Cuban flags upside down as a symbol of protest! That December, about 30 dissidents staged a protest march in Havana but, remarkably, none was arrested. It soon became apparent that this seeming tolerance did not represent a change in policy, however, for only a week later about a dozen leading dissidents were arrested and held for several days to discourage a planned demonstration marking the 51st anniversary of the Universal Declaration of Human Rights.

Meanwhile, international pressure against Castro's repression continued. The Inter American Press Association, the Committee to Protect Journalists and Reporters Sans Frontières in France all sent notes to Castro demanding he release jailed independent journalists and stop harassing others. One such independent journalist, Raúl Rivero, was named the recipient of the prestigious Maria Moors Cabot Award by Columbia University in September 1999, but of course the Cuban government refused to grant him a visa; his daughter, who lives in Miami, accepted the award for him. Another leading dissident, Elizardo Sánchez, formed the Commission for Human Rights and National Reconciliation, which monitors dissidents' arrests and reports them to the outside world.

The dissidents finally received some encouraging news in May 2000 when the government suddenly and unexpectedly

granted an early release to three of four dissidents who were imprisoned in July 1997 for criticizing a Communist Party document to foreign journalists, among other alleged sins. The sentences ranged from three and a half to five years, and the case had sparked international condemnation, even from Castro's friend, the Colombian Nobel Laureate Garbriel García Márquez. One of those released, Marta Beatríz Roque, an economist, had staged a two-month hunger strike in 1999. No reason was given for the early releases. It was not a harbinger of a Cuban *glasnost,* as it turned out. On February 24, 2001—the fifth anniversary of the shoot-down of the two Cuban exile planes—Cuban security forces rounded up about 40 known dissidents at various locations around the island to ensure there were no demonstrations marking the event. They were released a few hours later.

Not so with José González Bridón, leader of the dissident labor group Confederation of Democratic Workers. In 2000, he wrote an article reporting that a dissident had been killed by her ex-husband, which was published on the Web site of the Miami-based Cuba Free Press. He was jailed in December and tried in May 2001 for reporting "false news" about Cuba. In June he was sentenced to two years.

On a happier note, the baseball-loving Castro finally approved an exhibition game in Havana between the Baltimore Orioles and the Cuban All-Stars that had been in the works for three years. Castro

typical apartment housing in Havana

Photo by Sheila Curtin

attended the historic, invitation-only game on March 28, 1999, the first time a U.S. major league team had played in Cuba since 1959. Some observers compared the initiative with the "ping-pong diplomacy" in the early 1970s that presaged U.S. recognition of the People's Republic of China. Much to Castro's chagrin, the Orioles won the game in the 11th inning, 3-2. The All-Stars redeemed themselves in a second game in Baltimore on May 3, defeating the Orioles 12-6. The victory was muted, however, by yet another embarrassing defection; a 54-year-old pitching coach went to a Baltimore police station and requested political asylum. The Cuban team was abruptly ordered home, canceling a planned reception and tour of Baltimore.

Cuba has continued to experience a mix of triumph and embarrassment with its sports program, which, of course, is merely an appendage of the government-party apparatus. The Cuban baseball team won the championship at the 1999 Pan American Games in Winnipeg, Canada, but soon after the games ended three Cuban athletes were stripped of the medals they won at the games for alleged drug use. A high jumper reportedly tested positive for cocaine, while two weightlifters tested positive for anabolic steroids. Castro bitterly denounced the decision, using a typical argument that someone had put cocaine in the athlete's food to discredit the Cuban program. He said Cuban tests showed no steroids in the systems of the weightlifters—tests that could hardly be accepted as objective.

Then, in May 2000, Castro's baseball diplomacy led to another defection. A U.S. team from the University of St. Thomas in Minnesota had played an exhibition game in Cuba during the winter, and a team made up of University of Havana players flew to Minneapolis for a second game in May. Moments after the team arrived at the airport, one of the players, Mario Miguel Chaoui, hurriedly left with a Cuban-American uncle and asked for political asylum. He told journalists he hopes to play for the Florida Marlins.

Baseball was not the only sport plagued by defectors. In August 2002, two members of a 16-member fencing team went into hiding during a visit to Portugal and did not return to Cuba.

Meanwhile, dissent continued to grow at home. In December 2001, about two dozen people belonging to a group called the Pro-Human Rights Party, staged a march in a Havana neighborhood without apparent incident. On February 24, 2002, police staged preemptive moves to thwart the usual protests marking the anniversary of the 1996 shoot-down of two unarmed planes; 24 people were taken into custody. On May 5, 2002, Vladimoro Roca, the last of the "Group of Four" who had criticized the 1997 party congress to remain in prison, was released after four years and 10 months behind bars. However, the international watchdog group Human Rights Watch estimates that there are still 240 prisoners of conscience in Cuban jails.

Then there was the Varela Project, organized by Oswaldo Payá and named for Félix Varela, a priest who was a hero of independence, which was a petition drive calling for democratic reforms (see The Varela Project). Payá had himself been sentenced once to forced labor for his views.

The Elián González Controversy

In late 1999 and the first half of 2000, the attention of the entire world was focused on U.S.-Cuban relations because of an incident that demonstrated the passions that Castro excites among his adherents at home and his detractors among the exile community in Florida. On November 25, a five-year-old Cuban boy, Elián González, was found clinging to an inner-tube off the east coast of Florida. In the ensuing days, the boy was turned over to an uncle who lives in Miami, and it was learned that he was one of just three survivors of a raft that left Cuba with 11 people on board. Among those lost were the boy's mother and her boyfriend, who had organized the ill-fated venture.

The case immediately became a media sensation in the United States, while Castro quickly and predictably exploited the incident for its propaganda value. He declared that the boy, who turned six on December 6, had been "kidnapped" by his mother and demanded that he be returned immediately to his father in Cuba. He organized mass demonstrations to focus world attention on the case. Counterdemonstrations soon occurred in the exile community in Miami to demand that the boy be granted political asylum and be allowed to stay with his Miami relatives. (The difference between the mass demonstrations, of course, was that participation at the ones in Miami was purely voluntary.) Castro also paraded the boy's tearful father, Juan Miguel González, before television cameras, to plead for his son's return.

Legally, Castro had a strong case. Under U.S. and international laws, a surviving parent is the presumptive custodian. In January 2000 there began a tortuous legal battle, after the Immigration and Naturalization Service declared that the boy should be returned to his father. Attorney General Janet Reno supported that position a few days later, whereupon the Miami relatives filed suit in federal court seeking an immigration hearing.

Meanwhile, passions continued to rise, and the case became a political football in the United States. The Republican-controlled Congress suggested either granting the boy U.S. citizenship so he could not be deported to Cuba or granting resident alien status to the father if he chose to live with his son in the United States. Juan Miguel González, a Castro loyalist, indignantly refused, and Castro gleefully milked his refusal for its propaganda

Relaxing in Santiago *Photo by Wayne Thompson*

Cuba

Cuba's three propaganda "newspapers"

value. The case even became an issue in the U.S. presidential campaign when Vice President Al Gore, sensing an opportunity to carry Florida, dramatically broke with the position of the Clinton administration and advocated giving the boy resident alien status. Opinion polls, however, showed that a majority of Americans nationwide favored returning the boy to his father in Cuba.

Tensions increased after a U.S. district judge rejected the family's suit on March 21, 2000. The United States granted a visa to Juan Miguel González, who arrived in Washington on April 5 believing he would soon be reunited with his son. But his Miami relatives and their attorneys continued to file legal motions to delay surrendering Elián. Her patience wearing thin, Reno demanded that they surrender the boy so he could be reunited with his father, but still they stonewalled. Finally, in the pre-dawn hours of April 22, INS agents in SWAT gear stormed into the González house in Miami and hustled the terrified child into a waiting van. Cuba's totalitarian leader praised Reno for the forcible seizure, praise that must have made the attorney general squirm a bit. Elián was

flown to Washington, where father and son finally were reunited. They took up residence in a government-leased estate in Maryland, while waiting on the Miami relatives' appeal to be heard by the U.S. circuit court in Atlanta. On June 1, that court ruled that the INS had acted properly when it had rejected an asylum hearing for Elián and that only a parent should have the right to make such a decision for a child that age. Although the decision was what Elián's father (and Castro) wanted, Castro nonetheless summoned more mass demonstrations in Cuba to protest it. Why? Because Elián and his father could not return immediately but had to wait until the Miami relatives exhausted their appeals. On June 28, after the U.S. Supreme Court rejected the Miami relatives' appeal, Juan Miguel and Elián returned to Cuba to a heroes' welcome.

Cuba's Isolation Worsens

U.S.-Cuban relations turned decidedly chillier with the election of the new U.S. president, George W. Bush in 2000. The fact that Bush owed his razor-thin election victory to the overwhelming vote he re-

ceived from the Cuban exile community in Florida, thus giving him Florida's 25 electoral votes, was not lost on the Castro brothers.

On April 15, 2001, in an appearance commemorating the 40th anniversary of the Bay of Pigs invasion, Raúl Castro issued uncharacteristically strident remarks, accusing Bush of planning a new invasion of Cuba and vowing that it would be repulsed. Such paranoia seemed to dissipate somewhat later that month when Secretary of State Colin Powell stated publicly that Fidel Castro "had done good things for his people." That prompted Castro to compliment Powell for his audacity.

In May 2001, Senators Jesse Helms—coauthor of the Helms-Burton Act—and Joseph Lieberman—the losing Democratic vice presidential candidate in 2000—cosponsored a bill that would allocate $100 million to dissidents in Cuba over four years. It was unclear how they would receive the money or how it would be protected from seizure by the dollar-hungry Cuban government. In an apparent case of reverse psychology, Cuban Foreign Minister Felipe Pérez Roque endorsed the measure, saying it would demonstrate to the world that the United States is seeking to subvert Cuba.

Meanwhile, Cuba continued to experience triumphs and embarrassments in the diplomatic sphere. In November 1999, Castro proudly played host for the first time to the Ibero-American Summit. But the host soon became annoyed when some of the participants, including the king of Spain and the leaders of Portugal, Panama and even onetime defender Mexico, called for greater democratization on the island. Several leaders held meetings with leading dissidents, and Castro, accustomed to a controlled, obedient media, lashed out at the international media for what he termed disproportionate coverage of the dissidents. Whatever public relations value Castro may have gleaned from the summit was effectively nullified on April 18, 2000, however, when the U.N. Commission on Human Rights in Geneva approved a censure motion against Cuba for its repression of political dissent and religious freedom. The vote was 21–18, with 14 abstentions. Especially galling for Castro was the fact that two of Cuba's erstwhile allies, Poland and the Czech Republic, had sponsored the motion. Castro held a live, televised discussion the day after the vote that droned on for five hours, during which Castro vilified the countries that supported the censure as well as the dissidents at home.

Despite the perceived harder line toward Cuba of the Bush administration, on July 16, 2001, the new president angered Cuban exiles by doing the same thing that President Clinton had done every six months for four years: He exercised the executive prerogative granted under the Helms-Burton Act to block lawsuits against foreign companies occupying expropriated U.S. property in Cuba. Nonetheless, the Bush administration continued to tighten the screws in other areas, including stricter enforcement of the trade embargo and greater support for internal dissenters. Under a new initiative, the United States offered scholarships to Cuban prisoners of conscience, and the U.S. Interests Section in Havana has been distributing radios and information about free-market capitalism. Castro, of course, has bitterly denounced such activities as interference in Cuba's internal affairs and threatened to expel the U.S. diplomats. One explanation for the harsher U.S. stance: Bush had appointed Otto Reich, a Cuban exile and hard-line opponent of Castro, as assistant secretary of state for Western Hemisphere affairs. Still another: The president's brother, Jeb, was running for reelection as governor of Florida in 2002.

Surprisingly, despite souring bilateral relations, Castro was quick to condemn

Turning 15!
Photo by Gary Seldomridge

the September 11, 2001, terrorist attacks on the United States, and even more surprisingly, he was conciliatory toward the imprisonment of al-Qaeda and Taliban prisoners at Guantanamo Bay. Castro even offered to provide medical and sanitary support, and pledged to return any prisoners who escaped; it was a far cry from his attitude toward the detention there of Haitian and Cuban refugees. Perhaps in response to Castro's gesture, the Bush administration permitted the historic sale of food to Cuba in November 2001 as a hu-

manitarian gesture in the wake of Hurricane Michelle, which caused widespread suffering. Cuba purchased a total of $30 million worth of food, which was delivered in December. Both governments, however, noted that the sale did not herald a change in policy by either side. In January 2002, about 500 U.S. business leaders visited Cuba under the auspices of the Treasury Department.

As if Cuba did not have enough problems from its traditional nemesis, the United States, by 2002 Cuba was becoming increasingly isolated diplomatically and encountered serious problems in its relations with two traditional friends, Russia and Mexico. In October 2001, Russian President Vladimir Putin announced that Russia was closing its electronic surveillance station it had operated at Lourdes, 13 miles south of Havana, since 1964, at the height of the Cold War. In undiplomatic language, Castro angrily denounced the decision, saying he had not been asked for his "permission" to close the base and arguing it would create security problems for Cuba. He accused Putin—probably correctly—of trying to curry favor with President Bush, whom Putin needs far more than he needs Castro. What Castro probably lamented the most, however, was the loss of the $200 million annual rent Russia paid for the station.

In early February 2002, Mexican President Vicente Fox, the first opposition president in 70 years and a conservative businessman who enjoys a warm working relationship with President Bush, made his first state visit to Cuba. Fox and Castro engaged in cordial talks, aimed primarily at trade. During the visit, Mexican Foreign Minister Jorge Castañeda assured

Special show for children in Havana's National Museum of Fine Arts

Cuba

the Cubans that Mexico would neither "sponsor nor co-sponsor" a resolution before the U.N. Human Rights Commission in Geneva in April, implying that Mexico would abstain as it had in previous years. The visit turned sour when Fox, unlike previous visiting Mexican presidents, agreed to meet with Cuban dissidents, a distinct slap to Castro's face.

Later that month, Castañeda said during a visit to Miami that "the doors of the Mexican Embassy are open to all Cubans," a remark that was paraphrased by Radio Martí as an invitation to seek political asylum.

On 27 February, 25 young men crashed a bus through the embassy gates. Police moved in and forcibly prevented hundreds of others from entering the embassy compound; foreign journalists were pushed back, cursed or manhandled. The incident posed a ticklish diplomatic problem for Mexico and prompted a phone call from Fox to Castro. For one thing, some of the Cubans inside the compound yelled anti-Castro slogans from the roof. When the men did not seek asylum and refused to leave, Fox decided to allow Cuban security forces to enter the embassy grounds to arrest them.

Things grew worse in March when Fox hosted an international poverty summit in the city of Monterrey, which Castro decided at the last minute to attend, posing still another dilemma for Fox because Bush was scheduled to attend. Castro angrily left after his prepared speech to the conference on March 21, accusing Fox of asking him to leave; Fox denied the allegations.

But the final straw for Castro came on April 19, when Mexico joined eight other Latin American nations in voting for a resolution, proposed by Uruguay, calling on Castro to permit democratic reforms; the resolution passed 23–21, with nine abstentions. Castro angrily denounced Mexico for its "betrayal." For good measure, and in a stunning breach of diplomatic protocol, he called Fox a liar for denying Castro had been unwelcome at the Monterrey conference, and he played for international journalists a recording of his telephone conversation with Fox, which did imply that Fox was concerned about Castro's presence at the conference. Such a betrayal of confidence was grounds for Mexico to sever diplomatic relations, but it did not. (In fact, in May the two countries marked the 100th anniversary of their diplomatic relations.) However, in September 2002, Mexico replaced its ambassador in Havana, who was seen as too friendly with Castro for the Fox administration's taste.

Castro openly antagonized Uruguay for its role in the U.N. resolution by calling President Jorge Batlle a "lackey" of the United States. Batlle promptly responded by breaking diplomatic relations that had

Farm family in Viñales   *Photo by Wayne Thompson*

been reestablished in 1986 after a 25-year break, giving the Cuban ambassador 72 hours to leave the country.

Castro received another international rebuke in July 2002 when the European Union balked at an aid initiative by Barbados on behalf of Cuba, which had just joined the 63-member African-Pacific-Caribbean group of former European colonies. Under the Cotonou Agreement, signed between the EU and the APC countries in 2000, the EU is making a $12.7 billion aid package available to the APC over five years. But the EU demurred on speeding up Cuba's access to the aid funds, citing its lack of commitment to democracy and human rights. Cuba correctly labeled the EU decision a "humiliation and a slap in the face."

It was soon followed by another slap from the EU. In October, the European Parliament named Cuban dissident Osvaldo Payá, organizer of the Varela Project (see next section) and founder of the Christian Liberation Movement, the recipient of the 2002 Sakharov Award for Human Rights and Freedom of Thought. Other recipients for the prestigious award have included Nobel Peace Laureates Nelson Mandela of South Africa and Aung San Suu Kyi of Burma.

In December, Cuba for the first time hosted a meeting of the 15-member Caribbean Community (CARICOM), for which Cuba has only observer status. Castro announced that Cuba would reapply for inclusion in the Cotonou Agreement, and the CARICOM states pledged to support Cuba. The reapplication came in January 2003, and in March Poul Nielson, the EU

commissioner for development and humanitarian aid, spent five days in Cuba discussing the issue with Cuban authorities. Some Cuban dissidents favored Cuba's inclusion in Cotonou, believing that Cuba would be under more pressure to begin adhering to democratic principles, while others argued that it would merely reward Castro's government for its repression. Nielson concluded that Cuba's inclusion could help bring about democratic reform. However, within days the EU would suddenly see the prospects for Cuban democratization for what they are: an illusion (see The Crackdown of 2003).

Perhaps in response to its growing international isolation and alienation, in September 2002 Cuba suddenly declared it was willing to sign the Nuclear Non-Proliferation Treaty, which it had always refused to do on the grounds that it somehow needed to "defend" itself against nuclear aggression from the United States.

Castro witnessed first-hand just how isolated his archaic system is when he visited another old friend, China, in February 2003, his first visit in seven years. Castro confessed to his amazement at the changes he saw since his last visit, changes that have made China an economic powerhouse by virtue of market reforms. But Castro made it clear when he returned home that he did not intend to institute similar reforms.

The Varela Project

In early 2002, Castro stunned the world, as he had with the invitation to the pope in 1998, by inviting former U.S. President

Jimmy Carter to visit Cuba; Carter, long a champion of Latin American democracy, accepted.

Carter spent five days in Cuba in May, the highest-ranking American to visit Cuba since 1959. To his credit, Castro kept his word to allow Carter to address the Cuban people in his unpracticed Spanish without censorship. In his live address on radio and television, which was reported verbatim in the next day's issue of *Granma*, Carter denounced Cuba's restrictions on human rights, and he endorsed the Varela Project, a petition drive recently initiated by dissidents and signed by 11,020 Cubans, for a referendum on free elections and free expression. Of course, his puzzled listeners had read or heard nothing about the Varela Project through the Cuban media. At the same time, Carter called for an end to the U.S. economic embargo. After Carter's departure, Castro trumpeted Carter's call for an end to the embargo, while ignoring his calls for democratization.

Carter met with President Bush at the White House after his Cuban visit. Almost as if in response to Carter's call for an end to the embargo, however, Bush flew to Miami to deliver a policy address on the 100th anniversary of Cuban independence on May 20. In the address, Bush flatly rejected any notion of rescinding the embargo, and called on Castro to impose long-overdue reforms.

In a seeming response of his own to Bush's address, to Carter's calls for democratic reforms and to the Varela Project, Castro cynically launched a petition drive of his own, one calling for a constitutional amendment declaring the principles of the

Cuban Revolution "untouchable." In effect, it was like calling for a constitutional amendment forbidding constitutional amendments. In June, the government claimed that 8.2 million of the country's 11 million people—statistically, virtually everyone of voting age and then some— had signed the petition, which went before the National Assembly. On June 27, to no one's surprise, the 557 deputies present approved the amendment unanimously, without discussion. There was one major difference between the two petition drives, however: it did not require any courage to sign Castro's petition.

The fact that Castro launched his own petition drive to make the revolution "untouchable" was an indication that the dissidents' efforts were striking a raw nerve. The world would soon learn how raw that nerve is.

Crackdown and Aftermath

Undeterred by the predictable rejection of the Varela Project, the dissident movement in October 2002 organized the Assembly to Promote Civil Society. Organized by economist Marta Beatríz Roque, the new group is an umbrella organization of 321 discrete opposition movements and touted itself as a shadow parliament. Many of those in the new group did not support the Varela Project, arguing that it is merely lukewarm, which is the first indication of a schism within the opposition movement. In an address to the National Assembly, Castro ridiculed the opposition as "fish out of water" and accused the dissidents of receiving U.S. financial support. It was a harbinger of what was coming.

On October 31, 2002, Dr. Oscar Elías Biscet, the dissident sentenced to three years for hanging Cuban flags upside down, was released three months before his term was up, but he was rearrested in December for participating in a protest in Matanzas.

In December, Oswaldo Payá, the organizer of the Varela Project, was granted a travel visa at the last minute to go to Europe to receive the Sakharov Award from the European Parliament (see Cuba's Isolation Worsens), but not before his home was vandalized. The visa was granted apparently only after Spain, Cuba's window to the European Union, applied some diplomatic pressure on Cuba. During his 48 days outside Cuba, Payá visited eight countries and met with Pope John Paul II in Rome, Czech President Vaclav Havel, Mexican President Vicente Fox in Mexico City and U.S. Secretary of State Colin Powell in Washington, which did little to endear him to the Cuban government. Neither did Payá's nomination for the Nobel Peace Prize by Havel, himself a writer who had once opposed—and help topple—a Communist government.

Cuba held its latest "election" for the real parliament in January 2003. Voters elected 609 members of the National Assembly and 1,119 members of provincial assemblies. Of course, Communist Party candidates were the only ones on the ballot. Voter turnout was reported to be 97.6%, which the government and the party hailed as "proof" of the support for the Revolution. Among those elected to the National Assembly was Elián González's father. The newly formed Assembly to Promote Civil Society "monitored" the election, for whatever good that did. Dissidents also boycotted the election, and a few even courageously put up banners ridiculing it.

In February, the new chief of the U.S. Interests Section in Havana, James Cason, visited with 20 members of the Assembly to Promote Civil Society at Marta Roque's home and declared that the Castro government was "afraid" to grant civil liberties. He also called for Oscar Biscet's release. Castro denounced Cason's action as a "blatant provocation." The government also complained that Cason had traveled more than 6,000 miles around Cuba in the few months he had been there and accused him of promoting subversion.

In March 2003, the ax fell. On March 11, Roque and several other dissidents began a hunger strike. Almost simultaneously, during the five-day visit by EU Commissioner Nielson to discuss Cuba's inclusion in the Cotonou Agreement, by which Cuba stood to benefit by as much as $100 million, Vladimiro Roca and other leading dissidents petitioned the EU to deny Cuba's admission. Coincidentally or not,

Farming in Cuba

Photo by Katherine Dickson

Cuba

it was also the same week that the United States was preparing to invade Iraq. On March 18, as the attention of the world's media was focused on Iraq, authorities began rounding up some of the country's best-known dissidents, which the government referred to as "mercenaries," including Roque. When the roundup was completed a few days later, 78 people had been jailed, 21 of them independent journalists, including the best-known journalist, Raúl Rivero, and Hector Palacios, who had been active in the Varela Project. Many of those arrested had attended the meeting with Cason at Roque's house. The predictable charge: subversive activities. As significant as the list of those who had been arrested was those who had not: neither Payá nor Elizardo Sánchez was detained, though they reported their homes were under surveillance. Roca also remained free.

Meanwhile, the government imposed a new rule requiring foreign diplomats to obtain advance permission before traveling outside Havana, a move clearly directed at Cason. The United States imposed a similar restriction on Cuban diplomats a week later.

Justice would prove swift if not just. Trials began the first week of April, as U.S. forces moved on Baghdad, and prosecutors indicated at first they would seek life terms for some of the dissidents. Foreign journalists were barred from the kangaroo-court proceedings, but news quickly leaked out. Among the startling revelations was that one well-known independent journalist, Manuel David Orrío, was in fact an undercover agent assigned to infiltrate the dissident movement. He had attended meetings at the U.S. interests section, and he testified that Rivero and other journalists were conspiring with Cason to undermine the government.

The sentences were handed down behind closed doors as well, but news of them soon reached the international media. Roque and Rivero were both sentenced to 20 years, Palacios and Biscet to 25. The heaviest sentence, 27 years, was meted out to journalist Omar Rodríguez Saludes. His crime: launching Cuba's first independent magazine. The dissidents went immediately to prison. It was subsequently reported that about 60 of them were being held in solitary confinement. The Supreme Tribunal, the regime's highest court, upheld the verdicts.

Some Cuban dissidents continued to defy Castro despite the crackdown. According to a report in the *Miami Herald* in June 2003, as many as 40 independent Cuban journalists courageously continued to e-mail free-lance articles to foreign news organizations.

Coinciding with the crackdown and the sham trials was a wave of hijackings, two of airliners and one of a ferry. In the first airline hijacking on March 19, the plane was diverted from the Isle of Youth to Key West. Of the 31 passengers and crew, 15 elected to remain in the United States. U.S. authorities arrested the six hijackers for air piracy and returned the plane to Cuba. The second plane also was hijacked upon leaving the Isle of Youth but was forced to land in Havana because of low fuel. The hijacker then ordered the pilot to Key West. This time, 10 of the 19 passengers and crew chose not to return to Cuba. On April 2, eight hijackers commandeered a ferry with 50 passengers and attempted to take it to Florida, but low fuel forced it back to the port of Mariel. Two days of tense negotiations ensued, during which the hijackers threatened to kill their hostages; Castro himself went to Mariel to handle the crisis. Cuban troops stormed the ferry and arrested the hijackers, who were tried within days even as the trials of the dissidents were unfolding. Three were sentenced to death and executed by firing squad on April 11.

If Castro had thought that the world's preoccupation with war in Iraq would cause the crackdown, the trials of the dissidents and the executions of the hijackers to go unnoticed, he was quickly disillusioned and no doubt stunned by the ferocity of the reaction. The crackdown and subsequent trials were widely reported by U.S., European and Latin American media, and media groups like the Committee to Protect Journalists, Society of Professional Journalists, Inter American Press Association, American Society of Newspaper Editors and Reporters Sans Frontières all called on the Cuban government to release the independent journalists. International human rights groups like Amnesty International, Human Rights Watch and the Carter Center also denounced the arrests and stiff sentences handed down.

The Bush administration predictably condemned the crackdown and trials, which came as no surprise to Castro, but Bush was joined by the EU and Pope John Paul II; even longtime friend Canada angrily called upon Cuba to release the prisoners of conscience. The execution of the hijackers days later intensified the chorus of denunciations from countries where capital punishment is banned, including Mexico. Nonetheless, Castro defiantly shrugged off the world's condemnation.

As another indication of Castro's growing isolation, Costa Rica, a member of the U.N. Human Rights Commission, reversed its traditional opposition to a strongly worded resolution denouncing Cuba's human rights violations. Costa Rica, which in the past had supported resolutions that called only for a U.N. human rights monitor to visit Cuba, indicated that it would support a U.S.-backed resolution that expressed "deep concern" over the crackdown and that called on Cuba to release the dissidents. EU representatives also supported the resolution. But the 53-member commission is still dominated by countries with such despotic regimes as Sudan. On April 17, 2003, the commission rejected the harsh resolution 31–15. Instead, it approved 24–20 the same resolution it passed the year before for Cuba to allow a human rights monitor, French judge Christine Chanet, to visit the island. Castro had rejected Chanet's visit, calling her post "illegitimate." Cuban Foreign Minister Felipe Pérez Roque said Cuba would not abide by even the watered-down resolution. As had happened the year before when Castro alienated Uruguay, the Cuban delegate to the commission called Peru, Nicaragua, Uruguay and Costa Rica "repugnant lackeys" of the United States for voting for the weaker resolution. Peru summoned the Cuban ambassador in Lima to demand an explanation, while Nicaragua withdrew its charge d'affaires from Havana.

"The Cocktail War"

Twelve days later, Cuba was awarded one of Latin America's six seats on the commission, prompting the U.S. delegate to walk out in disgust. The 15-nation EU—later increased to 25—not only unanimously rejected Cuba's participation in the Cotonou Agreement but voted to impose a range of diplomatic sanctions that limited high-level visits to Cuba and reduced the EU's participation in Cuban cultural events. Even more galling to Castro, the EU announced it would begin inviting Cuban dissidents to receptions on European national days. The media quickly dubbed the Cuban-EU dispute the "cocktail war."

Defiant to the end, Castro alluded to the EU, which buys 35% of Cuba's exports and had provided about $160 million in aid to Cuba during the previous 10 years, as "a gang, a mafia" that had caved in to U.S. pressure. During a four-hour televised address on June 11, He called Spanish Prime Minister José María Aznar a "little Führer" and Italian Prime Minister Silvio a "Fascist" and a "clown." Spain for years had been Cuba's leading apologist before the EU, even under conservative governments like Aznar's. Italy summoned the Cuban ambassador in Rome to express "deep indignation" over Castro's offensive, undiplomatic remarks. The next day, Fidel and Raúl led hundreds of thousands of people in a mass protest outside the Spanish and Italian embassies. Cuba also annulled a 1997 agreement with Spain for a Spanish cultural center in Ha-

Cuba

vana. Castro used the occasion of the 50th anniversary of the July 26, 1953 attack on the Moncada Barracks, the spark of the Cuban Revolution, to reject any further aid from the EU under the Cotonou Agreement. He castigated Europe as the United States' "Trojan horse," and railed against its "shameful past" of colonization and exploitation.

Castro's tirades against the EU and Cuba's mother country served only to further alienate himself from the community of nations. On September 5, 2003, the European Parliament responded with a resolution formally condemning Cuba for its human rights abuses.

Another humiliation came in March 2004 when the U.N. Educational, Scientific and Cultural Organization (UNESCO) awarded the Guillermo Cano World Press Freedom Award to Raúl Rivero, the imprisoned journalist. The award, named for a murdered Colombian newspaper editor, includes a $25,000 cash prize. The Cuban foreign ministry denounced the award as "deplorable and embarrassing." Yes, but for whom? On May 3, the day Rivero received the award in absentia in Bosnia-Herzegovina, Cason and a delegation of European diplomats visited with Rivero's wife in her home.

In April 2004, the regime suddenly invited a delegation of international journalists to tour the prison where the dissidents are incarcerated, but they were allowed to speak only with inmates chosen by the government. They did not meet with Rivero himself.

On April 15, 2004, the U.N. commission once again voted, 22-21 with 10 abstentions, to call on Cuba to guarantee freedom of expression, to undertake dialogue with the dissidents and to allow Charet to visit Cuba. This time Honduras bore the brunt of Cuban fury for introducing the resolution, while Mexico's vote soured relations even further. Chile, Costa Rica, Guatemala and Peru also voted for the resolution. Mexico and Peru both recalled their ambassadors from Cuba after Castro denounced their votes in his annual May Day diatribe. Mexico's President Fox went further by ordering the Cuban ambassador to leave Mexico and declaring the Cuban political affairs attaché *persona non grata* for allegedly becoming involved in a scandal involving the Mexico City administration of the left-wing Party of the Democratic Revolution (see Mexico). The two countries came close to breaking diplomatic relations over the war of words that ensued, but in late May the two foreign ministers met and agreed to restore ambassador-level relations.

Cuba again cast itself in the role of outcast, unnecessarily, at the summit of 53 EU, Latin American and Caribbean countries in Guadalajara, Mexico, in May 2004, which Castro refused to attend. For once, Cuba was on the same side with the EU and its neighbors on a resolution condemning U.S. abuse of Iraqi prisoners. But the resolution wasn't harsh enough for Cuban Foreign Minister Pérez-Roque, who also accused the EU of scuttling a resolution condemning the U.S. trade embargo. Cuba was the only country at the summit not to vote in favor of the final declaration.

Even as Castro was alienating old friends, he managed to cultivate two new ones: newly elected presidents Luiz Inácio da Silva of Brazil and Néstor Kirchner of Argentina, who assumed office in January and May 2003, respectively. Castro attended both inaugurations. Kirchner reestablished diplomatic relations with Cuba in October 2003, which former President Fernando de la Rua had severed in 2001 because of Castro's insults. Da Silva, a longtime friend of Castro's, visited Havana in September 2003 and signed a number of bilateral agreements and a deal to stretch out Cuban repayment of its $40 million debt to Brazil. Both Argentina and Brazil abstained on the U.N. Human Rights Commission vote condemning Cuba in April 2004, and neither da Silva nor Kirchner expressed any qualms over Castro's 2003 crackdown.

Cuba's relations with Spain also improved dramatically with the election victory of the Socialists in March 2004, days after the devastating al-Qaeda terrorist attacks on the commuter trains in Madrid. José Luis Rodríguez Zapatero replaced Aznar as prime minister, and Zapatero began interceding on Castro's behalf with the EU. He argued that the freeze in diplomatic relations was not having the desired effect of improving human rights in Cuba. In December, Spain, Hungary and Belgium re-established normal relations with Cuba after Castro released five dissidents, including Rivero, on health grounds; Rivero chose to go into exile in Spain. Over the next three months, he would release nine more. On January 3, 2005, Austria, Britain, France, Germany, Greece, Italy, Portugal and Sweden also resumed full relations, and the rest of the EU followed suit a week later. It seemed the "cocktail war" was over.

Poland and the Czech Republic were the only EU members skeptical of appeasing Castro without asking anything in return; they would soon be proved right. When a meeting of EU foreign ministers announced on January 31 that the EU would continue to monitor Cuba for progress on human rights, Castro responded on February 2 with another of his arrogant four-hour speeches, in which he ridiculed the EU and said he had no intention of changing his policies. "What are they going to forgive us for?" he asked sarcastically, adding for good measure, "Cuba does not need Europe." Instead of improving his human rights record, Castro ordered Cubans to minimize the amount of time they spend associating with foreigners.

In early March, Bill Rammell, Britain's deputy foreign secretary for Latin America, visited Havana and urged Castro to release all the jailed dissidents. Castro bluntly told Rammell that while he welcomed improved relations with the EU, he would not release the dissidents and told the EU to stop interfering in Cuba's internal affairs. So much for appeasement.

On March 25, EU Development Commissioner Louis Michel, a Belgian, arrived in Havana for two days of talks, including with Payá and other dissidents. He is the highest-level EU official to date to visit Cuba, and Castro probably agreed because another vote was approaching on the U.N. Human Rights Commission. Since Rammell had failed with vinegar, Michel tried honey. After a four-hour meeting, Castro said the talks were "very frank," while Michel called them "very optimistic and positive." He proclaimed Castro "a very kind man" who, he said, had changed his position toward Europe. Michel noted that Castro had released 14 of the 75 dissidents and asked him politely to please release the remaining 61.

He did not, however, and Charet, still barred from visiting Cuba, submitted to the U.N. Human Rights Commission her scathing report on Cuba's refusal to free prisoners of conscience and its harassment of other dissidents. On April 14, 2005, for the sixth consecutive year, the commission voted to condemn Cuba. This time the vote was 21–17 with 15 abstentions. Instead of the usual vilification, Castro responded this time that he "couldn't care less" about the vote.

The EU and the United Nations were not his only targets. In May 2005, he called newly elected OAS Secretary-General José Miguel Insulza of Chile an "interventionist" for calling for reform in Cuba. Ironically, Insulza had worked in the government of Castro's good friend and fellow Marxist, Salvador Allende. Friction also developed between Castro and his friend, Argentine President Kirchner, in January 2005 when Castro denied Kirchner's personal request to allow a dissident Cuban neurosurgeon to visit her son and grandchildren in Buenos Aires.

Meanwhile, "Cocktail War II" erupted in May when Cuba expelled five European parliamentarians—three Spanish, one German and one Czech—who had gone there to attend a rally of the Assembly to Promote Civil Society, a dissident group, on May 20–21. Entry was denied to two Polish members of the European Parliament

Cuba

and four European journalists were arrested. The EU expressed its concern, while Italy and even Spain summoned the Cuban ambassadors to express their displeasure. With considerable understatement, the two Polish deputies who were denied entry to Cuba wrote to Spain's Javier Solana, the EU high representative, that "the change in European policy toward Cuba is not bringing results." Even the Spanish justice minister called the expulsions "disagreeable and serious." Castro had lost his best friend in Europe. EU policy was to be reviewed in June when the EU foreign ministers met.

The dissident movement has remained active as the diplomatic war of words swirls around them. Cuban authorities permitted the rally of the Assembly to Promote Civil Society in May, but forbade coverage by foreign journalists. About 200 people attended, led by Beatríz Roque. The group organized a 36-member steering committee and called for peaceful protests.

Not attending the assembly was Payá, who has become a rival of Roque's within the dissident movement. In February 2005, Payá called for a "National Dialogue" on the transition for post-Castro Cuba that included 57 exiles, but some anti-Castro hardliners opposed Payá's offer to include members of the government in the dialogue. Without them, of course, there is no "dialogue," but it is unlikely the government will agree anyway. Roque said the dialogue doesn't go far enough. Payá called her assembly a "smoke screen."

Meanwhile, the wives of the jailed dissidents have taken matters in their own hands. Nicknamed the "ladies in white," they have staged marches and candlelight vigils to focus attention on the plight of their husbands. Female government supporters physically broke up one such demonstration in March.

While relations with the EU went from bad to good to worse than ever, Castro hosted an amicable visit by his fellow autocrat, Chinese President Hu Jintao, in November 2004, during which the two countries signed new trade agreements. China accounts for 10% of Cuba's trade and is Cuba's third-largest trading partner after Venezuela and Spain. China also pledged to invest $500 million in a new nickel plant, while Cuba agreed to export 4,400 tons of nickel to China for its hungry industries.

Perhaps the only sign of a softening of the hard line came when Pope John Paul II died on April 2, 2005. The always unpredictable Castro declared three days of mourning and even attended a memorial Mass at Havana Cathedral—the first time he had entered the building since his sister's wedding in 1959.

An amusing episode in the on-going battle for human rights was the appearance in 2005 of an underground video, titled "Monte Roque," that satirizes the government's electronic surveillance of its citizens. Other underground videos have spoofed such things as chronic shortages, but this is the first that actually poked fun at official policy.

Growing Cuban-U.S. Tension

The crackdown of 2003 derailed, at least temporarily, the growing sentiment, even among Republican members of Congress, to lift the trade embargo. As a result of an easing of the embargo in 2000, Cuba had imported 600,000 tons of U.S. agricultural products, paid for in cash, beginning in November 2001. In August 2002, a shipment of $750,000 worth of brand-name grocery items arrived in Cuba, the first such transaction in 40 years. Despite objections from the Bush administration, U.S. agricultural executives held a food fair in Cuba in September 2002, also the first in 40 years. Cuba concluded $66 million in food contracts with the executives.

But a reminder of the tense political climate between Cuba and the United States came in November 2002, when the United States expelled two Cuban diplomats assigned to the United Nations, accusing them of spying. Days later, an almost comical incident exploded into another bilateral war of words when a Cuban airline pilot loaded seven family members into a Russian-built cropduster and flew it to Key West. Cuba labeled the theft an act of "terrorism" and demanded the return of the eight Cuban nationals and the plane. But the United States ruled the incident a defection and granted them political asylum, which caused Castro to hold one of his customary public rallies to vilify the U.S. decision. The Cubans were infuriated even more when the plane was sold for $7,000 as part of a $27 million civil judgment by a Florida court against the Cuban government.

The United States accused Cuba in September 2002 of seeking to undermine its efforts in the war on terrorism, which Cuba angrily denied. In March 2003, Cuba denounced the U.S.-led war on Iraq. On the eve of the crackdown on dissent, Cuba seized a shipment of 5,000 books ordered by the U.S. interests section to be distributed to independent libraries. Fourteen independent library operators were among the dissidents imprisoned in the crackdown. The authors of the seized books included John Steinbeck, Martin Luther King Jr.—even Groucho Marx! By May, after the U.S. victory over Iraq, Castro was accusing the United States of looking for a pretext to invade Cuba next. His paranoia was not

moderated when the United States stepped up airborne TV Martí broadcasts with digital satellite signals; there are an estimated 15,000 satellite disks in Cuba, and digital signals are more difficult to jam.

On a more positive note, aging U.S., Cuban and Russian political and military figures, including former Defense Secretary Robert McNamara, gathered in Havana to mark the 40th anniversary of the Cuban Missile Crisis in October 2002. Through an extraordinary exchange of declassified information, the former antagonists learned that the world had been even closer to nuclear war that they had believed in 1962.

Sales of U.S. food to Cuba have continued to escalate even as political relations have remained hostile. Cuba, however, still is barred from selling its products in the United States, such as its coveted cigars and rum. In July 2003, the first shipment of 140 head of Minnesota cattle arrived in Cuba. In September, U.S. Senator Max Baucus, a Montana Democrat, became the highest-level U.S. official to visit Cuba since the crackdown, and he signed an agreement for Montana to sell $10 million in agricultural products to Cuba over six months. However, he also visited Payá at his home. In April 2004, Cuba signed agreements with U.S. firms for the purchase of about $106 million worth of food, including powdered milk, corn and chicken. Clearly, the Bush administration was adroitly following a dual policy: a hard-line diplomatic one simultaneously with one of increased exports that appears humanitarian in nature, but in reality is benefiting money-minded businessmen who generally support the Republican Party.

Once again, Cuba was an issue in the 2004 U.S. presidential election. Bush reiterated his hard-line policy to please Cuban-American voters in Florida. In May, Bush unveiled a 500-page report by a presidential commission he had named to study the post-Castro succession in Cuba. Bush declared that he would not wait for Castro's death to begin planning for a democratic transition and would allocate $36 million toward that end. The commission recommended that the United States apply "pressure and attention on the ruling elite" to block the succession from Fidel to Raúl. To tighten the economic screws on the crippled regime, Bush changed the regulations for visits by Cuban Americans to family members in Cuba from one a year to one every three years, and he lowered the per diem allowance for expenditures during those visits from $160 to $50. He retained the current $1,200-a-year cap on remittances to the island, however. The changes took effect on July 1, 2004.

If Bush thought his tougher stance would cheer Cuban dissidents, he was quickly disappointed. The leading dissidents, including Payá, Sánchez and Gutiérrez, all denounced the idea as U.S. interference and argued that Cubans and Cubans alone should decide the succession. Meanwhile, Democratic presidential contender John Kerry came to Florida to charge that Bush had given only "lip service" to Cuban Americans over four years, while he promised to work "full-time" to bring about a democratic transition in Cuba.

Castro's response to Bush's pronouncements was swift. On May 11, 2004 he suspended sales of all but essential items at the island's 5,300 dollars-only stores, ostensibly for "inventory," thus inflicting a hardship on his own people that he conveniently blamed on the United States. On May 14, Castro called one of his trademark rallies to protest the U.S. changes, and hundreds of thousands of people dutifully showed up. It was largely a feel-good response, however. On May 24, Castro abruptly ordered the dollar stores reopened, but with prices about 15% higher than before. Of course, he blamed the increases on the United States.

On the eve of the U.S. election, and in an apparent attempt to influence the outcome, Castro went even further. On October 25, he ordered the Central Bank to declare that effective November 8, the U.S. dollar would no longer be accepted at Cuban stores, even the so-called dollar stores. Instead, only the "convertible peso" would be accepted. Castro also told his countrymen to ask relatives living abroad to begin sending remittances in euros, British pounds or Swiss francs. Cubans could still exchange dollars for pesos, but only with a 10% surcharge; other acceptable currencies were not subject to the surcharge.

Castro apparently was hoping the measure would intimidate Cuban Americans to vote for Kerry in the expectation that they would be able to resume sending dollars to their families in Cuba. If so, it backfired; Bush was reelected, and this time he carried Florida decisively.

The sometimes silly propaganda war between the United States and Cuba flared up again in December 2004, when the U.S. interests section in Havana put up a Christmas light display that contained the number "75," a reference to the dissidents arrested in 2003. The Cuban government demanded that the lights be removed; Cason refused. In retaliation, the Cubans erected a billboard containing one of the infamous photographs of U.S. soldiers abusing Iraqi prisoners at Abu Ghraib Prison. On the photo was a swastika and the legend, "Made in USA."

Even as the two governments continued to bicker, elected officials from both parties continued to visit Cuba to promote food sales from their home states. Baucus visited again in December 2004 as part of a 300-member delegation that concluded deals totaling $125 million. Castro met with the delegation and, never at a loss for words, spoke for several hours. Cuba bought another $45 million in food in January 2005. In March, Louisiana Governor Kathleen Blanco, also a Democrat, visited, as did two Republican U.S. representatives from California and Florida. As of February 2005, according to the Cuban government, purchases of U.S. food had passed the $1 billion mark. Although the U.S. government has permitted the sales as humanitarian exceptions to the embargo (and profitable for Republican campaign contributors), the Treasury Department made things tougher on Cuba. Effective March 31, Cuba had to pay for all shipments in cash in advance, before the ships are loaded, instead of upon delivery in Cuba. Baucus and other farm-state legislators of both parties howled in protest.

But the most serious U.S.-Cuban conflict since the Elián González controversy exploded in May 2005. The United States detained Luis Posada Carriles, a 77-year-old anti-Castro firebrand who had bribed his way out of a Venezuelan prison in 1985 while awaiting retrial for allegedly masterminding the 1976 bombing of a Cuban airliner that killed 73 people off Barbados. Arrested in Miami, where he has many supporters, Posada had apparently been in the United States for two months, entering illegally through Mexico. Reportedly, he had intended to seek political asylum, but went into hiding. He came out of hiding to hold a news conference, which led to Cuban and Venezuelan demands for his arrest. He was arrested on May 17.

Posada spent four years in prison in Panama, where he attempted to assassinate Castro during a summit in Panama in 2000; he was pardoned in 2004 (see Panama). Cuba also accuses him of the bombings of hotels in the 1990s, one of which killed an Italian tourist. Posada admitted the hotel bombings in an interview, then retracted it. He denies the airline bombing.

Venezuelan President Hugo Chávez immediately demanded that the United States extradite Posada back to Venezuela. He had already been twice acquitted of charges stemming from the airliner bombing. Posada, a renegade former CIA agent turned terrorist, holds Venezuelan citizenship, and the bombing was believed to have been planned in Caracas. Two other Venezuelans were convicted for their roles. Posada's supporters in Miami argued against extradition, saying Chávez could send him to Cuba, where he would face execution.

For his part, Castro termed Posada's arrest a "farce," questioning how such a high-profile fugitive could have entered and spent two months in the United States undetected. He also accused Bush of having a double standard toward terrorists. For once, Castro had not one but two valid points, and like the Elián González case, he began skillfully milking the Posada case for its propaganda value. What especially outraged Castro and Chávez was that Posada was arrested not as a fugitive from justice, but for illegally entering the country.

The U.S. government has played squarely into Castro's hands by its clumsy handling of the case. At first, authorities said they would decide what to do with Posada within 48 hours, then began stalling. When this book went to press, Posada was still being held in El Paso, Texas, while U.S. officials agonized over what to do with him (see Venezuela).

Culture: Cuba is an ethnic peculiarity in Latin America. The Spaniards largely exterminated the native Carib Indians, but the influx of blacks from the British West Indies has given Cuba a distinctive Euro-African culture. About 62% of Cubans today are black or mulatto. Although Roman Catholicism took root in colonial times and has survived the repression of the communist government, thousands of Cubans of African descent, both before and after the Revolution, practice a hybrid religion called *santería* that blends elements of Catholicism with ancient African tribal rites.

Although independence came to Cuba eight decades later than it did to its sister republics, some Creole writers and poets gained recognition during the 19th century. Best known of these is the poet José Martí (1853–95), a leader in Cuba's quest for independence, who was martyred in a battle against the Spanish. Cuba's best known 20th century poet was Nicolás Guillén (1902–87), whose verse celebrated the island's African cultural heritage.

Another celebrated 20th century Cuban writer in the Hispanic world and beyond was the novelist Guillermo Cabrera Infante (1929–2005), but the current Cuban government does not claim him because he fell out of favor with Castro in 1962 and did most of his acclaimed work after leaving Cuba in 1967. He won Spain's coveted Cervantes Prize in Literature in 1997. Most critics regard his most famous work as *Tres Tristes Tigres (Three Trapped Tigers)*, published in 1967, which was a sketch of pre-revolutionary Havana night life. Also well known were the autobiographical *Habana para un infante difunto (Infante's In-*

Cuba

"Gitano Tropical" by Victor Manuel García, 1929. In Museo National de Bellas Artes, Cuba

ferno) (1979) and *Mea Cuba* (1993) He obtained British citizenship and died in London on February 21, 2005.

Cuba's leading cultural export has been its music. The African-based rhythms of the mambo, the rumba and the cha-cha-cha were the rage in the United States and Europe during the 1940s and 1950s, and brought stardom to such bandleaders as Xavier Cugat and Desi Arnaz.

The Cuban Revolution has proved to be a cultural tradeoff. On the one hand, the repressiveness of the totalitarian system caused many of Cuba's most talented writers, artists, singers, musicians and actors to abandon Cuba for the United States, Spain or another Latin American country to more freely express themselves. None was better known than Celia Cruz, the acknowledged "queen of salsa." In prerevolutionary Cuba she won fame as the lead singer for the band, La Sonora Matancera. She resumed singing after she emigrated to the United States, eventually becoming a pop icon as salsa won acceptance among *anglos* as well as latinos. So great was her hemispheric recognition that when she died in New York City in July 2003, thousands turned out for her funeral, and her obituary was carried all

over Latin America—even, grudgingly, in the Cuban media.

Ironically, one of the people most responsible for renewing international interest in Cuban music was an American guitarist, Ry Cooder, an *aficionado* of Cuban sounds. He obtained permission to travel to Cuba in 1996 in quest of some of the aging figures of prerevolutionary music. He assembled pianist Rubén González, singer Ibrahim Ferrer and singers-guitarists Eliades Ochoa and Compay Segundo for a recording session under the name, the Buena Vista Social Club. The 1997 CD became a hit and won a Grammy Award, and the group's new fame led German director Wim Wenders to make a movie, "The Buena Vista Social Club," which received an Oscar nomination. Segundo's death in July 2003 and González's five months later made headlines all over Latin America as well as the United States.

While many cultural figures fled Cuba, previously banned leftist writers and other intellectuals were free to come. The Castro regime has taken great pride in its commitment to fostering arts and preserving the indigenous culture, particularly art, music, literature, theater and cinema. Several Cuban films have achieved international recognition in high-brow circles, but naturally they convey subtle—or not so subtle—ideological messages.

Some outstanding talent remained in Cuba after the Revolution, including the composer José Ardévol and Latin America's prima ballerina, Alicia Alonso. But other creative minds felt the heavy hand of the communist system. At least two cases of repression brought international condemnation upon the regime even from its sympathizers. When the writer Herberto Padilla was jailed in 1971, there was an outcry from such leftist intellectuals as Jean-Paul Sartre, Colombian novelist Gabriel García Márquez and the Mexican poet Octavio Paz. Castro ordered Padilla released, but only after the writer signed a confession of his "errors against the Revolution," which he was obligated to read before the Cuban Congress on Education and Culture.

As an indicator of post-revolutionary culture, the congress passed a resolution that said, in part, that the mass media, writers and artists "are powerful instruments of ideological education whose utilization and development should not be left to spontaneity and improvisation." Padilla worked in obscurity as a translator before being allowed to emigrate to the United States in 1980. In 1981, the poet Armando Valladares was imprisoned, provoking more international pressure. He, too, was allowed to resettle in the United States. Several intellectuals remain imprisoned in Cuba, although a visiting U.S. congressional delegation won the release of a few in 1996.

Cuba's literary community had cause to celebrate in July 2002 when one of its own, writer and poet Cintio Vitier, 80, received Mexico's coveted Juan Rulfo Literature Prize. He had received Cuba's National Literature Prize in 1988.

The history of the Cuban press is not a happy one, either before or since the Revolution. There was an eight-year period of relative press freedom during the constitutional administrations of Ramón Grau San Martín and Carlos Prío Socarrás prior to Batista's imposition of dictatorship in 1952. The Cuban government subsidized the press, which placed an economic sword of Damocles over newspapers critical of Batista. There were several independent dailies before the Revolution, the most prestigious being *Diario de la Marina*. By 1962, Castro had expropriated all the independent newspapers and magazines, and only one daily newspaper remained: *Granma*, the official *Communist Party* and government mouthpiece, named for the boat that brought Castro and his revolutionaries from Mexico in 1956. *Granma*, of course, is more of a propaganda organ than a genuinely informative newspaper.

The regime retained the name of one confiscated magazine, *Bohemia*, which is somewhat less propagandistic and more of a literary and artistic review.

All things considered, the term "revolutionary journalism" is an oxymoron, because everything that appears in print or is transmitted over the airwaves is tightly controlled by the regime. Meaningful intellectual freedom or pluralism of thought remains non-existent, and modern Cuban cultural expression has been rendered quadriplegic for nearly four decades.

Economy: Like so many Latin American countries, Cuba was condemned to a monocultural dependency on a given commodity, in Cuba's case, sugar cane. Nickel deposits and Cuba's famous black tobacco provided some economic diversity, but for the most part Cuba's prosperity or lack of it depended largely on the world market price for sugar. Even so, Cuba enjoyed a generally higher standard of living than did most of its sister republics, and it was somewhat ironic that Marxism took root here rather than in one of the more destitute nations.

The Marxist experiment has proved no more feasible in this tropical setting than it did in Eastern Europe. As industry minister in the early 1960s, the legendary Ché Guevara set out to convert Cuba into an industrialized state, with disastrous results. What Cuba became, and what it still is today, is an illusion of self-sufficiency, with housing, education and medical care all provided "free." But it was the infusion of nearly $1 million a day worth of Soviet aid for 30 years, and guaranteed Soviet purchases of Cuban sugar, that made this smoke-and-mirrors economy seem viable. The dependency on sugar continued, the difference being that with collectivized agriculture, crop yields dropped precipitously after the Revolution.

On paper, the Cuban peso was proclaimed to be worth more than the U.S. dollar, while in reality it was worthless. Official per capita GDP figures were disregarded by international economists, and largely still are (see below). The classic communist method of distribution of goods and services resulted in chronic food shortages, which the regime blamed solely on the U.S. embargo rather than face the reality of the system's design flaws.

When the Soviet sugar daddy (pun intended) began collapsing in the late 1980s and the aid stopped pouring in, the plight of the people became increasingly desperate. The unpredictable Castro suddenly shifted policy during what he euphemistically termed Cuba's "special period" of readjustment. In a desperate bid to alleviate the destitution, Castro decided to allow private agricultural plots and fruit markets and permitted some skilled workers, such as mechanics, to moonlight as entrepreneurs. The Cubans eagerly responded. When many of these small entrepreneurs and farmers began showing signs of bourgeois prosperity, Castro just as unpredictably terminated the experiment in limited capitalismtemporarily. At the Fourth Communist Party Congress in 1991, again motivated by desperation to alleviate food shortages, he resumed limited private and cooperative cultivation. He also permitted the U.S. dollar to circulate, in effect creating a dual currency system.

In 1993, Castro expanded limited entrepreneurship to 157 discrete areas of endeavor. For example, he permitted the licensing of mom-and-pop restaurants called *paladares*, and small pensions called *casas particulares*. By 1995, more than 200,000 tiny restaurants and hotels had been licensed, but they faced such stringent regulation and fees that the number dropped to 150,000 in 2001. Those that remained have proven popular with customers and modestly lucrative for their owners.

By 1997, the private agricultural plots and co-ops were providing more food than the state farms. By 2002, there were 65,000 such small farms, grouped into 1,116 cooperatives. In a remarkable concession to their success, the National Assembly voted in November 2002 to increase the amount of profits rebated to member farms from 50% to 70%.

In another seemingly counterrevolutionary move in 1994 that stemmed from raw desperation, Castro ordered the old decadent hotels, casinos and nightclubs to reopen under state tutelage. Cubans were not permitted to frequent such bourgeois establishments, of course, only to work there. The fun spots are reserved for foreign tourists, Canadians mostly, who are encouraged to pay with dollars. The gimmick to bring in desperately needed foreign exchange was successful, so much so that anti-Castro dissidents—whether from Florida or Cuba has not been determined—set off bombs in three of the hotels in September 1997, killing one tourist and injuring four, in an obvious attempt to frighten other tourists away.

Cuba remains the world's eighth-largest sugar producer, but the sugar industry has deteriorated dramatically in recent years, in part because of natural factors, but also because of outdated equipment and low world market prices. Hurricane Georges was a factor in the 24% drop in sugar production in 1998, from 4.2 to 3.4 million metric tons. The sugar crop was hit again in 2001 by Hurricane Michelle, which destroyed an estimated 35% of the crop.

Nonetheless, official figures released in June 2002 put the harvest at 3.61 million tons, up slightly from the record low of 3.53 million in 2000–01, but a far cry from the record of 8.1 million in 1989. Because of lower market prices, the 2002 crop brought in about $120 million less in export earnings than the $561 million from the 2001 crop. In mid-2002, faced with grim economic realities, the government grudgingly and quietly closed 71 of the island's 156 sugar mills and said it plans to modernize the remaining ones. It also announced plans to replace about half of the 3.5 million acres devoted to sugar cultivation with crops that will help feed the Cuban people, such as rice. On the remaining land, using improved techniques, the government hoped to increase the sugar yield from 16 tons per acre to 23. But the 2002–03 harvest showed a cataclysmic drop of 45%, to 2 million tons, a new record low. Still, Castro stubbornly clung to the collectiv-ist model. The 2003–04 harvest was up slightly to 2.5 million tons, but the worst drought in a century devastated the sugar crop of 2004–05. A glum Castro admitted the harvest would be no more than 1.7 million tons, possibly only 1.5 million, the lowest since 1909—before mechanization.

Cuba also is the world's sixth-largest producer of nickel and holds 30% of the world's reserves. Its exports of nickel and cobalt in 2001 exceeded $600 million. It produced 75,200 tons in 2002 and has the potential for 100 million, but because of the 2003 crackdown on dissent it has had difficulty finding European, Canadian or Australian mining firms willing to make the necessary $1.2 billion investment. In November 2004, Chinese President Hu Jintao visited Cuba and agreed to invest $500 million in Cuba's nickel industry, not out of the goodness of his heart but because China's booming industries need the nickel. China is to import 4,400 tons annually.

Cuba has hoped tourism would be its economic savior, and to a degree, it has been. In April 1999, Vice President Carlos Lage stated officially that the country was relying increasingly on foreign tourism for development. He said that tourism brought in $1.7 billion in badly needed foreign exchange in 1998 and that it showed a 30% increase in the first quarter of 1999. An estimated 1.8 million tourists visited Cuba in 2000, bringing in $1.9 billion, dwarfing the amount from sugar exports. In 2001, the number of tourists dropped by 5% to 1.7 million, reflecting the global drop in tourism as a consequence of the September 11, 2001 terror attacks on the United States, and in the first quarter of 2002 it was down by 14%. During the winter of 2001–02, several Cuban

Cuba

hotels actually closed up for lack of business, while prices at dollar stores skyrocketed. Most of Cuba's tourists are from Canada and Europe, and in response to that fact, Cuba officially began accepting the euro as well as the dollar at its main resort town of Varadero on June 1, 2002. By 2003, it seemed the crisis had been weathered, with 1.9 million tourists bringing in $2.1 billion. In January 2003, Castro himself presided at the opening of a 944-room resort on Cuba's northeast coast, the largest resort yet. The total number of hotel rooms on the island is now about 40,000. The government reported that in 2004, the number of tourists hit the 2 million mark, bringing in 15% more in foreign exchange than in 2003. The reports added tourism accounted for 4% of foreign exchange in 1990 and 41% in 2004.

So desperate has Cuba been for foreign exchange that Venezuela, about the best friend Cuba still has and the source of a third of its oil, was forced to suspend oil shipments in April 2002 when Cuba was unable to pay more than $63 million it owed for past shipments. The shipments resumed five months later under a deferred payments plan.

Cuba produces about 75,000 barrels of crude oil a day, about half its needs. Castro himself announced in December 2004 the discovery of an offshore oil deposit off the north coast containing an estimated 100 million barrels. He said production could begin in 2006.

Also dwarfing sugar earnings as a source of foreign exchange in recent years, now second only to tourism, have been remittances from Cubans living abroad, primarily the United States, Mexico and Spain. They are estimated at about $1 billion.

Since the collapse of the Soviet Union, Cuba has come to rely on foreign—i.e., capitalist—investors for economic development. By the end of 2001 there were nearly 400 joint ventures with the state, about 60% of them with Canadian, Spanish, French and Italian firms, specializing primarily in tourism, construction and biotechnology. Such investments have totaled an estimated $5 billion. But the drop in tourism, coupled with an unfavorable business climate, led to a dramatic decline in foreign investments. From an annual average of $268 million from 1996–2000, including $488 million in 2000, it plunged to only 38.9 million in 2001. The number of joint ventures dropped to about 300 in 2004, in part because the government abruptly began stiffening bureaucratic rules to drive out smaller businesses.

Economy Minister José Luis Rodríguez claimed at the end of 1998 that the country showed a 1.2% increase in GDP, the slowest since 1994. That was still well short of the 7.8% claimed in 1996. Since then, growth has averaged a respectable 4.7% per year, thanks almost wholly to foreign capitalist investors who are theoretically anathema to the Marxist-Leninist model. Growth was estimated at a robust 6.9% for 1999, 5.6% for 2000 and 3% for 2001, but plummeted to 1.1% in 2002 and 1.3% in 2003, largely as a result of the drops in tourism and sugar production. The government claimed growth in 2004 was 5%, while the Economist Intelligence Unit in London put it at 3%.

On paper, the country claimed a per capita income of $2,800 in 2003, which is suspicious considering that the average monthly wage is only about $20. This is accomplished through a smoke-and-mirrors technique called "purchasing power parity," which factors in such benefits as free rents and medical care.

Apparently in response to the dire state of the economy, Castro fired the ministers of transportation and of finance and prices in June 2003, replacing them with much younger technocrats. He retained Rodríguez as economy and planning minister—for the time being.

In 2004, Castro ordered one of his periodic crackdowns on entrepreneurship, which many Cubans must resort too to survive. Among those affected were private auto mechanics and even clowns who perform at birthday parties. He also froze new licenses for the popular *paladores*, or private restaurants, and *casas particulares*, a kind of Cuban bed-and-breakfast. He placed the existing establishments under onerous new restrictions and fees that could only be seen as disincentives. His logic in doing this was analogous to shutting off the engines once a plane had attained cruising altitude. Yet, in March 2005, he confidently declared an official end to the "special period" of austerity and readjustment following the Soviet collapse.

For a decade, Castro pragmatically allowed U.S. dollars to be spent at certain stores, appropriately tagged "dollar stores." That came to an abrupt end on November 8, 2004, when Castro ordered the Central Bank to prohibit circulation of the dollar at stores and businesses. In its place, there was the so-called "convertible peso," with an exchange rate to the dollar of 1:1. For government paychecks and most everyday uses, Cubans still used the regular peso, which Castro devalued in March 2005 from 27 to the dollar to 25. The Central Bank now levies a 10% surcharge to convert dollars to either kind of peso, while the euro and other hard foreign currencies are exempt.

In sum, Cuba today remains an economic basket case, a destitute society with an economy propped up only by a flourishing black market for almost everything, including parts for the pre-revolutionary Fords and Chevrolets that still chug along on Havana's streets as in a scene from a 1950s movie. Prostitution is rampant and uncontrollable despite revolutionary disapproval, and begging, something Castro once boasted he had eliminated, is back. A beggar, in fact, is what the entire country has become, totally reliant on pity from friendly countries, but even they are finding it increasingly difficult to ignore Castro's appalling abuse of human rights.

Although the U.S. government is under increased pressure from its friends abroad and from some members of Congress and businessmen at home to lift the 1960 economic embargo—the argument being that it penalizes the average Cuban more than it does the Castro regime—an end to the embargo would not prove to be the panacea that many assume. Only thorough economic reform, such as occurred in Hungary and other former East Bloc nations, will bring significant improvement. But, as the crackdown of 2003 proved once again, that will not happen as long as Castro is alive.

The Future: One of the world's great guessing games for years has been: How much longer can Castro last? With his people deserting the island like rats from a sinking ship, his Soviet benefactor consigned to the dustbin of history, his economy in shambles, one-time sympathizers like Spain, Canada, Mexico and the European Union turning against him, and his health questionable, he continues to amaze admirers and adversaries alike with his resilience—as well as with his arrogance. This author has given up predicting how much longer he will remain in power; I am now convinced that only death will end his rule.

Still, time is not on the side of the leader of one of the world's few remaining Marxist-Leninist systems. Castro is a living relic, but he cannot live forever. A dramatic reminder of his mortality came on June 23, 2001, when he briefly fainted while giving a speech under a blazing sun, something the Cuban people had never seen happen to their loquacious leader. Another came on October 20, 2004, when he tripped and suffered a nasty fall in a school gymnasium. He fell spreadeagle onto the floor, shattering his left kneecap as well as his dignity and fracturing his right arm. The tumble was shown around the world on television. There was something symbolic about that spill, signifying the Cuban economy and Castro's own deteriorating international prestige.

The brazen crackdown on dissent in 2003, in open defiance of world opinion, appeared to be as much an act of desperation as of repression. Far from being an indication that Castro is losing touch with reality, however, the crackdown was an overreaction to the reality that has begun crashing down about him. By lashing out at the world in response to growing demands for democratization, Castro has alienated many of the democratic countries that heretofore had been willing to turn a blind eye to his human rights abuses, including the EU and Cuba's chief advocate within it, Spain, as well as Canada, Sweden, Mexico, and Costa Rica. If Europeans and Canadians, who comprise the bulk of foreign tourists to Cuba, could just be offended enough by Castro's *gulag* system to vacation elsewhere, and if European and Canadian businessmen demur on further investments there, the effect on Cuba's economy would be devastating. It cannot afford any more devastation.

Another indication that Castro still has at least a finger-hold on reality is the fact that he has not dared to imprison Oswaldo Payá or Elizardo Sánchez, apparently acknowledging that they are too globally illustrious for him to risk turning them into martyrs.

Castro turned 79 on August 13, 2005. When he dies, there will be a monumental power vacuum, almost certainly filled in the short term by brother Raúl. But Raúl lacks the charisma and legendary aura of *el Comandante*. It will be interesting to see how long he can stand up to the inevitable and irresistible pressure, internal and external, that will be brought to bear on him to bring Cuba into the fellowship of the democratic nations of the 21st century.

Can the dissidents effect the transition on their own? The dissident movement in Cuba encompasses some very courageous individuals, who may form a cadre from which post-Castro leadership could be drawn, as was the case in Poland and the Czech Republic. But the internal squabble between Payá and Beatríz Roque is ominous. Others may return from Miami. But Raúl and the remaining revolutionaries are not likely to relinquish power willingly, and they still possess all the guns. If the succession turns into a bloodbath, and it well may, U.S. intervention along the lines of that in Haiti is not improbable.

Pride and joy, Santiago de Cuba   *Photo by Katherine Dickson*

The Dominican Republic

Panorama of Santo Domingo with the Presidential Palace in the foreground

Area: 18,811 square miles
Population: 8.8 million
Capital City: Santo Domingo (Pop. 2 million, estimated).
Climate: Tropical, tempered by sea breezes; moderate rainfall is heaviest from April to December.
Neighboring Countries: The Dominican Republic occupies the eastern two thirds of the island of Hispaniola, the second largest of the Greater Antilles; the Republic of Haiti occupies the western one-third of the island.
Official Language: Spanish.
Other Principal Tongues: There are small French and English-speaking groups.

Ethnic Background: Mixed European, African and Indian origin (73%), White (16%), Negro (11%).
Principal Religion: Roman Catholic Christianity.
Chief Commercial Products: Tourism, sugar, bananas, cacao, coffee, nickel, gold, textiles, clothing.
Currency: Peso.
Gross Domestic Product: U.S. $16.12 billion in 2003 ($1,896 per capita).
Former Colonial Status: Spanish Crown Colony (1492–1795); French Possession (1795–1808); Spanish Control (1808–1821); occupied by Haiti (1822–1844).
Independence Date: February 27, 1844.
Chief of State: Leonel Fernández Reyna (b. December 26, 1953), president (since August 16, 2004).
National Flag: Blue and red, quartered by a white cross.

The Dominican Republic occupies the eastern two-thirds of the island of Hispaniola, also known by its Indian name, *Hayti*, which means place of mountains. Majestically cresting at 10,000 feet in the center of the island, mountain spurs run south to the Caribbean Sea and to the east, dropping to rolling hills before reaching the coast. A separate range, with peaks reaching 4,000 feet, runs along the north coast of the Dominican Republic. The Cibao Valley, lying between the central range and north coast hills, and the southern coastal plains, are the most productive agricultural lands of the island and the most heavily populated regions. The slopes of the mountains, green throughout the year, are forested and well watered and are the locale of most of the country's coffee production.

The climate, while tropical, is moderated by invigorating sea breezes. During the dry season, December to March, the trade winds cool the air, making the southern coast beaches a major tourist attraction.

History: The island of Hispaniola was discovered by Columbus on his first voyage and selected as the site for his first colonization effort. The city of Santo Domingo, founded in 1496, is the oldest European-established city in the Americas. The native Indians were described as peaceful by Columbus and were absorbed into the Spanish population; they became virtually extinct as a race within 30 years of the Spanish discovery. Slaves from Africa were introduced in the 1520s. The discovery of more valuable domains on the mainland and the exhaustion of gold deposits on the island caused the Spanish to lose interest in Hispaniola at an early date after it was settled by them.

The island was frequently attacked by pirates and privateers—Santo Domingo was held for ransom by the English privateer Sir Francis Drake in 1585. Buccaneers took the western part of the island in 1630, and French settlers arrived shortly thereafter. The western portion of Hispaniola was ceded to France in 1697. With the outbreak of the French Revolution in 1789, a series of rebellions occurred on the island. The French section of the island, Haiti, was overrun by British and Spanish forces in 1791; they were expelled by the French in the same year and France was given possession of the entire island by treaty in 1795. Returned to Spain in 1806, the Spanish-speaking Dominicans declared themselves independent in 1821, but were conquered by the neighboring Haitians in the following year, and did not achieve final independence until 1844.

The independent history of the Dominican Republic has been a continuation of internal war, foreign intervention and misrule. From 1844 to 1861, the country was governed by a succession of military men who were put in office by various factions of the island's upper class. Constant unrest and invasions from Haiti caused General Pedro Santana to invite the Spanish to return in 1861; however, the Spanish discipline was no more welcome than it had been earlier, and the Spaniards were again ousted in 1865. The second republic was as restless as the first, and the government passed from one dictator to another in an unbroken series of corrupt administrations which had little or no governing ability.

By 1905, the Dominican Republic was largely bankrupt and threatened with occupation by European powers seeking to collect bad debts; the United States intervened under a 50-year treaty to administer the island's finances. There were more or less continuous revolts—in 1914 the United States landed Marines to bolster the government; nevertheless, the president was ousted in 1916. From 1916 to 1922, the country was administered by the U.S. Navy.

A provisional government was reestablished in 1922 and in 1924 U.S. troops were withdrawn. It soon became apparent that the Dominicans' political habits had not changed by the six years of military occupation; following a reasonably effective administration, revolt again broke out in 1930. General Rafael Leonidas Trujillo Molina, commandant of the military, seized power and brought a semblance of order to the country.

The Trujillo Era

The era of Trujillo provided a 31-year respite in a long history of violence and dissension. Ruthlessly suppressing all opposition, Trujillo dominated the island as its absolute ruler. Tyrannical as his rule was, no other dictator in Latin America approached his material benefits.

In 1930 he assumed control of a nation which had never known anything but lawlessness, banditry, bankruptcy and foreign intervention. With the treasury empty, the people poverty-stricken, the capital city destroyed by a hurricane and foreign debts almost three times the total annual income, Trujillo took on the herculean task of rebuilding his country. Twenty years later, internal and foreign debts had been paid; the national income had multiplied to 40 times the level of 1930 and the nation had a balanced budget for most of the period.

**General Rafael Leonidas
Trujillo Molina, 1930**

Schools, roads and numerous public buildings were constructed during the Trujillo years. *"El Benefactor"* also built a huge personal fortune, valued at an estimated $800 million and comprising 60% of all land in the nation. The cost of his rule was the total loss of personal liberty for the Dominican people, who were held in check by Trujillo's efficient and merciless secret police force. Trujillo's assassination in mid-1961 ended an era of one of Latin America's most brutal dictatorships. Attempts by his son to retain control of the country were unsuccessful and the family fled the island in late 1961.

The Balaguer 'Democracy'

Joaquín Balaguer, titular president at the time of the assassination, was able to maintain a semblance of order after the flight of the Trujillo family by promising to step down when provisions for elections could be made. Balaguer was overthrown by a military coup in early 1962 and a few days later, a counter-coup installed the vice president.

The first experiment in democratic government was undertaken in late 1962; Juan Bosch was chosen president in honest elections. He was inaugurated with feelings of optimism; honest, well-intentioned but politically inexperienced, he was overthrown by a military coup six months later as he attempted to limit the power of the armed forces.

A new regime was soon dominated by a former car salesman, but in April 1965 a civil war erupted when dissident elements in the armed forces sought to return Juan Bosch to office. As the toll in human lives quickly mounted (an estimated 2,000 were killed), fearing the imminent defeat of the conservative faction and creation of a new Castro-style government, the United States intervened with 22,000 combat troops.

Following considerable debate, the Organization of American States agreed to send in additional troops and take over the task of preserving order and conducting elections. Nevertheless, the fact that the United States intervened unilaterally—in apparent violation of existing inter-American agreements—caused wide-spread discontent among Latin American diplomats.

Carefully supervised by the OAS, free elections were held in mid-1966 and Balaguer, supported by a centrist coalition, won the presidency. He followed a moderate economic policy, satisfying few of the demands of the warring factions. The U.S. intervention solved none of the social or economic problems—it merely postponed the day when these questions would be resolved.

After amending the constitution so that he could succeed himself, President Bala-

Dominican Republic

guer was reelected to a second term in 1970. Unable to unite, the rival candidates provided only token resistance. Bosch boycotted the elections because he knew the military would overrule his liberal policies.

Under Balaguer, the economy achieved the most spectacular growth of any Latin America nation. Indeed, the gross national product rose by an impressive 12.5% in 1972–73—the world's highest rate in those years. Virtually every key sector of the economy set records in 1973, particularly agriculture, tourism and mining. Pacing the growth was the nation's revitalized sugar industry, where workers responded to a profit-sharing plan by increasing output.

The significant factor in the nation's economic boom was the political stability enforced by the soft-spoken Balaguer. The president's conservative Reformist Party pursued a policy called *continuísmo*, which meant a strong emphasis on law and order and economic development. However, opposition parties often received heavy-handed treatment in the name of political stability. The all-important loyalty of the armed forces was obtained by granting the military special favors.

During 1971, the administration was linked to a right-wing vigilante group called "The Gang," which terrorized and murdered several hundred suspected and real leftists. When a tiny group of 10 Cuban-trained guerrillas entered the country in early 1973, they were quickly eliminated by the efficient Dominican forces. Balaguer then used the occasion to polish off the rest of his opposition; political opponents were jailed, the university was closed and opposition newspapers and media were seized. Major political leaders were forced into hiding or exile.

The repression of political opponents set the stage for the 1974 elections. Although the opposition was divided among about 20 small parties, the two major groups (one liberal, the other conservative) formed a coalition and nominated Silvestre Antonio Guzmán Fernández, a wealthy cattle rancher.

Although Balaguer was at first regarded as a shoo-in for reelection despite his promise during the 1970 campaign to seek a constitutional change banning the reelection of presidents, a sudden groundswell of support for Guzmán clearly alarmed the administration. When Balaguer hurriedly implemented a new voting rule, the opposition boycotted the election, charging that the new rules would permit administration supporters to vote more than once.

With the opposition boycott and the military openly supporting his reelection, Balaguer coasted to an easy "victory."

Major problems facing him at the start of his third term were inflation, which had reached an annual rate of 20% by mid-1974, and high unemployment. A more fundamental problem was the fact that although the Dominican Republic was enjoying the most prosperous period in its history, the benefits of the boom were confined largely to the upper class, while fully 80% of the people remained trapped in poverty. The annual per capita income hovered at $350 while the population growth was increasing at a dangerous 3.6%.

Interregnum

Balaguer suffered a stunning upset in the 1978 presidential election when he was defeated by Guzmán of the Dominican Revolutionary Party (*PRD*). Balaguer supporters in the army temporarily halted vote tabulation when early returns showed him losing. However, strong protests at home and abroad, especially from the Carter administration, forced the military to allow the results to stand.

Guzmán's program to promote domestic peace and a strong economy was generally successful during the first three years of his term, with gains in health, education and rural development. However, a dramatic increase in the price of imported oil plus a sharp drop in sugar export earnings at the same time the United States and the Western Hemisphere were gripped by recession plunged the economy into a recession by late 1980. Guzmán announced he would not run for reelection in mid-1981—the first time in history that a Dominican chief of state had offered to step down *voluntarily*.

May 1982 elections saw the ruling *PRD* presidential candidate, moderate social democrat Salvador Jorge Blanco, win with 46% of the vote. His two main opponents were Balaguer (39.14%) and Bosch (9.69%).

Blanco, a 55-year-old constitutional lawyer affiliated with the Socialist International, saw his *PRD* also win control of Congress and most local governments. Although 12 people died in campaign violence, the election was generally the most honest and peaceful in the nation's history. Unhappily, however, the last victim proved to be President Guzmán himself, who committed suicide a month before leaving office.

At the insistence of the International Monetary Fund and creditor banks, Blanco imposed economic austerity, reducing luxury imports and limiting government expenditures. These measures contributed to a slow increase in GDP growth, which was slower than that of the population growth, and the per capita income fell slightly. The situation became tense in May 1984 when a series of popular demonstrations led to bloody confrontations with police. Because of adverse economic conditions, Blanco's popularity sagged badly in 1985. He granted government workers a small raise in mid-1985 and the resident IMF agent Congress called for expulsion of the IMF representative on the grounds that he was interfering with internal affairs.

Balaguer Returns

The elections in both 1986 and 1990 pitted an elderly Balaguer against an energetic opponent. Both campaigns were heated, replete with personal insults and slanderous statements. Notwithstanding an attempt by the military to halt ballot counting in 1986, Balaguer won even though his opponent was considered a shoo-in and in spite of the fact that Balaguer was virtually blinded by glaucoma.

The contest in 1990 was between Balaguer and Bosch, only four years younger than the president; Balaguer won by a margin of 22,000 votes out of 1.9 million. The reason for the two victories of the aging Balaguer was simple: relative prosperity.

Both elections were tainted with the usual irregularities. Balaguer carefully paved the way for yet another run for the presidency in 1994. This time, the favored opponent was José Francisco Peña Gómez, leader of the *PRD* and former Santo Domingo mayor. The campaign was extraordinarily dirty. Because Peña Gómez was black, and Dominicans harbor a deep fear and distrust of black Haitians, Balaguer successfully capitalized on these emotions. A video was used allegedly showing Peña Gómez practicing voodoo in Haitian style. Balaguer won by an estimated 30,000 votes amid charges of fraud. Many supporters of Peña Gómez somehow hadn't been registered even though they had.

The Clinton administration, backing an embargo of Haiti and needing Dominican help, chose to ignore the irregularities. Balaguer cooperated with the embargo, with the tacit understanding that the Clinton administration would not protest the 1994 election results. The matter quietly faded, and the 87-year-old Balaguer was inaugurated in August; by then he was totally blind.

Fernández and Mejía

Tacitly acknowledging irregularities, Balaguer, then 89, agreed to step down mid-way through his term and new elections were held in 1996. In the first round of voting in May, Peña Gómez of the *PRD* led with 46% of the vote to 39% for Leonel Fernández Reyna of Bosch's *PLD*. Balaguer, though the longtime rival of Bosch, disliked Peña Gómez even more, and threw his support behind Fernández, a 42-year-old lawyer who grew up in New York City. In the run-off election July 1, Fernández edged out Peña Gómez with 51.25% of the vote in a contest that international observers proclaimed fair and untainted by the traditional Balaguer trickery. The new president promised to take the Dominican Republic down a "new road."

Fernández found that "new road" a bumpy one. In the 1996 elections, his party won only one seat in the 30-member Senate and 12 of 120 seats in the lower house. In the May 1998 congressional elections, the *PRD* swept all but five seats in the Senate and won an absolute majority in the Chamber of Deputies. Peña Gómez, however, died before he could savor his party's triumph.

Tension among the political parties took a violent turn in January 1999. At issue was the election of a new secretary-general of the Dominican Municipal League, the organization that distributes revenues totaling 4% of the national budget to the local governments. The *PLD* and Balaguer's newly named Social Christian Reform Party (*PRSC*) joined forces once again to elect a secretary-general, prompting the dominant *PRD* to meet separately and "elect" its own candidate. Pro-*PRD* demonstrators surrounded the headquarters of the municipal league and soon clashed with police. In the ensuing melee, several demonstrators were injured by police shotgun pellets, including two *PRD* senators. Soldiers also surrounded the Congress building in a show of force, prompting the *PRD* to denounce Fernández as a would-be dictator.

A truly historic event occurred in August 1998 when Fidel Castro visited the Dominican Republic for the first time, shortly after Fernández reestablished diplomatic relations. Officially, Castro's visit was to attend the 14-nation Caribbean Fo-

Former President Hipólito Mejía

rum summit. Few were surprised when Castro paid a call on his old ally, Bosch, then 89. But Castro astonished everyone by also paying a visit to the 92-year-old Balaguer at his home. The two aging Cold War antagonists sat side-by-side on a sofa for nearly an hour and engaged in a cordial, even jocular conversation.

By 1999, the Fernández administration could boast a 40% increase in economic growth in its four years and Latin America's second-highest growth rate of 7% per year (see Economy). Such booms usually favor the party in power, but Fernández could not run for reelection himself, barred by the law aimed at Balaguer. Thus, he engineered the nomination of an economic adviser, Danilo Medina, 47, as the *PLD*'s standard bearer. Within the *PRD*, meanwhile, a 59-year-old agricultural economist, Hipólito Mejía, assumed Peña's mantle and became the party's nominee. The venerable and resilient Balaguer, by then 93, once again became the nominee of the *PRSC*.

Balaguer proved to be a spoiler for the *PLD*, dividing the conservative vote. Mejía, meanwhile, preached a populist message, vowing that the poor would begin enjoying the fruits of the burgeoning economy through expanded public works and improved education, a persuasive message to those who felt left out of the growing prosperity evident all around them. He fostered his image as a simple farmer, and charmed voters with Lincolnian folk wisdom and humor.

The campaign experienced an ugly incident on April 30 in the town of Moca. As Mejía's car passed the house of a local *PLD* official, gunfire erupted, and Mejía's bodyguards shot and killed the *PLD* official and another man, claiming an assassination attempt. The *PLD* maintained that the bodyguards had fired first.

In the vote results of May 16, certified as fair by more than 100 international observers, Mejía received 49.87% of the vote—tantalizingly close to a first-round victory. Medina and Balaguer finished in a dead heat for second place—but with Medina slightly ahead, 24.94% to 24.61%. On May 18, Balaguer announced he was accepting Mejía's election, meaning he would not endorse Medina in a runoff. Medina, faced with the near-impossibility of closing a 25-point gap with Mejía, withdrew, handing the presidency to Mejía. That same day, Balaguer graciously congratulated the president-elect when Mejía made a courtesy call at the nonagenarian's home. Scattered gunfire that night marred the celebrations of Mejía's victory.

Mejía was inaugurated on August 16, 2000.

Mejía inherited from Fernández the most robust economic growth in Latin

President Leonel Fernández

America, which benefited Mejía's *PRD* in the mid-term congressional elections of May 16, 2002. The party swept 29 of the 32 Senate seats, a gain of 10; strengthened its lead in the 150-member Chamber of Deputies; and won control of 104 of the 125 municipalities. Election-related violence was minimal by Dominican standards; "only" one person was killed and seven injured. Armed with these overwhelming majorities, the *PRD* amended the constitution to permit the immediate reelection of a president for a second term, largely because Mejía insisted that he was not interested in running again.

On February 7, 2002, the *PLD* lost its patriarch when Bosch died at the age of 92. He was buried with full military honors, and diplomatic representatives of six countries and Puerto Rico—but not the United States—attended the funeral, as did thousands of Dominicans. Bosch was followed in death five months later by his arch-rival, Balaguer, who died on July 14 at the age of 95. An colorful era in Dominican history was over.

Mejía's popularity began to plummet after the mid-term elections as the once-vibrant economy turned sour (see Economy). Power blackouts, created when the privatized power companies could not keep up with demand, led to protests in September 2002 that left two people dead and 50 injured. Mejía responded by renationalizing the power companies, which cost about $600 million, causing the IMF to cancel a loan for that amount in October 2002.

In February 2003, Mejía announced a series of austerity measures designed to halt an alarming increase in inflation and the decline in the value of the peso, which lost 40% of its value against the dollar in just the first two months of 2003. By February

Dominican Republic

2004, it was down by 65%. Among the austerity measures was a reduction in the number of government jobs and of government salaries. Unlike in other Latin American countries, where the opposition launches general strikes and confrontational street demonstrations to protest austerity measures, the opposition charged that the measures did not go far enough and called for street protests to demand even greater spending cuts.

The reeling economy was then delivered a knockout blow when Banco Intercontinental, or Baninter, the country's third-largest private bank, went bankrupt in April 2003 as the result of an embezzlement and fraud scandal. The central bank was legally obligated to pay only 500,000 pesos, or $12,000, to each depositor, but it generously compensated the depositors for their entire losses, a total of $2.4 billion that the economy could not absorb. The bank's owners went to jail, but that did not prevent the ripple effects of the bailout on the economy.

By early 2004, inflation was running at 42%, and unemployment was 16%. Dominicans began joining Cubans and Haitians in trying to reach the United States— or at least Puerto Rico—in search of a better life. It was a stark contrast to the boom times of the 1990s.

Fernández Makes a Comeback

Mejía made an abrupt about face and announced he planned to run again in May 2004. He met with immediate opposition from within his own *PRD*, whose rules still precluded immediate renomination. Mejía arrogantly pressed on with his reelection plans despite the factionalism it was causing in his party and despite polls that showed 73% of Dominicans opposing a second term.

He did not increase his popularity by contributing 370 Dominican troops to the allied coalition in Iraq. He began withdrawing them in April 2004, after Spain withdrew its troops following the al-Qaeda terror attacks in Madrid.

In December 2003, an anti-reelection faction chose *PRD* president Hatuey de Camps as its candidate, but in January, party regulars dutifully renominated Mejía at a convention boycotted by the de Camps faction. Mejía then attempted a Byzantine maneuver, pushing through Congress a bill that would allow each party to nominate up to five candidates, with the one receiving the most votes to receive all the party's votes. In the face of a public outcry, he arrogantly declared that "power is there to be exercised." This only inflamed public opinion further.

Former President Fernández, meanwhile, announced his own comeback bid

as the *PLD* candidate, and polls showed him a heavy favorite over Mejía. Rounding out the field was Eduardo Estrella of Balaguer's *PRSC*, who ran a distant third.

Mejía was so unpopular at that point he was booed at baseball games. Businessmen staged a two-day strike in late January, in which 20 people were injured. The IMF, meanwhile, reapproved the desperately needed loan, but parceled it out in increments. Gradually, however, as polls showed him ahead of the other factions in the *PRD*, they gradually coalesced around his candidacy as the only way to prevent a Fernández comeback.

There was a new twist to the 2004 campaign: The three candidates campaigned in Miami and New York, because Dominicans living abroad were allowed to vote for president for the first time; more than 52,000 were registered to do so. An estimated 1 million Dominicans reside in the United States, another 100,000 in Puerto Rico. Polling centers also were established in Montreal, Caracas, Madrid and Barcelona.

In the end, on May 16, Dominicans chose between a president who had presided over a boom and another who had presided over a bust. The turnout was 72% of the 5 million registered voters, compared with 76% in 2000. The results were pretty much what the polls had predicted:

Fernández	2,063,871	57.11%
Mejía	1,215,928	33.65%
Estrella	312,493	8.65%

Mejía was uncharacteristically gracious in conceding defeat. The leadership of the *PRD*-dominated Senate and Chamber of Deputies pledged they would not be obstacles to the new president. Mejía even allowed Fernández to represent the country at the Third European Union-Latin American-Caribbean Summit in Guadalajara, Mexico, a few days after the election. On the negative side, the *PRD* expelled de Camps from the party for "high treason."

Mejía proved far kinder to the president-elect than did Mother Nature. Days after the election, the worst torrential rains in recent Caribbean history hit the Dominican Republic and Haiti. The human toll on the Dominican side was 395 dead and 274 missing.

Fernández was inaugurated for his second term on August 16, 2004. He lost no time in creating controversy when he named four men to high-level posts who were under investigation for allegedly embezzling $100 million during Fernández's first term from a fund created to establish jobs and mediate strikes. Fernández dismissed the charges as "politically motivated."

Fernández devoted his first 100 days tackling the economic crisis with a series of painful austerity measures. He pushed

through the *PRD*-controlled Congress increases in various taxes, including telephone bills and cigarettes. He increased the VAT, or sales tax, from 12% to 16% to reduce a $490 million budget deficit and to prevent a default on the $7.9 billion debt. He also began ending subsidies on gas and electricity, but eased that blow by concluding an agreement for low-cost Venezuelan oil for electricity generation. Power blackouts remained a problem.

At the same time, he declared he would cut 20% from the budget, beginning with reducing the size of the bloated public payroll, which Mejía had increased by 30% to 400,000. Among those losing their jobs were 97 of the army's 202 generals; Fernández said the country didn't need, and couldn't afford, that many generals.

There was some grumbling over the austerity measures, but they apparently have begun turning the economy around. At the height of the economic crisis, the peso had dropped to 51 to the dollar; by the end of 2004, it was back up to 29. The country recorded a modest increase in the GDP for 2004 after posting a loss in 2003 (see Economy).

In February 2005, the corruption investigation shoe was on the foot of the other party. Charges were filed against two of Mejía's former ministers and several businessmen in an alleged scheme to divert $60 million worth of buses and minivans for the public transportation system into their own hands. The vehicles were then sold. In December 2004, police seized 1.4 tons of cocaine and arrested one of Mejía's friends and political fundraisers.

Culture: The succession of lengthy dictatorships since independence has not proven conducive to the development of Dominican culture. Ethnically, the island is a mix of European, Indian and African, and the domestic culture is a hybridization that has influenced its music. A dance that has won popular acceptance abroad is the *meringue*, with its contagious Caribbean rhythm.

The absence of educational reform and the resulting low literacy rate crippled the Dominican Republic's literary growth. The prose fiction writer Juan Bosch, who served briefly as president in the 1960s and remains influential in Dominican politics, is one of only a handful of Dominicans who have obtained international recognition in literature or the arts. Perhaps the country's most notable cultural contribution has been the fashion designer, Oscar de la Renta.

The independent Dominican press often has felt the pressure of dictators. The dean of the press is the daily *Listín Diario*, founded in 1889, which flourished until shut down by the Trujillo dictatorship. It resumed publication in 1963 and has followed a left-of-center editorial line, counterbalanced by the country's other "respectable" newspaper, *El Caribe*. *Listín Diario* was taken over by the government in 2003, not for criticizing the government but because its owner, Ramón Baéz, was arrested for fraud and embezzlement following the collapse of Banco Intercontinental, of which he was an owner (see History). A judge ruled in September 2004 that the newspaper was not connected to the bank collapse and ordered it returned to Baéz's family.

Sports is a national obsession, particularly soccer and baseball. Numerous Dominican baseball players have gone on to play in the U.S. major leagues, most notably Sammy Sosa of the Chicago Cubs, a source of great national pride, who along with Mark McGuire broke Roger Maris' single-season home run record of 61 in 1998; McGuire hit 70, Sosa hit 66.

Economy: The Dominican economy has been traditionally based on agriculture, with sugar being the main cash crop. However, now tourism produces more income than sugar as sugar prices fell and the U.S. reduced the Dominican quota allowed for importation. New hotels and tourist facilities have sprung up throughout the nation. In 2002, tourism revenue amounted to $2 billion. An aggressive government program to place unused farmland into production has increased the output of other cash products such as meat, coffee, tobacco and cacao.

Thanks to an ambitious irrigation program centering around a four-dam system on the Nizao River, some farm regions are now producing up to three crops a year in contrast to a single crop in previous years.

Also gaining in importance is the nation's mining industry. A Canadian-based consortium exports Dominican ferronickel ingots worth $75 million a year; other important exports include bauxite, salt and gypsum. Production of gold and silver has begun at newly developed mines. Three huge new oil refineries have also boosted the economy. Intensive efforts are being made to increase the output from the nation's own small oil fields. The Dominican Republic continues to attract record amounts of investment, partly because of the comparatively stable (at least on the surface) political conditions enforced by the government.

Foreign investment in luxury hotels and resorts, textiles, clothing and assembly-for-reexport plants, like Mexico's *maquiladoras*, created about 200,000 new jobs. The result was what could only be called a boom during the presidency of Leonél Fernández (1996-2000) of the conservative, business-oriented Democratic Liberation Party *(PLD)*.

Even as some of the major economies of the region slipped into recession after the Brazilian market meltdowns of 1998 and 1999, the Dominican Republic maintained the highest sustained GDP growth in Latin America: 7.3% in 1996, 8.2% in 1997, 7.3% in 1998, 8% in 1999 and 7.8% in 2000. Real GDP increased over those years from $13.5 billion in 1996 to $21,6 billion in 2001, and per capita GDP rose from $1,572 in 1996 to $2,486 in 2001.

In 2001, in the wake of the terrorist attacks in the United States, tourism dropped and the economy went into a slump. In 2002, inflation rose to 10.5%.

Mid-way through the presidency of Hipólito Mejía (2000-04), a populist of the Democratic Revolutionary Party *(PRD)*, the economy went into a tailspin. Unemployment jumped to 16% in 2003–04, inflation soared to 42% and the foreign debt more than doubled, from $3.7 billion to $7.6 billion. The value of the peso fell from 18 to the dollar in February 2003 to 51 in February 2004. The government generously paid out $2.4 billion to depositors in the bailout of Banco Intercontinental in 2003. The country's third-largest bank collapsed because of fraud and embezzlement, which exacerbated the crisis and caused an estimated $2 billion in foreign capital to be withdrawn from Dominican banks in the wake of the scandal. Real GDP growth slumped to 3% in 2001 and 4.1% in 2002, then declined by 0.4% in 2003. In real terms (adjusted for inflation), GDP plummeted from $21.7 billion in 2002 to $16.12 billion in 2003. Per capita GDP dropped to $2,320 in 2002 and $1,896 in 2003. Boom had turned to bust.

The downturn was largely responsible for the return to power in 2004 of former President Fernández. He quickly imposed a number of austerity measures, which turned the economy around (see History). GDP growth in 2004 was a modest 1.8%, a far cry from the boom years, but at least positive rather than negative.

Another major boost to the Dominican economy in recent years has been the remittances sent home by Dominican expatriates working abroad, primarily in the United States. In 2004, remittances were estimated at $2.7 billion, roughly 17% of GDP.

The Future: Hipólito Mejía's populist rhetoric in 2000 brought him to power, but his administration literally turned boom into bust. Not all was his fault, of course; he had no control over the worldwide market slump that began in 2000 or the drop in tourism that followed the September 11, 2001, terror attacks on the United States. There is no evidence he was involved in the Baninter scandal. But his erratic policies and his featherbedding of the government payroll by 30% deserved much of the blame. The voters threw him out in favor of former President Leonel Fernández, who at least had an economic success story to boast of.

He is trying to demonstrate that he can do it again, and in his first year he has had some success (see History, Economy). He has persuaded a *PRD*-controlled Congress to go along with some painful tax cuts and has kept the country in the good graces of the IMF.

If Fernández really wants to assure himself of a favorable place in Dominican history, he should now place a higher priority on reducing the country's ingrained corruption. That is a long shot, however.

Partial view of the port of Santo Domingo

The Republic of Ecuador

Fishermen out from Guayaquil, Ecuador

Area: 104,749 square miles.

Population: 13.2 million (2004 estimate).

Capital City: Quito (Pop. 1.5 million estimated).

Climate: The eastern lowlands are hot and wet; the coastal plains receive seasonally heavy rainfall; the highland climate becomes increasingly temperate with altitude.

Neighboring Countries: Colombia (north); Peru (east and south).

Official Language: Spanish

Other Principal Tongues: Quechua and Jívaro.

Ethnic Background: Predominantly Indian, with small groups of European and African origin.

Principal Religion: Roman Catholic Christianity.

158

Chief Commercial Products: Petroleum, coffee, bananas, cacao, shrimp, sardines.

Currency: U.S. Dollar (formerly the *sucre*).

Gross Domestic Product: U.S. $30 billion in 2004 ($2,304 per capita).

Former Colonial Status: Spanish Crown Colony (1532–1821); a state of *Gran Colombia* (1822–1830).

Independence Date: May 13, 1830.

Chief of State: Dr. Alfredo Palacio González (b. January 22, 1939), president (since April 20, 2005).

National Flag: A top yellow stripe, center blue stripe and a lower red stripe.

Because of disputes with Peru over boundaries, and territorial losses in the 1942 settlement of a war with Peru, no definite statement of Ecuador's area can be given with certainty. It has three distinct zones: the vast Andean highland, with lofty, snow-capped peaks and green valleys; the narrow coastal plain between the Andes and the Pacific, from 50 to 100 miles wide; and the *Oriente* (East), consisting of tropical jungles in the upper Amazon Basin. The high mountain valleys have a temperate climate, rich soils and moderate rainfall suitable for dairy farming and the production of cereals and vegetables. The Pacific coastal plains are tropical and devoted to plantation farming of bananas, cotton, sugar and cocoa. The *Oriente* is more than one third of the agricultural land of Ecuador and is a thick, virgin forest and jungle land containing valuable timber, although much of it cannot be transported to market at a profit.

Lying about 650 miles off the coastline are the Galapagos Islands, an archipelago situated on the Equator. Consisting of 14 islands and numerous islets, it is a haven for many species of waterfowl and giant turtles. With a population of 650, it is regularly visited by tour groups interested in its unspoiled setting.

History: Shortly before Spanish penetration of Ecuador, the ancient Inca Empire had been united under a single chief, Huayna Cápac, in 1526. Francisco Pizarro, the Spanish *conquistador*, touched along the coastline in 1528 at about the time Cápac died.

After returning temporarily to Spain, Pizarro came back to Ecuador with a larger force seeking the treasures he believed were in the interior. Huayna Cápac had divided his empire between two sons—Huáscar, who ruled the Cuzco area, and Atahualpa, who ruled over Quito.

After holding him for a huge ransom of gold and silver, Pizarro executed Atahualpa and mercilessly started the suppression of the Incas.

The invasion of Ecuador followed the pattern of other Spanish conquests. As the Incas and their subject tribes were defeated, the land was awarded in large grants to the successful leaders; the Indians were enslaved to work the estates and the Spaniards built strategically located cities to administer the territory. The low, unhealthy coastal plains had been shunned by the Incas, who lived in the temperate highland and valleys. The Spanish followed the same pattern building their cities of Quito, Ona, Cuenca and Loja above the 5,000-foot level.

The Spanish made little effort to improve the port of Guayaquil or to farm its valley, leaving the fever-ridden region to later arrivals and outcasts from the highlands. Thus, the colonial period continued a regionalism well established in the Inca period and which still divides the highlander from the coastal dweller.

Spanish rule was not challenged for several harsh, uneventful centuries. Antonio José de Sucre, a brilliant military leader under Simón Bolívar, united Ecuador with neighboring Colombia and Venezuela from 1822 to 1830. This union dissolved when Ecuador and Venezuela withdrew. Bolívar died at the age of 47 shortly thereafter.

Ecuador's history as an independent state has been an alternating swing from near anarchy under weak governments to the enforced peace established by dictators. The first president of Ecuador, Juan José Flores, a brave soldier but an indifferent governor, appealed to the Conservatives in Quito and aroused the opposition of the Liberals in Guayaquil. However, he worked out a scheme to alternate as president with Vicente Rocafuerte, a Guayaquil Liberal—a device which remained in effect until 1845.

In the next 15 years, Ecuador had 11 changes of administration, most of which carried the Liberal Party label; there were three constitutions and sporadic civil wars as well as border wars with Peru and Colombia. By 1860 there was little semblance of a central government—local strongmen ruled the communities with the support of their gunmen. Popular opposition to the cession of Guayaquil and the southern provinces to Peru in 1860 brought a Conservative to power, who established a theocratic Catholic dictatorship which lasted until his assassination in 1875. However, he did more for the unification of the country and for its economy than any other 19th century leader.

For 20 years, Ecuador returned to civil war and anarchy, banditry, and economic deterioration. Conservatives regularly won the elections and were regularly ousted by Liberals from Guayaquil until the revolution of 1895; this brought 50 years of Liberal rule to Ecuador, highlighted by three more constitutions, the passage of 28 presidents and uninterrupted political, social and economic crises. While the power of the Conservatives and the church were curtailed, the Liberal promises of free elections and honest government had little meaning, by and large. Galo Plaza Lasso (1948–52) was a notable exception to this pattern; he was installed as secretary-general of the Organization of American States in 1968.

From 1952–63, Conservatives alternated in power with Liberal José María Velasco Ibarra until a reform military government seized power; it was promptly overthrown by the liberals it sought to assist.

A constituent assembly elected an interim president in 1966; he was succeeded by Velasco, aging and cranky, who was elected president for a fifth time. Always controversial, he soon grew restless with his inability to win congressional approval for his economic policies. With the approval of the armed forces, he seized dictatorial power in mid-1970, dismissing the Congress and replacing the moderate constitution (Ecuador's 16th) with a more conservative 1946 version.

To the surprise of many, Velasco later vowed to surrender power to his legally elected successor by June 1972. But, fearing a free election would be won by Assad Bucaram, a left-leaning former mayor of Guayaquil, the armed forces seized power in early 1972 and installed General Guillermo Rodríguez Lara as president. Modeling itself after the reformist Peruvian military government, the new regime pledged its policies would be "revolutionary and nationalistic."

The regime concentrated on how best to spend the huge tax royalties pouring into the treasury from Ecuador's newly developed oil fields; most funds were spent on public works (education, highways and hospitals) and fancy military hardware.

Despite the oil boom, dissatisfaction arose against the center-right regime. Leftists denounced inaction of promised social and economic reforms, while Conservatives condemned swollen civil service rolls (one in every 10 workers) and new taxes on luxury imports. And everyone seemed annoyed by the oil revenue-fed inflation, high unemployment and continuing government corruption and repression.

Democracy, Ecuadorean Style

An unsuccessful attempt by soldiers to oust Rodríguez Lara in 1975 left 22 dead and 100 injured. But after widespread student and labor unrest in early 1976, the strongman was finally toppled by a three-man military *junta* headed by Admiral Alfredo Poveda. The new rulers moved promptly to restore civilian rule. In January 1978, voters approved another consti-

Ecuador

tution; elections were held six months later, followed by a run-off vote in April 1979.

Jaime Roldós Aguilera, a mild-mannered populist attorney from Guayaquil, was elected president by an amazing 59% of the vote. At 38, he was the youngest chief executive in Latin America. Although his own Concentration of Popular Forces party and the allied Democratic Left party won 45 of the 69 seats in the unicameral national legislature, the new president was unable to build a ruling coalition. Ironically, his most bitter foe was Assad Bucaram, his father-in-law and leader of Congress. Because Roldós rejected Bucaram's populist program in favor of a more conservative approach, the two quickly became enemies and the president's proposals in Congress were virtually all blocked.

Austerity measures further damaged Roldós' effectiveness; food and fuel prices rose, leading to widespread disorders and the threat of another military coup. A timely border clash with Peru in early 1981 temporarily diverted attention from Ecuador's economic problems. Although the basic dispute dates back to 1830, the latest crisis centered around the 1942 border treaty between the two nations, the settlement of which Ecuador later disavowed.

Roldós, his wife and seven others were killed in a plane crash while on a trip to the troubled border region. He was succeeded by the vice president, Osvaldo Hurtado, who maintained continuity in government by retaining most of the cabinet. Further, the late president's brother, León, was named vice president.

As in the rest of Latin America, the austere economic program demanded by the International Monetary Fund forced the government to take measures that not only affected its popularity, but threatened the social stability of the country. In May 1984, León Febrés Cordero, of the Social Christian Party, a businessman and candidate of the Front for National Reconstruction, was elected president.

The first year of Febrés Cordero's presidency saw modest economic growth, but accompanied by worker unrest and often bitter friction between the president and Congress. Febrés Cordero, an energetic, free-market capitalist, provided Ecuador with strong if heavy-handed leadership. He packed a .45 automatic pistol. When the choice of 18 members of the judiciary by the opposition legislature didn't suit him, he had the Supreme Court surrounded by tanks so they could not take

the oath of office. Eighteen others, more to his liking, were chosen. Dramatic efforts were taken to restrict the leftist revolutionary group, *Alfaro Vive, Carajo!*

Opposition members were fired from government positions and critical newspapers had a drop in advertising income. Difficulties with the military, punctuated by two attempts at mutiny, ultimately led to an unsuccessful effort to impeach Febrés Cordero for "disgracing the national honor."

Adverse economic conditions led Ecuadorians to turn to two leftists in 1988 elections. The contest was hot, with charges such as "alcoholic atheist" and "drug-trafficking fascist" commonplace. Rodrigo Borja ultimately won the contest.

Political bickering and infighting, corruption and a stale economy were the main features of the Borja years. Apparently tired of the "same old thing," the people turned to a conservative in the 1992 elections. Sixto Durán Ballén, a 71-year-old architect born in Boston, was elected after a campaign in which he promised basic reforms. After his election, he wasted no time in putting them into effect.

The currency was devalued by 27.5%, and state-owned enterprises, inefficient

Quito—the modern and the colonial

money-losers, were put on the auction block. Subsidies on commodities were sharply reduced or eliminated, but to prevent hardships caused by this measure, Durán raised wages modestly. Ecuador dropped its membership in OPEC and announced it would establish its own quotas to market its petroleum. Production rose 18% in 1993 over the previous year, but lower international oil prices meant decreased income.

Higher fuel and electricity prices, reduced state spending and a freeze on government employment combined to create serious unrest by the end of 1992. Payment on the $13 billion external debt was suspended, freezing international credit. Strikes and bomb attacks by terrorist groups added to Ecuador's difficulties.

There was a marked shift to the left in mid-1994 congressional elections; the president's party retained only nine of 65 locally elected seats. Payment of interest on the external debt was resumed, making IMF and private sector loans again possible.

Ecuadorians were abruptly distracted from their domestic economic woes on January 29, 1995, when the long-simmering border dispute with Peru finally erupted into open warfare in an isolated, mountainous area. Several times before there had been minor border clashes close to the anniversary of the January 29, 1942, Rio Accords by which Ecuador had been forced to cede nearly half its territory. This time, however, the incident quickly escalated into full-scale war with mortar attacks on the ground and air attacks from above. Ecuadorian gunners shot down a Peruvian helicopter and three jet fighter-bombers. Frightened civilians fled their villages. Two tentative cease-fires in February failed to hold. The four guarantor countries— Argentina, Brazil, Chile and the United States—finally succeeded in effecting a definite cease-fire on July 25. In the three weeks of heavy fighting at the outset of the hostilities, 73 people were killed and at least 200 wounded; each side took a number of prisoners, later expatriated.

The economy became generally better-organized during the Durán years, but scandal detracted from its successes and little attention was paid to the poor. This neglect was to have an impact on the 1996 election.

The Bucaram Fiasco

In the first round of voting in May, Jaime Nebot of the Social Christian Party led Abdalá Bucaram of the *Roldosista* Party, 30% to 26%. The runoff on July 7 thus presented voters with a clear choice: Nebot, a conservative who favored continuation of privatization of key economic sectors, and

Bucaram, a populist who opposed privatization or reform of the cumbersome social security system. Bucaram also displayed a flamboyance on the campaign trail that startled, and apparently amused, voters. He unabashedly proclaimed himself "*El Loco*." The unorthodox appeal to the unsophisticated masses for support worked: Bucaram defeated Nebot 54.1% to 45.9%.

What followed in the six months after Bucaram's inauguration in August 1996 marked the most bizarre episode in modern Ecuadorian political history, as the unpredictable Bucaram shocked Ecuadorians almost daily with his strange public antics and his even stranger governmental measures. He made international headlines when he invited Lorena Bobbitt, the Ecuadorian-born woman infamous for severing her husband's penis in the United States, to the presidential palace for lunch. He took to singing in a rock band, and the Associated Press distributed a photo of the president, clutching a microphone and flanked by buxom, scantily clad beauties, that was published all over the world. When a presidential helicopter crashed and burned in November, Bucaram denounced it as an assassination attempt.

On a governmental level, he shocked almost everyone by hiring Argentina's recently sacked economy minister, Domingo Cavallo, to be his economic adviser. More shocking still, he discarded his populist campaign promises and imposed an austerity program that included geometric price increases for public services, such as public transport (200%), electricity (more than 100%) and natural gas (250%). Bucaram's draconian measures sparked widespread protests, some of them violent, by teachers, students and labor unions. His approval rating dropped out of sight.

In February 1997, as Bucaram came under intense pressure to resign, Ecuador plunged into semi-chaos. The beleaguered president imposed a state of emergency that allowed him to take extra-constitutional measures, such as banning demonstrations and imposing press censorship. In a move that delighted the public but which totally disregarded the constitution, Congress removed Bucaram from office on February 6 on the grounds of "mental incapacity," despite the absence of any authoritative medical or psychiatric testimony.

Bucaram's peculiar behavior proved to be the least of his transgressions, however. He went into self-imposed exile in Panama (long a dumping ground for deposed and disgraced rulers), denouncing Congress for its unconstitutional actions. Evidence then surfaced that he may have absconded with as much as $26 million from the treasury. Some estimates placed the total that

Former President Jamil Mahuad

Bucaram and his entourage withdrew illegally from the treasury during his six months in power at $80 million. The Supreme Court formally charged Bucaram and four of his aides with corruption, influence peddling, embezzlement and nepotism, and the former president's extradition is still being sought. (Guatemala, it should be noted, has tried unsuccessfully since 1993 to extradite former President Jorge Serrano from Panama, who also allegedly stole millions from the treasury.) One of the aides was arrested in Peru, carrying $3.4 million. The full extent of the corruption of the ill-fated Bucaram administration remains under investigation.

Revolving-Door Presidency

The post-Bucaram transition also proved chaotic—and probably unconstitutional as well. At first, Vice President Rosalia Arteaga was duly sworn in as president, with the tacit blessing of the armed forces. But within days Congress "elected" one of its leaders, Fabián Alarcón, to serve as interim president until a new presidential election could be called. In a special referendum on May 25, 74% of Ecuadorian voters "ratified" Alarcón's interim presidency until August 1998. On another of the 14 referendum issues, 65% of voters indicated that they approved of Bucaram's removal from office. Interviewed by CNN in Panama, Bucaram ridiculed the plebiscite as a "political show."

Meanwhile, Ecuadorians once again were distracted from domestic concerns by renewed tensions along the border with Peru, which in July 1997 had begun

Ecuador

The main marketplace in Guayaquil

acquiring advanced Russian MiGs. Unlike 1995, however, sanity prevailed this time and the two countries sent representatives to Brasilia to negotiate a timetable for demarcation of the 50-mile stretch of disputed frontier. On January 19, 1998, the representatives signed an accord that set a deadline of May 30 for reaching a final agreement. Also signing were representatives of the four peace guarantors—Brazil, Argentina, Chile and the United States.

Ecuadorians went to the polls on November 30, 1997 to elect a constituent assembly charged with overhauling the 1978 organic law in the wake of the Bucaram fiasco and to prepare for the election of a new president. In the balloting, the conservative Social Christian Party of former President Febrés won a convincing plurality of 24 of the 70 seats. Former President Hurtado's Popular Christian Party was a distant second with nine seats, while 11 other parties split the remainder, ensuring that whatever emerged from the assembly would be by broad consensus.

The assembly convened in December 1997. In February 1998, it voted 60–7 to preclude anyone convicted of corruption, embezzlement or other misuse of public funds, from running for public office, a move aimed squarely at Bucaram, who already had announced from Panama that he planned to run in the presidential election scheduled for May 31.

Bucaram at first defiantly threatened to campaign from abroad. But in March, he relinquished his presidential bid and en-

dorsed the country's leading banana exporter, Alvaro Noboa, as the *Roldosista* candidate. As in 1996, the first round of voting became a free-for-all, with five other candidates vying with Noboa. The clear frontrunner was Quito Mayor Jamil Mahuad of the Popular Democracy movement. Surprisingly, the Social Christians, who did so well in the balloting for the constituent assembly and who narrowly lost the 1996 presidential election to Bucaram, opted not to field a candidate.

In the first round of balloting on May 31, Mahuad placed first with 36.6% and Noboa came in second with 29.7%. In the July 12 runoff, Mahuad pulled off a harrowingly narrow victory over the Bucaram stand-in, receiving 51% of the valid votes, or 2,242,836 to Noboa's 2,140,628. Noboa at first refused to concede defeat, but the 48-year-old Mahuad took office on schedule on August 10.

Ecuador's new president presented a sobering change from Bucaram; apparently the only thing they had in common is Lebanese ancestry. He was well prepared professionally, having served as labor minister under Roldós, then as a member of Congress before being elected mayor of Quito in 1992 and re-elected in 1996. In between, he managed to earn a master's degree in public administration from Harvard in 1989. His personal life was somewhat cloudier. He was the divorced father of a 20-year-old daughter, and acknowledged fathering a son out of wedlock while he was married.

In his first months in office, Mahuad could claim a major diplomatic achievement in reaching a peace agreement with Peru, but in coming to grips with the country's nagging economic woes he was faced with the same sort of public protests that had plagued Bucaram.

On the diplomatic front, Mahuad and Peruvian President Alberto Fujimori signed the peace accord in Brasilia on October 26, 1998, which definitively delineated the disputed 48-mile stretch of frontier that led to the 1995 war. The agreement was almost entirely along the lines Peru had demanded, that the border would follow the divide of the Cordillera del Condor range. As a gesture to Ecuador, however, Peru acquiesced Tiwintza Hill, which Ecuadorian soldiers had successfully defended against the Peruvians in 1995. As his own gesture of conciliation, Mahuad gave Fujimori a canteen used by an Ecuadorian soldier in the 1941 border war. The next step of the peace process came on January 18, 1999, when Mahuad and Fujimori met again along the border to dedicate the first border post at Lagartococha. The two leaders met again in Washington on February 4, where they worked out the final details of the peace agreement and of a $3 billion cross-border international loan package. Fujimori pledged not to buy any new weapons, while Mahuad announced he was cutting the draft by 60% and converting 8,000 soldiers—a fourth of the army—into policemen. Under the 10-year border development plan, the two countries were to make the border region accessible by new roads, integrate their electrical grids and embark on joint irrigation and resource-exploitation projects. Moreover, Peru was to allow Ecuador to use its oil pipeline. President Bill Clinton hosted the two presidents at the White House to toast them on their achievement, the peaceful resolution of the last major border conflict in Latin America.

Back at home, however, Mahuad was forced to face the ever-present economic crisis. No longer a member of OPEC, Ecuador could only watch helplessly as the price of oil on the world market plummeted in 1998, at one point diving to just over $11 a barrel. The price of Ecuador's other major export, bananas, also remained depressed. Ecuador then sustained $2.6 billion in damage from the floods of the 1997–98 *El Niño* and suffered financial fallout from Brazil's economic meltdown in late 1998. The day after his triumphant meeting along the border with Fujimori in January, Mahuad delivered grim economic news to his countrymen: a $1.5 billion budget deficit and a projected growth rate of 1.7 percent for 1999, with inflation estimated at a more merciful but still formidable 22%. Meanwhile, public discontent over the inevitable austerity measures erupted once again into street demonstrations.

In March 1999, several banks foundered. Mahuad declared a week-long bank holiday and the following day imposed a 60-day state of emergency. The value of the *sucre* went into a free-fall, losing 60% of its value at one point. As part of a new austerity plan, Mahuad decreed a price increase for gasoline from 89 cents to $2.33 a gallon and raised the value-added tax from 10% to 15%. Transit workers immediately went on strike, virtually paralyzing the country for five days. Street demonstrations led to 235 arrests. The Social Christian Party, the coalition partner of Mahuad's Popular Democracy party, denounced the austerity plan as "inhuman." Mahuad's public approval rating fell to 16% in one poll.

Mahuad caved in to the public outcry and struck a deal with the left-of-center parties in Congress for a watered-down austerity plan. The price of gasoline, for example, was rolled back to $1.20 a gallon, and in place of the VAT increase the Congress reinstated the income tax, with a 15% ceiling. This new coalition comprised 70 of the 121 seats in Congress but was shaky.

At the height of the crisis, there was another startling development in March: Former President Alarcón was arrested on charges that while president of the Congress he had padded congressional payrolls.

Over the next 10 months, the political and economic situations deteriorated from bad to worse to impossible. Every time Mahuad sought to impose austerity measures to win IMF approval for desperately needed capital, he would be faced with more public protests that forced him to back down. He sought a $1.2 billion bailout of 18 defunct banks, but then the head of one of the banks, who had been arrested for fraud, revealed he had donated more than $3 million to Mahuad's 1998 campaign.

In August, Mahuad announced that it could not make the $98 million interest payment on its $6 billion in Brady bonds, which the U.S. Treasury had extended to 18 countries to help them restructure their debts (Ecuador's total foreign debt by then was a ponderous $13.6 billion). A month later, Ecuador suffered the ignominy of becoming the first nation to default on its Brady bonds. By the end of the year, the *sucre* had fallen from 7,000 to 25,000 to the dollar; inflation had hit 61% for 1999; foreign creditors were pounding on the door; and military officers were publicly criticizing the civilian government's inaction, prompting rumors of an imminent coup. Moreover, a poll showed that 91% disapproved of Mahuad's performance and that 53% wanted him to resign.

Dollarization and Downfall

On January 9, 2000, the desperate president unveiled a desperate plan: He would replace the *sucre* with the U.S. dollar—not merely peg the *sucre* to the dollar as the Argentines had done, but make the dollar the official currency, as it is in Panama. For a few days, the dramatic proposal seemed to have a popular consensus. The Social Christian Party, *Roldosista* Party and Mahuad's own Popular Democracy party reached a rare agreement in support of dollarization, while one poll showed that 59% of the public supported the idea.

Apparently that survey neglected to poll the rural Indians who make up 40% of the population. Within days, the Ecuadorian Confederation of Indigenous Communities (*CONAIE*), reportedly the most powerful Indian-rights group in the Americas, not only declared its opposition to dollarization but demanded that Mahuad resign and mobilized thousands of peasants to march on Quito. Violence appeared imminent.

Matters came to a head on January 21. The *CONAIE* protesters actually stormed and occupied the Congress building. They were joined by about 150 field-grade military officers, led by Colonel Lucio Gutiérrez, who echoed the Indians' demand that the president resign. Faced with open rebellion, Mahuad fled the presidential palace and took refuge at a military base, but he steadfastly refused to resign. It didn't matter; his newly appointed defense minister, General Carlos Mendoza, announced that he was assuming power at the head of a three-man junta, which also included *CONAIE* leader Antonio Vargas and former Supreme Court Justice Carlos Solorzano. With the backing of the military, the ouster of Mahuad became a *fait accompli;* it was Latin America's first military *coup d'etat* since the overthrow of Jean-Bertrand Aristide in Haiti in 1991. After 22 years of tenuous democracy, Ecuador's constitutional system finally had broken down, a victim of mob rule.

For 24 tense hours, the rebel junta came under intense diplomatic pressure from the United States, Canada, the Organization of American States, the European Union, U.N. Secretary-General Kofi Annan and most of the Latin American presidents. Even Bucaram, who had long denounced Mahuad as a usurper, condemned his rival's overthrow. The following day, in a stunning turnabout, General Mendoza declared that he would yield power to the constitutional vice president, Gustavo Noboa, apparently to maintain some semblance of constitutional niceties; Vargas and Solorzano had little choice but to go along.

Though the transfer of power was undemocratic, the new president was at least a respectable figure. Noboa, then 62, was a lawyer and former dean of Catholic University, who gained fame as one of the negotiators of the border settlement with Peru. The hapless Mahuad, who still refused to resign, lamely expressed his backing for Noboa. "A deposed president doesn't resign," he said wanly, "he's just deposed." Congress duly confirmed Noboa to fill out the remainder of Mahuad's term, to 2003.

Ironically, Noboa almost immediately announced that he would push forward with the plan to replace the *sucre* with the dollar, which had precipitated Mahuad's downfall. In March, under pressure from the IMF and other international lending institutions, which had promised $2 billion in loans, Congress approved the dollarization plan. The IMF approved the first $304 million loan package in April, with the remainder contingent upon further concessions. Noboa announced that Ecuador would resume payments on its Brady bonds.

In another transparent and hypocritical attempt at constitutional window-dressing, the government moved quickly to "punish" the people who had brought about Mahuad's overthrow. Just six days after the coup, the defense ministry arrested four colonels and 12 lieutenant colonels for their roles in the event and began investigating the roles of hundreds more junior officers. The ministry narrowed the number to be court-martialed to 16 officers and one sergeant. The Supreme Court, meanwhile, brought charges against Vargas and Solorzano, together with two members of the Democratic Left party whom Congress had expelled for their involvement in the coup, for "attempts against the security of the state."

To bring this farce to an end, Noboa asked Congress to declare an amnesty to those who participated in the coup. The head of the Joint Chiefs of Staff and the commanders of the navy and the air force (but not the army) resigned their posts to protest the president's recommendation for amnesty for the rebellious soldiers. Nonetheless, Congress approved the amnesty for all 117 military rebels. Public opinion polls, which seem to govern Ecuador, showed that 67% of the public supported the amnesty.

Not so with the dollarization plan. A majority, according to the polls, opposed it. *CONAIE*, labor unions and students called a one-day strike to demand that the government revoke its agreement with the IMF, and the usual 10,000 demonstrators peacefully turned out in the streets of the capital. Teachers, hospital workers and other groups called for another, "indefi-

Ecuador

nite," strike in May, which closed schools and created some inconveniences before sputtering out after a few days.

The dollarization went into effect as planned in September 2000, and by year's end, the stability of the currency, coupled with the rising international price of petroleum and a $2 billion international loan package arranged by the IMF, led to a surprisingly rosy economic picture by the end of the year. Noboa consequently began enjoying a relative popularity few of his recent predecessors knew.

Nonetheless, Noboa had his problems. In August 2000, defections gave a center-left bloc a majority in Congress, which resisted Noboa's privatization plans for electricity, petroleum and telecommunications that the IMF—and foreign investors—expected. Moreover, the constitutional tribunal ruled 44 points of the privatization program unconstitutional. Then, in February 2001, when Noboa acceded to IMF demands and doubled the price of cooking gas and raised the price of gasoline by 22% to offset the reduction of subsidies, *CONAIE* and other groups took to the streets and roads again after months of dormancy, blocking the roads around the capital. Noboa declared a state of emergency, and in the ensuing violence four protesters were killed. To defuse the crisis, Noboa caved in to demands to scale back the increases. The IMF reluctantly agreed.

In March 2001, Congress thumbed its nose again at the IMF by rejecting an increase in the VAT from 12% to 15%. It also rejected other revenue-raising measures, virtually assuring a crushing budget deficit that would not please the IMF. In August 2001, the Constitutional Tribunal got into the act of hamstringing the president's efforts at fiscal reform by declaring unconstitutional a tax he had proposed to satisfy IMF demands; international financial markets reacted negatively.

To compound Noboa's domestic problems, in May 2000 members of a dissident faction of the Revolutionary Armed Forces of Colombia (*FARC*) encroached into Ecuadorian territory. Two of the rebels were killed in a firefight with the Ecuadorian army. Since then, drug-related violence has continued to spill over from Colombia. In February 2001, the army beefed up its 1,500-man border forces with an additional 2,000 troops. The border situation remains tense.

Then, in June 2002, as Noboa was negotiating a $240 million loan from the IMF in return for the usual unpopular austerity measures, his finance minister resigned in the midst of a major bribery scandal—major even by Ecuadorian standards. Allegedly, about 38% of $400 million in government funds transferred to local governments wound up in private pock-

Interim President Alferdo Palacio

ets. On the positive side, the dismal economic picture improved dramatically in 2001, although the improvement was in part illusionary.

The Elections of 2002

The presidential and congressional campaign of October 20 and November 24, 2002, turned into the customary Ecuadorian donnybrook. In July, former President Febrés Cordero surprised his Social Christian Party, still the country's largest, by announcing that he had decided against making a comeback bid because of ill health. A month later, the party nominated its congressional leader and former trade minister, Xavier Neira, after Febrés Cordero declared he would support him.

Within two weeks, the field became crowded as former presidents Borja of the Democratic Left and Hurtado both entered the race, as did banana millionaire Alvaro Noboa, no relation to President Noboa, who had narrowly lost to Mahuad in the 1998 runoff, and former ambassador to the United States Ivonne Juez de Baki. León Roldós, brother of the late president, entered as a Socialist. Another former president's brother, Jacobo Bucaram, became the *Roldosista* candidate.

But the race suddenly became unconventional with the entry of two leaders of the 2000 coup: Indian activist Antonio Vargas, and cashiered army Colonel Lucio Gutiérrez, who had spent time in jail and who became the candidate of the newly organized January 21 Patriotic Society. The parallels between Gutiérrez and Venezuela's Hugo Chávez were unmistakable, and as Gutiérrez suddenly began surging in the polls, the national and international media seized upon them.

Polls gave conflicting predictions. Thus, the results of the first round stunned everyone and sent a chill through Ecuador's political establishment—and the U.S. State Department. About 5.1 million, or 63%, of Ecuador's registered voters turned out. The results:

Gutiérrez	943,123	20.3%
Noboa	794,614	17.4%
Roldós	703,593	15.5%
Borja	638,142	14.1%
Neira	553,106	12.2%
Bucaram	544,688	11.9%

None of the other candidates received more than 4%.

Gutiérrez and Noboa then began trying to mend political fences with the losers for the November 24 runoff. Because both Noboa and Gutiérrez were political outsiders with populist messages, the political establishment was lukewarm to both of them. As the country's wealthiest man, Noboa appeared less frightening than Gutiérrez, who had the support of *CONAIE* and of Marxist-Leninist and other far-left elements.

The race came down to personalities. Noboa unconvincingly tried to persuade the country's impoverished masses that as a millionaire, he could serve their interests better than Gutiérrez by luring foreign investors to Ecuador. But like Chávez in Venezuela, the former rebel army officer excited voters with his pledge to combat Ecuador's notorious corruption as well as to increase funding for education and health. Polls showed Gutiérrez with a strong lead, and this time, they proved correct. Gutiérrez won a decisive mandate with more than 2.7 million votes, or 54.4%, to less than 2.3 million, or 45.6%, for Noboa.

Unlike his Venezuelan counterpart, President-elect Gutiérrez suddenly began sounding conciliatory and toned down his leftist rhetoric; he even apologized for saying that all the former presidents deserved to be in jail. He had little choice; Ecuador still desperately needed IMF and World Bank assistance. Moreover, the Social Christians and Democratic Left, both of which Gutiérrez had bitterly denounced during the campaign, formed a peculiar right-left opposition bloc of 62 members of the 100-seat Congress and elected an anti-Gutiérrez deputy as first vice president of Congress in a stormy session on the eve of his inauguration. Gutiérrez's party and its allies had but 17 seats.

Another Abortive Presidency

Gutiérrez, 45, a civil engineer by training and an erstwhile pentathlete, was sworn in as Ecuador's sixth president in as many years on January 15, 2003. His vice president was Alfredo Palacio, a 64-year-old heart surgeon and a populist who had served as health minister under Durán. The new president's task was unenviable: a $300 million budget deficit, $2.6 billion in foreign debt payments, an intransigent congressional opposition, a resentful military high command and a notoriously impatient and fickle electorate.

The new president bewildered his constituency by almost immediately undertaking a chameleon-like ideological transformation. He made some obligatory gestures to his Indian supporters, such as appointing Nina Picari, an Indian activist, as foreign minister, and reducing his own salary by 20%. But he also appointed Mauricio Pozo, a mainstream, investor-friendly economist, as finance minister.

Gutiérrez met with President Bush in Washington both before and after his inauguration and pledged Ecuador's cooperation against drug traffickers and terrorists. He also persuaded the IMF to make a $205 million loan available. Back home, he sought to placate the IMF by proposing tax increases; he also increased the price of gasoline by a third and of electricity by 10%, toward the aim of creating a $250 million budget surplus. A third of the $6.7 billion budget for 2003 was earmarked for debt reduction, only a fourth to promised social programs; it also increased military spending by 40.5%. Moreover, Gutiérrez pledged to retain the dollar, the proposed adoption of which was one of the root causes of his 2000 coup.

Gutiérrez's abandonment of the principles he had campaigned on began costing him allies. Vice President Palacio broke with him in January 2003, but did not resign. That August, *CONAIE*'s political arm, Pachakutik, withdrew its congressional support from Gutiérrez because of his cuts to the civil service and subsidies for basic commodities, leaving him with only six seats. He fired Pachakutik's cabinet ministers and turned to the conservative Social Christians for support. It was an unlikely match, but it held for a time. In June 2004, *CONAIE* and affiliated Indian groups sought to disrupt the summit of OAS foreign ministers in Quito to put pressure on Gutiérrez to resign.

In addition to the predictable complaints from the left, Gutiérrez was faced with hostility from high-ranking military officers, no doubt resentful over taking orders from a former colonel. Seventeen generals and admirals resigned before and after the inauguration, allowing Gutiérrez to appoint officers he could trust. He has not done as well in appointing civilian officials, however. Within months of his inauguration, five of his political appointees had to resign because of

Former President Lucio Gutiérrez

allegations of past unethical conduct, including his housing minister and his sister's brother, whom he had named to a post in a charitable organization.

As Gutiérrez's approval rating slid to 18% in November 2003, he himself became embroiled in a scandal. A former governor, César Fernández, was arrested on cocaine trafficking charges. Then it was reported that he gave $30 million to Gutiérrez's campaign. Gutiérrez denied being involved in drug trafficking. He also was accused of accepting illegal donations from Mexico's Labor Party. He responded to the charges by reshuffling his cabinet. Pozo remained as economy minister, but he resigned in June 2004, without stating a reason.

By mid-2004, Gutiérrez was faced with another crisis: the need to reform the woefully inefficient and money-losing state-run telecommunications and electricity companies. Those reforms were among those mandated by the IMF.

As if he didn't have enough problems with the IMF, opposition politicians, disgruntled generals, betrayed supporters and corruption accusations, Gutiérrez found himself in a nasty public controversy with his estranged wife, Ximena Bohorquez, a prominent physician and a member of Congress for Gutiérrez's January 21 Patriotic Society. Bohorquez complained in a newspaper interview that her husband had not lived up to his campaign promise to appoint well-qualified and uncorrupted officials. The president angrily responded that his wife was engaging in "cheap politics." It was reminiscent of the vocal opposition by the wives of former presidents Menem of Argentina and Fujimori of Peru; both of their husbands divorced them while in office. Bohorquez

chose to remain in the family's home rather than to move into the presidential palace with her husband. In September 2003, the couple announced a reconciliation, but then she began criticizing his economic policies. Their marriage to provided Ecuadorians with a real-life *telenovela*.

In August 2003, former President Noboa became the third former president to go into exile to avoid prosecution. Mahuad already had taken up residence in the United States, accused of corruption. Bucaram was still in Panama. Noboa was being investigated for allegedly scheming to use government bonds to shore up state-owned banks and for other alleged financial wrongdoing. He proclaimed his innocence, but asked for and received political asylum in the Dominican embassy. After the Supreme Court issued an arrest warrant, Noboa asked for and received from a grudging Gutiérrez a safe-conduct to the airport, and he flew to the Dominican Republic.

In October 2004, the Social Christian Party withdrew its support and announced it would seek to begin impeachment proceedings against Gutiérrez, ostensibly for misusing public funds for political purposes in the October municipal elections. The party collected the necessary 51-vote majority to begin impeachment hearings although it was well short of the necessary two thirds for removal. He received support from a heretofore unlikely source: the United States.

Gutiérrez began some cloakroom maneuvering, and by December he had forged an unusual new 52-member coalition in Congress with the *Roldosistas* and the party of millionaire Alvaro Noboa, whom he had defeated in the 2003 presidential runoff. This ended the impeachment effort, and Omar Quintana, a *Roldosista*, was elected president of Congress in January 2005. Gutiérrez was back in control, it seemed, and he should have left well enough alone. But he had Congress remove the 31 justices of the Supreme Court, most of them Social Christians, accusing them of being biased against him. He introduced a bill that would broaden his powers, including dissolving Congress. The move was widely regarded as revenge for the impeachment effort. He packed the court with "temporary" appointees and said he would call a referendum to choose a new method for selecting Supreme Court justices.

That smacked too much of dictatorship for the Ecuadorians, who already had enough grievances against him. On January 25, 2005 people staged a demonstration in Guayaquil to protest what they complained was Gutiérrez's failure to invest sufficient development funds in the country's major city. On February 17,

Ecuador

2005, tens of thousands of demonstrators massed outside the presidential palace in Quito, demanding that Gutiérrez resign for his perceived power play. It was reminiscent of January 2000.

Gutiérrez sought to defuse the mounting public outcry by welcoming a visit by a representative of the United Nations, which had expressed its grave concern over the attack on judicial independence. But the next day, Gutiérrez's interior minister resigned when the president declined to accept his proposal for a council to select new Supreme Court justices, rather than deciding the matter through a referendum. On March 3, the opposition in Congress attempted to revoke the dismissal of the justices, but the proposal fell three votes short. Congress, like the country itself, was becoming polarized.

The first indication that Gutiérrez was losing his congressional majority came on March 23 when nine members of the Gutiérrez coalition voted with the opposition to reject, 60-40, a list of possible nominees for attorney general. Opposition legislators before the vote had staged a sit-in, which police broke up by firing tear gas into the congressional chamber.

Feeling increasingly cornered, Gutiérrez asked the Constitutional Tribunal to review the constitutionality of the vote against the attorney general nominees. He called for outside mediation from the Andean Community of Nations to resolve the deadlock with the opposition. In an attempt at compromise, he suggested that Congress remove the temporary justices and establish an electoral college to appoint new ones, provided that the new body be approved by referendum. The opposition rejected the proposal.

On March 30, Gutiérrez's list of attorney general nominees came before Congress again. The two sides engaged in decidedly unparliamentary conduct, shouting insults, throwing coins and bottles and threatening to throw chairs. The list was rejected again, 56-44. Outside the building, pro-Gutiérrez demonstrators hurled eggs and sticks at opposition congressmen.

A new wrinkle developed the following day when Guillermo Castro, the head of the "temporary" Supreme Court and a *Roldosista,* suddenly declared all charges against former President Bucaram "null and void," paving the way for *"El Loco"* to return to the country. Castro also dropped pending charges against former President Noboa, and both exiled presidents returned to the country. Bucaram made his usual bombastic and eccentric statements, vowing to run for president in 2007 and lead a "revolution of the poor." The opposition immediately charged that Gutiérrez had sacked the Supreme Court just to permit Bucaram to return.

That same week, the mayor of Quito, a former army commander, urged the armed forces not to recognize Gutiérrez, in effect, calling for another coup. But the defense minister said the armed forces would continue to support the constitutional president.

Bucaram, a Gutiérrez ally, did his friend an unwitting disservice when in a radio interview he said cavalierly that Gutiérrez should dissolve Congress and declare a state of emergency. With friends like Bucaram, no Ecuadorian president needs any enemies. Rumors spread that Gutiérrez was planning to do just that, sparking a mini-panic in financial markets and causing the value of Ecuadorian bonds to drop. The interior minister made frantic denials that the president planned to dissolve Congress.

But the damage was done. Gutiérrez's opponents had the pretext they needed to fill the streets of Quito again on Friday, April 15, banging pots and pans and honking horns, demanding that the president resign. That night Gutiérrez declared a state of emergency, fired his hand-picked Supreme Court justices who were causing the crisis and vowed in an interview with the Reuters news agency that he would not resign. After all, he said with some validity, the economy was booming compared with the crisis that led to Mahuad's ouster in 2000 (see Economy).

Although the state of emergency empowered the military to break up the protests, it did not, thus avoiding a potentially bloody confrontation. On Saturday, April 16, in an attempt to pacify the demonstrators, Gutiérrez lifted the state of emergency after less than 24 hours. He addressed the nation on television, insisted he had achieved his primary objective of removing the Supreme Court and that "tranquillity is returning."

But it was not. The streets remained filled with thousands of unmollified, noisy but non-violent protesters—but no soldiers. On Monday, thousands of demonstrators also filled the streets of Guayaquil Back in Quito, the demonstrations dwindled down, but Congress began talking again of impeachment. On Tuesday, Gutiérrez reiterated to The Associated Press that he would not step down, which caused 30,000 protesters to take to the streets of the capital again that night, shouting *"Fuera, Lucio!"* ("Lucio, out!"). Police fired tear gas to drive them back from the presidential palace.

On Wednesday, April 20, Congress voted 62-0 to remove Gutiérrez from office on the peculiar pretext that he had "abandoned his post." Gutiérrez flew from the roof of the palace by helicopter and sought asylum at the Brazilian embassy. He flew to Brazil four days later, be-coming the latest of several Ecuadorian presidents to be forced into exile.

Transition to Palacio

Vice President Palacio, 66, a populist who had become critical of Gutiérrez's move to the right, was sworn in. But this still did not pacify some of the protesters, who trapped the new president in the building where he took the oath, demanding that he dissolve Congress and call new elections. Palacio said he would call for a referendum on constitutional reforms before calling any election, and he received the all-important pledge of support from the armed forces. He also met with the U.S. ambassador and promised to abide by existing treaties, while he promised to work with Palacio.

But the Organization of American States expressed concern whether Gutiérrez's removal was constitutional, and sent a high-level delegation to investigate. After three days of meetings with Palacio and the opposition, the OAS concluded that Palacio's government was legitimate.

Meanwhile, Bucaram, sensing the shifting political winds could be unhealthy for him, quickly fled to Peru and then back to Panama, which again granted him asylum. Noboa chose to remain in Ecuador, and in May he was placed under house arrest on the charges that he had mishandled debt negotiations.

At mid-year, Palacio was still in charge although there was speculation whether he would, or could, remain in office until Gutiérrez's term expires in January 2007. He demonstrated his constitutional muscle only days after assuming the presidency by appointing new armed forces commanders. Nineteen days later, without explanation, he replaced the army commander again. As an indication of the new president's populist tilt, his energy minister announced that he would review existing contracts with foreign oil companies to make sure they are "well formulated" and "within legal and ethical norms," whatever that means. As economy minister, Palacio named a leftist economist, Rafaél Correa, who announced that the government was reversing Gutiérrez's policy and would begin spending more oil revenue on social programs and less on debt servicing.

Culture: Ecuador is the quintessential *mestizo* country, with pure European and Indian descendants being heavily outnumbered by their ethnic hybrid. Of the two cultures, it is the Indian that has had the greater influence on the country's cultural identity. Ecuador is a remnant of the Inca Empire, and Quéchua is still widely spoken. The 200-odd Quéchua-based dialects serve as a unifying thread among the rural people. The Indian roots are visible and audible in the country's art and traditional folk music and dances.

Like other Bolivarian countries of northern South America, Ecuador has been whipsawed by dictatorship and political instability that has had a negative impact on cultural growth. Ecuadorian culture attracted little attention outside its borders until the 20th century. Its outstanding literary figure remains Jorge Icaza, whose 1934 novel, *Huasipungo*, is a Latin American classic and has been translated into at least 17 languages. Another prominent novelist was José de la Cuadra.

Ecuador's principal cultural contribution has come from its many talented artists, the best known of whom have been Oswaldo Guayasamín, a revolutionary painter in the style of Mexico's Diego Rivera, and Kingman Riofrío, whose works stress indigenous subjects. Guayasamín died in 1999, and a museum containing his works was dedicated in Quito in November 2002.

The high illiteracy rate has hampered development of the printed media. There are a number of mid-sized dailies, centered in Quito and Guayaquil. The oldest is the elite *El Telégrafo*, founded in 1884 and located in Guayaquil. The nation's circulation leader with about 200,000 daily is *El Universo*, which dates to 1921 and also is published in the port city. The capital's leading paper is *El Comercio*. There also are a number of magazines.

Economy: Ecuador's economy was always dependent upon the sale of agricultural products (bananas) and minerals abroad to pay for needed imports. It now is dominated by oil exportation (more than 385,000 barrels per day).

The agricultural/mineral exports are produced by illiterate, poorly paid labor in economic bondage to the land, who live on a per capita income of about $500 a year. Substantial resources in the form of fertile soils, valuable forests and mineral wealth have not been seriously exploited.

Ecuador's economic future improved dramatically with the discovery of rich oil deposits, estimated to total 5 billion barrels of high-grade petroleum, in the jungles east of the Andes. Oil income quadrupled government revenues with royalties reaching about $500 million by 1975. Nationalistic oil policies later forced most private firms to leave the country— thereby reducing exploration for new oil deposits. As a result, production declined; domestic oil consumption came close to outstripping production.

Although the government announced with much fanfare in 1981 that important new deposits were located, some observers feel that these would not greatly increase Ecuador's oil reserves. During 1981, oil output rose 27% to a total of 77 million barrels. However, the country's unfriendly attitude toward foreign oil companies prior to 1984 made it difficult to obtain foreign expertise needed to develop Ecuador's resources. This was remedied, however, by the administration of Febrés Cordero and as a result, additional exploration was underway in 1986.

But in 1985 another oil-related problem raised its ugly head: Saudi Arabia announced a rise in its production because other OPEC nations were cheating on their oil quotas. This allowed the price for the product to "float," and the worldwide market thus headed into a steep decline. The price descended to one-third of its 1980 level in 1986 (less than $10 a barrel), but rebounded to $17 by 1995. Production in existing fields was sufficient to last until 2000, but new discoveries have extended this.

A major earthquake in 1987 caused a severe economic setback. Remedial measures were not well coordinated.

During the 1990s, prices were depressed for bananas, cacao and coffee, but the price for the coffee doubled at the start of 1995 when killing frosts destroyed half of Brazil's trees. Ecuador, together with Peru and Bolivia, is a major producer of raw cocaine paste, which is processed into powder in Colombia. Numerous "factories" are located within Ecuador (owned by the Colombian cartels) where the paste is processed because of control measures within Colombia. Ecuador now imports four to five times as much of the chemicals needed to process cocaine than it would be able to use in the absence of that drug's production. Distribution is still via Colombia, equally to Europe and the United States.

The devastating effects of *El Niño* in 1997, the drastic drop in world oil prices in 1998 and the simultaneous meltdown of the Asian and Brazilian financial markets all contributed to an economic crisis that President Mahuad declared to be the worst in 70 years. The president told Congress in his state of the nation address in January 1999 that the country recorded real economic growth of only 0.8% in 1998, while inflation soared to 43.4%, the highest in Latin America.

OPEC's decision in March 1999 to boost the depressed price of oil augured well for Ecuador. In April, a panel of WTO experts meeting in Panama sided with the United States, Ecuador, Guatemala, Honduras and Panama in their complaint that the European Union's banana import policy was discriminatory. The five plaintiff countries had charged that the EU showed favoritism to bananas imported from former Caribbean colonies and against Latin American producers and U.S. distributors, in violation of international trading regulations. Ecuador exports 16% of its bananas to the EU, or $238 million of its $1.05 billion 1998 production, amounting to more than 650,000 tons.

In March 1999, Mahuad and the Congress reached an accord on a watered-down austerity plan that called for an income tax, a luxury tax on cars, more efficient collection of existing taxes and $100 million in spending cuts in an effort to cut the brutal budget deficit by $520 million. The plan also severely limited withdrawals from bank accounts. The IMF gave its approval to the plan, although Mahuad, faced with the opposition of the left-wing parties in his new coalition, was forced to abandon his privatization plan.

These painful measures deepened the recession, and the year-end figures for 1999 reflected the severity of the crisis that led a desperate Mahuad to recommend replacing the *sucre* with the dollar. Real GDP declined by a devastating 7.5%, unemployment jumped from 11.5% in 1998 to 16.9%, per capita income fell from $1,619 to $1,164, and inflation was officially the highest in Latin America: 50.4%.

The dollarization scheme led to massive public protests, which in turn led to Mahuad's ouster in January 2000, but his vice president and successor, Gustavo Noboa also embraced dollarization and put it into effect. The dollar replaced the *sucre* as Ecuador's legal tender that September. The resulting currency stabilization, coupled with the fortuitous rise in international oil prices, led to a much healthier than expected growth rate for 2000 of 2.0%. Inflation, however, nearly doubled to a crippling 96.6%, again the highest in Latin America, while unemployment dropped slightly to 14.7%.

The figures for 2001 were dramatically better, although deceptive. The good news was that real GDP increased by 5.6%, the fastest growth in all of Latin America In reality, of course, this only recovered the ground lost in 1999. Inflation, meanwhile, plummeted to "only" 22.4%.

There were two factors responsible for the strong showing in 2001. Noboa signed a $1.3 billion contract for an oil pipeline that is expected to create 50,000 jobs and, when completed, boost petroleum exports by 50%. But a more important factor was a peculiar demographic phenomenon. Since the 1999 economic meltdown, Ecuadorians have been abandoning the country in droves, legally and illegally, seeking work abroad in the United States, Spain, Italy and other countries. In 2001, the government actually created a program to expedite the exit visas of its citizens to work abroad; in March 2002 alone, 30,000 Ecua-

Ecuador

dorians signed up! Year-end figures for 2001 showed that this both cut domestic unemployment almost by half to 8.8% (although 40% are still considered underemployed) and generated $1.4 billion in remittances from abroad, accounting for an 8% of GDP, second only to oil exports. By 2003, the figure was $1.5 billion, or 5.6% of GDP.

The GDP grew by 3.3% in 2002 and 2.7% in 2003, small but steady. Inflation was only 6% in 2003, a record low. By 2004, the economy grew at a rate of 6%, among the highest in Latin America, while inflation was only 1.95%. The spike in international oil prices in 2004 was largely responsible for the growth. Income from oil exports totaled $2.13 billion, accounting for 43% of national revenue, definitely an over-reliance.

Tourism remains negligible, despite the popularity of the Galapagos Islands for foreign visitors. Tourism accounts for about $150 million a year, only about 5% of GDP.

Per capita GDP also has been rising steadily since the crisis, jumping from $1,450 per capita in 2002 to $2,304 in 2004. As often happens in South America, however, the robust economy did not enhance President Lucio Gutiérrez's popularity. Public protests forced him from office in April 2005 (see History).

Something Ecuador must address if it is ever to get a permanent handle on its economy is the entrenched corruption that costs the economy an estimated $2 billion a year—more than 10% of GDP. Tax evasion alone costs the public treasury an estimated $600-$800 million a year. There are encouraging signs, however, if they can be called that. Transparency International, the corruption watchdog group, rated Ecuador the third most corrupt country of the 20 Latin American republics in 2003; only Paraguay and Haiti were ranked worse. In 2004, Ecuador was "only" the seventh most corrupt, moving ahead of Guatemala, Bolivia, Venezuela and Honduras. President Gutiérrez made corruption the chief target of his 2002 campaign, but he was less than one year into his term before he himself was accused of corruption.

Another problem that needs to be addressed is illegal logging in Ecuador's rain forests, a precious natural resource. The government estimates that 370,000 acres of virgin forest fall to the saws each year, but environmental groups indicate it could be twice that. An estimated 70% of the lumber sold is cut illegally. In 1999, the government, unable to regulate the logging effectively itself, wisely contracted with a Swiss firm to monitor the logging and to tax legal logging. Under pressure from the logging industry, the Constitutional Tribunal overturned the outsourcing agreement in October 2003, for unclear legal reasons.

Environmentalists also are concerned with illegal shark fishing and harvesting of sea cucumbers in the Galapagos Islands, considered a world heritage site by the United Nations.

The Future: For the third time in less than eight years, either the Congress or the armed forces has ousted a duly elected Ecuadorian president. By most accounts, Ecuadorians should have been ecstatic with Lucio Gutiérrez for hauling its economy out of the abyss (see Economy), luring back foreign investors and balancing the budget. Yet, his approval ratings were themselves abysmal, about as low as Mahuad's, whom he helped topple five years earlier.

It is tough enough being president of Ecuador, who must perform a delicate high-wire act to appease the right and the left, the IMF and the indigenous Indians. Ecuadorians quickly turn on any president who does not prove to be Superman, which means all of them. But Gutiérrez squandered the capital (an appropriate metaphor) of a robust economy with his heavy-handed dismissal of the Supreme Court, a power play reminiscent of Hugo Chávez's in Venezuela. He brought his downfall upon himself.

Thus, the Ecuadorian presidency remains a greased pole. Indeed, in the perennial *Latinobarómetro* poll published by the British newsmagazine *The Economist*, the percentage of Ecuadorians who believe democracy is preferable to any other form of government has declined from 52% in 1996 to 46% in 2003 and 2004. Meanwhile, those who believe that authoritarian rule is sometimes preferable to democracy has jumped from 18% in 1996 to 34% in 2003; it dropped back to 30% in 2004—still the second-highest percentage in Latin America, after Paraguay. This does not auger well for the long-term prospects for democracy in Ecuador.

The man now on the greased pole, Alfredo Palacio, like Gustavo Noboa before him, appears to be a decent, non-controversial fellow who may be able to trump up public support if he can just avoid alienating too many people. That's not easy to do in Ecuador. A cardiologist who interned in Cleveland and who has a fondness for medical metaphors, Palacio has called Ecuador his "patient."

Unlike Noboa, however, Palacio at least has inherited a rebounding economy, with one of the highest growth rates in Latin America. With record high oil prices, Dr. Palacio should keep his patient on the road to economic recovery in 2005. But the real problem is not the doctor, nor the patient's past economic ills. The real problem is a quarrelsome patient with a history of chronic political complaints.

Giant tortoises of the Galápagos Islands

The Republic of El Salvador

Street scene in San Salvador

Area: 8,260 square miles.

Population: 6.6 million (including expatriates).

Capital City: San Salvador (Pop. 1.75 million, estimated).

Climate: Tropical in the coastal plain, becoming temperate at higher altitudes.

Neighboring Countries: Honduras (North and East); Guatemala (West).

Official Language: Spanish.

Ethnic Background: *Mestizo* (mixed Spanish and Indian).

Principal Religion: Roman Catholic Christianity.

Chief Commercial Products: Coffee, Cotton, Sugar.

Currency: U.S. Dollar (formerly the Colón).

Gross Domestic Product: U.S. $15 billion in 2003 ($2,258 per capita).

Former Colonial Status: Spanish Crown Colony (1524–1821).

Independence Date: September 15, 1821

Chief of State: Elías Antonio "Tony" Saca (b. March 9, 1965), president (since June 1, 2004).

National Flag: Blue, white and blue horizontal stripes with the national coat of arms on the white stripe.

El Salvador is the smallest and most densely populated of the Central American republics. Most of the country is a volcanic upland with two parallel rows of volcanos running east to west. Fourteen of the cones exceed 3,000 feet and three reach more than 7,000 feet. Lowlands lie north and south of the volcanic ranges. El Salvador's principal river, the Lempa, drains the northern lowlands by cutting through the volcanic region to reach the Pacific.

El Salvador's soils are rich and easily accessible from the Pacific coast; thus it is one of the few Latin American countries in which the whole of the national territory is settled. Various estimates are given for the percentages of European, Indian and African ancestry in the national population, but the most obvious facts are that there are no tribal Indians and few blacks, and that the white minority claiming pure European origins is indistinguishable from the admittedly *mestizo*, a mixture of Spanish and Indian. Cotton and sugar are raised on the coastal plains and the Lempa River valley, while the slopes of the volcanoes produce coffee. The climate is healthful and the rainfall abundant, with the rainy season running from May through October.

History: El Salvador was conquered by Pedro de Alvarado with a force from Mexico in 1524. Defeating the Indians and capturing their capital, Cuscutlán, he joined the region to the Captaincy-General of Guatemala. The small number of Spanish settlers intermarried with the Indians and established large agricultural and cattle-raising estates in the fertile valleys of the volcanic uplands, a pattern of land holding which exists today, and the root of most of El Salvador's present-day problems. The remnants of the Indian population still farm village-owned lands in the mountains.

El Salvador declared its independence from Spain on September 15, 1821, with the other countries of Central America. Joining in a short-lived federation until its breakup in 1838, El Salvador was a center for the liberal republican opposition to the conservatives of Guatemala. It sought admission to the United States at one time and participated in several attempts to

El Salvador

unite with Honduras and Nicaragua. As was true in most of the Central American republics, the political history of El Salvador during the 19th century after independence was one of turbulence, revolution, dictators, military governments and civil strife. Added to the internal difficulties of the nation were frequent periods of conflict with neighboring states.

The first quarter of the 20th century was relatively peaceful in El Salvador, but this was followed by virtual anarchy which did not end until the seizure of power by an absolute ruler, Hernández Martínez, from 1931 to 1944. The low point of his years in power came in 1932, when a peasant uprising in protest against the landed elite cost 20,000 lives, almost all of them peasants, an event remembered today as *"La Matanza"* (the slaughter).

Various factions have been labeled conservative (favoring central government and close church-state relations) and liberal (anti-clerical federalists); however, those represented only blocs within the elite landowning class and were not truly different political entities. A degree of political stability was evidenced by regimes in power from 1948 to 1960, but popular opposition to the elite domination of politics and continuing economic problems continued to center around a small number of wealthy and a comparatively huge number of poor. This led to minor change in October 1960.

A provisional military-civilian *junta* took power, promising to reform the nation's political structure and hold elections. A new constitution was adopted in 1962 and in presidential elections held the same year there was but one candidate, Adalberto Rivera of the *Partido de Conciliación Nacional (PCN)*, a movement controlled by the oligarchy and the military. Although he and his party were supposed to be "middle-of-the-road," there was no such thing in El Salvador. There were right-wing, elitist elements and communist-leftist rebels, with little in between. Providing capable and honest leadership, Rivera encouraged the development of light industry and supported the nation's participation in the Central American Common Market.

Starting about 1960, a culture of violence gripped the country. Right-wing vigilante groups, such as the White Warrior's Union, often joined with government forces—including rightist members of the army, the National Guard and the Treasury Police—to torture and execute peasant leaders and other advocates of social reform. Leftist groups—including Marxist-led guerrilla units such as the People's Revolutionary Army, the Popular Forces of Liberation, and the Armed Forces of National Resistance—responded in kind with attacks against military forces and their conservative supporters. Generally, leftist groups tended to pinpoint specific targets, while right-wing terrorists appeared less discriminatory. As a result, a large percentage of the political deaths in El Salvador have been linked to conservative forces.

Another *PCN* "moderate" candidate, Colonel Fidel Sánchez Hernández, won the 1967 election. His policies included an unheard-of land ownership reform proposal that infuriated conservatives, businessmen and wealthy landowners. The brief but bitter "Soccer War" was fought with Honduras in 1969 (see Honduras).

Great controversy surrounded the presidential elections of 1972. Christian Democrat José Napoleón Duarte, a nominal moderate, apparently outpolled *PCN* candidate Colonel Arturo Armando Molina. However, a subsequent "official" government count gave the ruling *PCN* party a 22,000 vote victory; Molina's "election" was confirmed by Congress, where the *PCN* enjoyed a two-thirds majority. The military used a similar tactic for the presidential elections of 1977 when the ruling *PCN* candidate, General Carlos Humberto Romero, was declared the winner by a two-to-one margin over his opponent, another right-wing officer. When riots broke out against the rigged elections, the government imposed martial law. Before order was restored, an estimated 100 protesters were killed.

A staunch conservative, Romero was involuntarily faced immediately with urgent problems of land reform, human rights and the Catholic Church, which had become reformist. He equated change from the old order with communism. Most of the fertile farmland in the valleys and lowlands (about 60% of the total) continued to be owned by a handful of families who were closely allied to the ruling armed forces. In contrast, more than 65% of the population lived in abject poverty. Backed by the military, the conservative aristocracy had traditionally blocked disorganized peasant demands for land and reform. Wealthy landowners (including military officers who owned large estates) feared a repetition of the unsuccessful peasant uprisings against the landed elite of 1932.

The pace of fighting between rightists and leftists rose dramatically after Romero became president. Hoping to wipe out all opposition, he launched a bitter campaign against leftists and their sympathizers.

Coup and Civil War

As the nation moved toward complete chaos, a group of liberal army officers led by Colonel Adolfo Arnoldo Majano ousted Romero in a bloodless coup in November 1979. Power then shifted to a progressive five-man *junta* that included Majano and two members of the "centrist" Christian Democratic Party. The new rulers promised sweeping economic and social reforms that provided: (1) nationalization of key parts of foreign trade industries, including coffee marketing, (2) nationalization of many banks (which traditionally provided loans only to the upper class, and (3) land reform.

On paper, the land reform proposal was comparable in scope to those of Mexico, Bolivia and Peru. The first phase, affecting 400 estates containing more than 1,235 acres each, would have redistributed about 600,000 acres of land (about 25% of the nation's arable land) to peasants. A second phase, planned for 1981, was to involve all farms larger than 370 acres.

A major catalyst for reform was the Carter administration in Washington, which supplied El Salvador with economic and military assistance. Washington feared that unless fundamental reforms were enacted, El Salvador would slide into a disastrous class war. Such a conflict might well be won by leftists, who could then be expected to combine with radicals in Nicaragua to force Marxist governments onto neighboring Honduras and Guatemala.

Conservative opposition to the *junta's* reforms proved overwhelming, however, and right-wing violence rose dramatically. The assassination of Archbishop Oscar Romero in 1980 shocked the nation, and in 1980 conservatives murdered the head of the country's Human Rights Commission (its report had embarrassed the government). The top six leaders of a "centrist" political front which included the Christian Democratic Party were killed in late 1980, and the following month four U.S. women missionaries were murdered. Early January was marked by the murder of two U.S. agricultural agents associated with the nation's land reform program.

Appalled by this violence, President Carter halted all aid to El Salvador in late 1980. The Salvadoran military responded by taking aim at the *junta*, but the result

José Napoleón Duarte

was unexpected. Majano was replaced by a new four-member *junta* under the leadership of José Napoleón Duarte of the Christian Democratic Party. A graduate of Notre Dame University, the 55-year-old civil engineer pledged to move forward with social reform while taking steps to control right-wing terrorism. Duarte quietly retired some right-wing military leaders while others were reassigned to isolated posts.

Convinced that the time was ripe for revolution, the guerrillas launched a full-scale "final assault" against government forces in January 1981. Although supplied with

Nicaraguan and Cuban arms, the rebels found no popular support in the countryside, and the offensive soon foundered.

In Washington, the new Reagan administration issued a hastily prepared report in February 1981 claiming to have "concrete" evidence that the Salvadoran guerrilla front was a part of a "worldwide communist conspiracy" masterminded by the Soviet Union. Insisting that it was necessary to "draw the line" against communism, President Reagan soon ordered a resumption of large-scale military and economic assistance to El Salvador. He also fired the Carter-appointed ambassador.

Despite such aid, Duarte's regime found itself increasingly dependent on the military for survival. To placate powerful right-wing critics in the country, Duarte predictably shelved many of his promised reforms. Hoping to increase domestic support for the government and to improve El Salvador's international image, Washington pressured Duarte to hold elections for a Constituent Assembly in March 1982 as the first step toward a return to constitutional government. While almost all leftists boycotted the elections—and the guerrillas sought to disrupt the balloting—voter turnout was heavy. Official returns showed 1.3 million votes cast.

Duarte's centrist-left Christian Democratic Party won 40% of the vote and 24 seats in the 60-seat Constituent Assembly, the largest total of any single party. But right-wing tickets led by the National Republican Alliance (*ARENA*) and the National Conciliation Party (*PCN*) gained nearly 60% of the vote and 34 seats in the Assembly.

Much to the chagrin of Duarte and his supporters in Washington, the rightists promptly formed a coalition and voted to exclude the Christian Democrats from participation in the new government. Named president of the Assembly was arch-conservative Roberto D'Aubuisson, an ex-army intelligence officer allegedly linked with the right-wing death squads. In 1980 he had been arrested for plotting a coup against the government.

Under strong pressure from the army's influential defense minister, General José Guillermo García, the Assembly elected a moderate U.S.-educated economist and banker as provisional president: Alvaro Alfredo Magaña, 56. The Assembly also named three vice presidents, one each for *ARENA*, *PCN*, and the Christian Democrats.

As the first democratically elected president in 50 years, Magaña was expected to have only a limited impact on the country's destiny. The rightist-controlled Assembly sought to strip the president of any real power while Assembly President D'Aubuisson tried to repeal many of the

Salvadoran guerrillas, Usulátan Province

El Salvador

A young rural mother does the family wash

reforms planned by the previous Duarte regime. In one of its first acts, the Assembly voted to dismantle Phases II and III of the land reform program longed for by the poor. (By mid-1982, provisional land titles had been given to more than 7,000 peasants under the program.) D'Aubuisson boasted he would wipe out the nation's guerrilla movement "in no more than six months."

Although weakened by the failures of its 1981 "final assault," the guerrillas were not dislodged. The insurgents controlled most of Chalatenango and Morazán provinces in the mountainous north part of the country near the Honduran border.

The nation's five major Marxist groups continued to quarrel among themselves, although their activities became coordinated under a single umbrella organization, the Farabundo Martí National Liberation Front (*FMLN*). Most of the groups, which trace their common roots to the communist-inspired peasant uprising in 1932, became active in the late 1960s and early 1970s. Both France and Mexico recognized the rebels in August 1981 as a "representative political force"—a move which could only alienate the United States.

Finding itself in the midst of a civil war, the Salvadoran government also began to improve its own military capabilities. Especially effective were the U.S.-trained battalions which used new tactics and sophisticated equipment provided by the United States.

The United States was drawn increasingly into the anti-communist war in El Salvador. A blank check was written to those in charge, a military establishment whose loyalty was consistently identified with the elite of the country. They faced an insurgency initially of poor guerrillas, who rapidly came to be supported by Soviet-via-Cuba resources, military and financial. A heavy infusion of U.S. aid was furnished during the Reagan years with a single instruction: win. American advisers took their place alongside the Salvadoran military, quickly training and developing rapid-response battalions that were virtually invincible, and which soon acquired the dubious label of "death squads."

Alongside the government forces, including these deadly battalions, there were private forces, capable of the worst atrocities to accomplish the desired goal: win. But it was not one-sided by any means; the communists also had a single goal: win. Both sides resorted to the worst sort of warfare, using any tactic or method necessary to instill total fear in innocent bystanders. Public torture, mutilation and murder of innocents, all became acceptable tools.

With the heavy infusion of U.S. aid, the Salvadoran military increasingly resembled the U.S. Army. Troops were armed with highly sophisticated equipment that was sometimes plagued with mobility, maintenance and cost problems. With the assistance of 55 U.S. military advisers (a number limited by the U.S. Congress) plus support personnel, government forces became more and more effective.

The U.S. Senate Foreign Relations Committee voted to cut $100 million from the Reagan administration's $226 million aid package in mid-1982. The U.S. House of Representatives passed a resolution requiring the president to certify that the Salvadoran government was making "good faith efforts" to prosecute five National Guard personnel accused of the 1980 murders of the three American nuns and a lay worker.

El Salvador's civil war increasingly spilled over into other parts of Central America. Thousands of Salvadoran peasants fled to Honduras to escape the terror from the guerrillas and the right-wing death squads, including *ORDEN*, a rural civil defense force feared even more than the regular army. An estimated 2 million Salvadorans lived outside the country; 1 million of them, mostly illegal immigrants, were in the United States.

Guatemala, Honduras, Costa Rica and El Salvador formed a common front to exchange intelligence and coordinate strategy against Nicaraguan and Salvadoran guerrillas. Both Honduras and Guatemala maintained large troop concentrations along their common borders with El Salvador. Honduran troops controlled a contested zone along the border of the two countries, partly to prevent the communist rebellion from spreading into its territory.

The *FMLN* sought to disrupt elections in 1984, but Salvadorans went to the polls under the eyes of scores of international observers. Duarte ultimately defeated D'Aubuisson for president, and immediately traveled to Washington to ask for more economic aid for social programs and military assistance. In 1985 legislative and municipal elections, the Christian Democratic Party, in an upset, captured a majority of seats in the National Assembly and municipal councils. The rightists hatched a scheme to list a single candidate as the choice of two parties, but the effort was voided by the Supreme Court.

An announcement by a Catholic Church official that it would try to mediate in the civil war eased the cautious attitude of the U.S. Congress, which in 1984 appropriated additional emergency and military aid to El Salvador. But in 1985, the communists kidnapped the daughter of Duarte as she was leaving the San Salvador University. The president had to agree to the release of 22 rebels and safe passage for 96 wounded guerrillas to Cuba (and then to Eastern Europe for medical treatment) before his daughter could be released. He sent his family to the United States to avoid further kidnappings. The military and rightists were furious at his apparent weakness, but talk about a coup rapidly faded. He was, after all, necessary for continued U.S. military aid.

The years 1986-87 saw a beefed up military achieve greater successes. Ultimately the conflict cost $6 billion in U.S. aid. Periodic negotiations failed, as both sides negotiated with ultimatums. In 1988 the FMLN flatly rejected a proposal that the organization participate in municipal and legislative elections. When it finally tried this in 1991, in spite of successfully blocking observation at 30 polling places it controlled, only one of its candidates was sent to the National Assembly.

But in 1989 the communists agreed to take part in and respect the outcome of presidential elections *if* they were postponed for six months. They demanded a multitude of other conditions that made the offer impossible. They resorted to terrorism to disrupt the electoral process, and the right-wing death squads retaliated, committing their own atrocities. As usual, the innocent suffered.

The Christian Democrats had unwisely divided into two factions. ARENA, well unified under D'Aubuisson, was able to mount an unexpected upset in local and legislative elections, and was the decisive victor in a contest marred by charges of ballot box stuffing.

Former President Armando Calderón Sol

Six candidates vied for office in 1989 presidential elections. The FMLN nominally supported one, but did its best to keep voters away from the polls. ARENA candidate Alfredo Cristiani won with almost 54% of the votes.

By late 1989, it was apparent that Soviet-Cuban aid was going to dry up. Deciding that negotiations were the best course, the FMLN tried two super-offensives-last-ditch efforts in 1989–90 to win as much territory as possible and thereby be in a better negotiating position. The guerrillas held parts of San Salvador for several days, but could not consolidate their gains. Nine members of a death squad murdered seven pro-guerrilla Jesuit priests in cold blood, together with their servant and her daughter in the melee. Two of the soldiers later were sentenced to 30 years imprisonment for following orders.

Peace at Last

After the last-gasp rebel offensive of 1989, both sides were forced to acknowledge a stalemate. Neither could achieve full victory, and each side was willing to make peace; all that was needed was an appropriate broker. In September 1991, the U.S. ambassador and his military group commander seized that initiative by traveling boldly into guerrilla territory in a four-wheel-drive vehicle to confront an astonished FMLN leadership. Essentially, the two U.S. officials asked what it would take for the FMLN to make peace. It turned out that two of the rebels' key expectations for a post-war El Salvador were relatively reasonable ones: rural electrification and an end to death-squad atrocities. The ambassador brought these and other bargaining points back to the capital. On December 31, the two sides signed a truce that ended 12 years of slaughter that had claimed an estimated 75,000 lives, a grim toll in a country of only 6 million people.

The formal signing of the peace accords followed on January 16, 1992. Under the terms of the peace agreement, guaranteed by the United Nations, the FMLN laid down their arms and agreed to participate in the democratic process. The army ceased its sponsorship of death-squad activities. Despite an occasional low-level violation, the desire for peace superseded the deep-seated class hatreds that had led to the bloodbath. Less realistic was the establishment of a "truth commission" to investigate the atrocities committed during the war. Among the recommendations in its 211-page report was that the entire Supreme Court be sacked. President Cristiani chose to ignore these and other recommendations, but the mood of the coun-

try was one of forgive and forget. Despite some pessimism and a few setbacks, the tenuous armistice took hold.

The first postwar elections revealed a great deal about the conflict in El Salvador. Both Duarte and D'Aubuisson had died of cancer since 1989. Armando Calderón Sol was the candidate of ARENA in the March–April 1994 contest; Rubén Zamora was the choice of a leftist coalition which included the FMLN. Campaigning was vigorous by all candidates. Calderón appeared as a mild-mannered moderate, although he had been a close adherent of D'Aubuisson. But Zamora, appearing with a narrow black beard and moustache, closely resembled the evil Mephistopheles; the comparative appearance of the two was not lost on the public.

The war had been fought largely on a local and regional basis, so the candidates of the left were immediately recognized even though their dress had been totally altered. The people were incredulous at the idea of seeing once-feared guerrillas suddenly soliciting their votes. In the first round, Calderón scored not quite 50% of the vote in balloting which was free of irregularities; Zamora received 25%. ARENA sailed to an easy victory in the runoff held in April.

ARENA and an allied party took 43 seats, a bare majority in the 84-seat Assembly, while the FMLN won 21 and the Christian Democrats fell to 18. In December 1994, the Christian Democrats fragmented, with nine of their deputies bolting to the Renewal Social Christian Movement and one becoming an independent.

While the elections were underway, the Clinton administration sliced the aid appropriation for El Salvador to 40% of what it received in 1993.

Nagging problems remained. FMLN guerrillas were promised jobs and stipends to enable them to live decently. But no one planned where the funds for this would come from. They split into numerous factions and groups, many of which practiced thievery, kidnapping and demolition of homes to obtain and extort money from small villages and the countryside. This illustrated an age-old problem: what is done with the revolutionaries when the revolution is over?

The lower echelon army troops went frequently unpaid, but were promised tracts in the rich, upper highlands, to be taken from the land barons. Anticipating this, many squatted on the large *estancias*, but were driven from them. They became embittered and restive.

The political and economic elites received a scare in the municipal and congressional elections of 1997. ARENA lost its absolute majority in the National Assembly, winning just 28 of the 84 seats,

El Salvador

Making *pupusas* (a *tortilla* made of cornmeal, onion, pork rinds, and shortening) at a sidewalk restaurant in San Salvador

Photo by the author

while the *FMLN* shocked the country—and the world—by winning 27. *ARENA* was forced to govern in coalition with small conservative parties. Moreover, the *FMLN* won the mayoralties of most of the major cities, including San Salvador. The winner in the capital was Hector Silva, a Boston-born gynecologist, who became highly popular for his public works improvements. The *FMLN* had an unlikely ally in President Calderón, who by 1998 had become unpopular because of a stagnant economy, allegations of corruption within his administration and an alarming increase in violent crime that he seemed impotent to control. By mid-1998, it seemed possible that the former guerrillas would win through the ballot box what they had failed for 12 years to win on the battlefield. But two things happened to blunt the pro-*FMLN* trend.

First, in March 1998, *ARENA* wisely decided to clean up its act by nominating as its presidential candidate Francisco "Paco" Flores, an unthreatening, 39-year-old former philosophy professor who had no link to the dark days of D'Aubuisson's death squads. In fact, he was an undergraduate at Amherst College in Massachusetts when the civil war erupted in 1979, then stayed in the United States to study for a year at Harvard before traveling to India to study Hindu philosophy. At the height of the civil war, he was studying Eastern philosophies at an obscure, unaccredited university in Ojai, California, from which he claims a master's degree. After returning to El Salvador, he taught at Central American University, where he became friends with the

Jesuit priests later slain by the army during the 1989 guerrilla offensive. He taught philosophy at a small college in the capital before becoming an adviser to President Cristiani. He was then elected to the National Assembly, where he became the chamber's president after the 1997 elections.

Second, the *FMLN* began disemboweling itself with nasty intra-party bickering between Marxist hardliners and moderates. In a party caucus in July 1998, the popular Silva, a moderate, deadlocked with another popular moderate, Victoria Aviles, who had served as U.N. human rights ombudsman. They deadlocked again in a second round of voting in October. Finally, they both acquiesced in favor of yet another moderate, Facundo Guardado, 44, a former commander-in-chief of the rebel army, who was best remembered for his seizure of the Sheraton Hotel during the 1989 offensive on the capital. But the public squabble within the *FMLN* ranks, which at times resembled a barroom brawl, was shown to the country on television, creating grave doubts about the party's ability to govern the country. Five other candidates entered the race, including Rubén Zamora again, and Rodolfo Parker for the Christian Democrats, which further fragmented the vote of the left. Polls showed the race would boil down to Flores and Guardado.

The Election of 1999

This author spent six days observing the election campaign in January 1999, interviewing both the major candidates and

other Salvadorans. The consensus among the people I interviewed on both right and left was that Guardado was handicapped by his image as a guerrilla commander, which stood out in especially sharp contrast with the intellectual and urbane Flores, as well as by the infighting within the *FMLN* ranks. Guardado did not help matters by choosing as his running mate Nidia Díaz, the *nom de guerre* for María Marta Valladares, whom the U.S. Justice Department still wants in connection with the killing of four U.S. Marines in a San Salvador restaurant in 1985.

Flores was forthright about *ARENA*'s own image problem, and insisted to me that he had turned it around in 10 months of campaigning. "People understand that there has been a deep change within *ARENA*," he said in English. "It's not only a generational change, but it's a change in the way we do things and the way we relate to other politicians, to other political parties and to the Salvadoran people."

In a separate interview in Spanish, Guardado agreed that the campaign has been respectful, but insisted that *ARENA* has not changed its spots and that the *FMLN* better represents the middle class.

"The danger of our losing is that the country will be prostrate for another decade," he said. "In five more years, *ARENA* will concentrate even more economic power in its hands, and use the power of the state to commit more abuses. Asked why *ARENA* is so successful if it represents only the upper class, Guardado replied, "*ARENA* has much greater access to information and they can manipulate it. The lower classes are much more easily manipulated. Also, (*ARENA* has) a lot of money for buying votes."

While Guardado was handicapped by his image as a guerrilla, Flores' own glowing academic credentials came under scrutiny. His résumé claims he did "postgraduate studies" in economics and philosophy at Harvard. But I called Harvard's Graduate School of Arts and Sciences, whose registrar told me there is no record of that. Flores then conceded to me in a subsequent telephone interview that he was enrolled in a "special student program" that was not degree-conferring. The registrar at Harvard's GSAS acknowledged that many Latin American students are admitted to such programs but that those records are kept separately, that it is not considered "post-graduate study" and that "his résumé should not state that." Flores also stated that he had studied at Oxford's Trinity College in the summer of 1980 as part of Amherst's honors program, but the Amherst registrar's office told me there was no record of his having received credit for going to Oxford. Flores then told me he attended Trinity College as part of the summer program of the University of Massachusetts at Amherst. As for his "master's degree" from World University of America in California, which in 1999 had only 78 students, Flores admitted the school lacks prestige. "I won't say I got took, but it wasn't what I expected," he said. His flirtation with Oriental religions became a campaign issue in Catholic El Salvador, to the point that Flores ran a campaign ad showing him attending Mass.

In the end, the polls and the pundits proved correct in their forecasts of the outcome. In the March 7 balloting, Flores avoided a runoff by receiving just under 52% of the vote, to 29% for Guardado; Zamora ran a distant third. Flores was inaugurated on June 1, 1999.

The Flores Presidency

The *FMLN* soon rebounded from its electoral loss. In the March 2000 congressional elections, they shocked the establishment once again by winning 31 seats in the National Assembly, while *ARENA's* seats remained unchanged at 29. The *FMLN* is now the largest bloc in the legislature, although *ARENA* still enjoys a small majority through a coalition with smaller conservative parties.

Two major but unrelated events occurred in January 2001. On January 1, El Salvador joined Panama and Ecuador in abandoning its currency and embracing the dollar. On January 13, the country was hit by a devastating earthquake that killed 1,200 people and caused an estimated $1 billion in damage—about half the national budget. A second quake struck exactly a month later, on February 13, which added to the damage but mercifully claimed far fewer lives.

A potentially significant political event occurred in November 2001. Salvador Sánchez Cerén, who under the *nom de guerre* Leonel González had commanded the largest of the *FMLN's* guerrilla factions during the civil war and who adheres to the party's traditional socialist roots, scored a decisive victory, 45% to 22%, over a reformist candidate to lead the *FMLN*. A third candidate, who had attempted to steer a middle course between the two factions, was second with 31%. In the wake of Sánchez's victory, some *FMLN* moderates, including six members of the Assembly, defected from the party to form their own movement, thus fragmenting the opposition to *ARENA.*

On January 16, 2002, Salvadorans marked the 10th anniversary of the signing of the peace accords that ended the civil war. Symbolically, President Flores attended a ceremony in the mountain village of Perquín, a former guerrilla stronghold. Although most Salvadorans still applaud the decade of peace, the hard-line Sánchez rained on the parade by complaining that peace had not eased the plight of the poor.

In March 2002, U.S. President George W. Bush included El Salvador on his itinerary for a three-nation visit to Latin America. His visit became the occasion for a summit with the other presidents of Central America, at which Bush preached his gospel of free trade. He also promised to increase U.S. aid for the 2001 earthquake from $67 million to $100 million.

Elections for the 84-seat Assembly and for municipalities were held on March 16, 2003. Despite an improvement in the economy, the *FMLN* won 31 Assembly seats to 27 for *ARENA,* recovering the six seats it had lost from defections. *ARENA* still enjoys a working majority through its alliance with the National Conciliation Party *(PCN),* which has 16 seats. The *FMLN* also retained the mayoralty of San Salvador under the candidacy of a political newcomer, Carlos Rivas Zamora.

In 2003, Flores dispatched a contingent of 380 troops to participate in the allied coalition in Iraq, under Spanish command. El Salvador decided to keep its troops in Iraq at least until August 2004, even after Spain withdrew its forces.

The waning days of the Flores administration were clouded by graft scandals at a private bank and a water company.

The Election of 2004

ARENA and the *FMLN* presented the voters with an even sharper choice in 2004 than they had in 1999. *ARENA* once again presented a youthful, post-civil war candidate by nominating Elías Antonio "Tony" Saca, 39, a former sportscaster who had become a media executive. The *FMLN*, which apparently had not learned anything about not frightening voters, chose Schafik Hándel, 73, a well-known leader of the Communist faction of the guerrilla movement. About the only thing the two men had in common was that they were born in the same neighborhood of Palestinian immigrant parents, who were from Bethlehem. Two minor candidates, including a Christian Democrat, rounded out the field.

In January 2004, polls showed Hándel pulling up to within a statistical tie of Saca. *ARENA* furiously used the usual scare tactics against the Communist Hándel, hinting that the United States could begin restricting remittances by Salvadorans living in the United States, as they do with remittances by Cuban Americans, if Hándel won. The *FMLN* candidate did little to downplay his past, pledging to establish diplomatic relations with Cuba

Former President Francisco Flores

and the People's Republic of China, to pull Salvadoran troops out of Iraq, to heavily tax businesses and the wealthy, to bring back the Colón to circulate alongside the dollar and to oppose a Central American free-trade agreement with the United States.

On March 21, 67.3% of the Salvadoran electorate turned out to vote, but despite the polls, the outcome was little different from that of 1999:

Saca	1,314,436	57.7%
Hándel	812,519	35.7%
Others	150,518	6.6%

Hándel, reflecting his antidemocratic background, ungraciously blamed his defeat on *ARENA's* "lies and blackmail."

Saca was sworn in on June 1, 2004. He continued Flores' commitment to the Allied Coalition in Iraq even after Honduras, Nicaragua and the Dominican Republic brought their troops home. Saca sent another contingent of 380 troops to Iraq in August 2004 to replace those who rotated home. That contingest was replaced in February 2005.

As another indication of El Salvador's pro-U.S. policy, the National Assembly voted 49–35 in December 2004 to ratify the proposed Central American Free Trade Agreement. It was the first country to do so.

A major multinational problem that Saca is being forced to deal with is the growing threat in El Salvador, the United States, Mexico, Guatemala and Honduras of *maras,* or street gangs. These groups, formed by Central American, mostly Salvadoran, emigrants in Los Angeles, now constitute a serious form of organized crime. Perhaps the most infamous is Mara Salvatrucha-13, or MS-13, which is believed to have 100,000 members in 31 states and five countries, including Ca-

El Salvador

nada. So serious is the threat that the FBI opened a special anti-gang office in San Salvador in May 2005, while Saca and Mexican President Vicente Fox called for an anti-gang summit.

Culture: The people of El Salvador are friendly, agricultural, Christian people. They have adopted European customs for the most part—pure Indians are hard to find in the Republic. Independent and fun-loving, their lives revolve around the family as the primary social, economic and political unit.

El Salvador (The Savior) has perhaps some of the most beautiful churches found in Latin America—the people devote a full 12 days of the year to a festival in honor of their Christian namesake.

Ancient ruins of Mayan civilization have yielded treasures from the countryside which are being intensely studied, and there are explorations in progress for traces of even earlier inhabitants. One invaluable site near San Salvador has been bulldozed for a housing development and a brand-new (bulletproof) American embassy.

A rising star in Latin American literature is the Salvadoran novelist Horacio Castellanos Moya, best known for *El asco* and *La diabla en el espejo*. His latest, published in 2003, was *Donde no estén ustedes*.

Economy: Agriculture is the dominant factor, with the major cash crops being coffee, sugar and cotton. Despite its small size, El Salvador ranks among the top five coffee producers in the world. Farming remains largely under the control of a small group of wealthy landowners; the large peasant population lives in virtual serf-dom. Serious overcrowding and limited economic opportunities in rural regions have caused many peasants to migrate to the already congested cities.

Since World War II, light industry has gained steadily, making El Salvador the most industrialized nation in Central America. The civil war was costly in spite of U.S. assistance and seriously undermined economic growth. Since 1982 the government has had serious cash flow problems. U.S. aid in 1992 was $82 million and $230 million in 1993. That was reduced to $94 million in 1994. The state banking industry has been privatized. A major portion of the federal budget formerly devoted to the military is now being used for health and welfare.

Salvadorans love to grumble about the state of their economy and to frighten the governing elite by voting for *FMLN* candidates for the National Assembly, but in relative terms, their lot is not that bad. While El Salvador is plagued by widespread poverty, and although its economy is far from booming, it is certainly nowhere near the basket cases of neighboring Honduras, which has about one third the per capita income of El Salvador, or Nicaragua, where it is one fifth as much. In reality, peace has brought greater foreign investment in the form of *maquiladora* assembly plants for textile products, which in turn have created jobs. Tourism has risen modestly since the killing stopped. Moreover, Salvadoran expatriates still living in the United States send an estimated $2 billion a year in remittances to their families back home, about 15% of GDP.

Real GDP growth has been sluggish for years, declining from 2.1% in 1997 to 1.4%

President Elias Antonio Saca

in 1998, 1.3% in 1999 and .5% in 2000 before rebounding to 2.5% in 2001 and 2.1% in 2002. It was back down to 1.8% in 2003. Some of the blame during those years can be attributed to the damage wrought by Hurricane Mitch in October 1998 and the twin earthquakes of January and February 2001.

Unemployment has remained about 7%. Inflation was 3% in 2000 and 3.5% in 2001. Prices have been stabilized as a result of replacing the Colon with the dollar on January 1, 2001. The dollarization made sound economic sense; tens of thousands of Salvadorans live and work in the United States, and the tens of millions of dollars in remittances they send home to their families annually have become an important pillar of the economy since the exodus of refugees during the civil war.

The Future: The conservative *ARENA* has now won four consecutive presidential elections. Perhaps by 2009 the former guerrillas of the *FMLN* will have learned to nominate a moderate instead of a bogeyman. Still, the *FMLN* has benefited greatly from its participation in the democratic process, becoming the largest party in the National Assembly and controlling numerous municipal governments, including the capital. Even the hard-line Marxists seem to acknowledge that that is preferable to the slaughter that ravaged the country before 1992.

It is too early to tell what kind of leader Tony Saca will be, but like all his predecessors, he has a daunting economic task cut out for him. Besides the chronically sluggish economy, he must now face the growing threat of *maras,* or street gangs. Perhaps the troops that have returned from duty in Iraq can be put to use closer to home.

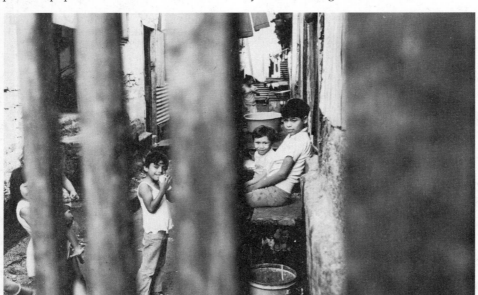

Children in an alleyway in San Salvador

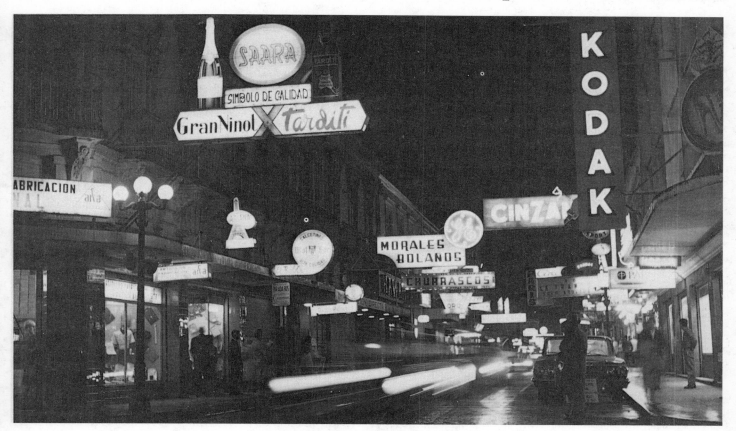

Guatemala City in the late evening

Area: 42,031 square miles.

Population: 14.3 million (2004 estimate).

Capital City: Guatemala City (Pop. 2.5 million, including surrounding areas).

Climate: Tropical on the coastal plains, temperate at the higher altitudes; heaviest rainfall is from May to October.

Neighboring Countries: Mexico (north and west); Belize (northeast); Honduras, El Salvador (east).

Official Language: Spanish.

Other Principal Tongues: Twenty distinct Maya-based dialects; Quiché is the most important.

Ethnic Background: Maya Indian origin (55%), *mestizo or Ladino* (mixed Spanish and Indian, (42%) European or African (3%).

Guatemala

Principal Religion: Roman Catholic Christianity. A substantial number of people have converted to evangelical Protestantism (about 25–30%).

Chief Commercial Products: Coffee, cotton, bananas, corn and other agricultural products.

Currency: *Quetzal.*

Gross Domestic Product: U.S.$23.3 billion in 2002 ($2,068 per capita, about $300 among those of Mayan descent).

Former Colonial Status: Spanish Crown Colony (1524–1821).

Independence Date: September 15, 1821.

Chief of State: Oscar Berger Perdomo (b. August 11, 1946), president (since January 14, 2004).

National Flag: Blue, white and blue vertical stripes with national crest in the center white stripe.

Guatemala, the most populous of the Central American republics, is a mountainous highland bordered by coastal plains in the North and South. The southern Pacific coast plain is a 200-mile ribbon of land reaching a maximum of 30 miles in width. The highland rises abruptly from this plain to an elevation of 8,000 to 10,000 feet with a string of volcanoes on the southern rim. Three of these volcanoes are above 13,000 feet and three of them are still quite active.

The highland is interspersed with basins ranging from 5,000 to 8,000 feet in elevation, which are the most heavily populated regions of Guatemala. The northeastern lowlands are more extensive than the southern, and include the valleys of the Motagua River, which originates in the southern volcanoes and flows 185 miles into the Gulf of Honduras; the Polochic River drains the more westerly mountains

along a 200-mile course into Lake Izabal, a salty lagoon extending some 50 miles west from the Gulf of Honduras.

The Petén, a low, poorly drained plain, extending north 100 miles into the Yucatán Peninsula, is heavily forested and sparsely populated.

History: Guatemala was conquered by Spanish forces from Mexico in 1523 and the first Spanish settlement was established in 1524. Finding little precious metal and a land peopled by a sedentary agricultural folk, the Spanish governor rapidly lost interest in the region. Left to their own devices, the Spanish settlers intermarried with the Indians. The missionaries sought to Christianize the Mayas, whose culture began many centuries before the birth of Christ. The fertile mountain valleys were developed into semi-independent estates worked by virtually enslaved Indians. The majority of the Maya, Quiché and other peoples of Mayan origin simply withdrew from the Spanish-speaking community and maintained their traditional way of life. The efforts of the missionaries to Christianize the Indians did not fully displace their pagan gods—rather, the Indians tended to add the Christian God to their own deities.

Before independence, the Captaincy-General of Guatemala included the modern Central American states and the southern provinces of present-day Mexico. Sparsely settled by the Spanish, the region contained subdued tribes in the highlands and poor settlements on the Pacific coast, while the Caribbean coast was in the hands of buccaneers, native Indians who had retained their independence and a few illegal British settlers.

Augustín de Iturbide, emperor of Mexico, invited the patriot committee of Guatemala to join Mexico in 1821. Despite considerable opposition, the Central American states were annexed in 1822; with Iturbide's abdication in 1823 they declared themselves independent. The northern state of Chiapas elected to remain with Mexico; Soconusco later joined that nation in 1842.

The independent states formed a federation known as the United Provinces of Central America. Two parties appeared in the formation of a government—the *Serviles* (conservatives) who wanted a strong central government and close ties with the Church, and the *Radicales*, who favored a federal republic and curtailment of the privileges of the landowners and the clergy. A constitution based on that of the United States was adopted and a liberal president was installed. The liberal-conservative conflict resulted in a series of wars, and the confederation collapsed in 1838.

Independence and Dictatorship

From the time of dissolution of the union to 1944, Guatemala was ruled by four dictators. The first was Rafael Carrera (1838–65), who was an illiterate but popular *mestizo* leader, beloved by the Indians, but a religious fanatic of conservative persuasion. Hating liberals, he intervened in neighboring countries, seeking the overthrow of liberal presidents. After his death, another conservative was elected, but liberal Justo Rufino Barrios gained control of the government in 1871 and ruled until his death in 1885 in the battle of Chalchuapa, El Salvador, while trying to reunite Central America by military force. A man of progressive ideas, Rufino fostered public education, built railroads and achieved a measure of economic development. He also curtailed the privileges of the landowners and destroyed the political power of the clergy. Manuel Estrada Cabrera (1897–1920), a cultured but ruthless man, ruled as a despot with no effort to conceal his absolute power. Jorge Ubico came to power in 1931 and ruled until 1944. Honest and hard-working, he suppressed the previous corruption in government, bolstered the economy and carried out many social reforms of benefit to the laboring classes.

Opposition to Ubico's strict discipline resulted in public disorder and he ultimately resigned in the so-called "October Revolution" in 1944. Following two short-lived military governments, a liberal intellectual, Juan José Arévalo, was elected president in a genuinely free election, taking office in 1945. He implemented a number of reforms, including social security, university autonomy and labor laws, and

Panorama of Guatemala City with the civic center in the foreground

is still remembered as one of Guatemala's most enlightened presidents.

In the elections of 1950, Jacobo Arbenz Guzmán won as the candidate for the Revolutionary Action and National Regeneration parties. Inexperienced, with a government infiltrated by communists, he was overthrown in 1954 by Colonel Carlos Castillo Armas in a coup promoted by the U.S. CIA. Basically corrupt and ineffective, the latter was assassinated in 1957 in the presidential residence.

Following inconclusive elections, Miguel Idígoras Fuentes was appointed president in 1958; also corrupt and arrogant, he was in turn overthrown by a military coup in 1963. Colonel Enrique Peralta Azúrdia, who assumed the power of chief of state, suspended the constitution, dismissed Congress and ruled by decree until 1966 when in free and apparently honest elections, Julio César Méndez Montenegro, a liberal, was elected. This was an effort to return constitutional government to Guatemala. In reality, it was the beginning of

General Jorge Ubico

20 years of military-dominated governments. It was also in the 1960s that a guerrilla insurgency began that lasted until 1996.

The single most impressive accomplishment of President Méndez Montenegro was his ability to stay in office until the end of his term. Beset by radicals and powerful conservatives, Méndez was forced to abandon reform programs and concentrate instead on pleasing traditionally powerful elements.

With virtual civil war between rightwing and leftist extremists continuing unabated, voters turned to conservative Colonel Carlos Arana in the 1970 presidential elections. Promising "bread and peace," the noted counter-insurgency expert nearly wiped out the leftist guerrilla movement by indiscriminately repressing all opposition political groups. His term

was marked by a reduction in political violence and improved economic conditions.

As the 1974 presidential elections approached, the military stipulated that any candidate would be acceptable—so long as he was in the armed forces. The ruling coalition thus nominated as its candidate the moderate former defense minister, General Kjell (pronounced "shell") Eugenio Laugerud García of the *Partido Institucional Democrático (PID)*. But when the early election returns gave National Opposition Front candidate Brigadier General Efraín Ríos Montt a formidable lead, the government suddenly halted the tabulation. Several days later the regime announced that its own candidate, Laugerud, had won with 41% of the vote. Although such blatant fraud caused an uproar, the military refused to permit a recount.

The election also catapulted Ríos Montt into national prominence and notoriety, where he remains to this day.

Relations between the new president and ultra-conservative elements in the ruling coalition—led by former President Arana and the right-wing *Movimiento de Liberación Nacional (MLN)*—soon began to sour when Laugerud suggested mild reforms to ease the plight of the impoverished highland Indians. The *MLN*, representing the wealthy landowners, bitterly accused the president of being a communist when he encouraged the formation of rural peasant cooperatives to increase production from inefficient, small peasant plots.

Guatemala was devastated in early 1976 by one of the worst natural disasters of the 20th century when a violent earthquake in 17 of the nation's 22 provinces killed 24,000 people. In addition, 76,000 were injured and 1.5 million left homeless. Worst hit were provincial towns and highland Indian settlements, where peasant dwellings were not built to withstand an earthquake. Although large amounts of foreign aid quickly poured into the country, little of it filtered down to the peasants because of bureaucratic bungling and political corruption.

None of the presidential candidates received a majority of votes in the 1978 general elections. The government-supported candidate, General Fernando Romeo Lucas García, was later named the winner by Congress. The outcome was no monument to the democratic process: (1) the race was limited to military candidates, (2) fully 60% of the electorate ignored or boycotted the balloting and (3) only 35 of the eligible lawmakers participated in the congressional runoff vote. The new president promptly ordered an about-face on the previous administration's policy of supporting limited reforms. Thus began an all-out campaign against both moderates and leftists—a strategy that had failed

ousted, ultra-conservative regimes in neighboring El Salvador.

Right-wing paramilitary "death squads" such as the Secret Anti-Communist Army—which drew most of their support from army and police units—systematically wiped out thousands of government opponents. Key targets included student, labor, peasant and political leaders. During its four years in office, Lucas García's regime was widely regarded as the most repressive and corrupt in Latin America. London-based Amnesty International even accused the regime of operating "murder and torture" chambers in an annex of the Presidential Palace!

A report released in 1981 by the Human Rights Commission of the Organization of American States found that the Lucas García regime was responsible for the "great majority" of political murders in the country at the time. Evangelical Church officials estimated in Guatemala that at least 11,000 civilians died from political violence in 1981. The Catholic Church there reported that 200,000 Guatemalan peasants fled to neighboring Central American countries to escape the violence.

Many of the country's human rights violations were linked to the government's counter-insurgency program. In an attempt to halt rural support for the guerrillas, Lucas García sought to wipe out key segments of the Indian population. Such repression, however, induced many peasants to join the insurgents. As a result, warfare spread to seven provinces and the number of guerrillas increased from 1,500 in 1980 to about 4,000 in 1982.

General Fernando Romeo Lucas García

179

Guatemala

Because of Guatemala's dismal human rights record, the Carter administration in Washington halted most military and economic aid to the country in 1977. Lucas García angrily responded by rejecting all U.S. military assistance. The subsequent election of Ronald Reagan in the United States was warmly applauded by the supporters of the Guatemalan president, who hoped that Washington would resume assistance to their country. Yet, the Reagan administration also kept its distance, although $3.2 million in military aid was provided in 1981.

Unbridled repression by the regime was not limited to its battle against peasants and leftists. When moderate Christian Democracy (*DC*) party members urged in late 1980 that all political groups be allowed to participate in upcoming March 1982 elections, right-wing terrorists responded by assassinating 76 DC party members.

Not surprisingly, only conservatives dared to run for president in the March 7, 1982 elections. When the balloting failed to produce a winner with a majority, Congress voted to elect the government-supported candidate, General Angel Aníbal Guevara—who had received a bare 16% of the popular vote. The three losing candidates were arrested when they protested that the election was a fraud.

The 1982 Coup

On March 23, 1982, as the political crisis escalated, a core group of 20 junior officers in the barracks decided to vote with their guns. Early in the morning, they surrounded the Presidential Palace, forcing Lucas García to flee from a side door.

The bloodless coup was attributed to a variety of factors: (1) the administration's heavy-handed treatment of opponents had offended nearly all segments of the population, (2) the president-elect was seen as a clone of the unpopular Lucas García and (3) the rising dissatisfaction of junior officers in the army. Indeed, while these men were being sent to the field to fight against the guerrillas, senior officers were frequently given cushy jobs away from battle zones. The widespread corruption that permeated the regime and the military high command was galling, even by Guatemalan standards. Vast public works projects initiated by the regime seemed to have been created for the sole purpose of providing a source of graft for top government officials. The military was also top-heavy with *chiefs*, with seemingly few *Indians* left to do any fighting. Of the 900 or so officers in the Guatemalan army, fully 240 were colonels or generals!

The sudden ouster of the president created a temporary political vacuum; on the day of the coup three different *juntas* were proclaimed before the military finally settled on one led by retired Brigadier General Ríos Montt, then 55. His participation tended to give the *junta* some legitimacy, since Ríos Montt had probably won the 1974 elections, only to see the prize stolen from him.

Within hours of assuming power, the new *junta* annulled the March elections, abolished Congress, suspended the 1965 constitution, barred activities by political parties, reaffirmed Guatemala's age-old claim to Belize, arrested various civilians for corruption, ruled out elections in the near future and announced that the new government would rule by decree. In the hope of dealing with the country's insurgency problems, the *junta* proposed an amnesty plan to leftist guerrillas. When the offer was rejected, Ríos Montt ordered an all-out "final assault" against the guerrillas in mid-1982, wiping out about 400 villages in the process.

Finding the three-member *junta* cumbersome, Ríos Montt fired his partners in mid-1982 and proclaimed himself president—breaking his pledge not to do so when he first joined with his cohorts.

The new president was a curiosity. A "born-again" evangelical Christian, he loved to quote the Bible to friends and foes alike when enunciating government policy. Thus, when asked about the nation's civil strife, he answered that the best way to combat it was with "love." On Sundays he gave spiritual pep-talks on national television. He was fond of saying that he "had lunch with God today."

His moralistic approach produced some positive results. He ordered a rare public campaign against corruption and cracked down on right-wing paramilitary vigilante groups. As a result, violent urban

General José Efraín Ríos Montt

General Oscar Humberto Mejía Victores

crime subsided somewhat, although political violence continued unabated in the countryside. Impressed by his efforts to reduce human rights violations, the Reagan administration offered Guatemala $4.5 million in military aid and $50 million in economic assistance in 1982.

Ríos Montt's grip on the presidency was tenuous. Some powerful elements in the military opposed his anti-corruption campaign which reduced lucrative supplementary income sources for high-ranking officials. Others disliked his moralistic approach, dubbing him "Ayatollah." His anti-Catholic stand made him extremely unpopular among members of that religion. General Oscar Humberto Mejía Victores overthrew the Ríos Montt regime in mid-1983 and proclaimed himself president.

Democracy Returns

Mejía promised a return to democracy. Elections for a constituent assembly were held in mid-1984; 71% of the electorate voted, which remains the record voter turnout. The *DC* appeared to be the most popular, although by a slim margin. A new constitution was adopted on May 31, 1985, and all political parties began preparing for congressional and presidential elections that November.

In honest elections, Vinicio Cerezo, a Christian Democrat who proclaimed himself "left of center", won the presidency—a dubious honor. During the military years, immense debts were run up and the treasury was empty. The International Monetary Fund suspended loan agreements. Military and state police death squads had caused the disappearance of about 100,000 people. Victorious leftists insisted on punishing the military, but Cerezo wisely established firm control and announced that although investigations would be conducted into violations of human rights, no punishments would result, infuriating many of his supporters. Mejía had decreed a general amnesty for the military during his final days in office. Underlining this, during the first three weeks of civilian government, five dozen bodies, some mutilated, were scattered throughout the country. More selective killings followed.

But "Vinicio," as the then-popular young president was known, carefully planned and executed a single raid and mass arrest of the Department of Technical Investigation, a military unit devoted to "counter-insurgency." Two hundred agents were fired and 400 were dispatched for "additional training." The message: the military was not always sacred. Substantial changes in military leadership were made in 1986–87.

A committee on human rights was formed. But the civilian government had the same problems experienced in Argentina and most lately in El Salvador: self-protection by the military. The matter was "resolved" when the Supreme Court issued more than a thousand writs of habeas corpus. As might have been expected, no one had any genuine desire to go around digging up dead bodies.

The right-wing military, police and vigilante groups did not have a monopoly on cruel violence. Three left-wing guerrilla groups joined into the Guatemalan National Revolutionary Union (*URNG*); in 1990 they moved their operations from remote, rural areas and were operating in the more populous regions around Guatemala City. They were bold enough to stop traffic on the Pan-American Highway to collect "taxes."

Talks were held in Madrid in 1987 between the government and rebel representatives. The rebels were down to 1,000 men (vs. a high of 10,000) and only operated in remote, rural areas where they were equally despised by local Indian inhabitants, who just wanted to be left alone by everyone. The talks lasted through 1988 and were inconclusive.

Military coups were aborted without violence in 1988 and 1989. But murders and disappearances at the hand of right-wing groups continued at the rate of more than 1,000 a year. Cerezo's popularity dwindled as his inability to control the military became increasingly apparent; further, he justifiably acquired the reputation of being a playboy, spending much of his time during the week away from the capital.

The country was in a state of near-anarchy by 1990. Countless paramilitary groups and the army operated freely, murdering at will virtually anyone suspected of being a leftist, the definition of which sometimes included anyone found outside after dark at night. In this setting, Ríos Montt campaigned in the 1990 elections on a "no-nonsense" platform; he was ruled ineligible under the 1986 constitution in a provision probably directed against him.

Jorge Serrano Elías, a fellow evangelical Protestant, was elected president in a January 1991. About one third bothered to vote, losing faith in the idea that things could be changed by the ballot box. He pledged to end the 30-year-old civil war. This proved to be impossible.

Moreover, while Cerezo had proved inept, Serrano proved venal and power-hungry. In May 1993, he attempted to effect a Fujimori-style "self coup" that initially had the backing of the armed forces. Serrano announced that he was dissolving Congress and ruling by decree on the familiar pretext that only in this way could he come to grips with the serious socioeconomic problems facing the country. To make sure the Guatemalan people received only the information he wanted them to, he imposed prior censorship on the print and broadcast media, which immediately began collaborating with one another to outwit the censors and get information to the public.

For a week, it appeared that Guatemala would experience a throwback to the bad old days of strongman rule. But thousands of demonstrators flooded the streets of the capital to protest Serrano's power grab, among them such eminent figures as 1992 Nobel Peace Prize Laureate Rigoberta Minchú and U.N. Human Rights Ombudsman Ramiro de León Carpio. Moreover, the U.S. State Department hinted not very subtly that aid to Guatemala would likely evaporate. Simultaneously, the Constitutional Court declared Serrano's actions illegal. The armed forces quickly realized that they were backing the wrong side and refused further to support the coup attempt. For a change, the military found itself hailed as a champion of democracy! Serrano fled the country to a life of luxurious exile in Panama with an estimated $20 million in "retirement funds" from the treasury. (Guatemala is still trying unsuccessfully to have Serrano extradited.) The Congress then named de León Carpio interim president, which proved to be a sound choice. As was the case with the interim presidency of Gerald Ford after the power abuses of Richard Nixon, de León Carpio proved fair and just, albeit a bit lackluster.

Legislative elections in mid-1994 (14% voted) resulted in a plurality for the Guatemalan Republican Front (*FRG*) led by Ríos Montt, who became president of the Congress. Four other parties split the remainder of the 80-seat body. But the *FRG* repeatedly found itself outmaneuvered by the other parties in Congress.

Most of the next two years in Guatemala were even more turbulent than ever. The president turned to the army for support, which may, itself, have tried to oust him in 1994. General fighting continued in spite of an agreement ending it—an agreement to keep on negotiating, in reality. The U.S. State Department warned tourists to avoid Guatemala; about 400 Peace Corps volunteers took shelter in Guatemala City. Torture and murder remained commonplace.

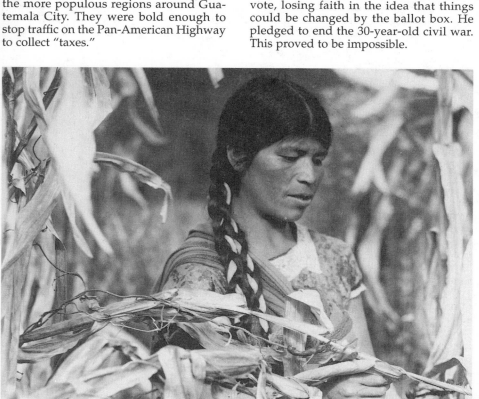

Woman picking corn World Bank Photo

Guatemala

Former President Ramiro de León Carpio

In November 1995, 12 candidates vied for president, whose term had been reduced from five to four years. The top two vote-getters were former Guatemala City Mayor Alvaro Arzú of the Party of National Advancement (*PAN*), and Alfonso Portillo of the *FRG*, the political vehicle of the still-popular Ríos Montt, whom the Constitutional Court again had ruled could not run. The court also prohibited the former strongman's wife from running, leaving Portillo as the stand-in candidate. Portillo unabashedly declared that Ríos Montt would serve in a high-level advisory capacity if he were elected.

Polls indicated that Arzú would win the January 1996 runoff in a landslide, but he squeaked into office with only 52% of the vote; he lost 18 of the 21 departments outside his power base in the capital, an indicator of the lingering popular appeal of Ríos Montt. Arzú's *PAN* won 43 of the 80 seats in the unicameral Congress, though Ríos Montt's *FRG* remained a potent opposition. The *URNG*, in its first test at the polls, elected two deputies.

The Arzú Presidency and Peace

The new president pledged to respect human rights and insisted, not altogether convincingly, that the armed forces would be subordinate to the civilian authority. However, Arzú was mainstream enough, coming from a wealthy and prominent business family, that he posed no threat to the generals and seemed adept at working with them.

Above all else, Arzú pledged to continue the peace talks and see them through to fruition. The two sides met throughout 1996 in Mexico City and finally reached an historic truce, though some grumbled over the amnesty given to members of the security forces for past human rights abuses. On December 27, 1996, several Latin American presidents and UN Secretary-General Boutros Boutros-Ghali came to Guatemala City to witness the momentous signing of the accords that ended Central America's longest civil war. The peace seems to have taken hold, with no serious violations by either side. The war-weary country at last had reason for some optimism regarding its future.

Arzú, smooth and charming while courting votes, proved ornery and arrogant as president. Days after his inauguration in January 1996, an incident occurred that soured his already stormy relationship with the press. While Arzú was horseback riding near Antigua, a milk truck suddenly headed toward him. Halted by the bodyguards, the driver fled from the vehicle. The bodyguards then opened fire, killing him. The presidential palace described the incident as an assassination attempt. But when the media looked deeper, they concluded that the driver was a drunken milkman who had panicked. A furious Arzú accused the media, most of which were critical of him, of attempting to discredit him.

The incident could have been dismissed as the tragi-comic case of a thin-skinned president, except that Arzú took measures aimed at curtailing the independent press. He used the government-subsidized television program, *Avances*, as a vehicle to vilify his editorial critics in the press and investigative reporting that had proved embarrassing to his administration.

Not content with rebutting criticism, which was his right in a democratic society, Arzú resorted to a more sinister method to silence his critics. According to the Inter American Press Association, Arzú cajoled wealthy friends to stop advertising in specified print media, particularly the country's leading daily, *Prensa Libre*, and the weekly newsmagazine *Crónica*. For business people who were not his friends, he extended a Godfather-like offer: Stop advertising, or face tax audits. For a time, he succeeded in driving away about 80 advertisers. *Prensa Libre* was too economically viable to be seriously hurt by the campaign, but *Crónica* was driven to the point of bankruptcy. In November 1998, *Crónica* was bought out by a group of businessmen loyal to Arzú; its editorial staff was fired and its editorial tone changed overnight.

On the positive side, the peace process took hold during the Arzú administration, although the public found itself polarized between those who demanded justice for past atrocities and those who preferred to forget the horrors of the past. Unfortunately, horrors kept occurring.

**Former President
Alvaro Enrique Arzú Irigoyen**

The Gerardi Murder

In April 1998, a Roman Catholic bishop, Juan José Gerardi Conedera, head of the church's human rights office, released a controversial report that laid the blame for most of the human rights abuses squarely at the feet of the army. Days later, on April 26, Gerardi was found bludgeoned to death in his quarters. The crime stunned the country and reverberated abroad.

The official, secular investigation into the murder resembled a Keystone Kops farce. First, a local drunk who had been a laborer for Gerardi was arrested, but eventually was released for lack of evidence. Then authorities arrested a priest and accused him of killing Gerardi in a homosexual crime of passion. At the same time, police arrested the bishop's cook and accused her of complicity in the crime. After five days, both were released. To make this comic-opera spectacle complete, the suspect priest's dog was "arrested" on suspicion of mauling Gerardi to death. However, Gerardi's body was exhumed for a second autopsy, which ruled out the canine theory. In a touch of irony worthy of a Greek comedy, Gerardi's successor as head of the church's human rights office was none other than Bishop Mario Ríos Montt, brother of the former strongman.

The Gerardi investigation ground on throughout 1999, largely because of intense public and media pressure, domestic and international. That August, authorities announced a break in the case, stating

The author interviews Nobel Laureate Rigoberta Menchú in Guatemala City, December 1999.

Photo by Mario Antonio Sandoval

that DNA from blood samples taken at the scene matched one of the suspects. Still, there were no arrests.

Guatemalan public opinion already had indicted the same culprit that Gerardi had named: the army. These suspicions were intensified in October, when the prosecutor in the case, who had been following the military lead, fled to the United States because of death threats. It wasn't until January 2000, days after the change of presidential administrations, that the priest and the cook were arrested again, along with three army personnel.

In January 2001, police arrested army Captain Byron Lima Oliva and his father, retired Colonel Disrael Lima Estrada, in connection with the Gerardi murder. Police also rearrested Gerardi's cook and issued a warrant for the priest, Mario Orantes, both of whom had been arrested and released in 1998. An intelligence NCO with the presidential guard, Sergeant Major José Obdulio Villanueva, was arrested the next day. It was Villanueva who had killed the milkman in 1996, for which he had been sentenced to five years in prison but arranged to pay a $1,500 fine instead. Orantes was arrested on February 9 when he returned from the United States to face the charges. A judge subsequently freed Villanueva on February 28 because of an apparently ironclad alibi. He was later rearrested, but another year passed before the four accused men went on trial in March 2002.

The trial absorbed Guatemala's attention—and that of human rights activists

around the world—before the historic verdicts were handed down on June 8, 2002: guilty! The judge sentenced the two Limas and Villanueva to 30 years and Orantes to 20; the cook was acquitted.

The elation of human rights groups over the conviction proved short-lived, however. Six weeks later, the judge fled the country because of death threats. In September 2002, the four convicted men formally appealed, and on October 8 an appeals court overturned their convictions and ordered a new trial, ostensibly because of questionable testimony from one eyewitness. They were not set free, however. On February 12, 2003, Villanueva was killed and decapitated when rival gangs of inmates at his prison north of the capital went on a rampage. It took 800 riot police to quell the disturbance.

Quest for Justice

Some measure of justice for past atrocities also was meted out in November 1998, when three former members of an army-organized civilian militia force were convicted and sentenced to death by lethal injection for their roles in the so-called Rio Negro Massacre in March 1982—during the first days of the Ríos Montt regime—in which 130 Indian peasants were slain. An appeals court overturned the sentences, but they were reinstated in October 1999.

Guatemala moved even closer to its long-sought catharsis on February 26, 1999, when the three-member Historical Clari-

fication Commission issued its report after 18 months of investigation into the human rights abuses committed during the civil war. The panel was headed by a German judge, Christian Tomuschat, and included a Guatemalan lawyer, Edgar Balsells, and a Mayan teacher, Otilia Lux de Coti. Among its more controversial findings, the commission concluded that more than 200,000 people had been killed during the course of the civil war; that there had been 42,000 individual human rights violations, 29,000 of them fatal; that 92% of these violations had been committed by the army; and that U.S. businesses and the CIA had pressured the successive Guatemalan governments into suppressing the guerrilla movement by ruthless means, particularly when Ríos Montt was in power.

When the commission presented its report at the National Theater before a crowd of about 2,000 people, mostly relatives of victims, the crowd chanted, *"justicia! justicia!"* President Arzú dutifully attended the ceremony and shook hands with the commission members, but studiously avoided accepting a copy of the report, citing "protocol." This led to catcalls from the crowd for him to accept the report. Some observers concluded that Arzú's actions were intended to distance the government from the report. Just days later, President Clinton visited Guatemala during his tour of countries affected by Hurricane Mitch and, while stopping short of a formal apology, expressed "regret" for the United States' role in the human rights abuses.

The quest for justice became an international issue in December 1999 when Guatemala's most illustrious human rights champion, 1992 Nobel Peace Laureate Rigoberta Menchú, flew to Madrid to file a lawsuit before the Spanish Supreme Court against eight past military and civilian figures, including former military strongmen Ríos Montt, Lucas García and Mejía Victores. It was the same court that had requested the extradition of former Chilean dictator Augusto Pinochet from Britain for alleged human rights abuses.

This author interviewed Menchú in Guatemala that December shortly before she returned to Spain to testify. She explained that she chose Spain because it had shown its commitment to human rights in the Pinochet case and others. (Ironically, Ríos Montt had served as Guatemala's military attaché to Spain during the 1970s, a consolation prize for having been cheated out of the presidency in the fraudulent 1974 election.) Asked whether her action prevents Ríos Montt from traveling abroad without facing arrest, she replied, "Well, Guatemala is a beautiful country. It's not a terrible punishment never being able to leave."

Guatemala

Alfonso Portillo addresses an *FRG* rally a week before the December 26, 1999, runoff.

Photo by the author

Among Menchú's complaints is the assault by security forces on the Spanish Embassy in Guatemala on January 31, 1980 after it was seized by guerrillas. In the ensuing fire, 39 Spanish diplomats and guerrillas perished, including Menchú's father. She also cites the deaths of her mother and two brothers between 1980 and 1982, and for the deaths of four Spanish priests during the same period. Menchú's eyes filled with tears as she explained that her mother's remains were never found. "I just want to recover my mother's bones and give her a decent burial," she said. Asked if a dialogue between her and Ríos Montt were possible, she said bitterly, "I'd have to wait 2,000 years."

Another milestone in the quest for justice was reached in October 2002 when Colonel Juan Valencia, a former assistant director of the presidential guard, was convicted and sentenced to 30 years for ordering the 1990 murder of U.S. anthropologist and human rights activist Myrna Mack. Two of his superiors, however, were acquitted, much to the chagrin of human rights advocates. In an astonishing and unprecedented gesture of atonement, the Guatemalan government officially acknowledged to the Inter-American Human Rights Commission in Costa Rica in February 2003 that the government bore "institutional responsibility" for Mack's death. However, the country's human rights record continued to come under international scrutiny.

The Elections of 1999

In politics, the country's attention was focused in 1999 on both a referendum, called the *"Consulta Popular,"* held on May 16 to ratify the constitutional changes agreed upon in the peace agreement between the government and the guerrillas, and on the upcoming presidential election. In the *Consulta Popular,* there was an almost unprecedented consensus reached among the *PAN*, the *FRG* and the *URNG*. About 50 complex issues were boiled down to four separate referendum items, including a restructuring of the role of the armed forces in society and the granting of far greater cultural and political autonomy to the indigenous Mayas. Voters were asked to vote *sí o no,* and the results stunned the country's political establishment. Only about 18% of the electorate bothered to vote, and those who did rejected all the initiatives by more than a 2–1 margin. The voters seemed to be saying they were not quite ready for their society to be overhauled by politicians. But with a turnout of 18%, it was clear most Guatemalans didn't care one way or the other.

In the presidential race, Alfonso Portillo, the Ríos Montt stand-in who almost upset Arzú in the 1996 runoff, was renominated as the *FRG*'s candidate. He had been campaigning for three years, as had Ríos Montt on his behalf. The aging strongman has demonstrated that he still has a charismatic appeal with the masses, albeit not among the rural Mayans against whom he had waged genocide.

The *PAN*, meanwhile, dutifully nominated Arzú's hand-picked choice, Guatemala City Mayor Oscar Berger, who quickly had a falling-out with the president when he demonstrated he intended to be his own man, not a puppet as Portillo was to Ríos Montt. Berger then withdrew his candidacy, declaring that his decision was "irreversible." Arzú huffily responded that he had plenty of candidates to choose from, but, in fact, he didn't, at least not one with any chance of winning. The party regulars prevailed upon Berger to reconsider.

The *URNG* experienced intra-party bickering between moderates and hardliners, eventually nominating a moderate, Alvaro Colom, an Indian rights advocate and nephew of a well-known leftist politician and mayor of Guatemala City who was assassinated during the presidency of Lucas García. An engineer, Colom himself is of pure Caucasian blood. The *URNG* became part of a left-wing coalition called the New Nation Alliance (*ANN*).

The campaign for the round of voting on November 7, 1999, took an interesting twist in July when Portillo was asked during a television interview about rumors that he had killed a man when he was living in exile in Mexico during the military regime. "That isn't true," he replied; "I killed two." He explained that while teaching at a school in the state of Guerrero in 1982 he had become involved in a local political dispute and that when two members of the rival faction attacked him with firearms, he killed them both with a pistol. The Mexican authorities eventually dropped the charges against Portillo.

Berger (pronounced bear-ZHAY), who is of Belgian descent, was quick to try to make political capital out of this confession, but the polls showed that it had no effect on public opinion. If anything, in fact, Portillo's candor (and perhaps the obvious *macho* factor of an outnumbered

Too young to vote, two children attend a campaign rally with their father

Photo by the author

Guatemala

man killing two assailants) may have helped him, because he pulled ahead of Berger in the polls.

This author spent 10 days in Guatemala during August observing the campaign and interviewing the three major candidates, as well as people from all social classes, as a free-lance journalist. It became obvious to me that voters were more concerned about the blatant corruption and cronyism of the Arzú administration and about the sour economy than they were about a 17-year-old incident in Mexico or the possible influence of Ríos Montt.

Portillo received a stunning endorsement in August when former President de León Carpio declared his support for him and said he would be a candidate for Congress on the *FRG*'s proportional representation list. In an interview at his home, de León conceded to me that the *FRG* is blemished by its association with Ríos Montt, "but above all I believe in Portillo's capacity to deal with the economic and social crisis. I am more for Alfonso Portillo than for the *FRG*. He has opened the doors of the party program and agenda, and he has a very sound policy." Of de León's endorsement of Portillo, Berger told me, "I think he has damaged himself more than us. I think it's a serious wound for him, a stain to his reputation."

Apart from the polls, I could sense unscientifically the shift in public opinion since the last election toward Portillo, whom the public called *"Pollo Ronco,"* or "Hoarse Chicken," because of his raspy, Godfather-like voice. When I asked people on the street in poor towns who they would vote for, most were too frightened to answer, but others replied simply, *"la manita,"* or the little hand, referring to the *FRG*'s blue party symbol of a hand with the thumb and first two fingers extended, representing "welfare, security and justice." Others responded by holding up a hand with the thumb and two fingers extended. (Party symbols appear on the ballot because of the high illiteracy rate.)

On November 7, an unexpectedly high 53% turned out to vote. Portillo almost won an outright victory, receiving 48% to 30% for Berger and 12% for Colom; nine lesser candidates split the remainder. The *FRG* won an absolute majority in the newly expanded Congress, winning 63 of the 113 seats and ensuring Ríos Montt's return to the president's chair. (His daughter, Zury, was No. 2 on the party's proportional representation list of deputies.) The *PAN* won 37 seats, the *ANN* but nine. In addition to former presidents Ríos Montt and de León Carpio, former President Cerezo was elected to Congress as one of the *DC*'s two deputies.

The campaign for the *segunda vuelta* on December 26 seemed almost anticlimactic,

as polls showed a Portillo victory inevitable. It drew international attention, however, because of Menchú's lawsuit against Ríos Montt and others. This author spent eight days in Guatemala in December and again interviewed the two candidates.

When I asked Portillo about what impact the lawsuit would have, he said, "None. None. It's a show. There's not a country in the world that can judge something that happened in Guatemala. Rigoberta Menchú doesn't even have followers in her hometown so she's looking for some in Europe. It's a show. Ask her people why I got 48 percent of the vote."

Portillo acknowledged candidly, however, that he was seen internationally as the surrogate of a former dictator. "The people in human rights circles don't believe my speeches," he said. "All I ask is, give me the benefit of the doubt. Judge me by my actions." He also assured me in the taped interview that he would "not tolerate harassment of the press" by members of his government, something for which Arzú was notorious. It was a promise he would break.

Although Berger spoke valiantly in public of scoring an upset, in the interview with me he appeared resigned to defeat. "We're going to be a constructive opposition," he said, adding prophetically, "not the kind of opposition they were. Anyway, it's only for four years, then the voters will do the same thing to them they did to us."

Because the runoff was held the day after Christmas, voter turnout was predictably much lower than it had been on November 7: 40.9% of the 4,458,744 registered voters. Nonetheless, Portillo won by the anticipated landslide: 1,184,932 of the valid votes, or 68.32%, to 549,407 votes, or 31.68% for Berger. A total of 4.79% of the votes cast had been blank or were voided. Portillo thus became the first Guatemalan presidential candidate to poll more than 1 million votes.

The Portillo Presidency

The 48-year-old Portillo was inaugurated on January 14, 2000, joining a growing list of Latin American presidents who won on their second attempts. In his address, he vowed to fulfill reforms promised in the peace accords, which the Arzú government had failed to implement, and he pledged to bring the killers of Bishop Gerardi to justice, calling the failure to do so after two years a "disgrace."

Just four days after his inauguration, Portillo stunned both the Guatemalan political and military establishments as well as the international community by appointing as defense minister a mere

Former President Alfonso Portillo

colonel, Juan de Dios Estrada, who had participated in the peace negotiations with the guerrillas, replacing a hardliner who was himself suspected of human rights abuses. In naming Estrada, Portillo bypassed 19 generals and one admiral. Under military regulations, a lower-ranking officer cannot give orders to a superior officer, meaning that the 20 officers of star rank on active service were forced to retire or to be placed on leave. However, he later appointed Ríos Montt's son to command the army.

Simultaneously, and equally as significant, Portillo announced that Estrada's appointment was only temporary, until Congress acted on a military reform package he had introduced that would allow him to appoint a civilian as defense minister. The reforms also would abolish the elite presidential guard, which had been blamed for numerous human rights abuses, including the shooting of the unfortunate milkman in 1996; it was also the prime suspect in Gerardi's murder. The reforms were assured of approval when Ríos Montt agreed to support them.

In March 2000, in another apparent effort to assert his sincerity on the human rights issue and to distance himself from Ríos Montt, Portillo proposed that Congress establish April 22—the anniversary of the Gerardi murder—as the National Day of Dignity for Victims of Violence. However, not only did this proposal meet immediate resistance from many *FRG* congressional deputies whose first loyalty was to Ríos Montt, but also from human rights groups. The Rigoberta Menchú Foundation ridiculed the proposal as a "political ploy."

Guatemala

As many had expected, Portillo and his mentor, Ríos Montt, soon became tangled in a power struggle within the *FRG*, in both the executive and legislative branches. In September 2000, Ríos Montt and 22 other *FRG* deputies were caught up in a scandal, gleefully reported in the press, involving the illegal altering of the percentage on a revenue bill on liquor from 20% to 10%—after it had passed. When the press reported the discrepancy, Ríos Montt and the other deputies vehemently denied they had changed the figure, but a reporter for the daily *Prensa Libre* produced an audio-tape of a committee meeting in which the amount had been set at 10%. The press immediately dubbed the scandal "Booze-gate." Portillo apparently was not involved, but the allegations against the members of his party embarrassed him

The power struggle continued into 2001. Portillo vetoed five bills supported by Ríos Montt; in apparent retribution, Congress slashed the appropriations for the ministries headed by members of the Portillo faction of the party.

Portillo's image was further tarnished in March 2002 when the daily newspaper *Siglo Veintiuno* and the Panamanian daily *La Prensa,* reported they had documentation that the president and Vice President Francisco Reyes had used dummy companies to open Panamanian bank accounts in 2001 designed to receive $1.5 million monthly in deposits. Days later, 3,000 protesters banging pots and pans demonstrated in front of the government palace demanding that Portillo and Reyes resign. Portillo denied the allegations, calling them a smear campaign by the oligarchy.

On April 16, 2002, former President de León Carpio died at an apartment he owned in Miami, apparently of a heart attack after he lapsed into a diabetic coma. He had created controversy in the 1999 election by being elected to Congress as a deputy of Ríos Montt's *FRG*. Just three weeks before his death, de León resigned from the *FRG* and publicly declared his affiliation to have been "a mistake."

Even as it seemed some degree of justice was beginning to be meted out for past atrocities with the convictions in the Gerardi and Mack murders (see Quest for Justice), those atrocities kept on surfacing—literally. In September 2002, the bodies of 47 people, apparently Indian peasants massacred during the civil war, were unearthed from a mass grave found beneath a school in Rabinal, 120 miles north of the capital.

Meanwhile, human rights advocates continued to fault Portillo for failing to keep his promise to abolish the presidential guard. At first, he merely embellished the guard with 70 trained civilians. Sensitive to criticism on the guard issue, Por-tillo used the occasion of the sixth anniversary of the signing of the peace accords in December 2002 to announce that the presidential guard had been reduced by 25%, that half the remaining members would be reassigned to other duties and that the guard would be removed from army control. The changes were to have been completed by July 2003. They were not.

Murders or death threats continued with seeming impunity against human rights advocates. In 2001, the international rights group Amnesty International told the Reuters wire service that threats against human rights workers in Guatemala had increased on Portillo's watch. The very next day, a member of Amnesty International was attacked in her hotel room. She was left gagged and drugged on a fire escape.

On April 29, 2002, Guillermo Ovalle, an administrator of the Rigoberta Menchú Foundation, was slain in a hail of automatic weapons fire in broad daylight at a takeout restaurant in the capital. Authorities maintained—as they had in the Gerardi murder almost four years to the day earlier—that it was a common crime, an apparent robbery attempt. That same month, human rights workers excavating the mass graves of victims of army massacres in the 1980s began receiving death threats. Then, in December 2002, two prominent Indian rights activists, Antonio Pop and Diego Velásquez Brito, were abducted and murdered. Also in December, Indian rights activist Amilcar Méndez was fired upon and robbed by assailants who knew his name. In January 2003, the UN Human Rights Commission in Geneva called on the Guatemalan government to bring the killers of Pop and Velásquez to justice.

According to Sergio Morales, the UN human rights ombudsman in Guatemala, there were 70 murders, attempted murders or death threats against human rights workers in 2002.

In 1999, Portillo had told this author that human rights groups should "judge me by my actions." They did.

On a brighter note, Pope John Paul II made his third—and last— visit to Guatemala in late July 2002 for the purpose of canonizing Pedro de San José Betancur (1619–67), son of a shepherd in the Canary Islands, who lived humbly in Antigua, Guatemala and who became a Franciscan brother and preached to prison inmates. He also raised money for orphans, established a hospital for the poor and founded the Antigua-based Bethlehemite Congregation. His grave in Antigua is a place of pilgrimage, and thousands have claimed miracles were granted after touching the tomb.

Ríos Montt was rudely reminded that he is not universally popular on June 14, 2003, when he traveled to the remote mountain town of Rabinal to attend an *FRG* meeting. His timing was unfortunate, but apparently deliberate, as local Mayas were preparing to rebury the remains of 66 people slain during the civil war that had recently been excavated from a mass grave. When Ríos Montt arrived, the furious Indians began hurling rocks at him. He escaped unhurt, and with a touch of bitter irony, his legislator-daughter Zury termed the stoning incident a "violation of human rights."

The Elections of 2003

Berger sought the *PAN* nomination again in 2003, with the business sector uniting behind him to try to stave off an-

Guatemalans queue up to vote in the town of Livingston on the Caribbean coast.
Photo by the author

186

other *FRG* victory. But the party broke up into three factions, with the party regulars nominating Leonel López Rodas, who had labored to keep the party afloat after Berger's poor showing in the 1999 runoff. A faction loyal to former President Arzú split off and resurrected an old party, the Unionist Party *(PU)*, choosing as its candidate Guatemala City Mayor Fritz Garcia-Gallont. Berger became the candidate of three tiny parties that comprised the Grand National Alliance *(GANA)*. Colom entered the race as well, this time as head of a coalition of left-wing parties called the National Union of Hope *(UNE)*. There were also six minor candidates.

That left the *FRG*. With the judicial appointments Portillo had made over three and a half years, Ríos Montt, by then 77, embarked on a Machiavellian maneuver to circumvent the constitution through the courts and run for the presidency. He declared his candidacy, but in June the Supreme Electoral Tribunal barred him from running, the courts already having declared him ineligible in 1990 and 1996. He appealed to the Supreme Court, which upheld the electoral tribunal's decision. He then appealed to the Constitutionality Court, which for the first time had a majority of *FRG* justices. In a stunning reversal, the Constitutionality Court voted 4-2 on July 14 to allow his candidacy.

Ríos Montt's opponents appealed that decision back to the Supreme Court, which granted a stay. What happened next shocked the country and the world, and may have turned the tide irreversibly against Ríos Montt. In an obviously well-orchestrated show of force, hundreds of pro-*FRG* peasants were bused to the capital from the country in exchange for a promise of $40 and three meals a day for two days. They were issued clubs and ski masks.

On Thursday, July 24, they went on a rampage, erecting barricades, burning tires, smashing store windows and demonstrating outside the Supreme Court and the Constitutionality Court. Without warning, they turned on the journalists covering the disturbances and began beating some of them or dousing them with gasoline. One, 65-year-old Héctor Ramírez, ironically with a pro-*FRG* television station, died of a heart attack while being chased by club-wielding goons. Through it all, the police failed to intervene. Under public pressure, President Portillo announced he would send in army troops to maintain order, but they never arrived. The disturbances, which the media named *Jueves Negro* (Black Thursday), spilled over into Friday. Then, Ríos Montt gave the order to end the demonstrations, and the goons dispersed.

Incredibly, the *FRG* insisted that it had not instigated *Jueves Negro*, even after

Indian women in traditional dress glance at a display for presidential candidate Oscar Berger in a shopping mall in Guatemala City in August 2003.   *Photo by the author*

newspaper photographers captured well-known *FRG* leaders, including Jorge Arévalo, a high-ranking congressman, and Ríos Montt's niece, on film; their images were published for all to see. Polls for years had suggested that Ríos Montt could win the presidency if he were allowed to run. Now, faced with the reality of his candidacy, voters began to get cold feet after *Jueves Negro*. He slipped to third, then fourth, then fifth place in the polls.

This author spent six days in Guatemala in August as a free-lance journalist to write about the campaign and interviewed Berger, López Rodas and the spokeswoman for the U.N. Verification Mission to Guatemala, who maintained

that the *FRG* was in fact responsible for the disturbances as well as threats against opposition journalists.

Ríos Montt, ever wary of foreign journalists, refused me an interview. But his daughter Zury, the *FRG*'s second-ranking figure in Congress after her father, agreed. She accused the "oligarchy" of manipulating the polls. She continued to insist that the *FRG* was blameless for *Jueves Negro*, saying that "the U.N. Mission has become very politicized."

Though Berger was leading in all the polls, he told me he was frankly worried because the *FRG* controlled not only the national government but many municipal governments in the interior.

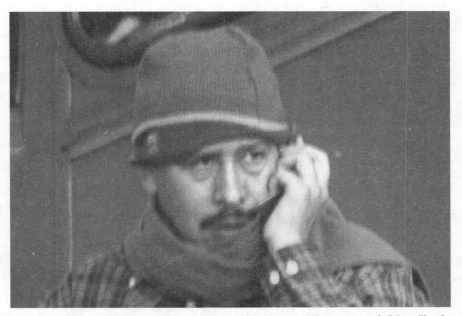

A photographer for the Guatemala City daily *Prensa Libre* snapped this tell-tale photo of Jorge Arevalo, the high-ranking *FRG* congressional deputy who successfully appealed the ban on Efrain Ríos Montt's candidacy, as he lifted his ski mask to use his cell phone during the bloody riots of *Jueves Negro*, July 24, 2003. The *FRG* had denied instigating the disturbances.   *Photo courtesy Prensa Libre*

Guatemala

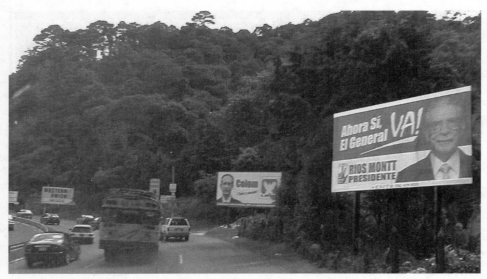

A billboard for former strongman Efrain Ríos Montt looms over the highway between Guatemala City and Antigua. In the background is a billboard for the left-wing presidential candidate Alvaro Colom, who bumped Ríos Montt out of the runoff in the November 9, 2003 election.

Photo by the author

"They have a very disciplined organization (in the interior), where they have undertaken public works," Berger said. "We don't worry that much about actual electoral fraud, but about intimidation. These are some very violent people, and (the Indians) are very timid people. They are easy to intimidate."

But my friend, political columnist Mario Antonio Sandoval of *Prensa Libre*, the leading daily, said that Ríos Montt "hanged himself when he announced the mob was going to withdraw, and they withdrew in five minutes. This proof of violence is what Guatemalans don't like. He *is* the violence. He *means* the violence." Meanwhile, the U.S. Embassy let it be known that the United States would not look favorably on a Ríos Montt victory.

The campaign continued to be marred by mysterious murders in the interior. Ríos Montt experienced a resurgence over the next three months, but not enough to recover the ground he lost from *Jueves Negro* to make it into the runoff. On November 9, a respectable 55.2% of the electorate went to the polls. The results:

Berger	904,533	34.5%
Colom	694,734	26.5%
Ríos Montt	503,994	19.2%
López Rodas	218,577	8.3%
García-Gallont	79,784	3.0%
Others	222,423	8.6%

Under the complicated proportional representation formula, Berger's new *GANA* coalition emerged as the largest movement in the newly enlarged Congress, with 48 of the 158 seats. The *FRG* was still a major force, finishing second with 42 seats. Colom's *UNE* won 33, the *PAN* won 15 and five other parties won 18. Clearly, there would have to be a coalition forged. But with which parties?

Ríos Montt refused to make a public concession, but the *FRG* publicly acknowledged its defeat. Berger and Colom shook hands and embarked on what was a gentlemanly campaign for the *segunda vuelta*, or runoff, on December 28. The turnout this time was 46.8%, and the results were almost exactly what polls had predicted:

Berger	1,235,303	54.13%
Colom	1,046,868	45.87%

It was the closest the Guatemalan left had ever come to tasting victory. Colom expressed disappointment, but graciously conceded. Two days after the runoff, Berger's *GANA*, Colom's *UNE* and the *PAN* announced that they had agreed on an unorthodox right-center-left legislative coalition, giving them a working majority of 96 seats. The *FRG* was once again in opposition, with Zury Ríos its leader in Congress. She made international headlines a year later by marrying U.S. Representative Jerry Weller, a Republican from Illinois; it was her fourth marriage. She still lives in Guatemala and serves in Congress, but goes to Washington when it is not in session.

After the elections, the reputations of both Colom and López Rodas were tarnished when it was disclosed that their parties had accepted campaign "donations" from the Portillo government, laundered through the national revenue agency. Apparently, the *FRG*, sensing Ríos Montt would not make the runoff, wanted to ingratiate itself with these two candidates in the event they did. Evidently, attempting to bribe Berger was not an option for Ríos Montt and Portillo.

Berger Makes Changes

Berger was sworn in as president on January 14, 2004, joining an ever-growing list of Latin American presidents elected on their second or subsequent attempts. His vice president is Eduardo Stein, who served as foreign minister in the Arzú administration. In his address, Berger promised to crack down on corruption and human rights abuses, something the jaded Guatemalans had heard time and again.

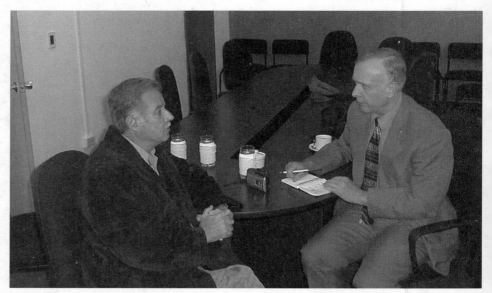

The author interviewing winning presidential candidate Oscar Berger in Guatemala City in August 2003.

Photo by Berger staff

The New York Times
La guerra en el Siglo 21

BÚSQUELO
EN ESTA
EDICIÓN

EDICIÓN DOMINICAL

PRENSA LIBRE

UN PERIODISMO INDEPENDIENTE, HONRADO Y DIGNO

AÑO LIV, NO. 17,538   Q3.00 LOS DOMINGOS   21 DE NOVIEMBRE DE 2004

EL FRG
DIVIDIDO Y AFECTADO POR CORRUPCIÓN

Analistas dicen que capturas y renuncias lo han debilitado

BODA
DE
POLÍTICOS

Jerry Weller y Zury Ríos se juraron amor eterno en ceremonia rodeada de lujos y 330 invitados guatemaltecos y de EEUU que se dieron cita en Antigua.

▶ Págs 2 y 3

DESESPERADOS POR UN HIJO

Cuando el deseo de ser padres encuentra barreras, la ciencia puede ayudar a la naturaleza

DEPORTES

Barsa fulmina

Catalanes derrotaron 3-0 al Real Madrid, ayer, en el Camp Nou. El Barsa es el superlíder.

The front page of *Prensa Libre* for November 21, 2004, was bittersweet for the Guatemalan Republican Front (*FRG*) of former strongman Efraín Ríos Montt. At right is a photo from the wedding of his daughter, Zury, the FRG's leader in Congress, who married U.S. Representative Jerry Weller of Illinois. At the left is a headline that reads, "The FRG: Divided and affected by corruption."

Guatemala

President Oscar Berger

In a gesture reminiscent of Andrew Jackson, he flung open the doors of the presidential palace on inauguration day, allowing thousands of ordinary people to visit.

Berger quickly set out to prove that he intended to make good on his promises. The day after his inauguration, he appointed Nobel Laureate Rigoberta Menchú as a "goodwill ambassador" to help monitor the 1996 peace accords, something that would have been unthinkable under Portillo. But Berger seems to be sensitive about his Belgian heritage and his reputation as a member of the ruling elite in the overwhelmingly Mayan country. He also appointed Frank LaRue, a leftist activist, as human rights commissioner.

On March 8, a court ordered Ríos Montt placed under house arrest, not for genocide, but for the death of the journalist Héctor Ramírez on *Jueves Negro*. Formal charges were filed on May 13, and he remains under house arrest.

In a move that seemed more like those of a Marxist and which once would have provoked a military coup, Berger cut the size of the army almost in half, from 27,000 to 15,500, with the savings used to boost welfare and education. Berger and members of his government received letters threatening their lives over the cuts. He also closed the notorious Santa Cruz de Quiché army base, which played a major role during the civil war, and he finally did what Arzú and Portillo were supposed to do but didn't: he disbanded the notorious presidential guard.

Under Berger, both the executive and legislative branches have declared war on the country's endemic corruption—a formidable enemy indeed. Transparency International ranked Guatemala as the third most corrupt country in the Western Hemisphere in 2004 (only Haiti and Paraguay were worse) and one of the 23 worst in the world. In March 2004, Congress fired its own comptroller when he fled the country to avoid answering allegations that he had channeled $447,000 in illegal campaign contributions to two parties in 2003. He was arrested in Nicaragua.

The government next launched an investigation into Portillo's Panamanian bank accounts. The U.S. government helped out by revoking the former president's visa. Portillo fled the country, surfacing in Mexico in August 2004 on a one-year work visa. He was living both in Mexico City and in the same town where he had killed the two men in 1982. In June, the government broadened the investigation to search for more corruption during the Portillo presidency. The government, and the country, got more than they bargained for. In December, the auditor released a report stating that $600 million in public funds was unaccounted for over a 12-year period, which also implicated the presidencies of Arzú and de León Carpio, as well as Serrano, whose crookedness was well known. The auditor said that about half that amount was bilked from the public health system.

In September 2004, a retired general serving in Congress filed a formal complaint alleging that four former defense ministers and Ríos Montt's son, who was army commander, diverted $100 million from army purchases to private bank accounts while Portillo was president. Prosecutors went to work on those allegations as well.

Racial discrimination had been officially outlawed in 2002 during Portillo's presidency, but no one had ever been prosecuted for it until September 2004. Five men with *FRG* ties, including Ríos Montt's grandson, were charged with abuse against Rigoberta Menchú in 2003 when she testified at a hearing against allowing Ríos Montt to run for president. They allegedly shoved her and verbally insulted her, saying, "Go back to selling tomatoes in the market, Indian." In April 2005, the five were convicted and sentenced to 38 months each in jail.

It was one sign that Guatemala was making progress on human rights, but U.N. Secretary-General Kofi Annan warned that the country still had a long way to go in providing rights to the Indian majority. Nonetheless, the U.N. Verification Mission for Guatemala was closed in December 2004.

Besides coming to terms with the corruption and rights abuses of the past, Berger has had to contend with the growing problem of street crime and an alarmingly high murder rate. It became so critical that he ordered 1,600 army troops to augment the police in patrolling the streets of the capital. He also fired his interior minister and police chief. Much of the crime is believed linked to the international *maras,* or street gangs, with roots in El Salvador and Los Angeles, California (see El Salvador).

The Congress ratified, and Berger signed into law, Guatemala's membership in the proposed Central America Free Trade Agreement (CAFTA) with the United States. El Salvador and Honduras have already ratified it; the U.S. Senate did in June 2005. The CAFTA vote was briefly delayed in Congress when 4,000 left-wing demonstrators outside the legislative building hurled rocks and bottles at police, who responded with tear gas. Nineteen people were injured and 16 were arrested. In a separate protest on a highway near the Mexican border, one demonstrator was killed in a clash with police.

Culture: The culture of modern Guatemala represents a composite of traditional Mayan and colonial Spanish. Although the mixing of the two bloods has produced a *mestizo* element called by the locals *"Ladino,"* the majority of the population remains unassimilated, pure-blood Indians of Mayan descent who speak a number of dialects, the most widely spoken being Quiché. The Mayan heritage has largely shaped the country's rich folklore in art and music, much to the benefit of the country's tourist industry. Guatemalans take special pride in their *marimba* bands, which often greet arriving visitors at the capital's airport.

Guatemala's religious practices are among the most curious in Latin America. Roman Catholicism never firmly took root, despite efforts by zealous colonial-era priests to force or entice the Indians away from their pagan practices. Eventually, the Church came to realize that it would have better results with a little more tolerance. Today, in towns such as Chichicastenango, visitors can see Indians practicing their tribal rites inside the Catholic cathedral. The shallow roots of Catholicism also made Guatemala a promising target for the proselytizing of U.S.-based evangelical Protestantism. Today an estimated one third of the population are zealous, "born-again" fundamentalists; among the converts were former strongman Efraín Ríos Montt and former President Jorge Serrano.

An abysmally low literacy rate, combined with chronic dictatorship and political violence, forced many of Guatemala's talented writers, artists and musicians to work abroad. But the cultural glass is far from empty. The country's most eminent writer was Miguel Angel Asturias (1899-1974), probably best remembered for his novel, *El Señor Presidente*. In 1967, Asturias became only the second Latin American to receive the Nobel Prize for Literature.

Former President Juan José Arévalo was a noted literary figure as well, and also served as ambassador to Israel.

Another internationally acclaimed literary figure was short story writer Augusto Monterroso, who went into exile to Mexico in 1944 during the Ubico dictatorship and remained there until his death in February 2003 at the age of 81. He received Spain's prestigious Prince of Asturias Award, and his story *El dinosaurio (The Dinosaur)* is reputed to be the shortest story in any language. It contained seven words: *"Cuando despertó, el dinosaurio todavía estaba allí."* ("When he awoke, the dinosaur was still there.")

Illiteracy and political violence also took its toll on the development of the Guatemalan press. Dozens of journalists, from newspaper publishers to reporters, were murdered by one side or the other during the 36-year civil war that ended in December 1996. There is only a handful of daily newspapers, all of them relatively young and all published in the capital, and even fewer magazines. The oldest, most prestigious newspaper, and the circulation leader until 2000, is *Prensa Libre*, founded in 1951. *Siglo Veintiuno* began publishing in 1991 and has become the country's second-ranking daily, winning high marks for its quality and reliability. Both papers now publish sensational, working-class tabloids as well. *Nuestro Diario*, published by *Prensa Libre*, has a circulation of 300,000, the greatest in Central America and a phenomenal number given the high illiteracy rate.

Radio is a popular, and influential, medium in Guatemala because of the poverty and illiteracy. The three privately owned over-the-air television stations are monopolized by a Mexican, Angel González, who is married to a Guatemalan; critics charge that his ownership, and the monopoly, are illegal, but he has managed to remain friendly with all the powers that be, no matter what their political leanings. In 2003, a new cable channel, Guatevisión, broke González's television monopoly and reaches 300,000 homes. Its independent news reporting is especially popular—so much so that it began receiving bomb threats during the presidency of Alfonso Portillo

Economy: Guatemala's economy is based almost entirely on agriculture. Major cash crops include coffee, bananas, beef and cotton. Most farmland is controlled by huge estates—the top 2% of the population owns more than 60% of the farmland.

A street vendor hawks copies of six different daily newspapers.   *Photo by the author*

The large Indian population lives outside the money economy on small plots in the highlands. The average per capita income is about $1,500 U.S., but among rural Mayans it is only about $300.

Light industry has grown in recent years, but economic development remains handicapped by the traditional, largely feudal economic system. Also impeding development are communications problems caused by the large number of Indian dialects used in Guatemala.

Although the devastating earthquake of early 1976 destroyed much of the nation's productivity by damaging roads, water facilities, power supplies, communications and the like, economic output survived largely intact. Major cash crops, produced mostly along the coastal regions, were unaffected by the quake. Light industries such as textiles, food processing and pharmaceuticals, located around the capital, also suffered only minor damage.

Like nearly all its neighbors in Central America, Guatemala has suffered from the high cost of foreign credit and from low export earnings from sugar and cotton. The economy went into a tailspin in 1981. Poor world prices and a low demand for Guatemalan products threaten economic gains, with the exception of coffee.

Efforts to root out corruption, a national pastime in Guatemala, have accomplished very little, if anything. Tax evasion, also another pastime, costs the government at least 50% of its intended revenue each year. By 2004, Transparency International ranked Guatemala the third most corrupt nation in the Western Hemisphere and one of the 23 most corrupt in the world.

Although not as seriously affected by Hurricane Mitch in 1998 as were Honduras and Nicaragua, Guatemala was far from unscathed. The human toll was 268 dead, 121 missing and 734,198 adversely affected. Ninety-eight bridges were destroyed, 60% of the roads were damaged and 45–60% of the corn crop, so vital for domestic consumption, was destroyed.

The hurricane could be only partially blamed for the grave downturn in the economy in 1999. Real GDP dropped from $19 billion in 1998 to $17.8 billion, a decline of 6.2%. Urban unemployment remained unchanged at 5.2%, while inflation was a merciful 5%. Figures do not reveal everything, however. During both of this author's visits to Guatemala in 1999, I heard several knowledgeable people discuss a financial crisis caused by the exodus of hard cash from the country as the victory of Alfonso Portillo of the Guatemalan Republican Front *(FRG)* appeared more certain. The wealthy elite, who control the Party of National Advancement *(PAN)*, feared the populist economic policies of Portillo and his mentor, Ríos Montt, and began stashing their money in foreign banks for the duration. No doubt the election of the pro-business Oscar Berger in 2003 will reverse that trend.

GDP has since shown steady growth of 3.3% in 2000, 2.3% in 2001 and 2.2% in 2002, which barely recovers the ground lost in 1999 and failed to keep up with population growth. It was expected to be about the same in 2003. Inflation in 2001 was a modest 6%. The government has been contemplating the possibility of following the lead of Ecuador and of neigh-

Guatemala

boring El Salvador in adopting the dollar as the official unit of currency and abandoning the *quetzal*. By 2003, the dollar was circulating alongside the *quetzal* and accepted as legal tender.

The Future: Guatemalans have now elected five presidents since the restoration of democracy and have been bitterly disillusioned with the first four. They have never returned a ruling party to power. It is hard to blame them. The first president was a playboy who showed little interest in improving the country. The second tried to become a dictator and remains in Panama after fleeing with $25 million from the treasury. The third succeeded in ending the civil war, but was disliked for his handling of the economy and for his aloofness. The fourth was the stand-in for a former dictator accused of genocide and is also in self-imposed exile, accused of enriching himself.

It is small wonder that in the periodic *Latinobarómetro* poll published in the British newsmagazine *The Economist*, the percentage of Guatemalans who say that democracy is preferable to any other form of government nosedived from 51% in 1996 and 49% in 2002 to just 33% in 2003, the last year of the corrupt and repressive Portillo presidency. Only Panama and Paraguay showed greater decreases in support for democracy. Perhaps the early impressive showing of President Berger is responsible for the modest rise to 35% in 2004.

There is cause for some cheer, however. The percentage who believe that authoritarianism can be preferable to democracy in certain circumstances also declined, from 21% in 1996 to 10% in 2003 and 11% in 2004, even though Guatemalans have been buffeted by "certain circumstances." In 2003, they had the chance to put former strongman Efraín Ríos Montt, whom they once revered for his crack-the-whip style

of government, back in charge, but when they deposited their ballots, only one in five chose that option.

Oscar Berger must now attempt to overcome his countrymen's cynicism and restore their faith in themselves. This author interviewed Alfonso Portillo on the eve of the 1999 runoff, and he gave me some assurances, such as respect for press freedom, that he didn't keep. In August 2003, Berger also gave me assurances that he would be different from the others. He struck me as more sincere than Portillo, however, and his first year and a half in office suggests he is serious about combating corruption and guaranteeing human rights. Given that he is himself an affluent, Caucasian businessmen with ties to the old oligarchy, his progress has been remarkable—and commendable. May he keep up the good work. Like the Guatemalans, whom I hold in high regard and affection, I'm keeping my fingers crossed.

The presidential palace in Guatemala City. *Photo by the author*

The Cooperative Republic of Guyana

A diver prepares to look for diamonds in the Essequibo River

Area: 82,978 square miles.

Population: 766,000.

Capital City: Georgetown (Pop. 210,000, estimated).

Climate: Tropically hot and humid; there are heavy rains from April to August and from November to January.

Neighboring Countries: Suriname (East); Brazil (South and West); Venezuela (West).

Official Language: English.

Other Principal Tongues: Various East Indian dialects.

Ethnic Background: East Indian (about 52%), African and mulatto (about 41%), European and mixed (about 7%).

Principal Religion: Christianity (Anglican Protestant).

Other Principal Religions: Roman Catholic Christianity, Hinduism, Islam.

Chief Commercial Products: Bauxite, sugar, rice, aluminum, shrimp, molasses, timber, rum, diamonds.

Currency: Guyana Dollar.

Gross Domestic Product: U.S. $656 million in 2002 ($840 per capita).

Former Colonial Status: Colony of the Dutch West India Company (1616–1796); British Colony (1796–1966).

Independence Date: May 26, 1966.

Chief of State: Bharrat Jagdeo (b. January 23, 1964), president (since August 11, 1999).

National Flag: A yellow field bordered in green with black, red and white triangles from top to bottom along the staff.

Guyana lies on the northeast coast of South America. A narrow (5 to 10 miles wide) ribbon of swampy plain extends along the 200-mile length of the coastline. Much of this land lies below sea level and is intersected by large rivers requiring a complex system of dikes and canals to protect it from both floods and drought. Annual rainfall averages 80 to 100 inches and the country is hot the year round; the daily temperature variation of 10° F is greater than the seasonal changes. This coastal region is the country's principal agricultural area and contains some 90% of the population.

Inland from the coastal plains, the land rises to natural grassy plains with poor soils and scrub bush. It is here that gold, diamonds and bauxite are found. Further inland, heavily forested hills rise to the base of the Guiana Highlands, with elevations of over 8,000 feet on the Guyana-Venezuela border, rising out of the forests in vertical red cliffs of 2,000 feet. Rivers flowing out of the highland produce spectacular falls as they drop to the lowlands.

Guyana's principal rivers, the Corantijn on the Suriname frontier, the Berbice and the Essequibo, which flow into the Atlantic at Georgetown, are navigable for only short distances because of falls and rapids—yet they are of major importance as means of communication in the roadless interior.

History: The Dutch first settled on the banks of the Essequibo River as early as 1596, but permanent settlements were not established until the Dutch West India Company started its operations about 1620. The Dutch drained the swamps and lagoons and initiated the system of dikes and canals which make the coastal plain habitable. The Spaniards and Portuguese conquerors of the lands to the west and south saw no apparent value in the Guianas and did not molest the British, French and Dutch settlers of the region. British forces captured the Dutch settlement in 1796, and the territory now incorporated into Guyana was ceded to the British in 1814. In 1831, the colony was officially named British Guiana. The British confined themselves to plantation operations along the coast and some lumbering along the rivers. Sugar, rice and cotton were the principal crops.

The population arrived in two different groups. The Africans came in the 17th and 18th centuries to work the plantations. With the abolition of slavery in 1830, Asian peoples migrated from India, China and southeast Asia, and they now account for the largest element in the population. During the 19th century, the British further developed the drainage system and built roads and railroads in an effort to open the interior for settlement and exploitation of the mineral wealth. However, few people moved to that area. Descendants of the African people have tended to gather in the urban areas as mechanics and tradesmen; the Asians have remained on the farms and plantations along the coast. Despite Guyana's size, the habitable land is overcrowded and the interior is uninhabited except for a few aboriginal Indians.

Politically, the British started tutoring the people of Guyana for independence after World War II. Self-government, which was planned for 1962, had to be postponed until 1966 because of bitter racial contro-

Guyana

versy between the Asian and African sectors of the population. Cheddi Jagan, leftist leader of the Asian people, was premier during most of these four years. His open sympathy with world communism and policies directed against those of African descent led to his defeat, and Forbes Burnham, of African descent, became prime minister. A constitutional change of 1965 provided for proportional representation of the two communities in the national legislature, and the election of moderate leaders in the 1964 elections made possible the granting of independence in 1966.

Under the leadership of Burnham, racial tensions were eased, although scattered disturbances surfaced from time to time. Burnham was reelected in 1968, easily defeating Cheddi Jagan. During his second term, he emphasized broadening the base of the economy and a neutral foreign policy. To reduce dependence on sugar exports, more attention was given to the development of other crops.

Burnham started moving toward the political left in 1970—he declared Guyana to be a "cooperative republic" whereby 1,200 small worker cooperatives were established. The government began taking over the nation's foreign-owned bauxite mining operations in 1971. Burnham was elected in 1973 to a third term, defeating Jagan. His People's National Congress (PNC) won 37 seats in the 57-member Parliament; the People's Progressive Party (PPP) of Jagan was reduced by five to a total of 14 members.

Burnham's main strength came from blacks who live in the cities, while Jagan dominated the East Indian vote in the rural areas. Although Asians comprised 52% of the population compared to 40% who were black, Burnham skillfully garnered his winning margins through political patronage and by espousing ideas originally proposed by his opponent.

Both Burnham and Jagan were dedicated Marxists. In May 1976, the government nationalized the huge British-owned sugar industry—the last remaining major foreign investment in Guyana. Steps were taken to control the insurance, banking and rum industries, so that the state ultimately owned 85% of the economy.

With Burnham continuing his swing to the left, he gained the unexpected endorsement of Jagan for his economic programs. This political accommodation brought an unfamiliar tranquility to Guyana, which was short-lived.

World attention of an unwanted sort was focused on Guyana in November 1978 when 913 members of a bizarre religious cult from California living in an isolated, newly constructed jungle settlement of Jonestown, named for its messianic leader, Jim Jones, committed suicide after drinking a concoction laced with cyanide.

Burnham decreed a new constitution in 1980 that gave him increased control over opposition political parties and the judicial system. Three months later, he won another five-year term in office.

The 140-year-old border dispute with Venezuela erupted anew in 1982 with Venezuelan incursions into Guyana. This latest dispute had been smoldering since 1962, when Venezuela suddenly declared the 1899 accords (which the United States helped to arrange between Britain and Venezuela) void. The dispute has quietly faded into the background since 1988, which marked state visits by the heads of the respective nations to each other.

Burnham died of heart failure in 1985 after minor throat surgery in Moscow. Although he had made plans for his family to take over Guyana, surprisingly the party endorsed his vice president, Desmond Hoyte. Balloting in a subsequent election gave the PNC 42 of the 53 seats in the National Assembly; Jagan claimed the contest was rigged.

President Hoyte, realizing that the collapsing Soviet Union offered no economic hope for Guyana, dropped all pro-Soviet rhetoric and traditional communist pronouncements and actively sought closer ties with Western nations. He personally visited the United States to encourage investment (without results). Energetic plans were put into execution to get the state out of business, of which it controlled 85%, and to drastically cut govern-

Guyana

ment personnel. Credit became available from the International Monetary Fund and the United States as a result. Hoyte wisely began including talented Asians at top levels within his administration.

Elections in October 1992, considered the fairest ever held in Guyana, ended the PNC's 28 years in power. The outcome was totally unexpected, because in 1991–92 Guyana's economy had hummed along well, and conditions had improved considerably. Usually in times of prosperity voters settle for what they have. CBut Jagan led the PPP to an upset victory, gaining a working majority of 35 seats in the Assembly. But this was *not* the old Cheddi Jagan. He also had dropped all illusions of Marxism and was able to portray himself as a moderate progressive rather than as a radical leftist.

With the typical zeal of the newly converted, Jagan implemented sweeping economic changes. From its high of 105% in 1989, inflation was reduced to 4.5% in 1996. That same year, he signed an agreement to reduce Guyana's debt to the Paris Club of creditor nations by two thirds. The erstwhile Marxist also opened Guyana's agricultural, mining and forestry sectors to foreign investors. Foreign economists praised Guyana's example as one of the most successful adjustments from a state-controlled to a free-market system. That legacy proved to be Jagan's requiem. On February 16, 1997, the 78-year-old president suffered a serious heart attack. He was taken to Walter Reed Hospital in Washington, where he died on March 6. Prime Minister Samuel Hinds was sworn in to succeed Jagan. Hinds then named Jagan's widow, Chicago-born Janet Rosenberg Jagan, as Guyana's first woman prime minister.

For the presidential and parliamentary elections of December 15, 1997, Hoyte again stood as presidential candidate for the PNC, but President Hinds stood aside to allow Mrs. Jagan to be the standard-bearer of the PPP. Mrs. Jagan insisted she was running reluctantly to fulfill a death-bed wish of her husband. But Hoyte accused her of nepotism and of seeking to establish a nation of "Jagana." Race also played a role in the campaign, with Hoyte supporters denouncing her as "that Caucasian old lady" and alleging that she still carries a U.S. passport. In reality, Mrs. Jagan's Guyanese credentials were impeccable. She had lived there for 54 years and had lost her U.S. citizenship when she voted in British Guiana in 1947. She had served time in jail with her husband during the independence struggle in the 1950s.

In balloting that the PNC immediately denounced as rigged, Mrs. Jagan unofficially received 191,332 votes to 144,359 for Hoyte. She was hastily inaugurated just

four days later, publicly defying a court injunction the PNC had obtained to block the ceremony. Hinds became prime minister. Although observers from the Organization of American States pronounced the elections fair, PNC loyalists embarked on a month of street protests, some quelled by army troops and police using tear gas. To help defuse the volatile situation, a negotiating team from the Caribbean Community (Caricom), headed by former Barbados Prime Minister Henry Forde, brokered an agreement between Mrs. Jagan and Hoyte that called for an end to street demonstrations and the institution of constitutional reforms.

The deal was a remarkable concession for Mrs. Jagan's government, because it called for new elections within three years, two years short of her constitutional mandate. Under the agreement, the constitutional reforms would be worked out within 18 months, and the elections would come within 18 months after that. Although the unrest quieted down, the personal animosity between Jagan and Hoyte lingered.

Hoyte and other critics of Jagan blamed her unreconstructed Marxism for discouraging badly needed foreign investments; her government, they noted, steadfastly refused to consider tax incentives, which drove potential investors to other, more inviting countries. Despite her life-long devotion to Marxism, however, Jagan pragmatically but grudgingly moved to privatize some cumbersome state-controlled enterprises, including the airline and a bauxite operation. Such economic reforms paid dividends in May 1999, when the World Bank and the IMF granted Guyana $256 million in relief for its $1.09 billion national debt under the Heavily Indebted Poor Countries initiative that rewards countries that implement painful but needed reforms. Guyana was only the third country to receive such debt relief under this program.

President Bharrat Jagdeo

A New Generation

A chronic heart condition forced Jagan to undergo treatment in the United States, as had her husband, and on August 11, 1999, she resigned. Although Prime Minister Hinds was in line to succeed her, he deferred in favor of the finance minister, Bharrat Jagdeo, a Hindu who, at 35, became the youngest head of state in the hemisphere. The departure of Jagan did little to defuse the tense political rivalry between the PNP and the PPP, however, as Hoyte refused to recognize Jagdeo's government either.

But in 2000, Jagdeo's main preoccupation was the long-simmering border disputes with both Venezuela to the west and Suriname to the east. In May, Venezuela issued a formal protest over a concession that Guyana had granted to a Texas company to construct a $100 million satellite launching facility in the disputed Essequibo region. In a strongly worded note to Foreign Minister Clement Rohee, Venezuelan Foreign Minister José Vicente Rangel called the concession an "unfriendly act" and called on the Guyanese government to "review" it. The site was chosen because of its proximity to the Equator, which makes it easier to launch heavy payloads into geosyncronous orbits. The European Space Agency has a similar facility in nearby French Guiana.

Then, on June 2, Suriname ordered a Canadian oil drilling company to tow its offshore platform from what it claimed was Surinamese territorial waters in the Atlantic Ocean. Like the Essequibo dispute with Venezuela, this dispute dates to colonial times. At issue is which bank of the Corantijn River forms the boundary between the two countries. The river empties into a V-shaped gulf, and the border is extended into the Atlantic Ocean. It was in that narrow disputed corridor that Guyana had granted a drilling concession to the Toronto-based company, which reluctantly towed its expensive platform into undisputed Guyanese waters and

Hugh Desmond Hoyte

195

Guyana

waited for the two countries to resolve the matter diplomatically. For a time, it seemed the matter would not be settled in a gentlemanly fashion, as each country accused the other of moving troops up to their common land border. The two governments then agreed to a series of talks, first in Georgetown, then in Paramaribo, June 13–18, which ended in failure. Another round of talks in July also failed, and further talks were put on hold because of the campaign for the March 19, 2001 election in Guyana. Meanwhile, each country made tragicomic attempts to build up its minuscule military force. Guyana, which has no navy, purchased two aging British and three U.S. warships, while Suriname beefed up its existing navy. There is far more at stake in the 7,700 square-mile disputed zone than water and fish; it sits atop an estimated 15 billion barrels of oil which, at a time of rising oil prices, could prove a jackpot for both of these impoverished nations—if they are willing to strike a deal.

The Elections of 2001

The general elections originally had been scheduled for January 2001, but an independent electoral commission, headed by the highly respected retired Major General Joseph Singh, concluded they could not be held before March. In December 2000, Jagdeo, after consulting with Hoyte, moved them back to March 19. Because of the ugliness of the disputed 1997 elections, the 2001 contest drew an unusual amount of international scrutiny: 170 observers from six separate organizations and 45 nationalities. For a time it appeared that the voter ID cards would not be ready in time, but the election was carried out with a minimum of discord.

The results were a resounding victory for the incumbent Jagdeo and his PPP, which had an electoral alliance with the small Civic Party: 209,031 votes, or 53% to 164,074, or 42%, for Hoyte's PNC. In the 65-seat Parliament, the PPP-C won an outright majority of 35 seats, the PNC won 27 and minor parties took the remaining three. Despite the clear-cut results, which the international observers termed fair and honest, the PNC filed a formal complaint with the electoral commission, claiming thousands of opposition voters had been turned away at the polls. Meanwhile, disgruntled PNC supporters vented some sour grapes on March 26 by going on a rampage in Georgetown, looting shops and torching a gas station. Police used tear gas to restore order. It was politics as usual in Guyana.

Not long after the election violence, the international human rights group Amnesty International accused Guyanese po-

lice of operating death squads that had allegedly summarily executed as many as 15 criminal suspects. The government denied the allegations. A few days after that negative international publicity, the United States ceased issuing visas to Guyanese citizens in reprisal for Guyana's refusal to repatriate 100 Guyanese nationals who had been arrested in the United States for various felonies.

Political violence erupted once again in July 2002 when pro-PNC demonstrators staged protests outside Jagdeo's office, apparently in an effort to embarrass the president, who was hosting a summit of leaders of the 14 Caribbean Community countries. In the ensuing violence, two protesters were killed and six wounded. Jagdeo called the incident an assassination attempt.

The political landscape changed dramatically with Hoyte's sudden death in December 2002. The partisan tension was evident even at his funeral, when Bagdeo magnanimously delivered a eulogy to his fallen rival but was sometimes drowned out by PNP hecklers.

Recent Developments

Early in 2003, the PNP members of Parliament staged a boycott that lasted several months. The stalemate between the two parties ended when the PNP elected Robert Corbin as leader of the opposition. On May 2, 2003, which President Bagdeo termed an "historic" day, he and Corbin sealed a pact that they termed "Constructive Engagement," by which the PNP ended its parliamentary boycott and Bagdeo appointed a nine-member Ethnic Relations Commission with powers to investigate and punish incidents of racial injustice.

It was not to last, however. In March 2004, the PNP staged a mass demonstration to investigate the mysterious killings of 40 black criminals by what is believed to be a death squad called the Phantom Gang, allegedly headed by Home Affairs Minister Ronald Gajraj. Supposedly, firearms and telephone records were traced to Gajraj's office. The United States and Canada, without explanation, revoked his visas. Gajraj denied the allegations and offered to step aside. Bagdeo at first declined his offer. Corbin, meanwhile, withdrew from the Constructive Engagement agreement in April and resumed the PNP's boycott of Congress.

In May 2004, Bagdeo agreed to appoint an investigative commission, but Corbin, still dissatisfied, refused to cooperate with it or to abide by its results. The situation became more volatile on June 24, 2004, when George Bacchus, an Afro-Guyanese rancher who had made the initial accusa-

tion of a death squad on national television, was shot to death at his home by unknown assailants. Bacchus was about to testify in the trial of two men accused of killing Bacchus' brother in January. Bacchus had claimed that his brother was slain by death-squad members who mistook his brother for him. Meanwhile, the magistrate hearing the case resigned because of death threats. The PNP immediately accused the government of complicity in Bacchus' death.

Gajraj eventually stepped down pending the outcome of the commission's inquiry. In April 2005, the commission formally exonerated Gajraj of any direct complicity in the death squads although it acknowledged he had an "unhealthy" relationship with organized crime figures and had illegally interfered with firearms licenses. He was reinstated as home affairs minister, which sparked complaints from the U.S. State Department, the European Union and the Guyana Human Rights Association.

Culture: The people of Guyana have adopted the culture of the British ruling elite of the past century. Schooled through the elementary grades, their literacy rate is higher than those in neighboring nations. There are few cultural traits reflecting the origin of the African community; the Asian community still retains some of its original customs, especially in marriage and family relations.

Economy: Despite large mineral and forest resources, Guyana's economy is agricultural and severely limited to foreign markets. Much of the nation's sparsely settled but potentially rich interior is also claimed by Venezuela. Efforts to populate this inhospitable region have been unsuccessful.

Although the ambitious Burnham sought to convert Guyana into a Marxist state, change was initially gradual in an attempt to avoid the disruptions that occurred in Cuba and in Chile during the communist interlude of the latter. But after 1982, all curbs in the march toward socialism disappeared—and Guyana commenced a more rapid disappearance down the economic drain. The result was disastrous. The purchasing power of the average citizen declined by 40% compared to 1976 figures.

The state-owned bauxite operation, called *Guybau*, showed a profit largely because of comparatively inflated world prices, which have since declined. Before the romance with communism, farm output was constant; rice and sugar exports initially rose after independence. Guyana reported a favorable balance of trade by 1975. In early 1977, Guyana applied for

Guyana

formal association with *Comecon*, the communist bloc's common market. Perhaps in order to emphasize its interest in trade rather than ideology, Guyana also became a member of the Inter-American Development Bank, a Washington-based organization of the OAS.

Critical of Guyana's close ties with Cuba, and adhering to its policy of encouraging the private sector, the United States in late 1983 vetoed a $40 million Inter-American Development Bank loan to increase Guyana's rice production because that plan actually would have created a lack of incentive for farm production; the loan was later approved.

Workers' strikes in late 1983 and 1984 resulted in a sharp decline in bauxite production. Guyana's economic situation deteriorated dreadfully in 1984–86. Negotiations with the International Monetary Fund were suspended and the IMF declared Guyana ineligible for further assistance. There initially was no improvement under Hoyte, but rather, further decline; he inherited an economy that had descended to primitive agriculture.

A substantial part of the Essequibo River had to be closed for a week in the summer of 1995 because of a leak of cyanide-contaminated slurry from the Omai gold mine. The huge mine is Guyana's largest enterprise, and is 95% owned by two Canadian firms.

The Hoyte administration brought some modest prosperity. Although strict conditions imposed by the IMF were resented, they were successful.

Throughout most of the 1990s, Guyana experienced extraordinary GDP growth averaging 7% a year. Unlike many of its Latin American neighbors that were cursed by dependence on one export commodity, Guyana was blessed with diversified exports, including bauxite (aluminum ore), gold, timber, sugar and rice. But the robust growth halted abruptly in 1998, when the Asian financial crisis and *El Niño* both hit Guyana. World market prices for timber, gold, bauxite and sugar all fell; timber exports alone dropped 35% because of the crisis in Asia, the major consumer of Guyanese wood. Only rice exports showed an increase. As a result, GDP growth for 1998 declined by 1.3% and grew only .3% in 1999 and another .5% in 2000, 2001 and 2002. Unemployment in 1999 was 11.9%; more recent figures are unavailable. Inflation in 2000 was a modest 5.9%.

In 2004, Guyana had the dubious distinction of having a public debt that was 200% of GDP, the highest in the entire world. However, when the so-called Paris Club of the wealthiest creditor nations met in June 2005 to discuss debt forgiveness, Guyana was one of the 18 countries—four of them in the Western Hemisphere—that qualified.

About the only thing sparkling in the Guayanese economy is its growing diamond production, which reached 250,000 carats in 2002.

The Future: Guyana has passed the torch, in President Kennedy's words, to a new generation of leaders. The two men who dominated the country since even before independence, Forbes Burnham and Cheddi Jagan, are dead. Janet Jagan retired at 79, while the PNC's Desmond Hoyte died in 2002 at age 73 and was replaced by the 55-year-old Robert Corbin. President Jagdeo is still just 41.

Jagdeo and Corbin almost made history on May 2, 2003 with their "Constructive Engagement" pact. It fell apart over the allegations of a government-sanctioned death squad that preys upon mostly black criminals who, the Indo-Guyanese complain, in turn have been preying upon them while the Afro-Guyanese-dominated military or constabulary do little or nothing to protect them.

To be sure, violent crime is a greater crisis in Guyana than even the dismal state of the economy. There were 160 murders in 2002 and 210 in 2003, an appalling number for such a sparsely populated country. Resentments between the two ethnic groups have been simmering dangerously for years, and unless the situation is defused, Guyana has no meaningful future.

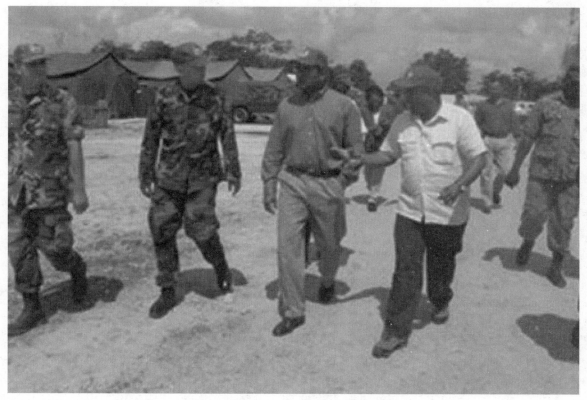

President Bharrat Jagdeo at New Horizons Timehri Base Camp.

197

The Republic of Haiti

Emperor Henri Christophe's *La Citadelle*, **the mountaintop fortress in the north that took 13 years and the labor of 200,000 men to build.**

Area: 10,711 square miles.
Population: 8.1 million (estimated growth rate 1.3% annually).
Capital City: Port-au-Prince (Pop. 1.2 million, estimated).
Climate: Tropical, moderate at higher elevations; rainy season from May to December.
Neighboring Countries: Haiti occupies the western third of Hispañola, the second-largest of the Greater-Antilles; the Dominican Republic occupies the eastern two thirds of the island.
Official Languages: French and Creole, a mixture of French and African origin spoken by almost all Haitians.
Other Principal Tongues: Creole, a dialect of French and African origin spoken by a majority of the rural Haitians.
Ethnic Background: African Negro (90%), mixed African and European (10%).

Principal Religion: Officially Roman Catholic Christianity, but a majority of Haitians practice *voodoo*, a variety of animism similar to African native religions, but with a greater emphasis on mysticism.
Chief Commercial Products: Coffee, light industrial products, sisal, sugar and textiles.
Currency: Gourde.
Gross Domestic Product: U.S. $3.5 billion in 2002 ($425 per capita).
Former Colonial Status: Spanish Colony (1492–1697); French Colony (1697–1804).
Independence Date: January 1, 1804.
Chief of State: Boniface Alexandre (b. January 31, 1936), president (since March 1, 2004).
Chief of Government: Gérard Latortue (b. June 19, 1934), prime minister (since March 9, 2004).
National Flag: Blue and red vertical stripes, coat of arms on white square in center.

The Haitian western one third of the island of Hispaniola is covered by tropically green mountains rising to heights of 9,000 feet. The narrow coastal plains and river valleys, one fifth of the total territory of the nation, are arable, but irrigation is necessary in many of the fields. Of these areas, the Artibonne River valley and the north coastal plains are most suited to agriculture. The mountains that divide Haiti and the Dominican Republic prevent the moisture-laden trade winds from reaching Haiti, thus its lands are generally drier than those of its neighbor.

History: Haiti was discovered by Columbus in 1492 and remained under Spanish control for the following 200 years. Because of the limited number of settlers, the Spanish exploited the eastern part of Hispaniola, neglecting the western portion, which became a popular base for French-speaking pirates. The western portion of the island was ceded to France in 1697, and ultimately became one of that country's most profitable colonies. African slaves had been brought in by the Spanish and their numbers increased during French rule. The slaves obtained their freedom during the period of the French Revolution in a confusion of slave rebellions and civil wars that involved blacks, mulattos, French, Spanish and English on the island of Hispaniola.

Toussaint L'Ouverture, a former slave, rose rapidly to the rank of general during this period. He fought with the Spanish against the French, later joined the French against the English, and ultimately forced them from the island. Napoleon sent a large force under his brother-in-law, General Victor-Emmanuel Leclerc, which cap-

Haiti

tured L'Ouverture and attempted to restore slavery. Independence was finally achieved in 1804 after a dozen years of bitter bloodshed when the French forces were defeated and expelled by the Haitians.

General Jean Jacques Dessalines, commander of the black army, was named governor-general for life. An ex-slave, illiterate, brutal and arrogant, he lacked the qualifications for ruling his newborn nation and was unable to secure aides capable of compensating for his ignorance. The few whites left in Haiti were slaughtered by Dessalines' order—the war had been fought not only to obtain freedom, but also to destroy anything that would remind the blacks of serfdom and forced labor.

Drafting a constitution abolishing slavery, prohibiting land ownership by whites and making the term *Negro* synonymous with Haitian, Dessalines was enthroned as Emperor Jacques I. By use of conscripted labor and enforced discipline, he made some progress in restoring order and in rebuilding the economy until he was assassinated in 1806 by his two trusted military commanders, Henri Christophe and Alexandre Pétion. Haiti then split into two states—the north ruled from Cap-Haitien by Henri Christophe and the south ruled as a republic by Alexandre Pétion. Christophe styled himself emperor; he constructed a massive castle and established an elaborate circle of courtiers, dukes, duchesses and barons who were former slaves. In contrast, Pétion governed the south as an independent republic, and his rule was relatively moderate and progressive. He was at war with Henri Christophe from 1811–18, when the latter, faced with rebellion caused by his cruelty, shot himself with a silver bullet.

Haiti was reunited between 1818 and 1820 by Jean Pierre Boyer, a French-educated mulatto who was able to dominate the entire island by 1822. Initially of moderate outlook, the declining economy and disruption of society induced Boyer to resort to harsh tactics to till the land and restore governmental authority. When he was overthrown in 1844, the Spanish-speaking eastern portion of the island regained its independence and Haiti again fell into the hands of illiterate leaders.

The period from 1843 to 1915 was one of disorder, tyranny and bloodshed under 22 dictators. It was a period of economic and social deterioration. The only occupants of the presidential palace who accomplished any beneficial acts were Fabre Geffrard (1859–67), who cut the army in half, built a few schools and signed a concordat with the Vatican to revitalize the church. Lysius Salomon (1879–88) created a national bank, built rural schools and imported French school teachers. The last, Florvil Hyppolite (1889–96), built bridges,

docks and public buildings and opened telephone and telegraph services.

U.S. Intervention, 1915–34

The country degenerated into anarchy in 1908, culminating in the killing and dismemberment of President Guillaume Sam by an angry mob on July 28, 1915. Sailors and Marines on a U.S. naval vessel offshore promptly seized Port-au-Prince to restore order. The occupation was to last for 19 years under five U.S. presidents of both parties, during which the military high commissioner, Marine Brigadier General John H. Russell, oversaw the successive "elections" of puppet presidents. The president from 1922–30 was Louis Borno, who collaborated so well with Russell that a U.S. financial adviser to Haiti called the arrangement a "joint dictatorship." The United States also imposed a new constitution on Haiti in 1918, written by the assistant secretary of the Navy— Franklin Delano Roosevelt. FDR later was to boast of its authorship. Under Russell's tutelage, there was no freedom of the press or other basic civil liberties. Several newspaper editors, in fact, were jailed in the name of establishing democracy, some-

thing that Thomas Jefferson would have frowned upon.

In 1919, the *cacos*, or peasants, under the leadership of the charismatic Charlemagne Peralte, revolted against U.S. rule. In an operation that has become part of Marine Corps folklore, Major Smedley Butler disguised himself, infiltrated Peralte's camp, killed him with his revolver and forced the other *cacos* to flee. The revolt was crushed, with more than 3,000 Haitians killed in the process.

On the positive side, the Marines greatly improved Haiti's infrastructure. From 1919–22 they built 365 miles of roads and improved 200 miles of existing road. Irrigation systems were repaired and experimental farms set up. The Marines also established the *Garde d'Haiti*, a constabulary that had American officers, to maintain law and order. This force, however, later would become little more than the personal goon squad for a succession of dictators. Moreover, the Americans made no effort to diversify the coffee-dependent economy or to train schoolteachers, with the result that Haiti remained the poorest and least literate nation of the Americas.

When a strike led to another outbreak of violence in 1929 that the Marines ruthlessly crushed, President Herbert Hoover dispatched an investigative commission to inspect the U.S. role in Haiti. In its report, the commission concluded: "The failure of the occupation to understand the social problems of Haiti, its brusque attempt to plant democracy there by drill and harrow, its determination to set up a middle class—however wise and necessary it may seem to Americans—all these explain why, in part, the high hopes of our good works in this land have not been realized."

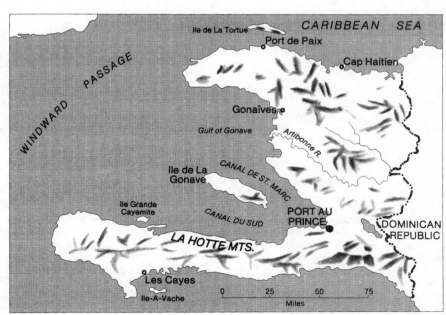

Haiti

A new legislative assembly was elected on October 14, 1930, General Russell resigned on November 1, and on the 19th legislators chose an opposition newspaper editor, Stenio Vincent, as president. Haitians reassumed control of key public agencies a year later. On August 15, 1934, President Roosevelt, who had once boasted of writing Haiti's constitution, withdrew the Marines. It would be 60 years, one month and four days before the next U.S. military intervention.

The departure of the U.S. Marines in 1934 was hailed as Haiti's second emancipation. Haitian politicians and military officers were restored to their former privileges, and the following three decades revealed that Haiti had profited little from U.S. military rule. The Marines had sought to place the educated *mulatto* minority in power, but the *Garde d'Haiti*, consisting principally of mulattos, emerged as the dominant force.

The Duvalier Era

The election of Dr. Francois "Papa Doc" Duvalier as president in 1957 began a new era of dictatorial rule. A devoted voodoo practitioner, Duvalier ruled Haiti by a combination of superstition and brutality. He created an incredibly cruel and imaginative force known as the *Tonton Macoutes* (rough translation: "Uncle's Boogeymen"), which had the capability of appearing out of nowhere to dispense instant justice (usually death or unbelievable torture). This force became an all-pervasive instrument of Haiti's "government." The single most significant accomplishment of his administration was his durability and longevity—he died apparently of natural causes in April 1971. Before his death, Duvalier named his portly, naïve, childish, fun-loving son, Jean-Claude ("Baby Doc") as Haiti's next president for life. Assuming a serious attitude not considered possible, the youthful ruler immediately proceeded to reshape Haiti's horror-filled image with a semblance of political stability and programmed economic growth under the tutelage of his older sister Simone and his mother. New foreign investments created more than 80,000 low-paying jobs.

Although Haiti received more per capita foreign aid than any other Western Hemisphere nation, most benefits were diluted by corruption. Half of all foreign loans and grants were funneled into secret accounts controlled by government leaders. The nation's stagnant economy prompted thousands to flee—often in unsafe boats—to the Bahamas and the United States in search of work. At one time, one out of every 10 persons in the Bahamas was said to be an illegal alien from Haiti.

To improve its international image, Haiti permitted limited free elections in 1979. The so-called "liberalization program" was short-lived; in November 1980 opposition political and intellectual leaders were arrested and deported in the worst government purge since 1963. Although it was not initially apparent to the outside world, "Baby Doc" apparently had become estranged from his mother and "divorced" his sister as the "first lady" of Haiti in favor of a very light-skinned charmer, Michèle Bennett. Her father, on the verge of bankruptcy, quickly became the coffee export baron on Haiti and the family attached itself firmly to the inner circles of government. Michèle tried to emulate the late Evita Perón of Argentina.

To outward appearances, Michèle Duvalier was the soul of charity and kindness, opening orphanages, providing relief for the poor and tirelessly working against injustice. But the palace life she created was another story. Luxuries piled upon luxuries and she "ran" Jean-Claude with an iron fist. Worst of all, she had television sets placed in every small town and settlement to (1) show all of her charitable works and, foolishly, (2) to broadcast the festivities from the marble palace. Her father and family graduated from the edge of bankruptcy to rich, elite exporters and businessmen. Goose liver paté contrasted sharply with garbage—anger started to smolder.

The Revolt of 1986

Perhaps the straw that broke Haiti's back occurred when Michèle went on a Paris shopping spree that cost more than $1 million! Among the items purchased in profusion were fur coats to be given as gifts to close friends. But alas, the palace was too hot for fur coats! The solution: install coolers. When this appeared on rural television (a charity ball!) it proved the beginning of the end.

The final insult came with the arrival of 1,200 money-laden passengers for the inauguration of a much celebrated and criticized new tourist haven on the island of Labadie at a resort developed under questionable financial circumstances. They were not to be exposed to Haiti's "backward" atmosphere, but rather, to luxury.

Rioting erupted in late January 1986. Duvalier made tentative efforts to disband the *Tonton Macoutes* and undertook some other reforms—all too late. The rioting continued and intensified. Amid chaos, "Baby Doc" and his wife were flown out of Haiti in a U.S. plane for France ("to spend eight days") in early February. Since no other country would receive him, he is still there. "Papa Doc's" tomb was raided (his body wasn't there) and others were broken open; skulls were paraded

through the streets. The Bennett family was all but wiped out. Shopkeepers had closed their shops, frozen with fear, in spite of governmental threats. Among the prime movers behind the revolt were the "liberation theology" priests of the Roman Catholic Church who from the pulpit regularly condemned the government.

A military regime under General Henri Namphy emerged to lead Haiti. Assets of the Duvaliers in various parts of the world, including the United States, France and Switzerland were frozen. However, enough remained untouched to apparently enable "Baby Doc" to live in comfort during his lifetime.

The ouster of Duvalier did not end violence in Haiti. Mobs sought out the members of the *Tonton Macoutes* and brutally murdered them. There were riots when the head of that organization was allowed to leave for Brazil instead of facing trial.

After a new constitution was adopted in 1987, there followed a procession of presidents averaging eight months in office before being overthrown. They all had initial approval of the military and the elite Haitians, which quickly soured as they tried to expand the bases of their popularity. The last one in early 1990 took the offensive: he had all significant rivals for power seized and beaten, then exiled to Florida. He also went there after the U.S. ambassador persuaded him that there was no choice—either he left or Haiti faced unbridled violence.

Elections were again attempted in late December 1990. Jean-Bertrand Aristide, a "liberation theology" priest who had been thundering anti-Duvalier, anti-elite rhetoric from his pulpit (defrocked by the Catholic Church for meddling in politics) was elected president. This was by a majority of 70%, despite the opposition of the army, the elite, the Catholic Church and what was left of the *Tonton Macoutes*. But he was revered by the poor. The army commander was able to coerce his men into inaction and silence to ensure free elections.

Lacking military support, President Aristide imported 60 Swiss officers to train a new palace guard loyal to him. Fearing loss of power, the military ousted him on September 30, 1991, and only the intervention of the United States, Canada, France and Venezuela prevented his assassination. He went initially to Venezuela, later entering the United States in early 1992, where he spent large sums of money from frozen Haitian assets without accounting for them.

French, EC and U.S. aid to Haiti was immediately suspended. An uneven trade embargo was imposed, dampened by President Bush and Europeans eager to make dollars from Haitian misfortune. Acting in spite of the embargo, they

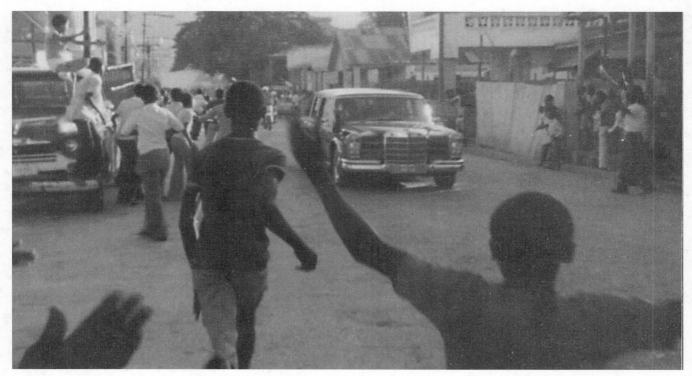

Haitians greet car of former president "Baby Doc" Duvalier, who is throwing money out of the car windows

Photo by Susan L. Thompson

shipped petroleum to Haiti, which was immediately snapped up by the military and the elite. The poor of the island became even more desperate, and began leaving by home-made boats for Florida and Guantanamo Bay, Cuba. The United States immediately blocked this with its Coast Guard, even though its activities were not within the coastal limits of the United States.

Of the Haitians who made it to the United States or Guantanamo, only about 11% were admitted as political refugees. Incredibly poor and uneducated, many of them infected with AIDS and other diseases, they were considered undesirables. Meanwhile, the Black Caucus of the U.S. Congress demanded that Aristide be returned and installed in office by U.S. troops, if necessary.

One of the cruelest hoaxes occurred during the U.S. presidential campaign of 1992. Democratic candidate Bill Clinton flatly promised that, if elected president, he would immediately admit refugee Haitians to the United States without limit. When Clinton was elected in November, countless numbers of Haitians began building boats, using any materials they could find, legally or illegally, awaiting the day of Clinton's inaugural so they could set sail from misery to hope. Literally within hours of taking the oath of office, Clinton decided that it was "wise" to continue the policies of his predecessor in office, whom he had defeated.

A substantial number of Haitians were quarantined at Guantanamo Bay because they were carriers of the HIV virus which develops into AIDS. A U.S. district judge ordered their release to the United States in mid-1993 because they had been in quarantine "too long." Although thousands of Haitians were returned to their country by the United States, there was no evidence that they were mistreated by the military led by General Raoul Cedras.

The question of Haiti appeared to have been solved in mid-1993 when an agreement was signed in New York by Aristide, Cedras and the head of the national police that Aristide would return by October 31. Training officers for the Haitian police appeared at Port-au-Prince aboard U.S. and Canadian vessels, but were prevented from landing by Haiti's informal military. Cedras did not abide by the agreement.

When President Clinton received black support in Congress on the NAFTA treaty and other measures, he was called upon to respond with more energetic action to remove the military from power in Haiti and to reinstall Aristide. On the refugee problem, the United Nations adopted di-

A wedding near Port–au–Prince

Haiti

Panoramic view of Port–au–Prince

rectives that they be received by all nations (actually meaning the United States).

To try to lower the pressures concerning Haiti, the U.S. Central Intelligence Agency was clumsily used in 1994 to float rumors that Aristide in his earlier life had experienced bouts of insanity. There was no proof of such a charge; what seemed to be a good reason to dump him became an acute embarrassment.

U.S. Intervention, 1994

Pressures for action mounted after mid-1994 and there was increased talk from Clinton threatening invasion of the island. Such a move was authorized by the U.N. Security Council in July. Troops were readied in September, and in a last-ditch effort, Clinton dispatched former President Jimmy Carter, Senator Sam Nunn and retired General Colin Powell to Haiti. They persuaded the military leadership to stand down and leave Haiti. Within days, the military leadership departed the island.

A force overwhelmingly of U.S. troops entered the island peacefully on September 19 and took up a triple role: janitors, policemen and, later, presidential guard after Aristide returned to the island. Little in their combat training prepared them for such roles. Both before and after his return on October 15, Aristide modified his former radical positions to become acceptable to the elite. A disarmament program was immediately organized, but for every weapon obtained, at least 10 were hidden by their owners. Almost 4,000 Haitian refugees were repatriated from Guantanamo Bay. The army, seen as an obstacle to democracy, was disbanded. That move would backfire on Aristide a decade later.

Aristide appointed Smarck Michel as prime minister; together they devised plans for election of a new Parliament in mid-1995. There were plans to withdraw U.S. forces by the fall of 1995, which proved impossible. Aristide's supporters started behaving as goons, not as saviors of their nation. A well-known opponent of Aristide was gunned down in March 1995. This was one of the first in an incalculable number of murders of anti-Aristide Haitians; his personal involvement was suspected.

The Préval Presidency

Aristide floated the idea of canceling presidential elections scheduled for the fall of 1995 so he could remain in office—a proposition that even liberals in the U.S. Congress shrank from in horror. René Préval won in an election with a light turnout; although Aristide hated him, he embraced him at his inauguration in February 1996.

Préval undertook the unenviable task of trying to govern a country still beset by economic, political and social conditions that have made it the basket case of the Western Hemisphere. As if he didn't have problems enough, he inherited a palace guard that was loyal to Aristide and who he did not trust. The United States dispatched a special security team to guard the president during the second half of the year.

Like so many other recent Latin American leaders, Préval faced economic reality and launched a program aimed at priva-

tizing the inefficient state-owned enterprises. He had the added incentive of meeting requirements of the International Monetary Fund to qualify for additional loans, which accounted for 60 percent of Haiti's budget. Part of the painful austerity program was the elimination of 7,000 of 43,000 public employees. As usually happens, the austerity measures sparked a series of protest demonstrations early in 1997. Préval also undertook an effort to distribute parcels of land to peasants, but the tracts were so tiny—1.2 acres—that they could not be commercially viable, and while he won meager appreciation from the recipients of the parcels, he was condemned by those who were left out.

A wave of political violence claimed about 50 lives in February and March 1997. Préval attributed the killings to remnants of the *Tonton Macoutes*, the paramilitary gang of thugs that enforced the will of the two Duvaliers.

The democratic process came close to total breakdown following Senate elections in April 1997. Aristide had established an offshoot of his *Lavalas* (Avalanche) Political Organization, or *OPL*, called the *Fanmi* (Family) *Lavalas*, apparently designed as a vehicle for his reelection in 2000. The Aristide faction was accused of rigging the election, which would have given *Famni* a majority in the Senate. Préval indefinitely postponed the runoff elections until the matter could be resolved. Prime Minister Rosny Smarth resigned in June to protest Aristide's alleged power play, but agreed to remain until Parliament confirmed a successor. In August, however, the 83-member Chamber of Deputies, in which the *OPL* was the largest bloc with 33, rejected Préval's nominee, Ericq Pierre.

In October, Préval nominated Hervé Denis, a 58-year-old economist committed to privatization of nine state-owned companies. In December, the Chamber voted 34–33 to confirm Denis, but abstentions

Former President René Préval

left him short of the needed majority. Préval stubbornly re-nominated Denis in March 1998, and the *OPL* just as stubbornly vowed not to confirm any nominee until the president dismissed the nine members of the electoral council and had the election results revised. Préval refused, and while this petty contest of wills continued, as much as $300 million in foreign aid packages was tied up because there was no one to negotiate them. It also frightened away whatever foreign investors who may have been bold enough to do business in Haiti.

U.S. Secretary of State Madeleine Albright visited Haiti in March and chided both sides for their failure to resolve the impasse. It seemed the logjam was broken in April when the Chamber finally confirmed Denis. But the nomination was blocked in the Senate when it received approval of eight of the 16 senators—not an absolute majority.

While the domestic crisis was unfolding, the three-year mandate of the U.N. peacekeeping force, composed of Canadians and Pakistanis, expired on November 30, 1997; the foreign troops withdrew the next day. It was the worst possible timing. Political violence and common street crime were engulfing the country, while drug traffickers began swarming into Haiti like cockroaches into a dark, filthy kitchen. Not only did the 5,200-member police force established under U.S. and U.N. auspices prove incapable of maintaining order, but the new police force had killed about 100 people, roughly half of them without any apparent justification. Two of Préval's bodyguards and two of his chauffeurs were gunned down (even his dog was stabbed to death), and he asked the United Nations to protect the presidential palace. Two days before the peacekeeping force left, the U.N. Security Council voted to establish a 290-member civilian police force with a one-year mandate. There also were 500 U.S. military "engineers" still in Haiti engaged in public works projects. They left in early 2000.

With the Denis nomination twice rebuffed by Parliament, Préval staged a strategic withdrawal in July 1998 and nominated as prime minister his minister of education, Jacques Edouard Alexis. For months, Parliament took no action, and the crisis rumbled on. Meanwhile, the Senate, facing the imminent expiration in January of the terms of eight of its remaining 16 elected members, simply voted in November to extend those terms until November 1999, apparently hoping that the impasse would be resolved and new elections called before then. It was an act of dubious constitutionality, and the Chamber of Deputies took no similar action to extend its own expiring mandate.

It suddenly seemed again that the logjam would be broken when, in December 1999, the Senate unexpectedly ratified Alexis 12–1, with three abstentions. Two days later, the Chamber followed suit, with 46 of the 78 remaining deputies voting to ratify Alexis. The president then promised to appoint a new electoral council by the end of December, and the country—as well as the United Nations and the U.S. government—breathed a collective sigh of relief.

Alas, Préval ignored his own deadline and failed to appoint the electoral council. The crisis flared up anew on January 11, 1999, the date of the expiration of parliamentary mandates. Declaring that in the absence of new elections there was no longer a parliamentary quorum, Préval announced that he would begin ruling by decree. The reaction was immediate and violent, as pro-*OPL* demonstrators, denouncing the move as a ploy by Préval to assume dictatorial powers, took to the streets. So did pro-Préval demonstrators, who blockaded local municipal councils on the pretext that their terms, too, had expired. Members of Parliament showed up for work in what was a largely symbolic gesture, because they found only one functioning telephone and the Finance Ministry had severed their operating funds.

The day after Préval's announcement, his sister was critically wounded in an ambush that killed her driver. Alexis, meanwhile, announced that he was assuming the post of prime minister and naming a cabinet in the absence of Parliament. Once again, Préval set a deadline of February 2, 2000, to name a new electoral council that would call new elections, and once again he let his own deadline pass, claiming he needed more time to choose a suitable council. Denying he was setting himself up as Haiti's latest dictator, he insisted, "It is democracy we are building."

The Electoral Farces of 2000

If so, the architect and carpenters should have been fired. Twice in mid-1999 the Provisional Electoral Council (*CEP*) set parliamentary election dates, first for November 28, then for December 19. Both were canceled. The CEP set a third date for March 19, 2000, but just two weeks before the elections the *CEP* declared a third postponement, which Préval ratified. The *CEP* then set April 9 and May 21 as the new dates for the first and second rounds, but Préval disapproved those dates.

At that point, the United States and the European Union impatiently reminded Préval that $500 million in aid that Haiti desperately needed was contingent upon his calling the long-overdue parliamentary elections. The Haitian people began show-

Former President Jean-Bertrand Aristide

ing their impatience as well with mass demonstrations on March 27 that left four people dead. According to the Organization of American States, there had been at least 50 separate incidents of politically related violence since the previous October. In a case of unfortunate timing, the last of the U.N. forces had withdrawn from Haiti just nine days before.

In April 2000, the *CEP* and Préval agreed on a fourth date: May 21, with runoffs on June 25, later moved to July 8. At stake were 19 of the 27 Senate seats and all 83 members of the Chamber of Deputies, plus about 7,500 local offices. During the six-week campaign that followed, at least 15 candidates or campaign workers for various parties were murdered, some hacked to death with machetes in traditional fashion. Another casualty, on April 3, was Jean Dominique, the country's most prominent radio commentator, who was gunned down as he arrived at work. Dominique had made enemies on both the far right and the far left. Six men believed to be the triggermen were arrested and eventually indicted two years later, but the investigation into who ordered Dominique's death was stymied by intimidation, including the murders of two witnesses.

Just two days before the voting, six opposition groups hastily formed an alliance in a last-ditch effort to prevent a predicted landslide by Aristide's *Lavalas* movement. It did not appear to have worked, although it was hard to tell. The election was marred by poor organization and outright manipulation. Many polling places opened late, and at others, the ballots had not yet arrived; they were still being printed.

In the department of Grand Anse, the election was postponed altogether because inter-party bickering had prevented voter registration. In some cases, workers

Haiti

refused to deliver election material unless they were paid in advance. OAS observers reported cases of vote fraud and intimidation of voters by pro-Aristide militants, which the U.N.-trained police force seemed uninterested in stopping. A policeman and a gunman were killed at one polling place. An opposition candidate for a local office was stoned to death. Some opposition pollwatchers reported they were denied entry by *Lavalas* partisans. Finally, as polls closed, armed goons, presumably from *Lavalas,* stormed several polling places and made off with the ballot boxes. Marked ballots, representing about 10% of those cast, were found lying in the street in front of the vote-counting center in the capital; workers swept up about 90% of them. It was Haitian "democracy" as usual.

The OAS official in charge of the 200 international observers, speaking with considerable understatement, termed the irregularities "most unfortunate." Former U.S. President Carter, whose Atlanta-based Carter Center also participated in observing the election, told this author in Caracas, Venezuela, six days later: "It is obvious to me that the election in Haiti was seriously flawed." About the only thing to cheer was the record voter turnout: An estimated 60% of the 4 million eligible voters—a far cry from the 5% who voted in the annulled 1997 elections. Unfortunately, not all their votes were counted.

According to the "results" released by the *CEP* days after the election, *Lavalas* won 16 of the 19 Senate seats and 23 deputy seats without a runoff. But on June 2, the deputy chief of the OAS observation mission reported that the *CEP* apparently had miscalculated the final percentages for the Senate by counting only the votes for the top four candidates for each seat. Eliminating the votes for lesser candidates gave several *Lavalas* candidates outright majorities that they did not actually have. The opposition and the observers claimed that 10 "winning" *Lavalas* Senate candidates should have faced a runoff. When the official results were finally announced, *Lavalas* held all but one of the 27 Senate seats and more than 80% of the seats in the Chamber of Deputies; it also controlled almost all the municipal governments.

This creative tabulating brought international demands that the *CEP* count the votes properly. In June, even U.N. Secretary-General Kofi Annan urged a clean vote count. But the government refused to budge. In fact, two weeks before the runoff elections, the president of the *CEP* fled to the Dominican Republic and then to the United States, saying that government officials had threatened him with death if he did not certify the flawed re-

sults. He had refused. The following day, Aristide supporters took to the streets to burn tires and to demand that the government release the results. It did—the flawed ones.

This farce was continued into the presidential election of November 26, 2000, which the major opposition parties boycotted to protest the parliamentary elections. (In a peripheral farce, two days before the election Parliament finally confirmed Alexis in the office he had held for 20 months.) Aristide, who almost certainly would have won anyway, was thus opposed only by six unknown candidates, and even they did not campaign because of threats of violence against them. In the usual pre-election violence, nine pipe bombings killed two people and injured at least 16. The United States, Canada and the European Union withdrew their observers rather than participate in a sham. In the balloting, Aristide predictably received 92% of the vote. The government declared that the turnout had been 60.5%, but more objective assessments put it at between 15% and 20%, depriving Aristide of a meaningful mandate.

Three weeks later, 15 opposition parties, calling themselves the Democratic Convergence, declared they would form an "alternative government" and even brashly called on *Lavalas* to join them. Certain of his position, however, Aristide brushed aside their call, and he was sworn in on February 7, 2001. Just as the opposition parties had boycotted the election, the international community largely snubbed the inauguration.

Governing a Cauldron

The opposition rebuffed Aristide's invitation to join his government, saying his election was illegitimate. It demanded new elections, and suggested Gerard Gourgue as an interim president. On March 14, 2001, an opposition demonstration in front of the local headquarters of the OAS, which had sought to broker a truce between the government and the opposition, was broken up by Aristide supporters. The ensuing violence left three people dead. In April, OAS Assistant Secretary-General Luigi Einaudi arrived in Haiti to attempt to jumpstart talks. Aristide supporters staged a tire-burning demonstration and blocked traffic, apparently to impress the OAS team that while Aristide is open to new talks with the opposition, they will be on his terms.

The talks dragged on, then broke down in July. Under U.S. and OAS pressure, *Lavalas* and the Convergence agreed to renew talks in October. They agreed in principle for a new parliamentary election to be held in November, but the opposition

rejected Aristide's "nonnegotiable" demand that the incumbent lawmakers be allowed to serve out their terms, which made new elections pointless. The talks collapsed after one day.

On December 17, 2001, a band of about 30 armed men stormed the National Palace in an attempted *coup d'etat*, killing two guards and two bystanders; they had first attacked the national penitentiary but were repulsed. Forces loyal to Aristide quickly recaptured the palace, killing one of the gunmen and capturing seven; another was apprehended as he attempted to cross the Dominican border. Two other men were arrested later, and Haiti demanded that the Dominican Republic extradite a former police captain believed to be hiding there; there also was evidence of involvement by Dominican soldiers in the attack.

Although the attackers appeared to be disgruntled former soldiers from the army that Aristide had disbanded in 1994, rather than Convergence activists, Aristide supporters around the country used the palace attack as a pretext to go on a rampage against the opposition, wielding machetes, erecting barricades and burning tires. A Convergence headquarters and the homes of three Convergence leaders were burned; four people were burned alive by mobs. Fearing for his life, Gourgue went into hiding. Pro-Convergence radio stations received threats. Much of the violence was believed linked to Aristide's personal goon squads, called *chimères*, or ghosts. They hacked to death another prominent radio journalist, Brignol Lindor, in February 2001 after he allowed opposition representatives on his talk show.

In March 2002, Prime Minister Jean-Marie Cherestal resigned amid mounting public pressure from Aristide supporters, who faulted him for not doing enough for the economy, which shrank by 1.2% in 2001. As his replacement, Aristide nominated, and Parliament approved, Senate President Yvon Neptune, who said his first priority would be to promote a dialogue with the opposition. In June, Aristide met with Convergence leaders for the first time in two years. The president assured the opposition that he would move to satisfy their demands, including reparations for the property destroyed by mobs in December. But the stalemate, and the public unrest, continued, with each side blaming the other for the continued freeze on $500 million in desperately needed international aid.

In May, Aristide ordered the imprisonment of Amiot Metayer, leader of one of his own *chimères*, which was called the "Cannibal Army." Metayer, who allegedly had burned down houses of a rival gang,

204

was charged with arson. Amiot then turned against Aristide, and in August Metayer's gang used a bulldozer to smash into his jail in Gonaives and free him and about 150 other inmates. Anti-Aristide demonstrations then broke out around the country, while Metayer disappeared—for 13 months.

International pressure increased on Aristide to clean up his act. Haiti joined the Caribbean Community (CARICOM) in July 2002, but at a summit in December the leaders of the other 14 member nations called for new elections to end the stalemate.

In March 2003, the OAS' Einaudi made yet another attempt to resolve the impasse and clear the way for a resumption of aid. Einaudi led a delegation of representatives from the United States, Canada, the European Union and OAS countries and insisted that Aristide take steps to disarm the *chimères*, respect human rights and overhaul the police. The delegation set a deadline of March 30 to set up a new electoral council to pave the way for new elections. The deadline was ignored.

Aristide Falls

Two events then set things in motion that would eventually bring down Aristide. The first was a scheduled meeting of representatives of 180 civic groups that were demanding Aristide's resignation in Cité Soleil, a teeming slum near the capital that is considered a stronghold of Aristide supporters. When the Aristide opponents sought to assemble on July 12, 2003, pro-Aristide mobs pelted them with rocks. Dozens were injured, including six journalists covering the event. The opposition countered with mass anti-Aristide demonstrations in Cap-Haitien, the second-largest city, on August 30 and September 14, both of which turned violent.

Then, on September 22, the body of Metayer was found near the coastal town of St. Marc. Metayer, who was believed to have been in hiding in his stronghold town of Raboteau, had been shot in the heart and through each eye. The identity of the assassins was a mystery, but Metayer's supporters were quick to accuse Aristide of silencing him because of his knowledge of the government's sins. Aristide denied complicity, but it was too late; a large, well-organized, well-armed band of thugs that had been loyal to him now took up arms against him.

Metayer's death sparked more than a week of tire-burning in the capital and in Gonaïves, the fourth-largest city, where gangs burned or ransacked four government buildings and captured weapons. Over the next three months, about 50 people died in sporadic political violence.

Then, in January 2004, even as the country observed the bicentennial of its independence, all hell began to break loose. Once again, the mandate of the Chamber of Deputies expired and no elections were forthcoming, so Aristide began ruling by decree as Préval had done. First came a general strike by shopkeepers. On January 18, the funeral of a student shot to death during an anti-Aristide demonstration the week before turned into yet another violent confrontation between demonstrators and police that left one person dead and six injured. Another violent confrontation on January 29 left an Aristide partisan dead.

Political attempts to resolve the impasse came to nothing. On January 20, a delegation of 14 opposition representatives, calling themselves the Democratic Platform, met with several Caribbean prime ministers during a CARICOM summit in the Bahamas. A CARICOM delegation came to Haiti for a fact-finding mission and on January 31, met with Aristide in Kingston, Jamaica. Aristide agreed to disarm his *chimères* and to reform the police. Now it was the opposition that became intransigent, saying Aristide must step down.

But it was the armed groups that were destined to determine the course of events. On February 5, armed insurrection broke out in at least a dozen towns, and rebels soon captured Gonaïves, symbolic as the cradle of Haitian independence. Metayer's brother, Butheur, declared himself the new police chief there. The first

week of the insurrection, 47 people were killed. Neptune admitted that the 5,000-man police force was incapable of dealing with the uprising—even if it had been so inclined. Many policemen simply fled as the rebels took town after town. The army, of course, had been disbanded in 1994—by Aristide. It literally became gang warfare, the rebels against the *chimères*.

The rebels, who named their movement the National Resistance Front for the Liberation of Haiti, were far from an army of liberation. They were a rag-tag, unappetizing and improbable collection of disgruntled Aristide loyalists, former soldiers from the army Aristide had disbanded for overthrowing him, even former members of the Duvaliers' *Tonton Macoutes*. Apparently the only thing they had in common was a belief in violence as a means for achieving their ends, and this they wielded skillfully. At first, the Democratic Platform disavowed the violence and distanced itself from the rebels, many of whose leaders were known killers. One was Louis-Jodel Chamblain, known as a former death squad leader under Baby Doc Duvalier, who was later convicted and sentenced to life while he was in exile for the 1993 murder of an Aristide associate. But when the rebels began achieving victories, they could not be ignored. Eventually, Guy Philippe, a more respectable former army officer and the former police chief in Cap-Haitien, emerged as their leader.

Meanwhile, U.S. Secretary of State Colin Powel admonished Aristide for con-

President Boniface Alexandre

Haiti

Palm trees along the northern coast of Haiti

tinuing to unleash gangs of thugs to attack peaceful demonstrations, but he insisted, for the time being, that the United States stood by the elected president. On February 21, Aristide finally yielded to a U.S.-brokered power-sharing plan that would have allowed him to remain in office. But the opposition, sensing imminent victory, turned it down.

That same day, 200 rebels overran Cap-Haitien, and looters went wild. The overall death toll rose to 80. The rebels began planning their attack on Port-au-Prince. A siege mentality gripped the capital as the Aristide gangs erected barricades. Foreign nationals left in droves. U.S. Marines entered Port-au-Prince to safeguard the embassy—much as they had in 1915. Philippe vowed to take the presidential palace and arrest Aristide. On February 27, the rebels captured Mirebalais, just 30 miles from the capital. There also was an

uprising in Les Cayes, the third-largest city, on the other side of Port-au-Prince.

Aristide remained defiant and pleaded for international troops to keep him in power, but by now Powell was questioning whether the man the United States had reinstalled in 1994 should in fact continue to misgovern his country. The United Nations said it would send peacekeeping forces only if Aristide and the opposition could agree on a power-sharing arrangement, which, of course, the opposition had no intention of, and no incentive for, accepting. Chaos reigned in Port-au-Prince, as Aristide's supporters even ransacked a hospital in search of wounded rebels. Looting was widespread.

On Sunday, February 29, 2004, Aristide resigned and fled the country, flying to the Central African Republic. The jubilation in the streets was immediate. Under the constitution, Supreme Court Chief Justice

Boniface Alexandre, 67, became interim president, but the menacing rebel gangs on the outskirts of the capital had not yet agreed to lay down their arms. Anti-Aristide mobs went in search of retribution, and exacted it. There were several execution-style slayings in the ensuing days. A contingent of 100 U.S. Marines and 300 French Legionnaires arrived in the capital as the vanguard of the latest U.N. peacekeeping mission, which had hastily been approved.

The rebel army entered Port-au-Prince on March 2, peacefully, as the U.S. Marines watched warily. Philippe announced that he was not interested in political power but wanted to be "military chief." Meanwhile, 1,500 more Marines entered Haiti, as did 500 more French and 130 Chilean troops, to maintain order and, unofficially, to prop up the new government. Philippe claimed he welcomed the foreign intervention.

Haiti

On March 9, Haiti moved a step closer to establishing a semblance of a government when a seven-member "Council of Sages" bypassed the leadership of the Democratic Platform to agree on a new prime minister to replace the detested Neptune. Their choice: Gérard Latortue, 69, a former U.N. official who had served briefly as foreign minister during one of the revolving-door presidencies in 1988, and who had been working as an international consultant in Boca Raton, Florida. Unlike Aristide's figurehead prime ministers, however, Latortue was given some genuine authority to run the government. He stated his top priorities were to establish law and order and to arrange for new elections. He also hinted he may re-establish an army. As interior minister he named Herard Abraham, one of the few respected retired generals from the Duvalier era.

Latortue also demonstrated political skills. On March 20, he addressed a rally of 3,000 cheering people in Gonaïves, his home town, to pay tribute to the rebels; he even praised the murdered gang leader Metayer as the catalyst for the overthrow of Aristide. Many of the rebels agreed to lay down their arms; many others did not, however, nor did the *chiméres*. Four of them were shot to death when they foolishly ambushed a Marine patrol.

Meanwhile, in a bizarre postscript, Aristide told journalists in his temporary exile that the United States had forcibly removed him from the presidential palace, in effect, not just abetting but staging a *coup d'etat*. The State Department denied the allegation, but its official declarations made it clear that the United States was glad to get rid of this embarrassment. CARICOM leaders, however, tended to accept Aristide's version and demanded that the U.N. General Assembly and the OAS investigate. They also were unhappy with what they saw as Latortue's kowtowing to the rebels. On June 8, despite objections from the United States and the new Haitian government, the OAS General Assembly voted to invoke Section 20 of the charter to determine whether the government of a member country was subverted through unconstitutional means.

Aristide stayed in Africa only a week before flying to Jamaica. There, on March 25, he announced his final destination: South Africa. He had developed a friendship with President Thabo Mbeke, who had tried to broker a dialogue with Aristide and the opposition at one point. Aristide arrived in Johannesburg on May 31, telling any reporters who would listen to him that he was still the legitimate president of Haiti and that the United States had forced him to leave. Latortue, meanwhile, flew to Washington to plead for renewed aid. The United States announced

in May it was increasing its aid to Haiti for the year by $60 million, bringing it to $160. That would not have happened, of course, had Aristide remained.

On June 1, the U.N. peacekeeping mission, 8,000 strong, set up its headquarters. The largest contingent was 1,200 Brazilian troops, so overall command was given to Brazilian General Augusto Ribeiro Pereira. There were also 500 Argentine troops, along with Canadians and Nepalese. The United States removed its troops by June 30. The United Nations authorized a force of 5,700, but by August there were only 2,300 U.N. peacekeepers left, far too few to deal with the lawlessness and political turmoil that was to come.

The new Haitian government let the foreigners know it was in no hurry for them to leave, especially after devastating floods in late May that killed 1,191 Haitians and left 1,484 unaccounted for. In September, Hurricane Jeanne slammed into Haiti, killing an estimated 3,000 people and leaving thousands more homeless. It seemed that Haiti was indeed living under a curse.

In July, a group of donor nations pledged $1.3 billion in aid for Haiti. But it has proven slow in disbursement.

Futile Quest for Stability

After a year and a half, the fall of Aristide has not proven to be the panacea for the country's ills that his opponents had hoped. The unelected Alexandre-Latortue interim government is viewed by many Haitians, and in some international circles, as illegitimate. Meanwhile, Aristide's *chimères* launched a low-grade insurgency roughly analogous to the insurgency in Iraq; indeed, they dubbed their effort "Operation Baghdad." Unlike the supporters of the deposed Saddam Hussein, the *chimères* are mercifully less well armed and apparently less well organized. Like the Iraqi insurgents, however, they hope for a return to the *ancien regime*.

The first major clash in the ongoing insurgency came in Port-au-Prince on September 30, 2004, when Aristide supporters demonstrated to commemorate the 13th anniversary of his 1991 overthrow. Three policemen were killed in a battle with the *chimères,* and by the time the violence subsided—temporarily—five days later, the overall death toll had reached 45. At least seven of them were policemen, three of whom were beheaded, in the style of the Iraqi insurgents. On October 24, Haitian police and Brazilian troops staged a counteroffensive by raiding *chimère*-controlled slums, in what proved to be little more than a show of force. Amnesty International charged that the interim government was little better than the insurgents,

accusing it of illegal detentions and at least 11 summary executions.

But the *chimères* were not the only threat to the interim government, or to U.N. peacekeepers. The former soldiers of the old army who had helped bring down Aristide, themselves still heavily armed, began demanding that the interim government reconstitute the army and restore them to their old positions—with back pay. In December 2004, Brazilian troops stormed an estate once owned by Aristide, which some of the former soldiers had converted into a fortress. The ex-soldiers surrendered peacefully and laid down their weapons. By March, hundreds of them had been allowed to join the new national police force, raising fears about the potential for human rights abuses.

By December, the U.N. contingent had been boosted to 7,400 to deal with the mounting violence. Brazil again played the leading role, but the force also included 1,000 Jordanians and some Chinese and Filipinos.

In a step toward legitimacy, Latortue announced on January 31, 2005, that elections would be held for president and Parliament on November 20 and that he would not be a candidate. The date was later changed to November 13, with runoffs to be held on December 18. Elections for 7,000 local offices were scheduled for October 9. A total of 91 parties have organized to contest the elections, including Aristide's *Lavalas*. The United States, Canada, the European Union and the United Nations have pledged to fund the elections. The new government would take charge in February 2006.

In April 2005, Aristide boldly declared from his exile that he wanted to be restored to power and that he would conduct free and fair elections; if so, it would be the first time. That same month, a U.N. fact-finding mission to Haiti cautiously predicted that the elections could be held on schedule despite the violence. But in May Secretary-General Kofi Annan said it would require 750 more troops and 275 more policemen to safeguard the electoral process.

Neither the call for the elections nor the concessions to the former soldiers was to stem the violence, however. On March 20, two U.N. peacekeeping troops—one from Nepal and one from Sri Lanka—were killed, and three others wounded in separate gun battles with former soldiers. Two of the former soldiers also were killed in the fierce firefights and 10 others wounded.

Since then, violence committed by rival gangs of pro- and anti-Aristide partisans has continued almost unabated, a lawless scenario reminiscent of the Lincoln County War in New Mexico of the 1870s, only with a much higher death toll. The U.N. peacekeepers and the 3,500 Haitian

Haiti

police have found themselves doing battle with both groups. On April 9, police killed Remissainthe Ravix, one of the key leaders of the former soldiers. Five days later, a Filipino army sergeant was killed in a clash with *chiméres*. The next day, police and Jordanian troops invaded Cité Soleil and clashed with the Aristide partisans, killing 10 of them. A new wave of violence in June 2005 left nine people dead, including a French diplomat, bringing the death toll since September 30, 2004, to about 750, of which 40 were policemen. The toll continues to mount daily. The Haitian Cabinet chief in June expressed displeasure over the capabilities of the U.N. peacekeepers and suggested U.S. troops may have to return to guarantee the electoral process. On June 22, the U.N. Security Council approved an additional 1,000 troops to safeguard the election.

One who did not die violently, as his brother did, was Butteur Metayer, one of the key instigators of the 2004 revolt against Aristide. He died of kidney failure on June 8, 2005. How his death might affect the complex equation in Haiti was uncertain.

Former Prime Minister Neptune, who had been arrested on June 27, 2004, ostensibly for ordering the massacre of Aristide opponents during the 2004 uprising, remains in jail without charges. In late February 2005, he began a hunger strike to protest his detention. When this book went to press, his condition was reported to be grave. Aristide's interior minister, Jocelerme Privert, also was arrested in 2004 without charges and went on a hunger strike. But in April 2005 the government filed specific charges that he had ordered the murders of Aristide opponents during the uprising of 2004.

Culture: Haiti's culture is a singular blend of African and European influences. A minority, the mulattos, relatively better educated in the French language schools, boast of their European culture and superiority. Educated in medicine and law, they patronize the arts and disdain most manual work. Most are Christian.

The Haitians are, for the most part, an illiterate peasant society. Poor and neglected, they practice *voodoo*, a type of animism with African roots with many spirits and deities, and great emphasis on the powers of evil and good spirits. Voodoo, or *voudou* as the Haitians spell it, was sanctioned in the 1987 constitution but was not officially recognized as a religion with legal authority to perform marriages and baptisms until 2003.

Their language is a dramatic indication of their culture. Called *Creole*, it is a blend of French, Spanish, English and Dutch, the foreign influences to which Haiti has been exposed, with a distinct basis in African dialects and tongues.

Creole is the basic language of the country; in addition to their French, the mulattos also speak this tongue. Some of its terms baffled troops sent by the United States to help Haiti. An important, wealthy person in Creole is a *gros neg*—"big nigger"—and a foreigner, regardless of race, is a *blanc*—"white." Most artistic expression has *voodoo* overtones. Traditional African designs blend with imaginative contemporary motifs in cloth, wood carving and basketry. Such crafts are valued internationally.

Economy: Haiti's economy, based on peasant survival at unbelievably low levels, is almost nonexistent. Deforestation, soil erosion and overpopulation all combine to limit agricultural production. The leading cash crops are coffee, cotton, sisal, cacao and sugar. Low wage scales are attracting foreign investment in light industry such as electronic assembly, finished leather goods and tourism. A new industry centered around clothes assembly is booming. Precut materials are sent from the United States and sewn into garments in Haiti. This substantially lowers import duties when the finished product is shipped to the United States.

When former President Bush watered down the embargo on Haiti, he did so not out of consideration of Haitians, but because of extreme pressure from the U.S. garment makers and merchants.

During the 1980s the economy suffered from expensive fuel imports, low prices for coffee exports and hurricane damage to crops. Continued U.S. assistance kept the nation economically afloat—barely—before 1987. The already prostrate economy was further stricken by Hurricane Georges in 1998. Aid in future years will depend on what shape the government takes under the new constitution. But the old system of granting monopolies in various imported articles to political favorites can hopefully be buried. It results in artificially high prices paid for goods by an impoverished people.

Beginning in the 1980s, the desperate economic conditions led to a massive exodus of economic refugees by boat, bound for Florida, the Bahamas, or anywhere they might find a better life; untold numbers died at sea. About the only cause for grim cheer in recent years was that in 1997 Haiti's per capita income of $458 exceeded that of Nicaragua by a few dollars, meaning Haiti was no longer officially the poorest country of the hemisphere. In 2001, the per capita figure had risen to $520, but unemployment remains an estimated 70%—by far the highest of the hemisphere. Economic growth declined by 1.2% in 2001 and another 0.9% in 2002. In 2002, the unemployment rate was 16%.

The Future: The Haitian people have discovered the cruel fact that political democracy is not a panacea for two centuries of tenacious poverty and political misrule. Haiti remains the Western Hemisphere's basket case: destitute, illiterate, lawless and virtually ungovernable. Haiti desperately needs an enlightened leader, but it has not found one.

Aristide, once heralded as the champion of the poor and the best hope for democracy, demonstrated in the electoral farce of 2000, in his intimidation of opponents through his *chimère* goon squads, and in his leasing of the country to drug traffickers in exchange for much more than 30 pieces of silver, that he was anything but enlightened. It ultimately proved his undoing. He had carefully planned ceremonies to mark the bicentennial of Haiti's independence from France on January 1, 2004, but his people decided to observe the bicentennial in their own way: they threw him out.

So, Aristide is gone. Ironically, the United States, which reinstalled him in 1994, facilitated his departure a decade later. Now what? President Boniface Alexandre and Prime Minister Gerard Latortue are by most accounts honorable men, which is at least a major improvement over any of the recent leaders, whether democrats or despots. But they are unelected leaders, governing without a Parliament, propped up only by U.N. troops. They have proven incapable of quelling the violence wrought by rival gangs of Aristide supporters and of former soldiers of the now-disbanded army who toppled Aristide—twice.

Now new elections have been called for November 13, 2005, with runoffs on December 18. It will be almost a miracle if the elections can take place as scheduled given the climate of violence. But even if they do, and even if the voter turnout is more than the usual 20%, what hope is there that these elections will bring about any more meaningful change than did the last three, which brought to power two presidents who were inept at best and corrupt and dictatorial at worst? In fact, corruption in Haiti is so ingrained that in Transparency International's 2004 rankings, Haiti tied with Bangladesh as the two most corrupt nations on the face of the Earth.

Once the U.N. troops leave, there is little room for optimism that the rule of law will take root in this unfortunate, hapless country.

God save Haiti.

The Republic of Honduras

Detail from a carved stone pillar at the Mayan ruins of Copán in western Honduras

Area: 43,266 square miles.
Population: 6.8 million (2004 estimate).
Capital City: Tegucigalpa (Pop. 725,000, estimated).
Climate: Tropical, with clearly marked wet and dry seasons. Heaviest rains occur from May to December.
Neighboring Countries: Nicaragua (Southeast); El Salvador (South); Guatemala (West).
Official Language: Spanish.
Other Principal Tongues: Various Indian dialects.
Ethnic Background: *Mestizo* (Mixed Spanish and Indian, 90%) African (5%), Indian (4%) European (1%).
Principal Religion: Roman Catholic Christianity.
Chief Commercial Products: Coffee, bananas, lumber, meats, petroleum products.
Currency: Lempira.
Gross Domestic Product: U.S. $8.3 billion in 2003 ($1,221 per capita).
Former Colonial Status: Spanish Colony (1524–1821).
Independence Date: September 14, 1821.

Chief of State: Ricardo Rodolfo Maduro Joest (b. April 20, 1946), president (since January 27, 2002).
National Flag: Blue, white and blue horizontal stripes, 5 blue stars in a cluster on the center stripe.

Honduras is the second largest of the Central American republics and one of the most thinly populated. Much of the country is mountainous; an irregular plateau in the southwest has peaks approaching 8,000 feet near Tegucigalpa and La Esperanza. The plateau drops to a narrow plain on the Pacific Coast (Gulf of Fonseca). To the north there also is a narrow coastal plain broadening to the east. The valleys of the Ulúa (N.W.) and Aguán (N.E.) rivers extending south from the Atlantic coast (Gulf of Honduras), are important agricultural regions. Running south from the Ulúa to the Gulf of Fonseca is an intermountain valley which is the principal route of communications from the Atlantic to the Pacific oceans. The eastern plains along the Patuca River are covered with jungle and only partially explored.

The central plateau descends into several basins at 2,000 to 4,000 feet, in which are located the principal urban centers. The southern and western highlands contain the majority of the native Indian societies. The black population is found in the banana-raising section along the Atlantic coast. Prevailing winds are from the east, and the Atlantic coastal plain, receiving heavy rainfall, is covered with forests that are also found on the eastern slopes of the plateau and mountains.

History: Honduras was settled by Spanish treasure seekers from Guatemala in 1524. The mainstream of movement and settlement was along the Guatemala trail, a pattern that today governs the population distribution. The Spaniards ignored the Atlantic coast and the region was untouched until the U.S. fruit companies set up banana plantations in the late 19th century.

Honduras achieved independence from Spain with the other Central American states in 1821, and joined with them in a short-lived federation. Going its own way as a separate state in 1838, Honduras has been subjected to interference from Guatemala, El Salvador and Nicaragua as these countries sought Honduran support in conflicts among and between them. Honduran politics has followed the Central American pattern—two-party conflict between liberal and conservative factions of the elite, little popular participation in the political process and a long list of ever-changing dictatorial regimes. However, Honduras' dictatorships have been somewhat more benign than those of its neighbors, and several governments have been committed to social and economic reform. Less inclined toward revolution than its neighbors, sparsely populated and with few roads, Honduras has been able to avoid the large-scale bloodshed of its neighbors. Still, during its first 161 years of independence, Honduras witnessed 385 armed rebellions, 126 governments and 16 constitutions. Generally regarded as the most capable presidents were Policarpo Bonilla (1894–99) and Tiburcio Carías Andino (1932–48). Neither made any pretense of democratic rule, governing instead as benevolent despots.

During his 16 years, Carías did more to advance the social and economic well-being of the country than any of his predecessors. Some roads and a few schools were built, and modern agricultural methods were introduced. His regime was maintained by jailing or exiling his critics.

After peacefully surrendering power following 1948 elections, Carías was followed by a series of mediocre presidents. The military seized power in 1963 in a coup led by General Oswaldo López. Hon-

Honduras

duras joined the Central American Common Market, trade was improved and an industrial development program was initiated in the northern plains region around San Pedro and Puerto Cortés. Presidential balloting held in 1965 resulted in López's election at the head of the National Party to a six-year term.

A long-simmering dispute between Honduras and El Salvador, stemming from the fact that tiny El Salvador is badly overpopulated, erupted into a brief, but bloody war in 1969. Since the 1940s, some 300,000 landless peasants have settled illegally on vacant land near the border inside under-populated Honduras. Some Salvadorans fled their homeland to escape the horrors of prolonged civil strife. Others came to Honduras in search of a better life. In time, these highly industrious people were living better than many native Hondurans in the region.

Alarmed by what it viewed as a growing flood of "squatters," Honduras enacted a new land reform law which, among other things, distributed to native Hondurans plots that had been cleared and brought under cultivation by the Salvadorans. All too often, the immigrants would be evicted just before their crops were ready for harvest. The mass deportation of 17,000 Salvadorans created such tension between the two countries that a disputed soccer game between them was all that was needed to cause a war in 1969.

Although the North American press tended to joke about the 100-hour "soccer war" between the two "banana republics," the conflict claimed more than 2,000 lives and devastated the economies of both countries. Because of the strife, Honduras withdrew from the Central American Common Market, causing further economic damage to both nations.

Capitalizing on his role as a "wartime" leader, President López sought to remain in office by amending the constitution to permit his reelection in 1971. When that effort failed, López persuaded the Liberal and National parties to divide equally most national offices. Under this "Pact of National Unity," Ramon Ernesto Cruz was elected president.

Unable to cope with the nation's growing economic and political problems, the elderly Cruz was ousted in a coup led by López in 1972. To gain popular support, he promised a major land reform program. The plan was opposed by both the landowners, who rejected any change in the tenure system, and by peasants, who felt the concept was too little, too late. López was himself ousted in a coup in 1975 as a result of a "bananagate" scandal in which high-level government officials were accused of accepting a $1.25 million bribe

from the U.S.-owned United Brands Company to lower taxes on banana exports.

The new chief of state, Colonel Juan Alberto Melgar Castro, sought to implement various social and economic development projects. Partly as a result of these efforts, the country enjoyed a healthy gross national product growth rate of 6%–8% annually until 1980. Pledging to enact the land reform program promised earlier by López, Melgar also found himself in a deadly crossfire between wealthy farmers and landless peasants.

The heart of the dispute was land. Much of Honduras is extremely mountainous; only 22% of the land is arable. A lion's share has traditionally been controlled by just 667 families (0.3% of the population) and by two U.S. banana firms. In contrast, the peasants (87% of the people) live as peons on small, difficult-to-till plots. The end result is often widespread malnutrition, particularly among the young. Still, the recent land reform program, while not meeting all expectations, has permitted a larger number of peasants to be resettled on their own property.

President Melgar was replaced in 1978 by a three-member *junta* headed by General Policarpo Paz García. Yielding to pressure from the Carter administration, Paz appointed a civilian-dominated cabi-

net to direct the transition to civilian government. Elections in April 1980 for the 71-seat constituent assembly gave the reform-minded Liberal Party 35 seats, while the conservative Nationalists took 33.

The Return to Democracy

General elections in 1981 marked the return of democracy to Honduras, resulting in the presidency of the Liberal Party's Roberto Suazo Córdova, who took office in early 1982. A country doctor, he tried to revive a patient that was suffering from backwardness, a declining economy and growing security problems caused by events in neighboring countries. More than 25,000 Salvadoran refugees flooded into Honduras to escape that nation's war. Many were relocated away from the border and were placed under the U.N. High Commissioner for Refugees.

After the Marxist *Sandinista* movement came to power in neighboring Nicaragua in 1979, Honduras unwillingly became a sanctuary for the Nicaraguan *Contra* forces opposed to the *Sandinistas*. During the 1980s, there were repeated raids into Honduras from Nicaragua as the *Sandinista* forces periodically tried to destroy *Contra* encampments in the remote, inaccessible mountains and jungle along the common border. The losses in coffee production in areas abandoned by farmers because of the conflict were substantial.

The Reagan administration in 1984–86 stepped up its military aid commitment to Honduras in response to the *Sandinista* threat from Nicaragua. In addition to weaponry, military personnel were sent. Economic aid in large amounts was insufficient to alleviate economic woes, however, associated with fluctuations in the prices of bananas and coffee.

Honduras

Cuba, meanwhile, used Honduras as a transport route to dispatch Soviet-bloc arms and munitions to the FMLN rebels in El Salvador, and to a lesser extent, Guatemala. By 1983, U.S. military advisers were training Salvadoran troops within Honduras. Friction with Nicaragua increased because of the *Contra* presence. In an effort to control the situation, a combined U.S.-Honduran military force established permanent American military bases close to the Nicaraguan border. Some thought this was an effort by President Reagan to provoke the *Sandinistas,* justifying direct intervention in Nicaragua.

An incident did occur—*Sandinista* troops entered Honduras in 1988 to wipe out a *Contra* base after a cease-fire had been negotiated between the warring parties. When 3,000 additional U.S. troops were sent into the country, the *Sandinistas* beat a hasty retreat.

President Arias of Costa Rica devised a peace plan for Central America which, although widely hailed, was impractical as long as the Soviets continued their support of the *Sandinistas.* With the collapse of the Soviet Union and the end of its support to the *Sandinistas,* a semblance of peace finally came to Central America.

But this left a burgeoning, expensive military in Honduras with little purpose after the end of the conflicts. Releasing them would not help in a country where the unemployment-underemployment rate has been close to 50% for more than a generation.

In spite of financial and security woes, democracy proceeded reasonably well in Honduras with the elections and peaceful transitions to power of José Azcona (Liberal) in 1985, Rafael Leonardo Callejas (Nationalist) in 1989 and Carlos Roberto Reina (Liberal) in 1993. All was not tranquil, however. Ethnic Indians, largely ignored by the government, became more politically aware and began expressing their dissatisfaction with their status. Vague guerrilla groups periodically appeared and disappeared, and there was an assassination threat against President Reina in early 1994 by a killer hired by a drug trafficker.

As U.S. aid dwindled to less than $100 million annually, other sources of funding were sought. The International Monetary Fund agreed to loans, but attached a host of conditions that were difficult, including reduction of the size of the legislature and military.

President Reina raised eyebrows in 1994 when he launched an anticorruption campaign that saw charges brought against 18 former officials, including none other than former President Callejas, who was immune from prosecution as a member of the Central American Parliament. But it

Former President Carlos Flores Facussé

was the paring of the once-omnipotent military that may be regarded as Reina's enduring legacy. He ended the draft, obtained executive control over the armed forces' budget, removed the national police from military control and reduced troop strength; some units are only 20% of their former size.

Moreover, there were Argentine-style efforts to hold the military accountable for human rights abuses during the 1970s and 1980s. In January 1998, days before Reina left office, a civilian judge ordered an investigation into the possible role of Armed Forces Commander General Mario Hung in the disappearance in 1988 of Roger González, a left-wing student leader. At the time, Hung was a lieutenant colonel in a special forces battalion.

The armed forces complained that the downsizing emasculated their ability to defend Honduras, but to defend Honduras against whom? The guerrilla wars in neighboring Nicaragua and El Salvador, which once threatened to embroil Honduras, had ended. More significantly, on January 18, 1998, nine days before leaving office, Reina signed a long-sought border agreement with Salvadoran President Armando Calderón Sol that formally delineated the disputed frontier areas that led the two countries to war in 1969.

Carlos Flores

The presidential and congressional elections of November 30, 1997, proved to be the most colorful yet for this fledgling democracy. To succeed the 71-year-old Reina, the Liberal Party made a generational leap to the president of the Congress, 47-year-old Carlos Flores Facussé, who lost an earlier bid to Callejas. The National Party, meanwhile, nominated Alba

Nora de Melgar, widow of erstwhile military strongman Juan Alberto Melgar Castro and a former mayor of Tegucigalpa. Her link to the days of dictatorship, plus her decision to hire as her campaign adviser Dick Morris, U.S. President Bill Clinton's onetime aide who resigned in disgrace in 1996 after admitting frequenting prostitutes, brought the campaign international attention. Three minor parties also fielded candidates.

Flores sought to distance himself from Reina and from the Liberal Party's traditional middle-class base and to reach out to the country's impoverished masses, although he has little in common with them. The scion of two of the country's wealthiest families, Flores was the son of journalist and Liberal activist Carlos David Flores, who in 1976 founded the daily newspaper *La Tribuna,* now the country's largest. His mother, Margarita Facussé, was the sister of Miguel Facussé, a Palestinian immigrant who amassed a fortune in food processing and textiles. The younger Flores received a degree in industrial engineering from Louisiana State University and held a master's degree in international economics and finance. His wife, Mary Flakes, still held U.S. citizenship. He held a cabinet post in the civilian government of Suazo Córdova.

While Mrs. Melgar pledged to promote economic growth by making Honduras a free-trade zone and by reducing illiteracy from 30% to 5% by 2001, Flores issued a 10-point New Agenda that stressed women's rights, child care and health improvement. A near-fatal helicopter crash during the campaign sidelined Flores for several weeks. Ultimately, his populist approach and youthful appeal proved successful, as he won a decisive victory over Mrs. Melgar, 53% to 42.4%. It was almost an exact replay of the two parties' results in the 1993 race. Flores was inaugurated on January 27, 1998.

Like his predecessors since the restoration of democracy, Flores found his will tested by the military. The armed forces commander promoted a list of officers without clearing them with the president—who objected to the men chosen and who nullified the promotions.

That problem, however, was trivial compared with the blow dealt to poverty-plagued and debt-ridden Honduras in late October 1998 by Hurricane Mitch, one of the most powerful storms in recorded history. Entire villages on the Caribbean coast were swept away by the winds and floods. The local governor compounded an already tragic situation by inflating the death toll to 9,000, for which the president fired her. In human terms, 5,657 Hondurans were confirmed dead, another 8,058 missing and uncounted thousands more left homeless. In terms of economic

Honduras

damage, the storm destroyed 170 bridges and damaged 70% of the country's roads; property losses were in the billions of dollars, and 90% of the vital banana crop was destroyed. International relief efforts to alleviate the immediate human misery were quick in coming, although an aid package for Honduras and neighboring countries affected by Mitch became a political football in the U.S. Congress. That December, the World Bank approved a $200 million loan, and in March 1999 the IMF extended a $215 million credit.

But these were little more than band-aids, and a bewildered President Flores declared to the world that Honduras's debt was "unpayable."

Ricardo Maduro

Hondurans were in the mood for change as they prepared to elect their sixth president since the establishment of democracy. The dominant Liberal Party nominated a party insider, Rafael Piñeda, 71, the president of the Congress, who had served as a deputy for 20 years. The opposition Nationalists, however, gambled on a 55-year-old businessman, Ricardo Maduro, whose only political office had

President Ricardo Maduro

been head of the Central Bank under the 1990–94 Nationalist administration of President Callejas. There was a handful of minor party candidates.

As both major parties are center-right, the campaign focused on personalities and the issues of who could better combat

crime and promote foreign investment. Maduro, whose own son had been killed in a kidnap attempt in 1997, made a crackdown on crime the centerpiece of his platform. He visited New York City and came home promising the "zero-tolerance" approach of then-Mayor Rudolph Giuliani, not only against violent crime but against such petty offenses as littering, vagrancy and defacing public property, all of which, Maduro argued, discourage tourism and foreign investment. Piñeda, a former elementary schoolteacher, countered that enhanced education was the solution to the crime problem, which had become exacerbated by violent gangs known as "maras."

In a country plagued by more than 2,000 murders a year, a staggering figure for a nation of only 6.2 million, Maduro's proposal enjoyed widespread support. The violence issue was underscored just two days before the election when a Nationalist candidate for Congress was assassinated; police later arrested three employees of a Liberal deputy.

On election day, November 25, voters gave Maduro a convincing mandate of 53% to Piñeda's 44%. It was only the second Nationalist victory since democracy was implemented in 1982. The National-

In this mountainous nation, passengers and freight share a flight

212

ists also won the mayoralty of Tegucigalpa, but minor parties kept either of the two major parties from gaining a majority in the 128-seat Congress.

That night, Maduro told his cheering supporters from the balcony of the party headquarters, "We are not just going to administer the country; we are going to effect significant reform." He also vowed "to enforce the laws as never before." In the days that followed, he also promised to reduce the bloated government payroll, to streamline the bureaucracy and to make it more efficient, and to crack down on abuses of privileges by government officials. For one thing, he said he would forbid public servants from flying first-class at taxpayer expense.

The gangs evidently took Maduro's promises seriously. In January, police foiled a plot by one gang to assassinate the president-elect two days before his

inauguration. He was sworn in on January 27, 2002.

On October 10, 2002, Maduro married a Spanish diplomat, Aguas Ocaña, Honduras' second consecutive foreign-born first lady. Maduro was divorced from his first wife in 1996. News reports soon circulated that the couple already had become estranged.

Maduro sought to reform the state-owned water utility in order to facilitate a line of credit from the International Monetary Fund, which was placed on hold in November 2002. As Congress considered the proposal, a demonstration by 10,000 people on August 26, 2002, became uncharacteristically violent. The crowd clashed with police, then stormed inside the Congress.

The president also created controversy in July 2003 when he agreed to contribute a contingent of 370 troops to the allied

coalition in Iraq for a one-year tour. However, after Spain withdrew its contingent following the terrorist attacks in Madrid, Maduro ordered the troops home in May 2004.

Gang-related violence remains the country's major problem, other than the endemic poverty that spawns it. But it has become apparent that the problem is not Honduras' alone. The gangs, organized by Central American expatriates in Los Angeles, mostly Salvadorans, have become a serious form of international organized crime, a Mafia with tattoos. The most infamous are the *Mara Salvatrucha*, better known as *MS-13*, and *Mara 18*. So serious have they become that the United States, Mexico and most Central American countries have launched a joint offensive against them (see El Salvador). In August 2003, the Honduran Congress passed a law that provides 12-year prison

Waiting to go into a stadium for a soccer game

213

Honduras

terms for gang membership. More recently, a bill was introduced to reinstitute the death penalty, which had been abolished in the 1950s.

In Honduras, such gangs have established control over local areas, posing a greater threat to the central government than did the guerrilla groups of the 1980s. They specialize in spectacular, grisly murders and even massacres to instill terror. On August 29, 2003, 13 people were killed and 17 wounded when gangs assaulted two buses in San Pedro Sula. In an even more shocking and senseless attack, the *MS-13* attacked a bus full of Christmas shoppers on December 23, 2004, in San Pedro Sula and killed 28 people, six of them children, and wounded 14. The gang's rationale for the attack, left on a note on the windshield: to protest the bill to reinstitute the death penalty! Three *MS-13* leaders were arrested; one of them escaped in January 2005 but was recaptured in Texas after illegally entering the United States. The government is now investigating possible links between the gangs and major drug-trafficking organizations.

The gang problem promises to dominate the campaign for the November 2005 presidential election, as it did the 2001 campaign. In the two parties' primaries on February 20, 2005, Porfirio Lobo Sosa, the president of the Congress and an advocate of capital punishment, defeated Tegucigalpa Mayor Miguel Pastor for the National Party nomination. Manuel Zelaya, a wealthy rancher who opposes the death penalty, easily won the Liberal Party nomination. For the first time, members of Congress will be elected directly instead of by proportional representation.

On March 3, 2005, Honduras became the second country, after El Salvador, to ratify the Central American Free Trade Agreement with the United States. More than 100 left-wing protesters briefly occupied the Congress building to protest the ratification.

Culture: Honduran culture is almost entirely based on that of its colonial conquerors. The ancient Mayan civilization, the subject of intensive research and archaeological exploration for more than 100 years, had declined many centuries prior to the arrival of the Spaniards. An isolated burial site with Spanish artifacts was supposed to belie this well-known fact, but it is most likely an isolated discovery of a burial site, not a civilization.

Moorish-Spanish architecture prevails throughout most of the nation, particularly in the beautiful churches built during

the centuries since the arrival of Roman Catholicism. Education is compulsory through the age of 15, but there is a serious shortage of trained teachers, a lack of schools and little effort to enforce the educational law. Higher education is available, including that offered by the National University of Honduras, established in the capital city in 1847. Only a small percentage of Hondurans engage in such studies.

The folklore and music of Honduras are not distinctive, bearing a close resemblance to those of the other Central American nations. Culture division exists between the bustling cities and the isolated, mountainous rural areas—the people of the lonely countryside have been almost completely bypassed by the civilization of the more mundane city people.

Economy: Honduras is a classic example of a "banana republic," with a small aristocracy, almost no middle class and a large peasant population that lives on a per capita income of less than $800 per year. Most of the nation's farmland is controlled by U.S.-owned banana firms and by a few huge cattle ranches. Mountainous terrain and periodic droughts limit farm output and methods are primitive. Most industry is foreign-owned. Coffee production has recently replaced bananas as the chief source of foreign exchange, followed by lumber, meat, sugar, cotton and tobacco. Continued balance-of-payments problems left the treasury nearly bankrupt by mid-1987 while the nation's debt has grown to $3 billion—the size of the annual gross national product. This is the highest ratio in Central America and indicates that substantial credit and borrowing will be required for years.

Honduras remains one of the three poorest countries of Latin America, along with Haiti and neighboring Nicaragua, and all three were buffeted by powerful hurricanes in 1998—Haiti by Georges and Honduras and Nicaragua by Mitch.

Largely because of the devastation caused to the banana crop, real GDP growth declined from 4.5% in 1997 to 3% in 1998, and for 1999 it was –3%. It rebounded to 6.3% in 2000 and tapered off to 4.0% in 2001, 2.5% in 2002 and 2003, and 4.2% in 2004. Per capita income has been rising steadily for years—$643 in 1998, $650 in 1999, $698 in 2000, $720 in 2001, $925 in 2002 and roughly $1,221 in 2003. But this is still desperately low, even by Latin American standards, and 53% of the population lives below the poverty line. Child prostitution is a growing social problem in Honduras.

Honduras also is saddled with a high external debt that is equal to 74.1% of GDP. It was one of 18 countries—and one of four in the Western Hemisphere—that qualified for a debt-forgiveness program when the so-called Paris Club of creditor nations met in June 2005.

Unemployment in 2004 was estimated at 28.5%. Compounding the economic woes is the country's crime problem, which was blamed for a devastating 30% decrease in foreign investments in 2001 alone. More than 200 business people have been the targets of kidnappers since 1997; several of them of them were murdered, including the son of current President Ricardo Maduro (see History).

The Future: Democracy seems to have taken root in this impoverished republic since 1982. The military has confined itself to its barracks, and the Liberal and National parties have demonstrated that they can alternate peacefully in power. Of course, there are few real philosophical differences between them.

The periodic *Latinobarómetro* survey published in the British newsmagazine *The Economist* shows that the percentage of Hondurans who believe that democracy is preferable to any other form of government has increased from 42% in 1996 to 55% in 2003, the greatest increase of any of the 17 Latin American countries in the survey. Although that support dropped to 46% in 2004, Honduras remains one of only three Latin American republics—Venezuela and Chile are the others—where support for democracy has increased rather than decreased since 1996.

However, Honduras must overcome two major problems: grinding poverty and gang-related violence. Only Paraguay, Haiti, Nicaragua and Bolivia have a lower per capita income among the 20 Latin republics. The gangs, or *maras*, are killing Hondurans and frightening away tourists and investors, needed more than ever since the devastation of Hurricane Mitch in 1998. Their growing strength has become a greater threat to the constitutional government than were the old guerrilla movements of the 1980s. The army, which had been scaled back because it had no one to fight, now does. It may well have to be pressed into battle against these increasingly bold and extremely well-armed gangs. It is a decision the next president, whether Nationalist Porfirio Lobo Sosa or Liberal Manuel Zelaya, will probably have to make soon after he takes over in January 2006.

Jamaica

Dunn's River Falls near Ocho Rios on the north–central coast, a 600–foot stairstep waterfall that is one of the island's favorite attractions.

Area: 4,470 square miles.

Population: 2.65 million; another 2–3 million live abroad.

Capital City: Kingston (Pop. 710,000, estimated).

Climate: The coastal climate is hot and humid; the uplands are moderate, variable and pleasant.

Neighboring Countries: This island state, the third largest of the Greater Antilles, lies about 100 miles south of Cuba and 100 miles west of the southwestern tip of Haiti.

Official Language: English.

Other Principal Tongues: A distinct variety of English spoken with a very rhythmic pattern.

Ethnic Background: African Negro and mulatto, with a very small European minority. There are prominent Chinese and East Indian minorities.

Principal Religion: Protestant Christianity (Anglican); the Roman Catholic Church and other Protestant sects are very active, as is Rastafarianism, which holds that former Ethiopian Emperor Haile Selassie was the reincarnation of Jesus Christ.

Chief Commercial Products: Alumina (partially refined bauxite), bauxite, sugar, bananas and other tropical fruits, rum. Tourism is a very important source of income

Currency: Jamaica Dollar.

Gross Domestic Product: U.S. $7.335 billion in 2002 ($2,771 per capita).

Former Colonial Status: Spanish Colony (1494–1655); British Colony (1655–1962).

Independence Date: August 6, 1962.

Chief of State: Queen Elizabeth II of Great Britain, represented by Sir Howard Cooke, governor-general.

Head of Government: Rt. Hon. Percival James "P.J." Patterson (b. April 10, 1935), prime minister (since March 1992).

National Flag: A gold diagonal Cross of St. Andrew, with black triangles at each side and green triangles at the top and bottom.

Jamaica is a picturesque, mountainous island about 145 miles long by 50 miles in width. The mountains run east and west, with spurs to the north and south reaching 7,420 feet in the east and descending in the west. The coastal plains are intensively cultivated and are the most densely populated. The Jamaican people are descendants of African slaves imported by Spanish and English planters. Rich soils and adequate rainfall encouraged sugar and cotton production during the colonial period, while the small valleys provided fruits and vegetables for local consumption. Jamaica possesses large deposits of bauxite and gypsum which are commercially exploited.

History: Jamaica's history is inextricably interwoven with the struggle between Spain and England for domination of Atlantic trade in the 16th and 17th centuries. The island was discovered by Columbus

Jamaica

in 1494 during his second voyage to the New World; the Spanish adventurer, Juan de Esquivel, settled the island in 1509, calling it Santiago. Villa de la Vega, (later, Spanish Town) was founded in 1523 and served as the capital until 1872. The native Arawak people were rapidly exterminated and Negro slaves were imported to provide labor. When Jamaica was taken by the British in 1655, the total population was about 3,000. The Spanish were completely expelled by 1660, at which time their slaves fled to the mountains. These people, known as *Maroons*, resisted all efforts to recapture them, and maintained a state of guerrilla warfare against the British through the 18th century. British title to Jamaica was confirmed in 1670, and from 1672 on, the island became one of the world's largest slave markets. By the end of the 18th century, Jamaica had a slave population in excess of 3 million, working 70 sugar, 60 indigo and 60 cacao plantations. With a profitable trade with London and an equally great illegal trade with Spanish America, the Jamaican planters were extremely wealthy. The prohibition of slave trade in 1807, freedom of the Spanish colonies by 1821 and the abolition of slavery in 1833–38, ended the plantation economy as the freed slaves took to the hills, occupying small plots of land, where their descendants are found today.

The 19th century was marked by increasing resistance to colonial rule as the economic situation deteriorated. Riots in 1865 brought about changes in the government, while disturbances in 1938 led to the establishment of dominion status in 1944 and an advance preparation for independence, granted in 1962.

Jamaica's history has also been influenced by natural disasters. A violent earthquake in 1692 destroyed Port Royal and led to the founding of Kingston. It in turn was destroyed by a 1907 earthquake, but was rebuilt. Hurricanes have also exacted their toll and revised the island's agricultural patterns. The island nation has a parliamentary system of government with a two-chamber legislature consisting of 21 senators and 60-member House of Representatives. The prime minister, selected from the majority party, chooses 13 senators and the remaining 8 are selected by the governor-general with advice from the leader of the opposition party. Technically, Jamaica is still a member of the British Commonwealth and a constitutional monarchy with the queen of Great Britain as the titular head of state. The queen appoints the governor-general (a Jamaican recommended by the prime minister) as her local representative.

By law, elections must be held every five years, but can be called by the party in power sooner. The two major political parties in Jamaica are the Jamaica Labour Party (JLP) and the People's National Party (PNP).

The Manley-Seaga Years

The ensuing two decades after 1972 were dominated by Michael Manley, whose father, Norman Manley, founded the PNP and played a key role in the independence movement, and Edward P.G. Seaga of the JLP. Both were Caucasian. Their policies were energetically directed toward improving Jamaica, and both tried a number of ideas to accomplish this, Manley from the left and Seaga from the right. Both, however, were hamstrung by the deep-seated problem of managing a poor country in deep economic water.

Manley, who won the 1972 elections, was at the time left-of-center. He swung all the way left quickly, and by 1976 had established a centrally planned economy and forged close ties with the Soviet Union via Castro's Cuba. Government spending increased tremendously and production fell sharply. By 1980, the prime minister's spending habits had all but bankrupted the country, and his popularity, even among the poor, plummeted. Although he counted on subsidies from the Soviet Union in the same manner that Cuba was receiving funds, the money and goods never seemed to make it beyond Cuba if, indeed, it had been sent at all by an overextended Soviet Union.

With political violence rampant, Manley scheduled elections for late 1982. A violent campaign took the lives of an estimated 650 people. Manley was opposed by the leader of the Jamaica Labour Party (JLP), Edward P.G. Seaga, who, despite of his party's liberal-sounding name, was right of center. Impoverished Jamaicans listened to his message and gave the JLP 51 of the 60 House seats.

Nine years of financial caution followed, coupled with slowly established close ties to the U.S. Slow financial growth

Michael Manley

Errol Harvey

resumed, but there was criticism of Seaga because of a devaluation of currency in late 1983. He called elections abruptly, catching the PNP off balance. It boycotted the contest and the JLP won all seats in the House. Another devaluation of the currency followed, but the Jamaican economy continued to falter. Export prices for bauxite (aluminum ore) dropped in large part because of widespread recycling of the metal. Discontent over the lack of progress led to a resurgence of Manley's party in 1986, when it captured all but one of the municipal elections.

Seaga was battling a new edition of Manley, who had the foresight to realize the imminent worldwide collapse of communism. He had discarded all the old rhetoric and concentrated on attacking Seaga's record, which actually was a by-product of the miserable state of the Jamaican economy. In national elections, Manley's party captured 44 seats in 1988. But discontent again swelled when there were two currency devaluations, rising unemployment and prices and a roaring hurricane in 1988 that left a half million homeless.

Jamaica

Edward P.G. Seaga
Elizabeth Marshall

Faced with growing discontent, and in failing health, the then 67-year-old Manley announced his imminent retirement. In spite of allegations of earlier questionable dealing, his deputy prime minister, Percival James "P.J." Patterson succeeded. Patterson, soft-spoken and well-educated, is the first post-independence black prime minister of Jamaica.

Elections were called for March 1993. Patterson and the PNP waged an openly racist campaign ("He is one of us"), appealing to the 75% black population of the island. He and his party won in a landslide, but the PLP charged that there was wholesale fraud in the contest. It initially boycotted the legislature, but returned to claim the eight seats it won.

The JLP fared little better in the general elections of December 19, 1997, in which it raised its number of seats only to 10. Overall, the PNP polled 56% of the vote to 39% for the JLP and 5% for the National Democratic Movement, which won no seats. Turnout was lower than usual, but so was the traditional politically motivated violence that in 1980 claimed 800 lives. A 60-member team of international observers, headed by former U.S. President Jimmy Carter, declared the elections generally fair, although Carter admitted there had been "serious problems." Chief among these was the peculiar Jamaican tradition of "garrison constituencies" controlled by one party or the other, a practice Carter said he had never seen in monitoring 22 elections in 15 countries. In several cases, all the ballots in a box were cast for one party.

A political era, and a dynasty, ended when Manley died of prostate cancer on March 6, 1997. Fidel Castro was among

those attending his funeral. Manley was buried next to his father.

In July 2001, Patterson was forced to mobilize the entire 3,000-man army to quell violence between gangs suspected of ties to the two major parties that left 28 dead in and around Kingston. He and Seaga held an unusual three-hour meeting in August aimed at reducing the partisan violence, but there were new outbreaks in September and October 2001 and in January 2002 that left scores dead, including several children. There was a total of 1,140 murders in Jamaica in 2001, a 28% increase over 2000, and the violence has affected the all-important tourism industry as hotels reported a wave of cancellations.

A special commission investigating the July 2001 outbreak concluded its work in March 2002, but the report was criticized by Amnesty International as one-sided because it relied solely on the testimony of the police and military forces. Not surprisingly, the report concluded that the security forces had acted properly. For his part, Seaga was called to testify before the commission but he refused.

Patterson also responded to the violence by advocating creation of a Caribbean Court of Justice, based in Trinidad, to replace Britain's Privy Council, currently the court of last resort for Jamaica and other British Commonwealth countries in the Caribbean. The new court is seen as a means of expediting hangings of murderers.

Recent Developments

Patterson called new elections for October 16, 2002. In the three months leading up to the balloting, there were 17 politically related deaths—relatively low for Jamaica. Both parties pledged to combat the alarming crime rate. The PNP vowed to seek a 6% growth in GDP, while the JLP stressed education. Polls showed the race to be a dead heat, and it was. Two days passed before the unofficial results confirmed that Patterson had won an unprecedented third term, but with a greatly reduced majority: 34 seats to 26. Patterson, 68, said he would retire before the end of his five-year mandate. Meanwhile, Seaga, 72, said before the election that he would step aside as opposition leader if the JLP lost again and make way for new leadership.

Patterson played a key role in early 2004 in the effort to effect a dialogue between Haitian President Jean-Bertrand Aristide and his opponents. When Aristide was forced into exile on February 29, 2004, he first went to the Central African Republic, then accepted Patterson's invitation to come to Jamaica. He remained there for two months before going into permanent exile in South Africa.

Prime Minister P. J. Patterson

Jamaica received an unsavory distinction on June 1, 2004, when two Jamaican nationals, Norris Nembhard and Leebert Ramcharan, were among a group of eight people from five countries placed on a sanctions list by the U.S. government as known international drug kingpins. A Jamaican court ordered Ramcharan extradited on June 7, while Nembhard was arrested and held without bail.

The murder of two prominent businessmen in May 2005 led to a one-day shutdown of Jamaican businesses to protest the crime problem. Meanwhile, the murder rate for 2004 was 50% higher than in 2003, exceeding 100 per month.

An old era ended and a new one began in Jamaican politics in early 2005. Keeping his promise, Seaga stepped down as leader of the JLP in January, and on February 24 Orrett Bruce Golding was elected to succeed him in a party convention. A former member of the House of Representatives who had become a senator, Golding had long been considered Seaga's heir apparent, but he had impatiently bolted the party several years earlier when Seaga declined to retire. However, Golding could not officially become leader of the opposition until he won a House seat, which he did in a by-election in West Kingston in April. He was sworn in as opposition leader on April 21. Seaga took a faculty position at the University of the West Indies. The PNP, meanwhile, was expected to name Patterson's successor as party leader at a convention in September.

Culture: The Jamaican people have inherited a vibrant culture. Their musical expression is found in the hypnotic rhythms of "reggae," a style popularized by Bob

Jamaica

Marley, Jimmy Cliff and Peter Tosh. Reggae, grounded in the Rastafarian religion, is the basis of a thriving recording industry in Jamaica and has achieved international acclaim.

Rastafarianism, or "Rasta," as its adherents call it, is a Christian cult with African roots. Its central tenet is that Haile Selassie, the late emperor of Ethiopia, was the reincarnation of Jesus Christ. The "dreadlock" hair style is a distinctive feature of this faith.

Performing arts have been exemplified by such groups as the National Dance Theatre and the Jamaica Folk Singers, which take the country's dance and song abroad. Kingston and almost all of the larger resort towns have excellent theatrical presentations.

The Daily Gleaner, established in 1834, is one of the oldest continually published newspapers in the hemisphere.

The National Gallery of Art, established in 1974, houses a collection of priceless works executed by Jamaican artists, but also contains representative works centuries old and new ones from many nations. Local artists, potters, sculptors and weavers produce works that encompass all schools and techniques. They range in price from $10 into the thousands. Many art galleries and craft shops are found throughout the island.

Lamentably, Jamaica is characterized by a culture of violence, some political, some common crime. Handguns abound in Jamaica and are the favored means of "settling" all disputes. A "Gun Court" was established more than a decade ago to hand down stiff sentences for illegal firearm activity. Capital punishment was discontinued in 1988, but it was reinstituted in 1999. All appeals must be completed within six months; execution is by hanging.

Economy: Rich bauxite deposits, sugar and tourism have dominated Jamaica's economy, and the financial conditions of the nation have been traditionally closely tied to these assets. The long-range outlook for the island's economy is linked to diversification and expansion. The Seaga government focused upon agricultural development. The goal was to become self-sufficient in food production as well as to capture a share in the lucrative U.S. market for winter vegetables. However, a winter vegetable plantation developed with Israeli cooperation was shut down because of lack of profits.

Although Jamaica's business community was buoyed by the election of pro-business Seaga and private investment did rise somewhat, foreign capital for economic development was slow in responding. A lowered annual inflation rate (5%) of the 1980s climbed back to 22% in the 1990s.

Marijuana is plentiful in Jamaica and is exported to the United States informally. Its availability is a large factor in the Jamaican crime rate, which is unacceptable by any standard.

An economic dilemma that has no immediate solution is the crushing external debt, which in 2000 stood at $3.1 billion, almost half of GDP. By 2004, the debt had reached about 140% of GDP, the fourth-highest percentage in the world! About 60% of government revenues are used just to service the debt.

The per capita GDP of $2,771 is deceptively high, because it is inequitably distributed. Moreover, unemployment has remained stubbornly high for years, and was 16% at the beginning of 2004. This is at least partially responsible for the alarming increase in crime; culture is another factor.

The gang culture has affected the economy as well as politics. An invisible economy revolves around the drug trade. Not only is marijuana produced in abundance for export, but Jamaica is a way station for an estimated 100-120 tons of cocaine per year en route to the United States, Canada and Europe. The gangs also engage in protection rackets, particularly in the construction sector, which increases construction costs by as much as 40%.

Tourism, the third largest industry after sugar and mining, is centered around all-inclusive resorts (meaning native Jamaicans are excluded). Tourism suffered a major slump in 2001–02, not only because of violent crime but because of the worldwide economic downturn and the general decline in tourism following the September 11, 2001 terror attacks. The number of tourists hit a record of 1.33 million in 2000, then dropped to 1.23 million in 2001 and 1.27 million in 2002. But figures for 2003 showed a 9.4% increase over 2002, 1.34 million tourists, who brought in $1.3 billion.

On a par with tourism as a source of foreign exchange are the remittances that the estimated 2-3 million Jamaicans living in the United States, Britain, Canada and other developing countries send home to their families. Remittances totaled $1.3 billion in 2002. However, that also means that the country's brightest minds are living and working elsewhere.

GDP growth has been dismal for years: –1.8% in 1996, –2.4% in 1997, 0.5% in 1998, –0.4% in 1999, 0.8% in 2000, 2.0% in 2001 and 1.1% in 2002.

A new venture that may prove successful is Excel Motors, which produced its first 22 automobiles in 2003.

The Future: A cynic might well ask, *what future?* Jamaica is plagued by a moribund economy based on market-sensitive commodities such as bauxite ore and sugar, a crushing external debt that is the fourth-highest in the world as a percentage of GDP, and a culture of political violence and common crime that is threatening the only other potential source of foreign exchange: tourism. Jamaica needs visionary leadership but doesn't have it. And even if it did, how could one leader transform an entire culture? It cannot happen under the imperfect democracy that Jamaica has.

However, change is on the horizon. The elections of 2002 were the last for the veteran leaders of the PNP and JLP, P.J. Patterson and Edward Seaga. Whether Seaga's successor, Bruce Golding, or whoever replaces Patterson will provide more effective leadership is an open question.

One bright spot in recent years has been a concerted effort by both government and the private sector to reverse decades of brain drain by luring back some of the thousands of Jamaicans who have earned advanced degrees elsewhere and have been working abroad. If this campaign is successful, it could create a badly needed young intelligentsia to infuse this troubled country with new ideas and approaches.

Netting a catch, Jamaica

The United Mexican States

STATES OF MEXICO

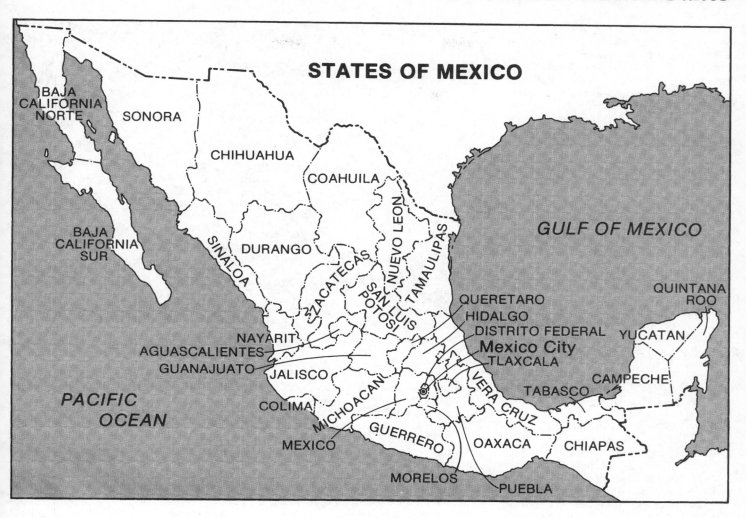

Area: 767,919 square miles.

Population: 105 million (2004 est.; growth, 1.8% per year).

Capital City: Mexico City (Pop. 20 million, estimated).

Climate: Hot, wet on the coast; milder winters, hot summers in the dry north; mild, dry winters in the central highlands.

Neighboring Countries: United States (North); Guatemala and Belize (South).

Official Language: Spanish.

Other Principal Tongues: Various Indian dialects (the census of 1960 identified 52 non-Spanish-speaking groups); English.

Ethnic Background: *Mestizo*, (mixed Spanish and Indian, 60%); Indian and predominantly Indian, (30%); White or predominantly white (9%); other (1%).

Principal Religion: Roman Catholic Christianity.

Chief Commercial Products: Petroleum, petroleum products, border assembly plants, tourism, cotton, coffee, non-ferrous metals, shrimp, sulfur, fresh fruit and vegetables, clothing.

Currency: Peso.

Gross Domestic Product: U.S. $615 billion in 2003, estimated ($5,945 per capita).

Former Colonial Status: Spanish Colony (1510–1821).

Independence Date: September 16, 1810 (observed); September 27, 1821 (achieved).

Chief of State: Vicente Fox Quesada (b. July 2, 1942), president (since December 1, 2000).

National Flag: Green, white and red vertical stripes with the national coat of arms (an eagle strangling a snake) in the white stripe.

Mexico is a vast upland plateau lying between the two branches of the Sierra Madre Mountains plus the low-lying Yucatán Peninsula. The Sierra Madre range enters Mexico in the south from Guatemala at elevations from 6,000 to 8,000 feet, then dips to low hills in the Isthmus of Tehuantepec and then rises abruptly to a jumble of scenic high peaks and intermountain basins. Mexico City is located in one of the most beautiful of these. From this point northward, the Sierra Madre Occidental (west) runs to Arizona in the U.S. and the Sierra Madre Oriental (east) proceeds northeast to the border of Texas. The eastern mountains are not as high as their counterparts in the west.

Mountains and their plateaus occupy two thirds of the land area of Mexico. The highest elevations are found south of Mexico City, where Citlaltepetl (the highest 18,696 feet) with an almost perfect conical shape, is reminiscent of Fujiyama in Japan. Mountains and plateaus drop gradually toward the north. The western range descends steeply to the Pacific Ocean with few passes, while the eastern range is

Mexico

more gentle, with gaps to the Gulf of Mexico at Tampico and Veracruz.

The western mountain slopes, the northern plateau and the peninsula of Lower California (*Baja California*) are arid; the southern inter-mountain valleys receive moderate rainfall; the eastern slopes and the Gulf of Mexico coast receive up to 100 inches of rainfall between the months of June and December.

The whole of Mexico lies in the tropical and subtropical zones; however, climatically, altitude is a more important influence than latitude. Temperatures are hot between sea level and 3,000 feet, temperate between 3,000 feet and 6,000 feet and cold above the latter height. The majority of Mexico's population is found in the southern part of the plateau at elevations between 3,000 and 7,000 feet.

History: Mexico has a rich, dramatic and colorful history that for the purposes of this chapter can be divided roughly into four periods: pre-Conquest, colonial, post-independence and post-revolutionary. Modern Mexico remains heavily influenced by its past, which must be explored if the current realities and dynamics there are to be understood.

The Pre-Conquest Period

A number of succeeding civilizations thrived in the land area that is now Mexico south of the Tropic of Cancer for more than a millennium before the arrival of the Spanish, among them the Toltecs, Mixtecs, Zapotecs and Olmecs. The Toltecs, who flourished on the central plateau in about the ninth and 10th centuries of the Christian era, are remembered for their development of metallurgy as well as for worshiping a deity known as Quetzalcoatl, or the feathered serpent. When the Toltec civilization collapsed, it was attributed to the departure of Quetzalcoatl to the lands beyond the eastern sea, though he promised to return one day to reclaim his dominions. Six centuries later, it was to become a self-fulfilling prophecy.

Perhaps the greatest of these early peoples, however, were the Mayas, whose empire extended from central Mexico as far south as modern-day Honduras. They were an advanced, if somewhat barbaric, people, paradoxically developing remarkable mathematical, astronomical, engineering, agricultural and medical knowledge even as they practiced rituals that included human sacrifice. The ruins of some of their greatest cities lie in present-day Mexico, such as Chichén Itzá on the Yucatán Peninsula and Palenque in the state of Oaxaca. This great empire suddenly and mysteriously disappeared in about the 15th century.

The ruins of the Maya civilization's temple of Chichen–Itza near Mérida, Yucatán.

To the north, even before the decline of the Mayas, another great civilization began to flower: the Aztecs. They, too, developed advanced knowledge in the sciences and medicine, but also practiced a barbaric cruelty to vassal tribes that eventually would lead to their undoing. According to legend, the Aztec god Huitzilopochtli instructed the tribal priests that their capital should be established where they found an eagle perched upon a cactus devouring a serpent. This omen was seen on an island in Lake Texcoco in the great central valley of Mexico in the early 14th century, and consequently the Aztecs began building their great city, Tenochtitlán, upon man-made islands in the lake connected by causeways to the mainland. With its network of canals for streets, the Spanish later dubbed Tenochtitlán, the "Venice of the New World," but the venue also explains why parts of modern-day Mexico City are sinking. The omen, of course, later became the basis for the modern-day symbol of the Mexican Republic, which graces the national flag.

The Aztec empire had reached its zenith by the end of the 15th century, and Tenochtitlán was as resplendent as any city of the Old World. In 1503, Moctezuma II ascended the throne, destined to be the last of the Aztec emperors. In February 1519, a force of 500 Spaniards landed first in Yucatán, then in Tabasco, and finally at Vera Cruz, on the Gulf coast. In command was a young nobleman and soldier-of-fortune determined to make himself rich and famous in this new, unexplored land: Hernán Cortés. Unlike earlier Spanish

freebooters who had robbed the coastal Indians, Cortés treated them benevolently and soon found in them willing allies against their oppressors, the Aztecs. Unknown to Cortés, he also had another ally in the legendary Quetzalcoatl. When this bearded, fair-skinned stranger from across the eastern sea landed in Mexico, the superstitious Indians immediately assumed that he was the reincarnation of the feathered serpent, returning as promised to reclaim his land.

Cortés and his band marched to Tenochtitlán, where Moctezuma, also in-

Moctezuma II

Retreat of the Spanish on *"la noche triste."*

fluenced by the legendary prophecy, greeted him almost as a deity. The wily Cortés, sensing an incredible opportunity, seized the emperor and, through him, issued orders to the Aztecs. The plan unraveled, however, when the Aztecs revolted against these uninvited "gods," and in the resulting melee Moctezuma was hit in the head by a rock and killed. On the night of June 30, 1520—remembered in Spanish and Mexican history as *la noche triste*—Cortés and his men had to fight their way across the narrow causeway to the mainland, suffering heavy losses. Reinforced by later arrivals from Cuba, however, he again marched on the Aztec capital with 900 men in early 1521. Meanwhile, Moctezuma had been succeeded by his 20-year-old nephew, Cuauhtémoc, who was to prove less amenable to the invaders than was his uncle. Cortés besieged the capital for three months, but despite starvation and disease, Cuauhtémoc refused to surrender. The Spaniards finally took Tenochtitlán by storm on August 13, 1521, and set it

ablaze; Cortés reportedly wept at the destruction of such a beautiful city. Cuauhtémoc was captured trying to escape by canoe and brought before Cortés, who angrily blamed him for the capital's destruction. Cuauhtémoc requested that Cortés kill him, and the conqueror complied. The remainder of Mexico was subdued quickly, and the Spanish would remain for precisely 300 years.

The Colonial Period

The viceroyalty of New Spain was a vast territory extending from Central America to modern-day California, Colorado and Texas. As was true in Spain's other American colonies, the colonial experience in Mexico differed sharply from that in England's colonies farther north. For example, the wealth of the English colonies lay primarily in their fertile agricultural land, which gave rise to a class of independent small-scale farmers. Mexico, too, had rich farmland in the central plateau, which attracted Spanish fortune-

seekers willing to work it. These were not small-scale farmers, however; they were the first of the *hacendados*, who ruled over vast estates like feudal lords.

Moreover, Mexico, like Peru, was blessed—or cursed, depending on one's standing in colonial society—with fabulously wealthy deposits of gold and silver, which filled the coffers of the royal treasury in Madrid and gave rise to a class of idle rich who occupied the top 1% of the social pyramid. Unlike their English counterparts, however, the Spanish did not drive the indigenous peoples from their lands and either exile or exterminate them and import African slaves or indentured servants to perform the heavy labor. Instead, the Spanish drove the Indians from their lands and enslaved them for labor on the *haciendas* and in the mines.

Besides the soldiers and the fortune hunters, the Spanish Crown had another ally in its quest to establish its dominion over this new territory: the Catholic Church. The first priests arrived in tandem with Cortés and set about converting

Mexico

the pagan inhabitants to Christianity. At first, the Indians were loathe to abandon their tribal gods in favor of the one worshiped by their oppressors, and they resented the destruction of their idols. At the same time, the veneration of saints and relics was not terribly unlike their pagan idolatry.

But in 1531, just 10 years after the Conquest, an event occurred that was to accelerate dramatically the conversion of the aborigines and would provide Mexico with an institution that remains part of its national identity. An Indian peasant named Juan Diego reported to the bishop that the Virgin Mary had appeared to him on a hillside outside the City of Mexico and had instructed him to return to gather the roses he would find there. Diego did as he was bidden and found roses lying among the cactus. He gathered them in his cloak and carried them to the bishop, but when the cloak was opened, the roses had disappeared and on the cloak was an image of the Virgin. At first skeptical, the church authorities accepted this version, which the Vatican later recognized as a bona fide miracle. The news that the Mother of God had appeared to a humble Indian peasant electrified the Indians and greatly facilitated the priests' job of bringing them into the bosom of the church. Below the hill where the roses were found was constructed the Shrine of Our Lady of Guadalupe, and over its altar still hangs the cloak of Juan Diego with the mysterious image that modern-day art experts have pronounced unexplainable. In December 2001, the Vatican canonized Juan Diego as a saint, which was a cause for national celebration. Pope John Paul II came to Mexico for the formal canonization in the Shrine of Guadalupe in August 2002.

Apart from the conversion of the Indians, there would be few changes in Mexico during the three centuries of Spanish colonial rule. There was, however, a gradual demographic change that was to have a major impact on the subsequent history of the country. Slowly, the Spanish conquerors began to pass their seed to their Indian subjects, and within a few generations a new, *mestizo* race began to grow and which would constitute a majority by the end of the colonial period. Yet, they were to be a race without any real identity, relegated by the Spanish to second-class citizenship, while resented by the Indians for their mixed ancestry. Although amorous dalliances with Indian women and the spawning of bastard children were commonly accepted, the Spanish men married women of their own race and social position, producing yet another class, the *criollos*, or creoles, people of pure European ancestry born in the New World.

The Spanish colonial experience in Mexico can only be described as exploitative. Her land and peoples were seen to exist only for the enrichment of the Crown. While England experienced the Renaissance, the Protestant Reformation, the Enlightenment and the Glorious Revolution, whose ideals were exported to its American colonies, Spain wallowed in the fear, tyranny and superstition of the Inquisition, which also was exported to America. Unlike the English colonies, there was no large middle class of well educated planters, merchants, craftsmen and intellectuals. Eventually the ideas of Locke, Rousseau and Voltaire did trickle into Mexico via a most unlikely source—the king himself. The sole exception to the succession of reactionary, divine-right monarchs was Carlos III, a reasonably enlightened sovereign who reigned from 1758–1788. Appalled when he learned of the abuses of power that characterized colonial rule in Mexico, Carlos instituted a number of reforms that improved local administration and facilitated trade. He also encouraged science and the arts, expanded education and appointed competent viceroys to carry out his ideas. At the same time, his French-inspired anticlericalism, exemplified by his expulsion of the Jesuits from Mexico, caused alarm within the church, which had heretofore enjoyed great wealth and privileges in the colony. As often happens when reforms are undertaken, there can be no turning back the clock. When Carlos died—on the eve of the French Revolution—he was succeeded by his pathetic son, Carlos IV, who was dominated by his wife who, in turn, was dominated by her unscrupulous paramour, Manuel de Godoy.

The misrule of Carlos IV contrasted so sharply with the enlightened rule of his

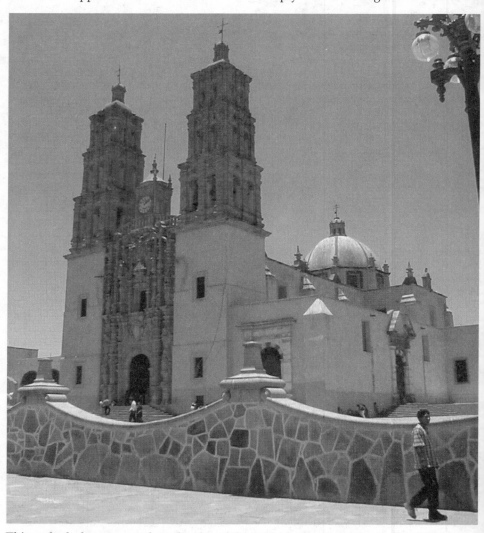

This cathedral was erected on the site of the humble church in the town of Dolores—now Dolores Hidalgo, Guanajuato—where on September 16, 1810, Father Miguel Hidalgo rang the bell to summon the peasants to take up arms against their Spanish oppressors.

Photo by the author.

Mexico

Father Miguel de Hidalgo

father that resentment soon set in. Mexico already had enough reason for resentment by the end of the 18th century. The *criollos* resented the social superiority of the Spanish-born elite, whom they referred to disparagingly as *gachupines,* or the ones with spurs. The *mestizos* and the Indians, meanwhile, chafed under the oppression of their Spanish masters. For 20 years after Carlos III's death, these resentments continued to ferment, while news of the American and French revolutions gave rise to talk of independence. Ironically, it was the French themselves, in the form of Napoleon Bonaparte, who were to become the catalysts for Mexican independence.

In 1808, the detested Carlos IV abdicated and was succeeded by his son, Fernando VII. Lured to Paris by Napoleon, both were imprisoned and replaced on the Spanish throne by Napoleon's brother, Joseph, whose "reign" was supported only by French bayonets. The resulting power vacuum in Madrid threw Mexico and all of Spain's American colonies into turmoil. For two years the various factions—the *gachupines* and the *criollos,* the liberals and conservatives—debated whether to maintain their allegiance to an imprisoned king or to rule themselves in his stead. Cells of independence-minded creoles sprang up in the major towns, and the one in the city of Querétaro included a liberal priest from the town of Dolores who had endeared himself to his Indian and *mestizo* parishoners: Miguel de Hidalgo. On September 16, 1810, as a Spanish force moved toward Querétaro to arrest Father Hidalgo and other conspirators, the priest rang the bells of the church in Dolores to assemble his parishioners and declared that the moment had come to take up arms against their oppressors. The date of the famous

Grito, or cry, of Dolores, has been observed ever since as Mexico's independence day.

As with the U.S. War of Independence, the struggle in Mexico was to be long, bloody, tedious and marked by discouraging reverses that would continue for 11 years. Father Hidalgo quickly assembled a rag-tag "army" of peasants who, motivated by a quest for social liberation as much as for independence, eagerly followed their creole leader. The rebels marched inexorably southward, gaining momentum, defeating the better-armed and trained but hopelessly outnumbered Spaniards. Yet, on the very threshold of Mexico City, Hidalgo lost his nerve and retreated. He would never regain the momentum. The Spanish counterattacked and defeated the rebel army at the Battle of Calderón, and Hidalgo fled to the northern mountains. There a trusted comrade betrayed him and other rebel leaders to the Spanish, who captured them. On July 31, 1811, the father of Mexican independence was defrocked and executed by firing squad in Chihuahua, and his head was sent to Guanajuato, where it remained on public display until independence was achieved.

However, the Spanish soon learned that the cause of independence did not die with Hidalgo. Another creole priest, José María Morelos, a man with more military skills than Hidalgo, raised a guerrilla army and took the offensive. Like Hidalgo before him, Morelos enjoyed the initiative for a time, scoring a succession of victories before he, too, was betrayed, captured and shot in 1815. Yet, still more leaders arose to take up the cause.

Meanwhile, the fall of Napoleon and the restoration of Fernando VII to the throne eliminated the issue of who was in charge in Madrid, but by then the movement for independence had taken on a life of its own. Fernando VII dispatched more troops to quell the uprising and, in a Byzantine maneuver, even negotiated with Mexican conservatives a scheme by which Fernando would leave Madrid and become the king of an independent Mexico. This occurred after Spanish liberals had forced him to swear to a constitution he abhorred. A pivotal moment in the war came when Agustín Iturbide, a competent officer in the Spanish army, defected and took up the cause of independence. He issued a decree, called the *Plan de Iguala,* under which an independent Mexico would be governed either by Fernando or another European monarch, the *gachupines* and *criollos* would become social equals, and the church would retain its Privileges. The two principal rebel generals, Vicente Guerrero and Guadalupe Victoria, embraced the plan, and one by one the major

cities fell in behind. Finally, faced with the inevitable, the newly arrived Spanish viceroy also accepted the *Plan de Iguala,* and on September 27, 1821, the Spanish abandoned Mexico City to Iturbide's army—300 years and one month after Cortés had taken it from Cuauhtémoc.

The Post-Independence Period

Just as the colonial period lasted exactly 300 years, the post-independence period would span 99, from 1821, when Iturbide triumphantly entered Mexico City, until 1920, when another military hero, Alvaro Obregón, would assume the presidency and begin to consolidate the gains of the Revolution. Those 99 years would prove to be the bloodiest and most contentious in the country's history, being marked by intrigue, betrayal, dictatorships and civil war. Few of the key players of this period would die quietly in their beds of old age.

The struggle for independence had found the various segments of Mexican society—the Privileged creoles, the *mestizos* and the Indians—fighting together in a peculiar alliance against a common enemy. With the departure of the Spaniards, however, the alliance became unraveled and friction inevitably developed among the classes. Moreover, as they fled, the *gachupines* took with them what little treasure remained, leaving the new country virtually bankrupt. Compounding Mexico's travails, the Spanish did not bequeath a strong governmental infrastructure the Mexicans could build upon

General Agustín Iturbide

Mexico

Mexico City street scene in the early 19th century

for self-rule. As was the case in other emerging Latin American republics, such as Chile and Colombia, Mexico's first century and beyond would be marked by a struggle between the forces of conservatism—the landed gentry and the clergy—and liberalism patterned after the ideals of the French and American revolutions.

The Liberals, understandably in the majority, counted on the support of the *mestizo* and Indian masses, whose cause they ostensibly championed. Fiercely anticlerical, the Liberals nonetheless were pragmatic enough to recognize that the devoutly Catholic masses would never accept such a radical concept as Protestantism. The Liberals' opposition to the properties and Privileges of the church led to the embrace of Freemasonry, a secret society with ancient roots in Europe and the Near East that remains influential among the governing elite to this day.

Unfortunately for the Liberals, the concept of Jeffersonian democracy was to prove unfeasible in a land where the vast majority of the population was illiterate, where there was no democratic tradition to build upon and where the lines of communication were too primitive for effective centralized government. That situation suited the outnumbered Conservatives just fine, many of them being local *caciques*, or strongmen, who wanted no interference from Mexico City. Also unfortunately for the Liberals, the generals who held the genuine power, backed by the cannon, the musket and the bayonet, opted to side with the Conservatives because it was they who possessed what wealth the country still had. The generals, quite simply, were bought off, rewarded for their services with land and treasure. As many a Mexican leader would discover over the next century, the lifespan of the generals' loyalty coincided with that of the payroll.

Iturbide, the conquering hero of the moment but also a man of unbridled ambition and pretentiousness, soon "amended" the *Plan de Iguala*. Instead of a European monarch, he himself would become emperor of Mexico, and he had the military forces to enforce that decision. The country was to witness the tragicomic spectacle of a woefully expensive coronation that the country could ill afford. Iturbide proved a less able administrator than he had a military commander, however. After a little more than a year, his governmental ineptitude, coupled with his profligate spending on the ridiculous trappings of monarchy, left the government bankrupt. That meant, of course, that he couldn't pay the army, which quickly overthrew him and sent the hemisphere's first "emperor" into exile. When he returned uninvited in 1823, he was arrested and shot.

With the fall of Iturbide, Mexico at last became a republic, the Liberals came to power, and in 1824 they promulgated the first of Mexico's three reasonably enlightened constitutions. Guadalupe Victoria (the inspirational *nom de guerre* of Félix

Fernández) became the first president, and he was succeeded in 1828 by the third great military hero of independence, Vicente Guerrero. Alas, as was the case with Iturbide before them, their proficiency on the battlefield proved of little value in the halls of government. Both were crude, abrasive men who alienated their own congress as well as the Conservatives. Mexico dissolved into chaos and in 1830 the Conservatives seized power in a *coup d'etat*. When Guerrero fled and took to the field to combat the usurpers, the deposed president was betrayed, captured and shot, like Hidalgo and Morelos before him. Also like Morelos, a southern state later was named in his honor.

General Antonio López de Santa Anna

Into this volatile situation was to stride a charismatic figure who was to dominate the country off and on for the next 30 years: Antonio López de Santa Anna. A former Spanish officer who, like Iturbide, had joined the independence movement, Santa Anna was the quintessential Latin American *caudillo*, the charismatic man on horseback who rules with an iron fist to maintain order. At the time of the Conservative coup, he was the commander of the garrison in Vera Cruz (today spelled Veracruz) where the all-important customs house was located. Santa Anna rebelled against the Conservative government in 1832. By the end of the year the grateful Liberals ill-advisedly made him president and Valentín Gómez Farías, a Zacatecan who would be the guiding force of Mexican Liberalism for 30 years, vice president. On the four occasions he would enjoy the supreme power of the republic, Santa Anna followed a curious practice of retiring to his *hacienda* in Vera Cruz and leaving the day-to-day responsibilities of gov-

erning the country to surrogates until such time as the situation demanded his strong hand.

Betraying the Liberals who had mistakenly hailed him as their champion, Santa Anna dissolved the Constitution of 1824, assumed dictatorial powers, and began calling himself the "Napoleon of the West." Liberals in the state of Zacatecas rose in revolt, and Santa Anna mercilessly suppressed them. Then the Anglo-American settlers of the far northern province of Texas, unaccustomed to being ruled by despots, also rebelled. In what is now a legendary epic in Texas history, Santa Anna marched into Texas in 1836 with an army of 6,000 men, killed the 187-man garrison at the mission fortress of the Alamo in San Antonio de Bexar after a desperate and bloody battle, ordered the execution of the 300 Texans who had surrendered the fort at Goliad, then swept eastward almost to the border of Louisiana. There he was defeated and captured by the army of General Sam Houston at the Battle of San Jacinto.

Houston, himself as skilled at politics as he was at war, bartered Santa Anna for Texan independence rather than hanging him, then sent the defeated dictator to Washington to meet with President Andrew Jackson. Santa Anna returned to Mexico in disgrace, retired again to his *hacienda*, and waited patiently for his country's call.

It came in 1838, when the French landed an invasion force to impose collection of debts. In the ensuing battle, Santa Anna's leg was shot off by a French cannon ball, and again he became a national hero. His leg was ceremoniously buried in the cathedral in Mexico City and in 1841, at the height of the latest Liberal-Conservative power struggle, he again became dictator. An efficient tax-collector, he was an equally extravagant spender. As had happened to Iturbide, the army deposed him in 1844 when he was unable to meet its payroll and sent him into exile in Cuba.

Meanwhile, a border dispute with the United States erupted into full-scale war in 1846, and Santa Anna was recalled from exile to take the field against the invaders from the north. Cunning as ever, Santa Anna slipped through the U.S. naval blockade by convincing American agents that he would make peace if he returned to Mexico. Instead, he was named acting president and took up arms against the Americans. Defeated by General Zachary Taylor at the Battle of Buena Vista near the city of Saltillo in February 1847, Santa Anna nonetheless sent back dispatches to Mexico City declaring that he had won a resounding victory.

Returning to the capital a hero, he again assumed dictatorial powers. He next opposed General Winfield Scott's army,

which had landed in Vera Cruz and was marching on Mexico City. Again Santa Anna was ignominiously defeated, and the capital fell to the Americans. Under the resulting Treaty of Guadalupe-Hidalgo, Mexico ceded nearly half its territory, from Texas to California. In return, the United States paid Mexico $15 million—a welcome deposit for the bankrupt treasury. Santa Anna again went into exile, this time to Venezuela.

There followed a few years of stable and efficient Liberal civilian governments, but in 1853 Santa Anna, this time the champion of the Conservatives, again was placed in power by *coup d'etat*. To raise money, he sold off another tract of land to the United States—the Gadsden Purchase, in what is today southern Arizona and New Mexico—for $10 million.

Of course, he quickly and frivolously squandered the money. The Liberals, under the leadership of Ignacio Comonfort, re-

Benito Juárez

belled against the dictator and published the *Plan de Ayutla*, which called for the drafting of a new constitution. Santa Anna fell from power for the fourth and final time in 1855 and spent most of the rest of his life in Cuba. Eventually allowed to return, he died in poverty and obscurity in 1876.

Mexico's second Liberal constitution was promulgated in 1857 under the presidency of Comonfort, but it was so anticlerical that the archbishop threatened to excommunicate anyone who took the required oath. By January 1858, the Conservatives had again overthrown the government, but this time the two sides found themselves in full-scale civil war, which was to last for three years and leave the country torn apart. Two Liberal champi-

Mexico

ons emerged during the conflict who would later play decisive roles in Mexican history.

One was a full-blooded Zapotec Indian who was governor of Oaxaca: Benito Juárez. It was he who would become the moral and spiritual guardian of Liberalism and social justice and become revered as the greatest of Mexico's leaders. The other was a *mestizo* guerrilla leader who would betray the cause of reform and become one of Mexico's most reviled villains: Porfirio Díaz.

After Comonfort was deposed, Juárez was named president and removed the constitutionalist government to the north, where it enjoyed the support of the United States. The Liberals won the civil war, and on January 11, 1861, Juárez became the newest hero to triumphantly enter Mexico City, but in keeping with his humble image he did so in a plain black carriage. He was reelected president, but the Conservatives were not yet ready to admit defeat. They resurrected the old idea of installing a European monarch on a Mexi-

Emperor Maximilian of Mexico

can throne, and they found a willing ally in France's Emperor Napoleon III.

Emboldened by the Americans' distraction with their own civil war, Napoleon landed an army at Vera Cruz and began the traditional march of conquerors to Mexico City. But at Puebla, the stubborn Mexican defenders dealt the French a stinging defeat on May 5, 1862, still commemorated as a national holiday—*el Cinco de Mayo*. The victory was fleeting, however, and the French soon captured the capital. Juárez again fled to the north with his government. In his place the Conservatives invited Archduke Maximilian, brother of the Hapsburg emperor of Austria, to reign as Mexico's second emperor.

Maximilian and his wife, Carlotta, a member of the Belgian royal family, are two of history's truly tragic figures. The Conservatives duped Maximilian into believing that he had been elected emperor in a plebiscite, and he and Carlotta arrived in Mexico expecting to be treated as beloved sovereigns. Instead, they found the country at civil war over his intervention. Ironically, Maximilian was himself something of a liberal, and he shocked the Conservatives by implementing some of the very reforms the Liberals had advocated. The Conservatives soon cooled toward their new emperor, and the *Juarista* army began scoring victories over the French and Conservative forces. With the end of the U.S. Civil War, the U.S. government warned Napoleon III to remove its forces from Mexico or the United States would intervene to enforce the Monroe Doctrine. To compound the woes of the beleaguered Maximilian, Carlotta began showing signs of mental instability. She was evacuated to Europe, where she sought unsuccessfully to win an audience with Napoleon III. Faced with the threat of war with the United States and lack of success on the battlefield, Napoleon III abandoned Maximilian to his fate. After a final defeat at Querétaro, the emperor and his army surrendered. Maximilian and two of his generals were executed by firing squad a few days later on June 19, 1867, atop the Hill of Bells, today a national landmark. Carlotta spent the remaining 60 years of her life in insanity.

Once again, Juárez triumphantly entered Mexico City and was soon reelected to a third term. By most accounts, the Juárez presidency was the most honorable and enlightened in Mexico's troubled history, before or since. There was no shameless self-enrichment such as Santa Anna and others had engaged in. The industrial base began to grow, and railroads were built. Juárez also began to implement the reforms of the Constitution of 1857, and he devoted special attention to secular education, particularly for the hapless In-

General Porfirio Díaz

dians who had long been treated as third-class citizens. This, of course, alienated Juárez from even the Liberal creoles. Moreover, in the name of economy and to guard against the praetorianism that had been the bane of Mexico since independence, Juárez had brusquely cashiered most of the officers and soldiers from the army with scant compensation for their services during 10 years of civil war. There were the inevitable military rebellions, which Juárez crushed as ruthlessly as his predecessors had. In the 1867 election, Juárez was opposed by one of his own generals, Porfirio Díaz.

Juárez was elected to a fourth term in 1871, which raised accusations that he hoped to become merely another dictator. In reality, the 1871 election was quite fair by Mexican standards, and Juárez failed to receive a majority, so his election was decided by Congress. Alas, Juárez died suddenly of a heart attack on July 18, 1872, and with him died Mexico's greatest hope for democracy with social reform. Vice President Sebastián Lerdo de Tejada, a respected and honest intellectual, succeeded him and was elected to a full term that fall, but when he chose to run again in 1876 Díaz issued a *pronuncamiento* that cynically purported to uphold the Liberal cause of "effective suffrage, no re-election." After a brief military struggle, the *Porfirista* forces captured the capital and forced Lerdo into exile. Díaz became provisional president, ushering in the longest dictatorship in Mexican history.

The Díaz dictatorship was a veritable yin-yang dichotomy of good and evil, darkness and light. On the one hand, Mexico was to experience unprecedented modernization and economic development during the 35 years he would control the country. On the other, Díaz ruled in the style of the classic Latin American *caudillo*, enjoying absolute power through a principle called *pan o palo* (bread or club). Díaz could be exceedingly generous in return for whole-hearted support, but those who refused his good offices faced imprisonment, economic deprivation, or worse. Turning his back on the Liberal principle of nationalism, he opened the doors to massive foreign investment, chiefly U.S. and British, which capitalized the country and expanded the middle class but left much of Mexico's land and wealth in foreign hands. Himself a *mestizo*, Díaz nonetheless abandoned Juárez's goal of improving the lot of the Indians, who were to continue to languish in the feudalism to which they had been consigned since the Conquest. Díaz surrounded himself with a cadre of creole technocrats, called *científicos*, who managed the economy *so* efficiently that in 1894 Mexico recorded the first budget surplus in its history. The dictator poured much of this revenue into much-needed public works projects and into the beautification of Mexico City, which he wanted to rival the grand capitals of Europe.

Because he had come to power on a platform opposing reelection, Díaz cleverly chose one of his sycophants, Manuel González, to be "elected" in 1880. During his single term, which of course was overshadowed by Díaz, González engaged in corruption on an unprecedented scale, even for Mexico. By 1884, the public was only too happy to forget about Díaz's supposed opposition to reelection and clamored for him to retake the presidency. He maintained himself in power thereafter through six rigged elections, in some of which he awarded himself a unanimous vote! In 1904, he also extended the presi-

Francisco I. Madero

dential term to six years. He concentrated all the patronage in his own hands, and enjoyed such power that he literally designated every state governor and member of Congress. Employing a system of divide-and-conquer, he pitted various factions against each other, and if one faction became too strong for his liking, he would undermine it by throwing his support to another. He did much the same thing with the officials in his government, so great was his fear of possible usurpation.

So jealous was he of possible rivals, he made absolutely no preparations for an eventual successor. By the time of his last "election" in 1910, he was 80 years old and showing signs of senility, raising concerns among the ruling elite. But there also was a restiveness among the lower classes who had been bypassed in the economic development of the Díaz years. Mexico was a social powder keg.

The spark that was to set off the inevitable explosion came from an unlikely source, a short, unassuming young man from a wealthy creole ranching family in the state of Coahuila: Francisco I. Madero. Díaz had indicated in an interview with a U.S. correspondent that he would not seek reelection in 1910, a statement that had been intended to mollify the democratic sensibilities of the U.S. government but which soon became reported in Mexico. Díaz then reneged on his promise not to stand again, and the idealistic Madero announced his own candidacy against him. Díaz at first tolerated the opposition of this seemingly insignificant upstart in order to perpetuate the myth of Porfirian democracy, but Madero's campaign appearances began attracting large, enthusiastic audiences. Madero was arrested on a trumped-up charge that he was conspiring to overthrow the regime, and he was kept behind bars until after Díaz had safely "reelected" himself. Symbolically, Díaz's latest power play had coincided with his grandiose centennial celebration of Father Hidalgo's *Grito de Dolores*.

Released from jail, Madero fled to the United States and issued a *pronunciamiento*. Suddenly there were spontaneous demonstrations against the dictatorship. Reentering Mexico, Madero found influential people flocking to his standard, but he also found himself the champion of the lower classes. Among his most important supporters was a legendary bandit from Chihuahua who had become a revolutionary: Francisco "Pancho" Villa. Meanwhile, in the southern state of Morelos, Emiliano Zapata organized a peasant army that seized the lands of the *hacendados* and engaged in battle with Díaz's federal army. The Mexican Revolution had begun.

Within months, the 35-year-old dictatorship began collapsing like the house of

Francisco "Pancho" Villa

Emiliano Zapata

Mexico

cards it was. When Villa's forces captured the border city of Ciudad Juárez in May 1911, Díaz made the traditional "withdrawal" from the treasury, fled to Vera Cruz and took ship to France. He died in Paris four years later. Madero, meanwhile, became the latest hero to enter the capital to the cheers of the masses.

Unfortunately, for all his noble ideals, Madero was no Benito Juárez. He proved an inept administrator and was easily manipulated by his family and their friends, some of whom had been among Díaz's *científicos*. The masses who had joined his movement expecting genuine social revolution were soon disillusioned. But a graver threat came in the traditional form of military uprisings, this time by counterrevolutionary *Porfiristas*. The Revolution took on the aspect of a free-for-all, with Villa and Zapata battling the counterrevolutionaries in the name of social justice and Madero's creole generals fighting essentially for themselves. The U.S. ambassador, meanwhile, angered by Madero's reversal of Díaz's *carte blanche* to foreign business interests, threw his support behind the counterrevolutionaries. Faced with the possibility of military defeat, Madero entrusted the defense of his government to a general he believed to be loyal: Victoriano Huerta. But in February 1913, with the complicity of the U.S. ambassador, Huerta arrested Madero and Vice President Pino Suárez and ordered them shot, allegedly while trying to escape. Huerta then seized the presidency for himself through a Machiavellian manipulation of the constitution.

Huerta, an alcoholic and drug addict and one of the most treacherous and repugnant figures in Latin American history, immediately found himself faced with formidable opposition. He had arrested Villa shortly before Madero's death, but the wily bandit bribed his way free and fled to the north. After Madero's murder became common knowledge, both Villa and Zapata took to the field against Huerta. In Coahuila, Governor Venustiano Carranza refused to recognize Huerta's regime and in time became the acknowledged leader of the constitutionalist forces. In Sonora, a laborer-turned-businessman-turned-general, Alvaro Obregón, raised yet another army to oppose the usurper.

Meanwhile, Woodrow Wilson became the U.S. president, and Huerta's naked power grab offended Wilson's democratic principles. He replaced the U.S. ambassador with one who applied pressure on the dictator. When Wilson learned a shipment of German arms was en route to Mexico, he ordered the Marines to seize the port of Vera Cruz in April 1914 to prevent the guns from reaching Huerta. This

Venustiano Carranza

intervention backfired, however, causing the various warring factions to unite temporarily in their denunciation of this new *gringo* invasion, even as the constitutionalists accepted shipments of U.S. arms.

In one of the most glorious and celebrated periods of Mexican history, the twin northern armies of Villa and Obregón literally raced each other southward, taking city after city from Huerta's forces, while Zapata's revolutionaries fought their way north toward the capital. In August 1914—the very month that Europe exploded into full-scale war—Huerta fled Mexico City and made his way to Texas, where he drank himself to death a year later.

All three revolutionary armies converged on the capital, and for a few days

Alvaro Obregón

there was near-anarchy. Order was restored as the various leaders met to discuss how Mexico was to be ruled, but peace was not yet at hand. Much to the displeasure of Villa and Zapata, Carranza was elected provisional president, and the two revolutionaries took to the field once again. This time, however, Villa met his match in Obregón, who employed modern concepts from the battlefields of Europe, such as massed machine guns and barbed wire, to decimate Villa's once-invincible cavalry at Celaya. Driven farther north, Villa was outflanked when President Wilson allowed constitutionalist forces to use Texas railroads for troop movements. Enraged, Villa captured some American engineers and had them shot, and in March 1916 he sacked the border town of Columbus, New Mexico, killing 19 Americans. Wilson ordered General John J. Pershing into Chihuahua in pursuit of Villa, a hopeless mission which, once again, served only to unite the warring factions against the invading *gringos*.

Even as the bloodshed droned on, Carranza summoned a constitutional convention that assembled in Querétaro in December 1916 and early the next year finalized the country's third liberal constitution. Unlike the earlier organic laws, this one guaranteed the rights of labor and decreed that property rights were secondary to the public good. The Constitution of 1917, which has decidedly socialist overtones, remains the oldest basic law in effect in Latin America. The constitution should be Carranza's legacy, but he is remembered as much for the rampant corruption that went on during his administration as for his role in the creation of a new Mexico.

The Mexican Revolution, which by most estimates claimed about 1 million lives, slowly wound down. A Carranza officer betrayed and assassinated Zapata in 1919. His armed struggle died with him, although the Morelos peasants were permitted to retain the lands they had seized from the *hacendados*. Villa, meanwhile, was bribed into passivity with an amnesty and a huge *hacienda* in Durango. Though he never took up arms again, he remained such a threatening force that he, too, was assassinated in 1923. In 1920, when Carranza sought to circumvent his own constitution's ban on reelection by hand-picking a puppet successor, Obregón and others turned against him. He was forced to abandon the capital and, a few days later, was murdered in his sleep by a trusted lieutenant. Obregón's army became the latest to enter Mexico City in triumph, and Obregón was duly elected president and took office in November 1920. After 10 years of Revolution, Mexico was at peace.

The Post-Revolutionary Period

Obregón, unlike earlier conquering generals who became president, proved both an able and enlightened leader, the best since Juárez. There was some of the inevitable corruption, but nothing on the scale of Díaz. Himself a former laborer who became a businessman before the call to arms, Obregón was friendly to labor but chose not to enforce some of the more radical aspects of the new constitution. He did, however, begin a modest land-redistribution program, Primarily to the Indian communal plots, called *ejidos*. He also allowed unprecedented press freedom and adhered to the constitution by stepping aside at the end of his term in 1924—although he essentially dictated who his successor would be.

Largely because of Obregón's guidance during those first critical post-revolutionary years, Mexico embarked on a nominally democratic path with guarantees of civil liberties, rather than embracing the totalitarian experiment of the Bolsheviks who had seized power in Russia the same year the Mexican constitution was drafted. And in 1924, the very year Lenin died and was succeeded by Stalin, Obregón duly relinquished power to another revolutionary general, Plutarco Elías Calles. Although this new president was to succumb to the temptations of near-absolute power, he was certainly no Stalin.

Calles served only one term, but he was destined to wield the actual power for 10 years. His administration basically was a continuation of Obregón's, with whom he maintained a close, harmonious personal relationship. It was suggested that the two men essentially were co-presidents. Calles, however, was even less committed to the social goals of the Revolution than was Obregón, and he slowed even the modest land distribution program.

On the subject of the church, however, Calles was deeply committed to the anticlerical principles that had been embodied in all three liberal constitutions. Both he and Obregón were practicing Freemasons, who are decidedly anti-Catholic and whose influence was believed to be even stronger after the Revolution. When the church opposed Calles' programs, he began enforcing all the radical anticlerical provisions of the constitution. The church's property, even the actual church buildings, were expropriated; priests were forbidden from engaging in political activity or even from wearing clerical garb on the street; foreign priests were expelled, and members of the clergy were required to register with the government. The clergy literally went on strike in 1926, refusing to say Mass for three years. Some fanatical Catholic laymen, called *cristeros*,

engaged in acts of terrorism. Church-state relations remained hostile for decades. Not until 1993 did Mexico establish diplomatic relations with the Vatican.

As the election of 1928 approached, Calles and Obregón found themselves unwilling to turn over power to a third man, so the constitution was amended to allow Obregón to run for a second term. Another amendment lengthened the presidential term, as Díaz had done, from four to six years. Obregón was elected over token opposition, but just three weeks later, on July 17, he was shot to death while dining in a restaurant by a young artist who apparently was a *cristero* acting on his own initiative. An eminent intellectual, Emilio Portes Gil, was named interim president until another election could be

Lázaro Cárdenas

held in 1929, although it was Calles who actually held the power. During this brief interregnum, however, an institution was established that was to be the dominant force in Mexican political life for the next 71 years. Calles and Portes Gil organized a new political party, the National Revolutionary Party, or *PNR*, that incorporated the revolutionary sectors of *campesinos*, or peasants, and organized labor under its umbrella. Its name would be changed in 1938 to the Party of the Mexican Revolution and yet again in 1946 to its current name, the Institutional Revolutionary Party, or *PRI*. Its candidate in 1929, Pascual Ortiz Rubio, won a suspiciously lopsided victory, a phenomenon that would be repeated over and over again.

Ortiz Rubio's three-year presidency is remembered as little more than a footnote because it was Calles who was really in charge. His control was so complete that when, in 1932, the president fired some officials who enjoyed Calles' support, Calles merely summoned a news conference to announce that Ortiz Rubio had resigned. The hapless president had no choice but to comply. Calles hand-picked Abelardo Rodríguez to fill out the last two years of what was to have been Obregón's term, then likewise designated a well-respected, 39-year-old former revolutionary general, Lázaro Cárdenas, as the official party's candidate for the 1934 election.

Cárdenas won by the predictable landslide, but before long the left-leaning president and the quasi-fascist Calles clashed over policy. A bloodless power struggle ensued, but this time it was Cárdenas who prevailed.

The Cárdenas administration is generally regarded as the most honest and socially conscious of the post-revolutionary period. During his six years in power, Cárdenas redistributed 45 million acres of land to the peasants, compared with 19 million that had been distributed from 1920–1934. He also gave unprecedented moral and official support to organized labor. He refused to recognize the government of the victorious Generalisimo Francisco Franco at the end of the Spanish Civil War and gave refuge to thousands of defeated Republicans. But the act for which Cárdenas is best remembered was the nationalization of foreign oil companies in 1937 after the companies refused the government's terms for settling a prolonged strike. Today, despite the privatization trend sweeping Latin America, oil drilling, refining and fuel retailing remain in the hands of the state monopoly, *Petroleos Mexicanos*, or *Pemex*.

Despite the near-absolute power Mexican presidents enjoy, there was less abuse under Cárdenas than under many of his predecessors or successors. Press freedom continued to grow, and Cárdenas tolerated the establishment of a conservative opposition movement, the National Action Party, or *PAN*, in 1939. It also was Cárdenas who finally and irrevocably established the revolutionary principle of "no reelection" by stepping aside at the end of his *sexenio*, or six-year term. Although he was to remain a respected and influential voice in Mexican politics until his death in 1970, Cárdenas made no effort to remain the power behind the throne as Calles and others had done.

However, Cárdenas chose to continue, and thus perpetuate, the decidedly undemocratic practice of Obregón and Calles of hand-picking his successor. Referred to in Mexico as *el dedazo*, or the tap of the fin-

Mexico

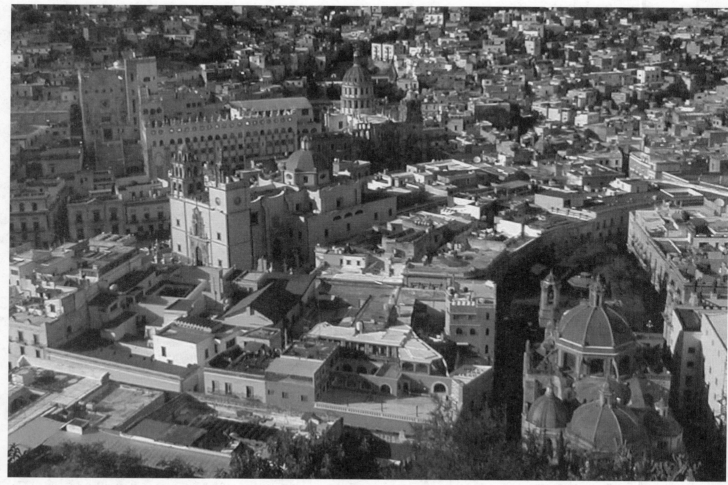

A panoramic view of the beautiful colonial city on Guanajuato, still a center of silver mining and a popular tourist destination. The triangular park in the right foreground is the Jardín de la Unión; the University of Guanajuato, one of the oldest and most prestigious learning institutions in Mexico, is the large white building on the hill at upper left.   *Photo by the author.*

ger, this practice was followed by all of Cárdenas' successors until Ernesto Zedillo disavowed it in 1999. By tradition, the incumbent conferred in secret about a year before the election with former presidents and a handful of top party leaders to discuss a list of possible candidates. At this stage, the heir apparent was referred to as *el tapado*, or the hidden one, whose identity became the focus of intense speculation by the public and the press. When the president announced his decision, the designated candidate was hailed by all sectors of the party and pro-*PRI* newspapers as a near-messiah and acclaimed as the greatest possible choice. The process more closely resembled the selection of a new pope by the College of Cardinals than the nomination of a presidential candidate in a supposedly democratic system; all that was missing was the emission of white smoke from the presidential palace to announce that a choice had been made. Some scholars have suggested the *PRI*'s selection process was based upon Masonic rites.

Cárdenas' choice was yet another revolutionary general, Manuel Avila Camacho, who had served as Cárdenas' defense secretary. This surprised many, because Avila Camacho was far to the right of Cárdenas. Moreover, he was a devout Catholic, which represented a sharp break with the anti-clericalism of the past. This transition established a precedent that would be seen again in the ensuing decades of alternating between presidents that were leftist and centrist, also between presidents who were dynamic and passive. Under Avila Camacho, land redistribution slowed to a glacial pace. On the other hand, World War II was to result in an economic boom for Mexico, which joined the Allies and declared war on Germany and Japan. Mexican industries churned out war supplies that were exported to the United States; relations in general between the United States and Mexico, strained since the beginning of the Revolution, finally began to improve. Avila Camacho hosted President Franklin D. Roosevelt at a meeting in Monterrey in 1943,

the first time a sitting U.S. president had crossed the southern border.

As his successor in 1946 Avila Camacho picked Miguel Alemán, his *secretario de gobernación*, usually translated as interior minister, the most powerful post in the cabinet, one that is roughly the combined equivalent of the secretary of the interior and White House chief of staff in the U.S. system. Whoever holds it is automatically placed on the "short list" to be nominated for president. Unlike earlier elections, however, this time there was a serious opposition candidate in the form of Foreign Minister Ezequiel Padilla, who was disgruntled over not being selected himself. Alemán, of course, was declared the winner with 80% of the vote. How honest that vote count was remains questionable, but for Mexico even 20% for an opposition candidate was extraordinary. The transition was a watershed in modern Mexican history because Avila Camacho was to be the last general to serve as president.

Like Avila Camacho, however, Alemán was a centrist who did little more than

Manuel Avila Camacho

give lip service to the socialist Principles of the Revolution, but he was more dynamic and more of a visionary than his predecessor. The Mexican economy was still growing, and Alemán chose to devote much of the increased revenues to mammoth public works projects like highways and dams. He also embarked on the greatest building program since the days of Díaz, and one of the chief beneficiaries of this program was the National Autonomous University of Mexico, or *UNAM*. Moreover, Alemán greatly improved the efficiency of state-owned enterprises like *Pemex*. On the negative side, corruption reappeared on a scale reminiscent of the days of Carranza and Díaz. The president himself escaped scandal, but it was noted that he and many of his appointees left office far wealthier than they had been before.

Apparently in response to the public discontent over the corruption, Alemán chose his interior secretary, Adolfo Ruíz Cortines, as the *PRI* presidential candidate in 1952. Once again, however, a *PRI* defector, a wealthy businessman and former general named Miguel Henríquez Guzmán, launched a serious independent candidacy. Ruíz Cortines supposedly defeated the popular Henríquez and minor candidates with 77% of the vote—still questionable, but it would be the smallest percentage the *PRI* would admit to for 36 years.

Ruíz Cortines restored an atmosphere of integrity to the presidency. Lacking Alemán's flamboyance and charisma, he often was derided as colorless. But he proved an aggressive, if not demonstrative, reformer. While Alemán had constructed grand projects, Ruíz Cortines focused on roads, irrigation, schools and hospitals. Among his lasting achieve-

ments was extending the suffrage to women in 1953, and in his last year in office Mexico became for the first time a net exporter of food.

Ruíz Cortines selected his young labor secretary, Adolfo López Mateos, as the *PRI* candidate in 1958. The *PAN* for the first time mounted a reasonably serious challenge, but López Mateos won by the usual landslide, about 90%. López Mateos swung the pendulum back to the left and toward more dynamic leadership. As labor minister he had earned the respect of the unions, and there were fewer strikes during his *sexenio* than in the previous three. Land distribution, which had tapered off steadily under his three predecessors, picked up dramatically. López Mateos parceled out about 22 million acres, making him second only to Cárdenas.

The pendulum then swung sharply back toward conservatism and drabness. As his successor, López Mateos picked his interior secretary, Gustavo Díaz Ordáz, a homely, most unpresidential-looking choice. For the first time, the *PAN* garnered more than 1 million votes in the 1964 election, and its percentage rose to just above 10%. There was nothing particularly breathtaking in the achievements of Díaz Ordáz other than the sports complex that was built for the 1968 Olympic Games. On the very eve of the games, however, something occurred that was to haunt the president until his death. The student unrest that had spread across Europe and the United States in 1968 arrived in Mexico that summer. Federal troops occupied the *UNAM* to quell a lengthy student strike. On the night of October 2, when students staged a peaceful demonstration in the Plaza de Tlatelolco in Mexico City, troops opened fire on the pretext that snipers had fired on them. Little or no evidence supports this, but as many as 300 people were killed, hundreds more wounded and more than 1,000 arrested. It was the greatest outbreak of violence

since the *cristero* revolt of the 1920s. More than 30 years later, the "Tlatelolco Massacre" remains a national controversy, with questions still unanswered.

Ironically, the man who was responsible for crushing the protests, Interior Secretary Luis Echeverría, was the man Díaz Ordáz selected to succeed him in 1970. This time the *PAN*'s percentage of the vote edged up to 13%. As if to atone for his role in the Tlatelolco incident, Echeverría swung the pendulum dramatically back to the left. Early in his term he freed hundreds of students who had been jailed for two years. He angered the United States by establishing diplomatic relations with the People's Republic of China and by speaking out against the war in Vietnam. He made a point of expressing support for Cuba's Fidel Castro and welcomed Castro on a state visit to Mexico. He refused to recognize the government of General Augusto Pinochet after the 1973 coup that overthrew and killed Marxist President Salvador Allende in Chile, and he granted asylum to thousands of Chilean leftists. He ordered his U.N. delegate to support a resolution condemning Zionism as racism, but when U.S. Jews launched a boycott of Mexican resorts, he abruptly reversed course. He made pretensions about being a leader of the so-called "Nonaligned Movement" and even sought to become U.N. secretary-general upon his retirement.

On the whole, Echeverría can be described as a fountain of hollow rhetoric. He denounced capitalism, and increased the number of state-owned enterprises from 50 to 750, but pragmatically did little to interfere with free enterprise in Mexico. He talked about democratizing the *PRI*, but didn't follow through. He encouraged the creation of left-wing publications, but when the leftist editor of the daily *Excélsior*, Julio Scherer García, became too critical for his taste, Echeverría used his influence to have him fired.

Former President López Portillo and family

Mexico

Scherer then launched a weekly newsmagazine, *Proceso,* which the president tried to strangle at birth by refusing to sell Scherer government-subsidized newsprint. *Proceso* survived, however, and today is the leading news weekly. Four months before he left office in 1976, Echeverría set a precedent for future presidents by making a dramatic economic move and leaving the consequences to his successor: he devalued the peso, from 12.5 to 20 to the dollar. He also bequeathed a 50% unemployment/underemployment rate and a 22% inflation rate.

That successor would be Echeverría's finance secretary, José López Portillo, who was elected without any meaningful opposition when the *PAN* refused to field a candidate in 1976 to protest what it called, not incorrectly, *PRI* electoral manipulations. In keeping with tradition, López Portillo swung the pendulum back to the right. The major departure from his predecessor's policy was to stop baiting big business, international lending institutions and the United States. He met with President Jimmy Carter, who was sworn in six weeks after himself, in Washington early in their terms and agreed to an emergency sale of Mexican natural gas to help the United States cope with the brutally cold winter of 1977. He also became the first Mexican president to address the U.S. Congress, to which he delivered a fatherly lecture about being good neighbors. Carter would later reciprocate the visit and become the first U.S. president to address the Mexican Congress—in Spanish. López Portillo later would exchange visits with Carter's successor, Ronald Reagan. López Portillo did not, however, distance himself from Fidel Castro. He also lent moral and financial support to the *Sandinista* regime in Nicaragua, which came to power on his watch in 1979, and opposed Reagan's support for right-wing regimes in El Salvador and Guatemala.

Still, he wisely mended fences with the International Monetary Fund and major foreign banks and succeeded in reassuring them that Mexico was a sound credit risk again. In this he was aided by the discovery in the early 1970s of vast deposits of petroleum, by some estimates rivaling the reserves of Saudi Arabia, in the southern states of Tabasco and Chiapas. *Pemex* brought the fields on line just in time to take full advantage of OPEC's quadrupling of the world market Price for oil. Mexico opted not to join OPEC, but the revenue from petroleum sales began to fill government coffers. López Portillo, like a poor man who has suddenly won the lottery, went on a wild spending spree. When the money ran out, he merely borrowed more from abroad on the assumption that the petroleum gravy train would

Former President de la Madrid and family

rumble on indefinitely. He would leave office before the full weight of his folly came crashing down upon his successor.

So, too, would the massive corruption committed by López Portillo and his top officials on a scale unseen since the time of Alemán. He became the embodiment of an old Mexican quip about the president: "The first two years he talks about corruption, the next two years he does nothing and the last two years he takes all he can." In López Portillo's case, he acquired a palatial estate called Dog Hill, with five mansions, swimming pools, stables, tennis courts and a gymnasium. On the positive side, he finally moved to give opposition parties a somewhat greater voice, while, of course, not actually jeopardizing the *PRI*'s grip on power. In the 1960s, the opposition had been reserved a maximum of 20 seats in the 197-seat Chamber of Deputies, the lower house of Congress, distributed by proportional representation. López Portillo enlarged the chamber to 400 seats, of which up to 100 could go to the opposition.

In 1982, López Portillo's final year in office, the world price of oil took a downturn and Mexico found itself in deep financial trouble. López Portillo was forced to implement a drastic—and exceedingly unpopular—austerity program that threw about 1 million bureaucrats out of work. He also was forced to devalue the peso again. In the midst of this crisis, he broke with convention by selecting as his successor his secretary of planning and budget, Miguel de la Madrid. Among other things, this shattered the long-accepted tradition of never picking a *PRI* candidate who speaks English. Not only that, de la Madrid had earned a master's degree in public administration from Harvard University. It was, moreover, to establish a new trend of selecting presidents who are technocrats who have never held elective office, reminiscent of Díaz's *científicos,* except that these new ones received their

training in the United States. In the July 1982 election, de la Madrid reportedly received 74.4% to 14% for the *PAN* candidate and 5.8% for the candidate of a coalition of left-wing parties. Just two weeks before he left office, López Portillo did something that not even the leftist Echeverría had dared to do—he nationalized the banks. On December 1, 1982, he turned over the mess he had created to de la Madrid and retired to Dog Hill. He was held in low esteem in public opinion right up until his death on February 17, 2004—and beyond.

De la Madrid was left to cope with the country's gravest economic crisis since the Depression of the 1930s. In 1983 the inflation rate was 60%, and the foreign debt continued to mushroom, from $65 billion in 1983 to $105 billion in 1988—among the greatest per capita debts in the world. Even as the president struggled to cope with this daunting challenge, the country was hammered by a dual blow in 1985. OPEC slashed the price for a barrel of petroleum by about two thirds, from roughly $30 to $10, a move that completely pulled the rug out from under the debt-ridden economy. Even nature seemed to be against Mexico; a disastrous earthquake struck Mexico City that year, killing an estimated 10,000 people and causing $3.5 billion in property damage—much of which was attributed to shoddy construction of government-sponsored projects. The peso began to plummet against the dollar, and the country faced the kind of hyperinflation that had once plagued Argentina, Brazil and Peru. Inflation soared to more than 100% on de la Madrid's watch, and the peso dropped from 24.5 to the dollar to 2,800 by 1990. Compounding the dilemma was Mexico's burgeoning birthrate of 3.2% annually. Even in the boom times the economy had barely been able to absorb the young new workers flooding the labor market, but in these lean times the situation became especially desperate. The cardboard shanty towns on the outskirts of Mexico City grew larger and larger, and more Mexicans than ever were seeking the traditional escape route from their misery—illegal entry into the United States. This, of course, served to strain bilateral relations.

Desperate times do indeed call for desperate measures, and de la Madrid employed them. He allowed the price of Mexican crude oil to "float" instead of pegging it at an artificial Price. He also began to sell off some of the government-owned enterprises whose payrolls had become bloated from *PRI* patronage. Attempts to renegotiate the foreign debt satisfied neither Mexico nor its creditors. Finally, de la Madrid succeeded in obtaining a $3.5 billion "bridging" loan from the Reagan administration in 1988.

As if de la Madrid did not have enough problems, early in his administration he was faced with still another—a scandal that erupted over the corruption committed under his predecessor. Among the high-level López Portillo officials accused of financial wrongdoing were the head of *Pemex*, who could not account for a missing 300,000 barrels of oil. Perhaps the most egregious case, one which especially outraged the public, was that of the Mexico City police chief, who had built himself an unbelievably ostentatious estate complete with air-conditioned doghouses! The chief was prosecuted and his property was expropriated and opened to the public as a "museum of corruption." López Portillo himself managed to escape prosecution (no such action has ever been taken against a former head of state since the Revolution), but the damage to his reputation wrought by his shameless nest-feathering was irreparable and today he remains a political outcaste even within the ranks of the *PRI*.

The lean economic times and the publicizing of outrageous cases of corruption took a serious toll on the *PRI*. Up to that point, the *PRI* not only had won every presidential election since 1929, but it had never lost an election for a state governorship or a federal Senate seat and rarely lost at any level. Now, for the first time, the *PAN* began winning municipal elections and even won some directly elected seats in the Chamber of Deputies, not merely the scraps the *PRI* reserved for the opposition under proportional representation.

In the 1988 presidential election, the *PRI* was to face the greatest threat to its power in its 60-year history, not from the right, but from the left. Cuauhtémoc Cárdenas, son of the revered former president and himself a member of the *PRI*, abandoned the party to organize a new left-wing movement, the Party of the Democratic Revolution, or *PRD*. As his successor, de la Madrid selected another technocrat who, like himself, spoke fluent English, was schooled at Harvard and had never held an elective office: Carlos Salinas de Gortari. The *PAN*, meanwhile, launched its most determined effort to date with the candidacy of Manuel Clouthier, a wealthy landowner from Sinaloa.

Polls showed that Salinas not only might fail to win an absolute majority, but even more unthinkable, might actually lose to Cárdenas. The campaign was the most contentious in living memory, and the actual election on July 6 remains the most controversial. As the polls had indicated, on election night early returns showed Cárdenas closing on Salinas. Then, suddenly, it was reported that the vote count had been delayed by a computer breakdown. Federal troops seized the ballot boxes. The results weren't announced until September 10, and it was reported that Salinas had neatly received a bare majority of 50.36% to 31.06% for Cárdenas and 16.81% for Clouthier. Both opposition parties cried foul, but Salinas was duly sworn in on December 1 under a cloud of suspicion and illegitimacy that haunts him to this day.

Just as Echeverría had sought to atone for the Tlatelolco Massacre by tilting heavily to the left, so Salinas attempted to neutralize the outrage over his suspicious election victory by portraying himself as a political reformer. The timing of the Salinas reforms, beginning in 1989, was especially symbolic. *Perestroika* and *glasnost* were in full flower in the Soviet Union; the democracy movement was underway in China, although it was to be crushed that June; the Berlin Wall came tumbling down in November, and the autocratic regime of Romania's Nicolae Ceaucescu came to a bloody end in December. Moreover, one Latin American dictatorship after another had given way to multi-party democracy.

With the temper of these times, Mexico's monopolistic political system suddenly looked like a man with his fly open at an elegant dinner party. Salinas put out the word that at least some elections must be fair and clean, if only to keep up appearances. As a result, the *PAN* began winning state governorships, first Guanajuato, then Baja California Norte, Jalisco, and Chihuahua. Both the *PAN* and the *PRD* began winning more directly elected seats in the Chamber of Deputies, and even the *PRI*'s monopoly in the 64-member Senate was finally broken.

Perhaps just as important as the electoral reforms, however, was the relaxation of controls on the media. Salinas abolished *Pipsa*, the government newsprint monopoly that offered paper at subsidized prices but which often had withheld it from overly critical publications. The virtual monopoly enjoyed by the giant pro-*PRI* television network *Televisa* also came to an end as rival network *TV Azteca* went on the air, although it, too, had pro-*PRI* owners. As a consequence, reporting became both more aggressive and more critical. Salinas, and the so-called "dinosaurs," or traditionalists within the *PRI*, soon discovered what Mikhail Gorbachev was to learn: that reforms after decades of repression gain momentum and take on a life of their own; once the forces of openness are placed in motion, they cannot be reversed without a violent reaction.

Meanwhile, Salinas sought to cope with the economic crisis he had inherited from his predecessor. He negotiated another "bailout" loan in 1990 from President George Bush, with whom he met several times and enjoyed a satisfactory working relationship. In addition, Salinas embraced the Latin American trend toward privatization of state-owned enterprises. The Mexican Revolution was essentially dead. In its place was a stampede toward free-market capitalism. No longer were

Former President Salinas de Gortari and family

Mexico

foreign, particularly U.S., businessmen viewed as bogeymen. Assembly plants, called *maquiladoras,* sprang up along the northern border. Hundreds of thousands of Mexicans found jobs in them, at wages well below U.S. levels but far above what they had before—nothing.

Slowly the economy began to improve, and Bush and Salinas discussed a grand scheme designed to benefit both economies—a North American Free Trade Agreement (NAFTA) that would encompass Canada, the United States and Mexico. NAFTA became a hot political issue in the U.S. presidential election of 1992, with organized labor vehemently opposed to it. But after some vacillation, Democratic candidate Bill Clinton also endorsed the concept. The independent candidate that year, tycoon H. Ross Perot, warned that NAFTA would create "a giant sucking sound" as U.S. jobs disappeared south of the border. After Clinton's victory, the U.S. Senate ratified the treaty in late 1993—after the Canadian Parliament and Mexican Congress already had done so—and it took effect on January 1, 1994. Modeled loosely after the European Common Market, in theory it benefits all three countries by eliminating tariffs, thereby stimulating trade and, indirectly, production. There has, indeed, been an explosion of trade. Tractor trailers flow in an endless stream across the Rio Grande in both directions, although in those heading north illegal drugs frequently ride piggy-back with legitimate cargo. The boom in northern Mexico was to be cut short, however, by yet another disastrous peso devaluation.

By the 1994 elections, Salinas' reforms had ricocheted on him, and the *PRI* was split more than ever between the reformers and the "dinosaurs." The traditionalists contemptuously regarded the reformers, most of whom had held only appointed offices by virtue of their advanced degrees, many of them from the United States, as upstarts who had not paid the necessary dues by coming up through party ranks. Despite his reforms, Salinas was not about to abandon the practice of the *dedazo.* According to tradition, he met Privately in September 1993 with a handful of influential party leaders before announcing he had selected yet another technocrat with a U.S. doctorate, Luis Donaldo Colosio, as the *PRI* candidate. Though he was a technocrat, the party elders regarded him as harmless and pledged to support him.

But Colosio soon demonstrated that he was his own man, not Salinas'. He campaigned as a populist and drew large, enthusiastic crowds, which led to a falling out with Salinas. The rift may have been Colosio's doom. On March 23, 1994, while pressing the flesh with a crowd of cheering supporters in Tijuana, Baja California

**Former President
Ernesto Zedillo Ponce de León**

Norte, Colosio was shot in the head by a man wielding a pistol and died on the spot. The killing sent shock waves through Mexico, because although violence is relatively commonplace in local politics, this was the highest-level assassination since the murder of President-elect Obregón in 1928. The lone gunman was apprehended, convicted and sentenced to 45 years in prison (Mexico does not have the death penalty), and although he never implicated anyone else in the assassination, there remains a widespread public belief that the killing was the result of a conspiracy.

Stunned, *PRI* officials met again with Salinas, who chose yet another technocrat, the Yale-educated Ernesto Zedillo Ponce de León. While Colosio had been perceived as shy, Zedillo was seen as colorless and reclusive. He had a flat, uninspiring speaking voice and initially showed no talent for leadership. He had spent his 21 years with the party hidden away from the public in various bureaucratic assignments. He received coaching to improve his style, but with dire results. In the spirit of Salinas' reforms, he agreed to meet the *PRD*'s Cárdenas and the *PAN* candidate, Diego Fernández de Cevallos, in a televised debate; his performance was disastrous. Polls after the event showed Fernández leading by 20%.

The well-oiled *PRI* machinery rushed to Zedillo's rescue. Although the "dinosaurs" were lukewarm about having a fourth Ivy League-trained bureaucrat as the party nominee, they rallied behind him to ensure victory through the *PRI*'s

time-honored methods. Zedillo likely would have won the August 21 vote even without creative vote counting, but like Salinas, he reportedly—and suspiciously—received the magic 50% majority. Fernández supposedly received 26%, while Cárdenas dropped to 17%. The *PAN* and the *PRD* made significant gains in the Congress. The *PRI* won an even 300 of the 500 seats in the Chamber of Deputies, while the *PAN* total rose to 119, the Workers Party (*PT*) had 10 and the *PRD* 7. In the expanded Senate, the *PRI* had 95 of the 128 seats, the *PAN* 25 and the *PRD* 8.

Like Echeverría before him, Salinas decided in the waning days of his administration to devalue the peso and let Zedillo deal with the consequences. The consequences were terrible; the economic recovery collapsed virtually overnight and the country plunged once again into recession. The trauma of this latest downturn on the newly emerging middle class was to have long-lasting political fallout for the *PRI*. Even today, young urban professionals from different states tell this author that they vote for the *PAN* because of Carlos Salinas.

Even before Zedillo could take office on December 1, 1994, the country would be shocked by yet another assassination, one that shook the government and the *PRI* to their very foundations. On September 28, *PRI* Secretary General José Francisco Ruíz Massieu, the No. 2 man in the party and a leader in the reform faction, was gunned down. Salinas, whose sister was once married to the slain politician, appointed Ruíz Massieu's brother Mario to investigate the murder. A few months later, after Zedillo had taken office, Mario Ruíz Massieu resigned, alleging that the *PRI* was obstructing the investigation. Ostensibly to ensure a non-partisan investigation, Zedillo appointed as attorney general a *PAN* loyalist, Antonio Lozano. In February 1995, Lozano stunned the nation again by ordering the arrest of former President Salinas' brother, Raúl, on charges of masterminding the Ruíz Massieu murder. A month later, Carlos Salinas—disgraced as much by his brother's arrest as by the recession already being blamed on him—absconded from the country, first to the United States, then to Canada, and finally to Ireland, which has no extradition treaty with Mexico. He remains a pariah in Mexico to this day, while the Ruíz Massieu assassination and the Salinas brothers' alleged links to it, as well as revelations they may have been linked to drug traffickers, remain grist for the Mexican media. In January 1999, Raúl Salinas was convicted of the murder and sentenced to 50 years' imprisonment. In June 2005, a three-judge appeal panel shocked the country by overturning the conviction. He walked out of prison a few days later.

The Political Earthquake of 1997

Mexico embarked on an uncharted political course with the midterm elections of July 6, 1997. At stake were all 500 deputies in the lower house of Congress, 300 of them elected directly by district and 200 by proportional representation, and 32 of the 128 senators, allocated by proportional representation. The *PRI* would have had to poll at least 42.2% to retain its absolute majority in the Chamber of Deputies, but it received only 39%.

Of the 300 deputies elected directly, the *PRI* won 164, the *PRD* won 70, the *PAN* took 65, and the *PT* had one. Proportionally, the *PRI* received 39% of the vote, *PAN* 27% and the *PRD* 25.5%. When the complicated formula was put into effect, the *PRI* fell about 10 seats short of a majority. Its majority in the Senate remained secure.

Buffeted by opposition from right and left, the *PRI* took an unprecedented drubbing in local races. In Mexico City, where the mayor was elected directly for the first time rather than appointed by the president, Cuauhtémoc Cárdenas, the *PRD* presidential candidate in 1988 and 1994, received a landslide victory, polling 47.1% of the vote to 25.6% for the *PRI*'s candidate and 15.3% for *PAN*'s. The *PRD* also captured 38 of the 66 seats in the Federal District's legislative assembly.

Of the six governorships at stake in the election, the *PAN* won decisive majority victories in both Nuevo León (Monterrey) and Querétaro. Those triumphs brought to six the number of states *PAN* had wrested from the *PRI* since 1989, after President Salinas' electoral reforms were implemented. In Nuevo León, *PAN* also swept 19 of the 26 seats in the state legislature, nine of the 11 seats for national deputy and held onto the mayoralties of Monterrey and four of its suburbs, which it had won in 1994. The *PRI* scored undisputed wins in San Luis Potosí and Colima states, but *PAN* claimed vote fraud cost it the governorship of Sonora, which borders Arizona, and of Campeche, in the southeast.

Apart from these charges, the election, which this author observed in Monterrey, apparently was carried out with unprecedented rectitude. Elections are now conducted under the auspices of the Federal Electoral Institute *(IFE)*, an independent, non-partisan entity, not a creature of *PRI* patronage as was the case in the past; each state has a similar body. Since 1994, each voter has a plastic ID card with photo and thumb Print, which is matched against a master list in each polling station. Each party is entitled to five accredited poll watchers at each station. Voters mark their ballots in secret, free from intimidation by *PRI* operatives. After a voter casts his bal-

Headlines in the Monterrey newspaper *El Norte* the morning of July 7, 1997, declare the opposition *PAN* candidate, Fernando Canales, the winner of the Nuevo León governor's race, as well as announcing that the opposition parties have broken the *PRI*'s domination of Congress and that the *PRD*'s Cuauhtémoc Cárdenas has won the mayor's race in Mexico City.

lot, his thumb is marked with indelible ink to thwart Chicago-style multiple voting. Alcohol sales are banned not only on election day but on election eve.

The business newspaper *El Financiero* had perhaps the most succinct headline the morning after the election: "END TO 70 YEARS OF HEGEMONY." Julio Castrillón, one of the victorious *PAN* candidates for national deputy from Nuevo León, had a prophetic assessment. "This is the death of the one-party system,"

Mexico

he proclaimed during an interview. "This is an historic turnover. The decisions in the Congress will have to be by consensus. The president will lose his absolute power."

The effect of this election went beyond Mexico finding itself in a U.S.-style situation of an opposition-controlled Congress, however. An examination of Mexico's electoral map showed a troubling polarization of the country between north and south, rich and poor, right and left. The *PAN* clearly is on the ascendancy in the northern half of the country, where proximity to the U.S. border has a positive correlation to the number of jobs generated by ubiquitous *maquiladora* assembly plants. The author was stunned by the increased affluence he found in Monterrey since his last visit 14 years earlier. With prosperity, it seems, had come political conservatism. In those states where *PAN* controlled the governorships, it scored lopsided victories in the races for federal deputies. In Baja California Norte, for example, the *PAN* won all six, in Chihuahua eight of nine, in Jalisco 18 of 19, in Guanajuato 11 of 14. The farther south one goes, however, the worse the poverty and the greater the voting strength of the *PRD*.

A learning process got underway in Mexico in the wake of the historic 1997 elections, as the *PRI*, the opposition parties, the media, the business community and the public in general all came to terms with the new political realities. For the first year, the *PAN* and the *PRD* put aside their obvious ideological differences in order to join forces to wrest control of key committees in the Chamber of Deputies

from the *PRI*. Cárdenas took office as mayor of Mexico City in December 1997, vowing in his inaugural address to combat the city's three major ills: crime, corruption and pollution.

But the euphoria of victory abruptly gave way to the grim realities of governing the world's most populous city. For one thing, the extent of *PRI* patronage and corruption proved to be even more mind-boggling than had been imagined. When Cárdenas' team took over city offices, it discovered that the outgoing *PRI* officials had erased the hard drives of all the computers—all, that is, except for the computers that had mysteriously vanished. The erasures apparently were less an act of sour-grapes sabotage by the losers against the winners than a matter of destroying evidence of criminal malfeasance. Meanwhile, scandal after scandal dominated newscasts and the front pages of newspapers throughout the country in 1998, most of them involving *PRI* officials or wealthy patrons.

The aftershocks of the political earthquake of 1997 continued to be felt through 1998 and 1999, when Mexico elected most of its governors. These races were closely watched bellwethers of the three major parties' electoral muscle heading into the crucial 2000 presidential election. Even before the campaigning got underway, however, the *PRI* was tarnished by yet another scandal.

In March 1998, President Zedillo startled the Chamber of Deputies with a cavalier proposal for the government to assume $65 billion in bad debts from the 1994–95 economic crisis. The debts were

held by the Bank Savings Protection Fund, the equivalent of the U.S. Federal Deposit Insurance Corporation, known by the acronym *Fobaproa*. Zedillo's plan amounted to a massive bailout of banks that went under during the crisis, with the taxpayers footing the bill. Soon, however, investigative journalists and opposition congressmen began disclosing that many of the bad debts resulted from incredibly stupid loans to multi-millionaires for high-risk ventures. Many of those businessmen, it turned out, had contributed millions of dollars to the *PRI*'s 1994 campaign chest.

The public outrage was immediate and intense. For months, the opposition *PAN* and *PRD* deputies joined forces to keep Zedillo's bailout bill hostage in the lower house, while the government made lame efforts to assuage public opinion by arresting more than 180 businessmen for fraudulent loans. That December, the logjam was broken when the *PAN* struck a compromise with the *PRI* on the 1999 budget, by which $55 billion of the *Fobaproa* debt would be converted into public debt. The *PRD* denounced the bailout as a travesty, signaling an end to the era of cooperation between the two opposition parties.

Prelude to 2000

With the *Fobaproa* scandal reverberating in the background, Mexicans proceeded to elect 17 of their 31 governors in 1998 and 1999. With the electoral reforms now firmly in place, the outcomes were no longer a foregone conclusion. The first major tri-cornered showdown came on July 5, 1998, in the contiguous north-central states of Chihuahua, Durango and Zacatecas. This author drove to Zacatecas to cover that election, considered the most newsworthy of the three, as a free-lance journalist. There, a former *PRI* whip in the Chamber of Deputies, Ricardo Monreal, had bolted the party when its kingpins refused to endorse his candidacy for governor. He then stood as the candidate for the *PRD*, while the *PRI* nominated a longtime party hack. The race was considered symbolic both because of Monreal's defection and because Zacatecas had long been a faithful *PRI* stronghold and had given President Zedillo the largest percentage of the vote of any state in 1994. Moreover, Zacatecans boasted a long tradition of rebelliousness.

The evening I arrived in the capital city, also named Zacatecas, thousands of Monreal supporters filled the Plaza de Armas for his closing rally. Hundreds *PRD* partisans carried lighted candles. "We're burying the *PRI*," an elderly woman explained. "These are for its wake." Monreal told the

A poll-watcher applies indelible ink to the thumb of a woman in Monterrey after she cast her ballots in the historic 1997 congressional elections, one of the many safeguards now in effect to prevent electoral fraud. The ruling *PRI* lost its majority in the lower house of Congress for the first time.   *Photo by the author*

Mexico

Thousands packed the Plaza de Armas in Zacatecas for the closing rally of the PRD gubernatorial candidate, Ricardo Monreal, in July 1998.
Photo by the author

cheering crowd, "We're about to witness the second taking of Zacatecas," alluding to the city's capture by Pancho Villa's rebel army in 1914. Pointing to the adjacent government palace, he declared, "That house is going to get a cleaning!" The same plaza was filled again a few nights later with even more euphoric Monreal supporters as election results confirmed his decisive victory, 43% to 36%, despite evidence of *PRI* vote tampering.

That same day, the *PRI* easily held onto the governorship of neighboring Durango, 40% to 28% for the *PAN* and 22.5% for the *PT*. But the *PRI* made history in Chihuahua with the first *recapturing* of a governorship from the *PAN*, which had won there in 1992.

From Zacatecas I drove 70 miles south to Aguascalientes, capital city of the like-named state, which was to elect its governor on August 2. Heavily industrialized, with a burgeoning middle class, Aguascalientes was as fertile a ground for the *PAN* as Zacatecas was for the *PRD*. It was. The *PAN* candidate, Felipe González won by about 10 percentage points.

The same day, the *PRI*'s Miguel Alemán, son and namesake of the former president, won by an even greater margin in Veracruz, while the *PRI* held onto the governorship of Oaxaca against a determined *PRD* challenge. The *PRD* cited incidents of vote fraud.

On October 25, 1998, the *PRI* easily won in Tamaulipas with 58% of the vote; the *PAN* was second with 25% and the *PRD* third with 14%. On November 8, the *PRI*

withstood stronger challenges from the *PAN* in Puebla, winning 51% to 34%, and in Sinaloa, where the margin was 47% to 32%. But in tiny Tlaxcala, a former *PRI* loyalist, Alfonso Sánchez Anaya, ran as the *PRD* candidate in that long-time *PRI* stronghold state. Sánchez pulled off a narrow upset victory, 45% to 43%.

Guerrero and Baja California Sur voted on February 7, 1999, in what were essentially two-way contests between the *PRI* and the ascendant *PRD*. In the former, a poor southern state where there had been guerrilla insurgency and where the *PRD* has a natural constituency, the *PRI* candidate was declared the winner by 49% to 47%. The *PRD* cried foul, alleging that the *PRI* had swapped votes for groceries. But in Baja California Sur, once again the *PRD* had nominated a *PRI* renegade, Leonel Cota Montana, who won by a landslide 55% to the *PRI* candidate's 36%.

Two weeks later, the *PRI* won in Hidalgo and even in Quintana Roo, where the incumbent *PRI* governor, Mario Villanueva Madrid, was under federal investigation for drug trafficking. In both states, the two opposition parties had failed to present a united front, thus dividing the opposition vote and assuring the *PRI* easy wins. In Hidalgo, the *PRI* received an absolute majority of 53%. But in Quintana Roo the *PRI* obtained a mere plurality of 43%, to 34% for the *PRD* and the remainder for the *PAN*. As a bizarre anticlimax to the Quintana Roo election, Governor Villanueva absconded the day before the inauguration of his successor

and disappeared. For two years he was an international fugitive before being arrested in Cancún in his home state on May 24, 2001.

On July 4, 1999, the nation's attention was riveted on two governor's races: in Mexico, the most populous state with 12 million people, which borders the Federal District, and in Nayarit, a small, impoverished state of 1 million on the Pacific coast. In Mexico, the *PAN* and a *PRD-PT* coalition both mounted strong candidates to face the *PRI*, thus dividing the opposition vote. But in Nayarit, to which this author drove to report on the campaign, the *PAN*, *PRD*, *PT* and the minuscule Socialist Revolutionary put aside their ideological differences to field a single candidate, Antonio Echevarría, a *PRI* defector. These two races underscored what a united opposition could achieve. In Mexico, the *PRI*'s Arturo Montiel won with a 41% plurality, to 31% for the *PAN* candidate and 21% for the *PRD-PT* candidate. But in Nayarit, Echevarría defeated the *PRI* candidate 50% to 44%, despite frantic *PRI* attempts to bribe opposition voters into surrendering their voter ID cards in return for a *dispensa*, or welfare package of groceries. "Remember," Echevarría had said when the bribe scheme became public, "a *dispensa* lasts for three days, but a bad government lasts for six years!" Similar charges surfaced in the Mexico election.

The same tricks also came into play before the gubernatorial election in the border state of Coahuila on September 26, 1999. While this author was in Saltillo to write about the campaign, one of the local newspapers carried a front-page photo montage of trucks carrying *dispensas* from a government warehouse to *PRI* precinct headquarters. Four parties—the *PAN*, the *PRD*, the *PT* and the small Environmental Green Party of Mexico (*PVEM*) had forged an alliance similar to the one in Nayarit. In Coahuila, however, the *PRI* candidate, Enrique Martínez y Martínez, a popular former mayor of Saltillo, was elected with 58% of the vote.

Thus, voters sent mixed signals in the governorship races of 1998–99. The major psychological winner was the *PRD*, which went into the races with no state governorships and emerged with three, Zacatecas, Tlaxcala and Baja California Sur. It also ran a strong second to the *PRI* in Oaxaca, Guerrero and Quintana Roo, and may have won in Guerrero except for possible *PRI* electoral trickery. The *PAN*, meanwhile, didn't quite break even, losing a large, powerful state (Chihuahua) while picking up a smaller, but still influential one (Aguascalientes); it still held six states. In Puebla, Sinaloa, Hidalgo and Mexico, it ran a strong second, garnering a third of the vote in all four, and received

237

Mexico

about a fourth of the vote in Durango and Tamaulipas, but second place just doesn't translate into power. An opposition alliance won the governorship of Nayarit but lost in Coahuila. The *PRI* could console itself that it won 13 of the 17 governorships, including the recapturing of Chihuahua, and that it still controlled 21 of the 31, but there was no escaping the mathematics that it suffered a net loss of four states and saw its electoral strength eroded in several more. Of the three parties, it clearly was the major loser.

The Elections of 2000

One of the potentially most important events in 20th century Mexico occurred in October 1998 when President Zedillo stated uniquivocably in a press interview that he was disavowing the *dedazo*, or tap, by which for 65 years the incumbent president had personally designated the next *PRI* candidate.

Seven candidates expressed interest in the *PRI* nomination. The earliest to enter the race, months even before Zedillo had disavowed the *dedazo*, was Manuel Bartlett, former governor of Puebla and interior secretary under de la Madrid. Bartlett was closely identified with the party's "dinosaur" faction, and his critics constantly badgered him by recalling that he was interior secretary during the infamous 1988 presidential election that Salinas allegedly stole at the expense of Cárdenas. Also declared was Humberto Roque Villanueva, Palacios' sacked predecessor as *PRI* chief. A late entry was Interior secretary Francisco Labastida, a former governor of Sinaloa, considered a reformist and unquestionably Zedillo's preferred choice. Tabasco Governor Roberto Madrazo, a dinosaur, also formally announced, and new Veracruz Governor Miguel Alemán, son and namesake of the former president, coyly expressed an interest without formally declaring his candidacy. Rounding out the field of likely precandidates were Foreign Secretary Rosario Green, who would have been the party's first female candidate and Mexico's first woman president; Social Development Secretary Esteban Moctezuma, and Génaro Borrego, director of the Social Security Institute.

Meanwhile, the *PRD*'s presumed candidate, Mexico City Mayor Cárdenas, who had been the frontrunner for president in most opinion polls throughout 1998, began to suffer a decline in public esteem for his perceived lack of progress. His prestige suffered a blow in April 1999 when the eminent political scientist Jorge Castañeda published a new book alleging that Cárdenas had met secretly with Carlos Salinas shortly after the highly suspect 1988 election and agreed not to challenge

A newly paved stretch of Highway 59 vaults through La Muralla, a notch-shaped pass through the rugged volcanic mountains north of Saltillo, Coahuila.   *Photo by the author*

Salinas' stolen victory. A prominent *PRD* leader, Porfirio Muñoz Ledo, harshly attacked Cárdenas and voiced his intention to challenge him for the presidential nomination.

In an historic eight-hour meeting on May 17, 1999, 328 members of the *PRI*'s 335-member National Political Council (*CNP*) approved the primary election process over a party convention by a vote of 307–21 and set November 7 as the date for the primary. The nominee would not be elected directly; the nomination would go to the candidate who polled a plurality of the vote in the largest number of the country's 300 districts for the Chamber of Deputies. This was seen as an effort to ensure that the candidates do not neglect the rural areas. Interestingly, the primary was opened to all voters regardless of party affiliation, apparently because the *PRI* does not have party membership cards. The *CNP* also set strict rules for campaigning, including a requirement that public officials had to resign their posts, an obvious dilemma for newly installed Governor Alemán.

The new rules winnowed the number of contenders to four: Labastida, Madrazo, Bartlett and Roque Villanueva. Labastida resigned his cabinet post, Madrazo went "on leave" as governor of Tabasco, and the *PRI*'s first-ever presidential primary was underway. It was a classic contest between the factions of traditionalists and

reformers, with Labastida emerging as the champion of the latter. Nonetheless, despite President Zedillo's public avowals of neutrality, Labastida's three opponents began grumbling that the *PRI* machinery and patronage power were being subtly used on Labastida's behalf. There was probably an element of truth to the charges. On election day, Zedillo claimed he had voted for all four candidates, thus nullifying his ballot, to demonstrate his neutrality.

True or not, Labastida scored a landslide victory in the historic November 7 showdown, which attracted worldwide media attention. Labastida received an outright majority of 5.3 million votes, or 55% of the 9.7 million votes cast, and in the vote that really mattered, carried 274 of the 300 districts for the Chamber of Deputies. Madrazo finished second with 2.7 million votes, or 27.8%, and 21 districts. He glumly congratulated Labastida and pledged to remain faithful to him during the coming campaign. Bartlett was third with 580,000 votes, or 6%, and five districts. He was not as gracious a loser as Madrazo. Roque Villanueva brought up the rear with 420,000 votes, or 4.3%; he carried no districts. The *dedazo*, it appeared, was not quite dead after all.

The campaign then began in earnest for the July 2, 2000 election. Mexico had never seen the likes of this race. Prior to the *PRI* primary, Fox had replaced Cárdenas as the frontrunner in all the major polls. But once Labastida's landslide primary victory was a fact, he quickly eclipsed Fox as the frontrunner, by varying margins. All attempts to forge an alliance between Fox, who had taken leave as governor of Guanajuato, and Cárdenas, who had resigned as mayor of Mexico City, ended in failure. Neither man, each known for an oversized ego, was willing to yield to the other.

In the first half of 2000, Fox chiseled away at Labastida's lead, and the race became essentially a contest between them. In December, the Green Party (*PVEM*) candidate withdrew from the race to endorse Fox, and the two parties forged a coalition called the Alliance for Change. Later in the campaign, the candidate of the small but venerable Authentic Party of the Mexican Revolution (*PARM*) also withdrew and endorsed Fox. The *PRD*, meanwhile, formed its own coalition with the *PT* and two smaller left-wing parties, called the Alliance for Mexico.

Fox effectively closed the gap with the April 25 debate, in which the flamboyant Fox was widely seen as the victor over Labastida and Cárdenas. His unorthodox campaign style, heretofore unknown to Mexicans, also seemed to strike a responsive chord, although his tendency to make outrageous statements against Labastida alienated some. For example, the six-foot, six-inch Fox, who enhances his image by wearing cowboy boots, took to deriding the five-foot-10 Labastida as "shorty;" once, he referred to him as *"La Vestida,"* the slang for cross-dresser, an unmistakable attack on his masculinity. He also committed what once would have been considered heresy by advocating scrapping the 1917 Constitution and drafting one more in line with the times.

The candidates failed to agree on the groundrules for a second debate among the top three candidates, but in May they squared off on *Televisa* from separate locations. Fox and Labastida dominated the so-called "mini-debate" by accusing each other of lying and by attacking the other's record. In June, Labastida was embarrassed by the revelation that his brother had benefited from the *Fobaproa* bank bailout.

Never had a *PRI* candidate faced such a determined and aggressive challenger. The *PRI* counterattacked with some unorthodox tactics of its own, such as a male strip show in a Mexico City suburb designed to attract female voters. It responded to the *"La Vestida"* remark by reminding voters that Fox's four children are adopted, in effect, questioning *his* masculinity. The usual charges surfaced that the *PRI* was attempting to bribe voters with groceries and building materials

and was leaning on government workers to vote for Labastida—or else. The Federal Electoral Institute (*IFE*) declined to take the charges seriously, however, stating that ballots are secret now and that even if charges of bribery were true the *PRI* would have no way of verifying how the "bribees" voted. Moreover, the opposition parties complained that Labastida was receiving a disproportionate amount of coverage in the media, especially television.

In June, Labastida (and Cárdenas) accused Fox of illegally accepting foreign campaign contributions, which Fox adamantly denied. (The *IFE* later confirmed they were true and levied a heavy fine on the PAN). Labastida even suggested that the devoutly Catholic Fox would impose his religious beliefs on the country.

By June 22, the last day legally to publish opinion polls, all the leading surveys

showed Labastida and Fox in a statistical tie. Cárdenas languished far behind.

Five days before the showdown vote, this author drove to Mexico to cover the final days of the campaign for several newspapers. Convinced that Fox was where the story was, I arrived in León, in Fox's home state of Guanajuato, for his closing rally in a huge soccer stadium on Wednesday, June 28. Enthusiastic *Panistas* began lining up in the hot sun nearly three hours before the rally began at 7 p.m. By starting time, the stands of the 60,000-seat stadium were overflowing, the crowds filled the playing field, and hundreds more waited outside, unable to enter. I spoke to several people, and was invariably given two reasons why they were supporting Fox: His positive record as governor, especially in education and exports, and the corruption of the *PRI*. But

The pre-election issue of the weekly newsmagazine *Proceso* carries irreverent caricatures of the three major candidates. At left is Vicente Fox, a Coca-Cola in one hand and an obscene gesture in place of his trademark "*Ya*" sign in the other; around his neck is a cross, symbolizing his devout Catholicism. In the middle is Francisco Labastida, carrying an enormous forefinger representing "*el dedazo*," meaning he was the favored candidate of President Ernesto Zedillo. On his lapel button is the unpopular former president, Carlos Salinas de Gortari. At right is Cuauhtémoc Cárdenas, portrayed as a moralistic reformer.

Mexico

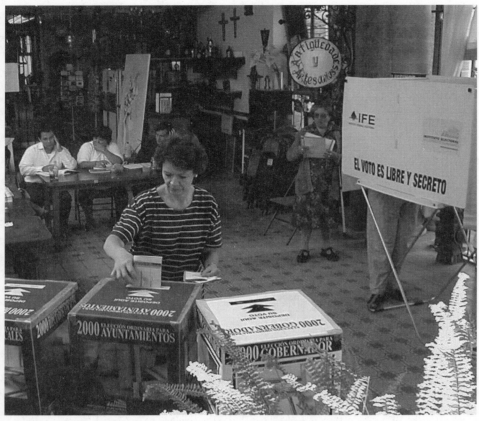

A woman casts her ballot in the city of Guanajuato on July 2, 2000. The sign on the voting booth at rights says, "The vote is free and secret." In the past, that wasn't always the case. That night, after the results began coming in, jubilant young supporters of *PAN* candidate Vicente Fox congregate in Avenida Venustiana Carranza in Saltillo to celebrate his victory—and the *PRI*'s first presidential defeat in 71 years.

Photos by the author

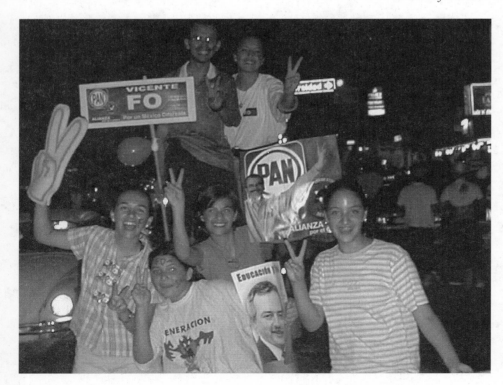

when I asked whether they thought he would win, many of them hesitated, then expressed their belief that the *PRI* would pull off a sneaky trick at the last minute to deprive Fox of victory, as it had Cárdenas in 1988.

In his speech, the candidate was surprisingly low-keyed, with none of the personal attacks on Labastida that had marked the campaign. Instead, he reiterated his goals for 7% annual economic growth that would generate 1.3 million new jobs a year, for an attack on corruption and narcotrafficking, for improvements in education, and for an elevation of the status of women. "If you are tired of the *PRI*, if you are sick of the corruption, if you want a government that is pluralist and inclusive, the only choice is to vote for the Alliance for Change!" he shouted. "Give me 10 seconds of your time, and I will give you six years working to give you a Mexico of grand opportunities. Vote for your children! Vote for Mexico! Don't hold back! With your vote you write your name in the book of history!" The crowd cheered as though Mexico had won the World Cup.

Labastida had closed his campaign that same day in his home state of Sinaloa, to a much smaller crowd, while Cárdenas chose to close his in the poor and troubled state of Chiapas. After more than a year of fevered campaigning, an eerie stillness settled over Mexico as her 60 million voters prepared to render their verdict.

If the mid-term elections of 1997 were a political earthquake, the elections of 2000 were a tidal wave. I observed some of the voting Sunday morning in the state capital, also called Guanajuato, and was struck by a new feature I had not seen in the elections in 1997 and 1998: there were plastic curtains on the voting booths to ensure secrecy! On the booths were the words, "The vote is free and secret." Would it make a difference?

From Guanajuato I drove north to Saltillo, Coahuila, arriving precisely as the polls closed at 8 p.m. On my car radio I heard the news that was once unimaginable: Exit polls showed Fox with 44%, Labastida with 38%, Cárdenas with 16%. Those figures fluctuated only slightly over the next two hours, as Fox's stunning and decisive victory became assured. The upset was of David-and-Goliath or hare-and-tortoise proportions.

Coahuila was a microcosm of the *PAN* victory. Not only did Fox carry the state with 55% of the vote, the *PAN* won two of the three directly elected Senate seats and four of the seven seats in the Chamber of Deputies; in the outgoing Congress, the *PRI* had held two Senate seats and six of the seven deputies. Along Saltillo's Boulevard Venustiano Carranza, thousands of jubilant *Panistas* honked horns, waved banners and posters and flashed the two-fingered symbol for Fox's campaign slogan, *"Ya!"* ("Right now!") There was a far larger explosion of jubilation around the Angel of Independence monument along the Paseo de la Reforma in Mexico City, which I watched on television. It was a euphoria I had witnessed only once before—the night in 1989 that Patricio Aylwin was elected president of Chile to end the 16-year dictatorship of Augusto Pinochet. For Mexico's opposition, the wait had been 71 years.

At midnight, a dour President Zedillo addressed his countrymen on television and acknowledged that "it appears unquestionable that the next president will be Licenciado Vicente Fox Quesada." He graciously congratulated Fox on his victory and pledged his cooperation for a smooth transition, but not as graciously spent considerably more time praising the losing Labastida, reminding his viewers what a positive force the *PRI* had been and pledging that the party would remain a vital force in the life of the nation. Soon thereafter, Fox appeared, and graciously praised Zedillo and Labastida. Ironically, July 2 also had been the victor's 58th birthday.

By morning, Mexico awoke not to a hangover but what seemed like another impossible dream. Not only had Fox carried 21 of the 31 states, but it appeared that the *PAN* would have near-parity with the *PRI* in the next Congress. Cárdenas carried only two states—Baja California Sur and his home state of Michoacán. To make the *PAN*'s night complete, it retained the governorship of Guanajuato, which Fox had relinquished, and picked up the governorship of the southern state of Morelos (the state of Emiliano Zapata) with an astounding 58% of the vote. It was the first time the *PAN* had won a governorship outside of its power base in the north. Meanwhile, the *PRD* candidate for mayor of Mexico City, Andrés Manuel López Obrador, narrowly won with 38% of the vote. What was surprising was that the *PAN* candidate finished a close second with 35%, while the *PRI* candidate was a distant third.

Overnight, it seemed, Mexico had been turned upside down, and a shell-shocked *PRI* began taking stock of the situation and wondering, as were all Mexicans, what the future would bring. One of my final images before leaving Mexico was a car with a sign painted on its back window that largely summed up the feelings of a decisive plurality of Mexicans: "GANO PAN, GANO MEXICO" ("PAN WON, MEXICO WON").

Final official tabulations by the non-partisan *IFE* were:

The front page of the Saltillo, Coahuila, daily newspaper *Vanguardia* proclaiming the stunning and decisive victory of Vicente Fox in the July 2, 2000, presidential election.

Fox	15,988,740	42.52%
Labastida	13,576,385	36.0%
Cárdenas	6,259,048	16.64%

Fewer than 1 million votes were scattered among three minor candidates, and 789,838 ballots were nullified. A total of 37,603,924 Mexicans had voted, a respectable turnout of 63.97%. The breakdown in the lower house after the allocation of the 200 seats by proportional representation was: The *PAN*, 208, and its

Mexico

partner, the *PVEM*, 15, for a total of 223 for the Alliance for Change, 27 seats short of a majority; the *PRI*, 209; the *PRD*, 52; the *PT*, 8; the Convergence for Democracy, 3; the Nationalist Society, 3; and the Social Alliance, 2. The breakdown of the 128 Senate seats was 58 for the *PRI*, 53 for the *PAN* and the *PVEM* and 17 for the *PRD*.

The new president was born on a ranch in Guanajuato on July 2, 1942, one of nine children of a Spanish mother and a father of U.S. descent. He received a Jesuit higher education at the Ibero-American Institute in Mexico City, then went into the family's business. He ran a boot manufacturing company and a frozen fruit and vegetable firm as well as becoming chief of Coca-Cola's Latin American division. He was elected to the Chamber of Deputies in 1988, and it is illustrative of his persuasiveness that as a member of the opposition he was instrumental in passing a constitutional amendment to allow citizens with one foreign-born parent to be elected president; previously, both parents had to be born in Mexico. (I heard a rumor from a *PRI* candidate for the Chamber of Deputies in Guanajuato that Fox had covered up the fact that his father really was born in the United States, which would have disqualified Fox for the presidency, but apparently there is no evidence to support that.) Fox was elected governor in 1995 and won high marks for his honesty, his work ethic and his administration. Despite his devout Catholicism, Fox is Mexico's first divorced president.

The Fox Presidency

It is not an exaggeration to state that a new era of Mexican history began when Vicente Fox was inaugurated as president on December 1, 2000. Not only was he the first president in 71 years who was not a member of the *PRI*, he also was the first unapologetically devout Catholic since Avila Camacho. The inaugural ceremony was attended by such ideologically diverse personalities as Cuban President Fidel Castro, Colombian Nobel Laureate Gabriel García Márquez, U.S. Secretary of State Madeleine Albright and Microsoft chairman Bill Gates.

After receiving the presidential sash from Zedillo before the Congress, still wearing cowboy boots, he kept a campaign promise by ordering an army withdrawal from Chiapas as his first official act. (see Armed Rebellions). He then did something no *PRI* president could have done: He went to the Basilica of Our Lady of Guadalupe to offer thanks to Mexico's patron saint, then delivered speeches before throngs of supporters in a soccer stadium and in the Zócalo. He proposed a breathtaking list of reforms: amending the constitution to permit referenda; a crackdown on corruption; greater environmental protection; streamlining, but not privatizing, *Pemex*; strengthening U.S.-style judicial review over laws passed by Congress; a code of ethics for cabinet secretaries; increased availability to university scholarships; increased incentives for savings and investments; greater government support for small businesses; universal health care; greater autonomy for the states; and the Indian rights bill demanded by the *Zapatistas*.

Fox's cabinet appointments also were symbolic of the new order and diversity of representation. As foreign secretary he appointed Jorge Castañeda, the noted political scientist; as attorney general, General Rafael Macedo, the army's prosecutor, who has a reputation for incorruptibility and has cashiered officers for

President Vicente Fox Quesada

corruption and collusion with drug traffickers; as interior secretary, the *PAN*'s leader in Congress, Santiago Creel. Fox stripped the interior and justice ministries of their domestic surveillance functions, concentrating them instead in a newly created law enforcement portfolio headed by the police chief in the *PRD* administration in Mexico City, Alejandro Gertz. As ambassador to the United States, Fox appointed veteran diplomat Juan José Bremer, a former ambassador to Spain, who was highly critical of the U.S. drug certification policy.

Mexican-U.S. relations began experiencing a dramatic improvement under Fox and the new U.S. president, George W. Bush, who is fluent in Spanish and who as governor of Texas became closely acquainted with Mexican affairs. It was his-
toric that for the first time ever, a U.S. president opted to make his first foreign visit to Mexico. Fox hosted his counterpart on his Guanajuato ranch for a one-day summit on February 16, 2001, less than a month after Bush assumed office. The two businesslike conservatives with ranching backgrounds got along well and covered the usual agenda: trade, drugs, immigration and energy. Even before he became president, Fox made regular appearances on U.S. interview programs, and he raised eyebrows by proposing that the U.S.-Mexican border be as open as the U.S.-Canadian frontier.

He made a symbolic gesture in April by opening the presidential palace of Los Pinos for the first time to the public. That gesture was to boomerang on him, however, when the media reported that the towels in the presidential bathrooms cost $400 and that the remote-controlled curtains cost $17,000. The media immediately labeled the first Fox mini-scandal "Towelgate."

In March, however, Mexicans learned that their new president was serious about cracking down on corruption. He fired 12 high-ranking government officials after they were caught taking bribes in a sting operation. Fox warned that there would be more such stings.

Fox obtained congressional support for his Indian rights bill, but he found less enthusiasm when he introduced an ambitious tax reform plan in April. Fox argued that the plan would encourage investments, create jobs and help redistribute wealth. Especially unpopular with the *PRI* and *PRD* legislators—and with the public—was his proposal to eliminate the value-added, or sales, tax exemptions on groceries and medicine. Fox countered that the plan would give $11 monthly rebates to the 27 million Mexicans below the poverty line and would provide an income tax exemption for those making less than 50,000 pesos (about $5,300) annually. The Green Party, which had been part of Fox's election coalition, broke with him over the tax reform scheme. In December 2001, Congress finally passed a watered-down version that focused on luxury taxes.

Fox stunned the nation, and allayed a possible personal scandal, by marrying his press spokeswoman, Martha Sahagún, on July 2, 2001, his 59th birthday and the first anniversary of his election victory. The nature of their relationship had been the subject of gossip for years, and she was known to be living in Los Pinos. It was reportedly she who had ordered the controversial towels and curtains. The press has not been kind to the first lady, criticizing her actions and her taste, much to the displeasure of her husband. However, she has remained popular with the public for her charitable works, and she has been hinted as a PAN presidential possibility in 2006.

In politics, the *PRI* continued to be plagued with problems since its 2000 defeat. As expected, an internecine battle for control of the party ensued between the reformers and the dinosaurs, and the party's separation from the reins of power has stripped it of its most powerful tool—patronage. Moreover, it has continued to lose governorships.

Just seven weeks after its presidential defeat, the *PRI* candidate for the governorship of troubled Chiapas was soundly defeated on August 20 by Pablo Salazar of the *PRD*, running as the candidate of a coalition of opposition parties. Salazar received 54% of the vote, and the *PRI* graciously conceded defeat.

The head of the *PRI*'s dinosaur faction, Tabasco Governor Roberto Madrazo, in true dinosaur fashion hand-picked the *PRI* candidate to succeed him as governor, Manuel Andrade. In the election on October 15, 2000, Andrade eventually was declared the winner, 44% to 43%, over the *PRD*'s Raúl Ojeda. The *PRD* appealed the decision to the *IFE*, citing the usual evidence of *PRI* vote-buying. On December 29, just three days before Andrade's inauguration, the *IFE* made the unprecedented decision to nullify the election results. The decision threw Tabasco into turmoil; at one point, the rival *PRI* factions in the state legislature chose two separate interim governors. Eventually, the new election was set for August 5, 2001. Andrade won narrowly, 50.5% to 46%, apparently fairly.

Another *PRI* dinosaur, Yucatán Governor Victor Cervera Pacheco, attempted to defy a federal court order that nullified his stacked state electoral commission, setting off a confrontation between the national and state executives. The *PAN* had challenged the state electoral commission as too partisan; the federal court agreed, and appointed its own commissioners. Heretofore, tradition had been to grant state governors virtual *carte blanche* over their fiefs. The two parties eventually reached a compromise. In the election on May 27, 2001, the *PRI* suffered yet another humiliating setback when the *PAN*'s Patricio Patrón defeated the *PRI*'s Orlando Paredes 51% to 46%. It brought to eight the number of states controlled by the *PAN*.

On July 8, the *PAN* easily retained control of the governorship of Baja California Norte for a third straight term under the candidacy of Eugenio Elorduy, a former mayor of Mexicali, who received 50% of the vote to 36% for the *PRI* candidate.

On November 11, the *PRI* suffered another defeat, for the governorship of Michoacán. There, Lázaro Cárdenas of the *PRD*, son of Cuauhtémoc and grandson and namesake of the illustrious former president, defeated *PRI* candidate Alfredo Anaya 41.8% to 36.7%. The victory brought to five the number of states, plus the Federal District, that the *PRD* controls. President Fox himself attended Cardenas' inauguration on February 15, 2002.

Fox's relationship with the Congress and the opposition parties continued its roller-coaster course. On October 7, 2001, the eight ideologically disparate parties signed a national accord whereby they agreed to work together to combat organized crime, terrorism and poverty and to implement overhauls of the tax system and the energy sector. But Congress then gutted Fox's tax overhaul; even his own *PAN* deserted him rather than risk voter retribution by taxing groceries and drugs.

The accord said nothing, however, about cooperating on uncovering corruption and human rights abuses. Fox had promised a fact-finding commission to investigate disappearances during the 1960s and 1970s, but took no action until the high-profile murder on October 19, 2001, of Digna Ortíz, a prominent human rights lawyer. He then commissioned the human rights ombudsman to prepare a report on past abuses, which could only prove an embarrassment to the *PRI*. The 3,000-page report, released on November 27, concluded that 532 people who disappeared during that period had been illegally detained by security forces, including the military, and that 275 were murdered and their bodies disposed of. Fox appointed an independent truth commission to investigate the abuses, ostensibly with the aim of bringing those responsible to justice. In June 2002, he ordered the declassification and release of 80 million intelligence files from the *PRI* period.

Oddly, however, Fox opposed resuming an inquiry into the 1968 Tlatelolco Massacre, saying it was time to focus on the future, not the past. The Supreme Court disagreed in January 2002 and upheld a lower court decision that overturned a decision by the justice department that the statute of limitations precluded an investigation. That July, former President Luis Echeverría (1970–76), then 80, was summoned before the commission and spent six hours being interrogated about Tlatelolco, which occurred while he was interior secretary, and about atrocities committed during his term as president, especially the so-called "Corpus Christi Day Massacre" on June 10, 1971, in which an undetermined number of leftists was slain. He refused to answer, saying he would give his responses in writing. The prosecutor then gave Echeverría 186 written questions to respond to; Echeverría refused to comply. Never before had a president or former

president been held accountable for his actions. A year later, on October 2, 2003, the 35th anniversary of the Tlateloleo massacre, declassified documents confirmed that the government had placed 360 snipers around the plaza and had opened fire on the demonstrators. A lower court dismissed the charges against Echeverría in the Corpus Christi Massacre in July 2004, ruling that the statute of limitations had expired, but federal prosecutors appealed. In June 2005, the Supreme Court ruled 3-2 that Echeverría could be tried, writing that the statute of limitations had to be dated to 1976, when he left office.

Still smarting from the human rights report, the *PRI* was outraged in January 2002 when Fox's comptroller general and attorney general announced that an investigation produced evidence that *Pemex* sent $120 million to the oil workers' union, which in turn channeled the funds to Labastida's 2000 presidential campaign. The interim *PRI* president, Dulce María Sauri, denounced the charges as politically motivated.

With the rightward, pro-U.S. shift in Mexican foreign policy under Fox, it was inevitable that the *PRI* and the parties of the far left sooner or later would find common cause against him. On September 8, 2001, just three days before the terrorist attacks on New York and Washington, Fox addressed a joint session of the U.S. Congress and stressed the need for mutual trust. He praised Bush as a friend and ally. After the terrorist attacks, Fox quickly pledged his cooperation with the United States in beefing up border security. Although the Mexican public was largely in agreement with Fox on the terrorism issue, the opposition parties favored a more neutral position. It was not to be; Fox delivered an address to the nation in which he denounced terrorism as a "war against humanity," and he made another visit to Washington in October. As a sop to the left, however, he made it his policy that no Mexican troops would be used in any U.N. action.

As another sop to the left, Fox visited Cuba in February 2002, which seemingly continued Mexico's tradition of friendship with the Castro regime. Foreign Minister Castañeda clearly stated in Havana that Mexico, as before, would not support a perennial resolution brought before the U.N. Human Rights Commission in Geneva urging Cuba to allow greater freedom of expression. But Fox outraged Castro—and the Mexican left—by breaking with tradition and meeting with Cuban dissidents. Relations were strained further when more than 20 dissidents invaded the Mexican Embassy in Havana (see Cuba).

Relations with Cuba came close to the breaking point that April. First, Fox hosted a U.N. conference on poverty in

Mexico

Mexico City's main thoroughfare, *Paseo de la Reforma*

Monterrey, which Castro decided to attend at the last minute. Castro left in a huff on the first day of the conference after making his speech, accusing Fox of pressuring him into leaving before Bush arrived; Fox flatly denied he had pressured Castro. A few days later, in Geneva, Mexico not only voted for the resolution critical of Cuba's human rights record, it co-sponsored it! An outraged Castro then broke with diplomatic courtesy and released a secretly recorded tape of his conversation with Fox concerning the Monterrey poverty summit that corroborated Castro's contention that Fox had pressured him into leaving; basically, Castro was calling Fox a liar.

The Mexican left rallied to Castro's side, and in an unprecedented action, the Mexican Senate denied Fox permission for a trip he had scheduled to the United States and Canada. Fox was humiliated, and argued that the Senate's action would damage Mexico's international prestige. But the *PRI* had its revenge for the corruption probe, petty as it was. (Fox later was given "permission" to attend the summit of Latin American and European Union leaders in Madrid in May.) In September 2002, Fox replaced the ambassador to Cuba, apparently because he was considered too friendly to the dictatorial regime for Fox's taste. His removal represented a major shift in foreign policy, one that the outgoing ambassador publicly criticized.

In politics, the power struggle between the dinosaurs and the reformers within the *PRI* erupted with a fury during the election for the new party president in February 2002. Tabasco's Roberto Madrazo, as

expected, was the candidate of the dinosaurs (who, not surprisingly, prefer the term *"tradicionalistas,"*) while Beatríz Paredes, speaker of the Chamber of Deputies, was the choice of the reform wing. During and after the bitter campaign, the two rivals came close to disemboweling their party. In the balloting on February 24, about 3 million *Pristas* voted, and the count was so close the final results weren't announced until March 3. Madrazo was declared the winner by a slim 52,000-vote margin, or 1.7 percentage points. The intra-party rivalry continued to fester as the 2003 midterm elections approached.

The *PRD* also elected a new leader in a campaign that also was rambunctious but mercifully less acrimonious. The contenders were former interim Mexico City Mayor Rosario Robles and Senator Jesús Ortega. The election on March 17, 2002, was marred from the start by poor organization and high abstention, and stained by such irregularities as stolen or stuffed ballot boxes and burned ballots. Fewer than 700,000 of the party's 4.2 million registered members participated. As with the *PRI* election, it took nearly a week to certify the results. In the end, Robles was declared the winner with 60.8% of the vote.

An event that had been intended to be spiritual turned out to be political. On July 31, 2002, Pope John Paul II arrived in Mexico for his fifth visit to formally canonize

Burros graze along a desert highway between Saltillo and Zacatecas.

Photo by the author.

244

the Indian peasant Juan Diego, to whom the Virgin of Guadalupe reportedly appeared in 1521 (see The Colonial Period). In the ceremony at the Shrine of Guadalupe on August 2, Fox broke with Mexico's long-standing anticlerical tradition and knelt and kissed the pope's ring. Perhaps more significantly, so did Mexico state Governor Arturo Montiel—a *Prista*. Fox received the inevitable criticism from anticlerical hardliners, but his action signaled an end to the stigma of openly practicing Catholicism. Fox made history again when John Paul II died in April 2005, becoming the first Mexican president to attend a papal funeral.

In July 2002, President Bush nominated a friend, Tony Garza, a member of the Texas Railroad Commission whose grandparents were born in Mexico, to be the new ambassador to Mexico. But two events soon cooled the warm relations that had developed between Mexico and the United States—and between Fox and Bush.

The first was the execution in Texas of a Mexican national, Javier Suárez Medina for the murder of a policeman. Mexico does not have capital punishment and has refused to extradite suspects to the United States who may be subject to the death penalty. The Mexican government had appealed to the U.S. Supreme Court on Suárez's behalf, arguing that he had not been given the right to consult a Mexican consul after his arrest as provided by international law. The Supreme Court rejected the appeal, and Fox personally appealed to Bush and to Texas Governor Rick Perry to grant a reprieve, but Suárez was executed on August 14, 2002. His death became a *cause celèbre* in Mexico, and Fox canceled a four-day visit he was to have made to Texas later that month, including a visit to Bush's ranch. The cancellation reportedly stunned Bush and no doubt created consternation at the State Department. When Perry visited Mexico City to lobby for San Antonio to be the site of the 2007 Pan American Games, Fox snubbed him. Fox's position won him the rare support of the majority opposition in Congress. Within a few weeks of the execution, Fox publicly renewed his call for a new immigration agreement with the United States saying, "For better or for worse, we are partners."

In January 2003, however, Mexico appealed to the World Court in The Hague to block the executions of 51 other Mexican nationals condemned to death in the United States. In February, the court in a 15–0 vote ordered the United States to temporarily stay three of the scheduled executions. In March 2004, the World Court formally ordered the United States to review the death sentences of the 51

Mexicans, who had been denied access to diplomatic counsel. In the past, states had often ignored the jurisdiction of the World Court, but in May the governor of Oklahoma commuted the death sentence of a Mexican about to be executed to life imprisonment. The issue lingered for two years, straining relations, until President Bush agreed in February 2005 to have the Justice Department review the 51 cases.

The second event that strained relations was the U.S. war against Iraq. Mexico currently holds one of Latin America's two rotating seats on the U.N. Security Council. Fox was caught between the need to maintain amicable relations with the United States in order to secure his open immigration agreement on the one hand and Mexican public opinion, which was overwhelmingly against a U.S. invasion of Iraq, on the other. As early as August, Fox signaled that Mexico did not intend to get involved in a possible U.S.-Iraqi war. In November, Mexico sided with France, a permanent member of the Security Council, in denying U.N. authorization for the United States to attack Iraq if Saddam Hussein did not account for his weapons of mass destruction. In March 2003, Mexico was one of the members that refused to commit itself to a U.S. resolution calling for use of force. Fox, who underwent back surgery as the critical vote approached, stated that he favored the disarmament of Iraq but preferred to exhaust diplomatic means to accomplish it. The United States was forced to withdraw the resolution and invade Iraq without a U.N. blessing. Fox said he regretted the U.S. position.

Citing his frustration over relations with the United States, Foreign Minister Castañeda resigned in January 2003 and was replaced by Economy Minister Luis Ernesto Derbéz, who has foreign affairs credentials as a former official of the World Bank. Nuevo León's Governor Fernando Canales became economy minister.

Whether or not Mexico's position on Iraq may have been a factor, a new wrinkle appeared in Fox's hoped-for immigration agreement when the Republican-controlled International Relations Committee of the U.S. House of Representatives voted in May 2003 to condition any new immigration agreement to Mexico's opening *Pemex* to foreign investment. Fox, echoing multipartisan sentiment in the Mexican Congress, tartly rejected any such *quid pro quo*.

The gridlock between Fox's *PAN* and the opposition majority in Congress led the president to make a plaintive plea for multipartisan cooperation for the good of the nation in his annual congressional address on September 1, 2002. There were three positive developments: First, the parties for the first time agreed to rotate the speakership of the Chamber of Deputies among the three major parties during the current legislative session. The *PRI*'s Beatríz Paredes was reelected to preside from September to December; a *PRD* deputy was speaker from December until March 2003, when a *PAN* deputy took over. Second, both houses passed Mexico's first genuine civil service law, which creates a five-tiered system of government employees free from the political patronage that the *PRI* had used and abused for

A scuffle breaks out on election night along Calle Rosales in Hermosillo, Sonora, between supporters of rival gubernatorial candidates Eduardo Bours of the *PRI* and Ramón Corral of the *PAN*, as a news photographer records the melee. Bours was the eventual winner of the cliffhanger election.   *Photo by the author*

Mexico

An enterprising woman sells iced *horchata*, a sweet rice-based beverage, and *duros*, a fried chip made from flour, outside a polling station set up in a *Pemex* station in Hermosillo, Sonora, on July 6, 2003. Hundreds of people were still waiting in sweltering heat to use one voting booth when the polls closed, but the voting continued.

Photo by the author

so long. Third, in June 2003 Congress enacted a U.S.-style freedom-of-information act that gives citizens—and especially journalists—unprecedented access to government records.

Midterm Elections

All the parties knew that they were facing the high-stakes midterm elections on July 6, 2003. The opposition was gleeful when the *PAN* itself came under investigation for allegedly receiving $14,000 in illegal funds from the United States for Fox's 2000 presidential campaign. The Federal Electoral Institute *(IFE)* verified a number of irregularities, giving the *PAN* an ill-timed image problem. (In October, the *IFE* fined the *PAN* $32 million).

The *PRI*, meanwhile, had its own problems in the ongoing intra-party wrangling between the dinosaurs and the reformers. The dinosaurs' Madrazo pulled off a skillful, but politically unwise, power play in May when he packed the party's list of candidates for the 200 federal deputies chosen through proportional representation with his own supporters. It will strengthen his hand heading to the party's next presidential primary, but it outraged the reformists, who cried foul. The chief loser was Mexico state Governor Montiel, a rival for the 2006 nomination.

At stake in the elections were all 500 members of the Chamber of Deputies, 300 of them directly elected from districts and 200 by proportional representation, and six governorships: Campeche, Colima, Nuevo León, Querétaro, San Luis Potosí and Sonora.

Fox was hoping to win an outright majority in both houses of Congress; even just increasing the *PAN*'s number of seats could be interpreted as approval of his presidency. The *PAN* was defending the governorships of Nuevo León and Queré-

taro, which it had won for the first time in the 1997 shakeup, against serious *PRI* challenges; polls showed José Natividad González, making a second bid as the *PRI* candidate in Nuevo León, with a 14-point lead over the *PAN*'s Mauricio Fernández Garza. Meanwhile, the *PAN* scented blood in Sonora, where it claimed it would have won in 1997 but for *PRI* fraud. Polls there showed the *PRI*'s Eduardo Bours ahead of the *PAN*'s Ramón Corral by less than the margin of error. The *PAN* also had hopes to win in Campeche in the southeast, where it had done well in 1997 and in San Luis Potosí.

This author chose to observe the midterm elections in Sonora, where I filed reports to two newspapers on a governor's race that proved to be even hotter than the polls had indicated.

The results of the nationwide voting were a cruel blow to Fox's quixotic dreams of a majority in the lower house. Not only did the *PAN* fail to win a majority and increase its number of seats, but it lost perhaps 58 of the 206 seats it had! The *PRI* proved it is still a force to be reckoned with, slightly increasing its representation. The major winner was the *PRD*, which doubled the size of its delegation.

At 11:30 p.m. local time on election night in Hermosillo, Sonora, where I was (1:30 a.m. in Mexico City), I watched a de-

Número 22,116 Año LXVI
66 páginas
$7.00 Hermosillo
$8.00 dominical
1.00 dólar en E.U.
Edición final

EL IMPARCIAL

Diario independiente de Sonora

Premios SIP
1992, 1993, 1994
1995, 1998 y 1999

Premios SND
1998, 1999, 2000,
2001 y 2002

Premio Nacional
de Periodismo
2002

Hermosillo, Sonora, México

FUNDADORES DE LA EMPRESA: JOSÉ S. HEALY (1895-1968) y JOSÉ A. HEALY (1928-1997)

www.elimparcial.com

Lunes 7 de julio del 2003

Presenta ligera ventaja el candidato del PRI

Al tú por tú Bours-Corral

Supera el priísta en 2.8 puntos porcentuales al panista Ramón Corral, revela PREP

Redacción (PH)

20
03

Hasta cerca de las 3:00 horas de este lunes el candidato de PRI a la gubernatura de Sonora, Eduardo Bours Castelo, iba a la cabeza en los resultados del PREP. Al cierre de esta edición los resultados preliminares eran los siguientes: Para el PRI el 47.0 por ciento, para el PAN el 44.2 y para el PRD el 7.1.

La diferencia entre los dos principales candidatos, Eduardo Bours y el panista Ramón Corral Ávila, era de 2.8 puntos porcentuales.

Las cifras preliminares del PREP significaban cerca del 28.92% de la lista nominal.

A su vez representaban alrededor del 63.18% de las casillas computadas.

Ayer por la tarde el candidato del PRI se declaró vencedor luego de conocerse los resultados de encuestas de salida de TV Azteca y de Televisa.

El CEN del PAN respondió declarando ganador a su candidato Corral Ávila.

Al final, ambos contendientes declararon que esperarán los resultados oficiales del Consejo Estatal Electoral.

En suspenso

De acuerdo al margen de error de la encuesta de salida aplicada por esta Casa Editorial (+-2.5%), el abanderado del PAN obtendría una votación que oscila entre el 44.5% y el 49.5%, en tanto que para el candidato del PRI/PVEM los porcentajes fluctuarían entre el 43.3% y el 48.3%.

FESTEJA EDUARDO... El abanderado tricolor festeja por fuera del PRI estatal los resultados de las encuestas de salida de Televisa y Televisión Azteca que lo ubicaron al frente hasta por 8 puntos.

Y TAMBIÉN RAMÓN El candidato del PAN anuncia en conferencia de prensa que él lleva la delantera y declara que esperará el conteo del Consejo Estatal Electoral para hacer oficial su triunfo.

An elderly *Panista* participates in premature street celebrations in Hermosillo, Sonora on election night, July 6, 2003.

Photo by Sherre Amire

jected Fox appear on television for a brief, terse statement acknowledging, "Once again, it is apparent that no single political force will have a majority in the Chamber of Deputies." I couldn't help but recall how an equally despondent Zedillo, three years earlier, had conceded that Fox had won the presidency. Such is the ebb and flow of democracy. In something of an understatement, Fox remarked, "The work now begins to build a consensus among us." He also focused on another significant outcome of the elections: the disturbingly low turnout of only 41%. "We hear the voices of those who did not express themselves at the polls," he said. "We all understand your silence."

In terms of raw votes, the *PRI* had received 34.4%, the *PAN* 30.5%, the *PRD* 17.1%. Four days after the election, the *IFE* released its final tally on the 300 directly elected seats: 163 for the *PRI*, 67 for the *PAN*, 56 for the *PRD*; two were still in doubt. After the complex formula was applied for the allocation of the 200 seats by proportional representation, the *PRI* increased the size of its total delegation from 211 deputies in the previous Congress to 224, 26 short of a majority. The *PAN* wound up with 155 seats, while the *PRD* jumped from 50 seats to 96. The Green Party *(PVEM)* had remained politically viable, taking 6.2% of the vote and winning an anticipated 14–16 seats through proportional representation, about the same as before. The *PT*

won only 2.4% of the vote and five to eight seats.

The *PAN* suffered another blow with the loss of Nuevo León, where González won in a landslide, 56.4%–33.9%. About the only cause the *PAN* had for cheer on election night was that it captured the governorship of San Luis Potosí for the first time, with Marcelo de los Santos besting the *PRI* candidate 44%–37%, and it retained the governorship of Querétaro with the candidacy of Francisco Garrido. The *PAN* almost captured Campeche, but the *PRI*'s Jorge Carlos Hurtado pulled off a narrow victory, 107,840 votes to 102,220 for the *PAN* candidate. The *PRI* also retained Colima, as expected.

Sonora, meanwhile, provided the country with some high political drama for a few days. On election night in Hermosillo, I witnessed a bizarre spectacle on the streets, as throngs of enthusiastic *Panistas* and *Priistas* both celebrated their perceived victory! The confusion was compounded by the four-page extra editions of the two morning dailies, *El Imparcial* and *Cambio*, which hit the streets about 10 p.m., four hours after the polls closed. *Cambio*'s front page trumpeted the exit polls of the two Mexican television networks, *Televisa* and *TV Azteca*, which showed Bours with leads of seven and eight points, respectively. *El Imparcial*, however, reported those exit polls as well as its own, which gave Corral a two-point edge.

In front of the library of the University of Sonora on broad Calle Rosales, the two groups of party enthusiasts took up positions on opposite sides of the street, waving banners and shouting taunts across the street. When a car bedecked with the banners of one of the candidates came down the "wrong" side of the street, it was sprayed with artificial snow and, occasionally and more maliciously, with paint (as was my shirt). The scene reminded me of downtown Dallas the night before a Texas-Oklahoma game. Some of the taunting was good-natured, but some scuffles inevitably broke out when one group would seize and trample a banner of the opposing candidate from a passing vehicle. Just as it seemed the confrontation would turn ugly, a pickup truck full of policemen arrived at the scene to maintain order, and there was no serious violence that night. I was then convinced that the much-criticized 48-hour dry law in effect in Mexico on election day and the day before is not such a bad idea.

Bours claimed victory that night, while Corral said both candidates should wait until the nonpartisan State Electoral Council *(CEE)* counted all the votes "one by one." On July 12, the *CEE* declared Bours the winner, 372,467 to 364,544.

The Ahumada Affair

By early 2004, it appeared from the polls that Mexico City Mayor Andrés Manuel

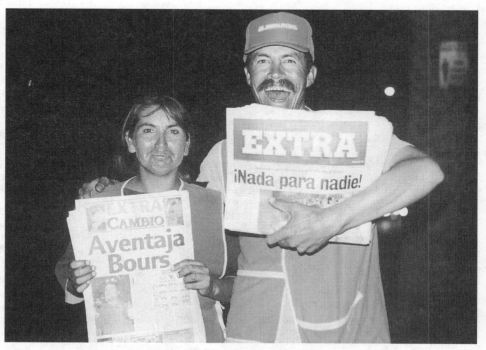

Vendors from the two Hermosillo dailies, *El Imparcial* and *Cambio*, hold up their respective papers' extra editions on election night. The headlines had conflicting results in the close governor's race between the *PRI*'s Eduardo Bours and the *PAN*'s Ramón Corral.

Photo by the author

Mexico

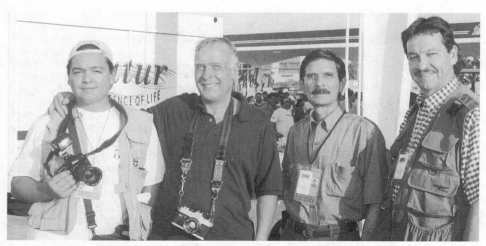

The author, second from left, with three photographers from the Hermosillo, Sonora, daily, *El Imparcial*, at a polling station on election day, July 6, 2003. *Photo by Sherre Amire*

López Obrador not only was the favorite for the *PRD* presidential nomination but that he was the frontrunner to win the 2006 election. He had compiled a favorable record as an honest and able administrator as mayor and was highly popular for implementing public works projects and a pension plan for the elderly. Suddenly, in March, he found himself the latest Mexican politician to have to confront a scandal.

Carlos Ahumada was a wealthy, politically connected, Argentine-born businessman who had lucrative paving contracts with the Mexico City government under López Obrador's predecessor, Rosario Robles. He videotaped himself offering a bribe to René Bejerano, the *PRD* floor leader in the Federal District's legislature.

Somehow, the videotape was leaked to the media, and on March 3 the country was treated to images of Bejerano stuffing money into his suit. Just two days earlier, similar videotapes had shown Mexico City's Finance Secretary Gustavo Ponce living it up gambling at a Las Vegas casino.

The mayor fired Ponce, who then went into hiding; he was arrested in Cuernavaca in October. López Obrador said Pnoce was later arrested in Cuernavaca in October that Ahumada was under investigation for receiving the paving contracts without bidding for them and for a $3 million fraud. Bejerano, meanwhile, lamely insisted that he had been collecting a "campaign donation" from Ahumada for a *PRD* legislative candidate, something that was itself illegal. Ahumada told the

media that the city government had extorted the money from him.

The Ahumada affair became an international incident when Ahumada fled to Cuba shortly after the videos were aired. While Ahumada was in Cuba, Mexico cast its second vote against Cuba on the U.N. Human Rights Commission in Geneva, again angering Cuba (see Cuba). At the request of Mexican officials, Ahumada was arrested in late April and dutifully deported to Mexico, but not before the Cuban government announced that Ahumada had "confessed" on videotape that the Fox administration had concocted the bribe in an attempt to damage López Obrador politically. Cuba also expelled an aide to Ahumada. A furious Fox not only denied the allegation and recalled the Mexican ambassador to Cuba, on May 2 he took the unusually harsh diplomatic step of ordering the Cuban ambassador to leave Mexico. He also declared the Cuban Embassy's political officer *persona non grata* for allegedly secretly engaging in political activities in Mexico. It seemed for a time that Mexico might break diplomatic relations with its old friend, but in late May the two foreign ministers met and decided to reestablish ambassador-level relations.

Jockeying for 2006

Despite the scandal, or perhaps because of it, López Obrador remained high in the polls. But his legal problems continued. He stood accused of contempt of court in 2001 for refusing to halt work on a road across expropriated private land that he

About 40,000 people turned out for the *"Fiesta del Triunfo,"* the closing rally for winning *PRI* gubernatorial candidate Jose Reyes Baeza, outside the Palacio de Gobierno in Chihuahua on June 30, 2004. National *PRI* President Roberto Madrazo appeared at the rally.

Photo by the author

Governor-elect Amalia Garcia of the *PRD* addresses cheering supporters on election night in Zacatecas July 4, 2004.   *Photo by the author*

insisted was needed for access to a public hospital. Then Fox's attorney general's office said López Obrador faced prosecution also for refusing to obey a court order to reinstate 39 city employees who were terminated when he became mayor in 2000 and to pay them back wages.

The mayor responded that the charges were politically motivated—not unthinkable under the Old Mexico. Faced with a possible congressional vote stripping him of his immunity, he called a mass demonstration on August 30, 2004, to declare his presidential candidacy, defying the courts, prosecutors, Congress and the president to stop him. It drew more than 150,000 supporters. As trivial as the charges were, they could have forced him from office and disqualify him from running for any public office if he were convicted.

The *PAN*, meanwhile, had its own problems. On May 31, 2004, Energy Secretary Calderón angrily resigned a day after Fox had publicly chastised him for attending a political rally in Guadalajara at which the governor of Jalisco endorsed Calderón for the *PAN* presidential nomination, even though Calderón had not yet declared his candidacy. Fox, whose own wife was believed to harbor presidential ambitions, testily declared that he expected his cabinet secretaries to occupy themselves with their duties. In his resignation letter, Calderón called Fox's remarks "unjust and excessive." Apparently recognizing that she was becoming a political liability to her husband and their party, Mrs. Fox

renounced her own presidential ambitions in July.

The first candidate to formally declare for 2006 was Jorge Casteñeda, the former foreign minister, but he is not connected with any of the parties and had only 1–2% in the polls.

As always, governor's races in the two years prior to presidential election were closely watched as gauges of the three parties' strength. On July 4, 2004, the states of Chihuahua, Durango and Zacatecas elected their governors; Aguascalientes and Oaxaca followed on August 1. Chihuahua was an especially crucial battleground, as the only state that the *PRI* had recaptured from the *PAN*. The *PRD* was defending Zacatecas for the first time, having won it from the *PRI* in 1998 (see Prelude to 2000). The *PAN*, meanwhile, was defending Aguascalientes for the first time, while the *PRI* was facing a strong challenge from a peculiar *PRD-PAN* coalition in Oaxaca.

In the balloting on July 4, which this author observed in Zacatecas, voters opted for the status quo in all three states. In Chihuahua, the *PRI* had entered into an alliance with the *PT* and the *PVEM*, while the *PAN* had formed the same right-left coalition with the *PRD* that it had in Oaxaca. The candidate of the *PRI*-led alliance, federal Deputy José Reyes Baeza, a former mayor of the capital city, crushed the *PAN*'s hopes of a comeback, winning 57% of the vote over Sen. Javier Corral. The voters I spoke with voiced the same sentiment, that *PRI* Gov. Patricio Martínez had done a

good job, while his *PAN* predecessor, Francisco Barrio, had been a do-nothing.

Durango, a long-time *PRI* stronghold, held little suspense. The *PRI* candidate, Ismael Hernández, received 56% to 29% for the *PAN* candidate and the rest went to the candidate of a *PRD-PT* coalition.

In Zacatecas, the voters returned the *PRD* to power, despite widespread grumbling I heard on the street that Gov. Monreal had focused too much on public works and not enough on social programs. The *PRD* candidate, Amalia García, a federal deputy, daughter of a popular former *PRI* governor of Zacatecas and former national *PRD* president (and one-time Communist Party member!), received 46% to 33% for the *PRI-PT-PVEM* candidate and 14% for the *PAN* candidate.

On August 1, the *PAN*'s Luis Armando, a former mayor of the capital, won easily over the *PRI*'s Carlos López Velarde in Aguascalientes. But the Oaxaca campaign erupted into scattered acts of violence in the week leading up to the election. In the balloting, the *PRI*'s Ulises Ruíz claimed victory, 47% to 45% for Gabino Cué of the *PRD-PAN* alliance. Cué immediately claimed vote fraud had cost him the election. Given the *PRI*'s track record in Oaxaca, that was not unthinkable. Ruíz belongs to the Dinosaur faction of *PRI* presidential aspirant Roberto Madrazo, and a *PRI* victory in Oaxaca was seen as crucial for Madrazo's chances of clinching the nomination. But the narrowness of Ruiz's win, and the cloud of suspicion hanging over it, effectively nullified any political value for Madrazo, who had campaigned for the *PRI* candidates in Oaxaca, Chihuahua and other states to rack up political IOUs.

The *PRI* could take some satisfaction over the victory of Jorge Hank Rhon, a controversial racetrack owner with alleged indirect ties to the Tijuana drug cartel, in the Tijuana mayor's race. The city, and the state of Baja California Norte, are *PAN* strongholds; in fact, the same day, the *PAN* retained control of the state legislature. Like Ruíz, Rhon is a Madrazo ally.

On September 5, the *PRI* marked another Pyrrhic victory in the Veracruz governor's race, where the *PRI*'s Fidel Herrera defeated the *PAN*'s Gerardo Burganza by less than one percentage point, with just 34.5% of the vote. A *PRD-PT* coalition garnered 28.3%. In 1998, the *PRI* had won by 20 points in what had been considered one of its bastions. If the *PAN* and the *PRD* had formed an alliance as they had in Oaxaca, the outcome likely would have been different. Any jubilation over Herrera's victory was further muted by the fact that the *PRI* lost its majority in the state legislature for the first time, while the *PAN* emerged as its largest party. The

Mexico

PAN contested the vote counts in Oaxaca and Veracruz, as well as in Tijuana, but the Federal Electoral Tribunal upheld all three *PRI* victories In November.

The *PRI* easily retained the governorships of its stronghold states of Tamaulipas and Puebla on November 14. It recaptured Tlaxcala that day from *PRD*, which ran a poor third. It was the first state the *PRI* had taken back from the *PRD*.

Mexico 2005. . .

The controversy over Mexico City Mayor López Obrador's supposed contempt of court and the effect it could have on his presidential ambitions dominated Mexicans' attention for months. What amounted to an impeachment effort in Congress led to an unholy alliance between the *PRI* and the *PAN*, both of which feared López Obrador would win. The opinion polls consistently have justified their fear. But to disqualify him for such a picayunish charge smacked of political opportunism at best and antidemocratic machinations, reminiscent of the old-style trickery of the *PRI*, at worst. Only this time, Fox and the *PAN* were parties to them. Even those within López Obrador's own *PRD* smelled blood; in January, Cuahtémoc Cardenas declared his intention to seek the presidency for a fourth time.

Meanwhile, three more gubernatorial elections were decided on February 5: Baja California Sur, held by the *PRD*, and Guerrero and Quintana Roo, held by the *PRI*. As expected, the *PRD* held onto Baja California Sur and the *PRI* to Quintana Roo. But in poverty-stricken Guerrero, the *PRI* lost for the first time. Like Oaxaca, there was some pre-election violence, but unlike Oaxaca, the vote was not even close. The *PRD* candidate, Zeferino Torreblanca, a popular former mayor of Acapulco and a successful businessmen with a centrist platform, received 55% to 42% for the *PRI*'s Hector Astudillo. His victory was seen as a major boost for López Obrador and a humiliation for Madrazo and his Dinosaurs, more than making up for the *PRD*'s loss of tiny Tlaxcala.

Later in February, the *PRI* retained the governorship of Hidalgo. When the *PRI* governor of Colima was killed in a plane crash, a special election was called for April 10. The *PAN*, which narrowly lost Colima in both 1997 and 2003, had high hopes of finally capturing it. But the *PRI*'s Silverio Cavazos defeated the *PAN* candidate 51.5% to 47.6%, about the same percentages as in 2003.

In February, López Obrador publicly called for "civil resistance" if he were arrested, in effect throwing down the gauntlet to the Congress with a thinly veiled threat of public unrest if what was considered the will of the people—his people—was thwarted. Polls backed up his threat, showing that upwards of 80% of Mexicans opposed his prosecution. He also declared he would campaign from a jail cell if necessary.

Unintimidated, the Chamber of Deputies voted 360-127, along party lines, on April 7 to strip López Obrador of his immunity from prosecution, paving the way for his removal from office pending trial. The *PRI* and the *PAN* joined forces to vote for *el desafuero*, the stripping of immunity. Pro-López Obrador demonstrators, 150,000 strong, filled the streets before the vote, while *"no al desafuero"* posters filled the capital. Others later protested outside Fox's ranch in Guanajuato, which led to minor scuffles with the presidential guards.

Legal authorities disagreed over whether the congressional vote meant that López Obrador could not perform his duties as mayor. For two weeks, the mayor waited at his home for an arrest warrant, but none was served. The two sides were involved in a literal Mexican standoff, which was not eased when Fox ruled out a presidential pardon for his political rival, saying that López Obrador was not above the law. However, Fox's interior secretary, Santiago Creel—the likely *PAN* candidate to face López Obrador—hinted that a "political solution" was possible. It appeared the *PAN* was becoming sensitive to charges that it was proving as heavy-handed toward opponents as the *PRI* once had been. Fox's reputation as a democratic reformer was clearly in jeopardy. Days later, the mayor was ordered to appear before a judge, but a deputy attorney general ruled out an arrest after a token amount was posted for bail. The judge, like Pontius Pilate, sent the case back to prosecutors because of a legal technicality.

On April 24, a "silent march" in support of the mayor drew 1 million people. López Obrador returned to his office the following day, defying those who said he could not continue as mayor. Finally, Fox capitulated and broke the crisis on April 28 by firing Attorney General Rafael Macedo de la Concha, the leading advocate for prosecuting López Obrador. Basically, Fox sacrificed Macedo on the altar of public opinion, replacing him with Daniel Cabeza de Vaca, who dropped the case against López Obrador. Both López Obrador and Fox issued conciliatory statements, and the country breathed a sigh of relief. The two men even had an amicable meeting in the Los Pinos presidential residence on May 6, a day after the charges were dropped.

Meanwhile, López Obrador's approval rating within Mexico City jumped in one poll from 76% to 84%, while national polls continue to show him with double-digit leads over any of his major rivals. On May 9, he announced that he would resign as mayor effective July 31 to devote himself full-time to his presidential campaign.

One of those potential rivals, Creel, declared his own candidacy on May 12 and resigned as interior secretary. That raises the specter of an internecine battle within the *PAN* between Creel and the moderate wing of the party and the traditionalists led by Felipe Calderón. Polls show Creel virtually tied for second place with the *PRI*'s Madrazo. Fox named Labor Minister Carlos Abascal to replace Creel.

U.S.-Mexican relations remain problematical. The tension over the U.S.-led war in Iraq eventually subsided, and relations warmed with the marriage of U.S. Ambassador Tony García to a Mexican heiress in February and President Bush's decision in March to accede to Mexican demands to review the death penalty cases of 51 Mexican nationals. But relations soured again over the immigration issue and with mutual finger-pointing over the alarming increase in drug-related violence on the Mexican side of the common border (see Other Current Issues: Drugs).

Bush and Fox had once been in accord on immigration, but the proposal for free immigration across the border went nowhere in the U.S. Congress. Bush then advocated a scaled-back, compromise version that would allow Mexicans who are offered jobs to work in the United States for up to three years, but they would not be eligible for U.S. citizenship and would be required to return to Mexico. Fox grudgingly endorsed the watered-down plan as better than nothing and lobbied the U.S. Congress for its passage, but Congress remained unenthusiastic. Then Bush announced the extension of a wall along the California-Baja California border and pushed for legislation requiring states to require proof of citizenship to obtain drivers licenses. The two measures were ostensibly aimed at thwarting terrorists from crossing the border, but they offended Fox and Mexicans in general. Fox's government sent a formal letter of protest regarding the wall.

At the height of the immigration controversy, Fox generated international media attention with an injudicious remark to a group of visiting Texas businessmen on May 13 that backfired on him. Voicing his frustration over the lack of progress on the immigration issue, he said that Mexican immigrants traditionally have taken jobs that "not even blacks want to do." That sparked a firestorm of criticism from U.S. black organizations, as well as providing grist for satirists and cartoonists on both sides of the border. The Revs. Jesse Jackson and Al Sharpton publicly demanded that Fox apologize, and both flew to Mexico City to meet with him. The president said he regretted that his remarks had been "misinterpreted," but he declined to make a formal apology, which only angered American blacks more. The Mexicans themselves rallied behind their president because of the criticism; to them, he had merely spoken the truth.

Other Current Issues

Drugs

Given the geographic reality of Mexico's 2,000-mile border with the United States, it was inevitable that Mexico would become a conduit in the traffic of illegal drugs from Colombia to the United States. It is estimated that 70%–80% of the cocaine and heroin entering the United States comes across that lightly guarded border. Apart from those two drugs of Colombian origin, vast quantities of Mexican-grown marijuana also stream across the border, as do methamphetamines. It was also inevitable that domestic drug cartels would arise in Mexico, further corrupting already corrupt governmental and law enforcement institutions.

Until 1997 there were three major drug cartels operating in northern Mexico: the Gulf Cartel on the eastern flank, based in Matamoros, Tamaulipas, and headed by Juan García Abregu; the Juárez Cartel, based in Ciudad Juárez in Chihuahua and headed by Amado Carrillo Fuentes; and the Tijuana Cartel in Baja California Norte, run by the Arellano Félix brothers, Ramón, Benjamín, Eduardo, Francisco Javier and Francisco Rafael. Of these five brothers—there were a total of 10 siblings—Benjamín was considered the brains behind the business, while Ramón was a bloodthirsty enforcer who was himself to die in a hail of bullets in 2002.

These three groups had unofficially "divided" the 1,200-mile frontier with the United States into operational zones. Occasionally, however, friction between them erupted into gangland-style violence. In one legendary case, a lieutenant of the Arellano Félixes infiltrated the Juárez Cartel in 1989, seduced the wife of a Carrillo Fuentes lieutenant, persuaded her to withdraw $7 million from her husband's account, then killed her and sent her head to her husband in a box. He also reportedly threw the couple's two children to their deaths from a bridge in Caracas, Venezuela.

Another spectacular incident was a 1993 shootout in the Guadalajara airport in which Cardinal Juan Jesús Posadas Ocampo was killed, supposedly in the crossfire. Some theories still contend that he was in fact a target because he knew too much of official complicity in the drug trade, and his death remains controversial to this day. Francisco Rafael Arellano Félix was convicted of his role in the archbishop's death, as was Joaquín Guzmán of the rival gang. Guzmán escaped in early 2001; Francisco Rafael Arellano Félix remains in prison.

In April 1996, the Gulf Cartel was beheaded when García Abregu was extradited to the United States and sentenced to 11 life terms by a federal court in Houston. García Abregu was known for his high-level influence, among others, it is reported, with Raúl Salinas, brother of the former president, and former federal prosecutor Mario Ruíz Massieu.

On July 4, 1997, Carrillo Fuentes, nicknamed "Lord of the Skies" because of his use of aging jetliners to ferry massive amounts of cocaine from Colombia and believed to have the largest of the three cartels, died while undergoing clandestine plastic surgery to alter his appearance. Reports surfaced in some Mexican media that his death was a "hit" by a rival drug gang, probably the Tijuana Cartel. Although the report never was officially confirmed, two of his surgeons later were found tortured and killed; a third was granted protection in the United States, where he insisted to investigators that Carrillo Fuentes' death was, indeed, due to nothing more than a botched medical procedure.

Carrillo Fuentes' brother, Vicente, for a time assumed leadership of the cartel, but he lacked his brother's genius for organization, logistics and control. The dead kingpin was not even in his grave before a monumental turf war erupted between his cartel and that of the Arellano Félix brothers. Both Juárez and Tijuana became war zones, averaging a killing every two days. Most of them were in imaginatively gruesome gangland fashion by strangulation, suffocation with plastic bags or multiple gunshot wounds. The bodies frequently were burned, dismembered or beheaded and found stuffed into suitcases, oil drums or automobile trunks. The violence continues to be beyond the capability of federal, state or local police to contend with.

For a time, the Tijuana Cartel gained the upper hand. It was the richest, most powerful, most feared and most bloodthirsty of the cartels. The Arellano Félix brothers maintained their power over public officials with a Godfather-like carrot-or-stick tactic called *"plata o plomo"* ("silver or lead"). They were Mexico's most wanted criminals, and Ramón was on the FBI's 10 Most Wanted List. In one incident, which garnered international news coverage, the gang massacred 19 members of a family in Ensenada who allegedly were competing for the local marijuana market. One

reason the heat on them became so intense was that they committed a serious tactical error: they began shooting crusading journalists.

Benjamín Flores, the young publisher of a small daily newspaper in Sonora along the border with Arizona, had regularly reported on alleged ties between drug traffickers and public officials or police. He was gunned down outside his office in July 1997. Four months later, Jesús Blancornelas, publisher of *Zeta*, a weekly magazine in Tijuana that has been a nemesis of the Arellano Félixes, was critically wounded in an ambush on his car that killed his bodyguard; one of the gunmen also was slain, either by the bodyguard or in the crossfire, and was identified as a hit man for the Tijuana Cartel. Another journalist from Sonora, Luis Mario García, was gunned down on a street in Mexico City in February 1998 minutes after leaving the office of the federal attorney general (*PGR*), where he had refused to divulge his sources for his story on police corruption. Since 1988, more journalists have been murdered in Mexico than in any other Latin American republic save Colombia, but the number of drug-related killings seems to be accelerating. The wounding of Blancornelas created a backlash against the Arellano Félixes, with other journalists vowing to create unbearable pressure on their cartel. As one of them told this author, "They can't kill all of us."

Because of the endemic corruption that riddles government at all levels and the parallel law enforcement agencies, efforts to combat drug trafficking have sometimes taken on the semblance of a comic opera. Frequent changes of top law enforcement officials, for example, hamstrung any serious attempt to combat the drug cartels prior to 2000. Mexico had seven attorneys general in eight years during the 1990s.

In 1994, then-President Salinas established the Institute to Combat Drugs (*INCD*), the equivalent of the U.S. Drug Enforcement Administration, but it, too, has had a revolving door, with four directors in as many years. One, Army General Jesús Gutiérrez Rebollo, was fired in March 1997 and arrested, accused of having taken bribes from Carrillo Fuentes. In March 1998 he was sentenced to 13 years and nine months in prison. The Gutiérrez case proved highly embarrassing to the Zedillo administration, coming at a time when the president was trying to prove to the United States that it is serious about drug enforcement. Gutiérrez was replaced by a lawyer, Mario Herrán Salvatti, but in May 1997, on the very eve of President Clinton's first state visit to Mexico, Zedillo abolished the *INCD* and returned its functions to the attorney general's office.

Mexico

National University of Mexico Library

Despite the Gutiérrez affair and the obvious continued influence of the drug cartels, the Clinton administration recertified Mexico as an ally in the war on drugs in February 1997, at the same time that it again decertified Colombia. The recertification provoked accusations of hypocrisy from the Republican majority in Congress; the House of Representatives passed a resolution opposing Mexico's recertification, but the Senate upheld Clinton's decision by a narrow margin.

Another battle between Clinton and Congress erupted in February 1998 when Clinton again recertified Mexico. This time, the head of Clinton's own Drug Enforcement Agency (DEA) publicly opposed recertification and became embroiled in a public dispute with retired General Barry McCaffrey, head of the White House Office of National Drug Control Policy, who supported it. There were leaks to the press that alleged even more high-level corruption than had been re-

ported. *The Washington Times* cited a CIA report that Interior Minister Francisco Labastida (who later became the *PRI's* presidential candidate) had dealt with drug traffickers when he was governor of Sinaloa from 1987–93. The Mexicans and McCaffrey disputed the report. Then the *New York Times* reported on a secret DEA document that said the Mexican army's links to drug traffickers were greater than had been previously known. The Mexicans grudgingly lobbied in favor of recertification, but they made it clear they regarded the recertification process as demeaning and insulting to Mexico's sovereignty. This time, despite the negative publicity, a resolution opposing decertification fell short in the House of Representatives.

Between these two certifications, President Clinton made a state visit to Mexico in May 1997, his first to any Latin American country. The visit was largely cosmetic, with few tangible results, but Clinton did succeed in ameliorating anti-U.S.

feeling by acknowledging that the root of the drug trade was not Mexican greed but the insatiable demand for drugs in the United States.

Whatever good will was gleaned from Clinton's visit evaporated in May 1998 as a result of a secret three-year-long sting operation by U.S. agents to nab Mexican bankers involved in money laundering. Called "Operation Casablanca," the sting involved U.S. agents acting clandestinely in Mexico without the knowledge or approval of Mexican authorities. The operation yielded 150 arrests and $110 million in laundered money, and three Mexican banks were indicted. The operation was hailed as a huge success north of the Rio Grande, but the Mexicans were outraged by what they regarded as a violation of their sovereignty. Clinton and Secretary of State Madeleine Albright offered lukewarm apologies for the failure to consult the Mexicans, but apart from the violation of the sovereignty issue there was the implicit unstated message: We don't trust you enough to tell you about undercover drug operations.

Bilateral relations appeared back on track when Clinton met with Zedillo in February 1999 for a one-day summit in Mérida, Yucatán, that focused mainly on drugs and trade. The two presidents worked out a new drug agreement that established performance measures of effectiveness (PMEs) for 16 areas of drug control—including reduction of demand in the United States. The United States also agreed to provide increased police training assistance in such areas as airport inspections. A few days after the summit, Clinton again recertified Mexico as an ally in the drug war.

That June, 13 cabinet-level officials from the two countries, including U.S. Attorney General Janet Reno, met in Mexico City and reached agreement on such topics as airline fares, immigration and splitting seized drug money. The talks were overshadowed, however, by embarrassing reports in *The New York Times* and *The Washington Post* that Reno and other U.S. officials suspected high-level Mexican officials, including Zedillo's Private secretary, of ties to drug traffickers.

In 2000, the newly inaugurated president, Vicente Fox, pledged a crackdown on corruption, which in Mexico is almost synonymous with drugs. In a meeting with his new U.S. counterpart, George W. Bush, in early 2001, Fox pledged continued and even heightened cooperation in the war on drugs, although like his predecessors he voiced his disapproval of the U.S. drug certification policy.

In its first year, the Fox administration scored some significant victories. One was the capture in May 2001 of the fugitive former governor of Quintana Roo, Mario Villanueva, who allegedly aided the Juárez Cartel in smuggling 200 tons of cocaine into the United States; he reportedly once flew 440 pounds into the United States aboard his private jet. He had been on the run for two years. In April, a Mexico City judge convicted Juan José Quintero, believed to be one of the leaders of the Juárez Cartel since Carillo Fuentes' death, and sentenced him to 17 years. Another of Carillo's suspected heirs, Ramón Alcides Magaña, known by the sobriquet "El Metro," was captured in Villahermosa, Tabasco, that June. It was he who was suspected of paying off Villanueva, $50,000 per shipment.

In April 2001, Mexican authorities arrested 21 alleged members of the Gulf Cartel, by then headed by Osiel Cárdenas, among them one of the suspected kingpins, Gilberto García, known as "El June." In May 2003 he was sentenced to eight years. Two months after García's arrest, Juan Manuel Garza, another of the alleged leaders of the Gulf Cartel, crossed the border from Reynosa into McAllen, Texas, and surrendered to the FBI. That September, six soldiers in an elite anti-drug unit were arrested in Mexico City, accused of protecting Cárdenas. They were convicted in 2003.

Cárdenas himself, nicknamed "El Loco" because he is so brazen that he once confronted DEA agents and ordered them out of "his" territory, and 22 accomplices were apprehended in March 2003 after a gun battle in Matamoros, across from Brownsville, Texas. Two weeks later, his second in command, Victor Manuel Vásquez, and seven other people were arrested in Veracruz.

Even before Cárdenas' arrest, there was an outbreak of drug-related violence in Nuevo Laredo, and since then what is believed to be a new turf battle has raged there to fill the latest vacuum at the apex of the Gulf Cartel. In October 2003, authorities announced that a band of deserters from the Mexican army, calling themselves "Los Zetas," had become established in Nuevo Laredo and was fighting for a piece of the turf.

The Arellano Félix organization suffered two major blows in 2002. First, Ramón was killed in a shootout, supposedly with police, in Mazatlán on February 10. He killed the policeman who killed him in the exchange of gunfire. Because the body was quickly cremated, there was speculation as to whether the corpse was actually that of the notorious drug kingpin or belonged to an imposter; it was reminiscent of the death of the Juárez Cartel's Carillo Fuentes in 1997.

Then, on March 9, Benjamín was arrested in a raid in Puebla. Benjamín confirmed that it was Ramón who had been killed in Mazatlán, although his credibility was suspect at best. However, police took blood and saliva samples from Benjamín, and DNA samples taken from the clothes of the man killed on February 10 proved they were a match.

There was a bizarre postscript to Ramón's death. The Associated Press, citing an anonymous "senior U.S. law enforcement official," reported that the police who killed Ramón were in fact part of a hit paid for by Ismael Zambada García, head of a rival drug cartel in Sinaloa. Mexican officials declined to comment on the report—but did not deny it.

Benjamín scored a courtroom victory a month after his arrest when a judge ruled that there was insufficient evidence to implicate him, along with his imprisoned brother Rafael, in Archbishop Posadas Ocampo's death in 1993. In February 2003, another judge dismissed a charge that Benjamín headed a drug-trafficking organization. Another brother, Eduardo, a surgeon, remains at large and is thought to hold a leadership role.

In June 2002, U.S. drug czar John Walters visited Mexico and praised the crackdown, calling the decapitation of the Tijuana Cartel the greatest victory in the drug war since the 1993 killing of Pablo Escobar in Colombia. But Mexican Attorney General Rafael Macedo de la Concha was more subdued in a speech to state attorneys general and prosecutors, warning that despite the arrests of 2,000 members of the cartel, it remained in business and its operations remained normal.

With the seeming downfall of the Arellano Félix brothers and the decapitation of the Gulf Cartel, the center of gravity in the drug trade shifted for a time to the state of Sinaloa—the original home of the Arellano Félixes. Sinaloa has a long history of involvement in the raising and trafficking of illicit drugs dating to the 19th century, when Chinese immigrants raised poppies for the production of opium, much of which was smuggled to the United States. At least two known rival cartels have been operating in Sinaloa. One is headed by the Guzmán brothers, Arturo, known as "the Chicken," and Joaquín, "El Chapo," who was serving a 20-year sentence for the accidental shooting death of Archbishop Posadas Ocampo in 1993 before he escaped in February 2001. He remains at large, but Arturo was arrested in September 2001. Arturo is believed to be responsible for an elaborate 1,400-foot tunnel under the U.S. border. Joaquín, meanwhile, is believed to be among the drug lords trying to fill the vacuum in Nuevo Laredo.

The other cartel is headed by Ismael "El Mayo" Zambada García, apparently the "rising star" in Mexican drug trafficking.

He reportedly had been attempting to muscle in on the Arellano Félixes' Tijuana operations for at least a decade, which helped fuel speculation he was responsible for Ramón's "execution" in Mazatlán. His organization became the target of a U.S.-Mexican investigation, code-named "Operation Trifecta" after the seizure of a 10-ton cocaine shipment at sea in December 2001.

An exceptionally violent territorial battle erupted between the two gangs. Within days of Ramón's death, a suspected Arellano Félix ally was gunned down, sparking a wave of gangland killings. The most spectacular was the abduction and subsequent execution-style slayings of 12 people in May 2002 by suspected Arellano Félix operatives.

In mid-2002, the bad news was that an estimated 9,500 tons of marijuana and seven tons of heroin were still being smuggled annually into the United States from Mexico. The good news was that the cocaine traffic had been disrupted, although not stopped, and that there had been more than 10,000 drug-related arrests, including soldiers and policemen, since Fox became president. Dozens of policemen—reports vary from 50 to 200—were arrested in Tijuana during a federal-state sting operation in April 2002, which also uncovered another tunnel under the border.

In October 2002, General Gerardo Vega García, the defense minister, revealed that 48 soldiers of a 600-member battalion based in Sinaloa that had been assigned to drug crop eradication were under investigation. Vega García admitted that the battalion was riddled with corruption. Days later, about two dozen current and former government bureaucrats, soldiers and federal policemen were arrested in Mexico City on suspicion of having sold classified material to drug traffickers. In November, two generals were convicted and sentenced to prison for having sold information to the late Carrillo Fuentes of the Juárez Cartel.

In a still larger anti-corruption operation within the Federal Special Prosecutor's Office for Drug Crimes, or FEADS, soldiers and police raided FEADS offices in 11 states on November 17, 2002, seizing supposedly incriminating documents. Seven FEADS agents were arrested in Tijuana, accused of extorting bribes from drug smugglers. In another sweep in April 2003, 700 drug agents arrested 41 state and local policemen in Ecatepec, near Mexico City, for allegedly selling drugs and protecting drug dealers.

In what could be a major development, growers in Guerrero state reportedly began replacing marijuana with high-grade opium poppies imported from Colombia.

Mexico

In the first such incident of its kind in Mexico, growers shot down two helicopters in Guerrero in March 2003 as they were spraying illegal crops, killing five crewmembers.

In August 2003, Attorneys General John Ashcroft and Rafael Maceda de la Concha announced simultaneously in Washington and Mexico City a "significant victory" in the battle against the Zambada García cartel. Zambada García was named in an unsealed U.S. indictment, along with two of his lieutenants; all three remain at large, however. Ashcroft and Macedo also announced that Operation Trifecta had yielded 240 arrests and indictments.

On June 1, 2004, President Bush announced that two Mexican cartels and eight individuals from Mexico and four other countries had been placed on a sanctions list, denying them access to U.S. financial institutions or from dealing with U.S. companies or individuals. Named were the Arellano Félix and Carrillo Fuentes organizations, and Mexicans Eduardo Arellano Félix, Francisco Javier Arellano Félix, and Armando Valencia Cornelio.

The two governments jointly launched a fugitive-hunting effort code-named Operation United Eagles in July 2003. To date probably the biggest catch was Gilberto Higuera Guerrero, a former operative in the Tijuana Cartel who bolted to join the Zambada gang in Sinaloa. He was apprehended in Mexicali, Baja California Norte, in August 2004. He had had a $2 million reward on his head.

In a major, and frightening, development, Juan José Esparragoza, who had been operations chief of the Juárez Cartel, took over the leadership from Vicente Carrillo Fuentes and began building alliances. He persuaded the rival Guzmán and Zambada cartels in Sinaloa to put aside their differences and to join the Juárez Cartel. With Benjamín Arellano

Félix of the Tijuana Cartel and Cárdenas of the Gulf Cartel both behind bars, this new alliance made the Juárez Cartel the largest in Mexico, and it began a two-front offensive against its rivals, with "El Mayo" Zambada the "general" in charge of battling the Tijuana Cartel for control of the drug routes into California and Arizona, and "El Chapo" Guzmán fighting the Gulf Cartel in Tamaulipas along the Texas border.

In an equally stunning development, however, Benjamín Arellano Félix and Cárdenas, jailed in the maximum-security La Palma federal prison near Mexico City, formed an unholy alliance of their own to defend their respective turfs against the onslaught from the Juárez Cartel. When the federal government got wind of their collusion, it launched a crackdown on the federal prison system, even dispatching troops to surround La Palma in January 2005. Cárdenas and Arellano Félix were separated, and many other prisoners were transferred to a prison in Matamoros, but not before their alliance was created.

Not surprisingly, this clash of the titans became spectacularly bloody, generating headlines on both sides of the border. Gangland-style killings are a daily occurrence, but the victims are not always members of the two gangs; law enforcement officers, journalists and innocent bystanders are being slain regularly as well. Figures are difficult to tabulate, but approximately 500 people were killed in drug-related violence in just the first five months of 2005. A comic-opera adjunct to this grim scenario has been the posting of "reward posters" by each gang for leaders of the rival gang, while each side has taken to hurling insults at the other over police band radios.

Nowhere is the violence worse than in Matamoros and Nuevo Laredo, both border cities in the state of Tamaulipas. *Los*

Zetas are believed to have become enforcers for the Gulf Cartel.

In a bold act that shocked both countries, six guards at the prison in Matamoros were seized by hit men when their shift ended on January 20, 2005, handcuffed, riddled with bullets execution-style and left in a car outside town. The killings were reportedly retribution for the crackdown on the federal prisons days earlier, and were interpreted as a challenge by the drug lords to the national government itself. The killings were probably carried out by *Los Zetas,* working for Cárdenas. President Fox responded by sending army troops to cordon off the prison. The prison killings also generated diplomatic friction between Mexico and the United States when U.S. Ambassador Tony García complained that Mexico was not doing enough to curtail the violence; the U.S. State Department also issued a travel advisory against U.S. citizens visiting the border area, which threatened Mexico's vital tourism industry. Fox responded testily that the United States bore much of the responsibility by not curtailing the demand for drugs. He vowed to wage "the mother of all battles" against the cartels.

In Nuevo Laredo, the lawless atmosphere is reminiscent of the Capone-Moran rivalry in Chicago in the 1920s—only bloodier. In the first two months of 2005, there were 21 drug-related killings in and around the city, prompting the Fox administration to dispatch 600 heavily armed federal policemen there in early March. In April, he added army troops to a force of 700 to help patrol the city, one step short of declaring outright martial law. In June 2005, the city finally filled the vacancy for police chief, a job no one was willing to take. Nine hours after the new chief assumed command, he was ambushed by drug traffickers and killed.

The drug traffickers loathe—and fear—crusading journalists only slightly less than they do law enforcement officials who can't be bought. In 2004, for the first time, more journalists were slain in Mexico than in Colombia. According to Reporters Without Borders, only Iraq, Bangladesh and the Philippines recorded more journalists killed than did Mexico. More have been killed in 2005. Most, but not all, of the killings have been close to the border.

In Tijuana, Francisco Ortíz Franco, an assistant editor for Jesús Blancornelas' crusading weekly *Zeta,* was gunned down in his car in the presence of his two children in June 2004. Two months later, Francisco Arratia Saldierna, a syndicated newspaper columnist in Matamoros who regularly attacked organized crime, was sadistically tortured and beaten to death.

Cancún, on the northeastern tip of the Yucatán Peninsula *Courtesy: Ann and Martin Shuey*

That November, Gregorio Rodríguez, a photographer with a newspaper in Sinaloa, was murdered after he took a picture of a drug dealer.

In strife-torn Nuevo Laredo, two of the city's best known journalists, both of whom reported on the drug cartels, have been murdered. Roberto Mora, news editor of *El Mañana*, was stabbed to death in March 2004, and Guadalupe García Escamilla, who hosted a radio crime program, was riddled with nine bullets outside the station in April 2005 and died 10 days later. That same week, Raúl Gibb Guerrero, director of a small newspaper in the state of Veracruz to the south, who had been unintimidated by death threats for reporting on the Gulf Cartel, was ambushed on his way home and killed, while Alfredo Jiménez, a crime reporter for *El Imparcial* in Hermosillo, Sonora, disappeared.

A suspect in Mora's murder was the only one arrested in any of the murders, and that suspect, a U.S. citizen, was stabbed to death in jail. Mexican journalists and international journalism organizations have demanded that the Fox administration do more to protect journalists and to apprehend journalists' killers.

But even the safety of Fox himself was called into question in February 2005 when Nahum Acosta, an employee of the presidential office, was arrested after police videotaped him meeting with a representative of "El Chapo" Guzmán. Acosta was accused of leaking information about presidential security to Guzmán, raising fears of a possible assassination plot.

But Fox's "mother of all battles" continues. On June 2, 2005, federal authorities arrested "El Chapo's" son, Ivan Archibaldo, on money laundering charges and jailed him at La Palma. A judge in Toluca ordered him released on bail, however, angering the government. The attorney general's office appealed his release. Days later, a third Guzmán brother, Miguel Angel, was arrested in Culiacán. A week later, the Mexican navy seized four tons of cocaine in a ship on the Pacific coast.

Bilateral relations in the drug war were strained, however, when the assistant DEA administrator for intelligence testified before a House committee that the greatest impediment to combating drug trafficking is corruption among Mexican law enforcement officials. Foreign Minister Derbéz dismissed his comments as "nonsense."

The Environment

Mexico City faces an air pollution crisis that is one of the worst of any of the world's major cities. Because the capital is located in a "bowl" surrounded by high mountains, with a population of 20 million and 3 million cars and trucks, there is literally no air circulation for about eight months a year. *Pemex*, the state-controlled petroleum monopoly, was notorious for producing poorly refined, pollutant-laden (particularly sulfur) gasoline, but unleaded fuel has become commonplace, which has led to a dramatic improvement in air quality. The Environment Ministry issued new guidelines in June 2005 aimed at providing even cleaner-burning gasoline and diesel fuel by 2008.

But smog remains a serious problem in the capital. The No. 1 diseases among the young are respiratory (chronic and debilitating). The response under a succession of presidential administrations has been inadequate. Factories have been suspended from operation, and autos (both domestic and foreign) are allotted certain days of the week on which they may be operated.

Mexico City's pollution is made worse by hundreds of tons of human and animal waste which, untreated, is dumped outside the city. It dries, and when the wind blows, it is picked up as a fine dust, further choking the air. Because of this and other pollution problems, educated and wealthy people have left the city for places such as San Luís Potosí and Cuernavaca.

Another environmental concern that has only recently attracted governmental attention is the alarming rate of deforestation through illegal logging. The Environment Ministry estimates that 1.3 million acres of forest are lost to illegal logging each year, even in the 133,000-acre preserve of El Rosario in the state of Michoacán, where the monarch butterflies spend the winter. In 2005, the winter population of the butterflies was only about a fourth what it was the year before. In December 2004, the ministry announced that 103 people had been arrested that year for illegal logging, triple the number of the year before, and that sophisticated surveillance had been undertaken to detect the poaching.

Until the government crackdown, the only effort to stem the logging had come from environmental activists, who often were met with violence and questionable charges brought by powerful local *caciques*, or political bosses. Perhaps the best-known group is the Peasant Ecologists of the Sierra Petatlán, in the state of Guerrero. Under national and international pressure, President Vicente Fox intervened to free two of the group's activists in 2001 after they were arrested on what were apparently trumped-up drug and weapons possession charges. Another member of the group, Felipe Arreaga, was arrested in November 2004 on questionable murder charges; domestic and international rights and environmental groups have demanded his release. In May 2005, yet another of the group's leaders, Albertano Penalosa, narrowly escaped death in an ambush that killed two of his sons, aged 19 and 9. The international environmental group Greenpeace estimates that 40% of the forest in the Sierra Petatlán was logged out between 1992 and 2000.

Also endangered is the Lacandón rainforest in the south, considered by ecologists to be the most biologically diverse jungle in the hemisphere after the Amazon, which also is threatened by illegal logging (see Brazil).

In a positive development, a private campaign by the U.S. group Nature Conservancy and Pronature of Mexico raised $3 million in 2004 purchase 370,000 acres of rain forest in Yucatán, which was added to the existing 1.8-million-acre Calakmul Biosphere Reserve. It was the largest private conservation project in Mexican history.

Armed Rebellions

For all its corruption and political violence, Mexico had not experienced actual armed insurrection since the Revolution. Thus, the country was shocked on New Year's Day 1994 when an organized band of rebels calling itself the *Zapatista* National Liberation Army (*EZLN*) launched a bloody offensive against federal institutions in Chiapas state. The group proclaimed itself the champion of the poor southern peasants, most of them full-blooded Indians, much like the revolutionary hero Emiliano Zapata after whom it is named.

Disputes between the wealthy ranchers and the impoverished masses had been festering in Chiapas for 175 years. The *EZLN*, whose strength was variously estimated at 200 to 2,000, denounced alleged electoral fraud by which the *PRI* had won the governorship of Chiapas. The army was sent in and for 10 days there was some skirmishing in which about 145 people were killed on both sides. Then the government and the rebels agreed to negotiate.

What followed was a media circus. The *EZLN* leader who emerged as its negotiator went by the *nom de guerre* "Subcomandante Marcos," who always appeared in ski mask and with bandoliers containing ammunition incompatible with the shotgun he brandished. This "guerrilla" subsequently was identified as Rafael Sebastián Guillén, son of a wealthy Caucasian family in Tampico in far-off northern Mexico and a former *Sandinista* activist. The unmasking of Subcomandante Marcos largely undermined the credibility of the *EZLN*.

Nonetheless, the *Zapatistas* made up in media savvy what they lacked in military expertise and proved to be skilled

Mexico

public relations practitioners. At first, they aroused sympathy, especially because many of their grievances were well-founded. But support began to wane in 1995 after the government engaged in a public relations counteroffensive that cynically blamed the rebels for frightening off foreign investments and thus contributing to the crippling recession. For the most part, the *EZLN* has engaged in what one political scientist wryly labeled "guerrilla theater."

Not so with a second group that burst on the scene—also in the south—in 1996. On June 28, peasants in Guerrero state held a memorial service to commemorate the first anniversary of the massacre of 17 peasants by Guerrero police. Dozens of hooded men and women showed up at the service, calling themselves the Popular Revolutionary Army (*ERP*). Unlike the *EZLN*, this group appeared to be well armed with AK-47s and clad more like serious guerrillas, with boots instead of sandals, for example. Alarmed, President Zedillo dispatched thousands of troops to Guerrero, provoking the wrath of many local officials who said the president was "militarizing" the state. Like Chiapas, Guerrero is characterized by a sharp division between extreme wealth (Acapulco and other posh Pacific resorts are in Guerrero) and abject poverty. It was the site of a minor insurgency in the 1960s and 1970s, led by the legendary, Robin Hood-like outlaw, Lucio Cabañas, who in the end was slain by security forces. After the June 28 memorial service, the Organization of American States sent a team of human rights workers to investigate charges of rights abuses in the state.

That August, the *ERP* stunned the country with a series of well-coordinated attacks against military garrisons and police stations, not only in Guerrero but in Chiapas and Oaxaca states as well. They killed at least 18 people, including two civilians, while suffering only two confirmed fatalities. The attacks led to unprecedented security for the annual Independence Day festivities in the capital on September 16, and President Zedillo vowed to suppress the "terrorists."

Since its first spectacular military strike, however, the *ERP* seemed to fade into the background. Unlike the *EZLN*, the *ERP* has called for the violent overthrow of the government and showed no appetite for negotiation. Also unlike the *EZLN*, it has failed to win public support, judging from opinion polls that showed two thirds of the public believe the *ERP*'s use of violence was unjustified. Subcomandante Marcos himself distanced the *EZLN* from the new group, saying in a public statement, "You fight for power. We fight for democracy, liberty and justice."

In February 1996, the government and the *EZLN* reached a tentative agreement in the town of San Andrés de Larrainzar, called the San Andrés accords, that would grant the Indians in the south greater autonomy from the institutionalized state and local governments, almost all of them controlled by the *PRI*. The *Zapatistas* broke off from talks with the government the following September, alleging the government was acting in bad faith by dragging its feet in implementing the accords. For 15 months the talks were in limbo; it took a shocking tragedy to get things moving again.

On December 22, 1997, about 70 armed members of a *PRI*-affiliated paramilitary group in Chiapas entered the village of Acteal, about 12 miles north of San Cristóbal de las Casas. Without provocation, they shot anyone who presented a target—men, women, children, even infants in their mothers' arms. People were gunned down as they desperately attempted to flee, others as they huddled in a church, an atrocity reminiscent of My Lai during the Vietnam War or the "ethnic cleansing" in the Balkans. When the firing stopped, 45 Indian peasants had been slain, all but nine of them women or children; four of the women were pregnant. At least 25 others were wounded.

The massacre made international headlines and presented President Zedillo with an instant public relations nightmare. With considerable understatement, the president denounced the massacre as a "cruel, absurd criminal act." In a clumsy effort at damage control, "investigators" from Mexico City hurried to Acteal and initially offered the lame explanation that the massacre had been motivated by a local family feud.

There was a time, before the emergence of viable opposition parties and press reforms, that the *PRI*'s version would have been accepted. Mexico's independent media and foreign journalists, however, interviewed survivors and reported that the gunmen, armed with AK-47s and dressed in blue uniforms, were members of a *PRI* paramilitary group from a neighboring village of Chanalho. One survivor stated that the gunmen fired in the direction of crying children. Eventually more than 30 men either were arrested, including the *PRI* mayor of Chanalho, or surrendered. Like the victims, the killers were Indians. The motive for the killings, they explained, was that the villagers were *Zapatista* sympathizers—including, presumably, the slain infants and fetuses.

The opposition *PRD* demanded the resignations of Interior Minister Emilio Chuayffet and the *PRI* governor of Chiapas, Julio César Ruíz Ferro. Chuayffet huffily refused to resign, but Zedillo soon

sacrificed his No. 2 man on the altar of public opinion and replaced him with Francisco Labastida. Ruíz Ferro yielded to public pressure and resigned in January 1998.

According to subsequent press reports, such killings of peasants by *PRI*-linked paramilitaries had occurred regularly on a smaller scale in Chiapas, but the Acteal massacre shocked the nation and the world and forced Zedillo to take action. Among other things, he pledged to reduce the army presence in Chiapas (the army was suspected of providing sophisticated weapons to the paramilitaries) and to crack down on paramilitary groups. Most importantly, however, Zedillo introduced sweeping constitutional reforms to Congress in an effort to jump-start the San Andrés accords. His proposal would recognize the rights of Mexico's 9 million indigenous people and permit them greater autonomy in their local affairs.

The rebels denounced the initiative as providing "the peace of tombs." Moreover, some lawmakers in the *PRI* and the *PAN* opposed the proposal as giving in too much to the rebels, while the *PRD* faulted it for not going far enough. To be enacted, the proposal would have to receive a two-thirds vote of Congress and ratification of 16 of the 31 state legislatures, a goal that seemed all but unattainable. If it failed, of course, Zedillo at least could say, "Well, I tried."

Apparently, he didn't try hard enough. A clash between army troops and a resurgent *EPR* in Guerrero on May 31, 1998, left 11 civilians dead. Three days later, in Chiapas, there occurred the worst violence since the so-called peace process began. The *EZLN* ambushed a combined army-police patrol and in the ensuing clash eight rebels and one policeman were killed.

Soon thereafter, Mary Robinson, the U.N. commissioner for human rights, rebuked the Mexican government for its alleged rights abuses in Chiapas. U.N. Secretary-General Kofi Annan touched off a diplomatic furor in June when he suggested the United Nations should play a role in the peace process. Mexico swiftly and vigorously denounced any outside interference in its internal affairs. Annan just as quickly backed off, and he made a three-day visit to Mexico in July to meet with Zedillo and Mexican human rights groups. Although Chiapas was not on the formal agenda, the two leaders discussed it at length. In the end, Annan said the government should exert more effort, but he also urged the rebels to return to the negotiating table, invoking the chiché, "It takes two to tango."

It appeared the "tango" might resume in November 1998 when 29 *Zapatista* delegates showed up in their trademark ski masks for a government-initiated meeting in San Cristobal de las Casas; Subcomandante Marcos was not among them. The government delegation included six congressmen from all three major parties. The rebels soon dashed any hopes the talks might resume in earnest. They accused the congressmen of being "racists" and refused to return to the bargaining table until the government met the five demands that led to the collapse of the talks two years earlier, including release of *EZLN* prisoners, democratic reforms, disbanding of paramilitary groups and demilitarization of much of southern Mexico. The rebels even complained about the accommodations the government had provided for them, saying they were being treated "like animals."

The *Zapatistas* attempted to regain the public relations initiative in March 1999 by staging a "national referendum" on their five demands. Of course, the wording of the referendum items was heavily slanted. It turned into a public relations debacle.

In April 1999, a potentially explosive incident ended peacefully. About 1,000 unarmed *Zapatistas* came down from the hills and "reoccupied" the city hall in San Andrés de Larrainzar, site of the first talks. The 150 outnumbered state policemen wisely fell back without opening fire. A few days later, 300 state policemen expelled the few remaining *Zapatistas* without violence or arrests.

For his part, Subcomandante Marcos finally came out of hiding on May 9, 1999 for the first time since November 1997, attending a meeting in the Chiapas village of La Realidad. There, he delivered the usual diatribe against the government, the *PAN*, the *PRD* and foreign investors.

The peace process remained moribund until after the 2000 presidential election, and it took the election of the conservative *PAN* candidate, Vicente Fox, followed a month later by the election of *PRD* candidate Pedro Salazar for governor of Chiapas, to get it moving again. Fox's first official act after being inaugurated on December 1, 2000, was to fulfill a campaign pledge to order the withdrawal of army troops from Chiapas as a sign of good faith. Fox also introduced a constitutional amendment to Congress in December that would accede to one of the *Zapatistas'* demands, to grant greater autonomy to Mexico's indigenous citizens. With the detested *PRI* out of power both in Mexico City and in Chiapas, and a president in power who seemed serious about peace, the ball was then in Subcomandante Marcos' court. He was now dealing with a president who was at least as astute a public relations practitioner as himself.

What occurred next was typical of Marcos' theatrics, and it garnered worldwide media attention. The *Zapatistas* staged a caravan to the capital in March 2001, reminiscent of the civil rights marches in the United States during the 1960s, which the media quickly labeled the "*Zapatour.*" Their stated goal was to lobby Congress directly for the indigenous rights bill. Traveling in trucks and buses, and leaving their weapons at home, Marcos and 23 other *EZLN* members and their entourage traveled through 12 states, receiving tumultuous welcomes from the impoverished Indians along the way, before arriving in the capital on March 11. They asked for permission to lobby the Chamber of Deputies. Fox was agreeable, although legislators of his own party adamantly opposed the idea.

The *Zapatistas* remained in the capital for 18 days and were threatening to return to Chiapas empty-handed on March 23 when they suddenly received the invitation to address the lower house. The *EZLN* leaders delivered not strident demands, but respectful requests to the country's lawmakers on March 28 during a meeting of several hours that was broadcast on national television; the always unpredictable Marcos did not appear. That same week, the army undertook the dismantling of its bases in Chiapas. The last base was dismantled in April.

After the dramatic appearance of the masked *Zapatistas*, which had turned into the inevitable media circus, Congress debated the indigenous rights bill in earnest. The original bill was based on the accords reached by the *EZLN* and the government in 1996 in San Andrés de Larrainzar. But there was grumbling by *PRI* legislators that the bill infringed on the traditional authority of state governors, and from *Panistas* that it conceded too much to the *Zapatistas*. The Senate unanimously approved an amended version on April 25. Three days later, the Chamber of Deputies passed it, 386–60. This time the opposition came from the *PRD* and the *PT* on the left, because of language that stresses the preeminence of national sovereignty over indigenous rights. The *EZLN* also opposed the watered-down version because it eliminated the guarantee of rights over land, water and natural resources.

The constitutional amendment then required ratification of a majority of the state legislatures, and the *Zapatistas* staged protests outside the various legislatures and blockaded highways—but did not shoot. Nonetheless, on July 12, Michoacán became the 16th state to ratify the amendment. It took effect on August 15, with the *EZLN* still complaining about "betrayal." The law was challenged, but the Supreme Court ruled 8–3 in September 2002 that it lacked jurisdiction over constitutional amendments.

On June 15, 2001, Fox announced an ambitious economic development program for southeastern Mexico and Central America, called *Plan Puebla-Panamá*. But the *Zapatistas* also denounced this plan as a capitalist ploy to force the Indians from their lands.

The world heard little more from the *Zapatistas* until June 22, 2005, when Marcos declared a "red alert" and ordered *Zapatista* fighters to assemble in their bases. For the next 24 hours, as *Zapatista* stronghold villages became deserted, Mexicans wondered whether they were about to launch a new offensive. The next day, however, Marcos issued a letter that declared the *Zapatistas* were not planning a return to violence, but were debating their next course of action. On June 28, they announced it: They would create a new political movement, composed of peasant Indians, laborers and students, and they would begin participating in the mainstream political system.

Culture: Appropriately symbolizing Mexico's ethnic composition is a park in Mexico City called *La Plaza de las Tres Culturas*. In Mexico as much as anywhere in the New World, the blending of the Spanish and Indian produced a third, separate race, the *mestizo*, which predominates today.

The giant of Spanish America in more ways than population size, Mexico had a rich cultural heritage centuries before the Spanish Conquest. The Aztec, Mayan, Toltec, Mixtec and other indigenous civilizations all have contributed much to Mexican folklore. Just as the mixing of bloods created a new race, so did the infusion of Spanish art, music, literature, food, and architecture, give rise to a new, discrete culture. It is Mexico's culture that most North Americans erroneously associate with all of Latin America: *mariachi* music, a spicy rice, bean and tortilla diet, red-tiled roofs and white stuccoed walls.

After independence, cultural development was slow owing to political instability, the crippling civil war between Liberals and Conservatives from 1857–61, the subsequent French intervention and general inattention to public education. Despite the Porfirio Díaz dictatorship rather than because of it, the late 19th and early 20th centuries were marked by the emergence of a distinctly Mexican literature. The most prominent writers of this period were Amado Nervo, Ramón López Velarde and Manuel Gutiérrez Nájera.

The demarcation line of Mexican culture, however, was the Revolution of 1910–20. Besides forever changing the political fabric of the country, the Revolution gave birth to a movement in realist art, appropriately called "revolutionary art," music and literature. Two classic revolu-

Mexico

tionary novels are Mariano Azuela's *Los de abajo* (1916), and Martín Luís Guzmán's *El aguila y la serpiente* ("The Eagle and the Serpent," 1928), both of which focus on social issues. The poetry of Alfonso Reyes, José Gorostiza and Jaime Torres Bodet and the novels of Agustín Yáñez also are identified with the post-revolutionary period.

Mexico's best-known novelists of the second half of the 20th century are Juan Rulfo (1917–1986), best remembered for *Pedro Páramo,* and Carlos Fuentes (1928–), whose classic remains *El gringo viejo,* adapted into the 1989 motion picture *The Old Gringo* with Gregory Peck and Jane Fonda. The acknowledged master of the short story was Juan José Arreola (1921–2001), a friend of Rulfo's, who developed a half-prose, half-poetry genre called *varia invención,* after the title of one of his stories. He published 16 books of stories, probably the most renowned being *La feria* and *Bestiario.*

But the titan of modern Mexican literature was the poet Octavio Paz (1914–98), who received the Nobel Prize in 1990, the fifth and most recent Latin American to be so honored. His verse was a critical, brutally honest examination of Mexico's hybrid Spanish-Indian culture, which alienated him from many of his leftist intellectual contemporaries. Yet, when he died at age 84 on April 19, 1998, his former detractors heaped praise on him, and the government accorded him a state funeral.

The premier figures of post-revolutionary art were Diego Rivera (1886–1957), José Clemente Orozco (1883–1949) and David Alfaro Siqueiros (1896–1974), whose heroic murals epitomize the social struggle of the Revolution. Rivera and Orozco

Diego Rivera

also were at home in the *avant-garde* art crowd of 1920s Paris, and were friends of Pablo Picasso, the influence of whose abstractionism can be detected in their paintings. Siquieros, a combat veteran of the Revolution, lived and painted for a time in Los Angeles, and fought on the republican side during the Spanish Civil War.

One of Rivera's four wives, Frida Kahlo (1907–54), carved out an international reputation as an artist in her own right and has posthumously become a feminist cultural icon in Europe and the United States. She was the subject of a 2002 U.S. motion picture, *Frida,* starring Mexican actress Salma Hayek (see below).

Probably Mexico's best-known artist today is the painter and sculptor Francisco Toledo, famed for his erotic shaman-based figures.

In photography, the premier figure was the internationally renowned Manuel Alvarez Bravo (1902–2002), whose photos ranged from street scenes to nude women.

Mexican music of the post-revolutionary period was dominated by Carlos Chávez, who founded the national symphony orchestra in 1928 and whose classical compositions were drawn from Mexico's Indian heritage. Popular music is characterized both by the *ranchero* style, a guitar-based sound that celebrates Mexico's *vaqueros,* (cowboys), and the quintessentially Mexican *mariachis.*

Mexico has long had a thriving popular music industry, one that blends the sounds of traditional Mexican music with the internationalized Latino sounds of the Caribbean. Mexican singers have achieved renown throughout Latin America and in the United States.

One of Mexico's leading pop icons is Gloria Trevi, the so-called "Madonna of Mexico." However, she has been more like the Michael Jackson of Mexico. For five years, she and her lover-manager were the focus of a tawdry international investigation of alleged kidnapping and raping of underage girls. She was jailed in Brazil (where she mysteriously became pregnant and gave birth) and extradited to Mexico, where she was finally acquitted by a judge in September 2004 in a court proceeding broadcast on national television. It generated much the same excitement as Michael Jackson's molestation trial and acquittal in the United States. She was 36 at the time of the acquittal and resumed her singing career.

Mexico City has a robust theatrical community, though the works of its playwrights to date have been primarily for domestic consumption.

Mexican cinema, on the other hand, developed parallel with that of the United States, and Mexican films have been exported for several decades now. Many

Frida Kahlo in 1932, sitting beneath her self-portrait

Mexican film stars went on to successful careers in Hollywood, such as Dolores del Río, Ramón Navarro, Anthony Quinn and Ricardo Montalbán.

But arguably Mexico's most revered film legend was María Félix (1914–2002), perhaps because she eschewed moving to Hollywood and devoted her career to her native country. Known as the "Marilyn Monroe of Mexico," she made 47 films between 1942 and 1970 and was a national icon. Her death in April 2002 brought thousands of mourners to the Palacio de Bellas Artes in Mexico City; President Vicente Fox extolled her as "a great shrine to our country."

Mexican cinema continues to thrive with several films that have achieved international acclaim in recent years. In 2001, for example, there were *De la calle, (On the street),* directed by newcomer Gerardo Tort, which is a searing glimpse of the lives of Mexico's street urchins; and *Amores perros (Love's a Bitch).* Another, and more controversial film that won notice abroad in 2002—and outraged the Roman Catholic hierarchy in Mexico—was *El crimen de Padre Amaro (The Crime of Father Amaro).* Adapted from a Portuguese novel, it is the story of a priest who seduces a 16-year-old girl. Another hit abroad was *Y tu mamá también* (*And Your Mama, Too.*)

Cinema also has been boosted by a new generation of actors, such as Salma Hayek, who was nominated for an Academy Award in 2003 for her title role in the U.S. movie *Frida,* based on the life of artist Frida Kahlo. Another is Gael García, who starred in *Amores perros, Y tu mamá también* and *Padre Amaro.* Both have become international sex symbols; in fact, the media have nicknamed García "Sex-Mex."

Mexico's television industry has been characterized by a mix of public-private cooperation. The privately owned *Televisa* network is today one of the world's largest, and Mexican programs, chiefly *telenovelas,* are the most popular in Latin America. By the mid-1990s, a new Privately owned channel, *TV Azteca,* was making inroads with daring new *telenovelas* that dealt frankly with formerly taboo subjects, such as women's sexuality and official corruption. Some programs began eclipsing *Televisa's* in the ratings.

The Mexican press is nominally independent, but for more than 60 years the Mexican government controlled the supply of newsprint through a subsidized public entity called *Pipsa.* This allowed the *PRI* to wield a powerful cudgel against overly critical newspapers, which often would find their supply of paper cut off. Meaningful reform came with the Salinas administration of 1988–94, but intimidation of the press continues. Mexico is second only to Colombia in the number of journalists murdered each year in Latin America. The press remains largely unbowed, however. About 30 dailies are published in the capital. The paper once regarded as the most prestigious was *Excélsior,* a cooperative owned by its employees, but in recent years its ties to the *PRI* have hurt the paper's credibility and its bottom line. The workers voted in June 2002 to sell the paper because of declining revenues—and lost wages. Newspapers with greater circulation and with better reputations of independence and aggressive reporting today are *El Universal* and *Reforma.*

Mexico has a more vigorous provincial press than do most Latin American countries; in fact, it is these smaller papers in the interior that frequently are the targets of violence by drug traffickers or corrupt local politicians or police officials who themselves have been targeted by aggressive reporters. Probably the most prestigious of these provincial papers is *El Norte* of Monterrey.

Mexico also has a sizable magazine industry, producing slick, high-quality, full-color magazines comparable with those in the United States or Europe. Probably the magazine most read abroad is the left-of-center *Proceso,* launched by Julio Scherer García in 1976 after the thin-skinned President Echeverría forced him from the editorship of *Excélsior* for his critical reporting and editorials.

The new role of the Mexican media in exposing corruption cannot be understated. Many, if not most, of the allegations of wrongdoing stem from journalistic rather than official investigations. A decade ago, this would have been unheard of. The government used the newsprint monopoly as a carrot and stick to keep the print media in line. The owners of the television giant Televisa, meanwhile, were loyal *PRI* partisans. The termination of the newsprint monopoly and the diversification of television with the new network, TV Azteca, with the resulting increase in aggressive, investigative journalism, has been as significant a factor in curtailing the power of the once-omnipotent *PRI* as has the rising electoral strength of the opposition parties. In fact, some have viewed the two parallel developments as a chicken-and-egg analogy—which led to what?

At the same time, investigative journalism in Mexico remains a notoriously high-risk endeavor. Journalists investigating links between drug traffickers and public officials have been murdered or intimidated at an alarming rate since 1997, and by 2004 the number of journalists killed in Mexico was the fourth highest in the world, exceeding the number in Colombia for the first time (see Drugs). This is not to say that all Mexican journalists are martyrs and saints, however. For decades, government officials and *PRI* leaders routinely paid bribes to low-paid reporters to ensure favorable news coverage, or—even better—no news coverage. This tawdry practice has been reduced with the election of opposition governors and an opposition president in 2000.

In addition, it must be conceded that too many Mexican journalists are overly subjective in their reporting and are not above slanting or even distorting the facts to make a story fit into that medium's particular agenda. Still, the fearless reporting of such Mexico City newspapers as *Reforma* and *El Universal,* as well as that of numerous feisty newspapers and magazines along the U.S. border, is a refreshing change from the old days when the press was either cowed or bought, and it has sent many a corrupt official scurrying for cover like cockroaches from a bright light.

Economy: The economy of Mexico is divided into three major sectors: agriculture (20%), industry (30%) and services (50%), a pattern generally associated with advanced nations.

The industrial sector, formerly centered around Mexico City and Monterrey, now is more clustered generally throughout the north, based on factories, called *maquiladoras,* that assemble finished products for export; most are owned by U.S. com-

panies, though joint ventures have become more common.

The quasi-socialist nature of the economy during the seven decades of domination of the *PRI,* and especially after the expropriation of foreign-owned oil companies in 1938, hung a "not welcome" sign for foreign investors. For decades, a foreign national or a foreign business could own only a 49% share of real estate or a business. After the 1960s, government participation in industry increased under the *PRI,* which viewed this as a means of extending party power, accompanied by inefficiency and corruption. In the 1990s this was reversed under former President Salinas. By 1993, more than 363 state-owned companies had been sold or shut down, bringing the government (and *PRI*) more than $22 billion.

The *maquiladora* movement greatly stimulated national development, at least in the north. Mexico's hourly wage was less than half that of the United States, and the workforce was literate. The lure of assembling finished goods just across the border at bargain-basement prices was irresistible to U.S. corporations. Of course, it was anathema to organized labor in the United States. The *maquiladoras* led to a veritable boom along the border, and stimulated growth of a middle class. (By 2000, *maquiladoras* accounted for about 48% of Mexico's exports, compared with 10% for oil exports). The North American Free Trade Agreement (NAFTA) of 1994 accelerated the boom and unquestionably helped the country emerge from the disastrous peso devaluation that year. By 2003, however, Mexico had lost more than 300 companies to China. Double-digit growth in exports returned briefly in 2004, but flattened out again at year's end, largely because of sluggish U.S. industrial output, to which *maquiladora* production is paired.

Petroleum remains the only major government monopoly, but it was a hotbed of *PRI* labor and management corruption. For a time there was talk of privatizing *Pemex,* which controls production from the well-head to distribution at the gasoline station, but public opinion was so vehemently opposed to it that not even the conservative, pro-business government of Vicente Fox pursued it. *Pemex* still accounts for about one third of the federal government's revenue.

In the 1980s, *Pemex* departed from production of sulphur-laden, sub-quality gasoline to include gasoline that meets U.S. standards. This was done to accommodate a burgeoning tourist trade.

Pemex currently is faced with the need to invest in discovery and deep-sea drilling as its existing fields become depleted. Production in 2004-05 was 3.38 million

Mexico

barrels per day, but this was expected to drop by 2006 unless new finds are made. Current reserves are estimated at 16-19 billion barrels, a dramatic drop from more than 28 billion in 1999. *Pemex* lacks deep-sea recovery technology, but contracting with foreign oil firms, even if it means keeping Mexico an exporter rather than an importer, is a political taboo in Mexico.

Mexico has profited enormously from Cuba's economic isolation, especially in tourist income. Various resorts offer complete package vacations to winter-weary neighbors to the north seeking the warm sun. The popularity of these soared in the late 1980s and 1990s as the peso plummeted in value against the dollar. Tourism suffered briefly from the September 11, 2001, terrorist attacks, but it has recovered and is booming. It may be affected again, however, by the proposal of the Bush administration to require Americans to have passports to travel to and from Canada, Mexico, and several Caribbean countries.

Agriculture is limited by a lack of arable land and division of what there is into small parcels. The official policy of the government after the Revolution favored redistribution of land, much of it into communal plots called *ejidos*, but the program moved forward at a glacial pace.

In 1993, Mexico's economy appeared to be blooming, but it was an illusion caused by increased U.S investment in anticipation of the results of the NAFTA treaty. In order to support this image of expansion, Mexico began printing more pesos—too many pesos—in the latter half of 1993 and 1994, diluting their genuine worth. Foreign investors began to demand more and more interest, as high as 33% per annum to compensate for what they decided was greater risk.

The break came on December 20, 1994 when the peso was devalued by 20% and then allowed to "float" four days later, all of which led to its decline of 50% by early 1995. The stock and bond markets panicked, contributing to the decline of the peso. The IMF revealed in 1995 that in the two weeks before the December 1994 devaluation of the peso, individuals and institutions quietly moved $6.7 billion out of Mexico.

The year 1995 was difficult for Mexicans. The peso, devalued by 50% in 1994 and floating in 1995, went down to 7.6 to the dollar (Prior to the devaluation the rate was 3.5). President Clinton proposed massive bailout loans to Mexico totaling $13.5 billion, which he got despite widespread opposition in Congress. More than 16,000 businesses ceased operation and more than 2 million Mexicans lost their jobs in 1995. Banks foreclosed on mortgages and repossessed autos at a record rate; more than 12% of bank loans were in

default (the rate is about 1.2% in the U.S.). The loans were guaranteed by the Mexican equivalent of the Federal Deposit Insurance Corporation, known as *Fobaproa*. An organization of creditors, *El Barzón*, entered the scene, correctly charging that the aid being received by Mexico is being used to help depositors, not debtors. *Fobaproa* became the focus of a major political scandal in 1998 when it was learned that many of the failed banks had made risky loans to *PRI* political cronies (see History).

In January 1997, amid much media hype, Mexico repaid the last installment of the $13.5 billion loan Clinton had authorized to see Mexico through its crisis. Mexico proudly noted that the loan was repaid two years ahead of schedule. What Mexico downplayed was the fact that the loan was repaid by borrowing the necessary amount from European sources.

Since the 1994–95 crisis, the Mexican economy rebounded into one of the healthiest in Latin America, weathering both the drop in oil prices in 1998 and the Brazilian market panic of January 1999. GDP growth since 1997 has averaged a respectable 4.3% per year. Mexico finished 2002 with a GDP of $637.2 billion, second only to Brazil, which was $5,910 per capita, third highest in Latin America after Argentina and Uruguay.

The drop in oil prices was probably responsible for a decline in GDP growth from 7% in 1997 to 4.8% in 1998 to 3.4% in 1999. Growth shot back up to 7.2% for 2000, thanks largely to the continued high price of oil. But the U.S. recession in 2001 and the September 11 terrorist attacks that year proved a double whammy for the Mexican economy. The recession caused trade to plummet, and the terrorist attacks caused a general decrease in tourism, compounded in Mexico's case by the inconveniences caused by tightened security along the border.

Consequently, GDP for 2001 declined by 0.3% and grew by only .9% in 2002, not enough to keep up with the growth in the labor market. In 2003, the economy grew by 1.3%, still sluggish, and in his state of the nation address to Congress in September 2004, a contrite President Fox admitted that the economy had not performed as he had hoped. Growth in 2004 was a far more encouraging 4.4%, and the spike in world oil prices in 2005 will probably have a beneficial effect for Mexico.

The NAFTA-generated boom in the north shrank the unemployment rate, from 5.5% in 1996, 3.7% in 1997, 3.2% in 1998 to a mere 2.8% in 1999 and 2.3% in 2000, the lowest (officially) in Latin America. In 2001, it crept back up to 2.8%. Inflation, meanwhile, declined gradually from 18.6% in 1998 to 13.7% in 2001.

One of the pillars of the Mexican economy for years has been the remittances that Mexican workers in the United States, whether legal or illegal, send home to their families. In the first half of 2003, remittances totaled $6.3 billion, for the first time surpassing direct foreign investment, which was $5.2 billion, or tourism, which was $4.9 billion. Remittances were second only to oil sales, which were $8 billion.

The Future: President Vicente Fox is approaching the final year of his term, largely dismissed as a lame duck who has failed to meet many of his own expectations. He has admitted as much.

Yet, despite failures and disappointments, Fox has assured himself of a place in Mexican—and world—history by ushering in the anticipated new era. Breaking the *PRI*'s stranglehold on the presidency was itself enough of an achievement to rank him with South Africa's Nelson Mandela or Poland's Lech Walesa. He has cracked down on official corruption and drug trafficking. He has held public officials accountable for their actions for the first time. He has diversified and decentralized his government. He has broadened Mexico's foreign policy. He has sought an accounting for past human rights abuses. He has removed the stigma of openly practicing one's Catholicism. Despite a sometimes stormy relationship with the media, he has not resorted to heavy-handed means of intimidation.

Sadly, Fox came close to sullying his own legacy when he stood idly by as the *PAN* deputies in Congress joined with the *PRI* deputies in April 2005 to strip Mexico City Mayor Andrés Manuel López Obrador of the *PRD* of his immunity from prosecution. His conviction on a minor contempt of court charge, a minuscule transgression compared with what *PRI* governors routinely used to get away with, would have disqualified the popular López Obrador from seeking the presidency. Thankfully, Fox saw the error of his ways and had his new attorney general drop the charges. To have done otherwise would have been shamelessly hypocritical for a democratic reformer.

Fox has been less than successful in passing major legislation through the Congress, such as his ambitious—and much needed—economic and energy reform proposals, but even this perceived shortcoming is itself transcendental for Mexico. Heretofore, the *PRI*-controlled Congress was merely a rubber stamp for the wishes of *PRI* presidents. Mexico at long last has an independent legislative branch, so vital for a true system of checks and balances.

So, too, is Mexico's first U.S.-style freedom-of-information act, which took effect in 2003. The law makes government records open to the public, and copies must be surrendered within 20 days of a request. Such openness would have been unheard of under the old *PRI* governments, and the new sunshine law hopefully will prove a boon to investigative journalists. Because of all these things, it will be virtually impossible to return to the Old Mexico, even if Roberto Madrazo and the Dinosaurs win the next election.

Moreover, the partial electoral comeback of the *PRI* in 2003 and 2004, such as its recapturing the governorship of Nuevo León from the *PAN* and of Tlaxcala from the *PRD*, is another reflection of the maturation of Mexico's young democracy. In a true democracy, strong, competitive parties alternate in power. The *PRI* benefited greatly from losing the presidency in 2000, and it cannot afford to abuse its power again in the future.

One troubling factor emerged from the 2003 and 2004 elections: a disturbingly high voter abstention rate. Still, this author remains confident of the long-term prospects for Mexican democracy. Why? Because of the dedication of those who *do* vote. I visited one polling place in a working-class housing development near Guaymas, Sonora, in 2003. Three ballot boxes had been set up under shade trees on a schoolyard. I saw scores of voters lined up under a blazing midday sun in 100-degree heat, patiently waiting to get into the shade to vote.

That evening, in Hermosillo, I visited a polling station set up under the canopy at a *Pemex* gas station, where more than 500 people stood in a serpentine queue in sweltering desert heat waiting to use *one* voting booth! At 6 p.m., when the polls closed, the election official unwisely announced that voting would be cut off. A hue and cry arose from the hundreds of outraged voters still waiting their turn. A heated discussion ensued, in which the election official was reminded that under national electoral law, anyone in line when the polls close must be allowed to vote. The official backed down, and the tedious process continued. This would not have happened in the Old Mexico. The voting continued until 9:30.

How many Americans, I wondered, would be willing to endure such an ordeal to exercise their franchise? I left Mexico more convinced than ever that democracy is taking root, and deeply moved by the grit of the Mexican voters. Thus, it was no surprise to me that the annual *Latinobarómetro* poll of 17 Latin American nations shows that Mexicans' belief that democracy is preferable to any other form of government has not wavered; the percentage was 53% in the first poll in 1996, and it remained at 53% in 2003 and 2004. Mexico is one of only three countries that have not shown a decrease since 1996. Meanwhile, the percentage who believe that authoritarianism can be preferable to democracy in certain circumstances declined from 23% in 1996 to 14% in 2003 and 2004. The peaceful transfer of power in 2000 was probably a factor.

Mexicans are now looking toward the July 2, 2006 presidential election. If polls are correct, the man to watch is López Obrador, who has excited Mexico's poor with his populist message and his competent administration as mayor of Mexico City, a post he relinquished on July 31 to devote himself full-time to his presidential campaign. Recent polls have consistently given him 35% to 40% of the vote. Pundits are speculating whether if he comes to power he will prove a leftist statesman like Brazil's Lula da Silva, or an erratic firebrand like Venezuela's Hugo Chávez. López Obrador himself dismisses the latter possibility, perhaps to calm the jitters of international investors.

If López Obrador wins, the ascension to power of the *PRD* will be almost as historic as Fox's toppling of the *PRI*. As López Obrador is unlikely to enjoy a congressional majority either, it will be his challenge to prove a better consensus-builder than Fox has been.

The polls show there are two tortoises trying to catch up with López Obrador's hare: the *PAN*'s Santiago Creel and the *PRI*'s Roberto Madrazo, who defeated López Obrador for governor of Tabasco in 1994. Creel and Madrazo are virtually tied for second place with about 25% each. But if one thing was learned from the 2000 and 2003 elections, it was that public opinion in Mexico can oscillate wildly, and today's frontrunner can become tomorrow's also-ran.

And let us not forget the moral from Aesop himself: in the end, the hare lost.

Except for the automobiles and the 21st Century clothing, this cobblestoned Plazas of Zacatecas looks much as it did in colonial times.   *Photo by the author*

The Republic of Nicaragua

A Saturday afternoon native dance in the countryside

Area: 49,163 square miles.

Population: 5.4 million

Capital City: Managua.

Climate: Tropical, with distinct wet and dry seasons. Rainfall is heavier on the Atlantic coast, with the heaviest downpours from May to December.

Neighboring Countries: Honduras (North); Costa Rica (South).

Official Language: Spanish.

Other Principal Tongues: English, Indian dialects.

Ethnic Background: *Mestizo* (A mixture of Spanish and Indian, 69%), Caucasian (17%), Negro (9%), Amerindian (5%).

Principal Religion: Roman Catholic Christianity.

Chief Commercial Products: Cotton, coffee, bananas, sugar.

Currency: Córdoba

Gross Domestic Product: US $4.0 billion in 2002 ($370 per capita).

Former Colonial Status: Spanish Colony (1519–1821).

Independence Date: September 15, 1821.

Chief of State: Enrique Bolaños Geyer (b. May 13, 1928), president (since January 10, 2002).

National Flag: Blue, white and blue horizontal stripes with a coat of arms on the white stripe.

Nicaragua is the largest and most sparsely settled of the Central American republics. It has three distinct geographic regions: a triangular mountain extension of the Honduran highlands, with its apex reaching to the San Juan River valley on the Costa Rican frontier; a narrow Pacific coastal plain containing two large lakes (Managua, 32 miles long and Nicaragua, 92 miles long); there is a wider Atlantic coastal plain.

The Pacific plain is part of a trough that runs from the Gulf of Fonseca in the northwest through the two scenic lakes and the San Juan River valley to the Atlantic. This is one of the most promising sites for a new interoceanic canal. There is considerable volcanic activity in the northwestern part of this region. Three volcanoes reaching to some 5,000 feet have emerged from Lake Nicaragua, another stands majestically on the north shore of Lake Managua and some 20 more

lie formidably between the lakes and the Gulf of Fonseca. The moist easterly winds from the Caribbean Sea drench the San Juan River valley and the Atlantic coastal plains, which are heavily forested.

The Pacific coastal plains receive less rainfall and in some parts require flood control and irrigation for agriculture. The majority of Nicaragua's population is found between the western slope of the highlands and the Pacific Ocean. The few settlements on the Atlantic coast were founded by the British and the population in this region is predominantly of African-West Indian origin, with a few pockets of native Miskito Indians.

History: The Spanish conquerors reached Nicaragua from Panama in 1519. They found a fairly dense population of agricultural Maya Indians on the shores of Lake Nicaragua, from whom gold ornaments were acquired. The Spaniards returned in 1524 and founded settlements at Granada and León. By 1570 the flow of gold had ceased, most of the settlers left and the two towns were put under the ad-

Nicaragua

ministration of the captaincy-general of Guatemala.

León, more accessible to the sea, was chosen as the administrative center rather than the larger and more wealthy Granada. The eastern coast was entirely neglected by the Spanish—the towns of Bluefields and Greytown (San Juan del Norte) were established by British loggers cutting mahogany and other valuable timber. By the time of independence, the Lake Nicaragua basin was the site of productive sugar and indigo plantations and the town of Granada was the center of political conservatism. León, the center of less valuable grain and food production and capital of the province, was the seat of anti-clerical political Liberalism.

Independence came to Nicaragua as a by-product of the movements in Mexico and in the South American states. Through the actions of Guatemala, Nicaragua joined Mexico under Iturbide and became a member of the Central American Confederation, but withdrew from it in 1838. The Liberal-Conservative conflict that marked the period was manifested in Nicaragua by an as-yet unsettled feud between the people of Granada and León. Other factors also entered into Nicaraguan problems. British interests established a protectorate over the Atlantic region, known as the Autonomous Kingdom of Miskitia, which was not incorporated into the national territory until 1860. During the 1850s and 1860s, Commodore Cornelius Vanderbilt's transit company became involved in ferrying California-bound gold prospectors across Nicaragua, and the Liberals of León invited William Walker, a U.S. soldier of fortune, to head up their army to crush the Granada Conservatives. At the same time, there were conflicts of British and North American interests who backed the various factions.

Walker's successes in León were such that Vanderbilt was induced to aid the Conservatives of Granada. Walker finally was captured and executed in 1860 and the Conservatives established their dominance, which would endure for 30 years. They quelled numerous uprisings, installed their presidents as became necessary and convenient and gave the country a semblance of stable government. During this period the cultivation of coffee and bananas was started, gold production was resumed and a few immigrants arrived from Europe. However, factional quarrels among the Conservatives made possible a Liberal coup in 1893 and the seizure of power by youthful José Santos Zelaya.

Sixteen years of tyrannical misrule by Santos Zelaya became notorious both at home and abroad. He persecuted his Conservative enemies, betrayed his Liberal supporters and systematically looted both public and private funds. He maintained his position with a ruthless system of spies and police, suppressing all critics. Despite his misrule, the economy prospered, railroads were built and public schools were increased.

His execution of two U.S. adventurers aroused the government of the United States and the dictator fled into exile in 1909; this left the country in a state of near anarchy—the government was bankrupt and foreign creditors were threatening intervention. The Conservatives appealed to Washington to intervene while New York financiers bought up foreign bonds and installed economic supervisors to manage the Nicaraguan economy and insure repayment of their investments.

Liberals revolted against a situation in which their country was the ward of foreign banks in 1912. United States warships landed a few Marines, suppressed the revolt and became involved in a 20-

year war for the elimination of banditry and the establishment of a stable government. While Washington supported Conservatives, Mexico supported Liberals in a see-saw contest. Larger forces of Marines were introduced in 1927 to control the country; the United States tried to resolve the internal Liberal-Conservative conflict through supposedly free and democratic elections. A guerrilla leader fighting against the Marines became a legendary figure in Nicaragua and most of Central America: Augusto César Sandino. A colorful character sporting a 10-gallon hat and six-shooter, he carried on lively correspondence with the commanders of his U.S. opponents.

The Somoza Dynasty

Hoping after six years that things were settled, the U.S. forces left Nicaragua in 1933, with the government in the hands of a Liberal president (Sacasa) and a peace guaranteed by a Marine-trained police force, the *Guardia Nacional*, under the command of Anastasio ("Tacho") Somoza. By 1934 it was obvious that true power lay with the *Guardia* and its commander. Sandino still maintained his guerrilla forces, but had agreed to a cease-fire once the Marines had gone. The government accepted a sweeping amnesty for Sandino's men, additionally offering them land and jobs.

Nicaragua

Augusto César Sandino

Things might have settled down if the Nicaraguan Congress had not voted to raise the salary of Sandino's 100-man personal guard and shortly afterwards to reduce the pay of the military. Further, Sandino's followers had not turned in all of their arms. The *Guardia* decided that Sandino had to be eliminated. A supposedly innocent President Sacasa invited Sandino to the presidential palace to discuss outstanding issues, where there were several meetings. But after a farewell following supper one evening, the *Guardia* met Sandino at the gate, took him and his men to the airfield, where they were executed and secretly buried.

Anastasio Somoza ruled until his assassination in 1955 and Congress named his son, Luis, to the presidency, which he occupied until 1963. The elections that year were relatively quiet and honest.

In 1967, Anastasio ("Tachito") Somoza Debayle became the third member of the family to occupy the presidency. Barred by law from succeeding himself, Somoza created a caretaker three-man *junta* in 1971 to rule until 1974, when he was elected to a second term with 91.7% of the vote. Somoza was a "Liberal" in name only. Nine small opposition parties were barred from the election.

Anastasio Somoza's second term would be his last. Resentment against the regime grew as increasing numbers of Nicaraguans objected to his heavy-handed tactics. His brutal treatment of political opponents convinced many that the regime would never tolerate democratic elections in the country. The business community was bitter and angry with Somoza's levying of kickbacks on the major commercial transactions conducted in the country. Residents of Managua were outraged by the *junta*'s blatant misuse of international aid earmarked for the city's reconstruction following a disastrous 1972 earthquake. Most Liberals and leftists were offended by the strongman's ostentatious display of wealth: his family owned a half billion dollars worth of investments and 8,260 square miles of Nicaragua, while 200,000 peasants were landless.

Revolution

For the first time, opponents of the regime began to unite—joined by one thing: *anti*-Somoza feelings (but little else). A broad-based coalition—ranging from Marxist guerrillas to conservative business leaders—was formed. While the business sector continued its strikes to dry up the economy, the guerrillas battled the National Guard.

Many groups which helped oust Somoza, wittingly or unwittingly, joined together with the Sandinista National Liberation Front (*FSLN*), named after the legendary nationalist guerrilla leader of the 1930s.

Actually, the origin of the group carrying this name was in the early 1960s under the auspices of Cuba's Fidel Castro. The *FSLN* grew rapidly when Anastasio Somoza became president. His brutal and corrupt rule pumped new life into the guerrilla movement. As the *Sandinistas* gained strength from association by noncommunist elements, Somoza retaliated with sweeping attacks against rural peasants suspected of aiding the guerrillas—ironically, a tactic that caused many peasants to join them. Mass support for the *FSLN* developed further following the violent earthquake that leveled Managua in December 1972 when it became known that Somoza was pocketing some of the international relief funds and buying up Managua real estate at fire-sale prices.

While the *Guardia* enjoyed a 4-to-1 manpower edge, the *Sandinistas* and associates boasted a force of 3,000 members by 1978. It was actually divided into three groups: two openly Marxist and a third—by far the largest—consisting of socialists and non-Marxist leftist trade unionists, Catholic Church members and a sprinkling of businessmen. Known as the *Terceristas* (Insurrectionists), this last group is best remembered for its daring 1978 occupation of the National Palace in Managua.

Collapse of the Regime

The crucial jolt in the long train of events leading to the overthrow of the Somoza regime came in January 1978, when assassins gunned down Pedro Joaquín Chamorro, longtime Conservative Party critic and publisher of the nation's leading newspaper, *La Prensa*. Although the identity of the killers remains unknown, most Nicaraguans attributed the murder to Somoza. Chamorro was widely respected—10,000 attended his funeral—and his death quickly touched off three days of bloody demonstrations throughout the nation. The *Guardia* responded in a heavy-handed manner; its ruthless mop-up operations in five major cities left 3,000 dead. The Chamorro murder, combined with the *Guardia*'s indiscriminate killing of many innocent bystanders, cost the regime the vital support of business leaders who then called for a general strike to demand Somoza's resignation. The strike brought more government reprisals. As the death toll mounted, the United States proposed a referendum to test national support for the Somoza regime. The plan was quickly rejected by the strongman in early 1979 because he insisted "If they want me to leave Nicaragua, they'll only get me out by force."

The *Sandinistas* were only too willing to oblige him. During its final two years in power, the Somoza regime faced a basic military problem: it seemed to be under attack throughout the country. The only significant Nicaraguan sector that continued to support the dictatorship was, as always, the *Guardia*. Meanwhile, the guerrillas continued to score important victories in rural areas, while major power groups in the cities were becoming more militant in their opposition to the strongman. One by one, rural areas began to fall under rebel control and by the spring of 1979 it was clear that Somoza could not endure much longer.

The Nicaraguan leader refused to budge. Secluded in his Managua bunker—a grim

Anastasio Somoza Debayle

264

Sandinistas **celebrate Somoza's overthrow, 1979**

reminder of the last days of World War II in Berlin—Somoza continued to direct the military activities of his *Guardia*. Curiously, Somoza made the same tactical error committed by Hitler during the battle for Stalingrad. Both men ordered heavy bombing of civilian areas in order to deny the enemy food and shelter. In both cases, however, the bombed-out buildings provided ideal concealment from which the defenders could fight back. In Nicaragua, the *Guardia*'s bombing of populated areas killed virtually no guerrillas—but it did further solidify public opinion against Somoza.

Along with the heavy shelling of civilian areas, Somoza also ordered the summary execution of suspected opponents of his regime. Many of these were youths, whose blindfolded and bound bodies were often found strewn along the shores of Lake Managua. During the final two years of fighting, thousands were killed and left homeless.

By late May 1979, ranking members of the regime began to flee the country. Somoza himself finally abandoned his bunker and flew to the United States, where he boarded a luxury yacht for a leisurely trip to Paraguay, to be given refuge by the Stroessner regime of that country. Thus ended one of the most durable dictatorships—46 years—in Latin American history.

He lasted only 14 months in Paraguay, however, before he was gunned down by three persons reported to be Argentine guerrillas. He had become depressed, drank to excess and grew fat. Before

his death, he was involved in a much-publicized love affair with a former Miss Paraguay—who also happened to be the mistress of Stroessner's son-in-law.

The Sandinista Era

On July 19, 1979, the *Sandinistas* took control of Managua—and a *new* revolution was about to start. Their non-communist allies in the revolution had little power within the new government.

After Somoza's ouster, the country was administered by a three-member *junta* called the Revolutionary Junta Government (*JRG*). One of the three was Violeta Barrios de Chamorro, widow of the assassinated journalist. This group, in turn, followed policy directives established by a nine-member *Sandinista* National Directorate, controlled by the *FSLN*. Power was shared with a Council of State, a *Sandinista*-dominated legislative body of 47 members representing various political and economic groups as well as the armed forces and the *FSLN*.

Although the Marxist influence was clearly in evidence—especially in the schools, the armed forces and the media—the government was initially primarily nationalistic. But in international relations, Nicaragua quickly joined the non-aligned bloc of Third World nations while also establishing close ties with communist-bloc nations. The regime refused to condemn the Soviet invasion of Afghanistan and in 1982 supported Argentina's invasion of the British Falkland Islands. Trade pacts were signed with various communist na-

tions, including Bulgaria, East Germany, the Soviet Union and Cuba.

Relations became particularly close with the Castro regime of Cuba. Almost all communist *Sandinista* leaders visited Havana and in mid-1980 Fidel Castro was guest of honor in Managua for the revolution's first anniversary celebration. As many as 6,000 Cuban "advisers" were stationed in Nicaragua; hundreds of Nicaraguan youths were sent to Cuba for educational programs that stressed Marxism.

Increased ties with communist nations led to strained relations with the United States. Some powerful members of the U.S. Congress regarded the *Sandinista* regime as a threat to Central America. Although the Carter administration provided some financial aid to Nicaragua in the hope of strengthening the prodemocratic forces there, the Reagan administration responded with a tough stance against what it concluded was a Soviet-sponsored client state within the Central American area.

Thus, Washington suspended all aid to Nicaragua in the spring of 1981 after the State Department accused the *Sandinistas* of aiding leftist guerrillas in El Salvador. In late 1981, the Reagan administration again denounced Nicaragua for "arms trafficking to El Salvador," and for building the largest military force "in the history of Central America." In early 1982, Reagan lectured Nicaragua's new ambassador to the United States against "adopting alien influence and philosophies in the hemisphere."

The Pentagon unveiled huge CIA aerial photos in 1982 to prove that Cuba and the

Nicaragua

Soviet Union were providing sophisticated military equipment to Nicaragua. Newly enlarged Nicaraguan airfields could be used for bombing raids against the Panama Canal, according to some U.S. officials. Several days later, a badly informed U.S. State Department staged a highly publicized press conference to display a Nicaraguan guerrilla who had been captured in El Salvador. But when the cameras started rolling, the Nicaraguan coolly accused his captors of torture. State Department officials, highly embarrassed by the incident, promptly deported the man to Nicaragua (where he received a hero's welcome). Later, Nicaraguan strongman Daniel Ortega Saavedra called an urgent meeting of the U.N. Security Council to protest "aggressive and destabilizing acts" by the United States against his country. In June 1982, Washington accused Nicaragua of firing on a U.S. helicopter over international waters near the Nicaraguan coast (The United States recognizes a 12-mile territorial limit; Nicaragua claims 200 miles).

Despite the running conflict, both countries made very unenthusiastic efforts to negotiate. In April 1982, Washington gave the *Sandinistas* a list of proposals for improved ties. When Managua promptly responded with its own set of counterproposals, the Reagan administration delayed two months before replying. The reason: Washington thought that deteriorating economic conditions at home and exile opposition from abroad might doom the *Sandinista* regime.

The "Stolen" Revolution

What had been envisioned by in some U.S. circles as a pluralistic revolution in Nicaragua was not correctly evaluated. There were many elements joined together in the anti-Somoza struggle, but only one had cohesiveness: the *FSLN*. It was natural that upon the departure of So-

moza this organization would assume a position of power. At first, other groups were allowed nominally to participate, but in 1982-83 the true nature of the *FSLN* became apparent, although during the revolutionary struggle the Marxist nature of the movement had a very low profile. There was no difficulty in initially enlisting the support of *La Prensa* and the Roman Catholic Church. Thus, although U.S. conservatives charged that the *Sandinistas* "stole" the revolution, such an accusation was not accurate. They simply filled a political vacuum and then refused to share it with any other Nicaraguan element. They insisted, on the contrary, that all Nicaraguans accept the *Sandinistas* as the only political force in the country—an expectation that was never met. In 1984, Ortega was elected president by a predictably wide margin. The opposition was divided and denied access to the media.

During more than 10 years in power, the *Sandinista* regime succeeded in generating widespread disillusionment and disappointment within Nicaragua. Anti-*Sandinista* rallies and meetings were broken up in 1981 and were later totally prohibited. A prominent leftist within the regime resigned, accusing the *Sandinistas* of planting "a reign of terror . . . a Soviet style Stalinist regime in Nicaragua."

The press that was not directly seized by the government was regularly harassed; *La Prensa* soon became the only non-government newspaper that quickly came to face daily government inspection and approval. Mrs. Chamorro, the publisher, resigned from the *junta* as a result. International credit quickly evaporated as the United States withdrew loan promises and private foreign banks balked at extensions of credit. The treasury had been emptied by Somoza, compounding the problems of the fledgling government.

Human rights violations sharply increased. Ultimately, an estimated 10,000 people, including former Somoza sup-

porters and former members of the *Guardia*, were jailed and other opponents were sent into exile. A dispute between the government and the Miskito Indians (who had been given a large measure of independence under Somoza) was provoked when the Miskitos were accused of aiding counter-revolutionary Somoza exiles living in Honduras. When the government attempted to resettle about 10,000 tribe members away from border areas, an estimated 20,000 fled to Honduras from where they started to harass the *Sandinistas*. The government responded by raiding Miskito settlements along the border in early 1982, leaving an estimated 105 dead. This would lead in the future to an alliance between the Indians and the "*Contras*."

Following a visit by Pope John Paul II in 1982, the Vatican adopted firm policies and selected personnel opposed to the regime.

Faced with acute money problems, the government desperately sought aid in 1982 from Cuba, the Soviet Union and other sources. The only response was inconsequential—it came from Libya.

For four years Nicaragua faced charges from abroad that a repressive dictatorship had taken hold of the country. In 1985, President Reagan requested military aid for the *Contras* ("antis"), a loosely-organized but relatively effective opposition to the regime. It had been armed by the CIA. Congress refused, but did allow $14 million for "humanitarian" aid. Ortega, meanwhile, received *pledges* of $200 million from Moscow, much to the embarrassment of Congress. Reagan imposed a total economic embargo on Nicaragua.

The state-controlled economy ultimately shrank to about one-third of the level that existed before *Sandinista* power. Crops were not harvested because of military pressures and the unwillingness of farmers to accept artificially low prices. Foreign aid and assistance dried up by

Daniel Ortega exhorts a group of students about the spirit of the *Sandinista* revolution

Nicaragua

Signing of the Summit Agreement

1987 when the final stages of a precipitous decline was underway in the former Soviet Union and its client, Cuba. Shortages were rampant and housing was shabby and crumbling.

Between 1985 and 1989 the U.S. Congress did not distinguish itself in dealing with the question of Central American "communism" and Nicaragua in particular. Reasons for its vacillating attitude were fashionable, but evasive: (1) "no more Vietnams," (2) we must *force* the *Sandinistas* to negotiate and (3) lack of *Contra* unity. At election time, aid for the *Contras* was provided lest there be an accusation that members of Congress were "soft on communism."

A last-ditch effort was made to overcome the *Contras* located in neighboring Honduras in 1988; the *Sandinista* effort was repulsed when two battalions of highly trained U.S. troops were sent to that country.

The Arias Plan

Signed by the leaders of Costa Rica, El Salvador, Guatemala, Honduras and Nicaragua meeting at Guatemala City on August 7, 1987, the Arias peace plan obligated the *Sandinistas* to negotiate a cease-fire with the *Contras*, allow freedom of the press and other media, cease political repression and allow free, open and democratic elections. Support of rebel forces in adjoining nations would be banned. It further provided for monitoring of all requirements by National Conciliation Commissions which would include government opposition, Church officials and Inter-American Human Rights Commission representatives. It appeared doomed to failure, since such conditions, if allowed to exist in Nicaragua, would lead to the replacement of *Sandinista* control.

Ortega, who signed the agreement, is an educated, but intellectually dishonest person, as were his cohorts of the *Sandinista* junta. He probably viewed the instrument only as a means to indefinitely lure the U.S. House of Representatives into continuing denial of military aid to the *Contras*, and to postpone the day of reckoning. Negotiations with the *Contras* and internal opposition groups began in early October 1987. They broke down immediately—the *Sandinistas* announced that "there will never, at any time or any place, be any direct *political* dialogue with the *Contras*." The impasse continued until Cardinal Obando y Bravo volunteered to mediate talks between the parties. His efforts were short-lived: the *Sandinistas* were firm in their ultimatum that they were present to receive a military surrender from the *Contras*, not to discuss politics. The Cardinal walked out in disgust in January 1988, accusing the *Sandinistas* of negotiating in bad faith.

La Prensa and *Radio Católico* were allowed to resume their activities during the first week in October 1987. But they were again shut down for 15 days in the spring of 1988.

The *Sandinistas* declared a unilateral cease-fire in early 1988, *not* because of the Arias peace plan, but because of dire economic conditions within Nicaragua and again, with the intent to lull the U.S. House of Representatives into inactivity. The cease-fire was extended repeatedly into 1990.

The Ortega strategy worked temporarily for the *Sandinistas*. When former President Reagan requested $37 million in aid for the *Contras*, 10% of which would be military, the House rejected it, voting in favor again of humanitarian aid. In 1989, the Bush administration didn't even bother to ask for military assistance for the

Contras, but had to settle for more humanitarian aid. To counter this, the administration linked world-wide arms reduction sought by the Soviet Union to reduced arms supply for Nicaragua.

Faced with economic and political bankruptcy, the *Sandinistas* engaged in a transparent effort to rig elections set for February 25, 1990, particularly insofar as it tried to control the media.

Chamorro Upsets Ortega

As the elections approached, it was clear that the *Sandinistas* were uneasy about the outcome. A cease-fire with the *Contras* was canceled, but the half-hearted military effort which followed was ineffective. Ortega took to the campaign trail. He discarded his khakis and appeared in a variety of costumes and said anything to please everybody, swinging his hips to rock music. Television and newspapers were full of propaganda extolling the party, and political rallies were held at which balloons and other trinkets were distributed. The *FSLN* outspent the opposition, the National Opposition Union (*UNO*), by at least 10–1.

The *UNO* candidate was Violeta Chamorro, widow of the publisher slain in 1978 under the Somoza regime. One observer labeled the *UNO* campaign as amateurish. *Sandinista* efforts were stepped up, including crude efforts such as bludgeoning those attending opposition rallies.

A Washington Post-ABC poll published on February 21, 1990 predicted a *Sandinista* triumph by a margin of 48% to 32%. Even though the headline read "Pre-Election Poll Shows Ortega Leads," there were, in the article, strong disclaimers as to the poll's accuracy. The pollsters might well have listened to a wizened farmer, who said "Only I know what I am going to do on my ballot."

Chamorro and the *UNO* won by 55.2% to 40.8%! Even the White House was startled. She was sworn in on April 25. After her inaugural, Nicaragua's slim hope for improved conditions evaporated swiftly. Much to the dismay of most participants in *UNO*, she appointed Humberto Ortega, brother of Daniel, to continue as defense minister. However, she reduced the army from about 80,000 to zero on the ground that it was no longer needed. There remained shadowy, informal armed forces, used to protect property seized by the *Sandinistas* by "law" between the time of Chamorro's election and the time she assumed office.

Following her inauguration, the disbanding of the army and the *Contras* added tremendously (almost 100,000) to the rolls of the unemployed, which rose to more than 50% of the workforce. Few Nicara-

Nicaragua

guan exiles returned; the wealthy ones in particular, who took much of their money with them, remained outside the country. Conditions on farms, prosperous in the 1970s, were—and still are—dreadful. Many that were split up and given to peasants and *Sandinista* fighters were idle, with little hope of restoring production. Potential investment capital was being withheld from Nicaragua.

Lower-level *Sandinistas* deserted the *FSLN,* as did former low-income supporters of the movement. The more affluent *Sandinistas* clung tenaciously to that which they acquired during their years in power. The *UNO* coalition in the National Assembly turned on Mrs. Chamorro, claiming she betrayed the elections of 1990. All she was able to speak about (vaguely) was "reconciliation" of Nicaragua.

With the *Sandinistas* in charge of the army, the police and the judiciary, Nicaragua was far from democratic. The president ignored the Assembly and formed an "inner cabinet" to rule the nation. She particularly relied on her son-in-law, Antonio Lacayo, in making crucial decisions that favored the top-drawer *Sandinistas.* The *Sandinista*-controlled Supreme Court nullified all actions of the National Assembly after September 2, 1992, on the dubious grounds that on that date it lacked a quorum! Its ruling was ignored.

The U.S. Congress appropriated $104 million in aid for Nicaragua to be released to it in 1992. Citing a U.S. law that forbids foreign aid to be granted to a country that has confiscated the property of U.S. owners without compensation, a senator demanded that the money be held up in the spring of 1992; it was. A team dispatched by the United States demanded the firing of army commander Ortega, discharge of the police chief and judicial reform, in addition to compensation, as the price for the aid. Chamorro did fire the police chief and said she would "discuss" compensation of U.S. owners, specifying no time limit for the latter. President Bush reluctantly released $50 million in December.

Following President Clinton's inauguration, Nicaraguan officials intensely lobbied the U.S. Congress for release of the remainder. On April 1, 1993, the Clinton administration sent the funds as requested, citing "important strides that have been made by the Nicaraguan government." An offended senator charged that the money was sent to a "government of thugs" and the decision was a "bad April Fool's joke come true."

The Chamorro government promised that Humberto Ortega would leave as army commander . . . in late 1995, by retirement. Continued U.S. pressure resulted in the announcement that Ortega would be removed in 1994 instead of 1995;

he was put under house arrest in early 1994 because of alleged involvement in a 1990 crime.

Humberto Ortega finally retired in early 1995, but his chief of staff was named to succeed him, thus continuing *Sandinista* control of the military. Six years after being elected by hopeful Nicaraguans who had "voted with their stomachs," Chamorro had proven totally incapable of raising Nicaragua out of its abject poverty.

The Alemán Presidency

Sensing an opportunity for a comeback, Daniel Ortega announced his candidacy for the October 20, 1996, presidential election. He entered the race an underdog behind the popular and conservative former mayor of Managua, Arnoldo Alemán, the candidate of the Liberal Alliance, like Ortega, 50 years old. Gone were Ortega's *Sandinista* uniform and his Marxist rhetoric, which he realized had helped defeat him in 1990. Six weeks before the election, the *Sandinistas* even softened the lyrics of their truculent anthem, removing the reference to "the Yankees, enemies of mankind."

Opinion polls indicated that the rehabilitated Ortega, preaching a more social democratic gospel, was running even with Alemán and might be given another chance to lead Nicaragua out of the mess he had helped to create. With 23 candidates on the ballot, there appeared little likelihood that any one of them could garner the necessary 45% to avoid a runoff. But once again, the Nicaraguan voters startled prognosticators by giving Alemán a decisive first-round victory of 48.4% to Ortega's 38.6%—even less than Ortega had obtained in 1990.

Ortega immediately—and unconvincingly—cried fraud. A delegation of observers from the Organization of American States—including longtime *Sandinista* apologist Jimmy Carter and former Secretary of State James Baker—concluded there was no evidence of any major irregularities. Carter was instrumental in persuading his friend Ortega to accept the results rather than resorting to mass protests as he had threatened to do.

The 1997 transition was to prove far more tense than that of 1990. Where Chamorro had pragmatically and almost with flattery sought to placate the *Sandinistas* whom she knew could easily overthrow her, Alemán was confrontational. But then, he had a personal score to settle with the *Sandinistas.* A onetime supporter of Somoza, Alemán had five farms confiscated by the *Sandinistas* in the 1980s. In 1989, while he was under house arrest, the *Sandinistas* refused even to allow him to accompany his wife, who was dying of can-

cer, to a hospital. Nor were the *Sandinistas* fond of Alemán.

A lawyer by profession, Alemán had been elected mayor of Managua in the same 1990 election that brought Chamorro to power. Like Guatemala's President Alvaro Arzú, Alemán compiled an impressive record of achievement as mayor of the capital city, which still felt the effects of the 1972 earthquake. He greatly improved the traffic engineering system and beautified the city. He also removed the *Sandinistas'* revolutionary art from walls and billboards.

Alemán was inaugurated on January 10, 1997 for a term that had been reduced to five years, marking the first time in Nicaraguan history that one duly elected civilian president had succeeded another. Seven Latin American presidents attended the ceremony, which was marred by the arrest of a former *Sandinista* security officer and two other men who were carrying four sticks of dynamite. Nonetheless, Alemán delivered a conciliatory inaugural address, offering a dialogue with the archrival *Sandinistas.* At first, the *Sandinistas* appeared resistant to his overtures and continued their bombastic threats to take their opposition into the streets. Yet, perhaps faced with the reality that they could no longer marshal the kind of public support they once enjoyed, the Ortega brothers met privately with Alemán in late January to discuss dialogue and conciliation.

Alemán displayed a take-charge attitude, promising to reverse the *Sandinistas'* opposition to free-market capitalism and to make Nicaragua more attractive to foreign investors in order to bring in desperately needed capital. He also proposed to

Former President Arnoldo Alemán

Street scene in Bluefields on the Caribbean Sea

greatly expand the free-trade zone Chamorro established in 1992, which attracted Mexican-style *maquiladora* assembly plants, mostly for apparel. Alemán said he hoped to greatly expand the output and create thousands of jobs to alleviate the country's punishing 52% rate of unemployment and underemployment.

Alemán's most controversial and divisive proposal was the plan to return land expropriated by the *Sandinistas* to its former owners, compensating the new owners with government bonds. After months of bickering between the Liberals and the *FSLN*, the two major parties came to realize the delay in resolving the title issue was hurting Nicaragua economically by discouraging foreign investment. Moreover, the United States was leaning on Alemán to resolve the issue because of the thousands of Nicaraguans displaced by the Revolution who were residing in the United States. By an overwhelming 70-4, the National Assembly approved a compromise measure that essentially verified the current ownership of most of the 1 million hectares the *Sandinistas* had seized. The new law granted title to those who received rural plots of less than 35 hectares or urban plots of less than 100 square meters. About 5,000 pre-revolutionary landowners thus were frustrated in their hopes of getting their property back.

In 1998, the *Sandinistas* continued to suffer reversals of fortune. In January, the official *FSLN* newspaper *Barricada*, which had been the pro-Somoza daily *Noticias* before it was expropriated in 1979, succumbed to the loss of government subsidies and ceased publication. Its editors accused the Alemán government of retribution through the withholding of government advertising, a time-honored practice of Latin American strongmen, but

their protests carried a hollow ring given the *Sandinistas'* own intimidation and censorship of the independent media when they were in power. *Barricada* subsequently reopened in March 2000.

Another blow, which threatened the very unity of the *FSLN*, came as a bombshell. In March 1998, Ortega's 30-year-old stepdaughter, Zoilamérica Narváez, publicly accused him in an interview in a daily newsletter of having sexually abused her for years, beginning when she was 11 and continuing into the years that

he was president. Narvaez's estranged husband, Alejandro Bendaña, like her a committed *Sandinista* and Ortega's former deputy foreign minister, denounced his former boss' "abuse of power."

Ortega immediately and adamantly denied the accusation, as did his common-law wife, Rosario Murillo, Narváez's mother. Ortega supporters inexplicably denounced the charges as "politically motivated" and even accused Narváez of participating in a CIA plot to undermine Ortega. The leader of the Liberals in the Assembly, Eliseo Nuñez, accused Ortega of hiding behind his legislative immunity and called on him to resign. With the storm of controversy swirling around him, Ortega issued a plea for party unity. It appeared to have worked; in May, he was reelected as *Sandinista* leader. Almost simultaneously, however, Narváez filed a formal civil suit against her stepfather and also accused high-level *Sandinistas* of aiding and abetting in the sex abuse. Ortega claimed parliamentary immunity, and for weeks the Nicaraguan media reported almost daily "no-I-didn't-yes-you-did" exchanges between Ortega and Narváez.

In April, Ortega attempted to divert attention from the sex scandal. In a mass demonstration, he called Alemán a "dictator" because of his move to re-establish a state security agency similar to that of the Somoza period. Ortega hinted darkly that if the president threatened human rights—as though he himself hadn't—the

Nicaraguan cowboy

Nicaragua

Sandinistas may be called upon "to take up arms." Alemán responded to this sinister suggestion on radio, calling on Ortega to "bury forever the hatchet of war and the rifle of death and let Nicaragua emerge from the poverty in which he left it."

In late October and early November 1998, Alemán faced a far greater adversary even than Ortega: Hurricane Mitch. The storm killed 2,863 Nicaraguans, 948 were missing and more than 867,000 were affected. Seventy-one bridges were destroyed, 70% of the roads were damaged and 30% of the banana crop was wiped out; Mitch also wiped out any hopes of immediate economic recovery. Only Honduras suffered greater devastation. International relief aid poured in to alleviate the appalling human suffering.

Although there was no evidence that this president profited from the disaster as Somoza had with the 1972 earthquake, Alemán was accused of enriching himself while on the public payroll. In February 1999, Comptroller General Agustín Jarquín, a member of the Social Christian Party and a longtime political rival of Alemán's, issued a report alleging that the president had increased his personal wealth by 900% between 1990, when he was elected mayor of Managua, and 1997, his first full year as president. Alemán did not dispute the increase but maintained it had come from property in Nicaragua and Miami that he had inherited from his parents and from his wife's family. He countered that Jarquín was merely out to get him.

Alemán counterattacked in November 1999, when the national police chief, before a crowd of journalists, arrested Jarquín and a well-known television journalist on supposed fraud charges. An appeals court subsequently dismissed the charges.

The Power-Sharing Accord

A major political development occurred in June 1999 whose long-term implications are still uncertain. The long-antagonistic Liberals and *Sandinistas* suddenly concluded an agreement by which they would cooperate in governing the country and would apportion seats on the Supreme Court and the electoral council between them. The agreement also would have the effect of reducing the number of frivolous individual presidential candidacies; 23 people had appeared on the 1996 ballot. On the surface, it seemed a welcome respite from the partisan bickering that had plagued the country. However, the minor parties charged—with some degree of justification—that the new pact was designed merely to divide the country's political spoils between the two major parties and exclude all others from a place at the public trough. Similar bipartisan pacts had existed in Colombia and Venezuela.

As Alemán entered the last year of his five-year term, he could point to a dramatically improving economy as foreign investment poured into the country and shopping malls began to spring up, a sign of a growing consumer economy. But the charges of corruption took a toll on the president's popularity and even his control over his party. A poll taken by a Swedish firm in April 2000 showed that 88% of Nicaraguans believed Alemán was corrupt.

Moreover, members of the president's party, now called the Constitutionalist

The Metropolitan Cathedral of León, considered the finest examples of colonial architecture in Central America

Liberal Party (*PLC*), voiced displeasure over the president's autocratic method of hand-picking party candidates for the November 2000 municipal elections. They also alleged that his call for a constitutional convention was aimed at allowing him to run for reelection. In May, Defense Minister Antonio Alvarado resigned, citing his disagreement with Alemán on the selection of candidates and his call for a constitutional convention. He also hinted he might run for president in 2001.

About the same time, Alemán's brother-in-law, Eddy Gomez, who reportedly was angered that he was not chosen as the Liberal candidate for mayor of Managua, resigned his seat in the Central American Parliament and joined the opposition Nationalist Liberal Party, which is identified with the defunct Somoza dictatorship. In the end, there was no constitutional convention, so Alemán was barred from seeking reelection.

The effect of the unholy political pact between the *PLC* and the *FSLN*, two parties with decidedly undemocratic ancestries, was seen clearly in the November 2000 municipal elections. The two major parties, through questionable challenging of the signatures of voters on party registration petitions, disqualified all parties but themselves from participating. In the voting, the *FSLN* won 11 of the 17 departments, and captured the mayoralty of Managua under the candidacy of Herty Lewites, one of the party's moderates.

The Elections of 2001

The *PLC* and the *FSLN* continued their heavy-handed treatment of other parties in the 2001 presidential race as well. Through their control of the Electoral Council, they denied registration to Jarquín's Social Christian Party, the National Unity Movement of former army commander Joaquín Cuadra and the fledgling party organized by former Defense Minister Alvarado, among others. Only the venerable Conservative Party was allowed to compete with the two major parties.

Denied registration for his own party, Jarquín made a bid to challenge Ortega for the *FSLN* presidential nomination. But in June 2001, the *Sandinistas* decided to stick with Ortega. The *PLC*, meanwhile, had nominated former Vice President Enrique Bolaños, then 73, who had resigned the previous October to make the run. The Conservatives' standard-bearer was Noel Vidaurre.

When Ortega formally began his fourth campaign for the presidency—symbolically, on July 19, 2001, the 22nd anniversary of the *Sandinistas'* defeat of Somoza—polls showed that he had a much better

than even chance to stage a dramatic political comeback. Bolaños, who himself enjoyed a reputation for personal honesty, was nonetheless tarnished by his association with the unpopular Alemán, who was stonewalling queries into how he had increased his personal wealth nine-fold between 1990 and 1997.

To further enhance his chances, Ortega broadened his political base by enticing prominent former *Sandinista* opponents to join his new coalition, called the Convergence. Chief among them was Jarquín, whom Ortega persuaded to become his running mate. Ortega also sought to sanitize his former guerrilla image even more than he had in 1996, abandoning the familiar black and red *Sandinista* colors in favor of the less threatening pink, and as a campaign slogan he adopted, "The Path to Love." He embraced the Liberals' free-market policies, and he even pledged to continue the Liberals' close ties with the United States. His victory appeared all but certain.

But as the November 4 election drew ever nearer, Ortega's lead in the polls shrank. Meanwhile, the Vidaurre, reportedly under U.S. pressure not to divide the anti-*Sandinista* vote, withdrew. After the September 11 terrorist attacks on the United States, Ortega vowed, if elected, to cooperate in the war against terrorism. Bolaños, however, effectively countered him with embarrassing televisions ads that showed then-President Ortega embracing Libyan leader Muammar Qadhafi and Iraqi dictator Saddam Hussein, both suspected of supporting Islamic terrorism. Ortega was stung further in October when two of his erstwhile protégés, Sergio Ramirez, who had been his vice president, and Father Ernesto Cardenal, his foreign minister, announced that they would boycott the election because, they complained, neither Ortega nor Bolaños was "worthy."

The U.S. ambassador, in a startling breach of protocol, appeared openly at Bolaños rallies and said in interviews that an

---

Nicaragua

Ortega victory could jeopardize the future of crucial U.S. aid. Even Florida Gov. Jeb Bush, brother of the U.S. president, got into the act by urging the thousands of resident Nicaraguans in Florida to vote for Bolaños.

On election day, Nicaraguan voters once again confounded the pollsters and handed Ortega his third successive humiliating defeat, 56% to 43.5%, prompting jubilant Liberals to take to the streets chanting, "Three strikes, you're out!" Ortega once again graciously conceded defeat, and an equally magnanimous Bolaños praised the *Sandinistas* as "worthy opponents."

In the balloting for the 90-seat National Assembly, the Liberals retained their majority with 49 seats to 40 for the *Sandinistas* and one for the Conservatives. In addition, under the Liberal-*Sandinista* pact, the retiring president (Alemán) and the losing presidential candidate (Ortega) both received seats in the Assembly—thus assuring Ortega continued immunity from his stepdaughter's molestation charges and Alemán from charges of illegal enrichment. Ortega subsequently renounced his legislative immunity—once the statute of limitations for prosecuting rape had expired.

The Bolaños Presidency

Bolaños was inaugurated on January 10, 2002. Almost immediately, he launched an anti-corruption campaign that soon had him at odds with his predecessor. Alemán was charged with involvement in a $1.5 million embezzlement scheme at the state-owned television station. Bolaños sought to have Alemán, who had been elected president of the National Assembly, stripped of his legislative immunity. Alemán lashed out at Bolaños as "inept" and called the investigation a "witch hunt" that was "politically motivated."

In August 2002, federal prosecutors unveiled additional evidence against Alemán and his associates that was of mind-boggling proportions. They allegedly had channeled nearly $100 million in public funds to a phantom foundation in Panama. At a time when Nicaragua was desperately trying to emerge from its economic straits, the revelations that the president and his cronies may have enriched themselves on such a scale stirred outrage. It also deepened the schism between the Bolaños faction of the *PLC* and the so-called *Arnoldistas*.

Yet, Bolaños stepped up his pressure on the Assembly to strip Alemán of his immunity, and the opposition *Sandinistas*—among them, ironically, Ortega—joined that chorus. But the *Arnoldistas* enjoyed a one-seat majority, and they stonewalled the attempts to prosecute their leader. As the damning evidence and the public outrage mounted, however, Alemán's support began to erode. On September 19, 2002, the Bolaños faction and the *FMLN* mustered 47 votes to remove Alemán as Assembly president; there was one abstention, while 44 *Arnoldistas* boycotted the session rather than face certain defeat.

In October, Bolaños suddenly found himself entangled in his own anti-corruption net when a federal prosecutor—who admitted being a friend of Alemán's—filed charges accusing the president of having illegally channeled foreign donations into his 2001 campaign fund. Like Alemán, Bolaños maintained his innocence and dismissed the charges as politically motivated, but unlike Alemán he voluntarily renounced his executive immunity and vowed to clear his name.

Over the next two months, several members of Alemán's family and former associates were charged on various counts of embezzlement and money-laundering. Among those implicated was his daughter, María Dolores, who also enjoyed immunity as a member of the Assembly. On December 12, the Assembly finally voted to strip Alemán of his immunity. The former president appeared in court the next day, claiming that he still enjoyed immunity as a member of the largely ceremonial Central American Parliament.

By mid-year 2003, some of the accused were beginning to go on trial, although Alemán remained under house arrest on his ranch, refusing to answer prosecutors' questions by still claiming legislative immunity. In June, prosecutors raised new charges, that he stole another $113 million from the treasury, theft on a Somoza-size scale. The *PLC* was hopelessly rent, with 38 Assembly members abandoning Bolaños, leaving him with only 10 loyal members. Meanwhile, civic organizations loyal to Bolaños launched a campaign to force a plebiscite on restructuring public institutions in an attempt to restore public confidence—which never really existed in the first place. The *Arnoldistas* and the *Sandinistas* responded with a call for a constituent assembly.

Alemán was eventually convicted and sentenced to 20 years. In March 2004, he went to prison, but he has continued to direct the *Arnoldistas*, who remain fanatically loyal to him.

Then, in a Machiavellian maneuver similar to the power-sharing accord of 1999, the *Sandinistas* and *Arnoldistas* joined in an improbable joint effort in October 2004 to form a special legislative committee to decide whether to impeach Bolaños on the old charge of receiving foreign campaign contributions. Between them, they had far more than the 60% needed for removal. Bolaños, hopelessly outnum-

President Enrique Bolaños

bered in the Assembly, lashed out at both Alemán and Ortega, accusing them of "a plot to carry out a coup d'etat." The move was motivated, apparently, by revenge on the part of the *Arnoldistas* and by fear on the part of the *Sandinistas,* who no doubt wondered whether the president would look next at their own sins.

Under pressure from both the United States and the Organization of American States, which warned against removing a constitutional president for politically motivated, trumped-up charges, the *FSLN* and the *PLC* backed off from impeachment, but in January 2005 they enacted a new law that curtailed Bolaños' appointment powers, especially the appointment of judges. The crisis eased in February when Ortega suddenly declared he would support Bolaños remaining in office until the end of his term. Ortega may have been playing the role of statesman; in March, he announced he would run again in the 2006 presidential election.

However, the crisis erupted anew in June 2005 when the Assembly named its own appointees to head the postal and telephone systems. Bolaños dispatched police to prevent the new appointees from entering their offices, while the Assembly threatened to impeach him for obstructing the law. The new OAS secretary-general, José Miguel Insulza, flew to Nicaragua himself to engage the two sides in dialogue. He left after four days, lamenting that he had been unable to bring the two sides to the bargaining table and expressing his concern for the impasse, which was continuing when this book went to press.

The *FSLN* was once again the major winner in the November 2004 municipal elections, retaining the mayoralty of Managua and winning in all the major cities.

Nicaragua

Friction between the *PLC* and Bolaños' Alliance for the Republic *(APRE)* erupted into a gunfight in the city of Juigalpa. A female reporter for *La Prensa* was killed in the crossfire.

The skyrocketing cost of petroleum in April 2005 sparked violent protests when Bolaños announced an increase in bus fares from 15 to 18 cents. When Bolaños attempted to address the thousands of student and peasant protesters, he was met with a barrage of rocks. He was uninjured, but his son was struck in the head and hospitalized. The high fuel prices also led the Spanish-owned power company to seek, and receive, an 11.3% increase in electric rates, which Bolaños restricted to major users. The resulting outcry prompted Bolaños to decree a state of economic emergency on May 30, which restricted the right of protest. He rescinded the decree three days later.

Culture: Though a substantial number of Nicaraguans lead a modern, urban life comparable to that of the large cities of Latin America, the majority live in rural simplicity. The culture closely resembles that of the rest of the Central American states. Upheavals associated with the post-revolutionary period have affected the lives of all, very adversely.

The music of the people, derived from their Spanish-Moorish conquerors, is used to accompany a wide variety of local dances and festivals. It was possible to see the latest dramatic and musical productions professionally performed in the busy capital of Managua, and after a short journey to also view a traditional *mestizo* comedy quaintly performed in a combination of *Hahuatl* (an Indian dialect), Spanish and *Mangue*, another Indian dialect.

Under the *Sandinistas*, most education heavily stressed communist principles and ideals—all alien to a basically politically unskilled people who are seldom politically intelligent and aware. Culturally, Nicaragua is currently (except in the rural countryside) a desert.

Nicaragua contributed one of the world's foremost poets, Rubén Dario (1867-1916).

Economy: Although Nicaragua is largely based on agriculture, which employed 65% of the work force, the increased development of light industry before the revolution gave Nicaragua's economy a degree of hope for a broader base than was found in most other Latin American countries. Underpopulated and with many unexploited natural resources, the nation has a substantial potential for tremendous economic growth with proper management.

Nicaragua's most important farm commodities are produced in the western region. Rich in volcanic soils, this section is the source of cotton, coffee and sugar. The cattle industry was also expanding in the western section. While the eastern region is largely devoted to banana production, some operations have been shifted to the west coast because of banana plant disease. Nationalization of large producing farms did not contribute to their efficiency, and the breakup of some into smaller peasant farms actually seriously lowered production.

The U.S. commercial embargo on Nicaragua was a serious long-range economic threat. Commercial relations between the two nations had been steadily declining since 1982. The 1985 total embargo had a devastating effect. The closing of U.S. ports and a ban on technological imports

Traditional Dance

273

Nicaragua

all but shut down the economy. As in Cuba—perhaps even worse than Cuba—Soviet economic difficulties and increasing limitations on its economic aid to socialist countries added a somber note to Nicaragua's possibilities for development. During 1986-90, virtually all that was exported was bananas, sold to the Soviet Union and Eastern Europe at inflated prices.

The Chamorro government, hamstrung by the ever-present threat of the *Sandinista* military, accomplished little at reducing unemployment and underemployment, which totaled more than 65%. Alemán, however, moved more aggressively to bring Nicaragua in line with International Monetary Fund demands and to make the country more attractive to foreign investors. GDP growth was a respectable 5% in 1997. Meanwhile, the IMF extended Nicaragua a three-year, $136 million loan package and praised Alemán for stabilizing the currency and reducing the bloated, featherbedded bureaucracy. The World Bank also granted a $70 million loan to help transform the financial sector from the old Marxist system.

Hurricane Mitch caused billions of dollars in damage to the economic infrastructure in 1998, a blow the country could ill

afford and which added another $300 million to the already oppressive $6.2 billion external debt. Surprisingly, however, Mitch did not derail the expanding economy. GDP growth was still 4% for 1998 and a respectable 6.2% for 1999. In 2000 it had tapered off slightly to 5.0%. It was 2.5% in 2001 and only 1% in 2002 and 1.4% in 2003.

Nicaragua's per capita income fell lower than Haiti's in 1997, to $436, making it for the first time the poorest country in the Western Hemisphere. By 2002 it had dropped even lower, to $370, compared with $440 for Haiti. Unemployment declined from 12.3% in 1998 to 11% in 1999 to 9% in 2000. It rose slightly in 2001 to 10.3%. Inflation remained steady at about 10% in 2000 and 2001.

The Future: Corruption is hardly a new phenomenon in Nicaragua. The Somoza dynasty was notoriously venal, and the *Sandinistas* demonstrated that they were not above seizing a few perks at public expense. The thievery from the treasury of the poorest nation in the hemisphere committed by Alemán and his cronies is monstrous even by Latin American standards. The amount, more than $100 million, is

tantamount to 4% of GDP being channeled into private bank accounts.

Nicaragua has been whipsawed from corrupt right-wing dictatorship to corrupt left-wing dictatorship to inept and corrupt democracy as if on an amusement park ride—only there is nothing amusing about it. Nothing has worked. What the Alemán affair may bode for Nicaragua's fragile democracy is uncertain, but it is difficult to be optimistic. Small wonder that in the annual *Latinobarómetro* surveys of 17 Latin American countries, Nicaragua ties with Paraguay as the two countries that have shown the greatest drop in public commitment to democracy over an eight-year span. In 1996, 59% of Nicaraguans and Paraguayans said that democracy was preferable to any other form of government; in 2004, that percentage had dropped to 39% in both countries.

Nicaragua now has a decent, reformist-minded president, but he has been hamstrung by the two major parties, who have no incentive for being reformed. One ray of hope for Nicaragua is that it is one of 18 countries designated as eligible for debt forgiveness by the Paris Club of major creditor nations. Nicaragua needs all the hope it can get.

The Republic of Panama

The almost completed Panama Canal—final blasting of a channel, October 1913

Area: 28,745 square miles.

Population: 3.2 million.

Capital City: Panama City (Pop. 1 million, estimated).

Climate: Tropical, with clearly marked wet and dry seasons. The heaviest rainfall is from May to December.

Neighboring Countries: Colombia (southeast); Costa Rica (northwest).

Official Language: Spanish.

Other Principal Tongue: English.

Ethnic Background: Mulatto (mixed African and European, 72%); African (14%); European (12%); Indians and other (2%).

Principal Religion: Roman Catholic Christianity.

Chief Commercial Products: Bananas, shrimp and apparel.

Currency: Balboa (in reality, the U.S. dollar is the legal tender).

Gross Domestic Product: U.S. $13.83 billion in 2004 ($4,320 per capita).

Former Colonial Status: Spanish Colony (1519–1821), Province of Colombia (1821–1903).

Independence Date: November 3, 1903.

Chief of State: President Martín Torrijos Espino (b. July 18, 1963), president (since September 1, 2004)

National Flag: A rectangle of four quarters; white with a blue star, blue, white with a red star, red.

Panama is a very narrow isthmus, 480 miles long and varying in width from 37 to 110 miles, connecting North and South America. Mountainous throughout, the highest elevation is the volcano Baru (11,397 feet) near the Costa Rican border. The Talamanca range continues southeast at an average elevation of 3,000 feet until it drops into the sea just west of Panama City. The San Blas range, rising east of Colón, runs southeast into Colombia; again the average elevation is 3,000 feet. A third range appears along the Pacific coast east of Panama City and runs southeast into Colombia. Both coasts have narrow plains cut by numerous small rivers running into the sea.

Lying in the tropical rainbelt, Panama's Atlantic coast receives up to 150 inches of rainfall—the Pacific coast receives about 100 inches. The dry season, or "summer," runs from December to April. Four fifths of Panama's territory is covered with jungle and one half lies outside effective con-

Panama

trol by the Panamanian government. The principal reason for Panama's existence as a nation and the principal source of its earnings is the geographical accident of the north-south gap between the Talamanca and San Blas ranges, which permitted the construction of a canal between the Atlantic and Pacific oceans. Now the site of the Panama Canal and the nation's major cities, more than half the population is found in a narrow corridor and along the Pacific coast west of the gap.

History: Panama was discovered by Columbus in 1498–1500 and called Veraguas. It assumed importance in 1513 when Vasco Nuñez de Balboa discovered the Pacific. Panama City was established on the Pacific coast in 1518 and connected to three Caribbean ports by trails and rivers.

Nombre de Dios (Name of God) and Portobelo were the principal Atlantic ports maintained by the Spanish. Panama became the base for the outfitting of expeditions into Peru and Central America; it later was a major link in the route over which the wealth of the region was shipped to Spain. This wealth, and Panama's strategic importance, attracted pirates, buccaneers and foreign armies.

The British privateer Sir Francis Drake burned Nombre de Dios in 1573 and 1598; Henry Morgan raided the isthmus, looting and burning Panama City in 1617; British Admiral Edward Vernon captured Portobelo in 1739 and San Lorenzo in 1740. Spain abandoned the Panamanian route in 1746 in favor of the trip around Cape Horn at the tip of Argentina and Chile to reach its colonies in western Latin America.

For nearly 100 years Panama was bypassed by trade and ignored during the wars for independence fought on the southern continent. After independence, Panama was a province of Colombia. The discovery of gold in California brought renewed interest in quick transit from the Atlantic to the Pacific coast of the United States. A railroad was constructed between 1850 and 1853, and the De Lesseps Company of France started work on a canal in 1882. The work was abandoned in 1893, in part because of yellow fever epidemics, and in 1904 the United States acquired the assets of the bankrupt company.

There ensued three years of fruitless negotiations between the United States and Colombia. Colombia was gripped by civil war during the period. Philippe Jean Bunau-Varilla, the French agent of the defunct canal company, with the knowledge of the United States, engineered a revolution in Panama with the understanding that the United States would intervene to establish Panama as an independent state and that U.S. financial interests would acquire the right to complete the interoceanic canal across the isthmus. President Theodore Roosevelt recognized the independence of Panama three days after its proclamation on November 3, 1903.

Treaty negotiations between the United States and Panama were brief. Bunau-Varilla represented Panama, and the two sides quickly reached an agreement giving the United States virtually sovereign rights "in perpetuity" over the Canal Zone, a 10-mile-wide swath of Panamanian territory from coast to coast. Panamanians were horrified when confronted with Bunau-Varilla's *fait accompli*, but there was little they could do. Construction on the canal started shortly thereafter—as did 70 years of wrangling between the United States and the Republic of Panama over the sovereignty issue. In August 1914, the 400-year-old dream of Spanish, French, British and North American adventurers was accomplished when a vessel sailed through the completed canal from the Atlantic to the Pacific Ocean.

Panama's political history as an independent state was in keeping with the pattern of the Central American and Caribbean nations. Power lay in the hands of a small, elite Caucasian group that exploited the geographic situation for its personal benefit. The population at the time of independence was concentrated in the terminal cities of the trans-isthmian railroad and dependent upon commerce for its income. The influx of labor for the construction completely overwhelmed the

Panama's Declaration of Independence

Lelcasco Viejo, **the old part of Panama City**

administrative capabilities of the small nation. A pattern ensued in which actual power was in the hands of the *Guardia Nacional*, whose head was infrequently the actual chief of state; more often he ruled through a figurehead president.

U.S. Patrimony

The United States took what measures it deemed necessary to achieve its purposes while Panama elected or appointed one ineffective government after another. The Panama Railroad, the United Fruit Company, which had established banana plantations during the late 1800s, and the Panama Canal Company, in consort with a small group of Panamanian families, exercised effective political and economic power in Panama. The steady influx of wealth supported a booming economy through the 1940s. Following World War II, the growing population exceeded the service demands of commerce and Panama began to feel the effects of 50 years of lack of direction and failure to invest its earnings in substantial industrial ventures.

Into this volatile political environment there appeared a charismatic and dema-

gogic figure who was to dominate Panamanian politics for the next half-century—and even beyond his death: Arnulfo Arias. The founder of the ultra-nationalist *Panameñista* Party, Arias exploited his people's near-xenophobic dislike of foreigners. He lashed out not only at the United States and the "Zonians" who enjoyed their suburban tropical paradise, but foreign immigrants as well, particularly those from Asia. On those rare occasions when the *Guardia Nacional* allowed Panamanians to vote in fair elections, Arias and his party did well—*too* well, for the *Guardia* and the elite. He was elected president in 1940 and in 1948, only to be deposed by the *Guardia* both times. He won again—and was deposed again—in 1968 and probably won two other elections, in 1964 and 1984, but was denied victory through creative vote-counting.

As the military, in league with the tiny clique of oligarchs, was the actual power in the country anyway, it "elected" one of its own, Police Chief José Antonio Remón, as president in 1952. Oddly enough, Remón was to prove one of Panama's more enlightened rulers, instituting long-overdue social reform, which estranged

him from the oligarchy, and cracking down on some of the more overt corruption. He also was friendlier to the United States than many of his predecessors had been, *too* friendly for some Panamanians. Nonetheless, his more rational policy succeeded in obtaining an increase in the rent for the Canal Zone in 1955 from a paltry $430,000 (it had been only $250,000 until 1939!) to a still-ridiculous $1.9 million. Remón was assassinated that same year, but whether his killers were motivated by social reactionism or anti-Americanism never has been determined.

Remón's antithesis, Ernesto de la *Guardia*, was elected president in a reasonably fair count in 1956 and began making strident demands on the United States. The war over the Suez Canal that year helped further fan Panamanian passions. Some of the demands were quite legitimate, such as elimination of the inequitable wage scales between Zonian and Panamanian canal employees. President Eisenhower, who had served in Panama as a young Army officer in the early 1920s, acceded to the wage demands, as well as to a demand to allow the Panamanian flag to fly in the Zone. But it seemed the more the Americans con-

Panama

ceded, the more antagonistic the de la *Guardia* government became. On Panamanian Independence Day in 1959, a well-orchestrated mob sought to "invade" the Zone, forcing U.S. troops to deter them with fixed bayonets. Ultra-nationalists and pro-Castro students exploited the incident for propaganda purposes. If nothing else, de la *Guardia* earned one important distinction for a Panamanian president: he served out his elected four-year term.

A far more moderate figure (and a member of the oligarchy), Roberto Chiari, was elected president in 1960 in what probably was the cleanest election Panama would ever have until 1994. Chiari enjoyed an amicable relationship with President Kennedy, who agreed to allow the Panamanian flag to fly alongside the U.S. flag in the Zone. Chiari also followed an anti-Castro line pleasing to Washington.

Nonetheless, toward the end of Chiari's term there occurred the worst incident of violence yet between Americans and Panamanians. In January 1964, foolhardy Zonian students at Balboa High School tore down the Panamanian flag flying next to the U.S. flag in front of the school and desecrated it. As word got out, Panamanians exploded in fury, and rioters flooded into the Zone, separated from Panama City only by the broad Fourth of July Avenue. In the resulting violence, 23 Panamanians and six Americans, most of them soldiers, were killed. Chiari broke diplomatic relations with the United States, and President Lyndon B. Johnson was faced with his first foreign policy crisis since succeeding the assassinated Kennedy two months earlier. Panama renamed Fourth of July Avenue *Avenida de los Mártires* (Avenue of the Martyrs), and to this day there are ceremonies marking each anniversary of the deadly riots.

In the election of May 1964, Chiari's cousin and fellow oligarch, Marco Aurelio Robles, narrowly defeated the fiery Arias, though the vote counting remains suspect to this day. Robles reestablished relations with Washington which, still shaken by the riots, began negotiating seriously about changes to the 1903 canal treaty. Robles withdrew government sanctioning on anti-U.S. demonstrations, and relations gradually improved—for a time.

The 1968 Coup

In the May 1968 elections, the perennial Arias won by a convincing margin that could not be denied. He was duly inaugurated on September 1, but just 11 days into his term, the *Guardia* overthrew him for a third time, ushering in 21 years of despotic military rule as heavy-handed as any in Latin America. For the first 13 of those years, absolute power rested with

President Jimmy Carter looks on as Panama's Omar Torrijos signs the 1977 Panama Canal Treaty

Colonel Omar Torrijos, who later promoted himself to brigadier general, a flamboyant and charismatic figure in the classic style of the Latin American *caudillo*.

Torrijos became a hero to the long-suppressed lower class as he established what amounted to a Panamanian version of a dictatorship of the proletariat. Political activity ceased, and a puppet legislative assembly rubber-stamped Torrijos' dictates. The egomaniacal Torrijos even had his heroic image emblazoned in a new frieze work on the legislative palace. Press freedom vanished as the government expropriated three newspapers owned by Arias' brother, Harmodio, and blackmailed the owner of the venerable and respected *La Estrella de Panama* into becoming a sycophantish parrot of the government line. Critics of the regime were tortured, and more than a few took a one-way helicopter

Brigadier General Omar Torrijos

ride over the Pacific Ocean. Those too prominent to kill were hustled off into exile, often after being beaten as a farewell gesture. Torrijos reestablished diplomatic relations with Cuba, and he engaged in *gringo*-baiting on a scale not seen since de la *Guardia*. He attacked traditional corruption long practiced by the elite, but a newer, more sinister version with ties to Colombian drug traffickers soon arose. Torrijos implemented lax banking regulations that attracted branches of major banks from every continent, while the drug traffickers found Panama a veritable paradise for money-laundering.

The New Canal Treaties

National politics was dominated in the 1970s by the lingering dispute with the United States over the canal. Most of this centered around the 1903 treaty which granted the United States virtual sovereignty "in perpetuity" over the 530-square-mile Canal Zone. Widespread resentment against what was regarded as an outdated treaty unified most Panamanian political factions in demanding a new treaty. Key changes sought by Panama included (1) increased rental payments, (2) a large-scale reduction of U.S. military presence in the zone, (3) a greater Panamanian role in operating the canal and (4) recognition of complete Panamanian sovereignty over the zone.

Although there was an effort to place some nationals in management positions within the Canal Company, Panamanians insisted they could, and should, be allowed an even greater role in running their nation's major industry. Panamanians employed in the Canal Zone were usually given menial tasks at low wages.

Panama

The Panama Canal at Miraflores locks

Since its opening in 1914, the canal was operated almost entirely by U.S. staff and supervisors. The zone itself resembled a "company town" as residents were provided with cradle-to-grave programs such as free schooling and medical care.

Because the 1903 treaty granted the United States territorial supremacy over the zone, Panama said the corridor represented a virtual foreign nation in its midst. It was a valid point. Zonians paid U.S. taxes. The Zone had its own police force. It had a U.S. federal district court, which was part of the 5th Circuit. It had U.S. post offices, although the Zone actually had its own postage stamps. Democrats in the Zone elected delegates to their party's national conventions. Panamanians could even be "deported" from the zone. It contended that U.S. control was a form of colonialism and insisted the 1903 treaty had to be replaced since it was forced on the tiny nation by U.S. "big stick" gunboat diplomacy.

An eight-point agenda for negotiators was signed early in 1974, during the waning days of the Nixon administration, and talks began shortly thereafter. The negotiations were continued into the Ford administration, and while they were not exactly secret, the administration certainly kept them low-key. In 1976, the canal talks became a campaign issue when Ronald Reagan, running for the Republican nomination against President Ford, assailed Ford for negotiating to surrender the vital U.S.-controlled waterway to a "tinpot dictator." Ford clumsily denied that he intended to give up the canal, an assertion

that immediately drew the ire of the Panamanians. Caught between a domestic political dilemma and an international powder keg, Ford then backtracked and acknowledged that canal negotiations were underway, but he denounced Reagan as "irresponsible" for opposing them. Ford narrowly defeated Reagan for the nomination, but lost the general election to Democrat Jimmy Carter.

Shortly after his inauguration in 1977, incoming President Carter gave a high priority to a new canal treaty. Ambassador Sol M. Linowitz was appointed to join Ellsworth Bunker as chief U.S. negotiators, and talks resumed in February 1977.

Completed in August, the new accord consisted of two separate treaties. The first one would permanently guarantee the canal's neutrality and use by all nations. In case of emergency, however, U.S. warships would be given priority over commercial traffic.

The second accord detailed a timetable for gradual transfer of the canal and the Zone from the United States to Panama. At noon on December 31, 1999, Panama would gain control of the whole works. Annual payments to Panama would also be boosted at once from $2.3 million to an estimated $60 million.

Although the two treaties incorporated a number of Panamanian demands, they left unsettled the question of a larger, deeper sea-level canal which President Carter said would be needed before the year 2000. The present facility employs the use of time-consuming locks. The Navy's largest warships and the new generation

of super-tankers are too large to pass through the canal's locks. The waterway is also subject to congestion. Both traffic and tonnage have been rising in recent years, placing additional burdens on the canal's facilities.

The new treaties were signed with a flourish when leaders from 23 Latin American nations gathered in Washington in September 1977 to witness the historic event. Still, the festive occasion could not hide the fact that the treaties faced a tough fight—both in the U.S. Senate (where critics said Washington gave up too much) and in Panama (where critics said Washington gave up too *little*).

The first test came in Panama, where the treaties were submitted to a national referendum. Despite vocal protests from both leftists and conservatives—who insisted that Torrijos should have held out for more money plus an earlier U.S. withdrawal—the treaties were approved by a comfortable 2–1 margin.

Attention next turned to Washington; for ratification, the agreements needed support from two thirds of the Senate—a tall order for an accord that public opinion polls said was still opposed by a majority of Americans. A campaign by retired and active high government figures was mounted in favor of the treaties. Ten weeks of debate ensued. Seventy-nine amendments were offered. The first treaty was approved in March by 68–32—just a one-vote margin above the necessary minimum. To gain approval, however, the president had to agree to an amendment permitting U.S. military intervention in

Panama

Panama should the canal be closed for any reason, including a strike or even technical problems. This amendment caused an immediate uproar in Panama. Nationalists protested that it was not only an affront to Panamanian dignity, but it would also violate previous U.S.-Latin American agreements that specifically prohibited the concept of unilateral intervention. As the Senate prepared to vote on the second treaty, Torrijos—subjected to a blast of pressure from critics at home—sent a message to 115 world leaders saying Panama could not accept the amendment.

In an 11th-hour attempt to save 14 years of painful negotiations with Panama, the White House and Senate leaders agreed to a new provision for the second treaty which promised that the United States would not interfere with Panama's "internal affairs" or "political independence." The lawmakers, obviously tired of the whole matter, voted in April by the same 68–32 margin in favor of the second treaty.

Behind the scenes, Carter had persuaded Torrijos that U.S. Senate ratification of the treaties would be impossible unless he sanitized his odious dictatorship. Torrijos pragmatically agreed to permit competitive elections and to ease restrictions on freedom of expression and of the press, which Carter trumpeted as proof of Torrijos' commitment to democracy. The seemingly close relationship between the U.S. president, who assailed right-wing Latin American military strongmen for their human rights abuses, and the Panamanian dictator who ordered the murders of political dissidents and confiscated newspapers, was most peculiar. This author was in Panama in June 1978 when Carter visited Panama to sign the instruments of ratification. At the public ceremony, Carter thrilled the Panamanian crowd by delivering a conciliatory address in his broken Spanish, in which he promised *"no intervención."* Torrijos, by contrast, was a disgrace. On this highly significant occasion in the life of his country, the representative of Panama was so drunk that his speech was badly slurred and he had to brace himself against the podium to keep from falling.

On October 1, 1979, an enormous Panamanian flag was raised atop Ancon Hill, which looms above Panama City and was the site of the U.S. Southern Command headquarters, and titular Panamanian sovereignty over the Canal Zone became a *reality.* Meanwhile, as window dressing, exiles were allowed to return. A new, more liberal press law was enacted, though the confiscated newspapers remained in government hands and *La Estrella* remained a faithful mouthpiece underneath its Sword of Damocles. The military established the Revolutionary Democratic Party (*PRD*)

Arístedes Royo

as its civilian political façade. In 1980, an ostensible "election" was held in which numerous parties participated, but the winner was predictable: Arístides Royo, candidate of the *PRD*.

That same year, a group of anti-Torrijos businessmen and intellectuals, headed by Roberto Eisenmann, who had been in exile for four years, put the new press law to the test by establishing a new daily newspaper, *La Prensa*, which soon became a constant irritant to the regime with its investigative reporting of government corruption, its biting editorials and its acidic satirical cartoons.

Numerous problems faced strongman Torrijos and his protege, President Royo. Many of the financial benefits expected to flow into Panama as a result of the new treaties were slow to materialize. In 1980 unemployment grew to 20% and growing inflation touched off two days of general strikes that crippled 80% of the country's industries.

The election of Ronald Reagan in 1980 caused shock waves in Panama, where Torrijos feared that the new President might try to sabotage the canal treaties. Given Reagan's long-standing opposition to the pacts, Panama felt it necessary to safeguard its position by obtaining (with the help of Cuba) a seat on the U.N. Security Council in 1980.

The Panamanian political landscape was altered abruptly and dramatically on July 31, 1981, when Torrijos was killed in a plane crash while on an inspection of *Guardia* units in western Panama. Bad weather was cited as the official cause of the crash, though persistent rumors began circulating almost immediately that it was no accident. Fidel Castro, of course, immediately accused the CIA, then headed by Reagan protege William Casey, of rubbing out his friend. Torrijos, or what little remained of him, was buried in an elaborate

masoleum on the parade ground of the former U.S. Army installation of Fort Amador. There was a frenzied outpouring of grief for the man who, whatever his shortcomings, had succeeded in reasserting Panamanian sovereignty over the Canal Zone. Command of the *Guardia* passed initially to Brigadier General Rubén Paredes, and democratic forces held their breath to see what course post-Torrijos Panama would take. Almost a year to the day after Torrijos' death, they found out. On July 30, 1982, Panama experienced a veritable night of the long knives as the military launched a widespread crackdown on dissent. President Royo was summoned to military headquarters and informed that he was resigning for "health reasons;" he readily complied. At the same time, a goon squad invaded the offices of *La Prensa*, vandalized it and beat several of its employees, including women. The paper was padlocked for several days; other independent publications and radio stations also were silenced.

Noriega Comes to Power

After two years of a behind-the-scenes power struggle, command of the *Guardia*, which had been renamed the Panama Defense Forces (*FDP*), passed to one of the most sinister figures in recent Latin American history: Colonel Manuel Noriega. The longtime chief of the *Guardia*'s G-2, or intelligence section, Noriega was no charismatic *caudillo* like Torrijos. He was squat and ugly, with a face heavily scarred by acne, which led his many detractors to give him the uncharitable sobriquet *"Cara de Piña,"* or "Pineapple Face." Where Torrijos had enjoyed the popularity of the masses, Noriega would rule by raw fear. Noriega was an alumnus of the U.S. Army's School of the Americas, then located at Fort Gulick, Panama, and had become a paid CIA operative. But he also acted as a double agent, providing intelligence to the Soviets and Cubans. Even more sinister, he enriched himself by providing protection to the Medellín Cartel of Colombia, which used Panama as a safe haven for its cocaine trafficking and money laundering. When this author served Army Reserve tours at the Southern Command in the 1970s and 1980s, Noriega's activities were well known, and his ascension to power was seen as the worst possible scenario. As *La Prensa*'s Eisenmann later told me, the difference between Torrijos and Noriega was that Torrijos merely ordered people tortured and murdered; Noriega participated in the torturing and killing and enjoyed it.

Noriega soon demonstrated the extent of his commitment to Torrijos' promise to Carter to ease human rights restrictions.

In 1984, he dutifully held open presidential elections for an expanded five-year term. As its candidate, the military-backed *PRD* selected Nicolás Ardito Barletta, a respected economist and graduate of the University of Chicago. The *Panameñistas* again nominated the resilient Arias, by then 83. When early tabulations, which were monitored by international observers, showed an unmistakable trend in favor of Arias, the *FDP* abruptly impounded the ballot boxes and continued the vote counting in secret. By independent estimates, Arias would have received a plurality of between 25,000 and 50,000 votes out of 900,000 cast, but through the *FDP*'s creative vote counting, Barletta was declared the winner by 1,700 votes.

Public opposition to Noriega's heavy-handed rule intensified. A curious coalition of the wealthy elite, leftist intellectuals and housewives took to the streets waving white handerkerchiefs. Some of the demonstrations were broken up by truncheon-wielding goon squads from *FDP*-backed groups euphemistically named "Dignity Battalions." Not all opponents of the regime fared that well, however.

One of the most prominent Noriega critics was Dr. Hugo Spadafora, a physician who once had served as Torrijos' vice minister of health. He had served both the Nicaraguan *Sandinistas* in their struggle against Somoza and then, when he became disillusioned with their human rights abuses once in power, he lent his support to the *Contras*. He contributed a regular column to *La Prensa*, in which he vilified the Noriega dictatorship, and he announced he would return to Panama from Costa Rica to lead an opposition movement. He never made it. In September 1985, his bus was stopped when it crossed the border and, according to witnesses, he was forcibly removed. Days later, his decapitated body was found stuffed in a mail bag in Costa Rica; the body bore unmistakable evidence of hideous torture.

This time Noriega had overplayed his hand, and the Spadafora murder would backfire on him the same way the murder of journalist Pedro Joaquín Chamorro had served as the catalyst for the downfall of Nicaragua's Somoza. News of this atrocious crime made headlines around the world, and domestic and international pressure mounted on the regime. A half-hearted investigation concluded that the murder had occurred in Costa Rica and that Panamanian authorities had no jurisdiction. The Costa Ricans disputed that claim, which only served to fuel the mounting public indignation in Panama. Trying to appease public opinion, President Barletta publicly vowed to bring the killers to justice, a declaration he had fool-

ishly made without consulting with Noriega. Like so many of his predecessors, the president was summoned to military headquarters and was informed he would not leave the building unless he resigned; he did. He was succeeded by the vice president, Eric Arturo Delvalle.

This author was stationed in Panama during the first half of 1986, when the outcry over the Spadafora murder reached a crescendo. The regime's response to the increasing number of protests was to cow the opposition with death threats. Graffiti accusing Eisenmann of treason began appearing all over Panama City, and the editor fled again to Miami for his life. That

General Manuel Antonio Noriega

June, Pulitzer Prize-winning reporter Seymour Hersh of the *New York Times* reported what insiders in Panama had known for years, that Noriega was involved in drug trafficking and that he was a double agent. I watched with amazement as a State Department spokesman testified on television before a congressional committee that there was no evidence to support Hersh's charges; apparently they hadn't been reading their intelligence cables for the past 10 years! Eventually, the U.S. government acknowledged that Noriega had once been a paid informant and was heavily involved in drug trafficking.

Noriega, of course, played the nationalist card, accusing the *gringos* of trying to undermine him. But in June 1987, one of his own former minions, Colonel Roberto Díaz Herrera, told the press not only that Noriega was a drug trafficker but that he had ordered Torrijos' fatal plane crash. The

opposition press gleefully published the charges. On July 26, 1987, Noriega cracked down hard. Díaz was arrested, and *La Prensa* and several other opposition papers and radio stations were shut down. The Reagan administration ostracized the Noriega regime economically. On February 25, 1988, President Delvalle attempted to salvage the country's devastated economy and to restore some degree of respect in the eyes of the world by firing Noriega as *FDP* commander. Noriega, of course, immediately fired Delvalle; Education Minister Manuel Solis Palma was installed to keep the president's chair warm until Barletta's term expired in 1989. That same year, a U.S. grand jury indicted Noriega on drug trafficking charges.

Incredibly, in May 1989, Noriega actually went ahead with yet another showcase election, as though anyone still believed Panama was a democracy. Arias had died in exile in Miami the previous August, and the *Panameñistas*, now renamed *Arnulfistas*, nominated a portly and uninspiring doctor, Guillermo Endara, as the sacrificial lamb to head a coalition opposition ticket that included the Christian Democrats. The *PRD* nominated Carlos Duque, a member of the family that published the regime's faithful mascot newspaper, *La Estrella*. Perhaps the most enduring image of this sham campaign was the attack on an opposition rally by Dignity Battalion goons. Guillermo Ford, one of the opposition's two vice presidential candidates, was badly beaten, and international news photographers and cameramen recorded him fleeing for his life, his white *guayabera* shirt drenched bright red with his own blood; these images were carried around the world. International observers were present for election day on May 7. Nevertheless, in a replay of the 1984 electoral farce, early returns showed Endara winning by a landslide, and once again the *FDP* halted the vote counting. This time, however, the observers knew Endara had won, so instead of merely proclaiming Duque the winner, the government nullified the election results. The justification: "Foreign interference"! When the term to which Barletta had been "elected" in 1984 expired on September 1, the Council of State, composed entirely of *FDP* officers and their *PRD* lapdogs, designated a close associate of Noriega's, Francisco Rodríguez, as the newest figurehead president.

Operation 'Just Cause'

Relations between the United States and Panama continued to deteriorate after the 1989 "election." Noriega suppressed a coup attempt by a group of *FDP* officers on October 3 and ordered them

Panama

summarily executed. The CIA made an abortive attempt to abduct Noriega, while President George Bush (who as CIA director in 1976 had been Noriega's "boss") issued an executive order banning Panamanian registered ships from entering U.S. ports. As Panama was second only to Liberia in the number of registries in world shipping, the order had potentially disastrous implications. But the bombastic Noriega soon proved to be his own worst enemy. Wielding a machete before a howling crowd of his adherents, he publicly "declared war" on the United States. In December, there were two separate incidents of off-duty U.S. service personnel—and one of their wives—being beaten by goons, and one U.S. serviceman was shot to death at a roadblock.

Faced with these provocations, Bush ordered the bombing of Noriega's headquarters on December 20, 1989, which was followed by an invasion by 9,500 U.S.-based paratroopers and Army Rangers in what was labeled Operation "Just Cause." Army forces stationed in Panama also moved to seize key installations. There were casualties on both sides as the *FDP* and the Dignity Battalions offered some futile resistance. Within days, order was

restored, and for once, U.S. troops were actually cheered by the Panamanians, a stark contrast to the riots of 1964. The day after the invasion, Endara was inaugurated as president. Panamanians suddenly found themselves with more individual freedom than they ever had experienced. *La Prensa* and other closed media were re-opened, the confiscated newspapers were returned to the widow and children of Harmodio Arias, the *FDP* was disbanded and replaced with a more benign civilian constabulary, and the country began building for the future.

Noriega went into hiding, changing his location every few hours. He sought and obtained refuge in the residence of the papal nuncio. A U.S. psychological warfare unit, in a move considered shrewd by some and crude by others, placed powerful loudspeakers outside the building and started broadcasting heavy metal rock at an overwhelming volume for the occupants of the building. The horrified nuncio told Noriega that the residence would be moved across the street and Noriega would not be welcome. Gloomily, the beaten man surrendered, to be taken to the United States with the assurance of no death penalty. He was sentenced to 40

years in 1992, but in 1999 a U.S. district judge ruled that he would be eligible for parole as early as 2000.

President Endara unsuccessfully tried to maintain a low profile to disguise his lack of talent. An opposition newspaper ridiculed him as "a non-musician leading an orchestra that does not play." Endara shrugged off chronic unemployment and rampant corruption as normal occurrences. By late 1993 his government became in fact a caretaker; influential cabinet members resigned to take part in 1994 presidential elections.

Ernesto Pérez Balladares

At the turn of the year, party reshuffling split Panamanian politics, enabling the organization that had supported Noriega, the *PRD*, to come to the fore. Its candidate was Ernesto Pérez Balladares, a former Citi-bank official with a U.S. education. He carefully distanced himself from Noriega, and won the election against an opposition that had split into numerous factions and parties. Running a strong second was Mireya Moscoso, the young widow of Arnulfo Arias, running as the *Arnulfista* candidate.

In June 1996, the *Miami Herald* and the *New York Times* carried reports linking top Panamanian government officials to an airline under indictment in the United States for its role in drug trafficking, including Panama City Mayor Alfredo Alemán, an adviser to the president; Foreign Minister Ricardo Alberto Arias, and intelligence chief Gabriel Castro. It also was reported that Pérez Balladares, like Colombia's Ernesto Samper, had received funds from drug traffickers for his presidential campaign. The president at first indignantly denied the allegations, and even threatened not to extend the work permit of Peruvian investigative journalist Gustavo Gorriti, recently named as editor of *La Prensa*. Pérez Balladares accused Gorriti of "masterminding a conspiracy" to undermine his government. A few days later, however, the president publicly made a contrite confession that the charges were true but insisted he had not known.

Gorriti continued to nettle the president. In 1997, *La Prensa* reported that Pérez Balladares had delayed passage of a new antitrust law to give his cousin time to acquire control of a second television station. This time the president followed through with his threat not to extend Gorriti's work permit, citing a provision in the labor law that media management positions must be held by Panamanians. The Interior Ministry ordered Gorriti to leave the country by August 28. The paper's lawyers went to court and succeeded in obtaining a delay of the deportation order.

Far from the capital's cosmopolitan life: Cuna Indians of the San Blas Islands

Meanwhile, Pérez Balladares became the center of a storm of international condemnation from journalism organizations and human rights groups; even Hillary Rodham Clinton discussed the Gorriti case during a state visit to Panama. Seeking to extricate himself from the tar baby he had struck, the president relented in October and agreed to extend Gorriti's work permit, while *La Prensa* agreed to the cosmetic change of giving the aggressive editor a different title. Panamanian press freedom thus survived a throwback to the days of Torrijos and Noriega.

Gorriti was not the only one who accused the president of nepotism and cronyism. International shipping companies expressed concerns that as the day inched ever closer for Panama to take over operation of the canal, Pérez Balladares was appointing friends and relatives to the Panama Canal Commission, now fully Panamanian. Even members of the president's own party criticized the appointments.

Although the effort to silence Gorriti failed, Panamanian officials resorted to yet another time-honored counterattack against media criticism: libel suits. Unlike the United States, Latin American countries have loosely defined defamation laws that allow public officials to sue for the expression of critical opinions, and Panamanian officials under both Endara and Pérez Balladares have resorted to it; Endara once sued a political cartoonist! By mid-1999, there were 85 such suits pending against the media in Panama, apparently more than in any Latin American country.

On the positive side, Pérez Balladares put the economy on a solid footing, nationally and internationally, through his program of privatization and fiscal discipline and pushed through a new bank law that should help crack down on the laundering of drug money, thus improving the country's image abroad.

Panama marked a major milestone in September 1997 when the U.S. Southern Command moved its headquarters from Quarry Heights to Miami, turning over the long-time U.S. nerve center atop Ancon Hill on the edge of Panama City to the Panamanians. Albrook Air Base also reverted to Panamanian control. It was something the Panamanians once dreamed of, but the Americans' departure also was a reminder that the payroll of the U.S. bases, which once pumped $370 million into the economy, was slowly drying up. Just three months after the Southern Command moved, Pérez Balladares announced that a multinational drug interdiction center would be established at Howard Air Force Base, one of the remaining bases under U.S. control. But in April 1998 the deal became unraveled when, in the view of the

Panamanian public, it infringed too much on Panama's sovereignty.

Mireya Moscoso

The transfer of U.S. bases to Panama continued on schedule during 1998 and 1999 as the election campaign heated up to select the president who would formally assume control of the canal on December 31, 1999. Pérez Balladares became the fourth Latin American president to seek to amend the constitution to permit him to run for immediate reelection. Constitutional amendments require only a majority vote in Congress, and the president had the votes needed for passage. But amendments then must be approved by the electorate. In a referendum on August 30, 1998, a resounding 64% voted "no" to Pérez Balladares' attempt to succeed himself, leaving the field wide open.

The opposition again coalesced around Mireya Moscoso of the *Arnulfista* Party, widow of Arnulfo Arias. After the referendum, the *PRD* decided to play the dynasty card as well by nominating Martín Torrijos, the 35-year-old illegitimate son of the former strongman, a businessman who earned an economics degree from Texas A&M and once managed a McDonald's franchise in Chicago.

Throughout most of the campaign, polls showed Torrijos leading by 10 to 15 percentage points. The two candidates differed little on major issues, with both pledging to maintain the canal efficiently and fairly, for the benefit of all nations. About the only issue that divided them was Moscoso's pledge to allay Pérez Balladares' moves to privatize utility companies. She also vowed to attack the rampant corruption that had been evident under Pérez Balladares; what could Torrijos say? Torrijos instead chided Moscoso for her lack of formal training; she had studied interior design at a junior college in Miami while married to the exiled Arias. Of course, there was another, unspoken handicap in a *macho* society: her gender.

In the last two weeks of the campaign, the underdog woman suddenly pulled abreast of Torrijos in the polls. In a pathetic attempt to minimize a possible bandwagon effect, *PRD* loyalists bought up 20,000 copies of the newspaper *La Prensa*, which carried a poll showing Moscoso ahead, and destroyed them.

On election day, May 2, 1999, Moscoso scored a upset, receiving a clear plurality of 44% to Torrijos' 38% and 18% for a third candidate. With voter turnout a heavy 75%, her mandate was reasonably solid despite winning only a plurality. The combined anti-*PRD* vote represented a dramatic rebuke to the ruling party. Both Pérez Bal-

Former President Mireya Moscoso

ladares and Torrijos graciously conceded defeat. Like the presidents of both neighboring countries—Miguel Angel Rodríguez in Costa Rica and Andrés Pastrana in Colombia—Moscoso had succeeded on her second try for the presidency.

Thus, from the grave, Arnulfo Arias finally achieved a sweet triumph, as his widow defeated the son of the man who had overthrown him in 1968. Moscoso, 52, had married Arias in exile in 1969, when he was 67 and she was 22, and was with him until his death in 1988. Very possibly it was his memory and his populist message, which she exploited, coupled with disturbingly high unemployment of 12.8%, that was responsible for her upset victory.

Another milestone in the transfer of the former Canal Zone to Panama was observed on July 29, 1999, when the U.S. Army departed Fort Clayton for the last time, ending a U.S. military presence of 96 years.

Moscoso was sworn in as Panama's first woman president on September 1, 1999, the 31st anniversary of her late husband's ill-fated inauguration in 1968. Pérez Balladares left office under an ethical cloud. She was only the second elected female president in Latin America, after Nicaragua's Violeta Chamorro. Just two days before the ceremony, *La Prensa* reported that Pérez Balladares and his secretary had sold hundreds of illegal visas to Chinese immigrants in the waning days of his administration for up to $15,000 each. The president, through a statement released by his justice ministry, angrily denied involvement in the scheme and effectively left his secretary to take the fall.

To compound the ugliness of the transition, Pérez Balladares had packed the Supreme Court with last-minute appointees, denied public funds for the open-air inau-

Panama

gural ceremony Moscoso had requested at a stadium, and even ramrodded legislation through the lame-duck Congress that restricted presidential powers, including even spending emergency funds allocated to the president. Moreover, he ungraciously demanded that Moscoso reserve half the tickets to the inaugural ceremony for his *PRD* supporters, "so we can both be booed." She refused, and Pérez Balladares declined to attend the ceremony to place the presidential sash on his successor's shoulders.

Moscoso received a sweet consolation for her predecessor's ungentlemanly actions when two small parties, Solidarity and National Liberal, withdrew from their coalition with the *PRD* and joined the *Panameñista Party* in a new coalition, giving it a one-seat majority in the 71-seat Congress.

Even before the inauguration, a controversy erupted in the United States and Panama when it was learned that a Hong Kong-based company, Hutchison Whampoa Ltd., had received a 20-year contract in 1997 to operate the port facilities at both entrances to the canal. This led U.S. Senate Majority Leader Trent Lott and other conservative Republicans in Congress to charge that the communist government in Beijing would be in a position to close the canal to U.S. shipping at will. Li Ka-shing, the billionaire owner of the company, denied any such intentions. The Clinton Administration also dismissed the idea of Chinese control as unfounded.

Because of fears of Y2K fears, the date for the ceremony transferring control of the canal was moved from December 31 to December 14, 1999. Representing the United States, appropriately enough, was former President Jimmy Carter, who had signed the new treaties in 1977. With his and Moscoso's signatures, Panama at last enjoyed full sovereignty over its territory and over the canal.

In November 2001, a two-year, $300 million project was completed that widened the Gaillard Cut, the "ditch" section of the canal, by 40 yards, increasing its traffic potential by 20 percent. But a far more ambitious $4.5 billion expansion project began in 2004. A Belgian-French consortium contracted to build a third lane of the canal, which will involve creating three more reservoirs.

In September 2002, canal tolls were raised 8%, the first increase since the Panamanian takeover; they were increased another 4% in 2003—the centennial year of the Bunau-Varilla Treaty. The pricing system also was changed from a per-ton basis to the type of ship and cargo. The increases were deemed necessary to keep the canal competitive. Long-term plans for upgrading the canal to accommodate larger ships

President Martín Torrijos

are expected to cost $8-$12 billion, and must be approved in a referendum.

In April 2002, the country experienced a catharsis of sorts when a special "truth commission" on disappearances and mysterious deaths during the 1968-89 military regimes presented its report to President Moscoso. The commission investigated 168 cases and reached conclusions on 110. Of those, 70 were found to be assassinations of political dissidents, most of them during the Torrijos period. Another 40 remain unsolved.

Moscoso unleased a hornet's nest when she fired Juan Jovane, the head of the social security fund, in September 2003, alleging he had mismanaged the fund. Unions countered that the government itself had mismanaged the fund and were using Jovane as a scapegoat. A coalition of unions, including doctors, staged Panama's first general strike in six years.

The last year of Moscoso's presidency was marred by various allegations of corruption in her government. The corruption issue was to prove an albatross around the *Arnulfista* Party's neck in the next election.

The Election of 2004

In March 2003, Martín Torrijos, still just 39, announced he would make his second bid for the presidency in the May 2004 election. He received the nomination of the *PRD* again and that of the Popular Party, the descendant of the Christian Democrats, forming an alliance called *Patria Nueva*. The *Arnulfistas* nominated Moscoso's personal choice, Foreign Minister José Miguel Alemán, who formed an alliance with two other parties called *Visión de País*. Former President Endara also entered the race as candidate of a

movement called *Solidaridad*. Rounding out the field was Ricardo Martinelli of *Cambio Democrático*.

Torrijos went into the campaign as the early favorite and stayed there. He promised to clean up the endemic corruption (neglecting to mention that it had been also rife in the Pérez Balladares administration, in which he served as a deputy government and justice minister). Unlike his father, he was not a gringo-baiter. Educated at Texas A&M, he is a practical businessman and advocated a free-trade agreement with the United States. He even cleaned up the *PRD*'s image for his generation of voters by purging it of some of the unsavory elements left over from the dictatorship. He was endorsed by the popular singer-actor Rubén Blades (see Culture).

On May 2, 76.9% of Panamanians voted, slightly more than in 1999. The results:

Torrijos	711,447	47.7%
Endara	462,766	30.9%
Alemán	245,845	16.6%
Martinelli	79,595	5.3%

Recent Developments

In the waning days of her administration, Moscoso provoked a diplomatic row with Cuba. On August 22, the Cuban government told Moscoso it understood she was considering pardoning four Cuban exiles imprisoned in Panama for planning an assassination attempt on Fidel Castro there in 2000 and warned that it would sever diplomatic relations if she did. The next day, Moscoso indignantly denied she had planned to pardon the four, condemned Cuba for its language, recalled Panama's ambassador to Cuba and ordered the Cuban ambassador to leave Panama. Then, on August 26, Moscoso abruptly pardoned the four for "humanitarian" reasons, saying she feared that Torrijos may extradite them to Cuba, where they would be executed. Cuba promptly broke diplomatic relations, calling Moscoso an "accomplice and protector of terrorism" and the pardons "repugnant and treacherous."

The most notorious of the four men is Luis Posada Carriles, who in 1985 escaped from prison in Venezuela where he was awaiting retrial for masterminding the bombing of a Cuban airliner in 1976 that killed 73 people. Consequently, Venezuela also severed diplomatic relations with Panama because of the pardons. Three of the men flew to Florida after their release, but Posada Carriles vanished. He eventually turned up in Miami, where he was arrested in May 2005, not on a fugitive warrant but for entering the country illegally.

Cuba and Venezuela are demanding he be extradited to Venezuela (see Cuba).

The pardons cast a cloud over the September 1, 2004 inauguration of Torrijos, who called them "unacceptable" and said he would restore diplomatic relations with both countries. Despite the tension, Moscoso was far more gracious to Torrijos at his inauguration than Pérez Balladares had been to her. She also had the satisfaction of serving out her full term, something her late husband was denied three times—the last time by the father of the man who succeeded her.

Just two months after Moscoso left office, the electoral tribunal revoked her immunity from prosecution. She is being asked to account for the alleged disappearance of $70 million in public funds during her presidency. She called the charges politically motivated, even though she brazenly admitted spending $ 3 million, which she said was justified to maintain her image!

Torrijos has taken a businesslike approach to solving pressing economic problems, especially a huge budget deficit and a bloated public pension system that was $100 million in the red. Torrijos has raised taxes, and his plan to increase the retirement age for men from 62 to 65 and to raise social security contributions led to violent protests, mostly by teachers and construction workers, in May 2005. Nonetheless, the National Assembly approved the changes 43–30. The reforms will allow Panama to borrow money at lower interest rates.

Torrijos then turned to expansion of the canal. He has called a referendum for November 20, 2005, on whether or not to reinvest $5 billion in canal revenue into expansion of the waterway.

Culture: Panama's culture is a reflection of its unique geographical situation as a crossroads of both terrestrial and maritime traffic between two oceans and two continents. There is a polyglot of ethnic groups, not one of which predominates: the indigenous Indians, many of them unassimilated, such as the Cuna tribe of the San Blas Islands on the Caribbean coast that contributed the distinctive *mola* tapestries that have become so identifiable with Panamanian culture; the Caucasians, not merely Spanish descendants but the scions of latter-day European, Arab and Jewish immigrants who today account for a disproportionate share of the country's wealth and political power; the *mestizos*, who outnumber the first two groups; blacks and mulattos, who are about equal in number to the *mestizos*, descended not from slaves as in Brazil, but from workers imported from the British West Indies to help construct the canal; and the sizable community of Orientals, principally Chinese, who have filtered into the

Carlota—a Panamanian beauty in native costume

country in the decades since the completion of the canal.

Because of this, Panama boasts a distinctive culture, particularly in its folk music, dances and costumes that its tourist industry has helped to preserve. In popular music it also has made some contributions. Its best-known singer, Rubén Blades, won a following in Latin America before appearing in a number of U.S. movies and receiving a U.S. Grammy Award. He ran for president of Panama in 1994 but ran third with 18% of the vote.

Literacy is relatively high in Panama, but the small population has not been sufficient to support much book or magazine publishing. Panama boasts one of Latin America's oldest daily newspapers, *La Estrella de Panamá*, founded in 1853. Unfortunately, *La Estrella's* owners were blackmailed into editorial support for dictators Torrijos and later Noriega, and the paper has never fully recovered from its reputation as a sycophant.

Until the U.S. invasion of 1989 that brought down the Noriega dictatorship, aggressive and critical journalism in Panama was a risky business. *El Panamá América*, expropriated from Harmodio Arias by Torrijos in 1968, was restored to his family and remains the second-leading daily. The country's leading daily today, *La Prensa*, was established in 1980 by Roberto Eisenmann and courageously stood up to both the Torrijos and Noriega

dictatorships. For this it was repeatedly vandalized and finally closed in 1987. The month after the U.S. invasion, its repaired presses began rolling again.

Economy: Panama's economy is based on trade brought to it by an accident of geography. Farm output is unable to feed the population; the major source of income (about 20% of the gross national product) is tied to the Canal. The Torrijos regime sought to diversify the economy—in addition to stressing rural development and road construction, the government established incentives to make Panama an international banking center. Passage of the Panama Canal treaties has had the effect of stimulating new industrial investments. An oil pipeline enables the transport of crude by supertankers ocean-to-ocean, compensating for their inability to fit through the narrow canal, providing substantial revenues to Panama.

In 1972 the government enacted a series of tariffs to protect local industries together with stringent worker protection laws at the request of the strong Panamanian labor movement. This had the effect of reducing competition from imports and raising the price of consumer goods. These moves were basically financed by foreign borrowing. By 1985 the International Monetary Fund insisted that these measures be sharply reduced as a condition to additional loans and assurances to

Panama

private banks, a move which met with widespread disapproval.

Much of the impetus for Panama becoming a major international banking center in the 1970s and 1980s stemmed from a Swiss-style banking law that made Panama a favored spot for the laundering of illegal drug money. Not until 1997 did Panama make a concerted effort to change the law and remove this stigma.

The prodigious economic spinoff from the canal, including the thousands of jobs generated by the canal itself and the numerous U.S. military bases, has long given Panama among the highest standards of living in Latin America; in 2004, Panama's per capita income was still the fourth-highest of the 20 Latin republics.

Moreover, Panama has avoided the hyperinflation that has plagued so many of \its neighbors. The reason: The official currency is called the Balboa, but in reality the U.S. dollar is the country's legal tender, which is a boon for international banking and provides monetary stability. (Panama has its own coins, which are identical in size and weight with U.S. denominations and thus are interchangeable in vending machines.) Largely because of the dollar-based economy, inflation has fluctuated between 1.7% and 1.0% for the past several years, remarkable for Latin America. For that reason, Ecuador and El Salvador have emulated Panama by replacing their currency with the dollar.

One of the country's greatest economic success stories is the Colón Free Zone, on the Caribbean side, created in 1948, which imports and re-exports products from all over the world. In 2002, turnover totaled about $10 billion.

On the negative side, Panama has one of the most cumbersome national debts per capita in the world, at present about $5.6 billion.

The Panamanian takeover of the canal on December 31, 1999, was historic, and while it was no economic panacea, Panama's stewardship has been far more successful than anticipated. When Panama took over, it generated $500 million in revenue; after five years, it brought in a record $1 billion, and a record operating profit of $183 million. It still accounts for 4.5% of all ocean-going trade, but 19% of cargo ships are too large to transit the century-old locks. President Martín Torrijos has called for reinvesting $5 billion in expanding the canal to increase its capacity, and Panamanian voters are to decide the issue in a referendum on November 20, 2005.

Panama's GDP growth in 2002 was only .9%, but it has since rebounded to 4.3% in 2003 and a robust 6.2% in 2004.

The Future: President Martín Torrijos went to great lengths to capitalize upon his father's name for those who still revere him (most Panamanians are now too young to remember him), while distancing himself from the dark side of his father's 13-year-long dictatorship. This author served in Panama in 1977, 1978 and 1979 during the Torrijos era. I remember him as a drunkard, a womanizer and a despot who closed down opposition media and who had political opponents tortured or killed by taking them on a "one-way helicopter ride" over the Pacific. I was at Fort Clayton in 1978 when President Jimmy Carter came to Panama to sign the instruments of ratification, and I watched the proceedings on television. Torrijos was so drunk at the ceremony

that he could barely stand at the podium, and his speech was slurred and sometimes incomprehensible.

By most accounts, his son, whom he did not even acknowledge until he was a teenager, is not from that mold. His performance in his first year as president suggests that the sins of the father have not been visited upon the son. He has promised to clean up the corruption and incompetence from the previous administration—just as Moscoso did. We will see whether a Texas Aggie who managed a McDonald's franchise will do a better job running the country than an interior decorator did.

Torrijos has correctly made the canal a priority, too, both expansion and security. More and more cargo ships are being built that are too large for the canal's 1,000-by-110-foot locks. New sets of locks would require building of new reservoirs. The only other option would be a new, parallel canal. Either way, the project would cost a minimum of $8 billion, and under the constitution would require approval in a referendum. That is scheduled for November 20, 2005, and the country's long-term economic progress hinges on that vote.

Security has become a more important consideration since September 11, 2001. It would be relatively easy for al-Qaeda terrorists to cripple one of the locks or to sink a ship in the still-narrow Gaillard Cut, closing the canal. Although such an attack would be aimed at the United States, its effect on the Panamanian economy—and world commerce—would be devastating. Panama still has no military establishment to protect the canal as the United States once did. It would be ironic if Torrijos called upon the United States to help safeguard the canal—even if his father turned somersaults in his tomb at Fort Amador.

Washing clothes at an outdoor sluice

The Republic of Paraguay

The unspoiled beauty of a whitewater river in Paraguay

Area: 157,047 square miles.

Population: 6.2 million.

Capital City: Asunción (Pop. 550,000).

Climate: The eastern section (*Oriental*) lies in a temperate zone; the western (*Occidental*) section is hot and oppressive. Rainfall is heaviest from February to May; most of Paraguay receives adequate water except for the western plains.

Neighboring Countries: Brazil (East and Northeast); Argentina (South); Bolivia (West and Northwest).

Official Language: Spanish.

Other Principal Tongues: Guaraní, a native Indian dialect, spoken as a first language by half the population.

Ethnic Background: *Mestizo* (mixed Spanish and Guaraní ancestry).

Principal Religion: Roman Catholic Christianity.

Chief Commercial Products: Cotton, soybean, timber, vegetable oils, coffee, light manufactured goods.

Currency: Guaraní.

Gross Domestic Product: U.S. $5.87 billion in 2003 ($1,019 per capita).

Former Colonial Status: Spanish Crown Colony (1537–1811).

Independence Date: May 14, 1811.

Chief of State: Nicanor Duarte Frutos (b. October 11, 1956), president (since August 15, 2003).

National Flag: Red, white and blue horizontal stripes. The white stripe displays the national seal on one side and the words *Paz y Justicia* (Peace and Justice) on the opposite side. This is the only flag in the world having different sides.

Although Paraguay lies almost in the geographic center of the continent and is one of South America's two interior nations, it is not landlocked. The Paraná river forms part of the boundary with Argentina and Brazil and links Paraguay with the Atlantic. The north to south Paraguay River, a Paraná tributary, divides the country into two regions with very different characters. Paraguay's third important river, the Pilcomayo, forms the southwest frontier with Argentina and joins the Paraguay opposite Asunción.

The eastern (*Oriental*) region of Paraguay, between the Paraguay and the Paraná rivers, is referred to as Paraguay proper. Containing approximately 40% of the nation's territory, the *Oriental* has fertile rolling plains with scattered hills in the south central portion, rising to the Amabay Mountains (2,700 feet) in the northeast along the Brazilian border. This is the most densely populated region of Paraguay.

The western (*Occidental*) region of the nation, commonly called the *Chaco*, is a hot, grassy prairie, interspersed with stands of hardwood known as *quebracho* (axe-breaker). Crossed by numerous unnavigable streams, its underground water is too salty for irrigation or human consumption; until recently this region was largely uninhabited. Today, through the impounding of rainwater, the Chaco is dotted with cattle ranches and the *quebracho* is harvested for tannin.

History: The history of Paraguay centers on the capital, Asunción, and on the villages within a 60-mile radius around that city on the eastern side of the Paraguay River. To the primitive people who roamed the area prior to the Spanish conquest, the lush plains lying between the Paraguay and the Paraná rivers were their traditional Garden of Eden. Of the many tribes which resided here, most were of the Tupi-Guaraní linguistic group. An amiable people, living by trapping, fishing and simple plantings, they offered little opposition to the Spaniards who explored the Paraná valley and established a fort at Asunción on August 15, 1537, some 70 years prior to the first English settlement in North America.

Though neglected by the Spanish crown, the colony prospered and at the end of 20 years boasted 1,500 Spanish residents, a cathedral, a textile mill and a

287

Paraguay

growing cattle industry. For two centuries, Asunción and its pleasant valley developed slowly while serving as the seat of Spanish authority in South America east of the Andes Mountains and south of the Portuguese colony in Brazil.

From Asunción, expeditions founded the cities of Santa Fé, Corrientes and Buenos Aires. Beginning in 1588, a company of Jesuit missionaries gathered some 100,000 Indians into mission villages and taught them better methods of farming, stock raising and handicrafts. The Jesuits protected their wards against enslavement by civil governors, settlers and Brazilian slave hunters; in the process, they helped to hold Paraguay and Uruguay for the Spanish. Unfortunately for the colony, the Jesuits were expelled in 1767.

Paraguay's transition from colonial status to independence was swift and unspectacular. In 1810, following the declaration of independence by Buenos Aires, Paraguay was invited to join with the Argentine ex-colony. The invitation was rejected and in 1811 Paraguay defeated a force sent from Buenos Aires to compel acceptance of Argentine leadership. A congress declared Paraguay to be a free and independent state and a five-man ruling council was established.

Dissension erupted; in 1814 a hopelessly deadlocked Congress voted full dictatorial powers to Dr. José Gaspar Rodríguez de Francia, who ruled until 1840. Austere, frugal, honest, dedicated and brutally cruel, he set the dictatorial pattern that persisted until 1989. Francia introduced improved methods in agriculture and in stock raising and was able to force the Paraguayan soil to produce more than ever before. Although dissent was ruthlessly suppressed, Paraguay was well ordered and well fed.

Francia's death created a power vacuum and a year of turmoil. The man who came to power, Carlos Antonio López, imposed a constitution, but one that let him rule with the same autocratic powers that Fran-

cia had. López established trade and diplomatic relations with other countries and groomed his son, Francisco Solano López, to succeed him. The son enjoyed playing soldier and built up Paraguay's army. After he succeeded his father, he gave himself the rank of *mariscal* (field marshal) and looked around for someone to fight. He foolishly declared war on Brazil, Argentina and Uruguay in 1865, a decision that was to decimate the country's male population. In the bloody, five-year War of the Triple Alliance, Paraguay's three enemies invaded the country and engaged in what today would be called genocide. Of a population of 520,000, at least 300,000 Paraguayans were slaughtered; only 28,746 males survived. It was a demographic cataclysm from which it took the country generations to recover. "Mariscal" López, for whom the main boulevard of Asunción is named today, was himself killed in a battle with the Brazilians in 1870, which ended the pointless struggle, the costliest in the history of post-colonial South America. It says something of the Paraguayan mentality that López still is revered as a national hero, as is Francia.

Between 1870 and 1932 Paraguay slowly recovered and remained at peace with its neighbors. However, internal turmoil persisted and presidents were put in office by gunplay rather than by elections. From 1870 until 1954, Paraguay had 39 presidents, most of whom were jailed, murdered or exiled before they completed

their term. As in many Latin American countries, the Conservative and Liberal parties competed for power, but there was little alternation between them; the Conservatives ruled from 1870–1904, when the Liberals gained power in a modest social revolution and governed until 1936. Economically, there was some progress. Immigrants from Italy, Spain, Germany and Argentina developed the agriculture, stock raising and forestry industries. Of the 800,000 population in 1928, the majority were illiterate and landless; profits from agriculture and industry went to foreign owners, mostly Argentine.

The Paraguay-Bolivia border remained undefined after the war of 1870. A humiliated Paraguay sought to extend its barren Chaco territory. Bolivia sought access to the Atlantic via ports on the Paraguay River. War broke out in 1932, ending in a 1935 truce that awarded Paraguay about 20,000 square miles at a cost of 36,000 dead, and a seriously damaged economy. Six of the Chaco War's heroes later became president.

A revolt by Chaco War veterans in February 1936 brought Colonel Rafael Franco into the presidency. Like his Spanish namesake who took power that very year, Franco initiated a quasi-fascist economic system that would endure for 50 years—some might argue it still exists. But he was deposed in August 1937 by Félix Paiva, and a decade of upheaval ensued. Paiva stood aside and allowed nominally democratic elections in 1939, which were won by the Liberals behind the candidacy of General Estigarribia, a Chaco War hero. But Estigarribia perished in a plane crash in 1940 and his war minister, Higinio Morínigo, seized power and ruled as dictator for eight years.

In 1947, the old Conservative Party renamed itself the *Colorado* Party and staged a coup that toppled the dictatorship and began an unbroken period of party dominance that continues to the present. Five presidents came and went during the next three years, until the election of the *Colorados'* Federico Chaves in 1950.

The Stroessner Era, 1954–89

In July 1954, the army revolted against Chaves and installed General Alfredo Stroessner in power. He was "re-elected" to the presidency by a large vote seven times, serving for 35 years. Although he initially allowed opposition elements to contest elections, they were subsequently eliminated by 1963. He later allowed the Liberal Party to field candidates in the elections in 1973 and 1978, but the outcomes of all the elections during his rule were preordained. Stroessner was able to arrange election victories by huge margins, which made the very use of the term "election" a farce.

In the 1973 election, for example, Stroessner received 681,306 votes over his opponent, Gustavo Riart of the Liberal Party, who got 198,096. Abstentions and blank ballots accounted for 35% of the vote. Elections for the new Senate and Chamber of Deputies were held at the same time. Since Stroessner's *Colorado* Party gained a majority in both houses, it was by law entitled to two thirds of the seats. The remaining one third was assigned to the opposition by a prescribed formula.

General Alfredo Stroessner

Two small opposition groups were actually similar in outlook to the *Colorado*s. All three favored free enterprise with minimal state intervention into the economy. However, the Liberals favored a more democratic government. Whenever any individual appeared to gain *too much* popularity during Stroessner's years, he was either jailed, exiled or simply disappeared.

With solid military backing, Stroessner ruled Paraguay as his personal fiefdom. He stressed political stability in the nation, his strong stand against communism and the regime's emphasis of road construction. Living standards did rise slowly, but steadily, during his years of power.

Political stability did attract foreign investment. Relations with the Catholic Church were generally poor, particularly when Stroessner sought to undermine the Marandú rural public housing program of the church. Supported with funds obtained in the United States, the effort attempted to provide the nation's impoverished Indian population with medical, legal and economic assistance. Nearly all of the estimated 100,000 Indians in Paraguay still live at the bottom of the nation's social and economic scales. The conservative elite viewed such attempts to help the Indians as a "communist conspiracy." Five Jesuit priests, leaders of the movement, were deported and others were jailed. (Even as recently as April 2005, the democratically elected Paraguayan Congress rejected a bill that would have established a 114,000-hectare reserve for the nomadic Ayoreo tribe in the Chaco, the last tribe outside the Amazon to have resisted contact with outsiders.)

The country was governed under Stroessner by "state of siege" legislation that suspended constitutional guarantees. It was renewed every 90 days.

Predictably, Stroessner was "re-elected" in 1983 and again in 1988. Corruption within the ruling *Colorado* Party was reported by the independent newspaper *ABC Color,* on the radio and by the Paraguayan Episcopal Conference in late 1984. The first two were closed down and the latter was ignored.

Stroessner was elected to his eighth term by a majority of 89% in 1988. There were the usual irregularities and voter apathy. The *Colorado* Party became mildly divided over the issue of what should happen after the president left the scene—the *tradicionalistas* wanted the aging dictator to step aside, while the *oficialistas* (also called *militantes)* thought Stroessner, barring ill health, should remain in office. The matter was postponed by Stroessner's candidacy for re-election. When opposition *Radio Ñanduti* became too vocal, it was jammed; the government claimed to know nothing about this.

Stroessner Falls

When in late 1988 Stroessner disappeared for 10 days there were rumors he had died. He underwent prostate surgery at an undisclosed location; his recovery was very slow. Sensing the time was right, the Commander-in-Chief of the military, General Andrés Rodríguez, staged a coup in February 1989, exiling the now-feeble Stroessner to Brazil without opposition. Low estimates of deaths during the coup were 50, high ones 300. Thus ended the 35-year rule of the son of a German brewmaster and a Guaraní Indian woman.

Taking the opposition by surprise, Rodríguez announced elections for May 1, 1989; Rodríguez became the *Colorado* candidate, assuring his election to a four-year term. He projected the image of a populist in contrast to the aloof, distant Stroessner.

Things didn't really change in Paraguay. Rodríguez received more than 74% of the vote; the *Colorado* Party received two thirds of the seats in the Chamber of Deputies and in the Senate. Periodic power struggles within the party occurred after the election between the "democratic" faction and the slightly more conservative "traditionalists;" Rodríguez favored the former. His daughter married Stroessner's son. Under Stroessner and Rodríguez, Paraguay had become a giant fencing operation, the largest in Latin America. If one wanted to buy or sell anything that had been stolen, Paraguay was (and still is, to a large degree) the place to go.

But even this enterprise was shaken in 1992 when a "whistle blowing" colonel disclosed that the army had a virtual monopoly on fencing expensive, stolen cars—its specialty. Surprisingly, this led to Rodríguez's removal of four top military figures; this was probably done to avoid a charge that he was also involved in the operation, although there is no known evidence that he was.

In late 1992, preparing for primary and general elections, the *Colorado* Party again became badly divided. The "democratic" faction prevailed and nominated Juan Carlos Wasmosy, a civil engineer and businessman. The conservatives, who had backed a charismatic army general named Lino Oviedo, ultimately joined to support him. Even today there are suspicions that Wasmosy and Oviedo resorted to stuffing ballot boxes, but Wasmosy's people managed to stuff more than did Oviedo's. Wasmosy was then opposed by two candidates in the May 1993 general election— Domingo Laino of the Authentic Radical Liberal Party *(PLRA)* and Guillermo Caballero Vargas of the National Encounter Party. As an encouraging sign of increased democratization and governmental decentralization, the governors of the 17 de-

Paraguay

Children celebrate Independence Day in a small town

partments were elected directly for the first time, and the Liberals captured Central Department, where Asunción is located. But Wasmosy won an expanded five-year term with more than 40% of the vote after campaigning on promises to improve the economy and employment.

The Oviedo Factor

The military had promised early in 1993 to continue "co-governing" with the *Colorado* Party. But the main political parties agreed upon a "governability pact" that excluded the police and military from party membership; the signing of it was postponed, however, after there were attacks by drunken *Colorado* Party supporters on opposition legislators.

A Liberal politician laid bare the existence of files of the secret police in December 1992 containing facts behind the disappearance of some 15,000 people during the Stroessner years. It also allegedly contained evidence supporting the existence of Operation Condor, a cooperative effort against leftists by Paraguay, Chile, Argentina and Uruguay during the 1980s that arranged disappearances of undesired people.

Democratic forces held their breath in late April 1996 when General Oviedo publicly called for Wasmosy to resign. It amounted to an attempted coup, but the rest of the armed forces failed to move against the civilian president. Wasmosy then summoned Oviedo to his office and ordered him to retire, promising him the cabinet post of defense secretary. For 27

tense hours, Oviedo demurred, provoking fears of a throwback to Paraguay's bad old days of military strongmen. In the end, he relented and retired, but public protests against his accepting the cabinet post led Wasmosy to withdraw the offer. Paraguay, at least, appeared to have established civilian control over the military. Wasmosy went even further in December 1996 by cashiering 207 cavalry officers who he said had supported Oviedo's short-lived rebellion. A judge overturned Wasmosy's order in January 1997, citing insufficient evidence. But an appeals court overturned the judge's decision and Wasmosy signed a decree dismissing the officers. Once again, civilian authority prevailed.

The Oviedo saga continued, however. In September 1997, the *Colorado* Party held its primary, in which Oviedo won the nomination for the May 10, 1998, presidential election. This infuriated Wasmosy, and relations between him and Oviedo went from poor to deplorable. In November, Oviedo publicly accused the president of incompetence and corruption; Wasmosy, falling back on his authority as commander-in-chief, ordered the general arrested for insubordination. Oviedo was a fugitive for 42 days before turning himself in. Wasmosy placed him under house arrest for 30 days.

There followed a series of legal battles between the two men in both civilian and military courts. In late December 1997, the nation's top electoral court rejected a plea from Wasmosy to disqualify Oviedo as the *Colorado* candidate. There was another

coup scare in January 1998 when, after a judge indicated he might order Oviedo's release because he had never been formally charged, tanks began rumbling in the streets. The military claimed, unconvincingly, that it had merely been a practice for a ceremony. Meanwhile, a determined Wasmosy assembled a special military tribunal in February that dutifully ordered Oviedo jailed for an "indefinite" term for his abortive coup in 1996. In March, the tribunal formally sentenced Oviedo, still a presidential candidate, to 10 years.

When it became apparent that Wasmosy might not be able legally to strip Oviedo of the *Colorado* nomination, and faced with polls that showed the Guaraní-speaking Oviedo in the lead, the president briefly pondered a decidedly undemocratic move: to postpone the May election. But Paraguay's *Mercosur* partners quickly reminded Wasmosy that democratic government was a condition of membership. The United States also issued a warning against postponing the election. Wasmosy was saved from being cast in the role of antidemocrat by the Supreme Court, which voted 5-4 to uphold Oviedo's prison term, effectively disqualifying his candidacy.

Oviedo vowed to campaign from jail, but the party, facing reality, nominated Oviedo's running mate, Raúl Cubas Grau, a 54-year-old businessman, to stand for president. To mollify the Wasmosy faction, they agreed on Luis María Argaña as the new vice-presidential candidate. The 11th-hour termination of Oviedo's candi-

Paraguay

Former President Raúl Cubas

A Paraguayan *alza prima* pulled by an ox.

dacy gave a boost to the perennial standard-bearer of the Liberals, Domingo Laino, running this time as candidate of the Democratic Alliance coalition. Now it was the *Colorado*s who called for a postponement of the election.

It was just as well for them that the vote wasn't delayed. Cubas received 54% to Laino's 42%; the Democratic Alliance immediately claimed fraud, a charge that appeared to be largely unsubstantiated. Just days before the election, Cubas declared unabashedly that if the *Colorado*s won, "Free, in jail, or wherever he is, Oviedo will have political power." He was to make good on that promise soon after he was inaugurated on August 15, 1998.

Assassination, Impeachment, Aftermath

Cubas' seven months in office were marked by Byzantine political intrigues that culminated in a high-level assassination, the president's impeachment and then his resignation and the ignominious flights into exile of both Cubas and Oviedo. These events sorely tested whether this fledgling democracy would long endure.

Just three days after his inauguration, Cubas pardoned Oviedo, which led to jubilant demonstrations by the general's supporters, who chanted, *"Lino presidente!"* Cubas then appointed a new military tribunal, packed with Oviedo sympathizers, which quickly dismissed all charges against the general. This brash action was to plunge Paraguay into a constitutional crisis, pitting the executive branch against both the legislative and judicial branches; under Stroessner's rule, of course, it would have been a short-lived contest. Days after the tribunal cleared Oviedo, members of Congress began threatening the president with impeachment.

On December 2, 1998, the Supreme Court ruled Cubas' pardon and the military tribunal unconstitutional and ordered Oviedo incarcerated again. Cubas merely ignored the order, which created a deep schism within the ranks of the *Colorado* Party. Heading the anti-Oviedo faction was Vice President Argaña, who prevailed in a vote by the *Colorado* leadership on December 5 to expel Oviedo from the party. The president and vice president had not even been on speaking terms since their inauguration.

The constitutional impasse rumbled on into 1999. By February, there were rampant rumors that Cubas was planning a Fujimori-style military takeover, which he adamantly denied. His opponents, meanwhile, denounced him at a *Mercosur* summit, a reminder to Cubas that membership in the trade bloc requires a democratic form of government. It was not an idle threat; about two thirds of Paraguay's exports are to its *Mercosur* partners.

On February 11, the lower house of Congress voted 71-37 to charge the president with abuse of power for his actions the previous August—just two votes shy of the two-thirds-plus-one-vote majority needed for formal impeachment. Several *Colorado* deputies joined with the opposition Liberals. To further complicate this Byzantine spectacle, the armed forces high command—loyal to Oviedo—dismissed the air force generals who had refused to participate in Oviedo's barracks revolt in 1996.

As this political drama reached a climax, Vice President Argaña was assassinated in broad daylight on March 23, 1999, as he ar-

rived at work. A vehicle containing three or four men in camouflage fatigues curbed Argaña's jeep. One of the men threw a grenade, while others opened fire, hitting the vice president in the heart. He died at the scene. His driver also was killed and his bodyguard gravely wounded. The killing threw the country into even greater turmoil and brought international denunciations. Both Cubas and Oviedo issued statements denouncing their rival's murder, but not before thousands of Argaña's supporters took to the streets in protest; security forces opened fire, leaving seven people dead.

The day after the assassination, the Chamber of Deputies overwhelmingly voted to impeach Cubas. The anti-Cubas *Colorado*s and opposition Liberals did not come across as champions of democracy, however; at least one pro-Cubas *Colorado* deputy was roughed up when he arrived at the Congress and prevented from entering. The case then went before the Senate, which took it up immediately. Conviction and removal were certain.

On March 28, Cubas abruptly resigned and boarded a waiting Brazilian air force plane that flew him into a comfortable exile; he owned a beach house in southern Brazil. Almost simultaneously, Oviedo fled the country in a light plane and flew to Buenos Aires, where he was briefly detained for not having the necessary immigration papers. Within a day, however, Argentina granted him asylum, giving him immunity from extradition. Paraguay requested it anyway.

In accordance with the constitution, Senate President Luis Angel González Macchi,

Paraguay

52, next in the line of succession after the president and vice president, was sworn in as interim president hours after Cubas' resignation. The army dispelled any lingering doubts about a peaceful transition when it pledged him its support. The new president, a former professional basketball player who had an unspectacular career as a legislator, appointed a new cabinet that included Argaña's brother and even some ministers from the opposition Liberal and National Encounter parties. Such power-sharing was unprecedented in the 52 years the *Colorado* Party has been entrenched in power.

The new government announced it would hold a new presidential election in six months and that a Liberal would be the running mate of the *Colorado* candidate. Later, however, the Supreme court ruled that González Macchi could serve the remainder of Cubas' five-year term.

Paraguay angrily recalled its ambassador from Argentina in July 1999 after the government of President Carlos Menem refused to extradite Oviedo. Simultaneously, Paraguay recalled its envoy from Uruguay, which refused to extradite Cubas' defense minister, José Segovia Boltes, in connection with the Argaña assassination. In October, however, the election to succeed Menem in Argentina was won by Fernando de la Rua, who had pledged to extradite Oviedo. Sensing he had overstayed his welcome, the wily general vanished shortly before de la Rua's inauguration on December 10.

Just after New Year's Day, 2000, Oviedo resurfaced, brazenly holding a news conference with a handful of reporters at an undisclosed location in rural Paraguay, which was reported by media throughout Latin America (this author read about it in the Chilean newspapers and saw it on television there). He maintained his innocence and alleged that his enemies had murdered Argaña to discredit him. Cocky as ever, he boasted again that he would one day return to Asunción as the people's champion.

Oviedo supporters in the military, the police and the Congress gave the country—and the world community—a scare on May 18, 2000, when three armored cars parked in front of the legislative palace and fired two shots at the building. A tense standoff ensued, as military unit commanders around the country publicly declared their support for González Macchi, who declared a 30-day state of siege. Denunciations of the revolt came pouring in from Argentina, Brazil, the United States and other democracies. The next morning, about 25 soldiers, a few retired officers, 12 policemen and three pro-Oviedo congressmen surrendered. The president of the Congress claimed in a televised interview that documents found after the revolt indicated that the mutineers planned to assassinate several *Colorado* Party leaders, including González Macchi and vice-presidential candidate Felix Argaña, the 42-year-old son of the slain vice president, who was running to

**Former President
Luis Angel González Macchi**

fill his father's vacant seat in an August election. González Macchi declared that the plotters would be duly punished. Oviedo, meanwhile, sent a communiqué from his hideout to the newspaper *ABC Color* denying he was involved in the short-lived revolt.

The whereabouts of the elusive general had become a national—and international—obsession even before the revolt. Besides Paraguay and Bolivia, Oviedo sightings were reported in Brazil, which turned out to be correct. In June 2000, acting on information from Paraguayan intelligence authorities who had been tapping and tracing Oviedo's numerous phone calls to supporters back home, Brazilian police arrested him in a posh apartment in Foz do Iguaçu, across the border from Ciudad del Este. Oviedo had grown a mustache and long hair. Police found 10 cellular phones in the apartment and a .38 pistol, which allowed them to charge him with illegal weapons possession.

For 18 months he languished in jail, until December 2001, when the 11 Brazilian Supreme Court justices unanimously rejected Paraguay's extradition request as "politically motivated" and ordered Oviedo released. The Paraguayan government was furious. A jubilant Oviedo, boastful as ever, vowed to return to Paraguay and run for president again. Ironically, Oviedo had been living with a cousin in an affluent neighborhood of Brasilia—a short distance from the home of the exiled Stroessner.

In domestic politics, González Macchi's tenuous coalition with the Liberals fell apart in February 2000 after the Liberals voted overwhelmingly to return to their role as an opposition party to protest al-

The water control spillways at Yacyretá

leged political corruption. The bone of contention between the two parties was a reform bill that would have streamlined and depoliticized Paraguay's cumbersome bureaucracy, which sucks up more than 80% of the national budget. Hardline *Colorado*s had resisted the reforms because patronage is a traditional tool by which the party had ensured support. The president also sought to privatize inefficient state-owned companies, which sparked a protest in front of the legislative palace by state workers, who were joined by landless peasants demanding free land. The atmosphere was such that González Macchi canceled a trip to Colombia, just as he had been forced to cancel earlier trips to Spain and Germany.

After the *Colorado*-Liberal alliance fell apart, the two parties fielded separate candidates in the special election called in August 2000, to fill the vacancy in the vice presidency. The *Colorado*s nominated Argaña's son, Félix, seemingly an unbeatable choice. But the political establishment was stunned when the Liberal candidate, Julio César "Yoyito" Franco, narrowly defeated Argaña. It was the *Colorado*s' first national-level defeat, a political event virtually on a par with the defeat of the *PRI* in Mexico's presidential election the month before. With the opposition in the vice presidency, pressure increased on the unpopular—and unelected—González Macchi to step aside. His position was not helped by the continued deterioration of the already sour economy (see Economy). Nor was the president bolstered by the embarrassing revelations in the media in April 2001 that his personal BMW, which was worth about $130,000 and for which he reportedly paid only $80,000, apparently had been stolen in Brazil and smuggled into Paraguay in time-honored fashion.

For the second year in a row, the United States "decertified" Paraguay in February 2000 as an ally in the war on drugs, citing the government's inaction at countering rampant smuggling. Paraguay's remote Chaco region is an important way station in smuggling coca from neighboring Bolivia. The United States likely was displeased also when Paraguay re-established diplomatic relations with Cuba in November 1999 after a 38-year break, the last Latin American nation to do so. The United States recertified Paraguay in 2001.

Paraguay, which has a large Arab community, primarily Lebanese and Jordanians, was back in the international spotlight following the September 11, 2001 terrorist attacks in the United States. A month later, Paraguayan police raided several Arab-owned businesses in Ciudad del Este, notorious as a smuggling center because of the porous borders with Brazil and Argentina, and detained several people. Police seized evidence of links with the Palestinian terrorist group Hezbollah. Even before September 11, the U.S. State Department had identified the so-called "Tri-Border" area as a hotbed of Islamic extremists.

González Macchi made himself even more unpopular in July 2002 by declaring a state of emergency in the wake of anti-government demonstrations in three cities that left two people dead. Riot police apparently overreacted. Rioting and looting erupted the following day in Ciudad del Este. The president lifted the state of emergency after only two days and freed 297 people who had been arrested. The president blamed the disturbances on Oviedo supporters and accused Vice President Franco of collaborating with them to bring down his government—an implausible scenario. Franco called for González Macchi's resignation, placing even greater stress on an already unpopular and crisis-wracked government.

Another public protest turned violent in September 2002, when 9,000 demonstrators, most of them Oviedo supporters, descended on the Congress to demand González Macchi's resignation. Police opened fire with tear gas, rubber bullets and water cannons; 67 people were injured. Days later, hundreds of farmers blocked roads to protest increases in taxes and fuel prices the government had imposed to obtain a $200 million IMF loan. The president relented and rescinded the increases.

Former President Cubas voluntarily returned to Paraguay in 2002 and placed himself at the disposition of the courts. He was placed under house arrest for a time, then released pending trial. He settled on a ranch in the Chaco, still awaiting trial.

González Macchi faced an impeachment trial in February 2003 over the stolen BMW and for allegedly mishandling $16 million in state funds. After a two-week proceeding, he was acquitted.

Nicanor Duarte Frutos

The country's electoral board set the presidential and congressional elections for April 27, 2003—the same day that neighboring Argentina was to elect its president. The *Colorado*s, now officially called the National Republican Alliance *(ANR)*, chose in a direct primary a man from the reformist wing of the party, Nicanor Duarte Frutos, 46, a lawyer and former journalist who had served capably as education minister under both Wasmosy and González Macchi. As his running mate he chose Luis Castiglioni Soria.

After two straight defeats, Laino stepped aside in favor of Vice President Franco for the *PLRA* nomination. Pedro Fadul, 49, a prominent banker, ran as the candidate of a new movement called *Patria Querida* (Beloved Fatherland). Oviedo hand-picked another lackey named Guillermo Sánchez to run as the stand-in as candidate of his whimsically named *Unión Nacional de Ciudadanos Eticos* (National Union of Ethical Citizens), or *UNACE*.

By 2003, the *Colorado* Party had been in power continuously longer than any party in the world save the North Korean Communist Party, which has ruled since 1945; the Chinese Communist Party came to power two years after the *Colorado*s did. Given the unpopularity of González Macchi and the 2000 election victory of Vice President Franco, it seemed logical that 2003 would be the year the opposition finally broke the *Colorado*s' 56-year grip on power. Logical in any other democracy, perhaps, but Paraguayan politics are not known for their logic. The fragmented field of candidates divided the opposition vote, and Paraguay, like Mexico and Panama, does not have runoff elections; a simple plurality wins. Moreover, all the candidates vowed to combat corruption.

On April 27, turnout was 64.5% of the 2.4 million registered voters, despite the fact that voting is mandatory, possibly a reflection of the widespread disenchantment with the democratic process in Paraguay (see The Future). In the end, voters opted for the status quo:

Duarte Frutos	574,232	37.1%
Franco	370,348	24%
Fadul	328,916	21.3%
Sánchez	208,391	13.5%

The *Colorado*s had little cause for gloating, however. They won the presidency by the smallest percentage yet, and they lost

President Nicanor Duarte Frutos

Paraguay

their majority in the Senate for the first time, losing nine seats. The Liberals also won the governorship of Caazguazú for the first time and retained the governorship of Central Department, where Asuncion is located. Oviedo was an even bigger loser, given his stand-in's poor showing. Oviedo sent gracious congratulations to Duarte from his refuge in Brazil, but he ordered the *UNACE* bloc in Congress not to join with the *Colorados* to form a majority coalition but to remain in opposition. *UNACE*, the *PLRA*, *Patria Querida* and National Encounter have since formed an uneasy but majority opposition coalition.

President-elect Duarte Frutos wasted little time in stepping on toes. In his victory speech, he vowed to overhaul the customs and internal revenue services, both notoriously corrupt and riddled with political patronage, which put him on an inevitable collision course with the *oficialista* wing of his own party. Moreover, he publicly vilified the country's Catholic priests as "a bunch of hypocrites" who, he charged, "had manipulated the faith" in favor of Fadul's candidacy. He also promised to renegotiate the $200 million IMF loan package that had been sacrificed the year before on the altar of public opinion.

Duarte Frutos and Castiglioni were inaugurated on Independence Day, August 15, 2003, at which time they inherited a bankrupt government, a stagnant economy, a $2.2 billion public debt and a population that had begun to long for the comparatively prosperous and stable days of dictatorship. Eight Latin American presidents attended the ceremony, including Chávez of Venezuela, Castro of Cuba, Da Silva of Brazil, Gutiérrez of Ecuador, Sánchez of Bolivia and Uribe of Colombia. Duarte sounded a populist theme, not only reiterating his vow to fight the "mafia" that controls smuggling and piracy, but also the "unproductive local oligarchy, who want the government to remain the lackey of its privileges." All the presidents except Castro and Chávez then signed a "Declaration of Asunción," pledging to cooperate on cracking down on drug trafficking.

Duarte Frutos met with President George W. Bush in the White House two months after the inauguration, the first Paraguayan president to do so. Although the United States was pleased with Duarte Frutos' role in the Declaration of Asunción, it was not pleased that Paraguay rejected a U.S. request to send a contingent of troops to Iraq, as the Dominican Republic, El Salvador, Honduras and Nicaragua did. Paraguay also abstained on the vote before the U.N. Human Rights Commission in Geneva in April 2004 to condemn Cuba for human rights violations. A large number of Paraguayans are now studying medicine in Cuba, while Cuba has provided many doctors to provide medical care in rural Paraguay.

Duarte Frutos also seemed eager to back up his populist rhetoric against the "oligarchy" in the case of an illegal land takeover during González Macchi's tenure. A group of armed peasants had invaded a large estate near San Lorenzo and established a colony called Marquetalia, named after the Colombian town where the Revolutionary Armed Forces of Colombia *(FARC)* was formed. González Macchi had timidly declined to take any action, but Duarte Frutos did him one better. He expropriated 25,000 hectares (62,000 acres) and issued titles to 1,300 peasant families, in effect telegraphing that the way to obtain free land was to arm oneself and become a squatter on someone else's property and the government would back him up. Thus emboldened, peasants invaded another 60 estates in September and October 2004. There are an estimated 300,000 landless peasants, and by some non-governmental estimates, 1% of the population owns 80% of the land. The issue continues to fester.

He also kept his promise to crack down on corruption, especially smuggling, and at the end of his first year the government reported that customs collections were up by 89%.

Former President González Macchi, who by contrast is still a pariah, has not had an enjoyable retirement. He has been charged with illegally diverting $16 million into a CitiBank account in New York, one of the charges for which he was acquitted in the Chamber of Deputies.

Recent Developments

The restless ghost of the assassinated Argaña has returned to haunt Paraguay. Oviedo embarked on a public relations campaign to clear his name in the murder, and found an ally in the daily newspaper *ABC Color* and the Brazilian newsmagazine *Isto É.* The paper quoted the chauffeur who survived the shooting as saying that Argaña had died of cancer the night before and the assassination was staged by the Argaña faction to discredit Oviedo. *Isto É* contended that Duarte Frutos, then head of the Colorado Party, was a party to this conspiracy. Another conspiracy theory floating about the country is that Argaña's own children rubbed out their ill father in an intra-family estate dispute. Casting doubts on the conspiracy theorists is the news videotape shot immediately after the shooting, which shows Argaña's body covered in blood, which would have been impossible if he had died the night before. The news footage also shows the body limp when it was placed on a stretcher; if he had died the night before, rigor mortis would have set in. This real-life whodunnit continues to absorb the country's attention.

Oviedo announced he would return to Paraguay on June 29, 2004, to face the accusations head-on. According to the local media, the announcement came only after several pro-Oviedo lawmakers met with Duarte to extract certain "guarantees." The president angrily pounded a table and shouted that he would not tolerate anyone "destabilizing" the country. Oviedo kept his promise and returned on June 29, turning himself in to authorities and vowing to clear himself. He was held in a military jail awaiting trial. In February 2005, he was cleared of charges that he had tried to overthrow González Macchi, but questions about his role in the Argaña assassination continue to hang over him.

In 2004 and 2005, the attention of Paraguayans has shifted to an alarming increase in street crime and kidnappings, something that they never experienced during Stroessner's iron-fisted regime. The climate of fear has had political repercussions. The highest-profile kidnapping was that of former President Cubas' 31-year-old daughter, Cecilia, who was abducted from her car in broad daylight near her home in September 2004 by assailants who riddled her car with bullets. Her kidnapping followed the discovery of the mutilated body of the kidnapped 10-year-old son of a wealthy tobacco merchant. Duarte Frutos fired his interior minister and a senior police official, apparently for failing to secure the boy's release.

Raúl Cubas paid an $800,000 ransom, while Paraguayans demonstrated for his daughter's release and put up "Free Cecilia" posters. But her decomposed body was found in February 2005, buried under a house near Asunción. Paraguayans, long inured to non-violent corruption, were horrified at the news, and the national police came under intense criticism for failing to save Cubas after receiving a credible tip as to her whereabouts; there were also suggestions of police complicity.

A leader of a tiny leftist group, *Patria Libre,* which is thought to have contacts with the *FARC* guerrillas of Colombia, was arrested in connection with Cubas' death. The president himself said that he believed the kidnapping was the work of common criminals using the guise of political terrorists, but he and his attorney general flew to Bogotá to meet with Colombian President Uribe about the case. Days after Cubas' funeral, Duarte Frutos fired his latest interior minister and forced 31 police officers into early retirement, apparently to appease public opinion. He retained the chief of the national police, however. It was the largest government reshuffle since the establishment of democracy in 1989; Paraguay has now had four interior ministers in less than two years.

Since then, the *FARC* has denied involvement with the kidnapping and murder. So has *Patria Libre*, which claims it is being used as a scapegoat to justify political repression. Duarte Frutos vowed to use the army if necessary to combat crime, and he promised to recruit 12,000 more policemen, without explaining how the country was going to pay for them. The investigation into the Cubas murder is ongoing.

The public does not appear to have been impressed with Duarte Frutos' efforts. The daily newspaper *La Nación* commissioned a poll in April 2005 that indicated that just 12% of respondents had confidence in him, down from 54% when he became president.

Between November 2004 and March 2005, a joint crackdown on pirated goods in the Tri-Border area, coordinated by Interpol, led to 79 arrests and the seizure of $2.5 million worth of contraband.

Culture: It is no exaggeration to state that Paraguay's unique culture is a product of geography and politics. Landlocked and cut off from contact with the outside world by a series of 19th century strongmen, Paraguay developed differently from its sister republics. To begin with, the indigenous inhabitants, the Guaraní, were culturally different from tribes on the fringes of the continent. Just as it took a special breed of native to subsist in this hot, dry climate, so it took a special breed of Spaniard to eschew the relative comforts of either coast to pioneer this inhospitable land.

Along with such pioneers came Jesuit priests, who effectively ran the colony in the 16th and 17th centuries, when the Spanish Crown expelled them. The ruins of their mini-civilization can be seen near modern-day Encarnación. Some scholars attribute the Paraguayan trait of obsequiousness to authority to this long-ago Jesuit influence, which inspired the motion picture, *The Mission*.

Because Paraguayan leaders placed little value on education, and in no small part because of the genocide committed during the War of the Triple Alliance of 1865–70, Paraguay never developed a European-based literary, artistic or musical tradition as did its neighbors. Paraguayan culture is derived almost wholly from the Guaraní, whose language still thrives; half the population learns Guaraní before Spanish. Several unassimilated Indian tribes still exist in Paraguay, providing tourists with cheap trinkets. But it is from the Guaranís that Paraguay developed the

Augusto Roa Bastos

beautiful lacework that is so identified with the country.

Probably the most identifiable element of Paraguayan culture, however, is its lovely harp-based folk music. During the Stroessner regime, law dictated that 50% of the music played on radio had to be domestic. One Paraguayan folk song in particular, *Recuerdos de Ipacaraí*, is so well known that guitarists or pianists can play it from memory in restaurants or piano bars from Mexico City to Buenos Aires to Madrid.

Paraguay's most internationally renowned literary figure—indeed, the only one—of the 20th century was Augusto Roa Bastos (1917–2005). He served as a medic during the 1932–35 Chaco War with Bolivia. Because of his leftist sympathies and his irreverence toward authority, Roa Bastos voluntarily went into exile in 1947, living and writing abroad for 49 years, first in Argentina, then France, and finally Spain, returning to Paraguay to live in 1996 and dying in Asunción. Unlike many writers who live in exile, however, Roa Bastos did not lose his Paraguayan identity, and he wrote primarily about his homeland. He was known for his use of basing his fiction on historical figures. His best-known work was the novel *Yo, el Supremo (I, the Supreme)*, published in 1974, which was based on the 19th century Paraguayan dictator José Gaspar Rodríguez de Francia (see History). Two other works, *El Hijo de Hombre (Son of Man)*, a 1960 collection of short stories, and *El Baldío (Vagabond)*, a novel published in 1966, were biting observations on Paraguay's often tragic history. Another, *Vigilia del Almirante (Vigil of the Admiral)*, a novel about Columbus, was published in 1992 to mark the 500th anniversary of the European discovery of the New World. His works were translated into 25 languages. He received Spain's prestigious Cervantes Prize in Literature in 1989, and he was often mentioned as a possible Nobel Laureate.

As in many of the Latin American republics, dictatorship and illiteracy combined forces to stifle the development of viable independent newspapers. A few dailies are published, but only in Asunción. One is the official *Colorado* Party mouthpiece, but beginning in the late 1970s the others courageously exposed the endemic corruption of the Stroessner regime—although they wisely avoided mentioning the president by name. The country's leading daily is *ABC Color*, founded by businessman Aldo Zucolillo in 1967, which became more and more critical of the dictatorship, until Stroessner ordered it closed in 1984. It didn't reopen until immediately after Stroessner's overthrow five years later. Other leading dailies are *El Diario, La Nación* and *Ultima Hora*.

Economy: The eastern (*Oriental*) region of Paraguay, with its favorable climate, is the country's primary source of economic wealth. The western (*Occidental* or *Chaco*) region contributes far less, particularly because of adverse geography and climatic conditions. Approximately 40% of Paraguay's income is from agriculture, cattle raising and forestry in which half of the people are employed; industry and commerce account for the remainder. Farm output remains comparatively low due in part to feudal land practices under which 1–3% of the population owns 80% of the usable land. Also, mechanization was slow to come to Paraguayan agriculture. In recent years, soybeans have been a major export, but there is little domestic processing. Paraguay's foreign trade is primarily with Argentina, the United States, the United Kingdom and Germany; other principal exports are vegetable oils, grains, cotton, tannin, forest products, meat and tobacco.

Paraguay has become a major banking center in recent years, partly because of political stability enforced by the Stroessner regime and partly because the nation is one of the few Latin American countries that places no exchange controls on the dollar. Because of liberal incentives to foreign investment, only 20% of the nation's industry is owned by Paraguayans. Explorations by three U.S.-owned firms in early 1975 in the bleak and desolate Chaco resulted in the discovery of modest amounts of petroleum.

The economy boomed in the 1970s and 1980s, bolstered by work on a huge hydroelectric dam: Itaipú (financed by Brazil). Paraguay is selling its share of electricity to Brazil. A contract was let for the construction of a second dam, Yacyretá, downstream on the Paraná River, financed by Argentina. This is the longest river dam in the world, extending 43 miles from the Paraguayan border to Argentina; it is now producing an abundance of electrical power.

Paraguay

Because of Paraguay's landlocked isolation, and its juxtaposition between two powerful neighbors, smuggling has traditionally been a major pillar of the economy. In recent years, traditional smuggling has been expanded to include drug trafficking, money laundering and copyright and trademark infringement. The United States at one point threatened Paraguay with economic sanctions because of the piracy of intellectual properties.

When Raúl Cubas assumed the presidency in 1998, he inherited a dismal economy and a budget deficit that totaled about 4% of the GDP of $10 billion. In his first month in office, he pledged to crack down on long-accepted tax evasion and black marketeering. He estimated that as much as 55% of taxes were not being paid (the figure today is estimated at 70%). The economy was imperiled even further by the market crisis in neighboring Brazil in late 1998.

Paraguay is one of the few remaining countries with diplomatic relations with Taiwan, but it paid off in 1999 when an appreciative Taiwan lent Paraguay $400 million, which kept the country afloat. The latest president, Nicanor Duarte Frutos, obtained a $73 million loan from the IMF, which prevented a possible default on the foreign debt.

Paraguay's GDP has shrunk for six of the past eight years. In 2002 it shrank by 2.3%, but showed positive growth of 2.6% in 2003. Per capita income has declined from $1,552 per capita in 1999 to only $1,019 in 2003, making Paraguay the fifth-poorest country in Latin America after Nicaragua, Haiti, Honduras and neighboring Bolivia. Recent figures indicate that 47% of Paraguayans live in poverty, and UNICEF reports that one child in seven suffers from chronic malnutrition.

Officially, unemployment is 17%, but unofficially it may be as high as 35%. These factors account for Paraguay's ongoing public discontent.

The Future: Nicanor Duarte Frutos, who took office at 46, is the youngest president in half a century and is the first born since the *Colorado* takeover of 1947. Although he is a *Colorado*, he once was a journalist with the daily newspaper *Ultima Hora*, which had been shut down for 30 days by the Stroessner regime for its aggressive reporting. Thus, he represents a new generation of Paraguayans, and of *Colorados*, and he seems serious about combating the institutionalized corruption that has made other Latin American countries look like paragons of official integrity by comparison. To do so, however, he has taken on some powerful, entrenched forces within his own party.

The corruption is so institutionalized that Paraguay enjoyed the unflattering distinction of being the second-most corrupt nation in the Western Hemisphere in 2004 after Haiti, according to Transparency International. It also ranked No. 140 among the 145 nations of the world (Haiti and Bangladesh tied for last place). Using an index score of 0-10.0, Paraguay had a score of 1.9 (Haiti and Bangladesh had a 1.5).

My contacts in Paraguay, however, question Duarte Frutos' commitment to combating corruption, asking how the son of an impoverished policeman from Coronel Oviedo had become so wealthy.

Another encouraging result of the 2003 elections, besides the change of generations, was the fourth-place finish of Lino Oviedo's stand-in candidate. Hopefully, the discredited Oviedo's star is now in permanent eclipse. But that is far from certain, as Paraguayans are still beset with an economy that remains stagnant.

A survey by a Latin American polling institution showed that the percentage of Paraguayans who would support an authoritarian form of government grew from 20% in 1995 to 42% in 1997, the period during which Oviedo staged his barracks revolt and became a political figure. Since then, the periodic *Latinobarómetro* survey of 17 Latin American countries for the British newsmagazine *The Economist* showed that the percentage of Paraguayans who think democracy is preferable to any other form of government has plummeted from 59% in 1996 to 45% in 2002 to 40% in 2003 to 39% in 2004. The 20-point drop tied with Nicaragua for the greatest of any nation in the survey. In the same survey, the percentage of Paraguayans who believe an authoritarian government can be preferable to a democracy "under certain circumstances" increased from 26% in 1996 to 44% in 2003 and 39% in 2004—by far the highest percentage in Latin America.

Like other peoples whose expectations for democracy after decades of dictatorship were unrealistically high, Paraguayans are growing disillusioned and impatient with their young democracy. This author lived in Paraguay from 1977–79, and I was struck by the Paraguayans' traditional obsequiousness to authority and the reverence they still bestow upon their *caudillos* of yesteryear, like Francia and Francisco Solano López. It is not difficult for me to understand why Paraguayans would be seduced by a charismatic figure like Oviedo.

That can only be prevented if Duarte Frutos is able to deliver on his promises. If he does, he will be the first post-Stroessner president who has.

An architect's sketch of Paraguay's new Congress building, which opened in June 2003. The government of Taiwan contributed $22 million toward its construction.

The Republic of Peru

Former Colonial Status: Spanish Colony (1532–1821).
Independence Date: July 21, 1821.
Chief of State: Alejandro Toledo Manrique (b. March 28, 1946), president (since July 28, 2001).
National Flag: Red, white and red vertical stripes.

Peru sits astride the majestic Andes mountains. The Sierra (upland plateau) is at an average invigorating elevation of 13,000 feet from which ranges of high peaks emerge. The highest, Huascarán, is 22,334 feet; 10 others exceed 20,000 feet and there are many volcanoes in the southern region. The Sierra occupies about one fourth of Peru's surface and is home to more than 60% of the population.

The Sierra is cut and crisscrossed with rivers; those flowing to the west frequently disappear in the desert before reaching the Pacific Ocean; rivers flowing to the east drop into the tropical jungles of the Amazon basin. Some of the eastern rivers have cut scenic gorges into the Sierra 5,000 feet in depth, with tropical climates and vegetation at the lower levels. The Pacific coastal shelf is a narrow ribbon of desert except for a few river valleys where there is sufficient water for irrigation.

The eastern slope of the Andes, known as the *selva* (jungle) contains over 60% of Peru's land and about 14% of the population. There are few roads into this region; travel is along the river valleys.

This area's resources are great, but inaccessibility hampers their exploitation. Peru's climate varies with altitude—tropical in the lowlands, it becomes temperate above the elevation of 3,000 feet and cold above 10,000–12,000 feet, with snow and bitter frost throughout the year on the highest peaks of the Andes. People with respiratory or coronary difficulties dare not venture into these heights—the air is too "thin" to support any but the hardiest of lives.

History: Peru has been host to civilized people from about the 3rd century A.D. Artistically sophisticated people have left pottery and textiles of excellent quality in the southern region which date from the 3rd to the 7th centuries. More primitive people lived in the vicinity of Lima, and a highly skilled culture existed in the north. The southern culture spread to the Sierra and gave rise to the Aymara society at Tiahuanaco, east of Lake Titicaca in the 10th to the 13th centuries. The Inca civilization began to develop in the Cuzco basin about the 11th century and by the end of the 15th century dominated the Andean Sierra and the Pacific shelf from Colombia to the Central Valley of Chile.

Peruvian school girls in Lima

Area: 482,122 square miles
Population: 27.9 million (2005 projection)
Capital City: Lima (Pop. 8 million, estimated)
Climate: The eastern lowlands are hot and humid; the coast is arid and mild; the highlands are increasingly temperate as the altitude rises.
Neighboring Countries: Ecuador (northwest); Colombia (northeast); Brazil (east); Chile (south).
Official Language: Spanish.
Other Principal Tongues: Quechua and Aymara.
Ethnic Background: *Mestizo* (a mixture of Indian and Spanish ancestry) and pure Indian, 88%; European, mostly Spanish, 12%.
Principal Religion: Roman Catholic Christianity.

Chief Commercial Products: Fish, fish-meal, cotton, sugar, copper, silver, lead, crude petroleum.
Currency: Sol.
Gross Domestic Product: U.S. $67.1 billion in 2004 ($2,305 per capita).

297

Peru

At the time of the Spanish invasion, a division had split the Inca rulers. The legitimate Inca Huáscar ruled the south from Cuzco while his half-brother, Atahualpa, ruled the northern provinces from Quito as a usurper challenging the legitimacy of Huáscar (see Ecuador).

When the explorers Francisco Pizarro and Diego de Almagro landed their small Spanish force in Ecuador in 1531, Atahualpa—apparently seeking allies to assist in his fight against his half-brother—allowed the Spaniards to reach the Sierra. The outnumbered Spanish tricked Atahualpa into an ambush, held him for ransom and killed him after it was paid. As Atahualpa had ordered the assassination of Huáscar, and his person was considered divine by the Incas, no one in the vast empire dared to raise a finger against the Spaniards as long as the emperor was a prisoner. Unopposed, the Spaniards moved into the interior of Peru, occupying the most strategic cities and, after the death of Atahualpa, ruled through puppet Incas until they felt strong enough to proclaim Spain's sovereignty.

Pizarro withdrew from Cuzco, the sacred capital of the Inca empire in 1535 and

Atahaulpa is ambushed by Spanish troops

founded Lima near the coast. Almagro was sent to conquer Chile, but the arid territory and Indian hostility forced him to return to Lima. A brief struggle for power followed and first Almagro and then Pizarro were killed. Spanish authorities intervened, restored peace and began organizing the new rich colony. Francisco de Toledo, one of the best viceroys Spain ever had, established a firm basis for colonial power. He ruled from 1568 to 1582, adopted many Inca traditions like the "*mita*" (annually every male member of the Inca empires had to work free for the emperor during a few months) for Spain's benefit, and the colony prospered. By the middle of the 17th century, Lima was a splendid city with cathedrals, palaces and a university and the viceroyalty of Peru had become the political and strategic center of the Spanish empire in South America.

Exasperated by the exploitation of the Indians in the mining area, a descendant of the last Inca adopted the name of Tupac Amaru in 1780 and raised the banner of rebellion. Intelligently, he appealed to the creoles (people of Peruvian mixed Spanish-Indian blood), ratified his Catholic faith and proclaimed that he was not fighting against the king, but against his "corrupt officials." The rebellion spread rapidly, but Tupac's Indian followers killed Spaniards and creoles indiscriminately. The alliance of both, plus the condemnation of the Catholic Church, sealed his fate. Thousands of Indians rallied around Spanish authorities (a testimony to Spain's colonial policies) and Tupac was defeated, captured and publicly executed. The rebellion, however, left a lingering fear among the creoles. As in Mexico and Cuba, they remained lukewarm toward an anti-Spanish struggle that could trigger another Indian uprising. The initiative for independence had to come from *outside*.

The arrival of General José de San Martín and his small army of Argentinians and Chileans opened the period of armed insurrection. Unable to defeat the Spaniards, who were supported by many creoles, San Martín awaited the arrival of

Tupac Amaru

General Simón Bolívar, whose victorious army was marching south from Venezuela and Colombia. After meeting with *el Libertador* in Guayaquil and failing to reach an agreement on the impending campaign, a disillusioned San Martín retired to private life. Bolívar and his second-in-command, Antonio José de Sucre, opened the campaign against colonial authorities and in 1824 the battle of Ayacucho put an end to Spanish dominion in South America.

After the battle, Bolívar made an energetic attempt to organize the country. Taxes were cut, convents were turned into schools and the most glaring abuses against the Indians were suppressed. Elected president-for-life, Bolívar could have accomplished much more, but growing resistance on the part of alarmed and conservative Peruvian creoles, and the progressive disintegration of his "Great Colombia" (the union of Venezuela, Colombia, and Ecuador) forced him to leave Peru in 1826. A period of relative stability followed while most of the government and military forces concentrated on solidifying a union with Bolivia in a "Confederation of the North." Unfortunately, Chile considered that union as a threat to its future and invaded Bolivia. Chilean victory at the battle of Yungay

forced the confederation to break up. The defeat plunged Peru into political turmoil until 1844, when a capable man, Ramón Castilla, seized power. President Castilla, who served until 1850 and again from 1855–60, united the country, mediated differences between the pro-church Conservatives and the anti-clerical Liberals, established government services, abolished black slavery, ended forced tribute from the Indians and built a few schools.

The national economy, however, was restored by sea birds, whose mountains of dung (guano) on the offshore islands, were highly sought after in European fertilizer markets. The guano trade also led to the discovery of the nitrate deposits in the southern deserts; the extraction of the mineral was largely in British hands.

The period following Castilla's rule was one of tension and war. Nine presidents occupied the office between 1862 and 1885, of which only two completed their terms. The most competent of these was Manuel Pardo (1872–1876), Peru's first civilian president and founder of the *Civilista* Party. A war with Spain (1862–66) and the War of the Pacific (1879–83) were brought on by the prosperity which Peru was enjoying. Spain sought to recover its past grandeur and lost; Chile, with British connivance, sought the wealth of the desert nitrate fields and won.

The War of the Pacific was a disaster for Peru—thousands of lives were lost, much property was destroyed, some territory and the port of Arica were ceded to Chile, and the national economy was reduced to a shambles. Huge foreign debts were accumulated, the nitrate beds were lost and the guano deposits were almost exhausted.

British interests funded the foreign debt in exchange for the national railways, the steamers of scenic Lake Titicaca, the exploitation of remaining guano deposits, free use of ports and other trade privileges. Peru's recovery was slow, but a measure of peace and order was established and trade resumed under a succession of *Civilista* presidents.

The major event of the early 20th century was the rule of Augusto B. Leguía from 1919 until 1930. Energetic and able, he gave impetus to mining and agriculture and restored Peru's international credit. Leguía called his regime "A New Fatherland," adopted a modern constitution and freed the church from state patronage. Initially an honest administrator, he succumbed to graft and corruption under the temptation of loans proffered by the United States banks during the 1920s. When the inevitable protests arose, there was wholesale jailing of critics, restriction of the press and the closing of universities.

APRA is Founded

By 1930, the Peruvian people were fed up with Leguía's terrorism and the subsequent failure of business during the worldwide depression, which caused widespread unemployment. A revolt caused him to flee; he was captured on the high seas and imprisoned on one of the offshore islands where he died.

During the last decade of the 19th century, there developed a movement for liberal reforms in Peru's higher society. Led by Manuel González Prada, a respected intellectual, demands were made to end feudalism, traditionalism and clericalism which González Prada declared enslaved the people to a handful of powerful men. Among the students attracted to González Prada was Victor Rául Haya de la Torre, a leader in the demand for educational-reforms, who founded the American Popular Revolutionary Alliance (*APRA*) in 1924.

Anti-communist, with ideas borrowed from Russian, Mexican and European models, *APRA* sought to integrate the Indian into Peru's social and economic structure and to terminate the monopoly of political power which had been held by the landowners and the clergy for more than 400 years. During the dictatorship of Leguía, *APRA* grew and became the spokesman for the Indian in the Sierra as well as the urban worker.

APRA won the 1931 elections, but Haya de la Torre was jailed and the party outlawed. Revolts which resulted were savagely repressed, and Peru's second dictatorship of the 20th century was launched. Marshal Oscar Benavides ruled somewhat moderately until 1939.

Manuel Prado, a moderate, was president from 1939–45. He made progress in trade, public health, education and sanitation, but simultaneously firmly repressed all popular challengers to the landowner-clergy domination of political power. His successor came to office by a change of *APRA* tactics; reorganizing as the People's Party, *APRA* supported the most liberal of the candidates, hoping to secure congressional seats and cabinet positions.

The *APRA* success in this effort brought on a conservative coup headed by General Manuel Odría, who ruled from 1948–56. No pretense of democracy was maintained; restoring order and suppressing *APRA*, the army ruled with firmness. From a managerial standpoint, the regime gave a good account of itself, restoring confidence in Peruvian industry. Legal elections again returned Prado to leadership, but conditions did not remain stable.

When *APRA* won substantial gains in 1962 elections, the army again intervened by setting aside the results; in more care-

Peru

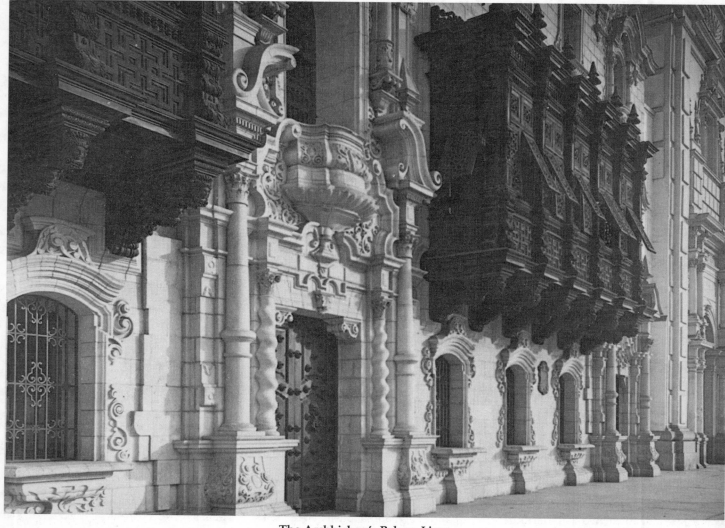

The Archbishop's Palace, Lima

fully staged elections in 1963, Fernando Belaúnde Terry of the Popular Action Party (*PAP*) won a bare plurality and was named president.

Leftist Military Rule, 1968–80

Charging that the nation's political leaders were insensitive to the needs of the masses, a military *junta* again ousted the civilian president in 1968 and replaced him with General Juan Velasco Alvarado, who served as president for the next seven years. The new regime promised to end the traditional political and economic control of Peru by the "top 40 families" and foreign corporations through a program of "social democracy," patterned loosely on the Yugoslav model, which (they said) would guide the nation on a path between capitalism and communism.

The first phase of the program, largely achieved by 1975, called for state control of strategic sectors of the economy. Thus, the regime nationalized the fishing industry, banks, communications facilities, most of the news media and U.S.-owned mining operations. A unique feature of the Inca Plan required major industries to grant half-ownership to the workers.

A cornerstone of the economic plan was one of the most extensive land reform programs in Latin America. Before the military seized power, fully 90% of all farmland was owned by just 2% of the population. To break the power of the landed aristocracy, the military seized 25 million acres from large private estates and redistributed them to worker-owned cooperatives and to peasant families.

In foreign affairs, the military government was nationalistic and leftist. Diplomatic ties were extended to many non-aligned and communist nations and Peru became the second nation in the Western Hemisphere to import Soviet weapons and advisers. At international conferences, Peru was a major advocate of Third World causes as well as a frequent critic of U.S. economic power.

These policies naturally strained relations with the United States. Although Peru agreed to pay for some of the seized property, the prices were largely dictated by it. A low point in U.S.-Peruvian relations came in late 1974 when the *junta* ousted 137 members of the Peace Corps and several U.S. Embassy officials on charges of spying for the CIA.

By combining a nationalistic foreign policy with a state-controlled economy, the *junta* hoped to build what it described as a "new Peruvian man." To speed up the process, the government expanded education programs, increased per capita incomes (predominantly of coastal residents), promised to spend new oil revenues on social programs and to turn over farms and factories to workers. The expected popular support, however, failed to materialize. Farm workers who

300

received land bitterly opposed sharing their gains with landless peasants. Factory workers continued to strike as often against state-owned industries as they had against the former owners. Part of the problem was rooted in the government's attempts to run Peru like a military barracks.

Congress was closed, most political parties were banned, and civilians were excluded from key government jobs. Professional organizations and free labor movements were suppressed and the press was censored. Compounding Peru's troubles were collapse of the fishmeal industry (the offshore anchovies disappeared), a plunge in world copper prices and the failure of new oil wells (in which the regime had gambled $1.5 billion) to produce as expected.

The government's economic program scared away badly needed foreign investment and poor management resulted in lowered production in nationalized industries. Benefits of the military revolution failed to filter down to the lower classes; unemployment and inflation cut the living standards of the people.

Velasco Alvarado, partially disabled from circulatory problems and a mild stroke, increasingly ruled by decree, jailing or deporting his critics. When he turned his wrath against fellow military officers, the armed forced finally stepped in and deposed him in a bloodless coup in 1975.

General Francisco Morales Bermúdez

Named as new president was General Francisco Morales Bermúdez, 54, a moderate and former prime minister. Although he pledged to follow the basic goals of the previous regime, he further stated that the revolution had entered a more conservative "consolidation phase." Faced with a bankrupt treasury, the regime turned away from a policy of rigid state control of industry. A number of major businesses (including the key fishing industry), nationalized by the previous administration, were returned to their former owners. At the same time, the role and power of labor unions were reduced.

Nevertheless, Peru's economy continued to decline during 1977. Hoping to prevent further labor unrest and related political violence, the *junta* announced in October 1977 that plans were being made to surrender power to constitutional government. The first election was set for June 4, 1978, when voters would name delegates to an assembly to rewrite the constitution. Under the plan, an elected president and congress would take control of the country by 1980. However, the military stipulated that the new constitution must embody basic nationalistic principles of the present government which had stressed social reforms and nationalization of major industries.

As an initial step toward the restoration of democracy, voters went to the polls in June 1978 for the first time in 11 years to elect representatives to a 100-seat Constituent Assembly, which would be given the task of drafting a new constitution. The biggest winner, with nearly 40% of the vote, was the *APRA* party, which campaigned on a slightly left-of-center platform. In second place were the leftists representing six Marxist parties with nearly 28%. The conservatives and moderates, led by the Popular Christian Party, were a close third with nearly 27%.

Panoramic view of Lima with the broad Avenida Alfonso Ugarte in the foreground

Peru

Return to Democracy

When presidential elections were held in May 1980, former president Fernando Belaúnde Terry of the *PAP* was an easy winner over 11 other candidates with 43% of the vote. *APRA* was second with 26%, while extremist parties fared poorly. Five leftist presidential candidates received 17% of the total and the center-right Popular Christian Party (*PCP*) won 11%.

Belaúnde became Peru's 102nd president in mid-1980, ending 12 years of military rule. The generals refused to attend the inauguration. Because his *PAP* won only 27 of the 60 Senate seats and 95 of the 180 seats in the Chamber of Deputies, Belaúnde had to have the cooperation of the *APRA* and the *PCP*. The new administration promised to respect the new constitution, create an independent judiciary, promote human rights, ensure freedom of the press (including return of newspapers and TV stations taken over by the previous military regimes), and to encourage economic development. Programs for construction of roads, housing, increased farm production and water resources and nurturing foreign investments (especially in oil production) were given a high priority on the government's agenda.

The Belaúnde administration faced severe political and economic problems, the aftermath of the military regimes' wasteful spending (for failing social programs, an oil pipeline for nonexistent oil and for unneccessary exotic Soviet arms) which brought the nation to the brink of financial insolvency. To combat the crippling 80% inflation, a 40% unemployment rate, and almost defaulting on its international loans, Peru had acceded to the harsh terms for aid from the International Monetary Fund in late 1978. Austerity measures were taken to lower the inflation rate and to stimulate financial investments for economic growth.

As usual, the real burden for these reforms, however, fell most heavily on the poor and middle class as the cost of living rose sharply while real wages dropped. From August 1978 to mid-1980, strikes—particular and general—closed down mines, mills, oil installations and schools as workers protesting price rises for rice, gasoline and fertilizer, clamored for wage increases to catch up with galloping inflation.

There were more strikes during the summer of 1981—involving an unlikely combination: copper miners, doctors and bank employees, all demanding higher pay! The volatile atmosphere heated up in September when acts of terrorism became commonplace. Although it is still unclear what group was responsible for the surge of violence, far more than 1,000 acts were

High school girls in a mountain village

reported, among them a bomb attack on the U.S. Embassy and others directed at four private companies with ties to the United States. Guerrillas boldly attacked three police stations and a penitentiary in 1982; 247 prisoners were freed. The government was forced to crack down hard by suspending constitutional guarantees in five towns southwest of Lima after terrorists had killed three people.

An important diplomatic event occurred for beleaguered Peru in late 1981—Javier Pérez de Cuellar was named to a five-year term as secretary general of the United Nations.

Terrorism—Counter-Terrorism

Peru's democracy remained frail and much political squabbling in Congress slowed down the legislative process. But President Belaúnde assured the public that the military would not attempt another coup. This was put to a severe test, however, by the activities of Maoist guerrilla bands calling themselves *Sendero Luminoso* ("Shining Path"—curiously a Lenin expression).

The movement consisted of cells rather than organized larger forces, making it extremely hard to deal with. Founded about 1970 by Professor Abimael Guzmán (b. 1935) of the University of Huamanga, in Ayacucho State, it spread quickly to colleges and universities of the highlands, attracting many of Indian ancestry. Its actions, and the government's struggle against it, took the lives of more than 25,000 people.

Guzmán went into hiding in 1975 but remained active. From sketchy accounts of his rigid beliefs and behavior (traditionalist Stalinist, Maoist "communism") it was suspected that he was mentally de-

ranged, becoming the leader of a mass cult which he mesmerized. One observer said he became "a Charlie Manson with an army to back him up."

Terrorism was committed not only by the *Sendero Luminoso* but also by elite military units sent to the impoverished region inhabited mostly by Indians. A group based in urban areas, the Tupac Amaru Revolutionary Movement, joined in the anti-government effort in 1984; it was named after the 18th century Peruvian Indian who revolted against Spanish rule. It knew how pipe bombs are made, and used them and heavier explosives to make life in Lima miserable. The city quickly came to be surrounded in the 1980s by "suburbs" of countless shacks and shanties where more than 8 million settled. It was easy in such a setting to bomb strategic locations—banks, businesses, embassies and the presidential palace—and disappear. The *Tupacs* shared their bomb talents with the *Senderistas*.

Further complicating life in Peru was the entry of coca production in the Upper Huallaga Valley which eventually became the source of 75% of coca used to produce illicit cocaine. The hirelings of drug traffickers were merciless and sometimes posed as revolutionaries to divert attention from their actual purposes.

Belaúnde rapidly declined in popularity (from 70% in 1980 to 20% in 1984). By mid-1984 the annual inflation rate reached 120% and Peru looked toward the presidential elections of 1985 with a mixture of hope and despair.

The contest was held April 14, 1985. *APRA* candidate Alan García received 46% of the votes, and the candidate of the United Left (which included communist elements), Alfonso Barrantes, popular mayor of Lima, got 21%. In order to discourage participation in the election, both the Shining Path and Tupac terrorists issued death threats and the Shining Path actually amputated the fingers of peasants to prevent them from voting. Police and military security at the polls was tight.

According to the Peruvian constitution, when none of the candidates obtains more than 50% of the votes, a second (runoff) election is obligatory. But before the date was legally determined, the president of the Electoral Tribunal was shot and gravely injured by members of the Shining Path. A few days later, Barrantes, probably trying to avoid a further decline of leftist votes, announced his withdrawal from the electoral contest.

García took the oath of office in July 1985. He immediately made dramatic and controversial promises. He stated that no more than an amount corresponding to 10% of Peru's export income would be used to "repay" a foreign debt of almost $16 billion, knowing that such an amount wouldn't even pay the interest on the indebtedness.

In order to deal with police and army corruption, García fired or retired many top figures in both organizations. He declared a state of emergency as lawlessness increased in Lima, ordering armored units from the military to patrol the streets. An American oil company was nationalized (assets: $400 million) without compensation. All U.S. aid was cut off as required by law. A new unit of currency, the *inti*, was introduced, which meant a devaluation of 64 to 1 in the national currency. It was later devalued several more times.

Peruvian conditions deteriorated severely after 1986. The Marxist-Maoist *Senderistas* were very active, promoting simultaneous riots at three prisons, including Canto Grande in Lima (which later became a training and indoctrination center for the *Senderistas* into which the guards were scared to enter). The army responded by executing almost 200 prisoners after they had surrendered. A public pronouncement was made by the movement that 10 *APRA* leaders would be killed for each guerrilla who died. Three universities were raided by 4,000 government troops, who located *Senderista* propaganda, violating the traditional security of such institutions. Violence escalated rapidly, with extreme measures pursued by the guerrillas—tying bombs to small children and burros to carry them to their target. The army responded with equally horrible acts.

There would have been a military coup, but the military didn't want to inherit an ungovernable Peru. Much of the country came under martial law. The *Senderistas*, then went into the upper Huallaga Valley in northeast Peru where most of the coca

is grown. They imposed a 10% "sales tax" on the farmers "for protection." Since they have no love for foreigners, the tourist trade all but dried up. The *Senderistas*, by then quite familiar with bomb fabrication and use, frequently disrupted the power supply of Lima, reducing it to three hours a day, if any.

People felt betrayed by García. More than half would have left the country if they could. He nationalized banks and insurance companies in 1987, creating economic havoc in Peru. Having defaulted on its external loans, Peru was on a cash-in-advance basis—as many as 50 ships at a time would lie in the harbor at Lima, laden with food, but awaiting payment in hard currency before unloading—while people in Peru were starving. Finally, after he left office, evidence surfaced that García had received a kickback for depositing Peru's reserves in BCCI, a shady bank that became the target of an international investigation, and from the construction of an Italian-built electric rail line. The charges were filed in 1992 but never were proved in court, because García fled into self-imposed exile in Colombia and stayed there for nine years—until the statute of limitations had expired.

The Fujimori Era

When 1990 elections approached, it was generally assumed that they would result in another traditional party victory. Polls showed the well-known novelist, Mario Vargas Llosa, the likely winner. But a surprise appeared on the horizon: Alberto Fujimori, soft-spoken son of Japanese immigrants, supported by a substantial number of Protestant evangelicals, entered the contest under the Cambio ("Change 90") banner. His supporters, going from door to door extolling his virtues, were persuasive. His popularity swelled from 3% in January to 60% in runoff elections a few months later.

A small element within the military, foreseeing the victory of Fujimori, attempted a coup just before the elections, replete with a plan to murder him. It failed—his intelligence received word of its time and place the week before.

Following his inauguration, Fujimori immediately dismissed the top echelon of the navy and air force, and in December 1990, of the army. He turned inward, trusting no one with basic decisions and policy. He ordered the reorganized military to commence a renewed campaign against the *Senderistas* and armed rural peasants.

The *Senderistas*, with their strength reaching about 15,000, launched a campaign in 1992 to gain control of Lima. Arms and munition supplies via Colom-

Alberto Fujimori

bia had become unreliable and they needed the support of the vast number of poor people surrounding the city in slums. At the same time, it became evident to Fujimori that the National Assembly, dominated by the traditional political elite, was obstructing him at every turn. He dismissed the body, as well as members of the judiciary, and assumed personal control by decree in April. He had the backing of the military for this so-called "self-coup."

Faced with grumbling from Washington and the OAS, Fujimori called for elections to be held in late 1992. The *Senderistas* immediately launched a campaign to disrupt them, but two months before the contest, Guzmán and other key members were nabbed by the military and police. Having avoided publicity and pictures, little was known of Guzmán; he turned out to be an obese, ordinary-looking person with remarkable powers of persuasion, not unlike Charles Manson and David Koresh. Violence had become an end, not a means, for his followers, who engaged in the worst sort of torture, maiming, mutilation

Peru

and murder of hapless victims. He was sentenced to a 40-year prison term.

Fujimori and his supporters drafted a new constitution, which was approved in late 1993 by a narrow margin.

Violence dwindled to less than 25% of what it had been in 1993. The *Senderistas* were reduced to a hard core of fewer than 1,000 who opposed Guzmán's surprising support from his jail cell of the new constitution. Fujimori's popularity soared.

Cambio 90 changed its name to *Nueva Majoría Cambio 90* ("New Majority for Change 90"). Political activity was on the rise in the latter half of 1994 in preparation for elections in April 1995. Discord in the presidential mansion surfaced—Fujimori's wife, Susana Higuchi, had been seized by political fever and separated from her husband. Forming a new political party, Harmony 21st Century, she announced she would run for president. The National Election Board declared that most of the signatures on her application were invalid; she accused it of "techno-fraud."

Fifteen candidates filed, including former U.N. Secretary-General Javier Pérez de Cuellar. A determined Higuchi aligned herself with the Police-Military Front. She was later excluded as a candidate, and they were divorced soon thereafter. Fujimori won 64% of the vote, and his party was assured of a comfortable margin in the Congress. He acquired the nickname "Chinochet," a reference to his Asian heritage and the name of Chile's General Pinochet. He declared that Peru needed order, discipline, the principle of authority and leadership, administration and honesty.

Because of severe unrest, Fujimori declared a state of emergency in Callao, the port city near Lima, in 1995. That same year, Peru fought a brief but bloody war with neighboring Ecuador over a border dispute that had simmered since 1942 (see Ecuador).

The Fujimori government soon faced a new guerrilla threat in 1996 from its other active guerrilla group, the Tupac Amaru Revolutionary Movement (*MRTA*). It differs from the *Senderistas* in that it is urban-based and far less bloodthirsty. Still, it demonstrated its ability to create mischief on December 17, 1996, when it raided a Christmas party at the Japanese ambassador's residence in Lima and took more than 400 diplomats and government officials hostage. The *MRTA* demanded release of prisoners, and gradually it released most of the hostages as tense negotiations unfolded with the Fujimori government.

The siege attracted worldwide media coverage. After four months, only 73 hostages remained in the compound, but Fujimori steadfastly refused to cave in to the demand to release prisoners. The standoff continued until April 22, 1997, when Peruvian commandos, acting on intelligence that the rebels were engaged in a soccer game, stormed the compound and killed all 14 of the remaining guerrillas, at a loss of only two commandos and one hostage, a Supreme Court justice. There was evidence that at least two women guerrillas attempted to surrender but were gunned down in cold blood, charges the government denied. The operation, and questions about whether guerrillas were summarily executed, remains controversial.

Fujimori sent up a trial balloon on the possibility of his running for a third consecutive term, on the pretext that his first election in 1990 had predated the new constitution. But in January 1997 the Constitutional Tribunal rejected the idea. Fujimori merely cajoled Congress, controlled by his allies, to remove three of the tribunal's justices.

By July 1997, Fujimori's tendency to play fast and loose with the constitution and with basic civil liberties erupted into a major scandal, which the opposition and its media allies played up to the hilt. A female army sergeant assigned to intelligence went public in a televised interview to reveal she had been tortured and another woman sergeant, Mariela Barreto, murdered for leaking information that military intelligence was wiretapping Fujimori's opponents in the Congress and the media and threatening some with physical violence. When Barreto's dismembered body was found, the public outcry reached a crescendo against the president and the two men who it was widely believed were ruling Peru with him as a triumvirate: intelligence chief Vladimiro Montesinos and General Nicolás Hermoza, chairman of the joint chiefs of staff. Foreign Minister Francisco Tudela, who had been one of the hostages held by the Tupac Amaru guerrillas, resigned to protest the government wiretapping campaign.

The embattled Fujimori responded to the crisis by revoking the Peruvian citizenship of Baruch Ivcher, the Israeli-born owner of *Frecuencia Latina* (Channel 2), the station that televised the interview, a flagrant violation of the constitution. Through a legal maneuver, control of the station passed to two pro-Fujimori minority shareholders. Fujimori pressured another station to fire a commentator who had been reporting on the alleged abuses

Machu Picchu

Courtesy: Heather Marion

Peru

of human rights. Spontaneous demonstrations erupted, and volunteers camped out at *Frecuencia Latina* to prevent an armed takeover by security forces. Fujimori's public approval rating nosedived to 19%, the lowest of his seven years in office.

There was more to come. For years, since Fujimori first ran in 1990, there had been rumors that he had been born in Japan and was thus constitutionally ineligible to serve as president. At the height of the crisis over the Ivcher case in 1997, *Caretas*, the country's most respected weekly newsmagazine, reported it had uncovered documents that raised further doubts about Fujimori's claim he had been born in Miraflores in 1938. The media began reprinting reproductions of the president's birth certificate, in which the place of birth obviously had been clumsily erased and the words "Miraflores, Lima" written over the erasure in a different handwriting.

Other documents arose, such as Fujimori's mother claiming two children when she immigrated in 1934; Fujimori is her second son. Peruvian officials stood by the president's denial that the documents had been falsified, and it boiled down to Fujimori's word against the media's. In that, of course, there was no contest as to who would prevail. The media also produced telephone records that suggested Fujimori had engaged in Watergate-style espionage of Pérez de Cuellar's 1995 campaign.

This tense situation took an even more bizarre twist in December 1997 with what was perceived as a showdown between Fujimori and the military. Fujimori published a book on the siege of the Japanese ambassador's residence, in which he played up his own role and downplayed that of Hermoza. Relations between the two were reported to be strained because the reelection-minded president had begun to see Hermoza as a drain on his popularity; rumors floated that Fujimori was on the verge of firing him. In an apparent test of his authority, Hermoza summoned all the country's generals to Lima, ostensibly to attend his birthday party, but rumors of an imminent coup began to fly. Fujimori quickly ordered the generals back to their posts; just as quickly, they went. Fujimori eventually reached an accord with Hermoza: the general kept his job, but the president cashiered a regional commander who was seen as more loyal to Hermoza than to the president and he named Fujimori loyalists to command two key units. Once again, the feisty little president had prevailed in a test of wills.

Meanwhile, Fujimori began to recuperate some of the fading esteem of his people by once again doing battle with a common enemy, not terrorists this time,

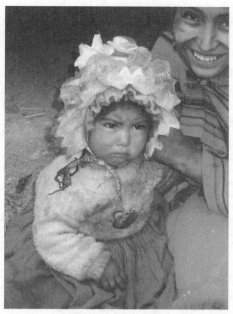

Mother and child in Andean village

but Mother Nature. *El Niño*, the periodic weather phenomenon that affects climate worldwide but which reserves its greatest fury for Peru, returned with a vengeance in December 1997 and continued for months. Torrential rains brought massive flooding that destroyed whole villages and killed about 300 people. Fujimori, a professional engineer, went to the affected areas and took personal charge of the efforts to contain the flood waters. He mingled with distraught, homeless survivors and gave them personal assurances that relief would soon be forthcoming. To Fujimori's critics, this was micromanagement at best and shameless grandstanding and exploitation of a tragedy at worst, but it was a take-charge gesture that was typically Fujimori.

In 1998, a popular movement called the Democratic Forum, backed by Fujimori's congressional opposition, collected 1.45 million signatures on a petition demanding a referendum on the issue of whether Fujimori could run again. The petition was presented to the electoral board, which voted 4–1 that only the Congress—controlled, of course, by Fujimori allies—could approve a referendum.

Congress took up the referendum issue and predictably voted it down. Pro-Fujimori and opposition legislators almost came to blows during the acrimonious debate. Police cordoned off the Congress building to repel demonstrators who chanted, "Death to the dictatorship." The vote effectively removed any remaining obstacle to a third-term bid except for one—the Peruvian voters themselves.

Perhaps one factor that improved Fujimori's popularity slightly in early 1999

was the signing of the long-sought peace agreement with Ecuador's President Jamil Mahuad in Brasilia in October, the dedication of the first border marker in January and the signing of bilateral economic development accords in Washington in February (see Ecuador).

On a darker note, Fujimori's government renewed its persecution of exiled television station owner Baruch Ivcher. In December 1998, a Lima court issued arrest warrants for Ivcher, his wife and daughter for allegedly altering the registration forms for his television station. Apparently stung by his growing image as a bully, Fujimori then shifted course and sought to reach an out-of-court settlement with Ivcher, arguing that the case was merely a legal battle between Ivcher and the pro-Fujimori shareholders who controlled the station. But the negotiations broke down when the two sides could not reach an agreement. Ivcher then took the case before the Inter-American Human Rights Commission, an organ of the OAS. Fujimori said he "regretted" Ivcher's appeal to the OAS body. The commission forwarded the case to the Inter-American Court of Human Rights, which already had seven outstanding cases against Fujimori's government. In Juy 1999, Fujimori resolved the matter in typical fashion: He simply withdrew Peru from the Court of Human Rights. At the same time, military intelligence officials adamantly opposed allowing Ivcher even to return to Peru, much less to resume control of *Frecuencia Latina*.

The "Elections" of 2000

The opposition to Fujimori grudgingly accepted the refusal of the Congress to call for a referendum on a third term and set out to defeat the president the only way left to them: at the ballot box. But three strong candidates emerged against him, thus dividing the opposition.

The early favorite was Lima Mayor Alberto Andrade, of *APRA*, who won a landslide reelection victory of 65% in October 1998 against a Fujimori ally. Then a second candidate, Luis Casteñeda, who had earned high marks as head of the social security system, moved up even in the polls to Andrade by early 2000. Fujimori, as usually happens when there is fragmented opposition, held a strong first place in virtually all the polls, but not the 50% needed to avoid a runoff.

Suddenly, the fourth-ranking candidate, Alejandro Toledo, a 54-year-old economist of pure Indian descent, broke from the rear of the pack and moved up on the outside. Three weeks before the April 9 election, he jumped from 16% to 25% in a poll, emerging as the man for Fujimori to beat.

Peru

The media made much of Toledo's humble farming background and how he had once shined shoes before going on to earn a doctorate at Stanford and to become an official at the World Bank.

Tension mounted as the election approached, as the opposition, the media and international election monitors began to uncover evidence that machinery was in place for possible vote-rigging. Fujimori adamantly insisted the vote would be clean. Nonetheless, the opposition was largely denied the access to the state-owned media that Fujimori enjoyed, and thugs suspected of being in the hire of security forces repeatedly pelted opposition rallies with rocks; no arrests were made. Moreover, the opposition candidates were the targets of scurrilous stories in tabloid newspapers.

The day after the election, it seemed that the worst fears would come to pass. Despite reliable exit polls that showed Fujimori well short of a majority, the first "official" count—suspiciously delayed until midday on April 10—showed Fujimori a hair short of a majority, 49.6%; Toledo was a strong second with 40.6%. It was apparent that as the count progressed, the president would go over the 50% mark. As the tedious vote counting progressed over the next three days, however, reports began surfacing of serious irregularities, such as soldiers preventing people from voting, ballots with Toledo's name torn off the bottom, pre-filled ballots, and Fujimori campaign officials inserting votes into the electoral commission's computer via an Internet café.

Domestic protests erupted, and the United States and other democracies warned Fujimori that they would take a dim view of a fraudulent election. Then, as if by magic, election officials "revised" the final vote count, giving Fujimori 49.89%, just 20,000 short of a majority. Toledo obtained 40.15%.

The opposition took heart from Fujimori's failure to steal the election outright and even more from the results in the congressional election. Fujimori's *Perú 2000* party lost its absolute majority, dropping from 67 seats in the 120-member Congress to 51. Toledo's *Perú Posible* was second with 28 seats. The rest were scattered among smaller parties, but the opposition soon alleged that Fujimori loyalists were offering $50,000 bribes for legislators to join an alliance with *Perú 2000*.

The eyes of the world were focused on the May 28 runoff election, especially as it seemed obvious that Fujimori did not intend to allow a trifle like the will of the people to stand in the way of his retaining power. As election day neared, it became apparent to both the domestic watchdog *Transparencia* and to inter-

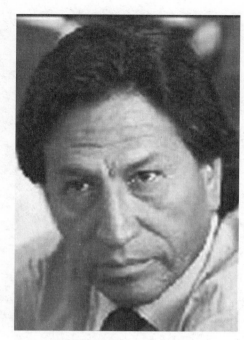

President Alejandro Toledo

national observers from the OAS and the Atlanta-based Carter Center, that it would be impossible to guarantee a fair and honest vote. Toledo proclaimed he would withdraw from the race unless the vote were postponed until June 18 to allow experts time to ensure there would not be the kinds of computer problems and irregularities that marred the first round. The international observers soon joined Toledo's call for a postponement. But Fujimori refused, countering that Toledo merely feared defeat.

The week before the election, Toledo withdrew, saying he refused to lend the appearance of legitimacy to a fraudulent election. Then the OAS and the Carter Center pulled out their observers, saying they could not guarantee the integrity of the vote unless it were delayed. The OAS mission declared that the process "was far from free and fair." The day before the election, this author spoke with Jimmy Carter in Venezuela, which had just postponed its election because of technical problems. "In Venezuela, the election has been postponed, but with integrity," he said. "In Peru, the election has been allowed to proceed without postponement, but without integrity." The Clinton administration warned Fujimori that Peru could face economic sanctions. Street violence broke out as Toledo supporters attacked Fujimori campaign offices. Toledo at first called on his voters to boycott the election, but the $33 fine for failing to vote is too stiff for most Peruvians. He then called on them to deface their ballots by writing, "No to fraud!"

Days before the election, Fabián Salazar, a columnist for the newspaper *La República*, was given videotapes from contacts in the National Intelligence Service that reportedly showed the intelligence chief, Vladimiro Montesinos, giving instructions to the head of the electoral commission on rigging the congressional elections to deny seats to certain candidates. As Salazar was viewing the tapes in his office, security agents broke in, confiscated the tapes and sawed Salazar's arm to the bone. (Salazar is a former executive at Ivcher's *Frecuencia Latina*.)

The outcome on May 28 was a foregone conclusion. Fujimori received only a bare majority of 51.1%. Toledo received 17.4%, and 30.3% of the ballots were voided as Toledo had requested.

International reaction was immediate. The U.S. State Department quickly branded Fujimori's victory as "illegitimate," and the presidents of several Latin American countries expressed their concern. Toledo flew to Madrid to ask for support from Spanish Prime Minister José María Aznar for a new election.

The tarnished election also headed the agenda of a meeting of OAS foreign ministers in Windsor, Ontario, June 4-6. But it soon became apparent that the Latin American representatives had no stomach for the U.S. position for strong hemispheric action. What emerged was a lukewarm Canadian resolution that called for former Colombian President César Gaviría and Canadian Foreign Minister Lloyd Axworthy to conduct a fact-finding mission to Peru to study ways to "strengthen democracy" there. There was no mention of sanctions or new elections. Axworthy, dashing any hopes among the Peruvian opposition, bluntly said that Fujimori's reelection was "reality." The Peruvian representative to the OAS meeting stated that Peru "welcomes" the mission's visit—so long as there were no discussion of a new election.

Fujimori Falls

Fujimori was inaugurated for his third term on July 28, 2000, an event largely snubbed by the international community and vigorously protested in the streets of Lima. Only two presidents, from neighboring Ecuador and Bolivia, attended, compared with nine in 1995. On inauguration eve, Toledo marshaled 80,000 demonstrators for a non-violent protest.

Inauguration day, however, was uglier, as riot police sought to disperse protesters with tear gas, which wafted toward the presidential palace and into the nostrils of the dignitaries. Uglier still, a bank was torched, and six security guards died in the blaze; each side blamed the other for starting it. In his address, Fujimori igwww.peru21.com

Perú.21

0,50

Tenga cuidado con el pescado en Semana Santa

La 'U' quedó fuera de la Libertadores

Rutas cercanas a Lima para disfrutar

No hubo autocrítica

▸ Toledo culpa del 'Pantelgate' a la mafia.
▸ Con mensaje por TV da por cerrado el caso.

▸ Solari pide que fiscalía y procuraduría evalúen iniciar juicio por difamación.
▸ Aceptaron renuncia del secretario de Prensa.

▸ Comisión de Fiscalización seguirá con la investigación y llamará a testigos.

▸ La oposición critica discurso y reacción tardía.

INFORME .21

LA ODISEA DE LA TRADUCCIÓN DEL EXPEDIENTE FUJIMORI

Tokio asumen la delicada tarea de pasar al idioma japonés 680 hojas con miras a la extradición. Cinco personas en

---

nored mention of the democratic reforms he had promised the OAS, focusing instead on economic growth. Meanwhile, as expected, several independent congressmen were "persuaded" to join the pro-Fujimori bloc, giving it a slim 63-57 majority.

If Fujimori believed the protesters would eventually relent and accept his stolen election as a *fait accompli*, he was soon disillusioned. For seven weeks, the protesters remained in the streets; usually the protests were non-violent, but occasionally there were clashes with riot police. Among the demonstrators' symbolic protests in front of the presidential palace: Washing the Peruvian flag in a tub of soap and water; using fumigation guns to spray the "rats" in the palace, and surrounding the palace with yellow police tape that bore the legend, "Caution! Mafia at work!" It was clever and effective nonviolent protest in the best tradition of Gandhi and Martin Luther King.

The protests proved little more than a minor annoyance for the thick-skinned and entrenched president. But in September, evidence became public that Montesinos may have been responsible for the transfer of arms through Peru to the *FARC* guerrillas in Colombia, which brought increased U.S. pressure on Fujimori. Then a television station broadcast a clandestine videotape that left little to the imagination: Montesinos was seen and heard at-

tempting to bribe a congressman in the anti-Fujimori faction into switching sides.

The resulting domestic and international pressure finally proved too much. On September 16, Fujimori stunned the nation in a televised address that he would order the disbanding of Montesinos' National Intelligence Service (whose Spanish acronym, *SIN*, is amusingly allegorical in English) and that he would call a new election—in which he would not be a candidate! He began talks with the opposition, brokered by the OAS, to effect a transition. Fujimori angered the opposition by agreeing to a new election on April 8, 2001, with the new president to succeed him on July 28, but only if the Congress approved an expanded amnesty law to protect members of the armed forces from prosecution in other than human rights cases. The opposition refused to go along, and it prevailed. Many in the opposition preferred Fujimori's immediate resignation, which the president at first refused to do, and they made the resignation of Montesinos the *sine qua non* for continued dialogue.

In September, the nation was shocked again by the news that Montesinos had fled to Panama, Latin America's traditional dumping ground for unpopular and venal political figures. Fujimori had just "fired" his intelligence chief under mounting pressure, but his escape abroad smacked of collusion. Others, however, were relieved he was gone. Montesinos sought political asylum in Panama, which demurred, despite pressure from the United States and some Latin American countries to allow him to remain, thus removing the possibility of his continuing as a player in Peru's complex power game.

With his tourist visa expiring and no charges awaiting him yet in Peru, Montesinos returned to Peru on October 23 just as suddenly and as unexpectedly as he had left, precipitating an immediate domestic crisis. Rumors flew that the armed forces chiefs, known to owe their first loyalty to Montesinos rather than to Fujimori, were planning to stage a *coup d'etat*. Fujimori went on television to assure the country that he was in "total control" of the armed forces. Montesinos went into hiding, and Fujimori made a widely publicized effort to "find" his intelligence chief, although most Peruvians believed the president actually was harboring him.

The opposition voiced its outrage over Montesinos' return and demanded Fujimori's resignation. Even First Vice President Francisco Tudela, long a Fujimori ally, resigned in protest—a decision he may have regretted a month later. Fujimori sought to mollify public opinion by

Peru

firing the heads of the three armed forces, all Montesinos loyalists. But his new army commander also was a *montesinista*.

Over the next eight months, Montesinos' whereabouts became an international guessing game; eyewitnesses reported seeing him in the Galapagos Islands of Ecuador, then in Costa Rica, then in Aruba; in January 2001, he was believed to have returned to Peru. By November, reports circulated in the media that Montesinos and Fujimori had been involved in money laundering, arms dealing and drug trafficking. A federal prosecutor alleged that Montesinos had $48 million in Swiss bank accounts (his monthly salary was just $337). By early 2001, an investigation had raised that figure to $70 million, and further probing brought evidence that Montesinos may have amassed as much as $264 million. Evidence surfaced later that some of the money may have been laundered by two front companies that had been set up in Singapore—by Fujimori.

Events then began to unfold rapidly, as often occurs when the rule of a long-entrenched ruler begins to unravel. On No-

vember 13, Fujimori flew to Brunei for a meeting of the Asia-Pacific Economic Cooperation (APEC) conference. By then, defections from Fujimori's bloc in Congress had given the opposition control. Hours after Fujimori departed, Congress deposed his loyal speaker and replaced her with Valentín Paniagua, a respected but relatively obscure 64-year-old lawyer from the now-tiny Popular Action Party. The country was jolted yet again on November 17, when Fujimori absconded to Japan, his family's homeland. Three days later, he faxed his resignation to Congress—which rejected it. Instead, Congress voted 62-9 to remove him from office as "permanently morally unfit."

At first, Second Vice President Ricardo Márquez sought to exercise his constitutional right to succeed the ousted president, but Congress was in no mood to have the presidency go to a Fujimori minion. Márquez resigned, and Congress appointed Paniagua as interim president. He vowed a "total house-cleaning" and appointed the respected former U.N. Secretary-General Javier Pérez de Cuellar as prime minister. Another positive step: *Fre-*

cuencia Latina was restored to its rightful owner, Baruch Ivcher, and the media were given free rein to report objectively on the upcoming election campaign, free of intimidation. Congress also restored the three judges Fujimori had sacked from the Constitutional Tribunal for ruling against his bid to run for a third term.

Thus, one of the most intriguing eras of *personalismo* in 20th century Peruvian—and Latin American—history had come to an end. In February 2001, Congress brought formal criminal charges against Fujimori for dereliction of duty and other specifications. But Japan granted him Japanese citizenship and has refused to extradite him. Nonetheless, Fujimori remains as much a fugitive as Montesinos was, unable to travel to countries that have extradition treaties with Peru.

He then faced murder charges at home. According to a former Japanese hostage, three of the guerrillas slain in the 1997 commando raid on the Japanese ambassador's residence were seen alive after the raid in commando custody. Fujimori had himself boasted of his micromanagement of that raid, making it unlikely that the prisoners could have been killed without his approval. It was a shabby end for a man once hailed as the country's savior.

Meanwhile, in early 2001, investigators seized from Montesinos' home about 2,400 videotapes on which the intelligence chief had unabashedly chronicled his bribes of a dazzling array of officials. Many of the so-called *"Vladivideos"* were released to the media, which kept the public spellbound—and further outraged. The public also learned that Montesinos had an escape tunnel under his bathtub.

Peruvian authorities then received word that Montesinos was in hiding in Venezuela, which the government of President Hugo Chávez denied for months. The Peruvians also learned that Montesinos had a secret bank account in Miami and asked the U.S. FBI to monitor it. Acting on irrefutable evidence from the FBI, the Peruvians confronted the Chávez government with the evidence of Montesinos' whereabouts, and on June 23, 2001, Venezuelan intelligence officials arrested Montesinos in a house in Caracas. Ironically, the Peruvian president-elect was in Caracas for the 13th Andean Summit, where Chávez announced that Montesinos was in custody.

In just 24 hours, Montesinos was hustled back to Lima, not on an extradition request, but as an undocumented alien! His appearance in court the following day, in handcuffs and a bulletproof vest, was a hemispheric media event, and the Peruvian public began waiting expectantly for new revelations of Montesinos' perfidy like they would an unfolding *telenovela*. Besides the money laundering, drug trafficking and arms smuggling charges, Montesinos also faced a murder charge in the death of the whistle-blowing female army sergeant in 1997.

It was widely believed Chávez had harbored Montesinos, in theory because Montesinos had once granted refuge to some of Chávez's henchmen after the failed 1992 Venezuelan coup, and it has soured bilateral relations. (see Venezuela).

New Election, New President

In January 2001, even as the special prosecutor was making public some of the 700 *"Vladivideos,"* no fewer than 10 candidates presented themselves for the April 8 election, including Toledo again. Perhaps the most surprising postulant was former President García, who returned home that month after nine years of self-imposed exile in Colombia—just after the statute of limitations on his kickback charges had expired. At first, the García candidacy on the *APRA* ticket was dismissed as a joke, a relic of the dreadful days of guerrilla warfare and rampant hyperinflation. For two

months, it seemed a foregone conclusion that the two candidates who would face each other in the runoff would be Toledo, candidate of the so-called *Perú Posible* movement, and Lourdes Flores, a veteran congresswoman from the conservative Popular Christian Party.

Toledo remained the favorite throughout the campaign with more than 30% in most polls, with Flores a strong second at 25%; García was a distant third. Toledo and Flores both sought to stake out the political center, with he slightly to the left, she slightly to the right, and García clearly to the left of Toledo. Suddenly, inexplicably, in March the polls began showing García moving up on the outside and closing in on Flores for the No. 2 spot. That sent a chill through domestic and international financial circles, which recalled that as president García had limited debt repayment to 10% of exports, thus sparking the hyperinflation that Fujimori was elected to combat. Nonetheless, García, an eloquent stump speaker, remained popular with the country's poor majority, who did not feel they had benefited appreciably from 10 years of *fujimorismo*. Still, he pragmatically toned down his fiery populist rhetoric so as not to frighten foreign investors and the ruling elite.

García also was aided by Toledo and Flores themselves, who began hurling mud at each other. Toledo was accused of fathering a child out of wedlock and refusing to take a paternity test. Also, *Caretas* magazine reproduced a medical report showing that he had tested positive for cocaine in 1998; Toledo countered that the *SIN* had abducted him and framed him. Race also became an issue. Toledo's Belgian-born wife, a U.S. citizen, who was referred to by Peruvians as a *"gringa,"* ridiculed Peru's white ruling elite. Flores' father, meanwhile, used a racial epithet to refer to Toledo, which cost her votes among the indigenous majority.

Peruvians should have become inured to shocks by this time, but they received another on April 8. Toledo, as expected, led the field with 36.5%, less than he had received the year before in the first round against Fujimori. García won the runoff spot with 26% to Flores' 24%.

Toledo was thought an easy winner in the June 3 runoff, as Flores' conservative voters obviously would prefer him to García. Both men frightened the money-changers; Toledo was seen as unknown and unpredictable, but García was *known* all to well. Toledo, with his Stanford degree in economics, appeared less of a bogeyman. But again, the grassroots voters astonished the pollsters. Toledo was elected by a slim 52% to 48%, making history as Peru's first full-blooded Indian president. García, at 52, was still young

enough to try again—and probably will. He received a major boost in July 2001 when the Supreme Court dismissed all pending charges against him, citing the statute of limitations.

Toledo's Troubled Presidency

Toledo was inaugurated on July 28, 2001. In his address, he pledged to combat the corruption left by Fujimori; to restructure the armed forces and police in the wake of Montesinos' departure; to create 400,000 jobs; and to continue cooperating with the United States in the war against drugs. The following day, in a symbolic demonstration of pride in his ethnic roots, Toledo participated in an Inca "inauguration" ceremony at the ruins of Machu Picchu. Fujimori's admirers had dubbed him *"El Chino;"* Toledo's nicknamed him "Pachacutec," after a 15th-century Inca emperor.

Peru rapidly began moving toward a catharsis to cleanse itself of the Fujimori legacy, a legacy the disgraced former president continued to defend from his safe haven in Japan. A week before Toledo's inauguration and the installation of the new Congress, the imprisoned Montesinos began singing like the proverbial canary bird. He alleged that Fujimori had ordered him to pay hundreds of thousands of dollars in bribes to key members of Congress to secure his reelection in 2000. Montesinos even named the members who had accepted the bribes, including several who had just been elected again.

In August 2002, Congress expelled two members of Fujimori's party for their role in his reelection maneuvers; they were seen plotting in a *"Vladivideo."*

Congress voted unanimously to strip Fujimori of his constitutional immunity from prosecution. Then the attorney general filed formal murder charges against him for his alleged knowledge and approval of two massacres of dissidents: the so-called "barbecue massacre" in the Lima neighborhood of Barrio Alto in 1991 that left 15 people dead, and another in 1992, in which 10 were killed. The massacres allegedly were committed by an infamous paramilitary death squad known as the "Colina Group." Fujimori also was charged with complicity in the 1997 murder and dismemberment of Mariela Barreto, the whistle-blowing intelligence service sergeant.

A few days later, a judge issued an international arrest warrant for Fujimori. Japan, however, continued to deny his extradition, which Peru called "unacceptable." The Peruvian cabinet formally asked Japan to extradite Fujimori in June 2002 to stand trial for the massacres. Congress, meanwhile, voted unanimously again in Oc-

Peru

In this editorial cartoon, President Toledo asks God, "Father, why have You forsaken me?" God replies: "Because of incompetence, frivolousness, insecurity, lying, erratic behavior, irresponsibility, indecisiveness, nepotism, for being dumb, for being a bad father. . ."

tober 2002 to strip Fujimori of immunity so he could be charged with embezzlement; Congress questioned the disappearance of $372 million, $260 million of which apparently went into accounts controlled by Montesinos. Another international arrest warrant was issued against Fujimori in January 2002 for an alleged $15 million payoff to Montesinos. In April 2002, Fujimori was formally charged with ordering the bribes of members of Congress to pave the way for his reelection.

Adding to Fujimori's woes, in May 2002 prosecutors cited forensic evidence that eight of the 14 guerrillas slain in the recapturing of the Japanese ambassador's residence in 1997 had been shot execution-style, not in combat as had been reported at the time. In March 2003, Interpol added Fujimori to its 10 Most Wanted list.

In June 2002, Montesinos was ordered to stand trial for his role in the killings. However, when police arrested a retired brigadier general, who was widely regarded as a hero in the hostage crisis, a public outcry quickly led to his release. A judge issued warrants for 11 other officers in the case, but none was detained.

Montesinos faces as many as 70 trials. His first conviction, of becoming intelligence chief in an illegal manner, was handed down in July 2002. He was sentenced to nine years. In March 2003 he was convicted of influence peddling and sentenced to five years, and in May 2003 he was convicted of embezzlement and sentenced to eight.

Meanwhile, former army commander Nicolás Hermoza, the third man in the so-called "triumvirate" with Fujimori and Montesinos, was eventually convicted in May 2005 of illegally amassing a $22 million fortune and sentenced to eight years.

In April 2002, the appointed Truth and Reconciliation Commission, which had been appointed the previous June by interim President Paniagua, began public hearings into human rights abuses committed during the 1980s and '90s. Peruvians were presented with horror stories of past atrocities. In September 2002, a team from the commission flew to Tokyo to interrogate Fujimori himself, who refused to meet with them.

Peruvians were abruptly reminded of another past horror that had led to the atrocities when, on March 21, 2002, a powerful car bomb exploded near the U.S. Embassy in Lima on the eve of a one-day visit by U.S. President George W. Bush, the first visit by a U.S. president. Ten people were killed and 30 injured. The purpose of the visit was a summit with the presidents of Peru, Colombia and Bolivia to discuss renewing the preferential U.S. tariff for Andean countries, the war on drugs and, ironically, the war on terrorism. One result of the meeting was the decision of Bush and Toledo to resume drug interdiction flights by the Peruvian air force, which had been suspended in 2001 after an air force fighter pilot, armed with bad information from the CIA, mistakenly fired on a light plane, killing a female U.S. Baptist missionary and her baby.

Police arrested four members of *Sendero Luminoso* in connection with the car bombing. The prospect of renewed violence by the once-feared group, whose size is estimated variously at 175 to 700, sent a chill through the country. So did the decision by the Supreme Couer in 2003 to overturn the conviction of *Sendero Luminoso* leader Guzmán. He was retried in November 2004, but that ended in a mistrial. He remains in jail awaiting yet another trial.

By March 2002, it became apparent that Toledo's honeymoon with the Congress and the public was over. Despite the fact that the economy was showing a brisk growth rate (see Economy), demonstrators took to the streets to denounce Toledo for failing to ease unemployment. In March his job approval rating in a major poll had plummeted to 25%, compared with 59% the previous August; 65% said they disapproved of him personally.

Toledo himself has contributed to his image problem, coming across as inartic-ulate, unpunctual and indecisive. For example, Toledo has changed his prime ministers, interior ministers and finance ministers with bewildering regularity, and he has replaced technocrats with political hacks. In 2001, he shelved a perfectly reasonable plan to purchase a helicopter to facilitate his travels around the mountainous country after critics complained loudly that the money would better be spent on alleviating poverty, as though one helicopter would make that much difference. Street protests in the capital and elsewhere remain a regular occurrence.

His efforts at privatization also came under attack. In June 2002, 700 soldiers and 1,000 riot police were dispatched to Arequipa to quell violent protests against plans to privatize two local electric companies. Leaders of the protest alleged that Toledo had broken a promise not to privatize the companies. When the protests continued, Toledo declared a 30-day state of siege, which prompted his interior minister to resign in protest. By the time the rioting died down a week later, two people had been killed and 200 injured. Toledo again backed down and called off the sale of the companies.

Former President Fernando Belaúnde, the acknowledged patriarch of Peru's new democracy, died June 4, 2002, at the age of 89. Toledo declared three days of national mourning and tearfully praised his predecessor as a "paradigm of democracy." The day of Belaúnde's funeral was a national holiday, and thousands filled the streets of the capital to honor him and to throw flower petals on his flag-draped casket as it was carried through the streets.

As a means of enhancing decentralization, Congress created 25 new federal-style regional governments. Elections for these new governorships and legislative assemblies were held on November 17, 2002. Toledo's *Perú Posible* party won only one governorship. *APRA* won 11 and independent candidates won 13. Alberto Andrade failed to win a third term as Lima's mayor, losing to Luis Castañeda of the center-right National Unity.

In a separate development, Toledo publicly acknowledged just two days before the election that confirmed what had been alleged by a former lover and widely believed by the public: that he was the father of a 14-year-old girl born out of wedlock.

Despite Peru's boasting the fastest economic growth rate in Latin America, large sectors of the work force continued to grumble that they were not feeling any of the benefits of it. In May 2003, teachers nationwide walked out of strike, and hundreds literally camped out outside the Congress to demand an increase in their $190-a-month salaries. The government

310

A religious procession in rural Peru

offered them a $29-a-month raise, which they angrily rejected. Meanwhile, farmers around the country, angered by taxes and by low prices they blamed on cheap imports, erected more than 60 barricades with boulders and burning tires on highways, especially along the 1,500-mile Peruvian segment of the Pan-American Highway, disrupting commerce and stranding travelers. Simultaneously, civil servants, health care workers and judicial employees went out on strike.

Toledo responded with a 30-day nationwide state of emergency. Troops and police moved in and forcibly but peaceably evicted the teachers from the Congress and began removing the barricades. Clashes between the farmers, troops and police led to 300 arrests and numerous injuries, including 16 policemen. On May 29, troops opened fire on protesting students in the southeastern city of Puno, killing one and wounding 36. The government claimed that *Senderistas* had instigated the violence.

Peace returned across the nation as the government and teachers renewed negotiations and reached a compromise on a salary increase. Largely as a public relations gesture, Toledo and his top cabinet ministers reduced their salaries by 30%. Toledo now receives "only"$8,000 a month.

Toledo has done little to enhance his popularity with the opulent lifestyle he follows. He angered Peruvians when he insisted on using the presidential jet to de-

liver the commencement address at his alma mater, Stanford, in May 2003, which cost $100,000, when the university had provided first-class commercial tickets for him and his wife. Toledo's response to his growing unpopularity: another cabinet shuffle! By August 2003, Toledo's approval rating had dropped to 12%, the lowest of any Latin American president; even Fujimori's was 31%! Toledo's popularity soon would drop even lower.

The Peruvian government stubbornly filed a 700-page extradition request with Japan on July 31, 2003, naming Fujimori as the intellectual author of the 1991 "barbecue massacre." Japan still has taken no action, although Fujimori retained a lawyer in Peru in February 2004 to represent him in connection with some of the charges, and he pluckishly announced his intention to run for president in 2006— even though he has been barred from holding office until 2010. In March 2005, Fujimori's brother and two sisters were arrested on charges that they has embezzled $21 million from a private charity.

The Truth and Reconciliation Commission presented its long-awaited report to Toledo in August 2003. It had spent two years and $13 million interviewing 17,000 witnesses and unearthing mass graves. Perhaps its most surprising conclusion was that 69,000 people had been killed during the guerrilla wars of the 1980s and '90s, more than twice as many as the 30,000 that had been generally believed. The commission laid the greatest blame

for the deaths at the feet of *Sendero Luminoso*, but also faulted the security services for human rights violations. It criticized the governments of former presidents Belaúnde and García as being inept and not responding forcefully enough, and Fujimori's for responding *too* forcefully.

Also in August 2003, the TV program "In the Wolf's Mouth" on *Frecuencia Latina*—the same station Fujimori had taken from its owner in 1997 for investigative reporting—aired a leaked audiotape in which Toledo could be heard speaking in earthy language about local authorities in Arequipa. The president reacted with fury, saying he would appoint a special commission to investigate the leak and that "heads will roll." But the embarrassment over his comments was secondary to the larger issue: That someone still had the capability to bug high-ranking officials and was doing it. Toledo had been alleging that people loyal to Montesinos and Fujimori were still operating clandestinely on their behalf to discredit him. Evidently, his paranoia was justified. The head that rolled eventually was Alfonso Panizo's, the latest intelligence chief. Even though he apparently had nothing to do with the taping, Toledo reasoned, he hadn't prevented it. He was replaced with Daniel Mora, a retired general whose primary qualification for the job apparently was loyalty to Toledo's party rather than experience in intelligence.

The embarrassment from the audiotape also was trivial compared to the series of

Peru

influence-peddling, nepotism and other scandals in late 2003 and early 2004, some of them brought to light by more clandestine tapes, which caused six cabinet ministers to resign. Vice President Raúl Diez Canesco also resigned in January 2004 for allegedly awarding a contract to a relative of his girlfriend when he was trade minister. Congress also forced out Interior Minister Fernando Rospigliosi in May 2004 for allegedly mishandling a riot in southern Peru in which angry Indian peasants beat a local mayor to death. The most recent casualty, Agriculture Minister José León, resigned in June after a television station exposé showed that a hotel owned by his family was being used as a brothel.

Another scandal was sparked in January 2004 by a leaked videotape that showed César Almeyda, Toledo's onetime personal attorney and his close aide, meeting in late 2001with Oscar Villanueva, a retired general suspected of being a key figure in Montesinos' bribery operations. In the tape, the men discuss influencing judges to release some of Montesinos' cronies. Villanueva subsequently committed suicide while under house arrest. Almeyda claimed that he was merely discussing a legal plea bargain. The scandal deepened when Fernando Olivera, leader of the Independent Moralizing Front (FIM), Perú Posible's main coalition partner, who was justice minister at the time of the meeting, admitted he had known of it. Olivera pulled his party out of the coalition on February 10, claiming he did so to give Toledo "a free hand."

The sleaze scandals not only caused Toledo's public approval rating to drop even lower, they brought increased pressure on him either to resign or to allow Congress more oversight of his appointments. In February 2004, the influential daily El Comercio carried a front-page editorial urging Toledo to salvage his presidency by consigning himself to a figurehead role and surrendering his authority to his prime minister. Others in Congress echoed that sentiment. Surprisingly, however, Congress voted 54-27 in June 2004 to require a two-thirds majority rather than a simple majority to remove the president. Supporters of the measure pointed out that a two-thirds majority is required to remove other officials, but the vote was seen as a move to ensure stability by preventing a frivolous removal, no matter how unpopular a president is.

Recent Developments

Faced with an approval rating that had sunk to 6%, the last thing Toledo needed was yet another scandal. But in January 2005, a judge ordered the arrest of Toledo's sister, Margarita, and 25 others for allegedly falsifying voters' signatures on the petitions to qualify Perú Posible for the ballot in the 2000 election. Rumors to that effect had been circulating for months, and a local TV station had aired yet another embarrassing video showing Toledo congratulating followers for collecting the signatures. An investigation produced evidence that 78% of the party's 520,000 signatures were forged. Toledo neither admitted nor denied the allegations, but remained silent. His only response: another cabinet shuffle.

Congress launched an investigation, and on May 3, a congressional committee, on a narrow 3–2 vote, concluded that Toledo was the "co-author" of the forgery scheme. This constituted grounds for impeachment and removal, but on May 20, Congress voted instead, 57–48, to forward the charges to a prosecutor for Toledo to face criminal charges. Because the president enjoys immunity from prosecution, however, the effect was to allow Toledo to serve out the remaining 14 months of his term. After he leaves office, the charges will be waiting for him.

If this succession of scandals weren't enough, the tabloid press for months reported rumors that Toledo was having an affair with a 23-year-old police lieutenant. A congressional committee subpoenaed her and questioned her behind closed doors in May about how she made a $47,000 land purchase when she makes $553 a month. She said the parcel was a family inheritance.

In April, Toledo signed a controversial law that doles out $30 a month to needy families, which his critics charge is merely a political gimmick in advance of the April 2006 elections. It did nothing to enhance the beleagured president's popularity; when this book went to press, his approval rating was still only 8%.

Violent protests continued to dog Toledo as well. In late May, peasants believed to be linked to Sendero Luminoso invaded the Tintaya copper mine and committed acts of vandalism, forcing it to suspend operations. Hundreds of police were dispatched to other key mines. Finance Minister Kuczynski warned mining companies that they need to provide more social spending for the poor local communities around the mines to allay protests.

In the drug war, the United Nations released figures showing that coca production in Peru had soared by 55% in 2004. Although the report conceded that Peru has eradicated more than 26,000 acres of coca, 42,000 acres of new coca were planted. Experts theorized that the crackdown on coca cultivation in Colombia had forced producers to shift operations to Peru, Ecuador and Bolivia. Peru's counter-drug agency vowed that drug seizures in 2005 would triple to 18 tons, the bulk of it cocaine.

Culture: The legacy of the Incas is evident in Peruvian folklore, art, music and architecture. Most of the population is full-blooded Indian today, and Quechua is the first language of millions of Peruvians. Still, the inevitable hybridization with Spanish culture produced something that is uniquely Peruvian.

Because Peru, like Mexico (New Spain), was a full-fledged viceroyalty that yielded dazzling amounts of gold and silver, the Spanish crown placed a higher value on this colony than on most. Consequently, a strong creole culture developed and along with it a literary tradition. Peruvian literary activity, however, never matched that of, say, Argentina or Chile. One of the most influential writers of the late 19th and early 20th centuries was Manuel González Prada, a journalist, poet and essayist who labored for reform and influenced later generations of idealistic Peruvian writers.

Many of Peru's best-known writers of the first half of the 20th century found their inspiration in politics, including the poet César Vallejo and the Marxist essayist José Carlos Mariátegui, who, like González Prada, was an major force in the Aprista movement. The most acclaimed novelists of that period and later years have all stressed indigenous themes, such as Ciro Alegría, Julio Ramón Ribeyra and José María Arguedas.

Without question Peru's most prominent contemporary writer is Mario Vargas Llosa. Born in 1936, he earned a doctorate in Madrid, and consequently his works are more cosmopolitan than those of his predecessors. His best-known novel, translated into several languages and the recipient of numerous international garlands, remains La guerra del fin del mundo (The War of the End of the World). One of his plays, La señorita de Tacna, also has been translated into English and other languages and received favorable reviews when performed on Broadway. His latest novel, released in 2003, is El paraíso en la otra esquina (The Paradise on the Other Corner). Vargas Llosa was Fujimori's opponent in the 1990 presidential election, and his electoral loss was seen as a victory for Peruvian literature. In November 2001, President Alejandro Toledo garlanded Vargas Llosa with the Order of the Sun, Peru's highest honor. In 2005 he was working on a new novel, Las travesuras de una niña mala (The Mischief of a Bad Girl), his first-ever love story.

Peruvians are as fanatically devoted to their two native musical styles, música criolla and Peruvian waltzes, as Argentines are to the tango. The same is true of the national folk dance, the *marinera*, subject of an annual festival in Ayacucho. Until her death in 1983, the singer Chabuca Grande conveyed these distinctly Peruvian sounds to audiences throughout Latin America.

Peruvian theater, cinema and television still lag behind those of such countries as Mexico and Argentina, though some works have achieved recognition abroad. Peru is producing more of its own *telenovelas*, and in 2005 it released Latin America's animated 3-D motion picture, Piratas de Callao (Pirates of Callao), produced by Hernán Garrido-Lecca, which has been distributed throughout Latin America as well as to the United States and China.

Peru can claim to be one of the birthplaces of Latin American journalism. Even before independence, the literary journal *Mercurio Peruano* appeared in 1791. The leading contemporary daily, *El Comercio*, (see below) was founded in 1839, losing to Chile's *El Mercurio* by two years the distinction of being Latin America's oldest continuously published newspaper. For most of Peru's troubled history, press freedom either was nonexistent or severely limited. During the peculiar social experimentation of the 1968–80 military regime, the major dailies were expropriated and turned over to various "social organizations," such as teachers and labor unions. The result was a journalistic disaster, and the first act of President Belaúnde when he returned to power in 1980 was to restore the newspapers to their rightful owners. Numerous dailies of stature, plus the usual sleazy tabloids, are published in the capital. A newspaper that has come to rival *El Comercio* in journalistic prestige since the restoration of democracy is the pro-*Aprista La República*. Some dailies also are published in the major provincial capitals. There also is a thriving magazine industry, the highest quality probably being *Caretas* and *Oiga*.

Peruvian cuisine is unique, owing to the great variety of seafood provided by the Humboldt Current and the cornucopia of foodstuffs from tropical and Andean ecospheres. Peruvian restaurants have begun cropping up in major cities in Europe and North America. The best known Peruvian dish abroad is *ceviche* (also spelled *cebiche*), raw fish marinated in lime juice. Pisco, a potent liquor distilled from grapes, is mixed with lime juice, sugar and egg whites to create the Pisco sour, one of South America's favorite cocktails.

Economy: Extraction and marketing of natural resources from mountain areas and the adjacent sea provides the basis of the Peruvian economy. Because the arid Pacific shelf and the high Andes restrict agricultural output, recent efforts have been made to open the eastern Andean slopes for farming. Water from the eastern slopes is also being used to irrigate former arid regions.

The ambitious land reform program implemented by the military government provided for the seizure of virtually all of the nation's large farms and their conversion into huge cooperatives rather than small, unproductive peasant plots. Relying on material incentives (profits were to go to the workers), the program was designed to increase farm output and bring—for the first time—larger numbers of peasants into the national money economy. However, because of poor management and a breakdown in the food distribution system, the land reform program fell far short of expectations. That failure, combined with a severe drought, caused widespread food shortages during 1979–80.

Abundant mineral resources provide the potential for sustained economic growth—with proper management. In 1981, Occidental Petroleum reported that new oil fields had been discovered in Peru's Amazon basin. Peru then reported early in 1982 that its proven oil reserves increased to 900 million barrels.

The inflation rate in 1989 was about 2,800%, creating a great deal of unrest among labor unions and an economically ruinous strike by the miners. The government began privatizing the nation's industry—the military had taken over more than 150 industries while in power. Peru's foreign debt is about $20 billion. To aid in its slow economic recovery, and under strict austerity requirements, the IMF in 1984 extended loans to the government; however, this was half as much as Peru hoped to receive.

When President Alan García demurred on payment of Peru's debts in the late

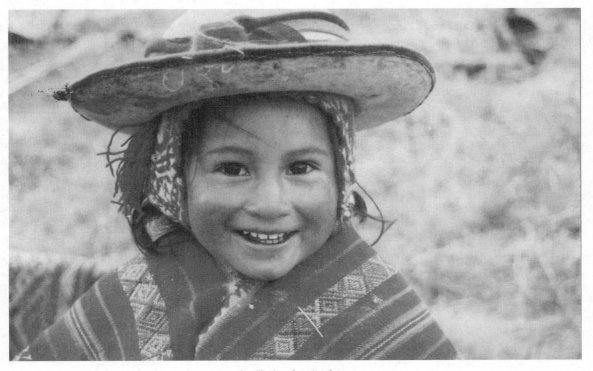

Smile in the Andes

Peru

1980s, the IMF declared Peru ineligible to receive further loans, and all other lenders followed suit. This meant that the nation was on a cash-in-advance status—an economic impossibility in a day and age when spare parts, machinery and manufacturing facilities are so vital to growth. It further meant that no government would honor Peruvian currency; the only substitute was foreign currency deposited in a foreign bank in advance to pay for imports.

All of this was reversed under President Alberto Fujimori. Peru again be-came credit-worthy and began receiving aid and investment from a number of sources. Approval of the constitution in late 1993 boosted available lending sources considerably.

Peru is the world's leading producer of raw coca leaf, from which refined cocaine is made, and second after Colombia in production of cocaine. Chewed by the Indians for millennia as a mild anesthetic to allay hunger, coca thrives in the remote Andean valleys. The illegal coca exports once accounted for an estimated $1 billion a year. But in 1996, Fujimori ordered his air force to begin shooting down planes crossing the border that refused to identify themselves. Total coca acreage that year dropped 18% as peasants, finding it impossible to market that product, willingly accepted a government plan, backed by $45 million in U.S. aid, that provided them with incentives to switch to such alternative crops as coffee, cocoa, yucca and peanuts.

Fujimori's much-touted privatization plan, his conquest of hyperinflation and his successful campaign to lure more foreign investors to Peru, received high marks in international financial circles, but they did little to alleviate Peru's grinding poverty. With the modernization that inevitably comes with privatization, industrial jobs were cut by the thousands. The streamlining of the bloated bureaucracy threw middle-class Peruvians out of work as well. The construction boom was concentrated in affluent sections of Lima, with little or no trickle-down effect. Meanwhile, the elimination of government subsidies drove up utility prices, which hit the poor the hardest.

Figures for real GDP were discouraging for several years. From a peak of $65.2 billion in 1997, which was a robust 7% growth from 1996, real GDP dropped to $51.6 billion in 1999. Per capita income also declined, from $2,675 in 1997 to $2,074 in 2001. Unemployment, which held steady at 7.7% in 1997 and 1998, jumped to 10% in 1999. It fell to 7.4% in 2000 and remained steady at 7.5% in 2001. Inflation dropped correspondingly, from 11.8% in 1996 to only 3.3% in 2001.

Despite the political uncertainty in 2000, real GDP grew by 3.1%, but it slowed to 0.6% in 2001, apparently because foreign investors held back to see what would happen when the dust from Fujimori's fall had settled. Fujimori's successor, Alejandro Toledo, has a doctorate in economics from Stanford and was once a World Bank official. He was elected on a moderately leftist platform, and was expected to be less enthusiastic about free-market economics and privatization than was Fujimori. However, Toledo surrounded himself with a retinue of U.S.-trained economists like himself, not unlike the "Chicago Boys" in Chile during the Pinochet years.

The new team has some cause for boasting. Peru's GDP growth for 2002 was 5.2%, the highest in Latin America, while inflation was only about 1.2%. The growth in 2003 was 3.8%, and in 2004 it was 5.07%; only Chile and Argentina recorded faster growth. For 2005 it was projected at 4.5-5%. Exports increased by about a third in 2004, one of the highest increases in the world.

In June 2004, Standard & Poor's raised Peru's foreign currency credit rating. Despite this, and the encouraging decline in inflation, an impatient public has repeatedly taken to the streets to demand more immediate improvements in the employment picture (see History). Critics on the left also complain that the impressive economic growth has not trickled down to the poor.

In August 2003, Peru signed a free-trade agreement with the *Mercosur* trade bloc (Argentina, Brazil, Paraguay and Uruguay), with tariff barriers to be gradually eliminated over a period of 13 years.

Much of the credit for the recent boom goes to the mining sector, which remains Peru's greatest export earner, accounting for 55% of the total, or $7 billion, in 2004. Peru ranks No. 2 in the world in silver production, No. 3 in copper and zinc, No. 4 in lead and No. 6 in gold. High world market prices in these metals have been a much-needed godsend for the economy.

So has the demand for natural gas, which Peru plans to begin exporting. In June 2005, Argentina, Brazil, Chile and Uruguay announced plans to begin buying $2.5 billion worth of gas from its new *Mercosur* partner, via a new pipeline to be built to Chile. Peru has estimated gas reserves of 13 trillion cubic feet in its Camisea field in the Amazon jungle in the south.

Peru was awash with good economic news in 2005. In June, the U.S. oil company Petro-Tech announced it had discovered an offshore field containing 10-50 million barrels of light crude, the largest discovery in Peru in 30 years. Days later, the Spanish oil and gas company Repsol YPF announced discovery of a smaller but onshore field in the Amazon jungle in the north that contains 70 million barrels of heavy crude, which is more difficult to refine than light crude. The discoveries coincided with the record high price of oil on international markets. Peru's known oil reserves are 320 million barrels.

The Future: Peru has one of Latin America's fastest GDP growth rates (5.07% in 2004) and among the lowest inflation rates (1.2%). Yet it has Latin America's most reviled president, with an approval rating of 8%. If this seems incongruous, it is.

President Toledo has been the target of strikes, street demonstrations, congressional investigations and editorials demanding his resignation or removal. Similar protests brought down the elected presidents of Ecuador in 2000 and 2005, Argentina in 2001 and Bolivia in 2003 and 2005. Granted, Toledo has brought much of the current discredit upon himself through bumbling and indecisive administration and his appointment of sleazy ministers. But Congress seems content now to let Toledo limp along through the final year of his five-year term. Just as well. If he had resigned or been removed, who would have replaced him, and would he or she have had any longer a honeymoon?

Meanwhile, former President Alan García, who narrowly lost to Toledo four years ago and whose party trounced Toledo's party in regional and municipal elections in 2002, waits his chance in the shadows like a hungry but patient jackal for the next election in April 2006. Peruvians seem to have forgotten that the last time García was president, from 1985-90, he wasn't given much of a honeymoon either, and his economic track record was far worse than Toledo's. In fact, it was nightmarish.

Peruvians, beware what you wish for; you may get it.

The Republic of Suriname

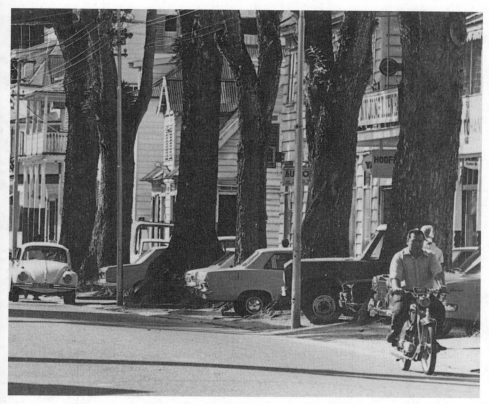

Street scene in the old section of Paramaribo

Area: 70,000 square miles

Population: 490,000

Capital City: Paramaribo (Pop. 190,000, estimated).

Climate: Very rainy, hot and humid.

Neighboring Countries: Guyana (West); French Guiana (Southeast); Brazil (South).

Official Language: Dutch

Other Principal Tongues: English, Spanish, Hindi, Javanese, Chinese and a local pidgin dialect called alternately *Sranan Tongo, Taki-Taki* or *Surinamese.*

Ethnic Background: Hindustani, 37%; creole (a person of mixed African and other ancestry) 31%; Asian, 15.3%; Bush Negro, 10.3%; Amerindian 2.6%; European and other, 3.8%. Figures are approximate.

Principal Religions: Hinduism, Roman Catholic Christianity, Islam, Protestant Christianity.

Chief Commercial Products: Refined aluminum ore, bauxite, aluminum, timber, rice, sugar, shrimp and citrus fruits.

Currency: Suriname Guilder.

Gross Domestic Product: U.S.$833 million in 2001 ($1,672 per capita).

Former Colonial Status: English Colony (1652–67); Dutch Colony (1667–1799); English-controlled (1799–1815); colony of the Netherlands (1815–1948); self-governing component of the Dutch Realm (1948–75).

Independence Date: November 25, 1975.

Chief of State: Runaldo Venetiaan (b. June 18, 1936), president (since August 12, 2000).

National Flag: Two green horizontal stripes, top and bottom, red horizontal stripe in the center, divided from the green by narrow white stripes; a gold five-pointed star is centered in the red stripe.

Separated from neighboring Guyana and French Guiana by large rivers, Suriname lies on the northeast coast of South America. Its 230-mile coastline is rather flat, a strip of marshy land lying mostly below sea level, which needs a series of dikes and canals to hold off the encroaching waters of the Atlantic Ocean. Along this fertile coast and stretching back about 50 of its 300 miles an inland extension is found where about 90% of the country's population lives.

Back from the coastal area, the land turns gradually into a grassland, becoming hilly and then densely forested with some 2,000 varieties of trees, 90% of the land area. This is a broad plateau land that reaches its highest point in the Wilhelmina Mountains. The land then dips down into the dense growth of the tropical rain forest where there are found hundreds of varieties of jungle birds, howler monkeys and all manner of wildlife typical to Brazil. In the interior is the 600-square-

mile W.J. van Blommestein Meer (lake), which provides hydroelectric power for the bauxite industry located downriver.

History: Although in 1499 the Spanish touched along the coast of what is now Suriname, no attempt at colonization was made. European explorers generally ignored the entire region—the land was not inviting and there were not wealthy native empires to subjugate or loot for the motherlands. Toward the close of the 16th century, the Dutch appeared on the coast, but the first large-scale colonization efforts were made in the early 1650s by the English governor of Barbados, who became the region's first governor. These English colonists established successful sugarcane plantations.

In 1667 the Dutch received Suriname from the English in exchange for the colony of New Netherlands (now New York). Early in the 1680s, workers were brought from Africa to work in the fields since there were few local natives.

The territory again fell to the British during the period of the Napoleonic Wars (1799–1815); a series of agreements between the three powers established the whole of Guiana, as it was then called, into English Guiana (now Guyana), Dutch Guiana (now Suriname) and French Guiana. The latter of these later became infamous for its offshore penal colony, Devil's Island.

The Netherlands emancipated the slaves in 1863 and many of them settled on small farms to cultivate their own produce. This created an immediate and critical labor shortage, which caused the Dutch to import cheap labor from India in the 1870s and from Java in the 1880s.

The territory was slow to develop any political awareness, but since World War II, Far Eastern groups have become increasingly insistent on playing a greater role in the destiny of the land in which they live. This has created a bitter rivalry between the largely agricultural creoles and the prosperous, business-oriented East Indians. The colony became a self-governing component of the Netherlands in 1948 and adopted the name Suriname—it had been called either Netherlands or Dutch Guiana—and after 1950 controlled its affairs with the exception of defense and foreign relations.

Border clashes between Suriname and the soon-to-be independent British Guiana (Guyana) occurred in 1970. Early in 1973, serious unrest erupted when the government refused to pay increased wages to trade union members. A bloody strike lasted for more than a month before order was gradually restored.

Elections in November 1973 for the Legislative Assembly resulted in a victory for

Suriname

an alliance of parties favoring independence. Known as the National Party Coalition (of which the strongest force is the National Party), it gained 13 seats. The Progressive Reform Party won three seats; this victory by the black-dominated National Party ended a long period of political control by a coalition of East Indians and Chinese.

With the National Party Coalition victory, the colony moved a step closer to independence. Although the Dutch appeared anxious to leave, the large East Indian (Hindustani) population feared that independence would bring serious racial problems similar to those that erupted in neighboring Guyana. The specter of violence soon sparked a mass migration to the Netherlands as independence day approached. All told, nearly a quarter of the population (140,000) fled Suriname.

Despite the damaging exodus, Suriname gained full independence after 308 years of colonial rule on November 25, 1975; the Netherlands agreed to help the new nation adjust to its status by giving it $100 million a year for the next decade—one of the most generous foreign aid programs on a per capita basis in history.

The new minister-president, Henck Arron, urged the nation's former residents to return. The appeal was indeed sincere since most of those who left were educated and skilled workers; their departure created a severe "brain-drain" for the new nation.

The principal political-economic controversy was the fate of the aluminum industry. Should it be nationalized, or should it remain in private hands, thus encouraging additional foreign investment? A decision was made to refrain from nationalization in spite of the fact that Arron's regime was initially leftist. Further complicating the political scene were ethnic differences and fears. The East Indian and Asiatic communities feared a black-dominated, oppressive regime.

Arron's policies gradually moderated and relative tranquility prevailed. But economic stability was in reality based on the $100 million annual Dutch subsidy; vital aluminum production was steadily declining. In 1980, however, non-commissioned officers ousted the government when it refused to allow them to form a Dutch-style military union. A nine-member National Revolutionary Council (RNC) was formed and backed the election of a government headed by Chin-A-Sen. The military, however, retained actual power; Lieutenant Colonel Desi Bouterse emerged as its leader. In December 1982 there was an attempted right-wing coup that led to assassinations of 22 military and civilian opponents of Bouterse. This "December Massacre" remains controversial to this day

and is one of Bourtese's lingering political liabilities.

The Dutch suspended aid and conditions rapidly worsened. Bouterse enlarged the military and conditions became extremely tense. Close relations with Cuba were established, to the extent that Cuba was viewed as a threat. The government was largely incompetent and inefficient. The "Cuban connection" was brief, ending after the United States invaded Grenada in 1983 (see Grenada).

Economically smarting because of the withdrawal of Dutch aid and lower world prices for aluminum products, Suriname announced a plan for "a return to democracy" in late 1984. A 31-member National Assembly consisting of 14 military officers, 11 trade unionists and six from the private sector were to draft a new constitution. The move did not satisfy the Dutch. Bouterse launched a mass political movement, *Stanvaaste*, in a move apparently intended to dominate any future democratically elected administration.

A U.N. report released in early 1985 accused the military of involvement in political murders and "suicides."

In mid-1986, Ronnie Brunswijk (*Brunsveek*) a Maroon (a descendant of escaped slaves) and former army sergeant, capitalized on the discontent of his people, about 50,000 strong, over the idea of being resettled in towns. They were used to living deep in the interior jungle, speaking their own language. The government had controlled little outside the capital. A group called the Jungle Commando began an armed resistance. The United Nations condemned fighting tactics of both sides, but the response was "when you fight, there will be victims."

Beset with this internal revolt in the interior and pressures from Washington,

Lt. Col. Desi Bouterse

Bouterse called for elections to an Assembly to be held in November 1987. Balloting was enthusiastic and the National Front for Democracy and Development, a coalition of three ethnic groups, won 41 of the 51 seats in the Assembly. It elected Ramsewak Shankar president for a five-year term in early 1988. Actual power, however, remained with Bouterse and the 7,000-man military until moves got underway to pass control to the civilian government. It was unable, however, to militarily best Brunswijk and his followers.

Dutch pressures, particularly in the form of denial of assistance under the 1975 treaty, continued to exert pressure on Suriname to settle its internal rivalries. Finally a vague, but written, agreement for a truce between the factions was reached in 1988. Bouterse alleged that the negotiations failed to end the rebellion. Many Maroons had fled to French Guiana to escape the conflict. The Dutch restored aid payments in generous amounts, but not enough to suit some Surinamese, particularly the military.

The Maroons began returning after assurances that the army would not occupy their traditional territories in the interior. Brunswijk, feeling safe, entered Paramaribo in March 1990 under a flag of truce. Feeling that at last his opportunity had arrived, Bouterse had the army arrest him. This was when the extent of Brunswijk's power (or lack thereof) was felt first-hand.

The following evening, all electrical power in Paramaribo was out; this included vitally needed sources to process aluminum. The Jungle Commando force announced that power would stay out until its leader was freed. President Ramsewak Shankar *ordered* Bouterse to release Brunswijk. After a few hours, Bourtese did so, steaming with resentment. The lights were promptly turned on.

In 1990, an investigation revealed Suriname was an important link in the Colombia-to-Europe cocaine traffic; both Bouterse and Brunswijk were accused of being heavily involved. When the drugs started reaching the Netherlands, the Dutch brought pressure, but Bouterse simply threw out President Shankar in a bloodless coup on Christmas Eve 1990 that was labeled the "Telephone Coup" because the president was told over the telephone to resign. The Dutch *again* suspended their annual aid.

Elections in 1991 resulted in the coalition selection of Runaldo Venetiaan, former education minister, as president, after five months of wheeling and dealing. Continued Dutch pressure brought about Bourtese's resignation as commander-in-chief in late 1992. As the government gained control over the military, it was also possible in 1992 to negotiate with the Surinamese Liberation Army Maroon and *Tucayana Amazonica* (native Indian) rebel movements, leading to a cease-fire in 1992.

Even though the coalition headed by President Venetiaan was successful in elections held in May 1996, Bouterse's National Democratic Party was the single most popular party.

Not unexpectedly, in elections held in September 1996, Jules Wijdenbosch of the National Democratic Party was elected as Suriname's new president. Venetiaan's New Front had won 24 of the 51 seats in the National Assembly in May general elections, falling short of the two-thirds majority needed to form a government. Thus, the choice for president fell to the United People's Conference (comprising members of the National Assembly and regional and district councils). By a vote of 438–407, Wijdenbosch won the office.

Wijdenbosch's *NDP* and its coalition partner, the Movement of Freedom and

Former President Jules Wijdenbosch

Democracy (*BVD*), initially held a majority of 29 seats in the National Assembly, but the coalition began showing signs of strain in August 1997 when the president fired Finance Minister Motilal Mungra of the *BVD* for criticizing government policy. The schism became more pronounced when Bouterse was charged in absentia in the Netherlands with drug smuggling and the Wijdenbosch government adopted an aggressive response toward the mother country, which still provided Suriname with $65 million a year in aid. In January 1998 four of the five members of the *BVD* abandoned the coalition to protest what they deemed the government's inclination toward dictatorship and for failing to consult with the *BVD* members on policy matters. The only *BVD* member who remained loyal to the coalition was the Assembly speaker, Indradevi Djwalapersad.

Bouterse, meanwhile, now a lumber executive, denied the Dutch charges that he had smuggled 1.3 tons of cocaine into Europe and had ties to Colombian cartels. He announced in December 1997 that he was considering running for president in 2001 and that he wanted to wean Suriname away from Dutch aid.

Bouterse was placed on the Interpol wanted list, and he was arrested in Trinidad in July 1998. But that country rejected a Dutch extradition request, and Bouterse returned to Suriname, where he continued to serve in Wijdenbosch's government with the euphemistic title of "presidential aide." In February 1999, a court in The Hague issued a summons for Bouterse to appear for trial in March, but he ignored the order; not even his attorney appeared to offer a defense. Apparently to appease the Dutch, whose aid was still welcome, Wijdenbosch fired Bourtese in April. The Dutch court then began trying Bourtese *in absentia*, and in July he was convicted, sentenced to 16 years in prison and fined the equivalent of $2.17 million.

To compound Bourtese's legal problems, in November 1999 the families of 15 of the dissidents slain after the December 1982 coup attempt filed a complaint with an Amsterdam court because Dutch prosecutors had not investigated the deaths. In November 2000, a Dutch appeals court ruled that prosecutors do have jurisdiction to investigate on the grounds that the 1982 killings constitute crimes against humanity. Bourtese faced an international arrest warrant, much as did Chile's former strongman Augusto Pinochet, but in September 2001 the Netherlands High Court dismissed the suit on the grounds that Dutch courts have no jurisdiction over Suriname and because Bourtese is neither a Dutch citizen nor a resident of the Netherlands. The court also ruled that Bourtese could not be tried under a U.N. conven-

Suriname

Boats tied up on the banks of the river at Paramaribo

Paramaribo's *De West*, March 28, 1990: "Military authority critizes Government's position." Insert shows Ronnie Brunswijk.

tion against torture that went into effect seven years after the 1981 incident. However, in December 2004 a Surinamese prosecutor announced that he would try Bourtese and 25 others for murder in the 15 deaths, but when this book went to press they had not yet gone on trial.

In late May 1999, violent street protests erupted against Wijdenbosch's handling of the economy, especially drastic price increases and a precipitous drop in the exchange rate of the guilder. On June 1, the opposition mustered 27 votes in the 51-seat National Assembly for a no-confidence motion against the president. Wijdenbosch refused to resign, and the constitution is ambiguous as to whether he can be removed. The consensus was that the National Assembly could call new elections by a two-thirds vote, or 34 members; Wijdenbosch's NDP has been reduced by defections to 16 seats, not quite enough to block the effort. In an attempt to defuse the move to unseat him, Wijdenbosch announced he would call for new elections no later than May 25, 2000, a year ahead of schedule.

Efforts by the opposition to replace Wijdenbosch with an interim president failed, so Wijdenbosch limped along as a lame-duck president for a full year. The May 25, 2000, election, in which 23 parties competed and 72% of the 265,000 registered voters participated, was a stinging rebuke both to him and to Bourtese. The New Front of former President Venetiaan won 33 of the 51 Assembly seats, one short of the two thirds needed to name a new president outright. Bourtese's Millennium Combination was second with 10 seats, while Wijdenbosch's Democratic National Platform 2000 won only three.

Venetiaan was inaugurated for a five-year term on August 12, 2000. He immediately inherited an international crisis from Wijdenbosch. Just days after the election, the outgoing government ordered a Canadian offshore oil rig towed from the disputed zone with Guyana at the mouth of the Corantijn River. Both countries moved troops to the area, as diplomats negotiated a peaceful solution.

Recent Developments

Internally, the issue of land rights for the black Maroons and indigenous Indian tribes (see Culture) resurfaced in May 2004. A legal representative of the Association of Village Leaders of Suriname appeared at a two-week meeting of the Permanent U.N. Forum on Indigenous Issues in New York to complain that mining operations had encroached upon the traditional lands of the Maroons and Indians. She said the government had done little to implement the guarantees contained in the 1992 peace agreement that ended the rebellion.

Despite the murder charges pending against him for the December 1982 massacre of his political opponents and his Dutch conviction for cocaine smuggling, Bourtese announced that he was standing for president again in the general elections of May 25, 2005, as the standard bearer of the NDP. Venetiaan has coyly avoided saying whether he would seek reelection. In the voting, Venetiaan's New Front again emerged with the most seats, 24, which was nine fewer than before and two short of a simple majority, much less the two-thirds majority needed to elect the president. Bourtese's NDP jumped from seven to 15 seats, while Wijdenbosch's latest vehicle, the People's Alliance for Development won only six. A new political organization representing the ethnic Maroons, the A-Combination, led by Bourtese's old nemesis Ronnie Brunswijk, won five seats and quickly agreed to join the New Front in a coalition. That still left the New Front five seats short of what it needed to elect a president, whether Venetiaan or someone else. Venetiaan had little choice but to swallow his pride and ask Bourtese to join his coalition; Bourtese refused.

The NDP and the People's Alliance for Development, meanwhile, have contested the vote count. When this book went to press, the wrangling was continuing, and if no candidate emerges with the needed 34 votes, the choice will fall to the 895-member United People's Conference as it did in 1996. Bourtese has stated publicly he expects Venetiaan to be unable to govern and thus to be forced to call new elections.

Culture: The majority of the people are found along the coastal, agricultural zone. Of this group, about a third live in the capital and chief port of Paramaribo, a picturesque city with palm-lined streets and colorful market areas.

The creole population is well represented in the civil service and mining industries; the East Indians tend to concentrate in commerce and farming activities. There are also about 12,000 native Indians in the Arawak, Carib, Trio and Wayana tribes. There are about 50,000 Surinamese descended from African slaves, called Maroons, who prefer to live in the interior.

Dutch is the official language, and there is a literacy rate of about 80%. Although most students of higher education go to the Netherlands, there are law and medical faculties in Paramaribo. Suriname boasts a cultural center, museums, active theatrical groups, a well known philharmonic orchestra and a modern sports stadium.

Economy: Alumina, aluminum and bauxite, the ore of aluminum, have accounted for as much as 70% of the country's exports and some 90% of its tax revenues. Production declined from 6.9 million tons in 1973 to 3.2 million tons in 1984 and only modest increases have occurred since then. The leading bauxite firm is U.S.-owned Suralco, a subsidiary of Alcoa. Although some bauxite is processed locally, aluminum is now shipped in a finished or semi-finished state to the United States. Panaram, the center of the vital industry, receives its hydroelectric power from Lake van Blommestein.

Offshore petroleum deposits have tremendous economic potential. In 2004, the state-owned oil firm, Staatsolie, was pumping 12,000 barrels a day from the Tambaredjo Field, and its refinery capacity is 7,000 bpd, but it was investing $350 million to expand production to 15,000 bpd and to expand refinery capacity. Current production meets domestic demands, but in April and May 2004 it signed contracts with Spanish and Danish firms to explore for oil in a 7,200-square-mile tract bordering the Tambaredjo Field, which could allow Suriname to become a net exporter.

There are few roads; rivers and aircraft provide most of the transportation. The majority of the people are employed in agriculture. The major cash crops are timber, citrus fruits, sugarcane, bananas and corn. Rice is the chief crop and food staple, accounting for half of all land under cultivation and is the source of valuable export income. Major problems facing the economy are high inflation and unemployment. The government is increasing its economic ties with Colombia, Venezuela and Brazil; with the aid of Venezuela it is hoped that new bauxite mines can be developed in the southern part of the country. In 2002, the government granted permits to a Canadian company to mine gold. The mine was expected to produce 6.7 tons of gold per year for eight years.

President Ronald Venetiaan devalued the guilder in 1993, which brought needed monetary stability, and by the end of his term in 1996 he had brought rampant inflation down to single digits.

Inflation and unemployment in 1998 were both 20%, which helps explain the voters' overwhelming decision to return Venetiaan to power in 2000. In 2001, the economy grew by a sluggish 1.9%. In 2004 growth was up to about 5%, but much of that was attributed to the high world market price for gold, bauxite and alumina.

The Future: Suriname, underpopulated and underdeveloped, is a land with great economic potential from natural resources and, recently, from ecotourism. But it must get a handle on its turbulent political situation. The confusing results of the May 25, 2005 election were not a step in the right direction. When this book went to press, the country's leadership was still in doubt.

Fishing off the coast of Suriname

The Republic of Trinidad and Tobago

Performs for spectators

Area: 1,864 square miles.
Population: 1.3 million.
Capital City: Port of Spain (Pop. 330,000, estimated).
Climate: Tropically hot and humid. The heaviest rainfall occurs from May to December.
Neighboring Countries: Trinidad forms the eastern edge of a shelf surrounding the Gulf of Paria on Venezuela's northeast coast, separated from the mainland by narrow channels. Tobago lies 18 miles north of Trinidad.
Official Language: English.
Other Principal Tongues: Hindi, French and Spanish.
Ethnic Background: African Negroid (43%), Asiatic (40%), European and other (17%).
Principal Religion: Protestant Christianity.
Chief Commercial Products: Petroleum, petroleum products, chemicals, tourism.
Currency: Trinidad Dollar.
Gross Domestic Product: U.S. $9.4 billion in 2002 ($6,490 per capita).

Former Colonial Status: Spanish Colony (1498–1797); British Colony (1797–1962).
Independence Date: August 31, 1962.
Chief of State: George Maxwell Richards, president (since March 17, 2003).
Head of Government: Patrick Manning, prime minister (since December 24, 2001).
National Flag: A diagonal black stripe bordered with white on a red field.

Trinidad and Tobago both have mountainous spines representing rounded extensions of the Venezuelan coastal ranges. Trinidad's mountains lie along the north coast. Plains extend to the south, rimmed with low, rolling hills. Petroleum and the famed asphalt lake are found in the south of the island. Tobago's mountains on the north are skirted with coral-dotted shelves. Trinidad's soils are rich and well suited to sugar and other crops. Sea breezes moderate the tropical climate and the annual rainfall of 65 inches is evenly distributed. Trinidad's asphalt has been of commercial significance since the colonial

period. The more recent discovery of oil and gas has fostered industrial development. Trinidad and Tobago's population is primarily African and Asian, with smaller groups of cosmopolitan people of Spanish, French and English ancestry.

History: Trinidad was discovered by Columbus in 1498 and colonized by the Spanish in the early 1500s. During the French Revolution, a large number of French families were settled on the land that in 1797 was captured from Spain by British forces. Ceded to Britain in 1802, Trinidad was joined by Tobago as a colonial unit in 1889.

The history of the dual-island nation has been rather uneventful. Administered as a British Crown Colony until 1962, its early value was in asphalt and sugar. Slaves had been introduced by the Spanish to work sugar and indigo plantations, and the British continued to add slaves until 1834. With the abolition of slavery, indentured East Indians and Chinese la-

Trinidad and Tobago

borers were imported to perform the manual labor. The decline of sugar markets hurt the island's economy, but the existence of asphalt and (later) petroleum cushioned the shock and led to a transformation of the economy.

The leasing of bases to the United States during World War II provided another source of income to bolster the economy. The transformation of Trinidad and Tobago from colonial dependency was relatively untroubled. Initially incorporated into the West Indian Federation, its reluctance to tie its healthy economy to the less well-endowed island dependencies was a major factor in the demise of the Federation.

The United States was drawn into the final phases of the negotiations for independence when Prime Minister Eric Williams sought to capitalize on the U.S. base at Chaguaramas as the site for a new capital city. The United States released part of the site in 1960, with the remainder reverting to Trinidad in 1977. Independence was attained in 1962.

When opposition parties boycotted the May 1971 elections to protest voting procedures, William's People's National Movement won all 36 seats in Parliament. Although generally a capable leader, Williams' popularity fell because of his heavy-handed methods. A major crisis developed in 1970 when labor unrest and rioting led to a mutiny by sections of the small army. Williams used government forces in 1975 to quell violent strikes by petroleum and sugar workers.

The dispute soon erupted into a more general strike, joined by transport and electrical workers. The prime minister sought to disorganize the strikers by jailing key

Former President Arthur Robinson

opposition leaders. Despite growing hostility by labor members and some sectors of the business community, Williams' political control seemed to remain firm, bolstered by the "mini-boom" caused by the enormous increases in oil prices.

The nation became a republic on August 1, 1976. Although the new constitution severed all ties to Great Britain, the country retains its membership in the British Commonwealth. Named as first president was Governor General Sir Ellis Clarke. In

the general elections held in September, Prime Minister Eric Williams won a fifth five-year term while his People's National Movement (PNM) took 24 out of the 36 seats in the House of Representatives. The Democratic Action Congress, traditionally the main opposition party, won only two seats. In contrast, a new Marxist-Leninist labor-oriented United Labor Front (UPF) won 10 seats. Representing sugar, oil and transport unions, the ULF had criticized Williams for failure to provide more jobs and housing and to control inflation. The group also opposed sections of the new constitution that vastly increase the power of the prime minister to restrict personal and political rights during emergencies. Despite the steady flow of oil revenues, stubbornly high unemployment fueled social unrest and persistent criticism of Williams. He died in 1981 at the age of 69. George Chambers, the minister of agriculture, was immediately named interim prime minister. Later, at the party convention, Chambers was designated Williams' successor.

In November 1981 elections, six political parties vied for the 36 parliamentary seats. Due to the splintered opposition, the PNM scored a major victory, winning 26

Prime Minister Patrick Manning

321

Trinidad and Tobago

Carnival in Port of Spain

seats in the House by the largest margin of votes in the nation's history (219,000).

Relations with Jamaica and Barbados, which had deteriorated in 1982 because of a trade war within the Caribbean Community, became further strained in late 1983 when Trinidad and Tobago opposed the multinational invasion of Grenada. A multi-nation Caribbean organization to promote free trade was created in 1979 in which Trinidad and Tobago joined. At its meeting in mid-1986, Prime Minister Chambers joined with the other member chiefs of state in criticizing the United States' Caribbean Basin Initiative because of its import restrictions on Caribbean products, principally textiles, footwear and oil products.

The collapse of international petroleum prices presented severe economic problems during 1984–87. The sugar industry also became non-existent except for production to meet local needs. The government started importing crude oil for refining because of decreased local production. Sagging world prices from 1986–88 further cut income despite increased production after 1984. Despite this, in the 1980s Trinidad and Tobago had one of the higher per capita annual incomes in the area.

The National Alliance for Reconstruction (NAR) led by Arthur Robinson won 33 of 36 seats in 1986 elections, ending the PNM's grip on power. Austerity and high unemployment led to an attempted coup in mid-1990 by a black Muslim group

called Jamaat al-Muslimeen. The prime minister was shot and beaten before the loyal army ended the affair, in which 24 people died. The courts gave amnesty to the rebels, much to the government's displeasure.

In late 1991, the PNM returned to power with 21 seats in the Parliament. Patrick Manning, the new prime minister, stressed economic improvement and lowered black-Indian tensions.

The pendulum swung again in 1995, this time in favor of the Indian community, when the United National Congress (UNC) won a two-seat majority and elected Basdeo Panday as prime minister. He pledged to be "the leader of all the people," but blacks still feared Indian domination. Panday also was faced with a burgeoning crime rate, a divided judiciary and police corruption related to drug trafficking. Trinidad made international headlines, and brought condemnation from human rights groups, in 1999 when it hanged nine convicted murderers, justified as a deterrent to rising crime. The public seemed to approve of the hard-line policy.

Trinidadian courts have continued to hand down death sentences, although the crime wave has continued, as have international protests. In July 2002, the Inter-American Court of Human Rights, an arm of the Organization of American States to which Trinidad and Tobago belongs, ordered the country not to carry out the exe-

cutions of 31 men and one women on the grounds that their rights had been violated.

Panday's UNC was narrowly returned to power in general elections on December 11, 2000, winning 19 of the 36 seats in Parliament to 16 for the PNM, still led by Manning. The NAR won the remaining seat.

In his second term, Panday succeeded in creating a business-friendly environment that attracted new foreign investment. But critics, including three of his own cabinet ministers, complained that Panday was becoming *too* friendly with business. Rumors circulated of kickbacks from an airport construction project. In September 2001, Attorney General Ramesh Maharaj and two other cabinet ministers publicly alleged corruption within the government. Panday fired Maharaj on October 1, precipitating a crisis that Panday unwisely sought to resolve by dissolving Parliament on October 9 and calling a new election for December 11, only a year after being returned to power. The election results led to a constitutional crisis when the UNC and the PNM each won 18 seats; the PAR was shut out.

A few days later, Panday and Manning struck a deal by which they would let President Robinson of the PAR, usually only a figurehead, decide who would be prime minister, who would then head a unity government. On December 24, 2001, Robinson, who like Manning is black, chose Manning to head the government, giving only a vague explanation for his reasons. A miffed Panday then reneged on his promise to cooperate in a unity government.

The Parliament did not meet until the first week of April 2002, barely beating a six-month deadline that would have forced a new election. For two days, the Parliament deadlocked on the election of a speaker, and the tension between the two parties—and hence the two ethnic groups—threatened to turn ugly.

On August 28, 2002 Panday dissolved Parliament and called elections for October 7, the third time in three years Trinidadians had gone to the polls. The campaign was predictably bitter, with the PNM pointing to the criminal charges that Panday allegedly had a secret London bank account in which he had stashed hundreds of thousands of dollars and the UNC running advertisements linking Manning to the black Muslim terrorist group that had attempted the 1990 coup. For good measure, a woman alleged that Manning had fathered her 2-year-old daughter. In the balloting, the voters broke the deadlock by giving the PNM 51% of the popular vote and a majority of 20 of the 36 seats, although the PNM won two constituencies

President George Maxwell Richards

by margins of only 244 and 247 votes. Voter turnout was 69.8% of 875,000 registered voters.

Within days, Panday announced he would step down as leader of the opposi-tion, saying he would soon be 70. However, in 2005 he was still leader of the UNC and has continued bedeviling Manning.

On May 31, 2005, Panday, his wife, his former works minister and a businessmen were arrested and charged with offering or accepting a $45,600 bribe for the airport construction contract. Thousands of UNC supporters demonstrated in support of Panday, who at first refused to post bail. After eight days, however, he paid the equivalent of $104,000 in bail and was released from jail pending trial.

On February 14, 2003, Parliament elected George Maxwell Richards, 71, a former dean of the University of the West Indies who is of African descent, to succeed Robinson as president. Sworn in on March 17, Richards, who is not a member of either party, pledged that he would govern without regard to race.

Culture: The people of Trinidad and Tobago, about 45% of black ancestry and 35% East Indian (Gujerat) have remained distinct ethnic groups, but have managed social and political integration during the period of British rule. Thus, people with many customs and origins live without restrictions of cultural variety. The Europeans find expression in sports clubs and in their business occupations. The African element has acquired renown for its *Calypso* music. The people learned that through hours of heating, tempering and pounding that the steel oil drums from World War II could be tuned into unique musical instruments that are world-familiar today. Although most speak English, it is with a unique lilt. Religious expression is unhampered, with popular participation in the *Carnival* of the Christians as well as the Islamic festival of Hosein.

Trinidadians felt a sense of pride in 2001 when Vidiadhar Surajprasad (V.S.) Naipaul, a Trinidad-born novelist, was named recipient of the Nobel Prize for Literature, only the second West Indian to be so honored. Their pride was muted somewhat by the fact that Naipaul had spent 50 of his 69 years in Britain and has ridiculed his homeland as "primitive." Scion of a literary family, Naipaul attended Oxford and opted to stay in Britain, vowing to "beat them (the British) at their own language." Yet, he used Trinidad as the setting for some of his novels, which include *A House for Mr. Biswas, The Suffrage of Elvira, The Mimic Men, Guerrillas,* and *In a Free State;* his first published novel, *The Mystic Masseur,* was made into a movie in 2001 and the filming was in Trinidad. The Nobel committee praised the iconoclastic Naipaul for his "incorruptible scrutiny" of the post-colonial West Indes, but he also had attracted notoriety for his attacks on Islam and for ridiculing such literary greats as C.S. Forrester and James Joyce.

Rural scene

Trinidad and Tobago

Economy: Although the nation contains rich soils and agriculture is important, the economy is based on oil and natural gas production. The only Caribbean country with oil deposits, Trinidad and Tobago was at one time the hemisphere's third-largest oil exporting nation. This has been declining since 1982, but in 2002 still accounted for 26.3% of GDP. Oil production rose for the first time in four years in 1984, allowing the government to purchase the assets of the Texaco-Trinidad, Inc. petroleum operation before the world price of oil plummeted in the mid-1980s.

The picture had brightened by 1996, when unemployment dropped from 21.5% to 16.5%, and inflation fell from 13% to 3.5%. The government has offered tax advantages to oil firms to encourage exploration. Liquefied natural gas (LNG) is increasingly being exploited and exported; the United States obtains 75% of its imported LNG from Trinidad and Tobago.

In July 2002, Prime Minister Patrick Manning announced plans for a gas pipeline under the Caribbean with branches to Cuba, Puerto Rico, Barbados, Guadaloupe, Martinique, Antigua and St. Kitts. The project was expected to take three years and cost $500 million.

During the days of the oil boom of the 1970s, per capita income was among the highest in the hemisphere, more than $7,000, but that plummeted to $3,800 at the depth of the recession of the late 1980s and early 1990s. By 2002 it had climbed back up to $6,490, although as is the case in many oil-rich countries, it is not equitably distributed.

A serious problem has the external debt, which in 1999 stood at $1.42 billion, nearly 25% of GDP. The government seems to have gotten it under control, as the debt service ratio has declined from 15.4% in 1997 to just 4.4% in 2002.

Real GDP declined for eight consecutive years, from 1988–95. Growth was respectable, between 3% and 4%, from 1996–98, and was a robust 7.1% in 1999 and 6.9% in 2000. In 2001, it was 3.3% and in 2002, 2.7%. Unemployment, however, has remained disturbingly high, although it declined steadily from 13.1% in 1999 to 10.4% in 2002. Inflation in 2000 was a manageable 3.5%, down from 5.6% in 1998.

Tourism, now principally on Tobago, would provide more profits than drug trafficking and would help diversify the oil-and-gas-dependent economy, but as in Jamaica, tourists are shunning this would-be tropical paradise because of an alarmingly high crime rate.

The Future: Unlike Guyana, where tension between the African and Indian communities has routinely erupted into political violence, Trinidadians have eschewed, thus far, the temptation to resort to violence. One can only hope that their traditional adherence to civilized norms of political behavior will continue, but the arrest of Panday in May 2005 on corruption charges, even if they prove to be true, will only heighten racial tension.

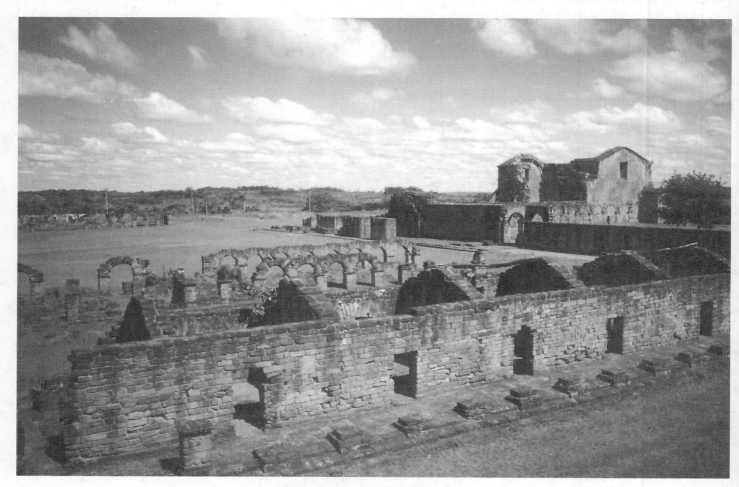

Jesuit Ruin of Trinidad

The Oriental (Eastern) Republic of Uruguay

Gauchos enjoy folk music in the countryside

Area: 72,150 square miles.

Population: 3.4 million.

Capital City: Montevideo (Pop. 1.7 million, estimated. Pronounced Mon-tay-vee-*day-oh*).

Climate: Temperate throughout the year. There is a warm season from November to April and a milder season from May through October. Rainfall is moderate and evenly distributed.

Neighboring Countries: Brazil (North); Argentina (West).

Official Language: Spanish.

Other Principal Tongues: Portuguese and English.

Ethnic Background: European (90%), *mestizo* (a mixture of European and Indian ancestry, 10%).

Principal Religion: Roman Catholic Christianity.

Chief Commercial Products: Hides, leather products, beef and other meat, wool, fish, rice.

Currency: New Peso.

Gross Domestic Product: U.S. $13.3 billion in 2004 (est.) ($3,900 per capita).

Former Colonial Status: Spanish Colony (1624–1680); contested between Spain and Portugal (1680–1806); captured by Great Britain (1806–1807); War for Independence (1807–1820); Portuguese Brazilian Colony (1820–1825); contested between Brazil and Argentina (1825–1828).

Independence Date: Independence was proclaimed on August 25, 1825, but Uruguay did not actually become independent until August 27, 1828, when a treaty was signed with Brazil and Ar-

gentina as a result of British intervention in the dispute between Uruguay's two neighboring countries.

Chief of State: Dr. Tabaré Ramón Vásquez Rosas (b. January 17, 1940), president (since March 1, 2005).

National Flag: Four blue and five white horizontal stripes; a rising sun of 16 alternating straight and wavy rays on a white square is in the upper left hand part of the flag.

Uruguay, the second smallest of the South American countries, is a land of rolling hills covered with lush grasses and a few scattered forests. The highest elevation is about 2,000 feet; the country is crossed by numerous small streams and is bounded by the Atlantic and several large rivers. The estuary of the Río de la Plata and the Uruguay River, separating Uruguay from Argentina, are navigable and provide an important means of transportation. The River Negro, which arises in Brazil and crosses Uruguay from northeast to southwest is also navigable for some distance.

The rich, black soils produce a high quality of grasses, which have encouraged cattle and sheep raising. Equally suited to agriculture, less than 10% of the land is used for farming. The climate is mild, though damp. Winter (June–August) temperatures average 57° to 60° F., with occasional frosts; summer (December–February) temperatures average 75° to 79° F. Rainfall is evenly distributed during the year, averaging 40 inches annually.

Nature and history have caused Uruguay to become a pastoral country.

History: The Spanish explorers of the Río de la Plata in the 16th century passed up the hills of Uruguay as unlikely to have treasure in gold and precious stones. The warlike Charrúa Indians also discouraged invasion. Military expeditions against the Indians were uniformly unsuccessful, but Jesuit and Franciscan missionaries were able to establish missions in 1624. Cattle are supposed to have been introduced by Hernando Arias in 1580 during one of the unsuccessful military expeditions. A counter-invasion by the Portuguese from Brazil came in 1680, following slave raids on the missions and cattle roundups of the wild herds that roamed the grasslands.

The Portuguese founded Colonia as a rival to Spanish Buenos Aires. The remainder of Uruguay's colonial history is one of war between the Spanish and Portuguese contenders for control of the La Plata River. Montevideo was planned by the Portuguese, built by the Spanish and taken by the British in 1806, but abandoned in 1807 when an attack on Buenos Aires failed. A Brazilian attack in 1811 was resisted by the Uruguayan cattleman and patriot José Artigas, who declared Uruguay's independence.

The struggle continued until 1820 when Montevideo fell to the Brazilians, and Artigas fled to Paraguay where he died in a comfortable self-imposed exile. A group of 33 exiles returned from Buenos Aires to take up the cause in 1825, and with Argentine assistance, they defeated the Brazilians

Uruguay

at Ituzaingo in 1827 (the city of Treinte y Tres is named in honor of that band of exiles). At this point, Great Britain intervened. Both Brazil and Argentina renounced their claims and Uruguay became independent in fact on August 27, 1828.

The settlement of Uruguay proceeded slowly from the first missionary stations. The *gauchos* (cowboys) who hunted the cattle in the 17th and 18th centuries were nomads and not interested in the land. Slaughtering the cattle for hides, they sold their wares to merchants from Argentina. By the time of independence, the nomads had disappeared and large ranches had taken up the land. Farming was practiced only around Montevideo, where a market for produce was assured. Following independence, Italian and Spanish immigrants settled in the farming belt where their descendants still live today.

The early history of the republic was a chaotic period of civil war as the factions fought for power. Two parties emerged—the *Blanco* (White), representing conservative ranchers, and the *Colorado* (Red), favoring liberal reforms. The parties and politics established in the 1830s have been hardened in more than 150 years of combat and still persist today. A 10-year civil war was fought between the factions with support from other powers that intervened, including French, English and Italian. The foreign intervention terminated with the unseating of Argentine dictator Rosas in 1852; however, the Uruguayans continued the civil war for another 10 years.

Further strife in 1863 led to Brazilian support for a *Colorado* despot who unseated his *Blanco* opponent in 1865. The Paraguayan dictator Francisco Solano-Lopez came to the aid of the *Blancos*, precipitating the Triple Alliance (Argentina, Brazil and Uruguay) war against Paraguay. The defeat of Paraguay left the *Colorados* in power, which they retained for nearly a century except for the military period.

The year 1870 marks a turning point in Uruguayan history. The rancher with his *gaucho* army was out of place. The demand for better quality meat, hides and wool required more modern methods and business-like management of the huge estates. Railroads were built, European immigrants settled in the cities and a middle class mercantile society developed. Clashes continued between the two parties through the remainder of the 19th century, but a growing group of responsible citizens emerged. Three *Colorado* dictators ruled from 1875 to 1890 with some degree of moderation. Two more ruled from 1890 to 1896 with such disregard for the law that civil war again broke out, resulting in the division of the country into *Colorado* and *Blanco* provinces. This uneasy arrangement lasted until 1903 and

the election of Uruguay's foremost statesman and leader, José Batlle y Ordóñez.

The Batlle Era

Uruguay's 20th century history has been dominated by Batlle—who assumed the leadership of a bankrupt, battle-torn and divided nation—even after his death. His first term, 1903–07, was spent in crushing civil war, uniting the country and securing popular support for sane, democratic govern-

ment. From 1911–15 he campaigned for his plan, which included replacing the powerful presidency with a council, an idea based loosely on the Swiss model but unheard of in Latin America. He encountered considerable opposition, but by 1917 a new constitution was adopted, and full franchise and progressive social legislation was enacted. Using the editorial pages of *El Día*, Montevideo's leading newspaper, Batlle pleaded his case and educated the people. By the time of his death in 1929, Uruguay was the most literate, democratic, well-fed state in Latin America. Batlle's unique plural executive system was in use until 1933.

Batlle's reforms did not, however, create the economic base needed to support the welfare state he had created. The next two presidents tried to carry out his programs, but they were restricted by the nine-member national council that wielded considerable power. Social and economic reforms were completely stopped when Uruguay went into an economic depression with the rest of the world in 1931.

Confusion, near-anarchy and no progress marked the years 1931 to 1951, replete with military dictators and corruption. Batlle's plural executive form of government was readopted as a result of a plebiscite in 1951 and its nine members functioned as the executive arm of government until March 1967. The long-dominant *Colorados* again were returned to power, but high inflation and other economic woes led to disenchantment. In the 1958 elections, the *Blancos* won for the first time since 1865. They were reelected in 1962. However, they proved no more capable of dealing with the economic crisis than had the *Colorados*, in no small part because neither party had the courage to deal with the bloated bureaucracy and overly generous retirement system that the welfare state had wrought.

Bankrupt and in desperate need of dynamic leadership, Uruguayans voted overwhelmingly to return to a presidential executive in elections and a plebiscite in 1966. The *Colorados*, in the minority for eight years, elected a former air force general, Oscar D. Gestido, to the presidency, bypassing Jorge Batlle, grand-nephew of the reformer. When Gestido died in 1967, he was succeeded by the vice president, Jorge Pacheco Areco, a civilian. Encumbered by an inefficient bureaucracy and runaway inflation, and lacking forceful leadership abilities, Pacheco proved no more capable than his predecessor in solving Uruguay's monumental problems of economic stagnation, corruption and rising urban terrorism by the *Tupamaros*—Latin America's most infamous urban guerrilla force in the 1960s.

Promising law and order and economic reform, the *Colorados* received another mandate in the 1971 elections with the presidential candidacy of Juan María Bordaberry. Most of the president's program was soon blocked in the Congress, however, where his party lacked a majority.

The *Tupamaros* achieved international notoriety by kidnapping and murdering an agricultural official with the U.S. Embassy, Dan Mitrione, whom the *Tupamaros* alleged was a CIA agent who was training the Uruguayan security forces in torture techniques. As the *Tupamaros* increased their terrorism, and under U.S. pressure because of the Mitrione incident, Bordaberry turned to a new power source: the armed forces. With stunning efficiency, the military systematically routed some 2,000 guerrillas by early 1973. Then, instead of returning to the barracks, the military demanded major reforms in the nation's welfare programs, which it believed had been the basis for rampant political corruption and economic decay.

Military Rule, 1973–85

On February 8, 1973, the armed forces staged a coup d'etat. The generals agreed to allow Bordaberry to remain in office, provided he agree to governmental reform and a crackdown on the *Tupamaros*. Five days later, Bordaberry agreed. Backed

by the armed forces, Bordaberry dissolved Congress, banned eight political parties, closed the nation's only university, broke up labor unions, instituted strict press censorship and jailed 6,000 political opponents. Under the new order, all power was vested in the military-controlled Council of the Nation, which ruled by decree. The Mitrione incident and the subsequent coup inspired the Costa-Gavras film, "State of Siege."

Bordaberry decided he wanted to become president-for-life with the military backing him in 1977, but the military, favoring a gradual return to democracy, ousted him in a bloodless coup in mid-1976. An interim president was named, who was chief of a 27-member Council of State formed to replace the dissolved Congress.

Under the military's master plan, the new president was to have served for three years, at which time a president selected in controlled elections was to have remained in office for another five years. Full democracy would then be restored at the end of this eight-year period. Further, the military was prepared to purge top leaders from the *Colorado* and *Blanco* parties before these groups would be permitted to participate in free elections set for 1984. All other parties would be banned.

The master plan went awry, however, when the new president unexpectedly refused to issue a decree abolishing the nation's top political leadership. The military ousted *him* and, after consultation with top conservatives, the generals recruited a new civilian president, Dr. Aparicio Méndez, 72. Installed in September 1976, Méndez dutifully canceled the political rights of 1,000 leaders from all existing parties for a 15-year period.

In foreign affairs, Uruguay's military government received increased criticism for its violation of human rights. In 1980, the military *junta*, ruling through a civilian "front" administration, felt secure enough to submit a new constitution for popular approval. Although it provided for free congressional elections, it also established a National Security Council, empowered with final approval of almost all governmental activity and limited the presidential election to a *single* candidate approved by the military. On November 30, 1980, the voters rejected the constitution by a margin of 58% to 42%—to the utter amazement of the *junta*.

Rival factions divided the military: hardliners urged an end to the liberalization policy initiated in 1977; others focused on the power struggle to name the presidential candidate. Meanwhile, leaders of the *Blanco* and *Colorado* parties demanded immediate removal of a ban on political activity and restoration of a free press. Despite these appeals and the pleb-

iscite, the military did not intend to surrender control, and as of January 1981, more than 1,200 political prisoners languished in Uruguayan jails.

After an investigation, without explanation, the *junta* announced the resignation of a group of senior officers in mid-1981. Included were those of the minister of the interior, commander of the Arms and Service School, the Montevideo police chief, the ambassador to Paraguay and several influential colonels. It was reported later that the officers had been involved in a get-rich-quick scheme with an unscrupulous broker, who used their money for loans to gamblers and for financing his own gambling. The broker disappeared, the officers lost hundreds of thousands of dollars and the *junta's* oft-proclaimed reputation for incorruptibility was tarnished. Ended, too, were the political careers of several generals.

General Gregorio Alvarez, former army commander, was appointed president and immediately began preliminary discussions with the political leaders of the two traditional parties for free general elections in 1984, that is, prior to March 1985 when his "term" expired. Negotiations stalled temporarily on the issue of membership of the commission to set rules for political activity and for framing a constitution to be submitted to a national referendum before the 1984 election.

By mid-1984, Uruguay's national attention was riveted on the dialogue between the government and the recognized political parties on the rules for the promised presidential election in November and several articles of a new constitution. The armed forces wanted guarantees that they would enjoy sufficient power under the new, legal regime, but the opposition insisted that the army's place is in the barracks.

On May 21, 1984, spokesmen for the armed forces hinted at the necessity of a "transitional period" between the military regime and return to democracy. Most political parties had either opposed the idea or stressed the brevity of such a "transitional period."

The tensions between the military and civilians reached their highest point when in June 1984 Wilson Ferreira Aldunate, leader of the *Blanco* Party, now generally known as the National Party, was imprisoned upon his return from exile. A wave of protests subsided as the elections approached; no group wanted to jeopardize Uruguay's return to democracy.

Return to Democracy

Held on November 25, 1984, the elections resulted in the victory of Julio María Sanguinetti, the *Colorado* candidate, who received 39% of the vote; the *Colorados*

Uruguay

also won a plurality in both houses of the National Assembly. Democracy was restored officially when the Assembly convened on February 15, 1985, and Sanguinetti was inaugurated on March 1. As in most of Latin America, the new president, considered a centrist, had to face the rising expectations of a population free of military rule, the political inexperience of many of his advisers and a serious economic situation. By mid-1985 strikes had multiplied in Uruguay—including one which for weeks completely paralyzed the port facilities of Montevideo. The government had suspended the activities of the Bank of Italy and Rio de la Plata, and reassured the public that the "restlessness" of the armed forces, provoked by a cut in the military budget and investigations into the actions of the past military regime, would be peacefully solved. An avowed agnostic in a nominally Catholic but traditionally secular country, Sanguinetti once stirred controversy by not kneeling to kiss the ring of Pope John Paul II during a papal visit.

A very delicate matter appeared to have been finally resolved in 1986: what to do with the military which, as in other Latin American countries, had committed numerous human rights violations. To try them would be an invitation to a military takeover. An oral agreement had been reached prior to the return to civilian rule that there would be no trials of either *Tupamaros* or the military. A reluctant but very practical assembly passed a general amnesty measure at Sanguinetti's request. In consideration of this, the military publicly acknowledged that some officers had committed "transgressions of human rights."

This, however, enraged a substantial number of people, including survivors of 50,000 persons who were slain or disappeared, presumably murdered. The matter was settled in April 1989 when in a referendum the amnesty was upheld by a margin of 57% to 43%.

A moderate *Colorado* candidate was expected to win 1989 elections, but Luis Lacalle of the *Blanco* Party captured a plurality of 37%. He had entered into a preelection coalition with the leftist *Frente Amplio* (Broad Front), the candidate of which received 21% of the vote. Thus a loose combination of leftists, including Communists, became a force to be reckoned with in Uruguayan politics, and it remains so today.

Although nominally leftist, President Lacalle followed a program of privatization of government enterprises, arousing substantial opposition from surplus employees of these industries. Privatization of the telephone system was halted by a 1992 referendum, in which 72% opposed the measure. On his watch, Lacalle made Uruguay a charter member of *Mercosur,* the free-trade bloc, with Argentina, Brazil and Paraguay. High inflation plagued Uruguay in 1993–94, which led to voter discontent.

The November 1994 election was virtually a three-way tie and left no party with a mandate. Former President Sanguinetti was returned to the presidency with a bare plurality of 631,025 votes, or 34.3%. The Blanco Party's Alberto Volonte was second with 607,388 votes, or 33%. An alliance of the left-wing Progressive Encounter with the Socialists and Communists, called Frente Amplio (Broad Front), fielded Montevideo Mayor Tabaré Vásquez, an oncologist by profession. He received 603,188 votes, or 32.8%, the left's strongest showing yet. The traditional two-party dominance of Uruguayan politics was effectively ended in the elections.

Largely because the vote had become so fragmented, the Assembly introduced a *segunda vuelta,* or runoff, for future presidential elections. Sanguinetti's second term was marked by continued emphasis on trade, especially within *Mercosur,* The economy experienced modest growth until late in his term, when the economic woes of neighboring Argentina and Brazil proved contagious.

The Elections of 1999

The party primaries of April 25, 1999, provided an interesting dress rehearsal for the elections scheduled for October 31 and November 28. About half of the country's

Former President Jorge Batlle

2.4 million voters participated and a clear plurality, just over 37%, voted in the *Colorado* primary. The winner was Senator Jorge Batlle, grand-nephew of the party's illustrious founder and son of Luis Batlle Berres, who served twice as president, in 1947–51 and 1954–58. A former journalist, Batlle had failed in four earlier presidential bids. The primary of the left-wing Progressive Encounter movement drew slightly more participants than did the *Blanco* primary, 30.5% to 29%. Making his second bid, Tabaré Vásquez received about 80% of the vote in the Progressive Encounter primary, while former President Lacalle was the easy winner in the *Blanco* primary.

Once again, the old Communist and Socialist parties coalesced around the Progressive Encounter to form the Broad Front. In the first round of voting on October 31, Vásquez scored a convincing first-place finish, with 854,170 votes, or 39.8%. Batlle received 694,617 votes, or 32.7%, while Lacalle trailed with 472,238 votes, or 22.2%. The other two candidates collected the remaining 4.8 Moreover, the Broad Front stunned the two traditional parties by emerging as the largest force in the new Congress, winning 40 of 99 seats in the Chamber of Representatives and 12 of the 30 seats in the Senate. Vásquez also carried Montevideo. Voter turnout was 91.8%.

Clearly, the Uruguayan left wing had come a long way since the 1973 coup, but the prospect of a Vásquez presidency alarmed the political establishment. The defeated Lacalle swallowed his pride and endorsed the candidate of the *Blancos*' arch-rivals, the *Colorados*. Batlle pledged to continue Sanguinetti's moderate free-market reforms and derided the "crazy ideas" of his leftist opponent. In the November 28 runoff, the results were:

Batlle	1,138,067	53.9%
Vásquez	972,197	46.1%

Thus, on his fifth try for the presidency, Batlle was inaugurated on March 1, 2000, at the age of 72. With 40% of the seats in both houses, the Broad Front forced the traditionally rival *Colorados* and *Blancos* to form a legislative marriage of convenience. This formal coalition ended in November 2002 when the Blanco cabinet ministers resigned, but the two parties continued to present a united front in the Assembly.

The Batlle government at first resisted the hemispheric trend toward wholesale privatization, then reluctantly began making moves to reform the large public sector in order to appease the International Monetary Fund (see Economy).

President Batlle found himself in the maelstrom of two international contro-

Uruguay

versies in 2002. In April, Uruguay co-sponsored a resolution before the U.N. Human Rights Commission that called upon Cuba to democratize and to respect human rights. When Cuban President Fidel Castro angrily lashed out and called Batlle a "lackey" of the United States, Batlle broke diplomatic relations with Cuba, which had been restored in 1986 after a 25-year break (see Cuba). In June, a television reporter asked Batlle at the end of an interview why he believed the Uruguayan economic situation was different from that of neighboring Argentina. Apparently thinking the formal interview had ended and the camera was turned off, Batlle replied that the Argentine government was "a band of thieves, from top to bottom." When he realized that his off-the-cuff remark would be broadcast, he shamefacedly rushed to Buenos Aires to personally apologize to President Eduardo Duhalde.

By early August 2002, there were signs that Uruguay was facing the same type of socioeconomic crisis that led to the chaos in Argentina eight months before. On July 19, the government had issued a surprise decision to let the peso float freely, and it plummeted in value from 17 to the dollar to 28. When Uruguayans began withdrawing their savings in a panic, and bank deposits dropped from $13 billion at the end of 2001 to just $8.8 billion, Batlle declared a "temporary" bank holiday on July 30. Newly appointed Economy Minister Alejandro Atchugarry announced the next day that the holiday would be extended until August 2, and violence and looting broke out on August 1 in a working-class neighborhood of Montevideo. On August 4, the Bush administration authorized a $1.5 billion emergency loan, the first time Bush had approved a direct loan to a Latin American country. Within days, the loan was repaid when the IMF approved a $3.8 billion loan.

The economic crisis continued into 2003, however, and despite international predictions of a default, Uruguay managed to service its debt through painful austerity measures that led to some rare street protests, but that even the leftist opposition Broad Front proclaimed necessary.

Faced with grim economic choices, the Blancos and Colorados boldly voted to slaughter the sacred cow of state-owned monopolies by approving a bill late in 2003 that dismantled the inefficient state oil monopoly, ANCAP, and opened it up to badly needed foreign investors. But the Broad Front had enough votes to force a referendum on the law on December 7. In a replay of the 1992 referendum on telephone privatization, 62% of the electorate voted to repeal the privatization.

In April 2004, the Chamber of Deputies passed a controversial bill that would have legalized abortion, making Uruguay the only Latin American country other than Cuba to do so, as well as providing for sex education and distribution of contraceptives. The Senate rejected the bill on May 5, 17–13.

The Elections of 2004

In 2004, the country geared up for the October 31 presidential election. The Broad Front renominated Vásquez, the Colorados nominated former Interior Minister Guillermo Stirling, and in a party primary in June the Blancos rejected former President Lacalle in favor of Jorge Larrañaga, a former governor and senator. By then the economy was rebounding, but it was too late for either of the now-discredited major parties, especially the Colorados.

Like Presidents Ricardo Lagos of Chile and Luiz Inácio da Silva of Brazil, Vásquez suddenly moderated his long-standing socialist rhetoric and emerged as a pragmatic, statesmanlike figure. He rejected a radical approach, pledging to couple an emphasis on social programs with moderate economic policies. It was a message the recession-weary Uruguayans, who were still reluctant to scrap their

Uruguay

overly generous social welfare system, wanted to hear. Polls showed that Vásquez could win without a runoff, and they proved right on target:

Vásquez	1,121,622	50.5%
Larrañaga	762,715	34.3%
Stirling	230,434	10.4%

Vásquez was inaugurated on March 1, 2005, Uruguay's first leftist president; the 170-year grip on power by the *Colorados* and the *Blancos* was finally broken. The Broad Front also emerged with a working majority in Congress. The inauguration itself was something of a fiesta for the South American left. Da Silva and Lagos were there, as were Venezuela's Hugo Chávez and Argentina's Néstor Kirchner. Cuba's Castro was uncharacteristically absent, but Vásquez's first act as president was to restore diplomatic relations with Cuba, three years after Batlle's spat with Castro.

In keeping with his campaign promises, Vásquez, himself a physician, announced a $100 million social program to provide medical care and nutrition. At the same time, he has continued the grudging efforts toward, if not outright privatization, a mixed economy that has created partnerships between the state and private industry. It was much the approach he followed as mayor of Montevideo. He already has enjoyed success in satisfying the IMF and the World Bank (see Economy).

Following the lead of Argentina and Chile, Vásquez quickly made an effort for Uruguay to come to terms with the human rights abuses of the 1973-85 military dictatorship. In April he struck a deal with the military by which he agreed to abide by the amnesty law, while the military would cooperate in recovering the bodies of those who disappeared during the dictatorship to give their families some closure.

In gubernatorial elections on May 9, the Broad Front did better than expected, winning eight of the 19 departments. The *Blancos* won 10, while the *Colorados* took only one.

Culture: Almost entirely Caucasian, Uruguay in many ways resembles an extension of Europe, and this certainly is true in its culture. Like Chile, highly literate and prosperous Uruguay has made cultural contributions far out of proportion to its small size. Also as in Chile, this cultural development was made possible by a climate of political stability and virtually unlimited freedom of expression.

Uruguay's contributions to art and music are not insignificant, but it is in the field of literature that the country has attained its greatest recognition beyond its borders. One of the most distinguished writers was

President Tabaré Vásquez
Source: BBC

José Enrique Rodó, whose 1900 essay, *Ariel*, extolled Latin American culture and denounced the United States as lacking in appreciation for cultural values. Needless to say, this essay was revered by latter-day Marxists and *dependentistas* throughout Latin America. Regarded as leading representatives of the romantic period in Uruguay were the novelists Eduardo Acevedo Díaz and Carlos Reyes; the poet Juan Zorilla de San Martín bridged the gap between romanticism and modernism. Two women of the post-modernist period, Delmira Agustini and Juana de Ibarbourou, also achieved international recognition. Some of Uruguay's leading contemporary writers abandoned the country during the military regime of 1973–86, the best known being the novelists Juan Carlos Onetti and Mario Benedetti.

Uruguayan journalism is highly developed but also highly politicized. The leading daily remains *El Día*, founded in 1886 by the future President of the Republic José Ordóñez y Batlle as a mouthpiece for his *Colorado* Party, which it still is today. Ordóñez's picture remains on the editorial page like the image of a patron saint. The *Blanco* Party has its own organ, *El País*, founded in 1918. The third major daily is *El Diario*, also pro-*Blanco*.

Economy: Uruguay's economy is almost totally dependent on its cattle and sheep-raising industry, which accounts for more than 40% of all exports. Because of heavy taxation on farm products, as well as inefficient state management of the economy, the gross national product actually declined between 1955 and 1975. Inflation has also been a serious problem. Prices rose by an incredible 1,200% in the decade following 1968. To help control inflation, the government imposed new tax and credit policies. Steps were also taken to increase farm output, stimulate exports and begin offshore oil exploration.

Economic growth declined for several years during the country's economic crisis of 1999–2002 (see History). Real GDP shrank 3.2% in 1999, 1.3% in 2000, 3.4% in 2001 and 10.8% in 2002. It finally grew by 2.5% in 2003 and 12.3% in 2004, which did not even recover the ground lost during the recession. Unemployment has remained stubbornly in the double-digits for several years: 11.3% in 1999, 13.4% in 2000 14.3% in 2001, 20% in 2002, 16% in 2003 and 14% in 2004. Inflation dropped from 5.1% in 2000 to 4.5% in 2001, then spiraled back to 26% in 2002. It has since moderated.

Much of the blame for the 1999–2002 crisis could be placed on the dire economic situation in neighboring Argentina. Argentines who once crowded the beautiful beaches at Punta del Este stayed home in droves in the summer of 2002. Even worse, they began withdrawing millions they had deposited in Uruguayan banks for safekeeping. The crucial beef industry was simultaneously affected by an outbreak of mad cow disease, which caused exports to nosedive.

Uruguay's seemingly enviable cradle-to-the-grave social welfare system and generous retirement benefits helped to give Uruguay one of the hemisphere's best standards of living for decades, and the per capita income for years was second only to Argentina's among the Latin American republics. It was $6,300 in 1998, but it dropped steadily during the devastating recession of 1999–2002. The per capita income of $3,300 in 2004 ranked seventh in the region. In 2004, about a third of Uruguayans lived below the poverty line.

The long-cherished social welfare system has come at a high price; external debt in 1999 was $6.3 billion, about 30% of GDP, even then a heavy burden for such a small country, and by the end of 2004 it was about 90% of GDP, the ninth highest in the world.

In February 2002, the international rating for Uruguayan bonds was reduced, thus making it more costly to borrow money. The Batlle administration responded with an economic austerity plan, which included privatization of state-owned utilities, telecommunications, airports and even highways, and a cut in the bloated civil service pensions. Batlle also promised to reduce the budget deficit, which was 4.2% of GDP in 2001, to 2.5% in 2002 and to balance the budget by 2004. The move was popular with the International Monetary Fund, which approved $743 million in loans in March 2002, another for $1.5 billion in May and $3.8 billion in August. Uruguay and the IMF agreed to restructure its bond indebtedness, thus extending the term of its bonds. But a law privatizing the state-owned oil company, *ANCAP*, proved unpopular with the voters; 62% of them voted to repeal it in a referendum on December 7, 2003.

Despite his leftist tilt, newly elected President Tabaré Vásquez bent over backward before his election to reassure foreign investors and creditors that he would honor Uruguay's debt commitment (about $11 billion when he took office in March 2005), and he moderated his long-standing opposition to free trade. Thus, he more closely resembles Brazilian President Luiz Inácio da Silva and Chilean President Roberto Lagos, two socialists who pragmatically moved to the center, than the confrontationist Presidents Néstor Kirchner of Argentina and Hugo Chávez of Venezuela. His pragmatism has paid off, literally; in June 2005, the IMF approved a $1.13 billion loan and the World Bank approved an $800 million, five-year loan to help the country recover from the recession.

The Future: Uruguay is the embodiment of Churchill's comment that democracy is the worst possible form of government— except for all the others. Even faced with grim economic realities that threaten their once-enviable standard of living, Uruguayans are reluctant to abandon their cherished welfare state and state-owned monopolies, which have become luxuries the economy cannot afford. They have punished any party at the polls that sought to do so.

Now, it is the turn of Dr. Tabaré Vásquez, who finally succeeded in accomplishing at the ballot box what the *Tupamaros* failed to do with terror. But like so many other erstwhile Latin American firebrands, the 65-year-old oncologist has moderated his Marxist rhetoric and eschewed a radical approach. This will be a revolution dressed in suit and tie (and perhaps a surgical gown) rather than

combat fatigues. Like Dr. Alfredo Palacio, the cardiologist who became president of Ecuador a month after Vásquez was inaugurated, Dr. Vásquez will have to prescribe some of the same bitter medicine to his spoiled countrymen as did his now unpopular predecessors. They spat it back in his predecessors' faces. It will be interesting to see if he can persuade them to swallow it.

Punta Del Este

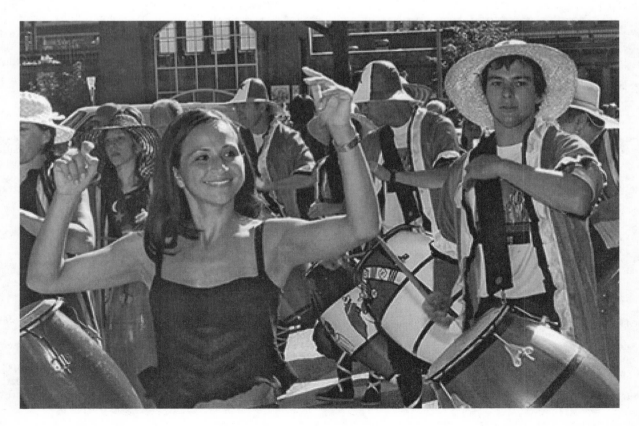

The Bolivarian Republic of Venezuela

Caracas and the mountains

Area: 352,150 square miles.
Population: 24.7 million (2004 estimate).
Capital City: Caracas (Pop. 5 million, estimated).
Climate: Tropical in the coastal lowlands, increasingly temperate at higher elevations in the interior. Heaviest rainfall is from June to December.
Neighboring Countries: Guyana (East); Brazil (Southeast and South); Colombia (Southwest and West); Trinidad and Tobago are islands lying a short distance from the northeast coast.

Venezuela

Official Language: Spanish
Other Principal Tongue: English.
Ethnic Background: Mulatto-*mestizo* (mixed European, African and Indian ancestry, 83%); European (10%); African (5%); Indian (2%).
Principal Religion: Roman Catholic Christianity.
Chief Commercial Products: Petroleum and petroleum products, aluminum, alumina and bauxite, agricultural products, small manufactured products.
Currency: Bolívar.
Gross Domestic Product: U.S. $115 billion in 2004 ($4,400 per capita).
Former Colonial Status: Spanish Colony (1498–1811).
Independence Date: July 5, 1811. Venezuela seceded from *Gran Colombia*, also known as New Granada, on September 22, 1811.
Chief of State: Hugo Chávez Frías (b. July 28, 1954), president (since February 2, 1999).
National Flag: Yellow, blue and red horizontal stripes with seven yellow stars in a semi-circle on the red stripe.

Venezuela has four distinct geographic regions: the Venezuelan Highlands to the west and along the coast, the Maracaibo Lowlands around freshwater Lake Maracaibo, the *Llanos* or plains of the Orinoco River and the Guiana Highlands. The Venezuelan Highlands are an extension of the eastern mountains of Colombia and are Venezuela's most densely populated region, with Caracas, Maracay and Valencia located in the fertile inter-mountain basins. The northern slope of the Highlands is relatively arid, but the basins receive adequate rainfall and because of elevation, are temperate and suited to agriculture.

The Maracaibo Lowlands, encircled by mountains, are windless and one of the hottest regions in South America, famous for the great lake (129 miles long and 60 miles wide) under whose water are some of the most extensive oil deposits in the world. Rainfall in this region is heavy along the slopes of the highlands, gradually diminishing toward the coast.

The *Llanos* of the Orinoco are the great treeless plains of the Orinoco River valley, which run east and west between the Venezuelan Highlands and the Guiana Highlands. Extending some 600 miles in length and 200 miles across, these plains are low and wet; intersected with slow moving streams, this region has been plagued with periodic floods and drought, but the poor soil has supported cattle raising. Presently, the government is undertaking flood control and irrigation projects to make this land available for agriculture and to support the development of new breeds of cattle.

The Guiana Highlands, south of the Orinoco, comprise more than half of Venezuela's territory. Rising in steep cliffs from the *Llanos*, this area is a flat tableland that extends to the Brazilian border. Heavily forested in part, it contains vast deposits of iron ore and bauxite. Gold and diamonds also exist in this region, which has been explored only superficially.

History: At the time of the Spanish conquest, Venezuela was inhabited by warlike tribes of Carib and Arawak Indians who offered brave but ineffective resistance to the invaders; the first landing was in the Gulf of Paria, where pearls were discovered. Under Spanish direction, Indian divers soon stripped the beds of the Gulf. The first settlement was established at Cumaná in 1520, with additional settlements at Coro (1520), Barquismeto (1551), Valencia (1555) and Caracas (1567).

Indians were utilized to pan the rivers for gold, but the results were disappointing and the settlers turned to agriculture. The wealth found in Peru and Mexico caused the Spanish government to lose interest in Venezuela, and options to explore its potential were leased to Dutch and German adventurers. The Spanish settlers gradually consolidated their small holdings, but it was nearly a century later before a serious attempt was made to explore the interior. The enslaved Indian laborers perished on the coastal plantations, and Negroes from Africa were imported to work the sugar and indigo crops. The neglected planters, with little merchandise to ship to the Spanish markets and forbidden to trade with the growing American markets, revolted against Spanish authority in 1796.

Two additional abortive attempts to set up an independent government were made in 1806 and 1811 under the leadership of Francisco de Miranda. At his urging, a republican congress declared independence on July 5, 1811, but the so-called First Republic lasted only a year. Venezuela's national hero, Simón Bolívar, took up the struggle after 1811 and fought a limited, but deceptive, guerrilla war against local armies in the pay of Spain until his capture of Angostura in 1817. Here he was joined by British veterans of the Peninsular War in Spain and by cattlemen from the *Llanos* with whom he made a dramatic march on Bogotá. The Spanish were finally expelled from northern Latin America in 1819 and the country achieved full independence, becoming a part of the Republic of Gran Colombia, led by President Simón Bolívar and Vice President Francisco de Paula Santander, and including present-day Colombia and Ecuador. Dissension and the subsequent illness of Bolívar led to the dissolution of Gran Colombia; Venezuela withdrew from the Republic in 1830.

General José Antonio Páez, the country's first president and a hero of independence, dominated Venezuelan politics from 1830 to 1848. He later returned as a dictator from 1861 to 1863. A capable and popular leader, he was effective in restoring order to war-torn Venezuela and in the establishment of governmental services and control. He was followed in 1848 by 13 years of repressive dictatorship by the Monagas brothers, who forced him into exile.

Returning to the *Llanos* in 1861, Páez raised another force of cattlemen to regain liberty in Venezuela. He ruled for two years, but was less tolerant of opposition than he had been during his first tenure; he was ousted in 1863 and intermittent civil war wracked the country until 1870 as young liberals fought conservatives.

Antonio Guzmán Blanco emerged from the chaos of civil strife; as strongman, he served as president or ruled through puppets for 18 years. Well educated, arrogant and completely unscrupulous, he enforced honesty among his ministers while converting a substantial part of the national treasury to his personal use. A careless despot who enjoyed living in Paris, he left his office in the hands of a puppet once too often and was overthrown in 1888.

Eleven years of confusion ensued, punctuated by violence and short-term presidents. An illiterate soldier of fortune who had been exiled to Colombia, Cipriano Castro, captured the presidency with the help of a private army in 1899. His nine-year rule was certainly the most repressive in Venezuela's troubled history. His high-handed dealing with European powers resulted in a blockade of the Venezuelan coastline by British, German and Italian naval units. After intervention by President Theodore Roosevelt, the matter was settled by arbitration. Castro turned the government over in 1909 to Juan Vincente Gómez, who ruled until 1935.

Gómez gave Venezuela its most able and its most savage administration. Oil had been discovered and he arranged lucrative contracts with American, British and Dutch interests for its extraction and processing. Simultaneously, he fostered agriculture and public works, established sound foreign relations and paid off the national debt. He also mechanized the army to support his regime and built a personal fortune. By comparison with his predecessors, Gómez left Venezuela in a prosperous condition when he died, but totally bereft of qualified leaders to administer the wealth which he had accumulated or to control the army which he had enlarged and modernized.

333

Venezuela

From 1935 to 1948 a series of moderate, but ineffective presidents occupied the office; during this period, political parties were allowed to organize, the largest being the *Acción Democrática* (Democratic Action), a popular, leftist party which had attempted to consolidate rural labor into a mass organization. Fearful of a rigged election in 1945, the party revolted and named Rómulo Betancourt as provisional president.

Venezuelans were delighted with democratic government—action was taken to recover some of the wealth from Gómez's estate and from others who had privately benefited during his rule. In the first free and honest elections in its history, Rómulo Gallegos, a well-known novelist, was chosen as president in 1947. Moving too fast to accomplish his goals, he frightened the army, which feared loss of its power and position in the government; he was ousted by a coup within three months of his inauguration. The army declared that it would save the country from communism, and exiled Gallegos and Betancourt, establishing another dictatorship under General Marcos Pérez Jiménez. He loosed a reign of terror and with reckless abandon spent the income from oil on public works in the city of Caracas and on poorly planned industrial ventures, with a handsome cut to friends and to the army. By late 1957 Venezuelans had had enough—resistance increased to the point that even the pampered army refused to oppose the popular will. Pérez Jiménez fled in January 1958, and a combined military and civilian committee took over the government.

Democracy Takes Root

Three moderate parties vigorously competed for the presidency in free elections that December: Democratic Action, or *AD*; the Democratic Republican Union (*URD*), and a social Christian movement with a cumbersome name that is better known by the acronym *COPEI*. The *AD*'s Betancourt was returned to the presidency with a 47% plurality and was sworn in for a five-year term on February 13, 1959, beginning an unbroken line of nine presidential administrations that has continued to the present, an enviable record of stability for Latin America.

An enlightened leader, Betancourt oversaw the adoption of a liberal constitution in 1961, but he also had to deal with a leftist insurgency incited by Cuba's Fidel Castro. Nonetheless, left-wing political parties such as the Movement to Socialism (*MAS*) were allowed to compete under Betancourt's tolerant constitution. One of the fundamental tenets of that document, designed to guard against another Gómez

or Pérez Jiménez, was that no president could be reelected for 10 years after leaving office. Thus, the popular Betancourt was succeeded in 1964 by Raúl Leoni, also of *AD*, who received a 33% plurality. In the December 1968 election, *COPEI*'s Rafael Caldera was elected with only a 29% plurality. Caldera was instrumental in establishing the Organization of Petroleum Exporting Countries (OPEC).

AD was returned to power in 1973 elections in which Carlos Andrés Pérez won a landslide (by Venezuelan standards) 48% of the vote over his principal opponent. Both candidates had run on almost identical center-left platforms. Voters firmly rejected both the radical left and right— the Marxist-Socialist candidate received only 4.2% of the vote and the right-wing candidate, a former associate of former dictator Pérez Jiménez, got less than 1%. In congressional races, *AD* won 24 of 49 seats in the Senate and 102 out of 200 seats in the Chamber of Deputies. The new president launched new, ambitious programs in agriculture and education, which amazed even his own supporters.

Venezuela took charge of the U.S.-operated iron mines near Ciudad Guyana in 1975, offering $101.3 million in compensation rather than the $350 million sought by the companies. The most important nationalization occurred at the beginning of 1976 when control of the oil industry was assumed. The 40 private firms, most of them U.S.-based, were granted compensation of $1.2 billion, which Venezuela asserted was equal to the book value of their assets. The companies claimed the true value to be between $3.5 and $5 billion.

Although Pérez maintained that nationalization of the oil industry would now make Venezuelans "masters of their destiny," in actual fact the nation continued to depend heavily on the foreign oil companies to refine, transport and market the oil. In addition, the oil firms provided technical assistance to the state-owned oil organization, *Petroven*. Ironically, the fees

charged by the private oil firms for these services were almost as high as the profits made by them before nationalization. Such a lucrative arrangement led to criticism of the Pérez administration by those who claimed that "oil nationalization needed more nationalization."

In 1973, when it joined OPEC in raising prices by more than 400%, Venezuela experienced windfall profits. With its oil income rising from $2 billion in 1972 to $10.4 billion in 1974 and $14.5 billion in 1983, Venezuela earned more from oil during the two years following the price hike than in the previous 56 years it had been exporting oil.

The gush of petrodollars swamped the nation with more money than could be realistically absorbed. To control the resulting inflation, which rose from the usual rate of 2–3% to 20% in 1974, the government channeled half the money out of the country. Some was invested in international lending agencies while other funds were loaned to developing nations, particularly in the Caribbean region. To further reduce the cash inflow, and to conserve the nation's dwindling oil reserves (now estimated at 12–15 billion barrels), Venezuela cut production from an average of 3.3 million barrels a day in 1973 to 2.2 million barrels in 1976.

The huge oil income vastly increased Venezuelan influence in Latin America. By raising contributions (and therefore voting power) in international lending organizations, it hoped to make these agencies less subject to "humiliating vetoes" of loans to nations out of favor with the United States. Venezuela has also helped to finance the establishment of cartels— such as in banana and coffee production and marketing—so that developing nations may charge more for raw materials sold to industrialized countries.

In foreign relations, Venezuela tried to become a leading advocate for the "Third World" causes and for Latin American economic independence. The Pérez ad-

The house in Caracas where Simón Bolívar, *"El Libertador,"* was born.

Photo by the author

334

Venezuela

Caracas boasts an ultra-modern skyline, but the makeshift vendors' stalls in the foreground are a reminder of the disparity between the elite and the poor in Venezuela.

Photo by the author

ministration played a major role in advocating greater respect for human rights in the region. Thus, it strongly condemned the use of torture by the military regime in Chile.

Relations with the United States remained cordial. In late June 1977, President Pérez visited the United States, where he praised the Carter administration's campaign for greater respect for human rights in Latin America. Washington regarded Venezuela as a valuable bridge between North America and the Third World. Venezuela also was given high marks for its refusal to join a 1973 OPEC oil embargo against the United States arising out of the Arab-Israeli conflict, and for shipping extra quantities of oil to North America during the unusually cold winter of 1976–77.

Although the government tried to channel petrodollars into development projects, highly visible luxuries proved more tempting. Venezuela had one of the highest per capita incomes in Latin America, but most of that income was concentrated in the upper class (5%) and the middle class (15%), both of which literally went on a spending spree. Signs of the "good life" abounded—swimming pools, comfortable homes and beach villas. A 350% tax on new luxury cars didn't even slow demand. Although domestic car production reached record levels, there was a long waiting list for buyers. Further prestige was associated with the commencement of *Concorde* supersonic service in 1976.

In this jewel of opulence, fully 80% of the people lived in poverty (and still do), with attendant malnutrition afflicting half of the youth of the nation. Almost none of the oil money filtered down to the poor. Pérez warned, "Our country is rich, but our people are poor." Ironically, he at the time was one of the "fat cat" class engaged in open thievery.

The search for jobs and a better life lured 80% of the nation's population to urban areas, where they settled in filthy slums surrounding traditional city areas. This caused not only a costly drop in farm output and a jump in food prices, but created immense problems of how to provide basic services to this population encircling the cities. More than 70% of the population of Caracas, then and now, lives in sordid *ranchos*, where even the police hesitate to go, in sharp contrast to the gleaming skyscrapers of the city. Incentives encouraging slum dwellers to move back to the country failed.

Investment during the first Pérez administration centered on the oil, steel and electrical industries, traditional sources of income for the super-rich of Venezuela.

Such massive economic development projects also led to massive economic problems. In 1978, Venezuela suffered its largest balance of payments deficit in its history ($1.7 billion). Exports (mostly oil) were down 7.5% from the previous year. (During the five years that Pérez was in office, Venezuelan imports rose by more than 230%).

As is often common during periods of rapid economic expansion, there were also widespread reports of government fraud, inefficiency, administrative waste and a relative decrease in social services. The industrialization program seemed to benefit a fortunate few, while living standards actually declined for the lower-income masses. Although Pérez did boast that unemployment had been largely eliminated, the inflation rate ranged between 10% (officially) and 20% (more accurate). Urban residents also complained of inadequate basic services, including overcrowded schools, a shortage of water and electric power and declining health facilities.

Increased economic problems set the stage for late 1978 presidential elections when voters turned to Luis Herrera Campíns, candidate of the *COPEI*. He won with 46.6% of the 5.5 million votes cast. The ruling *AD*'s candidate trailed with 43%. During the campaign, Herrera Campíns repeatedly charged that the nation's oil income had been squandered through government corruption, waste and deficit spending. All in all, the campaign was not an especially exciting one for the public, which found neither of the major candidates particularly inspiring.

The new president, a former journalist, was widely regarded as an intellectual. He promised in his inaugural speech in 1979 to emphasize state development of major industries while also encouraging greater private investments. He also pledged to pay more attention to the problems of the poor as well as to expand the nation's school system.

Like his predecessor, Herrera Campíns spent a considerable amount of time dealing with the country's economic development, and making efforts to diversify it from its great dependence on oil. He tried to steer Venezuela on a steady course, grappling with growing economic problems.

Herrera Campíns criticized the Reagan administration for its policies in Latin America—for its "treatment" of Nicaragua, its support of the appointed government in El Salvador and for its backing of Britain in the Falkland Islands invasion by Argentina. There was one matter brought out and set on the front burner: Venezuela's long-simmering border dispute with neighboring Guyana. Venezuela claimed a full five eighths of Guyana's territory! There was strong anti-British feeling running deep in Venezuela—exacerbated by the Falklands dispute. Venezuelans have not forgotten that British warships shelled Venezuela's ports early in the 20th century when Venezuela failed to repay loans to British banks. Herrera Campíns wanted to settle the border dispute through negotiation. However, the amount of territory claimed makes a solution almost impossible to reach. The area claimed is rich in timber—and potentially rich in oil, minerals and precious gems.

Venezuela's oil wealth attracted a flood of immigrants from its poorer Latin American neighbors. Government efforts to register the newcomers were inadequate. The ethnic picture of the country was also changed by the presence of about 1 million Europeans who settled permanently, usually engaging in the higher technological aspects of petroleum production.

By 1981 it was clear that Venezuela's governments had not been able to fol-

Venezuela

low the wise advice of Rómulo Betancourt "to sow the oil," which meant to diversify the economy and avoid the country's increasing dependence on oil exports. Limited industrialization, declining agricultural production and a lack of serious planning made the Venezuelan economy highly vulnerable to any change in the price of oil.

Consequently, the oil gluts of 1979–80 and 1986 hit Venezuela immediately. In 1982, the country suffered from a severe cash crisis produced by falling oil revenues, a sharp decline in international reserves and a lack of confidence of potential investors. The government was forced to reevaluate its gold holdings and to place the state oil company under central bank jurisdiction, somewhat ameliorating the burden of a foreign debt that had swelled in a few short years to $18.5 billion. Unaccustomed to austerity, the Venezuelans reacted with mounting criticism to the erratic policies of the administration.

Presidential and congressional elections in late 1983 demonstrated the general discontent with *COPEI*. Jaime Lusinchi, the presidential candidate of *AD*, won easily, receiving more than 50% of the vote over the respected former President Rafael Caldera of *COPEI*. *AD* also received a majority in Congress.

Those who thought austerity measures would be eased were bitterly disappointed. The currency was devalued by almost one half, fuel prices were increased more than 100% to eliminate what amounted to an annual subsidy of $85 million and wage-price freezes were instituted in large sectors of the economy. An increase in the minimum wage was later allowed, unless an industry could show that paying the higher amount would result in a loss.

Venezuela had placed a moratorium on the repayment of its foreign debt in 1983, but under pressure from international banks, it renegotiated the obligation and agreed in February 1986 to resume payment. Although large reserves indicated the ability to maintain payments, at the same time the debt payment resumption was finally negotiated, Venezuelan oil was in the process of dropping from $28 per barrel to less than $10 in the face of increased Saudi Arabian and world production. The pressure was not direct—Venezuela and Mexico were competitors for the petroleum import needs of the United States. Mexico, too, was saddled with an immense foreign debt ($104 billion, Venezuela $30 billion; figures include public and private debt). Increases in the price of oil from $17 a barrel were beneficial, but the trade balance during 1986–88 was again in the red for the first time since 1982.

The 1988 campaign for the presidency was lively, but, as usual, centered around the two powerful political parties. The American expression "there's not a dime's worth of difference between them" applied to Venezuela much more than to the United States. *COPEI* was still dogged by popular association of it with the early 1980s sharp economic fall.

Within *AD*, Lusinchi opposed the nomination of former president Pérez, but Pérez accurately accused the president of maintaining the illusion of prosperity by emptying out the treasury. Further, Lusinchi divorced his wife in order to marry his secretary, which did not endear him to the predominantly Roman Catholic population. Pérez had been convicted of theft during his first term, but departed for Spain to avoid going to prison. The voters' memory didn't reach back that far, and he received a majority of 53% over 40% for the *COPEI* candidate.

Rather than leave the task to his successor, Lusinchi announced yet another moratorium on debt principal repayment on the last day of the year. At the same time, Pérez negotiated additional aid from the International Monetary Fund, at the cost of imposing reforms on Venezuela. He waited a month before announcing them: an increase in gasoline by 90% (from 15 cents to 25 cents a gallon), doubled bus fares, unfroze prices on almost everything and ended numerous subsidies.

Suddenly, the poor were faced with the brutal realization that the free lunch they had been enjoying was over. Riots broke out in Caracas during Pérez's inauguration in 1989 and quickly spread to other cities. Common criminals took advantage

Former President Carlos Andrés Pérez

of the unrest to loot stores. The president declared martial law and ordered the army to crush the rioters. At least 300 people were killed and more than 2,000 injured in what came to be called the "*Caracazo*." It remains controversial to this day, just as the 1968 Tlatelolco Massacre is in Mexico.

In his first administration, Pérez was elitist, clumsy and dishonest. Conditions deteriorated swiftly in 1988 in spite of nominally improved economic conditions, and Caracas became a city owned by criminals, with homicides occurring at the rate of 1,500 and more per year. Drug trafficking became rampant, with associated criminal involvement. Wages for all but the elite were incredibly low. The mass of people enveloped by abject poverty began to fully realize who had benefited from more than a half century of oil exportation.

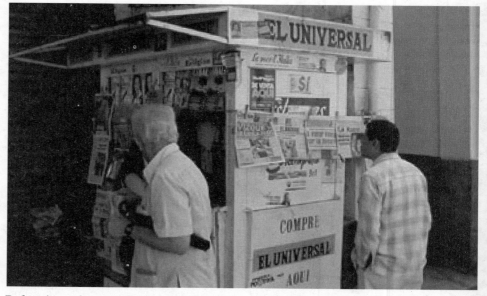

Pedestrians glance at the morning headlines at a news kiosk near Plaza de Bolívar in Caracas. Venezuela supports a multitude of newspapers and magazines, but press freedom has been under pressure under President Hugo Chávez. *Photo by the author*

Crisis and Corruption

In 1992, Venezuela's once-admired democracy was shaken to its very foundations. There were two abortive military coups, one of which was nearly successful but collapsed when commanders of key units failed to join the effort to oust Pérez. The instigator, a charismatic paratrooper named Lieutenant Colonel Hugo Chávez, was sentenced to two years in prison. The same year, Pérez was accused of pilfering $17 million in public funds. He issued a clumsy, unconvincing, almost arrogant denial, and public opinion turned harshly against him.

Pérez's party, his majority in the legislature and his hand-picked Supreme Court, turned on him in 1993. The court voted to allow his impeachment if ordered by the upper house, which voted unanimously in favor of the measure. He was forced to step down; a 76-year-old centrist was named by the Senate in June 1993 to head an interim government for the rest of his term—until February 1994. For good measure, Pérez was convicted in a criminal court and served 28 months in prison, being released in September 1996. But in April 1998, now 74, Pérez was again placed under house arrest when he and his mistress were charged with "illegal enrichment" for depositing large sums of undisclosed origin in U.S. banks.

In December 1993 elections the voters rejected the two principal political parties, voting for Caldera, now 80, who had ended his association with *COPEI*. He was the candidate of a 17-party coalition, the *Convergencia Nacional* (CN—"National Convergence"). His first term of office had been uncontroversial and somewhat uneventful during a period of relative Venezuelan wealth. This time, he inherited an absolute nightmare.

In spite of decades of oil money, Venezuela was in dire financial straits. A controversial value added tax (VAT) was initially extended, then canceled because of popular opposition in 1994. The second-largest bank collapsed in February, with fallout in the form of a run on all banks. The cause: massive thievery—83 were arrested.

Venezuela's years of drunken-sailor spending had given it a foreign debt in excess of $27 billion, more than half of GDP, which threatened the country with insolvency. The crisis was so severe that in 1996 Caldera was forced to eat crow and signed a reform package with the IMF, something he once vowed he would never do. Among other things, the package eliminated the gasoline subsidy and abolished price controls. The measures were annoying to Venezuela's small, crybaby middle class but were especially painful to Venezuela's poor, who account for 80% of the population.

The crisis lumbered on into 1997. The state-owned airline, *Viasa*, went bankrupt in February. At the end of the year, Caldera, the one-time populist, privatized the money-losing state-owned steel company, *Sidor*, and announced plans to sell off the state's aluminum company. In early 1998, the government was hit with a new fiscal blow when the price of oil, on which the government pegs its budget estimates, suddenly dropped. The government had drawn up a $23 billion budget based on an estimate of $15.50 a barrel, but the price fell to $12.80. Moreover, despite efforts to reduce the size of the cumbersome bureaucracy (see Economy), the public payroll in 1997 actually *increased* by 4%! On a positive note, however, inflation was reduced to a still-high 38% in 1997, the highest in Latin America, due mostly to a 75% pay increase for public employees in February 1997.

The Elections of 1998

Like a retreaded tire, the second Caldera administration blew out and the country lumbered along for the last year of his term, as Venezuelans desperately searched for a mechanic. So eager were they for a fresh face offering dynamic new leadership that for a time it seemed they would entrust their future to Irene Sáez, the 1981 Miss Universe, who had compiled a respectable record as mayor of the Caracas suburb of Chacao. After she declared her independent candidacy in 1997, polls showed the 35-year-old Sáez with a commanding lead over any candidate from one of the traditional parties. After a few months, however, her poll figures began to drop when she failed to offer any substantive solutions for the country's ills; she was, it seemed, little more than a still pretty face and name recognition.

Not so Hugo Chávez, leader of the abortive coup of 1992, who declared his own independent candidacy in early 1998 under the banner of the Fifth Republic Movement. His candidacy sent chills through the heavily entrenched political and economic establishments, but he soon gained a following among the downtrodden masses; polls soon showed him eclipsing Sáez.

Unquestionably homelier than the erstwhile beauty queen, Chávez nonetheless was a dynamic speaker, whose *macho*, charismatic mien and populist rhetoric were reminiscent of Latin American *caudillos* of old. Instead of a white horse and fringed epaulets, however, this late 20th-century savior had his red paratrooper's beret. Born into the middle class in 1954, he is the son of two schoolteachers. As a boy, he sold fruit on a street corner, and the army recruited him because of his skill as a baseball pitcher. Besides the appeal of his humble beginnings, his vow to clean up the country's cumbersome, corrupt political system, to wrest power away from the elite and to effect genuine socioeconomic reforms electrified Venezuela's destitute, long-suffering and resentful masses. As his bandwagon gained inertia, more alienated political groupings jumped aboard, forming an alliance called Patriotic Pole. At the same time, Chávez's open admiration for Fidel Castro alarmed the business and political elite, as well as foreign investors.

The months leading up to the November congressional and regional elections and the December presidential election witnessed the most bizarre campaign in the history of Venezuela's 40-year-old democracy. As Chávez's lead in the polls widened, the two traditional parties panicked and grasped for ways to stop this juggernaut. In May, adopting an if-you-

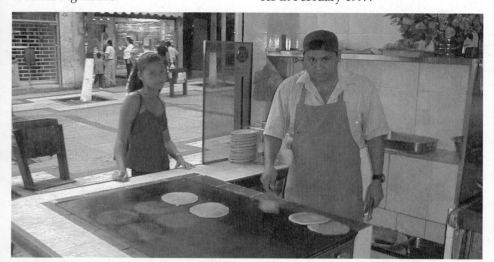

A short-order cook prepares a batch of *cachapas*, a popular corn-based Venezuelan pancake, at one of Caracas' many sidewalk cafes. *Photo by the author*

Venezuela

The Cienpies Exchange, Caracas

can't-beat-'em-join-'em strategy, *COPEI* offered its nomination to Sáez, who foolishly accepted. Now identified with one of the establishment parties blamed for the country's woes, she began to fall even further behind Chávez. *AD*, meanwhile, showed even less political sense, initially nominating Luis Alfaro, a 76-year-old party hack. Filling out the race was another independent, Henrique Salas, a respected 62-year-old businessman and Yale graduate, who formed a movement called Project Venezuela.

In the November 8 elections, Patriotic Pole became the largest force in the new Congress, winning 34% of the seats in the 48-member Senate and 189-member Chamber of Deputies. *AD* was a distant second with 22%; Salas' Project Venezuela won 12% of the seats, and *COPEI* won a pitiful 11%. Patriotic Pole also won seven of the 23 governorships; Chávez's own father, also named Hugo, was elected governor of Barinas. *AD* fell from 11 governorships to eight.

Chávez then surprised almost everyone by suddenly softening his fiery populist, anti-establishment rhetoric. Evidently aware that he was on the brink of full power, he seemed to be reassuring the foreign investors and domestic financial kingpins on whose support he would depend to resuscitate the moribund economy.

Meanwhile, the two traditional parties took heart from the fact that Patriotic Pole fell well short of a majority and clung to the hope that Chávez might still be defeated. In an unprecedented maneuver that can be described only as Machiavellian, *AD* and *COPEI* abruptly and unceremoniously jettisoned their own candidates on November 20 and rallied behind Salas, who by now was running second

in all the polls. Sáez and Alfaro bitterly vowed to continue on their own. Chávez, meanwhile, sneered that this only proved that *AD* and *COPEI* had conspired all along to share power.

But this last-ditch ploy failed. On December 6, an uncharacteristically high 65% of the electorate turned out to vote. Chávez polled a landslide 56.5%, to 39.5% for Salas; Sáez was a microscopic third. Hours after his victory, the flamboyant Chávez appeared humble and conciliatory, insisting that neither he nor the Venezuelan people view him as a messiah, and reaching out to *AD* and *COPEI* for a consensus on how to solve the country's problems. He also reassured the business establishment that he did not seek to dismantle the capitalist system. Ironically, after all the fears Chávez had generated in financial circles, the Caracas stock market actually *rose* after Chávez's victory, perhaps in acknowledgment that drastic reforms were indeed needed to save the terminally ill economy.

Chávez put his imprint on the new Congress that was installed on January 23, 1999. Elected president of the Senate was retired Colonel Luis Dávila of the Patriotic Pole, who participated with Chávez in the unsuccessful 1992 coup. *COPEI*'s Enrique Capriles, only 26, was elected president of the Chamber of Deputies, marking the first time in the 40 years of Venezuela's democracy that *AD* had been shut out of congressional leadership posts. Even before Congress was installed, however, the president-elect declared his intention to call for a referendum dissolving Congress and the judiciary and calling for the installation of a constituent assembly to rewrite the 1961 constitution. The traditional parties vowed to block Chávez's initiative, prompting

Chávez to denounce what he called a "conspiracy" and to threaten to dissolve Congress and rule by decree. It was to be the first of many bombastic threats to circumvent democratic institutions.

New President, New Constitution

Chávez was inaugurated on February 2, 1999. He reiterated his plans to scrap the 1961 constitution he had just sworn to uphold, deriding it as "moribund," and proclaimed what he called the "Bolivarian revolution." He set April 25 as the date for the first of three referenda on constitutional reform. Among his proposals for the new basic law: removal of the ban against immediate reelection, saying he needed at least 10 years to put Venezuela's house in order.

Like a weary parent trying to placate a willful child, Congress acceded to Chávez's persistent demands and approved an "enabling law" giving him the power to make sweeping economic decisions without congressional approval for six months. Chávez announced he would veto the new law for not going far enough, and he threatened again to dissolve Congress and rule by decree. Then he cooled down and signed it into law.

The April 25 referendum erased any doubt about who the masses were siding with. With a 60% turnout, a stunning 90% voted "*sí*" for a constituent assembly.

The next step was the election of the 131 members of the constituent assembly, which was held on July 25, 1999. Predictably, 121 of the 131 members elected were members of Patriotic Pole, including Chávez's wife, Marisabel, and his brother. A prominent loser for one of the seats from Tachira State: former President Pérez. The results were a dramatic rebuke of the *AD* and *COPEI* parties and an equally dramatic public ratification of Chávez's "Bolivarian revolution." Almost immediately,

President Hugo Chávez Frías

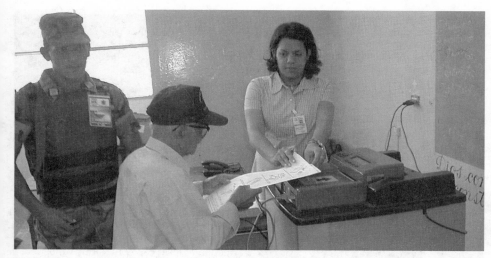

Under the watchful eye of a soldier assigned to maintain order, and with the assistance of a polling official, an elderly voter casts his ballot in a computerized tabulation machine in Caracas on July 30, 2000. Malfunctions in the machines delayed the voting for several hours past the scheduled time to close the polls.   *Photo by the author*

the assembly moved to usurp the powers of the Congress and the judiciary, even though the Supreme Court had ruled that the assembly had to confine itself to drafting the new constitution.

In late August, the assembly formally voted to strip the Congress of its remaining powers and sealed off the gold-domed capitol building, which sparked protests by Chávez opponents. Several opposition members of Congress scaled the fence around the *Capitolio* in defiance of the assembly's decision, while pro- and anti-Chávez factions clashed in the street outside. Violence appeared imminent.

Chávez resisted the temptation to use force to evict the aggrieved lawmakers from the building, which the assembly also was using. The Catholic Church mediated a peaceful solution on September 10, thus preventing what could have escalated into another bloody *Caracazo* that would have benefited neither side. The agreement stipulated that Congress would continue to serve as the law-making body, including the power to approve the budget, until after the referendum on the new constitution. (Chávez later broke that promise.)

The assembly soon renewed its attack on the judiciary. It appointed a special judicial investigative committee, which summarily removed 130 judges who had been under investigation for taking bribes and for other sins. Few had any sympathy for the sacked judges, as the judiciary had become notoriously corrupt, but the lack of due process was troubling. The Supreme Court meekly upheld the judges' dismissal.

The assembly moved like a steamroller on the new constitution. The final document had Chávez's fingerprints all over it. It renamed the country the Bolivarian Re-

public of Venezuela. It established a new 165-member unicameral National Assembly, abolishing the Senate. The presidential term was increased from five to six years, and immediate reelection was permitted. The president was to enjoy far greater authority than under the old constitution. The state and local governments were replaced by regional and municipal councils. Active-duty members of the military were given the right to vote for the first time. There was no prohibition against abortion, which drew fire from the Catholic Church. It reduced the work week from 48 to 40 hours, which upset businessmen. It declared that Venezuelans have a right to "free, truthful, uncensored information," but left unsaid who would determine what is "truthful," a clause seen as an attempt to silence Chávez's critics in the media. The cries of naysayers that the new organic law was drafted too hastily and concentrates too much power in the president's hands were drowned out in an avalanche of public approval. On December 15, 1999, voters overwhelmingly ratified it.

It was not the only deluge to occur that day in Venezuela. The coast was pounded by cataclysmic rains that swept away entire communities. The death toll could only be estimated at from 5,000 to 30,000; if closer to the latter, it would be the worst natural disaster in terms of loss of life in recorded Latin American history. The monetary damage was estimated at $20 billion, dealing the already desperately ill economy a cruel relapse.

Renewed Mandate

Before Christmas, the constituent assembly, emboldened by the new constitu-

tion, formally abolished the old Congress and the Supreme Court. It then created a 23-member standing committee, nicknamed the "*Congresillo*," to act as the legislative authority pending the election of the new National Assembly. Elected president of the *Congresillo* was Luis Miquilena, a close Chávez ally who was widely regarded as the second most powerful man in the country.

Chávez then announced that he would subject himself to the will of the electorate under the new constitution to seek a renewed mandate. All other officials established under the new constitution would be selected in the same "*Megaelecciones*," scheduled for May 28, 2000.

In February 2000, the first schism appeared in Chávez's Bolivarian revolution. To mark the eighth anniversary of the 1992 coup attempt, three of Chávez's former comrades-in-arms broke with the president, accusing him of corruption and of betraying the goals of their revolutionary movement. They cited 46 specific cases of corruption, involving Chávez and Miquilena, among others.

Among the three dissidents was Francisco Arias Cárdenas, governor of Zulia State, widely regarded as the intellectual author of the 1992 coup attempt. Though not as charismatic or brash as Chávez, Arias was generally respected for his more reasoned, moderate approach. To use a Steinbeckian metaphor, Arias played the role of George to Chávez's Lenny. An even unkinder metaphorical cut for Chávez came, symbolically, on March 15—the Ides of March—when Arias declared that he would run for president against his former friend and chief. A former mayor of Caracas, Claudio Fermín, also declared his candidacy.

As the campaign progressed, polls showed Chávez with a lead over Arias. Chávez steadfastly—and wisely—eschewed the intellectually superior Arias' invitation to a debate. Capitalizing on what he termed Chávez's cowardice, Arias aired a television commercial in which he "debated" a hen, which represented, of course, his "chicken" opponent. A white hen quickly became the unofficial symbol of the Arias campaign. Both major candidates crisscrossed the country, speaking to large, enthusiastic crowds.

But there was an ominous cloud over the campaign. The five-member National Electoral Council, or *CNE*, all of them Chávez appointees, warned that it was unsure it could resolve computer problems in time for the election. The *CNE* blamed the problems on a U.S. firm that had the contract to tabulate the votes, while the company complained that the *CNE* had made 11,000 last-minute changes to the database. This prevented the com-

Venezuela

pany from having the flashcards needed to program the computers that would be used in more than half the 8,400 polling stations ready in time. Less than a week before the election, Chávez dispatched an air force jet to Omaha, Nebraska, to receive the necessary flashcards.

This was the milieu when this author flew to Caracas on May 24 to cover the elections the following Sunday as a freelance journalist. Arias had held his closing rally in the Avenida Bolívar the previous day, and Chávez's closing rally was in full sway that night, also in the Avenida Bolívar. The president's electrically charged voice was blaring from a radio in the lobby of my hotel, sounding more like that of a soccer announcer than a politician. It was easy to understand from hearing him how he could so work up a crowd. I walked the four blocks to the rally just as it was breaking up. The atmosphere resembled a Louisiana Mardi Gras more than a political rally. A majority of those in the almost entirely working-class multitude—many of them wearing Chávez's trademark red beret—showed signs of advanced inebriation, and crushed beer cans carpeted the streets.

At noon the following day, May 25, the bombshell struck. The *CNE* postponed the election because of technical difficulties. Chávez met with journalists and expressed his support for the delay; from Maracaibo, Arias cautiously did the same, although he called for the dismissal of the *CNE* on grounds of incompetence. Reaction I heard on the street ran the gamut from anger to nonchalant acceptance. Within hours of the announcement, Chávez supporters surrounded the *CNE* headquarters, protected by a phalanx of police and national guardsmen in riot gear. Evidently, the Chávez backers felt cheated out of a victory they regarded as inevitable. For amusement, they decapitated a white hen.

On May 27, former U.S. President Jimmy Carter, who has become a sort of self-appointed guardian of Latin American democracy in recent years, held a news conference in Caracas to declare his support for the postponement which, he said, "was for a good reason." In response to my question, he drew a contrast with the obviously rigged election in Peru that would be held the following day and predicted that the Venezuelan election ultimately would be held and would "accurately reflect the will of the Venezuelan people."

On one point, there was almost universal agreement among the Chávez supporters, Arias, the OAS observers and the U.S. election software company: the *CNE* had botched its job. On May 29, Chávez sacked the five members and replaced

Thousands of jubilant supporters of President Hugo Chávez crowd under the balcony of the Miraflores Palace in Caracas late on July 30, 2000, to hear him proclaim his landslide reelection victory.
Photo by the author

them, at Carter's suggestion, with a group that was less partisan and more representative of the discrete sectors of society. It contracted with a Spanish firm to conduct the election, and waited for computer experts to reach a consensus on how long it would take to resolve the glitches before announcing a new election date. That date was July 30, 2000.

Chávez was resoundingly reelected with 59.2% of the vote, a mandate even greater than his 1998 landslide. His Fifth Republic Movement (*MVR*) received 57.6% of the votes for the new National Assembly, which translated into 92 of the 165 seats. That fell short of the two-thirds majority needed for constitutional amendments and confirmation of judicial appointments, but it gave Chávez the three-fifths majority needed to pass emergency legislation that would allow him to rule by decree. Ironically, the much-maligned

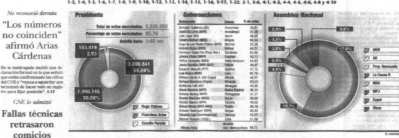

The Caracas daily *El Universal* reports the landslide reelection victory of President Chávez on July 30, 2000.

and discredited *AD* was second with 19.7%, giving it 35 seats. Arias' *Proyecto Venezuela* was a distant third with 4.9%, or eight seats, while *COPEI* was a poor fifth with a mere 2.4%, or four seats. The *MVR* and its ally, the Movement to Socialism (*MAS*), won 15 of the 23 governorships. The Carter Center criticized apparent irregularities that occurred throughout the country and the failure of election officials to investigate them. But Chávez's mandate was unassailable.

An International Loose Cannon

Almost immediately after his overwhelming vote of confidence, Chávez set out to make Venezuela—in reality, himself—a player on the world stage. Just 11 days after the election, Chávez raised diplomatic eyebrows around the world when he became the first head of state since the 1991 Gulf War to pay a state visit to Iraq's Saddam Hussein. Ostensibly, the visit was for bilateral talks between two OPEC members, but apparently the trip had no other purpose than for Chávez to poke his finger in the eye of the United States.

In September 2000, Chávez enthusiastically hosted a meeting of OPEC heads of state in Caracas. There, his was the loudest voice in favor of curtailing production to drive up world oil prices. At the time, they were above $30 a barrel, the highest since the Gulf War. His motive may have been partially global, but more likely it was primarily domestic, as every $1 increase in the price of a barrel of oil adds $1 billion a year to his government's revenue. As 60% of that revenue comes from oil, he desperately needed the money to fund his "social revolution" and to bring the economy out of recession. Moreover, it was another way to irritate the United States, although high oil prices hurt poor countries the most. Chávez seemed to recognize that, too; Venezuela sells oil to Cuba and Central America at discount prices.

Chávez annoyed the United States again a month later by hosting a five-day state visit by Fidel Castro. The two long-winded orators spoke to Venezuelans on a live national broadcast from the Carabobo battlefield, site of one of Bolívar's victories. Chávez railed against what he called a world market economy dominated by the United States, while Castro told Venezuelans that their country is considerably larger than Cuba and thus also could resist U.S. domination. Castro returned in August 2001 to celebrate his 75th birthday.

Meanwhile, Chávez strained relations with both Colombia and Peru. In March 2001, he met with a miffed President Andrés Pastrana of Colombia, after Venezu-ela had arrested, then released, a Colombian guerrilla wanted in an airplane hijacking (see Colombia). Chávez is known to be sympathetic to the guerrillas, which has strained bilateral relations. Nonetheless, Chávez and Pastrana announced that their intelligence services would begin exchanging information.

That deal seemed ludicrous in November 2001 after Diego Serna, a member of the Revolutionary Armed Forces of Colombia (*FARC*), admitted in a television interview in Colombia that he had helped provide security for Chávez during a recent state visit to Colombia. Even more embarrassing, a captured video showed Chávez and Serna together. At any rate, Chávez failed to keep his promise of intelligence-sharing, and relations with Colombia grew even worse under its tough new president, Alvaro Uribe, who took office in August 2002.

During the first half of 2001, Chávez and then-Foreign Minister Rangel adamantly denied reports that the fugitive former Peruvian intelligence chief, Vladimiro Montesinos, was hiding in Venezuela (see Peru). In June, even as Chávez was hosting the 13th Andean Summit, Peruvian authorities presented him with conclusive evidence from the U.S. FBI that Montesinos was, in fact, in the country. Chávez's intelligence service then obligingly arrested Montesinos in Caracas without any apparent difficulty.

Chávez had the audacity to boastfully announce the arrest during the summit; among those attending was Peruvian President-elect Alejandro Toledo. Chávez promised Toledo that Montesinos would be returned to Peru "faster than a rooster crows." He kept his word; Montesinos was flown back to Peru within 24 hours, not as an international fugitive, but as an undocumented alien!

In the ensuing days, the opposition parties and media began asking pointed questions about how Montesinos could have entered Venezuela and remained there for several months without the knowledge of the intelligence agency—meaning, of course, of Chávez himself. The international wire services suggested that Chávez was beholden to Montesinos because the latter had provided refuge for some of the plotters of the failed 1992 coup. Chávez's response to these queries was an uncharacteristic and stony silence, and each country temporarily withdrew its ambassador from the other.

In April 2001, Chávez again relished being in the international spotlight at the third Summit of the Americas in Quebec. There, he was the only one of the 34 heads of state who opposed the idea of establishing a Free Trade Area of the Americas (FTAA) by the end of 2005. Chávez ar-gued, with some validity, that little had been done to implement the lofty goals of alleviating poverty in Latin America that had been advanced during the second summit in Chile in 1998. He also argued that subregional integration should come before hemispheric integration, and he warned that the FTAA would be dominated by the United States. He also irked his fellow presidents by balking at the requirement that signatories to the FTAA be "representative democracies;" he said he preferred the term "participatory democracy," which apparently could be more loosely construed. The new U.S. president, George W. Bush, snubbed Chávez by avoiding a one-on-one meeting, as he held with most other presidents.

The deterioration in U.S.-Venezuelan relations further accelerated in August 2001 when the U.S. military mission was ordered to vacate its offices in the Venezuelan military headquarters and relocate elsewhere. The defense minister insisted that the Venezuelans needed the space.

Then came September 11, 2001. Chávez dutifully denounced the terrorist attacks on the United States as "abominable," but two weeks later, in a speech to Congress, Chávez defended his close ties with Iraq, Iran and Libya, calling them "our brothers and partners." He claimed there was insufficient proof of U.S. assertions that they abetted international terrorists. Chávez made trips to Iran and Libya again as part of a three-week tour of Europe and Algeria in October.

During his tour, he also managed to irritate the French by expressing, as he had in 1999, his concern over the welfare of the Venezuelan-born terrorist Ilyich Ramírez, better known by the sobriquet Carlos the Jackal, who was incarcerated in a French prison after two decades as an international fugitive.

Back home, Chávez then criticized the U.S. bombing campaign in Afghanistan as "using terror to fight terror." The U.S. State Department responded that it was "surprised and deeply disappointed" by the remark, a diplomatic euphemism that meant U.S. policymakers were mad as hell, and noted that his comments were not consistent with Venezuela's support for two U.N. resolutions recognizing the United States' right to self-defense. Three days later, the United States recalled its ambassador for consultation, a diplomatic move just short of breaking relations, which led the foreign minister to hurriedly reiterate Venezuela's support for the war on terrorism. The ambassador returned the following week, and Chávez insisted that Venezuela and the United States were "allies and friends."

But relations were strained again in March 2003, when Chávez condemned the

Venezuela

U.S. invasion of Iraq. At about the same time, media reports began circulating that the large Arab community on the Venezuelan island of Margarita had become a haven for Hamas and Hezbollah terrorists.

Chávez turned down an opportunity to perform on the world stage in September 2003 when he declined to give the traditional address by heads of state at the United Nations, claiming there was a plot to kill him in New York. Besides, he said, the addresses served no purpose and he called them a "dialogue of the deaf."

In late 2003, it was Chile's turn to become annoyed with Chávez's loose tongue. He commented that he dreamed of one day visiting a Bolivian beach, a reference to Bolivia's ongoing quest to regain the seacoast it lost to Chile in the 1979-84 War of the Pacific (see Bolivia, Chile). Chile protested the comment and recalled its ambassador for consultation.

Chávez served as naysayer again at the Fourth Summit of the Americas in Monterrey, Mexico, in May 2004. This time, however, he had two new adherents, presidents Luiz Inacio da Silva of Brazil and Néstor Kirchner of Argentina, both of whom are skeptical of FTAA.

In February 2004, Chávez hosted a summit of the so-called Group of 15, a group of developing nations. The summit was marred by protests by Chávez opponents who were trying to focus international attention on their frustrated efforts to force a recall election (see The Recall Movement). Police broke up the demonstrations with tear gas and shotguns.

Dissent and Repression Grow

Chávez also had to contend with pressing domestic issues, not the least of them declining living standards. One solution: Create a new labor organization to replace the Confederation of Venezuelan Workers (*CTV*), long affiliated with the discredited *AD*. The new organization had the predictable name Bolivarian Workers' Force. As usual, he put the idea up for a vote in yet another referendum, held on December 3, 2000. Critics warned that this was merely another attempt to concentrate more power in Chávez's own hands and to curtail, rather than enhance, the strength of organized labor. Chávez received the expected lop-sided majority for his plan, but he was stunned by the anemic 25% voter turnout, a fraction of what he had grown accustomed to for his rubber-stamp plebiscites. Moreover, only two thirds of those who did vote cast ballots on the union issue, with the remaining third voting only in municipal elections. In those contests, the *MVR* won 40% of the seats. It was a diluted victory for Chávez, his first real electoral defeat and a warn-

ing that his honeymoon with the working class was ending.

That assessment was underscored in February 2001 when a frustrated Chávez reshuffled his cabinet, something he has continued to do with bewildering regularity. Among the most controversial changes: Foreign Minister José Vicente Rangel, an erstwhile journalist and longtime leader of the *MAS*, became the first civilian defense minister in 70 years; the switch did not go over well with the corps of general officers. Miquilena, the former president of the *Congresillo*, at age 81 became interior minister.

In March 2001, schoolteachers, oil workers and university students staged a strike to protest the state of the economy. For the first time, the National Guard was sent into the streets to disperse the protesters, and Rangel warned that although the right of assembly was a constitutional one, henceforth demonstrators would have to "get permission" before using the streets. The next day, state employees and aging pensioners staged a peaceful protest outside the presidential palace to plead with their president for their overdue paychecks and pension payments; he did not appear.

There were other signs that Chávez was growing increasingly impatient with dissent, something he no doubt picked up from his friend in Havana. He long has assailed the Venezuelan press as controlled by the oligarchy. In one case of legalized suppression, Pablo López, editor of the gadfly Caracas weekly *La Razón*, went into hiding in August 2000 rather than face house arrest for charges he had defamed Tobías Carrero, a wealthy friend and financial benefactor of Chávez's and Miquilena's. López already had been arrested once for refusing to testify in his defamation case. He went into hiding

when he refused again to testify, after the judge had refused to allow López to introduce evidence that the articles published in *La Razón* about Carrero's influence peddling were true. In many countries with a Hispanic legal tradition, truth is not a defense in libel or defamation cases, as it is in the United States; all that must be proven is that the plaintiff was offended. López's lawyer took his case to the Inter-American Commission on Human Rights (ICHR) in Washington, an organ of the Organization of American States. In February 2001, the ICHR ruled in López's favor and ordered the Venezuelan government to stop the persecution of López. Chávez responded that the matter is a judicial one, and López remains in self-imposed exile in Costa Rica.

Addressing a meeting of the small Communist Party in June 2001, Chávez renewed his commitment to an anti-imperialist revolution, threatened to confiscate the property of tax evaders and absentee landowners and threatened to declare a state of emergency and rule by decree if necessary. The next day, he stirred international condemnation when he addressed a seminar of ambassadors and foreign businessmen and declared he would expel any foreigner who "criticizes" Venezuela. He insisted that he had no objection to internal dissent, however. Such a threat contravened the U.N. Declaration of Human Rights, to which Venezuela is a signatory.

Just one day later, Rangel announced the establishment of pro-Chávez neighborhood groups called "Bolivarian Circles." Rangel denied that these circles were patterned after Cuba's Committees for the Defense of the Revolution, insisting they were for political association, not for internal intelligence. Another parallel with Cuba has been the application of a clause

Oil derricks, Lake Maracaibo

in the new constitution to teach "Bolivarian principles" in the public schools; critics contend that the nebulous term is a euphemism for pro-Chávez propaganda.

In September 2001, in a move reminiscent of Salvador Allende's land reform program in Chile, Chávez presented the deeds to 105,000 acres of idle land to small farmers, and he warned large landowners that they should "donate" unused land to the state for redistribution or face confiscation. Chávez touted his agrarian reform plan as a means of relieving the crowded, squalid conditions in the slums around Caracas, something chillingly reminiscent of the Khmer Rouge in Cambodia.

Chávez next lashed out at the independent television station *Globovisión*, known for hard-hitting reporting that often embarrasses the government. He accused the station and its director of engaging in "terrorism," called them "enemies of the revolution" and threatened to revoke their license. Days later, the station was notified that it was being investigated under a broad provision of the new constitution that prohibits "false or misleading" information. The station was accused of inaccuracies in a news report on crimes against taxi drivers that supposedly led the drivers to strike.

Chávez stunned the nation in November 2001 with a list of 49 decrees affecting virtually all economic sectors, especially the all-important oil industry. One decree doubled royalties on foreign oil companies from 16.5% to 30%, a move that would drive away badly needed capital investment. The president's brash action had the unintended effect of forging an unlikely alliance between *Fedecamaras*, the country's main business lobby, led by Pedro Carmona, and the *CTV*, still smarting from Chávez's attempt to scuttle it the year before, whose president, Carlos Ortega, defeated Chávez's hand-picked candidate.

By December 2001, Venezuela had become irrevocably polarized between passionate pro-Chávez and anti-Chávez camps. The president's approval ratings had slipped below 50% for the first time, and few Venezuelans remained ambivalent about Chávez and his revolution *Fedecamaras* called for a 12-hour general strike on December 10, and the *CTV* supported it. Chávez ridiculed the strike and its organizers, saying "nothing can stop Venezuela." He had to eat his words; millions participated in the work stoppage, and the degree of its success surprised even its organizers.

By the end of 2001, there was growing dissent as well within the ranks of the military, which apparently had become riddled with corruption as the administrator of Chávez's $100 million social program, Plan Bolivar 2000. The president was acutely embarrassed by revelations that his hand-picked army commander, General Victor Cruz, had pocketed millions from the fund; Chávez fired him on December 22, while refusing to give the reason. Yet, when the auditor-general uncovered still more examples of embezzlement of funds destined for the poor, Chávez responded by firing the auditor-general.

By early 2002, Chávez's popularity had dropped to 30%. Emboldened by the success of the December 2001 general strike and by the defections of Chávez loyalists, the opposition organized a demonstration scheduled, symbolically, for January 23, the anniversary of the fall of the Pérez Jiménez dictatorship in 1958. This time, Chávez confidently organized a counter-demonstration, but again was embarrassed when the anti-Chávez crowd, estimated at 200,000, was several times larger than his own.

Chávez was stunned even more in February 2002 when an air force colonel and a National Guard captain publicly called on Chávez to resign. The colonel was forced to retire and the captain was jailed for 15 days.

Suddenly, the always enigmatic Chávez began to sound conciliatory. In a televised address, he agreed to moderate some of his more radical economic decrees. He also announced budget cuts as a response to falling oil prices, and declared that the Bolívar would be allowed to float freely. He called for understanding from the opposition, and said he hoped he could "sheath my sword." He met with a group of priests in an effort to mend fences with the church. He even condemned Colombia's *FARC* guerrillas and applauded President Pastrana's decision to suspend peace talks. But this era of good feeling proved fleeting.

In late February 2002, events began to unfold quickly and dramatically. It began when Chávez unexpectedly fired General Gauicaipuro Lameda as president of the state-owned oil company, Petroleos de Venezuela (*PDVSA*) and replaced him with a leftist economist, Gastón Parra. *PDVSA* white-collar workers protested the change with marches, but held off on calling a strike that would halt oil exports. Chávez refused to change his mind.

Then two high-ranking officers, Vice Admiral Carlos Molina Tamayo and Air Force General Roman Gómez Ruíz, publicly declared their opposition to their commander-in-chief for what they regarded as corruption and mismanagement of the armed forces; Gómez Ruíz called on Chávez to resign.

Rumors of an imminent coup began to fly, and the media reported that dissident officers had approached U.S. diplomats to ask whether the United States would back such an effort. The State Department issued a statement expressing its firm support for democratic institutions. The crisis escalated on March 5 when *Fedecamaras* and the *CTV* issued a plan for a post-Chávez Venezuela, without explaining how they planned to unseat the president. Meanwhile, the protests at *PDVSA* continued, threatening to upset the world oil market; production dropped by 450,000 barrels a day—about 20%. Venezuelans and the world watched anxiously to see what would happen next.

Coup and Counter-Coup

On Tuesday, April 9, 2002, *Fedecamaras* and the *CTV* declared a one-day general strike, which was successful. *Fedecamaras* and the *CTV* then extended the strike indefinitely—meaning, until Chávez resigned. On Thursday, April 11, about 150,000 people poured into the streets to demand Chávez's resignation, and pro-Chávez goons opened fire on them, killing 17 and wounding at least 100. The armed forces high command declared later that Chávez had ordered them to implement "*Plan Avila*," the code name for the use of deadly force to protect the Miraflores Palace, but that they had refused to fire on unarmed civilians; a leaked audiotape corroborated their account.

After midnight on Friday, April 12, the generals acted, using the violence against the peaceful demonstrators as justification to restore order. The president was taken into "protective custody" and hustled off to the island of La Orchila; accounts leaked later to the media revealed that Chávez broke into tears when he surrendered. By Chávez's own account later, he was told to sign a resignation statement, but he refused. Nonetheless, General Efraín Vásquez, the army commander, announced to the nation and the world that Chávez had stepped down. As interim president, they named *Fedecamaras*' Pedro Carmona. Meanwhile, the U.S. State Department issued a statement, which would later backfire, suggesting that the forcible removal of Chávez was the will of the Venezuelan people. The United States also sought to allay an OAS resolution denouncing "the alteration of the constitutional order," but in the end it grudgingly supported it.

Few anticipated what would happen next. First, Carmona unwisely said he was abrogating Chávez's 1999 constitution and dissolving the Assembly and the Supreme Court; he called for new congressional elections in eight months. This was too much even for those delighted by Chávez's ouster, and it brought international rebuke—even from the Bush administration, which directed its new am-

Venezuela

bassador to try to dissuade Carmona from dissolving the institutions. Mexican President Vicente Fox, meanwhile, refused to recognize the interim government. To make matters worse, Carmona did not name any representatives of the *CTV* in his interim cabinet. Within hours, the new "government" unraveled.

On Saturday, April 13, hundreds of thousands of furious *chavistas* poured into the streets around the country and rioted to demand Chávez's reinstatement. Fighting broke out, and at least 50 people were killed and hundreds injured. Some of the *chavistas'* rage was directed against the opposition media. Suddenly, a schism appeared within the ranks of the armed forces, which had been thought to be almost solidly opposed to Chávez. Loyalist mid-ranking unit commanders rebelled against the rebellion and stormed the Miraflores Palace; among them were the paratroopers, whence Chávez had sprung. On Saturday night, Carmona resigned; to fill the power vacuum, the high command agreed to allow Chávez's vice president, Diosdado Cabello, to take charge until Chávez returned. Carmona was placed under house arrest. An estimated 80 officers also were detained.

On Sunday, April 14, Chávez was back in power. Although brief, his forcible removal marked only the third military coup in more than 20 years of democratic reforms in Latin America, following that in Haiti in 1991 and Ecuador in 2000. In the days following the coup and countercoup, Chávez appeared chastened and, again, conciliatory toward his opponents.

"Let's put our house in order," Chávez said at a news conference, and promised not to seek revenge for his ouster. He lamented that "We have sown hatred." He also announced that he had accepted the resignations of Parra and the entire *PDVSA* board and that he was willing to compromise to settle the dispute with the *PDVSA* management. Oil production quickly returned to normal. On April 20, Chávez appointed Ali Rodríguez, the OPEC secretary-general and a former Venezuelan oil minister, as president of *PDVSA*. He also replaced Vice President Cabello with Defense Minister Rangel. Meanwhile, Chávez relieved Vásquez from command of the army.

The U.S. government, meanwhile, denied that it had abetted the coup attempt. Presidential security adviser Condoleezza Rice did little to quell international suspicions when she stated in a televised interview that she hoped Chávez had received the "message" of the Venezuelan people and that he "takes advantage of this opportunity to right his own ship, which has been moving, frankly, in the wrong direction for quite a long time."

Political Stalemate

OAS Secretary-General Cesar Gaviría, a former Colombian president, flew to Caracas to meet with Chávez and leaders of the umbrella opposition body, Democratic Coordinator, urging the two sides to effect a reconciliation. But the opposition remained intransigent. Admiral Molina called the government "illegitimate." The opposition party *AD* declared it did not recognize Chávez as president. Other opposition members of the Assembly called on Chávez to resign, or for a referendum on his remaining in power.

On May Day, thousands of supporters of both sides took to the streets again—this time peacefully. Meanwhile, an opinion poll suggested that the coup attempt had boosted Chávez's approval rating by 10 points, to 44%—still a far cry from the 90% he once enjoyed. Emboldened, he dropped the conciliatory tone and vilified those who instigated the coup as "Nazis." In a separate development, Carmona escaped from house arrest and sought asylum at the Colombian Embassy. Colombian President Pastrana, no doubt delighted to repay Chávez for his support of the *FARC*, granted it, and days later Carmona left for Bogotá. Carlos Fernández succeeded him as *Fedecamaras* president.

On June 15, 2002, tens of thousands of anti-Chávez demonstrators filled the streets to demand he resign. As if he didn't have enough pressure from critics, his government admitted it couldn't account for $2 billion that was supposed to have been deposited in a contingency fund to stabilize the economy.

Chávez invited former President Carter to Caracas in July to broker an agreement, but those talks ended in failure.

The next scene of this political drama opened in August 2002 and was fraught with irony. First, it pitted Chávez against a Supreme Court that he had packed with his own appointees. Second, Chávez, the erstwhile rebel lieutenant colonel who spent two years in jail for leading an abortive coup against an elected president, now sought to prosecute four officers involved in the April coup against him. The officers—two navy admirals and an army and an air force general—appealed to the Supreme Court to block their trial, arguing that Chávez's own constitution makes it lawful to disobey orders from an authoritarian government, in this case, an order to fire on unarmed civilians. They also argued that they had acted to prevent anarchy when they believed Chávez had resigned. The court twice delayed a decision, as Chávez supporters and opponents demonstrated outside the Supreme Court building; violent clashes ensued. Chávez himself declared that he

and the armed forces would not respect any ruling that the four officers would not have to stand trial, in effect, saying that he would not respect the independence of his own judicial branch. On August 14, the court voted 11–8 to dismiss the charges, citing insufficient evidence. Furious Chávez supporters tried to storm the court building but were repulsed by security forces.

The ever-erratic Chávez then said he accepted the decision and appealed to his supporters to remain calm. He sent mixed signals at a *chavista* rally, telling his backers they all had to "swallow the decision like a fish with bones," but he called on them to stage a "nonviolent" protest against the decision. Tens of thousands of them turned out on August 24. Pro-Chávez congressmen threatened an "investigation" of some of the justices, while Chávez called for "reforms" to his own constitution that would allow him to govern as he chooses.

Animated by the court decision, opposition leaders initiated a variety of criminal charges against Chávez, including abuse of power and accepting illegal campaign contributions. Chávez also came under criticism from international journalism organizations for his harsh rhetoric against the opposition media and for the alarming number of physical attacks on journalists working for anti-Chávez media. In September 2002, representatives of the Inter American Press Association and the Vienna-based International Press Institute visited Caracas and warned that Venezuela could become another Cuba. Vice President Rangel assured the IAPA and the IPI that the Venezuelan media operate without censorship.

Chávez next found himself in a test of wills with Alfredo Peña, the opposition mayor of Caracas. Chávez accused the Caracas police of treating pro-Chávez demonstrators more harshly than anti-Chávez demonstrators; Peña alleged that his police were ambushed by *chavistas* when they responded to a disturbance call. In retaliation, Chávez grounded Peña's helicopter. In October 2002, fighting broke out between the police and *chavistas*. Pro-Chávez policemen began a strike, dividing the police force and making a volatile situation even more combustible.

Chávez invited disinterested international representatives to mediate a solution between him and the Democratic Coordinator. On September 9, 2002, representatives of the United Nations, the OAS and the Carter Center arrived in Caracas to jump-start the dialogue. Chávez reiterated that he was agreeable to a referendum, but not before August 2003, the mid-point of his term, as specified in the constitution. The talks ended in failure.

Chávez had good reason to stall; his approval rating was down to 30%, and anti-Chávez demonstrations had become an almost daily occurrence. In October, OAS Secretary-General Gaviría returned to make another attempt at brokering an accord. After three days, he left in despair. The principal stumbling block was the timing of the referendum, with the opposition demanding an early, if non-binding, vote. Gaviría urged both sides to be more compromising.

Gaviría's plea fell on deaf ears. The opposition called another mass rally, attended by an estimated 1 million people, at which the *CTV*'s Ortega and *Fedecamaras*' Fernández issued Chávez an ultimatum: Resign, or face a general strike on October 21. Chávez responded with another huge rally of his own three days later, which he claimed was attended by 2 million people but was probably half that. On October 21, the opposition followed through with its threat of a 12-hour general strike, which brought the country to a standstill and cost the economy an estimated $300 million.

On October 23, coup fears resurfaced when 14 anti-Chávez officers urged their comrades to rise up and depose the president, but their calls went unheeded. Some officers joined the rebellious group, however, displaying again the divisions within the ranks. Within a week, the number of rebels, led by General Enrique Medina, had swelled to 120, and they camped out in Plaza Altamira in eastern Caracas, continuing to demand Chávez's resignation. They again invoked the clause of Chávez's own constitution, which legitimizes rebellion against an authoritarian government. Many of them were already facing court-martial for participating in the April coup. Thousands of civilians soon joined the protest.

The plaza became the focal point for a petition drive to force a December referendum. The opposition claimed it had the necessary 1.2 million signatures, or 10% of registered voters as required by Chávez's constitution for a nonbinding referendum, and Ortega threatened an indefinite general strike if Chávez refused. Gaviría began to favor an electoral solution as a way out of the crisis, but he urged Ortega to drop the strike threat as counterproductive.

Events turned uglier on November 4, the day the opposition staged a march to the National Electoral Council to present petitions containing 2 million signatures calling for a referendum on December 4. *Chavistas* attacked the marchers, and Caracas police intervened. In the resulting melee, dozens of people were injured, more than 20 of them by gunfire.

Chávez refused to call the referendum. Tensions between the pro-Chávez and anti-Chávez factions of the police force erupted into violence that left two people dead and dozens wounded. Chávez ordered a federal takeover of the Caracas police force, sending in national guardsmen to serve alongside the municipal police. Peña and the rest of the opposition were outraged by this power play, which the Supreme Court declared unconstitutional. Demonstrators banging pots and pans filled the streets almost every day, and there were the usual outbreaks of violence. Venezuela, it seemed, was on the brink of anarchy.

General Strike

Fedecamaras and the *CTV* called for an indefinite general strike, to begin December 2, 2002. At first it was not universally observed. The vital oil industry continued functioning, and some sections of the capital operated normally. The government proclaimed the strike a failure. But it continued day after day, and the economy soon felt the pinch. Pot-banging demonstrators continued to take to the streets in cities and towns around the country. Tear gas and rubber bullets were used on the protesters with increasing frequency. On December 6, *chavista* gunmen fired into an opposition rally, killing three and wounding 28. *Chavistas* also stepped up their vandalism against *Globovisión* and other anti-Chávez media, egged on by the president, who called his media opponents "terrorists." At almost the same time, Chávez disavowed the violence and appealed to both sides to refrain from further bloodshed.

On December 5, rebels seized a government oil tanker; Chávez ordered the navy to retake it. By the fourth day of the strike, striking port workers had brought oil exports from the world's fifth-largest producer almost to a halt. Production dropped from 3 million barrels a day to 400,000, then to 200,000, and the world oil market began to shiver. The price of crude jumped accordingly, to more than $30 a barrel. Chávez no longer dismissed the strike as a failure, but assailed the opposition as "fascists," "traitors," "terrorists," "saboteurs," "coup-plotters" and "hijackers." He broke off the OAS-sponsored negotiations until the strike ended, and he fired striking *PDVSA* executives and tanker captains. He dispatched troops to retake another struck tanker and to arrest the crew. Meanwhile, he began using foreign reserves to import food, medicine and, ironically, fuel.

The nation remained paralyzed for weeks. Neither side was willing to budge, and the economy languished. The opposition now set February 2, 2003, as a date for the referendum. Gaviría, Jimmy Carter,

the Bush administration and the European Union all advocated early elections as the only way to defuse the crisis. Chávez left the door open to negotiations over a *binding* referendum after August 2003, but vowed he would not resign under duress. The divided army declared its support for Chávez, saying the strike was threatening the national well-being. The country spent a peaceful but uneasy Christmas. The demonstrators soon returned to the streets and threatened a tax revolt. Chávez threatened to revoke the broadcast licenses of the anti-Chávez radio and television stations, and he began restructuring *PDVSA*.

On January 3, 2003, violence erupted during an opposition march on armed forces headquarters when *chavistas* pelted the marchers with rocks and bottles; two people died, five were wounded by gunfire and 73 were injured. Chávez accused the opposition of firing on the crowd to discredit the government. The two dead turned out to be *chavistas*. Vice President Rangel was among the high-ranking officials who served as pallbearers.

The demonstrations continued. Chávez ordered the army to seize the heavy weapons of the Caracas police, and later disarmed all 500 motorcycle policemen. He used troops to keep banks and schools open. On January 23, he announced temporary controls on foreign currency exchanges to try to protect the value of the Bolívar, which at that point had declined by 25%.

Chávez flew to New York in January to meet with U.N. Secretary-General Kofi Annan to discuss a diplomatic solution. Meanwhile, newly inaugurated Brazilian President Luiz Inacio da Silva offered his intercession and invited the United States, Spain, Portugal, Chile and Mexico to form a "Friends of Venezuela" group to mediate an end to the crisis. Annan also agreed to send an emissary. Carter returned to Caracas and met with both sides and with Gaviría against the backdrop of violent demonstrations.

Suddenly, the general strike began losing its steam as small businesses, faced with bankruptcy, began reopening. By the end of January, oil production was back up to about 1 million barrels a day. Private banks reopened on February 3. The same week, the non-oil sector was operating normally. Chávez claimed victory and threatened to prosecute the strike's organizers. In reality, there were no winners, as the strike had cost $6 billion and left the economy in a shambles (see Economy), not to mention the lives lost. Perhaps Finance Minister Tobías Nobrega summed it up best when he called the 61-day general strike a "kamikaze attack."

Venezuela

The Recall Movement

The opposition returned to petition-gathering, this time claiming 4 million signatures. Chávez hung tough, saying there could be no vote before August 19, 2003.

In February 2003, Gaviría and the "Friends of Venezuela" finally persuaded the two sides to agree to an eight-point resolution that renounced violence. It also called for the government to respect freedom of expression and for the media to show restraint in their rhetoric.

Just three days later, it came unraveled when Fernández was arrested on charges of treason and inciting violence. Ortega also was ordered to surrender, but he received diplomatic asylum at the Costa Rican Embassy. The government granted him safe-conduct in March to go to Costa Rica, apparently preferring to send him into exile rather than risk his becoming a martyr in a prison cell in Venezuela. (Ortega later returned to Venezuela clandestinely, and was arrested while playing bingo in March 2005.)

The opposition threatened to resume the general strike, and international condemnation poured in on Chávez. The president accused the United States and Spain of siding with the opposition and even reprimanded Gaviría, who had spent three months patiently trying to effect an agreement, for meddling in Venezuela's internal affairs.

Two days later, bombs exploded minutes apart at the Spanish Embassy and Colombian Consulate, injuring four people. Suddenly turning conciliatory again, Chávez warned the Colombian guerrillas not to enter Venezuelan territory, as though that would magically resolve the issue. Bilateral relations became even worse when Colombia accused Venezuela of providing close-air support for *FARC* rebels in March. (see Colombia).

The logjam again appeared to break in April when the two sides finally agreed on the terms for a referendum. The opposition agreed to wait until after August 19, 2003 (in reality, there was no other choice), and Chávez pledged not to try to delay the vote and to resign if he lost. He predicted he would win, however. At the same time, he said the signatures collected earlier were invalid and that the opposition would have to go through the petition process again after August 19. Chávez soon reneged on the agreement, raising a new condition that the opposition's elected officials also face a recall referendum.

Gaviría went back to work, and in May the two sides again announced they had reached a consensus on a referendum, for both Chávez and some opposition legislators. The agreement also included a civilian disarmament plan to curtail further bloodshed. The agreement was signed on May 29, 2003. Moreover, the National Assembly, in which the *chavistas* enjoy a small majority, would have to appoint a new National Electoral Council *(CNE).* Then Chávez suddenly reneged again, suggesting that the terms did not specify that he *must* call a referendum.

Still, the Democratic Coordinator pressed on with plans for a binding referendum, which would require 20%, not just 10%, of the more than 12 million registered voters, or 2,436,083 valid signatures. If the opposition succeeded in forcing a recall election, the turnout would have to be at least 25% and the votes to remove Chávez would need to match or exceed the 3.76 million votes Chávez received in his 2000 reelection. Also key would be the date. If held before August 19, 2004, the fourth anniversary of Chávez's reelection, the *CNE* would be required to call a new election within 30 days. If after that date, Vice President Rangel would serve out the remainder of his term, with Chávez in all probability pulling the strings.

On August 20, 2003, one day after the mid-point of Chávez term as required in the constitution, the Democratic Coordinator presented the *CNE* with petitions containing 3.4 million signatures. Chávez immediately declared the signatures invalid, not explaining how he could know that, and ridiculed his opponents as "crazy."

But the terms of the *CNE* members had expired, and the Assembly obviously was not inclined to appoint new ones. Five days later, the Supreme Tribunal appointed a new five-member *CNE*, which surprisingly met with the approval of Chávez, the Democratic Coordinator, Gaviría and the United States. The members were seen as balanced, two pro-Chávez, two favoring the opposition and one neutral. Soon, however, it became apparent that the "neutral" member was in the government's corner.

In September, Chávez complicated matters by threatening not to bide by the *CNE's* decision if it validated the petition, saying his sources assured him thousands of signatures were fraudulent, either phantoms or dead people. He sent a squad of armed police into *CNE* headquarters to search, unsuccessfully, for proof of fraud, a move widely seen as designed merely to intimidate the *CNE*.

If so, it apparently worked. The *CNE* declared that the petitions were invalid because the signatures were collected *before* the August 19 mid-point. It said the Democratic Coordinator would have to collect the needed signatures again, but during a four-day window. This was a hurdle the *CNE* perhaps believed to be in-surmountable, but in late November the opposition succeeded in collecting 3.4 million signatures; Gaviría came to observe the process. The petitions were presented to the *CNE* in December.

By law, the *CNE* was supposed to validate the petition within 30 days and issue a ruling, but it kept delaying action until March 2, 2004, when it ruled that only 1.83 million signatures were valid, 140,000 were invalid and 1.1 million more were in doubt. Changing the rules in the middle of the game, the *CNE* announced that the Democratic Coordinator had the burden of confirming the signatures of enough of the questioned signatures to reach the necessary number, or about 600,000, and gave it four days to do so. Riots erupted throughout the country, which left six people dead.

The Democratic Coordinator, meanwhile, took the *CNE* decision to court, appealing to the Supreme Tribunal's electoral chamber. In a stunning decision, the chamber on March 15 upheld the validity of the petitions and ruled that a recall election must be held. The government quickly appealed to the Supreme Tribunal's constitutionality chamber, which just as quickly overturned the electoral chamber's decision on March 23.

Apparently miffed by the unpredictability of the Supreme Tribunal, Chávez introduced a bill that would allow him to increase the size of the court from 20 justices to 32 and would reduce the requirement for Assembly confirmation from two-thirds (which Chávez did not have) to a simple majority (which he barely had). For weeks, the opposition tried to filibuster this naked power grab to death, but in the end, it passed on April 30.

The stalemate continued for two more months, when the two sides agreed that the verification of signatures would begin on May 27.

Before then, a bizarre spectacle unfolded on May 9, when security forces raided a farm near Caracas owned by a Cuban exile and arrested about 50 people the government said were Colombian right-wing paramilitaries sent to Venezuela to "destabilize" the country. Another 27 people were arrested later. Colombian President Uribe disavowed any knowledge of a plot, and commended Chávez for arresting what he called "criminals."

During the four-day verification process, signers of the petition were required to come forward and verify their signatures. The process drew international scrutiny, and Jimmy Carter returned to Caracas on May 29 to act as an observer. He pronounced the process fair.

Again the Democratic Coordinator presented its petitions to the *CNE,* and again the country and the world held their breaths. This time, although it disallowed about 110,000 signatures the opposition insisted were valid, the *CNE* could not escape reality. On June 3, it announced that the Democratic Coordinator had collected 2,451,821 valid signatures—15,738 more than required!

Instead of his usual defiance, Chávez declared he accepted the *CNE's* conclusion and insisted that he "welcomes the challenge" of the recall election, predicting he would win. His followers were less conciliatory and went on a violent rampage in Caracas, attacking Mayor Peña's office and the offices of several opposition media and beating an opposition legislator outside the Assembly. One policeman was killed in the disturbances.

The two sides had agreed on Sunday, August 8, 2004, as the date for the referendum, but the *CNE* arbitrarily postponed it one week to August 15, claiming the new computer system could not be in place until then. In June, Carter returned to Caracas to meet with Chávez and one of Chávez's fiercest media foes, Gustavo Cisneros of *Venevisión*, whom Chávez had accused of conspiring to kill him. Carter apparently extracted a pledge from Chávez that the referendum would go forward fairly, democratically, and without intimidation or trickery. Based on past experience, Carter has reason to be wary.

Conflicting polls made it difficult to predict the outcome. After a tempestuous but relatively non-violent campaign, hundreds of international observers and foreign journalists descended on Caracas to observe the climax of the two-year-long recall effort. A total of 70% of Venezuela's 14 million registered voters participated, voting "*Sí*" to remove Chávez, or "*No.*" The results stunned both sides:

Sí	3,989,008	40.74%
No	5,800,629	59.25%

In a replay of two earlier election nights in 1998 and 2000, Chávez claimed victory before jubilant supporters at the Miraflores Palace. Becoming a bit messianic, he declared that "the will of the people is the will of God."

The disgruntled opposition, meanwhile, immediately claimed that computer fraud had robbed it of victory and called on international observers to investigate. Some called for a return to street protests.

Carter and Gaviría rejected the claims of fraud; even the Bush administration said it respected the result and called for reconciliation. However, Carter and Gaviría called for an audit of 150 randomly selected polling stations to look for signs of fraud. The Democratic Coordina-

tor refused in advance to recognize the audit, thus nullifying its own argument.

The opposition suffered another stinging defeat in state and municipal elections on October 31, 2004, losing control of Caracas and losing 20 of the 23 state governorships.

Recent Developments

The opposition eventually acquiesced to its losses, and for the first time in more than two years it seemed as though the violence, turmoil and economic upheaval in Venezuela would subside at last and that peace, albeit an uneasy one, would return. Those hopes were suddenly jarred on November 19, 2004, when a car bomb killed Danilo Anderson, a high-level government prosecutor who was in charge of the cases against about 400 opposition figures implicated in the 2002 coup attempt. The assassination caused Chávez to cancel his trip to Costa Rica for the Ibero-American Summit. The killing remains unsolved.

Emboldened by his mandate at the polls, Chávez quickly began to consolidate more and more power in his hands. A new law placed municipal and state police forces under unified national—meaning his—control. The addition of 12 new justices to the Supreme Court took effect in December 2004. He appointed another loyalist to the *CNE*, giving it a lop-sided 4-1 majority. He stepped up seizures of privately owned rural land under the 2001 land reform act. He ingratiated himself to the armed forces with a 50-60% pay increase in June 2005.

Chávez also moved to tighten the screws on privately owned broadcast stations that have opposed him. In December 2004, he signed the Radio and Television Social Responsibility Law, which has such vague language that domestic and international media organizations and even the OAS's Inter-American Human Rights Commission have denounced it as an attempt to censor content. The law, ostensibly designed to protect children, states that images of sex or violence, including news coverage of violent demonstrations, cannot be aired between 7 a.m. and 11 p.m. It also provides for 70 minutes of government programming per week. Violators can be fined or have their licenses revoked for carrying programming that is deemed slanderous, that "incites disruption of public order" or that is "contrary to national security," all defined by the government on a case-by-case basis.

By March 2005, several journalists had been charged with one violation or another. In May, the government's taxing agency levied a $2.5 million fine against *Globovisión*, one of Chávez's most persistent critics, not under the terms of the new law but for allegedly airing opposition

propaganda for free during the general strike of 2002-03 and for back taxes. The station insisted it owed no back taxes and appealed to Chávez's court system.

Equally onerous were Chávez's revisions to the penal code, which in effect outlawed peaceful dissent. It subjects journalists to up to 12 months in jail for criminal defamation, which is loosely defined, and five years for "causing panic" by disseminating "false information," not just by the mass media but by e-mail or other means; the presumption of innocence in such cases was eliminated. Demonstrators engaging in banging pots and pans in the traditional Latin American form of protest may now be arrested for "intimidating" public officials.

Even as he clamped down on domestic media critics, Chávez got his government into the mass media business itself with the creation of a regional all-news television channel, *Telesur*, in conjunction with the friendly governments of Argentina and Uruguay; Brazil and Cuba are providing technical support. The first experimental transmission was sent in May 2005, and it was to have begun operation in late July. While Chávez extolled the new channel as a counterweight to the domination of U.S. and European all-news channels, critics complained that the programming was little more than left-wing, anti-U.S. propaganda.

In foreign affairs, relations with Colombia and the United States remained rocky, while those with Spain improved markedly.

On December 14, 2004, the Colombian government announced that it had arrested Rodrigo Granda, considered the *FARC's* "foreign minister," in the Colombian city of Cucuta. That was partly true; Colombian authorities did take him into custody there that day. But soon Chávez charged that Granda had been abducted in Caracas and whisked across the border by Venezuelan national guardsmen who, Chávez said, had been "bribed" by the Colombian government. At first, President Uribe denied the allegations, then suddenly admitted them, but he called the payment for Granda's abduction a "reward."

Chávez angrily denounced what he called a Colombian violation of Venezuelan sovereignty and demanded an apology from Uribe, who not only refused to apologize but accused Chávez of having harbored a representative of what the world community regards as a terrorist organization and was thus threatening the security of Colombia. Chávez recalled his ambassador from Bogotá and canceled a recent bilateral agreement to build a $200 million gas pipeline. He also contended that Colombia should have asked his gov-

Venezuela

ernment to arrest Granda. But Uribe no doubt recalled how Chávez had insisted to Peru in 2001 that the fugitive Vladimiro Montesinos was not in Venezuela. Eight national guardsmen involved in the abduction were arrested and charged with treason.

The war of words escalated during January and February 2005, with the Colombian and opposition Venezuelan media reporting that Granda held a Venezuelan passport and had voted in the August referendum. The obvious question was, how could Granda have obtained Venezuelan citizenship and operated freely in Venezuela (he was abducted in a café) without the knowledge of Venezuelan intelligence personnel and, logically, Chávez himself? Chávez invited Uribe to discuss the matter directly. Uribe at first said he would meet with Chávez only in conjunction with other Latin American presidents. Eventually, Uribe flew to Caracas, where the two presidents met behind closed doors on February 15. They emerged to announce that the crisis had been resolved, that the pipeline deal was back on, and that Venezuela was mindful of Colombia's security concerns. There was no apology from Uribe.

The two presidents would meet again in Puerto Ordaz, Venezuela on March 30 together with Brazilian President da Silva and Spanish Prime Minister José Luis Rodríguez Zapatero. Venezuelan relations with Spain improved immediately with the election victory of Zapatero's Socialist Party following the Madrid terror bombings in March 2004. The new Spanish prime minister has steered a foreign policy 180 degrees from that of the conservative government of José María Aznar, whom Chávez had accused of complicity in the 2002 coup attempt. Zapatero used the summit as the opportunity to sign a $1.7 billion arms deal by which Venezuela purchased four coastal patrol ships, four corvettes, 10 transport planes and two surveillance planes. The two leaders also announced that Spain would sell Venezuela an oil tanker and that Repsol, Spain's oil company, would increase its investments in Venezuela.

The Spanish arms purchase came on the heels of the announcement that Venezuela was buying 100,000 AK-47 assault rifles and 40 Mi-35 assault helicopters from Russia, which drew a quick protest to Russia from the United States Secretary of State Condoleezza Rice (whom Cháves has deridingly referred to as "Condolencia") called Chávez a "negative force" in the region. Meanwhile, Defense Secretary Donald Rumsfeld openly questioned during a visit to Brazil why Venezuela needs 100,000 AK-47s and darkly suggested that the arms would wind up in the hands of the Colombian rebels. They could have another use: in March, training began for pro-Chávez paramilitary units, called "Popular Defense Units," which have the stated mis-

sion of resisting a U.S. invasion. Chávez also has doubled the size of the army reserve, to more than 100,000.

Venezuelan-U.S. relations did not improve with the arrest in the United States in May 2005 of Luis Posada Carriles, an anti-Castro Cuban exile who bribed his way out of a Venezuelan prison in 1985. Posada was awaiting retrial for the bombing of a Cuban airliner off Barbados in 1976 that killed 73 people. Venezuela formally requested his extradition, after assuring the United States that Posada would not be sent to Cuba. Chávez at first hinted that he would close the Venezuelan embassy in Washington if Posada were not extradited, then just as quickly declared that he would not. In June, the United States refused to extradite Posada on the grounds that the extradition request did not contain the required evidence against Posada, who already had been acquitted in Venezuela of the bombing.

Posada had illegally entered the United States after serving time in a Panamanian prison for an alleged plot to assassinate Castro there in 2000. When outgoing Panamanian President Mireya Moscoso pardoned Posada days before she left office, both Cuba and Venezuela broke diplomatic relations with Panama. When this book went to press, Posada was being held in a federal detention center in El Paso, Texas, as an illegal alien. His case continues to strain U.S. ties not just with

Angel Falls

348

Venezuela but with Latin America in general, which regards it as hypocritical for the United States to seek support for its war on terror while refusing to extradite a suspected terrorist.

U.S. concerns over Venezuela's purchase of rifles, ships and planes suddenly paled when Chávez announced in May that he planned to enter into talks with Iran to begin a Venezuelan nuclear program. That was too much even for friendly Brazil, which said it would not cooperate in helping Venezuela establish a nuclear energy program if Iran were involved.

Culture: Venezuela's ethnic makeup is an intriguing blend of European, Indian, *mestizo*, black and mulatto. The crippling succession of dictatorships took a heavy toll on cultural development, however.

Its two most distinguished men of letters both spent many of their most productive years abroad. The 19th century intellectual and writer Andrés Bello (1781–1865), left Venezuela at the age of 19 in 1810, then spent 19 years in London and the remainder of his life in Chile.

In the 20th century, Rómulo Gallegos (1884–1969) spent two decades in Spain during the Gómez dictatorship. His best known novel, *Doña Bárbara*, was published in 1929—in Madrid, not in Caracas. Two more of Gallegos' best known works were written in Barcelona: *Cantaclaro* (1934) and *Canaima* (1935). Returning to Venezuela after Gómez's death in 1935, Gallegos wrote *Pobre negro* (1937) *and El forestero* (1942), but they never achieved the critical acclaim of his novels written in Spain. Perhaps that was because he was more absorbed by his political activities; he was elected president of the republic in 1948 (see History). He went into exile again during the Pérez Jiménez dictatorship of the 1950s, this time to Mexico. The Romulo Gallegos International Novel Prize, now one of the most prestigious in Latin America, was created in his honor in 1965.

In art, Venezuela has produced a few figures with a regional reputation, but in classical music and theater it still largely borrows from abroad.

In popular music, however, Venezuela has produced at least two singers who have achieved acclaim throughout Latin America and beyond. One is a regional megastar of pop-rock, José Luís Rodríguez (b. 1943), also known by the sobriquet *El Puma*. He recorded his first hit in Venezuela in 1978 and for more than two decades has remained one of Latin America's most popular crooners. His three-volume *"Inolvidable"* album, released between 1997 and 2001, has been among his most popular.

The other singer is Simón Díaz (b. 1928), who specializes in the genre of the *tonadas*, or Venezuelan folk ballads. He has composed and sung hundreds of *tonadas*, which celebrate the bygone lifestyle of the farmers and cowboys of Venezuela's high plains, much as Woody Guthrie did with his folk ballads about the common man in the United States. His signature song is a love ballad, *"Caballo viejo,"* which the French group Gipsy Kings co-opted for its international smash hit *"Bamboleo"* in 1989. Díaz later received a copyright infringement settlement. Long a popular television personality in Venezuela, Díaz became famous throughout Latin America, and in 2004 he released a CD in the United States, *"Mis canciones."*

Venezuela's fledgling film industry continues to show promise, and a few Venezuelan *telenovelas* are marketed abroad.

Beauty contests are a national passion in Venezuela, where special schools that groom young women for competition, and plastic surgeons who enhance their looks, have become thriving industries. Five Venezuelans have won the Miss World title since its inception in 1951, the most recent in 1995. Four Venezuelans have won the Miss Universe title since it was created in 1953, in 1979, 1981, 1986 and 1996. One, Irene Sáez (1981), later went into politics and ran for president in 1998 (see History).

The absence of free expression before the advent of democracy in 1958 also hamstrung the press. Since then, press freedom has caused the number of newspapers and magazines to mushroom. The capital's two prestigious dailies are the venerable *El Universal*, founded in 1909, and *El Nacional*, which dates to 1943. High-quality magazines include *Resúmen, Momento, Bohemia, Elite, Auténtico* and *Zeta*.

Economy: Venezuela's economy is completely dominated by petroleum production. Oil revenues account for more than two-thirds of all government income and more than 90% of the nation's exports; Venezuela is the world's fourth-largest oil producer. As a hedge against the day when oil reserves are depleted, recent governments sought to "sow the oil"—to invest oil revenues into other segments of the economy, with but limited success. To date, investments have increased output of industry and development of other mineral resources, including iron and aluminum. The program has produced two new cities: Ciudad Guyana (iron and hydroelectric power) and El Tablazo (a petrochemical center near Lake Maracaibo).

With the largest proven heavy oil reserves in the world, how to extract it from the tar-like deposits led to an $8 billion project to develop resources of the Orinoco oil belt. An even brighter note on the oil scene was the discovery of a large field in the eastern state of Monagas with an estimated 8.6 billion barrels in late 1987. Total reserves, including "heavy" oil, are about 300 billion barrels. In April 2003, the state oil company announced the discovery of still another new field in Monagas containing an estimated 350 million barrels of light crude and 870 million cubic feet of natural gas.

One bright spot on the economic horizon is renewed oil drilling in the Maracaibo area. Twenty-one years after Venezuela nationalized its oil industry, it began inviting oil companies to come back in 1996 to explore in promising areas. The contracts signed would give the government a generous 90 percent of the oil pumped, a veritable no-lose arrangement. International experts agree that Venezuela will never put its economic house in order until it comes to grips with its most insidious problem: its bloated, featherbedded, indolent, inefficient and corrupt bureaucracy, which has become the horror story of Latin America. Of Venezuela's 24 million population, 1.35 million, or 6.1%, are government employees, compared with 4.5% in Brazil and 2.2% in Colombia. As just one anecdotal example, when the state-owned airline Viasa went bankrupt in 1997, it was learned that it had employed 291 pilots for its 12-plane fleet, or 24 pilots per plane! If society had received the benefits from such a huge public workforce, it would be one thing, but the bureaucracy was padded with phantom employees and real employees who are notoriously lazy and inefficient. The effect has been to discourage foreign investors and lenders and to drive up inflation. Despite President Caldera's effort to reduce the public sector, the workforce actually *increased* by 50,000 in 1997. Why? Because of decentralization, laid-off federal workers entered the payrolls of state and local governments. But another reason may be linked to that traditional dark side of democracy: spoils and patronage. To gain or keep power, politicians swap jobs for votes. It will not be easy to dismantle something so institutionalized, but until it is done, the bureaucracy, will remain, in the words of Caldera's own planning minister, "A huge leech sucking society dry."

President Hugo Chávez was elected in 1998 to rescue the economy and battle the corruption that was such a drain. Economic statistics confirmed the severity of the crisis he inherited. Real GDP growth in 1997 was an illusionarily rosy 5.1%, but that gain followed negative growth of –0.4% the year before. In 1998, the year of the free-fall in world oil prices, growth declined by –0.3%, and in 1999, Chávez's first full year in office, it plummeted by a

Venezuela

devastating −6.1% despite skyrocketing oil prices. In 2000, Venezuela showed positive growth of only 3.2%, almost entirely the result of the continued high price of oil on the international markets, something Chávez had pushed at the September 2000 OPEC summit in Caracas, but it was not enough to overcome the losses of the previous three years. Growth in 2001 was 3.0%, but in 2002, largely because of the abortive coup and a crippling general strike that began on December 2 (see History), GDP fell again by 8.9%. Growth in 2003 was about 9% and in 2004 was a robust 16%, the highest in Latin America, but the growth was the result of the spiraling world price of petroleum. This should continue to benefit the economy in 2005; growth of 5% is forecast.

Unemployment rose steadily from 10.6% in 1997 to 13% in 1998 to 14.5% in 1999. It then began to taper off, to 13.2% in 2000 and 13% in 2001, still almost the highest in Latin America after Colombia and Argentina. In 2003, it was almost 20%, and in 2004 it was still 17%.

Inflation has declined from a paycheck-stealing 103.2% in 1996 to 12% in 2001. In 2003 it was back up to 27%, the highest in Latin America.

Oil wealth once gave Venezuela among the highest standards of living in the region, but inflation and negative economic growth have steadily eroded it. In 2004 it still had a per capita income of $4,400, the third-highest of the 20 Latin American republics, but it is inequitably distributed; 80% of the population lives below the poverty line. The public debt, meanwhile, has risen from 29% of GDP when Chávez became president to 39% in 2005.

It is small wonder that poverty-stricken Venezuelans, as well as a middle class that has seen its standard of living steadily erode, turned in desperation in 1998 to a charismatic demagogue who promised to rescue them. He has not; the percentage of Venezuelans living in extreme poverty has actually increased from 54% when Chávez became president to 60% in 2005. Even so, they voted against removing him in August 2004, apparently in the

hope that he will eventually rescue them in the long run.

The oil sector, as always, remains the country's greatest hope, indeed, its only one, because of its over-dependence on it. In 2004, oil accounted for 85% of total export value, $29 billion, which in turn accounted for 52% of government revenue. Three decades after oil production was nationalized, however, the state oil company, *PDVSA*, has become increasingly dependent on foreign companies once again to maintain production, which in 2005 was between 2.7 million and 3.1 million barrels per day, the fifth-highest in the world; about 1 million bpd was accounted for by foreign companies. Part of the reason for this is that Chávez largely politicized *PVDSA* after the crippling general strike of 2002–03; he fired more than 40% of *PDVSA* managers and workers and replaced them with political loyalists. The change has not improved efficiency. *PDVSA* has entered into joint ventures with U.S., British, Dutch, Spanish and Brazilian oil firms to bring production up to 5 million bpd by 2009. With the price of oil at $60 in mid-2005, it has also become economically feasible to exploit the heavy crude in the Orinoco tar belt. Foreign firms will also engage in offshore exploration, and natural gas production is expected to increase as well.

The Future: President Chávez confounded his opponents at home and in Washington by surviving the long-sought effort to recall him at the ballot box. His winning margin in the August 2004 referendum, 59%, was identical to that of his reelection victory in July 2000. Love him or loathe him, he is what the majority of Venezuelans clearly want, having received three convincing mandates in six years. The opposition will now gear up for his next reelection in July 2006. With the economy rebounding, largely by virtue of skyrocketing world oil prices, it seems doubtful he will lose much if any popularity between now and then, and the opposition is now in such disarray that it is unlikely it can field a meaningful challenge anyway.

Chávez is reminiscent of Argentina's Juan Perón, a charismatic military man who became what can only be called a democratically elected populist despot, who used legal and economic maneuvers to intimidate political opponents and the independent opposition press. The so-called Radio and Television Social Responsibility Law Chávez signed into effect in December 2004 is just one more nail in the coffin of free expression in Venezuela. As has happened under other repressive regimes, the Venezuelan broadcast media now will likely begin censoring themselves. Under the vaguely worded law, a legitimate exposé of government corruption could be construed as "inciting disruption of public order," thereby justifying the revocation of a station's license. Media owners brought some of their troubles upon themselves by unquestionably biased and sometimes irresponsible reporting, but as *The Economist* observed in a report in its March 12, 2005, edition, "the government's cure is worse than the disease." The crackdown on peaceful forms of protests, even the traditional banging of pots and pans, is equally disturbing.

An intriguing thing about turbulent Venezuela is that it is one of only two countries in Latin America where support for democracy has *increased* since 1996 in the perennial *Latinobarómetro* survey of 17 countries for *The Economist*. In 1996, 62% of Venezuelans said they believed that democracy was preferable to any other form of government. In 2003, at the height of the turmoil over the economy and the recall drive, that figure was 67%. In 2004, during the recall referendum campaign, it jumped to 74%. The 12-point increase is the greatest in Latin America. By the same token, the percentage of those who believe that an authoritarian form of government is sometimes preferable to democracy declined, from 19% in 1996 to 15% in 2003 and just 11% in 2004.

Venezuelans evidently still have faith in democracy; the question is, is Venezuelan democracy becoming a "tyranny of the majority" with little regard for opposition rights and viewpoints?

**Wall of the Thousand Columns
(top of the Auyán-Tepui)**

Smaller Nations and Dependent Territories of Latin America

HAITI

DOMINICAN REPUBLIC

PUERTO RICO

CARIBBEAN SEA

COLOMBIA

ARUBA (Neth.)

BONAIRE (Neth.)

CURACAO (Neth.)

VENEZUELA

0   100 Miles

CARICOM

Many of the smaller nations and dependent territories of Latin America lie in the Caribbean area and in Central America. They grouped together into the Caribbean Community, or CARICOM, in 1973. Originally intended as a common market encompassing member nations, the organization has become largely ineffective as a political confederation.

CARICOM now includes 15 members in the political community: Antigua and Barbuda, the Bahamas, Barbados, Belize, Dominica, Grenada, Guyana, Haiti, Jamaica, Montserrat, St. Lucia, St. Kitts and Nevis, St. Vincent and the Grenadines, Suriname and Trinidad and Tobago. The Bahamas is not a member of the common market. Associate members are Anguilla, Bermuda, the British Virgin Islands, the Cayman Islands and the Turks and Caicos.

What was supposed to be a mutually tariff-free organization has been beset, particularly in the 1980s, by trade limitations made necessary by adverse economic conditions generally and, more particularly, within member nations. Member nations have a common currency, the East Caribbean dollar; the exchange rate is officially pegged at $1.00 U.S. = EC$2.70. There are fluctuations from one country to another, however. Since most members produce large quantities of sugar, they have been hurt by lower import quotas allowed by the United States, which traditionally had been their biggest customer. More recently, the European Community also has stopped buying sugar at favorable prices.

At a meeting in October 1992 held in Trinidad, chiefs of state discussed means of lowering intra–member tariffs. Although the purpose of the organization was originally to lower rates, they had been gradu-

ally inched higher by members who individually sought trade advantages. Initial reductions from 45% to 35% were agreed upon, with annual reductions to follow in years to come.

ST. THOMAS

BRITISH VIRGIN ISLANDS

ST. JOHN

U. S. VIRGIN ISLANDS

ST. CROIX

ANGUILLA

ST. MARTIN

ST. BARTHELEMY (Fr.)

SABA (Neth.)

ST. EUSTATIUS (Neth.)

ST. KITTS

NEVIS

REDONDA

BARBUDA

ANTIGUA

MONTSERRAT

ATLANTIC

OCEAN

GUADELOUPE

MARIE GALANTE

DOMINICA

MARTINIQUE

ST. LUCIA

Plans were made in 1993 for a pact between member nations that would provide for taxation of income at the place of its origin rather than the location where it is received; the agreement has not been finalized. Further complicating the economic picture has been the NAFTA treaty (Mexico, U.S., Canada) and the General Agreement on Tariffs and Trade (GATT), both lowering and/or abolishing tariffs.

Because of the relative political stability of most CARICOM countries and the success with offshore banking on many of them, they tended to enjoy favorable credit ratings, which led many of them to overborrow and to become heavily indebted. Of the 10 countries in the world with the highest debt as percentage of GDP in 2004, six are CARICOM members. In order of percentage, they are Guyana, St. Kitts and Nevis, Antigua and Barbuda, Dominica, Grenada and Belize.

Most of the members are heavily dependent on tourism for foreign exchange, and thus suffered from the fall in tourism following the September 11, 2001 terrorist attacks on the United States. That sector has recovered, but violent crime is frightening away tourists from such idyllic destinations as Barbados, St. Kitts and Nevis, and Trinidad and Tobago.

In 2001, 12 of the English-speaking countries and dependencies signed a treaty to establish the Caribbean Court of Justice in Port-of-Spain, Trinidad, which would replace the British Privy Council as the region's court of last resort. The court was formally established on April 16, 2005, although only two of the signatories, Barbados and Guyana, have enacted the necessary legislation to forward cases to the new court.

SOVEREIGN NATIONS

Antigua and Barbuda (Independent November 1, 1981)

The Bahamas (Independent July 10, 1973)

Barbados (Independent November 30, 1966)

Grenada (Independent February 7, 1974)

Dominica (Independent November 3, 1978)

St. Kitts and Nevis (Independent September 19, 1983)

St. Lucia (Independent February 22, 1979)

St. Vincent and the Grenadines (Independent October 27, 1979)

THE DEPENDENT TERRITORIES

British Virgin Islands (colony)

Anguilla (British Crown colony)

Cayman Islands (British colony)

ST. VINCENT

BARBADOS

GRENADINES

GRENADA

Falkland Islands (British colony)

Turks and Caicos (British colony)

Montserrat (British colony)

French Guiana (French overseas department)

Guadeloupe (French overseas department)

Martinique (French overseas department)

Puerto Rico (U.S. commonwealth)

U.S. Virgin Islands (territory)

TO

TRINIDAD

The Commonwealth of the Bahamas

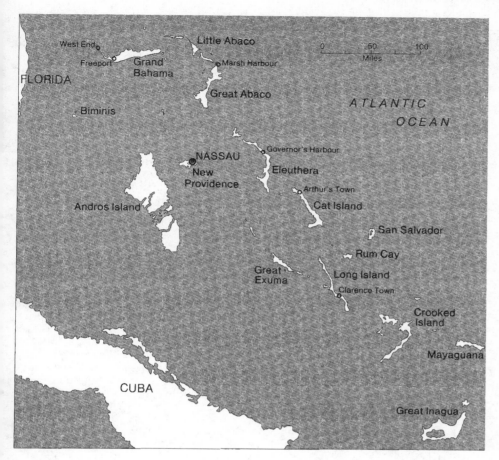

group of businessmen then in control of political and economic life on the islands ("The Bay Street Boys"). Continually gaining strength, the PLP was voted into office in 1967, and in 1972 it won 29 of 38 seats in the House of Assembly.

In July 1977, Bahamians voted in the island's first elections since independence in 1973. Although Prime Minister Lynden O. Pindling ("Black Moses") had been severely criticized for his economic policies, voters gave his PLP 31 of the 38 House seats. The government's "black power" image hurt the all-important tourist industry.

Pindling followed a trend found throughout the Caribbean: increased state control over the economy. The government forced many businesses to hire local workers to replace foreigners. New taxes were placed on foreign workers and on the sale of property to non-Bahamians. The government claimed that these programs produced a black middle class.

One impact of these measures was an end to the Bahamas' former status as a tax-free haven for the rich. Many of the so-called suitcase companies moved from the Bahamas to the Cayman Islands, where taxes remain low.

General elections in mid-1982 saw Prime Minister Pindling's PLP win with 53% of the vote and a majority in the House of Assembly. A similar victory occurred in 1987, despite repeated accusations that the prime minister was involved in drug trafficking, including eyewitness testimony linking him to Everette Bannister. The latter was known as "Mr. Fixit" of the Bahamas, and widely suspected as a drug smuggler.

In August 1992, elections resulted in victory for the opposition Free National

Area: 5,389 square miles, encompassing about 700 islands and islets only 35 of which are inhabited. In addition, there are over 2,000 cays which are low reefs of sand or coral.

Population: 310,000 in 2002.

Capital City: Nassau, on New Providence Island (Pop. 160,000, estimated).

Climate: Sunny and semi-tropical, with prevailing sea breezes; there is a hurricane season from June to October.

Official Language: English.

Ethnic Background: African (80%), White (10%), Mixed (10%).

Chief Commercial Ventures: Tourism, gambling, banking and drug smuggling.

Gross Domestic Product: U.S. $5.2 billion in 2002 ($17,000 per capita).

Former Colonial Status: Crown Colony of Great Britain, 1717–1964; self governing colony 1964–73.

Independence Date: July 10, 1973.

Chief of State: Queen Elizabeth II of Great Britain, represented by Governor-General Dame Ivy Dumont.

Head of Government: Perry Christie (b. August 21, 1943), prime minister (since May 2002).

Like the fragments of a broken piece of pottery, the Bahama Islands spread their natural beauty over about 100,000 square miles of ocean, making a gently curving arc 700 miles long from a point off the Florida coast down to the islands of Cuba, Haiti and the Dominican Republic. Only 35 of the islands are inhabited, with New Providence Island having more than half of the nation's population.

History: In October 1492 Christopher Columbus first sighted his New World at the island he promptly named San Salvador—"the Savior"—lying on the eastern edge of the island group. The Arawak Indians who populated these islands were exterminated over a brief period of years by Spanish slave traders, who shipped them off to the large Spanish-owned islands to work on the sugarcane plantations.

Thinly populated, the islands were virtually ignored for a century and a half until 1647 when a former governor of the English island of Bermuda sailed south and landed on the long, narrow strip of land called Eleuthera. He and his party were seeking greater religious freedom than was found on Bermuda. In the late 1930s and early 1940s the tourist boom started; today the islands receive more than a million and a half vacationers annually.

The Progressive Liberal Party (PLP) was formed in 1953 by Bahamians (pronounced Ba-haim-yans) who resisted rule by a small

**Former Prime Minister
Hubert A. Ingraham**

Bahamas

Prime Minister Perry Christie

Movement (FNM) and selection of Hubert Ingraham as prime minister, ending the 27-year rule of Pindling. An investigation of corruption in state owned enterprises during the Pindling years ensued. Ingraham's government also has stressed economic development through inviting foreign investment. The FNM was returned to power in general elections in March 1997, winning 35 seats to only four for the PLP.

In the general elections of May 2002, the PLP returned to power, winning 29 of 40 seats. Perry Christie became prime minister.

Culture: The people of the Bahamas, approximately 90% of whom are of African ancestry, are good-humored and generally prosperous. Most derive their living from the tourist trade. Among their many festivals is a special holiday—Junkanoo—a carnival not unlike the New Orleans Mardi Gras, which takes place during Christmas week. A sportsman's paradise, the islands provide excellent fishing, first-rate golf courses, a lively night life, visiting ballet companies, concerts and other theatrical productions. Goombay is a musical sound which is exclusively Bahamian; it blends a combination of goatskin drums, maracas and saws scraped with nails. The rhythm is fast-paced, exciting and non-stop.

Economy: Tourism is the number one industry, accounting for 60% of GDP. Most visitors are from the United States on excursion cruises out of Miami who stay one or two days. Europeans, who stay for an average of two weeks, spend much more, and strong efforts are being made to cultivate this trade. New hotels and vacation facilities have been constructed in the

"outer" islands. Tourism could be negatively affected by a new U.S. regulation in 2005 requiring U.S. citizens to have a passport to visit the Bahamas.

Ranking second to tourism is the international banking industry (15% of GDP), with more than 350 banks located on the islands. Because there is no income tax and great secrecy of financial transactions, the Bahamas has traditionally been a major tax haven and scene of widespread "laundering" of money from illegal drugs. The government has attempted to broaden the base of the economy by lowering import duties and other attractive incentives. Production of bauxite is important. Oil refining and transshipment from large ships to smaller vessels at new terminals is a major source of income, together with cement production.

Another source of income is "dummy" registration of ships, which can be returned to U.S. registry in the event of a war. Better terms are being offered than those of Liberia; Bahamian registry includes huge supertankers. Commercial fishing is also being expanded. Lavish and lively gambling casinos, in operation around the clock, see millions of dollars changing hands each week, but they have

felt the effect of U.S. state lotteries and legalized gambling.

Although new building developments are encroaching on the limited arable farmlands, "double cropping" each year in this warm climate makes most food plentiful, but imports have increased. Citrus fruit groves have replaced dairy farming as the most important sector of agriculture. Huge groves were planted to take advantage of severe frosts in Florida in the 1980s. Oranges, limes and other tropical fruit are plentiful and some are shipped to the United States. Other major exports include rum and salt.

Limitations on the economy include the presence of a large number of unskilled Haitians requiring high levels of social services.

The Bahamas posted a GDP in 2002 of $5.2 billion, a growth rate of 0.1% over 2001.

The Future: Blessed with the highest annual per capita income in Latin America, the Bahamas is very prosperous; this does not include a considerable amount of money generated by illicit drug trafficking. As in most prosperous places of the world, prices are high, including items that attract tourists.

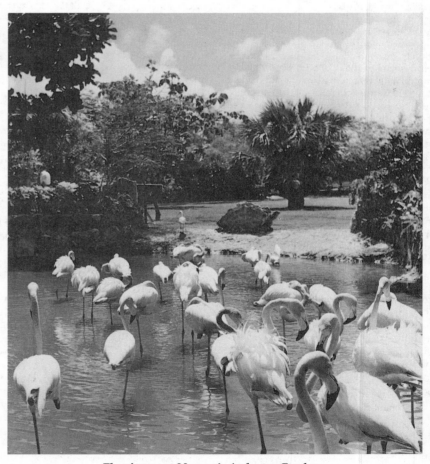

Flamingos at Nassau's Ardastra Gardens

Barbados

Prime Minister Owen Arthur

Area: 166 square miles.
Population: 276,607 in 2003.
Capital City: Bridgetown (Pop. 110,000, estimated).
Climate: Tropical, but pleasant, with moderate rainfall from June to December.
Ethnic Background: African (77%); mixed races (17%); European (6%).
Chief Commercial Products: Sugar, molasses, rum.
Gross Domestic Product: U.S.$2.6 billion in 2003 ($12,000 per capita).
Former Colonial Status: Colony of Great Britain, 1627–1966.
Independence Date: November 30, 1966.
Chief of State: Queen Elizabeth II of Great Britain, represented by Governor General Sir Clifford Husbands.
Head of Government: Rt. Hon. Owen Arthur (b. October 17, 1949), prime minister (since September 1994).

Barbados is an island 21 miles in length and 14.5 miles at its greatest width, lying in the Atlantic Ocean 100 miles east of the Lesser Antilles. The island is surrounded by colorful coral reefs and has but one natural harbor, Carlisle Bay, on the southwestern coast; the island's high elevation is Mt. Hillaby (1,115 feet) on the northern part. The land slopes to the south in gentle terraces. Temperatures of the tropical climate are moderated by sea breezes. Fertile soils and adequate rainfall have favored sugar production.

History: Barbados was occupied by the British in 1625 and remained continuously

in British control until its independence in 1966. Until the mid-19th century, sugar produced great wealth for the planters. The abolition of slavery in 1838 disturbed, but did not destroy, the island's economy. By comparison with other West Indian islands, Barbados' history has been tranquil. Riots occurred in 1876 and in 1937 because of efforts to federate the island with other British possessions. Ministerial government with partial self-rule was granted in 1954 by Britain. In 1961 Barbados became internally self-governing within the British Commonwealth. Full independence was achieved in 1966. The House of Assembly is the second-oldest legislative body in the Western Hemisphere, having first met in 1639.

Elections in 1971 were won by Prime Minister Errol Walton Barrow's Democratic Labor Party. Disturbed by the decline in the national economy, voters in 1976 turned to the Barbados Labor Party headed by J.M.G. (Tom) Adams. But in 1986 elections, in the presence of a declining economy, the people again turned to Barrow, who won a landslide victory in mid-1986, but died in June 1987. He was succeeded by his deputy, Erskine Sandiford.

Winning half the vote in January 1991, the DLP captured 18 of the 28 seats in the House of Assembly. Sandiford, who continued as prime minister, had promised to carry out the policies of his predecessor. The BLP had revitalized itself under the leadership of Owen Arthur since 1993 and promised competition based on the flagging economy in the next election.

Tax reforms, including a value-added tax, highlighted 1993, as did the development of tax reductions and incentives intended to boost export of small manufactured goods, including clothing.

In elections held in September 1994, the BLP ended the eight-year rule of the Democratic Labor Party winning 18 of the 28 seats in the House of Assembly, and Arthur became prime minister. Arthur and the BLP won a landslide reelection victory in January 1999, winning 26 seats. Two seats were added to the Assembly before the May 21, 2003 elections, which the BLP won again, taking 23 of the 30 seats.

Crime has become such a serious problem, threatening the vital tourism industry, that the Arthur government has followed Trinidad and Tobago's and Jamaica's lead in reinstating death by hanging. The last hanging was in 1984, but the British Privy Council, which has a five-judge panel that hears Caribbean appeals, commuted several sentences. In response, on April 16, 2005, 12 Caribbean members of the British Commonwealth established a new Caribbean appeals court of last resort, which will sit in Port-of-Spain Trinidad that will replace the Privy Council. So far, only Barbados and Guyana have ratified this change.

In February 2005, Prime Minister Arthur went a step further and advocated abolishing Barbados' recognition of the queen as chief of state and establishing a republic. He said the change would be submitted to voters in a referendum.

Barbados

Culture: The people of Barbados are descendants of British colonists and African slaves. They have a typically West Indian culture with a blend of English tradition. Their rhythmic dances and Calypso music, backed by steel drum bands (see Trinidad and Tobago), are in strange contrast to their love of cricket, always the joy of the British upper classes, but in Barbados the game of the people. African influence is as dominant as British, except in political and economic institutions, where the latter is maintained. Barbados is densely populated, with more than 1,500 people per square mile.

Economy: Sugar production and tourism account for a large percentage of the nation's foreign exchange earnings. Fish, fruit and beef output barely meet domestic needs of the nation, one of the world's most densely populated regions. In addition, a lack of mineral wealth hampers economic growth. To help reduce unemployment and racial tensions, the government has been making a concerted effort to involve its large, literate (97% adult literacy rate) black population in tourism to offset a decline in sugar production. Production of sugar has been steadily declining in the face of falling world prices.

The tourism boom of the 1990s has made Barbados a relatively prosperous little country, with an estimated per capita income in 2001 of $9,444, well above that of most of the 20 "Latin" republics. GDP grew by 3.7% in 2000, well above the 0.7% annual population growth rate. But it declined by .6% in 2001 and another 0.4% in 2002, reflecting the global drop in tourism in the wake of the September 11, 2001 terrorist attacks on the United States.

Unemployment remains stubbornly high: 12% in 1998, 10.6% in 1999, 9.3% in 2000, 9.9% in 2001 and 10.8% in 2002. Inflation was only 1.6% in 1999 and 2.4% in 2000, but shot up to 20.17% in 2002. The income tax rate, 25%, is one of the highest in the region, and Arthur promised in the 2003 election to reduce it to 22.5%.

Tourism, which now accounts for three-fourths of GDP, has helped offset the serious balance of trade deficit. In 2000, Barbados imported $1.03 billion in goods and exported only $286 million. However, the country's over-reliance on tourism became an issue in the 2003 elections, in which Prime Minister Owen Arthur pledged to diversify by encouraging small arts and crafts enterprises.

The Future: Persistent unemployment led to an increase in crime in the 1990s. Tourism has not been growing as rapidly as might be expected because of this problem. Establishing a republic may give Barbadians a greater sense of identity, but it will not solve their economic problems.

The Village of Bathsheba

Grenada

Area: 133 square miles, including the islets of Carricou and Petit Martinique in the Grenadines.

Population: 100,800 in 2004.

Capital City: St. George's (Pop. 34,000, est.).

Climate: Tropically rainy and dry, hot, with prevailing ocean breezes.

Official Language: English.

Ethnic Background: African.

Chief Commercial Products: Nutmeg, tropical agricultural products.

Gross Domestic Product: 734.33 million in Eastern Caribbean dollars in 2004, about US$273 million (EC$9,053 per capita, or US$3,365).

Former Colonial Status: Ruled alternately by French and British, 1650–1783; colony of Great Britain, 1783–1974.

Independence Date: February 7, 1974.

Chief of State: Queen Elizabeth II of Great Britain, represented by Governor-General Sir Daniel C. Williams.

Head of Government: Rt. Hon. Keith Mitchell (b. November 12, 1946), prime minister (since June 1995).

Prime Minister Keith Mitchell

Like a large pearl, Grenada (pronounced Greh-NAY-dah) is the southernmost of the Windward Island chain, lying peacefully at the edge of the Caribbean Sea and the Atlantic Ocean. Blessed with beautiful beaches, clear water and a pleasant (but tropical) climate, the island is 21 miles long from north to south and only 12 miles horizontally at its widest point. Grenada has heavily wooded mountains watered by many streams that feed the quiet, lush valleys. There is the calm of smooth beaches and the rockbound coasts where the surf pounds and churns endlessly.

History: Discovered in 1498 by Columbus, Grenada was originally inhabited by the Carib Indians. In the 1650s the island was colonized by the French, who established large tobacco plantations. England acquired Grenada in 1763 by the Treaty of Paris, under which (among other exchanges of territory) France ceded Canada to the English. The new rulers of the island imported slaves from Africa to work the sugarcane plantations.

For over 200 years, Grenada basked peacefully in obscurity, harvesting its crops and almost oblivious to the rest of the world. During this period it was administered as a separate British Colony until its membership in the short-lived West Indian Federation (1958-72). The federation collapsed partly because one key member, Trinidad, did not want to tie its own healthy economy to that of its poorer federation neighbors.

Elections held in 1972 brought an overwhelming victory to the Grenada United Labor Party of Premier Eric Gairy (13 out of 15 seats in the House of Representatives), whose major platform during the election was the complete independence of the island nation. As a result of talks in London soon afterward, a constitutional conference was set for May 1973.

Grenada gained its independence in 1974. The most prominent figure in the nation's politics since 1962, Gairy continued to control Grenada through his domination of powerful labor unions. However, his corrupt and brutal rule generated widespread resentment at home, while abroad he generated notoriety over his stated belief in UFOs. Opponents, led by the "new left" black-power New Jewel Movement, ousted him in 1979.

The new regime, headed by London-educated Maurice Bishop, 34, promptly dissolved Parliament and promised a new constitution that would make the island a "socialist democracy." Although it restricted personal liberties (no press freedom, no elections), the regime somewhat improved living conditions for the poor. Private enterprise remained largely intact.

In foreign affairs, Bishop embraced the Castro regime. Cuba responded with technical and military assistance for Grenada's new "People's Revolutionary Army."

The Reagan administration viewed the Grenada regime as a tool of Moscow via Cuba and imposed a blackout of the island. The government collapsed and anarchy ensued which was ended when a force of U.S. Marines and troops from other Caribbean nations and territories invaded. Several hundred Cuban troops were taken prisoner and returned to Cuba; vast amounts of Soviet and Cuban military equipment was found. The occupying force was withdrawn after elections were held in December 1984.

Herbert Blaize, leader of the New National Party, was selected prime minister over a coalition government that split in 1989; Blaize died shortly thereafter. Inconclusive elections in 1990 resulted in Nicholas Braithwaite being selected to lead yet another coalition government. He stumbled badly in 1993, failing to find economic measures acceptable to the media and people, and his resignation was demanded. He vowed to stay until 1995 elections, but in 1994 resigned as head of the National Democratic Congress.

Contrary to his promise, Braithwaite resigned on February 1, 1995. In June elections, the New National Party (NNP) led by former Works and Communications Minister Keith Mitchell, defeated the NDC, taking eight of the 15 seats in the House of Representatives.

As prime minister, Mitchell embarked on a successful campaign to lure foreign investors to the island, but there were signs that his government corrupted itself in the awarding of public works contracts. When two of his ministers defected to the opposition in late 1998 over the allegations of corruption, Mitchell lost his one-seat majority and was forced to call general elections 18 months early. In the election held on January 18, 1999, voters resoundingly indicated they were more concerned about the jobs Mitchell had brought to the island than with the corruption charges: The NNP won all 15 seats in the House. Mitchell himself received 89% in his district. The leader of one opposition party complained that with the snap election and short six-week campaign, "We were caught with our pants down."

The latest election was held on November 27, 2003, and the NNP was returned

357

Grenada

to power but with only a one-seat majority of 8–7.

Grenada was hit harder than any other country by Hurricane Ivan in September 2004, the most powerful storm in the Caribbean in at least 20 years. An estimated 85% of the homes and other buildings on the island, including Mitchell's home and the prison, were destroyed or damaged.

Culture: The people of Grenada, 95% of whom are black or mulatto, are a fun-loving and hard-working group. Grenada's capital and main port, St. George's, rises steeply from the bay and the red-roofed houses are painted in pastel shades of pink and green. Nightlife in the city is often punctuated by continuous music from colorful Calypso bands.

Economy: Grenada is called the Isle of Spice, and for centuries its economy has been based on its nutmeg. It is presently the world's second-largest exporter of this product. Other exports include bananas, sugar, cacao and mace. The tourist industry is vital to the island's economic health. Most exports go to EC countries. An annual U.S. assistance package will be necessary indefinitely. Grenada and the Windward Islands were greatly favored by EC import limitations on bananas from other Caribbean sources.

GDP grew by only 0.6% in 2002, due in part to the general downturn in tourism following the September 11, 2001, terrorist attacks on the United States. By 2004 it was back up to 4%. Grenada has a public debt that in 2004 was 112% of GDP, the eighth highest in the world. The devastation of Hurricane Ivan in September 2004 was an economic catastrophe that is still being calculated.

The Future: Grenada observed the 20th anniversary of the 1983 invasion in October 2003. Few question that the country is better off now than it was then, and Parliament paid homage to former President Ronald Reagan when he died in June 2004. However, the sluggish economy and corruption remain problems that need to be addressed. Hurricane Ivan was a blow the country could ill afford, and it may take several years to recover.

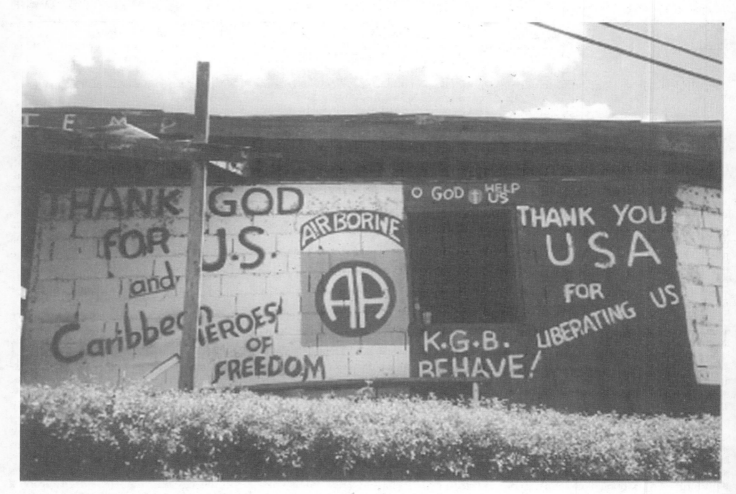

Graffiti in Grenada following U.S. invasion in 1983

Photo by Susan L. Thompson

THE DEPENDENT TERRITORIES

The dependencies in Latin America have a wide variety of relationships with the nations controlling them. Those of Great Britain have various degrees of internal self-government. In the Caribbean area, the British attempt to unite several territories into the West Indian Federation failed, and Barbados, Guyana and Jamaica became sovereign nations shortly thereafter.

The islands of Guadeloupe and Martinique, and mainland French Guiana, are governed as *départments* of France. The Netherlands Antilles are internally self-governing. Puerto Rico is a commonwealth within the United States that possesses internal autonomy, and the U.S. Virgin Islands are federally administered territories of the United States. The Falkland Islands, lying off the coast of Argentina, are governed by the British and claimed by the Argentines.

Fort-de-France, Martinique; Mt. Pelee looms behind the capital. *Photo by Miller B. Spangler*

British dependencies

CAYMAN, TURKS AND CAICOS ISLANDS

Area: 269 square miles.
Population: 28,000 (estimated).
Administrative Capital: Georgetown (Pop. 4,700, estimated).
Heads of Government: Michael Gore (Caymans); Michael Bradley (Turks and Caicos), Governors.

These two groups of islands were administered by the Governor of Jamaica until 1962 when they were placed under the British Colonial Office. With the closing of the Colonial Office, administration passed to the Commonwealth Relations Office. The Cayman Islands lie midway between Jamaica and the western tip of Cuba. Turks and Caicos Islands are geographically a portion of the Bahamas. There are some 35 small islands in these groups, of which only eight are populated. The predominantly black and mulatto people eke a meager existence from fishing and the production of salt. Because of their limited resources, these islands cannot sustain themselves as independent nations. The Cayman Islands have become increasingly popular as a tax haven since the Bahamian government ended tax exempt status there for foreign corporations. There are numerous banks catering to "commerce," which means "laundering" money, the source of which is desired to be secret—usually narcotics. Crime associated with drug trade is increasing sharply. There are 532 banks, 80 of which actually have offices in the islands—one for every 53 people; more than 25,000 companies are registered to do business.

A five-member executive council is elected in the Caymans; political activity is minimal. Turks and Caicos Islands have a 20-member Legislative Council and an eight-member executive council.

FALKLAND ISLANDS

Area: 4,618 square miles.
Population: 2,600 (estimated).
Administrative Capital: Port Stanley
Head of Government: William H. Fullerton, Governor.

The Falkland Islands are made up of two large and 200 small islands, treeless, desolate and windswept, which lie off the southern tip of Argentina in the Atlantic Ocean.

The British discovered and named the islands in 1690; the French established a small colony on one of the larger islands in 1764 and the British started a settlement on the other large island in the following year. France gave up its possession to Spain in 1767 and the Spanish drove the British from the island they occupied. The territory was abandoned by the Spanish in 1811, and Argentina, after gaining independence, established a small colony on the islands in 1824. This settlement was destroyed by the U.S. Navy in 1831 in retaliation for Argentine harassment of whaling ships from Boston.

The British again gained possession of the islands in 1833 and have held them since that time. Argentina claims the islands based on its effort of 1824. Originally of strategic importance because of their closeness to the Atlantic-Pacific sea route around the Cape, with the opening of the Panama Canal their value greatly decreased. However, the British Navy successfully struck from the islands against the German Navy in both world wars.

The islands are an economic liability to Britain, but are still a symbol of its sovereignty, not to be relinquished. When Argentina suddenly invaded the Falklands in April 1982, Britain met the challenge head on . . . successfully. A later dispute was resolved when Britain and Argentina agreed upon a joint, 200-mile fishing boundary around the islands calculated to exclude Japan, Russia and Taiwan.

Development of oil deposits within the 200-mile radius, and a new Argentine constitution reaffirming sovereignty over what it calls the *Islas Malvinas*, have created problems that will be difficult to solve.

French dependencies

FRENCH GUIANA

Area: 34,740 square miles.
Population: 125,000 (estimated).
Administrative Capital: Cayenne (Pop. 32,000, estimated).
Head of Government: Jean-François Corden, Prefect.

French Guiana lies on the north coast of South America, north of Brazil and east of Suriname. The land consists of fertile, low plains along the coast, rising to the Tumuc-Humac Mountains on the Brazilian frontier. The Isles of Salut (Enfant Perdu, Remire and Ile du Diable—Devil's Island), lying off the coast, form part of the territory administered as a French *département*. The climate is tropical, with an average temperature of 80°F. The rainy season is from November to July, with the heaviest downfall in May.

Guiana was awarded to France in 1667, attacked by the British in the same year, taken by the Dutch in 1676 and retaken by France in the same year. In 1809 it was seized by a joint British-Portuguese effort based in Brazil, and remained under Brazilian occupation until 1817, when the French regained control. Gold was discovered in 1853, inspiring disputes with Brazil and Suriname which were not set-tled until 1915. The colony is best known for its infamous prison colony, which was closed in 1945.

Guiana has fertile soils, 750,000 acres of land suitable for stock raising, vast resources of timber and coastal waters abounding in shrimp and fish. However, only some 12,000 acres are cultivated and most foodstuffs are imported. The population consists of creoles (descended from African black ancestors), Europeans, Chinese and a few native Indians. The principal products are shrimp, gold, hardwood and rum. French Guiana has adequate resources to support itself as an independent state, but little or no effort has been made to exploit these resources.

For a brief interval, French Guiana loomed in France as a 20th century *El Dorado*. During a three-day visit to Guiana in 1975, Olivier Stirn, minister of territories, announced a resettlement plan for the French colony, one part of which would initially require 10,000 settlers to develop a pulp and lumber industry. The plan was adversely received by Guiana local leadership and was condemned by 11 Caribbean chiefs of state. Nevertheless, French immigration to the territory proceeded. A satellite-launching base was constructed at Kourou, and continental French now constitute about a third of the population of Guiana. They have gathered in an ultra-conservative political movement, the *Front National*, and, of course, oppose independence; the local movement for this faded quickly.

Political expression is mainly through the Guianese Socialist Party affiliated with the Socialist Party in France and the opposition Rally for the Republic, a Gaullist party affiliated with that of France. The prefect governs with the advice and consent of a General Council and a Regional Council.

Vast unused resources remain under the dense rain forest that covers more than 70% of the land area. Intense farming is done by the industrious Hmong people of Laos who were transplanted here more than three decades ago. Timber and fish are the most important exports. Hydro-electric installations completed in 1993 provide all electricity needed, albeit at a substantial cost in local animal and bird life. As in so many other tropical settings of the region, social and economic unrest is at a high level and probably has no "cure."

GUADELOUPE

Area: 657 square miles.
Population: 400,000 (estimated).
Administrative Capital: Basse-Terre (Pop. 21,000, estimated).
Head of Government: Franck Perriez, Prefect.

Guadeloupe consists of two islands separated by a narrow channel. Five small French islands in the Lesser Antilles are administered as a part of the Department of Guadeloupe (Marie Galante, Les Saintes, Desirade, St. Barthelemy and one-half of St. Martin).

Guadeloupe dependencies are occupied by the white descendants of Norman and Breton fishermen (and pirates) who settled there 300 years ago—the population is predominantly of mixed European and African derivation. The climate is tropical, with the rainy season extending from July to December.

Guadeloupe's principal products are bananas, sugar, rum, coffee, cocoa and tourism. Although this is an island of call for Caribbean cruises, it has excellent accommodations for extended vacations. The balance of trade is unfavor-able and the *département* has little hope for independence.

The people are apparently content with a Regional Council and a General Council, the latter of which exercises executive power. Elections are on a party basis and are spirited; the one in 1992 had to be voided because of "irregularities." The right wing prevailed in a re-run.

A new World Trade Center opened on Guadeloupe in 1994 and is the seat of numerous efforts to boost Euro-Caribbean trade.

MARTINIQUE

Area: 420 square miles.
Population: 380,000 (estimated).
Administrative Capital: Fort-de-France (Pop. 120,000, estimated).
Head of Government: Michel Morin, Prefect.

Martinique has been in French possession since 1635 except for two short periods of British occupation. Mountainous, with Mt. Pelee reaching 4,800 feet, its climate is tropical; the rainy season extends from July to December; violent hurricanes are frequent during this period. An eruption of Mt. Pelee in 1906 killed 10,000 people. The population is predominantly of mixed European and African origin.

Martinique's principal products are sugar, rum, bananas and other tropical fruits. This island also is an attractive tourist haven, with modern facilities available widely. Cattle raising is a steady industry, but presently produces enough for local consumption only. Politics in the 1990s have been dominated by conservatives.

NETHERLANDS ANTILLES

Area: 395 square miles.
Population: 260,000 (estimated).
Administrative Capital: Willemstad (Pop. 75,000, estimated).

The Netherlands Antilles consist of two groups of three islands each—one group lies off the north coast of Venezuela; the other lies just east of the Virgin Islands. Fully autonomous in internal affairs since 1954, the islands are organized into four self-governing communities—Aruba, Bonaire, Curaçao, and the Leeward Islands (southern portion of St. Martin, St. Eustatius and Saba). The population consists of about one third European ancestry and two thirds of mixed blood. Dutch is the official language. Spanish, English and a local *lingua franca* called Papamiento are

also spoken. All of the islands are popular calls for cruise ships, and have, with the exception of St. Eustatius and Saba, have good facilities for extended vacations.

The economy of the Netherlands Antilles is based on the large oil refineries on Curaçao and Aruba. Almost all articles for consumption must be imported because fishing does not fill local needs and an arid climate coupled with poor soil do not support agriculture. The islands of Bonaire, St. Martin, St. Eustatius and Saba are of little economic importance. Despite some discontent among the non-European population, it is not likely that the islands will seek independence. Aruba was granted separate status from the other islands in 1986, with full independence set for 1996.

The lingering question of independence was probably laid to rest by balloting in 1993 on Curaçao and in 1994 on the remaining islands. Voters chose to remain a Dutch territory by a large majority, rejecting even the semi-independence that had been granted to Aruba. They undoubtedly wished a continuation of benefits derived from an annual Dutch subsidy of U.S. $160 million. Aruba, originally scheduled to become completely independent in 1996, instead continues in "special status."

The island of Curaçao has evidently been chosen as a drug outlet by Colombian, Surinamese and Dutch traffickers—rivals and their hired thugs fought pitched battles in late 1993.

Willemstad, Curaçao

United States dependencies

El Morro fortress for centuries guarded the entrance to the harbor at San Juan.

PUERTO RICO

Area: 3,423 square miles.
Population: 3,808,610 (2000 census).
Capital: San Juan (Pop. 2,450,292 in 2000, greater metropolitan area).
Per capita annual income: U.S. $8,000.
Head of Government: Governor Aníbal Acevedo Vila (since January 2, 2005).

The easternmost and smallest island of the Greater Antilles, Puerto Rico is somewhat rectangular in shape, measuring 111 miles from east to west and about 36 miles north to south at its widest point; it includes four offshore islands, two of which are populated. Centrally located at almost the middle of approximately 7,000 tropical islands, most of them very tiny, hardly more than atolls, much of the island is mountainous or hilly—three quarters of the terrain is too steep for large-scale, mechanized cultivation. Puerto Rico is a *commonwealth* of the United States—while not a state, it is legally within the territorial jurisdiction of the U.S. The people are by language and culture part of the Caribbean and Latin America. Since it is not a state, Puerto Rico has no voting representation in Congress, but does have an elected resident

commissioner with a four-year term who holds a seat, can speak out on issues, but does not have a vote. Otherwise, he enjoys the same privileges and immunities of other congressmen.

History: Puerto Rico was discovered by Christopher Columbus in 1493. There were at least three native cultures on the island, mostly of Arawak origin from the South American mainland. They were a peaceful group, quickly enslaved by the Spaniards and eventually died out as a

race. The explorer claimed the island for Spain and named it San Juan Bautista (St. John the Baptist). After many years of colonization, the island was given the name Puerto Rico (Rich Port) and its capital city became San Juan.

Its first governor was Juan Ponce de León, who was later to discover Florida in his fabled search for the Fountain of Youth. Almost from the time of early colonization, Puerto Rico was a military target due to its strategic location. The French, British and Dutch were repelled

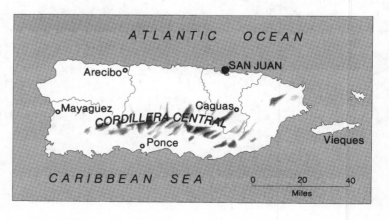

362

over the centuries and massive fortifications were erected by Spain to guard the harbor at San Juan. The 1700s up until the early 1800s were rather uneventful, and during Latin American wars for independence, Puerto Rico remained faithful to Spain. Sugar, tobacco and coffee produced on the island found a ready market in the United States, as did its flourishing rum industry. Toward the middle of the 1800s Puerto Rican social consciousness came slowly to life. In 1868 there was a revolution against Spain, which was quickly snuffed out.

Slavery was finally abolished in 1873. As the 19th century came to a close, Spain granted Puerto Rico broad powers of self-rule, but only days after the new government began to assume its duties the Spanish-American war broke out. The U.S. public had been appalled by the stories of harsh treatment of Cuban revolutionaries, which caused a growing anti-Spanish sentiment in the United States, carefully fed by the press, which printed sensational stories of supposed atrocities. After the battleship *U.S.S. Maine* was mysteriously blown up in Havana harbor on February 15, 1898, the United States declared war on Spain. One of the operations was the invasion of Puerto Rico by American forces under General Nelson A. Miles the following July.

The treaty of peace signed in Paris in December after the brief conflict forced Spain to withdraw from Cuba, and ceded to the United States were Puerto Rico, Guam and the Philippines. The Spanish-American war established the United States as a world power. A military government was set up in Puerto Rico, but in 1900 the first civil government was established. It gave the federal government full control over island affairs, with the president appointing the governor, the members of the Executive Council (legislature) and the island's Supreme Court. Members of the House of Delegates, which functioned as a second legislative branch, were popularly elected. All trade barriers with the United States were removed as Puerto Rico was placed within existing U.S. tariff walls. The island, the Philippines and Guam, were collectively designated an "unincorporated territory."

With the advent of civil government, men were again allowed the right to vote as they had under Spain. Also, the island was made exempt from paying federal taxes, duties and excise taxes collected in Puerto Rico on foreign products and on Puerto Rican products sold in the United States, all of which were handed over to the island treasury. Between 1900 and 1925, foreign trade increased from $16 million to $178 million annually; it now is a healthy $13.2 billion. A corresponding population increase occurred: from some 950,000 in 1905 to 1.3 million in 1921.

There was a rapid extension of the school system, accompanied by a reduction in illiteracy from about 90% to less than 50%. A more worrisome condition was the gradual concentration of wealth in fewer hands. Two half-mile tunnels were opened in 1909 through the mountains that provided irrigation for the south side of the island, very dry due to the constant trade winds. On the eve of World War I, Congress granted U.S. citizenship to Puerto Ricans and replaced the appointed Executive Council with a popularly elected Senate. However, the island remained exempt from federal taxes and was allowed to design its own tax system and raise its own revenues. Trade with the United States grew by leaps and bounds so that the island became one of the top consumers of U.S. goods in Latin America.

When the United States declared war on Germany in 1917, the Selective Service Act was extended to Puerto Rico by request of the island's government and some 18,000 men were inducted into service. As a result, Puerto Ricans were granted U.S. citizenship that same year. During the first decades of the 20th century, Puerto Rico developed its sugar production, but most of the profits went to the absentee landlords in the United States. By the time of the Great Depression of 1929, most Puerto Ricans were caught up in a web of poverty. There was mass unemployment, malnutrition and deteriorating health conditions. By 1930, unemployment stood at a frightening 60%. When the Roosevelt administration came into office in 1933, it began to extend a large measure of relief to the stricken land. Because of poor economic conditions, a strong nationalist movement emerged seeking complete independence from the United States. The movement reached its peak when in 1937 police fired on a nationalist demonstration in the southern city of Ponce, killing 20 people.

Commonwealth Status

Puerto Rico played an important defense role in the Caribbean region during World War II. President Truman appointed a Puerto Rican governor for the island in 1946 and one year later signed a law permitting it to elect its own governor. In 1948, voters elected Luis Muñoz-Marín of the Popular Democratic Party (*PDP*). Further, in 1950 an act of the U.S. Congress allowed the island to draft its own constitution, which was approved with amendments by the Congress and then accepted in a plebiscite by the people in 1952. Governor Muñoz-Marín claimed the constitutional process and plebiscite were an act of self-determination of the Puerto Rican people, thus marking an end to American colonial rule. The Commonwealth was officially established on July 25, 1952, the 54th anniversary of the day the U.S. forces landed in 1898.

Despite the move toward self-determination, a small but aggressive minority of "nationalists" clamored for full independence, eventually resorting to terrorism. A band of nationalists attempted to assassinate President Truman in a bloody shootout in Washington in 1951. Three years later, nationalist terrorists opened fire from the gallery of the U.S. House of Representatives, wounding five congressmen. Militant nationalism resurfaced in the 1970s with the creation of the so-called Armed Forces of National Liberation, or *FALN*. Between 1974 and 1983, the *FALN* was believed responsible for 130 terrorist bombings in the continental United States that killed six people and wounded dozens of others. The worst bombing, on a tavern in New York's Greenwich Village in 1975, killed four.

The government of Muñoz-Marín laid the foundations for the industrial development of the island, aided by important incentives at home and aggressive promotion abroad. The program, called "Operation Bootstrap," was one of the 20th century's great success stories—Puerto Rico's economy was transformed from one based on a single crop (sugar) to a broadly-based manufacturing one, creating a strong middle class and one of the highest standards of living in all of Latin America. Per capita income has grown from about $120 per year in 1940 to more than $8,000 today. Further, university and college enrollment soared from about 5,000 students in 1945 to about 150,000 by the mid-1980s.

Former Governor Pedro J. Rosselló

Puerto Rico

Street scene in Ponce, Puerto Rico's second largest city

Photo by Miller B. Spangler

In a 1967 plebiscite, 60% of the voters favored continuation and improvement of the commonwealth status with the United States while 38% voted for statehood. The major independence groups boycotted the plebiscite. The pro-statehood New Progressive Party (*PNP*) won the governorship in 1968, winning again in 1976 and 1980. The pro-commonwealth *PDP* won in 1972, 1984 and 1988. These frequent changes in power produced a virtual stalemate on the political status of the island. This still goes on; the effect is to discourage investment in job producing facilities in Puerto Rico that otherwise would occur.

In spite of then-President Bush's support for Puerto Rican statehood, the matter was bottled up in Congress in 1989–91; the Republicans did not wish to give Democrats an opportunity to tighten their hold on both houses of Congress. In a gesture of defiance, Puerto Rico enacted a measure providing that Spanish was the *only* official language. It was later repealed by a measure in 1993 recognizing both Spanish and English. Only the wealthy and middle-class educated are genuinely bilingual.

Roselló and Referendums

In the 1992 elections, the *PNP* and its candidate for governor, Pedro J. Rosselló, again ran on a platform advocating statehood. The *PDP* favored continuing commonwealth status, and was soundly trounced in its worst defeat in its 54-year history. The victors promised and delivered another referendum (non-binding) on statehood, which was held in November 1993. Fully 73% of the electorate participated and the result was 48.4% for commonwealth status and 46.2% for an application for statehood. Less than 5% favored independence. Rosselló, ignoring the result, insisted that the struggle for statehood would go on.

Rosselló was reelected in November 1996, which he interpreted as a mandate to continue his quest for statehood. Responding to his persistent efforts, the U.S. House of Representatives voted in March 1998 for a *binding* referendum that ostensibly would decide the issue once and for all; the measure passed by only one vote, however, and the Senate failed to follow up.

Marking the 100th anniversary of U.S. occupation in July 1998, Rosselló then called for yet another non-binding referendum for December 13. Five options were listed on the complicated ballot: statehood, independence, an ambiguous "free association," continued commonwealth and "none of the above." The opposition *PDP*, however, advocated instead what it called an "enhanced commonwealth" by which Puerto Rico could enter into treaties with other nations and would have the power to annul federal laws, def-

initely the best of both worlds but which likely would never win congressional approval. As its "enhanced commonwealth" was not on the ballot, the *PDP* campaigned vigorously for "none of the above." The 1998 referendum was a near-duplicate of the 1993 plebiscite, only this time "none of the above" won a slim but absolute majority of 50.2%, while the vote for statehood was virtually unchanged at 46.5%. Independence received 2.5%, "free association" 0.3% and commonwealth only 0.1%. This sent the ambiguous message that Puerto Ricans were ready to change their status, but didn't yet know what that status should be.

Meanwhile, a corruption scandal exploded in March 1999 that tarnished Rosselló's reputation and credibility and was to prove a major political liability for the *PNP* in the 2000 elections. The former comptroller of the San Juan AIDS Institute—an entity Rosselló had approved in 1987 when he was health director of San Juan—pleaded guilty to conspiracy and testified that $2.2 million in federal funds intended for AIDS victims had been diverted to the political campaigns of both the *PNP* and *PDP*, including Rosselló, who allegedly received $250,000 for his 1992 campaign. Rosselló dismissed the allegations as a "character assassination." Although the governor himself was never indicted, he was forced to undergo the ignominy of appearing on the witness stand in the trials that ended in 2000 with the convictions of two high-ranking officials.

Then, in August 2000, 18 *PNP* officials, including two mayors, were indicted on federal charges that they received $800,000 in campaign donations in exchange for $56 million in government contracts. Several of them also were convicted in 2001.

Rosselló also stood accused by pro-*PDP* newspapers of employing the time-honored cudgel of Latin American dictators of withholding government advertising from them. *El Nuevo Día*, which lost its government advertising after several investigative articles on corruption, sued the government in 1997. In May 1999, the paper and the government reached a settlement by which the government restored the advertising, established a policy for distributing advertising fairly and expressed its respect for press freedom, but admitted no wrongdoing; the paper, meanwhile, agreed to offer the government discounted rates.

In September 1999, President Clinton sparked controversy with the unexpected announcement that he had offered clemency to 12 convicted members of the *FALN* and another militant group, the *Macheteros*, or machete wielders, in exchange for their promise to renounce terrorism. None had been convicted of any of the bombings of the 1970s and '80s, but on charges of seditious conspiracy and weapons possession. Nine of the prisoners accepted the clemency offer, and returned to heroes' welcomes in Puerto Rico. Even Governor Rosselló supported Clinton's offer. Not so the Republican-controlled Congress, which passed a stinging censure resolution against the president for his perceived softness on terrorists. Other critics alleged the president offered the clemency bid in order to help his wife, Hillary, win Puerto Rican votes in her successful campaign for the U.S. Senate from New York in 2000.

Independence activists seized the national spotlight again in 1999 and 2000 with their support for the 9,100 residents of the island of Vieques, who were protesting the island's use by the U.S. Navy as a bombing and gunnery range. The Navy had bombarded Vieques since 1941, but residents now complained that they were endangered by the exercises and by unexploded ordnance. Public protests began when a resident of the island was killed by a stray bomb in April 1999. In December, President Clinton announced a five-year withdrawal plan to placate the islanders. But they were not placated. In May 2000, 200 residents staged a nonviolent occupation of the range, forcing federal agents to take them into custody for trespassing on federal property. The occu-

Former Governor Sila María Calderón

pation and arrests became the focus of national and international media attention.

The Vieques controversy continued into 2001, with more protesters being arrested and others seeking redress in federal court to enjoin the Navy from using the range. But in May 2001, a federal court ruled in favor of the Navy, which resumed target practice. Even pro-commonwealth Puerto Ricans were offended by the Navy's arrogance in disregarding the wishes of the island's residents. Also in May, the Rev. Al Sharpton, a controversial civil rights activist from New York City, who like Mrs. Clinton is believed to be currying favor among Puerto Rican voters there for a possible presidential run, was among several protesters arrested on Vieques for trespassing on the range.

A referendum was held in July 2001, in which the island's residents voted 68% for the Navy to leave immediately. President George W. Bush announced that the Navy would abandon Vieques in 2003—not soon enough for many critics.

First Woman Governor

The corruption scandals of the Rosselló administration forced him to decide, wisely, not to seek a third term. Instead, the wounded *PNP* nominated Carlos Pesquera, a former secretary of transportation and public works, while the *PDP* nominated a woman, Sila María Calderón; the Puerto Rican Independence Party (*PIP*) nominated Rubén Berrios.

Despite the corruption scandals, polls showed the race a dead heat between Pesquera and Calderón. The Vieques issue overshadowed the campaign, with Pesquera largely avoiding it, Berrios trumpeting it and Calderón making only vague statements in support of the island's residents.

An extraneous issue was interjected into the campaign in July when a pro-statehood federal judge in San Juan ruled in favor of 11 residents who demanded the right to vote in the U.S. presidential election between Al Gore and George W. Bush. The *PDP* and the *PIP* challenged the ruling, and in October the 1st U.S. Circuit Court of Appeals in Boston ruled that Puerto Ricans did not have that constitutional right.

The gubernatorial election was another reminder of how divided Puerto Ricans are on the statehood issue, and the results were a virtual replay of the 1998 referendum: Calderón narrowly won with 48.5% of the vote to 46.1% for Pesquera and 4.9% for Berrios. The *PDP* also won clear majorities in the House and Senate. However, the *PNP*'s Jorge Santini recaptured the mayoralty of San Juan after 12 years of *PDP* control, making him a rising star in the party.

After her inauguration on January 2, 2001, as Puerto Rico's first woman governor, Calderón suddenly became far more strident in demanding that the Navy leave Vieques. She discussed the issue with President George W. Bush in Washington soon after his own inauguration.

The Vieques controversy continued to simmer for two years. In August 2002, the Navy notified Calderón that it would resume bombing exercises on the island, which brought a tart rebuke from the governor. But in October, the Navy did an about-face and announced that it would abandon Vieques the following May. It kept its word, and on May 1, 2003, the Navy's bombing range—along with six decades' worth of unexploded ordnance—reverted to Puerto Rican control. Jubilant celebrations, some of which turned ugly, marked the transition. The island already had begun attracting tourists before May 1; in February 2003 the Wyndham hotel chain opened a 256-room resort. Calderón sought federal help in cleaning up the old bombing range.

Political scandals continued to stain both major parties. In October 2001, the FBI arrested the *PDP* mayor of the San Juan suburb of Vega Alta on charges of extortion, embezzlement and money laundering. But a far greater scandal tainted the *PNP* in January 2002, when the FBI arrested 17 people for money laundering and extortion in a $4.3 million kickback scheme involving private computer contractors and the department of education under the Roselló administration. Once again, federal funds destined for a worthy cause—the computer training of teachers—allegedly had gone into private pockets; $1 million reportedly went into the *PNP*'s 2000 campaign fund. Among those arrested were Victor Fajardo, Roselló's edu-

Puerto Rico

cation secretary from 1994–2000; his deputy secretary; the former *PNP* speaker of the House of Representatives; and the president of the Puerto Rico Chamber of Commerce. All were subsequently convicted.

The commonwealth-statehood-independence debate continued to raise controversy between elections and referenda; even license plates became an issue. The new license plates issued under the Calderón administration contained the legend, "Free Associated State," and supposedly were issued to mark the 50th anniversary of the commonwealth's 1952 constitution. But both the *PNP* and the *PIP* denounced the plates as a *PDP* political statement.

Then, in June 2002, *PNP* president Carlos Pesquera sought to make a political statement of his own by forcing his way through a crowd to plant a U.S. flag alongside the Puerto Rican flag in the Office of Women's Affairs, whose director had insisted on displaying only the Puerto Rican flag. Pesquera was arrested and charged with inciting to riot.

2004 Electoral Deadlock

Governor Calderón opted not to seek reelection in 2004, and the *PDP* nomination went to Aníbal Acevedo Vila, Puerto Rico's resident commissioner to the U.S. Congress. Despite the past scandals, the *PNP* nominated former Governor Roselló instead of Pesquera. The *PIP* again ran Berrios as its candidate. It was the usual spirited campaign, with Acevedo scoring points by raising the corruption issue and by promising to come to terms with the alarming increase in crime that was frightening and angering Puerto Ricans. Governor Calderón had been compelled to put the National Guard on the streets of San Juan in July 2004 to complement the police force. By year's end, Puerto Rico experienced a record 789 murders, up from 780 the year before. Acevedo also pledged to call a constituent assembly in 2005 to discuss revising Puerto Rico's status to allow for greater autonomy.

Puerto Ricans had become accustomed to closely divided elections, but the November 2, 2004 contest was closer than ever. In the preliminary vote count, Acevedo led Roselló by a mere 3,880 votes out of 1,990,372 cast. Acevedo received 48.38% to Rosello's 48.18%. By law, when the difference is less than 0.5 percentage points, a recount is mandatory. The results of the recount by the elections commission reconfirmed Acevedo's razor-thin margin:

Acevedo Vila	963,303	48.40%
Roselló	959,737	48.22%
Berrios	54,551	2.74%

Governor Aníbal Acevedo Vila
Source: BBC

In an eerie replay of the contested 2000 presidential vote count in Florida, the *PNP* then disputed about 7,000 ballots that had been ambiguously marked for both the *PIP* as a party and for Acevedo for governor. Roselló went to U.S. district court in San Juan to have the votes disallowed. The *PDP* argued in the commonwealth court system that the ballots were valid votes for Acevedo. The Puerto Rico Supreme Court ruled that the ballots should be counted, while the federal judge said they should be counted pending his review of them. The *PDP* appealed to the 1st Circuit Court of Appeals in Boston, arguing that the election was a commonwealth, not federal, matter. On December 15, a three-judge panel agreed that the Puerto Rico Supreme Court has jurisdiction over elections. On December 28, just five days before the inauguration, the elections commission certified Acevedo's 3,566-vote margin.

Roselló grudgingly said that he would not contest the election further and contribute to "the uncertainty and anxiety of the people of Puerto Rico," but he added that he still considered the election results "irregular and unjust." He could console himself that Acevedo would have to face a legislature with a *PNP* majority of 18 of the 27 Senate seats and 34 of 51 House seats. A Roselló protégé, Luis Fortuno, was narrowly elected the new resident commissioner to Washington. It is the first time the governor and commissioner have been from different parties.

At his January 2, 2005, inauguration, Acevedo called for an end to the partisan bitterness that has so sharply divided Puerto Ricans. He also declared that he favored a U.S. withdrawal from Iraq within six months. At the time, 23 Puerto Ricans had been killed in the war.

In March, Acevedo laid off more than 23,000 public employees in an effort to reduce a mounting budget deficit. In April, the *PNP*-controlled legislature passed

a vague law that called on Washington to abide by any future decision by Puerto Ricans on the island's status. Acededo vetoed it.

Culture: For centuries the Spanish presence in Puerto Rico left an indelible imprint on the island, but it also has been a true melting pot, a blend of the Spanish with Indians and Africans. Color lines are thus blurred and racial tensions hardly exist.

The abundant literature of Puerto Rico emphasizes its colonial past and the island's fight to retain its Hispanic identity. Leading authors include Luis Rafael Sánchez, Pedro Juan Soto, José Luis González and Enrique Laguerre.

In art, José Campeche (1752–1809) produced some magnificent portraits and points of historical and religious themes. Francisco Oller (1833–1917) was influenced by the great figures of French impressionism—two of his paintings hang in the Louvre Museum in Paris. Today the island is particularly strong in silk screening and plastic arts, with recognized masters such as Lorenzo Homar, Rafael Tufiño, Julio Rosado del Valle, Manuel Hernández Acevedo, Carlos Raquel Rivera and later, Antonio Martorell, Myrna Baez and Luis Hernández Cruz. Also, Francisco Rodón has emerged as one of Latin America's leading portrait artists.

In the mainland United States, Puerto Rican performers in the movies, popular music, television and legitimate theater have included José Ferrer, Rita Moreno, Chita Rivera, Raúl Julia, Erik Estrada, Justino Díaz and Pablo Elvira, to mention only a few.

In recent years, Puerto Rican *salsa* singers like Ricky Martin have carved out a niche in U.S. and Latin American popular music. A new, underground musical genre on the island is called "raggaeton," a peculiar combination of Latin and hip-hop. Tego Calderón was the first raggaeton singer to sign a contract with a U.S. recording label, in 2005.

Puerto Rico's favorite sport is baseball, and it has contributed many dozens of players to the major leagues—in 1984 Willie Hernández of the Detroit Tigers was the American League's Most Valuable Player. The unforgettable Pittsburgh Pirate Roberto Clemente shares company in Baseball's Hall of Fame with such greats as Babe Ruth and Hank Aaron.

On the bleak side, Puerto Rican slums and housing projects are comparable to the worst in the United States. The murder rate rose to more than any of the 50 states during the 1990s (but not as high as Washington, D.C.), forcing the Governor Roselló in 1993 and Governor Calderón in 2004 to call out the National Guard with assault weapons to reduce street violence. Most of it is related to drug trafficking and use. It has grown even worse; by 2004, the island recorded 200 homicides more than New York City, which has twice the population.

Economy: Although the Puerto Rican economy is reasonably strong, it has its problems. The main pillar of the economy is manufacturing. The island has nearly 2,000 plants, the majority of which are subsidiaries of U.S. companies attracted to Puerto Rico mainly because of tax advantages. The 1987 tax reforms, however, altered these incentives. These industries are geared to producing export items—the famous Bacardi Rum, for example, is produced on the island. Puerto Rico is a favorite location for U.S. pharmaceutical manufacturers because of particular tax advantages derived from locating on the island.

With industrialization, agricultural production, the dominant sector of the economy, commenced a decline starting in the 1950s. Agricultural workers first went to San Juan and then immigrated to the United States in search of jobs. As a result, about 3 million people of Puerto Rican heritage are now living in the United States.

Puerto Rico attracts tourists from all over the world; tourism, after manufacturing and agriculture, has been one of the mainstays of the economy. It now stands seriously threatened by crime directly connected to a burgeoning drug traffic from Colombia to the United States. It is relatively easy to get cocaine to the island and difficult to prevent it from entering the mainland United States since Puerto Ricans are citizens and need pass no more than the security check for weapons on flights to the United States, particularly New York. An area in which there could be much improvement is government employment: fully 28% of the people work for the government, a figure about 15% too high, at an enormous, unnecessary cost.

If Puerto Rico were independent, its per capita income of about $8,000 would be the highest in Latin America. In relative terms, that is only about one third the per capita income of the U.S. mainland, but it is four times as much as Puerto Rico's closest sovereign neighbor, the Dominican Republic. Because wages are so much higher than in other Caribbean countries, however, Puerto Rico is at a disadvantage in the competition for tourism.

Although Puerto Ricans pay no federal income tax, they qualify for welfare and unemployment benefits; unemployment at this writing was about 14%, compared with less than 5% on the U.S. mainland. Moreover, the island receives about $10 billion in aid from the mainland. In other words, the Puerto Ricans have the best of both worlds, which helps explain why a clear majority of them continues to eschew both statehood and independence.

The Future: The 2004 elections showed just how polarized Puerto Ricans remain over their unique status. Under these circumstances, there can be no consensus for any dramatic changes for years to come. Puerto Ricans had best stop worrying about statehood and start working to reduce crime, which is a cancer gnawing at the island's society.

U.S. VIRGIN ISLANDS

Area: 132 square miles
Population: 140,000 (estimated).
Administrative Capital: Charlotte Amalie (Pop. 14,000, estimated).

The U.S Virgin Islands lie about 40 miles east of Puerto Rico and consist of three major islands (St. Croix, St. Johns and St. Thomas) and some 50 small islands and cays, mostly uninhabited. The islands were acquired by purchase from Denmark in 1917 and are administered as a Federal Territory by the U.S. Department of the Interior. Although voters turned down a proposed new constitution in 1978, attempts are being made to write a new charter. Most residents seem to prefer commonwealth status—rather than independence or statehood—with the United States.

The islands are hilly, with arable land given to small farms. The climate is tropical, with a May to November rainy season.

The population is about 20% North American and European descent; the remainder is of African and mixed heritage. The principal products for export are rum and bay rum, the fragrant distilled oil of the bayberry leaf. Cattle raising and truck farming are important for local consumption. The islands do not possess resources adequate for support as an independent entity.

Prosperity in the 1970s brought a tremendous influx of immigrants—now only about 40% of the islanders are natives. The ethnic derivation of these "newcomers" was about 75% black from neighboring Caribbean nations, including Haitians, and 25% white U.S. mainlanders. Because the Virgin Islands in the past relied principally on rum taxes for government expenses, tax changes have seriously undermined this scheme. The response was increased taxes on just about everything in the last several years—very unpopular to say the least. Tourism has been a mainstay of the economy and is being promoted. Unemployment remains very low by Caribbean standards—about 5%.

Charles W. Turnbull was elected governor in November 1998, succeeding Roy L. Schneider.

A referendum of the islands' future relationship with the United States was held in late 1993 after being postponed because of a hurricane. Ninety percent voted for continued or enhanced status—the *status quo*. But only 27% of the electorate bothered to participate in the balloting; it thus did not meet validation requirements.

Selected Bibliography of Key English Language Sources

WEB SITES
Useful General Web Sites:

www.un.org (Web site for United Nations. Many links.)

www.unsystem.or (Official UN website)

http://europa.eu.int (EU server site)

www.oecd.org/daf/cmis/fdi/statist.htm (OECD site)

www.wto.org (World Trade Organization site)

www.worldbank.org/html/Welcome.html (World Bank news, publications with links to other financial institutions)

www.ceip.org (Carnegie Endowment for International Peace, using a fully integrated Web-database system)

www.cia.gov/index.html (Central Intelligence Agency)

www.odci.gov/cia (Includes useful CIA publications, such as *The World Factbook* and maps)

www.state.gov/www/ind.html (U.S. Department of State, including country reports)

http://usinfo.state.gov (U.S. Department of State)

lcweb2.loc.gov/frd/cs/cshome.html (Library of Congress with coverage of over 100 countries)

WWW.embassy.org/embassies (A site with links to all embassy web sites in Washington D.C.)

www.psr.keele.ac.uk\official.htm (Collective site for governments and international organizations)

Newspapers, Journals and Television with good coverage on Latin American affairs:

www.chicagotribune.com (Named best overall U.S. newspaper online service for newspapers with circulation over 100,000.)

www.csmonitor.com (*Christian Science Monitor*. Named best overall U.S. newspaper online service for newspapers with circulation under 100,000.)

www.dallasnews.com (*The Dallas Morning News*)

www.diariolasamericas.com (*Diario las Américas*, Miami)

www.economist.com (British weekly news magazine)

www.miami.com/mld/miamiherald/news/world/americas/ (*The Miami Herald*)

www.nytimes.com

www.washingtonpost.com

www.washingtontimes.com

www.foreignaffairs.org (One of best-known international affairs journal)

www.cnn.com (Latest news with external links)

www.news.BBC.co.uk (British Broadcasting Corporation site)

www.c-span.org (Includes C-SPAN International)

www.sun-sentinel.com (South Florida Sun-Sentinel, Fort Lauderdale)

General

Adelman, Jeremy, ed. *Colonial Legacies: the Problem of Persistence in Latin American History*. New York: Routledge, 1999.

Alvarez, Sonia E. *Cultures of Politics, Politics of Cultures: Revisioning Latin American Social Movements*. Boulder, CO: Westview Press, 1998.

Appelbaum, Nancy P., Anne S. Macpherson, and Karin Alejandra Rosemblatt, eds. *Race and Nation in Modern Latin America*. Chapel Hill:University of North Carolina Press, 2003.

Arnson, Cynthia. *Comparative Peace Processes in Latin America*. Stanford, CA: Stanford University Press, 1999.

Atkins, G. Pope. *Latin America and the Caribbean in the International System*. Boulder, CO: Westview Press, 1998.

Atkins, G. Pope. *Latin America in the International Political System*. Boulder, CO: Westview Press, 3rd. ed. 1995.

Barham, Bradford L. and Oliver T. Coomes. *Prosperity's Promise: the Amazon Rubber Boom and Distorted Economic Development*. Boulder, CO: Westview Press, 1996.

Barton, Jonathan R. *A Political Geography of Latin America*. London: Rutledge, 1997.

Beezley, William H. and Linda Curcio-Nagy, eds. *Latin American Popular Culture: an Introduction*. Wilmington, DE: Scholarly Resources, 2000.

Bethell, Leslie, ed. *A Cultural History of Latin America: Literature, Music and the Visual Arts in the 19th and 20th Century*. New York: Cambridge University Press, 1998.

Bethell, Leslie, ed. *Latin America since 1930*. New York: Cambridge University Press, 1994.

Black, Jan Knippers, ed. *Latin America: Its Problems and Its Promise*. (3rd Edition) Boulder, CO: Westview Press, 1998.

Blake, Charles H. *Politics in Latin America*. St. Charles, Il: Houghton Mifflin, 2004.

Bonilla, Frank, et al., eds. *Borderless Borders: U.S. Latinos, Latin Americans, and the Paradox of Interdependence*. Philadelphia, PA: Temple University Press, 1998.

Britton, John A. *The United States and Latin America: a Select Bibliography*. Langham, MD: Scarecrow Press, 1997.

Brysk, Alison. *From Tribal Village to Global Village: Indian Rights and International Relations in Latin America*. Stanford, CA: Stanford University Press, 2000.

Bulmer-Thomas, Victor. *The Economic History of Latin America since Independence*. New York: Cambridge University Press, 1994.

Burkholder, Mark A. and Lyman L. Johnson. *Colonial Latin America*. New York: Oxford University Press, 3rd ed. 1998.

Castañeda, Jorge G. *Utopia Unarmed: the Latin American Left after the Cold War*. New York: Random House, 1993.

Centeno, Miguel Angel, *Blood and Debt: War and the Nation-State in Latin America*. University Park: The Pennsylvania State University Press, 2002.

Chasteen, John Charles. *Born in Blood and Fire: a Concise History of Latin America*. New York: W.W. Norton & Company, 2000.

Chomsky, Noam. *Latin America: from Colonization to Globalization*. Hoboken, NJ: Ocean Press, 1999.

Cockcroft, James D. *Latin America: History, Politics, and U.S. Policy*. Chicago, IL: Nelson-Hall, 2nd ed. 1996.

Cleary, Edward L. and Timothy J. Steigenga, eds. *Resurgent Voices in Latin America: Indigenous Peoples, Political Mobilization and Religious Change*. New Brunswick: Rutgers University Press, 2004.

Craske, Nikki. *Women and Politics in Latin America*. Piscataway, NJ: Rutgers University Press, 1999.

Davis, Darien J. *Slavery and Beyond: the African Impact on Latin America and the Caribbean*. Wilmington, DE: SR Books, 1995.

De la Campa, Romban. *Latin Americanism*. Minneapolis, MN: University of Minnesota Press, 1999.

Dent, David W. *Monroe's Ghosts*. Westport, CT: Greenwood Publishing Group, 1999.

Diamond, Larry et al. *Democracy in Developing Countries: Latin America*. Boulder, CO: Lynne Rienner, 1999.

Dominguez, Jorge I. *Democratic Politics in Latin America and the Caribbean*. Baltimore, MD: Johns Hopkins University Press, 1998.

Dominguez, Jorge I., ed. *Latin America's International Relations and Their Domestic Consequences: War and Peace, Dependency and Autonomy, Integration and Disintegration*. New York: Garland Publishing, 1994.

Dominguez, Jorge I., ed. *Race and Ethnicity in Latin America*. New York: Garland Publishing, 1994.

Early, Edwin. *A History Atlas of South America*. Old Tappan, NJ: Macmillan Publishing Company, 1998.

Fagg, John E. *Latin America: a General History*. New York: Macmillan Publishing Company, 3rd ed 1977.

Fauriol, Georges A. *Fast Forward: Latin America on the Edge of the Twenty-First Century*. New Brunswick, NJ: 1997.

Ferman, Claudia, ed. *The Postmodern in Latin America Cultural Narratives: Collected Essays and Interviews*. New York: Garland Publishing, 1996.

Fitch, John S. *The Armed Forces and Democracy in Latin America*. Baltimore, MD: Johns Hopkins University Press, 1998.

Foders, Frederico and Manfred Feldsieper, eds. *The Transformation of Latin America.* Northampton, MA: Edward Elgar Publishing, 1999.

Foster, Dean. *The Global Etiquette Guide To Mexico and Latin America.* New York: John Wiley & Sons, Inc, 2002.

Fowler, Will, ed. *Ideologues and Ideologies in Latin America.* Westport, CT: Greenwood Publishing Group, 1997.

Franco, Jean, et al. *Profane Passions: Politics and Culture in the Americas.* Durham, NC: Duke University Press, 1999.

Garreton, Manual Antonia et al. *Latin America in the Twenty-First Century: Toward a New Sociopolitical Matrix.* Boulder, CO: Lynne Rienner, 2003.

Garreton, Manuel Antonia and Edward Newman, eds. *Democracy in Latin America.* Washington D.C.: Brookings, 2002.

Gilderhus, Mark T., et al., eds. *The Second Century: U.S.-Latin American Relations since 1889.* Wilmington, DE: Scholarly Resources, 1999.

Gill, Anthony. *Rendering Unto Caesar: The Catholic Church and the State in Latin America.* Chicago: University of Chicago Press, 1998.

Goodwin, Paul Jr. *Latin America* (10th Ed). Guilford, CN: The Dushkin Publishing Group, Inc., 2003.

Green, Roy E., ed. *The Enterprise for the America's Initiative: Issues and Prospects for a Free Trade Agreement in the Western Hemisphere.* New York: Praeger, 1993.

Gutteridge, William F. *Latin America and the Caribbean: Prospects for Democracy.* Brookfield, VT: Ashgate Publishing Company, 1997.

Gwynne, Robert N. *Latin America Transformed: Globalization and Modernity.* New York: Oxford University Press, 1999.

Halebsky, Sandor and Richard L. Harris, eds. *Capital, Power, and Inequality in Latin America.* Boulder, CO: Westview Press, 1995.

Hamill, Hugh M., ed. *Caudillos: Dictators in Spanish America.* Norman, University of Oklahoma Press, 1992.

Hartlyn, Jonathan et al. Eds. *The United States and Latin America in the 1990s: Beyond the Cold War.* Chapel Hill: The University of North Carolina Press, 1992.

Harvey, Robert. *Liberators: Latin America's Struggle for Independence.* New York: The Overlook Press, 2000.

Henderson, James D., et al. *A Reference Guide to Latin American History.* Armonk, NY: M.E. Sharpe, 2000.

Hillman, Richard S., ed. *Understanding Contemporary Latin America.* Boulder, CO: Lynne Rienner Publishers, 2001.

Hofman, André A. *The Economic Development of Latin America in the Twentieth Century.* Northampton, MA: Edward Elgar Publishing, 2000.

Jorge, Antonio, et al., eds. *Capital Markets, Growth and Economic Policy in Latin America.* Westport, CT: Greenwood Publishing Group, 2000.

Kanellos, Nicolas and Cristelia Perez. *Chronology of Hispanic-American History.* Detroit, MI: Gale Research, 1995.

Keen, Benjamin and Mark Wasserman. *A History of Latin America (6th Edition).* Boston: Houghton Mifflin Company, 2000.

Kelly, Philip. *Checkerboards & Scatterbelts: The Geopolitics of South America.* Austin: The University of Texas Press, 1997.

Landau, Saul. *The Guerrilla Wars of Central America: Nicaragua, El Salvador, and Guatemala.* New York: Saint Martin's Press, 1993.

Langley, Lester D. *The Americas in the Age of Revolution: 1750–1850.* New Haven, CT: Yale University Press, 1996.

Lombardi, Cathryn L. and John V. *Latin-American History. A Teaching Atlas.* Madison, WI: The University of Wisconsin Press, 1983.

Loveman, Brian. *For la Patria: Politics and the Armed Forces in Latin America.* Scholarly Resources, 1999.

Lynch, John, ed. *Latin American Revolutions, 1808–1826: Old and New World Origins.* Norman, OK: University of Oklahoma Press, 1994.

MacDonald, Scott B. and Georges A. Fauriol. *Fast Forward: Latin America on the Edge of the Twenty-First Century.* Piscataway, NJ: Transaction Publishers, 1998.

Mainwaring, Scott, ed. *Presidentialism and Democracy in Latin America.* New York: Cambridge University Press, 1997.

Maldifassi, José and Pier A. Abetti. *Defense Industries in Latin American Countries: Argentina, Brazil, and Chile.* New York: Praeger, 1994.

Manzetti, Luigi. *Privatization South American Style.* New York: Oxford University Press, 2000.

Margheritis, Ana, ed. *Latin American Democracies in the New Global Economy.* North South Center Press, Miami: University of Miami, 2003.

Martz, John D., ed. *United States Policy in Latin America: a Decade of Crisis and Challenge.* Lincoln, NE: University of Nebraska Press, 1995.

Mendez, Juan E., et al., eds. *The (Un)Rule of Law and the Underprivileged in Latin America.* Notre Dame, IN: Notre Dame Press, 1999.

Millett, Richard L. and Michael Gold-Biss, eds. *Beyond Praetorianism: The Latin American Military in Transition.* North South Center Press, University of Miami, 1996.

Mills, Kenneth and William B. Taylor, eds. *Colonial Spanish America: a Documentary History.* Wilmington, DE: Scholarly Resources, 1998.

Morales, Juan Antonio and Gary McMahon, eds. *Economic Policy and the Transition to Democracy: the Latin American Experience.* New York: Saint Martin's Press, 1996.

Morley, Samuel A. *Poverty and Inequality in Latin America: the Impact of Adjustment and Recovery in the 1980s.* Baltimore, MD: Johns Hopkins University Press, 1995.

O'Brien, Thomas F. *Century of U.S. Capitalism in Latin America.* Albuquerque, NM: University of New Mexico Press, 1999.

Orr, Bernadette M, and Cruz. *Americas: Study Guide.* New York: Oxford University Press, 1993.

Park, James William. *Latin American Underdevelopment: a History of Perspectives in the United States, 1870–1965.* Baton Rouge, LA: Louisiana State University Press, 1995.

Payne, Leigh A. *Uncivil Movements: the Armed Right Wing and Democracy in Latin America.* Baltimore, MD: Johns Hopkins University Press, 2000.

Peeler, John. *Building Democracy in Latin America.* Boulder, CO: Lynne Rienner Publishers, 1998.

Peeler, John. *Building Democracy in Latin America.* Second Edition. Boulder, CO: Lynne Rienner, 2004.

Ramsey, Russell, *Guardians of the Other Americas: Essays on the Military Forces of Latin America.* Lanham, MD: University Press of America, Inc., 1997.

Roberts, Paul. *The Capitalist Revolution in Latin America.* New York: Oxford University Press, 1997.

Rochlin, James F. *Vanguard Revolutionaries in Latin America: Peru, Colombia, Mexico.* Boulder, CO: Lynne Rienner, 2003.

Roseberry, William, ed. *Coffee, Society, and Power in Latin America.* Baltimore, MD: Johns Hopkins University Press, 1995.

Rosenberg, Kincaid and Logan, eds. *Americas, an Anthology.* New York: Oxford University Press, 1992.

Rosenberg, Tina. *Children of Cain.* New York: Penguin Books, 1991.

Scheina, Robert L., *Latin America's Wars (Vol. 1)—The Age of the Caudillo, 1791–1899.* Washington: Brassey's Inc., 2003.

Schoultz, Lars. *Beneath The United States: A History of US Policy Toward Latin America.* Cambridge: Harvard University Press, 1998.

Schoultz, Lars, et al., eds. *Security, Democracy, and Development in U.S.-Latin American Relations.* North South Center Press, University of Miami, 1996.

Schwaller, John F., et al., eds. *The Church in Colonial Latin America.* Wilmington, DE: Scholarly Resources, 2000.

Silva, Patricio, ed. *The Soldier and the State in South America.* Great Britain: Palgrave, 2001.

Skidmore, Thomas and Smith, Peter. *Modern Latin America.* (5th Edition). New York: Oxford University Press, 2001.

Smith, Gaddis. *The Last Years of the Monroe Doctrine: 1945–1993.* New York: Hill & Wang/Farrar, Straus & Giroux, 1994.

Smith, Peter H. *Talons of the Eagle: Dynamics of U.S.-Latin America Relations.* New York: Oxford University Press, 1996.

Smith, William C., ed. *Politics, Social Change, and Economic Restructuring in Latin America.* Coral Gables, FL: University of Miami, North/South Center Press, 1997.

Stallings, Barbara and Wilson Peres. *Growth, Equity and Employment: the Impact of the Economic Reforms in Latin America and the Caribbean.* Washington, DC: Brookings Institution Press, 2000.

Taylor, Lance, ed. *After Neoliberalism: What Next for Latin America?* Ann Arbor, MI: University of Michigan Press, 1998.

Tenenbaum, Barbara A. *Encyclopedia of Latin American History and Culture.* New York: Scribner, 1996.

Thorp, Rosemary. *Progress, Exclusion and Poverty: an Economic History of Latin America in the 20th Century.* Washington, DC: Inter-American Development Bank, 1998.

Tulchin, Joseph S., and Ralph H. Espach, eds. *Combating Corruption in Latin America.* Baltimore: Woodrow Wilson Center Press, 2000.

Tulchin, Joseph S. and Ralph H. Espach, eds. *Latin America in the New International System.* Boulder, CO: Lynne Rienner, 2001.

Turner, Barry. *Latin America Profiled: Essential Facts on Society, Business and Politics in Latin America.* New York: Saint Martin's Press, 2000.

Ungar, Mark. *Elusive Reform: Democracy and the Rule of Law in Latin America.* Boulder, CO: Lynne Rienner, 2002.

Valtmeyer, Henry and James F. Petras. *Dynamics of Social Change in Latin America.* New York: Saint Martin's Press, 2000.

Vargas Llosa, Alvaro. *Liberty For Latin America.* New York: Farrar, Strauss and Giroux, 2005.

Vera, Leonardo. *Stabilization and Growth in Latin America: a Critique and Reconciliation.* New York: Saint Martin's Press, 2000.

Von Mettenheim, Kurt and James M. Malloy. *Deepening Democracy in Latin America.* Pittsburgh, PA: University of Pittsburgh Press, 1998.

Youngers, Coletta A. and Rosin, Eileen, eds. *Drugs and Democracy in Latin America. The Impact of U.S. Policy.* Boulder, CO: Lynne Rienner, 2004.

Andes Region

Crandall, Russell, et al, eds. *The Andes in Focus: Security, Democracy, and Economic Reform.* Boulder, CO: Lynne Rienner, 2005.

Caribbean

Allahar, Anton, ed. *Caribbean Charisma: Reflections on Leadership, Legitimacy, and Populist Politics.* Boulder, CO: Lynne Rienner, 2001.

Beckles, Hilary M. and Verene Shepherd, eds. *Caribbean Freedom: Economy and Society from Emancipation to the Present.* Princeton, NJ: Markus Wiener Publishers, 1998.

Braveboy-Wagner, Jacqueline and Dennis J. Gayle, eds. *Caribbean Public Policy Issues of the 1990s.* Boulder, CO: Westview Press, 1997.

Braveboy-Wagner, Jacqueline, et al. *The Caribbean in the Pacific Century: Prospects for Caribbean-Pacific Cooperation.* Boulder, CO: Lynne Rienner Publishers, 1993.

Braveboy-Wagner, Jacqueline A. *The Caribbean in World Affairs: the Foreign Policies of the English-Speaking States.* Boulder, CO: Westview Press, 2000.

Carvajal, Manuel J. *The Caribbean, 1975–1980: a Bibliography of Economic and Rural Development.* Lanham, MD: Scarecrow Press, 1993.

Craton, Michael. *Empire, Enslavement and Freedom in the Caribbean.* Princeton, NJ: Markus Wiener Publishers, 1997.

Desch, Michael C., et al., eds. *From Pirates to Drug Lords: the Post-Cold War Caribbean Security Environment.* Albany, NY: State University of New York Press, 1998.

Dominguez, Jorge I., ed. *Democracy in the Caribbean: Political, Economic, and Social Perspectives.* Baltimore, MD: Johns Hopkins University Press, 1993.

Dominguez, Jorge I. *Democratic Politics in Latin America and the Caribbean.* Baltimore, MD: Johns Hopkins University Press, 1998.

Granberry, Julian, ed. *An Encyclopaedia Caribbeana: a Research Guide.* Detroit, MI: Omnigraphics, 2000.

Griffith, Ivelaw L. *The Political Economy of Drugs in the Caribbean.* New York: Saint Martin's Press, 2000.

Griffith, Ivelaw L. *The Quest for Security in the Caribbean: Problems and Promises in Subordinate States.* Armonk, NY: M.E. Sharpe, 1993.

Grugel, Jean. *Politics and Development in the Caribbean Basin: Central America and the Caribbean in the New World Order.* Bloomington, IN: Indiana University Press, 1995.

Hillman, Richard S. and Thomas D'Agostino, eds. *Understanding the Contemporary Caribbean.* Boulder, CO: Lynne Rienner, 2003.

Maingot, Anthony P. *The United States and the Caribbean: Challenges of an Asymmetrical Relationship.* Boulder, CO: Westview Press, 1994.

Marshall, Don D. *Caribbean Political Economy at the Crossroads: NAFTA and Regional Developmentalism.* New York: Saint Martin's Press, 1998.

Meditz, Sandra W. and Dennis M. Hanratty. *Islands of the Commonwealth of the Caribbean: a Regional Study.* Washington, DC: U.S. GPO, 1989.

Palmer, Ransford W., ed. *U.S.-Caribbean Relations: Their Impact on Peoples and Cultures.* Westport, CT: Greenwood Publishing Group, 1998.

Payne, Anthony and Paul Sutton, eds. *Modern Caribbean Politics.* Baltimore, MD: Johns Hopkins University Press, 1993.

Portes, Alejandro, ed. *The Urban Caribbean: Transition to the New Global Economy.* Baltimore, MD: Johns Hopkins University Press, 1997.

Sheperd, Verene, ed. *Women in Caribbean History.* Princeton, NJ: Markus Wiener Publishers, 1999.

Smith, Robert Freeman. *The Caribbean World and the United States: Mixing Rum and Coca-Cola.* Boston, MA: Twayne Publishers, 1994.

Stallings, Barbara and Wilson Peres. *Growth, Equity and Employment: the Impact of the Economic Reforms in Latin America and the Caribbean.* Washington, DC: Brookings Institution Press, 2000.

Taylor, Patrick. *Nation Dance: Religion, Identity and Cultural Difference in the Caribbean.* Bloomington, IN: Indiana University Press, 2000.

Tulchin, Joseph S. and Ralph H. Espach, eds. *Security in the Caribbean Basin: the Challenge of Regional Cooperation.* Boulder, CO: Lynne Rienner Publishers, 2000.

Central America

Alexander, Robert J. *Presidents of Central America, Mexico, Cuba and Hispaniola: Conversations and Correspondence.* New York: Praeger, 1995.

Booth, John A. and Thomas W. Walker. *Understanding Central America.* (3rd Edition) Boulder, CO: Westview Press, 1999.

Brockett, Charles D. *Land, Power and Poverty: Agrarian Transformation and Political Conflict in Central America.* Boulder, CO: Westview Press, 1998.

Coatsworth, John H. *Central America and the United States: the Clients and the Colossus.* Boston, MA: Twayne Publishers, 1994.

Dominguez, Jorge I., ed. *Democratic Transitions in Central America.* Gainesville, FL: University Press of Florida, 1997.

Foster, Lynn V. *A Brief History of Central America.* New York: Facts on File, 2000.

Krenn, Michael L. *The Chains of Interdependence: U.S. Policy toward Central America, 1945–1954.* Armonk, NY: M.E. Sharpe, 1996.

Langley, Lester D. and Thomas Schoonover. *The Banana Men: American Mercenaries and Entrepreneurs in Central America, 1880–1930.* Lexington, KY: University Press of Kentucky, 1995.

Lentner, Howard H. *State Formation in Central America: the Struggle for Autonomy, Development, and Democracy.* Westport, CT: Greenwood Publishing Publishing, 1993.

LeoGrande, William M. *Our Own Backyard: the United Stated in Central Amer-*

ica, 1977–1992. Chapel Hill, NC: University of North Carolina Press, 1998.

Moreno, Dario. *The Struggle for Peace in Central America*. Gainesville, FL: University Press of Florida, 1994.

Paige, Jeffery M. *Coffee and Power: Revolution and the Rise of Democracy in Central America*. Cambridge, MA: Harvard University Press, 1997.

Scott, Peter D. *Cocaine Politics: Drugs, Armies and the CIA in Central America*. Berkeley, CA: University of California Press, 1998.

Torres-Rivas, Edelberto. *History and Society in Central America*. Austin, TX: University of Texas Press, 1993.

Walker, Thomas W. and Ariel C. Armony, eds. *Repression, Resistance and Democratic Transition in Central America*. Wilmington, DE: Scholarly Resources, 2000.

Weaver, Frederick Stirton. *Inside the Volcano: the History and Political Economy of Central America*. Boulder, CO: Westview Press, 1994.

Woodward, Ralph L. Jr. *Central America: a Nation Divided*. New York: Oxford University Press, 1999.

Argentina

Adelman, Jeremy. *Republic of Capital: Buenos Aires and the Legal Transformation of the Atlantic World*. Stanford, CA: Stanford University Press, 1999.

Alonso, Paula. *Between Revolution and the Ballot Box: the Origins of the Argentine Radical Party*. New York: Cambridge University Press, 2000.

Armory, Ariel C. *Argentina, the United States, and the Anti-Communist Crusade in Central America*. Athens, OH: Ohio University Press, 1997.

Balze, Felipe A.M. de la. *Remaking the Argentine Economy*. New York: Council on Foreign Relations, 1995.

Biggins, Alan. *Argentina*. Santa Barbara, CA: ABC-CLIO, 1991.

Cavarozzi, Marcelo. *Argentina*. Boulder, CO: Westview Press, 1999.

Deutsch, Sandra McGee and Ronald H. Dolkart, eds. *The Argentine Right: Its History and Intellectual Origins, 1910 to the Present*. Wilmington, DE: Scholarly Resources, 1993.

Erro, Davide G. *Resolving the Argentine Paradox: Politics and Development, 1966–1992*. Boulder, CO: Lynne Rienner Publishers, 1993.

Escude, Carlos. *Foreign Policy Theory in Menem's Argentina*. Gainesville, FL: University Press of Florida, 1997.

Feitlowitz, Marguerite. *A Lexicon of Terror: Argentina and the Legacies of Torture*. New York: Oxford University Press, 1998.

Foster, David W. and Melissa F. Lockhart. *Culture and Customs of Argentina*. Westport, CT: Greenwood Publishing Group, 1998.

Horvath, Laszlo. *A Half Century of Peronism, 1943–1993: an International Bibliography*. Stanford, CA: Hoover Institution Press, 1993.

Ivereigh, Austen. *Catholicism and Politics in Argentina, 1810–1960*. New York: Saint Martin's Press, 1995.

Keeling, David J. *Contemporary Argentina: a Geographical Perspective*. Boulder, CO: Westview Press, 1997.

Manzetti, Luigi. Institutions, Parties, and Coalitions in Argentine Politics. Pittsburgh, PA: University of Pittsburgh Press, 1993.

Munck, Gerardo L. *Authoritarianism and Democratization: Soldiers and Workers in Argentina, 1976–1983*. University Park, PA: Pennsylvania State University Press, 1998.

Rein, Monica. Translated by Martha Grenzeback. *Politics and Education in Argentina, 1946–1962*. Armonk, NY: M.E. Sharpe, 1998.

Rock, David. *Authoritarian Argentina: the Nationalist Movement, Its History and Its Impact*. Berkeley, CA: University of California Press, 1993.

Sawers, Larry. *The Other Argentina: the Interior and National Development*. Boulder, CO: Westview Press, 1996.

Shumway, Nicolas. *The Invention of Argentina*. Berkeley, CA: University of California Press, 1996.

Tulchin, Joseph S., ed. *Argentina: the Challenge of Modernization*. Wilmington, DE: Scholarly Resources, 1998.

Barbados

Beckles, Hilary McD. *A History of Barbados: from Amerindian Settlement to Nation-State*. New York: Cambridge University Press, 1990.

Belize

Merrill, Tim L., ed. *Guyana and Belize: Country Studies*. Washington, DC: U.S. GPO, 2nd ed. 1993.

Sutherland, Anne. *The Making of Belize: Globalization in the Margins*. Westport, CT: Greenwood Publishing Group, 1998.

Wright, Peggy and Brian E. Coutts. *Belize*. Santa Barbara, CA: ABC-CLIO, 2nd ed. 1993.

Bolivia

Gallo, Carmenza. *Taxes and State Power: Political Instability in Bolivia, 1900–1950*. Philadelphia, PA: Temple University Press, 1991.

Gill, Lesley. *Teetering on the Rim: Global Restructuring, Daily Life and the Armed Retreat of the Bolivian State*. New York: Columbia University Press, 2000.

Hudson, Rex A. and Dennis M. Hanratty, eds. *Bolivia: a Country Study*. Washington, DC: U.S. GPO, 3rd ed. 1991.

Lehman, Kenneth D. *Bolivia and the United States: a Limited Partnership*. Athens, GA: University of Georgia Press, 1999.

Leons, Madeline B. and Harry Sanabria, eds. *Coca, Cocaine, and the Bolivian Reality*. Albany, NY: State University of New York Press, 1997.

Morales, Waltraud. *Bolivia: Land of Struggle*. Boulder, CO: Westview Press, 1992.

Morales, Waltraud Q. *A Brief History of Bolivia*. New York: Checkmark Books, 2004.

Brazil

Baronov, David. *The Abolition of Slavery in Brazil: the "Liberation" of Africans through the Emancipation of Capital*. Westport, CT: Greenwood Publishing Group, 2000.

Boxer, C.R. *The Golden Age of Brazil: Growing Pains of a Colonial Society*. New York: Saint Martin's Press, 1995.

Bresser Pereira, Luiz Carlos. *Economic Crisis and State Reform in Brazil: toward a New Interpretation of Latin America*. Boulder, CO: Lynne Rienner Publishers, 1996.

Burns, E. Bradford. *A History of Brazil*. New York: Columbia University Press, 3rd ed. 1993.

Capistrano de Abreu, João. *Chapters in Brazil's Colonial History, 1500–1800*. New York: Oxford University Press, 1997.

Cavalcanti, Clovis de Vasconcelos, ed. *The Environment, Sustainable Development and Public Policies: Building Sustainability in Brazil*. Northampton, MA: Edward Elgar Publishing, 2000.

Cavaliero, Roderick. *The Independence of Brazil*. New York: Saint Martin's Press, 1993.

Chaffee, Wilber A. *Desenvolvimento: Politics and Economy in Brazil*. Boulder, CO: Lynne Rienner Publishers, 1997.

Eakin, Marshall C. *Brazil: Once and Future Country*. New York: Saint Martin's Press, 1997.

Fausto, Boris. *A Concise History of Brazil*. New York: Cambridge University Press, 1999.

Goertzel, Ted G. *Fernando Henrique Cardoso: Reinventing Democracy in Brazil*. Boulder, CO: Lynne Rienner Publishers, 1999.

Gordon, Lincoln. *Brazil's Second Chance. En Route toward the First World*. Washington, D.C.: Brookings, 2003.

Hanchard, Michael. *Racial Politics in Contemporary Brazil*. Durham, NC: Duke University Press, 1999.

Hecht, Tobias. *At Home in the Street: Street Children in Northeast Brazil*. New York: Cambridge University Press, 1998.

Hudson, Rex A., ed. *Brazil: a Country Study*. Washington, DC: U.S. GPO, 5th ed. 1998.

Hunter, Wendy. *Eroding Military Influence in Brazil: Politicians against Soldiers*. Chapel Hill, NC: University of North Carolina Press, 1997.

Kingstone, Peter R. and Timothy J. Powers, eds. *Democratic Brazil: Actors, Insti-

tutions and Processes. Pittsburgh, PA: University of Pittsburgh Press, 2000.

Kinzo, Maria, ed. *Brazil under Democracy. Economy, Polity, and Society since 1985*. Washington, D.C.: Brookings, 2003.

Lesser, Jeff. *Negotiating National Identity: Immigrants, Minorities, and the Struggle for Ethnicity in Brazil*. Durham, NC: Duke University Press, 1999.

Levine, Robert M. *Brazilian Legacies*. Armonk, NY: M.E. Sharpe, 1997.

Levine, Robert M. and John J. Crocitti, eds. *The Brazil Reader: History, Culture, Politics*. Durham, NC: Duke University Press, 1999.

Levine, Robert M. *Father of the Poor? Vargas and His Era*. New York: Cambridge University Press, 1998.

Mainwaring, Scott. *Rethinking Party Systems in the Third Wave of Democratization: the Case of Brazil*. Stanford, CA: Stanford University Press, 1999.

Page, Joseph A. *The Brazilians*. Reading, MA: Addison-Wesley, 1995.

Power, Timothy J. *The Political Right in Postauthoritarian Brazil: Elites, Institutions and Democratization*. University Park, PA: Pennsylvania State University Press, 2000.

Purcell, Susan K. *Brazil under Cardoso*. Boulder, CO: Lynne Rienner Publishers, 1997.

Ribeiro, Darcy and Gregory Rabassa. *The Brazilian People: the Formation and Meaning of Brazil*. Gainesville, FL: University Press of Florida, 2000.

Robinson, Roger. *Brazil*. Des Plaines, IL: Heinemann Library, 1999.

Skidmore, Thomas E. *Brazil: Five Centuries of Change*. New York: Oxford University Press, 1999.

Topik, Steven C. *Trade and Gunboats: the United States and Brazil in the Age of Empire*. Stanford, CA: Stanford University Press, 2000.

Von Mettenheim, Kurt. *The Brazilian Voter: Mass Politics in Democratic Transition*. Pittsburgh, PA: University of Pittsburgh Press, 1995.

Weyland, Kurt Gerhard. *Democracy without Equity: Failures of Reform in Brazil*. Pittsburgh, PA: University of Pittsburgh Press, 1996.

Willumsen, Maria J., ed. *The Brazilian Economy: Structure and Performance*. Coral Gables, FL: University of Miami, North/South Center Press, 1997.

Chile

Bosworth, Barry P., ed. *The Chilean Economy: Policy and Challenges*. Washington, DC: Brookings Institution Press, 1994.

Collier, Simon and William F. Sater. *A History of Chile, 1808–1994*. New York: Cambridge University Press, 1996

Constanble, Pamela and Arturo Valenzuela. *A Nation of Enemies: Chile under Pinochet*. New York: W.W. Norton, 1993.

Davis, Madeleine, ed. *The Pinochet Case*. Washington, D.C.: Brookings, 2003.

Hachette, Dominique and Rolf Luders. *Privatization in Chile: an Economic Appraisal*. San Francisco, CA: ICS Press, 1993.

Franceschet, Susan. *Women and Politics in Chile*. Boulder, CO: Lynne Rienner, 2005.

Hojman, David E. *Chile: the Political Economy of Development and Democracy in the 1990s*. Pittsburgh, PA: University of Pittsburgh Press, 1993.

Hudson, Rex A., ed. *Chile: a Country Study*. Washington, DC: U.S. GPO, 3rd ed. 1994.

Lomnitz, Larissa Adler and Ana Melnick. *Chile's Political Culture and Parties: an Anthropological Explanation*. Notre Dame, IN: University of Notre Dame Press, 2000.

Lonregan, John B. *Legislative Institutions and Ideology in Chile*. New York: Cambridge University Press, 2000.

Monteon, Michael. *Chile and the Great Depression: the Politics of Underdevelopment, 1927–1948*. Tempe, AZ: Arizona State University, Center for Latin American Studies, 1998.

Oppenheim, Lois Hecht. *Politics in Chile: Democracy, Authoritarianism, and the Search for Development*. Boulder, CO: Westview Press, 2nd ed. 1998.

Oxhorn, Philip. *Organizing Civil Society: the Popular Sectors and the Struggle for Democracy in Chile*. University Park, PA: Pennsylvania State University Press, 1995.

Petras, James, et. al. *Democracy and Poverty in Chile: the Limits to Electoral Politics*. Boulder, CO: Westview Press, 1994.

Pietrobelli, Carlo. *Industry, Competitiveness and Technological Capabilities in Chile: a New Tiger from Latin America*. New York: Saint Martin's Press, 1998.

Puryear, Jeffrey. *Thinking Politics: Intellectuals and Democracy in Chile, 1973–1988*. Baltimore, MD: Johns Hopkins University Press, 1994.

Roberts, Kenneth M. *Deepening Democracy? The Modern Left and Social Movements in Chile and Peru*. Stanford, CA: Stanford University Press, 1999.

Siavelis, Peter. *The President and Congress in Post-Authoritarian Chile: Institutional Constraints to Democratic Consolidation*. University Park, PA: Pennsylvania State University Press, 1999.

Sigmund, Paul E. *The United States and Democracy in Chile*. Baltimore, MD: Johns Hopkins University Press, 1993.

Silva, Eduardo. *The State and Capital in Chile: Business Elites, Technocrats, and Market Economics*. Boulder, CO: Westview Press, 1996.

Solimano, Andres. *Distributive Justice and Economic Development: the Case of Chile and Developing Countries*. Ann Arbor, MI: University of Michigan Press, 2000.

Spooner, Mary Helen. *Soldiers in a Narrow Land: the Pinochet Regime in Chile*. Berkeley, CA: University of California Press, 1994.

Valdes, Juan Gabriel. *Pinochet's Economists: the Chicago School in Chile*. New York: Cambridge University Press, 1995.

Verdugo, Patricia. *Chile, Pinochet, and the Caravan of Death*. Boulder, CO: Lynne Rienner, 2001.

Wheelan, James R., *Out of the Ashes: Life, Death and Transfiguration of Democracy in Chile, 1833–1988*. Washington: Regnery Gateway, 1989.

Colombia

Crandall, Russell. *Driven By Drugs: U.S. Policy Toward Colombia*. Boulder, CO: Lynne Reinner, 2002.

Davis, Robert H. *Historical Dictionary of Colombia*. Lanham, MD: Scarecrow Press, 2nd ed. 1993.

Drexler, Robert W. *Colombia and the United States: Narcotics Traffic and a Failed Foreign Policy*. Jefferson, NC: McFarland & Company, 1997.

Duzan, Maria Jimena. Translated and edited by Peter Eisner. *Death Beat: a Colombian Journalist's Life inside the Cocaine Wars*. New York: HarperCollins, 1994.

Hanratty, Dennis M. and Sandra W. Meditz, eds. *Colombia: a Country Study*. Washington, DC: U.S. GPO, 4th ed. 1990.

Kirk, Robin. *More Terrible Than Death: Massacres, Drugs, and America's War in Colombia*. New York: Public Affairs, 2003.

Kline, Harvey F. *Colombia: Democracy under Assault*. Boulder, CO: Westview Press, 2nd ed. 1995.

Kline, Harvey F. *State Building and Conflict Resolution in Colombia, 1986–1994*. Tuscaloosa, AL: University of Alabama Press, 1999.

McFarlane, Anthony. *Colombia before Independence: Economy, Society, and Politics under Bourbon Rule*. New York: Cambridge University Press, 1993.

Menzel, Sewall H. *Cocaine Quagmire: Implementing the U.S. Anti-Drug Policy in the North Andes-Colombia*. Lanham, MD: University Press of America, 1997.

Mohan, Rakesh. *Understanding the Developing Metropolis: Lessons from the Study of Bogota and Cali, Colombia*. New York: Oxford University Press, 1994.

Posada-Carbo, Eduardo. *Colombia*. New York: Saint Martin's Press, 1997.

Rabasa, Angel and Peter Chalk. *Colombian Labyrinth: The Synergy of Drugs and Insurgency and Its Implications for Regional Stability*. Santa Monica: Rand Corp, 2001.

Rausch, Jane M. *The Llanos Frontier in Colombian History, 1830–1930*. Albuquerque, NM: University of New Mexico Press, 1993.

Safford, Frank and Marco Palacios. *Colombia: Fragmented Land, Divided Society*. New York: Oxford University Press, 2002.

Thorpe, Rosemary. *Economic Management and Economic Development in Peru and*

Colombia. Pittsburgh, PA: University of Press, 1991.

Thoumi, Francisco E. *Political Economy and Illegal Drugs in Colombia.* Boulder, CO: Lynne Rienner Publishers, 1995.

Wade, Peter. *Blackness and Race Mixture: the Dynamics of Racial Identity in Colombia.* Baltimore, MD: Johns Hopkins University Press, 1993.

Costa Rica

Basok, Tanya. *Keeping Heads above Water: Salvadorean Refuges in Costa Rica.* Toronto: University of Toronto Press, 1993.

Booth, John A. *Costa Rica: Quest for Democracy.* Boulder, CO: Westview Press, 1998.

Colesberry, Adrian and Brass McLean. *Costa Rica: the Last Country the Gods Made.* Helena, MT: Falcon Press, 1993.

Creedman, Theodore S. *Historical Dictionary of Costa Rica.* Lanham, MD: Scarecrow Press, 2nd ed. 1991.

Edelman, Marc. *Peasants against Globalization: Rural Social Movements in Costa Rica.* Stanford, CA: Stanford University Press, 2000.

Helmuth, Chalene. *Culture and Customs of Costa Rica.* Westport, CT: Greenwood Publishing Group, 2000.

Honey, Martha. *Hostile Acts: U.S. Policy in Costa Rica in the 1980s.* Gainesville, FL: University of Florida Press, 1994.

Miller, Eugene D. *A Holy Alliance? The Church and the Left in Costa Rica, 1932–1948.* Armonk, NY: M.E. Sharpe, 1996.

Rottenberg, Simon, ed. *Costa Rica and Uruguay.* New York: Oxford University Press, 1993.

Stansifer, Charles L. *Costa Rica.* Santa Barbara, CA: ABC-CLIO, 1991.

Wilson, Bruce M. *Costa Rica: Politics, Economics, and Democracy.* Boulder, CO: Lynne Rienner Publishers, 1998.

Yashar, Deborah J. *Demanding Democracy: Reform and Reaction in Costa Rica and Guatemala, 1870s–1950s.* Stanford, CA: Stanford University Press, 1997.

Cuba

Arbdeya, Jesus. Translated by Rafael Betancourt. *The Cuban Counterrevolution.* Athens, OH: Ohio University Press, 2000.

Baloyara, Enrique and James A. Morris. *Conflict and Change in Cuba.* Albuquerque, NM: University of New Mexico Press, 1993.

Benjamin-Alvarado, Jonathan. *Power to the People: Energy and the Cuban Nuclear Program.* New York: Routledge, 2000.

Blight, James G, et al. *Cuba on the Brink: Castro, the Missile Crisis, and the Soviet Collapse.* New York: Pantheon Books, 1993.

Bunck, Julie Marie. *Fidel Castro and the Quest for a Revolutionary Culture in Cuba.* University Park, PA: Pennsylvania State University, 1994.

Corbett, Ben. *This is Cuba.* Boulder, CO: Westview, 2002.

Diaz-Briquets, Sergio and Jorge Perez-Lopez. *Conquering Nature: the Environmental Legacy of Socialism in Cuba.* Pittsburgh, PA: University of Pittsburgh Press, 2000.

Fernandez, Damian J. *Cuba and the Politics of Passion.* Austin, TX: University of Texas Press, 2000.

Fursenko, Alexandr and Timothy J. Naftali. *"One Hell of a Gamble": Khrushchev, Castro and Kennedy, 1958–1964.* New York: W.W. Norton & Company, 1997.

Gonzalez, Edward and McCarthy, Kevin F. *Cuba After Castro. Legacies, Challenges, and Impediments.* Santa Monica, CA: Rand, 2004.

Gott, Richard. *Cuba: A New History.* New Haven: Yale University, 2004.

Halperin, Maurice. *Return to Havana: the Decline of Cuban Society under Castro.* Nashville, TN: Vanderbilt University Press, 1994.

Hernandez, José M. *Cuba and the United States: Intervention and Militarism, 1868–1933.* Austin, TX: University of Texas Press, 1993.

Ibarra, Jorge. *Prologue to Revolution: Cuba, 1898–1958.* Boulder, CO: Lynne Rienner Publishers, 1998.

Jordan, David C. *Revolutionary Cuba and the End of the Cold War.* Lanham, MD: University Press of America, 1993.

Kirk, John M. *Canada-Cuba Relations: the Other Good Neighbor Policy.* Gainesville, FL: University Press of Florida, 1997.

Kornbluh, Peter, ed. *Bay of Pigs Declassified: the Secret CIA Report.* New York: New Press, 1998.

Leonard, Thomas M. *Castro and the Cuban Revolution.* Westport, CT: Greenwood Publishing Group, 1999.

Luis, Julio Garcia. *Cuban Revolution Reader: a Documented History of 40 Years of the Cuban Revolution.* Hoboken, NJ: Ocean Press, 2000.

Mesa-Largo, Carmelo, ed. *Cuba after the Cold War.* Pittsburgh, PA: University of Pittsburgh Press, 1993.

Moses, Catherine. *Real Life in Castro's Cuba.* Wilmington, DE: Scholarly Resources, 2000.

Oppenheimer, Andres, *Castro's Final Hour: The Secret Story Behind the Coming Downfall of Communist Cuba.* New York: Simon & Schuster, 1992.

Paterson, Thomas G. *Contesting Castro: the United States and the Triumph of the Cuban Revolution.* New York: Oxford University Press, 1994.

Perez, Louis A., Jr. *On Becoming Cuban: Identity, Nationality and Culture.* Chapel Hill, NC: University of North Carolina Press, 1999.

Perez-Lopez, Jorge F. *Cuba at a Crossroads: Politics and Economics after the Fourth Party Congress.* Gainesville, FL: University of Florida Press, 1994.

Perez-Lopez, Jorge F. *Cuba's Second Economy: from behind the Scenes to Center State.* New Brunswick, NJ: Transaction Publishers, 1995.

Perez-Stable, Marifeli. *The Cuban Revolution: Origins, Course, and Legacy.* New York: Oxford University Press, 2nd ed. 1999.

Purcell, Susan Kaufman and David Rothkopf, eds. *Cuba: the Contours of Change.* Boulder, CO: Lynne Rienner Publishers, 2000.

Quirk, Robert E. *Fidel Castro.* New York: W.W. Norton, 1993.

Ritter, Archibald R.M. and John M. Kirk, eds. *Cuba in the International System: Normalization and Integration.* New York: Saint Martin's Press, 1995.

Roy, Joaquín. *Cuba, the United States, and the Helms-Burton Doctrine: International Reactions.* Gainesville, FL: University Press of Florida, 2000.

Santi, Enrico Mario, ed. *Cuban Studies XXIV.* Pittsburgh, PA: University of Pittsburgh Press, 1994.

Schwab, Peter. *Cuba: Confronting the U.S. Embargo.* New York: Saint Martin's Press, 2000.

Schulz, Donald E. *Cuba and the Future.* Westport, CT: Greenwood Press, 1994.

Skoug, Kenneth N. *The United States and Cuba under Reagan and Shultz: a Foreign Service Officer Reports.* New York: Praeger, 1996.

Stubbs, Jean, et al. *Cuba.* Santa Barbara, CA: ABC-CLIO, 1996.

Suchlicki, Jaime. *Cuba: from Columbus to Castro and Beyond.* McLean, VA: Brassey's, Inc.: 4th ed. 1997.

Szulc, Tad. *Fidel. A Critical Portrait.* NY: Avon Books, 1986.

Tulchin, Joseph S., et al., eds. *Cuba and the Caribbean: Regional Issues and Trends in the Post-Cold War Era.* Wilmington, DE: Scholarly Resources, 1997.

Dominican Republic

Atkins, G. Pope. *The Dominican Republic and the United States: from Imperialism to Transnationalism.* Athens, GA: University of Georgia Press, 1998.

Baud, Michiel. *Peasants and Tobacco in the Dominican Republic, 1870–1930.* Knoxville, TN: University of Tennessee Press, 1995.

Haggerty, Richard A., ed. *Dominican Republic and Haiti: Country Studies.* Washington, DC: U.S. GPO, 2nd ed. 1991.

Hall, Michael R. *Sugar and Power in the Dominican Republic: Eisenhower, Kennedy and the Trujillos.* Westport, CT: Greenwood Publishing Group, 2000.

Hartlyn, Jonathan. *The Struggle for Democratic Politics in the Dominican Republic, 1961–1996.* Chapel Hill, NC: University of North Carolina Press, 1998.

Howard, David. *Dominican Republic: a Guide to the People, Politics and Culture.*

Northampton, MA: Interlink Publishing Group, 1999.

Roorda, Eric. *The Dictator Next Door: the Good Neighbor Policy and the Trujillo Regime in the Dominican Republic, 1930–1945.* Durham, NC: Duke University Press, 1998.

Sagás, Ernesto. *Race and Politics in the Dominican Republic.* Gainesville, FL: University Press of Florida, 2000.

Ecuador

Alchon, Suzanne Austin. *Native Society and Disease in Colonial Ecuador.* New York: Cambridge University Press, 1991.

De la Torre, Carlos. *Populist Seduction in Latin America: the Ecuadorian Experience.* Athens, OH: Ohio University Press, 2000.

Gerlach, Allen. *Indians, Oil, and Politics: A Recent History of Ecuador.* Wilmington: Scholarly Resources, Inc, 2003.

Goffin, Alvin M. *The Rise of Protestant Evangelism in Ecuador, 1895–1990.* Gainesville, FL: University Press of Florida, 1994.

Hanratty, Dennis M., ed. *Ecuador: a Country Study.* Washington, DC: U.S. GPO, 3rd ed. 1991.

Herz, Monica and J.P. Nogueira. *Ecuador vs. Peru: Peacemaking Amid Rivalry.* Boulder, CO: Lynne Rienner, 2002.

Hey, Jeanne A.K. *Theories of Dependent Foreign Policy and the Case of Ecuador in the 1980s.* Athens, OH: Ohio University Press, 1995.

Isaacs, Anita. *The Politics of Military Rule and Transition in Ecuador, 1972–92.* Pittsburgh, PA: University of Pittsburgh Press, 1993.

Muratorio, Blanca. *The Life and Times of Grandfather Alonso: Culture and History in the Upper Amazon.* New Brunswick, NJ: Rutgers University Press, 1991.

Selverston-Scher, Melina. *Ethnopolitics in Ecuador: Indigenous Rights and the Strengthening of Democracy.* North South Center Press, Miami: University of Miami, 2001.

El Salvador

Angel, José, et al. Strategy and Tactics of the Salvadoran FMLN Guerrillas: Last Battle of the Cold War, Blueprint for Future Conflicts. New York: Praeger, 1995.

Beirne, Charles Joseph. *Jesuit Education and Social Change in El Salvador.* New York: Garland Publishing, 1996.

Didion, Joan. *Salvador.* New York: Vintage, 1994.

Doggett, Martha. *Death Foretold: the Jesuit Murders in El Salvador.* Washington, DC: Georgetown University Press, 1993.

Grenier, Yvon. *The Emergence of Insurgency in El Salvador: Ideology and Political Will.* Pittsburgh, PA: University of Pittsburgh Press, 1999.

Haggerty, Richard A., ed. *El Salvador: a Country Study.* Washington, DC: U.S. GPO, 2nd ed. 1990.

Hammond, John L. *Fighting to Learn: Popular Education and Guerrilla War in El Salvador.* New Brunswick, NJ: Rutgers University Press, 1998.

Hassett, John and Hugh Lacey, eds. *Toward a Society that Serves Its People: the Intellectual Contribution of El Salvador's Murdered Jesuits.* Washington, DC: Georgetown University Press, 1991.

Marenn, M.J. *Salvador's Children: a Song for Survival.* Columbus, OH: Ohio State University, 1993.

Pelupessy, Wim. *The Limits of Economic Reform in El Salvador.* New York: Saint Martin's Press, 1997.

Popkin, Margaret L. *Peace without Justice: Obstacles to Building the Rule of Law in El Salvador.* University Park, PA: Pennsylvania State University, 2000.

Quizar, Robin O. *My Turn to Weep: Salvadoran Women in Costa Rica.* Westport, CT: Greenwood Publishing Group, 1998.

Ucles, Mario L. Translated by Amelia F. Shogun. *El Salvador in the 1980's: Counterinsurgency and Revolution.* Philadelphia, PA: Temple University Press, 1996.

Williams, Philip J. *Militarization and Demilitarization in El Salvador's Transition to Democracy.* Pittsburgh, PA: University of Pittsburgh Press, 1998.

Wood, Elisabeth Jean. *Insurgent Collective Action and Civil War in El Salvador.* Cambridge: Cambridge University Press, 2003.

Grenada

Heine, Jorge, ed. *A Revolution Aborted: the Lessons of Grenada.* Pittsburgh, PA: University of Pittsburgh Press, 1990.

Guatemala

Benz, Stephen Connely. *Guatemalan Journey.* Austin, TX: University of Texas Press, 1996.

Dosal, Paul J. *Doing Business with the Dictators: a Political History of the United Fruit in Guatemala, 1899–1944.* Wilmington, DE: Scholarly Resources, 1993.

Dosal, Paul J. Power in Transition: the Rise of Guatemala's Industrial Oligarchy, 1871–1994. New York: Praeger, 1995.

Grandin, Greg. The Blood of Guatemala: a History of Race and Nation. Durham, NC: Duke University Press, 2000.

Handy, Jim. Revolution in the Countryside: Rural Conflict and Agrarian Reform in Guatemala, 1944–1954. Chapel Hill, NC: University of North Carolina Press, 1994.

Hendrickson, Carol. *Weaving Identities: Construction of Dress and Self in a Highland Guatemalan Town.* Austin, TX: University of Texas Press, 1995.

Jonas, Susanne. *Of Centaurs and Doves: Guatemala's Peace Process.* Boulder, CO: Westview Press, 2000

Jones, Oakah L. *Guatemala in the Spanish Colonial Period.* Norman, OK: University of Oklahoma Press, 1994.

Levenson-Estrada, Deborah. *Trade Unionists against Terror: Guatemala City, 1954–1985.* Chapel Hill, NC: University of North Carolina Press, 1994.

Lovell, George W. *A Beauty That Hurts: Life and Death in Guatemala.* Austin, TX: University of Texas Press, rev. ed 2000.

McCleary, Rachel M. *Dictating Democracy: Guatemala and the End of Violent Revolution.* Gainesville, FL: University Press of Florida, 1999.

McCreery, David. *Rural Guatemala, 1760–1940.* Stanford, CA: Stanford University Press, 1994.

Nelson, Diane M. *A Finger in the Wound: Body Politics in Quincentennial Guatemala.* Berkeley, CA: University of California Press, 1999.

Perera, Victor. *Unfinished Conquest: the Guatemalan Tragedy.* Berkeley, CA: University of California Press, 1993.

Schirmer, Jennifer. *The Guatemalan Military Project: a Violence Called Democracy.* Philadelphia, PA: University of Pennsylvania Press, 1998.

Shea, Maureen E. *Culture and Customs of Guatemala.* Westport, CT: Greenwood Publishing Group, 2000.

Stoll, David. *Between Two Armies: in the Ixil Towns of Guatemala.* New York: Columbia University Press, 1993.

Stoll, David. *Rigoberta Menchu and the Story of All Poor Guatemalans.* Boulder, CO: Westview Press, 1998.

Trudeau, Robert H. *Guatemalan Politics: the Popular Struggle for Democracy.* Boulder, CO: Lynne Rienner Publishers, 1993.

Woodward, Ralph Lee. *Guatemala.* Santa Barbara, CA: ABC-CLIO, rev. ed. 1992.

Woodward, Ralph Lee. *Rafael Carrera and the Emergence of the Republic of Guatemala.* Athens, GA: University of Georgia Press, 1993.

Yashar, Deborah J. *Demanding Democracy: Reform and Reaction in Costa Rica and Guatemala., 1850s–1950s.* Stanford, CA: Stanford University Press, 1997.

Wilkinson, Daniel. *Silence On The Mountain: Stories of Terror, Betrayal, and Forgetting in Guatemala.* Boston: Houghton Mifflin Company, 2002.

Zimmerman, Marc. *Literature and Resistance in Guatemala: Textual Modes and Cultural Politics from El Señor Presidente to Rigoberta Menchu.* Athens, OH: Ohio University Press, 1995.

Guyana

Da Costa, Emilia Viotti. *Crowns of Glory, Tears of Blood: the Demerara Slave Rebellion of 1823.* New York: Oxford University Press, 1994.

Gibson, Kean. *The Cycle of Racial Oppression in Guyana.* Lanham, MD: University Press of America, 2003.

Merrill, Tim L., ed. *Guyana and Belize: Country Studies.* Washington, DC: U.S. GPO, 2nd ed. 1993.

Williams, Brackette F. *Stains on My Name, War in My Veins: Guyana and the Politics* of Struggle. Durham, NC: Duke University Press, 1991.

Williams, David P., et al., eds. Privatization vs. Community: the Rise and Fall of Industrial Welfare in Guyana. Lanham, MD: Rowman & Littlefield, 1998.

Haiti

Chambers, Frances, ed. Haiti. Santa Barbara, CA: ABC-CLIO, 2nd ed. 1994.

Fatton, Robert Jr. Haiti's Predatory Republic: The Unending Transition to Democracy. Boulder, CO: Lynne Rienner, 2002.

Gibbons, Elizabeth D. Sanctions in Haiti: Human Rights and Democracy under Assault. Westport, CT: Greenwood Publishing Group, 1999.

Fatton, Robert J. Haiti's Predatory Republic: The Unending Transition to Democracy. Boulder: Lynne Reinner Publishing, 2002.

Haggerty, Richard A., ed. Dominican Republic and Haiti: Country Studies. Washington, DC: U.S. GPO, 2nd ed, 1991.

Hein, Robert Debs and Hein, Nancy Gordon. Revised and Expanded by Hein, Michael. Written in Blood. The Story of the Haitian People 1492-1995. Lanham, MD: University Press of America, 1996.

Kumar, Chetan. Building Peace in Haiti. Boulder, CO: Lynne Rienner Publishers, 1998.

Laguerre, Michel S. The Military Society in Haiti. Knoxville, TN: University of Tennessee Press, 1993.

Langley, Lester D. The Americas in the Age of Revolution, 1750–1850. New Haven, CT: Yale University Press, 1996.

Perusse, Roland I. Haitian Democracy Restored, 1991–1995. Lanham, MD: University Press of America, 1995.

Rotberg, Robert I., ed. Haiti Renewed: Political and Economic Prospects. Washington, DC: Brookings Institution Press, 1997.

Stotzky, Irwin P. Silencing Guns in Haiti: the Promise of Deliberative Democracy. Chicago: University of Chicago Press, 1997.

Weinstein, Brian and Aaron Segal. Haiti: the Failure of Politics. New York: Praeger, 1992.

Zephir, Flore. Haitian Immigrants in Black America: a Sociological and Sociolinguistic Portrait. Westport, CT: Bergin & Garvey, 1996.

Honduras

Euraque, Dario A. Region and State in Honduras, 1870–1972: Reinterpreting the "Banana Republic." Chapel Hill, NC: University of North Carolina Press, 1996.

Merrill, Tim L. Honduras: a Country Study. Washington, DC: U.S. GPO, 3rd ed. 1995.

Meyer, Harvey Kessler and Jessie H. Meyer. Historical Dictionary of Honduras. Lanham, MD: Scarecrow Press, 2nd ed. 1994.

Jamaica

Butler, Kathleen Mary. The Economics of Emancipation: Jamaica and Barbados, 1823–1843. Chapel Hill, NC: University of North Carolina Press, 1995.

Gray, Obika. Radicalism and Social Change in Jamaica, 1960–1972. Knoxville, TN: University of Tennessee Press, 1991.

Heuman, Gad. The Killing Time: the Morant Bay Rebellion in Jamaica. Knoxville, TN: University of Tennessee Press, 1994.

Hewan, Clinton G. Jamaica and the United States Caribbean Basin Initiative: Showpiece or Failure? New York: Peter Lang Publishing, 1994.

Ingram, K.E. Jamaica. Santa Barbara, CA: ABC-CLIO, Inc., revised ed. 1997.

Keith, Nelson W. and Novella Z. Keith. The Social Origins of Democratic Socialism in Jamaica. Philadelphia, PA: Temple University Press, 1992.

Lundy, Patricia. Debt and Adjustment: Social and Environmental Consequences in Jamaica. Brookfield, VT: Ashgate, 1999.

Mordecai, Martin and Pamela Mordecai. Culture and Customs of Jamaica. Westport, CT: Greenwood Publishing Group, 2000.

Moser, Caroline and Jeremy Holland. Urban Poverty and Violence in Jamaica. Washington, DC: The World Bank, 1997.

Payne, Anthony J. Politics in Jamaica. New York: Saint Martin's Press, rev. ed. 1994.

Zips, Werner. Translated by Shelley L. Frisch. Black Rebels: African-Caribbean Freedom Fighters in Jamaica. Princeton, NJ: Markus Wiener Publishers, 1999.

Mexico

Alonso, Ana Maria. Thread of Blood: Colonialism, Revolution, and Gender on Mexico's Northern Frontier. Tucson, AZ: University of Arizona Press, 1995.

Aspe, Pedro. Economic Transformation in the Mexican Way. Cambridge, MA: MIT Press, 1993.

Bondi, Loretta. Beyond the Border and Across the Atlantic. Mexico's Foreign and Security Policy Post-September 11. Washington: Brookings, 2004.

Bosworth, Barry P., et al., eds. Coming Together? Mexico-U.S. Relations. Washington, DC: Brookings Institution Press, 1997.

Britton, John A. Revolution and Ideology: Images of the Mexican Revolution and the United States. Lexington, KY: University Press of Kentucky, 1995.

Brunk, Samuel. Emiliano Zapata: Revolution and Betrayal in Mexico. Albuquerque, NW: University of New Mexico Press, 1995.

Bulmer-Thomas, Victor, et al., eds. Mexico and the North American Free Trade Agreement: Who Will Benefit? New York: Saint Martin's Press, 1994.

Butler, Edgar. Mexico and Mexico City in the World Economy. Boulder, CO: Westview Press, 2000.

Castañeda, Jorge G. The Mexican Shock: Its Meaning for the U.S. New York: New Press, 1995.

Chand, Vikram K. Mexico's Political Awakening. Notre Dame, IN: University of Notre Dame Press, 2000.

Cope, R. Douglas. The Limits of Racial Domination: Plebeian Society in Colonial Mexico City, 1660–1720. Madison, WI: University of Wisconsin Press, 1994.

Crandall, Russell, et al, eds. Mexico's Democracy at Work: Political and Economic Dynamics. Boulder, CO: Lynne Rienner, 2004.

Davidow, Jeffrey. The U.S. and Mexico: The Bear and the Porcupine. Markus Weiner, 2004.

Davis, Diane E. Urban Leviathan: Mexico City in the Twentieth Century. Philadelphia, PA: Temple University Press, 1994.

Dominguez, Jorge I. and James A. McCann. Democratizating Mexico: Public Opinion and Electoral Choices. Baltimore, MD: Johns Hopkins University Press, 1996.

Dominguez, Jorge I. and Alejandro Poire, eds. Toward Mexico's Democratization: Parties, Campaigns, Elections and Public Opinion. New York: Routledge, 1999.

Eisenhower, John S.D. Intervention! The United Stated and the Mexican Revolution, 1913–1917. New York: W.W. Norton, 1993.

Erfani, Julie A. The Paradox of the Mexican State: Rereading Sovereignty from Independence to NAFTA. Boulder, CO: Lynne Rienner Publishers, 1995.

Fehrenbach, T.R. Fire and Blood: a History of Mexico. New York: Da Capo Press, 1995.

Foster, Lynn V. A Brief History of Mexico. New York: Facts on File, 1997.

Garber, Peter M., ed. The Mexico-U.S. Free Trade Agreement. Cambridge, MA: MIT Press, 1994.

Gledhill, John. Neoliberalism, Transnationalism and Rural Poverty: a Case Study of Michoacan, Mexico. Boulder, CO: Westview Press, 1995.

Hamnett, Brian. Juarez. White Plains, NY: Longman Publishing, 1994.

Harvey, Neil, ed. Mexico: Dilemmas of Transition. London: British Academic Press, 1993.

Johns, Christina Jacqueline. The Origins of Violence in Mexican Society. New York: Praeger, 1995.

Jones, Richard C. Ambivalent Journey: U.S. Migration and Economic Mobility in North-Central Mexico. Tucson, AZ: University of Arizona Press, 1995.

Katz, Friedrich. The Life and Times of Pancho Villa. Stanford, CA: Stanford University Press, 1998.

Krauze, Enrique. Mexico-Biography of Power: a History of Modern Mexico, 1810–1996. New York: HarperCollins Publishers, 1997.

Krooth, Richard. Mexico, NAFTA and the Hardships of Progress: Historical Patterns and Shifting Methods of Oppression. Jefferson, NC: McFarland & Company, 1995.

Markiewicz, Dana. The Mexican Revolution and the Limits of Agrarian Reform, 1915–1946. Boulder, CO: Lynne Rienner Publishers, 1993.

Merrell, Floyd. The Mexicans. A Sense of Culture. Boulder, Co: Westview, 2003.

Merrill, Tim L. and Ramon Miro, eds. Mexico: a Country Study. Washington, DC: U.S. GPO, 4th ed. 1997.

Meyer, Michael C., et al. The Course of Mexican History. New York: Oxford University Press, 1998.

Middlebrook, Keven J., ed. Dilemmas of Political Change in Mexico. Washington: Brookings, 2004.

Oppenheimer, Andres. Bordering on Chaos: Guerrillas, Stockbrokers, Politicians and Mexico's Violent Struggle. New York: Little, Brown, 1996.

Peters, Enrique Dussel. Polarizing Mexico: the Impact of Liberalizatio n Strategy. Boulder, CO: Lynne Rienner Publishers, 2000.

Preson, Julia and Dillon, Samuel. Opening Mexico: The Making of a Democracy. New York: Farrar, Straus and Giroux, 2004.

Purcell, Susan K. and Luis Rubio, eds. Mexico under Zedillo. Boulder, CO: Lynne Rienner Publishers, 1998.

Rodriguez, Victoria E. and Peter M. Ward. Opposition Government in Mexico. Albuquerque, NM: University of New Mexico Press, 1995.

Roett, Riordan, ed. Political and Economic Liberalization in Mexico: at a Critical Juncture? Boulder, CO: Lynne Rienner Publishers, 1993.

Rubio, Luis and Purcell, Susan Kaufman, eds. Mexico Under Fox. Boulder, CO: Lynne Rienner, 2004.

Ruiz, Ramon E. On the Rim of Mexico: Encounters of the Rich and Poor. Boulder, CO: Westview Press, 1998.

Schulz, Donald E. and Edward J. Williams, eds. Mexico Faces the 21st Century. Westport, CT: Greenwood Publishing Group, 1995.

Sernau, Scott. Economies of Exclusion: Underclass Poverty and Labor Market Change in Mexico. New York: Praeger, 1994.

Shirk, David A. Mexico's New Politics: The PAN and Democratic Change. Boulder, CO: Lynne Rienner, 2004.

Staudt, Kathleen A. Free Trade? Informal Economies at the U.S.-Mexican Border. Philadelphia, PA: Temple University Press, 1998.

Thomas, Hugh. Conquest: Montezuma, Cortes, and the Fall of Old Mexico. New York: Simon & Schuster, 1994.

Tulchin, Joseph S. and Andrew D. Selee, eds. Mexico's Politics and Society in Transition. Boulder, CO: Lynne Rienner, 2002.

Wise, Carol. The Post-NAFTA Political Economy: Mexico and the Western Hemisphere. University Park, PA: Pennsylvania State University Press, 1998.

Womack, John Jr. Rebellion in Chiapas: an Historical Reader. New York: New Press, 1999.

Netherlands Antilles

Brown, Enid. Suriname and the Netherlands Antilles: an Annotated English-Language Bibliography. Lanham, MD: Scarecrow Press, 1992.

Sedoc-Dahlberg, Betty, ed. The Dutch Caribbean: Prospects for Democracy. New York: Gordon and Breach, 1990.

Nicaragua

Biondi-Morra, Brizio N. Hungry Dream: the Failure of Food Policy in Revolutionary Nicaragua, 1979–1990. Ithaca, NY: Cornell University Press, 1993.

Gambone, Michael D. Eisenhower, Somoza and the Cold War in Nicaragua, 1953–1961. Westport, CT: Greenwood Publishing Group, 1997.

Hale, Charles R. Resistance and Contradiction: Miskitu Indians and the Nicaraguan State, 1894–1987. Stanford, CA: Stanford University Press, 1994.

Kagan, Robert. A Twilight Struggle: American Power and Nicaragua, 1977–1990. New York: Free Press, 1996.

Luciak, Ilja A. The Sandinista Legacy: Lessons from a Political Economy in Transition. Gainesville, FL: University Press of Florida, 1995.

Merrill, Tim L., ed. Nicaragua: a Country Study. Washington, DC: U.S. GPO, 3rd ed. 1994.

Miranda, Roger and William Ratliff. The Civil War in Nicaragua: Inside the Sandinistas. New Brunswick, NJ: Transaction, 1993.

Prevost, Gary. The Undermining of the Sandinista Revolution. New York: Saint Martin's Press, 1997.

Randall, Margaret. Sandino's Daughters: Feminism in Nicaragua. New Brunswick, NJ: Rutgers University Press, 1994.

Ryan, David. US-Sandinista Diplomatic Relations: Voice of Intolerance. New York: Saint Martin's Press, 1995.

Sabia, Debra. Contradiction and Conflict: the Popular Church in Nicaragua. Tuscaloosa, AL: University of Alabama Press, 1997.

Spalding, Rose J. Capitalists and Revolution in Nicaragua: Opposition and Accommodation, 1979–1993. Chapel Hill, NC: University of North Carolina Press, 1994.

Vanden, Harry E. and Garry Prevost. Democracy and Socialism in Sandinista Nicaragua. Boulder, CO: Lynne Rienner Publishers, 1993.

Walker, Thomas W. Nicaragua. Living in the Shadow of the Eagle. Boulder, Co: Westview, 2003.

Walker, Thomas W., ed. Nicaragua without Illusions: Regime Transition and Structural Adjustment in the 1990s. Wilmington, DE: Scholarly Resources, 1997.

Walter, Knut. The Regime of Anastasio Somoza, 1936–1956. Chapel Hill, NC: University of North Carolina Press, 1993.

Whisnant, David E. Rascally Signs in Sacred Places: the Politics of Culture in Nicaragua. Chapel Hill, NC: University of North Carolina Press, 1995.

Panama

Conniff, Michael L. Panama and the United States: the Forced Alliance. Athens, GA: University of Georgia Press, 1992.

Donnelly, Thomas, et al. Operation Just Cause: the Storming of Panama. New York: Lexington Books, 1991.

Guevara Mann, Carlos. Panamanian Militarism: a Historical Perspective. Athens, OH: Ohio University Press, 1996.

Johns, Christina Jacqueline and P. Ward Johnson. State Crime, the Media, and the Invasion of Panama. New York: Praeger, 1994.

Leonard, Thomas M. Panama, the Canal and the United States: a Guide to Issues and References. Claremont, CA: Regina Books, 1993.

Major, John. Prize Possession: the United Stated and the Panama Canal, 1903–1979. New York: Cambridge University Press, 1993.

Meditz, Sandra W. and Dennis M. Hanratty, eds. Panama: a Country Study. Washington, DC: U.S. GPO, 4th ed. 1989.

Noriega, Manuel and Peter Eisner. America's Prisoner: the Memoirs of Manuel Noriega. New York: Random House, 1997.

Pearcy, Thomas L. We Answer Only to God: Politics and the Military in Panama, 1903–1947. Albuquerque, NM: University of New Mexico Press, 1998.

Perez, Orlando J., ed. Post-Invasion Panama: the Challenges of Democratization in the New World Order. Lanham, MD: Lexington Books, 2000.

Ward, Christopher. Imperial Panama: Commerce and Conflict in Isthmian America, 1550–1800. Albuquerque, NM: University of New Mexico, 1993.

Paraguay

Gimlette, John, At the Tomb of the Inflatable Pig: Travels Through Paraguay. New York: Alfred A. Knopf, 2003.

Hanratty, Dennis and Sandra W. Meditz, eds. Paraguay: a Country Study. Washington, DC: U.S. GPO, 2nd ed. 1990.

Kracy, Hendrick, and Thomas Whigham, eds., I Die With My Country: Perspectives on the Paraguayan War, 1864-70. Lincoln: University of Nebraska Press, 2004.

Lambert, Peter and Andrew Nickson, eds. Transition to Democracy in Paraguay. New York: Saint Martin's Press, 1997.

Leis, Paul H. Political Parties and Generations in Paraguay's Liberal Era, 1869–1940. Chapel Hill, NC: University of North Carolina Press, 1993.

Miranda, Carlos R. *The Stroessner Era: Authoritarian Rule in Paraguay.* Boulder, CO: Westview Press, 1990.

Nickson, R. Andrew. *Historical Dictionary of Paraguay.* Lanham, MD: Scarecrow Press, 2nd ed. 1993.

Whigham, Thomas, *The Paraguayan War (Vol. 1)—Causes and Early Conduct.* Lincoln: University of Nebraska Press, 2002.

Peru

Cameron, Maxwell, A. *Democracy and Authoritarianism in Peru: Political Coalitions and Social Change.* New York: Saint Martin's Press, 1994.

Clayton, Lawrence A. *Peru and the United States: the Condor and the Eagle.* Athens, GA: University of Georgia Press, 1999.

Gootenberg, Paul. *Imagining Development: Economic Ideas in Peru's "Fictitious Prosperity" of Guano, 1840–1880.* Berkeley, CA: University of California Press, 1993.

Gorriti, Gustavo. *The Shining Path: a History of the Millenarian War in Peru.* Chapel Hill, NC: University of North Carolina Press, 1999.

Hudson, Rex A., ed. *Peru: a Country Study.* Washington, DC: U.S. GPO, 1993.

Jacobsen, Nils. *Mirages of Transition: the Peruvian Altiplano, 1780–1930.* Berkeley, CA: University of California Press, 1993.

Klaren, Peter Flindell. *Peru: Society and Nationhood in the Andes.* New York: Oxford University Press, 2000.

Lockhart, James. *Spanish Peru, 1532–1560: a Social History.* Madison, WI: University of Wisconsin Press, 1994.

Masterson, Daniel M. *Militarism and Politics in Latin America: Peru from Sanchez Cerro to Sendero Luminoso.* Westport, CT: Greenwood Publishing Publishing, 1991.

Kirk, Robin. *The Monkey's Paw, New Chronicles From Peru.* Amherst: University of Massachusetts Press, 1997.

Palmer, David Scott, ed. *The Shining Path of Peru.* New York: Saint Martin's Press, 1992.

Peña, Milagros. *Theologies and Liberation in Peru: the Role of Ideas in Social Movement.* Philadelphia, PA: Temple University Press, 1995.

Quiroz, Alfonso W. *Domestic and Foreign Finance in Modern Peru, 1850–1950: Financing Visions of Development.* Pittsburgh, PA: University of Pittsburgh Press, 1993.

Roberts, Kenneth M. *Deepening Democracy? The Modern Left and Social Movements in Chile and Peru.* Stanford, CA: Stanford University Press, 1999.

Seligmann, Linda J. *Between Reform and Revolution: Political Struggles in the Peruvian Andes, 1969–1991.* Stanford, CA: Stanford University Press, 1995.

Sheahan, John. *Searching for a Better Society: the Peruvian Economy from 1950.* University Park, PA: Pennsylvania State University Press, 1999.

Starn, Orin, Carlos Ivan Degregori, and Robin Kirk, eds. *The Peru Reader: History, Culture, Politics.* Durham: Duke University Press, 1995.

Stern, Steve J. *Peru's Indian Peoples and the Challenge of Spanish Conquest: Huamanga to 1640.* Madison, WI: University of Wisconsin Press, 2nd ed. 1993.

Stern, Steve J., ed., *Shining And Other Paths.* Durham: Duke University Press, 1998.

Tarazona-Sevillano, Gabriela. *Sendero Luminoso and the Threat of Narcoterrorism.* New York: Praeger, 1990.

Tulchin, Joseph S. and Gary Bland, eds. *Peru in Crisis: Dictatorship or Democracy?* Boulder, CO: Lynne Rienner Publishers, 1994.

Watters, R.F. *Poverty and Peasantry in Peru's Southern Andes, 1963–90.* Pittsburgh, PA: University of Pittsburgh Press, 1994.

Puerto Rico

Dietz, James L. *Puerto Rico: Negotiating Development and Change.* Boulder, CO: Lynne Rienner, 2003.

Suriname

Brown, Enid. *Suriname and the Netherlands Antilles: an Annotated English-Language Bibliography.* Lanham, MD: Scarecrow Press, 1992.

Dew, Edward M. *The Trouble in Suriname, 1975–1993.* New York: Praeger, 1994.

Hoefte, Rosemarijn. *In Place of Slavery: a Social History of British Indian and Javanese Laborers in Suriname.* Gainesville, FL: University Press of Florida, 1998.

Hoefte, Rosemarijn. *Suriname.* Santa Barbara, CA: ABC-CLIO, 1991.

Trinidad and Tobago

Anthony, Michael. *Historical Dictionary of Trinidad and Tobago.* Lanham, MD: Scarecrow Press, 1997.

Regis, Louis. *The Political Calypso: True Opposition in Trinidad and Tobago, 1962–1987.* Gainesville, FL: University Press of Florida, 1998.

Yelvington, Kelvin A. *Trinidad Ethnicity.* Knoxville, TN: University of Tennessee Press, 1993.

Uruguay

Gillespie, Charles Guy. *Negotiating Democracy: Politicians and Generals in Uruguay.* New York: Cambridge University Press, 1991.

Gonzalez, Luis E. *Political Structures and Democracy in Uruguay.* Notre Dame, IN: University of Notre Dame Press, 1991.

Hudson, Rex A. and Sandra W. Meditz, eds. *Uruguay: a Country Study.* Washington, DC: U.S. GPO, 2nd ed. 1992.

Preeg, Ernest H. *From Here to Free Trade: Essays in Post-Uruguay Round Trade Strategy.* Chicago: University of Chicago Press, 1998.

Rottenberg, Simon, ed. *Costa Rica and Uruguay.* New York: Oxford University Press, 1993.

Sosnowski, Saul. *Repression, Exile, and Democracy: Uruguayan Culture.* Durham, NC: Duke University Press, 1992.

Venezuela

Canache, Damarys J. and Michael R. Kulisheck, eds. *Reinventing Legitimacy: Democracy and Political Change in Venezuela.* Westport, CT: Greenwood Publishing Group, 1998.

Coppedge, Michael. *Strong Parties and Lame Ducks: Presidential Partyarchy and Factionalism in Venezuela.* Stanford, CA: Stanford University Press, 1994.

Coronil, Fernando. *Magical State: Nature, Money and Modernity in Venezuela.* Chicago: University of Chicago Press, 1997.

Ellner, Steve and Hellinger, Daniel, eds. *Venezuelan Politics in the Chávez Era: Class, Polarization, and Conflict.* Boulder, CO: Lynne Rienner, 2004.

Enright, Michael J., et al. *Venezuela: the Challenge of Competitiveness.* New York: Saint Martin's Press, 1996.

Goodman, Louis W., et al., eds. *Lessons of the Venezuelan Experience.* Baltimore, MD: Johns Hopkins University Press, 1995.

Haggerty, Richard A. *Venezuela: a Country Study.* Washington, DC: U.S. GPO, 4th ed. 1993.

Hillman, Richard S. *Democracy for the Privileged: Crisis and Transition in Venezuela.* Boulder, CO: Lynne Rienner, 1994.

Rudolph, Donna K. and G.A. Rudolph. *Historical Dictionary of Venezuela.* Lanham, MD: Scarecrow Press, 1996.

A Peruvian Indian and his llama keep a lonely vigil in some of the highest country in the western Andes